Themes and Writers Series

G. Robert Carlsen
General Editor

About the Editors of the Themes and Writers Series

G. Robert Carlsen, Professor of English and Professor of Education at the University of Iowa, has taught English in the public schools of Minneapolis and at the universities of Minnesota, Colorado, Texas, Hawaii, and Iowa. He has served as consultant in curriculum revision to a number of school systems in Texas, Iowa, Colorado, California, Oklahoma, and Virginia. For many years he was book review editor of young people's books for the *English Journal* and was coauthor of an edition of *Books for You.* Dr. Carlsen is a past president of the National Council of Teachers of English. He has written some seventy articles for professional journals and is coauthor of *The Brown-Carlsen Test of Listening Comprehension* and of the National Council of Social Studies' publication entitled *Social Understanding Through Literature.* He is also an author of *Books and the Teen-Age Reader.*

Anthony Tovatt is Professor of English at Burris Laboratory School of Ball State University. Dr. Tovatt has been the director of an extended research study on the teaching of composition under the Program for English of the United States Office of Education. He has been cited by the National Council of Teachers of English and the Indiana Council of Teachers of English for outstanding contributions to the teaching of English in the secondary school. Since 1955 he has been a column editor of the *English Journal.* His articles have been published in many professional journals, and his poetry has appeared in magazines and newspapers.

Edgar H. Schuster, Assistant Professor of English at Beaver College, has taught in both urban and suburban high schools in the Philadelphia area, as well as at the college level. He has written articles for many professional journals, including *Educational Leadership* and the *English Journal.* Mr. Schuster is author of *Grammar, Usage, and Style,* a high school language text; is coauthor of McGraw-Hill's *American English Today,* a junior high and high school language and composition series; and is a contributing author of a new McGraw-Hill elementary language arts program.

Gabriele L. Rico, Instructor of English at the University of Santa Clara, has taught English and German at high schools, junior colleges, and colleges in California. At San Jose State College she was also a supervisor of student teachers and teaching interns. During the years that she taught at the high school level, she was instrumental in setting up the curriculum for the innovative Advanced Placement in English. She recently served as a consultant for McGraw-Hill's *Today: A Text-Workbook for English Language and Composition.*

Robert L. Donald, Assistant Professor of English at Oakland University, Rochester, Michigan, prepared the words study program for *Insights* and *Encounters.* He is a former John Hay Fellow at the University of California at Berkeley.

Don L. Wulffson, teacher of English at San Fernando High School in Los Angeles, prepared the words study program for *American Literature* and *Western Literature* and assisted in the preparation of resource guide material.

Themes and Writers Series

Second Edition

INSIGHTS

Themes in Literature

G. Robert Carlsen
Anthony Tovatt

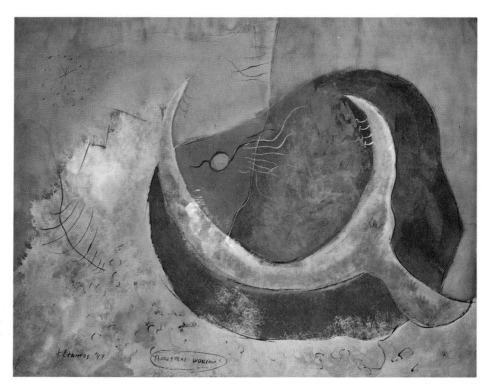

ANCESTRAL WORSHIP
Theodore Stamos
Pastel, gouache,
and ink, Collection,
Whitney Museum
of American Art

Webster Division, McGraw-Hill Book Company
New York, St. Louis, San Francisco, Dallas, Atlanta

ST. GEORGE
AND THE DRAGON
Raphael

Library of Congress Cataloging in Publication Data

Carlsen, G. Robert, 1921–   comp.
  Insights: themes in literature.

  (Themes and writers series)
  SUMMARY: A thematically arranged anthology of poems, short stories, plays, and novellas for the ninth-grade reader.
  1. Literature—Collections. [1. Literature—Collections] I. Tovatt, Anthony, joint comp. II. Title.
[PN6014.C318 1973]   808.8   72-641
ISBN 0-07-009903-0

ISBN 07-009903-0

Editorial Development: Susan Gelles; Editing and Styling: Linda Epstein; Design: John Keithley; Production: Richard E. Shaw.

CALL TO ADVENTURE

WITH WHAT YOU HAVE

THE INNER CIRCLE

THE WAYS OF A POET

THE POET FEELS

THE POET TELLS A STORY

BIRD IN SPACE *Constantin Brancusi*

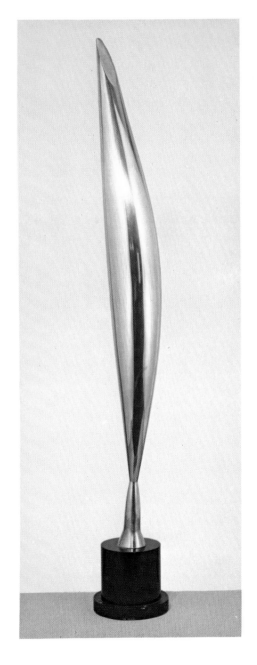

IDENTITY

THE STRANGE AND EERIE

CANVASSING FOR A VOTE
George Caleb Bingham

MOMENTS OF DECISION

How many a man
has dated a new era in his life
from the reading of a book.
The book exists for us, perchance,
which will explain our miracles and reveal new ones.
The, at present, unutterable things
we may find somewhere uttered.
These same questions that disturb and puzzle and confound us
have in their turn
occurred to all the wise men: not one has been omitted;
and each has answered them according to his ability,
by his word,
and his life.

HENRY DAVID THOREAU

CALL TO ADVENTURE

Kansas Boy

This Kansas boy who never saw the sea
Walks through the young corn rippling at his
    knee
As sailors walk; and when the grain grows
    higher
Watches the dark waves leap with greener
    fire
Than ever oceans hold. He follows ships,
Tasting the bitter spray upon his lips,
For in his blood up-stirs the salty ghost
Of one who sailed a storm-bound English
    coast.
Across wide fields he hears the sea winds
    crying,
Shouts at the crows—and dreams of white
    gulls flying.

RUTH LECHLITNER

KANSAS BOY first appeared in *Poetry*, November 1931.
Was copyrighted 1931 by The Modern Poetry Association,
and is reprinted by permission of the Editor of *Poetry* and
the author, Ruth Lechlitner.

A young man stands on a high and desolate cliff; his face is ruddy in the setting sun of an England 1,000 years ago. His rough cloak flies outward from his shoulders in the whipping sea wind. With restless eyes he searches the distant horizons of the sea and sky, like the modern day "Kansas Boy" who never saw the sea, but "follows ships,/Tasting the bitter spray...."

The sound of the angry waters crashing and tumbling on the rocky coast fills the young man with an intense yearning. He dreams of testing himself in a crude sailing ship against the strength of the endless seas.

The youth asks himself, what lies beyond the sunset? He dreams of adventure:

> Oh, wildly my heart
> Beats in my bosom and bids me to try
> The tumble and surge of seas tumultuous,
> Breeze and brine and the breaker's roar.
> Daily, hourly, drives me my spirit
> Outward to sail, far countries to see.
> Liveth no man so large in his soul,
> So gracious in giving, so gay in his youth,
> In deeds so daring, so dear to his lord,
> But frets his soul for his sea adventure,
> Fain to try what fortune shall send.

The call to adventure is an old one. It comes from deep within mankind. In every age, both the great and the unknown have heard it and have answered. Odysseus heard it on the shores of the Aegean Sea over 3,000 years ago, before he set sail for the war at Troy. Columbus heard it when he struck out across uncharted waters in search of new lands and riches. The men and women who pioneered the American wilderness heard it. Matthew Henson heard it when he wrote: "The lure of the Arctic is tugging at my heart; to me the trail is calling!" Charles Lindbergh heard it on the morning of May 20, 1927, when he set out to cross the vast Atlantic in his tiny plane, *The Spirit of St. Louis*. And today our spacemen continue to hear it as they explore the universe.

But travel is only one of the many dimensions of adventure. Adventure can be found in all kinds of experiences and situations. Adventure is all around you if the spirit of adventure is within you. It is as near as the book you hold in your hand.

In the stories in CALL TO ADVENTURE you will visit a tropical island where an evil hunter rules, face lurking danger in the Little Jackpine Valley along with Nathan Stemline, and pioneer on the planet Mars. You will meet such real adventurers as Matthew Henson, Raymond Ditmars, Charles Lindbergh, and John Wise. In addition, you will meet the master sleuth of fiction, Sherlock Holmes. Finally, you will share the experiences of Odysseus, the mighty Greek warrior, whose journey home to Ithaca was so filled with danger that it remains one of the greatest adventure stories of all times.

This is a lighthearted depiction of one kind of adventure.

"Alberto Santos-Dumont, Brazilian, 1906"
Otto Nielsen

From Old English Poetry, "Seafarer," p. 145, by J. Duncan Spaeth. Copyright 1921 by Princeton University Press.

A mysterious island
looms to the right of the ship—an island
whose very name suggests evil!
What adventure lies ahead? What will prove
to be "the most dangerous game"?

The
Most Dangerous
Game

RICHARD CONNELL

"Off there to the right—somewhere—is a large island," said Whitney. "It's rather a mystery——"

"What island is it?" Rainsford asked.

"The old charts call it 'Ship-Trap Island,'" Whitney replied. "A suggestive name, isn't it? Sailors have a curious dread of the place. I don't know why. Some superstition——"

"Can't see it," remarked Rainsford, trying to peer through the dank tropical night that was palpable as it pressed its thick, warm blackness in upon the yacht.

"You have good eyes," said Whitney, with a laugh, "and I've seen you pick off a moose moving in the brown fall bush at four hundred yards; but even you can't see four miles or so through a moonless Caribbean night."[1]

"Nor four yards," admitted Rainsford. "Ugh! It's like moist black velvet."

"It will be light enough in Rio,"[2] promised Whitney. "We should make it in a few days. I hope the jaguar guns have come. We'll have some good hunting up the Amazon.[3] Great sport, hunting."

"The best sport in the world," agreed Rainsford.

"For the hunter," amended Whitney. "Not for the jaguar."

"Don't talk rot, Whitney," said Rainsford. "You're a big-game hunter, not a philosopher. Who cares how the jaguar feels?"

"Perhaps the jaguar does," observed Whitney.

"Bah! They've no understanding."

"Even so, I rather think they understand one thing—fear. The fear of pain and the fear of death."

"Nonsense," laughed Rainsford. "This hot weather is making you soft, Whitney. Be a realist. The world is made up of two classes—the hunters and the hunted. Luckily, you and I are hunters. Do you think we've passed that island yet?"

"I can't tell in the dark. I hope so."

"Why?" asked Rainsford.

"The place has a reputation—a bad one. It's gotten into sailor lore, somehow. Didn't you notice that the crew's nerves seemed a bit jumpy today?"

"They were a bit strange, now you mention it. Even Captain Nielsen——"

"Yes, even that tough-minded old Swede, who'd go up to the devil himself and ask him for a light. All I could get out of him was: 'This place has an evil name among seafaring men, sir.' Then he said to me, very gravely: 'Don't you feel anything?'—as if the air about us was actually poisonous. Now, you mustn't laugh when I tell you this—I did feel something like a sudden chill.

"There was no breeze. The sea was as flat as a plate-glass window. We were drawing near the island then. What I felt was a—a mental chill; a sort of sudden dread."

---

1. **Caribbean**\ˈkă·rə ᐱbē·ən, kə ᐱrĭ·bē·ən\ of or pertaining to the arm of the Atlantic Ocean between the West Indies islands and the American mainland.

2. **Rio,** short for Rio de Janeiro\ˈrē·ō də zhə ᐱnā·rō\ the large seaport in southeast Brazil.

3. **Amazon**\ᐱă·mə ˈzŏn\ the huge river flowing in an easterly direction through Brazil, called the largest river in the world.

"Pure imagination," said Rainsford. "One superstitious sailor can taint the whole ship's company with his fear."

"Maybe. But sometimes I think sailors have an extra sense that tells them when they are in danger. Sometimes I think evil is a tangible thing—with wave lengths, just as sound and light have. An evil place can, so to speak, broadcast vibrations of evil. Anyhow, I'm glad we're getting out of this zone. Well, I think I'll turn in now, Rainsford."

"I'm not sleepy," said Rainsford. "I'm going to smoke another pipe up on the afterdeck."

"Good night, then, Rainsford. See you at breakfast."

"Right. Good night, Whitney."

There was no sound in the night as Rainsford sat there but the muffled throb of the engine that drove the yacht swiftly through the darkness, and the swish and ripple of the wash of the propeller.

Rainsford, reclining in a steamer chair, indolently puffed on his favorite brier. The sensuous drowsiness of the night was on him. "It's so dark," he thought, "that I could sleep without closing my eyes; the night would be my eyelids——"

An abrupt sound startled him. Off to the right he had heard it, and his ears, expert in such matters, could not be mistaken. Again he heard the sound, and again. Somewhere, off in the blackness, someone had fired a gun three times.

Rainsford sprang up and moved quickly to the rail, mystified. He strained his eyes in the direction from which the reports had come, but it was like trying to see through a blanket. He leaped upon the rail and balanced himself there, to get greater elevation; his pipe, striking a rope, was knocked from his mouth. He lunged for it; a short, hoarse cry came from his lips as he realized he had reached too far and had lost his balance. The cry was pinched off short as the blood-warm waters of the Caribbean Sea closed over his head.

He struggled up to the surface and tried to cry out, but the wash from the speeding yacht made him gag and strangle. Desperately he struck out with strong strokes after the receding lights of the yacht, but he stopped before he had swum fifty feet. A certain cool-headedness had come to him; it was not the first time he had been in a tight place. There was a chance that his cries could be heard by someone aboard the yacht, but that chance was slender, and grew more slender as the yacht raced on. He wrestled himself out of some of his clothes, and shouted with all his power. The lights of the yacht became faint and ever-vanishing fireflies; then they were blotted out entirely by the night.

Rainsford remembered that the shots had come from the right; and doggedly he swam in that direction, swimming with slow, deliberate strokes, conserving his strength. For a seemingly endless time he fought the sea. He began to count his strokes; he could do possibly a hundred more and then——

Rainsford heard a sound. It came out of the darkness, a high, screaming sound, the sound of an animal in an extremity of anguish and terror.

He did not recognize the animal that made the sound; he did not try to; with fresh vitality he swam toward the sound. He heard it again; then it was cut short by another noise, crisp, staccato.

"Pistol shot," muttered Rainsford, swimming on.

Ten minutes of determined effort brought another sound to his ears—the most welcome he had ever heard—the muttering and growling of the sea breaking on a rocky shore. He was almost on the rocks before he saw them; on a night less calm he would have been shattered against them. With his remaining strength he dragged himself from the swirling waters. Jagged crags appeared to jut up into the opaqueness; he forced himself upward, hand over hand. Gasping, his hands raw, he reached a flat place at the top. Dense jungle came down to the very edge of the cliffs. What perils that tangle of trees and underbrush might hold for him did not concern Rainsford just then. All he knew was that he was safe from his enemy, the sea, and that utter weariness was on him. He flung himself down and tumbled head-long into the deepest sleep of his life.

When he opened his eyes, he knew from the position of the sun that it was late in the afternoon. Sleep had given him new vigor; a sharp hunger was picking at him. He looked about him, almost cheerfully.

"Where there are pistol shots, there are men. Where there are men, there is food," he thought. But what kind of men, he wondered, in so forbidding a place? An unbroken front of snarled and ragged jungle fringed the shore. He saw no sign of a trail through the closely knit web of weeds and trees; it was easier to go along the shore, and he floundered along by the water. Not far from where he had landed, he stopped.

Some wounded thing, by the evidence a large animal, had thrashed about in the underbrush; the jungle weeds were crushed down and the moss was lacerated; one patch of weeds was stained crimson. A small, glittering object not far away caught Rainsford's eye and he picked it up. It was an empty cartridge.

"A twenty-two," he remarked. "That's odd. It must have been a fairly large animal, too. The hunter had his nerve with him to tackle it with a light gun. It's clear that the brute put up a fight. I suppose the first three shots I heard was when the hunter flushed his quarry and wounded it. The last shot was when he trailed it here and finished it."

He examined the ground closely and found what he had hoped to find—the print of hunting boots. They pointed along the cliff in the direction he had been going. Eagerly he hurried along, now slipping on a rotten log or a loose stone, but making headway; night was beginning to settle down on the island.

Bleak darkness was blacking out the sea and jungle when Rainsford sighted the lights. He came upon them as he turned a crook in the coast line, and his first thought was that he had come upon a village, for there were many lights. But as he forged along he saw to his great astonishment that all the lights were in one enormous building—a lofty structure with pointed towers plunging upward into the gloom. His eyes made out the shadowy outlines of a palatial château;[4] it was set on a high bluff, and on three sides of it cliffs dived down to where the sea licked greedy lips in the shadows.

"Mirage," thought Rainsford. But it was no mirage, he found, when he opened the tall spiked iron gate. The stone steps were real enough; the massive door with a leering gargoyle[5] for a knocker was real enough; yet about it all hung an air of unreality.

He lifted the knocker; and it creaked up stiffly, as if it had never before been used. He let it fall, and it startled him with its booming loudness. He thought he heard steps within; the door remained closed. Again Rainsford lifted the heavy knocker, and let it fall. The door opened then, opened as suddenly as if it were on a spring, and Rainsford stood blinking in the river of glaring gold light that poured out. The first thing his eyes discerned was the largest man he had ever seen—a gigantic creature, solidly made and black-bearded to the waist. In his hand the man held a long-barreled revolver, and he was pointing it straight at Rainsford's heart. Out of the snarl of beard two small eyes regarded Rainsford.

"Don't be alarmed," said Rainsford, with a smile which he hoped was disarming. "I'm no robber. I fell off a yacht. My name is Sanger Rainsford of New York City."

The menacing look in the eyes did not change. The revolver pointed as rigidly as if the giant were a statue. He gave no sign that he understood Rainsford's words, or that he had even heard them. He was dressed in uniform, a black uniform trimmed with gray astrakhan.

"I'm Sanger Rainsford of New York," Rainsford began again. "I fell off a yacht. I am hungry."

The man's only answer was to raise with his thumb the hammer of his revolver. Then Rainsford saw the man's free hand go to his forehead in a military salute, and he saw him click his

---

4. **château**\shə ˄tō\ the French word for castle; also a large country house.
5. **gargoyle**\˄gar 'gȯil\ a protruding ornament in the shape of a fantastic animal.

heels together and stand at attention. Another man was coming down the broad marble steps, an erect, slender man in evening clothes. He advanced to Rainsford and held out his hand.

In a cultivated voice marked by a slight accent that gave it added precision and deliberateness, he said: "It is a very great pleasure and honor to welcome Mr. Sanger Rainsford, the celebrated hunter, to my home."

Automatically Rainsford shook the man's hand.

"I've read your book about hunting snow leopards in Tibet,[6] you see," explained the man. "I am General Zaroff."

Rainsford's first impression was that the man was singularly handsome; his second was that there was an original, almost bizarre quality about the general's face. He was a tall man past middle age, for his hair was a vivid white; but his thick eyebrows and pointed military mustache were as black as the night from which Rainsford had come. His eyes, too, were black and very bright. He had high cheekbones, a sharp-cut nose, a spare, dark face, the face of a man used to giving orders, the face of an aristocrat. Turning to the giant in uniform, the general made a sign. The giant put away his pistol, saluted, withdrew.

"Ivan is an incredibly strong fellow," remarked the general, "but he has the misfortune to be deaf and dumb. A simple fellow, but I'm afraid, like all his race, a bit of a savage."

"Is he Russian?"

"He is a Cossack,"[7] said the general, and his smile showed red lips and pointed teeth. "So am I."

"Come," he said, "we shouldn't be chatting here. We can talk later. Now you want clothes, food, rest. You shall have them. This is a most restful spot."

Ivan had reappeared, and the general spoke to him with lips that moved but gave forth no sound.

"Follow Ivan, if you please, Mr. Rainsford," said the general. "I was about to have my dinner when you came. I'll wait for you. You'll find that my clothes will fit you, I think."

It was to a huge, beam-ceilinged bedroom with a canopied bed big enough for six men that Rainsford followed the silent giant. Ivan laid out an evening suit, and Rainsford, as he put it on, noticed that it came from a London tailor who ordinarily cut and sewed for none below the rank of duke.

The dining room to which Ivan conducted him was in many ways remarkable. There was a medieval magnificence about it; it suggested a baronial hall of feudal times with its oaken panels, its high ceiling, its vast refectory table where two score men could sit down to eat. About the hall were the mounted heads of many animals—lions, tigers, elephants, moose, bears; larger or more perfect specimens Rainsford had never seen. At the great table the general was sitting alone.

Rainsford noted the table appointments were of the finest—the linen, the crystal, the silver, the china.

They were eating *borsch,* the rich, red soup with sour cream so dear to Russian palates. Half apologetically General Zaroff said: "We do our best to preserve the amenities of civilization here. Please forgive any lapses. We are well off the beaten track, you know. Do you think the champagne has suffered from its long ocean trip?"

"Not in the least," declared Rainsford. He was finding the general a most thoughtful and affable host, a true cosmopolite. But there was one small trait of the general's that made Rainsford uncomfortable. Whenever he looked up from his plate he found the general studying him, appraising him narrowly.

"Perhaps," said General Zaroff, "you were surprised that I recognized your name. You see, I read all books on hunting published in English, French, and Russian. I have but one passion in my life, Mr. Rainsford, and that is the hunt."

---

6. **Tibet**\tə ▲bĕt\ central Asian country between China and India.
7. **Cossack**\▲kŏ 'sək\ one of a warlike people from the plains of southeast Russia. They are noted for their horsemanship.

"You have some wonderful heads here," said Rainsford as he ate a particularly well-cooked filet mignon. "That Cape buffalo is the largest I ever saw."

"Oh, that fellow. Yes, he was a monster."

"Did he charge you?"

"Hurled me against a tree," said the general. "Fractured my skull. But I got the brute."

"I've always thought," said Rainsford, "that Cape buffalo is the most dangerous of all big game."

For a moment the general did not reply; he was smiling his curious red-lipped smile. Then he said slowly: "No. You are wrong, sir. The Cape buffalo is not the most dangerous big game." He sipped his wine. "Here in my preserve on this island," he said in the same slow tone, "I hunt more dangerous game."

Rainsford expressed his surprise. "Is there big game on this island?"

The general nodded. "The biggest."

"Really?"

"Oh, it isn't here naturally, of course. I have to stock the island."

"What have you imported, general?" Rainsford asked. "Tigers?"

The general smiled. 'No," he said. "Hunting tigers ceased to interest me some years ago. I exhausted their possibilities, you see. No thrill left in tigers, no real danger. I live for danger, Mr. Rainsford."

The general took from his pocket a gold cigarette case and offered his guest a long black cigarette with a silver tip; it was perfumed and gave off a smell like incense.

"We will have some capital hunting, you and I," said the general. "I shall be most glad to have your society."

"But what game——" began Rainsford.

"I'll tell you," said the general. "You will be amused, I know. I think I may say, in all modesty, that I have done a rare thing. I have invented a new sensation. May I pour you another glass of port, Mr. Rainsford?"

"Thank you, general."

The general filled both glasses, and said: "God makes some men poets. Some He makes kings, some beggars. Me He made a hunter. My hand was made for the trigger, my father said. He was a very rich man with a quarter of a million acres in the Crimea,[8] and he was an ardent sportsman. When I was only five years old, he gave me a little gun to shoot sparrows with. When I shot some of his prize turkeys with it, he did not punish me; he complimented me on my marksmanship. I killed my first bear when I was ten. My whole life has been one prolonged hunt. I went into the army—it was expected of noblemen's sons—and for a time commanded a division of Cossack cavalry, but my real interest was always the hunt. I have hunted every kind of game in every land. It would be impossible for me to tell you how many animals I have killed."

The general puffed at his cigarette.

"After the debacle in Russia I left the country, for it was imprudent for an officer of the Czar[9] to stay there. Many noble Russians had lost everything. Luckily, I had invested heavily in American securities, so I shall never have to open a tea room in Monte Carlo or drive a taxi in Paris. Naturally, I continued to hunt—grizzlies in your Rockies, crocodiles in the Ganges,[10] rhinoceroses in East Africa. It was in Africa that the Cape buffalo hit me and laid me up for six months. As soon as I recovered I started for the Amazon to hunt jaguars, for I had heard they were unusually cunning. They weren't." The Cossack sighed. "They were no match at all for a hunter with his wits about him, and a high-powered rifle. I was bitterly disappointed. I was lying in my tent with a splitting headache one night when a terrible thought pushed its way into my mind. Hunting was beginning to bore me! And hunting, remember, had been my life. I have heard that in America businessmen often go to pieces when they give up the business that has been their life."

---

8. **Crimea**\krai ▲mē•ə\ a peninsula jutting into the Black Sea from southwestern Russia.
9. The general here refers to the overthrow of the Czar's (Tsar) government in Russia, 1917, with confiscation of the estates of the old Russian nobility.
10. **the Ganges**\▲găn•jēz\ the great river flowing south in northern and northeastern India.

"Yes, that's so," said Rainsford.

The general smiled. "I had no wish to go to pieces," he said. "I must do something. Now, mine is an analytical mind, Mr. Rainsford. Doubtless that is why I enjoy the problems of the chase."

"No doubt, General Zaroff."

"So," continued the general, "I asked myself why the hunt no longer fascinated me. You are much younger than I am, Mr. Rainsford, and have not hunted as much; but you perhaps can guess the answer."

"What was it?"

"Simply this; hunting had ceased to be what you call 'a sporting proposition.' It had become too easy. I always got my quarry. Always. There is no greater bore than perfection."

The general lit a fresh cigarette.

"No animal had a chance with me any more. That is no boast; it is a mathematical certainty. The animal had nothing but his legs and his instinct. Instinct is no match for reason. When I thought of this it was a tragic moment for me, I can tell you."

Rainsford leaned across the table, absorbed in what his host was saying.

"It came to me as an inspiration what I must do," the general went on.

"And that was?"

The general smiled the quiet smile of one who has faced an obstacle and surmounted it with success. "I had to invent a new animal to hunt," he said.

"A new animal? You're joking."

"Not at all," said the general. "I never joke about hunting. I needed a new animal. I found one. So I bought this island, built this house, and here I do my hunting. The island is perfect for my purposes—there are jungles with a maze of trails in them, hills, swamps——"

"But the animal, General Zaroff?"

"Oh," said the general, "it supplies me with the most exciting hunting in the world. No other hunting compares with it for an instant. Every day I hunt, and I never grow bored now, for I have a quarry with which I can match my wits."

Rainsford's bewilderment showed in his face.

"I wanted the ideal animal to hunt," explained the general. "So I said: 'What are the attributes of an ideal quarry?' And the answer was, of course: 'It must have courage, cunning, and, above all, it must be able to reason.' "

"But no animal can reason," objected Rainsford.

"My dear fellow," said the general, "there is one that can."

"But you can't mean—" gasped Rainsford.

"And why not?"

"I can't believe you are serious, General Zaroff. This is a grisly joke."

"Why should I not be serious? I am speaking of hunting."

"Hunting? General Zaroff, what you speak of is murder."

The general laughed with entire good nature. He regarded Rainsford quizzically. "I refuse to believe that so modern and civilized a young man as you seem to be harbors romantic ideas about the value of human life. Surely your experiences in the war——"

"Did not make me condone cold-blooded murder," finished Rainsford stiffly.

Laughter shook the general. "How extraordinarily droll you are!" he said. "One does not expect nowadays to find a young man of the educated class, even in America, with such a naïve, and, if I may say so, mid-Victorian[11] point of view. Ah, well, doubtless you had Puritan ancestors. So many Americans appear to have had. I'll wager you'll forget your notions when you go hunting with me. You've a genuine new thrill in store for you, Mr. Rainsford."

"Thank you, I'm a hunter, not a murderer."

"Dear me," said the general, quite unruffled, "again that unpleasant word. But I think I can show you that your scruples are quite ill-founded."

"Yes?"

---

11. **mid-Victorian**\ˈmĭd ˈvĭk ▲tō·rē·ən\ suitable to the times of Queen Victoria of England, whose reign (1837–1901) was marked by ideas now regarded as narrow and limited.

"Life is for the strong, to be lived by the strong, and, if needs be, taken by the strong. The weak of the world were put here to give the strong pleasure. I am strong. Why should I not use my gift? If I wish to hunt, why should I not? I hunt the scum of the earth—sailors from tramp ships—lascars,[12] blacks, Chinese, whites, mongrels—a thoroughbred horse or hound is worth more than a score of them."

"But they are men," said Rainsford hotly.

"Precisely," said the general. "That is why I use them. It gives me pleasure. They can reason, after a fashion. So they are dangerous."

"But where do you get them?"

The general's left eyelid fluttered down in a wink. "This island is called Ship-Trap," he answered. "Sometimes an angry god of the high seas sends them to me. Sometimes, when Providence is not so kind, I help Providence a bit. Come to the window with me."

Rainsford went to the window and looked out toward the sea.

"Watch! Out there!" exclaimed the general, pointing into the night. Rainsford's eyes saw only blackness, and then, as the general pressed a button, far out to sea Rainsford saw the flash of lights.

The general chuckled. "They indicate a channel," he said, "where there's none: giant rocks with razor edges crouch like a sea monster with wide-open jaws. They can crush a ship as easily as I crush this nut." He dropped a walnut on the hardwood floor and brought his heel grinding down on it. "Oh, yes," he said, casually, as if in answer to a question, "I have electricity. We try to be civilized here."

"Civilized? And you shoot down men?"

A trace of anger was in the general's black eyes, but it was there for but a second; then he said, in his most pleasant manner: "Dear me, what a righteous young man you are! I assure you I do not do the thing you suggest. That would be barbarous. I treat these visitors with every consideration. They get plenty of good food and exercise. They get into splendid physical condition. You shall see for yourself tomorrow."

"What do you mean?"

"We shall visit my training school," smiled the general. "It's in the cellar. I have about a dozen pupils down there now. They're from the Spanish bark San Lucar[13] that had the bad luck to go on the rocks out there. A very inferior lot, I regret to say. Poor specimens and more accustomed to the deck than to the jungle."

He raised his hand, and Ivan brought thick Turkish coffee. Rainsford, with an effort, held his tongue in check.

"It's a game, you see," pursued the general blandly, "I suggest to one of them that we go hunting. I give him a supply of food and an excellent hunting knife. I give him three hours' start. I am to follow, armed only with a pistol of the smallest caliber and range. If my quarry eludes me for three whole days, he wins the game. If I find him"—the general smiled—"he loses."

"Suppose he refuses to be hunted?"

"Oh," said the general, "I give him his option, of course. He need not play that game if he doesn't wish to. If he does not wish to hunt, I turn him over to Ivan. Ivan once had the honor of serving as official knouter to the Great White Czar,[14] and he has his own ideas of sport. Invariably, Mr. Rainsford, invariably they choose the hunt."

"And if they win?"

The smile on the general's face widened. "To date I have not lost," he said.

Then he added, hastily: "I don't wish you to think me a braggart, Mr. Rainsford. Many of them afford only the most elementary sort of problem. Occasionally I strike a tartar.[15] One almost did win. I eventually had to use the dogs."

"The dogs?"

---

12. **lascar**\▲läs·kər\ a native East Indian sailor.
13. **San Lucar**\'san 'lū ▲kar\.
14. The Great White Czar was Alexander III, who reigned from 1881 to 1894. Ivan punished criminals and opponents of the Czar by flogging them with the knout, a leather and metal whip.
15. **to strike a tartar** is to meet with an opponent who shows unexpected strength or resistance.

"This way, please. I'll show you."

The general steered Rainsford to a window. The lights from the windows sent a flickering illumination that made grotesque patterns on the courtyard below, and Rainsford could see moving about there a dozen or so huge black shapes; as they turned toward him, their eyes glittered greenly.

"A rather good lot, I think," observed the general. "They are let out at seven every night. If anyone should try to get into my house—or out of it—something extremely regrettable would occur to him." He hummed a snatch of a gay French song.

"And now," said the general, "I want to show you my new collection of heads. Will you come with me to the library?"

"I hope," said Rainsford, "that you will excuse me tonight, General Zaroff. I'm really not feeling at all well."

"Ah, indeed?" the general inquired solicitously. "Well, I suppose that's only natural after your long swim. You need a good, restful night's sleep. Tomorrow you'll feel like a new man, I'll wager. Then we'll hunt, eh? I've one rather promising prospect——"

Rainsford was hurrying from the room.

"Sorry you can't go with me tonight," called the general. "I expect rather fair sport—a big, strong black. He looks resourceful—— Well, good night, Mr. Rainsford; I hope you have a good night's rest."

The bed was good, and the pajamas of the softest silk, and he was tired in every fiber of his being; nevertheless Rainsford could not quiet his brain with the opiate of sleep. He lay, eyes wide open. Once he thought he heard stealthy steps in the corridor outside his room. He sought to throw open the door; it would not open. He went to the window and looked out. His room was high up in one of the towers. The lights of the château were out now, and it was dark and silent, but there was a fragment of sallow moon, and by its wan light he could see, dimly, the courtyard; there, weaving in and out in the pattern of shadow, were black, noiseless forms; the hounds heard him at the window

and looked up, expectantly, with their green eyes. Rainsford went back to the bed and lay down. By many methods he tried to put himself to sleep. He had achieved a doze when, just as morning began to come, he heard, far off in the jungle, the faint report of a pistol.

General Zaroff did not appear until luncheon. He was dressed faultlessly in the tweeds of a country squire. He was solicitous about the state of Rainsford's health.

"As for me," sighed the general, "I do not feel so well. I am worried, Mr. Rainsford. Last night I detected traces of my old complaint."

To Rainsford's questioning glance the general said: "Ennui. Boredom."

Then, taking a second helping of crêpes suzette,[16] the general explained: "The hunting was not good last night. The fellow lost his head. He made a straight trail that offered no problems at all. That's the trouble with these sailors; they have dull brains to begin with, and they do not know how to get about in the woods. They do excessively stupid and obvious things. It's most annoying. Will you have another glass of Chablis, Mr. Rainsford?"

"General," said Rainsford firmly, "I wish to leave this island at once."

The general raised his eyebrows; he seemed hurt. "But, my dear fellow," he protested, "you've only just come. You've had no hunting——"

"I wish to go today," said Rainsford. He saw the dead black eyes of the general on him, studying him. General Zaroff's face suddenly brightened.

He filled Rainsford's glass with venerable Chablis from a dusty bottle.

"Tonight," said the general, "we will hunt—you and I."

Rainsford shook his head. "No, general," he said. "I will not hunt."

The general shrugged his shoulders and delicately ate a hothouse grape. "As you wish, my

---

16. **crêpes suzette** \\▲krāp sū ▲zĕt\\ thin, sweet pancakes rolled with various sauces.

friend," he said. "The choice rests entirely with you. But may I not venture to suggest that you will find my idea of sport more diverting than Ivan's?"

He nodded toward the corner to where the giant stood, scowling, his thick arms crossed on his hogshead of a chest.

"You don't mean——" cried Rainsford.

"My dear fellow," said the general, "have I not told you I always mean what I say about hunting? This is really an inspiration. I drink to a foeman worthy of my steel—at last."

The general raised his glass, but Rainsford sat staring at him.

"You'll find this game worth playing," the general said enthusiastically. "Your brain against mine. Your woodcraft against mine. Your strength and stamina against mine. Outdoor chess! And the stake is not without value, eh?"

"And if I win——" began Rainsford huskily.

"I'll cheerfully acknowledge myself defeated if I do not find you by midnight of the third day," said General Zaroff. "My sloop will place you on the mainland near a town."

The general read what Rainsford was thinking.

"Oh, you can trust me," said the Cossack. "I will give you my word as a gentleman and a sportsman. Of course, you in turn must agree to say nothing of your visit here."

"I'll agree to nothing of the kind," said Rainsford.

"Oh," said the general, "in that case——But why discuss that now? Three days hence we can discuss it over a bottle of wine, unless——"

The general sipped his wine.

Then a businesslike air animated him. "Ivan," he said to Rainsford, "will supply you with hunting clothes, food, a knife. I suggest you wear moccasins; they leave a poorer trail. I suggest, too, that you avoid the big swamp in the southeast corner of the island. We call it Death Swamp. There's quicksand there. One foolish fellow tried it. The deplorable part of it was that Lazarus followed him. You can imagine my feelings, Mr. Rainsford. I loved Lazarus; he was

the finest hound in my pack. Well, I must beg you to excuse me now. I always take a siesta after lunch. You'll hardly have time for a nap, I fear. You'll want to start, no doubt. I shall not follow till dusk. Hunting at night is so much more exciting, don't you think? *Au revoir*,[17] Mr. Rainsford, *au revoir*."

General Zaroff, with a deep, courtly bow, strolled from the room. From another door came Ivan. Under one arm he carried khaki hunting clothes, a haversack of food, a leather sheath containing a long-bladed hunting knife; his right hand rested on a cocked revolver thrust in the crimson sash about his waist. . . .

Rainsford had fought his way through the bush for two hours. "I must keep my nerve. I must keep my nerve," he said through tight teeth.

He had not been entirely clear-headed when the château gates snapped shut behind him. His whole idea at first was to put distance between himself and General Zaroff; and, to this end, he had plunged along, spurred on by something very much like panic. Now he had got a grip on himself, had stopped, and was taking stock of himself and the situation.

He saw that straight flight was futile; inevitably it would bring him face to face with the sea. He was in a picture with a frame of water, and his operations, clearly, must take place within that frame.

"I'll give him a trail to follow," muttered Rainsford, and he struck off from the rude path he had been following into the trackless wilderness. He executed a series of intricate loops; he doubled on his trail again and again, recalling all the lore of the fox hunt, and all the dodges of the fox. Night found him leg-weary, with hands and face lashed by the branches, on a thickly wooded ridge. He knew it would be insane to blunder on through the dark, even if he had the strength. His need for rest was imperative and he thought: "I have played the fox, now I must

---

17. **au revoir**\ō rə ▲vwar\ French for "good-bye; till I see you again."

play the cat of the fable."[18] A big tree with a thick trunk and outspread branches was nearby, and, taking care to leave not the slightest mark, he climbed up, and stretching out on one of the broad limbs, after a fashion, rested. Rest brought him new confidence and almost a feeling of security. Even so zealous a hunter as General Zaroff could not trace him there, he told himself; only the devil himself could follow that complicated trail through the jungle after dark. But, perhaps, the general was a devil——

An apprehensive night crawled slowly by like a wounded snake, and sleep did not visit Rainsford, although the silence of a dead world was on the jungle. Toward morning when a dingy gray was varnishing the sky, the cry of some startled bird focused Rainsford's attention in that direction. Something was coming through the bush, coming slowly, carefully, coming by the same winding way Rainsford had come. He flattened himself down on the limb, and through a screen of leaves almost as thick as tapestry, he watched. The thing that was approaching was a man.

It was General Zaroff. He made his way along with his eyes fixed in utmost concentration on the ground before him. He paused, almost beneath the tree, dropped to his knees and studied the ground. Rainsford's impulse was to hurl himself down like a panther, but he saw that the general's right hand held something metallic—a small automatic pistol.

The hunter shook his head several times, as if he were puzzled. Then he straightened up and took from his case one of his black cigarettes; its pungent incenselike smoke floated up to Rainsford's nostrils.

Rainsford held his breath. The general's eyes had left the ground and were traveling inch by inch up the tree. Rainsford froze there, every muscle tensed for a spring. But the sharp eyes of the hunter stopped before they reached the limb where Rainsford lay; a smile spread over his brown face. Very deliberately he blew a smoke ring into the air; then he turned his back

18. **the cat of the fable,** Rainsford has used the craft of a fox and now he must watch patiently like a cat at a mousehole.

on the tree and walked carelessly away, back along the trail he had come. The swish of the underbrush against his hunting boots grew fainter and fainter.

The pent-up air burst hotly from Rainsford's lungs. His first thought made him feel sick and numb. The general could follow a trail through the woods at night; he could follow an extremely difficult trail; he must have uncanny powers; only by the merest chance had the Cossack failed to see his quarry.

Rainsford's second thought was even more terrible. It sent a shudder of cold horror through his whole being. Why had the general smiled? Why had he turned back?

Rainsford did not want to believe what his reason told him was true, but the truth was as evident as the sun that by now had pushed through the morning mists. The general was playing with him! The general was saving him for another day's sport! The Cossack was the cat; *he* was the mouse. Then it was that Rainsford knew the full meaning of terror.

"I will not lose my nerve. I will not."

He slid down from the tree, and struck off again into the woods. His face was set and he forced the machinery of his mind to function. Three hundred yards from his hiding place he stopped where a huge dead tree leaned precariously on a smaller, living one. Throwing off his sack of food, Rainsford took his knife from its sheath and began to work with all his energy.

The job was finished at last, and he threw himself down behind a fallen log a hundred feet away. He did not have to wait long. The cat was coming again to play with the mouse.

Following the trail with the sureness of a bloodhound, came General Zaroff. Nothing escaped those searching black eyes, no crushed blade of grass, no bent twig, no mark, no matter how faint, in the moss. So intent was the Cossack on his stalking that he was upon the thing Rainsford had made before he saw it. His foot touched the protruding bough that was the trigger. Even as he touched it, the general sensed his danger and leaped back with the agility of an ape. But he was not quite quick

enough; the dead tree, delicately adjusted to rest on the cut living one, crashed down and struck the general a glancing blow on the shoulder as it fell; but for his alertness, he must have been smashed beneath it. He staggered, but he did not fall; nor did he drop his revolver. He stood there, rubbing his injured shoulder; and Rainsford, with fear again gripping his heart, heard the general's mocking laugh ring through the jungle.

"Rainsford," called the general, "if you are within sound of my voice, as I suppose you are, let me congratulate you. Not many men know how to make a Malay man-catcher. Luckily, for me, I, too, have hunted in Malacca.[19] You are proving interesting, Mr. Rainsford. I am going now to have my wound dressed; it's only a slight one. But I shall be back. I shall be back."

When the general, nursing his bruised shoulder, had gone, Rainsford took up his flight again. It was flight now, a desperate, hopeless flight that carried him on for some hours. Dusk came, then darkness, and still he pressed on. The ground grew softer under his moccasins; the vegetation grew ranker, denser; insects bit him savagely. Then, as he stepped forward, his foot sank into the ooze. He tried to wrench it back, but the muck sucked viciously at his foot as if it were a giant leech. With a violent effort, he tore his foot loose. He knew where he was now. Death Swamp and its quicksand.

His hands were tight closed as if his nerve were something tangible that someone in the darkness was trying to tear from his grip. The softness of the earth had given him an idea. He stepped back from the quicksand a dozen feet or so and, like some huge prehistoric beaver, he began to dig.

Rainsford had dug himself in in France when a second's delay meant death. That had been a placid pastime compared to his digging now. The pit grew deeper; when it was above his shoulders, he climbed out and from some hard saplings cut stakes and sharpened them to a fine point. These stakes he planted in the

19. **Malacca**\mə ˈlă·kə\ an area on the southwestern coast of Malaya in extreme southeastern Asia.

bottom of the pit with the points sticking up. With flying fingers he wove a rough carpet of weeds and branches, and with it he covered the mouth of the pit. Then, wet with sweat and aching with tiredness, he crouched behind the stump of a lightning-charred tree.

He knew his pursuer was coming; he heard the padding sound of feet on the soft earth, and the night breeze brought him the perfume of the general's cigarette. It seemed to Rainsford that the general was coming with unusual swiftness; he was not feeling his way along, foot by foot. Rainsford, crouching there, could not see the general, nor could he see the pit. He lived a year in a minute. Then he felt an impulse to cry aloud with joy, for he heard the sharp crackle of the breaking branches as the cover of the pit gave way; he heard the sharp scream of pain as the pointed stakes found their mark. He leaped up from his place of concealment. Then he cowered back. Three feet from the pit a man was standing, with an electric torch in his hand.

"You've done well, Rainsford," the voice of the general called. "Your Burmese tiger pit[20] has claimed one of my best dogs. Again you score. I think, Mr. Rainsford, I'll see what you can do against my whole pack. I'm going home for a rest now. Thank you for a most amusing evening."

At daybreak Rainsford, lying near the swamp, was awakened by a sound that made him know that he had new things to learn about fear. It was a distant sound, faint and wavering; but he knew it. It was the baying of a pack of hounds.

Rainsford knew he could do one of two things. He could stay where he was and wait. That was suicide. He could flee. That was postponing the inevitable. For a moment he stood there, thinking. An idea that held a wild chance came to him, and, tightening his belt, he headed away from the swamp. The baying of the hounds drew nearer, then still nearer, nearer, ever nearer. On a ridge Rainsford climbed a tree. Down a watercourse, not a quarter of a mile away, he could see the bush

moving. Straining his eyes, he saw the lean figure of General Zaroff; just ahead of him Rainsford made out another figure whose wide shoulders surged through the tall jungle weeds; it was the giant Ivan, and he seemed pulled forward by some unseen force; Rainsford knew that Ivan must be holding the pack in leash.

They would be on him any minute now. His mind worked frantically. He thought of a native trick he had learned in Uganda.[21] He slid down the tree. He caught hold of a springy young sapling and to it he fastened his hunting knife, with the blade pointing down the trail; with a bit of wild grapevine he tied back the sapling. Then he ran for his life. The hounds raised their voices as they hit the fresh scent. Rainsford knew now how an animal at bay feels.

He had to stop to get his breath. The baying of the hounds stopped abruptly; and Rainsford's heart stopped, too. They must have reached the knife.

He shinned excitedly up a tree and looked back. His pursuers had stopped. But the hope that was in Rainsford's brain when he climbed died, for he saw in the shallow valley that General Zaroff was still on his feet. But Ivan was not. The knife, driven by the recoil of the springing tree, had not wholly failed.

Rainsford had hardly tumbled to the ground when the pack took up the cry again.

"Nerve, nerve, nerve!" he panted, as he dashed along. A blue gap showed between the trees dead ahead. Ever nearer drew the hounds. Rainsford forced himself on toward that gap. He reached it. It was the shore of the sea. Across a cove he could see the gloomy gray stone of the château. Twenty feet below him the sea rumbled and hissed. Rainsford hesitated. He heard the hounds. Then he leaped far out into the sea.

---

20. **The Burmese**\'bər ▲mēz\ **tiger pit** is a deep pit covered over with light brush wood and used to trap tigers in Burma\ ▲bər•mə\, the country in southeastern Asia between India and Thailand.

21. **Uganda**\'ū ▲gan•də\ an area in East Africa north of Lake Victoria.

When the general and his pack reached the place by the sea, the Cossack stopped. For some minutes he stood regarding the blue-green expanse of water. He shrugged his shoulders. Then he sat down, took a drink of brandy from a silver flask, lit a perfumed cigarette, and hummed a bit from *Madame Butterfly*.

General Zaroff had an exceedingly good dinner in his great paneled dining hall that evening. With it he had a bottle of his rarest wine. Two slight annoyances kept him from perfect enjoyment. One was the thought that it would be difficult to replace Ivan; the other was that his quarry had escaped him; of course the American hadn't played the game—so thought the general as he tasted his after-dinner liqueur. In his library he read, to soothe himself, from the works of Marcus Aurelius.[22] At ten he went up to his bedroom. He was deliciously tired, he said to himself, as he locked himself in. There was a little moonlight; so, before turning on his light, he went to the window and looked down at the courtyard. He could see the great hounds, and he called: "Better luck another time," to them. Then he switched on the light.

A man, who had been hiding in the curtains of the bed, was standing there.

"Rainsford!" screamed the general. "How did you get here?"

"Swam," said Rainsford. "I found it quicker than walking through the jungle."

The general sucked in his breath and smiled. "I congratulate you," he said. "You have won the game."

Rainsford did not smile. "I am still a beast at bay," he said, in a low, hoarse voice. "Get ready, General Zaroff."

The general made one of his deepest bows. "I see," he said. "Splendid! One of us is to furnish a repast for the hounds. The other will sleep in this very excellent bed. On guard, Rainsford."

He had never slept in a better bed, Rainsford decided.

I

THE HUNTER BECOMES THE HUNTED

"Who cares how a jaguar feels?" says Rainsford, at the beginning of the story. He seems to agree with General Zaroff's philosophy: "Life is for the strong. . . . The weak in the world were put here to give the strong pleasure." The meaning of such a philosophy is brought home to Rainsford when he himself becomes the "weak," the hunted.

1. In what ways are Rainsford and Whitney different from each other? How does the author reveal Rainsford's attitude toward the animals he hunted? In what two situations does Rainsford feel that Whitney is not a "realist"—one who sees things as they really are? How is Whitney proved right in both cases?

2. Why does General Zaroff recognize Rainsford's name? The author establishes Zaroff as an evil man by a series of clues and revealing statements. What convinces us of this beyond question?

3. Authors often take advantage of the fact that a word can have more than one meaning. An excellent example of this is the title of this story. What two meanings of "game" make sense in this title?

4. How does Rainsford show his wide knowledge of hunting tactics? Although you are not told how Rainsford disposed of General Zaroff, you do know that he gave him a chance to fight for his life. Why do you think Rainsford gives him this chance? What might Rainsford have done instead?

II

IMPLICATIONS

Many times, after you have read a story, you realize that it suggests some puzzling or debatable ideas about how people act and think. Throughout this book you will find these implied ideas set forth in statements for you to consider and discuss. You

---

22. **Marcus Aurelius**\ˈmar·kəs ɔ ˈrē·lē·əs\ a Roman emperor (A.D. 161–180) and famous stoic philosopher, who attempted to govern Rome and himself by stern standards and indifference to pleasure and pain.

do not have to agree. These statements or propositions may be true or they may be false. You may even decide that you do not have enough evidence to make any decision at all.

The propositions are meant to provide an *adventure in thinking*. They ask you to probe for deeper, broader meanings in literature, to think carefully about ideas. Such discussion should lead to a better understanding of people and of what you read.

Now that you have read "The Most Dangerous Game," consider and discuss these propositions. Remember: You are free to disagree!

1. Men in history have actually held General Zaroff's point of view. His beliefs would have been accepted in ancient Sparta or in Nazi Germany.

2. Hunting, just for thrill and adventure, should be outlawed. It makes no difference what animal is being hunted.

III
TECHNIQUES

Suspense and Foreshadowing

1. Even before General Zaroff and Ivan appear, Rainsford has seen and heard a number of things that arouse apprehension in the reader. Discuss what these things are.

2. The introduction of Ivan and his master increases concern for Rainsford's safety. Describe Zaroff and Ivan. When do you first suspect that Zaroff is evil? What feature of his face makes him seem like a beast of prey?

3. Why is suspense increased when Rainsford indicates that if he returned to the mainland he would not remain silent about the general's activities?

Conflict

1. What is the main conflict in "The Most Dangerous Game"? Are the two opposing forces evenly matched? Is there a conflict of ideas or beliefs in this story? What is it?

2. Conflict cannot be resolved or settled without *action*. The moment of most crucial action is usually the high point of interest and suspense. This moment is called the *climax* of the story. "The Most Dangerous Game" has several episodes, and each episode has its own climax. What is the most im-

portant climax or turning point in the story? Which moment of action finally settles the conflict?

Imaginative Language

Much of the imagery in this short story is made up of *similes* and *metaphors*. Both simile and metaphor are used to suggest a likeness or resemblance in things which are unlike or dissimilar. While the simile compares one thing with another and uses the words *like* or *as*, the metaphor states directly that one thing is another. Thus, from "The Most Dangerous Game" an example of simile would be: ". . . giant rocks with razor edges crouch *like* a sea monster with wide-open jaws. They can crush a ship *as* easily as I crush this nut."

Metaphor is used in the sentence: ". . . the sea licked greedy lips in the shadows."

1. Locate five examples of imagery expressed in simile or metaphor in the selection you have just read.

2. Richard Connell's choice of verbs in combination with other descriptive words makes his imagery especially vivid. Locate and discuss those word combinations in the following quotations which appeal most strongly to the senses.

a. The cry was pinched off short as the blood-warm waters of the Caribbean Sea closed over his head.

b. . . . the dank tropical night . . . pressed its thick, warm blackness in upon the yacht.

c. . . . and on three sides of it cliffs dived down to where the sea licked greedy lips in the shadows.

d. . . . there, weaving in and out in the pattern of shadow, were black, noiseless forms; . . .

e. He shinned excitedly up a tree and looked back.

f. Twenty feet below him the sea rumbled and hissed.

g. An apprehensive night crawled slowly by like a wounded snake.

Suspense, Conflict, Foreshadowing, Imaginative Language

The great American writer Emerson said, "'Tis the good reader that makes the good book." The more you read, the more you will become aware of the devices writers use to make their effects. A good writer has something to *communicate* to his reader—a story, an argument, a joke, a way of feeling. The writer is speaking to you through the printed page. It is your job to listen carefully. You must learn to hear what the author is really saying. The task of this book is to help you become a more critical reader, but not so critical that you lose the joy of reading. In fact, knowing how to appreciate good writing increases your reading pleasure.

Adventure is the general theme uniting this first group of selections. The study notes are concerned with elements that make good adventure stories exciting: *Suspense, Conflict, Foreshadowing,* and *Imaginative Language.*

Suspense is a state of excited uncertainty. The reader intensely wants to know *what* is going to happen? *Who* is going to appear? *How* will the hero escape? The adventure writer deliberately withholds the answers as long as he can.

One moment of high suspense in "The Most Dangerous Game" comes on page 13 when Rainsford is hiding in a tree. General Zaroff is standing directly beneath him: "The general's eyes had left the ground and were traveling inch by inch up the tree. . . ."

Foreshadowing is one of the chief means of creating suspense. The writer plants hints of dangers and perils that lie ahead. In "The Most Dangerous Game," even the title foreshadows the excitement. The mood of the story is set immediately by the name of the mysterious island (Ship-Trap Island) and by the description of the "dank tropical night that was palpable as it pressed its thick, warm blackness in upon the yacht."

Conflict is the struggle between opposing forces. Without conflict there is no drama, no interest, no suspense—no story. The conflicting action may be between a man and—

1. other men or animals,

2. forces of nature, such as a storm or a flood,

3. society, or groups of men who hold opposing ideas,

4. himself.

The last item, the conflict within a single man, is the basis for much of the world's best literature. Sometimes a man may feel two ways about a problem; the conflict comes as he decides how to act.

In real life, a person usually has more than one problem or conflict to handle. So it is in most stories. There is more than one conflict involved. Usually, however, there is a central conflict which is the most important. It is the unraveling of this main conflict that makes for the *plot.*

Plot is the series of related incidents put together in a planned order so that a solution to the conflict is reached. If the plot is closely knit, no incident can be removed or changed in position without destroying the story's unity.

Many modern stories are simply a series of incidents loosely held together by a central character. These are stories without plot. They simply begin at one place and end at another without any sort of satisfactory solution, however interesting the story may be.

The tightly plotted story, then, has a beginning, a middle, and an end. Somewhere near the end, the action builds to a high point of interest. At this point the reader can see that the conflict must be resolved. This high point is called the *climax.*

In *Imaginative Language,* words are used so that they arouse the reader's feelings. One sees, hears, smells, touches, tastes with the author. A word picture can be as vivid as a photograph or drawing. Sometimes a vivid image appeals to more than one sense at a time. An example of this is Rainsford's description of the tropical night: "moist black velvet."

As you read again the descriptions of Rainsford's arrival at the castle, let the pictures take shape in your mind:

". . . Rainsford stood blinking in the river of glaring gold light that poured out. The first thing his eyes discerned was the largest man he had ever seen—a gigantic creature, solidly made and black-bearded to the waist. . . . Out of the snarl of beard two small eyes regarded Rainsford."

Nathan could not rid himself
of the feeling of dread
he had whenever he thought
of the Little Jackpine Valley. What could
be lurking there that filled him with
such apprehension?

The Woods–Devil

PAUL ANNIXTER

For the four days since his father's accident, it had snowed intermittently. The slate-black clouds of winter had banked up in the north and west. They were motionless, changeless, remote, and ridged like banks of corrugated metal. For days during this north Maine winter, the only sun the family had seen had been a yellowish filter at midday that came in the cabin window like a thin sifting of sulphur dust.

Nathan was just bringing the night's wood, enough short logs to burn till morning; with another pile of wood chunks beside the daubed clay fireplace they would last the following day if need be. His face and ears burned from laboring in a temperature of thirty below. He was dressed in brown linsey-woolsey; on his feet were shoes of heavy felt, stuffed with coarse, gray socks against the cold. A cap of worn coonskin crowned his shagbark hair that had not been cut in many weeks. He had reached the gangling age of fifteen and a half, when the joints are all loose and clumsy. His lean face was drawn and pinched, the dark eyes sullen from overwork.

His mother sat darning a sock over an egg,

From *Pride of Lions* by Paul Annixter. Copyright © 1960 by Hill and Wang, Inc. Reprinted by permission of Hill and Wang, Inc.

rising now and then to stir the pot of mush or turn the cooking rabbit. His father lay in the cord bunk in the corner of the cabin, his injured leg raised high beneath the blankets. His gaunt, unshaven face was etched with the memory of the pain he had endured before the settlement doctor had come to set the broken bone. Worry showed in his black eyes turned up to the ceiling poles. Little food was left for the family—a bit of jerked venison in the smokehouse, a side of bacon, some beans, and meal. The Stemlines were true woodsies.[1] They'd been eking along, waiting for the fur season. All that they ate, spent, and wore came from their traps and rifles.

Nathan went out for the final log, and the door creaked behind him on its crude hinges. The snow in the clearing was almost knee-deep. The forest surrounded it on all sides broken only where a road cut a black tunnel through the balsams[2] toward the settlement down to the south.

A sudden wind rose with the darkness. Nathan could hear it far off and high, a growing roar above the forest. Abruptly it snatched at the clearing, whirling the snow in eddies; the serried[3] pine tops bent in rhythm. Because his impulse was to hurry in and close the door against it, Nathan stood for several minutes, his face straight into it, letting the cold and darkness and emptiness sink into him.

Indoors, he eased down his log and took off his sheepskin coat and cap, baring his mop of brown hair. He sat down beside Viney, his eight-year-old sister, playing with the endless paper people she cut out of the mail order catalogue. The wind made hollow bottle noises down the chimney, and the driven snow made a dry *shish-shish* against the log walls.

"Listen to that," said Nathan's mother. "The

1. **woodsies**\ˈwʊd·sēz\ people whose lives are built around the woods.
2. **balsams**\ˈbɔl·səmz\ evergreen trees having small needles and cones more than two inches long.
3. **serried**\ˈsĕr·ēd\ pressed together in rows.

Almanac was right. We're due for another cold spell. 'A stormy new moon. Keep a good fire,' Father Richard says for the ninth. 'Colder. Expect snow,' it says for the tenth."

Nathan's voice had a manly note. "It's getting colder all right, but it won't snow. It's too darned cold to snow. A fellow'd soon be stiff if he didn't keep working."

"Is the ax in?" his father asked.

"Yes." Nathan fetched it and put a keen, shining edge on it with the whetstone. Then he ran a greased rag through each of the rifle barrels. He could feel his father's approving gaze on his back as he sighted through each barrel into the firelight. "Bright's a bugle," he copied his father's invariable comment.

Then he sat waiting, his hands clasped tightly between his knees, for what he knew must come.

"Nathan," his father said presently, and the boy went over and stood dutifully by the bunk. "Do you think you can cover the trapline tomorrow, son?"

"Yes, I guess I can."

He was prickling with trepidation. The wind shook the cabin door as he spoke, and he thought of all that lay up in the far pine valley—things to be felt, if not seen or heard.

"It's a long ways, I know, and it's mortal cold. . . ." His father's voice was drained and tired, and for a moment Nathan glimpsed the naked misery and worry in his mind. "But money's scarce, son. We've got to do what can be done."

"I don't mind the cold or the snow." Nathan stared down at his feet until that look should leave his father's face.

"I'll be laid up three, four weeks, maybe more. It's four days since we laid out the line. Varmints may have got most of our catch by now. You've got to go, Nathan. If you start at daylight you can make the rounds and be back by night."

"Shucks, yes." Nathan forced a smile.

When he dared lift his eyes, he saw his father's face had hardened again in coping with the problem.

"You needn't try to bring in the catch," he said. "You can hang some of it on high boughs, then reset the traps. Main thing's to find what kind of range we got in there. Later on, you may have to spend a night in the valley. Think you'll be a-scairt to sleep alone in the deep woods?"

"Not me." Nathan's tone discounted all concern, but misgivings quickly crowded in. "Anyhow I'd have an ax and a rifle and plenty cartridges," he said.

His father managed a smile. "Might have to sleep in there once every week till I'm up again. So you'd best look at that log cache[4] we built to store traps in. It's plenty big enough to sleep a man."

Pride filled Nathan. This was real man's work he was detailed to do.

"You'd best eat now and turn in early," his father said, "so's you can start at dawn."

"All right."

"You're a brave boy, Nathan," his mother said. "You're the provider for this family now. What a blessing it is you're big enough to cover the line while your father's down. Last year you could never have done it."

"He's near about as good as any man now," his father said. "Knows the woods and critters as well as I."

Young Nathan grew more stolid than usual, holding himself against the rushing tide of feeling. He wished he were all they said of him. Inside he was frightened whenever he thought of the Little Jackpine Valley where their trapline had been laid out. For three days the vision of the valley and what he had felt there had lurked before his mind's eye, filling him with dread, even when he tried to put his mind to something else.

Methodically, Nathan ate the man's share of food his mother set before him on the hewn-log table. Soon after, he climbed the sapling ladder to the small quarter loft where he slept. He lay quiet, pretending to sleep, but long after the lamp went out he was still

---

4. **log cache**\kăsh\ a hiding place built of logs, used for storing things necessary for life in the wilderness.

grappling with his thoughts. Storm gripped the cabin. The snow crept up against the walls and the night was full of voices. Once far in the forest a wolf howled. Nathan's skin prickled and his two hands made fists underneath the blankets.

Now and again he could hear his father stirring and knew that he, too, was thinking the same thoughts.

Dawn had not yet come when Nathan descended the ladder. He built up the fire, made coffee, and ate a hurried breakfast. He took down his old wool sweater to wear under his sheepskin coat.

"Make sure you don't forget anything," his father said. "Have you got plenty cartridges ... matches? Belt ax? Bait?"

"Yes, pa."

"Best take my rifle," his father said.

Nathan took down his father's finely balanced rifle with its curly walnut stock and held it proudly in his hands. It was a far better weapon than the old Sharps Nathan usually carried.

"I wouldn't take the sled," his father was saying. "It's heavy, and I want you should be back by night. Be right careful, won't you, son?" he called as Nathan lifted the latch.

The cold bit deep. It was scarcely light yet in the clearing. The storm had died down in the night, and there was no wind now, but the air cut Nathan's cheeks like a razor. It was colder than anything he had ever known.

After twenty minutes of tramping he thought of turning back. His face and hands were numbing; his joints seemed to be stiffening. Each breath was agony. He snatched up some of the hard, dry snow and rubbed it against his stiffened face till a faint glow of feeling came. Then he ran for a long way—beating his arms, one, then the other, against his body, shifting the rifle, till his thin chest was heaving. Again his face was like wood. He was terrified, but he would not give up, would not turn back.

He covered the three miles to the mouth of the Little Jackpine in a daze. He did not know what he could do with his numbed hands if he did find a catch in the traps; he could not even use the rifle if the occasion arose. He would have cried had he been a year younger, but at fifteen you do not cry. He started into the valley.

The Little Jackpine lay at the foot of old Shakehammer Mountain, and through it a small stream rushed and snarled like a wildcat, its bed choked with almost inaccessible jungles of windfalls. It was an appalling wilderness.

Both Nathan and his father could read the silent speech of place and time in the outdoors, and what the valley had said to them had been vaguely antagonistic from the first—almost a warning. Nathan remembered how they had threaded the valley bottom, in single file, silent. The breeze had droned its ancient dirge in the treetops, but not a breath of it had stirred along the stream bed. The hiss of the water had created an intense hush.

He remembered how he had spat in the boiling waters to show his unconcern, but it hadn't done much good. Several times as they headed homeward, Nathan's father had stopped abruptly in his tracks to look behind and to all sides. "Queer," he had muttered. "A full hour past I had a right smart feelin' we were bein' watched and followed. I still got it."

"I had it, too, Pa," Nathan had said. "It's mighty fearsome back yonder, ain't it?"

"It ain't a bear." His father had evaded the question. "May be some young lynx cat, figurin' he'd like to play with us. A lynx is a tomfool for followin' humans."

They had backtracked to the top of a rise to look, but they saw nothing. Then the valley struck its first blow. A perfectly placed boulder that had lain poised for untold years had toppled at that exact moment to crush the older Nathan's leg as he scambled down a rocky ledge. . . .

Nathan passed the spot, but he did not pause. Something seemed to listen behind each tree and rock, and something seemed to

wait among the taller trees ahead, blue-black in the shadows. After a while it felt warmer, perhaps because he was climbing. Then he came to the first trap and forgot wind, cold, and even fear.

A marten, caught perhaps two days before, lay in the set. Its carcass had been partially devoured, its prime pelt torn to ribbons as if in malice. Roundabout in the snow were broad, splayed tracks, but wind and sleet had partly covered them, so that their identity was not plain. But they told Nathan enough. Neither fox nor wolf had molested this trap, nor was it a bear. Nathan knew what it was, but he wasn't admitting it yet—even to himself.

He stood up, his eyes searching for a glimpse of a secret enemy, but the valley gave back nothing. Except for the soughing of the balsam boughs far overhead, the stillness was complete.

He moved on between the endless ranks of trees and again had the feeling of being watched. At intervals he stopped to glance

back along his trail, but saw nothing. The trunks of the dark trees seemed to watch him as he approached, slipping furtively behind him as he passed.

The next trap had been uncovered and sprung, the bait—a frozen fish—eaten, and the trap itself dragged off into the brush and buried in the snow. It took nearly half an hour of floundering and digging to uncover trap and clog. Hard by was another set, and there Nathan saw a thing that made his skin crawl. The remains of a porcupine lay in the trap, and the creature had been eaten—quills, barb, and all. Blood from the jaws of the eater was spattered all around. Only a devil could have done that! Beneath a spruce he saw clearly the despoiler's trail—splayed, hand-shaped tracks like those of a small bear, each print peaked with fierce claw marks.

These were the tracks of a giant wolverine, the woods-devil, bane of all hunters and trappers.

For long minutes Nathan stood in the dusky shadows, fighting down his fear. He had heard about the evil fortune that fastens upon trappers molested by a wolverine. Then he thought of what awaited him at home—that stricken look on his father's face. His fear of that was greater than his fear of the valley.

He hung his sack of frozen bait on a high bough. Useless to reset any of the traps now, for the creature he was pitted against could smell cold steel, unbaited, through two feet of snow, and, in sheer deviltry, would rob and destroy wherever it prowled.

Nathan plodded on again, his chest hollow with hopelessness, not knowing what he could do.

The snow became deeper. One after another he came upon six more sets that had been robbed. Each had held a catch, and each ravaged pelt meant the loss of food and clothing to his family.

Then Nathan gave a whimpering cry. He had come to the seventh trap and that one had contained treasure, a pelt worth a whole season's work to the Stemlines. This was a black fisher marten, always a trapper's prize. If only he could have carried home such a pelt on this first day of his rounds! How smoothed and eased his father's worried face would have become! But the woods-devil had destroyed it—an even more thorough job than on any of the others, as if he had sensed the value of this catch.

The boy whimpered again as he crouched there in the snow. Then anger flooded him, fought back the tears. He rose and began the endless plodding again, peering into every covert for the dark, skulking shape. He did not know the size of a wolverine. He'd never seen one. He recalled old Laban Knowles's tale of the wolverine that had gnawed his walnut rifle stock in two and scored the very rifle barrel. And Granther Bates told of a woods-devil that had killed his two dogs, then knawed through a log wall to rob him of his grub cache.[5]

It was afternoon when Nathan neared the farthest limit of the trapline. Of twenty-odd traps, only two had been unmolested. Abruptly

he came upon a fresh trail in the snow: the same hand-shaped tracks and demon claws, no more than an hour old. Grimly he turned aside to follow their twisting course.

He was descending a steep wooded slope, when on a sudden impulse he doubled back on his own tracks and plunged up the grade through deep snow. As he reached the crest, a dark, humped shape took form beneath the drooping boughs of a spruce—a ragged, sooty-black and brown beast, some three and a half feet long, that lumbered like a small bear; it was lighter colored along its back and darker underneath, in direct contrast to all other forest beings. It saw him, and its green-shadowed eyes fixed on those of the boy beneath a tree some hundred feet away. The black jaw dropped open, and a harsh grating snarl cut the stillness. The utter savagery of this challenge sent a shiver through Nathan's body. His rifle flew up, and without removing his mitten he fired. The whole valley roared. In the same instant, the wolverine disappeared.

Nathan rushed forward, reloading as he ran. Under the spruce were several drops of blood in the snow, but the wolverine had vanished completely. Because of his haste and the clumsiness of his mittened hand, Nathan had only grazed the animal; he'd lost his one big chance.

Panting, stumbling, sobbing, the boy plunged along the trail, bent low, ducking under the drooping limbs of the trees, sometimes crawling on hands and knees. He saw other drops of blood. They gave him heart. He had a lynx eye, his father had often said. He would follow on to the very Circle[6] if need be; he would not miss a second time. His one hope now was to settle with the beast for good and all.

The trail led down along the stream bed, twisting through tangles of windfalls, writhing masses of frost-whitened roots, and branches

---

5. **grub cache**, hidden food.
6. **Circle**, that is, the Arctic Circle.

that seemed caught in a permanent hysteria. Twice he fell, but each time he thrust high the rifle as he went down to keep the snow from jamming its snout. He plunged on again; he did not know for how long or how far, but he was aware at last of the beginning of twilight. And the end of light meant the end of the trail. Victory for the enemy.

The way had grown steeper. He was coming to the narrow throatlatch of the valley's head, a place where hundreds of great trees, snapped off by storm and snowslide from the slopes above, had collected in a mighty log jam, a tangle of timber, rock, and snow that choked the stream bed from bank to bank. Countless logs lay crisscrossed helter-skelter with two- and three-foot gaps between. The great pile was acre large, fifty feet high, rank with the odor of rotted logs and old snow.

Into this maze led the trail of the woods-devil. Nathan skirted the pile. The trail did not come out!

Trembling, he squeezed his way between two logs into the great jam. The wolverine might be fifty yards inside, but somehow it must be ferreted out. In and in Nathan wormed his body, pausing to watch, to listen, his rifle thrust carefully before him. Then down and down into the twisting chaos of dead and dying trunks, led by his nose, for the rank odor of the devil's den now filled the air. Coming upward from the very bottom of the jam, it was fouler than any skunk taint.

Nathan stopped short, his body tensing like a spring. To his ears came a harsh and menacing growl, but from which direction he could not tell. He waited but could see nothing. He loosened the safety on his rifle and wriggled forward again, and again the air was filled with that ominous challenge. This time it seemed to come from behind him. He whirled in panic, but there was nothing. His terror mounted. The creature must be watching him, and he could not see it. And might not there be *two* of them? Then a movement caught his eye, and he glimpsed a soot-dark shape in the lower shadows.

The boy wriggled on his belly along a slanting log, maneuvering for a shot through the intervening timbers. He braced himself, craning far downward. . . . Then in the very instant he took aim, he slipped on the snow-sheathed log. The gun roared; the shot went wild; and, as Nathan caught himself, the rifle slid from his ice-slick grasp. It clattered downward, striking against log after log before it lodged at the bottom of the jam, snout down in snow, its barrel clogged and useless.

In that instant all the craft that has made man master of the wild fell away, and Nathan was reduced to first principles. The wolverine clambered slowly upward. Inexorably it advanced upon him. He screamed at it, but there was no vestige of fear in the beast. Nathan's hand went to his light belt ax; he gave no ground.

With a panicking shout he leaned and swung at the low flat head, but missed because of hindering logs. He swung again and again, and the blade struck, but with no apparent effect, for the creature's advance never checked. Its small, implacable eyes shone blue-green.

It lunged suddenly for Nathan's dangling legs. He flung himself up and over the log, then slipped on the icy sheath, grasped desperately for another log, and slipped again to a point eight feet below. He flung around with a cry of desperation, expecting to meet open jaws, as the demon was almost upon him. But the animal was logy. Its power lay in its indomitability—a slow, irresistible power.

In it came again, above him now. He stood upright, braced on two logs, to meet it. He was crying now, sobbing and unashamed.

He struck again, yelling with each blow of the belt ax, but hack and cut as he would, the beast bore in and in, maneuvering along the undersides of logs to avoid the ax blows.

Then as Nathan slipped again, he avoided the traplike jaws. He fell to the bottom of the jam, biting snow as he screamed. He was on his feet again before the creature above released its claw hold and dropped upon him like a giant slug.

Flinging an arm up over his throat, he jerked back blindly. Spread saber claws tore open his heavy coat. Then the ax fell again, blow after blow with all his strength; he shouted with every blow. No longer cries of terror, but of war.

The thing would not die. The jaws clamped on Nathan's leg above the knee, and he felt his own warm blood. Then his hand found the skinning knife at his belt, and the blade sank into the corded neck—turned till the clamp of jaws released.

Nathan climbed up out of the abatis[7] till half his body emerged from the top of the great jam, and there he rested—panting, spent. He whimpered once, but there were no tears now. Instinctively, his eyes lifted skyward. Overhead, as night drew on, a great rift appeared in the leaden canopy of cloud, and a few stars shone through. He fixed his eyes on the brightest star until chaos left him; then his vision steadied, as if his head were higher than ever it had been before, in a realm of pure air. His brain was almost frighteningly clear.

The trickle of warm blood down his leg roused him. He pressed his heavy pants leg around his wound till he felt the bleeding stop. Painfully, he turned down into the maze of logs again and brought up the rifle. Then down again to struggle upward, dragging the woods-devil by its short and ragged scut.[8] He laid it out on the snow and pulled out his bloody knife. He wasn't tired now, he wasn't cold, he wasn't afraid. His hands were quick and sure at the skinning; even his father had never lifted a pelt with smoother, defter hand. Darkness shut down, but he needed no light. There was no hurry. The head he cut from the body, leaving it attached to the hide.

He thought of the proud fancy that made the far northern Indians covet a garment made of a wolverine's skin. Oh, there would be talk in the cabin tonight; they would set at the table long after their eating was done,

as great folk were supposed to do. He'd recount all the details of the day and the fight before he brought his trophy in to show.

He rose at last and rolled up his grisly bundle, fur side out, and moved away through the blackness of the trees, sure of tread, for he had the still hunter's "eyes in the feet." Reflection from the snow gave a faint light. He was limping a bit.

Off in the black woods, a wolf howled dismally, and Nathan smiled. Never again would the night dogs make his skin crawl. Never again would he be afraid of anything above ground.

I
NATHAN CONQUERS HIS FEAR

1. What traits does the wolverine have that would cause woodsmen to think of him as a "woods-devil"?

2. Why doesn't Nathan go back home when he realizes the kind of animal that is destroying his furs?

II
IMPLICATIONS

Agree or disagree with the following.

1. Fear is usually greater when one cannot see his enemy or adversary.

2. Man is actually as malicious and wasteful as the wolverine.

III
TECHNIQUES

Conflict

Three of the four kinds of conflict between opposing forces can be seen in this story. Discuss what they are.

Suspense and Foreshadowing

Find and discuss two illustrations of foreshadowing early in the story.

---

7. **abatis**\\ˈab-ə-tē\\ a defensive obstacle formed by felled trees with sharpened branches facing the enemy.
8. **scut**\\ˈskət\\ a short erect tail, as of a hare, rabbit, or deer.

"I dare you!"
is a phrase commonly used by children at play.
As people grow older
they may not voice such a challenge,
but they still imply it. In this next story,
Jerry never actually hears anyone taunt him
with "I dare you," but he still undergoes
a terrible trial of endurance.
From what does the challenge come?

Through the Tunnel

DORIS LESSING

Going to the shore on the first morning of the holiday, the young English boy stopped at a turning of the path and looked down at a wild and rocky bay, and then over to the crowded beach he knew so well from other years. His mother walked on in front of him, carrying a bright striped bag in one hand. Her other arm, swinging loose, was very white in the sun.

The boy watched that white, naked arm, and turned his eyes, which had a frown behind them, toward the bay and back again to his mother. When she felt he was not with her, she swung around.

"Oh, there you are Jerry!" she said. She looked impatient, then smiled. "Why, darling, would you rather not come with me? Would you rather—" she frowned, conscientiously worrying over what amusements he might secretly be longing for which she had been too busy to imagine.

He was very familiar with that anxious, apologetic smile. Contrition sent him running after her. And yet, as he ran, he looked back

over his shoulder at the wild bay; and all morning, as he played on the safe beach, he was thinking of it.

Next morning, when it was time for the routine of swimming and sunbathing, his mother said, "Are you tired of the usual beach, Jerry? Would you like to go somewhere else?"

"Oh, no!" he said quickly, smiling at her out of that unfailing impulse of contrition—a sort of chivalry. Yet, walking down the path with her, he blurted out, "I'd like to go and have a look at those rocks down there."

She gave the idea her attention. It was a wild-looking place, and there was no one there, but she said, "Of course, Jerry. When you've had enough, come to the big beach. Or just go straight back to the villa, if you like."

She walked away, that bare arm, now slightly reddened from yesterday's sun, swinging. And he almost ran after her again, feeling it unbearable that she should go by herself, but he did not.

She was thinking. Of course he's old enough to be safe without me. Have I been keeping him too close? He mustn't feel he ought to be with me. I must be careful.

He was an only child. . . . She was a widow. She was determined to be neither possessive nor lacking in devotion. She went worrying off to her beach.

As for Jerry, once he saw that his mother had gained her beach, he began the steep descent to the bay. From where he was, high up among red-brown rocks, it was a scoop of moving bluish green fringed with white.

As he went lower, he saw that it spread among small promontories and inlets of rough, sharp rock, and the crisping, lapping surface showed stains of purple and darker blue. Finally, as he ran sliding and scraping down the last few yards, he saw an edge of white surf, and the shallow, luminous movement of water over white sand, and, beyond that, a solid, heavy blue.

He ran straight into the water and began swimming. He was a good swimmer. He went out fast over the gleaming sand, over a middle region where rocks lay like discolored monsters under the surface, and then he was in the real sea—a warm sea where irregular cold currents from the deep water shocked his limbs.

When he was so far out that he could look back not only on the little bay but past the promontory that was between it and the big beach, he floated on the buoyant surface and looked for his mother. There she was, a speck of yellow under an umbrella that looked like a slice of orange peel. He swam back to shore, relieved at being sure she was there, but all at once very lonely.

On the edge of a small cape that marked the side of the bay away from the promontory was a loose scatter of rocks. Above them, some boys were stripping off their clothes. They came running, naked, down to the rocks.

The English boy swam toward them, and kept his distance at a stone's throw. They were of that coast, all of them burned smooth dark brown, and speaking a language he did not understand. To be with them, of them, was a craving that filled his whole body. He swam a little closer; they turned and watched him with narrowed, alert dark eyes.

Then one smiled and waved. It was enough. In a minute, he had swum in and was on the rocks beside them, smiling with a desperate, nervous supplication. They shouted cheerful greetings at him, and then, as he preserved his nervous, uncomprehending smile, they understood that he was a foreigner strayed from his own beach, and they proceeded to forget him. But he was happy. He was with them.

They began diving again and again from a high point into a well of blue sea between rough, pointed rocks. After they had dived and come up, they swam around, hauled themselves up, and waited their turn to dive again.

They were big boys—men to Jerry. He dived, and they watched him, and when he swam around to take his place, they made way for him. He felt he was accepted, and he dived again, carefully, proud of himself.

Soon the biggest of the boys poised himself, shot down into the water, and did not come up.

The others stood about watching. Jerry, after waiting for the sleek brown head to appear, let out a yell of warning; they looked at him idly and turned their eyes back toward the water.

After a long time, the boy came up on the other side of a big dark rock, letting the air out of his lungs in a sputtering gasp and a shout of triumph. Immediately, the rest of them dived in. One moment, the morning seemed full of chattering boys; the next, the air and the surface of the water were empty. But through the heavy blue, dark shapes could be seen moving and groping.

Jerry dived, shot past the school of underwater swimmers, saw a black wall of rock looming at him, touched it, and bobbed up at once to the surface, where the wall was a low barrier he could see across. There was no one visible; under him, in the water, the dim shapes of the swimmers had disappeared. Then one, and then another of the boys came up on the far side of the barrier of rock, and he understood that they had swum through some gap or hole in it. He plunged down again.

He could see nothing through the stinging salt water but the blank rock. When he came up, the boys were all on the diving rock, preparing to attempt the feat again. And now, in a panic of failure, he yelled up, in English, "Look at me! Look!" and he began splashing and kicking in the water like a foolish dog.

They looked down gravely, frowning. He knew the frown. At moments of failure, when he clowned to claim his mother's attention, it was with just this grave embarrassed inspection that she rewarded him.

Through his hot shame, feeling the pleading grin on his face like a scar that he could never remove, he looked up at the group of big brown boys on the rock and shouted *"Bonjour! Merci! Au revoir! Monsieur, monsieur!"*[1] while he hooked his fingers round his ears and waggled them.

---

1. Commonplace French phrases: **bonjour**\\'bȯn ▲zhür\\ "good day"; **merci**\\'mȧr ▲sē\\ "thank you"; **au revoir**\\'ō rə ▲vwȧr\\ "good-bye"; **monsieur**\\mə ▲sur\\ "mister," "sir."

Water surged into his mouth; he choked, sank, came up. The rock, lately weighted with the boys, seemed to rear up out of the water as their weight was removed. They were flying down past him, now, into the water; the air was full of falling bodies. Then the rock was empty in the hot sunlight. He counted one, two, three. . . .

At fifty, he was terrified. They must all be drowning beneath him, in the watery caves of the rock! At a hundred, he stared around him at the empty hillside, wondering if he should yell for help.

He counted faster, faster, to hurry them up, to bring them to the surface quickly, to drown them quickly—anything rather than the terror of counting on and on into the blue emptiness of the morning. And then, at a hundred and sixty, the water beyond the rock was full of boys blowing like brown whales. They swam back to the shore without a look at him.

He climbed back to the diving rock and sat down, feeling the hot roughness of it under his thighs. The boys were gathering up their bits of clothing and running off along the shore to another promontory.

They were leaving to get away from him. He cried openly, fists in his eyes. There was no one to see him, and he cried himself out.

It seemed to him that a long time had passed and he swam out to where he could see his mother. Yes, she was still there, a yellow spot under an orange umbrella. He swam back to the big rock, climbed up, and dived into the blue pool among the fanged and angry boulders. Down he went, until he touched the wall of rock again. But the salt was so painful in his eyes that he could not see.

He came to the surface, swam to shore and went back to the villa to wait for his mother. Soon she walked slowly up the path, swinging her striped bag, the flushed, naked arm dangling beside her. "I want some swimming goggles," he panted, defiant and beseeching.

She gave him a patient, inquisitive look as she said casually, "Well, of course, darling."

But now, now, now! He must have them this minute, and no other time. He nagged and pestered until she went with him to a shop. As soon as she had bought the goggles, he grabbed them from her hand as if she were going to claim them for herself, and was off, running down the steep path to the bay.

Jerry swam out to the big barrier rock, adjusted the goggles, and dived. The impact of the water broke the rubber-enclosed vacuum, and the goggles came loose.

He understood that he must swim down to the base of the rock from the surface of the water. He fixed the goggles tight and firm, filled his lungs, and floated, face down on the water.

Now he could see. It was as if he had eyes of a different kind—fish-eyes that showed everything clear and delicate and wavering in the bright water.

Under him, six or seven feet down, was a floor of perfectly clean, shining white sand, rippled firm and hard by the tides. Two grayish shapes steered there, like long, rounded pieces of wood or slate.

They were fish. He saw them nose toward each other, poise motionless, make a dart forward, swerve off, and come around again. It was like a water dance.

A few inches above them, the water sparkled as if sequins were dropping through it. Fish again—myriads of minute fish, the length of his fingernail, were drifting through the water, and in a moment he could feel the innumerable tiny touches of them, against his limbs. It was like swimming in flaked silver.

The great rock the big boys had swum through rose sheer out of the white sand, black, tufted lightly with greenish weed. He could see no gap in it. He swam down to its base.

Again and again he rose, took a big chestful of air, and went down. Again and again he groped over the surface of the rock, feeling it, almost hugging it in the desperate need to find the entrance.

And then, once, while he was clinging to the black wall, his knees came up and he shot his feet out forward and they met no obstacle. He had found the hole.

He gained the surface, clambered about the stones that littered the barrier rock until he found a big one, and, with this in his arms, let himself down over the side of the rock. He dropped, with the weight, to the sandy floor.

Clinging tight to the anchor of the stone, he lay on his side and looked in under the dark shelf at the place where his feet had gone. He could see the hole.

It was an irregular, dark gap, but he could not see deep into it. He let go of his anchor, clung with his hands to the edges of the hole, and tried to push himself in.

He got his head in, found his shoulders jammed, moved them in sidewise, and was inside as far as his waist. He could see nothing ahead.

Something soft and clammy touched his mouth. He saw a dark frond moving against the grayish rock, and panic filled him. He thought of octopuses, or clinging weed.

He pushed himself out backward and caught a glimpse, as he retreated, of a harmless tentacle of seaweed drifting in the mouth of the tunnel. But it was enough.

He reached the sunlight, swam to shore, and lay on the diving rock. He looked down into the blue well of water. He knew he must find his way through that cave, or hole, or tunnel, and out the other side.

First, he thought, he must learn to control his breathing. He let himself down into the water with another big stone in his arms, so that he could lie effortlessly on the bottom.

One, two, three. He counted steadily. He could hear the movement of blood in his head. Fifty-one, fifty-two. . . .

His chest was hurting. He let go of the rock and went up into the air. He saw that the sun was low. He rushed to the villa and found his mother at her supper. She said only, "Did you enjoy yourself?" and he said, "Yes."

All night, the boy dreamed of the water-filled cave in the rock, and as soon as breakfast was over he went to the bay.

That night, his nose bled badly. For hours he had been underwater, learning to hold his breath, and now he felt weak and dizzy. His mother said, "I shouldn't overdo things, darling, if I were you."

That day and the next, Jerry exercised his lungs as if everything, the whole of his life, all that he would become, depended upon it. Again his nose bled at night, and his mother insisted on his coming with her the next day.

It was a torment to him to waste a day of his careful self-training, but he stayed with her on that other beach, which now seemed a place for small children, a place where his mother might lie safe in the sun. It was not his beach.

He did not ask for permission, on the following day, to go to his beach. He went, before his mother could consider the complicated rights and wrongs of the matter.

A day's rest, he discovered, had improved his count by ten. The big boys had made the passage while he counted a hundred and sixty. He had been counting fast, in his fright. Probably now, if he tried, he could get through that long tunnel, but he was not going to try yet.

A curious, most unchildlike persistence, a controlled impatience, made him wait. In the meantime, he lay underwater on the white sand, littered now by stones he had brought down from the upper air, and studied the entrance to the tunnel. He knew every jut and corner of it, as far as it was possible to see. It was as if he already felt its sharpness about his shoulders.

He sat by the clock in the villa, when his mother was not near, and checked his time. He was incredulous and then proud to find he could hold his breath without strain for two minutes. The words "two minutes," authorized by the clock, brought the adventure that was so necessary to him close.

In another four days, his mother said casually one morning, they must go home. On the day before they left, he would do it. He would do it if it killed him, he said defiantly to himself. But two days before they were to leave—a day of triumph when he increased his count by fifteen —his nose bled so badly that he turned dizzy and had to lie limply over the big rock like a bit of seaweed, watching the thick red blood flow onto the rock and trickle slowly down to the sea. He was frightened.

Supposing he turned dizzy in the tunnel? Supposing he died there, trapped? Supposing— His head went around in the hot sun, and he almost gave up. He thought he would return to the house and lie down, and next summer, perhaps, when he had another year's growth in him —then he would go through the hole.

But even after he had made the decision, or thought he had, he found himself sitting up on the rock and looking down into the water, and he knew that now, this moment, when his nose had only just stopped bleeding, when his head was still sore and throbbing—this was the moment when he would try. If he did not do it now, he never would.

He was trembling with fear that he would not go, and he was trembling with horror at that long, long tunnel under the rock, under the sea. Even in the open sunlight, the barrier rock seemed very wide and very heavy; tons of rock pressed down on where he would go. If he died there he would lie until one day—perhaps not before next year—those big boys would swim into it and find it blocked.

He put on his goggles, fitted them tight, tested the vacuum. His hands were shaking. Then he chose the biggest stone he could carry and slipped over the edge of the rock until half of him was in the cool, enclosing water and half in the hot sun.

He looked up once at the empty sky, filled his lungs once, twice, and then sank fast to the bottom with the stone. He let it go and began to count. He took the edges of the hole in his hands and drew himself into it, wriggling his shoulders in sidewise as he remembered he must.

Soon he was clear inside. He was in a small rock-bound hole filled with yellowish-gray water. The water was pushing him up against the roof. The roof was sharp and pained his back. He pulled himself along with his hands— fast, fast—and used his legs as levers.

His head knocked against something; a sharp pain dizzied him. Fifty, fifty-one, fifty-two. . . .

He was without light, and the water seemed to press upon him with the weight of rock. Seventy-one, seventy-two. . . . There was no strain on his lungs. He felt like an inflated balloon, his lungs were so light and easy, but his head was pulsing.

He was being continually pressed against the sharp roof, which felt slimy as well as sharp. Again he thought of octopuses, and wondered if the tunnel might be filled with weed that could tangle him. He gave himself a panicky, convulsive kick forward, ducked his head, and swam.

His feet and hands moved freely, as if in open water. The hole must have widened out. He thought he must be swimming fast, and he was frightened of banging his head if the tunnel narrowed.

A hundred, a hundred and one. . . . The water paled. Victory filled him. His lungs were beginning to hurt. A few more strokes and he would be out. He was counting wildly; he said a hundred and fifteen, and then, a long time later, a hundred and fifteen again. The water was a clear jewel-green all around him. Then he saw, above his head, a crack running up through the rock. Sunlight was falling through it, showing the clean dark rock of the tunnel, a single mussel shell, and darkness ahead.

He was at the end of what he could do. He looked up at the crack as if it were filled with air and not water, as if he could put his mouth to it to draw in air. A hundred and fifteen, he heard himself say inside his head—but he had said that long ago.

He must go on into the blackness ahead, or he would drown. His head was swelling, his lungs cracking. A hundred and fifteen, a hundred and fifteen pounded through his head, and he feebly clutched at rocks in the dark, pulling himself forward, leaving the brief space of sunlit water behind.

He felt he was dying. He was no longer quite conscious. He struggled on in the darkness between lapses into unconsciousness. An immense, swelling pain filled his head, and then the darkness cracked with an explosion of green light. His hands, groping forward, met nothing, and his feet, kicking back, propelled him out into the open sea.

He drifted to the surface, his face turned up to the air. He was gasping like a fish. He felt he would sink now and drown; he could not swim the few feet back to the rock. Then he was clutching it and pulling himself up onto it.

He lay face down, gasping. He could see nothing but a red-veined clotted dark. His eyes must have burst, he thought; they were full of blood. He tore off his goggles and a gout of blood went into the sea. His nose was bleeding, and the blood had filled the goggles.

He scooped up handfuls of water from the cool, salty sea, to splash on his face, and did not know whether it was blood or salt water he tasted. After a time, his heart quieted, his eyes cleared, and he sat up.

He could see the local boys diving and playing half a mile away. He did not want them. He wanted nothing but to get back home and lie down.

In a short while, Jerry swam to shore and climbed slowly up the path to the villa. He flung himself on his bed and slept, waking at the sound of feet on the path outside. His mother was coming back. He rushed to the bathroom, thinking she must not see his face with bloodstains, or tearstains, on it. He came out of the bathroom and met her as she walked into the villa.

"Have a nice morning?" she asked, laying her hand on his warm brown shoulder a moment.

"Oh, yes, thank you," he said.

"You look a bit pale." And then, sharp and anxious, "How did you bang your head?"

"Oh, just banged it," he told her.

She looked at him closely. He was stained. His eyes were glazed-looking. She was worried. And then she said to herself, "Oh, don't fuss! Nothing can happen. He can swim like a fish."

They sat down to lunch together.

"Mummy," he said, "I can stay under water for two minutes—three minutes, at least." It came bursting out of him.

"Can you, darling?" she said. "Well, I shouldn't overdo it. I don't think you ought to swim any more today."

She was ready for a battle of wills, but he gave in at once. It was no longer of the least importance to go to the bay.

I

A BOY PROVES HIMSELF

This story actually moves along at two levels. On the surface, the most obvious action is a boy's successful attempt to swim through a dangerous underwater tunnel. But there are other and deeper currents in the story.

1. Jerry's relationship to his mother has great influence on his actions at the seashore. What kind of mother is she? Discuss whether you think she really understands Jerry.

2. Why doesn't Jerry wish to stay and swim with his mother? With whom does he wish to swim and make friends? How does he discover the existence of the underwater tunnel?

3. How did Jerry prepare himself for the ordeal of swimming through the hole? Why did he need goggles? How did he make use of the large stones?

4. What gave him a sense of false victory before he really reached the end of the tunnel? What psychological effect did this have on Jerry?

II

IMPLICATIONS

The directions for these propositions will usually ask you to "consider and discuss." Remember that the *considering* is just as important as the *discussing*—perhaps even more so. It is pointless to speak or write before you have decided *what* you want to say and *how* you want to say it. Before you begin to speak, make a mental note of three or four points you want to make, and arrange your points in a logical order. *Consider*, then discuss:

1. A person benefits from any test he forces on himself.

2. It is a good idea to be suspicious of foreigners.

3. One of the cruelest ways to treat people is to be indifferent to them.

4. Often after a person works hard to achieve something, it no longer seems important to him.

III

TECHNIQUES

Suspense

By the time the boy has made the decision that the moment has come when he will try to swim through the tunnel, the author has carefully acquainted the reader with the dangers involved.

1. What two dangerous possibilities particularly frightened Jerry?

2. List other possibilities of danger which the author mentioned earlier in the story.

Conflict

This story is rich in elements of conflict. Jerry's desire to test himself results from conflicting feelings which struggle within him. He loves his mother, but he is in rebellion against the restraint and "safeness" she represents.

1. Jerry takes action to prove his own worth. What is the opposing force against which he chooses to struggle?

2. The notes above suggest that the main conflict of the action (the boy against the dangers beneath the sea) may not be the story's most important conflict. Where is the climax or turning point of the action? How is the conflict inside the boy settled?

Imaginative Language

Although British author Doris Lessing does not use many unusual ideas or words for the imagery of this selection, there are two noteworthy examples. What comparisons does she make (p. 27) as she describes Jerry's pleading grin, and what comparisons tell what it was like to swim among myriads of fish?

Sometimes a simple statement about the shape and color of a thing invokes vivid imagery. Notice Lessing's descriptions such as "the blue emptiness of morning," "[his mother] was still there, a yellow spot under an orange umbrella." "the great rock . . . rose sheer out of the white sand, black, tufted lightly with greenish weed."

The previous selections have been about individuals deliberately seeking adventure. But adventure can also come without warning— as it did to young Raymond Ditmars in his own home. This is a true account of his meeting with a deadly bushmaster, the largest poisonous snake of the Western Hemisphere.

Episode of the Bushmaster

RAYMOND DITMARS

There had been an event of great importance. The family had moved to a large house and the upper floor was mine! Moreover, I had been given permission to have some snakes.

Simultaneously with the permission a carpenter appeared and placed a powerful spring on the door of the room where the serpents were to be kept. I suggested that if anyone were to go into that room and allow the spring to *slam* the door, the vibration would frighten the more nervous snakes. The family countered by declaring that nobody would go into that room unless chaperoned by me, and I could thus regulate the closing of the door to suit reptilian temperament.

My first step was to investigate a near-by grocery and take stock of empty boxes. One grocery store did not suffice. I accumulated twenty good cases of the starch-box variety.[1] "Chips"[2] at the museum knocked apart some old packing cases, smoothed the boards, and

---

1. These are wooden boxes.
2. **Chips** is a nickname often given to a carpenter.

Reprinted with permission of The Macmillan Company from *Thrills of a Naturalist's Quest* by Raymond L. Ditmars. Copyright 1932 by The Macmillan Company, renewed 1960 by Gladys Ditmars and Beatrice D. Stanchfield.

cut them to dimensions, so that I could assemble some larger cages at home. Night after night I staggered homeward with these loads, having grave troubles with guards on the Elevated,[3] but usually managing to induce them to allow me to ride on the platform, where my lumber projected to the roof. I had decided on six big cages, requiring such knocked-down material. The family had been told they were not to see the room until it was ready—and I carried the key in my pocket. Their only hint of developing details was the nightly hammering.

When it came to buying the sliding glass panels for the twenty small cases and the six big ones, there was a halt. I had to wait for the bi-monthly pay check at the museum, and the glass absorbed most of it. The cases were tinted with a walnut stain, were scraped very smooth inside with sandpaper, and finally the insides were rubbed with powdered wax. This rendered them non-absorbent. . . .

Everything in the snake room was made spick and span. The six-foot cases, these two feet high and the same depth, were on a platform six inches above the floor. They formed a double-story frontage eighteen feet long. Six of the smaller cages were arranged in double column on each side of the big cases. This made a total frontage of about twenty-two feet, or close to the length of the room. The additional eight small cases were ranged on the tops of the big ones. It was an imposing array—although as yet destitute of snakes.

The family was invited for inspection. I held back the strongly sprung door as they came in. I shall never forget the utter silence which greeted my wave of hand toward the glistening rows of glass. My father's attitude was that he had sowed the wind, and our home would reap the whirlwind[4]—when enough reptilian life had been gathered to fill those cages. The murmurings of the family also indicated that never had they imagined there could be so many kinds of snakes. . . .

My first big specimen cost me nothing. It was a six-foot Florida diamond-back rattlesnake, which had been pining in a coal bin in New

Formal portrait of Raymond Ditmars with one of his snakes, photographed by Edward Steichen, copyright 1932.

York. It belonged to Dr. C. Slover Allen, who had been experimenting with serpent poison, but had completed his work. . . .

My next unusual specimen was a young boa constrictor, barely a yard long, sent to the museum from a tropical fruit boat. I was permitted to keep it when we checked the fact that the museum had already pickled several boas from similar sources. Here was a lead! I asked for an

---

3. New York City used to have elevated trains, running on raised tracks above Third, Lexington, Sixth, and Ninth Avenues.
4. The reference is to the Scriptures: "For they have sown the wind, and they shall reap the whirlwind," King James Version, Hosea 8:7; indicating that he who acts foolishly sets off a disaster.

afternoon off, went to the place where the boa came from, found that reptiles often came to the North with fruit, and was referred to some other places. Everybody explained that most of the specimens were killed when discovered, but everybody promised that somehow or in some way they would try to save immigrant specimens if I would call for them. Linen bags were sent to these people, and some very pretty tropical reptiles of harmless kinds were thus obtained.

The collection was materially increased by a vacation trip. This collecting brought in some timber rattlers, copperheads, blacksnakes, milk snakes, water snakes, and spreading adders. . . .

Coming home one evening and going to the snake room, I saw a long envelope on the teak-

Green tree snakes wound around a branch —emerald colored, Ditmars calls it, "our most beautiful arboreal species."

wood table. It bore Trinidad stamps.[5] Ripping it open, I found a long, official-looking paper and a letter. The letter read (in part): ". . . I delayed shipment principally, thinking I might get you a fair bushmaster, and on a plantation not far distant, one was caught without it being injured. It is a beautiful creature and rather young (about eight feet long). The case I have dispatched, per SS *Irawaddy*, of the Trinidad line, contains:

One bushmaster (be extremely careful in liberating)
Two fer-de-lance
Four coral snakes
Two cribos (yellow rat snakes)
One black and yellow rat snake
Two emerald tree snakes (our most beautiful arboreal species)
One Cook's tree boa
Two boa constrictors (six and ten feet long respectively).

Bills of lading are enclosed, mailed per *Irawaddy*. I hope the specimens do well with you."

"Mailed per *Irawaddy*." That meant the snakes were in port! I had a very restless night. . . .

Rushing home next day, I found the case was there. Two sweating and protesting expressmen, carrying it at arms' length, had managed to swing it around the stairways to my upper floor. It wouldn't go through the door. So they had left it outside the snake room. This, I figured, was just as well. If they had entered the room, banged the door, and started the rattlers buzzing, they might have dropped the case and fled.

Dinner was a mere gesture, but my mother insisted upon my joining the family before I started on the job upstairs. Everybody was excited; but I was the only enthusiastic member of the circle. I insisted upon being alone during the unpacking. My mother wanted to look on.

---

5. **Trinidad**\\ˈtrĭ·nə'dăd\\ a British island of the West Indies lying off the coast of Venezuela.

There was anxiety in her eyes. My only way out of it was continued insistence on giving them a big surprise. They had not been burdened with details as to the devilish contents of that case.

Taking hammer and pry bar, I went upstairs and at it. My chief anxiety, in removing the cover, was the thought that I might find the odor of dead specimens. There is always a hazard in distance shipment of serpents. They can go for weeks without food, but some suffer from thirst. The careful shipper is particular to supply his specimens liberally with water before packing them, but reptiles are temperamental, drink when they feel like it, and may not be so inclined for days. Packing for shipment is liable to occur during such passive periods. Specimens thus dispatched may suffer from thirst during long travel. It is difficult to provide snakes with water during travel, unless they are accompanied by a skilled attendant, and particularly difficult, and highly dangerous, to attempt any such provision with poisonous snakes. Hence shipments of snakes often go thousands of miles without attention of any kind, like this case from Trinidad. The greatest hazard to such a shipment is exposure to low temperature.

The boards of the cover were off and laid aside. There was no odor or hint of any loss among the specimens.

. . . The tray on the top was about fourteen inches deep, showing that the bottom portion was considerably deeper. There were three compartments in the top, loosely filled with straw. Burlap bags containing the specimens were nested in this. Each bag was tagged with the name of its contents. Lifting the bags out of the straw I found the cribos, rat snake, tree snakes, tree boa, coral snakes, and fer-de-lance. The fer-de-lance were in separate bags. It was thrilling to know that here were living examples of things I had read about with fascinated interest. The bags from the top portion were carried into the room.

Lifting the now empty tray disclosed a sight which caused me to set it back abruptly. The boas were not in bags. One raised its head to stare up at me. In the glance into this lower section, I could see one third of it was partitioned off and in that was a large bag of coarsely woven material. It certainly contained the bushmaster, and it was alive; I saw it move!

Going to my bedroom I obtained a bathrobe, removed the tray, and dropped the robe over the boas. This eliminated the probability of their striking at me. I had certain misgivings as to how, alone, I was going to get the big boa into the room, but that could wait. I removed the bushmaster's bag and put the tray back.

I was disappointed in the weight of the bushmaster. My thought was that the bag would be quite heavy. I was soon to learn that the bushmaster was quite different from the pictures I had seen in natural-history books—and I was within a few moments of learning something of its dangerous habits, which had not appeared in books.

"Everything all right up there?" called my father.

"Everything fine. Don't anybody come up until things are in the cages; then I'll give you a grand show."

The rat snakes, tree snakes, and tree boa gave no trouble. Placed in the cages, they glided over to the water pans, and drank long and copiously.

The coral snakes were lovely, deceptively slender and quiet. They were lifted into the cages on a piece of telegraph wire, bent at the end like a poker.

It was thrilling to cut the cord on a bag containing a fer-de-lance. The bag was placed on the cage floor before this was done. Then it was inverted by hooking the bend of the wire beneath it. A sage-green, chevron-marked serpent slid out. It was rather slender—not more than an inch and a half in diameter at the thickest part. It snapped back its anterior third into a loop like a lateral S. Its tongue flashed with such vigor of oscillation that its head jiggled. The glass was slid shut with the bent wire. . . .

The great moment had arrived. I was going to see a bushmaster! As I said before, it seemed rather light for the length specified in the letter —eight feet—but it made considerable displacement in the bag, and where its sides pressed outwardly upon the cloth, rough scales showed through, like the surface of a pine cone. It was to occupy one of the long cages, and as it was in a very deep bag I reached for one of the staffs to invert the bag. There were several of these staffs in handy corners. They were mop handles, with a piece of heavy wire at the end bent like a shepherd's crook. They were very useful in transferring a poisonous snake from one cage to another, as the crook could be shoved under a snake, without greatly disturbing it, then the reptile could be slid forward or lifted, if the crook had been worked to about the center of its body, so it hung balanced upon it.

Getting the point of the crook under the end (or bottom) of the bushmaster's bag, the receptacle was lifted higher and higher, which meant that the snake was sliding nearer and nearer to the mouth of the bag, which had been untied. But the nearer it came, the more its coil expanded until it was tight across the bag, which stopped its outward progress. Yet it was moving. I could see that by the roughened scale surface rippling beneath the fabric.

This tussling with the bushmaster's bag had brought it closer to the front of the cage, as I naturally could exert more effort with the staff in a vertical, than a horizontal, position. Looking now, almost downward on the bag, the cage being on the lower tier, part of a coil could be seen issuing from the bag, moving as steadily as the rim of a wheel. Its color was startling—alternate salmon pink and jet black. I was so astonished and impatient to see more that I reached down with my hand, grasped the bag, and whisked it away from this amazing creature.

The eye and the brain are like a camera lens and a photographic plate. The lens flashes the impression. The plate retains it. My glance at the bushmaster was not more than a flash, before things started to happen, but from that flash I could have sat down and written a fairly detailed, academic description of the creature. It is enough to say here that the serpent was far

longer than its weight implied and about three inches in diameter at the central part, and gradually, gracefully tapering. Its head was large and very blunt at the snout. What impressed me most was its exceedingly rough surface, caused by the projecting center of each scale, yet this roughness was symmetrical in diagonal lines, like the surface of a wood rasp. The coloration, from head to tail, was the boldest imaginable, salmon hue crossed with well-separated bars of black. A curious impression formed in my mind. The creature looked as though it were of wax. The pinkish hue might have been responsible for this; then the protuberances of the scales were polished, and glistened, as if they had been rubbed clear of that indefinable, powdery surface of molded wax; and with the exception of these raised and polished points the greater area of the body had the dull glow of wax.

This turmoil of impressions might have consumed a second, or as much as five seconds; certainly no longer. It terminated in attention to the serpent's eyes, quite large and set above pinkish jowls. They were particularly prominent from their hue, which was reddish-brown, so dark the pupil was indistinguishable. My attention had concentrated on the eyes because the bushmaster's head was coming toward me. This was done by the creature forming a great striking loop of the whole anterior half of his body and edging forward at the same time. I stepped well back, as it looked as if he could strike a full four feet. My backward progress bumped me into one of the big chairs, so I shoved the crook of the staff against the snake, which was out of the cage by this time.

Pushing the staff against a part of its loop, so I could get around the chair and gain more distance, I saw that it had an alarming way of flowing forward of the staff. As fast as I pushed it back, it gained in footage. The condition was dangerous. I hadn't realized a viper[6] could prepare to strike so far, nor that any viperine snake was deliberately aggressive. There was no rushing or quick glide forward. The disturbing

―――――――
6. **viper,** a poisonous snake, any of a related group.

thing was this continuous motion, so dexterous I couldn't stop it. I wasn't taking any chances of being anywhere but at arm's length of that staff. My thought was of the horribly long fangs and great amount of poison accredited to the bushmaster. . . .

It had backed me halfway round the place when I spied the broom. I had passed it, but it was within reach of the crook of the staff. Giving it a hard jerk it clattered behind me. The snake was coming between the rungs in the rear of one of the chairs. Braced as it was and constantly surging forward, its loops reared in an oblique plane, I sought more distance before picking up the broom. So taking a quick step backward I kicked it a bit farther behind me, then picked it up.

Thrusting it forward, I shoved it squarely in the bushmaster's face. It didn't strike, but pulled its head back and shook it. I followed this with several more jabs, which changed the snake's tactics. It pulled its body into a tight coil and was satisfied for the moment to do no more than to beat a tattoo on the floor by shaking its tail.

I figured it had received one of the surprises of its life—and it had certainly given me the worst jolt of mine. So advancing on the now much modified striking loop, I gave the serpent more of the broom treatment; it turned, glided beneath the chairs, and, fortunately, toward the cages. By pushing the crook of the staff under its head, it was not difficult to guide the reptile upward, and it went into the cage. I was perspiring profusely when the glass panel was slid shut.

I

A DANGEROUS HOBBY

Not many families would be as cooperative as Raymond Ditmars' if a son were to bring home such an assortment of deadly and unpredictable playmates. From a young hobbyist, however, Ditmars went on to become one of the world's authorities on reptiles.

1. What may have been Ditmars' motives for taking up the collecting of snakes?

2. What marks of character and personality were revealed by Ditmars in the moments he struggled with the bushmaster?

3. In what sense was young Ditmars an adventurer?

4. Ditmars' parents had reasons for relying on his carefulness in carrying through his hobby. What indications of this are in the story?

II

IMPLICATIONS

Defend or attack the following propositions:

1. Ditmars' parents were very foolish to have allowed their son to have a "snake room" in the house.

2. Parents should allow children to pursue their interests even when an element of danger is present.

III

TECHNIQUES

Suspense and Foreshadowing

1. Show how the attitudes of each of the following people foreshadow the excitement to come: (a) the author's mother, (b) his father, (c) the expressmen, and (d) the author's correspondent in Trinidad.

2. At exactly what point in this article did you begin to experience a sensation of suspense?

Imaginative Language

"Episode of the Bushmaster" is a piece of factual writing. Its style is for the most part precise and objective. For this reason, when Ditmars uses a metaphor or simile, the imaginative language strikes the reader with great force. Discuss the simile (p. 36) in the following sentence: "The eye and brain are like a camera lens and a photographic plate." How is this comparison appropriate at the point where Ditmars uses it? How does it control the writing in the rest of the paragraph?

CALL TO ADVENTURE

The stirring call to adventure, the urge for conquest and mastery, the
excitement of uncertainty can be shared through paintings and sculpture as well
as in stories and poems. This gallery depicts adventures that will speak
differently to each of us, but it should remind us that the excitement of adventure
is as old as mankind.

THE BRONCO BUSTER
Frederic Remington
The St. Louis Art Museum
Gift of J. Lionberger Davis

From the most ancient mythologies comes the great hero who can overcome incredible monsters. Odysseus, Beowulf, and St. George are heroes in this tradition. This famous version of ST. GEORGE AND THE DRAGON comes from the great Italian painter of Madonnas, Raphael. It is an example of the art that developed during the Renaissance, in the fifteenth century.

SAINT GEORGE AND THE DRAGON
Raphael
National Gallery of Art,
Washington, D.C., Andrew Mellon Collection

A more recent hero is the cowboy of the American West. THE BRONCO BUSTER records in bronze the fierce battle between man and mustang. This piece is by a nineteenth century New Yorker, Remington, whose private adventure was the making of an artistic record of life on the Western plains. Long before the cowboy and the storyteller came the hunter, whose hazardous pleasure was really a duty to his community. The American Indian continued in this drama until a hundred years ago. Here, an unknown artist catches the thrill known to THE BUFFALO HUNTER.

THE BUFFALO HUNTER
unknown American artist
Santa Barbara Museum of Art

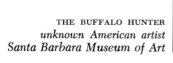

One of the famous paintings of the Western world is this panel section of THE ROUT OF SAN ROMANO by the vigorous Uccello. This battle scene vibrates with color and strong form in a way literally unknown in painting before the work of this early fifteenth century Florentine. Lautrec's THE JOCKEY captures the excitement of a different kind of battle—the battle of a horse race. The creator of this vital lithograph was a deformed and tormented little man.

LE JOCKEY
Henri de Toulouse-Lautrec

ARAB ON HORSEBACK ATTACKED BY A LION
Eugène Delacroix

BAYEAUX TAPESTRY,
Queen Mathilda, Bayeaux Castle, Normandy, France

Sometimes it was
the animal who attacked man,
as in the stirring encounter
between lion and Arab at left.
The romantic French painter
of the nineteenth century,
Eugène Delacroix, painted
this bold and moving contest.
But not all the adventurous
contests were between men
and animals; just as often
they were between men themselves,
as can be seen in the embroidered
tapestry from the twelfth century,
depicting the Norman Conquest
of England in 1066.

41

Long before airplanes, adventurous men risked their lives in balloons. NADAR ELEVATING PHOTOGRAPHY TO A HIGH ART is a visual joke as the picture puns on the fact that altitude rather than fine style is being achieved. The master printmaker, Daumier, made his living as a political cartoonist of the early nineteenth century. Winslow Homer in BREEZING UP depicts another kind of adventure—the enchantment and pleasure of sailing on the open sea. In contrast to Daumier, Homer illustrates this adventure in a serious and realistic manner. In this way he shares with us his love of the sea and sailing.

NADAR ELEVATING PHOTOGRAPHY TO A HIGH ART
Honoré Daumier

BREEZING UP
Winslow Homer
National Gallery of Art, Washington, D.C.,
Gift of the W. L. and May T. Mellon Foundation

THE CONQUEST OF THE AIR, 1913 is a joyous painting
that points to man's adventures in the air. It is a
celebration not only of its subject matter but also of the
cubist style in which Roger de La Fresnaye worked. The
basic geometric rather than natural shapes are easy to see
as you study the design and patterns of color that make
up this French tribute to the early days of flight.

There is adventure to solving any mystery—
whether it's a simple neighborhood puzzle
or a complicated international plot.
The hero of "The Red-Headed League"
is Sherlock Holmes, the classic sleuth
of all detective fiction. His power
of observation is keen; his reasoning is sharp.
Both are put to the test as Holmes fits together
an odd assortment of clues which lead him
to a daring and clever criminal.
The story is set in London
three-quarters of a century ago. Some of the words
and expressions used in the story may be puzzling.
Glancing at the footnotes or using the glossary
will be helpful in gaining a clearer picture
of what is happening. Much of the pleasure
of a detective yarn comes in being alert
to the clues the writer gives along the way.
Read with a detective's eye for details.

The
Red-Headed
League

A. CONAN DOYLE

I had called upon my friend, Mr. Sherlock Holmes, one day in the autumn of last year, and found him in deep conversation with a very stout, florid-faced, elderly gentleman, with fiery red hair. With an apology for my intrusion, I was about to withdraw, when Holmes pulled me abruptly into the room and closed the door behind me. "You could not possibly have come at a better time, my dear Watson," he said, cordially.

"I was afraid that you were engaged."

"So I am. Very much so."

"Then I can wait in the next room."

"Not at all, Watson. Mr. Wilson, I would like you to meet Dr. Watson, my partner, friend, and helper in many of my most successful cases.

The stout gentleman half rose from his chair and gave a bob of greeting, with a quick, little, questioning glance from his small, fat-encircled eyes.

"Try the settee," said Holmes, relapsing into his armchair, and putting his finger-tips together, as was his custom when in judicial moods. "I know, my dear Watson, that you share my love of all that is bizarre and outside the conventions and humdrum routine of everyday life. You have shown your relish for it by the enthusiasm which has prompted you to chronicle, and, if you will excuse my saying so, somewhat to embellish so many of my own little adventures."

"Your cases have indeed been of the greatest interest to me," I observed.

"You will remember that I remarked the other day, just before we went into the very simple problem presented by Miss Mary Sutherland, that for strange effects and extraordinary combinations we must go to life itself, which is always far more daring than any effort of the imagination."

"A proposition which I took the liberty of doubting."

"You did, doctor, but none the less you must come round to my view, for otherwise I shall keep on piling fact upon fact on you, until your reason breaks down under them and acknowledges me to be right. Now, Mr. Jabez[1] Wilson here has been good enough to call upon me this morning, and to begin a narrative which promises to be one of the most singular which I have listened to for some time. You have heard me remark that the strangest and most unique things are very often connected not with the larger but with the smaller crimes, and occasionally, indeed, where there is room for doubt whether any positive crime has been committed. As far as I have heard, it is impossible

Reprinted by permission of the Estate of Sir Arthur Conan Doyle.

1. **Jabez**\\ˈjā ˈbĕz\\.

for me to say whether the present case is an instance of crime or not, but the course of events is certainly among the most singular that I have ever listened to. Perhaps, Mr. Wilson, you would have the great kindness to recommence your narrative. I ask you, not merely because my friend, Dr. Watson, has not heard the opening part, but also because the peculiar nature of the story makes me anxious to have every possible detail from your lips. As a rule, when I have heard some slight indication of the course of events, I am able to guide myself by the thousands of other similar cases which occur to my memory. In the present instance I am forced to admit that the facts are, to the best of my belief, unique."

The portly client puffed out his chest with an appearance of some little pride, and pulled a dirty and wrinkled newspaper from the inside pocket of his greatcoat. As he glanced down the advertisement column, with his head thrust forward, and the paper flattened out upon his knee, I took a good look at the man, and endeavored, after the fashion of my companion, to read the indications which might be presented by his dress or appearance.

I did not gain very much, however, by my inspection. Our visitor bore every mark of being an average, commonplace British tradesman, obese, pompous, and slow. He wore rather baggy gray shepherd's check trousers, a not overclean black frock-coat, unbuttoned in the front, and a drab waistcoat with a heavy, brassy Albert chain,[2] and a square pierced bit of metal dangling down as an ornament. A frayed top-hat and a faded brown overcoat with a wrinkled velvet collar lay upon a chair beside him. Altogether, look as I would, there was nothing remarkable about the man save his blazing red head, and the expression of extreme chagrin and discontent upon his features.

Sherlock Holmes's quick eye took in my occupation, and he shook his head with a smile as he noticed my questioning glances. "Beyond the obvious facts that he has at some time done manual labor, that he takes snuff, that he is a Freemason,[3] that he has been in China, and

that he has done a considerable amount of writing lately, I can deduce nothing else."

Mr. Jabez Wilson started up in his chair, with his forefinger upon the paper, but with his eyes upon my companion. "How, in the name of good fortune, did you know all that, Mr. Holmes?" he asked. "How did you know, for example, that I did manual labor? It's as true as gospel, for I began as a ship's carpenter."

"Your hands, my dear sir. Your right hand is quite a size larger than your left. You have worked with it, and the muscles are more developed."

"Well, the snuff, then, and the Freemasonry?"

"I won't insult your intelligence by telling you how I read that, especially as, rather against the strict rules of your order, you use an arc-and-compass breastpin."

"Ah, of course, I forgot that. But the writing?"

"What else can be indicated by that right cuff so very shiny for five inches, and the left one with the smooth patch near the elbow where you rest it upon the desk?"

"Well, but China?"

"The fish that you have tattooed immediately above your right wrist could only have been done in China. I have made a small study of tattoo marks, and have even contributed to the literature of the subject. That trick of staining the fishes' scales of a delicate pink is quite peculiar to China. When, in addition, I see a Chinese coin hanging from your watchchain, the matter becomes even more simple."

Mr. Jabez Wilson laughed heavily. "Well, I never!" said he. "I thought at first that you had done something clever, but I see that there was nothing in it, after all."

"I begin to think, Watson," said Holmes, "that I make a mistake in explaining. '*Omne ignotum pro magnifico*,'[4] you know, and my poor little

---

2. **Albert chain,** a heavy metal watch chain named for Prince Albert, the husband of Queen Victoria.
3. **Freemason,** a member of the secret order commonly called the Masons in America. The arc-and-compass design that Holmes refers to later is used on jewelry worn by members of this society.
4. **Omne ignotum pro magnifico,** Latin, "whatever is not understood seems greater than it really is."

reputation, such as it is, will suffer shipwreck if I am so candid. Can you not find the advertisement, Mr. Wilson?"

"Yes, I have got it now," he answered, with his thick, red finger planted halfway down the column. "Here it is. This is what began it all. You just read it for yourself, sir."

I took the paper from him, and read as follows:

To the Red-Headed League:

On account of the bequest of the late Ezekiah Hopkins,[5] of Lebanon, Pa., U. S. A., there is now another vacancy open which entitles a member of the League to a salary of four pounds a week for purely nominal services. All red-headed men who are sound in body and mind, and above the age of twenty-one years, are eligible. Apply in person on Monday, at eleven o'clock, to Duncan Ross, at the offices of the League, 7 Pope's Court, Fleet Street.[6]

"What on earth does this mean?" I ejaculated, after I had twice read over the extraordinary announcement.

Holmes chuckled, and wriggled in his chair, as was his habit when in high spirits. "It is a

"What on earth does this mean?"

little off the beaten track, isn't it?" said he. "And now, Mr. Wilson, off you go at scratch,[7] and tell us all about yourself, your household, and the effect which this advertisement had upon your fortunes. You will first make a note, doctor, of the paper and the date."

"It is *The Morning Chronicle* of April 27, 1890. Just two months ago."

"Very good. Now, Mr. Wilson?"

"Well it is just as I have been telling you, Mr. Sherlock Holmes," said Jabez Wilson, mopping his forehead; "I have a small pawnbroker's business at Coburg Square, near the City.[8] It's not a very large affair, and of late years it has not done more than just give me a living. I used to be able to keep two assistants, but now I only keep one; and I would have a job to pay him, but that he is willing to come for half wages, so as to learn the business."

"What is the name of this obliging youth?" asked Sherlock Holmes.

"His name is Vincent Spaulding, and he's not such a youth, either. It's hard to say his age. I should not wish a smarter assistant, Mr. Holmes; and I know very well that he could better himself, and earn twice what I am able to give him. But, after all, if he is satisfied, why should I put ideas in his head?"

"Why indeed? You seem most fortunate in having an employee who comes under the full market price. It is not a common experience among employers in this age. I don't know that your assistant is not as remarkable as your advertisement."

"Oh, he has his faults, too," said Mr. Wilson. "Never was such a fellow for photography. Snapping away with a camera when he ought to be improving his mind, and then diving down into the cellar like a rabbit into its hole to

---

5. Ezekiah\\ĕ·zə ᴀkai·ə\.
6. Pope's Court is a short street leading from Fleet Street, the latter being an important thoroughfare running off Strand Street parallel to the Thames Embankment in historic old London.
7. **at scratch**, from the very beginning.
8. **Coburg Square**, Doyle here suggests the area near St. Pancras Station. **The City**, the heart of metropolitan London.

develop his pictures. That is his main fault; but, on the whole, he's a good worker. There's no vice in him."

"He is still with you, I presume?"

"Yes, sir. He and a girl of fourteen, who does a bit of simple cooking, and keeps the place clean—that's all I have in the house, for I am a widower, and never had any family. We live very quietly, sir, the three of us; and we keep a roof over our heads, and pay our debts, if we do nothing more.

"The first thing that put us out was that advertisement. Spaulding, he came down into the office just this day eight weeks, with this very paper in his hand, and he says:

" 'I wish to the Lord, Mr. Wilson, that I was a red-headed man.'

" 'Why that?' I asks.

" 'Why,' says he, 'here's another vacancy on the League of the Red-headed Men. It's worth quite a little fortune to any man who gets it, and I understand that there are more vacancies than there are men, so that the trustees are at their wits' end what to do with the money. If my hair would only change color, here's a nice little crib⁹ all ready for me to step into.'

" 'Why, what is it, then?' I asked. You see, Mr. Holmes, I am a very stay-at-home man, and as my business came to me instead of my having to go to it, I was often weeks on end without putting my foot over the door-mat. In that way I didn't know much of what was going on outside, and I was always glad of a bit of news.

" 'Have you never heard of the League of the Red-headed Men?' he asked, with his eyes open.

" 'Never.'

" 'Why, I wonder at that, for you are eligible yourself for one of the vacancies.'

" 'And what are they worth?' I asked.

" 'Oh, merely a couple of hundred a year, but the work is slight, and it need not interfere very much with one's other occupations.'

"Well, you can easily think that that made me prick up my ears, for the business has not been over-good for some years, and an extra couple of hundred would have been very handy.

" 'Tell me all about it,' said I.

Sir Arthur Conan Doyle

While he actually began his career as a doctor of medicine, Arthur Conan Doyle soon found a greater fascination in writing about the adventures of Sherlock Holmes than in treating patients.

The character of Sherlock Holmes, the model of so many fictional detectives who have followed him, was so realistically drawn that many people have thought he actually existed. At one time, the author decided to put an end to Holmes and had him killed in a plunge from a cliff. The protest from readers was so great that in order to quiet the storm, the author wrote another story in which it turned out that Holmes had not really perished, but had merely eluded the criminals chasing him. In this way, Sherlock Holmes has become a sort of legend existing in the half-world between fiction and reality and is one of the most famous characters in the popular literature of England.

" 'Well,' said he, showing me the advertisement, 'you can see for yourself that the League has a vacancy, and there is the address where you should apply for particulars. As far as I can make out, the League was founded by an American millionaire, Ezekiah Hopkins, who was very peculiar in his ways. He was himself red-headed, and he had a great sympathy for all red-headed men; so, when he died, it was found that he had left his enormous fortune in the hands of trustees, with instructions to apply the interest to the providing of easy berths to men whose hair is of that color. From all I hear it is splendid pay, and very little to do.'

" 'But,' said I, 'there would be millions of red-headed men who would apply.'

" 'Not so many as you might think,' he answered. 'You see it is really confined to Londoners, and to grown men. This American had started from London when he was young, and he wanted to do the old town a good turn. Then,

---

9. **crib,** an easy berth or position.

Actor Basil Rathbone in his most famous role as detective Sherlock Holmes.

west every man who had a shade of red in his hair had tramped into the City to answer the advertisement. Fleet Street was choked with red-headed folk, and Pope's Court looked like a coster's orange barrow. I should not have thought there were so many in the whole country as were brought together by that single advertisement. Every shade of color they were—straw, lemon, orange, brick, Irish-setter, liver, clay; but, as Spaulding said there were not many who had the real vivid flame-colored tint. When I saw how many were waiting I would have given it up in despair; but Spaulding would not hear of it. How he did it I could not imagine, but he pushed and pulled and butted until he got me through the crowd, and right up the steps which led to the office. There was a double stream upon the stair, some going up in hope, and some coming back dejected; but we wedged in as well as we could, and soon found ourselves in the office."

"Your experience has been a most entertaining one," remarked Holmes, as his client paused and refreshed his memory with a huge pinch of snuff. "Pray continue your very interesting statement."

"There was nothing in the office but a couple of wooden chairs and a deal table, behind which sat a small man, with a head that was even redder than mine. He said a few words to each candidate as he came up, and then he always managed to find some fault in them which would disqualify them. Getting a vacancy did not seem to be such a very easy matter, after all. However, when our turn came, the little man was much more favorable to me than to any of the others, and he closed the door as we entered, so that he might have a private word with us.

"'This is Mr. Jabez Wilson,' said my assistant, 'and he is willing to fill a vacancy in the League.'

"'And he is admirably suited for it,' the other answered. 'He has every requirement. I cannot recall when I have seen anything so fine.' He took a step backward, cocked his head on one side, and gazed at my hair until I felt quite

again, I have heard it is no use your applying if your hair is light red, or dark red, or anything but real bright, blazing, fiery red. Now, if you cared to apply, Mr. Wilson, you would just walk in; but perhaps it would hardly be worth your while to put yourself out of the way for the sake of a few hundred pounds.'

"Now, it is a fact, gentlemen, as you may see for yourself, that my hair is of a very full and rich tint, so that it seemed to me that, if there was to be any competition in the matter, I stood as good a chance as any man that I had ever met. Vincent Spaulding seemed to know so much about it that I thought he might prove useful, so I ordered him to put up the shutters for the day, and to come right away with me. He was very willing to have a holiday, so we shut the business up, and started off for the address that was given us in the advertisement.

"I never hope to see such a sight as that again, Mr. Holmes. From north, south, east, and

bashful. Then suddenly he plunged forward, wrung my hand, and congratulated me warmly on my success.

" 'It would be injustice to hesitate,' said he. 'You will, however, I am sure, excuse me for taking an obvious precaution.' With that he seized my hair in both his hands, and tugged until I yelled with the pain. 'There is water in your eyes,' said he, as he released me, 'I perceive that all is as it should be. But we have to be careful, for we have twice been deceived by wigs and once by paint. I could tell you tales of cobbler's wax which would disgust you with human nature.'

"He stepped over to the window, and shouted through it at the top of his voice that the vacancy was filled. A groan of disappointment came up from below, and the folk all trooped away in different directions, until there was not a red head to be seen except my own and that of the manager.

" 'My name,' said he, 'is Mr. Duncan Ross, and I am myself one of the pensioners upon the fund left by our noble benefactor. Are you a married man, Mr. Wilson? Have you a family?'

"I answered that I had not.

"His face fell immediately.

" 'Dear me!' he said, gravely, 'that is very serious indeed! I am sorry to hear you say that. The fund was, of course, for the propagation and spread of the red-heads as well as for their maintenance. It is exceedingly unfortunate that you should be a bachelor.'

"My face lengthened at this, Mr. Holmes, for I thought that I was not to have the vacancy after all; but, after thinking it over for a few minutes, he said that it would be all right.

" 'In the case of another,' said he, 'the objection might be fatal, but we must stretch a point in favor of a man with such a head of hair as yours. When shall you be able to enter upon your new duties?'

" 'Well, it is a little awkward, for I have a business already,' said I.

" 'Oh, never mind about that, Mr. Wilson!' said Vincent Spaulding. "I shall be able to look after that for you.'

" 'What would be the hours?' I asked.

" 'Ten to two.'

"Now a pawnbroker's business is mostly done of an evening, Mr. Holmes, especially Thursday and Friday evenings, which is just before payday, so it would suit me very well to earn a little in the mornings. Besides, I knew that my assistant was a good man, and that he would see to anything that turned up.

" 'That would suit me very well,' said I. 'And the pay?'

" 'Is four pounds a week.'[10]

" 'And the work?'

" 'Is purely nominal.'

" 'What do you call purely nominal?'

" 'Well, you have to be in the office, or at least in the building, the whole time. If you leave, you forfeit your whole position forever. The will is very clear upon that point. You don't comply with the conditions if you budge from the office during that time.'

" 'It's only four hours a day, and I should not think of leaving,' said I.

" 'No excuse will avail,' said Mr. Duncan Ross. 'Neither sickness nor business nor anything else. There you must stay, or you lose your billet.'

" 'And the work?'

" 'Is to copy out the *Encyclopedia Britannica*. There is the first volume of it in that press.[11] You must find your own ink, pens, and chair. Will you be ready tomorrow?'

" 'Certainly,' I answered.

" 'Then, good-by, Mr. Jabez Wilson, and let me congratulate you once more on the important position which you have been fortunate enough to gain.' He bowed me out of the room, and I went home with my assistant, hardly knowing what to say or do, I was so pleased at my own good fortune.

"Well, I thought over the matter all day, and by evening I was in low spirits again for I had quite persuaded myself that the whole

10. At the time of this story the English pound was worth almost five American dollars, and in general prices were much lower than they are now.
11. **press**, a shelved cupboard, or a case.

affair must be some great hoax or fraud, though what its object might be I could not imagine. It seemed altogether past belief that anyone could make such a will, or that they would pay such a sum for doing anything so simple as copying out the *Encyclopedia Britannica*. Vincent Spaulding did what he could to cheer me up, but by bedtime I had reasoned myself out of the whole thing. However, in the morning I determined to have a look at it anyhow, so I bought a penny bottle of ink, and with a quill pen and seven sheets of foolscap paper, I started off for Pope's Court.

"Well, to my surprise and delight, everything was as right as possible. The table was set out ready for me, and Mr. Duncan Ross was there to see that I got fairly to work. He started me off upon the letter A, then he left me; but he would drop in from time to time to see that all was right with me. At two o'clock he bade me good-day, complimented me upon the amount that I had written, and locked the door of the office after me.

"This went on day after day, Mr. Holmes, and on Saturday the manager came in and planked down four golden sovereigns for my week's work. It was the same next week, and the same the week after. Every morning I was there at ten, and every afternoon I left at two. By degrees Mr. Duncan Ross took to coming in only once of a morning, and then, after a time, he did not come in at all. Still, of course, I never dared to leave the room for an instant, for I was not sure when he might come, and the billet was such a good one, and suited me so well, that I would not risk the loss of it.

"Eight weeks passed away like this, and I had written about Abbots and Archery and Armor and Architecture and Attica, and hoped with diligence that I might get on to the B's before very long. It cost me something in foolscap, and I had pretty nearly filled a shelf with my writings. And then suddenly the whole business came to an end."

"To an end?"

"Yes, sir. And no later than this morning. I went to my work as usual at ten o'clock, but the door was shut and locked, with a little square of cardboard hammered on to the middle of the panel with a tack. Here it is, and you can read for yourself."

He held up a piece of white cardboard about the size of a sheet of note-paper. It read in this fashion:

THE RED-HEADED LEAGUE
IS DISSOLVED
OCTOBER 9, 1890

Sherlock Holmes and I surveyed this curt announcement and the rueful face behind it, until the comical side of the affair so completely overtopped every other consideration that we both burst out into a roar of laughter.

"I cannot see that there is anything very funny," cried our client, flushing up to the roots of his flaming head. "If you can do nothing better than laugh at me, I can go elsewhere."

"No, no," cried Holmes, shoving him back into the chair from which he had half risen. "I really wouldn't miss your case for the world. It is most refreshingly unusual. But there is, if you will excuse my saying so, something just a little funny about it. Pray, what steps did you take when you found the card upon the door?"

"I was staggered, sir. I did not know what to do. Then I called at the offices round, but none of them seemed to know anything about it. Finally, I went to the landlord, who is an accountant living on the ground-floor, and I asked him if he could tell me what had become of the Red-headed League. He said that he had never heard of any such body. Then I asked him who Mr. Duncan Ross was. He answered that the name was new to him.

" 'Well,' said I, 'the gentleman at No. 4.'

" 'What, the red-headed man?'

" 'Yes.'

" 'Oh,' said he, 'his name was William Morris. He was a solicitor,[12] and was using my room as a temporary convenience until his

---

12. **solicitor,** a business representative, or law-agent.

new premises were ready. He moved out yesterday.'

" 'Where could I find him?'

" 'Oh, at his new offices. He did tell me the address. Yes, 17 King Edward Street, near St. Paul's.'[13]

"I started off, Mr. Holmes, but when I got to that address it was a manufactory of artificial kneecaps, and no one in it had ever heard of either Mr. William Morris or Mr. Duncan Ross."

"And what did you do then?" asked Holmes.

"I went home to Saxe-Coburg Square, and I took the advice of my assistant. But he could not help me in any way. He could only say that if I waited I should hear by post. But that was not quite good enough, Mr. Holmes. I did not wish to lose such a place without a struggle; so, as I have heard that you were good enough to give advice to poor folk who were in need of it, I came right away to you."

"And you did very wisely," said Holmes. "Your case is an exceedingly remarkable one, and I shall be happy to look into it. From what you have told me I think that it is possible that graver issues hang from it than might at first sight appear."

"Grave enough!" said Mr. Jabez Wilson. "Why I have lost four pounds a week."

"As far as you are personally concerned," remarked Holmes, "I do not see that you have any grievance against this remarkable league. On the contrary, you are, as I understand, richer by some thirty pounds, to say nothing of the minute knowledge which you have gained on every subject that comes under the letter A. You have lost nothing by them."

"No, sir. But I want to find out about them, and who they are, and what their object was in playing this prank—if it was a prank—upon me. It was a pretty expensive joke for them, for it cost them two-and-thirty pounds."

"We shall endeavor to clear up these points for you. And, first, one or two questions, Mr. Wilson. This assistant of yours who first called your attention to the advertisement—how long had he been with you?"

"And the door was shut and locked."

"About a month then."

"How did he come?"

"In answer to an advertisement."

"Was he the only applicant?"

"No, I had a dozen."

"Why did you pick him?"

"Because he was handy, and would come cheap."

"At half wages, in fact?"

"Yes."

"What is he like, this Vincent Spaulding?"

"Small, stout-built, very quick in his ways, no hair on his face, though he's not short of thirty. Has a white splash of acid upon his forehead."

Holmes sat up in his chair in considerable excitement. "I thought as much," said he.

---

13. **St. Paul's Church,** a famous cathedral.

"Have you ever observed that his ears are pierced for earrings?"

"Yes sir. He told me that a gypsy had done it for him when he was a lad."

"Hum!" said Holmes, sinking back in deep thought. "He is still with you?"

"Oh, yes, sir; I have only just left him."

"And has your business been attended to in your absence?"

"Nothing to complain of, sir. There's never very much to do of a morning."

"That will do, Mr. Wilson. I shall be happy to give you an opinion upon the subject in the course of a day or two. Today is Saturday, and I hope that by Monday we may come to a conclusion."

"Well, Watson," said Holmes, when our visitor had left us, "what do you make of it all?"

"I make nothing of it," I answered, frankly. "It is a most mysterious business."

"As a rule," said Holmes, "the more bizarre a thing is, the less mysterious it proves to be. It is your commonplace, featureless crimes which are really puzzling, just as a commonplace face is the most difficult to identify. But I must be prompt over this matter."

"What are you going to do, then?" I asked.

"To smoke," he answered. "It is quite a three-pipe problem, and I beg that you won't speak to me for fifty minutes." He curled himself up in his chair, with his thin knees drawn up to his hawk-like nose, and there he sat with his eyes closed and his black clay pipe thrusting out like the bill of some strange bird. I had come to the conclusion that he had dropped asleep, and indeed was nodding myself, when he suddenly sprang out of his chair with the gesture of a man who has made up his mind, and put his pipe down upon the mantelpiece.

"Sarasate[14] plays at the St. James's Hall this afternoon," he remarked. "What do you think, Watson? Could your patients spare you for a few hours?"

"I have nothing to do today. My practice is never very absorbing."

"Then put on your hat and come. I am going through the City first, and we can have some lunch on the way. I observe that there is a good deal of German music on the program, which is rather more to my taste than Italian or French. It is introspective, and I want to introspect. Come along!"

We traveled by the Underground[15] as far as Aldersgate;[16] and a short walk took us to Saxe-Coburg Square, the scene of the singular story which we had listened to in the morning. It was a poky, little, shabby-genteel place, where four lines of dingy, two-storied brick houses looked out into a small railed-in enclosure, where a lawn of weedy grass and a few clumps of faded laurel-bushes made a hard fight against a smoke-laden and uncongenial atmosphere. Three gilt balls and a brown board with JABEZ WILSON in white letters, upon a corner house, announced the place where our red-headed client carried on his business. Sherlock Holmes stopped in front of it with his head on one side, and looked it all over, with his eyes shining brightly between puckered lids. Then he walked slowly up the street, and then down again to the corner, still looking keenly at the houses. Finally he returned to the pawnbroker's, and, having thumped vigorously upon the pavement with his stick two or three times, he went up to the door and knocked. It was instantly opened by a bright-looking, clean-shaven young fellow, who asked him to step in.

"Thank you," said Holmes, "I only wished to ask you how you would go from here to the Strand."[17]

"Third right, fourth left," answered the assistant, promptly, closing the door. "Smart fellow, that," observed Holmes, as we walked away. "He is, in my judgment, the fourth smartest man in London, and for daring, I am

---

14. **Pablo de Sarasate**\ˈsä•rə ˈsä ˈtē\ a Spanish violinist (1844–1908).
15. Londoners call their subway system the Underground.
16. **Aldersgate,** a section of London a little north of St. Paul's.
17. **The Strand** is a famous London street.

not sure that he has not a claim to be third. I have known something of him before."

"Evidently," said I, "Mr. Wilson's assistant counts for a good deal in this mystery of the Red-headed League. I am sure that you inquired your way merely in order that you might see him."

"Not him."

"What then?"

"The knees of his trousers."

"And what did you see?"

"What I expected to see."

"Why did you beat the pavement?"

"My dear doctor, this is a time for observation, not for talk. We are spies in an enemy's country. We know something of Saxe-Coburg Square. Let us now explore the parts which lie behind it."

The road in which we found ourselves as we turned round the corner from the retired Saxe-Coburg Square presented as great a contrast to it as the front of a picture does to the back. It was one of the main arteries which convey the traffic of the City to the north and west. The roadway was blocked with the immense stream of commerce flowing in a double tide inward and outward, while the foot-paths[18] were black with the hurrying swarm of pedestrians. It was difficult to realize, as we looked at the line of fine shops and stately business premises, that they really abutted on the other side upon the faded and stagnant square which we had just quitted.

"Let me see," said Holmes, standing at the corner, and glancing along the line, "I should like just to remember the order of the houses here. It is a hobby of mine to have an exact knowledge of London. There is Mortimer's, the tobacconist, the little newspaper shop, the Coburg branch of the City and Suburban Bank, the Vegetarian Restaurant, and Mc-Farlane's carriage-building depot. That carries us right on to the other block. And now, doctor, we've done our work, so it's time we had some play. A sandwich and a cup of coffee, and then off to violinland, where all is sweetness and delicacy and harmony, and there are

The Sherlock Holmes exhibition, London, 1951; the living room of 22b Baker Street reconstructed by Michael Weight for St. Marylebone Borough Council.

no red-headed clients to vex us with their conundrums."

My friend was an enthusiastic musician, being himself not only a very capable performer, but a composer of no ordinary merit. All the afternoon he sat in the stalls[19] wrapped in the most perfect happiness, gently waving his long, thin fingers in time to the music, while his gently smiling face and his languid, dreamy eyes were as unlike those of Holmes, the sleuth-hound, Holmes, the relentless, keen-witted, ready-handed criminal agent, as it was possible to conceive. In his singular character the dual nature alternately asserted itself, and his extreme exactness and astuteness represented, as I have often thought, the reaction against the poetic and contemplative mood which occasionally predominated in him. The swing of his nature took him from extreme languor to devouring energy; and, as I knew well, he was never so truly formidable as when, for days on end, he had been lounging in his

---

18. **foot-paths,** British for *sidewalks*.
19. **stalls,** theater seats nearest the orchestra on the ground floor.

armchair amid his improvisations and his black-letter editions. Then it was that the lust of the chase would suddenly come upon him, and that his brilliant reasoning power would rise to the level of intuition, until those who were unacquainted with his methods would look askance at him as on a man whose knowledge was not that of other mortals. When I saw him that afternoon so enwrapped in the music at St. James's Hall, I felt that an evil time might be coming upon those whom he had set himself to hunt down.

"You want to go home, no doubt, doctor," he remarked, as we emerged.

"Yes, it would be as well."

"And I have some business to do which will take some hours. This business at Coburg Square is serious."

"Why serious?"

"A considerable crime is in contemplation. I have every reason to believe that we shall be in time to stop it. But today being Saturday rather complicates matters. I shall want your help tonight."

"At what time?"

"Ten will be early enough."

"I shall be at Baker Street[20] at ten."

"Very well. And, I say, doctor, there may be some little danger, so kindly put your army revolver in your pocket." He waved his hand, turned on his heel, and disappeared in an instant among the crowd.

I trust that I am not more dense than my neighbors, but I was always oppressed with a sense of my own stupidity in my dealings with Sherlock Holmes. Here I had heard what he had heard, I had seen what he had seen, and yet from his words it was evident that he saw clearly not only what had happened, but what was about to happen, while to me the whole business was still confused and grotesque. As I drove home to my house in Kensington[21] I thought over it all from the extraordinary story of the red-headed copier of the *Encyclopedia* down to the visit to Saxe-Coburg Square, and the ominous words with which he had parted from me. What was this nocturnal expedition,

and why should I go armed? Where were we going, and what were we to do? I had the hint from Holmes that this smooth-faced pawn-broker's assistant was a formidable man—a man who might play a deep game. I tried to puzzle it out, but gave it up in despair, and set the matter aside until night should bring an explanation.

It was a quarter past nine when I started from home and made my way across the Park, and so through Oxford Street to Baker Street.[22] Two hansoms were standing at the door, and, as I entered the passage, I heard the sound of voices from above. On entering his room I found Holmes in animated conversation with two men, one of whom I recognized as Peter Jones, the official police agent, while the other was a long, thin, sad-faced man, with a very shiny hat and oppressively respectable frock-coat.[23]

"Ha! our party is complete," said Holmes, buttoning up his pea-jacket,[24] and taking his heavy hunting crop[25] from the rack. "Watson, I think you know Mr. Jones, of Scotland Yard?[26] Let me introduce you to Mr. Merry-weather, who is to be our companion in tonight's adventure."

"We're hunting in couples again, doctor, you see," said Jones, in his consequential way. "Our friend here is a wonderful man for starting a chase. All he wants is an old dog to help him do the running down."

---

20. Holmes lived on Baker Street. This Baker Street is between Regent's Park and Hyde Park. London has several other Baker Streets.
21. **Kensington,** a well-to-do residential section west of Hyde Park in London.
22. The Park is Hyde Park east of Kensington. Oxford Street is a major street running from Hyde Park to Baker Street.
23. **frock-coat**\frŏk\ a long double-breasted dress overcoat.
24. **pea-jacket,** a short, loose, heavy, double-breasted coat.
25. **crop,** a short riding whip.
26. **Scotland Yard,** the headquarters of the London police, especially its detective division, located on Scotland Street near Whitehall.

"I hope a wild goose may not prove to be the end of our chase," observed Mr. Merryweather, gloomily.

"You may place considerable confidence in Mr. Holmes, sir," said the police agent, loftily. "He has his own little methods, which are, if he won't mind my saying so, just a little too theoretical and fantastic, but he has the makings of a detective in him. It is not too much to say that once or twice, as in that business of the Sholto murder and the Agra treasure,[27] he has been more nearly correct than the official force."

"Oh, if you say so, Mr. Jones, it is all right," said the stranger, with deference. "Still, I confess that I miss my rubber.[28] It is the first Saturday night for seven-and-twenty years that I have not had my rubber."

"I think you will find," said Sherlock Holmes, "that you will play for a higher stake tonight than you have ever done yet, and that the play will be more exciting. For you, Mr. Merryweather, the stake will be some thirty thousand pounds; and for you, Jones, it will be the man upon whom you wish to lay your hands."

"John Clay, the murderer, thief, smasher,[29] and forger. He's a young man, Mr. Merryweather, but he is at the head of his profession, and I would rather have my bracelets[30] on him than on any criminal in London. He's a remarkable man, is young John Clay. His grandfather was a royal duke, and he himself has been to Eton and Oxford.[31] His brain is as cunning as his fingers, and though we meet signs of him at every turn, we never know where to find the man himself. He'll crack a crib[32] in Scotland one week, and be raising money to build an orphanage in Cornwall[33] the next. I've been on his track for years, and have never set eyes on him yet."

"I hope that I may have the pleasure of introducing you tonight. I've had one or two little turns also with Mr. John Clay, and I agree with you that he is at the head of his profession. It is past ten, however, and quite time that we started. If you two will take the first

hansom,[34] Watson and I will follow in the second."

Sherlock Holmes was not very communicative during the long drive, and lay back in the cab humming the tunes which he had heard in the afternoon. We rattled through an endless labyrinth of gas-lit streets until we emerged into Farringdon Street.

"We are close there now," my friend remarked. "This fellow Merryweather is a bank director, and personally interested in the matter. I thought it as well to have Jones with us also. He is not a bad fellow, though an absolute imbecile in his profession. He has one positive virtue. He is as brave as a bulldog, and as tenacious as a lobster if he gets his claws upon anyone. Here we are, and they are waiting for us."

We had reached the same crowded thoroughfare in which we had found ourselves in the morning. Our cabs were dismissed, and, following the guidance of Mr. Merryweather, we passed down a narrow passage and through a side door, which he opened for us. Within, there was a small corridor, which ended in a very massive iron gate. This also was opened, and led down a flight of winding stone steps, which terminated at another formidable gate. Mr. Merryweather stopped to light a lantern, and then conducted us down a dark, earth-smelling passage, and so, after opening a third door, into a huge vault, or cellar, which was piled all round with crates and massive boxes.

"You are not very vulnerable from above,"

---

27. The Sholto murder and the Agra treasure were referred to in a mystery story called "The Sign of the Four," another Sherlock Holmes story.
28. **rubber,** a game of whist or bridge.
29. **smasher,** a person who passes counterfeit money.
30. **bracelets,** handcuffs.
31. **Eton** \ˈē·tən\ a famous English preparatory school at Eton on the Thames west of London. **Oxford,** one of England's two most famous universities.
32. **crack a crib,** break into a building.
33. **Cornwall,** the southwestern county in England.
34. **hansom** \ˈhăn·səm\ a one-horse, two-wheeled, covered carriage with the coachman's seat above and behind the passenger's cab.

Holmes remarked, as he held up the lantern and gazed about him.

"Nor from below," said Mr. Merryweather, striking his stick upon the flags which lined the floor. "Why, dear me, it sounds quite hollow!" he remarked, looking up in surprise.

"I must really ask you to be a little more quiet," said Holmes, severely. "You have already imperiled the whole success of our expedition. Might I beg that you would have the goodness to sit down upon one of those boxes, and not to interfere?"

The solemn Mr. Merryweather perched himself upon a crate, with a very injured expression upon his face, while Holmes fell upon his knees upon the floor, and, with the lantern and a magnifying lens, began to examine minutely the cracks between the stones. A few seconds sufficed to satisfy him, for he sprang to his feet again, and put his glass in his pocket.

"We have at least an hour before us," he remarked; "for they can hardly take any steps until the good pawnbroker is safely in bed. Then they will not lose a minute, for the sooner they do their work the longer time they will have for their escape. We are at present, doctor—as no doubt you have divined—in the cellar of the City branch of one of the principal London banks. Mr. Merryweather is the chairman of directors, and he will explain to you that there are reasons why the more daring criminals of London should take a considerable interest in this cellar at present."

"It is our French gold," whispered the director. "We have had several warnings that an attempt might be made upon it."

"Your French gold?"

"Yes. We had occasion some months ago to strengthen our resources and borrowed, for that purpose, thirty thousand napoleons[35] from the Bank of France. It has become known that we have never had occasion to unpack the money, and that it is still lying in our cellar. The crate upon which I sit contains two thousand napoleons packed between layers of lead foil. Our reserve of bullion is much larger at present than is usually kept in a single branch office, and the directors have had misgivings upon the subject."

"Which were very well justified," observed Holmes. "And now it is time that we arranged our little plans. I expect that within an hour matters will come to a head. In the meantime, Mr. Merryweather, we must put the screen over that dark lantern."

"And sit in the dark?"

"I am afraid so. I had brought a pack of cards in my pocket, and I thought that, as we were a *partie carrée*,[36] you might have your rubber after all. But I see that the enemy's preparations have gone so far that we cannot risk the presence of a light. And, first of all, we must choose our positions. These are daring men, and though we shall take them at a disadvantage, they may do us some harm unless we are careful. I shall stand behind this crate, and do you conceal yourself behind those. Then when I flash a light upon them, close in swiftly. If they fire, Watson, have no compunction about shooting them down."

I placed my revolver, cocked, upon the top of the wooden case behind which I crouched. Holmes shot the slide across the front of his lantern, and left us in pitch darkness—such an absolute darkness as I have never before experienced. The smell of hot metal remained to assure us that the light was still there, ready to flash out at a moment's notice. To me, with my nerves worked up to a pitch of expectancy, there was something depressing and subduing in the sudden gloom, and in the cold, dank air of the vault.

"They have but one retreat," whispered Holmes. "That is back through the house into Saxe-Coburg Square. I hope that you have done what I asked you, Jones?"

"I have an inspector and two officers waiting at the front door."

"Then we have stopped all the holes. And now we must be silent and wait."

---

35. **napoleon,** a French gold coin worth about twenty francs.
36. **partie carrée** 'pär 'tē ka ▲rā\\ a party of four.

What a time it seemed! From comparing notes afterwards it was but an hour and a quarter, yet it appeared to me that the night must have almost gone, and the dawn be breaking above us. My limbs were weary and stiff, for I feared to change my position; yet my nerves were worked up to the highest pitch of tension, and my hearing was so acute that I could not only hear the gentle breathing of my companions, but I could distinguish the deeper, heavier in-breath of the bulky Jones from the thin, sighing note of the bank director. From my position I could look over the case in the direction of the floor. Suddenly my eyes caught the glint of a light.

At first it was but a lurid spark upon the stone pavement. Then it lengthened out until it became a yellow line, and then, without any warning or sound, a gash seemed to open and a hand appeared; a white, almost womanly hand, which felt about in the center of the little area of light. For a minute or more the hand, with its writhing fingers, protruded out of the floor. Then it was withdrawn as suddenly as it appeared, and all was dark again save the single lurid spark which marked a chink between the stones.

Its disappearance, however, was but momentary. With a rending, tearing sound, one of the broad, white stones turned over upon its side, and left a square, gaping hole, through which streamed the light of a lantern. Over the edge there peeped a clean-cut, boyish face, which looked keenly about it, and then, with a hand on either side of the aperture, drew itself shoulder-high and waist-high, until one knee rested upon the edge. In another instant he stood at the side of the hole, and was hauling after him a companion, lithe and small like himself, with a pale face and a shock of very red hair.

"It's all clear," he whispered. "Have you the chisel and the bags? Great Scott! Jump, Archie, jump, and I'll swing for it!"[37]

Sherlock Holmes had sprung out and seized the intruder by the collar. The other dived down the hole, and I heard the sound of rending cloth as Jones clutched at his skirts. The light flashed upon the barrel of a revolver, but Holmes's hunting crop came down on the man's wrist, and the pistol clinked upon the stone floor.

"It's no use, John Clay," said Holmes blandly. "You have no chance at all."

"So I see," the other answered, with the utmost coolness. "I fancy that my pal is all right, though I see you have got his coat-tails."

"There are three men waiting for him at the door," said Holmes.

"Oh, indeed! You seem to have done the thing very completely. I must compliment you."

"And I you," Holmes answered. "Your red-headed idea was very new and effective."

"You'll see your pal again presently," said Jones. "He's quicker at climbing down holes than I am. Just hold out while I fix the derbies."[38]

"I beg that you will not touch me with your filthy hands," remarked our prisoner, as the handcuffs clattered upon his wrists. "You may not be aware that I have royal blood in my veins. Have the goodness, also, when you address me always to say 'sir' and 'please.'"

"All right," said Jones, with a stare and a snigger. "Well, would you please, sir, march upstairs, where we can get a cab to carry your highness to the police-station?"

"That is better," said John Clay, serenely. He made a sweeping bow to the three of us, and walked quietly off in the custody of the detective.

"Really, Mr. Holmes," said Mr. Merryweather, as we followed them from the cellar, "I do not know how the bank can thank you or repay you. There is no doubt that you have detected and defeated in the most complete manner one of the most determined attempts at bank robbery that has ever come within my experience."

---

37. **swing for it,** be hanged or pay some other penalty for it.
38. **derbies**\ˈdär·bēz\ handcuffs.

"I have had one or two little scores of my own to settle with Mr. John Clay," said Holmes. "I have been at some small expense over this matter, which I shall expect the bank to refund, but beyond that I am amply repaid by having had an experience which is in many ways unique, and by hearing the very remarkable narrative of the Red-headed League."

"You see, Watson," he explained, in the early hours of the morning, as we sat over a glass of whisky-and-soda in Baker Street, "it was perfectly obvious from the first that the only possible object of this rather fantastic business of the advertisement of the League, and the copying of the *Encyclopedia*, must be to get this not over-bright pawnbroker out of the way for a number of hours every day. It was a curious way of managing it, but, really, it would be difficult to suggest a better. The method was no doubt suggested to Clay's ingenious mind by the color of his accomplice's hair. The four pounds a week was a lure which must draw him, and what was it to them, who were playing for thousands? They put in the advertisement, one rogue has the temporary office, the other rogue incites the man to apply for it, and together they manage to secure his absence every morning in the week. From the time that I heard of the assistant having come for half wages, it was obvious to me that he had some strong motive for securing the situation."

"But how could you guess what the motive was?"

"Had there been women in the house, I should have suspected a mere vulgar intrigue. That, however, was out of the question. The man's business was a small one, and there was nothing in his house which could account for such elaborate preparations and such an expenditure as they were at. It must, then, be something out of the house. What could it be? I thought of the assistant's fondness for photography, and his trick of vanishing into the cellar. The cellar! There was the end of this tangled clue. Then I made inquiries as to this mysterious assistant, and found that I had to deal with one of the coolest and most daring criminals in London. He was doing something in the cellar—something which took many hours a day for months on end. What could it be, once more? I could think of nothing save that he was running a tunnel to some other building.

"So far I had got when we went to visit the scene of action. I surprised you by beating upon the pavement with my stick. I was ascertaining whether the cellar stretched out in front or behind. It was not in front. Then I rang the bell, and, as I hoped, the assistant answered it. We have had some skirmishes, but we had never set eyes upon each other before. I hardly looked at his face. His knees were what I wished to see. You must yourself have remarked how worn, wrinkled, and stained they were. They spoke of those hours of burrowing. The only remaining point was what they were burrowing for. I walked round the corner, saw the City and Suburban Bank abutted on our friend's premises, and felt that I had solved my problem. When you drove home after the concert, I called upon Scotland Yard and upon the chairman of the bank directors, with the result that you have seen."

"And how could you tell that they would make their attempt tonight?"

"Well, when they closed their League offices, that was a sign that they cared no longer about Mr. Jabez Wilson's presence—in other words, that they had completed their tunnel. But it was essential that they should use it soon, as it might be discovered, or the bullion might be removed. Saturday would suit them better than any other day, as it would give them two days for their escape. For all these reasons I expected them to come tonight."

"You reasoned it out beautifully," I exclaimed, in unfeigned admiration. "It is so long a chain, and yet every link rings true."

"It saved me from ennui,"[39] he answered, yawning. "Alas! I already feel it closing in upon me. My life is spent in one long effort to

---

39. **ennui**\ɔn ▴wē\ boredom.

escape from the commonplaces of existence. These little problems help me to do so."

"And you are a benefactor of the race," said I.

He shrugged his shoulders. "Well, perhaps, after all, it is of some little use," he remarked. "'L'homme c'est rien—l'œuvre c'est tout,' as Gustave Flaubert wrote to George Sand."[40]

I
THE FASCINATION OF A MYSTERY

Conan Doyle has carefully woven a series of telltale clues into this detective story. Unless close attention is paid to detail, the reader does not have the full satisfaction of understanding how Holmes arrived at his solution of the mystery.

1. Why did Holmes discuss with Watson the exact location of the businesses which were in the block behind the pawnshop?

2. Who was Mr. Merryweather? Why did Holmes scold him for tapping on the floor of the vault?

3. Dr. Watson does not seem to be much of a detective, but he is in the story for a definite purpose. Discuss what you think this to be.

4. Are you satisfied with Holmes's explanation of how he solved the mystery? Was everything explained satisfactorily? What do you suppose the criminals did with the dirt taken from the tunnel?

5. The following quotations are all spoken by Sherlock Holmes. What do they suggest about the lure of adventure to him?

a. ". . . my love of all that is bizarre and outside the conventions and humdrum routine of everyday life."

b. ". . . for strange effects and extraordinary combinations we must go to life itself, which is always far more daring than any effort of the imagination."

---

40. L'homme c'est rien—l'œuvre c'est tout, "man is nothing—his work is all." **Gustave Flaubert**\ˈgus ˈtav ˈflō ˈbär\ (1821–1880), French novelist. **George Sand** \jȯrj sand\ pen name of Madame Dudevant\dü•də-ˈvän\ another French novelist (1804–1876).

c. "It is most refreshingly unusual."

d. "It saved me from ennui," he answered, yawning. "Alas! I already feel it closing in upon me. My life is one long effort to escape from the commonplaces of existence. These little problems help me to do so."

II
IMPLICATIONS

Writers of mystery stories usually picture the police as bungling, stupid, and inefficient. The implication is that more difficult crimes can be solved only by a "supersleuth" or a private individual outside the police organization. Discuss why this idea has such popular appeal, and why it has become a recurrent theme for countless short stories, novels, and dramas.

III
TECHNIQUES

Conflict

Discuss the main conflict in "The Red-headed League." With whom or what is Sherlock Holmes matching wits?

Suspense and Foreshadowing

1. Holmes says: "This business at Coburg Square is serious." What does he tell Watson to bring with him for their meeting that night? How does this emphasize the element of danger?

2. Early in the story, Conan Doyle arouses questions about the character of Vincent Spaulding. How is this done? How does Holmes reveal in his first conversation with Wilson that the man called Spaulding is known to him?

Imaginative Language

1. Midway through the story, Holmes requests Dr. Watson not to speak to him for fifty minutes while he smokes and thinks about the mysterious Red-headed League. Here the author presents the reader with a picture of Holmes curled up in his chair. What two features always associated with the image of Sherlock Holmes, detective, are mentioned here?

2. What similes does Holmes use to tell you why he wishes to have Peter Jones with them as they go after the criminal?

The Pole

Introduction

Inside the warm igloos of the Eskimos of North Greenland at feast time, the name *Miy Paluk*, which means "brother," is still heard in song and story. It stands for a man whose warm, hearty laughter and skill at hunting and fishing made him a hero these people like to remember. *Miy Paluk's* formal name was Matthew Alexander Henson. He was the black man who accompanied Navy Commander Robert E. Peary on all but one of his hazard-filled expeditions to the Arctic.

Had it not been for *Miy Paluk's* extraordinary intelligence, ingenuity, and dependability, it is quite possible that Peary might never have achieved his goal. It was Henson who quickly learned the language of the Eskimos and acted as trader and hunter for the expeditions, Henson who designed and built the sledges used for the final dash to the Pole, Henson who trained the dogs to pull the sledges, and Henson whose unfailing good humor and quiet courage served as a continuing source of inspiration for the other expedition members.

Left an orphan at seven, Matthew Henson was only thirteen when the desire for adventure became so strong within him that he could no longer resist it. He left his job in Washington, D.C., and walked to Baltimore to ship aboard the towering three-masted merchantman *Katie Hines* as cabin boy. After his first voyage he became a seaman and for the next four years sailed all over the world.

When Captain Childs died, Henson took a job ashore as a stock clerk in a clothing store in the nation's capital. After his years at sea, he did not find this work to be very exciting. When a young civil engineer named Peary came into the store one day and offered Henson the chance to go with him to Nicaragua on a surveying expedition for the Navy, Henson accepted eagerly.

Between 1891 and 1909, Peary led eight expeditions to the frozen North, each of the last ones bringing him a little closer to finding out what lay at the uppermost axis of the earth. On July 8, 1908, the final expedition left New York on the specially built icebreaker, the S.S. *Roosevelt*. Struggling through ice-filled Arctic waters, the *Roosevelt* made it to Cape Sheridan, a base where the party spent the long winter of continuous darkness. From there they embarked by sled on February 18, 1909, across the ever-moving and drifting ice of the Arctic Ocean, to make their last attempt to reach the North Pole.

At this time Arctic night still prevailed, but to the south a thin band of twilight was beginning to show. Each day the period of light would lengthen. Every minute counted if the trip to the North Pole were to be accomplished and the return to land made before the ice floes became impassable. And, if the ship were to be able to take advantage of the breakup of the ice to make the voyage back to the states, the party had to return to the *Roosevelt* by midsummer.

In their race against time, designated support teams moved ahead to break trail and carry supplies. On a planned schedule, the teams turned back, eventually to reassemble at the ship to await Peary's return. By March 30, all of the teams had turned back except for the two headed by Bartlett, captain of the *Roosevelt*, and Matthew Henson. They awoke that morning to find open water all around them, and it was not until 5 P.M., with the temperature at 43 degrees below zero, that they were able to move ahead. The ice was so thin in places that it undulated beneath them. As this account begins it is April 1, and Captain Bartlett, who has broken trail ahead to a point 87°48′ north latitude,[1] the farthest north thus far reached by man, has just turned back.

---

1. **87°48′ north latitude.** Latitude measures distance north and south of the Equator.

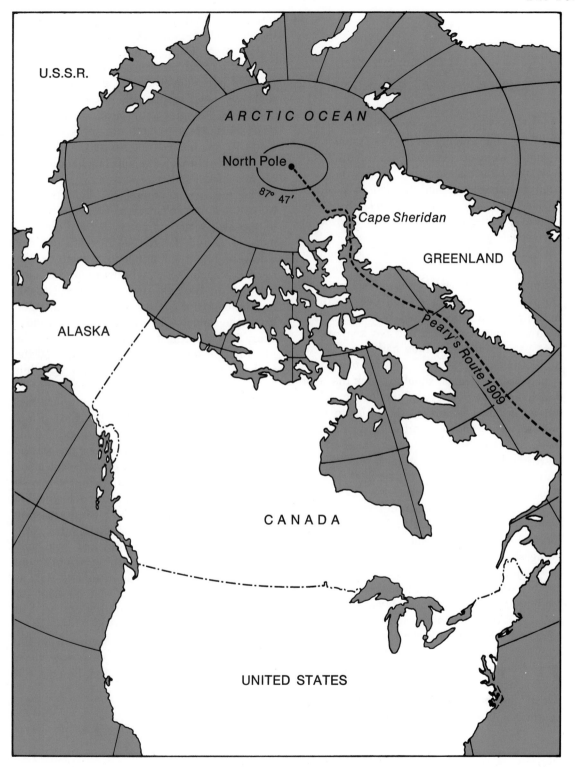

U.S.S.R.

ARCTIC OCEAN

North Pole

87° 47'

Cape Sheridan

GREENLAND

ALASKA

Peary's Route 1909

CANADA

UNITED STATES

The Pole

MATTHEW A. HENSON

Day and night were the same. My thoughts were on the going and getting forward, and on nothing else. The wind was from the southeast, and seemed to push us on, and the sun was at our backs, a ball of livid fire, rolling his way above the horizon in never-ending day.

Captain Bartlett had gone. Commander Peary and I were alone (save for the four Eskimos, Ootah, Egingwah, Seegloo and Ooquah), the same as we had been so often in the past years. As we looked at each other, we realized our position and we knew without speaking that 'the time had come for us to demonstrate that we were the men who, it had been ordained, should unlock the door which held the mystery of the Arctic. Without an instant's hesitation, the order to push on was given, and we started off in the trail made by the captain to cover the Farthest North he had made and to push on over one hundred and thirty miles to our final destination.

The captain had had rough going, but, owing to the fact that his trail was our track for a short time, and that we came to good going shortly after leaving his turning point, we made excellent distance without any trouble, and only stopped when we came to a lead[2] barely frozen over, a full twenty-five miles beyond. We camped and waited for the strong southeast wind to force the sides of the lead together. The Eskimos had eaten a meal of stewed dog, cooked over a fire of wood from a discarded sledge, and, owing to their wonderful powers of recuperation, were in good condition. Commander Peary and myself, rested and invigorated by our thirty hours in the last camp, waiting for the return and departure of Captain Bartlett, were also in fine fettle,[3] and accordingly the accomplishment of twenty-five miles of northward progress was not exceptional. With my proven ability in gauging distances, Commander Peary was ready to take the reckoning as I made it and he did not resort to solar[4] observations until we were within a hand's grasp of the Pole.

The memory of those last five marches, from the Farthest North of Captain Bartlett to the arrival of our party at the Pole, is a memory of toil, fatigue, and exhaustion, but we were urged on and encouraged by our relentless commander, who was himself being scourged by the final lashings of the dominating influence that had controlled his life. From the land to 87° 48′ north, Commander Peary had had the best of the going, for he had brought up the rear and had utilized the trail made by the preceding parties, and thus he had kept himself in the best of condition for the time when he made the spurt that brought him to the end of the race. From 87° 48′ north, he kept in the lead and did his work in such a way as to convince me that he was still as good a man as he had ever been. We marched and marched, falling down in our tracks repeatedly, until it was impossible to go on. We were forced to camp, in spite of the impatience of the commander, who found himself unable to rest, and who only waited long enough for us to relax into sound sleep, when he would wake us up and start us off again. I do not believe that he slept for one hour from April 2 until after he had loaded us up and ordered us to go back over our old trail, and I often think that from the instant when the order to return was given until the land was again sighted, he was in a continual daze.

---

2. **lead**\lēd\ a narrow channel of water through a field of ice.
3. **fettle**\ˈfĕt·əl\ good spirits.
4. **solar**\ˈsō·lər\ pertaining to the sun.

Reprinted by permission of the Publisher, Walker and Company, New York.

Onward we forced our weary way. Commander Peary took his sights from the time our chronometer watches[5] gave, and I, knowing that we had kept on going in practically a straight line, was sure that we had more than covered the necessary distance to insure our arrival at the top of the earth.

It was during the march of the third of April that I endured an instant of hideous horror. We were crossing a lane of moving ice. Commander Peary was in the lead setting the pace, and a half hour later the four boys and myself followed in single file. They had all gone before, and I was standing and pushing at the upstanders of my sledge when the block of ice I was using as a support slipped from underneath my feet, and before I knew it the sledge was out of my grasp, and I was floundering in the water of the lead. I did the best I could. I tore my hood from off my head and struggled frantically. My hands were gloved and I could not take hold of the ice, but before I could give the "Grand Hailing Sigh of Distress," faithful old Ootah had grabbed me by the nape of the neck, the same as he would have grabbed a dog, and with one hand he pulled me out of the water and with the other hurried the team across.

He had saved my life, but I did not tell him so, for such occurrences are taken as part of the day's work, and the sledge he safeguarded was of much more importance, for it held, as part of its load, the commander's sextant,[6] the mercury, and the coils of piano wire that were the essential portion of the scientific part of the expedition. My *kamiks* (boots of sealskin) were stripped off, and the congealed water was beaten out of my bearskin trousers, and with a dry pair of *kamiks* we hurried on to overtake the column. When we caught up, we found the boys gathered around the commander, doing their best to relieve him of his discomfort, for he had fallen into the water also, and while he was not complaining, I was sure that his bath had not been any more voluntary than mine had been.

When we halted on April 6, 1909, and started to build the igloos, the dogs and sledges having been secured, I noticed Commander Peary at work unloading his sledge and unpacking several bundles of equipment. He pulled out from under his *kooletah* (thick, fur outer garment) a small folded package and unfolded it. I recognized his old silk flag, and realized that this was to be a camp of importance. Our different camps had been known as Camp Number One, Number Two, etc., but after the turning back of Captain Bartlett, the camps had been given names such as Camp Nansen, Camp Cagni, etc., and I asked what the name of this camp was to be—"Camp Peary"? "This, Matthew, is to be Camp Morris K. Jesup, the last and most northerly camp on the earth." He fastened the flag to a staff and planted it firmly on the top of his igloo. For a few minutes it hung limp and lifeless in the dead calm of the haze, and then a slight breeze, increasing in strength, caused the folds to straighten out, and soon it was rippling out in sparkling color. The stars and stripes were "nailed to the Pole."

A thrill of patriotism ran through me and I raised my voice to cheer the starry emblem of my native land. The Eskimos gathered around and, taking the time from Commander Peary, three hearty cheers rang out on the still, frosty air, our dumb dogs looking on in puzzled surprise. As prospects for getting a sight of the sun were not good, we turned in and slept, leaving the flag proudly floating above us.

This was a thin silk flag that Commander Peary had carried on all of his Arctic journeys, and he had always flown it at his last camps. It was as glorious and as inspiring a banner as any battle scarred, bloodstained standard of the world—and this badge of honor and courage was also bloodstained and battle scarred, for at several places there were blank

---

5. **chronometer watches**\krə ˈnŏm•ət•ər\ exceptionally precise timepieces.
6. **sextant**\ˈsĕk•stənt\ an instrument for measuring altitudes of celestial bodies from a moving ship or airplane in order to determine longitude and latitude.

squares marking the spots where pieces had been cut out at each of the "farthests" of its brave bearer and left with the records in the cairns[7] as mute but eloquent witnesses of his achievements. At the North Pole a diagonal strip running from the upper left to the lower right corner was cut, and this precious strip, together with a brief record, was placed in an empty tin, sealed up and buried in the ice as a record for all time.

Commander Peary also had another American flag, sewn on a white ground, and it was the emblem of the "Daughters of the Revolu-

tion Peace Society." He also had and flew the emblem of the Navy League and the emblems of a couple of college fraternities of which he was a member.

It was about 10 or 10:30 A.M., on the seventh of April, 1909, that the commander gave the order to build a snow shield to protect him from the flying drift of the surface snow. I knew that he was about to take an observation, and while we worked I was

---

7. **cairns**\kā(ə)rnz\ piles of stone erected as memorials or landmarks.

nervously apprehensive, for I felt that the end of our journey had come. When we handed him the pan of mercury the hour was within a very few minutes of noon. Lying flat on his stomach, he took the elevation and made the notes on a piece of tissue paper at his head. With sun-blinded eyes, he snapped shut the *vernier* (a graduated scale that subdivides the smallest divisions on the sector of the circular scale of the sextant) and with the resolute squaring of his jaws, I was sure that he was satisfied, and I was confident that the journey had ended. Feeling that the time had come, I ungloved my right hand and went forward to congratulate him on the success of our eighteen years of effort, but a gust of wind blew something into his eye, or else the burning pain caused by his prolonged look at the reflection of the limb of the sun forced him to turn aside; and with both hands covering his eyes, he gave us orders to not let him sleep for more than four hours. Six hours later he purposed to take another sight about four miles beyond, and he wanted at least two hours to make the trip and get everything in readiness.

I unloaded a sledge, and reloaded it with a couple of skins, the instruments, and a cooker with enough alcohol and food for one meal for three, and then I turned into the igloo where my boys were already sound asleep. The thermometer registered 29 degrees below zero. I fell into a dreamless sleep and slept for about a minute, so I thought, when I was awakened by the clatter and noise made by the return of Peary and his boys.

The commander gave the word, "We will plant the stars and stripes—*at the North Pole!*" and it was done. On the peak of a huge paleocrystic floeberg[8] the glorious banner was unfurled to the breeze, and as it snapped and crackled with the wind, I felt a savage joy and exultation.

---

8. **paleocrystic floeberg**\\'pā·lē·ō ᴬkrĭs·tĭk ᴬflō·bərg\\ a massive slab of ice of ancient origin formed on the surface of a body of water.

I
THE UNKNOWN BECKONS

In the opening years of this century, when Peary made up his mind that he was going to be the man to discover the North Pole, most people thought he was foolhardy. At this time aviation had not developed to the point where aerial surveys or rescues could be made. No one even knew whether there was land at the North Pole or only shifting ice floes. There wasn't even radio to keep in touch with the outside world. But even though the danger was great, Matthew Henson said that Peary seemed to inspire confidence in all who worked with him.

1. What evidence do you find in the account you have read to show that Peary, in turn, places great confidence in Matthew Henson?

2. Describe Matthew Henson's instant of "hideous horror."

II
IMPLICATIONS

1. Matthew Henson ended his book, first published in 1912, with the words: ". . . the lure of the Arctic is tugging at my heart; to me the trail is calling." From this the conclusion could be drawn that a real adventurer continues to feel a desire for adventure throughout his life, while the ordinary person does not have this feeling.

2. The achievements of most great explorers are built on the labors of those who accompany and aid them.

III
TECHNIQUES

Conflict

In the concluding chapters of *A Black Explorer at the North Pole* are found the words: "Commander Peary had taken the North Pole by conquest, in the face of almost insuperable natural difficulties. . . . The winning of the North Pole was a fight with nature." From your reading, discuss at least three illustrations of the explorers fighting nature in order to achieve their purpose.

Some people look out
over the water and wish for a ship.
Johnny Wise looked up into the sky and
wished for a way to sail among the clouds.

The Wild Flight of John Wise

LYMAN M. NASH

On a warm day in the summer of 1822, a housewife on the outskirts of Lancaster, Pennsylvania, straightened up from her gardening and very nearly swooned. Floating 100 feet in the air was a large wicker basket.

She shut her eyes, shook her head, and took a second look. The basket was still there, all right, and now she could see it contained young Johnny Wise, busily engaged in shoving straw into a small stove. Above the stove was a cloth bag, inflated with hot air, and the entire assemblage was proceeding leisurely toward Lancaster.

Midway over the city Johnny ran out of straw. The hot air in his homemade fire balloon began to cool. Down it came, slowly at first, and then more rapidly.

It was Johnny's misfortune to land with a thud on the roof of a house, highly susceptible to ignition. Hot coals, still in the stove, spilled out, and in moments the roof was ablaze. Fortunately, Johnny escaped. Unfortunately, the house did not.

After that ill-fated jaunt, there were some who said Johnny's ingenious flight showed promise of a great future in ballooning. Others swore he would come to no good end. In a way both factions were correct.

Almost from the moment of his birth in

1808, it seemed John Wise was destined to take to the air. He scarcely learned to walk before he was flying kites. When he learned to read, he ignored children's stories, instead poring over his father's technical magazines, devouring every article on ballooning. At night he dreamed of the time he would be old enough to soar aloft. That day came sooner than anyone expected.

At fourteen he collected all the old shirts he could find and sewed them into a balloon. With a small stove to provide hot air and his mother's laundry basket to ride in, Johnny sailed off to burn down that house.

When nothing but ashes remained, an irate Lancasterian stormed up to the boy. Shaking his finger under Johnny's nose, he thundered, "A little more wind and the whole town might have gone up in flames."

"But if there had been more wind," the boy aeronaut[1] answered, "I would have been carried beyond town, and this wouldn't have happened."

Sound as Johnny's reasoning was, it failed to save him from getting a good tanning and grounded him for thirteen years. Meanwhile, he finished school, becoming an apprentice pianoforte tuner. Since pianofortes were considered racy instruments in those days, they were in short supply, and pianoforte tuners were in even shorter demand.

He pursued his profession diligently, but with little zeal, saving every cent he could. By 1835 he had enough money to build another balloon.

His second flight began as disastrously as the first had ended. Early on the morning of May 2, he rose from the corner of Ninth and Green streets, in Philadelphia, not far from where Jean Blanchard made the first balloon flight in American history. John's takeoff was completely unintended.

Crawling into the wicker car to check the progress of his hydrogen generating machine, John was about to announce that the balloon

Reprinted by permission of Lyman M. Nash and *Boy's Life*, published by the Boy Scouts of America.

1. **aeronaut**\ˈăr·ə ˈnɔt\ navigator of a balloon.

needed another hour's inflating. He didn't get a chance to open his mouth. The ground crew, fully as inexperienced as he, let go of the mooring lines. With a mighty shove, they sent balloon and ballonist shooting high into the sky.

Weighted down with sandbags, picnic lunch, and John Wise, and only partially inflated, the balloon reached housetop level. There it began a swift horizontal journey, bumping into roofs, knocking over chimneys, and scaring late sleepers out of their wits. Finally, it came to earth half a dozen blocks away.

An excited crowd bore down on the hapless adventurer, expecting to find him more dead than alive. But rounding a corner, they saw him tossing ballast, lunch, hat, and topcoat out of the basket. Considerably lighter, the balloon resumed its flight, rising to an altitude of 1,000 feet.

On a gentler wind, it soared off over Philadelphia, continued on to New Jersey, and landed in the middle of a forest. Late that night John Wise returned to civilization with a tremendous appetite and an even greater enthusiasm for ballooning.

His third flight, a few weeks later, nearly ended his career and his life at the same time. Twenty-five hundred feet in the air, the lower portion of his balloon burst. Down he plunged. Luckily, enough gas remained trapped in the upper half to avert complete disaster. Not wishing to land ignominiously on the heads of spectators, he waited until the last moment before dumping his sand. With renewed lift, he was able to swoop off and crash in privacy.

Undismayed, John Wise kept right on ballooning. In the course of some 200 flights, he experienced explosions, storms, accidents, and animosity in about equal proportions. Frequently, he was forced to tune pianofortes for months before earning enough to invest in another balloon. Then he would take to the air again.

With each new flight, he became more convinced that man's destiny lay in the air. More important, John Wise discovered a river of air, flowing constantly west to east, thousands of feet above earth. Prior to this discovery, a balloonist could control only his rise and descent. Where he went depended pretty much on luck.

By making use of this aerial river, a balloonist could virtually bank on traveling eastward. Sailing over the countryside one sunny afternoon, Wise asked himself: Why not build large commercial balloons, capable of carrying passengers and freight cross-country to the Atlantic seaboard or across the ocean to Europe? Once arrived at their destinations, the balloons could be deflated and shipped back to their starting point by fast freight.

The more he pondered the question, the fewer objections he could find. Thus was born his magnificent idea, the wonderful Trans-Atlantic Balloon Company.

It is, however, a long way from idea to reality. The money he made passing the hat at ascensions would never be enough to put his dream into action. So John Wise set out to find a backer.

Prospect after prospect listened bemusedly. Prospect after prospect turned him down.

Dejected, but not discouraged, Wise took off on an exhibition tour through New England. In Vermont he met a shrewd businessman named Oliver A. Gager. Bowled over by Wise's fiery oratory, Gager reluctantly agreed to discuss financing the proposed company while going for a balloon ride.

Up they went. At 5,000 feet Gager said, "The idea sounds feasible." At 6,000 feet he said, "Yes, it sounds fine." At 7,000 feet he said, "Count me in." Wise lost no time in valving out hydrogen and returning his benefactor to earth.

Back on the ground, Gager coerced three friends into investing in what he called "this momentous undertaking." With the matter of financing solved, Wise turned his attention to publicizing the newly formed company.

At a meeting with Gager, he suggested placing ads in the large newspapers.

"No," Gager said, exercising his Yankee know-how, "what we need is something spectacular, like an exploit. And it has to be so breathtaking, the name of our company will be on everyone's lips."

"Spectacular, eh?" Wise answered. "Well, suppose we make a flight from St. Louis to New York. On our way we could pass over Chicago, Cleveland, maybe even Pittsburgh, and shout greetings to the folks below. That should be spectacular enough for anybody."

It was so ridiculously simple. You merely ascended in St. Louis and came down in New York, letting the west-east wind do the work. Struck by the excellence of his inspiration, Wise turned immediately to making plans.

The balloon would be the most advanced ever designed and carry the latest meteorological instruments, navigational aids, and scientific doodads. It would be so huge that all previous balloons would look like children's playthings. With a stroke of pure genius, he decided to name it *Atlantic*.

The voyage would commence from Washington Square, St. Louis, on the afternoon of July 1, 1859. That much was certain. Wise wished he could set a time of arrival in New York, but that, of course, depended on the wind.

As the great day approached, Wise began to worry. Newspapers might look on the flight as just another balloonist's harebrained scheme. There had been enough stunts recently—men going up hanging by their teeth or going up to set off fireworks. One even went up sitting astride a horse. Such foolishness gave ballooning a bad name. Wise wanted no part of it.

This flight, Wise determined, would demonstrate ballooning's practical side and, at the same time, blaze a trail for the company's regularly scheduled passenger flights later.

To keep it out of the silly category, Wise announced that Oliver Gager would accompany him as scientific observer. Another investor, John LaMountane, would accompany them as cosmical navigator, although exactly what he would navigate remained obscure, for the balloon, floating free, could go only where the wind directed.

July 1, 1859, was a perfect day. The St. Louis Gaslight Company honored the occasion by laying a special pipeline to the scene, and inflating began in midmorning. But long before that time Washington Square was swarming with spectators. Whole families had driven in from surrounding farms during the night and now stood agog as the great balloon took form.

By late afternoon it was fully inflated with 60,000 cubic feet of illuminating gas. Large enough to envelope a five-story building, *Atlantic* stood 60 feet high and had a 50-foot diameter. Thirty-six shroud lines were needed to distribute the giant's lift. These were secured to the concentrating ring, from which a dozen heavier ropes descended to support the car, 10 feet below. And a dozen feet below the car hung a wooden lifeboat.

Originally, the lifeboat was intended only as a safety precaution, in the event the balloon was forced down over the Great Lakes. But by the time all the provisions, ballast, instruments, and suitcases had been stowed in the car it was discovered that the only way the three men would fit in was by sitting on each other's shoulders. Gager and LaMountane, therefore, were assigned to the boat with some of the ballast.

Shortly before takeoff time the boat also became a cargo hold. An American Express wagon fought its way through the crowd, bringing bundles of newspapers, packages, and letters to be carried to New York as airmail.

Promptly at 6:30, John Wise climbed to the basket and squeezed in amid the sandwiches, sandbags, thermometers, barometers, compasses, sextants, transits, and telescopes. Gager and LaMountane boarded the lifeboat. At the last moment a young reporter, eager for a firsthand story, volunteered to join the adventurers. Wise motioned him aboard as publicity director. Then ground lines were

cast off, and with a gentle lurch the *Atlantic* struggled aloft.

Almost from the beginning nothing went right. Rising upward, with the crowd cheering wildly below, Wise noticed the balloon was dangerously out of trim. The extra man and unexpected mail had shifted its center of gravity. Instead of thirty-six shroud lines sharing the weight, only six were doing the job. The other thirty hung loose.

Wise considered landing, correcting the trim, and starting off again. Rather than create a needless stir, he decided to carry on as if nothing were wrong. When safely out of sight, the trim could be corrected.

Over Illinois the *Atlantic's* condition grew worse. Something had to be done immediately. Wise called to Gager. Gager took one glance at the fast fading landscape below, looked up at the threatening bulges in the ballon above, gulped twice, and proceeded to climb, hand over hand, to the basket. Then he and Wise crawled over the network of retaining ropes, pushing and shoving the varnished silk back

into place. This done, with the *Atlantic* in good trim, Gager returned to the lifeboat, his hands raw and bloodied.

At nightfall the cosmical navigator, La-Mountane, glanced at the setting sun, surveyed the heavens, and called out, "Right on course." Presumably he meant they were headed for Chicago, as planned. He was wrong; they were far to the south and whipping briskly along.

A little later Wise called down to the men below that since all was in order, he was going to sleep. Hours passed. Near Lafayette, Indiana, the balloon started descending. Alarmed, Gager ordered some ballast dumped. As Wise slept, the *Atlantic* shot upward, much faster and much higher than expected.

The cooling air distended the balloon, so much so that the gas escape nozzle worked out of position, dropped inside the car, and hung a few inches above Wise's nose.

Sound asleep, Wise could not hear the steady hiss of escaping illuminating gas. In the boat the three men were frightened by the alarming increase in altitude and chilled by the corresponding drop in temperature. Through chattering teeth they called to Wise but got no answer.

For the second time Gager climbed to the basket, his bleeding hands pulling him up inch by inch. He found Wise not only asleep but unconscious and very close to asphyxiation. Working fast, Gager got the nozzle back in place and slapped Wise into consciousness. Somewhat groggily, the commander valved out sufficient gas to bring them down to a comfortable altitude. Then Gager rejoined the lifeboat.

Dawn found the trailblazers starting out over Lake Erie. In his log Wise noted that he could see Toledo on his left and Sandusky on his right. He also noted that they were barreling along at 60 miles an hour and heading into a hurricane.

Any other man would have landed immediately. Not John Wise. If they could tag on to that hurricane, he figured, there'd be no reason to stop at New York. They could sail on to Europe and be there in a day's time.

Elated by this sudden change in plans and wanting the world to know, he valved out more gas and dropped low to pass the word to a fishing trawler. At 60 miles per hour his stirring message was lost to the winds, and watching the speed at which the vessel disappeared behind, he raised his estimate of their speed to 80 miles an hour.

Oddly enough, the only indication of their breakneck pace was the waves slipping by below. Since they were moving as fast as the wind, there was utter silence, with not a breeze to flutter the pages of Wise's log.

While Wise thoroughly enjoyed their rapid progress, the three men below had entirely opposite feelings. They were not only terrified, but also seasick. At that low altitude there was a violent turbulence, and the balloon would zoom up 150 feet, shoot down 100, then zoom up again.

They begged Wise to ascend to quieter air. Leery of valving out any more gas lest they

not have enough to make Europe, he ordered them to dump more ballast. They were so pleased at the prospect of rising above the turbulence that they dumped every bag of sand. A few minutes later they were zipping over Niagara Falls, 10,000 feet high and traveling 90 miles an hour.

Leaving Niagara far behind, they whipped along, dropping closer and closer to the ground. The gas escape valve had jammed, and they were losing gas. Soon they were low enough to hear earth sounds. They heard the crash of uprooted trees, saw small buildings bowled over, but felt not the slightest breeze.

Aware of their perilous position, Wise called down, "Toss out everything you can."

Turning to with a gusto not expected of the desperately ill, the hapless aerial mariners gleefully jettisoned newspapers, packages, and letters. Then they threw the oars overboard. Still not satisfied, they ripped out the seats.

The *Atlantic* climbed rapidly and streaked out across Lake Ontario. "Next shoreline a hundred miles ahead," Wise yelled down. "We're making good time. Should be there in little over an hour." Somehow his voice had lost the ring of enthusiasm.

Again the balloon started sinking. Wise tossed out his suitcase, his cigars, and the expensive instruments. The lifeboat crew started ripping up the floorboards. The *Atlantic* regained a little lost altitude.

With the shoreline coming up fast, Wise faced an important decision. Should he valve out gas and attempt a landing on the lake or take a chance on coming down over dry land? One look at the foaming waves gave him his answer. "Join me in the basket," he shouted. "We'll cut the boat loose." Reaching Europe was now out of the question.

Their strength stemming from pure panic, the scientific observer, cosmical navigator, and publicity director scrambled up to the chief balloonist. Free of the boat, the *Atlantic* bounced upward, but not for long.

Careening through the storm-darkened sky,

dropping steadily, the four aeronauts could hear the wind ripping into the forest and growing ominously louder. All they could do was hang on for dear life, which they were certain wouldn't be with them long.

Eyes shut, they flinched at the sickening sound of a tree limb scraping the bottom of the car.

"To the rigging, men," Wise shouted. "We'll be safer there." Hardly had they clambered out before a branch slashed through the wickerwork. Caught for an instant, the *Atlantic* suddenly jerked free, tossing them back into the shattered remains of the wicker gondola.[2]

The climax came moments later. Whipping along nearly horizontally, the gas bag impaled itself on a tree. The car plunged to earth, tumbling its human contents like dice from a cup.

They landed in a heap at precisely 2:20 in the afternoon, July 2, 1859, not far from Henderson, New York. They had been aloft nineteen hours and fifty minutes and had traveled 1,200 miles.

Newspapers said it was the greatest balloon flight ever made. In 100 years there has been no reason to challenge that label. Not until 1910 did a balloon fly farther, but none has ever flown faster.

The ride was so wild, so dangerous, and proved such a fiasco, it was a miracle anyone survived. The only casualty, however, was the Trans-Atlantic Balloon Company, which couldn't weather the publicity and had to suspend operations.

As soon as the young reporter returned to St. Louis, he asked to be transferred to the society beat. Gager, convinced that ballooning was not conducive to longevity, withdrew his backing and never again climbed higher than the top of his stepladder. LaMountane made one more ascension, landing in the wilds of Canada, and had to walk 300 miles, putting an end to his desire to fly.

Wise alone remained a staunch advocate of balloons. In 1879, aged seventy-one, he made his four hundred and forty-sixth ascension, which was one too many. Rising from Chicago, he sailed over Lake Michigan and vanished forever.

I
AN EARLY AERONAUT

1. How old is Johnny when he builds his first balloon? Describe it and the flight he makes.

2. What is funny about Johnny's second balloon venture? Why does it increase his enthusiasm for ballooning?

3. What happens to him in his third flight? Does this discourage him? What important discovery does he make in later flights? What wonderful idea does he get from this?

4. Why do he and Gager plan the trip from St. Louis to New York? Why are Gager and LaMountane assigned to the lifeboat?

II
IMPLICATIONS

Can you find support for all of these generalizations about this story? Discuss each.

1. Things that seem ridiculously simple in the planning usually turn out to be much more complicated in the doing.

2. A hasty judgment is seldom an accurate one.

3. Even the most serious predicaments of men can be very funny.

III
TECHNIQUES

Foreshadowing

1. What two things about Johnny's future are foreshadowed in the fifth paragraph of the story?

2. On page 68, the author states: "It was so ridiculously simple." What is your immediate reaction?

3. In what way does the author's mention of the cargo and passengers aboard the *Atlantic* foreshadow the success or failure of the venture?

---

2. **gondola**\ˈgŏn·də·lə\ a basket or enclosure attached to and carried aloft by a balloon.

It was 1903. The new century was alive
with the bustle of discovery.
Balloon ascensions were commonplace.
On the ground the world clamored
for wheels. In that year, Henry Ford
sold over seventeen hundred two-cycle,
eight-horsepower automobiles
from his new factory in Detroit.
In late fall, at Dayton, Ohio,
two brothers bought tickets for
Kitty Hawk, North Carolina, and
loaded a strange-looking crate aboard
a train. It was this journey to the barren,
windswept dunes of the Carolina coast
which finally brought flight from the realm
of speculation to reality. Man moved
one step closer to his destiny in the sky.

How
I Learned
To Fly

ORVILLE WRIGHT

as told to Leslie Quirk

I suppose my brother and I always wanted
to fly. Every youngster wants to, doesn't he?
But it was not till we were out of school that
the ambition took definite form.

We had read a good deal on the subject, and
we had reverently studied Otto Lilienthal's[1]
tables of figures. He was the greatest aeronautical engineer in Europe. Then one day, as it
were, we said to each other: "Why not? Here
are scientific calculations, based upon actual
tests, to show us the sustaining powers of
planes. We can spare a few weeks each year.

Suppose, instead of going off somewhere to
loaf, we put in our vacations building and flying gliders." I don't believe we dared think beyond gliders at that time—not aloud, at least.

That year—it was 1900—we went down to
North Carolina, near Kitty Hawk. There were
hills there in plenty, and not too many people
about to scoff. Building that first glider was the
best fun we'd ever had, too, despite the fact
that we put it together as accurately as a
watchmaker assembles and adjusts his finest
timepiece. You see, we knew how to work because Lilienthal had made his tables years before, and men like Chanute,[2] for example, had
verified them.

To our great disappointment, however, the
glider was not the success we had expected. It
didn't behave as the figures on which it was
constructed vouched that it should. Something
was wrong. We looked at each other silently,
and at the machine, and at the mass of figures
compiled by Lilienthal. Then we proved up on
them to see if we had slipped somewhere. If
we had, we couldn't find the error; so we
packed up and went home. We were agreed
that we hadn't built our glider according to
the scientific specifications. But there was another year coming and we weren't discouraged.
We had just begun.

We wrote to Chanute, who was an engineer
in Chicago at the time. We told him about our
glider; we drew sketches of it for him; we set
down long rows of figures. And then we wound
up our letter by begging him to explain why
the tables of Lilienthal, which he had verified
by experiments of his own, could not be proved
by our machine.

Chanute didn't know. He wrote back that it
might be due to a different curve or pitch of
surfaces on the planes, or something like that.
But he was interested just the same, and when
we went down to Kitty Hawk in 1901, we invited him to visit our camp.

---

1. **Otto Lilienthal**\ˈlē·lē·ən 'tal\ (1848–1896) was a
pioneer German aeronautical engineer.
2. **Octave Chanute**\ŏk ˈtāv shə ˈnūt\ (1832–1910) was
an early leader in aeronautical thought.

By permission of *Boy's Life,* published by the Boy Scouts of
America.

Chanute came. Just before he left Chicago, I recall his telling us, he had read and O.K.'d the proofs of an article on aeronautics which he had prepared for the *Encyclopædia Britannica,* and in which he again told us of verifying Lilienthal's tables.

Well, he came to Kitty Hawk for a visit, and after he looked our glider over carefully, he said frankly that the trouble was not with any errors of construction in our machine. And right then, all of us, I suspect, began to lose faith in Lilienthal and his gospel figures.

We had made a few flights the first year, and we made about seven hundred in 1901. Then we went back to Dayton to begin all over. It was like groping in the dark. Lilienthal's figures were not to be relied upon. Nobody else had done any scientific experimenting along these lines. Worst of all, we did not have money enough to build our glider with various types and sizes of planes or wings, simply to determine, in actual practice, which was the best. There was only the alternative of working out tables of our own. So we set to work along this line.

We took little bits of metal and we fashioned planes from them. I've still a deskful in my office in Dayton. There are flat ones, concave ones, convex ones, square ones, oblong ones, and scores and scores of other shapes and sizes. Each model contains six square inches. When we built our third glider the following year, ignoring Lilienthal altogether and constructing it from our own figures, we made the planes just 7,200 times the size of those little metal models back at Dayton.

It was hard work, of course, to get our figures right, to achieve the plane giving the greatest efficiency—and to know before we built that plane the exact proportion of efficiency we could expect. Of course, there were some books on the subject that were helpful. We went to the Dayton libraries and read what we could find there; afterward, when we had reached the same ends by months and months of study and experiment, we heard of other books that would have smoothed the way.

But those metal models told us how to build. By this time, too, Chanute was convinced that Lilienthal's tables were obsolete or inaccurate, and was wishing his utmost that he was not on record in an encyclopedia as verifying them.

During 1902 we made upward of fourteen hundred flights, sometimes going up a hundred times or more in a single day. Our runway was short, and it required a wind with a velocity of at least twelve miles an hour to lift the machine. I recall sitting in it, ready to cast off, one still day when the breeze seemed approaching. It came presently, rippling the daisies in the field, and just as it reached me, I started the glider on the runway. But the innocent-appearing breeze was a whirlwind. It jerked the front of the machine sharply upward. I tilted my rudder to descend. Then the breeze spun downward, driving the glider to the ground with a tremendous shock and spinning me out headfirst. That's just a sample of what we had to learn about air currents; nobody had ever heard of "holes" in the air at that time. We had to go ahead and discover everything for ourselves.

But we glided successfully that summer, and we began to dream of greater things. Moreover, we helped Chanute to discover the errors in Lilienthal's tables, which were due to experimental flights down a hill with a descent so acute that the wind swept up its side and out from its surface with false buoying power. On the proper incline, which would be one parallel with the flight of the machine, the tables would not work out. Chanute wrote the articles on aeronautics for the last edition of that encyclopedia again, but he corrected his figures this time.

The next step, of course, was the natural one of installing an engine. Others were experimenting, and it now became a question of who would be the first to fly with an engine. But we felt reasonably secure, because we had worked out all our own figures, and the others were still guessing or depending upon Lilienthal's or somebody else's that were inaccurate. Chanute knew we expected to try sustained

Above, the first flight at Kitty Hawk, North Carolina,
December 17, 1903. Several flights
were made that day ranging from 12 seconds
to nearly one minute.
Center right, portrait of Orville Wright, 1906.
Far right, Wilbur Wright, 1906.

flights later on, and while abroad that year mentioned the fact, so we had competition across the water, too.

We wrote to a number of automobile manufacturers about an engine. We demanded an eight-horse one of not over two hundred pounds in weight. This was allowing twenty-five pounds to each horsepower, and did not seem to us prohibitive.

Several answers came. Some of the manufacturers politely declined to consider the building of such an engine; the gasoline motor was comparatively new then, and they were having trouble enough with standard sizes. Some said it couldn't be built according to our specifications, which was amusing, because lighter engines of greater power had already been used. Some seemed to think we were demented—"Building a flying machine, eh?" But one concern, of which we had never heard, said it could turn out a motor such as we wanted, and forwarded us figures. We were suspicious of figures by this time, and we doubted this concern's ability to get the horsepower claimed, considering the bore of the cylinders, etc. Later, I may add, we discovered that such an engine was capable of giving much greater horsepower. But we didn't know that at the time; we had to learn our ABC's as we went along.

Finally, though, we had a motor built. We

had discovered that we could allow much more weight than we had planned at first, and in the end the getting of the engine became comparatively simple. The next step was to figure out what we wanted in the way of a screw propeller.

We turned to our books again. All the figures available dealt with the marine propeller—the thrust of the screw against the water. We had only turned from the solution of one problem to the intricacies of another. And the more we experimented with our models, the more complicated it became.

There was the size to be considered. There was the material to be decided. There was the matter of the number of blades. There was the delicate question of the pitch of the blades. And then, after we had made headway with these problems, we began to scent new difficulties. One pitch and one force applied to the thrust against still air; what about the suction, and the air in motion, and the vacuum, and the thousand and one changing conditions? They were trying out the turbine engines on the big ocean liners at that time, with an idea of deter-

74

mining the efficiency of this type. The results were amazing in the exact percentage of efficiency developed by fuel and engine and propeller combined. A little above 40 per cent efficiency was considered wonderful. And the best we could do, after months and months of experimenting and studying, was to conceive and build a propeller that had to deliver 66 per cent of efficiency, or fail us altogether. But we went down to Kitty Hawk pretty confident, just the same.

There were the usual vexatious delays. But finally, in December, 1903, we were ready to make the first flight. My brother and I flipped a coin for the privilege of being the first to attempt a sustained flight in the air. Up to now, of course, we had merely taken turns. But this was a much bigger thing. He won.

The initial attempt was not a success. The machine fluttered for about a hundred feet down the side of the hill, pretty much as gliders had done. Then it settled with a thud, snapping off the propeller shaft, and thus effectually ending any further experiments for the time being.

It was getting late. Already the gales off Hatteras[3] were beginning to howl. So I went back to Dayton personally to get a new shaft and to hurry along the work as rapidly as I could.

It was finished at last. As I went to the train that morning, I heard for the first time of the machine constructed by Langley, which had dropped into a river the day before. You see, others were working just as desperately as we were to perfect a flying machine.

We adjusted the new shaft as soon as I reached Kitty Hawk. By the time we had finished, it was late in the afternoon, with a stiff wind blowing. Our facilities for handling the machine were of the crudest. In the past, with our gliders, we had depended largely upon the help of some men from a lifesaving station, a mile or two away. As none of them happened to be at our camp that afternoon, we decided to postpone the next trial till morning.

It was cold that night. A man named Brinkley—W. C. Brinkley—dropped in to warm himself. He was buying salvage on one or more of the ships that had sunk during a recent storm that raged outside Kitty Hawk Point. I remember his looking curiously at the great framework, with its engine and canvas wings, and asking, "What's that?" We told him it was a flying machine which we were going to try out the next morning and asked him if he thought it would be a success. He looked out toward the ocean, which was getting rough, and which was battering the sunken ships in which he was interested. Then he said, "Well, you never can tell what will happen—if conditions are favorable." Nevertheless, he asked permission to stay overnight and watch the attempted flight.

Morning brought with it a twenty-seven mile gale. Our instruments, which were more delicate and more accurate than the government's, made it a little over twenty-four; but the official reading was twenty-seven miles an hour. As soon as it was light, we ran up our signal flag for help from the lifesaving station. Three men were off duty that day and came pounding over to camp. They were John T. Daniels, A. D. Etheridge, and W. S. Daugh. Before we were ready to make the flight, a small boy of about thirteen or fourteen came walking past.

Daniels, who was a good deal of a joker, greeted him. The boy said his name was Johnny Moore and he was just strolling by. But he couldn't get his eyes off the machine that we had anchored in a sheltered place. He wanted to know what it was.

"Why, that's a duck-snarer," explained Daniels soberly. North Carolina, of course, is noted for its duck shooting. "You see, this man is going up in the air over a bay where there are hundreds of ducks on the water. When he is just over them, he will drop a big net and snare every last one. If you'll stick around, Johnny, you can have a few ducks to take home."

---

3. **Cape Hatteras**\ˈhă·tə·rəs\ is located on an island off the North Carolina coast. The area often has severe gales.

So Johnny Moore was also a witness of our flights that day. I do not know whether the lack of any ducks to take away with him was a disappointment or not, but I suspect he did not feel compensated by what he saw.

The usual visitors did not come to watch us that day. Nobody imagined we would attempt a flight in such weather, for it was not only blowing hard, but it was also very cold. But just that fact, coupled with the knowledge that winter and its gales would be on top of us almost any time now, made us decide not to postpone the attempt any longer.

My brother climbed into the machine. The motor was started. With a short dash down the runway, the machine lifted into the air and was flying. It was only a flight of twelve seconds, and it was an uncertain, wavy, creeping sort of a flight at best; but it was a real flight at last and not a glide.

Then it was my turn. I had learned a little from watching my brother, but I found the machine pointing upward and downward in jerky undulations. This erratic course was due in part to my utter lack of experience in controlling a flying machine and in part to a new system of controls we had adopted, whereby a slight touch accomplished what a hard jerk or tug made necessary in the past. Naturally, I overdid everything. But I flew for about the same time my brother had.

He tried it again the minute the men had carried it back to the runway and added perhaps three or four seconds to the records we had just made. Then after a few secondary adjustments, I took my seat for the second time. By now I had learned something about the controls and about how a machine acted during a sustained flight, and I managed to keep in the air for fifty-seven seconds. I couldn't turn, of course—the hills wouldn't permit that —but I had no very great difficulty in handling it. When I came down, I was eager to have another turn.

But it was getting late now, and we decided to postpone further trials until the next day. The wind had quieted, but it was very cold.

In fact, it had been necessary for us to warm ourselves between each flight. Now we carried the machine back to a point near the camp and stepped back to discuss what had happened.

My brother and I were not excited nor particularly exultant. We had been the first to fly successfully with a machine driven by an engine, but we had expected to be the first. We had known, down in our hearts, that the machine would fly just as it did. The proof was not astonishing to us. We were simply glad, that's all.

But the men from the lifesaving station were very excited. Brinkley appeared dazed. Johnny Moore took our flights as a matter of course and was presumably disappointed because we had snared no ducks.

And then, quite without warning, a puff of wind caught the forward part of the machine and began to tip it. We all rushed forward, but only Daniels was at the front. He caught the plane and clung desperately to it, as though thoroughly aware as were we of the danger of an upset of the frail thing of rods and wings. Upward and upward it lifted, with Daniels clinging to the plane to ballast it. Then, with a convulsive shudder, it tipped backward, dashing the man in against the engine, in a great tangle of cloth and wood and metal. As it turned over, I caught a last glimpse of his legs kicking frantically over the plane's edge. I'll confess I never expected to see him alive again.

But he did not even break a bone, although he was bruised from head to foot. When the machine had been pinned down at last, it was almost a complete wreck necessitating many new parts and days and days of rebuilding. Winter was fairly on top of us, with Christmas only a few days off. We could do no more experimenting that year.

After all, though, it did not matter much. We could build better and stronger and more confidently another year. And we could go back home to Dayton and dream of time and distance and altitude records, and of machines for two or more passengers, and of the practical value of the heavier-than-air machine.

For we had accomplished the ambition that stirred us as boys. We had learned to fly.

I

SUCCESS AT KITTY HAWK

To be the first, the very first men to fly a machine driven by an engine! After all the centuries that man had dreamed of such an achievement, one would imagine that the two brothers would have been jubilant. They had constructed a vehicle that was a match for the legendary Pegasus.

But were these conquerors exultant? Not particularly. There were no newsmen on the scene, and the brothers did not bother to notify the press of their feat. Instead, they sent a simply worded telegram to their father in Dayton telling of their success and asking him to inform the press. Read again Orville Wright's statement on page 438 describing how they felt, then discuss the following as possible explanations for their matter-of-fact reactions:

1. They had already built successful gliders.

2. They were careful, exacting workmen who checked and rechecked all their figures and calculations.

3. They were more concerned with proving their theories than in achieving personal glory.

II

IMPLICATIONS

Consider these statements. Do you agree or disagree?

1. There is no substitute for hard personal work.

2. Most people do not like to risk the unfamiliar.

3. If you would know success, you must be able to endure failure.

III

TECHNIQUES

Suspense and Conflict

From the first sentence, "I suppose my brother and I always wanted to fly," to the last two sentences, "For we had accomplished the ambition that stirred us as boys. We had learned to

fly," Orville Wright's story is told with such remarkable simplicity that the unique effort of the Wright brothers seems unexceptional and almost routine. Notice the apparently uncomplicated steps they took in gathering information and developing their flight plans and equipment. All of the detail and scientific planning is mentioned only as "hard work" necessary "to get our figures right," and the "usual vexations."

The effect of this restraint coupled with the conversational approach gives the story a directness and unpretentiousness that is refreshing. Nevertheless, the author does not overlook a common technique employed by any good storyteller to keep the reader's or listener's interest alive. As he goes along, he casually mentions items and incidents that will alert the listener's or reader's mind to possibilities of conflict or danger. An example of this is found on page 75 in Wright's observation: "As I went to the train that morning, I heard for the first time of the machine constructed by Langley, which had dropped into a river the day before. You see, others were working just as desperately as we were to perfect a flying machine."

1. Describe the scene in which W. C. Brinkley comes to their camp the night before they are to make the crucial test on the following morning. How do his actions and words arouse suspense?

2. As was indicated by the last sentence in the preceding quotation, the Wright brothers were competing against other inventors in their determined effort to be the first to construct a successful flying machine. This made the testing of their machine that December an almost absolute necessity. How were they in conflict with nature in attempting to achieve this goal?

3. After Orville Wright had managed to keep the plane in the air for fifty-seven seconds and had landed it, an unexpected incident took place involving one of the men from the lifesaving station. What suspense was aroused here?

IV

WORDS

A. New words enter the language through numerous processes. One process is the combining of Greek and Latin forms to create new words which are largely technical and scientific. A fairly recent word, *astronaut,* the name given a man who travels in a spacecraft, is a typical example of this process of word making. Of Greek origin, *astro* means "star" and *naut* means "sailor." Thus, an astronaut is literally "a sailor to the stars." The airborne ancestors of today's astronauts were the *aeronauts,* men who piloted the lighter-than-air balloons of yesteryear. And, even though their flying machines were heavier than air, the Wright brothers were at first probably regarded as aeronauts too. The form *aero* means "air." Another example of a word made from two forms is *altimeter,* referring to the instrument that measures the altitude of an aircraft. Each word is a Latin form—*alti* means "high," and *meter* means "measure." Also the result of two combining forms are *cosmonaut* (from a Russian word), "an astronaut," *aerospace,* "the earth's atmosphere and the space beyond," and *astrophysics,* "the science of the physical properties and phenomena of the celestial bodies." What combining forms have been used in the creation of the following scientific and technical terms and what do they mean: *aquanaut, megalopolis, astrosphere, aerosol, cardiogram, audiometer,* and *seismograph?*

B. Another process of word formation is the addition of prefixes or suffixes or both to words already in use. As a case in point, two new words have been created from *plane*; a word appearing a number of times in "How I Learned To Fly," *deplane,* "to disembark from an airplane," and *enplane,* "to board an airplane." To the word *ecology,* "the study of the relationship between organisms and their environment," the suffix *ize* has been added to create *ecologize,* "to conserve organisms and their environment." Note that in both examples the affixes (a term covering both suffixes and prefixes) actually change the meaning of the word as well as the part of speech to which it belongs. *Plane,* in the sense of aircraft, is a noun, whereas *deplane* and *enplane* are both verbs. Similarly, *ecology* is a noun, but *ecologize* is a verb. Other examples of affixational word formation are *belittle,* "to speak slightingly of," *debrief,* "to elicit information from someone who has returned from a mission," *inductee,* "one who has been inducted into the armed forces," and *de-energize,* "to stop the flow of current or energy through." What affixes can you add to these words: *final, rich, draft, large, saline, grudge, human, luxury, person,* and *noble?*

The morning of May 20, 1927,
had dawned gray in mists and falling rain.
A few minutes before eight o'clock
the sky was still overcast,
but the rain had stopped
and the mists had lifted.
Weather stations reported clear skies
over New England and outward
over the Atlantic Ocean.
On the western end of the soggy runway
of New York's Roosevelt Field
a slim, resolute, 25-year-old airmail pilot
stood by his silver monoplane.
For a moment he studied the drooping
white flag near the far end of the runway,
marking the point of no return,
then with one last look at the sky
he climbed into the tiny cockpit
of the *Spirit of St. Louis.*

The Flight

KENNETH S. DAVIS

He signaled the ground crew. The propeller was turned; the motor coughed, then caught.

He opened the throttle wider, wider, until the ultimate of roaring power was reached, his gaze fixed anxiously on the round dial of the tachometer.[1] The needle quivered, steadied. Mulligan was right: the propeller was making forty fewer turnings per minute than it had made when he last tested the engine. This

1. **tachometer**\tă ▲kŏm·ĕ·tər\ an instrument that measures the speed of engine rotation in revolutions per minute.

wasn't much, of course; he was being denied only a little over two per cent of the power he should have had, but it reduced by another tiny fraction the margin of safety on which he had counted.

He closed the throttle, let the engine idle, and leaned back for a moment, adding up the hazards one last time in his mind. A slow wet runway. A heavier load than the *Spirit of St. Louis* had ever lifted before. An engine delivering slightly less power than it should. A tail wind instead of a head wind. A brain whose judgments might soon become blurred with fatigue. . . . He turned when Frank Tichenor[2] came up to speak to him.

"Are you taking only five sandwiches?" Tichenor asked, curiously.

The question seemed, at that moment, absurdly trivial. It opened wider the gulf between Lindbergh and those who stood safely upon the earth and were certain they'd still be alive ten minutes from now, five minutes from now. But Lindbergh answered, grinning crookedly.

"Yes, five," he said. "That's enough. If I get to Paris I won't need any more. If I don't— well, I won't need any more either." He did have with him Army emergency rations in case he were forced down at sea and managed to stay afloat on the rubber raft he carried. . . .

Tichenor stepped back. Lindbergh beckoned to Mulligan.

"What do you think?" he asked.

Mulligan hesitated, then said: "Rev her up again. We'll listen once more."

Lindbergh opened the throttle. Mulligan and Boedecker[3] leaned close to the motor, listening with ears trained to detect and interpret the slightest variation of motor noise, while the deadly propeller sliced air only inches away from them. Then they backed away, looking at one another and nodding slightly. Lindbergh again closed the throttle.

"She sound okay?"

Mulligan cleared his throat, swallowed. Weighing his words carefully, he said in a flat tone: "The engine's doing as well as you can expect in this weather."

Lindbergh looked at him intently for a second. Then he looked down the long runway, seeing the pools of water standing on it and how narrow it looked, narrower than ever before, and how high the telephone wires looked at the runway's end, higher than ever before, and he said, matter-of-factly: "Well, then, I might as well go."

As if he were driving over to town. . . .

"So long," he called to Blythe.[4] He smiled and waved, as the blocks were pulled from in front of the wheels.

Leaning forward, he once again opened the throttle wide. He grasped the stick. Slowly, sluggishly the plane moved forward, pushed by men who were lined up along each wing.

Reporters took note of the precise time. It was 7:52 A.M.

Slowly, with agonizing slowness, the plane gathered speed. The men beside the wings were running now. Then some of them fell behind. Then the last of them fell behind. Still Lindbergh held the tail down (with all the gas in it, the *Spirit of St. Louis* was slightly nose heavy; he didn't want to risk nosing over before the speed was up), roaring toward a curtain of mist which blurred the far horizon, roaring faster, faster toward the point of no return.

Now, *now* the tail was up.

But how sluggish and heavy the plane felt as the white cloth on its stick rushed nearer, nearer! He gave that cloth a fleeting glance. Should he cut the motor, or go on? He couldn't be sure, but it seemed to him that the odds were slightly in his favor as the cloth flashed by and he committed himself, forever, to this attempt.

The plane lurched as it hit a rough spot, lurched again, and then was thrown by a bump into the air. He pulled back slightly on the stick, then let it come forward again; the plane

---

2. **Frank Tichenor,** writer for the publication *Aero Digest.*
3. **Mulligan and Boedecker,** engineers assigned to the flight by the manufacturer of the engine in the plane.
4. **Blythe,** "public relations counsel" assigned to the flight.

came down, as if it would cling stubbornly to the muddy earth, but he could feel its lightness now. He eased the stick back, gently, gently. . . .

And to those who watched, breathless, on the ground, it seemed that he *willed* his plane into the air, lifting it with a terrific spiritual effort. He was only a few feet off the ground when he passed a group of men near the runway's end. . . . They said later that his face was white and strained, that he leaned forward tensely, that his gaze was fastened on the tachometer.

He was airborne now, but he could sense that he was barely so. He was so delicately balanced upon the propeller's blast that the slightest jerk or swerve would bring him down again. He must *feel* his flight carefully; he must shape his feeling into a precise calculation. He must climb just enough to clear obstacles. To climb too fast, or try to, would be to stall.

Ah! He'd cleared a tractor beyond the runway by a scant ten feet. He was over the gully into which he might have crashed.

Now for the telephone wires. They were flashing toward him. Was his climb fast enough? He eased the stick back, very gently, and the muscles of his abdomen grew stiff with his effort to lift, lift the plane.

Now! The wires were under him, behind him! He'd cleared them by twenty feet!

He pushed the stick forward a little, letting the plane dip to gather speed before he pulled back again, lifting the nose. He was climbing again as he turned the plane slightly to the right . . . in order to fly over the lowest point in the tree line. Another tense moment, and the job was done!

The trees were behind him. White faces stared up at him from the rolling golf course. Then they were behind him, too.

He leaned back for a moment, letting his breath out in a long aching sigh while the plane continued its slow steady climb into the mist-wreathed sky. When a ray of sunlight broke through the clouds above him, he grinned to himself exultantly. He was on his way. He was alone.

No, he wasn't! His smile froze.

For the first time he noticed that a plane was flying not far from him and at the same height. Then he saw another plane. Photographers were leaning from the cockpit, pointing cameras at him. The sight stirred in him a sudden powerful gust of anger.

Couldn't they leave him alone, even now? Must they spoil even this shining moment?

He turned his face away, letting the stick come forward, leveling out his flight. The tachometer recorded 1825 rpm. He throttled down to 1775 rpm, then to 1750. With this terrific load, imposing the necessity of a high angle of attack upon his wing with a consequently high wind resistance, he could still fly over one hundred miles an hour at 1750 rpm! Later, when the load was reduced, he would cut his air speed to around ninety miles an hour, for fuel economy. By then, too, his angle of attack would be diminished, making for less drag and more miles per gallon of gasoline. He felt a glow of pride in the *Spirit of St. Louis*. So far as the fuel factor was concerned, he could make Paris now for sure!

There came another tense moment when the plane passed over the Long Island shore. Almost always there was rough air where land and sea met, and for an instant, as the *Spirit of St. Louis* rocked and bumped, he feared the air might become turbulent. With the load he was carrying, turbulent air could break his wing. . . .

But it didn't happen. Suddenly the air was as smooth as glass.

He leaned back again and looked around him. The gray skies were empty; the newspaper planes had turned back.

At long last, he was truly alone.

Beyond the mountain guardians of St. John's harbor, Lindbergh eased the stick back and climbed slowly, with a minimum loss of forward speed, into the evening sky. By now the overload on his plane was mostly gone; he'd used a third of his fuel, some 150 gallons, and the *Spirit of St. Louis* was nearly 920 pounds lighter than it had been when it narrowly cleared those wires at the edge of Roosevelt Field. He could maneuver easily now and make well over one hundred miles an hour, with the wind behind him, while throttling down to 1600 rpm and leaning out his gasoline mixture until the engine's smooth roar grew slightly roughened.

Behind him (he turned in his seat to take a farewell look), Newfoundland's mountains, blackly silhouetted against the western sky, seemed to be sinking slowly, steadily into the sea. Below him, that sea, already black with the coming of night, was streaked with gray threads moving from west to east, as though unraveled from a spool where the wind brushed the waters. Ahead of him the dark air was mottled with white where, here and there, floated islands of fog. Then, all at once, it seemed to him that the sky mirrored the sea (or did the sea mirror the sky?), for he saw that there were white islands floating below him, too, in the water.

Icebergs!

At first he saw only a few craggy islands of ice. Then there were many of them; the sea was dotted with them as far as he could look in every direction. And as the icebergs multiplied, so did the fog islands ahead of him. He saw, with a faint but rising apprehension, that the wisps of fog were flowing together, forming banks; soon they formed a solid layer which masked the sea as he climbed. Slowly and steadily he climbed, but the fog rose with him. After a while there was not only a floor of cloud beneath him, there was also a pillar of cloud beside him, and another ahead of him, then another beside and another ahead—great towering masses of cloud. Still he climbed.

Night rose out of the east to cover him. Stars twinkled in the blackest sky he'd ever seen.

He came at last to a wall of cloud so high he could not top it, so wide he could not detour around it without serious loss of time and gas (and who could know but what there'd be another wall to the left or right?). He tightened his safety belt. He pushed forward on the stick, lowering slightly the plane's nose. He plunged straight into the black turbulence of the cloud, feeling the bump and jar of angry air buffeting his plane, flying wholly by instruments in pitch darkness two miles above the sea.

His gaze flicked from altimeter to turn and bank indicator and then to the dial indicating air speed. He turned his flashlight upon the cylinder where rode, delicately balanced, the compass and level, for the radium figures on this instrument glowed too faintly for him to read them without the flash's beam. He counted heavily, now, upon all his instruments; he had to repress his body's instincts when these were contradicted by what he read upon the glowing dials.

He became aware of the cold; he buttoned up his flying suit. When you got above ten thousand feet in that latitude, and especially at night, you could expect the air to grow icy cold.

Ice!

Quickly he jerked his glove off and, through the cockpit window, thrust his bare hand out into the screaming wind stream. Quickly he drew his hand back; slivers and pellets of ice had stung his flesh. He switched on his flashlight and sent its beam glancing along a wing strut and along the lower leading edge of the wing. The entering wedge of the strut glittered and showed roughness; it was coated with ice; and when he sent the beam straight out he saw that the whole of the black air was streaked with sleet. The veil of fatigue which had been blurring his perceptions was abruptly stripped away.

He was in danger! He was in mortal danger! Ice not only weighted down a plane, it could so change the curve of a wing as to plunge a plane into the sea within minutes.

Fighting down a tide of panic, he began to turn his plane around, for he must fly straight back into that portion of the sky where he *knew* the air was clear. He must, at once! Only by great effort of will did he make a long slow turn (fear told him the turn indicator was icing up, that the plane might soon go out of

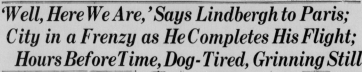

'Well, Here We Are,' Says Lindbergh to Paris; City in a Frenzy as He Completes His Flight; Hours Before Time, Dog-Tired, Grinning Still

Captain Charles A. Lindbergh wearing decorations for his transatlantic flight.

Above, The banner headlines in the New York World, May 22, 1927.

control) instead of a swift curve, which might have caused him to skid dangerously down the air. Again and again he flashed his light upon the liquid compass (the untried earth inductor was not to be trusted, he felt, in this crisis) and checked his altitude carefully, leveling out when at last the instruments told him that he was indeed going back the way he had come. Yet still he flew blind and still the ice coated, ever more quickly, the wing struts and the leading edges of the wing itself. Would he never——?

Then he burst out of the cloud. He was under stars again, out of the ice storm, but headed toward Newfoundland, not Ireland.

And so again he turned his plane, 180 degrees in a long curve.

Thereafter he flew around the great thunderheads which towered above the tumbled floor of cloud as he headed eastward. In the dim light of stars he saw a world of wild, weird beauty, awesome, coldly indifferent to him (how tiny, how insignificant he felt amidst those mountains and canyons and pillars of cloud!), yet inspiring to him as no other beauty had ever been. How grand these dreamlike mountain ranges! How awesome their turmoil as they opened up or closed down, in stupendous rolling waves, the paths his plane might follow! How vast the space across which, at 186,000 miles per second for thousands of years, had traveled most of the starlight which now, this instant, struck his eyes! He shivered a little, drawing himself together in the cockpit. Terror and exaltation mingled in his soul.

He remembered how, as a boy, in those far-off summers on the Minnesota farm, he had gone alone into the field of tall timothy or redtop, had lain down upon his back, hidden from all eyes in a cozy nest of grass, and had gazed for hours up into the blue sky where great white cumulus clouds were floating. What was it like up there? he had wondered. How delicious it would be, he had thought, to ride up and down those billowing slopes of cloud or dive deep into their cool and secret hearts! In that strange lovely upper world a man might know many truths denied the earthbound; a man, up there, might be truly free.

Well, the boy become a man knew that the freedom of the upper air must be paid for in coins of danger. He knew that clouds, which had a peaceful abstract beauty for those who viewed them from the ground, had hearts of darkness and were often harsh with danger for those who challenged them in the air. Yet even now he could feel something of what the boy on the farm had felt on those long-ago summer afternoons: the cockpit of the *Spirit of St. Louis* ("this little box with fabric walls," he called it) was like that nest of grass in which the boy had huddled, hidden and alone, under the enormous sky. So warm it was, even with its windows open, compared to the coldness of infinity. A warm, cozy nest. . . .

And then he had to jerk his head back and slap his cheeks briskly, driving away the sleep which, denied him last night, now gathered around him in fatal waves of blackness, threatening to overwhelm him. Sleep, which would have been his greatest friend last night, was tonight his greatest enemy.

He was grateful, in a way, for the clouds. They broke the monotony which might have lulled him to sleep; they forced him to pay attention. Whenever he deviated from the line of flight he had drawn in San Diego (how long ago *that* seemed!) on maps of the North Atlantic he had obtained there, he must make precise calculations of times and distances. If he flew thirty degrees to the south of that line for ten minutes, in order to avoid an icy cloud, he must correct the error by flying thirty degrees to the north of the line for ten minutes, and at the same speed. Moreover, he must make allowances for the fact that air speed and ground (or sea) speed were by no means identical. When he made eighty-five miles an hour air speed, which is what the indicator said he made at that moment (he was climbing a little), he made well over one hundred miles an hour over the waves far below—for the air moved in the same direction as he moved at something more than thirty miles an hour. . . . Yes, he must pay attention; it was the price of his survival.

But his aching tiredness remained constant. Out of it came, as had come the night before, a fear undefined in itself which, fastening first on one thing, then another, was defined for the moment by each of these.

In the dusk of the evening he had worried about splashes of mud on the underside of the wing; they would slow his air speed slightly. In the darkness of night he worried about the ice coating which, though evaporating from struts and wing, did so very slowly. And from time to time all through the night he had spasms of acute anxiety over his navigation. Something might have happened to the compasses to throw their readings completely off! Of course those readings *seemed* to check against the constellation overhead; the North Star seemed to stand where it ought to stand, high in the sky at his left, if he were on course. He couldn't be certain he'd not made a mistake, however, and if his total flight were very far off course—if he had failed to make accurately just one of hundreds of swift calculations—he might be headed for Africa, or Norway, instead of toward Ireland, England, France.

He was experiencing, he knew, the shortest night any man in that latitude had ever experienced. Because the earth turned from west to east and he was flying west to east, he flew toward a rising sun. He had, for his night, less than two hours of full darkness. Those hours seemed to him, however, very long.

After a while, he noticed a strange thing. The clouds at his left were more sharply defined than those at his right. Why? The answer came to him at once, bringing relief to his anxious soul; the moon was rising (he had forgotten the moon), soon to be followed by the sun, and it was being heralded by a wash of reddish silver over the clouds.

But his relief ended abruptly in panic. The moon was rising at his *left!* Shouldn't it be rising at his right? Wasn't he headed far to the south of his proper course?

His drooping mind, jerked taut, shaped the wave of panic into a solid and limited object of reason. He recognized the problem. Swiftly he solved it.

The North Star, the constellation overhead, the instruments—all told him he might be heading as much as ten degrees south of the route he had mapped, but no more than that. What he must remember was that his route was the Great Circle, and that he therefore crossed each meridian at a slightly different angle from the one before and must expect that heavenly bodies which rose at his right when he left New York would rise at his left as he approached Paris.

Not that he was approaching Paris now. He was not halfway across the ocean. But he had gone far enough on his journey to justify a moonrise somewhat to the left of his line of flight.

He smiled to himself. He felt that he had gone far enough, also, to justify a conviction that he belonged now more to Europe than America. Theretofore his mind had had as its point of reference the scene of his departure; it had cast back along the way he had come. Now it had as its reference point the approaching scene of his arrival; it cast forward along the way he would go.

The moon rose above the clouds, lighting with its glow a weirdly lovely skyscape. His became a world of stupendous silver forms, of magnificent silver vistas, stretching infinitely on all sides of him under a sky no longer black but deeply, darkly purple. Then, as he flew into a thin mist, came the twilight of dawn, and he saw far below through breaks in the clouds a gray Atlantic streaked with foam where a gale must be blowing. He exulted. The tail wind sped him faster on his way than he had dared hope for, provided he made no grave errors of navigation.

He was less vulnerable now to a fatal shortage of fuel. He was also less vulnerable to his great enemy, sleep. Monotony, a dull sameness or absence of sensation—this was a weapon strengthened in the hands of his enemy by the darkness of night. It was weakened by the light of day. As the rising sun burnt away the mists, the width and variety of his visual world increased, and variety was what he needed for wakefulness. Novelty of sensation was as spur and whip to his flagging attention.

Thereafter he used this spur and whip deliberately. He refrained from placing in their cockpit frames the panes of glass which would have walled out the cold and muffled the roar of the engine. He varied the height of his flight, sometimes climbing miles above the ocean, sometimes skimming barely ten feet above the waves. Once he took smelling salts from his first-aid kit and, holding them to his nose, was dismayed to find that (his senses being so dulled by fatigue) he couldn't smell them. He played games with his mind, speculating on everything he noticed, carefully calculating and recalculating his fuel consumption, his direction, the probable effect of wind drift; keeping an hour-by-hour log of his voyage, and remembering in vivid detail (as he would record long afterward) scenes from his past life.

And so the long hours passed. Morning passed. Afternoon came on and advanced, the sun sinking behind him more rapidly than it had ever done before, and he began to pray that he might see land before that sun went down.

In the twenty-seventh hour of his flight he noticed below him and to his right some black spots upon the water. He focused on one of them. It was a boat! He was over a fleet of small fishing boats! Instantly his every sense was alert; this could only mean that he was approaching land, and the sun still stood high behind him in the west. Now, for the first time, he might check absolutely his navigation.

He turned and dove down across one of the boats, seeing on it no sign of life. Then, very low, he circled another. Its deck was empty, too, but he glimpsed a man's head thrust through a porthole below deck. He circled back, closed the throttle, and, passing the man's head less than fifty feet away, shouted as loudly as he could: "Which way is Ireland?" The man's face remained expressionless and silent. Lindbergh circled and tried again, and again received no response. Puzzled, half-angry, he again climbed the air, determined to waste no more minutes and gasoline. Anyway, he was near land, he told himself. He *must* be.

And in the twenty-eighth hour of his flight, he saw land!

At first it looked like a dark cloud on the northeastern horizon (he had been flying through rain squalls). Then he saw that it was solid, stationary, and he veered to the left, off course, to look at it. It rose slowly out of the sea as he approached—a rugged coastline, rocky islands guarding inlets, high green hills—and with it rose both his spirit and his plane as he climbed to gain a wider perspective. He checked what he saw below against what he saw upon the chart spread out upon his knees. He gasped with joyful amazement.

That was Ireland, all right! Not only that, but he had hit the southwestern coast almost precisely where, according to the line on his chart, he should have done so! That was Dingle Bay[5] down there.

He had done this despite all the detours he had had to make in the night, despite the fact that his compass needles had for long periods wavered so widely that he must guess at their readings. He had accomplished a masterpiece of navigation—one worthy of that genius of dead reckoning, Christopher Columbus—and he could know, in his exultancy, that it would be recognized as such by fellow professional fliers, the men whose opinions he most respected. ("To have stayed within fifty miles of his course to Ireland would have been luck," one such man would say. "To hit it within twenty-five miles of course would show remarkable navigating ability. To hit it at Dingle Bay was sheer genius!") He was now only 600 miles from Paris, and hours ahead of schedule. Heavy fog over southern England might force him back to Ireland; or, if England was clear, heavy fog over the English Channel or northern France might force him back to that country. Otherwise it would be easy from now on. The *Spirit of St. Louis* performed perfectly, and he wasn't sleepy any more.

He flashed across the high hills of County Kerry and out into Saint George's Channel in

less than an hour. Less than two hours after that he was over Cornwall, England, seeing below him in clear air toylike houses and tiny fields separated by hedges. Soon he saw, beneath his left wing, Plymouth, from whose harbor the Pilgrims had sailed in the *Mayflower*. From Plymouth, Massachusetts, he had flown to Plymouth, England, accomplishing in less than thirty hours a voyage which had required of the Pilgrims two stormy months.

Then he was over the English Channel, headed for Cherbourg eighty-five miles away. He was over the Cherbourg peninsula, which was the farthest western coast of France, in a little more than three quarters of an hour. (He knew then that he had broken the world's record for long-distance nonstop flying. If he were forced down now, he would still be eligible for the Orteig Prize,[6] having journeyed through air from New York to the shores of France.) He followed the coastline to Deauville; he turned up the valley of the Seine; and not 'til then, as he looked down upon French peasants running out into the streets of the village over which he passed, did he remember that he'd had no food since he left New York.

As he opened the bag of sandwiches, he glanced at the clock in his cockpit. Fourtwenty, it said. This meant that it was ninetwenty in the evening by the clocks of France. The sun had set behind him. He flew through twilight (it lasted long in late May in this latitude) as he held the stick between his knees and tried to eat. It was difficult. Though he'd had no food for thirty-two hours, he had, he found, no appetite: his mouth was dry, the bread and meat tasteless. He ate only one of the five sandwiches he carried. . . .

Night rose up out of the earth ahead of him, shoving the twilight back, back into the west. The earth below became gray, then black, jeweled with lights. No longer did he count

---

5. **Dingle Bay,** located in the southwest corner of Ireland.
6. **Orteig Prize,** a $25,000 prize offered for the first transatlantic flight.

A ring of Paris policemen attempt to hold back the crowd after Lindbergh's arrival at Le Bourget airfield.

time in hours. Within minutes, now, he'd see a glow in the eastern sky as of a rising moon and know that Paris was there, Le Bourget[7] was there.

Was that it?

Yes, a pool of light was reflected there on the horizon, rising slowly, then swiftly to meet him. Soon he was over a portion of it, seeing the solid pool fragmented into individual pin points of light. A few minutes later he was over the Eiffel Tower,[8] circling it before heading to the northeast where the airfield was.

From an altitude of four thousand feet he saw a black square framed by regularly spaced beads of light but having at one side a mass of lights jammed together. Was that Le Bourget? It must be, according to his map. He flew over it, then circled slowly and flew back, slanting downward in a slow glide. Three thousand feet, said the altimeter. Two thousand. He was again over that huge black square, circling it. Yes, it was an airfield. There were hangers at one end, and floodlights, though the latter seemed to him woefully feeble, lighting an area not large enough to land in.

He circled again and again, losing altitude, then turned for the straight glide downward. He knew an instant of panic as he began his glide; for the first time in his flying experience, being numb with fatigue, he had completely lost the feel of his plane during a landing. He must do everything, not according to a felt sense of distance and speed and balance, but according to calculations from what he saw on his instrument panel and what he saw when he stuck his head out the windows. He forced himself to do so, with a last effort of will. Panic, pierced by logic, died as he slanted down over the hangars into the wind, into the floodlit area, easing back on his stick, then forward, then back again, kicking first the left rudder and then the right.

He was near the outer edge of the floodlit area, with only blackness ahead of him, when —gently, gently—his wheels touched earth and the tail came down. He was again a creature of earth, after thirty-three and one-half hours in the air; the time in Paris was precisely 10:24 P.M. on Saturday, May 21, 1927. He rolled into the darkness beyond the lighted ground, slowing as quickly as he could (it was nervous work, plunging forward blindly) until at last he could swing his plane around and head it back toward the hangars.

But he had barely begun to taxi back when, staring in amazement out the window, he cut his motor.

Toward him, across the lighted space, surged a sea of humanity. It engulfed his plane. And even through the deafness caused by long hours of the motor's roar he heard shouted over and over again by thousands of voices in strange accents: *Lindbergh! Lindbergh! Lindbergh!*

7. **Le Bourget**\lə ˈbur·zhā\ the principal airport for the city of Paris.
8. **The Eiffel**\ˈai·fəl\ **Tower,** an iron tower in Paris that was at the time the tallest structure in the world.

I

A NEW WORLD HERO

Charles Lindbergh's feat captured the imaginations of people everywhere. The tall, serious-minded airman, who had been a relatively unknown mail pilot a few days before, suddenly became an international hero. His wild reception at the airport in Paris was only a beginning. Everywhere he went, people lined the streets to cheer and to catch a glimpse of the young man who had expanded the frontiers of flight.

Governments decorated him. Organizations honored him. From every part of the globe, people sent letters, telegrams, and gifts by the hundreds of thousands. Hundreds of poems and songs were composed in tribute.

Despite the wild acclaim, Lindbergh remained much the same unassuming person. Huge sums of money sent to him by various governments were returned with the young flier's expressed hope that the money would be used for the families of airmen lost in flight or for some other purpose which would advance aviation. Compare his accomplishment with the accomplishment of some of the present-day astronauts who have traveled to the moon. Was Lindbergh's adventure as danger filled?

II

IMPLICATIONS

In addition to providing us with a vivid, suspenseful description of the action before and during the lift-off, the long flight, and the landing in Paris, the author tries to give us his estimate of Lindbergh as a person by revealing his reactions and feelings.

1. Consider and discuss the following as clues to Lindbergh's character:

a. His adding up of the hazards facing him before the takeoff.

b. His response to the question about the number of sandwiches he carried.

c. His manner of announcing that he was ready to begin the flight.

d. His feelings when he discovered the photographers alongside his plane.

e. His feelings as he flies among the threatening clouds two miles above the Atlantic.

f. His reaction to the discovery that the moon seemed to be rising on the wrong side of his plane.

g. His feelings when he arrived over Dingle Bay on the Irish coast.

2. Do you agree or disagree with the following statements:

a. Success demands taking calculated risks.

b. People must have heroes.

III

TECHNIQUES

Suspense

Many accounts of Charles A. Lindbergh's historic flight have been written. Each has in some way tried to recapture the drama of the event; however, few have the sustained suspense of this selection. With his first words, the author begins to build suspense, and he keeps us in suspense until the very last line. How does he accomplish this?

1. Suspense is built on uncertainty. In the first three paragraphs, what are those circumstances the author mentions that increase suspense?

2. Discuss how the author's use of the italicized words in the following help to build suspense:

a. "...his gaze *fixed anxiously* on the round dial. ..." (p. 78)

b. "Slowly, *with agonizing slowness,* the plane gathered speed." (p. 79)

c. "But how sluggish and heavy the plane felt as the white cloth rushed *nearer, nearer!*" (p. 79)

d. "*Now* for the telephone wires." (p. 80)

e. "Yet *still* he flew blind and *still* the ice coated, ever more quickly. ..." (p. 82)

f. "... *staring in amazement* out the window, he cut his motor." (p. 86)

Imaginative Language

The author uses language skillfully in building the drama of the flight. Discuss his imaginative use of language in the following instances:

1. "... gray threads moving from west to east, as though unraveled from a spool where the wind brushed the waters." (p. 81)

2. "The veil of fatigue which has been blurring his perceptions was abruptly stripped away." (p. 81)

3. "... the freedom of the upper air must be paid for in coins of danger." (p. 82)

4. "Night rose up out of the earth ahead of him, shoving the twilight back, back into the west." (p. 85)

Have you ever dreamed
of being a space pioneer? Would you like
to live on another planet? This story tells
what kind of adventure it might
turn out to be.

Dark
They Were,
and Golden-Eyed

RAY BRADBURY

The rocket metal cooled in the meadow winds. Its lid gave a bulging *pop*. From its clock interior stepped a man, a woman, and three children. The other passengers whispered away across the Martian meadow, leaving the man alone among his family.

The man felt his hair flutter and the tissues of his body draw tight as if he were standing at the center of a vacuum. His wife, before him, seemed almost to whirl away in smoke. The children, small seeds, might at any instant be sown to all the Martian climes.

The children looked up at him, as people look to the sun to tell what time of their life it is. His face was cold.

"What's wrong?" asked his wife.

"Let's get back on the rocket."

"Go back to Earth?"

"Yes! Listen!"

The wind blew as if to flake away their identities. At any moment the Martian air might draw his soul from him, as marrow comes from a white bone. He felt submerged in a chemical that could dissolve his intellect and burn away his past.

They looked at Martian hills that time had worn with a crushing pressure of years. They saw the old cities, lost in their meadows, lying like children's delicate bones among the blowing lakes of grass.

"Chin up, Harry," said his wife. "It's too late. We've come over sixty million miles."

The children with their yellow hair hollered at the deep dome of Martian sky. There was no answer but the racing hiss of wind through the stiff grass.

He picked up the luggage in his cold hands. "Here we go," he said—a man standing on the edge of a sea, ready to wade in and be drowned.

They walked into town.

Their name was Bittering. Harry and his wife Cora; Dan, Laura, and David. They built a small white cottage and ate good breakfasts there, but the fear was never gone. It lay with Mr. Bittering and Mrs. Bittering, a third unbidden partner at every midnight talk, at every dawn awakening.

"I feel like a salt crystal," he said, "in a mountain stream, being washed away. We don't belong here. We're Earth people. This is Mars. It was meant for Martians. For heaven's sake, Cora, let's buy tickets home!"

But she only shook her head. "One day the atom bomb will fix Earth. Then we'll be safe here."

"Safe and insane!"

Tick-tock, seven o'clock sang the voice-clock; *time to get up.* And they did.

Something made him check everything each morning—warm hearth, potted blood-geraniums—precisely as if he expected something to be amiss. The morning paper was toast-warm from the 6 A.M. Earth rocket. He broke its seal and tilted it at his breakfast place. He forced himself to be convivial.

"Colonial days all over again," he declared. "Why, in ten years there'll be a million Earthmen on Mars. Big cities, everything! They said we'd fail. Said the Martians would resent our invasion. But did we find any Martians? Not a living soul! Oh, we found their empty cities, but no one in them. Right?"

A river of wind submerged the house. When the windows ceased rattling, Mr. Bittering swallowed and looked at the children.

"I don't know," said David. "Maybe there're Martians around we don't see. Sometimes nights I think I hear 'em. I hear the wind. The sand hits my window. I get scared. And I see those towns way up in the mountains where the Martians lived a long time ago. And I think I see things moving around those towns, Papa. And I wonder if those Martians *mind* us living here. I wonder if they won't do something to us for coming here."

"Nonsense!" Mr. Bittering looked out the windows. "We're clean, decent people." He looked at his children. "All dead cities have some kind of ghosts in them. Memories, I mean." He stared at the hills. "You see a staircase and you wonder what Martians looked like climbing it. You see Martian paintings and you wonder what the painter was like. You make a little ghost in your mind, a memory. It's quite natural. Imagination." He stopped. "You haven't been prowling up in those ruins, have you?"

"No, Papa." David looked at his shoes.

"See that you stay away from them. Pass the jam."

"Just the same," said little David, "I bet something happens."

Something happened that afternoon.

Laura stumbled through the settlement, crying. She dashed blindly onto the porch.

"Mother, Father—the war, Earth!" she sobbed. "A radio flash just came. Atom bombs hit New York! All the space rockets blown up. No more rockets to Mars, ever!"

"Oh, Harry!" The mother held onto her husband and daughter.

"Are you sure, Laura?" asked the father quietly.

Laura wept. "We're stranded on Mars, forever and ever!"

For a long time there was only the sound of the wind in the late afternoon.

Alone, thought Bittering. Only a thousand of us here. No way back. No way. No way. Sweat poured from his face and his hands and his body; he was drenched in the hotness of his fear. He wanted to strike Laura, cry, "No, you're lying! The rockets will come back!" Instead, he stroked Laura's head against him and said, "The rockets will get through someday."

"Father, what will we do?"

"Go about our business, of course. Raise crops and children. Wait. Keep things going until the war ends and the rockets come again."

The two boys stepped out onto the porch.

"Children," he said, sitting there, looking beyond them, "I've something to tell you."

"We know," they said.

In the following days, Bittering wandered often through the garden to stand alone in his fear. As long as the rockets had spun a silver web across space, he had been able to accept Mars. For he had always told himself: Tomorrow, if I want, I can buy a ticket and go back to Earth.

But now: The web gone, the rockets lying in jigsaw heaps of molten girder and unsnaked wire. Earth people left to the strangeness of Mars, the cinnamon dusts and wine airs, to be baked like gingerbread shapes in Martian summers, put into harvested storage by Martian winters. What would happen to him, the others? This was the moment Mars had waited for. Now it would eat them.

He got down on his knees in the flower bed, a spade in his nervous hands. Work, he thought, work and forget.

He glanced up from the garden to the Martian mountains. He thought of the proud old Martian names that had once been on those peaks. Earthmen, dropping from the sky, had gazed upon hills, rivers, Martian seas left nameless in spite of names. Once Martians had built cities, named cities; climbed mountains, named mountains; sailed seas, named seas. Mountains melted, seas drained, cities tumbled. In spite of this, the Earthmen had felt a silent guilt at putting new names to these ancient hills and valleys.

Nevertheless, man lives by symbol and label. The names were given.

Mr. Bittering felt very alone in his garden under the Martian sun, anachronism bent here, planting Earth flowers in a wild soil.

Think. Keep thinking. Different things. Keep your mind free of Earth, the atom war, the lost rockets.

He perspired. He glanced about. No one watching. He removed his tie. Pretty bold, he thought. First your coat off, now your tie. He hung it neatly on a peach tree he had imported as a sapling from Massachusetts.

He returned to his philosophy of names and mountains. The Earthmen had changed names. Now there were Hormel Valleys, Roosevelt Seas, Ford Hills, Vanderbilt Plateaus, Rockefeller Rivers, on Mars. It wasn't right. The American settlers had shown wisdom, using old Indian prairie names: Wisconsin, Minnesota, Idaho, Ohio, Utah, Milwaukee, Waukegan, Osseo. The old names, the old meanings.

Staring at the mountains wildly, he thought: Are you up there? All the dead ones, you Martians? Well, here we are, alone, cut off! Come down, move us out! We're helpless!

The wind blew a shower of peach blossoms.

He put out his sun-browned hand, gave a small cry. He touched the blossoms, picked them up. He turned them, he touched them again and again. Then he shouted for his wife.

"Cora!"

She appeared at a window. He ran to her.

"Cora, these blossoms!"

She handled them.

"Do you see? They're different. They've changed! They're not peach blossoms any more!"

"Look all right to me," she said.

"They're not. They're *wrong*! I can't tell how. An extra petal, a leaf, something, the color, the smell!"

The children ran out in time to see their father hurrying about the garden, pulling up radishes, onions, and carrots from their beds.

"Cora, come look!"

They handled the onions, the radishes, the carrots among them.

"Do they look like carrots?"

"Yes . . . no." She hesitated. "I don't know."

"They're changed."

"Perhaps."

"You know they have! Onions but not onions, carrots but not carrots. Taste: the same but different. Smell: not like it used to be." He felt his heart pounding, and he was afraid. He dug his fingers into the earth. "Cora, what's happening? What is it? We've got to get away from this." He ran across the garden. Each tree felt his touch. "The roses. The roses. They're turning green!"

And they stood looking at the green roses.

And two days later Dan came running. "Come see the cow. I was milking her and I saw it. Come on!"

They stood in the shed and looked at their one cow.

It was growing a third horn.

And the lawn in front of their house very quietly and slowly was coloring itself like spring violets. Seed from Earth but growing up a soft purple.

"We must get away," said Bittering. "We'll eat this stuff and then we'll change—who knows to what? I can't let it happen. There's only one thing to do. Burn this food!"

"It's not poisoned."

"But it is. Subtly, very subtly. A little bit. A very little bit. We mustn't touch it."

He looked with dismay at their house. "Even the house. The wind's done something to it. The air's burned it. The fog at night. The boards, all warped out of shape. It's not an Earthman's house any more."

"Oh, your imagination!"

He put on his coat and tie. "I'm going into town. We've got to do something now. I'll be back."

"Wait, Harry!" his wife cried.

But he was gone.

In town, on the shadowy step of the grocery store, the men sat with their hands on their knees, conversing with great leisure and ease.

Mr. Bittering wanted to fire a pistol in the air.

What are you doing, you fools! he thought. Sitting here! You've heard the news—we're stranded on this planet. Well, move! Aren't you frightened? Aren't you afraid? What are you going to do?

"Hello, Harry," said everyone.

"Look," he said to them. "You did hear the news, the other day, didn't you?"

They nodded and laughed. "Sure. Sure, Harry."

"What are you going to do about it?"

"Do, Harry, do? What *can* we do?"

"Build a rocket, that's what!"

"A rocket, Harry? To go back to all that trouble? Oh, Harry."

"But you *must* want to go back. Have you noticed the peach blossoms, the onions, the grass?"

"Why, yes, Harry, seems we did," said one of the men.

"Doesn't it scare you?"

"Can't recall that it did much, Harry."

"Idiots!"

"Now, Harry."

Bittering wanted to cry. "You've got to work with me. If we stay here, we'll all change. The air. Don't you smell it. Something in the air. A Martian virus, maybe; some seed, or a pollen. Listen to me."

They stared at him.

"Sam," he said to one of them.

"Yes, Harry?"

"Will you help me build a rocket?"

"Harry, I got a whole load of metal and some blueprints. You want to work in my metal shop on a rocket, you're welcome. I'll sell you that metal for five hundred dollars. You should be able to construct a right pretty rocket, if you work alone, in about thirty years."

Everyone laughed.

"Don't laugh."

Sam looked at him with quiet good humor.

"Sam," Bittering said. "Your eyes—"

"What about them, Harry?"

"Didn't they used to be grey?"

"Well now, I don't remember."

"They were, weren't they?"

"Why do you ask, Harry?"

"Because now they're kind of yellow-colored."

"Is that so, Harry?" Sam said, casually.

"And you're taller and thinner—"

"You might be right, Harry."

"Sam, you shouldn't have yellow eyes."

"Harry, what color eyes have *you* got?" Sam said.

"My eyes? They're blue, of course."

"Here you are, Harry." Sam handed him a pocket mirror. "Take a look at yourself."

Mr. Bittering hesitated, and then raised the mirror to his face.

There were little, very dim flecks of new gold captured in the blue of his eyes.

"Now look what you've done," said Sam a moment later. "You've broken my mirror."

Harry Bittering moved into the metal shop and began to build the rocket. Men stood in the open door and talked and joked without raising their voices. Once in a while they gave him a hand on lifting something. But mostly they just idled and watched him with their yellowing eyes.

"It's suppertime, Harry," they said.

His wife appeared with his supper in a wicker basket.

"I won't touch it," he said. "I'll eat only food from our Deepfreeze. Food that came from Earth. Nothing from our garden."

His wife stood watching him. "You can't build a rocket."

"I worked in a shop once, when I was twenty. I know metal. Once I get it started, the others will help," he said, not looking at her, laying out the blueprints.

"Harry, Harry," she said, helplessly.

"We've got to get away, Cora. We've *got* to."

The nights were full of wind that blew down the empty moonlit sea meadows past the little white chess cities lying for their twelve-thousandth year in the shallows. In the Earthmen's settlement, the Bittering house shook with a feeling of change.

Lying abed, Mr. Bittering felt his bones shifted, shaped, melted like gold. His wife, lying beside him, was dark from many sunny afternoons. Dark she was, and golden-eyed, burnt almost black by the sun, sleeping, and the children metallic in their beds, and the wind roaring forlorn and changing through the old peach trees, the violet grass, shaking out green rose petals.

The fear would not be stopped. It had his throat and heart. It dripped in a wetness of the arm and the temple and the trembling palm.

A green star rose in the east.

A strange word emerged from Mr. Bittering's lips.

"*Iorrt. Iorrt.*" He repeated it.

It was a Martian word. He knew no Martian.

In the middle of the night he arose and dialed a call through to Simpson, the archeologist.

"Simpson, what does the word *Iorrt* mean?"

"Why, that's the old Martian word for our planet Earth. Why?"

"No special reason."

The telephone slipped from his hand.

"Hello, hello, hello, hello," it kept saying while he sat gazing out at the green star. "Bittering? Harry, are you there?"

The days were full of metal sound. He laid the frame of the rocket with the reluctant help of three indifferent men. He grew very tired in an hour or so and had to sit down.

"The altitude," laughed a man.

"Are you *eating*, Harry?" asked another.

"I'm eating," he said, angrily.

"From your Deepfreeze?"

"Yes!"

"You're getting thinner, Harry."

"I'm not!"

"And taller."

"Liar!"

His wife took him aside a few days later. "Harry, I've used up all the food in the Deepfreeze. There's nothing left. I'll have to make sandwiches using food grown on Mars."

He sat down heavily.

"You must eat," she said. "You're weak."

"Yes," he said.

He took a sandwich, opened it, looked at it, and began to nibble at it.

"And take the rest of the day off," she said. "It's hot. The children want to swim in the canals and hike. Please come along."

"I can't waste time. This is a crisis!"

"Just for an hour," she urged. "A swim'll do you good."

He rose, sweating. "All right, all right. Leave me alone. I'll come."

"Good for you, Harry."

The sun was hot, the day quiet. There was only an immense staring burn upon the land. They moved along the canal, the father, the mother, the racing children in their swim suits. They stopped and ate meat sandwiches. He saw their skin baking brown. And he saw the yellow eyes of his wife and his children, their eyes that were never yellow before. A few tremblings shook him, but were carried off in waves of pleasant heat as he lay in the sun. He was too tired to be afraid.

"Cora, how long have your eyes been yellow?"

She was bewildered. "Always, I guess."

"They didn't change from brown in the last three months?"

She bit her lips. "No. Why do you ask?"

"Never mind."

They sat there.

"The children's eyes," he said. "They're yellow, too."

"Sometimes growing children's eyes change color."

"Maybe *we're* children, too. At least to Mars. That's a thought." He laughed. "Think I'll swim."

They leaped into the canal water, and he let himself sink down and down to the bottom like a golden statue and lie there in green silence. All was water-quiet and deep, all was peace. He felt the steady, slow current drift him easily.

If I lie here long enough, he thought, the water will work and eat away my flesh until the bones show like coral. Just my skeleton left.

And then the water can build on that skeleton—green things, deep water things, red things, yellow things. Change. Change. Slow, deep, silent change. And isn't that what it is up *there*?

He saw the sky submerged above him, the sun made Martian by atmosphere and time and space.

Up there, a big river, he thought, a Martian river, all of us lying deep in it, in our pebble houses, in our sunken boulder houses, like crayfish hidden, and the water washing away our old bodies and lenghthening the bones and——

He let himself drift up through the soft light.

Dan sat on the edge of the canal, regarding his father seriously.

"*Utha*," he said.

"What?" asked his father.

The boy smiled. "You know. *Utha's* the Martian word for 'father.'"

"Where did you learn it?"

"I don't know. Around. *Utha*."

"What do you want?"

The boy hesitated. "I—I want to change my name."

"Change it?"

"Yes."

His mother swam over. "What's wrong with Dan for a name?"

Dan fidgeted. "The other day you called Dan, Dan, Dan. I didn't even hear. I said to myself, That's not my name. I've a new name. I've a new name I want to use."

Mr. Bittering held to the side of the canal, his body cold and his heart pounding slowly. "What is this new name?"

"Linnl. Isn't that a good name? Can I use it? Can't I, please?"

Mr. Bittering put his hand to his head. He thought of the silly rocket, himself working alone, himself alone even among his family, so alone.

He heard his wife say, "Why not?"

He heard himself say, "Yes, you can use it."

"Yaaa!" screamed the boy. "I'm Linnl, Linnl!"

Racing down the meadowlands, he danced and shouted.

Mr. Bittering looked at his wife. "Why did we do that?"

"I don't know," she said. "It just seemed like a good idea."

They walked into the hills. They strolled on old mosaic paths, beside still pumping fountains. The paths were covered with a thin film of cool water all summer long. You kept your bare feet cool all the day, splashing as in a creek, wading.

They came to a small deserted Martian villa with a good view of the valley. It was on top of a hill. Blue marble halls, large murals, a swimming pool. It was refreshing in this hot summertime. The Martians hadn't believed in large cities.

"How nice," said Mrs. Bittering, "if we could move up here to this villa for the summer."

"Come on," he said. "We're going back to town. There's work to be done on the rocket."

But as he worked that night, the thought of the cool blue marble villa entered his mind. As the hours passed, the rocket seemed less important.

In the flow of days and weeks, the rocket receded and dwindled. The old fever was gone. It frightened him to think he had let it slip this way. But somehow the heat, the air, the working conditions——

He heard the men murmuring on the porch of his metal shop.

"Everyone's going. You hear?"

"All going. That's right."

Bittering came out. "Going where?" He saw a couple of trucks, loaded with children and furniture, drive down the dusty street.

"Up to the villas," said the man.

"Yeah, Harry. I'm going. So is Sam. Aren't you, Sam?"

"That's right, Harry. What about you?"

"I've got work to do here."

"Work! You can finish that rocket in the autumn, when it's cooler."

He took a breath. "I got the frame all set up."

"In the autumn is better." Their voices were lazy in the heat.

"Got to work," he said.

"Autumn," they reasoned. And they sounded so sensible, so right.

"Autumn would be best," he thought. "Plenty of time, then."

No! cried part of himself, deep down, put away, locked tight, suffocating. No! No!

"In the autumn," he said.

"Come on, Harry," they all said.

"Yes," he said, feeling his flesh melt in the hot liquid air. "Yes, in the autumn. I'll begin work again then."

"I got a villa near the Tirra Canal," said someone.

"You mean the Roosevelt Canal, don't you?"

"Tirra. The old Martian name."

"But on the map—"

"Forget the map. It's Tirra now. Now I found a place in the Pillan mountains—"

"You mean the Rockefeller range," said Bittering.

"I mean the Pillan mountains," said Sam.

"Yes," said Bittering, buried in the hot, swarming air. "The Pillan mountains."

Everyone worked at loading the truck in the hot, still afternoon of the next day.

Laura, Dan, and David carried packages. Or, as they preferred to be known, Titl, Linnl, and Werr carried packages.

The furniture was abandoned in the little white cottage.

"It looked just fine in Boston," said the mother. "And here in the cottage. But up at the villa? No. We'll get it when we come back in the autumn."

Bittering himself was quiet.

"I've some ideas on furniture for the villa," he said after a time. "Big, lazy furniture."

"What about your encyclopedia? You're taking it along, surely?"

Mr. Bittering glanced away. "I'll come and get it next week."

They turned to their daughter. "What about your New York dresses?"

The bewildered girl stared. "Why, I don't want them any more."

They shut off the gas, the water, they locked the doors and walked away. Father peered into the truck.

"Gosh, we're not taking much," he said.

"Considering all we brought to Mars, this is only a handful!"

He started the truck.

Looking at the small white cottage for a long moment, he was filled with a desire to rush to it, touch it, say good-by to it, for he felt as if he were going away on a long journey, leaving something to which he could never quite return, never understand again.

Just then Sam and his family drove by in another truck.

"Hi, Bittering! Here we go!"

The truck swung down the ancient highway out of town. There were sixty others traveling the same direction. The town filled with a silent, heavy dust from their passage. The canal waters lay blue in the sun, and a quiet wind moved in the strange trees.

"Good-by, town!" said Mr. Bittering.

"Good-by, good-by," said the family, waving to it.

They did not look back again.

Summer burned the canals dry. Summer moved like flame upon the meadows. In the empty Earth settlement, the painted houses flaked and peeled. Rubber tires upon which children had swung in back yards hung suspended like stopped clock pendulums in the blazing air.

At the metal shop, the rocket frame began to rust.

In the quiet autumn Mr. Bittering stood, very dark now, very golden-eyed, upon the slope above his villa, looking at the valley.

"It's time to go back," said Cora.

"Yes, but we're not going," he said quietly. "There's nothing there any more."

"Your books," she said. "Your fine clothes."

"Your *lles* and your fine *ior uele rre,*" she said.

"The town's empty. No one's going back," he said. "There's no reason to, none at all."

The daughter wove tapestries and the sons played songs on ancient flutes and pipes, their laughter echoing in the marble villa.

Mr. Bittering gazed at the Earth settlement far away in the low valley. "Such odd, such ridiculous houses the Earth people built."

"They didn't know any better," his wife mused. "Such ugly people. I'm glad they've gone."

They both looked at each other, startled by all they had just finished saying. They laughed.

"Where did they go?" he wondered. He glanced at his wife. She was golden and slender as his daughter. She looked at him, and he seemed almost as young as their eldest son.

"I don't know," she said.

"We'll go back to town maybe next year, or the year after, or the year after that," he said, calmly. "Now—I'm warm. How about taking a swim?"

They turned their backs to the valley. Arm in arm they walked silently down a path of clear-running spring water.

Five years later a rocket fell out of the sky. It lay steaming in the valley. Men leaped out of it, shouting.

"We won the war on Earth! We're here to rescue you! Hey!"

But the American-built town of cottages, peach trees, and theaters was silent. They found a flimsy rocket frame rusting in an empty shop.

The rocket men searched the hills. The captain established headquarters in an abandoned bar. His lieutenant came back to report.

"The town's empty, but we found native life in the hills, sir. Dark people. Yellow eyes. Martians. Very friendly. We talked a bit, not much. They learned English fast. I'm sure our relations will be most friendly with them, sir."

"Dark, eh?" mused the captain. "How many?"

"Six, eight hundred, I'd say, living in those marble ruins in the hills, sir. Tall, healthy. Beautiful women."

"Did they tell you what became of the men and women who built this Earth-settlement, Lieutenant?"

"They hadn't the foggiest notion of what happened to this town or its people."

"Strange. You think those Martians killed them?"

"They look surprisingly peaceful. Chances are a plague did this town in, sir."

"Perhaps. I suppose this is one of those mysteries we'll never solve. One of those mysteries you read about."

The captain looked at the room, the dusty windows, the blue mountains rising beyond, the canals moving in the light, and he heard the soft wind in the air. He shivered. Then, recovering, he tapped a large fresh map he had thumbtacked to the top of an empty table.

"Lots to be done, Lieutenant." His voice droned on and quietly on as the sun sank behind the blue hills. "New settlements. Mining sites, minerals to be looked for. Bacteriological specimens taken. The work, all the work. And the old records were lost. We'll have a job of remapping to do, renaming the mountains and rivers and such. Calls for a little imagination.

"What do you think of naming those mountains the Lincoln Mountains, this canal the Washington Canal, those hills—we can name those hills for you, Lieutenant. Diplomacy. And you, for a favor, might name a town for me! Polishing the apple. And why not make this the Einstein Valley, and further over . . . are you *listening*, Lieutenant?"

The lieutenant snapped his gaze from the blue color and the quiet mist of the hills far beyond the town.

"What? Oh, *yes*, sir!"

I
A PEOPLE TRANSFORMED

Now that the moon is being explored, a colony on Mars is not an impossible dream. After the moon, the planet nearest to Earth is Venus, but Venus is believed too hot for manned exploration. The next nearest is Mars, and scientists believe there is possibility that some form of life may exist there. But while the moon is never further than 250,000 miles from earth, Mars is never closer than 35 million miles. For this reason, it would take months to reach Mars. Making such a trip would take a hardy pioneer.

1. In the beginning of the story, how do the man and woman differ in their reactions to the new environment? Discuss whether you feel the man or the woman is weaker in character.

2. What happens on earth that causes Mr. Bittering to decide that he should build a rocket? Where does he get the material? What is the attitude of the other colonists?

3. When the Bitterings and their neighbors leave the town, where do they go? How do they come to feel about the town and earth people?

II
IMPLICATIONS

Consider and discuss the following statements.

1. Flowers and vegetables could change because of different chemical qualities in the soil and air of Mars. It is not unreasonable to believe that human beings would also change.

2. As new Martians, the colonists' lives were more satisfying than they had been on earth.

3. Eventually the new Martians would disappear just as the first Martians had.

III
TECHNIQUES

Suspense and Foreshadowing

Ray Bradbury depends heavily upon foreshadowing to maintain suspense and give his story impact at the end. In discussion, trace the way he foreshadows the fate of the Bitterings and of others from earth who would continue to colonize Mars. How is mention of the wind used effectively throughout the story?

Imaginative Language

From the very beginning of this story, the reader is conscious of a quality of mystery that overshadows all activity. In part, this is a result of the fact that the author does not give a detailed account of the family's daily life on Mars. Time is shifted with only momentary glimpses of story developments, and this vagueness adds to the mysterious quality of the story. However, the mysterious quality is largely due to the author's choice of words. For example, in the first paragraph the word *whispered* appears in an out of the ordinary way, telling how the family's fellow passengers disappeared across the Martian meadow. Find and discuss two other examples in the story where language is imaginatively used to add to the impression of mystery.

Can you see
in this poem another
kind of adventure . . .

I AM A

Cosmonaut
Cradled in dangers
Orbiting a garden universe
Snipping cosmos, probing Venus,   5
Sighting summer's end blindly,
Weightily weightless
Spinning out of reach,
      out
        of   10
          reach
Signaling strangers.

LENORE MARSHALL

Reprinted from *Latest Will,* New and Selected
Poems, by Lenore Marshall. By permission of
W. W. Norton & Company, Inc. Copyright ©
1969 by Lenore Marshall.

SUMMING UP

Call to Adventure

Adventure is possible for anyone who, like Sherlock Holmes, refuses to let "the commonplaces of existence" overwhelm him. Adventure can be found anywhere if you have an adventurous spirit. Its call can be heard in the roar of the sea, the whistle of a train, or the silence of a classroom. Adventure is where you find it!

THE IDEA OF ADVENTURE

Consider each of the following statements before you decide whether you agree or disagree. Most of these statements would make a good topic for a brief essay or talk. If you choose to use one of them for this purpose, remember that your talk or paper will be more interesting and convincing if you refer as often as possible to *specific* points in the selections in CALL TO ADVENTURE.

1. Reading stories of adventure satisfies the basic human need to have some variety in the pattern of everyday existence.

2. To hear the call to adventure, you must be an original and independent thinker.

3. People's actions are largely determined by the way they think about themselves.

4. A hero is simply a person who happens to be in the right place at the right time.

5. A person dares all in achieving some objective. Once he has achieved it, he is often no longer interested in what originally challenged him. Thus, one could conclude that the whole affair was not worth the trouble.

6. In making up the true image of a hero, honor should be the first qualification, with courage and daring secondary considerations.

TECHNIQUES

When you think back over some of the adventures in this group of selections which were true accounts, such as Charles Lindbergh's flight over the Atlantic, you realize that nonfiction can be just as exciting as fiction. In fact, in many respects, fiction and nonficition are alike. Explain. this statement after considering the following questions:

1. What makes fictional or imaginary adventure seem real?

2. Do you understand characters in stories better if they talk and act like people you know?

Conflict

All of the adventures in this section have centered around conflict of one kind or another. In some selections, the opposing forces are easily seen; in others there are many elements of conflict and some of them are rather hard to identify.

Discuss the following statements and tell why you think they are true or untrue.

1. "The Most Dangerous Game" centers about conflict of man against man; but it also shows inner conflict where one idea struggles against another, and a third kind of conflict, man against nature.

2. "The Red-Headed League" deals with the conflict of man against man but also shows man against society.

3. "Through the Tunnel" shows only one type of conflict.

4. In Ray Bradbury's story, "Dark They Were, and Golden-Eyed," it is difficult to decide whether the central characters are actually *in conflict* with nature.

Suspense and Foreshadowing

Foreshadowing action is one of the many ways an author has of building the suspense which makes an audience or reader wonder what is going to happen.

1. In which of the preceding selections did you continue to feel suspense *after* the conflict had been resolved? Is this many times true in a mystery or detective story? Why?

2. What is to come in aviation is foreshadowed by Orville Wright in the concluding paragraph of "How I learned To Fly," page 76. Reread this paragraph. Name another individual you read about in this unit who fulfilled one of Wright's dreams. Which story among the selections do you think goes beyond anything Wright may have imagined as being in the future for heavier-than-air machines?

Imaginative Language

At the beginning of the section, imaginative language was defined as the combining of words in such a way that they arouse the feeling of the reader, or evoke an experience of the senses.

1. Think back to "The Most Dangerous Game." In this story, the author, Richard Connell, made a definite effort to imprint images upon the reader's mind, to give an experience of the senses. What character, or characters, described by Connell return to you most vividly?

2. Which of the writers from this section do you consider the greatest master of imaginative language? Why? Thinking back over the section, list some of the imaginative language that remains in your mind. Try to give the reasons why these images have remained with you.

HOMER'S

Odyssey

THE GREAT

ADVENTURE

Introduction

Nearly thirty centuries ago (roughly 800 B.C.), Homer, a blind minstrel in ancient Greece, is thought to have put together two of the world's great adventure stories. One story, the *Iliad*,[1] tells of the war between Greece and Troy.[2] It was a war which dragged on for ten long years, until finally a crafty Greek warrior named Odysseus[3] thought of a plan which brought victory to his people. The other story, the *Odyssey*,[4] tells of the many adventures of this same hero, Odysseus, as he struggles to sail home to Greece after the war is over.

The Epic

These ancient adventure tales, the *Iliad* and the *Odyssey*, are called *epics*. One of the oldest of literary forms, the *epic* is a story-poem about some great hero who performs daring deeds that require superhuman courage. In the Greek epics, the gods take an active part in helping or hindering the hero. For example, in the *Odyssey*, the god of the sea, Poseidon,[5] is Odysseus' enemy; while Athene,[6] the goddess of wisdom, helps the courageous Greek.

Recited from memory by minstrels who wandered from one lord's banquet hall to another, epics were passed along from minstrel to minstrel for many centuries.

Every epic took one hero, a man anyone could be proud to claim as an ancestor, through a series of separate adventures. When all of these separate stories were strung together into a long story-poem, they became an epic. The fate of the hero is usually bound up with the fate of a whole nation or race. Like most ancient peoples, the Greeks of Homer's time and later believed that their ancestors had been supermen, great in physical strength and unusually keen in mind. These superbeings supposedly found their greatest glory in battle.

By the time the *Odyssey* was written, the pattern of the Greek epic was well established. The verse form used was the hexameter. The prefix *hexa* indicated that there were six poetic measures to a line.

The Epic Poet

The epic poet did not "create" his story in the same way as a modern writer. The Greeks called an epic singer a *rhapsode*. This means "song-stitcher," which describes a minstrel very well. He felt free to borrow from legends and epics which were already well known to him and to his audience, but characters and places might be changed to suit a particular story. Since the epics were sung or told aloud, they had to be clear and readily understood. The minstrel-poet drew from a large store of phrases and descriptions from familiar epics, all of which had been repeated so often they were

---

1. **Iliad**\\ˈĭ·lē·əd\\.
2. **Troy**\\troi\\ an ancient city of northwest Asia Minor south of the mouth of the **Dardanelles**\\'dard·ən ˈĕlz\\, straits connecting the **Aegean Sea**\\ə ˈjē·ən\\ with the Sea of Marmara.
3. **Odysseus**\\ə ˈdĭ·sē·əs\\.
4. **Odyssey**\\ˈŏ·də· 'sē\\.
5. **Poseidon**\\pə ˈsai·dən\\ the Earth-Shaker, called **Neptune**\\ˈnĕp 'tūn\\ by the Romans.
6. **Athene**\\ə ˈthē·nə\\ the goddess of wisdom, industry, and arts, and protector of civilized life. She has always helped Odysseus. Called **Minerva** by the Romans.

quickly recognized by his listeners. Above all, the epic singer had to make his stories as uncomplicated for his listeners as possible. Thus he dealt with only one thing at a time.

Homer

Within the set epic pattern, there was still opportunity for the poet-singer to display originality of idea, expression, and effect. Here Homer outshone the other epic singers. He had the ability to bring his heroes alive. His epics were the ones which the Greeks valued enough to save for future generations.

Reading
the Odyssey

The lines of the following poem flow smoothly, much as a person would speak. This, however, is an English translation of the original Greek poetry. It does not use the hexameter verse form which fit the Greek language perfectly but which usually seems heavy and clumsy when attempted in English. To allow the action to move ahead rapidly, this translation is written in a verse form which has four measures to the line, is unrhymed, and has a certain marked rhythm. If it is read aloud, as it was meant to be, the reader can avoid the sing-song which robs any poetry of its vitality if he will *pause only briefly* at the end of each line in which the thought runs into the line following.

In this abridgement of Bates' translation of *The Odyssey of Homer,* many episodes and details have necessarily been omitted. If you enjoy these adventures of Odysseus, you will probably be interested in reading the whole book.

The War
at Troy

No one really knows the reasons the Trojan War was fought. Some classical scholars believe that it came about when the Greeks decided to control the trade route between the Aegean Sea and the Black Sea and thus spent many years both blockading and attacking Troy

and towns along the coast of Asia Minor that were friendly to the Trojans.

According to ancient myth, however, the bitter fighting at Troy all began when the Trojan prince, Paris, kidnapped Helen, the beautiful queen of Sparta, and carried her across the sea to Troy.

Gathering a huge army and a thousand ships, the angry Greeks sailed over the Aegean Sea. There they anchored their vast fleet by the shore before Troy and prepared to assault the forbidding walls of the city. However, the Trojans had prepared for the coming of the Greeks and they put up a stiff resistance. The result was that instead of the quick victory the Greeks had expected there was a long, drawn-out war in which the gods and goddesses took sides.

An Adventure in Archaeology

The search for and the eventual discovery of the ruins of Troy was in itself a thrilling adventure. The man who made the first great excavation, Heinrich Schliemann,[1] had become so intrigued with Homer's stories that, as a boy in a small German village, he vowed some day to find the great ruins. Schliemann amassed a fortune before he was forty and began his search for the ancient Greeks in earnest. In 1868, he went to what is now Turkey to dig.

Using the descriptions of Troy which Homer gives in the *Iliad,* Schliemann located a vast mound of earth on the shore of the Dardanelles. There he began his excavation.

Within the mound he found many levels of cities which over the centuries had been built one atop the ruins of another. He also unearthed a great store of priceless gold and silver ornaments. Most important of all, he established that there was a historical basis to the *Iliad.*

The Unlikely Hero, a book by Alan Honour, is an especially interesting account of Schliemann's life and discoveries.

1. **Heinrich Schliemann**\ˈhīn ˈrïkh ˈshlē ˈman\.

For nine long years the struggle went on with fortune favoring first one side, then another. The Greeks could not batter down the Trojan walls; the Trojans could not destroy the Greek fortifications or their ships along the shore.

In the tenth year of the war, Odysseus, who was famous for his craftiness, devised a plan which brought about the fall of the Trojan stronghold. The Greeks built a huge, hollow wooden horse and left it in view of Troy. Odysseus and a picked band of men were hidden inside the horse. Then the Greek armies, pretending to give up the long struggle, sailed off to a hiding place down the coast to await the coming of the night.

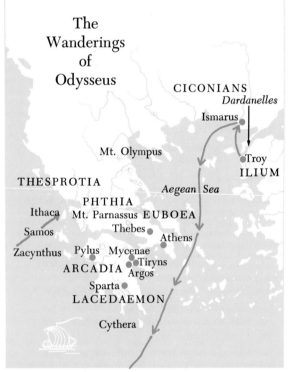

The Aegean Sea and the islands of Greece.

Overjoyed that their enemies had gone at last, the Trojans poured from the city. They surrounded the great horse, and thinking it their spoils of battle, pushed the great wooden structure inside the walls of their city. In the darkest hour of night, Odysseus and his men slipped from the horse and opened the gates to the returning Greek armies.

Caught off guard and hopelessly outnumbered, the Trojans were slaughtered and their beautiful city sacked and burned.

With the ruins of Troy smoking behind them, the Greeks sailed for home rejoicing that the ten years of war were over. But many were never to reach their homelands, for in destroying the Trojan city they had offended many of the most powerful gods. Not only had the victorious violated certain of the Trojan temples, but they also had failed to make suitable offerings to the gods after the fighting was ended.

These angry gods caused great storms to wreck many Greek ships. Scores of men were drowned. Great numbers were killed in other ways. Since Odysseus was the one who had suggested the plan for taking Troy, the gods decreed that he should spend ten more years wandering before he reached his home.

Homer begins the *Odyssey* with a traditional plea to the muse of poetry. He begs her to help him tell the story of the hero whom the gods sent wandering over the seas and who found that even after he reached his homeland and his loved ones his struggles were not over.

To make certain that his audience knows what story he is to tell, Homer also sings in the opening lines about some of the places Odysseus visited and of the gods and people the hero met. The modern reader might think this strange and repetitious, but the ancient Greeks never tired of the story. Here was a Greek to make every Greek proud. Where, indeed, could one find a hero as handsome, as courageous, and as clever as Odysseus? Where could one hope to match such a clear-voiced poet as Homer to tell the story of The Great Adventure!

Homer need not be afraid of "giving away" his story in the opening lines by telling what will happen. The audience already knew the tale of Odysseus. They were more interested in *how* Homer told the ancient stories than in *what* the plot would be.

THE ODYSSEY OF HOMER

TRANSLATED INTO ENGLISH VERSE BY HERBERT BATES

PART I

The Wanderings of Odysseus

BOOKS I–IX

PROLOGUE

Tell me the tale, Muse, of that man
Of many changes, he who went
Wandering so far when he had plundered
Troy's sacred citadel. And many
The men whose cities he beheld, 5
Whose minds he learned to know, and many
The sorrows that his soul endured
Upon the deep the while he strove
To save himself from death and bring
His comrades home.

> Of these things now, 10
Daughter of Zeus,[1] O goddess, tell us,
Even as thou wilt, the tale.

> Ere this
Those others who escaped death's stroke

Had reached their homes at last, delivered
From battle and the sea. But him 15
And him alone—though still he longed
For home and wife—the nymph Calypso,[2]
A mighty goddess, kept imprisoned
Within her hollow caves, and longed
To make him there her husband. No, 20
Not when the day came when the gods
Granted, as circling seasons passed,
That he might once again return
To Ithaca[3]—not even then,
With those that loved him, might he find 25
A rest from strife. And all the gods
Felt pity for him, all but one—
Poseidon.[4] Still, with wrath unceasing,
He strove against the good Odysseus
Until he reached his home. 30

ODYSSEUS TELLS HIS STORY

[Ten years have passed since the Greeks destroyed Troy. At this point in the story, Odysseus has been shipwrecked and has made his way to shore half-drowned. He has been taken in as a

Selections from *The Odyssey of Homer*, translated by Herbert Bates. Copyright, 1929, by McGraw-Hill Book Company, Inc.; renewed, 1957, by Chaloner Bates. Reprinted by permission of McGraw-Hill, Inc.

1. **Zeus**\zūs\ god of the sky, wielder of the thunderbolt, and leader of all the gods, called **Jupiter**\ˈjū·pə·tər\ by the Romans.
2. **Calypso**\kə ˈlĭp ′sō\ sea nymph of the island Ogygia.
3. **Ithaca**\ˈĭ·thə ′kə\ one of the Ionian islands off the coast of northwestern Greece, Odysseus' homeland.
4. **Poseidon**\pə ˈsaid·ən\ god of the sea, called Neptune\nĕp tyūn\ by the Romans.

guest at the palace of King Alcinoüs. At a feast
in the palace, he sits among the guests as
a stranger. The King and his lords do not know
he is the famous hero, Odysseus.

The feasting is ended. The minstrel has sung
so vividly of the ruin and death at Troy that
Odysseus is greatly moved. The King notices
this and asks the handsome stranger to tell his
story. Odysseus answers:]

"Mighty Alcinoüs,[1]   30
Honored of all men, good indeed
It is to hear the minstrelsy
Of such a singer, for he sings
Even as a god. Never, I think,
Can man attain a fairer goal   35
Than this:—when all a people meet
In joy and friendship. Side by side
They sit in the great hall at feast
And hear the minstrel's song. Beside them
Stand tables heaped with meat and bread.   40
While ever he who serves the wine
Dips from the mixing-bowl and fills
The feasters' cups. Such scenes I deem
Of all scenes, sweetest.
            But your heart
Now urges you to ask what sorrow   45
Brings forth these sighs—though this but
  leads me
To sigh and weep the more. Nay, then—
What shall I tell you first, and what
Leave to the last? For many a sorrow
The gods that dwell on high have given   50
To be my lot.
        And first of all
I will tell forth my name that you,
Like all, may know it; and at last,
When I have shunned death's cruel day,[2]
We may be friends still, host and guest,   55
Though I dwell far away.
             I am
Odysseus, great Laërtes'[3] son,
For cunning plans of every kind
Known among men; and even to heaven
Has spread my fame. My native land   60
Is Ithaca, a sun-bright island
Where rises Neriton,[4] a mountain
Far-seen, with wind-stirred woods. About it

Lie many an island, close together—
Doulichium, wooded Zacynthus,[5]   65
And Same.[6] Ithaca itself
Is low of shore and lies far out
To sea and toward the west: the others
Lie toward the dawn and sunrise. Rugged
It is, this land of mine, yet breeds   70
A sturdy youth, and I can find
No land more sweet to me than this,
My native land.
            But come,
For I will tell the many sorrows
Zeus sent upon me as I traveled   75
Homeward from Troy.

ADVENTURE
OF THE LOTUS-EATERS

Great Zeus, who guides the clouds, sent forth
Against our ships a wild north wind,
A raging tempest, and enshrouded
In dark clouds land and sea. Deep night   80
Came rolling from on high. Our ships
Drove headlong, while their sails were riven
Asunder by that gale; but these
We stored beneath the decks, still toiling
In dread of death, and striving ever,   85
Rowed on and reached the land
Where dwell the Lotus-eaters,[7] men
Whose food is flowers. And we all
Here went ashore and drew us water,
And by the sides of their swift ships   90
My men prepared their meal. And now
When we at last had had our fill
Of meat and drink, I sent forth men
To learn what manner of mankind
That live by bread might dwell here. Two   95
I chose to go and sent with them

---

1. **Alcinoüs**\ˈăl ˄sĭ·nō·əs\ king of the **Phæacians**
\ˈfē ˄ā·shəns\, an island or coastal people who help
the shipwrecked Odysseus.
2. Escaped death by reaching home.
3. **Laërtes**\lā ˄ər·tēz\.
4. **Neriton**\˄nā·rə·tən\.
5. **Doulichium**\ˈdū ˄lĭ·kē·əm\.
Zacynthus\zə ˄kĭn·thəs\.
6. **Same**\ˈsa·mā\.
7. **Lotus**\˄lō·təs\ the lotus eaters ate the fruit of the
lotus tree, which supposedly had magical properties.

A third, a herald. And these quickly
Went forth into that land and mingled
Among the Lotus-eaters. Never
Did these men, eaters of the lotus,   100
Plan evil to my men, and yet
They gave them of the lotus flower
And bade them eat of it, and lo,
Whatever man of them but tasted
That blossom strange and honey-sweet,   105
Naught cared he then to hasten back
With tidings to the ships, or ever
Turn homeward any more, but longed
To dwell there with the Lotus-eaters,
And pluck and eat the lotus blossoms   110
And think no more of home.
                              But these
I brought back to the ships by force,
Though they lamented, and I dragged them
Aboard the hollow ships and bound them
Beneath the benches. Then I bade   115
The rest, my true companions, hasten
Aboard the ships, lest one of them
Taste of the lotus, too, and lose
All memory of home. So straightway
They came aboard and sat them down   120
In order on the thwarts and smote
The foaming sea with oars.
                              So thence
We sailed upon our way sad-hearted.

ADVENTURE
OF THE CYCLOPS

And now we came unto the land
Where dwell the Cyclops[8]—arrogant   125
And lawless beings, who, with trust
In the undying gods, plough not
Nor plant with hands a single plant.
Yet crops spring up for them unsown
On fields untended—wheat and barley   130
And vines that bear full-clustered grapes
To make them wine. The rain of Zeus
Still brings increase in all. These men
Have neither meeting-place for council
Nor settled laws. They live apart   135
On lofty mountain ridges, dwelling
In hollow caverns. Each makes laws

For wife and child, and gives no heed
To any save himself.

                    There lies,
Facing the Cyclops' land, an island,   140
Sheltering the haven's outer side,
Not near, nor yet far out.
                              Thither we sailed
Seeking the land. Surely it was
Some god that gave us guidance thither
Through the dense night, for we could see   145
Nothing before our eyes: the mist
Shut close about the ships; no moon
Showed forth in heaven, for clouds en-
    closed it.
So no man with his eyes beheld
That isle or saw the long seas rolling   150
Against the land till we had beached
Our well-benched ships.
                              We drew our ships
Forth on the sands and lowered sail,
And we ourselves went up beyond
The breaking of the seas, and there   155
We fell asleep, and lay awaiting
The sacred dawn.
                              But when the dawn
Came, early-born and rosy-fingered,
We went forth, roaming through the island,
Gazing in wonder.
                              Now we looked   160
And saw not far away the mainland
Where dwelt the Cyclops. And we saw
Smoke rise, and heard the speech of men
And bleat of sheep and goats.
Then I called together   165
My men and spoke to all:
                              'Rest here,
Dear comrades, while with my own ship
And my own men I go to learn
What men these are—if wild and cruel
And ignorant of right, or kind   170
To every stranger and with hearts
That fear the gods.'
                              I spoke and went

———
8. **Cyclops**\▲sai 'klŏps\.

Reconstructed helmet with ram's head design from ancient Greece.

That land that lay hard by, we saw
Upon its utmost point a cave
Close to the sea: high-roofed it was,　　180
With laurel overhung, and many
The flocks of sheep and goats that there
Found shelter in the night. Around it
A courtyard lay, high-walled with stones
Set deep in earth, with lofty pines　　185
And high-leaved oaks.

　　　　　　　Within this lair
A man was wont to sleep, a monster
Who grazed his sheep far off, alone,
Nor ever mingled with his kind,
But lonely dwelt—lawless and evil.　　190
And marvelously was he shapen—
This monstrous being, not like mortals
That live by bread, but like a peak
That rising rough with woods stands forth
Apart from other hills.

　　　　　　　　And I　　195
Now bade my trusty men to bide
Close by the ship and guard the ship,
But twelve I chose, the best of all,
And we set forth.

　　　　　　　I bore with me
A goatskin filled with dark sweet wine,　　200
Which Maron, priest of Phœbus,[9] gave me,
Sweet and unmixed, a drink for gods.
As I set forth, I bore besides
Food in a leathern sack. For now
My fearless heart foresaw a meeting　　205
With a strange man of monstrous might—
A savage, scornful of the gods
And of man's law.

　　　　　　　Straightway we reached
His cave and entered, but we found not
The man within. For far away　　210
He herded, while they grazed at pasture,
His goodly flock. So on we passed
Far into that great cave and marveled
At all we saw within. Here stood
Crates heaped with cheese and here were pens　　215
Crowded with lambs and kids; all these

Aboard my ship and bade my men
Embark and loose the cables. Quickly
They came aboard and sat them down　　175
Each in his place and smote with oars
The whitening sea.

　　　　　Now when we reached

---

9. **Maron**\ˈmā·rən\. **Phœbus**\ˈfē·bəs\ (or **Phœbus Apollo**\ˈfē·bəs a ˈpŏ ′lō\), the god of the sun.

Were penned in pens apart; in one
Were kept the eldest, in another,
The younger; in a third, the youngest;
And all the well-wrought vessels used   220
For milking—pails and bowls—stood full,
Brimming with whey.

         And now my men
Besought me eagerly to carry
The cheeses thence, and come again
And loose the kids and lambs and drive
   them   225
In haste to our swift ship, then sail
Away o'er the salt sea. But this
I would not grant, though better far
Had I but done so! For I hoped
To look upon this man—he might   230
Give gifts of friendship. But, alas,
When he appeared, he was to bring
My poor men little joy!

         So there
We kindled fire and of that cheese
We made an offering, and ate   235
Ourselves thereof, and sat and waited
Until at last he entered, driving
His flock before him.

         He bore in
Dry wood to cook his meal, a load
Of wondrous weight, and down he flung it   240
Within the cave, with such a crash
We cowered back with fear and crouched
In the cave's corner. Then he drove
Into that spacious cave the sheep
That he must milk, and left the others—   245
The rams and goats—without, to roam
The high-walled court.

         Then in its place
He set the massive rock that closed
The doorway of the cave; he raised it
Lightly aloft, a weight so vast   250
That never two and twenty wagons,
Four-wheeled and firmly built, might stir it
From where it lay on earth—so great
That towering crag was that he set
To close his door.

         Now sat he down   255
And milked his sheep and bleating goats
All in due order, and he set

Her young by each. Half the white milk
He curdled and then gathered it
And set it by in wicker baskets;   260
And half he left there in the bowls
That he might sup thereon. And now,
When he had labored busily
And finished every task, he stayed
And kindled up the fire and saw us   265
And asked us:

         'Strangers, who are you,
And whence do you come sailing hither
Over the sea's wet ways? What errand
Can bring you hither? Or perchance
You wander purposeless, like robbers   270
Who rove the seas and venture life
To bring to strangers in far lands
An evil fortune.'

         So he spoke,
And at his words our hearts within us
Were crushed and broken, for we feared   275
The man's deep voice and monstrous body.
Yet I spoke up and answered, saying:
'We are Achæans[10] come from Troy;
We wander blown by every wind
Over the sea's great gulf, still striving   280
To reach our homes, yet ever go
On alien ways, by paths we never
Have willed to travel—so it pleases
Zeus to decree. We boast we once
Were warriors under Atreus' son,   285
Great Agamemnon,[11] he whose fame
Is highest under heaven—so great
A city he laid low, so many
The men he slew there. Now we come
Hither before your knees to pray you   290
Give welcome to your guests and grant us
Such gifts as guests should have. Respect,
O mighty one, the gods, for we
Are suppliants, and Zeus avenges
The suppliant and stranger: he   295

---

10. **Achæans**\ə ⁴kē·əns\ a people thought to have
migrated down into Greece from Danube regions in
the thirteenth century B.C.; in Homer's works, any
people living in what is now Greece.
11. **Atreus**\⁴ā·trē·əs\ father of **Agamemnon**\⁴ă·gə-
'mĕm·nŏn\ a Greek leader in the Trojan War.

Is god of strangers, watching over
Each worthy wanderer.'
                          So I spoke,
And pitiless of heart, he answered:
'Stranger, you either are a fool
Or come from a far land, to bid me   300
Fear or beware the gods! We Cyclops
Fear not your ægis-wielding[12] Zeus
Nor any god above. For we
Are mightier far than they. I would not
Show mercy to your men or you   305
To shun the wrath of Zeus, nay, never
Unless my own heart bade. But come,
Tell me, where left you your good ship
When you came hither? Was it near
Or at the land's far end? Nay, tell me,   310
For I would know.'
                          So asked he, striving
To trap the truth from me, but caught not
My tried mind unaware. So thus
With crafty words I spoke:
                          'The god
Who shakes the earth, Poseidon, broke   315
My ship asunder, for he drove her
Upon the cliffs that line your land
And dashed her on the rocks. A tempest
Had blown us in from sea and I
And these my comrades here but barely   320
Escaped sheer death.'
                          So I replied.
He, cruel-hearted, made no answer,
But springing up, reached forth his hands
And seized my comrades. Two at once
He snatched up in his grasp and dashed
  them   325
To earth like helpless puppies. Forth
The brains flowed, moistening the ground.
Then limb from limb he tore their bodies
And made his meal, devouring them
Savagely as a lion bred   330
Among the mountains. Naught of them
He left uneaten—flesh or entrails
Or marrowy bones. And we cried out
In lamentation and uplifted
Our hands to Zeus, to see a deed   335
So horrible. Numb terror laid
Hold on our hearts.

              And now the Cyclops,
When he had filled that monstrous belly
With flesh of men, and followed this
With draughts of unmixed milk, lay
  stretched   340
Full length upon the cavern floor
Among his flock.

                  And now I formed
This plan within my daring heart—
To venture nearer and to draw
My keen sword from my thigh and thrust it   345
Deep in his breast, straight to the spot
Where lay his liver, feeling first
To seek the place; and yet a thought
Withheld me, for we all, each man,
Must then have met sheer death; for never   350
Could our strength stir from that high
  door
The massive stone he set there. So
Lamenting there we sat and waited
The sacred dawn.

                  And when the dawn
Came, rosy-fingered, then once more   355
He kindled fire and milked his flock
Of wondrous sheep, in order due,
Setting her young by each; and now
When he had labored busily
And finished every task, he seized   360
Once more upon two men and made
His morning meal. And after this,
His breakfast done, he drove away
His goodly flock, moving with ease
The mighty door-stone thence, then set it   365
In place as lightly as a man
Would set the lid upon a quiver.
So with a mighty whoop the Cyclops
Went driving his fat flock away
Off to the mountains.

                  There he left me   370
Pondering evil—how I best
Might find revenge, if but Athene
Would hear my prayer. And this plan
  seemed

---

12. **ægis-wielding**\ˈē·jĭs\ shield-handling; the Cyclops
claim not to fear the power of Zeus' protection.

Best to my mind at last:
There lay
Close by the pens, a mighty staff   375
Cut by the Cyclops. Olive wood
It was, still green, for he had cut it
To use when it had dried: it seemed,
As we stood gazing, the great mast
Of some broad ship of twenty oars,   380
Laden with cargo, a black ship
That sails the great gulf of the sea,
So long and thick it seemed. So there
I took my stand by it and cut
A fathom's length away, and this   385
I gave my men and bade them shape it.
They made it smooth, while I stood by
And brought it to a point and charred it
In glowing fire; and then I took it
And hid it in the dung that lay   390
In heaps about the cave.
I bade then
My company cast lots to see
Which men of them would dare to join me
And lift that stake and bore it deep
Into his eye when gentle slumber   395
Should come upon him. And the lot
Fell on the four I should have chosen,
And I myself became the fifth
To share the venture.
And now came
The Cyclops home at evening, herding   400
His well-fleeced flocks. Straightaway he
  drove
Into that cavern, one and all,
His goodly flocks, nor left he any
In the wide court without. He felt,
Perhaps, some sense of coming evil;   405
Perhaps some god had warned him. Next
He set in place the massive door-stone,
Lifting it lightly, and sat down
And milked his sheep and bleating goats
All in due order, and he set   410
Her young by each; and when at last
With busy labor he had finished
His every task, then once again
He seized on two of my companions
And made his evening meal.
And now   415

I stood before him, and thus spoke,
The while I held forth in my hands
An ivy bowl, filled with dark wine:
'Here, Cyclops, take this wine, and drink
After your feast of human flesh,   420
And learn how good a drink we kept
Hidden within our ship. I brought it
An offering to you, in hope
You might have pity on my sorrows
And help me home. But you, alas,   425
In rage exceed all patience! Madman!
How shall there ever come hereafter
Another stranger here to seek you
From any land on earth, if you
Thus scorn all human laws!'
So said I.   430
He took the wine and drank it. Vastly
That sweet drink pleased him. And again
He begged of me:
'In goodness give me
Yet more, I pray. And tell me now
Your name, and quickly! I will give you   435
A gift to make your heart rejoice.
Indeed the Cyclops' fertile fields
Yield noble wine from mighty clusters,
And Zeus sends rain to speed their
  growing,
But this you give me is a cup   440
Of nectar and ambrosia mingled.'
So spoke he, and once more I bore him
That glowing wine. Aye, thrice I bore it
And gave it him, and thrice in folly
He drained it off. Then when the wine   445
Had stolen round his wits, I spoke
And said in honeyed words:
'O Cyclops,
You ask my far-famed name, and this
I now will tell you. Give me therefore
The stranger's gift, as you have promised.   450
My name is Noman; aye, and Noman
My father and my mother called me
And all my comrades.'
So I spoke,
And he with cruel heart replied:
'Noman, of all his company,   455
I shall eat last; and all the others
I'll eat before him. This shall be

My gift to you—my guest.'
                        So spoke he,
Then down he sank and on his back
Lay flat, his thick neck bent aside,   460
And from his throat there poured forth
  wine
And fragments of men's flesh.

                        And now
Deep under heaped-up coals I thrust
That stake till it grew hot, and stirred
The courage of my men with speech   465
Lest one of them should shrink with fear
And fail my need.
                        And now that stake
Of olive wood, green as it was,
Was ready to burst forth in flame,
All glowing with fierce heat. I drew it   470
Forth from the fire, while round about me
My men stood ready. Then—for surely
Some god had breathed into our hearts
High courage—they laid hold upon
That sharpened olive stake and thrust it   475
Deep in his eye, the while above them
I leaned upon its top and turned it
As one who with an auger bores
A great ship timber. Those below him
Twist it by thongs on either side,   480
And still it ever turns unceasing.
So holding that huge stake of wood
Deep in his eye, we kept it turning.

Two-handled Greek vase depicting the blinding
of Polyphemus—from the collection
of the Staatliche Museum, Berlin.

Round that hot brand, forth poured the
  blood;
And round it all his brows and lashes   485
Were singed off by the blast that came
Out of that burning eye. Its roots
Seethed in the fire. As when a smith
Dips a great axe or adz in water
To temper it, and loud it hisses—   490
For so steel gets its strength—even so
His eye hissed round that olive stake.
And loud his cry and terrible
Till the rocks echoed and we fled
Away in fear. Then from his eye   495
He wrenched away that stake, thick
  clotted
With his own blood and raging hurled it
Out of his hands. Then loud he shouted
To all the Cyclops who dwelt round him
In caves upon the windy heights.   500

They heard his shout and straggling
  gathered,
One here, one there, from every side,
And standing all about his cave
They asked what grieved him.
                        'What can ail you,
O Polyphemus,[13] that so loudly   505
You cry out in the heavenly night
And keep us sleepless? Is some man,
Some mortal, driving off your flocks
Against your will; or is some man
Now slaying you by force or cunning?'   510
And thus in answer from his cave
Spoke mighty Polyphemus:
                        'Friends,
Noman is slaying me by cunning,
Nor uses force at all!'
                        And they
With wing'd words thus replied:
                        'Since no man   515
Now does you violence, while you
Are there alone, this illness sent
By mighty Zeus, no man may shun

---

13. **Polyphemus**\ˈpŏ·lə ▲fē·məs\ son of Poseidon.

In any way. But pray you now   520
To your great father, Lord Poseidon.'

So said they and then went their way.
And in my heart I laughed to think
How with that name and my shrewd plan
I had deceived them.
                          But the Cyclops,
Groaning in agony and anguish,   525
Went groping with his hands, and lifted
The great rock from the door and there
He sat athwart the doorway, stretching
His hands, to catch, if it might be,
Any who sought to pass the door   530
Among the sheep; for in his heart
He hoped that I might prove so foolish
As thus to venture. But I still
Sat planning how to bring this peril
To a good end and win us all—   535
My men and me—escape. Full many
The plan and trick I fashioned, striving
For life itself, for great the peril
And close at hand. And at the last
This, as I deemed, was of them all   540
The wisest plan.
                     There in the cave
Were well-grown rams of thickest wool,
Fair beasts and great, and dark of fleece.
These silently I bound together
With twisted willow withes, whereon   545
The Cyclops slept, that savage monster
Who knew no law nor right. I bound them
By threes together and the midmost
Bore under him a man; the others,
One on each side, were to conceal   550
And save my comrades: so there went
A man to each three sheep. And I,
Myself, now seized upon a ram,
The best of all that flock, and grasped
His back from underneath, and lay   555
Beneath his shaggy belly; there
Twisting my fingers deep within
That wondrous fleece, I hung, face
  upward,
With steadfast heart. And so, lamenting,
We waited sacred dawn.
                          And now,   560

When earliest dawn came rosy-fingered,
Then forth the rams went to the pasture,
But all the unmilked ewes went bleating
About their pens with swollen udders.
Their lord, though torn by cruel pain,   565
Yet, ere each ram passed, made him stand
And felt along his back. He guessed not
In his dull mind, that there beneath
Those fleecy breasts, were bound my men.

Now to the door, last of them all,   570
The great ram slowly came, weighed down
With heavy fleece and with the burden
Of me and my shrewd plans. Upon him
The mighty Polyphemus then
Laid searching hands, and said:
                                    'Dear ram,   575
Why do you cross the cave so slowly,
Last of the flock? Till now, you never
Lagged thus, but ever first of all
Sped forth with mighty strides to crop
The soft bloom of the grass, and ever   580
Were first to reach the running waters,
And first, when evening came, to long
To turn back home. And yet you now
Come last of all. Surely you sorrow
Over your lord's lost eye! A villain   585
Has quenched its sight—he and his crew
Of wretched fellows, mastering
My wits with wine, this fellow Noman!
Not yet, I say, has he escaped
The death that waits him. Would but you   590
Could know my thought and had the power
To speak in words and let me know
Where he is skulking from my wrath!
For I should smite him down and dash
His brains about the cave—here, there,   595
Aye, on the ground! By such a deed
My heart might find some ease from all
The evils that this worthless Noman
Has brought upon me.'
                          So he spoke,
And sent the ram forth through the
  doorway.   600

And now, when we were safe outside
That cavern and its yard, I loosed

111

My grip upon the great ram's fleece
And then unbound my men in turn,
Setting them free. And then in haste   605
We drove that flock before us—sheep
Most rich in fat, most long of stride—
And yet we often turned our heads
To glance behind us ere we came
Safe to our ship. Welcome indeed   610
We were to our dear comrades, snatched
From death itself; and yet they wept
Lamenting those we lost. But this
I would not suffer, but forbade,
With lifted brows, all lamentation,   615
And bade them quickly bear aboard
Into the ship those many sheep
So fine of fleece, and sail away
Across the salt sea waves. And they
Went then aboard and took their seats   620
Each in his place, and smote with oars
The whitening sea.

           And now, when yet
A shout might reach the land, I called
To Cyclops, taunting him:

               'O Cyclops,
You were not, then, to find that man   625
A helpless weakling—him whose men
You ate there in your hollow cave
With might and cruel strength. For surely
These evil deeds of yours are doomed
To overtake you. O mad fool   630
Who felt no shame, but must devour
Your guests in your own home! May Zeus
And all the other gods send vengeance
Upon you for such deeds!'

              So spoke I,
And he in heart grew angrier yet   635
And tearing off a hill's great summit,
He hurled it. And it fell beyond
Our dark-bowed ship: the sea surged high
As that great rock crashed down. A wave
Came rolling back, a mighty billow   640
Out of the deep, and swept our ship
In toward the land. Swiftly I grasped
A great pole in my hands and thrust
The ship from shore and bade my men,
Nodding my brows, fall to and pull   645
Their best upon the oars and flee

Out of that danger; and they all
Bent to their oars.

              But when we now
Were twice as far from shore as we
Had been before, once more I called   650
Unto the Cyclops, but my men
With pleading words came all about me
And begged me stay:

           'Why, like a madman,
Will you enrage this savage monster
Who made but now so great a cast   655
He drove our ship, then far at sea,
Back to the land. We thought that we
Were lost indeed there. Had he heard
A man of us but stir or speak,
He would have shattered all our heads   660
And our ship's timbers, too, so rugged
A rock he would have cast, so strongly
He sends it on its way!'

             So spoke they.
But did not move my lordly spirit,
And once again with angry heart   665
I called back, saying:

             'If, O Cyclops,
A mortal man shall ever ask you
How it befell your eye was blinded
So hideously, then answer thus:
It was Odysseus blinded you,   670
Taker of Troy, Laërtes' son,
Who dwells in Ithaca.'

             So spoke I,
And with a groan he spoke and answered:
'Alas, for now are come upon me
The ancient oracles.[14] A prophet   675
Once dwelt here, a great man and good,
And he foretold me everything
That time should bring to pass—that I
Should lose my sight here at the hand
Of one Odysseus. But I ever   680
Watched for the coming of a man
Tall, handsome, armed with wondrous
   strength;
And now this little worthless fellow
Has robbed me of my eye by craft,

---

14. **oracles**\ˈȯ·rə·kəls\ messages of advice from the gods.

First mastering me with wine. Yet now   685
Come hither, O Odysseus, come!
For I would give my guest his gifts
And would implore the far-famed god
Who shakes the shores to give you help
Upon your way. I am his son: 690
He owns himself my father. He,
And he alone, can make me whole
If so he will, but this no other
Can do, no other of the gods
On high or mortal men who perish.'   695

So spoke he and I answered thus:
'Would I could be as sure that I
Could strip you bare of soul and being,
And send you to Death's house, as I
Am sure of this:—that none shall ever   700
Restore your eye, not even he
Who makes earth tremble!'[15]

           So I spoke,
And he with hands upraised in prayer
To starry heaven, thus besought
The lord Poseidon:

          'Hear me now,   705
Thou dark-haired god who mak'st earth
  tremble!
If I be verily[16] thy son
And thou wilt own thyself my father,
Grant that Odysseus, he who took
The towers of Troy, come never home.   710
Yet, should it be his fate to see
His friends once more and come at last
To his good house and native land,
Late may he come, in evil fortune,
With loss of all his men, and borne   715
Within a stranger's ship, and meet
In his own home affliction.'

              So
He spoke in prayer, and to his words
The dark-haired god gave ear.

          Once more
He stooped and lifted up a rock   720
Far greater than before, and swung it
And summoned all his monstrous strength
And hurled it. And it fell behind
Our dark-bowed ship and barely missed
The rudder's end. Up surged the sea   725

As that huge rock came down: the wave
Drove us upon our way and toward
The farther shore.

          And so we came
Back to the isle where our good ships
Were lying side by side, and here   730
Beside them sat our comrades weeping
And watching for our coming.

          So all that day
Until the sun went down, we sat
And feasted there on meat in plenty
And pleasant wine; and when the sun   735
Went down and darkness came upon us,
There slept we by the breaking sea.
But when the earliest dawn appeared
Rose-fingered, then I roused my men
And bade embark and loose the cables.   740
Then quickly they embarked and took
Their seats upon the thwarts, in order,
And smote with oars the whitening sea.
So sailed we on with aching hearts,
Glad we were saved from death, yet sad   745
To think how our dear comrades perished."

I
THE GREEK HERO

Homer's listeners must have found Odysseus an ideal figure—a hero. Nearly everyone is a hero worshiper to some extent: We admire men who exemplify an ideal. Odysseus was daring, strong, intelligent, decisive.

1. The Greeks looked upon Odysseus' ideas and actions as fitting and proper to a leader. And they *were* fitting and proper—in Homer's day. Today, however, we might regard some of Odysseus' actions in a different light. Recall the following sections of the poem and discuss whether you would consider Odysseus' behavior proper for a hero today:

    a. The way Odysseus introduced himself to Alcinoüs (ll. 56–60)

    b. Odysseus' first thought on entering the Cyclops' cave (ll. 229–231)

---

15. **Poseidon,** the father of Polyphemus, was called the "Earth-Shaker."
16. **verily,** truly.

c. His taking of the Cyclops' sheep (ll. 541–607)

d. His taunting the blind Polyphemus (ll. 624–634)

2. How does Polyphemus reply to Odysseus when the latter says the Greeks are suppliants and are thus protected by Zeus?

3. What does Odysseus gain by not telling Polyphemus the location of his ship and by giving a false name?

4. How do you feel toward the blinded Polyphemus as he talks to his prized ram before sending it to the pasture?

5. How did the coming of Odysseus fulfill the prophecy given to Polyphemus through the oracle?

II
TECHNIQUES

Conflict

1. The *Odyssey* is a tale of conflict: Odysseus struggles against one foe after another in his effort to reach his home and family. Who is his chief enemy? Why?

2. What conflict did Odysseus have to face in the land of the Lotus-eaters?

Foreshadowing

1. Discuss the foreshadowing in the Prologue (ll. 21–26). Which lines foreshadow continued trouble after Odysseus reached Ithaca?

2. Polyphemus prays to his father, Poseidon, the dark-haired god of the sea, to curse Odysseus. What punishment does the Cyclops ask for the Greek? Which line indicates that this prayer will be answered?

Imaginative Language

A noteworthy feature of Greek epic poetry is the use of word combinations known as *epithets*. These are names or descriptions applied to persons or things over and over again. Homer uses epithets when he speaks of "ægis-wielding Zeus" or "wing'd words." Sometimes an epithet can provide a particularly vivid image. The famous Homeric epithet "rosy-fingered dawn" paints a picture of the morning sky streaked with lines of crimson fire.

Locate and discuss other epithets found in the *Odyssey* so far. Be on the lookout for this type of imagery as you continue Odysseus' adventures.

114

PART II

The Odyssey

BOOKS X–XII

ADVENTURE OF THE WINDS

And now we came unto the isle
Æolia. Here Æolus,[1]
Dear to the deathless gods was dwelling.
His island floated on the deep,   750
And round it rose on every side
A brazen wall unbreakable,
In sheerest cliff. And here were born
Twelve children to him; six were
  daughters,
And six, grown sons. And these beside   755
Their father and their honored mother
Sit at unending feast. Before them
Are set fine foods innumerable,
And all day long the house is fragrant
With steam of feasting, and reëchoes   760
With music to its gates. At night
They sleep beneath soft coverings
In smooth-strung beds.
                And now we came
To this their city and fair mansion,
And here a month he made me welcome   765
And questioned me of all: he asked
Of Ilium and the Argive[2] ships,
And the Achæans sailing homeward,
And I of each, in order due,
Told him the tale. But when I asked him   770
Which way to sail for home, and prayed him

---

1. Æolia\'ē ᴬō·lĭ·ə\. Æolus\ᴬē·ō·ləs\ the god of the wind. Since the ancient Greeks believed that all the land rested on the sea, it was not hard for them to imagine that Æolus' domain was a floating island.
2. Ilium\ᴬĭ·lĭ·əm\ another name for Troy. Argive \ᴬar·jaiv\ Greek.

To aid me on my road, naught then
Did he refuse me, but was ready
To help me onward. For he gave me
A sack, the whole hide of an ox   775
Nine winters old. In this he tied
The roaring winds from every quarter,
For mighty Zeus had made him keeper
Of all the winds, to still or rouse them,
Even as he would.

    This sack he gave me   780
To carry in my hollow ship:
A shining cord of silver bound it
That not a breath could pass. And with me
He sent a fair west wind to bear
My ships and men along. Far other   785
Must be our journey's end, alas,
For through our own rash deed we came
To utter ruin.

    Thence we sailed
Nine days, both day and night, and spied
On the tenth morning, plain before us,   790
The fields of our own land, so near
We saw men tending fires.

      That instant
Upon me, worn with weariness,
Sweet sleep seized suddenly, for ever
In my own hand I had held fast   795
The corner of the sail, nor dared
Entrust this charge to any other
Of all my men, for I would quickly
Come to my own dear land.

     But now
As I lay slumbering, my men   800
One with another spoke, and whispered
That what I homeward bore was treasure,
Silver and gold, gifts given me
By noble Æolus. For one,
With meaning glances to his neighbor,   805
Would say:

   'Ah me, how strange it is
That wheresoever this man wanders,
In every land and every city
He gets from all men love and honor!
A fine big treasure this he carries   810
From plundered Troy, while we, alas,
Who labored on the same hard road

*Vase from Thebes, 700 B.C., picturing oarsmen
in a long boat of a style that may have been
contemporary with Odysseus.*

Sail home with empty hands. Nay, come
 now
And quickly! Let us see what lies
Hid in this sack—what gold, what silver!'   815
So spoke they, and their evil plotting
At last prevailed. They loosed the cord;
The sack was opened. From it burst
The bound winds, all, at once. Down
 swirled
A swooping gust and swept them seaward   820
Far from their own dear land, lamenting.

Then I awakened. In my heart,
Though free from blame, I wondered
 whether
It were not best at once to leap
Forth in the sea and so to perish,   825
Or whether I should yet remain
Among the living and endure.
Yet I remained there and endured,
Laying me down within my ship,
My mantle round my head.

     So we   830
And all our ships once more were driven,
Swept back by stormy blasts, the while
My men lamented, to the island
Of Æolus.

   Thither we came
And went ashore, and here my men   835

115

Drew water, and they made them ready
By the swift ships a hasty meal.
And then, when we had satisfied
Our need of food and wine, I chose me
A herald and a man to follow,   840
And forth we went to seek the famed
Palace of Æolus. We found him
Sitting at feast, and there beside him
His wife and children. And we entered
Into his house, and by the pillars,   845
We sat us down as suppliants
Upon his threshold.
                        In amazement
They saw us, and they asked:
                              'How came you
Thus here again, Odysseus? Tell us
What evil power of the gods   850
Has wrought against you? For we sent you
Safe on your way with every care
That you might reach your land, wherever
Your heart's desire might lead.'
                              So said they,
And I with sorrowing heart replied: 855
'My men turned utterly to evil,
And cruel sleep betrayed me. Friends,
Help now, for you have power!'
                              So said I,

*Odysseus in the land of
the Lestrigoni (cannibal giants),
a Roman fresco, second century B.C.*

116

Beseeching with soft words. But they
All sat in silence. Then the father   860
Answering, spoke:
                        'Hence quickly! Get you
Out of this island, man most luckless
Of all men living. Heaven itself
Forbids we shelter here or help
Upon his way a man so hated   865
By the blest gods. Hence! for it was
The hatred of the gods that brought you
Back to this island!'
                        So he spoke,
And sent me from his house lamenting.

Thence on we sailed with aching hearts,   870
And each man's soul was spent with toiling
Hard at the oar, a toil we owed
To our own folly, but no wind
Now came to help us."

[After this disheartening adventure, Odysseus
and his men go to another land where even greater
disaster comes to them. There gigantic cannibals
destroy the ships and kill the men. Only Odysseus
and the crew of the one ship escape. They make
their way to the island of the goddess Circe,
where they stay for a year. At the end of this
time, she sends Odysseus to the Land of the Dead
where he learns what he must do to reach his
home. After this adventure, he returns briefly to
Circe's island before sailing on.

Just before he leaves, Circe takes Odysseus
aside and warns him of some of the dangers he
will meet in his journey. She tells him what
precautions to take so that he and his men will
not fall prey to the sweet-singing Sirens, whose
marvelous voices have lured so many to their
deaths on the rocky shores. She describes the
dreadful Clashing Rocks and the horrible
monsters, Scylla and Charybdis, that will rob him
of more of his men. Finally, she tells him that
he must at all costs avoid harming the sacred
cattle of the Sungod.]

ADVENTURE OF THE SIRENS

                              "And now I said,
Sad-hearted, to my men:
                              'Unfitting   875

It is, friends, that but one or two
Should hear the sacred prophecies
Of that dread goddess, Circe.[3] These
I now shall tell you, for then either
We die foreknowing what shall fall,   880
Or we escape and shun the death
And doom that wait us.

            This she first
Bids us:—to shun the wondrous Sirens,[4]
With their sweet voices and their meadows
Abloom with flowers. For she bade   885
That I alone should hear their song.
So bind me fast in bonds—aye, lash me
Upright against the mast, that thence
I may not stir, and cast strong ropes
About me, too. If I entreat you   890
And bid you set me free, then bind me
Yet tighter than before.'

              And so
I told them all she said. And ever
Our good ship sailed on swiftly, nearing
The Sirens' island, for the wind   895
Blew fair and drove her on. And now
The wind ceased suddenly; there came
A calm without a breath: some god
Laid all the sea to sleep. So now
My men rose, furled the sail, and stowed it   900
Within the hollow ship, and sitting
In order on the thwarts, they smote
With polished oars the whitening sea
But I, with my keen blade, now cut
A great round lump of wax, and kneaded   905
The fragments with my hands, till swiftly
The wax was softened, for my strength
Had warmed it and the shining rays
Of the great Sun, the mighty lord
Who rides on high. With this, I stopped   910
The ears of all my crew, in turn;
Then fast they bound me, hand and foot
Upright in my swift ship, my back
Against the mast, with ropes cast round me.
Then once again they sat and smote   915
The foaming sea with oars.

               And now.
When we were but so far away
As a man's cry may reach, and lightly
Went driving on—our ship's swift flight,

*Red-figured Greek vase from the fifth century B.C.
Odysseus in the house of Circe.*

As close to land she sped, escaped not   920
The Sirens' sight, and they upraised
At once their clear, sweet song:

                  'Come hither,
O famed Odysseus, mighty glory
Of the Achæans. Turn your ship
But hither to the shore and hearken   925
The song we sing, for no man ever
Has steered his black ship hence till he
Has heard the honey-sweet delight
Of music from our lips; then forth
He went upon his way with joy   930
And fuller wisdom. For we know
All that the Argives and the Trojans
Endured on Troy's wide plains; we know
All that befalls mankind on earth,
The nourisher of all.'

               So sang they,   935
Uttering their sweet song. My heart
Yearned to hear further, and I bade
My men to loose me, and I frowned
My bidding with my brows, but they

3. **Circe**\\ˈsər ˈsē\\ an island sorceress whose magic
turned men into beasts.
4. **Sirens**\\ˈsai·rəns\\ womanlike creatures whose en-
chanting songs lured sailors to their deaths.

*Odysseus tied to the mast
to hear the Sirens' song—
classical Greek vase.*

Bent busier to their oars, and two,   940
Eurylochus and Perimedes,[5]
Arose and bound me ever faster
With double lashings. But at last,
When we had passed them and no more
Might hear the song those Sirens sang   945
And their sweet voices, then my men
Took quickly from their ears the wax
Wherewith I stopped them, and they loosed
The bonds that bound me.

ADVENTURE OF SCYLLA AND CHARYBDIS

           And we now
Had left that isle behind, but soon   950
I saw the smoke of flying spray,
And huge seas rolling, and I heard
The boom of breakers. From the hands
Of my affrighted men the oars
Fell and trailed idle, roaring through   955
The running sea beside us. Quickly
The ship lost way and stopped, for now
My men no longer toiled, with hands
Upon the tapered oars. Now swiftly
I passed through all the ship and paused   960
By each in passing, cheering him

With gentle words:
            'We are not, friends,
Untried in danger. This new peril
That lies before us is no greater
Than when the Cyclops caught and held us   965
Fast in his hollow cave. Yet thence
We found escape—all through my valor
And wit and shrewdness; and I think
That we shall live to tell the tale
Of this day too. But rouse you now.   970
Do as I bid you. Take your seats
Upon the thwarts and drive your oars
Deep in the sea whose billows roll
So steep against us. We shall see
If Zeus will grant us to escape   975
Out of this place of death. And you,
Helmsman, I charge you, fix my words
Fast in your heart, for you alone
Hold in your hand the helm that guides
Our hollow ship. Steer boldly forth   980
Out of these smoking seas and head her
Straight for yon crag, and take good heed
Lest she swing wide and sweep us all
Into sore peril!'
           So I spoke,
And they obeyed my order quickly,   985
And yet I did not speak of Scylla,[6]
That monster none may face, in fear
Lest they from terror drop their oars
And hide within the hold.
                Slight heed
I gave to Circe's hard command   990
I should not arm me. I put on
My glorious armor and I grasped
Two spears in hand and took my station
On the decked prow, for there I thought
I first should see appear this Scylla   995
That dwelt within the rock, to bring
My men destruction.
           And yet nowhere
Could I behold her, and my eyes
Wearied with wandering up and down
That shadowy wall of stone.

---

5. **Eurylochus**\yə ˈrĭ·lə·kəs\, **Perimedes**\pə ˈrĭ·mə ˈdēz\ sailors.
6. **Scylla**\sĭ·lə\ a hazardous rock on the Italian coast mythically thought of as a female monster.

So onward 1000
Into that strait we sailed lamenting—
On one side Scylla, on the other
Dreadful Charybdis.[7] Terribly
She swallowed down the salt sea-water
Then spewed it forth till all 1005
Was tossed and whirling like a caldron
Above a raging fire; and spray
Flew high and fell upon the tops
Of the tall crags. But when once more
She sucked the salt sea down, we saw 1010
The whirl's wild depths laid bare; the
 waters
Roared loud about the rocks; far down
We saw the bottom of the deep
Blackened with sand.
           Pale terror then
Laid hold on us: we saw the monster 1015
And feared death near.
              And on that instant
Scylla reached forth and snatched my men
Out of my hollow ship—six men,
My best in strength and courage. Lo,
Even as I looked along the ship 1020
To seek them, there I saw, above me,
Their hands and feet as up she swung them
Aloft in air. And loud they cried,
Calling, for the last time, my name,
In agony of heart. And even 1025
As one who fishes from a rock
That juts far out to sea, casts down
His bait to lure small fish and tosses
Into the deep a bit of horn
From kine of his own field—aye, even 1030
As he, if then he takes a fish,
Flings it aloft out of the sea
All quivering, even so she swung them
All quivering up to her high crag.
There she devoured them, one and all, 1035
Before her doorway, while they shrieked
And still stretched out their hands to me
In dying agony. That sight
Was saddest of all sights my eyes
Have ever seen, while through sore trials 1040
I wandered the sea's ways.
          So now
We had escaped the Clashing Rocks,

And Scylla and the dread Charybdis,
And quickly came to the fair isle
Of the great Sun."

[On the island of the Sungod, Odysseus' men disobeyed him and killed some of the sacred cattle for a feast. Odysseus knew that the gods would punish them. He tells how that punishment came.]

THE SHIPWRECK

        "And now, 1045
When we had left the isle behind us,
And yet no other land appeared—
Nothing but sea and sky, then Zeus,
The son of Cronus,[8] set in heaven
Over our hollow ship, a cloud 1050
Of sullen blue which darkened all
The deep below. And now our ship
Sped on, yet not for long; for swiftly
Out of the west there burst a gale
Shrieking in raging blasts. A gust 1055
Snapped the two forestays[9] of the mast.
Back fell the mast upon the stern,
And all its tackle lay entangled
In the ship's hold. And as it fell,
Striking the stern, it struck the helmsman[10] 1060
Upon the head and broke and shattered
Each bone within. Down he fell headlong,
As falls a diver, from the deck:
His proud soul left his body. Zeus
Now thundered from on high and hurled 1065
His bolt upon the ship. She quivered
Through all her length, struck by the bolt
Of Zeus: a smoke of sulphur filled her;
And straightway from the ship my men
Fell to the sea, and breakers swept them 1070
On past the black ship's side, like sea-birds.
And so now God forever ended
Their hopes of home.

---

7. **Charybdis**\kə ˈrĭb ˈdĭs\ a whirlpool opposite Scylla; passage between the two "monsters" was impossible.
8. **Cronus**\ˈkrō·nəs\ a Titan who had dethroned his father Uranus before him. Uranus was the primary god of the sky and husband to the Earth.
9. **forestays,** oxhide ropes supporting the mast. The Greek ship had one large square sail attached to the mast.
10. **helmsman,** the one who steered the ship.

                    Still to and fro
I hastened through the ship. At last
A great wave tore her keel[11] away   1075
Out of her frame, and on the billows
It floated bare. The mast had broken
Clear from the keel, but still the backstay
Kept it close by. And with this stay,
Twisted of oxhide, I made fast   1080
The two together, mast and keel.
And seated on them both, I drifted
Before that deadly storm."

[Odysseus goes on to tell King Alcinoüs and the banquet guests how he had been cast ashore on an island where the goddess Calypso (kə **lĭp·sō) held him prisoner seven long years. At the end of that time the goddess Athene persuaded Zeus to order Calypso to free the lonely wanderer. But Poseidon wrecked the raft Calypso gave Odysseus, and he nearly drowned before he swam ashore and came to the palace of Alcinoüs. Thus Odysseus completes the telling of his adventures up to this time.

All are moved by Odysseus' story, and the good king not only orders a swift ship to carry Odysseus to his homeland, but he also presents the weary wanderer with many valuable gifts.]

I
A MAN WHO WOULDN'T GIVE UP

After escaping the Cyclops, Odysseus and his men continue to suffer misfortune. Gradually the noble Greek loses his followers. Any man of lesser courage might have given up when faced with the hardships Odysseus endured.

1. While Æolus is happy to help Odysseus the first time, he fears to give him aid the second time. Why? Of what dangers does Circe warn Odysseus? How did Odysseus bring his ship safely by the Sirens?

2. Although Circe has warned Odysseus of Scylla, he does not tell his men what to expect. Why? What do we mean when we say that someone is caught between Scylla and Charybdis?

---

11. **keel,** the long, heavy timber extending along the bottom of a vessel and supporting the frame.

3. What final act of folly brings destruction to Odysseus' men? How does Odysseus manage to save himself? How long does the goddess Calypso hold him prisoner? What goddess intervenes to force Calypso to release him so that he can start homeward once more?

4. Homer shows his understanding of human nature in the naturalness of the actions and words of his characters. Reread (ll. 806–15) the words spoken by Odysseus' men before they loosed the bag of winds. What common traits of men make these words natural in such a situation?

5. Odysseus often reproaches himself for actions that are too hasty. Does this make him seem to be less of a hero? How would it affect his appeal to the ordinary listener or reader? Should a hero be less than perfect? Discuss.

II
TECHNIQUES
Conflict and Foreshadowing

As you continue reading, you realize that although Odysseus struggles valiantly, he is also at the mercy of the gods. He accepts their whims and punishment with little complaint and continues to battle toward his objective.

1. Which of the gods sent the destruction which took the last of Odysseus' men? Is there any indication thus far in the story that this god does not hold a permanent grudge?

2. After Odysseus tells how Æolus tied the roaring winds (the storm winds) into a bag which he gave to him, he says:

> And with me
> He sent a fair west wind to bear
> My ships and men along. (ll. 783–85)

How do the lines immediately following these foreshadow disaster?

Imaginative Language

1. There is an exceptionally sharp piece of imagery in lines 1025–34 beginning: "And even/ As one who fishes . . ." Discuss the picture it contains by rephrasing it in your own words. What is the literary term used to identify this kind of comparison?

2. Look back over the episodes you have read thus far. What epithets and word combinations have you found repeated often enough that you have become familiar with them?

PART III

The Homecoming of Odysseus

BOOKS XIII–XX

ARRIVAL IN ITHACA

[Swiftly and safely the ship brings Odysseus to his homeland from which he has been gone for twenty years. He rejoices to be back in Ithaca. But his joy is short-lived, for on the shore he is met by Athene who warns him he cannot go at once to his home because he would surely be murdered. Three years ago, she tells him, many suitors came to his great house. They came to convince Odysseus' wife, Penelope (pə ▲nĕ·lə 'pē), that her husband is dead and that she should marry one of them. The faithful Penelope still hopes for her husband's return and has constantly refused the suitors. However, she has been unable to get rid of them because the men loyal to Odysseus had gone with him to war. Her servants are mostly women and a few men advanced in age. Even now, Athene says, the suitors sit in Odysseus' banquet hall drinking, feasting, wasting his wealth and plotting to kill his son Telemachus (tə ▲lĕ·mə·kĕs) who is just growing into manhood. With Telemachus dead, the suitor who married Penelope would gain all of Odysseus' wealth.]

And then spoke
Keen-eyed Athene:
  "Think now well,
Noble Odysseus, shrewd in counsel, 1085
How you may lay your hands in vengeance
Upon these shameless wooers, men
Who for three years have ruled as masters
Here in your hall, the while they wooed
Your noble wife, with proffered gifts, 1090

While she, her heart still sorrowing
Because you come not, holds forth hope
To every one and gives her promise
To each in turn and sends to each
Her messages; though all her mind 1095
Is set on other hopes."
  Then answered
Crafty Odysseus:
  "Come, fashion now
Some crafty plot that I may take
My vengeance on them. Stand you now
Yourself beside me! Fill my heart 1100
With courage to dare all—aye, even
As once you did of old, when we
Brought low Troy's shining crown.[1] If you,
O keen-eyed goddess, stand beside me
Eager as then, I could do battle 1105
Against three hundred men—would you,
O mighty goddess, but vouchsafe
To be my helper!"
  Then thus answered
Keen-eyed Athene:
  "Surely I
Will be beside you. You shall never 1110
Be from my mind when we begin
This mighty task. Aye, some, I think,
Of these same wooers that devour
Your substance now, with blood and brains
Shall spatter the broad earth. But come, 1115
For I will change you now, that mortals
Shall know you not. For I will wither
The fair flesh from your pliant limbs,
And pluck from off your head the locks
That now shine yellow, and will clothe you 1120
In such a wretched garb that he
Who sees shall shrink away in loathing
From him that wears it. I will dim
The luster of your eyes that once
Were beautiful to see, till you 1125
Shall seem most foul to all the wooers,
Aye, even to your own wife's sight
And to the son you left behind you,
An infant in your hall.
  Now first

---

1. Athene had helped Odysseus in the Trojan War.

Seek out the swineherd who keeps watch   1130
Over your swine, for he is loyal,
True to your son and steadfast wife,
Penelope. And you will find him
Sitting beside his swine that pasture
Close by the Raven Rock.[2]
              There   1135
Stay you awhile and sit beside him
And question him of all. And I
Will go, meanwhile, my way to Sparta,[3]
Land of fair women, and will summon
Telemachus—your own dear son,   1140
Odysseus!—home again, for he
Went forth to wide-wayed Lacedæmon,[4]
To Menelaüs[5] house, to seek
Tidings of you, to learn if you
Were yet alive."
          So spoke she,   1145
And with her wand clothed him
In a vile cloak and tunic—tattered,
Unclean, stained foul with smoke, and o'er
  them
A great hide, a swift stag's, its hair
All worn away. A staff she gave him   1150
And a poor beggar's scrip[6] with many
A rent therein, its only strap
A wretched cord.
        So the two made
Their plans and parted. Off she sped
Hasting to sacred Lacedæmon   1155
To find Odysseus' son.

TELEMACHUS MEETS HIS FATHER

[In Sparta, Athene finds Telemachus and warns
him that some of the wooers lie in wait for his
ship in order to murder him on his voyage home.
She tells him where to steer his vessel in order
to avoid the suitors and advises him that as soon as
he reaches Ithaca he should go to the hut of the
faithful swineherd, Eumæus ('yū ᴧmē·əs).

Meanwhile Odysseus has already met the
swineherd and has been given food and
lodging. He is very careful not to reveal his
identity. Instead, he tells Eumæus and the
other swineherds that he is a wanderer who had
fought at Troy and had known Odysseus.]

Odysseus and the goodly swineherd
Together in the hut at dawn
Prepared their breakfast, kindling fire,
When they had sent the men away   1160
To drive the swine afield. And now
Telemachus drew near. The dogs,
Though wont to bark, now wagged their
  tails
Nor barked at all; and great Odysseus
Saw how they wagged their tails, and
  heard   1165
The sound of footsteps, and spoke quickly
With wing'd words to Eumæus:
            "Surely,
Eumæus, there comes hither now
A friend or one you know! The dogs
Bark not, but wag their tails, and faintly   1170
I hear the fall of steps."
          And scarcely
Had he thus said, when his dear son
Stood in the doorway. Then the swineherd
Sprang up surprised, and from his hands
Let fall the bowl with which he labored   1175
Mingling the glowing wine. He hastened
To greet his master. . . .
         And said:
"So you are come, Telemachus,
Sweeter than light. I thought I never
Should see you more when you went sail-
  ing   1180
Away to Pylus.[7] Come, come in!"
          So he spoke,
And took the young man's brazen spear.
So in now stepped Telemachus
Over the sill of stone. His father
Rose from his seat to give him place,   1185

---

2. **Raven Rock,** A great jutting rock still bears this
name in Ithaca.
3. **Sparta**\ᴧspar·tə\ an ancient city state in southern
Greece.
4. **Lacedæmon**\ˈlă·sə ᴧdē·mən\ another name for
Sparta.
5. **Menelaüs**\ˈmĕ·nə ᴧlā·əs\ king of Sparta; Helen of
Troy had been his queen.
6. **scrip,** a bag or wallet carried by beggars.
7. **Pylus**\ᴧpai·ləs\ a city at which Telemachus stopped
on his way to Sparta.

But this he would not have, and stayed
  him,
And said:
        "Nay, stranger, sit. For we,
Here on this farm of ours, with ease
Shall find a seat, and this man here
Will soon provide one."
                So he spoke.   1190
Back to his seat then turned Odysseus,
And the good swineherd heaped fresh
  bushes
And spread a fleecy skin upon them
And here now sat Telemachus.
                        And now,
When food and drink had stayed their
  hunger,   1195
He said to the good swineherd:
                        "Whence,
Good father, comes this stranger? . . .
                        Then,
Swineherd Eumæus, thus you[8] answered:
"From Crete,[9] he told me, but through
  many
A city of mankind he passed   1200
In wandering hither. . . . He has come
To my own house, and to your charge
I give him now. Do with him, then,
Whate'er you will. He is, he says,
Your suppliant."
                Then thus replied   1205
Prudent Telemachus:
                        "Eumæus,
Your words pierce to my heart. How can I
Receive a guest at home? . . . And yet,
Since he has come here to your house,
I'll give him garments, cloak and tunic, 1210
Besides a two-edged sword and sandals
To bind upon his feet, and send him
Where he would go. Or keep him here
With you upon your farm, and I
Will send him clothing, aye, and food   1215
Of every kind, lest he prove costly
To you and yours. But to my house
Among the wooers, he shall never
Go by my will, for they are filled
With sin and insolence. . . . But go,   1220
Quickly, my good old friend—go tell

Prudent Penelope that I
Am safe here, come from Pylus." . . .
                        So
Then spoke Telemachus, and sent
The swineherd on his way. He took   1225
His sandals and he bound them on,
And set off for the town. And yet
He did not go his way unseen
By great Athene, for she came,
In form a woman, fair and tall,   1230
And skilled in dainty crafts, and stood
Close by the door. Odysseus saw her;
His son beheld her not, though standing
Before his face, nor knew her presence,
For not to all men do the gods   1235
Appear in open sight. Odysseus
Saw, and the dogs saw too; they barked
  not,
But whimpering slunk off in fear
Across the farmland. With her brows
She signed to him. Odysseus saw   1240
And understood, and forth he came
By the great courtyard wall and there
He stood before her. Then to him
Thus spoke Athene:
                "Shrewd Odysseus,
Laërtes' son, now you shall tell   1245
Your son your secret; now no longer
Need you keep silence. And you twain
Shall plan together death and doom
For the proud wooers. Then go forth
Together to your glorious city.   1250
I shall not be far off. My soul
Looks forward to the battle."[10]
                        So
Athene spoke, and upon his body
She put a fresh new cloak and tunic,
And mightier she made him seem   1255

---

8. Homer uses the second person pronoun, the form
for direct address, to show an especially kindly feeling
toward the old and faithful servant.
9. **Crete**\krēt\ a large island in the eastern Mediter-
ranean. Odysseus had made up a story to tell the
swineherd.
10. Athene is a warlike goddess often found in the
thick of battle.

And fairer, and the deeper hue
Of youth came back; his cheeks once more
Were rounded, and upon his chin
His beard was darkened. This she did,
Then went her way.
                          And now Odysseus   1260
Entered the lodge, and his son marveled
Beholding him, and turned his eyes
Away in awe, lest this might be
A god before him, and he spoke
In wing'd words:
                    "You are changed, O stranger,   1265
From what you seemed but now. Your gar-
      ments
Are not the same; your very flesh
Is altered. Surely you are one
Of the immortal gods that have
Wide heaven for home. Then look upon us   1270
In kindness while we offer you
A welcome offering and bring you
Gifts finely wrought of gold. Show, now,
Compassion on us!"
                        Then replied
Noble, long-tried Odysseus:
                                  "Nay,   1275
I am no god! Why liken me
To those that die not! I am he
Whom you so long have wept, for whom
You bore men's violence."
                              But his son,
Who could not yet believe that this   1280
Could be his father, answered him
And said:
          "No, you are not Odysseus;
My own dear father!
                      A moment past
You were an old man, meanly clad,
Now you are like the gods who dwell   1285
In the wide heavens."
                        Then Odysseus
Answered and said:
                      "Telemachus,
It is unworthy of you thus
To stare and marvel beyond measure
At your own father, when at last   1290
He stands before you! No Odysseus
But I will ever come! For I

It is, I that you see before you,
Who have borne perils and have wandered
In many lands, and now at last   1295
Come, after twenty years, again
To my own native land."
                          So said he,
And sat him down. Then round his neck
His son cast both his arms and sobbed
And poured forth tears. Upon them both   1300
Came longing and wild weeping.
                                  At last thus spoke
Noble Odysseus:
                    . . . "Hither now
I come at counsel of Athene,
That you and I may plan the slaying
Of all our enemies. But tell me   1305
The number of these wooers—tell me
That I may know how many men
They are and of what sort. I then
May ponder in my heart, and find
Whether we two may fight them here   1310
With no man's aid, or needs must call
For aid on others."
                      Then thus answered
Discreet Telemachus:
                        "Dear father,
Long have I heard of your great name—
A warrior strong of arm, and wise   1315
When men hold council. But this thing
You speak of—this is far too great!
Awe takes me at the thought, for never
Could two men fight against so many,
All mighty warriors. They number   1320
Not ten, nay, not twice ten, but more.
Bitter for us and terrible
May prove this vengeance that you seek,
Now you are come. Nay, rather think
As best you may, what men will fight   1325
Upon our side, or will in friendship
Give us their help."
                        Then thus replied
Noble, long-tried Odysseus:
                                  "Nay,
But I will tell you of such helpers.
Heed then and listen! Think you, now,   1330
That Father Zeus and great Athene
Are aid enough, or must I seek

For more to help us!"
          Then replied
Telemachus:
        "Strong helpers truly
Are these you name, who sit on high   1335
Among the clouds and rule there ever
O'er men and deathless gods."
          Then spoke
Noble Odysseus thus:
        "Not long
Will those two keep them from that battle
And its wild tumult, when we two   1340
In our own hall shall meet those wooers
In the dread strife of war. But go you
Tomorrow morning home; there join
The haughty wooers. And the swineherd
Shall bring me in, an aged beggar.   1345
Then, if they treat me with foul insult
In my own home, still let your breast
Endure it all. Nay, though they drag me
About the hall, and hurl their missiles,
Look on in patience: speak smooth words   1350
And bid them cease, but they will heed
  not,
For on them comes their fated day.
And this I say now: mark it well:
If you are truly mine, the son
Of my own ancient blood, let no one   1355
Learn that Odysseus is returned—
No, not Laërtes, not the swineherd
Nor any of the house, nay, not
Penelope herself!"
        And now, at evening,
Back came the swineherd to Odysseus   1360
And his brave son, and there they made
Their supper ready. But Athene
Had first drawn near.
         And once again
She made him agèd to behold
And meanly clad, lest the good swineherd   1365
Should look upon his face and know him,
And go to wise Penelope
And tell his tidings.
         Now they turned them
From toil and feasted, and when hunger
Was stayed with food and drink, their
  hearts   1370

Terracotta relief from Greece, fifth century B.C., pictures the return of Odysseus.

Then thought of rest, and so upon them
There came the gift of sleep.

ODYSSEUS COMES TO HIS OWN HOME

And now Telemachus went forth
Across the farmland. Fast he walked
With hurrying feet, still planning evil   1375
Against the wooers.
         And at last
He reached the stately house and set
The spear he carried in its place
By a great pillar. Then he entered
O'er the stone threshold. First of all   1380
To see him was old Eurycleia,[11]
His nurse, as she was spreading fleeces
Upon the carven chairs. And swiftly
She came with flowing tears to meet him.
And now there came forth from her room   1385
Penelope, like Artemis,[12]
Or golden Aphrodite.[13] Weeping,
She cast her arms about her son

---

11. **Eurycleia**\ˈyu̇·rə ᐱklē·ə\.
12. **Artemis**\ᐱar·tə·məs\ goddess of the moon and hunting, called **Diana**\ᐱdai ᐱă·nə\ by the Romans.
13. **Aphrodite**\ˈă·frə ᐱdai·tē\ goddess of love and beauty, called **Venus**\ᐱvē·nəs\ by the Romans.

And kissed his face and his fair eyes,
And then amid her sobs she spoke 1390
And said, in wing'd words:
                    "Now at last
You come, Telemachus, more welcome
Than the sun's light. I thought my eyes
Should never see you more, when you
Went off so secretly to Pylus 1395
Aboard your ship, to seek for tidings
Of your dear father."
                    But meanwhile
Before Odysseus' door the wooers
Were all at play: on level ground
They hurled their spears and cast the
  discus 1400
As they had done before, so great
Their reckless insolence. Now came
The time for supper, and the flocks,
Driven by those whose wont it was,
Came home from pasture. Then up spoke 1405
Before them Medon,[14] the good herald
Who ever pleased them most, and ever
Was present at their feasts:
                    "Come, now,
Young masters, since you all have taken
Your pleasure in the sports, come hither 1410
Within the house, and we shall make
Our good meal ready. Naught is better
Than food at feasting-time!"
                    So spoke he,
And up they sprang and hastened in,
Heeding his words. So they all came 1415
Into that stately house and cast
Their cloaks upon the chairs and couches,
And slew great sheep and fatted goats
And killed a fat hog and a heifer
And so prepared their feast.
                    Meanwhile 1420
The herdsman guided toward the city
His lord and master, like a beggar
Wretched and old, and leaning ever
Upon a staff, his body clad
In wretched garments.
                    At last Odysseus 1425
And the good swineherd stayed their steps
As they drew near, for all about them
Came music of the hollow lyre,

For Phemius[15] within was singing
And struck the strings. And now Odysseus 1430
Took the good swineherd by the hand
And said:
                    "This is, indeed, Eumæus,
Odysseus' house. Aye, easily
A man might tell it, though full many
Stood all about. For building here 1435
Is joined to building, and the courtyard
Is closed about with walls and coping,
And double gates protect it. None
Could capture it by force. And this
I see, moreover: many a man 1440
Is gathering for a feast. The savor
Of roast fat rises. In the hall
I hear the lyre, a gift the gods
Have given us, the fit companion
Of the glad feast."
                    And thus you answered, 1445
Swineherd Eumæus:
                    "Aye, you know it,
And readily. You are in nowise
Of sluggish wit. But come, consider
How we shall best contrive! Will you
Go first into the stately dwelling 1450
And join the wooers, while I wait
Without the door? Or, if you will,
Wait here, while I go first. Yet linger
Not overlong, lest some one spy you
Lingering without, and hurl things at you 1455
Or drive you hence with blows. I bid you
Think warily of this."
                    Then answered
Long-tried Odysseus:
                    "Nay, I know;
I see your meaning, for you speak
To one who understands. Go first 1460
And I will wait behind. For I
Am not unused to blows and missiles.
I have a sturdy spirit: many
The cruel hardships I have suffered
From war and wave; be this but added 1465
To swell the tale."
                    So spoke they

---

14. **Medon**\ˈmē·dən\.
15. **Phemius**\ˈfē·mĭ·əs\ a minstrel.

One to another.

        Now a dog
Lay near, and heard, and straightway lifted
His head and ears. For this was Argos,[16]
Steadfast Odysseus' dog—a dog   1470
He reared long since, but never used,
For ere he used him, he went thence
To sacred Ilium. Young men,
In days now gone, would take the dog
To chase wild goats and deer and hares, 1475
But now, his master far away,
He lay despised upon the dung
Left by the cattle and the mules
Heaped high before the doors.
                There
Argos, this dog, now lay, all foul   1480
With vermin. Yet when he beheld
Weak though he was, Odysseus near him,
He wagged his tail and dropped both ears,
Though he had now no strength to move
Nearer his master.
          And Odysseus   1485
Saw him, but drew not near. He wiped
A tear away before Eumæus
Might see he wept; then thus he spoke
And said:
        "Now this is strange, Eumæus,
Why should a dog like this lie here   1490
Upon a dunghill? For this dog
Is finely formed: I cannot say
Whether his speed can match his beauty,
Or if he be but of those dogs
That masters keep for show at table."   1495
Then, good Eumæus, you replied:
"Aye, he who owned this dog has perished
In a far land. Were this dog now
What he was once, in grace of form
And feats of hunting—on the day   1500
His master went to Ilium
And left him here—you would be seized
With sudden wonder did you see
His swiftness and his strength. No beast
That he once started from his lair   1505
In the dense forest depths escaped him;
Keenly he followed scent. But now
His evil days have come. His master
Has perished far away; the women
Care not and let him lie untended.   1510
For slaves, when masters pass from power,
Give no more heed to toil. When once
Ill fortune brings a man to bondage
Far-thundering Zeus then takes from him
Full half his worth."
          So spoke Eumæus,   1515
Then entered that fair house and passed
Straight down the hall and through the
  midst
Of those proud wooers. Then on Argos
Death's dark end came, when he had seen
Odysseus, gone for twenty years.   1520

Noble Telemachus first saw,
Long ere the rest, the swineherd coming
Across the hall, and nodded to him
And called him thither. And the swine-
  herd,
Glancing about him, took a chair   1525
That stood hard by, the chair from which
The carver sent forth meat in plenty
Among the wooers when they feasted
There in the hall. This chair the swineherd
Borne to the table where he faced   1530
Telemachus, and sat him down.
A herald brought him food and served it
With bread out of the basket.
                Now,
A little after him, Odysseus
Entered the house. He seemed a beggar 1535
Wretched and old, and wretched too
The clothing that he wore. And there
He sat him on the ashen threshold
Within the doorposts. . . .

PENELOPE MEETS ODYSSEUS IN DISGUISE

[The haughty and treacherous suitors treat the
"beggar" roughly. One hits him with a stool.
Others curse him. Odysseus holds his anger in
check and plans how he will deal with these evil
men. Penelope treats the beggar graciously and,

---

16. **Argos**\ˈär·gōs\.

since she believes he has some news of her husband, takes him aside and says:]

"Alas,
O stranger, but now all wherein   1540
I once excelled, in form or face,
The gods laid waste that day the Argives
Embarked for Ilium; for with them
My husband went away, Odysseus!
Would he might come again to watch   1545
Over my life here: better far
Would be my fame, and fairer. Now
I can but suffer. Such the evil
Some power from on high has sent
For my affliction. So I give   1550
But little heed to wanderers
Or suppliants or heralds serving
The people's need, but ever long
After Odysseus, wasting ever
My heart away.

      These men would hasten   1555
My marriage day, so I must spin
A skein[17] of trickery. And first
Some power whispered to my heart
That I should build me in my hall
A great loom, and should weave me here   1560
A robe, a garment rich and wide.
So then I said to all:

      'Young men
Who come to woo me—this I pray you:
Though great Odysseus now lie dead,
Forbear to urge this marriage. Wait   1565
But till this robe I weave is finished—
I would not have its threads all wasted!
This is a shroud for lord Laërtes[18]
When the dread doom of death shall take him
And leave long sorrow. I must do this   1570
Lest some Achæan woman blame me
In my own land, if he should lie
Without a shroud, who once was lord
Of wealth so great.'

      So then I spoke,
And their proud hearts agreed. And so   1575
Each day I wove at my great web,
But every night I bade them bring
Torches to light me, and unraveled

All I had wrought by day. And thus
Three years I did, unseen, and ever   1580
Deceived the wooers. But at length,
When the fourth year came round, my maids,
Ungrateful, like base dogs, betrayed me.
The wooers came and caught me. Harshly
They railed against me. So, compelled,   1585
And through no will of mine, I brought
That weaving to its end. And now
I can no longer put off marriage
Or shape me a new plan. My son
Grows angry that these men devour   1590
His very livelihood, for now
He knows what passes: he is now
A man indeed, and fit to watch
The fortunes of his house, a man
Whom Zeus grants honor."

      And then indeed   1595
Odysseus' heart was filled with pity
At his wife's weeping. But now,
When she with many a tear had taken
Her fill of sorrow, once again
She spoke and told him:

      "Now I mean   1600
To try you, stranger. I would know
If you in truth[19] received my husband
As guest in your own hall, and all
His noble comrades with him there
As you have said. So come now—tell me   1605
What clothing did he wear? How looked he?
And tell me too of his companions
Who followed after."

      Thus then answered
The wise Odysseus:

      "Noble lady,
This is a hard thing to tell rightly   1610
After so long a time, for now

---

17. **skein**\skān\ a quantity of spun yarn off the reel in a twisted loop; a metaphor for any twisted arrangement.
18. **shroud for Lord Laërtes** a corpse wrapping for Odysseus' aged father.
19. **in truth,** actually; Odysseus has told Penelope the story he told the swineherd: that he was of the noble family of Crete who had played host to Odysseus years ago.

Full twenty years have gone their way
Since he set forth and left my land.
Yet I will tell you how my heart
Still sees his picture. Great Odysseus   1615
Then wore a cloak of purple wool
In double fold. Upon it shone
A brooch of gold: two clasps it had,
And thus its front was carved:—a dog
Held with its paws a dappled fawn   1620
Struggling, and gripped it in its jaws;
And all who saw it marveled how,
Though wrought of lifeless gold, that dog
Held the fawn gripped, and strangled it,
While, striving to escape, the fawn   1625
Still struggled with its feet. I marked
His tunic, too, that shone as bright
Upon his body as the skin
That gleams upon a sun-dried onion,
So smooth it was, and shining like   1630
The sun itself. And many a woman
Gazed at him wondering. And this
I say besides; mark well: I know not
If he was wont to wear this clothing
At home, or if some comrade gave it   1635
When he embarked in his swift ship,
Or if some host had given it him,
For he was loved by many, few
So loved as he. And I myself
Gave him a sword of bronze, a cloak   1640
With double fold, of fairest purple,
And a fringed tunic, and so sent him,
With love and honor, on his way
In his good ship."

        So he spoke,
And once again he waked in her   1645
The need of weeping, for she knew
So well each token that Odysseus
Told her so clearly. But at length
She answered:

        "From this moment, stranger,
You who have been a sight for pity,   1650
Shall be beloved and honored. I
It was, with my own hand, who gave him
Those garments you have told of. First
In my own room, I folded them
And fixed upon them the bright brooch,   1655
That precious jewel. Yet I never

Shall greet him now, returning hither
To his own land."

        And thus Odysseus
Answered her saying:

        "Honored wife
Of great Odysseus, mar no more   1660
Your lovely flesh, nor waste away
Your heart with weeping for your husband,
And yet I blame you not. No woman
But weeps to lose her lord, the man
She loved, whose children she has borne—   1665
Aye, even though he were far other
Than was Odysseus who, men say,
Is like the gods. But cease your weeping
And heed my words, for I will speak
Truth only and will hold back naught   1670
Of all I lately heard: Odysseus,
They say, is near at hand and safe.
I say that he is safe. Already
He is at hand: no longer now
Will he delay and linger far   1675
From friends and native land. Nay, more,
I add my oath. Be witness, now,
Zeus, highest of the gods and best,
And let this hearth of good Odysseus,
Where I now stand, be witness too   1680
That now, this very year, Odysseus
Shall come here, aye, as this moon passes
And the new moon begins."

        Then spoke
Prudent Penelope:

        "Alas,
I would, O stranger, that your words   1685
Might but be true. Then you would learn
My kindness to the full, and many
The gifts that I should give, and all
You met would call you happy. Yet
This thought is ever in my heart: 1690
That thus it all must end—that he
Will nevermore come home.

        But come,
I have an aged woman here.
Her heart is prudent. It was she
Who in his childhood nursed and tended   1695
My luckless lord and took him up
In her own arms the very day
His mother bore him. And this woman,

129

*Odysseus returning to Penelope
while he is disguised as a beggar.
The fresco is from Pompeii.*

Though weak with years, shall wash your
  feet.
So rise now, trusty Eurycleia,   1700
And wash this stranger's feet—a man
Old as your master. Aye, Odysseus
May be already as this man,
With aged hands and feet: men soon
Grow old in evil fortune."
                    So said she.   1705
Therewith the aged woman took
The shining bowl they ever used
To wash the feet. First into it
She poured cold water freely, then
She added hot.
             Meanwhile Odysseus   1710
Was sitting by the hearth, but quickly
Turned toward the darkness, for the
  thought
Now rose within his mind, she might
When she should lift his foot, behold
The scar and know it, and then all   1715
Would come to light.
                And now she drew
Nearer her master and made ready
To wash his feet. And straightway then
She knew the scar. It was the scar
A boar's white tusk made long ago   1720

Upon a day Odysseus went
To far Parnassus.[20] And now
As the old woman put her hand
Upon his leg, and laid the palm
Upon the scar, at once she felt it   1725
And knew it well. She let the leg
Fall as it would. Down dropped the foot
Into the basin, and the bowl
Of copper rang aloud and tilted
Upon its side till all the water   1730
Ran on the ground. Joy suddenly,
And sorrow, both together, seized
Upon her heart. And her two eyes
Were filled with tears. Her eager voice
Faltered, and on Odysseus' beard   1735
She laid her hand, and said:
                    "Yes, truly,
You are Odysseus, my dear child,
And yet I knew not it was you
Until I felt the wound that told me
It was my master."
                Swiftly Odysseus   1740
Drew her close to him and said:
"Good mother, why are you so eager
To bring me ruin? It was you
Who nursed me long ago and held me
To your own breast. And now I come,   1745
When twenty years are past, far struggling
Through many perils, once again
To my own land. Be silent,
Nor let one person here be wiser."

And then answered   1750
The prudent Eurycleia:
                "Child, you know
How steadfast is my soul, a spirit
That naught can shake. I shall stand firm
As stubborn rock or iron!"

                    And now,
When she had washed him and anointed   1755
His body with smooth oil, once more
Odysseus moved his bench and sat
Still nearer to the fire, but covered

---

20. **Parnassus**\par ˄nă·səs\ a mountain in central
Greece.

The scar beneath his rags. Then thus
Prudent Penelope began: 1760
"Already there draws near that morning
Of evil omen that shall part me
From my Odysseus' home. Today
I hold a contest for the wooers,
The contest with the axes. These,   1765
He used, when he was here, to set
All in a row, twelve axes, ranged
Like frames to build a ship, and then,
Standing far off, he shot an arrow
Straight through them all.[21] This is the trial   1770
That I have set before the wooers.
He who most easily shall bend
The bow with his two hands and shoot
His shaft through those twelve axes—him
I then will follow, and forsake   1775
This house to which I came a bride,
A house so beautiful, so filled
With all that makes life good. I know
That oft hereafter, in my dreams,
I shall remember it."
          And thus   1780
Odysseus spoke:
          "Delay no longer,
O honored wife of great Odysseus,
But hold here straightway in your hall
This trial with the bow. For here
Odysseus, with his ready counsel,   1785
Will be at hand before the wooers
Can take the polished bow in hand,
And stretch the string and speed an arrow
Straight through the iron."
          Then again
Prudent Penelope replied: 1790
"If you were only willing, stranger,
To sit here in my hall and give me
Delight like this,[22] then sleep would never
Fall on my eyes again. And yet
No man can live on without sleep   1795
So spread your bed here on the ground
Or let the maids bring bedding."
          So
She spoke and to her shining room
She went her way.

So there Odysseus laid him down   1800

To slumber in the porch. He spread
A rough hide on the ground, and on it
Laid many a fleece stripped from the sheep
The wooers slew. But Odysseus
Lay sleepless, ever pondering   1805
Evil against the wooers.

I
HOME IN ITHACA

Even though Odysseus, with the ship and crew furnished him by Alcinoüs, is at last able to reach his beloved Ithaca after twenty years away, he finds himself confronted with many problems.

1. Why does Athene warn Odysseus not to go to his home? Where does she instruct him to go instead?

2. Why had Telemachus gone to Sparta? Why is he in danger from the suitors?

3. To whom does Odysseus first reveal his identity? Why is Telemachus doubtful that they can slay all of the suitors? What two helpers does Odysseus tell him that they can depend upon? How does Odysseus describe his home to Eumæus?

4. Describe Argos. How had he changed in appearance during the absence of Odysseus? What happens to him after he has once again looked upon his master?

5. What treatment does Odysseus receive at the hands of the suitors? What reception is given him by Penelope? How had she deceived the suitors for three years? What ended her deception?

6. Odysseus is now approaching the most personal and dramatic conflict of his adventurous life. Soon he and Telemachus will face some three hundred enemies in hand-to-hand combat. This seems like terrific odds until you consider that he has the guidance and aid of Athene and now, surprisingly enough, of her father Zeus.

Locate that passage in lines 1097–1108 which indicates that through all his experiences, even

---

21. **an arrow . . . through them all.** Many ancient Greek axes had a large round opening in their iron blades.
22. **delight like this.** Penelope enjoys the "beggar's" talk of Odysseus' return, but she thinks it idle chatter.

Bronze helmeted warrior from the ancient Etruscans of Italy. Their art of 700–500 B.C. showed Greek influence.

the fighting at Troy, Odysseus has depended greatly on Athene. Discuss how the request which Odysseus makes of Athene as he plans for the coming conflict does not make him any the less of a hero to his admirers.

II
TECHNIQUES

Suspense

To quicken the pulses of his listeners, Homer, the master storyteller, resorts to a trick which has always increased anticipation of coming action. His hero is disguised so that his enemies fail to recognize him until that dramatic moment when he chooses to reveal his identity.

1. Describe how Athene changes Odysseus in appearance. Even though the goddess ages the Greek hero, what is the one identifying sign which might betray him that she does not erase? Does anyone recognize him from this mark, and does it place him in danger?

2. What test does Odysseus encourage Penelope to demand of her suitors? Why does this increase interest as to what *may* happen?

PART IV

The Contest with the Bow

BOOK XXI

[When morning comes, Penelope sets about preparing for the contest with the great bow.]

S o she came,
This noble lady, to the wooers,
And took her stand close by a pillar
Of that great hall. Before her face
She held a fair-wrought veil, and thus 1810
She spoke to the proud wooers:
"Come, then, you wooers,
Here stands your prize! And here before you
I now set forth the mighty bow
Of great Odysseus, and the man 1815
Who with his hands most readily
Shall bend it, and shall send an arrow
Through the twelve axes, he shall be
The man I follow; for I then
Will leave this house of my first bridal, 1820
So beautiful, so filled with all
That makes life good! Always in dreams
I shall remember it."

  So spoke she,
And bade Eumæus, the good swineherd,
Set forth the bow and the grey iron 1825
Before the wooers. He with tears
Took them and set them down; the herdsman[1]
Wept too, in his own place, to see
His master's bow.
Now spoke Telemachus before them 1830
In might and honor:

---

1. The herdsman **Philœtius**\\'fī ▲lē·tĭ·əs\\ is loyal to Odysseus.

"Come, you wooers,
Here stands your prize, and such a woman
As is not found in all Achæa,[2]
In holy Pylus—not in Argus
Nor in Mycenæ.[3] But all this   1835
You know already. Why should I
Thus praise my mother? Hold not back
With vain excuse, but bend the bow
And learn how this will end. I too
Would try the bow, for if I bend it   1840
And send my arrow through the iron,
I need not suffer shame that now
My honored mother leaves our house
To follow a new lord, while I
Remain behind; for I should be   1845
A man, then, able to perform
My father's glorious feats."
                              So said he,
And up he sprung full height and cast
His scarlet mantle from his shoulders,
And from his shoulders laid aside   1850
His keen-edged sword. And first of all
He set the axes: one long furrow
He dug for all and laid it straight
With a stretched line, and stamped the
   earth
About them on both sides. And wonder   1855
Laid hold on all who saw, so fitly
He set them up, though ne'er before
Had he beheld them. Then he went
And took his stand upon the threshold
And tried the bow. And as he strove   1860
To bend and string it, thrice indeed
He made it tremble, and thrice stayed
To rest his strength, but still he hoped
To stretch the string and send the arrow
Straight through the axes. And he yet,   1865
Straining the fourth time, might have
   strung it,
But now Odysseus shook his head
And staved his eager strength. Then thus
Spoke the great lord Telemachus:
"Alas, must I, then, ever be   1870
Worthless and weak! Or am I yet
Too young to trust these hands of mine
To win me justice if a man
Assails me unprovoked! But come,

You who are stronger; try the bow   1875
And end the contest!"

[One by one the suitors try vainly to string the
great bow. At last they decide to let the contest go
until the next day when they will hold a great
feast in honor of Apollo, the god of archery.
They believe Apollo will thus allow one of them
to string the bow and send an arrow through
the axes. While they are thus engaged, Odysseus
goes out of the hall and tells Eumæus and the
faithful herdsman who he is. He convinces them
by showing them the great scar on his leg.
Eumæus and the herdsman are overjoyed their
master has returned and agree to help him fight
the suitors. They return to the hall where the
suitors are drinking wine.]

                    Now
When each man to his heart's desire
Had poured and drunken, wise Odysseus,
With crafty purpose spoke:
                              "Now hearken,
Wooers of our famed queen! A boon   1880
I beg now of Eurymachus
And great Antinoüs[4]—for rightly
He counseled that we now lay by
The bow and leave the gods to settle
The issue of the strife. Tomorrow   1885
Let God grant mastery as he will!
But give me now the polished bow
And let me try before you here
My skill and strength—whether there yet
Dwells in these supple limbs the might   1890
That once was theirs, or if already
With wandering and want it now
Is brought to nothing."
                    So he spoke,
But when they heard him, all broke out
In furious anger, for they feared   1895

---

2. **Achæa**\ə ˈkē·ă\ ancient Greece.
3. **Argus . . . Mycenæ**\ˈmai ˈsē·nə\ cities in ancient
Greece.
4. **Eurymachus**\ˈyū ˈrĭ·mə·kəs\ and **Antinoüs**\ˈăn ˈtĭ-
nō·əs\ were the two chief suitors who had plotted to
kill Telemachus (Book XV); Athene had saved him
with a warning.

That he might bend the polished bow.
Then thus Antinoüs rebuked him
And said:
            "O wretched stranger, surely
Your wits have left you! Are you not
Content to eat at ease among us,   1900
Men rightly proud, here where you miss
Naught of our feast, but hear our words
And noble speech? No other beggars
Or strangers—you alone—can listen
To all we say. It is the wine   1905
Distracts you thus, the honeyed wine,
That often has brought grief to others
Drunk greedily and out of measure! . . .
And this I prophesy: if you
Shall bend that bow, then sore indeed   1910
Shall be your sufferings, for no one
In all this land will ever hail you
With friendly greeting: we will send you
In a black ship to Echetus,[5]
The king who murders all mankind;   1915
Thence you shall not escape. So sit
And drink in peace, and do not try
To strive with younger men."
                        Then answered
Prudent Penelope:
            "Unfitting
It is, Antinoüs, and unjust   1920
Thus to deny the right of strangers,
Guests of Telemachus, who come
Here to this house. What, do you think
That if this stranger proves he rightly
Trusts his arms' strength and power, and
  bends   1925
Odysseus' mighty bow—that he
Would lead me straightway to his home
And take me for his wife! The man
Has never in his inmost bosom
Had such a thought. Let none of you   1930
Who sit at feast here vex your spirit
With thoughts like these. Never, I say—
Never could that befall."
                        Then spoke
Polybus'[6] son, Eurymachus,
And answered:
            "Wise Penelope,   1935
Icarius'[7] daughter, we have never

Once thought this stranger here would
  wed you,
For that could never be. And yet
We shame to think what might be said
By men and women—how some fellow,   1940
One of the baser sort among us,
Should say: 'These men who came to woo
That great lord's wife were all too weak:
They could not bend his polished bow.
And yet another came, a beggar,   1945
A vagabond—and he with ease
Bent the great bow and sent an arrow
Straight through the iron.' Even so
The tale will run, and this will bring us
Reproach forever!"   1950
                Then replied
Prudent Penelope:
            "You cannot,
Eurymachus, win any honor
Here in this land by eating all
A great man's wealth the while you bring
Dishonor to his house. Why lay, then,   1955
Such weight on the reproach! This stranger
Is big of body and well-built,
And is, he says himself, the son
Of a good father. Come, then, give him
The polished bow, and let us see   1960
What he can do! For this I say,
And as I say, so shall it be:
If great Apollo grant his prayer
And let him bend the bow, I then
Will give him clothing—cloak and tunic— 1965
And a sharp spear to ward away
Both dogs and men, and a good sword,
Two-edged, besides; and I will give him
Sandals upon his feet; and hence
I then will send him wheresoever   1970
His heart and soul may wish."
                        Then spoke
The wise Telemachus and answered:
"Mother, no man of the Achæans

---

5. **Echetus**\ˈĕ·kə·təs\ a Greek king who had ordered
a dreadful punishment for his daughter and her lover.
Here Antinoüs belittles Odysseus as if he were a small
child — threatening to send him to the hobgoblins.
6. **Polybus**\ˈpŏ·lə·bəs\.
7. **Icarius**\ī ˈkă·rē·əs\.

Has greater right than I to give
This bow or hold it back.
                        But go   1975
Now to your room. There busy you
With woman's proper work, the loom
And distaff; give your maids commands
And let them ply their tasks. A bow
Is matter fit for men—for all men—   1980
But most of all for me, for I
Am master in this house."
                        And she,
Astonished at his words, went thence
Up to her room, and laid to heart
Her son's wise words. So she ascended   1985
To her own room, among her maidens,
And wept her own dear lord Odysseus
Until at last keen-eyed Athene
Sent on her eyes sweet sleep.

                        And now
The swineherd took the bow in hand   1990
To bear it to his lord. The wooers,
Beholding, each and all broke out
With clamor in the hall, and one
Of the proud youths thus spoke:
                        "Now where,
You worthless swineherd, are you taking   1995
That curved bow? O you idle rascal,
I wish that those swift dogs you breed
Might eat you, off there all alone
Among your swine! Would but Apollo
Might grant us this!"
                        These words he spoke, 2000
And in his fear the swineherd quickly
Laid the bow down where he was
  standing,
For many a man, through all the hall,
Cried out against him. Loudly then
From where he sat, Telemachus   2005
Called, threatening:
                        "Go on, good father,
Take him the bow! But I shall teach you,
And soon, you must not take your orders
From every man.
                        Ah, would I were
As surely, stronger than these men,   2010
These wooers in this house! For soon

Would I send some of them in sorrow
Off home, out of our house! Their deeds
Are all of evil!"
                        So he spoke,
And all the wooers laughed thereat   2015
With merry laughter, and forgot
The bitter wrath they felt before
Against Telemachus. And now
Down through the hall the swineherd
  came
Bearing the bow, and by Odysseus   2020
He halted, and he gave the bow
Into his hand. And then he called
Nurse Eurycleia from within
And said:
                        "Telemachus thus bids you,
Wise Eurycleia. Lock you now   2025
The close-set doors between the chambers
And the great hall. If any woman
Hear there within the sound of groans
Or combat from the men without
In the great hall, let her not look   2030
Forth from the door, but bide within
And ply her task in silence."
                        So
He spoke to her. His words unwing'd
Rested unanswered and she fastened
The doors of that fair hall. And softly   2035
Philœtius sped forth from the house
And barred the gates of the walled court.
Then back he went and sat him down
Where he had sat before; and ever
He fixed his eyes upon Odysseus.   2040
And now Odysseus held the bow
And turned it, side to side, and tried it
In every part, lest worms, the while
Its lord was far away, had eaten
Into the horn. And one who watched   2045
Would say, quick glancing at his neighbor:
"This fellow must be used to bows,
A clever rascal. He may have
A bow like this laid by at home
Or studies how to make one. Look: 2050
See how the idle beggar turns it
This way and that with ready hands,
Well tried in mischief!"
                        And another

Of the proud youths would say:

"May he
Meet ever such good luck as now   2055
Will be his lot, when he shall fail
To bend the bow!"

So spoke the wooers.
But wise Odysseus, who had handled
That mighty bow, testing each part,
At once as easily as a man,   2060
A singer, skillful with the lyre,
Stretches a string in place and fits it
To its new peg, and at each end
Makes fast the twisted gut—even so
With ready ease Odysseus bent   2065
And strung that mighty bow.

He took it
In his right hand and tried the bowstring,
And at his touch it rang out loud,
Clear as a swallow's cry.

Then fell
A deadly dread on all the wooers,   2070
And every face turned pale. Zeus sent
His sign from heaven in loud thunder,
And great Odysseus, who so long
Had suffered and endured, rejoiced
To hear this signal from the son   2075
Of artful Cronus.

Now he took
A swift shaft in his hand: it lay
Before him, drawn, upon the table;
For in the hollow quiver yet
The rest lay waiting—as the Achæans   2080
Ere long should learn.

And now he laid
The arrow in the rest, and seated
There on the bench, he drew the string
And the notched arrow. Straight he aimed,
And loosed the shaft.

And not one axe   2085
Of all it missed. Through every one
From the first axe, that bronze-tipped
 arrow
Went speeding to the very last
And out beyond. Then thus Odysseus
Spoke to Telemachus:

"This stranger,   2090

Telemachus, who as your guest
Sits in your hall, has not, you see,
Brought shame on you. I have not missed
The mark nor made a mighty labor
Of stringing the great bow. My strength   2095
Is even as of old, nor fails me now
As these in insult deemed.

At last
The time is come, the destined hour
To bid these wooers sup with us,
Though yet it is full day! And we   2100
Have sport for them besides—the dance
And twanging of the lyre, to crown
This coming feast!"

So spoke Odysseus,
And gave, with bended brows, the signal.
And, on the instant, his dear son   2105
Telemachus girt by his side
His keen-edged sword and took his stand
Beside his father's seat, all armed
In glittering bronze.

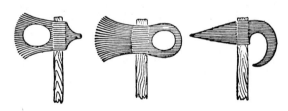

Three ancient Greek axes.

I
THE CONTEST

1. Prudent and beauteous Penelope promises to leave the home she loves and follow the suitor who can string Odysseus' bow and send a shaft through the center holes of the twelve axes. Before any of the suitors can try, however, Telemachus announces that he wishes to test himself and see if he can perform the feat. What reason does he give?

2. Even though Telemachus does not complete the test, his subsequent actions show that he is eager to assume the responsibilities of a grown man. Give two illustrations of such actions which show this.

II
TECHNIQUES

Suspense

From the time Penelope first announces the contest of the bow, Homer arranges the action which follows so that it builds anticipation toward the satisfying moment when Odysseus will reveal his identity.

1. Discuss those incidents which take place between the time the contest is announced until Odysseus has the fateful bow in his hands which prolong the coming of the awaited moment and increase the listeners' suspense.

2. An author sometimes makes use of what is known as *irony* to draw his audience or readers closer to him and increase their interest in what is going to happen. After all, anything is more fun if you feel that you're "in the know" or "on the inside" as to what is taking place. *Irony* occurs when what appears to be true really isn't so at all. For example, when Penelope says to the suitors that even if the stranger strings the bow and sends an arrow through the axes, he has no thought of making her his wife, this is ironical. Explain.

Conflict

Finally, after a fitting buildup, the moment arrives! Odysseus "who so long had suffered and endured" is at last to get revenge.

What sign from a god does the courageous hero get to show him that the time has come for taking action? What precautions had been taken to see that the suitors did not flee from the hall? Who took his stand beside Odysseus to fight along with him? How many other men could he count upon to help him in the fighting?

Foreshadowing

There is another kind of irony which is found in the epic. This is the kind of irony which lies not in the situation, but directly in the choice of words which have more than one meaning. They may seem, on the surface to mean one thing, but they actually mean another. Thus Odysseus' closing words in which he speaks of the feast in store for the wooers are indeed ironical. What do you think he actually means by "sport," the "dance," and the "twanging of the lyre"?

PART V
The Battle in the Great Hall

BOOK XXII

Now wise Odysseus stripped away 2110
His ragged garments. Up he sprang
To the great threshold with the bow
And the full quiver, and poured forth
The swift shafts at his feet. Then thus
Before the wooers he spoke:
        "So now 2115
Ends this dread contest. And again
I aim, at a new mark, a mark
No man has hit before. And may
My aim be true, and great Apollo
Grant me the glory!"
        So he spoke, 2120
And at Antinoüs he aimed
His piercing arrow. Now this man
Was just then lifting to his lips
A fair gold cup of double handle
And held it high in both his hands 2125
Ready to drink the wine. Of death
No thought was in his heart. For who
Could think that here among these men,
Sitting at feast, one man, alone
Among so many, though his strength 2130
Were great indeed, could bring upon him
Dread death and fate's black end?
        Odysseus
Took steady aim and drove the arrow
Straight to the throat: the keen point sped
Through the soft neck. The man sank
  down: 2135
Sidelong he bent: out of his hand
As he fell smitten, dropped the cup;
Forth from his nostrils sprang the blood
In a thick stream.

And when the wooers
Saw the man fall, they rose in tumult   2140
Through all the hall. Up sprang each man
Out of his place and ran about
Searching in terror every side
Of those strong walls; but there they found
No shield or warlike spear.[1] And thus   2145
They spoke, then, and in angry words
Rebuked Odysseus:
                    "This, O stranger,
Will bring you evil, thus to turn
Your shafts on men!
                    You have slain
The first and foremost man of all   2150
The youth of Ithaca!"
                    But Odysseus
Spoke, frowning sternly on them:
                                    "Dogs,
You told yourselves that I should never
Come back again to my own home
Out of the land of Troy. And so   2155
You have devoured my house,
                            And though I
Myself was living, sought like traitors
To woo my wife. You neither fear
The gods that dwell in the high heavens
Nor yet the wrath of man that ever   2160
Follows with vengeance. Round you all
Death's cords are tightening!"
                            So spoke he,
And at his words their knees grew weak,
And weak their hearts within. And then
Eurymachus at once spoke out   2165
Before them all:
                "Never, my friends,
Will this man stay his ruthless hand
Now that he holds the polished bow
And quivered arrows; but will stand there
On that bright threshold and will smite us   2170
Till he has slain us all. So summon
Your spirit to the fight. Draw swords!
Hold up the tables as a shield
Against these shafts of death, and rush
Upon him swiftly, all at once,   2175
Locked close together. So perhaps
We yet may thrust him from the threshold
And from the door, and so flee forth

And reach the town and there raise quickly
Our cry for aid. And then this man   2180
Will soon shoot his last shaft!"
                            So said he,
And with these words he drew his sword,
Keen, double-edged, and rushed upon him,
Shouting a dreadful shout!
                        That instant
Noble Odysseus loosed his arrow.   2185
It struck him in the breast.
                        Out of his hand
His sword flew. Lifeless, limp, he sank
Across the table, and fell headlong,
O'erturning food and cup. His head
Beat on the ground in agony;   2190
He writhed, and thrusting with both feet
Spurned back the chair and threw it over,
And dark upon his eyes then fell
The mists of death.
                    Telemachus sped
To his dear father's side, and there   2195
He stood and with wing'd words he said:
"Now, father, I will bring you hither
A shield, and I will bring two spears
And a good helmet all of bronze
Fitting your brows, and I myself   2200
Will get me armor, and will arm
The swineherd and the herdsman; armor
Will make us safer."
                    Then replied
The wise Odysseus:
                    "Run, then, fetch them,
While I have arrows yet remaining   2205
To hold our foemen off, or they,
When I am left alone, may drive me
Out of the doorway."
                    So he spoke,
And good Telemachus obeyed
His father's bidding. Forth he hastened   2210
Up to the room wherein lay hidden
Those glorious arms, and thence he took
Four shields, eight spears, and four good
  helmets
Brazen, with horsehair crests. And these

----

1. **no shield or warlike spear.** Earlier, Telemachus had
locked their weapons in a room off the banquet hall.

He bore with him, and quickly came 2215
Back to his father's side. And first
Round his own body he girt on
The brazen mail, and then those two,
His servants, armed them like himself
In that fair armor. There they stood 2220
Beside their lord, the wise Odysseus,
Ready of counsel.
                    Now so long
As he had shafts wherewith to hold
His foes afar, he still smote down
A wooer with each shaft; they fell there 2225
One by another. But at length
The mighty archer's arrows failed him.
Then he set down his bow and leaned it
Close by a pillar of the hall
Against the shining wall's bright surface, 2230
Then round his shoulders slung a shield
Of four-fold hide and on his head
He set a helmet, finely fashioned,
And terribly its horsehair crest
Nodded above it; and he took 2235
Two bronze-tipped spears in hand.
                            There was,
It chanced, a postern door that pierced
The massive wall, just at the level
Of the great threshold of the hall.
Through this a man might reach the pas-
  sage 2240
That ran without, but this was barred
By well-joined doors. And here Odysseus
Bade the good swineherd take his stand
And keep good watch, for here alone
Might those within pass forth. And now 2245
Thus to his comrades Agelaüs[2]
Made plain his thought:
                  "Friends, might not one
Climb up and reach that little door,
And so pass forth and tell our people
And raise the cry for help? This man 2250
Would soon shoot his last shaft."
                        Then answered
Melanthius[3] the goatherd:
                        "Never
Can that be done, great Agelaüs.
It lies too near the fine great doors
That lead forth to the court, and hard 2255

It is to pass these; for one man,
If stout of heart, might hold the passage
Against us all. But look, now—I
Will bring you from the upper room
Arms for each man, for there, I think, 2260
Odysseus and his valiant son
Have stored the arms away."
                        So spoke
Melanthius the goatherd; straightway
He clambered up and through the holes
That aired the hall, slipped forth and
  reached 2265
Odysseus' inner room. And thence
He chose out twelve good shields and
  spears
And helmets with high crests of horsehair,
And back he brought them all in haste
And gave them to the wooers.
                        So they stood 2270
Breathing fierce breath of battle, ready
Upon the threshold, four alone
While those who faced them in the hall
Were many, tried in arms.
                        And Agelaüs,
Son of Damastor,[4] now urged forward 2275
The wooers to the fight, and with him
Eurynomous, Amphimedon,[5]
And Demoptolemus: Peisander,
Polyctor's[6] son, and Polybus,
Famed for his wisdom. These men stood 2280
Highest in worth among the wooers
Who yet were left alive and battled
For life itself. The rest, the bow
And those thick-flying shafts already
Had struck with death.
                        And Agelaüs, 2285
Son of Damastor, now spoke out
Before the wooers, and made clear
His thought to all:

---

2. **Agelaüs**\\'ă·jə ▲lā·əs\\ one of the wooers.
3. **Melanthius**\\mə ▲lăn·thē·əs\\ one of the household servants who threw in his lot with the wooers.
4. **Damastor**\\də ▲măs·tər\\.
5. **Eurynomous**\\yū ▲rĭn·ə·məs\\, **Amphimedon**\\'ăm ▲fĭ·mə·dən\\ wooers.
6. **Demoptolemus**\\də 'mŏp ▲tō·lə·məs\\, **Peisander**\\'pai-▲săn·dər\\, **Polyctor**\\▲pŏ·lĭk·tər\\.

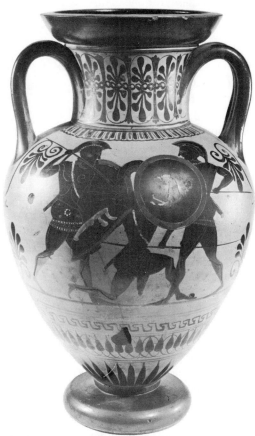

Black Figured Vase or Amphora showing warriors fighting over a kneeling comrade, from Attica about 540 B.C.

"Now cast
All your long spears, yet not together.
Come, let six cast at once and learn   2290
If Zeus will let us now lay low
Odysseus and win glory. Heed not
The others, so he fall!"

        So said he,
And at his word all cast their spears
And mightily. But great Athene   2295
Made them of no avail. One struck
A pillar that upheld the roof
Of the great hall; another smote
The firm-set door, and a third spear,
With ashen shaft and brazen head,   2300
Drove deep into the wall. So now
When every spear the wooers hurled

Had missed its mark, then spoke Odysseus,
So sorely tried:

        "Now, friends, I tell you
We too must cast our spears and aim them   2305
All at that throng of wooers, men
Who madly long to strip our bodies
And add to their foul score."

          He spoke,
And each of them took aim and cast
His keen spear at the man who faced him.   2310
Odysseus with his flying spear
Struck Demoptolemus; his son
Smote down Euryades;[7] the swineherd
Slew Elatus;[8] and the good herdsman
Struck down Peisander. And they all   2315
Fell there together and their teeth
Bit the broad earth. Back up the hall
Shrank all the wooers to the far
Sheltered recesses, and those others
Sprang forward and plucked forth the
  spears   2320
From those that lay there slain.

         Once more
The wooers then all hurled together
Their pointed spears, and mightily,
But great Athene made them all
Of no avail. For one but struck   2325
A pillar that upheld the roof
Of the great hall; another smote
The firm-set door; and a third spear,
With ashen shaft and brazen head,
Drove deep into the wall. But one,   2330
Amphimedon's long spear, struck lightly
Telemachus upon the wrist,
Grazing the skin; and now Ctesippus,[9]
Sending his spear above the shield,
Just touched Eumæus' shoulder: onward   2335
It sped and fell to earth.

         Once more
The men who fought beside their wise
And crafty lord Odysseus, cast
Their keen spears all together, aiming
Into the throng. And now Odysseus,   2340
Taker of Troy, struck with his spear

7. **Euryades**\ˈyu ▲rē•ə ˈdēz\.
8. **Elatus**\▲ĕ•lə•təs\.
9. **Ctesippus**\▲tĕ•sə•pəs\.

Eurydamas; Telemachus
Smote down Amphimedon; the swineherd
Slew Polybus, and the good herdsman
Struck, full upon the breast, Ctesippus.   2345
                Then on their hearts
Came panic; through the hall they fled
Like kine some darting gadfly follows
And stings to madness in the springtime
When days grow long. And as the vultures 2350
Come down from mountain heights and
  swoop
Upon the lesser birds that cower
Beneath the clouds and flit their way
Upon the levels, as they pounce
Upon them, slaying, where no help   2355
Or hope of flight is found, while men
Look on and see the sport with gladness—
Even so these men came rushing down
Upon the wooers, and they drove them
Through all the house on every side   2360
And smote them down. And horrible
Arose the groans of men who fell
With shattered heads, and all the floor
Was red with blood.
             And now
The son of Terpes, Phemius,[10]   2365
The minstrel whom the wooers forced
To sing before them, still was seeking
How he might shun black death. He stood
Close by the postern door; his hands
Held his clear lyre. . . .
             And now he set   2370
His hollow lyre upon the floor . . .
And he himself sprang forth and clasped
Odysseus' knees, and with wing'd words
Besought him thus:
            "A suppliant,
I clasp your knees, Odysseus. Honor   2375
And pity a poor minstrel. Sorrow
May seize you later if you slay
A singer who has made sweet music
For gods and men.
          So do not seek
To smite my head from me. Your son,   2380
Your own Telemachus, will tell you
That not of my own will, nor seeking
For gain thereby, did I come hither

To sing my songs here in your house
While these men sat at feast. For they   2385
Were mightier than I and many,
And forced me to their will."
           So said he,
And the great prince Telemachus
Heard him and by his father's side
Thus quickly spoke:
         "Nay, hold your hand,   2390
Nor slay this man with your bronze blade,
For he is blameless. Let us spare, too,
Medon, the herald. For when I
Was still a child, here in our home
He had me ever in his keeping.   2395
Spare him, unless Philœtius slew him
Or the good swineherd, or he fell
Before your hand as you swept raging
Through all the house."
         He spoke, and Medon,
A man of wisdom, heard, for crouching   2400
He lay beneath a chair, all hidden
In a raw oxhide, so escaping
From fate's black end. And now he quickly
Came from beneath the chair, and rose,
And cast the hide aside, and ran   2405
Straight to Telemachus and clasped
His hands about his knees and spoke
Beseeching in wing'd words:
          "Yes, friend,
Here I am now! So stay your hand,
And speak, I pray you to your father,   2410
Lest in his strength he smite me dead
With his sharp sword in his great anger
Against these wooers—these who wasted
His wealth here in his halls, too foolish
To heed your words."
         Then smiling spoke   2415
The wise Odysseus:
         "Have good courage,
For he has snatched you from your peril
And saved you. Lay this truth to heart:
Aye, and tell others: he who does
Good deeds will find far better fortune   2420
Than he whose deeds are evil. Go you
Forth from the hall now. Sit you down

---

10. **Terpes**\\ˈtər ˈpēz\\.

Out in the court, far from this slaughter,
You and yon minstrel, rich in music,
While in the house I do the work   2425
I yet must do."
          He spoke, and they
Passed quickly from the hall and sat them
Beside the altar of great Zeus,
Peering about on every side
In dread of death.

          And now Odysseus   2430
Went through the house and searched about
To see if anywhere remained
A man yet left alive and hiding
To shun black death. But he beheld
Them one and all, each man, all lying   2435
In blood and dust.

[Odysseus now sends for Eurycleia to help in
placing the hall back in order.]

          And Eurycleia,
When she beheld those bodies there,
And that dread flow of blood, was ready
To cry aloud for joy, beholding
How great a deed was done. But he   2440
Stayed her and bade her to refrain
Her eager longing, speaking thus
In wing'd words:
          "Let your heart rejoice,
Old woman, but refrain, nor cry
Aloud in triumph. It is evil   2445
To glory o'er the slain. Their fate
Has brought them to this end, the fate
The gods have shaped them, and their own
Foul deeds of sin. These men respected
No man on earth, or good or evil,   2450
Who came among them. So they now,
Through their own evil deeds, are fallen
A prey to dreadful death."
          And now
He called to him Telemachus
And called the swineherd and the herds-
  man,   2455
And in wing'd words he said:
          "Begin, now
The work of bearing out the dead."

          Now Odysseus
Spoke to his good nurse Eurycleia:
"Bring hither brimstone now, old woman,
To keep off harm; bring fire besides   2460
To purify the hall, then go
And bid Penelope come hither
With all her maids: bid all the women
Within the house to come."
          So said he,
And Eurycleia, his dear nurse,   2465
Failed not to heed his words. She brought
  him
Brimstone and fire besides; with these
Odysseus purified the hall,
The buildings and the court.
          And now
Up through the fair house the old woman   2470
Went hastening to tell the women
And speed them on. And forth they came
Out of their room, and in their hands
They all bore torches, and they thronged
About Odysseus and with joy   2475
Welcomed him home.

I

THE GREAT BATTLE

1. The suitors seemed unable to organize themselves effectively to fight Odysseus, Telemachus,
and the two loyal servants. Discuss how the following factors contributed to their confusion.

  a. Shock effect of the "beggar's" true identity

  b. Suitors' lack of shields and spears

  c. Suitors' lack of physical fitness and battle experience

  d. Suitors' indifference to the gods

  e. Early deaths of Antinoüs and Eurymachus

2. How do the suitors later obtain spears,
shields, and helmets?

3. What reasons does Phemius the minstrel give
that Odysseus should spare his life? What insight
does this give you into the regard with which the
minstrel was held in Odysseus' time?

4. The Greeks looked upon arrogance or insolence toward gods and men as lawlessness, and

the word they had for such conduct was *hybris*. Those guilty of *hybris* were bound to be punished or destroyed. Discuss in what ways the suitors were guilty of *hybris*.

II
TECHNIQUES

Conflict

In considering conflict in the other selections in this section, you have been concerned with the four basic types: (1) Man struggles against another man or animal; (2) Man struggles against the forces of nature; (3) Man struggles against society or groups of people who represent certain ideas or beliefs; (4) Man is torn by conflict within himself. There is, also, a fifth type of conflict. This is the struggle of man against Fate or destiny. When the gods actively enter into a conflict, the odds are heavy against the men they oppose. These men are fated to be punished. This fifth type of conflict is that which is seen throughout *The Odyssey*, and it is especially notable in this episode which brings to a high point the conflict between Odysseus and the suitors.

1. While the suitors actually do not see Athene, how does her aid to Odysseus become obvious to them each time after they have cast their spears?

2. Describe how Medon escaped "fate's black end." What grim humor can be seen in this incident? How does it help the story?

Imaginative Language

Within some of the last episodes read, there have been a number of similes which bring vivid pictures to mind. One of the most detailed of these is that in lines 2346–64 in which the poet tells how the suitors fled in panic through the halls pursued by Odysseus and his supporters. Put the picture contained in this simile into your own words. To what two kinds of creature are the avengers likened? To what are the suitors likened?

Odysseus and Penelope—terracotta and gold.

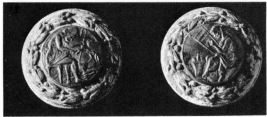

PART VI
The Reunion of Odysseus and Penelope

BOOK XXIII

Now the old woman went her way,
Laughing for joy, up to the room
Where lay her mistress, with the tidings
That her dear lord was come. Her knees   2480
Grew strong with joy; her feeble feet
Ran faster than their wont. She halted
There by her lady's head and thus
She spoke to her:
        "Awake, dear child,
Penelope, and see at last   2485
With your own eyes what you have hoped for
Day after day. For now Odysseus
Is come again, to his own home;
Long looked for, he has come at last,
And he has slain the haughty wooers   2490
Who troubled all his house and wasted
His wealth away and threatened evil
To his dear son."
        Then thus replied
The wise Penelope:
        "Dear nurse,
The gods have made you mad;   2495
Your mind, till now, was ever steady.
Why do you mock me, now my spirit
Is heavy with its grief, to tell me
Such tales as this?"
        Then replied
Her dear nurse Eurycleia:
        "Nay,   2500
Dear child, I do not mock you. Here

In very truth, Odysseus now
Is with us, he himself. For he
Was the poor stranger every man
Insulted in the hall. Long since   2505
Telemachus knew well that he
Was here among us, but with foresight
He hid his knowledge, that his father
Might all the better take his vengeance
For all the cruel wrongs these men   2510
Have wrought in arrogance."
                  Then replied
Prudent Penelope:
            "Dear nurse,
Now be not over-quick to boast
And laugh with joy. You know indeed
How welcome he would be to all   2515
In his own house, and most to me
And to the son I bore him. Yet
This tale you tell cannot be true:
Alas, it is some god came hither
And slew those haughty wooers, angered   2520
At the rash insults of their pride
And all their evil deeds.
               So for their crimes
They met this end. But far away
Odysseus now has lost forever
All hope of his returning hither—   2525
Nay, he himself is lost!"
               Then answered
Her dear nurse Eurycleia:
               "Child,
What words are these that now have
  passed
The portal of your teeth! To say
That your own husband, he who now   2530
Stands here upon his hearth, will never
Come home again. Your heart is ever
Slow to believe. Yet I can tell you
Another sign, a sign yet surer,
The scar of the deep wound the boar   2535
Once gave with his bright tusk. I spied it
That day I washed his feet, and longed
To tell you what I saw. But he
Laid hand upon my mouth and so
With his wise foresight, stopped my
  speech.   2540
But come, now, follow me."

Then wise Penelope replied:
"Dear nurse, wise as you are, 'tis hard
To guard against the secret purpose
Of the eternal gods. And yet   2545
Let us go down and seek my son
And see these wooers who lie slain
And him that slew them."
               So she spoke,
And down she passed then from her room,
And sorely was her heart divided   2550
Whether to stand far off and question
Her own dear lord, or stand beside him
And kiss his face and clasp his hand.
But when she entered and passed over
The threshold of carved stone, she went   2555
And sat her down, facing Odysseus,
In firelight, by the farther wall.
And he still sat with downcast eyes
By the tall pillar and awaited
In wonder if his stately wife   2560
Would speak to him when she should turn
Her eyes and see him. A long time
She sat in silence, and amazement
Was in her heart; then for a time
She gazed upon him face to face,   2565
And then again she knew him not,
For he still wore upon his body
A beggar's raiment.
               And her son,
Telemachus, now spoke, and said,
Reproaching her:
            "Mother of mine,   2570
Unmotherly, why is your heart
So hard? Why do you ever keep
Far from my father?
            Your heart is ever
Harder than stone!"
            Then thus replied
Prudent Penelope:
            "My son,   2575
My spirit is amazed within me.
I have no power to speak or question
Or look upon his face. And yet,
If this can be Odysseus' self,
And he has now come home, we two   2580
May know each other far more surely
Than any other may, for we

Have secret tokens known to us,
Hidden from all besides."
                    So said she,
And great Odysseus smiled and quickly   2585
Thus to Telemachus he spoke
In wing'd words:
                    "Go, Telemachus,
And leave your mother in the hall
To test me. She shall learn ere long
More surely what I am. But now,   2590
Because I am unclean to see,
And wear base garments on my body,
She holds me in dishonor, saying
That I am not her lord!"

[Odysseus leaves to bathe and to dress in
more fitting clothing. At that time Athene
restores his handsome appearance.]

                    So he came
Forth from the bath, and seemed in
    presence   2595
Like the immortal gods. And thus
He came once more back to the seat
Whence he had risen, and there sat
Facing his wife, and spoke to her
And said:
                    "O most perplexing woman,   2600
Surely the dwellers on Olympus
Have given you a harder heart
Than other tender women. Nay,
There is no other woman living
Would stand aside thus, hardening   2605
A stubborn heart against her husband
Who after many a peril past
Comes, in the twentieth year, once more
To his own land."
                    And thus answered
The wise Penelope:
                    "O man   2610
Perplexing to my soul—nay, I
Am not held off by pride, nor scorn you,
But I am lost in wonder. Well
I know what you were once when, sailing
Away in your oared ship, you left   2615
Your home in Ithaca. But come
Now, Eurycleia, and make ready

His firm-built bed. Make it outside
The room he built him himself. Aye, move
His firm-built bedstead forth and strew   2620
Upon it bedding—fleeces, covers,
And bright-hued rugs."
                    All this she said
To try her husband. But Odysseus
Was angered at her words, and thus
He spoke to his true wife:
                    "What, woman!   2625
What words are these you now have said
To pierce my heart! Who can have set
My bed in a new place?
                    No mortal man
Of living men, in his full strength,
Could ever move it easily   2630
Out of its present place. For in it,
Wrought in its very frame, is hidden
A secret token, and no other
Wrought this, but I alone.
                    There grew
Within our yard an olive tree,   2635
Long-leaved and thriving, strong of
    growth,
Thick as a pillar. Round its trunk
I shaped my room and built it thus
Till all was finished, walling it
With massive stone, and well I fashioned   2640
The roof to cover it and hung
And fitted its joined doors. And then,
From that long-leaved tall olive tree
I cut the crown away and squared,
Using my axe, the stem remaining   2645
Above the roots; then with the adz
I smoothed it and made true the line,
And thus I made my bed-post. Next
I bored it all with a keen auger
And, so beginning, ever worked   2650
On to the end, and it stood finished.
I decked it all with gold and silver
And ivory, and across it stretched
Long strips of oxhide bright and red.
This is the token that I mean.   2655
Now, wife, I do not know if still
That bed is standing there, or whether
Some one has cut that olive stem
And moved it elsewhere."

145

So he spoke,
And at his words her knees grew weak 2660
And all her soul within, for well
She knew this token that Odysseus
Had told so plainly. And she wept,
And straight to him she ran, and cast
Her arms about her husband's neck 2665
And kissed his face and said:
                              "Odysseus,
Pray be not angry with me. You
Have ever been, through every fortune,
Wisest of men. The gods have sent
Sore grief upon us, for they grudged us 2670
That we should side by side together
Share the delight of youth and cross
The threshold of old age. Yet be not,
I pray you, wroth with me or blame me,
Because I did not when I saw you, 2675
Run thus to greet you! For my heart
Within my breast was shuddering ever
Lest some strange man should come and
  cheat me
With lying words. For many a man
Will plot base deeds for gain. But now, 2680
Since you have made so plain the secret
Of this our bed
              —lo, now
You quite convince this heart of mine,
Stubborn what though it be!"
                          So spoke she,
And stronger still there came upon him 2685
A yearning need of tears, and there,
Holding his wise and faithful wife,
He wept with joy. And she beside him,
Like men that see the land with gladness—
Seamen whose sturdy ship Poseidon 2690
Has smitten on the deep and shattered
With storm and mighty seas, and few
Are they who from the foaming waters
Escape to swim to shore: their skin
Is crusted with the brine, but happy 2695
They step to land once more, delivered
Out of their danger—with such gladness
She gazed upon her husband.

The Odyssey

SUMMING UP

I

AN ADVENTURER FOR ALL TIMES

For Homer, life was filled with many hazards, but it was still a heroic adventure to be undertaken with joy and courage. The Homeric hero was not discouraged by the fact that he could unknowingly be condemned to destruction by the gods or by the Fates. His joy of living was apparent in the way he faced each new experience.

The poetry of Homer has continued to appeal to readers through the years because his characters are true to the fundamentals of human nature.

1. Think over this last statement carefully, then list what you feel to be some of the fundamental characteristics of human nature.

2. Discuss, with specific illustrations from the *Odyssey*, whether or not you feel Homer's characters to be basically true to life.

II

IMPLICATIONS

Reflect on the following statements, then discuss each as it applies to the *Odyssey*.

1. The person who really mattered in the ancient Greek world was the king or chief.

2. Men were not considered unmanly if they cried when moved by joy or grief.

3. The position of Penelope was similar in many ways to that of women today.

III

TECHNIQUES

1. The Homeric story-poems, or epics, have continued to be admired throughout the centuries for three reasons:

    a. The action moves rapidly.

    b. The language is simple.

    c. Noble actions or deeds are glorified.

What relationship can you see between these three characteristics and the fact that the epic was first sung as entertainment?

2. Characterization is of great importance in the epic. In various ways, Homer told his listeners enough about each of the important persons appearing in his songs that his audience was interested in hearing what happened to them.

Write a brief essay on one of the following topics:

a. The character of Penelope

b. My opinion of Odysseus

c. Telemachus as the ideal son

IV
WORDS

A. The procedure of attempting to use context clues to find the meaning of unfamiliar words may be used with any kind of writing—poetry or prose, narrative or exposition, new styles or old, simple or difficult. When ancient Homer says, "Good indeed it is to hear the minstrelsy of such a singer," we have a fair idea of what *minstrelsy* means. Guess at the meanings of the italicized words in the following contexts; then look up the words in your dictionary.

1. Within this lair a man was *wont* to sleep . . .

2. And we cried out in *lamentation.*

3. As one who with an *auger* bores a great ship timber . . .

4. Groaning in agony and *anguish* . . .

5. If I *entreat* you and bid you set me free . . .

6. . . . would you, O mighty goddess, but *vouchsafe* to be my helper.

However, the method of context clues—like anything else—has its limitations. Consider the lines "But this you give me is a cup of nectar and ambrosia mingled." Guess at the meanings of *nectar* and *ambrosia* and then look them up in your dictionary.

B. The English language has, of course, many prefixes that are not negative. A second group of prefixes might be labeled *situational* prefixes, in that they suggest situation, location, or direction. Perhaps the simplest prefixes of this kind are *a-,* as in *abed,* which suggests the meaning of *up, in, on, to; be-,* as in *beset,* roughly meaning *around, about;* and *for-,* as in *forsake,* suggesting *away, off, from.* But prefixes are often general and unstable in their meanings. To what extent do the comments made above apply to these words from the Homer selection: *await, arise, amid, aloud, athwart, aloft, asunder; beseech, befall, behold; forbid, forbear.*

C. In the process of finding verbs that serve as companion forms to nouns, one finds that the English language has an unexpected number of patterns for noun-verb relationships. For instance, the word *fear* is both noun and verb, but the word *fright* is usually a noun, with *frighten* as its companion form. What nouns serve as companion forms for the following verbs: *expect, realize, approve, lament, deliver, appear, seize, guide?*

D. Simple words can sometimes teach us as much about our language as more complicated ones. We have been noticing the importance of accent position in words, such as the difference between *minute* in "wait a minute" and *minute* in "a minute particle hardly visible to the naked eye." Now what happens when we take some of the simple words in these selections and give companion forms: *medicine-medicinal, modern-modernity, prepare-preparation?* What has happened to the position of the main stress or accent? What happens to the stress when you form adjectives from the nouns *history, tempest, herald, courage, oracle, palace, substance,* or when you form nouns from the adjectives *public, simple, mortal, human, fertile?* Incidentally, all of the words in this exercise have come into the English language as borrowings from French or from Latin.

BIOGRAPHICAL NOTES
Richard Connell

Richard Connell (1893–1949), son of a New York newspaper editor and congressman, was born in Poughkeepsie, New York. City editor of the *Poughkeepsie News Press* at sixteen, Connell further pursued his interest in writing at Harvard University. He was editor of two Harvard student publications, the *Daily Crimson* and the *Lampoon.* After graduating from Harvard in 1915, Connell served stints as a newspaperman, advertising copy editor, and soldier in World War I. In 1919, he became a free-lance fiction writer, concentrating chiefly on short stories, with an occasional novel, motion picture story, or screenplay. By the time of his death, more than three hundred of his short stories had been published in American and English magazines.

Paul Annixter

Paul Annixter (1894–   ), who lives in Pasadena, California, left school at eighteen and took to the open road, roaming over much of the United States and Canada. From his experiences he has published over 500 short stories in magazines in the United States, Canada, and England. He believes that the head and hands should work together and "that the best ideas that come to a writer are apt to drip off the end of a shovel or trowel." Mr. Annixter does not confine himself to short stories. One of his most popular novels is *Swiftwater*.

Doris Lessing

Doris Lessing (1919–   ), whose parents were English, was born in Kermanshah, Persia. When her father tired of the graft and corruption in Persia at the time, he moved the family to southern Rhodesia where he bought a corn farm. A short story collection, *This Was the Old Chief's Country*, and *In Pursuit of the English*, her autobiography, are her best-known works. Many of her stories center around South Africa. She is considered one of Britain's foremost writers.

Raymond Ditmars

Raymond Ditmars (1876–1942), zoologist and science writer, was born in Newark, New Jersey. After graduating from Barnard Military School in New York, he was employed by New York's American Museum of Natural History. He then served two years as a court reporter for *The New York Times*. In 1899, he became curator of reptiles in the New York Zoological Park, and, in 1910, became curator of mammals as well. His books on zoology include: *Snakes of the World*, *The Book of Living Reptiles*, and *Confessions of a Scientist*.

Sir Arthur Conan Doyle

Arthur Conan Doyle (1859–1930) was born at Picardy Place, Edinburgh, Scotland. While working toward his Bachelor of Medicine degree at Edinburgh University, Doyle became acquainted with Joseph Bell, Edinburgh Infirmary surgeon, who may have become the model for Sherlock Holmes. In 1902, Doyle was knighted and became Sir Arthur as a reward for writing *The Great Boer War* in which he defended the British cause.

Matthew A. Henson

Matthew A. Henson (1866–1955) was born in Charles County, Maryland. His book, *A Black Explorer at the North Pole,* touches only lightly on the hardships of his childhood. Although he did not have the advantage of many years of formal schooling, he had an active, inquiring mind, and he became well educated. In the years after he and Peary had reached the North Pole, Henson was made a member of the famous Explorer's Club, granted honorary Master of Science degrees from Howard University and Morgan College, and, in his eighty-eighth year, invited to the White House to be honored by President Eisenhower.

Lyman M. Nash

Lyman M. Nash (1926–   ), was born in Wisconsin and moved to Minnesota at an early age. He went to sea and later served in the Army. After his discharge from the Army he married. Since then he has twice lived in Madrid, Spain and is now living in Chicago where he is a free-lance writer.

Orville Wright

Orville Wright (1871–1948), airplane inventor, was born in Dayton, Ohio. While operating a bicycle shop with his brother, Wilbur, Orville began experimenting with gliders. On December 17, 1903, he and Wilbur made their first flights in an airplane with an engine at Kitty Hawk, North Carolina. After serving in World War I as a major in the Aviation Corps, Orville became an aeronautical researcher.

Kenneth S. Davis

Kenneth S. Davis (1912–   ) was born in Salina, Kansas. He holds degrees from Kansas State University and the University of Wisconsin. He has been a newspaper reporter, a correspondent in Europe during World War II, a journalism instructor, a United States Department of Agriculture specialist, and editor of the Newberry Library Bulletin. He has written *The Experience of War* and several biographies.

Ray Bradbury

Ray Bradbury (1920–   ), science-fiction writer, was born in Waukegan, Illinois. Descendent of a long line of American editors and publishers, Bradbury became interested in science fiction and fantasy at an early age. He religiously followed the comic strip adventures of Buck Rogers and Tarzan. After writing for obscure magazines for several years, Bradbury made his first quality sale to the *American Mercury* in 1945. Since then, his stories have appeared in numerous national magazines and short story anthologies. His best-known books are *The Illustrated Man, The October Country, The Martian Chronicles,* and *Dandelion Wine.*

Lenore Marshall

Lenore Marshall (1899–1971) was born in New York City and lived there and in New Hope, Pennsylvania, most of her life. A graduate of Barnard College, she was married to James Marshall, a lawyer and political scientist. She published novels, short stories, poetry, and articles. Her work appeared in such magazines as *Saturday Review, Harper's, The New Yorker,* and *The New Republic.*

Homer

There is actually very little known about Homer, who may have lived about 800 B.C. There are no facts to prove that such a person even existed. However, the ancient Greeks believed that an old, blind, wandering poet named Homer composed the two great Greek epics, the *Iliad* and the *Odyssey,* and that he went about from place to place reciting these stirring tales.

So great was the honor accorded these stories that no fewer than seven cities of the ancient Greek world claimed to be Homer's birthplace. For centuries Greek schoolboys learned to know by heart some version of these Homeric poems. Groups of men devoted their lives to preserving, reshaping, and reciting these verses of the deeds and legends of the men who fought at Troy.

Some scholars, probing the mists of antiquity, believe that the two epics were the works of many men. Other scholars simply accept the legend that such a person as Homer did exist. The question of the authorship is really not too important. What is important is the fact that we have these great stories that are still the basis of Western classical education in every part of the world.

WITH WHAT YOU HAVE

Phizzog

This face you got,
This here phizzog you carry around,
You never picked it out for yourself, at all,
    at all—did you?
This here phizzog—somebody handed it to
    you—am I right?
Somebody said, "Here's yours, now go see
    what you can do with it."
Somebody slipped it to you and it was like a
    package marked:
"No goods exchanged after being taken
    away"—
This face you got.

CARL SANDBURG

From *Good Morning, America,* copyright, 1928, 1956, by Carl Sandburg. Reprinted by permission of Harcourt Brace Jovanovich, Inc.

Without eyes to help him, the blind botanist continues his work by means of the senses he still has. Here the fingering of the thorny plant symbolizes this act of continuing courage.

"The Blind Botanist" by Ben Shahn. Courtesy of the Wichita Art Museum.

"Make the most of yourself, for that is all there is of you."—Ralph Waldo Emerson

A boy in a city ghetto is shamed by his teacher because he wants to prove that he has a father like everyone else. An infant girl is left blind and deaf by a searing fever. A small slave child, ruthlessly kidnapped, is redeemed for a broken-down race horse.

When he grows older, Dick Gregory, the boy shamed by his teacher, gains fame as a comedian and author. The infant girl, Helen Keller, grows into an outstanding woman who "sees" and "hears" with more perception than many persons who have perfect sight and hearing. The kidnapped child, George Washington Carver, because of his great knowledge about growing things and his ability to "make something from nothing," becomes one of America's foremost scientists.

Each of us is born with particular physical characteristics. Each of us is born into a particular environment. Each of us must take "what we have" and go from there.

Some people seem to be able to do everything quite easily. They never seem to have any real problems. They are popular and good-looking. They are good in sports or smart in class, or both. They can sing or play musical instruments. Their clothes look "right," and they have money to buy the things they want. Others do not seem to be that fortunate. They may have so many handicaps, real or imagined, that it seems unlikely that their natural abilities will ever be developed. But these handicaps can become assets in that they force people to work harder to find a place for themselves—a place where they feel useful and secure. Also, many of the people who seem to have everything going for them really have problems that trouble them a great deal.

The lives of individuals who struggle to cope with themselves in their environments and who take "what they have" and manage to achieve some triumph, great or small, are found in biography, short stories, plays, and poems. The young person who reads of the longings, hopes, fears, frustrations, and triumphs of such people knows that he has feelings in common with others— in dreaming his dreams, he is not alone.

◆

"...man has two ways out
in life—laughing or crying."
Dick Gregory, well-known black comedian and
author, was brought up to believe that
crying will get you
nowhere.

Not Poor, Just Broke

DICK GREGORY

Like a lot of Negro kids, we never would have made it without our Momma. When there was no fatback to go with the beans, no socks to go with the shoes, no hope to go with tomorrow, she'd smile and say: "We ain't poor, we're just broke." Poor is a state of mind you never grow out of, but being broke is just a temporary condition. She always had a big smile, even when her legs and feet swelled from high blood pressure and she collapsed across the table with sugar diabetes. You have to smile twenty-four hours a day, Momma would say. If you walk through life showing the aggravation you've gone through, people will feel sorry for you, and they'll never respect you. She taught us that man has two ways out in life—laughing or crying. There's more hope in laughing. A man can fall down the stairs and lie there in such pain and horror that his own wife will collapse and faint at the sight. But if he can just hold back his pain for a minute she might be able to collect herself and call the doctor. It might mean the difference between his living to laugh again or dying there on the spot.

So you laugh, so you smile. Once a month the big gray relief truck would pull up in front of our house and Momma would flash that big smile and stretch out her hands. "Who else you know in this neighborhood gets this kind of service?" And we could all feel proud when the neighbors, folks who weren't on relief, folks who had Daddies in their houses, would come by the back porch for some of those hundred pounds of potatoes, for some sugar and flour and salty fish. We'd stand out there on the back porch and hand out the food like we were in charge of helping poor people, and then we'd take the food they brought us in return.

And Momma came home one hot summer day and found we'd been evicted, thrown out into the streetcar zone with all our orange-crate chairs and secondhand lamps. She flashed that big smile and dried our tears and bought some penny Kool-Aid. We stood out there and sold drinks to thirsty people coming off the streetcar, and we thought nobody knew we were kicked out—figured they thought we *wanted* to be there. And Momma went off to talk the landlord into letting us back in on credit.

But I wonder about my Momma sometimes, and all the other Negro mothers who got up at 6 A.M. to go to the white man's house with sacks over their shoes because it was so wet and cold. I wonder how they made it. They worked very hard for the man, they made his breakfast and they scrubbed his floors and they diapered his babies. They didn't have too much time for us.

I wonder about my Momma, who walked out of a white woman's clean house at midnight and came back to her own where the lights had been out for three months, and the pipes were frozen and the wind came in through the cracks. She'd have to make deals with the rats: leave some food out for them so they wouldn't gnaw on the doors or bite the babies. The roaches, they were just like part of the family.

I wonder how she felt telling those white kids she took care of to brush their teeth after they ate, to wash their hands. She could never

From the book *Nigger: An Autobiography* by Dick Gregory with Robert Lipsyte. Copyright © 1964 by Dick Gregory Enterprises, Inc. Published by E. P. Dutton & Co., Inc. and used with their permission.

tell her own kids because there wasn't soap or water back home.

I wonder how my Momma felt when we came home from school with a list of vitamins and pills and cod liver oils the school nurse said we had to have. Momma would cry all night, and then go out and spend most of the rent money for pills. A week later, the white man would come for his eighteen dollars rent and Momma would plead with him to wait until tomorrow. She had lost her pocketbook. The relief check was coming. The white folks had some money for her. Tomorrow. I'd be hiding in the coal closet because there was only supposed to be two kids in the flat, and I could hear the rent man curse my Momma and call her a liar. And when he finally went away, Momma put the sacks on her shoes and went off to the rich white folks' house to dress the rich white kids so their mother could take them to a special baby doctor.

Momma had to take us to Homer G. Phillips, the free hospital, the city hospital for Negroes. We'd stand on line and wait for hours, smiling and Uncle Tomming every time a doctor or a nurse passed by. We'd feel good when one of them smiled back and didn't look at us as though we were dirty and had no right coming down there. All the doctors and nurses at Homer G. Phillips were Negro, too.

I remember one time when a doctor in white walked up and said: "What's wrong with him?" as if he didn't believe that anything was.

Momma looked at me and looked at him and shook her head. "I sure don't know, Doctor, but he cried all night long. Held his stomach."

"Bring him in and get his clothes off."

I was so mad the way he was talking to my Momma that I bit down too hard on the thermometer. It broke in my mouth. The doctor slapped me across my face.

"Both of you go stand in the back of the line and wait your turn."

My Momma had to say: "I'm sorry, Doctor," and go to the back of the line. She had five other kids at home and she never knew when she'd have to bring another down to the city hospital.

And those rich white folks Momma was so proud of. She'd sit around with the other women and they'd talk about how good their white folks were. They'd lie about how rich they were, what nice parties they gave, what good clothes they wore. And how they were going to be remembered in their white folks' wills. The next morning the white lady would say: "We're going on vacation for two months, Lucille, we won't be needing you until we get back." Two-month vacation without pay.

I wonder how my Momma stayed so good and beautiful in her soul when she worked seven days a week on swollen legs and feet, how she kept teaching us to smile and laugh when the house was dark and cold and she never knew when one of her hungry kids was going to ask about Daddy.

I wonder how she kept from teaching us hate when the social worker came around. She was a nasty woman with a pinched face who said: "We have reason to suspect you are working, Miss Gregory, and you can be sure I'm going to check on you. We don't stand for welfare cheaters."

Momma, a welfare cheater. A criminal who couldn't stand to see her kids go hungry, or grow up in slums and end up mugging people in dark corners. I guess the system didn't want her to get off relief, the way it kept sending social workers around to be sure Momma wasn't trying to make things better.

I remember how that social worker would poke around the house, wrinkling her nose at the coal dust on the chilly linoleum floor, shaking her head at the bugs crawling over the dirty dishes in the sink. My Momma would have to stand there and make like she was too lazy to keep her own house clean. She could never let on that she spent all day cleaning another woman's house for two dollars and carfare. She would have to follow that nasty woman around those drafty three rooms, keeping her fingers crossed that the telephone hidden in the closet wouldn't ring. Welfare cases weren't supposed to have telephones.

But Momma figured that some day the Gregory kids were going to get off North Taylor Street and into a world where they would have to compete with kids who grew up with telephones in their houses. She didn't want us to be at a disadvantage. She couldn't explain that to the social worker. And she couldn't explain that while she was out spoon-feeding somebody else's kids, she was worrying about her own kids, that she could rest her mind by picking up the telephone and calling us—to find out if we had bread for our baloney or baloney for our bread, to see if any of us had gotten run over by the streetcar while we played in the gutter, to make sure the house hadn't burnt down from the papers and magazines we stuffed in the stove when the coal ran out.

But sometimes when she called there would be no answer. Home was a place to be only when all other places were closed.

I never learned hate at home, or shame. I had to go to school for that. I was about seven years old when I got my first big lesson. I was in love with a little girl named Helene Tucker, a light-complected little girl with pigtails and nice manners. She was always clean and she was smart in school. I think I went to school then mostly to look at her. I brushed my hair and even got me a little old handkerchief. It was a lady's handkerchief, but I didn't want Helene to see me wipe my nose on my hand. The pipes were frozen again, there was no water in the house, but I washed my socks and shirt every night. I'd get a pot, and go over to Mister Ben's grocery store, and stick my pot down into his soda machine. Scoop out some chopped ice. By evening the ice melted to water

for washing. I got sick a lot that winter because the fire would go out at night before the clothes were dry. In the morning I'd put them on, wet or dry, because they were the only clothes I had.

Everybody's got a Helene Tucker, a symbol of everything you want. I loved her for her goodness, her cleanness, her popularity. She'd walk down my street and my brothers and sisters would yell, "Here comes Helene," and I'd rub my tennis sneakers on the back of my pants and wish my hair wasn't so nappy and the white folks' shirt fit me better. I'd run out on the street. If I knew my place and didn't come too close, she'd wink at me and say hello. That was a good feeling. Sometimes I'd follow her all the way home, and shovel the snow off her walk and try to make friends with her Momma and her aunts. I'd drop money on her stoop late at night on my way back from shining shoes in the taverns. And she had a Daddy, and he had a good job. He was a paper hanger.

I guess I would have gotten over Helene by summertime, but something happened in that classroom that made her face hang in front of me for the next twenty-two years. When I played the drums in high school it was for Helene and when I broke track records in college it was for Helene and when I started standing behind microphones and heard applause I wished Helene could hear it, too. It wasn't until I was twenty-nine years old and married and making money that I finally got her out of my system. Helene was sitting in that classroom when I learned to be ashamed of myself.

It was on a Thursday. I was sitting in the back of the room, in a seat with a chalk circle drawn around it. The idiot's seat, the troublemaker's seat.

The teacher thought I was stupid. Couldn't spell, couldn't read, couldn't do arithmetic. Just stupid. Teachers were never interested in finding out that you couldn't concentrate because you were so hungry, because you hadn't had any breakfast. All you could think about was noontime, would it ever come? Maybe you could sneak into the cloakroom and steal a bite of some kid's lunch out of a coat pocket. A bite of something. Paste. You can't really make a meal of paste, or put it on bread for a sandwich, but sometimes I'd scoop a few spoonfuls out of the paste jar in the back of the room. Pregnant people get strange tastes. I was pregnant with poverty. Pregnant with dirt and pregnant with smells that made people turn away, pregnant with cold and pregnant with shoes that were never bought for me, pregnant with five other people in my bed and no Daddy in the next room, and pregnant with hunger. Paste doesn't taste too bad when you're hungry.

The teacher thought I was a troublemaker. All she saw from the front of the room was a little black boy who squirmed in his idiot's seat and made noises and poked the kids around him. I guess she couldn't see a kid who made noises because he wanted someone to know he was there.

It was on a Thursday, the day before the Negro payday. The eagle always flew on Friday. The teacher was asking each student how much his father would give to the Community Chest. On Friday night, each kid would get the money from his father, and on Monday he would bring it to the school. I decided I was going to buy me a Daddy right then. I had money in my pocket from shining shoes and selling papers, and whatever Helene Tucker pledged for her Daddy I was going to top it. And I'd hand the money right in. I wasn't going to wait until Monday to buy me a Daddy.

I was shaking, scared to death. The teacher opened her book and started calling out names alphabetically.

"Helene Tucker?"

"My Daddy said he'd give two dollars and fifty cents."

"That's very nice, Helene. Very, very nice indeed."

That made me feel pretty good. It wouldn't take too much to top that. I had almost three dollars in dimes and quarters in my pocket. I stuck my hand in my pocket and held onto the money, waiting for her to call my name. But the teacher closed her book after she called everybody else in the class.

I stood up and raised my hand.

"What is it now?"

"You forgot me."

She turned toward the blackboard. "I don't have time to be playing with you, Richard."

"My Daddy said he'd . . ."

"Sit down, Richard, you're disturbing the class."

"My Daddy said he'd give . . . fifteen dollars."

She turned around and looked mad. "We are collecting this money for you and your kind, Richard Gregory. If your Daddy can give fifteen dollars you have no business being on relief."

"I got it right now, I got it right now, my Daddy gave it to me to turn in today, my Daddy said . . ."

"And furthermore," she said, looking right at me, her nostrils getting big and her lips getting thin and her eyes opening wide, "we know you don't have a Daddy."

Helene Tucker turned around, her eyes full of tears. She felt sorry for me. Then I couldn't see her too well because I was crying, too.

"Sit down, Richard."

And I always thought the teacher kind of liked me. She always picked me to wash the blackboard on Friday, after school. That was a big thrill, it made me feel important. If I didn't wash it, come Monday the school might not function right.

"Where are you going, Richard?"

I walked out of school that day, and for a long time I didn't go back very often. There was shame there.

Now there was shame everywhere. It seemed like the whole world had been inside that classroom, everyone had heard what the teacher had said, everyone had turned around and felt sorry for me. There was shame in going to the Worthy Boys Annual Christmas Dinner for you and your kind, because everybody knew what a worthy boy was. Why couldn't they just call it the Boys Annual Dinner, why'd they have to give it a name? There was shame in wearing the brown and orange and white plaid mackinaw the welfare gave to 3,000 boys. Why'd it have to be the same for everybody so when you walked down the street the people could see you were on relief? It was a nice warm mackinaw and it had a hood, and my Momma beat me and called me a little rat when she found out I stuffed it in the bottom of a pail full of garbage way over on Cottage Street. There was shame in running over to Mister Ben's at the end of the day and asking for his rotten peaches, there was shame in asking Mrs. Simmons for a spoonful of sugar, there was shame in running out to meet the relief truck. I hated that truck, full of food for you and your kind. I ran into the house and hid when it came. And then I started to sneak through alleys, to take the long way home so the people going into White's Eat Shop wouldn't see me. Yeah, the whole world heard the teacher that day, we all know you don't have a Daddy.

It lasted for a while, this kind of numbness. I spent a lot of time feeling sorry for myself. And then one day I met this wino in a restaurant. I'd been out hustling all day, shining shoes, selling newspapers, and I had goo-gobs of money in my pocket. Bought me a bowl of chili for fifteen cents, and a cheeseburger for fifteen cents, and a Pepsi for five cents, and a piece of chocolate cake for ten cents. That was a good meal. I was eating when this old wino came in. I love winos because they never hurt anyone but themselves.

The old wino sat down at the counter and ordered twenty-six cents worth of food. He ate it like he really enjoyed it. When the owner, Mister Williams, asked him to pay the check, the old wino didn't lie or go through his pocket like he suddenly found a hole.

He just said: "Don't have no money."

The owner yelled: "Why did you come in here and eat my food if you don't have no money? That food cost me money."

Mister Williams jumped over the counter and knocked the wino off his stool and beat him over the head with a pop bottle. Then he stepped back and watched the wino bleed. Then he kicked him. And he kicked him again.

I looked at the wino with blood all over his face and I went over. "Leave him alone, Mister Williams. I'll pay the twenty-six cents."

The wino got up, slowly, pulling himself up to the stool, then up to the counter, holding on for a minute until his legs stopped shaking so bad. He looked at me with pure hate. "Keep your twenty-six cents. You don't have to pay, not now. I just finished paying for it."

He started to walk out, and as he passed me, he reached down and touched my shoulder. "Thanks, sonny, but it's too late now. Why didn't you pay it before?"

I was pretty sick about that. I waited too long to help another man.

I remember a white lady who came to our door once around Thanksgiving time. She wore a woolly, green bonnet around her head, and she smiled a lot.

"Is your mother home, little boy?"

"No, she ain't."

"May I come in?'

"What do you want, ma'am?"

She didn't stop smiling once, but she sighed a little when she bent down and lifted up a big yellow basket. The kind I saw around church that were called Baskets for the Needy.

"This is for you."

"What's in there?"

"All sorts of good things," she said, smiling. "There's candy and potatoes and cake and cranberry sauce and"—she made a funny little face at me by wrinkling up her nose—"and a great big fat turkey for Thanksgiving dinner."

"Is it cooked?"

"A big fat juicy turkey, all plucked clean for you...."

"Is it cooked?"

"No, it's not...."

"We ain't got nothing in the house to cook it with, lady."

I slammed the door in her face. Wouldn't that be great, to have a turkey like that in the house with no way to cook it? No gas, no electricity, no coal. Just a big fat juicy raw turkey.

I remember Mister Ben, the grocery-store man, a round little white man with funny little tufts of white hair on his head and sad-looking eyes. His face was kind of gray-colored, and the skin was loose and shook when he talked.

"Momma want a loaf of bread, Mister Ben, fresh bread."

"Right away, Richard," he'd say and get the bread he bought three days old from the bakeries downtown. It was the only kind he had for his credit-book customers. He dropped it on the counter. Clunk.

I'd hand him the credit book, that green tablet with the picture of the snuff can on it, to write down how much we owed him. He'd lick the tip of that stubby pencil he kept behind his ear. Six cents.

"How you like school, Richard?"

"I like school fine, Mister Ben."

"Good boy, you study, get smart."

I'd run home to Momma and tell her that the bread wasn't fresh bread, it was stale bread. She'd flash the big smile.

"Oh, that Mister Ben, he knew I was fixin to make toast."

The peaches were rotten and the bread wasn't fresh and sometimes the butter was green, but when it came down to the nitty-gritty you could always go to Mister Ben. Before a Jewish holiday he'd take all the food that was going to spoil while the store was shut and bring it over to our house. Before Christmas he'd send over some meat even though he knew it was going on the tablet and he might never see his money. When the push came to the shove and every hungry belly in the house was beginning to eat on itself, Momma could go to Mister Ben and always get enough for some kind of dinner.

But I can remember three days in a row I went into Mister Ben's and asked him to give me a penny Mr. Goodbar from the window.

Three days in a row he said: "Out, out, or I'll tell your Momma you been begging."

One night I threw a brick through his window and took it.

The next day I went into Mister Ben's to get some bread for Momma and his skin was shaking and I heard him tell a lady, "I can't understand why should anybody break my window for a penny piece of candy, a lousy piece of candy, all they got to do is ask, that's all, and I give."

THERE'S MORE HOPE IN LAUGHING

Discuss the incidents about the church basket, Mister Ben, and the candy bar. How do you know from these incidents that Dick Gregory might easily have become different?

II

IMPLICATIONS

1. "Poor is a state of mind you never grow out of, but being broke is just a temporary condition."

2. "If you walk through life showing the aggravation you've gone through, people will ... never respect you."

III

TECHNIQUES

Characterization

1. How does "Momma" keep her kids from feeling shame when the relief truck comes?

2. What did she do when the family was evicted?

3. Why might she have been bitter and filled with hate?

TECHNIQUES

Characterization

A person who appears in a piece of literature, whether it is fiction or nonfiction, is referred to as a character. A writer who wants to tell you what a character is like has five commonly used ways to do this. He may tell you:

1. What the character looks like;
2. What the character says and thinks;
3. What others say and think about the character;
4. The way the character acts in a given situation;
5. The way others act toward the character.

Some of the most vivid characterizations are found in fiction—made up stories, poems, and plays. Usually, when a character in fiction seems real and alive, it is because he or she is like someone the reader knows or knows about in real life.

In a nonfiction autobiographical account, such as "Not Poor, Just Broke," the writer has the task of showing his own character. Dick Gregory does this by making frequent use of the second characterization technique listed above—what the character says and thinks. As an example, see if you can recall what Dick thought about when he went to school hungry and the teacher put him in the troublemaker's seat. Discuss what the teacher thought of Dick when she looked at him and his behavior. Discuss the author's description of the scene in the classroom when Dick tries to buy himself a Daddy. Discuss how he reveals much about the teacher's character as well as his own. How many of the characterization techniques listed above are used in this scene?

Significant Details

A character cannot be developed into a memorable person, nor can a story be written so that it seems real without the use of details. However, a writer, either of fiction or nonfiction, cannot tell every real or imagined event in the lives of his characters. He must select only those details that will have the most meaning or give the best insight. For example, in "Not Poor, Just Broke," Dick Gregory chooses to tell about his experience with the old wino in the restaurant.

Note how in his relating of this experience, Dick Gregory provides additional insight into his own character. Describe the wino's reaction after Dick offers to pay the twenty-six cents the wino owes. With what significant comment does Dick Gregory conclude his telling of this experience?

AUTO | BIO | GRAPHY
self | life | to draw

Take the prefix *bio*, meaning "life," and add to it the stem *graph*, meaning "to draw" or "to write." Biography, then, means the drawing or writing of someone's life. Now take another prefix, *auto*, which means "self," and place it before "biography." What do you think "autobiography" means? Why is "Not Poor, Just Broke" an autobiography?

How the autobiographer handles his material is a matter of personal choice. Since he is writing about his own life, he may be very selective and share with the reader only those things he wishes known about himself. He may fictionalize his story to the extent that he re-creates scenes by recalling conversations, thoughts, and actions as accurately as possible, or he may use an entirely factual approach and include actual documents to substantiate any statements he makes. Which method is found in "Not Poor, Just Broke"?

How the biographer handles his material is a matter of personal choice just as it is for the autobiographer. He may limit himself to facts alone—actual records, diaries, letters, interviews, authentic documents. The factual biographer never puts words into his characters' mouths unless he has evidence that they really spoke those words. Factual biography, however, is less popular than biography that is fictionalized to some extent. In fictionalizing biography, the author does painstaking research about his subject, then puts his information together with imagination. He may invent possible incidents and make up conversations in order to have his biography read like a story. If the author is successful, the reader gains much insight into the individual about whom he is reading.

The collection WITH WHAT YOU HAVE speaks of the hope and courage with which handicaps and hardships are overcome and great things achieved. Quiet strength and determined purpose are the stuff of which these records of human victories are made.

TWO YOUNG WOMEN PLAYING CAT'S CRADLE
Suzuki Harunobu
The Metropolitan Museum of Art,
Bequest of Mrs. H. O. Havemeyer, 1929,
The H. O. Havemeyer Collection

Although these works of art are widely removed in time and mood, both of them reflect the special quality of children to imaginatively use unimpressive things. The Japanese girls in the quiet Harunobu woodcut are engrossed in a game of cat's cradle. With a simple piece of string they create a serene world of their own. In contrast, the children in Shahn's painting are playing in a ravaged world, but they have not been able to achieve a feeling of serenity in their play.

LIBERATION
Ben Shahn
Tempera on composition board,
Collection, James Thrall Soby

161

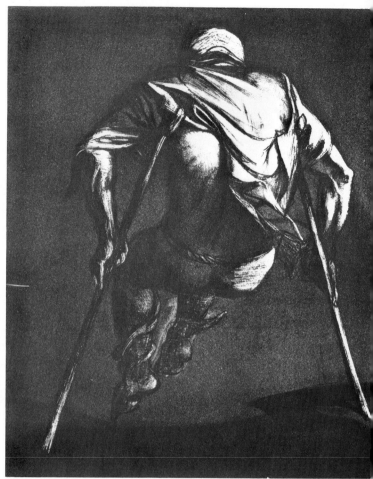

THE BLIND GIRL
Ejnar Nielsen
Hirshsprung Collection, Copenhagen

RABBIT
Rico Lebrun

The dignity, power, and inner resourcefulness with which physical handicaps are often faced is reflected in the serene painting BLIND GIRL and in the forceful lithograph of a cripple. In a different vein, FOLK SINGER illustrates how a person can make use of a particular talent that he may have for his own and others' enjoyment.

FOLK SINGER
Charles White

STILL LIFE WITH OIL-LAMP
Juan Gris

These two artists are not bound by a literal interpretation of reality. They have the ability to take ideas or simple objects and transform them through their imaginative vision. Juan Gris, a Spaniard, was a member of the French Cubist movement earlier this century. Josef Albers was a member of a renowned German design school, the Bauhaus. His paintings which explore the possibilities of the square create movement, depth, and endless change from the simplest forms.

HOMAGE TO THE SQUARE: "ASCENDING."
Josef Albers
Oil on composition board, Collection,
Whitney Museum of American Art, New York

Porfirio Díaz ruled as a heartless
dictator in Mexico from 1876 to 1910.
Although he may have loved his country
and promoted its modernization and industrial
growth, he did so at the expense of the
common laborer and landholder.
During his rule, a small portion of the
people became even wealthier than
before and the rest became even more
desperately poor. Díaz muzzled the press and
used his own police force and government
troops to shoot down striking laborers and
control those who dared to criticize him.
Some of the country's intellectual and
political leaders began planning secretly to
overthrow Díaz. For safety, they set up
administrative offices for their council, or
junta (ˈhʊn·tə), in Los Angeles. It was to this
junta, in this story, that a boy named
Felipe Rivera reported one day.

The Mexican

JACK LONDON

1

Nobody knew his history—they of the
junta least of all. He was their "little mystery,"
their "big patriot," and in his way he worked
as hard for the coming Mexican Revolution as
did they. They were tardy in recognizing this,
for not one of the junta liked him. The day he
first drifted into their crowded, busy rooms
they all suspected him of being a spy—one of
the bought tools of the Díaz secret service.
Too many of the comrades were in civil and
military prisons scattered over the United
States, and others of them, in irons, were even

Reprinted by permission of the Jack London Ranch. Permission granted by Irving Shepard copyright owner. Last copyright 1941.

then being taken across the border to be lined
up against adobe walls and shot.

At the first sight the boy did not impress
them favorably. Boy he was, not more than
eighteen and not overlarge for his years. He
announced that he was Felipe Rivera, and
that it was his wish to work for the revolution. That was all—not a wasted word, no
further explanation. He stood waiting. There
was no smile on his lips, no geniality in his
eyes. Big, dashing Paulino Vera felt an inward shudder. Here was something forbidding, terrible, inscrutable. There was something venomous and snakelike in the boy's
black eyes. They burned like cold fire, as with
a vast, concentrated bitterness. He flashed
them from the faces of the conspirators to the
typewriter which little Mrs. Sethby was industriously operating. His eyes rested on hers
but an instant—she had chanced to look up—
and she, too, sensed the nameless something
that made her pause. She was compelled to
read back in order to regain the swing of the
letter she was writing.

Paulino Vera looked questioningly at Arrellano and Ramos, and questioningly they
looked back and to each other. The indecision
of doubt brooded in their eyes. This slender
boy was the Unknown, vested with all the
menace of the Unknown. He was unrecognizable, something quite beyond the ken of
honest, ordinary revolutionists whose fiercest
hatred for Díaz and his tyranny after all was
only that of honest and ordinary patriots.
Here was something else, they knew not what.
But Vera, always the most impulsive, the
quickest to act, stepped into the breach.

"Very well," he said coldly. "You say you
want to work for the revolution. Take off your
coat. Hang it over there. I will show you—
come—where are the buckets and cloths. The
floor is dirty. You will begin by scrubbing it,
and by scrubbing the floors of the other
rooms. The spittoons need to be cleaned.
Then there are the windows."

"Is it for the revolution?" the boy asked.

"It is for the revolution," Vera answered.

Rivera looked cold suspicion at all of them, then proceeded to take off his coat.

"It is well," he said.

And nothing more. Day after day he came to his work—sweeping, scrubbing, cleaning. He emptied the ashes from the stoves, brought up the coal and kindling, and lighted the fires before the most energetic one of them was at his desk.

"Can I sleep here?" he asked once.

Aha! So that was it—the hand of Díaz showing through! To sleep in the rooms of the junta meant access to their secrets, to the lists of names, to the addresses of comrades down on Mexican soil. The request was denied, and Rivera never spoke of it again. He slept they knew not where, and ate they knew not where or how. Once Arrellano offered him a couple of dollars. Rivera declined the money with a shake of the head. When Vera joined in and tried to press it upon him, he said:

"I am working for the revolution."

It takes money to raise a modern revolution, and always the junta was pressed. The members starved and toiled, and the longest day was none too long, and yet there were times when it appeared as if the revolution stood or fell on no more than the matter of a few dollars. Once, the first time, when the rent of the house was two months behind and the landlord was threatening dispossession, it was Felipe Rivera, the scrub boy in the poor, cheap clothes, worn and threadbare, who laid $60 in gold on May Sethby's desk. There were other times. Three hundred letters, clicked out on the busy typewriters (appeals for assistance, for sanctions from the organized labor groups, requests for square news deals to the editors of newspapers, protests against the high-handed treatment of revolutionists by the United States courts), lay unmailed, awaiting postage. Vera's watch had disappeared—the old-fashioned gold repeater that had been his father's. Likewise had gone the plain gold band from May Sethby's third finger. Things were desperate. Ramos and Arrellano pulled their long moustaches in

despair. The letters must go off and the post office allowed no credit to purchasers of stamps. Then it was that Rivera put on his hat and went out. When he came back he laid a thousand two-cent stamps on May Sethby's desk.

"I wonder if it is the cursed gold of Díaz?" said Vera to the comrades.

They elevated their brows and could not decide. And Felipe Rivera, the scrubber for the revolution, continued, as occasion arose, to lay down gold and silver for the junta's use.

And still they could not bring themselves to like him. They did not know him. His ways were not theirs. He gave no confidences. He repelled all probing. Youth that he was, they could never nerve themselves to dare to question him.

"A great and lonely spirit, perhaps. I do not know, I do not know," Arrellano said helplessly.

"He is not human," said Ramos.

"His soul has been seared," said May Sethby. "Light and laughter have been burned out of him. He is like one dead, and yet he is fearfully alive."

"He has been through a lot," said Vera. "No man could look like that who has not been through a lot—and he is only a boy."

Yet they could not like him. He never talked, never inquired, never suggested. He would stand listening, expressionless, a thing dead, save for his eyes, coldly burning, while their talk of the revolution ran high and warm. From face to face and speaker to speaker his eyes would turn, boring like gimlets of incandescent ice, disconcerting and perturbing.

"He is no spy," Vera confided to May Sethby. "He is a patriot—mark me, the greatest patriot of us all. I know it, I feel it, here in my heart and head I feel it. But him I know not at all."

"He has a bad temper," said May Sethby.

"I know," said Vera with a shudder. "He has looked at me with those eyes of his. They do not love; they threaten; they are savage as a wild tiger's. I know, if I should prove unfaithful to the cause, that he would kill me. He has no heart. He is pitiless as steel, keen and cold as frost. He is like moonshine in a winter night when a man freezes to death on some lonely mountain top. I am not afraid of Díaz and all his killers; but this boy, of him am I afraid. I tell you true. I am afraid. He is the breath of death."

Yet Vera it was who persuaded the others to give the first trust to Rivera. The line of communication between Los Angeles and Lower Califronia had broken down. Three of the comrades had dug their own graves and been shot into them. Two more were United States prisoners in Los Angeles. Juan Alvarado, the federal commander, was a monster. All their plans did he checkmate. They could no longer gain access to the active revolutionists, and the incipient ones, in Lower California.

Young Rivera was given his instructions and dispatched south. When he returned, the line of communication was reestablished, and Juan Alvarado was dead. He had been found in bed, a knife hilt-deep in his breast. This had exceeded Rivera's instructions, but they of the junta knew the times of his movements. They did not ask him. He said nothing. But they looked at one another and conjectured.

"I have told you," said Vera. "Díaz has more to fear from this youth than from any man. He is implacable. He is the hand of God."

The bad temper, mentioned by May Sethby, and sensed by them all, was evidenced by physical proofs. Now he appeared with a cut lip, a blackened cheek, or a swollen ear. It was patent that he brawled, somewhere in that outside world where he ate and slept, gained money, and moved in ways unknown to them. As the time passed he had come to set type for the little revolutionary sheet they published weekly. There were occasions when he was unable to set type, when his knuckles were bruised and battered, when his thumbs were injured and helpless, when one arm or the other hung wearily at his side while his face was drawn with unspoken pain.

"A wastrel," said Arrellano.

"A frequenter of low places," said Ramos.

"But where does he get the money?" Vera demanded. "Only today, just now, have I learned that he paid the bill for white paper—$140."

"There are his absences," said May Sethby. "He never explains them."

"We should set a spy upon him," Ramos propounded.

"I should not care to be that spy," said Vera. "I fear you would never see me again, save to bury me. He has a terrible passion. Not even God would he permit to stand between him and the way of his passion."

"I feel like a child before him," Ramos confessed.

"To me he is power—he is the primitive, the wild wolf, the striking rattlesnake, the stinging centipede," said Arrellano.

"He is the revolution incarnate," said Vera. "He is the flame and the spirit of it, the insatiable cry for vengeance that makes no cry but that slays noiselessly. He is a destroying angel moving through the still watches of the night."

"I could weep over him," said May Sethby. "He knows nobody. He hates all people. Us he tolerates, for we are the way of his desire. He is alone . . . lonely." Her voice broke in a half sob and there was dimness in her eyes.

Rivera's ways and times were truly mysterious. There were periods when they did not see him for a week at a time. Once he was away a month. These occasions were always capped by his return, when, without advertisement or speech, he laid gold coins on May Sethby's desk. Again, for days and weeks, he spent all his time with the junta. And yet again, for irregular periods, he would disappear through the heart of each day, from early morning until late afternoon. At such times he came early and remained late. Arrellano had found him at midnight, setting type with fresh-swollen knuckles, or mayhap it was his lip, new split, that still bled.

2

The time of the crisis approached. Whether or not the revolution would be depended upon the junta, and the junta was hard-pressed. The need for money was greater than ever before, while money was harder to get. Patriots had given their last cent and now could give no more. Section-gang laborers—fugitive peons[1] from Mexico—were contributing half their scanty wages. But more than that was needed. The heartbreaking, conspiring, undermining toil of years approached fruition. The time was ripe. The revolution hung on the balance. One shove more, one last heroic effort, and it would tremble across the scales to victory. They knew their Mexico. Once started, the revolution would take care of itself. The whole Díaz machine would go down like a house of cards. Díaz could not resist. The people would rise. The defenses of city after city would crumple up. State after state would totter down. And at last, from every side, the victorious armies of the revolution would close in on the city of Mexico itself, Díaz's last stronghold.

But the money. They had the men, impatient and urgent, who would use the guns. They knew the traders who would sell and deliver the guns. But to culture the revolution thus far had exhausted the junta. The last dollar had been spent, the last resource and the last starving patriot milked dry, and the great adventure still trembled on the scales. Guns and ammunition! The ragged battalions must be armed. But how? Ramos lamented his confiscated estates. Arrellano wailed the spendthriftness of his youth. May Sethby wondered if it would have been different had they of the junta been more economical in the past.

"To think that the freedom of Mexico should stand or fall on a few paltry thousands of dollars," said Paulino Vera.

Despair was in all their faces. José Amarillo, their last hope, a recent convert who had promised money, had been apprehended at his hacienda[2] in Chihuahua[3] and shot against his own stable wall. The news had just come through.

Rivera, on his knees, scrubbing, looked up, with suspended brush, his bare arms flecked with soapy, dirty water.

"Will 5,000 do it?" he asked.

They looked their amazement. Vera nodded and swallowed. He could not speak, but he was on the instant invested with a vast faith.

"Order the guns," Rivera said, and thereupon was guilty of the longest flow of words they had ever heard him utter. "The time is short. In three weeks I shall bring you the 5,000. It is well. The weather will be warmer for those who fight. Also, it is the best I can do."

Vera fought his faith. It was incredible. Too many fond hopes had been shattered since he had begun to play the revolution game. He believed this threadbare scrubber of the revolution, and yet he dared not believe.

"You are crazy," he said.

"In three weeks," said Rivera. "Order the guns."

He got up, rolled down his sleeves, and put on his coat.

"Order the guns," he said. "I am going now."

3

After hurrying and scurrying, much telephoning and bad language, a night session was held in Kelly's office. Kelly was rushed with business; also, he was unlucky. He had brought Danny Ward out from New York, arranged the fight for him with Billy Carthey,

---

1. **peons**\\ˈpē·ŏnz\\ unskilled farm workers.
2. **hacienda**\a ˈsyĕn·da\ a large estate or ranch, or the house of the owner of the estate.
3. **Chihuahua**\chē ˈwa·wa\ the capital city of the state of Chihuahua in northeast Mexico.

the date was three weeks away, and for two days now, carefully concealed from the sporting writers, Carthey had been laid up, badly injured. There was no one to take his place. Kelly had been burning the wires east to every eligible lightweight, but they were tied up with dates and contracts. And now hope had revived, though faintly.

"You've got some nerve," Kelly addressed Rivera, after one look, as soon as they got together.

Hate that was malignant was in Rivera's eyes, but his face remained impassive.

"I can lick Ward," was all he said.

"How do you know? Ever see him fight?"

Rivera shook his head.

"He can beat you up with one hand and both eyes closed."

Rivera shrugged his shoulders.

"Haven't you got anything to say?" the fight promoter snarled.

"I can lick him."

"Who'd you ever fight, anyway?" Michael Kelly demanded. Michael was the promoter's brother, and ran the Yellowstone Poolrooms, where he made goodly sums on the fight game.

Rivera favored him with a bitter, unanswering stare.

The promoter's secretary, a distinctively sporty young man, sneered audibly.

"Well, you know Roberts," Kelly broke the hostile silence. "He ought to be here. I've sent for him. Sit down and wait, though from the looks of you, you haven't got a chance. I can't throw the public down with a bum fight. Ringside seats are selling at $15; you know that."

When Roberts arrived it was patent that he was mildly drunk. He was a tall, lean, slack-jointed individual, and his walk, like his talk, was a smooth and languid drawl.

Kelly went straight to the point.

"Look here, Roberts, you've been braggin' you discovered this little Mexican. You know Carthey's broken his arm. Well, this little yellow streak has the gall to blow in today and

say he'll take Carthey's place. What about it?"

"It's all right, Kelly," came the slow response. "He can put up a fight."

"I suppose you'll be sayin' next that he can lick Ward," Kelly snapped.

Roberts considered judicially.

"No, I won't say that. Ward's a topnotcher and a ring general.[4] But he can't hash-house Rivera in short order. I know Rivera. Nobody can get his goat. He ain't got a goat that I could ever discover. And he's a two-handed fighter. He can throw in the sleep-makers from any position."

"Never mind that. What kind of a show can he put up? You've been conditioning and training fighters all your life. I take off my hat to your judgment. Can he give the public a run for its money?"

"He sure can, and he'll worry Ward a mighty heap on top of it. You don't know that boy. I do. I discovered him. He ain't got a goat. He's a devil. He'll make Ward sit up with a show of local talent that'll make the rest of you sit up. I won't say he'll lick Ward, but he'll put up such a show that you'll all know he's a comer."

"All right," Kelly turned to his secretary. "Ring up Ward. I warned him to show up if I thought it worthwhile. He's right across at the Yellowstone, throwin' chests and doing the popular." Kelly turned back to the conditioner. "Have a drink?"

Roberts sipped his highball and unburdened himself.

"Never told you how I discovered the little cuss. It was a couple of years ago he showed up out at the quarters. I was getting Prayne ready for his fight with Delaney. Prayne's wicked. He ain't got a tickle of mercy in his makeup. He'd chopped up his pardners something cruel, and I couldn't find a willing boy that'd work with him. I'd noticed this little starved Mexican kid hanging around, and I was desperate. So I grabbed him, slammed on

4. **ring general,** an experienced fighter who can take full control in a boxing match.

the gloves, and put him in. He was tougher'n rawhide, but weak. And he didn't know the first letter in the alphabet of boxing. Prayne chopped him to ribbons. But he hung on for two sickening rounds, when he fainted. Starvation, that was all. Battered? You couldn't have recognized him. I gave him half a dollar and a square meal. You oughta seen him wolf it down. He hadn't had a bite for a couple of days. That's the end of him, thinks I. But next day he showed up, stiff an' sore, ready for another half and a square meal. And he done better as time went by. Just a born fighter, and tough beyond belief. He hasn't a heart. He's a piece of ice. And he never talked eleven words in a string since I know him. He saws wood and does his work."

"I've seen'm," the secretary said. "He's worked a lot for you."

"All the big little fellows has tried out on him," Roberts answered. "And he's learned from 'em. I've seen some of them he could lick. But his heart wasn't in it. I reckoned he never liked the game. He seemed to act that way."

"He's been fighting some before the little clubs the last few months," Kelly said.

"Sure. But I don't know what struck 'm. All of a sudden his heart got into it. He just went out like a streak and cleaned up all the little local fellows. Seemed to want the money, and he's won a bit, though his clothes don't look it. He's peculiar. Nobody knows his business. Nobody knows how he spends his time. Even when he's on the job, he plumb up and disappears most of each day soon as his work is done. Sometimes he just blows away for weeks at a time. But he don't take advice. There's a fortune in it for the fellow that gets the job of managin' him, only he won't consider it. And you watch him hold out for the cash money when you get down to terms."

It was at this stage that Danny Ward arrived. Quite a party it was. His manager and trainer were with him, and he breezed in like a gusty draught of geniality, good nature, and all-conqueringness. Greetings flew about, a

joke here, a retort there, a smile or a laugh for everybody. Yet it was his way, and only partly sincere. He was a good actor, and he had found geniality a most valuable asset in the game of getting on in the world. But down underneath he was the deliberate, cold-blooded fighter and businessman. The rest was a mask. Those who knew him or trafficked with him said that when it came to brass tacks he was Danny on the Spot. He was invariably present at all business discussions, and it was urged by some that his manager was a blind whose only function was to serve as Danny's mouthpiece.

Rivera's way was different. Indian blood, as well as Spanish, was in his veins, and he sat back in a corner, silent, immobile, only his black eyes passing from face to face and noting everything.

"So that's the guy," Danny said, running an appraising eye over his proposed antagonist. "How de do, old chap?"

Rivera's eyes burned venomously, but he made no sign of acknowledgment.

Danny protested facetiously to the promoter, "You ain't expectin' me to fight a deef mute." When the laughter subsided he made another hit. "Los Angeles must be on the dink when this is the best you can scare up. What kindergarten did you get 'm from?"

"He's good, Danny, take it from me," Roberts defended. "Not as easy as he looks."

"And half the house is sold already," Kelly pleaded. "You'll have to take 'm on, Danny. It's the best we can do."

Danny ran another careless and unflattering glance over Rivera and sighed.

"I gotta be easy with 'm, I guess. If only he don't blow up."

Roberts snorted.

"You gotta be careful," Danny's manager warned. "No taking chances with a dub[5] that's likely to sneak a lucky one across."

"Oh, I'll be careful all right, all right,"

---

5. **dub**\dəb\ a clumsy, unskillful person.

Danny smiled. "I'll get 'm at the start an' nurse 'm along for the dear public's sake. What d'ye say to fifteen rounds, Kelly—an' then the hay for him?"[6]

"That'll do," was the answer. "As long as you make it realistic."

"Then let's get down to biz.' Danny paused and calculated. "Of course, 65 per cent of gate receipts, same as with Carthey. But the split'll be different. Eighty will just about suit me." And to his manager, "That right?"

The manager nodded.

"Here, you, did you get that?" Kelly asked Rivera.

Rivera shook his head.

"Well, it's this way," Kelly explained. "The purse'll be 65 per cent of the gate receipts. You're a dub, and an unknown. You and Danny split, 20 per cent goin' to you, an' 80 to Danny. That's fair, isn't it, Roberts?"

"Very fair," Roberts agreed. "You see, you ain't got a reputation yet."

"What will 65 per cent of the gate receipts be?" Rivera demanded.

"Oh, maybe 5,000, maybe as high as 8,000," Danny broke in to explain. "Something like that. Your share'll come to something like 1,000 or 1,600. Pretty good for takin' a licking from a guy with my reputation. What d'ye say?"

Then Rivera took their breaths away.

"Winner takes all," he said with finality.

A dead silence prevailed.

"It's like candy from a baby," Danny's manager proclaimed.

Danny shook his head.

"I've been in the game too long," he explained. "I'm not casting reflections on the referee or the present company. I'm not sayin' nothing about bookmakers an' frame-ups that sometimes happen. But what I do say is that it's poor business for a fighter like me. I play safe. There's no tellin'. Mebbe I break my arm, eh? Or some guy slips me a bunch of dope." He shook his head solemnly. "Win or lose, 80 is my split. What d'ye say, Mexican?"

Rivera shook his head.

Danny exploded. He was getting down to brass tacks now.

"Why, you dirty little greaser! I've a mind to knock your block off right now."

Roberts placed his body between them.

"Winner takes all," Rivera repeated sullenly.

"Why do you stand out that way?" Danny asked.

"I can lick you," was the straight answer.

Danny half started to take off his coat. But, as his manager knew, it was grandstand play. The coat did not come off, and Danny allowed himself to be placated by the group. Everybody sympathized with him. Rivera stood alone.

"Look here, you little fool," Kelly took up the argument. "You're nobody. We know what you've been doing the last few months— putting away little local fighters. But Danny is class. His next fight after this will be for the championship. And you're unknown. Nobody ever heard of you out of Los Angeles."

"They will," Rivera answered with a shrug, "after this fight."

"You think for a second you can lick me?" Danny blurted in.

Rivera nodded.

"Oh, come; listen to reason," Kelly pleaded. "Think of the advertising."

"I want the money," was Rivera's answer.

"You couldn't win from me in a thousand years," Danny assured him.

"Then what are you holding out for?" Rivera countered. "If the money's that easy, why don't you go after it?"

"I will, so help me!" Danny cried with abrupt conviction. "I'll beat you to death in the ring—you monkeyin' with me this way. Make out the articles, Kelly. Winner take all. Play it up in the sportin' columns. Tell 'em it's a grudge fight. I'll show this fresh kid a few."

Kelly's secretary had begun to write, when Danny interrupted.

"Hold on!" He turned to Rivera. "Weights?"

---

6. **then . . . for him,** then I'll finish him.

"Ringside," came the answer.

"Not on your life, fresh kid. If winner takes all, we weigh in at 10 A.M."

"And winner takes all?" Rivera queried.

Danny nodded. That settled it. He would enter the ring in his full ripeness of strength.

"Weigh in at ten," Rivera said.

The secretary's pen went on scratching.

"It means five pounds," Roberts complained to Rivera. "You've given too much away. You've thrown the fight right there. Danny'll be as strong as a bull. You're a fool. He'll lick you sure. You ain't got a chance."

Rivera's answer was a calculated look of hatred.

4

Barely noticed was Rivera as he entered the ring. Only a very slight and very scattering ripple of halfhearted handclapping greeted him. The house did not believe in him. He was the lamb led to slaughter at the hands of the great Danny. Besides, the house was disappointed. It had expected a rushing battle between Danny Ward and Billy Carthey, and here it must put up with this poor little tyro.[7] Still further, it had manifested its disapproval of the change by betting two, and even three, to one on Danny. And where a betting audience's money is, there is its heart.

The Mexican boy sat down in his corner and waited. The slow minutes lagged by. Danny was making him wait. It was an old trick, but ever it worked on the young, new fighters. They grew frightened, sitting thus and facing their own apprehensions and a callous, tobacco-smoking audience. But for once the trick failed. Roberts was right. Rivera had no goat. He, who was more delicately coordinated, more finely nerved and strung than any of them, had no nerves of this sort. The atmosphere of foredoomed defeat in his own corner had no effect on him. His handlers were strangers. Also they were scrubs—the dirty driftage of the fight game, without honor, without efficiency. And they

were chilled, as well, with certitude that theirs was the losing corner.

"Now you gotta be careful," Spider Hagerty warned him. Spider was his chief second. "Make it last as long as you can—them's my instructions from Kelly. If you don't, the papers'll call it another bum fight and give the game a bigger black eye in Los Angeles."

All of which was not encouraging. But Rivera took no notice. He despised prizefighting. He had taken up with it, as a chopping block for others in the training quarters, solely because he was starving. The fact that he was marvelously made for it had meant nothing. He hated it. Not until he had come in to the junta had he fought for money, and he had found the money easy. Not first among the sons of men had he been to find himself successful at a despised vocation.

He did not analyze. He merely knew that he must win this fight. There could be no other outcome. For behind him, nerving him to this belief, were profounder forces than any the crowded house dreamed. Danny Ward fought for the money and for easy ways of life that money would bring. But the things Rivera fought for burned in his brain—blazing and terrible visions, that, with eyes wide open, sitting lonely in the corner of the ring and waiting for his tricky antagonist, he saw as clearly as he had lived them.

He saw the white-walled, waterpower factories of Rio Blanco.[8] He saw the 6,000 workers, starved and wan, and the little children, seven and eight years of age, who toiled long shifts for ten cents a day. He saw the perambulating corpses, the ghastly death's heads of men who labored in the dye rooms. He remembered that he had heard his father call the dye rooms the "suicide holes," where a year was death. He saw the little patio, and his mother cooking and toiling at crude housekeeping and finding time to caress and love

---

7. tyro\ˈtair·ō\ a beginner in learning.
8. **Rio Blanco**\ˈrē·ō ˈblaŋ ˈkō\ a town in the state of Vera Cruz in eastern Mexico.

him. And his father he saw, large, big mustached, and deep chested, kindly above all men, who loved all men and whose heart was so large that there was love to overflowing still left for the mother and the little *muchacho*[9] playing in the corner of the patio. In those days his name had not been Felipe Rivera. It had been Fernandez, his father's and mother's name. Him had they called Juan. Later he had changed it himself, for he had found the name of Fernandez hated by prefects of police, *jefes políticos*,[10] and *rurales*.[11]

Big, hearty Joaquin Fernandez! A large place he occupied in Rivera's visions. He had not understood at the time, but, looking back, he could understand. He could see him setting type in the little printery, or scribbling endless hasty, nervous lines on the much-cluttered desk. And he could see the strange evenings, when workmen, coming secretly in the dark like men who did ill deeds, met with his father and talked long hours where he, the *muchacho*, lay not always asleep in the corner.

As from a remote distance he could hear Spider Hagerty saying to him: "No layin' down at the start. Them's instructions. Take a beatin' an' earn your dough."

Ten minutes had passed, and he still sat in his corner. There were no signs of Danny, who was evidently playing the trick to the limit.

But more visions burned before the eye of Rivera's memory. The strike, or, rather, the lockout, because the workers of Rio Blanco had helped their striking brothers of Puebla.[12] The hunger, the expeditions in the hills for berries, the roots and herbs that all ate and that twisted and pained the stomachs of all of them. And then the nightmare; the waste of ground before the company's store; the thousands of starving workers; General Rosalio Martinez and the soldiers of Porfirio Díaz; and the death-spitting rifles that seemed never to cease spitting, while the workers' wrongs were washed and washed again in their own blood. And that night! He saw the flatcars, piled high with the bodies of the slain, consigned to Vera Cruz,[13] food for the sharks of the bay. Again he crawled over the grisly heaps, seeking and finding, stripped and mangled, his father and mother. His mother he especially remembered—only her face projecting, her body burdened by the weight of dozens of bodies. Again the rifles of the soldiers of Porfirio Díaz cracked, and again he dropped to the ground and slunk away like some hunted coyote of the hills.

To his ears came a great roar, as of the sea, and he saw Danny Ward, leading his retinue of trainers and seconds, coming down the center aisle. The house was in wild uproar for the popular hero who was bound to win. Everybody proclaimed him. Everybody was for him. Even Rivera's own seconds warmed to something akin to cheerfulness when Danny ducked jauntily through the ropes and entered the ring. His face continually spread to an unending succession of smiles, and when Danny smiled he smiled in every feature, even to the laughter wrinkles of the corners of the eyes and into the depths of the eyes themselves. Never was there so genial a fighter. His face was a running advertisement of good feeling, of good-fellowship. He knew everybody. He joked, and laughed, and greeted his friends through the ropes. Those farther away, unable to suppress their admiration, cried loudly: "Oh, you Danny!" It was a joyous ovation of affection that lasted a full five minutes.

Rivera was disregarded. For all that the audience noticed, he did not exist. Spider Hagerty's bloated face bent down close to his. "No gettin' scared," the Spider warned.

---

9. **muchacho**\mū ▲cha·chō\ boy.
10. **jefes políticos**\▲hĕ·fās pō ▲ lē·tē 'kōs\ political bosses.
11. **rurales**\rū ▲ra·lās\ rural police.
12. **Puebla**\▲pŭĕb·la\ capital of the state of Puebla in southeast central Mexico; one of Mexico's oldest and most famous cities.
13. **Vera Cruz**\'vĕr·a ▲krūs\ a port city in the state of Vera Cruz located on the Gulf of Mexico.

"An' remember instructions. You gotta last. No layin' down. If you lay down, we got instructions to beat you up in the dressingrooms. Savvy? You just gotta fight."

The house began to applaud. Danny was crossing the ring to him. Danny bent over him, caught Rivera's right hand in both his own and shook it with impulsive heartiness. Danny's smile-wreathed face was close to his. The audience yelled its appreciation of Danny's display of sporting spirit. He was greeting his opponent with the fondness of a brother. Danny's lips moved, and the audience, interpreting the unheard words to be those of a kindly-natured sport, yelled again. Only Rivera heard the low words.

"You little Mexican rat," hissed from between Danny's gaily smiling lips, "I'll fetch the yellow outa you."

Rivera made no move. He did not rise. He merely hated with his eyes.

"Get up, you dog!" some man yelled through the ropes from behind.

The crowd began to hiss and boo him for his unsportsmanlike conduct, but he sat unmoved. Another great outburst of applause was Danny's as he walked back across the ring.

When Danny stripped, there were ohs! and ahs! of delight. His body was perfect, alive with easy suppleness and health and strength. All grace, and resilience, and power resided therein. He had proved it in scores of battles. His photographs were in all the physical culture magazines.

A groan went up as Spider Hagerty peeled Rivera's sweater over his head. His body seemed leaner because of the swarthiness of the skin. He had muscles, but they made no display like his opponent's. What the audience neglected to see was the deep chest. Nor could it guess the toughness of the fiber of the flesh, the instantaneousness of the cell explosions of the muscles, the fineness of the nerves that wired every part of him into a splendid fighting mechanism. All the audience saw was a brown skinned boy of eighteen

with what seemed the body of a boy. With Danny it was different. Danny was a man of twenty-four, and his body was a man's body. The contrast was still more striking as they stood together in the center of the ring receiving the referee's last instructions.

Rivera noticed Roberts sitting directly behind the newspapermen. He was drunker than usual, and his speech was correspondingly slower.

"Take it easy, Rivera," Roberts drawled. "He can't kill you, remember that. He'll rush you at the go-off, but don't get rattled. You just cover up, and stall, and clinch. He can't hurt you much. Just make believe to yourself that he's choppin' out on you at the trainin' quarters."

Rivera made no sign that he had heard.

"Sullen little devil," Roberts muttered to the man next to him. "He always was that way."

But Rivera forgot to look his usual hatred. A vision of countless rifles blinded his eyes. Every face in the audience, as far as he could see, to the high dollar seats, was transformed into a rifle. And he saw the long Mexican border arid and sun washed and aching, and along it he saw the ragged bands that delayed only for the guns.

Back in his corner he waited, standing up. His seconds had crawled out through the ropes, taking the canvas stool with them. Diagonally across the squared ring, Danny faced him. The gong struck, and the battle was on. The audience howled its delight. Never had it seen a battle open more convincingly. The papers were right. It was a grudge fight. Three-quarters of the distance Danny covered in the rush to get together, his intention to eat up the Mexican lad plainly advertised. He assailed with not one blow, nor two, nor a dozen. He was a gyroscope of blows, a whirlwind of destruction. Rivera was nowhere. He was overwhelmed, buried beneath avalanches of punches delivered from every angle and position by a past master in the art. He was overborne, swept back against the ropes, separated by the referee, and swept back against the ropes again.

It was not a fight. It was a slaughter, a massacre. Any audience, save a prizefight one, would have exhausted its emotions in that first minute. Danny was certainly showing what he could do—a splendid exhibition. Such was the certainty of the audience, as well as its excitement and favoritism, that it failed to notice that the Mexican still stayed on his feet. It forgot Rivera. It rarely saw him, so closely was he enveloped in Danny's man-eating attack. A minute of this went by, and two minutes. Then, in a separation, it caught a clear glimpse of the Mexican. His lip was cut, his nose was bleeding. As he turned and staggered into a clinch the welts of oozing blood, from his contacts with the ropes, showed in red bars across his back. But what the audience did not notice was that his chest was not heaving and that his eyes were coldly burning as ever. Too many aspiring champions, in the cruel welter of the training camps, had practiced this man-eating attack on him. He had learned to live through for a compensation of from a half a dollar a go up to fifteen dollars a week—a hard school, and he was schooled hard.

Then happened the amazing thing. The whirling, blurring mix-up ceased suddenly. Rivera stood alone. Danny, the redoubtable Danny, lay on his back. His body quivered as consciousness strove to return to it. He had not staggered and sunk down, nor had he gone over in a long slumping fall. The right hook of Rivera had dropped him in mid air with the abruptness of death. The referee shoved Rivera back with one hand and stood over the fallen gladiator counting the seconds. It is the custom of prizefighting audiences to cheer a clean knockdown blow. But this audience did not cheer. The thing had been too unexpected. It watched the toll of the seconds in tense silence, and through this silence the voice of Roberts rose exultantly:

"I told you he was a two-handed fighter!"

By the fifth second Danny was rolling on his face, and when seven was counted he rested on one knee, ready to rise after the count of nine and before the count of ten. If his knee still touched the floor at "ten" he was considered "down" and also "out." The instant his knee left the floor he was considered "up," and in that instant it was Rivera's right to try and put him down again. Rivera took no chances. The moment that knee left the floor he would strike again. He circled around, but the referee circled in between, and Rivera knew that the seconds he counted were very slow. All were against him, even the referee.

At "nine" the referee gave Rivera a sharp thrust back. It was unfair, but it enabled Danny to rise, the smile back on his lips. Doubled partly over, with arms wrapped about face and abdomen, he cleverly stumbled into a clinch. By all the rules of the game the referee should have broken it, but he did not, and Danny clung on like a surf-battered barnacle and moment by moment recuperated. The last minute of the round was going fast. If he could live to the end he would have a full minute in his corner to revive. And live to the end he did, smiling through all desperateness and extremity.

"The smile that won't come off!" somebody yelled, and the audience laughed loudly in its relief.

"The kick that greaser's got is something awful," Danny gasped in his corner to his adviser while his handlers worked frantically over him.

The second and third rounds were tame. Danny, a tricky and consummate ring general, stalled and blocked and held on, devoting himself to recovering from that dazing first round blow. In the fourth round he was himself again. Jarred and shaken, nevertheless his good condition had enabled him to regain his vigor. But he tried no man-eating tactics. The Mexican had proved a tartar.[14] Instead he brought to bear his best fighting

---

14. tartar\ˈtar·tər\ an unexpectedly powerful person.

powers. In tricks and skill and experience he was the master, and though he could land nothing vital, he proceeded scientifically to chop and wear down his opponent. He landed three blows to Rivera's one, but they were punishing blows only, and not deadly. It was the sum of many of them that constituted deadliness. He was respectful of this two-handed dub with the amazing short-arm kicks in both his fists.

In defense Rivera developed a disconcerting straight left. Again and again, attack after attack he straight-lefted away from him with accumulated damage to Danny's mouth and nose. But Danny was protean.[15] That was why he was the coming champion. He could change from style to style of fighting at will. He now devoted himself to infighting. In this he was particularly wicked, and it enabled him to avoid the other's straight left. Here he set the house wild repeatedly, capping it with a marvelous lock-break and lift of an inside uppercut that raised the Mexican in the air and dropped him to the mat. Rivera rested on one knee, making the most of the count, and in the soul of him knew the referee was counting short seconds on him.

Again, in the seventh, Danny achieved the diabolical inside uppercut. He succeeded only in staggering Rivera, but in the ensuing moment of defenseless helplessness he smashed him with another blow through the ropes. Rivera's body bounced on the heads of the newspapermen below, and they boosted him back to the edge of the platform outside the ropes. Here he rested on one knee, while the referee raced off the seconds. Inside the ropes, through which he must duck to enter the ring, Danny waited for him. Nor did the referee intervene or thrust Danny back.

The house was beside itself with delight.

"Kill 'm, Danny, kill 'm!" was the cry.

Scores of voices took it up until it was like a war chant of wolves.

Danny did his best, but Rivera, at the count of eight, instead of nine, came unexpectedly through the ropes and safely into a clinch.

Now the referee worked, tearing him away so that he could be hit, giving Danny every advantage that an unfair referee can give.

But Rivera lived, and the daze cleared from his brain. It was all of a piece. And in the worst of it visions continued to flash and sparkle in his brain—long lines of railroad track that simmered across the desert; *rurales* and American constables; prisons and calabooses; tramps at water tanks—all the squalid and painful panorama of his odyssey after Rio Blanco and the strike. And, resplendent and glorious, he saw the great revolution sweeping across his land. The guns were there before him. Every hated face was a gun. It was for the guns he fought. He was the guns. He was the revolution. He fought for all Mexico.

The audience began to grow incensed with Rivera. Why didn't he take the licking that was appointed him? Of course he was going to be licked, but why should he be so obstinate about it? Very few were interested in him, and they were the certain, definite percentage of a gambling crowd that plays long shots. Believing Danny to be the winner, nevertheless they had put their money on the Mexican at four to ten and one to three. More than a trifle was up on the point of how many rounds Rivera could last. Wild money had appeared at the ringside proclaiming that he could not last seven rounds, or even six. The winners of this, now that their cash risk was happily settled, had joined in cheering on the favorite.

Rivera refused to be licked. Through the eighth round his opponent strove vainly to repeat the uppercut. In the ninth Rivera stunned the house again. In the midst of a clinch he broke the lock with a quick, lithe movement, and in the narrow space between their bodies his right lifted from the waist. Danny went to the floor and took the safety of the count. The crowd was appalled. He

---

15. **protean** \ˈprōt·ē·ən\ flexible, able to change and adjust to new situations.

was being bested at his own game. His famous right uppercut had been worked back on him. Rivera made no attempt to catch him as he arose at "nine." The referee was openly blocking that play, though he stood clear when the situation was reversed and it was Rivera who required to rise.

Twice in the tenth Rivera put through the right uppercut, lifted from waist to opponent's chin. Danny grew desperate. The smile never left his face, but he went back to his man-eating rushes. Whirlwind as he would, he could not damage Rivera, while Rivera, through the blur and whirl, dropped him to the mat three times in succession. Danny did not recuperate so quickly now, and by the eleventh round he was in a serious way. But from then till the fourteenth he put up the gamest exhibition of his career. He stalled and blocked, fought parsimoniously,[16] and strove to gather strength. Also he fought as foully as a successful fighter knows how. Every trick and device he employed, butting in the clinches with the seeming of accident, pinioning Rivera's glove between arm and body, heeling his glove on Rivera's mouth to clog his breathing. Often, in the clinches, through his cut and smiling lips he snarled insults unspeakable and vile in Rivera's ear. Everybody, from the referee to the house, was with Danny and was helping Danny. And they knew what he had in mind. Bested by this surprise box of an unknown, he was pinning all on a single punch. He offered himself for punishment, fished, and feinted, and drew, for that one opening that would enable him to whip a blow through with all his strength and turn the tide. As another and greater fighter had done before him, he might do—a right and left, to solar plexus[17] and across the jaw. He could do it, for he was noted for the strength of punch that remained in his arms as long as he could keep his feet.

Rivera's seconds were not half caring for him in the intervals between rounds. Their towels made a showing but drove little air into his panting lungs. Spider Hagerty talked

advice to him, but Rivera knew it was wrong advice. Everybody was against him. He was surrounded by treachery. In the fourteenth round he put Danny down again, and himself stood resting, hands dropped at side, while the referee counted. In the other corner Rivera had been noting suspicious whisperings. He saw Michael Kelly make his way to Roberts and bend and whisper. Rivera's ears were a cat's, desert-trained, and he caught snatches of what was said. He wanted to hear more, and when his opponent arose he maneuvered the fight into a clinch over against the ropes.

"Got to," he could hear Michael, while Roberts nodded. "Danny's got to win—I stand to lose a mint. I've got a ton of money covered—my own. If he lasts the fifteenth I'm bust. The boy'll mind you. Put something across."

And thereafter Rivera saw no more visions. They were trying to job[18] him. Once again he dropped Danny and stood resting, his hands at his side. Roberts stood up.

"That settled him," he said. "Go to your corner."

He spoke with authority, as he had often spoken to Rivera at the training quarters. But Rivera looked hatred at him and waited for Danny to rise. Back in his corner in the minute interval, Kelly, the promoter, came and talked to Rivera.

"Throw it," he rasped in a harsh low voice. "You gotta lay down, Rivera. Stick with me and I'll make your future. I'll let you lick Danny next time. But here's where you lay down."

Rivera showed with his eyes that he heard, but he made neither sign of assent nor dissent.

"Why don't you speak?" Kelly demanded angrily.

"You lose anyway," Spider Hagerty supplemented. "The referee'll take it away from you. Listen to Kelly and lay down."

---

16. **parsimoniously**\\\'par·sə ▲mō·nē·əs·lē\\ in a manner marked by extreme stinginess.
17. **solar plexus**\\▲sō·lər ▲plĕks·əs\\ the pit of the stomach.
18. **job,** to swindle or trick.

"Lay down, kid," Kelly pleaded, "and I'll help you to the championship."

Rivera did not answer.

"I will, so help me, kid."

At the strike of the gong Rivera sensed something impending. The house did not. Whatever it was, it was there inside the ring with him and very close. Danny's early surety seemed returned to him. The confidence of his advance frightened Rivera. Some trick was about to be worked. Danny rushed, but Rivera refused the encounter. He sidestepped away into safety. What the other wanted was a clinch. It was in some way necessary to the trick. Rivera backed and circled away, yet he knew, sooner or later, the clinch and the trick would come. Desperately he resolved to draw it. He made as if to effect the clinch with Danny's next rush. Instead, at the last instant, just as their bodies should have come together, Rivera darted nimbly back. And in the same instant Danny's corner raised a cry of foul. Rivera had fooled them. The referee paused irresolutely. The decision that trembled on his lips was never uttered, for a shrill, boy's voice from the gallery piped, "Raw work!"

Danny cursed Rivera openly and forced him, while Rivera danced away. Also Rivera made up his mind to strike no more blows at the body. In this he threw away half his chance of winning, but he knew if he was to win at all it was with the outfighting that remained to him. Given the least opportunity, they would lay a foul on him. Danny threw all caution to the winds. For two rounds he tore after and into the boy who dared not meet him at close quarters. Rivera was struck again and again; he took blows by the dozens to avoid the perilous clinch. During this supreme final rally of Danny's the audience rose to its feet and went mad. It did not understand. All it could see was that its favorite was winning after all.

"Why don't you fight?" it demanded wrathfully of Rivera. "You're yellow! You're yellow!" "Open up, you cur! Open up!" "Kill 'm, Danny! Kill 'm!" "You sure got 'm! Kill 'm!"

In all the house, bar none, Rivera was the only cold man. By temperament and blood he was the hottest passioned there; but he had gone through such vastly greater heats that this collective passion of 10,000 throats, rising surge on surge, was to his brain no more than the velvet cool of a summer twilight.

Into the seventeenth round Danny carried his rally. Rivera, under a heavy blow, dropped and sagged. His hands dropped helplessly as he reeled backwards. Danny thought it was his chance. The boy was at his mercy. Thus Rivera, feigning, caught him off his guard, lashing out a clean drive to the mouth. Danny went down. When he arose Rivera felled him with a down-chop of the right on neck and jaw. Three times he repeated this. It was impossible for any referee to call these blows foul.

"Oh, Bill! Bill!" Kelly pleaded to the referee.

"I can't," that official lamented back. "He won't give me a chance."

Danny, battered and heroic, still kept coming up. Kelly and others near to the ring began to cry out to the police to stop it, though Danny's corner refused to throw in the towel. Rivera saw the fat police captain starting awkwardly to climb through the ropes, and was not sure what it meant. There were so many ways of cheating in this game. Danny, on his feet, tottered groggily and helplessly before him. The referee and the captain were both reaching for Rivera when he struck the last blow. There was no need to stop the fight, for Danny did not rise.

"Count!" Rivera cried hoarsely to the referee.

And when the count was finished Danny's seconds gathered him up and carried him to his corner.

"Who wins?" Rivera demanded.

Reluctantly the referee caught his gloved hand and held it aloft.

There were no congratulations for Rivera. He walked to his corner unattended, where his seconds had not yet placed his stool. He leaned backwards on the ropes and looked his hatred at them, swept it on and about him till the whole 10,000 were included. His knees trembled under him, and he was sobbing from exhaustion. Before his eyes the hated faces swayed back and forth in the giddiness of nausea. Then he remembered they were the guns. The guns were his. The revolution could go on.

I

AN IMPLACABLE FOE

It is far along in the story before the reader finds out what is driving Felipe Rivera to take almost unbelievable punishment in order to get the money to keep the revolution going.

1. What happened to his family that causes him to have such hatred for Díaz? Why did he change his name from Fernandez?

2. How does the junta test the boy in the beginning to see if he is really sincere in his desire to work for the revolution?

3. What is the continual and pressing need of the junta? What are the suspicions of the junta members when the scrub boy begins to give help financially?

4. When the junta is desperate for money, what does Rivera promise?

5. Why does Rivera get a chance to fight a boxer with the reputation of Danny Ward?

6. Explain why Rivera insists that "winner takes all."

7. What trick does Ward use before the fight to try to unnerve Felipe?

8. Why don't the unfriendly faces in the audience disturb the boy?

9. Describe the beginning of the fight. How does the referee give Danny unfair advantage?

10. In what round does Felipe finally win the fight? Why does Felipe have to avoid a clinch with Danny for the last three rounds?

II

IMPLICATIONS

Are all of the following generalizations either stated or implied in "The Mexican"? Discuss each.

1. The more you know about a person, the better you like him.

2. A person who holds himself aloof from other people arouses resentment and suspicion.

3. The eyes are a true index of a person's character.

4. A person can accomplish the impossible if he knows he must.

III

TECHNIQUES

Characterization

1. How does the author use a description of one of the boy's facial features to characterize him early in the story?

2. Vera describes Rivera as "the breath of death." How does the whole paragraph in which these words appear build the image of the boy as someone to be feared?

3. To what other creatures does Arrellano compare Rivera?

4. How does the author describe Roberts? Contrast Roberts with Kelly.

5. How does Danny Ward contrast with Rivera in personality? Is Ward sincere?

Significant Details

The reader must remain alert or he may become confused about what is taking place in a story. Just as settings are changed in a play, so they may be shifted in a story. Many times an author does not state directly that such a change has taken place. He leaves it to the reader to discover the change from details he places in the story. Part 3 of this story opens in a different setting from parts 1 and 2. What is it and what does this reveal about Rivera's mysterious absences from the junta offices?

When George Washington Carver arrived
at Tuskegee Institute in 1896, the laboratory
was a barren room and there was no equipment
and no money to buy any.
But the quiet scientist, who had learned
early in life to make something from nothing,
set about constructing laboratory equipment
from the scrap heaps and junk piles
in the community. He had something more
important than money and shining equipment.
Discover what he had and what he did with it.
This account was written a few years
before Dr. Carver's death.

A Boy
Who Was Traded
for a Horse

JAMES SAXON CHILDERS

The stooped old Negro trudged along
through the dust of an Alabama road at a curiously rapid rate. He was carrying an armful of
sticks and wild flowers.

The sticks I could understand—he would
use them for kindling—but I had never before
seen an old black man ambling along a road at
nine o'clock in the morning with swamp roses,
wild geranium, and creeping buttercups mingled with a lot of dry sticks.

When I got a little closer to him I saw that
he was wearing a saggy coat which originally
might have been a green alpaca, but which the
sun had faded until I couldn't be sure about the
color; there were so many patches that I
couldn't even be certain about the material.

The old man was walking towards a large
brick building, one of the buildings of Tuske-

gee Institute, the famous school for Negroes at
Tuskegee, Alabama.[1] His thin body bent by the
years, his hair white beneath a ragged cap, he
seemed pathetically lost on the campus of a
great modern educational institution.

At the entrance of the building toward which
we were both walking, the old Negro turned in.
"He's probably the janitor," I told myself, "and
I'm sincerely glad that they've given him a job
of some kind."

I stepped into the hallway. I saw a trim little
secretary hurry toward the bent old Negro. I
heard her say to him, "That delegation from
Washington is waiting for you, Doctor Carver."

Dr. George Washington Carver, the very
man I had come to see! Fantastic and unbelievable as it seemed, this old man with his
armful of sticks and wild flowers was none
other than the distinguished Negro scientist of
Tuskegee Institute. A discoverer renowned far
and wide for his chemical wizardry in creating
useful new products from such stuff as peanut
shells and fallen leaves which most of us waste
and throw away. An inventor acclaimed for his
genius in transforming such common things as
peanuts, sweet potatoes, and even the clay of
the earth, into things of uncommon value for
our everyday needs.

That saggy alpaca coat covered a Bachelor
of Science, Master of Science, Honorary Doctor of Science, winner of the Spingarn Medal
for Negro achievement, member of the Royal
Society for the Encouragement of Arts, Manufactures and Commerce of Great Britain.

Yet as I looked at him, studied his kindly
face, and recalled what I had heard of the story
of his life, I saw that the figure of the man himself was not half so fantastic or unbelievable as
is the record of his achievement.

Dr. George Washington Carver started with
nothing. He never had anything. Yet out of
nothing he has created inestimable wealth for
fellow human beings to whom he has devoted
his life.

1. **Tuskegee**\\'təs ᴀkē•gē\\ **Institute** is in the city of Tuskegee in eastern Alabama.

Born a slave child, he began life without even so much as a name. He never knew his father. He never knew his mother. To this day he doesn't know just when he was born, though he figures his age at somewhere close to seventy. Without a red cent he worked out his own early schooling, then his higher college education, then the postgraduate work for his Master of Science degree. All his life he has been joyously at work with common, everyday things, making something out of nothing, or next to nothing. During the thirty-six years in which he has been Director of Agricultural Research at Tuskegee Institute, that has been his work. And out of it have come scientific marvels:

From wood shavings he has made synthetic marble.

From peanut shells he has made insulating walls for houses.

From the muck of swamps and the leaves of the forest floor he has made valuable fertilizers.

From cow dung he has made paint.

From the common, ordinary peanut he has made 285 useful products, including milk, butter, cheese, candies, instant coffee, pickles, sauces, oils, shaving lotions, wood stains, dyes, lard, linoleum, flour, breakfast foods, soap, stock foods, face powder, tan remover, shampoo, printer's ink, and even axle grease!

From the lowly sweet potato he has made 118 products, among them flour, meal, starch, library paste, vinegar, shoe blacking, ginger, ink, rubber compound, chocolate compound, dyes, molasses, wood filler, caramels.

From clays of the earth he has made nonfading paints and pigments.

From worn-out sandy soil he has produced paying crops.

Something from nothing. And this is only a portion of his work. Experts say that he has probably done more than any other living man to rehabilitate agriculture in the South.

And more still. Doctor Carver is also an artist, especially skilled in painting flowers. His paintings have been exhibited at world fairs, and at least one is going to the Luxembourg Gallery in Paris after his death. He makes all his own paints, using Alabama clays. The paper he paints on he makes from peanut shells, and the frames for his pictures he makes out of corn husks. His work in embroidery and crochet has won prizes in various exhibits. He has woven gorgeous rugs with fibers he had made from cotton stalks. He is a skilled musician, too— once he toured the Middle West as a concert pianist. And last, but not least, he is an expert cook. His recipes are used today in some of the leading hotels of the country.

All this does sound a bit incredible, doesn't it? I confess that when I set out for Tuskegee to see and talk with Doctor Carver, I was more than skeptical of many of the stories I had heard about him. And so, after he had entertained the visiting delegations from Washington, I returned to see him, in his office in the big brick building, with many doubts lingering in my mind.

He was sitting behind a desk cluttered inches high with letters and papers. On top of the papers were the sticks and wild flowers that I had seen him carrying that morning. As I went in, he was looking through a microscope at the stems of a wild rose.

"I beg your pardon," I said.

The old man raised his head and looked at me; then, taking hold of the edge of the desk to steady himself, he pushed himself up from his squeaky swivel chair. He wore a long canvas apron that was splotched and stained. His gold-rimmed spectacles rested far down on his nose. Standing there so tall despite his noticeable stoop, he peered over the tops of his spectacles and smiled at me.

"Good morning," he said and the quiet tone of his voice blended with the gentle sincerity of his smile.

In slight confusion, then, I explained why I had called on him. "People tell me that I couldn't possibly write a story about Tuskegee unless I wrote a lot about you," I added.

The old Negro grinned with the genuine shyness that has kept him so long hidden from the public. "People are too kind to me," he insisted. "I'm really a very small part of this institution. Won't you sit down?"

I was touched by his gentleness, and by an unmistakable spiritual quality in the glow of his face. Frankly, I was confused. To open the conversation, I remarked on the numerous Maxfield Parrish[2] paintings that hang on his office walls. "Somehow they seem a little out of place in the office of a scientist," I said lamely.

"But can't a scientist be a lover of the beautiful?" he asked. "There is no one of the moderns who uses blue half so well as Maxfield Parrish uses it."

And then he was off. For forty-five minutes he walked about his office, showing me how Maxfield Parrish uses blue, and telling how the ancients used the color. Quietly he told how the Egyptians loved it, how they had adorned their homes and tombs with it.

Then he led me from his office across the hall into his laboratory, a room about thirty by twenty feet. It was filled with racks and shelves and tables, bottles and tubes and retorts. He picked up a jar and carried it to the window. "See"—and he held it to the sun.

And I saw the richest, the purest blue that I have ever seen.

Doctor Carver was talking quietly as he tilted the jar one way and the other, giving the sun its full chance to mate with the glorious color. "I believe," he went on, "that it's a rediscovery of the old Egyptian blue. A number of chemists have come to see it, and they agree with me. At present I'm working on the Egyptian purple; I believe that soon we shall have that, too.

"I get my dyes," the old man continued, "from Alabama clays. You remember what the Bible says"—Doctor Carver has built his life on what the Bible says—"you remember that the Bible says, 'Look to the hills from whence cometh your help.'[3] I did it; I looked to these Alabama hills, and I made these dyes from the clays that I found there. All these dyes and paints"—he waved toward thirty-six boards, each of which was colored differently—"all of

them were made from Alabama clay—all," he added, "except this one; it was made from rotten sweet potatoes; and this one, which was made from cow dung; and this one, a much finer paint, was made from horse dung."

After I had been an hour in Doctor Carver's laboratory, after I had seen rope made from okra fiber, baskets from wistaria, and dyes from dandelion, black oak, wood ashes, sweet gum, swamp maple, sweet potato, pomegranate, peanut, Osage orange, muscadine grape, onion, velvet bean, and tomato vine—after I had seen those discoveries, among a few hundred others, I was willing to believe almost anything possible to this kindly man to whom apparently brick without straw would be a simple problem.

"When you do the common things of life in an uncommon way," Doctor Carver once said to his students, "you will command the attention of the world." In that sentence lies the secret of his own achievement.

He was born in a rude slave cabin on the farm of Moses Carver near Diamond Grove, Missouri. Moses Carver owned his mother, and a neighbor owned his father. When he was a baby six months old, night riders swooped down on his master's plantation and carried away a number of slaves, among them the baby and his mother.

In their flight, the raiders took no care of the child; he developed whooping cough and was dying when emissaries sent out by Moses Carver arrived from Missouri to buy back the stolen slaves.

But the mother had already been disposed of; no one ever learned what became of her. Indeed, there is only one thing of hers that is left: In Doctor Carver's room in one of the dormitories at Tuskegee is a battered old spinning wheel on which his mother spun flax when she was a slave. A friend of Doctor Carver's

---

2. **Maxfield Parrish,** born in 1870, American illustrator and muralist.
3. . . . **from whence cometh your help,** paraphrased from Psalms 121:1.

said to me, "I've seen him touch that wheel; he touches it like a priest reverently touching an altar. I sometimes feel that if I could be in his room when he retires, I should hear the old man say 'Good night' to that wheel."

The emissaries sent to ransom the stolen slaves finally struck a bargain with the night riders. The baby was evaluated and traded back to his owner; he was traded for a broken-down race horse worth about $300!

The Carvers reared the sickly child, and from them he took his surname, according to the practice common among slaves. It is told that they bestowed the given name "George Washington" upon him because of his youthful honesty and industry. Because he was a frail and undersized lad and could do no heavy work, he performed household chores, getting in the wood, tending the fires, and helping Mrs. Carver with the meals. He became an excellent cook and also learned to sew and mend clothes.

When the chores were done, his favorite playground was in the woods near by, where his companions were the birds, the flowers, the trees, and the small animals.

As a boy he had only one book. It was Webster's blue-back speller.

"With that book," he said to me, "I began my education. Even as a boy I realized that life requires a thorough preparation; there is no short cut to achievement; veneer isn't worth anything. And so I studied that book until I knew every word of it."

When he was about ten years old, having mastered the speller, he determined to get further schooling. He heard of a school in the village of Neosho, Missouri, eight miles away. The Carvers wanted him to have an education, but offered him no money. So, without a cent in his pockets, he set out over the hills for Neosho. Arriving there, alone among strangers, he slept at first in an old horse barn. Soon he picked up odd jobs about the village and entered the school. It wasn't much of a school—an old log cabin equipped with hard, high benches for the pupils. Within a year he had mastered all that the teacher could tell him and

more. But he had learned enough to be eager for more knowledge.

One day, while walking along the road, he met a mule-team outfit headed for Fort Scott, Kansas. In true hitch-hike fashion, he asked the travelers if he could go along with them. After several day's journey they reached Fort Scott, where he got a job in a home as cook, dishwasher, and all-round housekeeper.

In this way, and by washing clothes, he earned his keep while he attended classes in high school. Still frail in physique and small for his age, he was continuing to make something out of nothing. Seven years passed, and he completed his high school course. He was now in his early twenties. And, almost miraculously, he began suddenly to grow in body. Within a year or so he developed from a weakling into a strapping six-footer.

Without accepting financial aid, he had struggled through his schooling; now he determined to make his way through college. But first he paid a summer visit to his old home with the Carvers back in Missouri. They gave him his mother's spinning wheel, which he carried back with him to Fort Scott.

In the fall he mailed an application to a college in Iowa, and by mail he was accepted. But when he arrived at the college, they refused to admit him because he was a Negro. He had spent most of his money for railway fare, and there was not enough left to take him out of town. But he was undismayed. Again he worked at odd jobs—cooking, cleaning carpets, and doing other chores. Before long he had accumulated enough money to open a small laundry, which was patronized by college students and townspeople. For a time he worked as a hotel cook.

The next year he entered Simpson College at Indianola, Iowa. After he had paid his entrance fee he had ten cents left, which he invested in five cents' worth of corn meal and five cents' worth of suet. On this fare he lived for nearly a week. For three years he worked his way at Simpson; then in 1890 he enrolled at Iowa State College. Four years later he was graduated, taking his degree in agriculture, having earned every penny of his expenses.

Two years after graduation he won his Master of Science degree. His work in agricultural chemistry so impressed the authorities of the college that they appointed him to a place on the college faculty—this boy who only a few years before had been traded for a horse!

While Carver was teaching at Iowa State College, the late Booker T. Washington, the great Negro educator, heard of him and asked him to come to Tuskegee.

"He asked me to come here and to let down my bucket,"[4] Doctor Carver told me one day as I watched him busy in his laboratory. Turning from his work, he looked out of the window, and I saw that he was looking back through the years. "I did come here. I did let down my bucket. And every time I've pulled it up, it has been brimful and running over—running over," he repeated.

In accepting Doctor Washington's call, Carver saw a great opportunity to serve his own people in the South, an opportunity for which he had fully prepared himself by his work in agriculture and chemistry. He saw that the valuable cotton lands of the South, where for years cotton had been the chief paying crop, were wearing out through neglect of simple scientific methods of farming, such as proper fertilizing and rotation of crops. He saw small farmers overburdened by debt and facing poverty. He saw a way to help lift their burden.

Carver's first job when he arrived at Tuskegee in 1896 was to create an efficient department of agriculture, which had barely been started in the school. The department was housed in an old building and was almost entirely lacking in laboratory equipment. At once he put into practice what he had learned about making something out of nothing. He and his students went out into back alleys and searched trash piles collecting old bottles and jars, bits of rubber and wire and other odds and ends. Out of these he built laboratory apparatus—later to be replaced by new equipment.

His next big job was to take over and work nineteen acres of the worst land in Alabama. He used this plot of ground as an experiment station, where he proceeded to prove to the Alabama farmers that coarse sand, fine sandy loam, and clay loam could be worked profitably. If crops could be developed successfully on this patch of land, he argued, they certainly could be grown in any part of the South.

In 1897, when Carver began this work, the best methods of farming, combined with abundant use of fertilizer, had produced a net loss of $16.25 an acre on this land. Within a year he had treated the soil until it showed a net gain of $4 an acre. Seven years later he produced eighty bushels of sweet potatoes on an acre of sandy loam; and that same year he produced another crop on the same acre. The profit was $75. The next year he raised a 500-pound bale of cotton on that acre, and in Alabama there aren't many acres that will bear a 500-pound bale.

Profits out of barren soil. In these experiments in crop rotation during his first twelve years at Tuskegee Institute, Doctor Carver demonstrated something of inestimable value to the farmers—that by intelligence and industry and simple understanding of the ways of Nature it was possible to make a great deal out of nothing and turn waste and loss into gain. One of the incidental results of the experiments, he pointed out, was to prove that the world allows to go to waste an almost unlimited supply of valuable fertilizer that most soils need—the muck from swamps and the leaves from forests.

---

4. "... let down my bucket." Dr. Carver is referring to one of Booker T. Washington's favorite stories: A ship lost at sea for several days signaled another ship that the crew was out of water and the men were dying of thirst. The other vessel responded: "Cast down your bucket where you are." When the captain of the vessel in distress finally cast down his bucket, it came up full of fresh water. His ship was in the mouth of the Amazon River.

Carver's third big job, which continues unceasingly to this day, was to serve as a scientific pilot to the Southern farmers in the face of disaster. That disaster was the coming of the boll weevil, the insect pest which attacked and devastated the cotton fields.

Thirty years ago Carver witnessed the arrival of the boll weevil in Alabama. He saw the almost total destruction of the cotton crop. He set himself to two tasks: He would assist in fighting the pest, and he would preach a gospel of native money crops other than cotton.

After study, and thought, and experiment, he decided that the Southern farmer could get his money with more surety, and with less damage to his soil, by growing peanuts and sweet potatoes than by attempting any other crop. Doctor Carver began to write bulletins proving his contentions. He made speeches arguing his beliefs. After a time, a number of Southern farmers increased their peanut and sweet potato acreage. And then, suddenly, and sadly, Doctor Carver awoke to what he had done. He had increased the supply without increasing the demand. The peanut and the sweet potato were rotting; the Southern farmer was not only losing the money that he had hoped to make, but he was losing the cost of production and the cost of labor as well.

Almost fiercely the Negro scientist set about the work that the centuries will probably declare to be his greatest contribution to knowledge. He had made a great mistake. He felt that he had done a great personal injustice. Days and nights he spent in his laboratory, seeking to develop new commercial uses for the peanut and for the sweet potato. Slowly, one product at a time, this man forced Nature to give up her secrets; and as each of them was learned, Doctor Carver gave them freely to the world, asking only that they be used for the benefit of mankind.

"He cares nothing about marketing his products," I was told. "He merely discovers them, then gives them away to anyone who wants them."

Inevitably Doctor Carver's work in agriculture, in chemistry, and in other sciences brought him offers to leave Tuskegee and go elsewhere. One of these offers was made by Thomas A. Edison. On the walls of Doctor Carver's office are two autographed pictures from Edison.

"He sent me one of them when he asked me to come to his laboratory and work with him," Doctor Carver explained. "He sent me the other, the larger one, when I told him that my work was here in the South, and that I didn't think God wanted me to leave it."

The aged Dr. George Washington Carver working in a greenhouse at Tuskegee Institute, Tuskegee, Alabama.

Another offer tempted the old Negro—him who once had been valued and traded for $300—tempted him with an annual salary of $100,000. He refused it. He stayed in Tuskegee, where his meager salary is quickly consumed in anonymously paying the bills of worthy boys, both white and black, who are trying to get an education. He stayed in Tuskegee and continued to wear the old alpaca coat which he himself has so often mended, the black trousers which he has so frequently patched, the old shoes which are just a little too large for him, and which he has patched until the patches overlap. Neckties, too, are expensive: so he knits his own out of fibers that he makes himself.

"Money means nothing to him," a friend told me. "Some wealthy peanut growers in Florida were suffering terribly from a diseased crop. They sent Doctor Carver some specimens. He told them what was wrong and how to cure it. After his diagnosis and treatment had proved correct, they sent him a check for $100, promising that they would send him the same amount monthly as a retainer's fee. He sent back the check, telling them that God didn't charge them anything for growing the peanut and that he shouldn't charge them anything for curing it."

I had known Doctor Carver for two days when, at ten o'clock one morning, he took off his spectacles, put the cover on his microscope, and said, "I should be greatly honored if you would come to my rooms with me. I should like you to see some of my pictures."

On the morning that Doctor Carver and I started out to walk to his rooms, we were interrupted by an eight-year-old boy who had caught a fluffy young wood thrush and brought it to Doctor Carver. The old man took the bird, soothed it, and with long black fingers stilled its feeble fluttering. Once the bird no longer darted its little yellow-marked head about, Doctor Carver began to describe its habits, telling the lad how the bird lived, the things it ate, where it loved best to sit and sing; the old man softly whistled the song of the bird. "And now take it back and turn it loose, my boy; take it back to its mother. It's terrible when a young bird is taken from its mother. You wouldn't want to be taken from your mother, would you?"

The lad shook his head.

"That's right"—the great scientist looked away—"of course you wouldn't—none of us would."

When at last we arrived at Doctor Carver's rooms, he unlocked the outer door and bowed me in. "I'm just a little crowded here," he admitted, waving his arm toward a living-room that is in reality a confused combination of library, picture gallery, hothouse, and museum.

There are bookshelves from the floor almost to the ceiling—books on geology, agriculture, botany, chemistry, physics, astronomy, butterflies, mushrooms, frogs; books in English, German, and other languages. In the corners are stacks of scientific journals.

In the center of the room and almost filling the place is a table on which are piled rocks and stones and stalactites and stalagmites and scores of other formations known only to the trained geologist. Outside the window is a great shelf on which stand fifty pots of plants and flowers with which Doctor Carver is constantly experimenting.

On one wall of the room is a glass case four feet wide and six feet high. It is filled with embroidery, tatting, and crochet work. Even an absolute layman can recognize their exceeding delicacy and beauty.

"But how do you find time to do it all?" I asked.

"Chiefly because I've made it a rule of my life to get up every morning at four o'clock. Winter and summer, I wake at that hour; and I get up. I go out into the woods. Alone there with the things I love most, I gather specimens and study the great lessons that Nature is so eager to teach me. I return to my laboratory at nine o'clock, and I work there all day. Every night, and regardless of what kind of entertainment or celebration is going on, I go to bed at nine o'clock."

He hesitated a moment, then went on: "But don't talk as if I had accomplished very much. What I've done may seem a lot, though I"— he shook his head sorrowfully as he turned away—"though I know that it's mighty little when compared to all that I should have done, all that I want to do."

Doctor Carver's belittlement of his own achievements is an unobtrusive indication of his sincere humility. A few years ago he made a trip to Washington. After he returned to Tuskegee, he said nothing about what had happened.

"A week passed before we learned what he had done," an official of the institute told me. "We heard about it first from some newspaper clippings that were sent us."

When the Hawley-Smoot tariff bill[5] was being considered, Southern farmers sent plea after plea to Congress asking that the peanut be named as an article on which import duty was to be charged. Congress saw no reason for acceding to the pleas; but the Ways and Means Committee granted a hearing, and named a day.

On that day, a dozen men appeared before the committee, each man in his turn consuming his allotted ten minutes. In the background, standing alone, Doctor Carver, with his trembling hands, awaited his time to speak. Last on the list of speakers, he finally came forward to address congressmen who were thoroughly tired of harangues about the peanut.

The old man took his place behind the table, where stood scores of bottles and cases containing products that he had made from the peanut. Smiling his humble smile, he explained that he had been brought to Washington by a group of Southern peanut growers; he apologized for taking up the time of his hearers; he thanked them for listening. Then simply, and with an occasional reference to God, he told the tired congressmen the story of the peanut. He told the congressmen merely of how he had asked, "God, what is a peanut and why did you make it?" Then he told how he had sought the answer to his question, and how in his searching he had discovered products ranging from face powder to chocolate wafers. As he talked, he pointed to each product that he had made in his Alabama laboratory.

Exactly at the end of ten minutes, Doctor Carver thanked the committee for allowing him to appear before them. But the congressmen would not let him go; they demanded that he continue his story.

He spoke for one hour and forty-five minutes

before the most important committee of Congress. And when he finished, the committee adjourned to the next room and wrote the peanut into the tariff bill of the United States.

No one can adequately report the strange feeling of spiritual betterment that one constantly feels while with this unusual man; nor can one even intimate one's regret at the time of saying good-by—when Doctor Carver, his smile itself a God-speed, places his trembling hand on your shoulder and says, "Good-by, my boy, good-by. And may God bless you". . . . It is a benediction from a simple, a kindly, a noble heart.

I

HE BLAZED NEW TRAILS

Few lives so exactly illustrate the central theme of this group of selections, WITH WHAT YOU HAVE, as does that of George Washington Carver. His was an amazing ability to overcome obstacles and to make use of what he had. Over and over in his life, he quietly moved forward when the path seemed closed to him.

In building the department of agriculture at Tuskegee Institute from a bare room to a widely respected research laboratory, Dr. Carver discovered many ways to put to use things most people wasted. Recognition came from all over the world. He was sought after by foreign governments for help with their agricultural problems. He was made a consultant to the United States Department of Agriculture. He was elected a member of the British Royal Society of Arts. He was given medals and honors and degrees. A ship and several schools were named for him. Active until the end, the scientist died quietly at Tuskegee in 1943.

1. Under what kinds of handicaps did Dr. Carver work at Tuskegee?

---

5. **Hawley-Smoot tariff bill,** passed in 1930, was the last general tariff. It had the highest rates ever enacted into a United States tariff bill. Four years later, legislation brought about the gradual reduction of many of these tariffs.

2. By what means did he win the respect of others?

II

IMPLICATIONS

1. Ingenuity and creativity are far more important in helping a person accomplish something than are abundant equipment and materials.

2. No job is "beneath" one.

3. The most satisfying thing in life is a job into which one can throw heart and soul.

4. Dr. Carver's spirit and personality are more important to humanity than his discoveries in the realm of science.

III

TECHNIQUES

Characterization

Writers are well aware that people judge others by what they say, as well as by the way they act. Think about each of the following quotations carefully and tell what each reveals about Dr. Carver's character:

1. "He's probably the janitor," I told myself, "and I'm sincerely glad that they've given him a job of some kind."

2. "People are too kind to me," he insisted. "I'm really a very small part of this institution."

3. "But can't a scientist be a lover of the beautiful?" he asked.

4. "When you do the common things of life in an uncommon way, you will command the attention of the world."

5. "Even as a boy I realized that life requires a thorough preparation; there is no short cut to achievement; veneer isn't worth anything."

6. "He sent back the check, telling them that God didn't charge them anything for growing the peanut and that he shouldn't charge them anything for curing it."

IV

WORDS

A. The meaning of a word will often change with the context in which it is used. Note, for instance, the different meaning of *make* (the past form of which is *made*) in each of these three sentences from the story about Dr. Carver:

"He *makes* all his own paints, using Alabama clays."

"He *made* speeches arguing his beliefs."

". . . the Southern farmer was not only losing the money he had hoped to *make*, but he was losing the cost of production and the cost of labor as well."

In the first sentence, *makes* means "creates," in the second, *made* means "delivered," and in the third, *make* means "to earn." In other contexts, *make* may mean "to bring about or cause," "to cause the success of," "to develop into," or "to use or adopt for a specified purpose." Of the seven different definitions—and these are not all there are—that have been given for *make*, try to determine which one applies to each of the following sentences:

1. The over-supply of peanuts and sweet potatoes *made* Dr. Carver unhappy.

2. Who could have guessed that the slave child would one day *make* a great agricultural chemist?

3. Dr. Carver's remarkable work at Tuskegee *made* him a national figure.

4. Despite numerous offers to go elsewhere, Dr. Carver *made* Tuskegee his base of operation.

5. Dr. Carver's speech to the congressmen *made* them want to hear more.

B. After he received an honorary Doctor of Science degree, the agricultural wizard from Tuskegee was called Dr. Carver. His title was altogether appropriate, since the word *doctor* is derived from the Latin word *docere*, meaning "to teach." From the same Latin source comes the word *docile*, meaning "teachable; easily formed or shaped." Originally, *doctor* applied to any man of great learning. It was during the Middle Ages that the title became associated especially with a man of medicine. Today, the original meaning of the word is reflected in the title *Doctor* that is given to a person with a Ph.D. degree.

The needle's eye that does supply,
The thread that runs so true,
Many a beau have I let go,
Because I wanted you.

Jesse Stuart, now a well-known writer, heard these familiar words sung with a circle game the first day he taught school in his mountain region of Kentucky. Later he chose the second line as the title for his popular book from which the following selection is taken.

Jesse Stuart was only 17 at the time he taught his first school and had only three years of high school training. After he had finished high school and worked his way through college, he took another teaching assignment. This was at Winston, where the newly established high school was a dilapidated old lodge hall tumbling into decay and inhabited by bats, birds, and wasps. He was the whole faculty. There were fourteen pupils who would not otherwise have had a chance to attend high school.

While he had little in the way of books or equipment, Jesse Stuart soon realized that he had some exceptional students. Among these was Budge Waters, a tall, gangling, blue-eyed boy who had a photographic memory. He read not by the sentence but by the paragraph and retained nearly everything he read. All of the books which Jesse Stuart had brought for his own reading, his pupils read in the first two weeks. He made frequent trips to Landsburgh, the county seat, to get books for them, sometimes carrying back forty-pound loads in his old suitcase.

After school one December day, he made the trip to the county seat to procure new reading material and to see about entering his students in the state scholastic contest. In the fury of a winter storm, he lost his way and was forced to sleep overnight in some fodder shocks pulled together for shelter. As soon as it was light next morning, he continued to Landsburgh where he got a fresh supply of books and made arrangements for his school to enter the contest.

Landsburgh High expected to win the contest. What competition could Winston offer? It was only . . .

A Little Mudhole in the Road

JESSE STUART

When I told my pupils about a scholastic contest with Landsburgh High School, I watched their expressions. They were willing and ready for the challenge. The competitive spirit was in them.

"We must review everything we have covered in our textbooks," I told them. "We must cover more territory in our textbooks too. Hold up your right hands if you are willing!"

Every pupil raised his hand.

Right then we started to work. In addition to regular assignments, my pupils began reviewing all of the old assignments we had covered.

Despite the challenge ahead and all the reviewing and study we planned to do, we never stopped play. The Tiber River was frozen over. Then ring of skates and merry laughter broke the stillness of the winter nights. We skated on the white winding ribbon of ice beneath the high, cold winter moon. Often we'd skate until midnight. We'd hear the wind blow mournfully over the great white silence that surrounded us and sing lonesome songs without words in the barren branches of the bankside trees. And we'd hear the foxes' barking, high upon the walls of sheltering cliffs, mocking the music of our ringing skates.

Over the week ends we'd go to Tiber where

Reprinted with the permission of Charles Scribner's Sons from *The Thread That Runs So True*, pp. 95–101, by Jesse Stuart. Copyright 1949 Jesse Stuart.

we'd cut holes in the ice and gig fish.[1] The boys and I would rabbit-hunt up and down the Tiber Valley in the old stubble fields now covered with snow and swept by wind. We'd track minks, possums, raccoons, weasels, and foxes to their dens. We'd climb the mountains and get spills over the rocks into the deep snow. This took our minds from books and taught us another kind of education. It was as much fun as reading books. Now that a big contest was before us, we needed diversion. And we got it. Our state was not usually cold enough for winter sports. This winter was an exception, and we took full advantage of it.

When we hunted, the girls didn't go with us, but when we skated, fished, and rode sleighs they went along. There was a long, gentle slope not far from the schoolhouse we found ideal for our sleighs. It was almost a mile to the end of our sleigh run. We went over the riverbank and downstream for many yards on the Tiber ice. We rode sleighs during the noon hour, before and after school.

On winter days when the snow had melted,

leaving the dark earth a sea of sloppy mud, we designed floor games for our little one-room school. They were simple games, such as throwing bolts in small boxes. And we played darts. We also played a game called "fox and goose." We made our fox-and-goose boards, and we played with white, yellow, and red grains of corn. We had to make our own recreation. I never saw a distracted look on a pupil's face. I never heard one complain that the short, dark winter days were boresome because there wasn't anything to do. I think each pupil silently prayed for the days to be longer. We were a united little group. We were small, but we were powerful. We played hard, and we studied hard. We studied and played while the December days passed.

That day in early January, we dismissed school. This was the first time we had dismissed for anything. We had never lost an hour. I had actually taught more hours than was required.

---

1. **gig fish,** to spear fish in schools with a series of hooks attached to a kind of fishing rake called a gig.

This was the big day for us. It was too bad that another blizzard had swept our rugged land and that a stinging wind was smiting the valleys and the hills. But this didn't stop the boys and me from going. Leona Maddox, my best Latin pupil, couldn't go along. Her father, Alex Maddox, wouldn't let her ride a mule seventeen miles to Landsburgh to compete in a contest on a day like this. I couldn't persuade him to let her go.

On that cold, blizzardy morning, Budge Waters rode his mule to school very early and built a fire in the potbellied stove. When the rest of us arrived on our mules at approximately seven o'clock, Budge had the schoolroom warm. We tied our mules to the fence, stood before the fire, and warmed ourselves before we started on our journey. Then we unhitched our mules from the fence and climbed into the saddles. Little clouds of frozen snow in powdery puffs arose from the mules' hoofs as six pupils and their teacher rode down the road.

Though the force of wind in the Tiber Valley was powerful, it was at our backs. The wind was strong enough to give our mules more momentum. We made good time until we left the valley and climbed the big hill. Here, we faced the wind. It was a whipping wind—stinging, biting wind on this mountain—that made the water run from our eyes and our mules' eyes, but for us there was no turning back. We were going to Landsburgh High School. That was that. We were determined to meet this big school; big to us, for they outnumbered us twenty-six to one. Soon we were down in Hinton Valley. Then we rode to the top of the Raccoon Hill, where we faced the stinging wind again.

"Mr. Stuart, I have been thinking," Budge Waters said, as we rode along together, "if you can sleep in a fodder shock when it's twelve degrees below zero, we can take this contest from Landsburgh High School! I've not forgotten how you walked seventeen miles to carry us books. All of your pupils remember. We'll never let you down!"

Budge Waters thought of this because we were riding down the mountain where I had slept that night. Then we rode down into the Raccoon Valley, and Billie Leonard, only thirteen years old, complained of numbness in his hands, feet, and lips. He said he felt as if he was going to sleep. I knew what he was talking about. I had had the same feeling the day Ottis Baylor had put my hands and feet in cold water. We stopped at a home, tied our mules to the fence, and went in and asked to warm. Bert Patton, a stranger to us, piled more wood on the open fire until we were as warm as when we had left the schoolhouse. We told him who we were and where we were going.

"On a day like this!" he said, shaking his head sadly.

We climbed into the saddles again. We were over halfway now. The second hitch would put us at Landsburgh High School. We had valley all the way to Landsburgh, with walls of rugged hills on each side for windbreaks.

At eleven o'clock we rode across the Landsburgh High School yard, and hitched our mules to the fence around the athletic field. There were faces against the windowpanes watching us. Then we walked inside the high school, where Principal Ernest Charters met and welcomed us. He told us that he was surprised we had come on a day like this and that we had been able to arrive so soon.

In the principal's office my pupils and I huddled around the gas stove while we heard much laughter in the high-school corridors. The Landsburgh High School pupils thought we were a strange-looking lot. Many came inside their principal's office to take a look at us. We were regarded with curiosity, strangeness, and wonder. Never before had these pupils seen seven mules hitched to their schoolyard fence. Never before had they competed scholastically with so few in number—competitors who had reached them by muleback. The Landsburgh High School principal didn't feel about the contest the way we felt. To him, this was just a "setup" to test his pupils for the district contest which would soon be held. He told me this when he went after the sealed envelopes that

The author, Jesse Stuart, in his homemade "office," formerly a tool shed and smokehouse.

held the questions. We warmed before the gas stove while he made arrangements for the contest.

"These questions were made out by the state department of education," he said when he returned. "I don't know how hard they are."

My pupils stood silently by the stove and looked at each other. We were asked to go to one of the largest classrooms. A Landsburgh High School teacher had charge of giving the tests. When the Landsburgh High School pupils came through the door to compete against my pupils, we knew why Principal Charters had selected this large classroom. My pupils looked at each other, then at their competitors.

I entered redheaded Jesse Jarvis to compete with ten of their plane-geometry pupils. I entered Billie Leonard against twenty-one of their selected algebra pupils.

"Budge, you'll have to represent us in grammar, English literature, and history," I said.

"And I believe I'll put you in civil government. Is that all right?"

"Yes," he agreed. Budge had never had a course in civil government. All he knew about it was what he had read in connection with history.

"Robert Batson, you enter in history and grammar.

"Robin Baylor, you enter in algebra.

"Snookie Baylor, you enter in algebra and plane geometry.

"Sorry, Mr. Charters," I said, "we don't have anyone to enter in Latin. My best Latin pupil, Leona Maddox, couldn't make this trip."

After the contest had begun, I left the room. Miss Bertha Madden was in charge. I took our mules to Walter Scott's barn on the east end of Landsburgh, where I fed and watered them.

With the exception of an interval when the contestants ate a quick lunch, the contest lasted until 2:30 P.M. I had one pupil, Budge Waters, in four contests. I had planned to enter him in two. Just as soon as Budge finished with civil government, we started grading the papers. All the pupils were requested to leave the room.

We graded the papers with keys. Mr. Charters, Miss Madden, and two other teachers, and I did the grading. Mr. Charters read the answers on the keys, and we checked the answers. Once or twice we stopped long enough to discuss what stiff questions these were. We wondered how far we would have gotten if we—all of us college graduates—had taken the same test. One of the teachers asked me, while we graded these papers, if Budge Waters had ever seen these questions before.

When we were through grading the papers, Mr. Charters called the contestants into the classroom.

"I want to read you the scores of this contest," Principal Charters said. His voice was nervous.

"Budge Waters, winner in English literature.

"Budge Waters, winner in grammar.

"Budge Waters, winner in history with almost a perfect score.

"Budge Waters, winner in civil government.

"Why didn't you bring just this one boy?" Principal Charters asked me.

"Because I've got other good pupils," I quickly retorted.

"Billie Leonard, winner in algebra, with plenty of points to spare.

"Jesse Jarvis, second in plane geometry, lost by one point.

"Snookie Baylor and Robin Baylor tied for second place in algebra.

"Congratulations," said Principal Charters, "to your pupils and to you, on your success. It looks as though Winston High will represent this county in the district scholastic contest. I've never heard of such a remarkable thing."

When we left the Landsburgh High School we heard defeated pupils crying because "a little mudhole in the road like Winston beat us."

In a few minutes our mule cavalcade passed the Landsburgh High School. Faces were against the windowpanes, and many pupils waved jubilantly to us as we rode by, our coat tails riding the wind behind our saddles, and the ends of our scarfs bright banners on the wind. We rode victoriously down the main street of Landsburgh on our way home.

I

TWENTY-SIX TO ONE

Jesse Stuart believed that it was up to every schoolteacher in America to try to inspire and teach his students in such a way that they would make the greatest citizenry the United States had ever had. Each teacher had to do his share, and the building of a solid citizenry began with each unit of teacher and students—no matter how small or isolated the school might be.

1. What evidence is there that Jesse Stuart inspired his students to do their best?

2. In what way were the odds against them? What "advantages" did they have over students in the larger schools?

3. Compare the feelings displayed by the pupils of Landsburgh High when the Winston students arrived and when they left.

II

IMPLICATIONS

Do you agree or disagree with these propositions?

1. Teaching can only be as good as the pupils being taught.

2. Appearances can be deceiving.

3. The outcome of a contest depends on the contestants, not the odds.

4. Landsburgh High wasn't a very good school.

III

TECHNIQUES

Characterization

Mr. Stuart's first book, *Man with a Bull-Tongue Plow*, was a volume of poetry. Even though he tells this story in a straightforward, matter-of-fact way, there are passages to show the reader his poetic use of language.

1. How does the author describe the wind when they were skating on winter evenings? What does he have to say about the barking of the foxes?

2. Although in this autobiographical account, attention is centered upon what the students did, much is revealed indirectly about the author. You know, for example, that while he is matter-of-fact, he has poetic feelings. What other traits of character are suggested? Do you think he has determination, concern for the feelings of others, and ambition? Support all claims of character traits with evidence taken from the selection. In what traits does he resemble George Washington Carver? How does his character differ? How were their problems similar?

Significant Details

Jesse Stuart's writing is filled with small but significant details which help the reader to picture each situation he describes. For instance, when he tells you about the games, he specifies that they threw bolts into small boxes and played "fox and goose" using white, yellow, and red grains of corn.

Find five or more examples from the selection to show the author's habit of supplying specific details rather than being indefinite.

An *unspoken* "Thank you"
is often the most sincere.

Thank You, M'am

LANGSTON HUGHES

She was a large woman with a large purse that had everything in it but a hammer and nails. It had a long strap, and she carried it slung across her shoulder. It was about eleven o'clock at night, dark, and she was walking alone, when a boy ran up behind her and tried to snatch her purse. The strap broke with the sudden single tug the boy gave it from behind. But the boy's weight and the weight of the purse combined caused him to lose his balance. Instead of taking off full blast as he had hoped, the boy fell on his back on the sidewalk and his legs flew up. The large woman simply turned around and kicked him right square in his blue jeaned sitter. Then she reached down, picked the boy up by his shirt front, and shook him until his teeth rattled.

After that the woman said, "Pick up my pocketbook, boy, and give it here."

She still held him tightly. But she bent down enough to permit him to stoop and pick up her purse. Then she said, "Now ain't you ashamed of yourself?"

Firmly gripped by his shirt front the boy said, "Yes'm."

The woman said, "What did you want to do it for?"

The boy said, "I didn't aim to."

She said, "You a lie!"

By that time two or three people passed, stopped, turned to look, and some stood watching.

Reprinted by permission of HAROLD OBER ASSOCIATES INCORPORATED. Copyright © 1958 by Langston Hughes.

"If I turn you loose, will you run?" asked the woman.

"Yes'm," said the boy.

"Then I won't turn you loose," said the woman. She did not release him.

"Lady, I'm sorry," whispered the boy.

"Um-hum! Your face is dirty. I got a great mind to wash your face for you. Ain't you got nobody home to tell you to wash your face?"

"No'm," said the boy.

"Then it will get washed this evening," said the large woman, starting up the street, dragging the frightened boy behind her.

He looked as if he were fourteen or fifteen, frail and willow-wild, in tennis shoes and blue jeans.

The woman said, "You ought to be my son. I would teach you right from wrong. Least I can do right now is to wash your face. Are you hungry?"

"No'm," said the being-dragged boy. "I just want you to turn me loose."

"Was I bothering *you* when I turned that corner?" asked the woman.

"No'm."

"But you put yourself in contact with *me*," said the woman. "If you think that that contact is not going to last awhile, you got another thought coming. When I get through with you, sir, you are going to remember Mrs. Luella Bates Washington Jones."

Sweat popped out on the boy's face and he began to struggle. Mrs. Jones stopped, jerked him around in front of her, put a half nelson about his neck, and continued to drag him up the street. When she got to her door, she dragged the boy inside, down a hall, and into a large kitchenette-furnished room at the rear of the house. She switched on the light and left the door open. The boy could hear other roomers laughing and talking in the large house. Some of their doors were open, too, so he knew he and the woman were not alone. The woman still had him by the neck in the middle of her room.

She said, "What is your name?"

"Roger," answered the boy.

"Then, Roger, you go to that sink and wash your face," said the woman, whereupon she turned him loose—at last. Roger looked at the door—looked at the woman—looked at the door—*and went to the sink.*

"Let the water run until it gets warm," she said. "Here's a clean towel."

"You gonna take me to jail?" asked the boy, bending over the sink.

"Not with that face, I would not take you nowhere," said the woman. "Here I am trying to get home to cook me a bite to eat, and you snatch my pocketbook! Maybe you ain't been to your supper either, late as it be. Have you?"

"There's nobody home at my house," said the boy.

"Then we'll eat," said the woman. "I believe you're hungry—or been hungry—to try to snatch my pocketbook!"

"I want a pair of blue suede shoes," said the boy.

"Well, you didn't have to snatch *my* pocketbook to get some suede shoes," said Mrs. Luella Bates Washington Jones. "You could of asked me."

"M'am?"

The water dripping from his face, the boy looked at her. There was a long pause. A very long pause. After he had dried his face and not knowing what else to do, dried it again, the boy turned around, wondering what next. The door was open. He could make a dash for it down the hall. He could run, run, run, *run!*

The woman was sitting on the day bed. After a while she said, "I were young once and I wanted things I could not get."

There was another long pause. The boy's mouth opened. Then he frowned, not knowing he frowned.

The woman said, "Um-hum! You thought I was going to say *but,* didn't you? You thought I was going to say, *but I didn't snatch people's pocketbooks.* Well, I wasn't going to say that." Pause. Silence. "I have done things, too, which I would not tell you, son—neither tell God, if He didn't already know. Everybody's got something in common. So you set down while I fix us something to eat. You might run that comb through your hair so you will look presentable."

In another corner of the room behind a

screen was a gas plate and an icebox. Mrs. Jones got up and went behind the screen. The woman did not watch the boy to see if he was going to run now, nor did she watch her purse, which she left behind her on the day bed. But the boy took care to sit on the far side of the room, away from the purse, where he thought she could easily see him out of the corner of her eye if she wanted to. He did not trust the woman *not* to trust him. And he did not want to be mistrusted now.

"Do you need somebody to go to the store," asked the boy, "maybe to get some milk or something?"

"Don't believe I do," said the woman, "unless you just want sweet milk yourself. I was going to make cocoa out of this canned milk I got here."

"That will be fine," said the boy.

She heated some lima beans and ham she had in the icebox, made the cocoa, and set the table. The woman did not ask the boy anything about where he lived, or his folks, or anything else that would embarrass him. Instead, as they ate, she told him about her job in a hotel beauty shop that stayed open late, what the work was like, and how all kinds of women came in and out, blondes, redheads, and Spanish. Then she cut him a half of her ten-cent cake.

"Eat some more, son," she said.

When they were finished eating, she got up and said, "Now here, take this ten dollars and buy yourself some blue suede shoes. And next time, do not make the mistake of latching onto *my* pocketbook *nor nobody else's*—because shoes got by devilish ways will burn your feet. I got to get my rest now. But from here on in, son, I hope you will behave yourself."

She led him down the hall to the front door and opened it. "Good night! Behave yourself, boy!" she said, looking out into the street as he went down the steps.

The boy wanted to say something other than, "Thank you, m'am," to Mrs. Luella Bates Washington Jones, but although his lips moved, he couldn't even say that as he turned at the foot of the barren stoop and looked up at the large woman in the door. Then she shut the door.

I

A CLEAN FACE

When Roger left the apartment of Mrs. Luella Bates Washington Jones, his dirty face had been washed, and this large woman had given him much—probably much more than even he realized then. Yet Mrs. Jones would seem to most people to have little to share with others. Although she gave to Roger from her limited supply of money, what other things did she give him that are of greater value?

When Roger told her why he wanted the money, what *didn't* Mrs. Jones do that he expected her to do? Do you think this increased his respect for her? Why?

II

IMPLICATIONS

Consider and discuss the following statements.

1. The more one has to give, the more willingly he shares.

2. A person should think of his own welfare first. If you don't think of yourself first, nobody else will.

III

TECHNIQUES

Characterization

Roger could have been any dirty, neglected boy off the streets, but Mrs. Jones is an individual of great force. As she told Roger: "When I get through with you, sir, you are going to remember Mrs. Luella Bates Washington Jones."

Describe her actions in dealing with the boy that show her physical strength. What adjective does the author use twice in the opening paragraph that gives the reader the central clue in understanding this woman's character? Discuss how this word applies to her entire treatment of Roger.

◆ Do you have pictures
in your memory? For example,
have you ever seen . . .

A Clown at Ten

We should have guessed—
When he pounced home in a flailing dance,
Clucking like a hen possessed,
Elbows flapping in a sidelong prance,
Grinning grimly,   5
Mocking primly
A saucy schoolmate's slur—
The deepdown bite of her.

We should have known
His pull-ups on the closet pole,   10
His swimming in the kitchen zone,

His pugilistic body roll
On the church pew
And museum queue
Were ways to storm the pass   15
For the smallest in his class.

Each noon he licked his silly grin
And ate beyond our discipline.
We called him fool
And fed him shame,   20
This little giant
With our name.

JAMES A. EMANUEL

A COMIC WITH A PURPOSE

It is easy to see this "clown at ten" when you read the poet's words and make an effort to picture, in your mind's eye, a boy going through all the antics described in order to establish his importance. His handicap is his size.

1. How do you imitate a hen? Discuss.

2. What did he do to try to build up his chest and general physique?

3. The poet uses the expression, "he licked his silly grin." What common association is made with the gesture of licking the lips?

Characterization

After reading this poem or hearing it read, think over the people you know at school or in the community. Is there a particular one you can think of who plays a role or assumes a kind of character in order to make himself or herself more important? Do you associate a certain way of talking or certain characteristic actions with this individual? You may wish to write a brief paragraph or a poem in which you try to picture this person.

What does he have—
this old black man—that raises him above
the miseries and pain of living?

Jazz Poem Two

there he stands. see?
like a black Ancient Mariner[1] his
wrinkled old face so
full of the wearies of living is
turned downward with   5
closed eyes. his frayed-collar
faded-blue old shirt turn
dark with sweat & the old
necktie undone drops
loosely about the worn   10
old jacket see? just
barely holding his
sagging stomach in. yeah.
his run-down shoes have
paper in them & his   15
rough unshaven face shows
pain
in each wrinkle

but there he stands. in
self-brought solitude head   20
still down eyes
still closed ears
perked & trained upon
the bass line for
across his chest lies an old   25
alto saxophone—
supported from his neck by
a wire coat hanger.

---

1. **Ancient Mariner,** a reference to a
poem, "The Rime of the Ancient
Mariner," by Samuel Taylor Coleridge
in which a seaman shoots an alba-
tross, a bird of good omen, and
suffers supernatural punishment. The
seaman is compelled to tell his story
repeatedly.

gently he lifts it now
to parted lips. see? to   30
tell all the world that
he is a Black Man. that
he was sent here to preach
the Black Gospel of Jazz.

now preaching it with words of   35
screaming notes & chords he
is no longer a man. no not even
a Black Man. but (yeah!)
a Bird!—
one that gathers his wings & flies   40
  high
    high
      higher
until he flies away! or
comes back to find himself   45
a Black Man
again.

CARL WENDELL HINES, JR.

_____

Originally appeared in *American Negro Poetry*, ed. by Arna Bontemps. Hill and Wang, 1963.

A GOSPEL WITHOUT WORDS

Like the ancient mariner in Coleridge's poem, the old jazz musician feels he has a message for the people of the world. He is a pitiable figure, but he is also a commanding one. He has the power to speak in a way that makes men listen— a gift that many people richer in worldly goods do not possess. He speaks eloquently through his music; it is this act of creation that lifts him above the squalor of his surroundings. Coleridge's ancient mariner felt compelled to travel from land to land to preach love and reverence for all forms of life, great and small. Discuss whether you think this message might also be found in the "preaching" of the old jazz musician.

Characterization

Carl Wendell Hines, Jr., wants the reader to "see" the old man clearly, and he manages to give a vivid picture without waste of words.

1. What are you told about the old man's face, his clothing, his shoes? How do you know he isn't much interested in talking to those around him? What instrument is his "voice"?

2. Why are the last ten words of the poem significant?

In evaluating what they have
most people feel especially blessed if
they were born with no physical handicaps.
Is this really as much
a blessing as it would seem?

The Basement

PÄR LAGERKVIST

We have all seen him and see him nearly every day. We don't take much notice of him. Now and then we pass him as he lies there but pay little attention; it is as though he should be here, as though he belonged to our world. I mean Lindgren, the little old man with the withered legs, the one who drags himself along the streets and in the parks with the help of his hands. He wears leather gloves; his legs, too, are covered with leather. The short-bearded face is marked by suffering which it cannot quite express; the eyes are small and submissive. We have all met him, meet him continually. It is as though he were a part of ourselves. In passing we put a coin in his worn-out hand; he, too, must live.

But few know much about him other than that he exists. So I am going to tell you a little more about the old man, for I know him.

I had often stopped and talked to the old chap for a while. There was something soothing and good about him which I seemed to need. I had done this so often that people must have thought he was an unfortunate relative of mine. It is not so. There is no distress in our family; only a grief which is ours and

none other's, which we bear erectly. But I felt I had to stand and talk to him sometimes: for his sake, so that he would not feel like an outcast, but also for my own, because he had something to tell me. And there didn't seem to be any gulf between us. I often thought that if I had not had any legs to walk with, had had to drag myself along the ground as he did, it would not have suited me so badly either. I should have had no reason to think it strange that this had fallen to my lot. In this way there was, after all, something we had in common.

One evening in the late autumn I came across him in a park where lovers used to meet. He was lying under a lamp in order to be seen, stretching out his worn hand though nobody came. No doubt he thought that love makes people generous. Actually he didn't know much about this world, but just lay stretching out his hand somewhere, just lived here all the same. It had been raining; he was muddy from the sodden ground and looked tired and ill.

"Hadn't you better be getting home, Lindgren?" I said. "It's late."

"Yes," he replied, "I suppose I had."

"I'll walk part of the way with you," I said. "Where do you live?"

He told me, we found that we lived not far from each other and went the same way.

We crossed a street.

"Isn't it risky," I asked, "when you want to get from one side to the other?"

"Oh no," he replied. "They're on the lookout for me. Yesterday a policeman stopped the entire traffic for me to cross. But he said I'd have to hurry, and you can't wonder. Oh no, everybody here knows me; they seem to think I belong here."

We went slowly on. I had to shorten my steps and even stop occasionally so that he could keep up. It started to drizzle. He shuffled along at my feet, the muddy hands scratching against the pavement, the body moving up and down. It was like an animal dragging itself home to its lair. Yet it was a human being like myself. I heard him talking and breathing down there as I was doing, but the street lamps shone feebly through the mist and I could hardly see him. I was filled with such pity as I heard him down there, struggling to keep up.

"Don't you think you have a hard lot to bear, Lindgren?" I said. "You must often feel it's unfair."

"No," he answered from below. "The odd thing is that it is not so bad as people think. You get used to it. And I was born with it; it's not as if a healthy grown man suddenly meets with something unexpected. No, I can't say I have anything to complain of, if I really come to think of it. There must be many who are worse off than I am. I am spared much that others have to go through. My life is quiet and secure; the world has been merciful to me. You must remember that I only come in contact with the good in it."

"Oh?" I said wonderingly.

"Yes, I only come in contact with good people; they're the only ones who stop and give me a coin. I know nothing about the others. They just walk past."

"Well, Lindgren, you know how to make the best of things," I answered with a smile.

"But it's true," he said seriously, "and it's something to be thankful for." I also took it seriously; in fact, realized that he was right. What a great blessing it was getting to know only the good in life!

We went on. Light was coming from a shop in a basement. "I'm going to buy bread here," he said, creeping up to the window and knocking. A girl came up with the parcel, which was all ready. "Good evening, Lindgren," she said. "Ugh, what weather! You ought to be getting home."

"Yes, I'm going," the old chap answered. They nodded good-bye to each other, and she closed the door after her.

"I always do my shopping in the basement," he said as we proceeded.

"Yes, I suppose so," I answered.

"People there are always so kind."

"Oh? Yes, perhaps."

"But they *are*," he said decidedly.

We struggled through one or two dark, hilly lanes.

"I live in the basement, too, as you can imagine," he continued. "It suits me best. Our landlord arranged it. He is a remarkable man."

Then we went through one street after the other, groping our way along. It had never occurred to me that it was such a long way home. I felt tired, exhausted. It was as if I, too, were dragging myself along in the darkness, heavily and wearily, though I was no cripple. I walked erect, as one should walk. By the street lamps I saw him crawling down there; then he disappeared again. I merely heard his panting breath.

At last we turned into his street, and came up to the house where he lived. It was large and splendid; nearly all the windows were lighted. There seemed to be a party on the first floor. The chandeliers glistened, music penetrated out into the dismal autumn night and dancing couples could be seen flitting past. He crept forward to the three or four steps which led down to where he lived. Beside them was a window with a piece of curtain and a sardine tin with flower bulbs. "You'll come down, won't you, and have a look at my room?" he said.

I had not thought of that. I had not realized I would have to. I felt strangely heavy at heart. Why should I go down? We were not close enough friends to warrant it. I had come with him part of the way because we lived in much the same direction; I'd had no intention of going home with him. Why should I go down? But I had to.

It occurred to me that actually I knew the family up there who were giving the party. It was strange that they had not invited me; they must have forgotten.

"You don't mind my asking you down, do you?" the old chap asked, as though remarking on my silence.

"No," I said.

He had misunderstood me. I wanted to go down and see how he lived; that was why I had come along. I wanted to go where I was asked.

He shuffled down the steps, got out the key and put it in the lock. I noticed that this had been moved lower down so that he could reach it.

"Our landlord had it done," he said. "He thinks of everything." The door opened and we went in. When the light had been put on I looked around the room. It was small and bare. The floor was cold stone with one or two bits of carpet on it. In the middle was a table which had part of the legs sawn off, and two low chairs. In one corner was the stove, which he could also use for cooking, apparently. Beside it was a shelf that served as a pantry. The tins were arranged according to height, with labels on. Pieces of bread he had evidently saved for dipping in his coffee stood in a row. Around the shelf was a white, paper lace edging. At one end of the room was his

bed, consisting of a bunk raised off the floor; the bedcover was clean and nice. Despite all the poverty, every corner of the room was neat and tidy. I don't know why, but this orderliness distressed me. Why did he have it like this? Had I been in his shoes I should have had it dirty and horrible—just a hole to creep into and hide, like an animal. It would have been easier then, I thought, to hold out. But it was clean and tidy everywhere.

It seemed a cozy little home as he crept about busily, reached up for the flower vase on the table and filled it with water, slid down again, got a cloth out of a little blue-painted chest, spread it, got out cups and saucers. It cut me to the heart to see him doing these homely things. He had taken off the leather gloves; his hands were flat with thick skin on the palms. He then lit the fire, blowing on it so that the flames roared up the pipe; added coal, took down the coffeepot and put it on. I was not allowed to help him; no, he knew best how it should be. He did it all with such a deft and practiced hand that you could see he enjoyed it, that he had grown fond of these little tasks. Now and then he would look up at me good-naturedly. There was something so warm and secure about him here in his home; he was not as he was in the street. Soon the coffeepot was simmering on the fire and the aroma filled the room. When it was ready he crept up laboriously onto his chair and settled down, beaming and contented. He poured out the coffee and we began to drink. It was nice and warming. He thought I should eat some bread too, but I didn't want to take it from him. He himself ate with a marked solemnity, slowly breaking piece after piece and carefully picking up all the crumbs. There was such reverence about his meal. His eyes shone; never have I seen a face so radiant as his, never transfigured in such a tranquil way.

I felt at once moved and oppressed at seeing him like this in the midst of his affliction. How could he? I, who lived the real life, who merely sat here as a temporary guest in order to see what it was like down here in his lair—I had no peace. Well, I thought to myself, he probably has something else he hopes for. He must be one of those who believe in God and the like, and then anything can be endured, nothing is hard. And I remembered that I was going to ask him about this very thing, which forever weighed me down, which never gave me any peace, which dragged me down into the depths where I did not want to be. That was why I had come home with him, to ask him about it. I didn't belong down here, was only going to ask him about it.

"Tell me, Lindgren," I said, "when one's life is like yours, when one has to suffer as you do, I suppose one feels, more strongly than the rest of us, the need of believing that there is something outside this world, that there is a prevailing God who has a higher purpose with what He lays upon us?"

The old man pondered a moment.

"No," he replied slowly, "not when one's life can be like mine."

I thought this was strange, distressing to hear. Was he not aware of his misery, did he not know how rich and glorious life should be?

"No," he said, lost in thought, "it is not we who need Him. Even if He existed He could not tell us more than we already know and are grateful for.

"I have often talked to our landlord about it," he went on. "He has taught me a great deal. Perhaps you don't know our landlord here in the house, but you should; he is a strange man."

"No, I don't know him."

"No, of course not—I see that—but you should."

Oh, I thought, yes, maybe. I didn't know this remarkable landlord he was talking about; he might well be something out of the ordinary, but I lived in another house. I kept my thoughts to myself, however.

"I wonder," the old chap answered me. "He has many houses—nearly all of them. He owns yours, too, I think.

"Yes," he went on, "he's a great one for managing and arranging everything. When I came and asked if he could perhaps house me here, as I, too, had to live somewhere, he eyed me narrowly for a long time.

" 'Well, I shall have to put you in the basement,' he said. 'You can't live up in the house itself.'

" 'No,' I answered, 'I see that.'

" 'I think the basement will suit you,' he said. 'I hope I'm not mistaken about you? What's your own opinion?'

" 'I think it would do nicely for me there.'

" 'Yes. You know, don't you, that I won't have just anyone there. No bitterness and hatred, no wicked or undependable people. Upstairs I have to take in all kinds, many whom I know very little about, but in the basement I want good, reliable people, people I know and like. What do you think—do you belong here?'

" 'I'd like very much to think so,' I answered happily.

"'Well and good. But can you pay the rent?' he said, for he's strict, too—that he is. 'Everyone must pay; there's no getting out of it, however wretched you are. You can have it cheaply, as you're not fit for much. But you must pay something at all events. How will you scrape it together?'

"'I shall have to live on the good people in the world.'

"'Are there any?' he asked, looking at me sharply.

"'There must be many, surely.'

"'That is right,' he said. 'That is easy to work out for anyone who really wants to. You are a man of sense; you shall live with me.'

"Yes, he is remarkable, though so simple and natural. He has helped me over much. I couldn't get on without him. Every now and then he looks in and sits for a while, talking. It's such a help. It cheers one up being appreciated. 'You're a worthwhile man, Lindgren,' he says. It does one good to hear that."

He looked at me in glad content. "Are you a worthwhile man?" he asked.

I made no answer, but looked down at the floor, not wanting to meet his eyes.

"One should be," he said. "It helps one over a lot to know that one is."

The room about us was plain but snug. The lamplight shone over the low table with its sawed-off legs, over the cloth where his saved-up bread lay, over the bed on which he took his rest. He paid no attention to my silence. He was sitting with his own thoughts, I could see.

Then he got down from the chair, saw to the fire, washed up the cups and put them on the shelf where they belonged; crept to the bunk and made it ready, folding up the bedcover. But when he had folded it across the seat of the chair and smoothed it, he remained kneeling there.

"It's good when the day is over," he said. And one could see that he was tired.

"Is it, Lindgren? When life is so full and means so much to you?"

"Yes," he answered, looking quietly in front of him, "life is full. I know that so well, I feel it so surely and firmly inside me. But each day is heavy to bear.

"I tell you this because I think we understand one another so well. And one mustn't pretend to be better than one is."

He drew a deep breath. Seeing him huddled together there on his knees, one might have thought he was praying, but he was just made like that.

I got up quietly to go, went up and thanked him, said good night. He thought I should come back when I felt like it, and I said I should like to. Then he crept with me to the door and I was standing out in the street again.

The whole house was in darkness now. Even the first floor where the chandeliers had blazed just now. It could not have been a real party if it was already over. The old man's lamp was the only one burning; it lighted me nearly all the way home.

I

WHO IS THE MORE FORTUNATE?

"The Basement" is a story that leaves the reader with more questions than answers. On the surface what takes place seems quite simple. Three people are involved: the storyteller or narrator, apparently a normal, average person; Lindgren, a cripple who drags himself along the streets with his hands; and Lindgren's landlord, a kind and just man.

1. Where does the narrator find Lindgren that evening in late autumn? How does he happen to go home with him?

2. What reasons does Lindgren give for believing his life to be better than that of many other persons?

3. How does the narrator feel about Lindgren's neat, cozy, little basement home? What evidence is there here that the landlord cares about Lindgren?

4. What is the question that the narrator feels compelled to ask Lindgren? What is Lindgren's answer? Why had Lindgren's landlord placed him in the basement?

5. In this story, which man gives comfort to the other? Which man seems the most secure? In what way is the normal person inferior to the physically handicapped person?

II

IMPLICATIONS

The depth of this story lies in the meaning that might be found in many of the lines. Discuss the following as examples:

1. "It is as though he were a part of ourselves." (p. 203)

2. "But I felt I had to stand out and talk to him sometimes . . . because he had something to tell me." (p. 203)

3. " 'Yes, I only come in contact with good people; they're the only ones who stop and give me a coin. I know nothing about the others. They just walk past.' " (p. 204)

4. " 'He [the landlord] has many houses—nearly of them. He owns yours, too, I think.' " (p. 206)

5. " 'Everyone must pay; there's no getting out of it, however wretched you are.' " (p. 207)

6. " 'You are a man of sense; you shall live with me.' " (p. 207)

7. "He looked at me in glad content. 'Are you a worthwhile man?' he asked." (p. 207)

8. "The whole house was in darkness now. . . . It could not have been a real party of it was already over. The old man's lamp was the only one burning; it lighted me nearly all the way home." (p. 207)

III

TECHNIQUES

Significant Details

When an author feels he has something very important to say and wishes to say it in a story that his readers will remember, he may use an allegory, one of the oldest literary forms. An allegory is a symbolic story in which people and things really represent something in addition to what they seem to be.

To decide whether "The Basement" has some allegory in it, the class may wish to divide into three groups. The purpose of each group would be to check details in the story that might be significant in revealing who or what each of the three important characters represents. One group should be concerned with Lindgren, the second with the narrator, and the third with the landlord. To facilitate sharing of ideas, each group may subdivide into units of no more than five or six people. Before beginning discussion, the members of all groups should look back over the story to note lines they believe significant in revealing information about their assigned character's identity. After sufficient time has been given for the various groups to reach conclusions, a central discussion leader may call for the findings of each group. These findings may then be discussed by the whole class.

SUMMING UP

With What You Have

The people you have been reading about in the foregoing selections could have been guided by the advice of Ralph Waldo Emerson given in the introduction to this unit: "Make the most of yourself, for that is all there is of you."

If you look around at school or in your community at the people who are successful, you will discover that they spend little time envying others or complaining about what they do not have. They are people like Dick Gregory or Budge Waters who use "what they have" and make it count.

Discuss people you know personally in your community, or those you may know about only through reading books and newspapers or watching television, who you believe have achieved despite handicaps. What have they achieved and how?

IMPLICATIONS

Discuss the following statements as they relate to your reading in this unit:

1. The ability to laugh at oneself is important to success.

2. A true measure of a man's worth is his achievement.

3. Many commonly accepted customs reflect hypocrisy and discrimination.

4. Taking on an impossible task strengthens character.

5. Humility is one sign of greatness.

6. Hatred is as great a spur to achievement as love.

7. Most people are blind to the opportunities for greatness that are present around them.

TECHNIQUES

Characterization

In your daily contact with others, perhaps you have noticed that at times a few chance words or a gesture will reveal something significant about someone's personality or character. If a friend loses the contest for the class presidency, does he laugh and say, "Better luck next time," snarl that his opponent used dirty tactics, or refuse to comment? The particular reaction can be revealing.

A writer of fiction or nonfiction, whose principal interest is setting forth clearly and vividly the personality of his subject, knows the value of such "character indicators." He uses five common ways to tell you what an individual is really like. In review, these are:

1. What the character looks like;

2. What the character says and thinks;

3. What others say and think about the character;

4. The way the character acts in a given situation;

5. The way others act toward the character.

Consider the following and discuss what is revealed about the character of the person whose name precedes the quotation.

1. *Dick Gregory:* "I love winos because they never hurt anyone but themselves." (page 157)

2. *Felipe Rivera:* "'A great and lonely spirit, perhaps. I do not know, I do not know,' Arrellano said helplessly." (page 168)

3. *Lindgren:* "The odd thing is that it is not so bad as people think. You get used to it. And I was born with it; it's not as if a healthy grown man suddenly meets with something unexpected. No, I can't say I have anything to complain of, if I really come to think of it. There must be many who are worse off than I am. I am spared much that others have to go through. My life is quiet and secure; the world is merciful to me. You must remember that I only come in contact with the good in it." (page 204)

Significant Details

Specific details are the very life of good biographical or autobiographical writing. They give reality to the situations through which the central figure passes. A few specific details can tell the reader more than many vague generalities. For example, Dick Gregory, in describing the period of numbness he experienced after the teacher said everyone knew he didn't have a father, tells you how he felt about his welfare mackinaw, Mister Ben's rotten peaches, and the sugar borrowed from Mrs. Simmons. The inclusion of these details makes the incident far more vivid and memorable for the reader than if Gregory had just written, "After that I felt ashamed of being on welfare."

The following are statements which the author might have used if he had omitted the significant details. Supply three details, in each case, with which the author added reality and vividness. Do not look up the incident in the selection until after you have tried to supply the details from memory.

1. Dr. Carver made many products from plants ("A Boy Who Was Traded for a Horse," p. 183).

2. Jesse Stuart's students took part in the scholarship contest at Landsburgh ("A Little Mudhole in the Road," p. 194).

3. Mrs. Jones caught the boy who tried to snatch her purse and took him home with her ("Thank You M'am," p. 196).

Homeless Annie Sullivan
spent a good part of her childhood
in a state almshouse, with rats to play with
instead of toys. It might seem
that there would be little she could give
to a pampered child surrounded with comfort.
Yet Annie had courage, compassion,
and fighting spirit. With "what she had,"
she worked a miracle.

The
Miracle Worker

Introduction

In the evening of October 19, 1959, an opening night audience at the Playhouse on New York's Broadway watched in fascination as the talented cast of William Gibson's play, *The Miracle Worker*, brought to life a stirring chapter from the early life of Helen Keller. When the final curtain came down, the audience responded with thunderous applause. They had been through a moving and memorable experience. Their emotions had been drawn taut as they witnessed the mind and soul of the deaf, blind, and mute seven-year-old Helen being pulled from an animal-like existence into a world she could at last understand.

Mark Twain, who met Helen Keller when she was still quite young, said that she was one of the two outstanding personalities of the nineteenth century. (The other was Napoleon.) She has traveled to all parts of the globe, lectured to thousands, written books, and made friends with most of the leading figures of her time. Yet had it not been for the efforts of Annie Sullivan, her teacher and her constant companion for nearly fifty years, the brilliant mind of Helen Keller might have remained forever isolated on an island of darkness.

Two years before she graduated from Radcliffe College with honors, Miss Keller completed an autobiography, *The Story of My Life.* The story of her early life was an immediate success and became required reading for students at various colleges and high schools over the United States. This story of her triumph has inspired millions of people, among them playwright William Gibson, who was moved to write *The Miracle Worker.*

In the beginning, Mr. Gibson wrote *The Miracle Worker* for television. Following its presentation in February of 1957, the response from viewers was so enthusiastic that he was asked to rewrite it for the Broadway stage. It appeared later as a successful motion picture.

When he had completed the original script, Mr. Gibson had it typed in Braille and sent to Miss Keller for corrections. She returned it with four pages of notes to aid him in avoiding factual errors. While the incidents in the play are basically accurate, the writer was forced to use imaginative devices introducing background information to explain the actions of the characters. The offstage voices which Anne Sullivan hears during the play are part of such a device.

The most persistent of these voices out of Annie's past is that of her little brother Jimmie. Since there is a flesh-and-blood Jimmie in the play, as Helen's half-brother James is sometimes called, the reader will need to be alert not to confuse the two.

As you read the first act of *The Miracle Worker*, watch for lines which give you clues to the personality of each character.

On Reading a Play

Plays are written primarily to be translated by actors into speech and action on a stage. When we read a play, then, we obviously miss certain dimensions. We cannot actually hear the voices of the actors speaking the lines. We do not see the movements, the gestures, the costumes, the color—all of the reality of a performance. Too, we miss the shared dramatic experience of being in a darkened theater, the hurry and scurry of our everyday lives shut out for a time, our attention focused on the stage where trained performers are bringing a written script to life.

In order to make up for the things in a live production that we miss, we must make special demands on our imaginations as we read a play. One of the best ways to get the most from reading drama is to "stage" the play in our minds. In this way, we take the script, or the blueprint, of the playwright and build our own production. From their descriptions, we picture the characters and we visualize the sets. We imagine the movements, the gestures, the tone of voice of each actor. Actually, there is an advantage in doing this. We can avoid some of the disappointments we have in the theater when the sets and lighting are poor, or when some actors are stiff or weak in their parts. Too, we can halt the action of the play any time that we wish to reflect over the significance of a speech or action, something impossible at a real performance.

However, in order to stage our own ideal production as we read, we must follow carefully the blueprint of the playwright's stage directions.

A spoon went flying over the footlights and into the audience on opening night during the breakfast-room struggle between Anne Bancroft (Annie Sullivan) and Patty Duke (Helen) on Broadway. Director Arthur Penn gave these versatile performers free reign in the interpretation of this episode, and it was never played exactly the same way twice. The pantomime siege was of such sustained length and violence that some theatergoers conjectured wryly whether or not understudies might be needed for the rest of the performance.

When the show opened, both Miss Bancroft and Patty Duke were fitted with knee pads and elbow pads. Before many performances had been given, they realized that they needed even more protection: shin guards, arm guards, and pads for the fronts and backs of their legs were added, along with padding sewed to the insides of their dresses. For this very real battle, Patty Duke found the high button shoes of her costume were a decided help.

THE MIRACLE WORKER

A play in three acts by
W I L L I A M   G I B S O N

"At another time she asked, 'What is a soul?' 'No one knows,' I replied; 'but we know it is not the body, and it is that part of us which thinks and loves and hopes. . . . [and] is invisible.' . . . 'But if I write what my soul thinks,' she said, 'then it will be visible, and the words will be its body.'"

—ANNIE SULLIVAN, 1891

Characters

A DOCTOR	JAMES
KATE	ANAGNOS
KELLER	ANNIE SULLIVAN
HELEN	VINEY
MARTHA	BLIND GIRLS
PERCY	A SERVANT
AUNT EV	OFFSTAGE VOICES

Time: The 1880's.

Place: In and around the Keller homestead in Tuscumbia, Alabama; also, briefly, the Perkins Institution for the Blind, in Boston.

The Miracle Worker, a play by William Gibson. Copyright © 1956, 1957 by William Gibson; Copyright © 1959, 1960 by Tamarack Productions, Ltd., and George S. Klein and Leo Garel as trustees under three separate deeds of trust. Reprinted by permission of the author and Atheneum Publishers.

CAUTION: The Miracle Worker is the sole property of the above named copyright Owners and is fully protected by copyright. It may not be acted by professionals or amateurs without written permission and the payment of a royalty. All rights, including professional, amateur, stock, radio broadcasting, television, motion picture, recitation, lecturing, public reading, and the rights of translation into foreign languages are reserved. All inquiries should be addressed to the Owners' agent, LEAH SALISBURY, INC., 790 Madison Avenue, New York, New York 10021.

The playing space is divided into two areas by a more or less diagonal line, which runs from downstage right to upstage left.

The area behind this diagonal is on platforms and represents the Keller house; inside we see, down right, a family room, and up center, elevated, a bedroom. On stage level near center, outside a porch, there is a water pump.

The other area, in front of the diagonal, is neutral ground; it accommodates various places as designated at various times—the yard before the Keller home, the Perkins Institution for the Blind, the garden house, and so forth.

The convention of the staging is one of cutting through time and place, and its essential qualities are fluidity and spatial counterpoint. To this end, the less set there is, the better; in a literal set, the fluidity will seem merely episodic. The stage therefore should be free, airy, unencumbered by walls. Apart from certain practical items—such as the pump, a window to climb out of, doors to be locked—locales should be only skeletal suggestions, and the movement from one to another should be accomplishable by little more than lights.

Act I

It is night over the Keller homestead.

Inside, three adults in the bedroom are grouped around a crib, in lamplight. They have been through a long vigil, and it shows in their tired bearing and disarranged clothing. One is a young gentlewoman with a sweet girlish face, KATE KELLER; *the second is an elderly* DOCTOR, *stethoscope at neck, thermometer in fingers; the third is a hearty gentleman in his forties with chin whiskers,* CAPTAIN ARTHUR KELLER.

DOCTOR. She'll live.

KATE. Thank God.

(The DOCTOR *leaves them together over the crib, packs his bag.)*

DOCTOR. You're a pair of lucky parents. I can tell you now, I thought she wouldn't.

KELLER. Nonsense, the child's a Keller, she has the constitution of a goat. She'll outlive us all.

DOCTOR [*amiably*]. Yes, especially if some of you Kellers don't get a night's sleep. I mean you, Mrs. Keller.

KELLER. You hear, Katie?

KATE. I hear.

KELLER [*indulgent*]. I've brought up two of them, but this is my wife's first, she isn't battle-scarred yet.

KATE. Doctor, don't be merely considerate, will my girl be all right?

DOCTOR. Oh, by morning she'll be knocking down Captain Keller's fences again.

KATE. And isn't there anything we should do?

KELLER [*jovial*]. Put up stronger fencing, ha?

DOCTOR. Just let her get well, she knows how to do it better than we do.

(He is packed, ready to leave.)

Main thing is the fever's gone, these things come and go in infants, never know why. Call it acute congestion of the stomach and brain.

KELLER. I'll see you to your buggy, Doctor.

DOCTOR. I've never seen a baby with more vitality, that's the truth.

(He beams a good night at the baby and KATE, *and* KELLER *leads him downstairs with a lamp. They go down the porch steps, and across the yard, where the* DOCTOR *goes off left;* KELLER *stands with the lamp aloft.* KATE *meanwhile is bent lovingly over the crib, which emits a bleat; her finger is playful with the baby's face.)*

KATE. Hush. Don't you cry now, you've been trouble enough. Call it acute congestion, indeed, I don't see what's so cute about a congestion, just because it's yours? We'll have your father run an editorial in his paper, the wonders of modern medicine, they don't know what they're curing even when they cure it. Men, men and their battle scars, we women will have to—

(*But she breaks off, puzzled, moves her finger before the baby's eyes.*)

Will have to—Helen?

(*Now she moves her hand, quickly.*)

Helen.

(*She snaps her fingers at the baby's eyes twice, and her hand falters; after a moment she calls out, loudly.*)

Captain. Captain, will you come—

(*But she stares at the baby, and her next call is directly at her ears.*)

Captain!

(*And now, still staring,* KATE *screams.* KELLER *in the yard hears it, and runs with the lamp back to the house.* KATE *screams again, her look intent on the baby and terrible.* KELLER *hurries in and up.*)

KELLER. Katie? What's wrong?

KATE. Look.

(*She makes a pass with her hand in the crib, at the baby's eyes.*)

KELLER. What, Katie? She's well, she needs only time to—

KATE. She can't see. Look at her eyes.

(*She takes the lamp from him, moves it before the child's face.*)

She can't *see!*

KELLER [*hoarsely*]. Helen.

KATE. Or hear. When I screamed she didn't blink. Not an eyelash—

KELLER. Helen. Helen!

KATE. She can't *hear* you!

KELLER. *Helen!*

(*His face has something like fury in it, crying the child's name;* KATE *almost fainting presses her knuckles to her mouth, to stop her own cry.*)

The room dims out quickly.

Time, in the form of a slow tune of distant belfry chimes which approaches in a cre-

scendo and then fades, passes; the light comes up again on a day five years later, on three kneeling children and an old dog outside around the pump.

The dog is a setter named Belle, and she is sleeping. Two of the children are Negroes, MARTHA *and* PERCY. *The third child is* HELEN, *six and a half years old, quite unkempt, in body a vivacious little person with a fine head, attractive, but noticeably blind, one eye larger and protruding; her gestures are abrupt, insistent, lacking in human restraint, and her face never smiles. She is flanked by the other two, in a litter of paper-doll cutouts, and while they speak* HELEN's *hands thrust at their faces in turn, feeling baffledly at the movements of their lips.*)

MARTHA [*snipping*]. First I'm gonna cut off this doctor's legs, one, two, now then—

PERCY. Why you cuttin' off that doctor's legs?

MARTHA. I'm gonna give him a operation. Now I'm gonna cut off his arms, one, two. Now I'm gonna fix up—

(*She pushes* HELEN's *hand away from her mouth.*)

You stop that.

PERCY. Cut off his stomach, that's a good operation.

MARTHA. No, I'm gonna cut off his head first, he got a bad cold.

PERCY. Ain't gonna be much of that doctor left to fix up, time you finish all them opera—

(*But* HELEN *is poking her fingers inside his mouth, to feel his tongue; he bites at them, annoyed, and she jerks them away.* HELEN *now fingers her own lips, moving them in imitation, but soundlessly.*)

MARTHA. What you do, bite her hand?

PERCY. That's how I do, she keep pokin' her fingers in my mouth, I just bite 'em off.

MARTHA. What she tryin' do now?

PERCY. She tryin' *talk.* She gonna get mad. Looka her tryin' talk.

(HELEN *is scowling, the lips under her fingertips moving in ghostly silence, growing more and more frantic, until in a bizarre rage she bites at her own fingers. This sends* PERCY *off into laughter, but alarms* MARTHA.)

MARTHA. Hey, you stop now.

(*She pulls* HELEN'S *hand down.*)

You just sit quiet and—

(*But at once* HELEN *topples* MARTHA *on her back, knees pinning her shoulders down, and grabs the scissors.* MARTHA *screams.* PERCY *darts to the bell string on the porch, yanks it, and the bell rings.*

Inside, the lights have been gradually coming up on the main room, where we see the family informally gathered, talking, but in pantomime: KATE *sits darning socks near a cradle, occasionally rocking it;* CAPTAIN KELLER *in spectacles is working over newspaper pages at a table; a benign visitor in a hat,* AUNT EV, *is sharing the sewing basket, putting the finishing touches on a big shapeless doll made out of towels; an indolent young man,* JAMES KELLER, *is at the window watching the children.*

With the ring of the bell, KATE *is instantly on her feet and out the door onto the porch, to take in the scene; now we see what these five years have done to her, the girlish playfulness is gone, she is a woman steeled in grief.*)

KATE [*for the thousandth time*]. Helen.

(*She is down the steps at once to them, seizing* HELEN'S *wrists and lifting her off* MARTHA; MARTHA *runs off in tears and screams for momma, with* PERCY *after her.*)

Let me have those scissors.

(*Meanwhile the family inside is alerted,* AUNT EV *joining* JAMES *at the window;* CAPTAIN KELLER *resumes work.*)

JAMES [*blandly*]. She only dug Martha's eyes out. Almost dug. It's always almost, no point worrying till it happens, is there?

(*They gaze out, while* KATE *reaches for the scissors in* HELEN'S *hand. But* HELEN *pulls the scissors back, they struggle for them a moment, then* KATE *gives up, lets* HELEN *keep them. She tries to draw* HELEN *into the house.* HELEN *jerks away.* KATE *next goes down on her knees, takes* HELEN'S *hands gently, and using the scissors like a doll, makes* HELEN *caress and cradle them; she points* HELEN'S *finger housewards.* HELEN'S *whole body now becomes eager; she surrenders the scissors,* KATE *turns her toward the door and gives her a little push.* HELEN *scrambles up and toward the house, and* KATE *rising follows her.*)

AUNT EV. How does she stand it? Why haven't you seen this Baltimore man? It's not a thing you can let go on and on, like the weather.

JAMES. The weather here doesn't ask permission of me, Aunt Ev. Speak to my father.

AUNT EV. Arthur. Something ought to be done for that child.

KELLER. A refreshing suggestion. What?

(KATE *entering turns* HELEN *to* AUNT EV, *who gives her the towel doll.*)

AUNT EV. Why, this very famous oculist in Baltimore I wrote you about, what was his name?

KATE. Dr. Chisholm.

AUNT EV. Yes, I heard lots of cases of blindness people thought couldn't be cured he's cured, he just does wonders. Why don't you write to him?

KELLER. I've stopped believing in wonders.

KATE [*rocks the cradle*]. I think the Captain will write to him soon. Won't you, Captain?

KELLER. No.

JAMES [*lightly*]. Good money after bad, or bad after good. Or bad after bad—

AUNT EV. Well, if it's just a question of money, Arthur, now you're marshal you have this Yankee money. Might as well—

KELLER. Not money. The child's been to specialists all over Alabama and Tennessee, if I thought it would do good I'd have her to every fool doctor in the country.

KATE. I think the Captain will write to him soon.

KELLER. Katie. How many times can you let them break your heart?

KATE. Any number of times.

(HELEN *meanwhile sits on the floor to explore the doll with her fingers, and her hand pauses over the face: this is no face, a blank area of towel, and it troubles her. Her hand searches for features, and taps questioningly for eyes, but no one notices. She then yanks at her* AUNT's *dress, and taps again vigorously for eyes.*)

AUNT EV. What, child?

(*Obviously not hearing,* HELEN *commences to go around, from person to person, tapping for eyes, but no one attends or understands.*)

KATE [*no break*]. As long as there's the least chance. For her to see. Or hear, or—

KELLER. There isn't. Now I must finish here.

KATE. I think, with your permission, Captain, I'd like to write.

KELLER. I said no, Katie.

AUNT EV. Why, writing does no harm, Arthur, only a little bitty letter. To see if he can help her.

KELLER. He can't.

KATE. We won't know that to be a fact, Captain, until after you write.

KELLER [*rising, emphatic*]. Katie, he can't.

(*He collects his papers.*)

JAMES [*facetiously*]. Father stands up, that makes it a fact.

KELLER. You be quiet! I'm badgered enough here by females without your impudence.

(JAMES *shuts up, makes himself scarce.* HELEN *now is groping among things on* KELLER's *desk, and paws his papers to the floor.* KELLER *is exasperated.*)

Katie.

(KATE *quickly turns* HELEN *away, and retrieves the papers.*)

I might as well try to work in a henyard as in this house—

JAMES [*placating*]. You really ought to put her away, Father.

KATE [*staring up*]. What?

JAMES. Some asylum. It's the kindest thing.

AUNT EV. Why, she's your sister, James, not a nobody—

JAMES. Half sister, and half—mentally defective, she can't even keep herself clean. It's not pleasant to see her about all the time.

KATE. Do you dare? Complain of what you *can* see?

KELLER [*very annoyed*]. This discussion is at an end! I'll thank you not to broach it again, Ev.

(*Silence descends at once.* HELEN *gropes her way with the doll, and* KELLER *turns back for a final word, explosive.*)

I've done as much as I can bear, I can't give my whole life to it! The house is at sixes and sevens[1] from morning till night over the child, it's time some attention was paid to Mildred here instead!

KATE [*gently dry*]. You'll wake her up, Captain.

KELLER. I want some peace in the house, I don't care how, but one way we won't have it is by rushing up and down the country every time someone hears of a new quack. I'm as sensible to this affliction as anyone else, it hurts me to look at the girl.

KATE. It was not our affliction I meant you to write about, Captain.

(HELEN *is back at* AUNT EV, *fingering her dress, and yanks two buttons from it.*)

AUNT EV. Helen! My buttons.

(HELEN *pushes the buttons into the doll's face.* KATE *now sees, comes swiftly to kneel, lifts* HELEN's *hand to her own eyes in question.*)

KATE. Eyes?

(HELEN *nods energetically.*)

She wants the doll to have eyes.

(*Another kind of silence now, while* KATE *takes pins and buttons from the sewing basket and attaches them to the doll as eyes.* KELLER *stands, caught, and watches mo-*

---

1. **at sixes and sevens,** in a state of neglect and confusion.

rosely. AUNT EV *blinks, and conceals her emotion by inspecting her dress.*)

AUNT EV. My goodness me, I'm not decent.

KATE. She doesn't know better, Aunt Ev. I'll sew them on again.

JAMES. Never learn with everyone letting her do anything she takes it into her mind to—

KELLER. You be quiet!

JAMES. What did I say now?

KELLER. You talk too much.

JAMES. I was agreeing with you!

KELLER. Whatever it was. Deprived child, the least she can have are the little things she wants.

(JAMES, *very wounded, stalks out of the room onto the porch; he remains here, sulking.*)

AUNT EV [*indulgently*]. It's worth a couple of buttons, Kate, look.

(HELEN *now has the doll with eyes, and cannot contain herself for joy; she rocks the doll, pats it vigorously, kisses it.*)

This child has more sense than all these men Kellers, if there's ever any way to reach that mind of hers.

(*But* HELEN *suddenly has come upon the cradle, and unhesitatingly overturns it; the swaddled baby tumbles out, and* CAPTAIN KELLER *barely manages to dive and catch it in time.*)

KELLER. *Helen!*

(*All are in commotion, the baby screams, but* HELEN *unperturbed is laying her doll in its place.* KATE *on her knees pulls her hands off the cradle, wringing them;* HELEN *is bewildered.*)

KATE. Helen, Helen, you're not to do such things, how can I make you understand—

KELLER [*hoarsely*]. Katie.

KATE. How can I get it into your head, my darling, my poor—

KELLER. Katie, some way of teaching her an iota of discipline has to be—

KATE [*flaring*]. How can you discipline an afflicted child? Is it her fault?

(HELEN's *fingers have fluttered to her mother's lips, vainly trying to comprehend their movements.*)

KELLER. I didn't say it was her fault.

KATE. Then whose? I don't know what to do! How can I teach her, beat her—until she's black and blue?

KELLER. It's not safe to let her run around loose. Now there must be a way of confining her, somehow, so she can't—

KATE. Where, in a cage? She's a growing child, she has to use her limbs!

KELLER. Answer me one thing, is it fair to Mildred here?

KATE [*inexorably*]. Are you willing to put her away?

(*Now* HELEN's *face darkens in the same rage as at herself earlier, and her hand strikes at* KATE's *lips.* KATE *catches her hand again, and* HELEN *begins to kick, struggle, twist.*)

KELLER. Now what?

KATE. She wants to talk, like—*be* like you and me.

(*She holds* HELEN *struggling until we hear from the child her first sound so far, an inarticulate weird noise in her throat such as an animal in a trap might make; and* KATE *releases her. The second she is free* HELEN *blunders away, collides violently with a chair, falls, and sits weeping.* KATE *comes to her, embraces, caresses, soothes her, and buries her own face in her hair, until she can control her voice.*)

Every day she slips further away. And I don't know how to call her back.

AUNT EV. Oh, I've a mind to take her up to Baltimore myself. If that doctor can't help her, maybe he'll know who can.

KELLER [*presently, heavily*]. I'll write the man, Katie.

(*He stands with the baby in his clasp, staring at* HELEN's *head, hanging down on* KATE's *arm.*

The lights dim out, except the one on KATE *and* HELEN. *In the twilight,* JAMES, AUNT EV, *and* KELLER *move off slowly, formally, in separate directions;* KATE *with* HELEN *in her arms remains, motionless, in an image which overlaps into the next scene and fades only when it is well under way.*

Without pause, from the dark down left we hear a man's voice with a Greek accent speaking:)

ANAGNOS. —who could do nothing for the girl, of course. It was Dr. Bell[2] who thought she might somehow be taught. I have written the family only that a suitable governess, Miss Annie Sullivan, has been found here in Boston—

(*The lights begin to come up, down left, on a long table and chair. The table contains equipment for teaching the blind by touch— a small replica of the human skeleton, stuffed animals, models of flowers and plants, piles of books. The chair contains a girl of 20,* ANNIE SULLIVAN, *with a face which in repose is grave and rather obstinate, and when active is impudent, combative, twinkling with all the life that is lacking in* HELEN's, *and handsome; there is a crude vitality to her. Her suitcase is at her knee.* ANAGNOS, *a stocky bearded man, comes into the light only towards the end of his speech.*)

ANAGNOS. —and will come. It will no doubt be difficult for you there, Annie. But it has been difficult for you at our school too, hm? Gratifying, yes, when you came to us and could not spell your name, to accomplish so much here in a few years, but always an Irish battle. For independence.

(*He studies* ANNIE, *humorously; she does not open her eyes.*)

This is my last time to counsel you, Annie, and you do lack some—by some I mean *all*— what, tact or talent to bend. To others. And what has saved you on more than one occasion here at Perkins is that there was nowhere to expel you to. Your eyes hurt?

ANNIE. My ears, Mr. Anagnos.

(*And now she has opened her eyes; they are inflamed, vague, slightly crossed, clouded by the granular growth of trachoma, and she often keeps them closed to shut out the pain of light.*)

ANAGNOS [*severely*]. Nowhere but back to Tewksbury,[3] where children learn to be saucy. Annie, I know how dreadful it was there, but that battle is dead and done with, why not let it stay buried?

ANNIE [*cheerily*]. I think God must owe me a resurrection.

ANAGNOS [*a bit shocked*]. What?

ANNIE [*taps her brow*]. Well, He keeps digging up that battle!

ANAGNOS. That is not a proper thing to say, Annie. It is what I mean.

ANNIE [*meekly*]. Yes. But I know what I'm like, what's this child like?

ANAGNOS. Like?

ANNIE. Well— Bright or dull, to start off.

ANAGNOS. No one knows. And if she is dull, you have no patience with this?

ANNIE. Oh, in grownups you have to, Mr. Anagnos. I mean in children it just seems a little —precocious, can I use that word?

ANAGNOS. Only if you can spell it.

ANNIE. Premature. So I hope at least she's a bright one.

ANAGNOS. Deaf, blind, mute—who knows? She is like a little safe, locked, that no one can open. Perhaps there is a treasure inside.

ANNIE. Maybe it's empty, too?

ANAGNOS. Possible. I should warn you, she is much given to tantrums.

ANNIE. Means something is inside. Well, so am

---

2. Captain Keller appealed to Alexander Graham Bell (1847–1922), who became famous as developer of the telephone but who had come to America from Scotland as a teacher of speech to the deaf. Bell referred Captain Keller to Mr. Anagnos, Director of Perkins Institution for the Blind in Boston.

3. **Tewksbury**\ˈtŭks ˈbĕ·rĭ\ location of the state (Massachusetts) almshouse where Annie and her brother were sent as young children after her mother died and her father became an alcoholic.

I, if I believe all I hear. Maybe you should warn *them*.

ANAGNOS [*frowns*]. Annie. I wrote them no word of your history. You will find yourself among strangers now, who know nothing of it.

ANNIE. Well, we'll keep them in a state of blessed ignorance.

ANAGNOS. Perhaps *you* should tell it?

ANNIE [*bristling*]. Why? I have enough trouble with people who don't know.

ANAGNOS. So they will understand. When you have trouble.

ANNIE. The only time I have trouble is when I'm right.

(*But she is amused at herself, as is* ANAGNOS.)

Is it my fault it's so often? I won't give them trouble, Mr. Anagnos, I'll be so ladylike they won't notice I've come.

ANAGNOS. Annie, be—humble. It is not as if you have so many offers to pick and choose. You will need their affection, working with this child.

ANNIE [*humorously*]. I hope I won't need their pity.

ANAGNOS. Oh, we can all use some pity.

(*Crisply*)

So. You are no longer our pupil, we throw you into the world, a teacher. *If the child can be taught.* No one expects you to work miracles, even for twenty-five dollars a month. Now, in this envelope a loan, for the railroad, which you will repay me when you have a bank account. But in this box, a gift. With our love.

(ANNIE *opens the small box he extends, and sees a garnet ring. She looks up, blinking, and down.*)

I think other friends are ready to say goodbye.

(*He moves as though to open doors.*)

ANNIE. Mr. Anagnos.

(*Her voice is trembling.*)

Dear Mr. Anagnos, I—

(*But she swallows over getting the ring on her finger, and cannot continue until she finds a woe-begone joke.*)

Well, what should I say, I'm an ignorant opinionated girl, and everything I am I owe to you?

ANAGNOS [*smiles*]. That is only half true, Annie.

ANNIE. Which half? I crawled in here like a drowned rat, I thought I died when Jimmie died, that I'd never again—come alive. Well, you say with love so easy, and I haven't *loved* a soul since and I never will, I suppose, but this place gave me more than my eyes back. Or taught me how to spell, which I'll never learn anyway, but with all the fights and the trouble I've been here it taught me what help is, and how to live again, and I don't want to say goodbye. Don't open the door, I'm crying.

ANAGNOS [*gently*]. They will not see.

(*He moves again as though opening doors, and in comes a group of girls, 8-year-olds to 17-year-olds; as they walk we see they are blind.*[4] ANAGNOS *shepherds them in with a hand.*)

A CHILD. Annie?

ANNIE [*her voice cheerful*]. Here, Beatrice.

(*As soon as they locate her voice they throng joyfully to her, speaking all at once;* ANNIE *is down on her knees to the smallest, and the following are the more intelligible fragments in the general hubbub.*)

CHILDREN. There's a present. We brought you a going-away present, Annie!

ANNIE. Oh, now you shouldn't have—

CHILDREN. We did, we did, where's the present?

SMALLEST CHILD [*mournfully*]. Don't go, Annie, away.

CHILDREN. Alice has it. Alice! Where's Alice? Here I am! Where? Here!

(*An arm is aloft out of the group, waving a present;* ANNIE *reaches for it.*)

---

4. In order to lend reality to this scene, these children in the original cast of the play were actually blind.

ANNIE. I have it. I have it, everybody, should I open it?

CHILDREN. Open it! Everyone be quiet! Do, Annie! She's opening it. Ssh!

(*A settling of silence while* ANNIE *unwraps it. The present is a pair of smoked glasses, and she stands still.*)

Is it open, Annie?

ANNIE. It's open.

CHILDREN. It's for your eyes, Annie. Put them on, Annie! 'Cause Mrs. Hopkins said your eyes hurt since the operation. And she said you're going where the sun is *fierce*.

ANNIE. I'm putting them on now.

SMALLEST CHILD [*mournfully*]. Don't go, Annie, where the sun is fierce.

CHILDREN. Do they fit all right?

ANNIE. Oh, they fit just fine.

CHILDREN. Did you put them on? Are they pretty, Annie?

ANNIE. Oh, my eyes feel hundreds of per cent better already, and pretty, why, do you know how I look in them? Splendiloquent.[5] Like a race horse!

CHILDREN [*delighted*]. There's another present! Beatrice! We have a present for Helen, too! Give it to her, Beatrice. Here, Annie!

(*This present is an elegant doll, with movable eyelids and a momma sound.*)

It's for Helen. And we took up a collection to buy it. And Laura[6] dressed it.

ANNIE. It's beautiful!

CHILDREN. So don't forget, you be sure to give it to Helen from us, Annie!

ANNIE. I promise it will be the first thing I give her. If I don't keep it for myself, that is, you know I can't be trusted with dolls!

SMALLEST CHILD [*mournfully*]. Don't go, Annie, to her.

ANNIE [*her arm around her*]. Sarah, dear. I don't *want* to go.

SMALLEST CHILD. Then why are you going?

ANNIE [*gently*]. Because I'm a big girl now, and big girls have to earn a living. It's the only way I can. But if you don't smile for me first, what I'll just have to do is—

(*She pauses, inviting it.*)

SMALLEST CHILD. What?

ANNIE. Put *you* in my suitcase, instead of this doll. And take *you* to Helen in Alabama!

(*This strikes the children as very funny, and they begin to laugh and tease the smallest child, who after a moment does smile for* ANNIE.)

ANAGNOS [*then*]. Come, children. We must get the trunk into the carriage and Annie into her train, or no one will go to Alabama. Come, come.

(*He shepherds them out and* ANNIE *is left alone on her knees with the doll in her lap. She reaches for her suitcase, and by a subtle change in the color of the light, we go with her thoughts into another time. We hear a boy's voice whispering; perhaps we see shadowy intimations of these speakers in the background.*)

BOY'S VOICE. Where we goin', Annie?

ANNIE [*in dread*]. Jimmie.

BOY'S VOICE. Where we goin'?

ANNIE. I said—I'm takin' care of you—

BOY'S VOICE. Forever and ever?

MAN'S VOICE [*impersonal*]. Annie Sullivan, aged nine, virtually blind. James Sullivan, aged seven—What's the matter with your leg, Sonny?[7]

ANNIE. Forever and ever.

MAN'S VOICE. Can't he walk without that crutch?

(ANNIE *shakes her head, and does not stop shaking it.*)

Girl goes to the women's ward. Boy to the men's.

---

5. **splendiloquent**\ˈsplĕn▲dĭ·lə·kwənt\ a made-up word meaning something like splendid and excellent.

6. Laura Bridgman, a blind deaf-mute who had been taught to communicate with those about her by Dr. Samuel Gridley Howe, former Director of Perkins Institution. She remained at Perkins Institution because she was never able to adapt herself to any other kind of life. Annie first learned the manual alphabet in order to talk with Laura.

7. Jimmy suffered from a tubercular hip and died in agony four months after he and Annie were sent to the State Infirmary at Tewksbury.

BOY'S VOICE [*in terror*]. Annie! Annie, don't let them take me—Annie!

ANAGNOS [*offstage*]. Annie! Annie?

(*But this voice is real, in the present, and* ANNIE *comes up out of her horror, clearing her head with a final shake; the lights begin to pick out* KATE *in the* KELLER *house, as* ANNIE *in a bright tone calls back.*)

ANNIE. Coming!

(*This word catches* KATE, *who stands half turned and attentive to it, almost as though hearing it. Meanwhile* ANNIE *turns and hurries out, lugging the suitcase.*

The room dims out; the sound of railroad wheels begins from off left, and maintains itself in a constant rhythm underneath the following scene; the remaining lights have come up on the KELLER *homestead.* JAMES *is lounging on the porch, waiting. In the upper bedroom which is to be* ANNIE'S, HELEN *is alone, puzzledly exploring, fingering and smelling things, the curtains, empty drawers in the bureau, water in the pitcher by the washbasin, fresh towels on the bedstead. Downstairs in the family room* KATE *turning to a mirror hastily adjusts her bonnet, watched by a Negro servant in an apron,* VINEY.)

VINEY. Let Mr. Jimmie go by hisself, you been pokin' that garden all day, you ought to rest your feet.

KATE. I can't wait to see her, Viney.

VINEY. Maybe she ain't gone be on this train neither.

KATE. Maybe she is.

VINEY. And maybe she ain't.

KATE. And maybe she is. Where's Helen?

VINEY. She upstairs, smellin' around. She know somethin' funny's goin' on.

KATE. Let her have her supper as soon as Mildred's in bed, and tell Captain Keller when he comes that we'll be delayed tonight.

VINEY. Again.

KATE. I don't think we need say *again*. Simply delayed will do.

(*She runs upstairs to* ANNIE'S *room,* VINEY *speaking after her.*)

VINEY. I mean that's what he gone say. "What, again?" (VINEY *works at setting the table. Upstairs* KATE *stands in the doorway, watching* HELEN'S *groping explorations.*)

KATE. Yes, we're expecting someone. Someone for my Helen.

(HELEN *happens upon her skirt, clutches her leg;* KATE *in a tired dismay kneels to tidy her hair and soiled pinafore.*)

Oh, dear, this was clean not an hour ago.

(HELEN *feels her bonnet, shakes her head darkly, and tugs to get it off.* KATE *retains it with one hand, diverts* HELEN *by opening her other hand under her nose.*)

Here. For while I'm gone.

(HELEN *sniffs, reaches, and pops something into her mouth, while* KATE *speaks a bit guiltily.*)

I don't think one peppermint drop will spoil your supper.

(*She gives* HELEN *a quick kiss, evades her hands, and hurries downstairs again. Meanwhile* CAPTAIN KELLER *has entered the yard from around the rear of the house, newspaper under arm, cleaning off and munching on some radishes; he sees* JAMES *lounging at the porch post.*)

KELLER. Jimmie?

JAMES [*unmoving*]. Sir?

KELLER [*eyes him*]. You don't look dressed for anything useful, boy.

JAMES. I'm not. It's for Miss Sullivan.

KELLER. Needn't keep holding up that porch, we have wooden posts for that. I asked you to see that those strawberry plants were moved this evening.

JAMES. I'm moving your—Mrs. Keller, instead. To the station.

KELLER [*heavily*]. Mrs. Keller. Must you always speak of her as though you haven't met the lady?

(KATE *comes out on the porch, and* JAMES *inclines his head.*)

JAMES [*ironic*]. Mother.

(*He starts off the porch, but sidesteps* KELLER'S *glare like a blow.*)

I said mother!

KATE. Captain.

KELLER. Evening, my dear.

KATE. We're off to meet the train, Captain. Supper will be a trifle delayed tonight.

KELLER. What, again?

KATE [*backing out*]. With your permission, Captain?

(*And they are gone.* KELLER *watches them offstage, morosely.*

Upstairs HELEN *meanwhile has groped for her mother, touched her cheek in a meaningful gesture, waited, touched her cheek, waited, then found the open door, and made her way down. Now she comes into the family room, touches her cheek again;* VINEY *regards her.*)

VINEY. What you want, honey, your momma?

(HELEN *touches her cheek again.* VINEY *goes to the sideboard, gets a tea-cake, gives it into* HELEN'S *hand;* HELEN *pops it into her mouth.*)

Guess one little tea-cake ain't gone ruin your appetite.

(*She turns* HELEN *toward the door.* HELEN *wanders out onto the porch, as* KELLER *comes up the steps. Her hands encounter him, and she touches her cheek again, waits.*)

KELLER. She's gone.

(*He is awkward with her; when he puts his hand on her head, she pulls away.* KELLER *stands regarding her, heavily.*)

She's gone, my son and I don't get along, you don't know I'm your father, no one likes me, and supper's delayed.

(HELEN *touches her cheek, waits.* KELLER *fishes in his pocket.*)

Here. I brought you some stick candy, one nibble of sweets can't do any harm.

(*He gives her a large stick candy;* HELEN *falls to it.* VINEY *peers out the window.*)

VINEY [*reproachfully*]. Cap'n Keller, now how'm I gone get her to eat her supper you fill her up with that trash?

KELLER [*roars*]. Tend to your work!

(VINEY *beats a rapid retreat.* KELLER *thinks better of it, and tries to get the candy away from* HELEN, *but* HELEN *hangs on to it; and when* KELLER *pulls, she gives his leg a kick.* KELLER *hops about,* HELEN *takes refuge with the candy down behind the pump, and* KELLER *then irately flings his newspaper on the porch floor, stamps into the house past* VINEY *and disappears.*

The lights half dim on the homestead, where VINEY *and* HELEN *going about their business soon find their way off. Meanwhile, the railroad sounds off left have mounted in a crescendo to a climax typical of a depot at arrival time, the lights come up on stage left, and we see a suggestion of a station. Here* ANNIE *in her smoked glasses and disarrayed by travel is waiting with her suitcase, while* JAMES *walks to meet her; she has a battered paperbound book, which is a Perkins report,*[8] *under her arm.*)

JAMES [*coolly*]. Miss Sullivan?

ANNIE [*cheerily*]. Here! At last, I've been on trains so many days I thought they must be backing up every time I dozed off—

JAMES. I'm James Keller.

ANNIE. James?

(*The name stops her.*)

I had a brother Jimmie. Are you Helen's?

JAMES. I'm only half a brother. You're to be her governess?

ANNIE [*lightly*]. Well. Try!

JAMES [*eyeing her*]. You look like half a governess.

(KATE *enters.* ANNIE *stands moveless, while*

---

8. **Perkins report,** a report of work done by the Perkins Institution for the Blind in Boston.

JAMES *takes her suitcase.* KATE's *gaze on her is doubtful, troubled.*)

Mrs. Keller, Miss Sullivan.

(KATE *takes her hand.*)

KATE [*simply*]. We've met every train for two days.

(ANNIE *looks at* KATE's *face, and her good humor comes back.*)

ANNIE. I changed trains every time they stopped, the man who sold me that ticket ought to be tied to the tracks—

JAMES. You have a trunk, Miss Sullivan?

ANNIE. Yes.

(*She passes* JAMES *a claim check, and he bears the suitcase out behind them.* ANNIE *holds the battered book.* KATE *is studying her face, and* ANNIE *returns the gaze; this is a mutual appraisal, southern gentlewoman and working-class Irish girl, and* ANNIE *is not quite comfortable under it.*)

You didn't bring Helen, I was hoping you would.

KATE. No, she's home.

(*A pause.* ANNIE *tries to make ladylike small talk, though her energy now and then erupts; she catches herself up whenever she hears it.*)

ANNIE. You—live far from town, Mrs. Keller?

KATE. Only a mile.

ANNIE. Well. I suppose I can wait one more mile. But don't be surprised if I get out to push the horse!

KATE. Helen's waiting for you, too. There's been such a bustle in the house, she expects something, heaven knows what.

(*Now she voices part of her doubt, not as such, but* ANNIE *understands it.*)

I expected—a desiccated spinster. You're very young.

ANNIE [*resolutely*]. Oh, you should have seen me when I left Boston. I got much older on this trip.

KATE. I mean, to teach anyone as difficult as Helen.

ANNIE. *I* mean to try. They can't put you in jail for trying!

KATE. Is it possible, even? To teach a deaf-blind child *half* of what an ordinary child learns—has that ever been done?

ANNIE. Half?

KATE. A tenth.

ANNIE [*reluctantly*]. No.

(KATE's *face loses its remaining hope, still appraising her youth.*)

Dr. Howe did wonders, but—an ordinary child? No, never. But then I thought when I was going over his reports—

(*She indicates the one in her hand.*)

—he never treated them like ordinary children. More like—eggs everyone was afraid would break.

KATE [*a pause*]. May I ask how old you are?

ANNIE. Well, I'm not in my teens, you know! I'm twenty.

KATE. All of twenty.

(ANNIE *takes the bull by the horns, valiantly.*)

ANNIE. Mrs. Keller, don't lose heart just because I'm not on my last legs. I have three big advantages over Dr. Howe that money couldn't buy for you. One is his work behind me, I've read every word he wrote about it and he wasn't exactly what you'd call a man of few words. Another is to *be* young, why, I've got energy to do anything. The third is, I've been blind.

(*But it costs her something to say this.*)

KATE [*quietly*]. Advantages.

ANNIE [*wry*]. Well, some have the luck of the Irish, some do not.

(KATE *smiles; she likes her.*)

KATE. What will you try to teach her first?

ANNIE. First, last, and—in between, language.

KATE. Language.

ANNIE. Language is to the mind more than light is to the eye. Dr. Howe said that.

KATE. Language.

(*She shakes her head.*)

We can't get through to teach her to sit still. You *are* young, despite your years, to have such—confidence. Do you, inside?

(ANNIE *studies her face; she likes her, too.*)

ANNIE. No, to tell you the truth I'm as shaky inside as a baby's rattle!

(*They smile at each other, and* KATE *pats her hand.*)

KATE. Don't be.

(JAMES *returns to usher them off.*)

We'll do all we can to help, and to make you feel at home. Don't think of us as strangers, Miss Annie.

ANNIE [*cheerily*]. Oh, strangers aren't so strange to me. I've known them all my life!

(KATE *smiles again,* ANNIE *smiles back, and they precede* JAMES *offstage.*

The lights dim on them, having simultaneously risen full on the house; VINEY *has already entered the family room, taken a water pitcher, and come out and down to the pump. She pumps real water. As she looks offstage, we hear the clop of hoofs, a carriage stopping, and voices.*)

VINEY. Cap'n Keller! Cap'n Keller, they comin'!

(*She goes back into the house, as* KELLER *comes out on the porch to gaze.*)

She sure 'nuff came, Cap'n.

(KELLER *descends, and crosses toward the carriage; this conversation begins offstage and moves on.*)

KELLER [*very courtly*]. Welcome to Ivy Green, Miss Sullivan. I take it you are Miss Sullivan—

KATE. My husband, Miss Annie, Captain Keller.

ANNIE [*her best behavior*]. Captain, how do you do.

KELLER. A pleasure to see you, at last. I trust you had an agreeable journey?

ANNIE. Oh, I had several! When did this country get so big?

JAMES. Where would you like the trunk, father?

KELLER. Where Miss Sullivan can get at it, I imagine.

ANNIE. Yes, please. Where's Helen?

KELLER. In the hall, Jimmie—

KATE. We've put you in the upstairs corner room, Miss Annie, if there's any breeze at all this summer, you'll feel it—

(*In the house the setter Belle flees into the family room, pursued by* HELEN *with groping hands; the dog doubles back out the same door, and* HELEN *still groping for her makes her way out to the porch; she is messy, her hair tumbled, her pinafore now ripped, her shoelaces untied.* KELLER *acquires the suitcase, and* ANNIE *gets her hands on it too, though still endeavoring to live up to the general air of propertied manners.*)

KELLER. *And* the suitcase—

ANNIE [*pleasantly*]. I'll take the suitcase, thanks.

KELLER. Not at all, I have it, Miss Sullivan.

ANNIE. I'd like it.

KELLER [*gallantly*]. I couldn't think of it, Miss Sullivan. You'll find in the south we—

ANNIE. Let me.

KELLER. —view women as the flowers of civiliza—

ANNIE [*impatiently*]. I've got something in it for Helen!

(*She tugs it free;* KELLER *stares.*)

Thank you. When do I see her?

KATE. There. There is Helen.

(ANNIE *turns, and sees* HELEN *on the porch. A moment of silence. Then* ANNIE *begins across the yard to her, lugging her suitcase.*)

KELLER [*sotto voce*]. Katie—

(KATE *silences him with a hand on his arm. When* ANNIE *finally reaches the porch steps she stops, contemplating* HELEN *for a last moment before entering her world. Then she drops the suitcase on the porch with intentional heaviness,* HELEN *starts with the jar, and comes to grope over it.* ANNIE *puts forth her hand, and touches* HELEN'S. HELEN *at once grasps it, and commences to explore it, like reading a face. She moves her hand on to* ANNIE'S *forearm, and dress; and* ANNIE *brings her face within reach of* HELEN'S *fingers, which travel over it, quite without timidity, until they encounter and push aside the smoked glasses.* ANNIE'S *gaze is grave, unpitying, very attentive. She puts her hands on* HELEN'S *arms, but* HELEN *at once pulls away, and they confront each other with a distance between. Then* HELEN *returns to the suitcase, tries to open it, cannot.* ANNIE *points* HELEN'S *hand overhead.* HELEN *pulls away, tries to open the suitcase again;* ANNIE *points her hand overhead again.* HELEN *points overhead, a question, and* ANNIE, *drawing* HELEN'S *hand to her own face, nods.* HELEN *now begins tugging the suitcase toward the door; when* ANNIE *tries to take it from her, she fights her off and backs through the doorway with it.* ANNIE *stands a moment, then follows her in, and together they get the suitcase up the steps into* ANNIE'S *room.*)

KATE. Well?

KELLER. She's very rough, Katie.

KATE. I like her, Captain.

KELLER. Certainly rear a peculiar kind of young woman in the north. How old is she?

KATE [*vaguely*]. Ohh— Well, she's not in her teens, you know.

KELLER. She's only a child. What's her family like, shipping her off alone this far?

KATE. I couldn't learn. She's very closemouthed about some things.

KELLER. Why does she wear those glasses? I like to see a person's eyes when I talk to—

KATE. For the sun. She was blind.

KELLER. Blind.

KATE. She's had nine operations on her eyes. One just before she left.

KELLER. Blind, good heavens, do they expect one blind child to teach another? Has she experience at least, how long did she teach there?

KATE. She was a pupil.

KELLER [*heavily*]. Katie, Katie. This is her first position?

KATE [*bright voice*]. She was valedictorian—

KELLER. Here's a houseful of grownups can't cope with the child, how can an inexperienced half-blind Yankee schoolgirl manage her?

(JAMES *moves in with the trunk on his shoulder.*)

JAMES [*easily*]. Great improvement. Now we have two of them to look after.

KELLER. You look after those strawberry plants!

(JAMES *stops with the trunk.* KELLER *turns from him without another word, and marches off.*)

JAMES. Nothing I say is right.

KATE. Why say anything?

(*She calls.*)

Don't be long, Captain, we'll have supper right away—

(*She goes into the house, and through the rear door of the family room.* JAMES *trudges in with the trunk, takes it up the steps to* ANNIE'S *room, and sets it down outside the door. The lights elsewhere dim somewhat.*)

Meanwhile, inside, ANNIE *has given* HELEN *a key; while* ANNIE *removes her bonnet,* HELEN *unlocks and opens the suitcase. The first thing she pulls out is a voluminous shawl. She fingers it until she perceives what it is; then she wraps it around her, and acquiring* ANNIE'S *bonnet and smoked glasses as well, dons the lot: the shawl swamps her, and the bonnet settles down upon the glasses, but she stands before a mirror cocking her head to one side, then to the other, in a mockery of adult action.* ANNIE *is amused, and talks to her as one might to a kitten, with no trace of company manners.*)

ANNIE. All the trouble I went to and that's how I look?

(HELEN *then comes back to the suitcase, gropes for more, lifts out a pair of female drawers.*)

Oh, no. Not the drawers!

(*But* HELEN *discarding them comes to the elegant doll. Her fingers explore its features, and when she raises it and finds its eyes open and close, she is at first startled, then delighted. She picks it up, taps its head vigorously, taps her own chest, and nods questioningly.* ANNIE *takes her finger, points it to the doll, points it to* HELEN, *and touching it to her own face, also nods.* HELEN *sits back on her heels, clasps the doll to herself, and rocks it.* ANNIE *studies her, still in bonnet and smoked glasses like a caricature of herself, and addresses her humorously.*)

All right, Miss O'Sullivan. Let's begin with doll.

(*She takes* HELEN'S *hand; in her palm* ANNIE'S *forefinger points, thumb holding her other fingers clenched.*)

D.

(*Her thumb next holds all her fingers clenched, touching* HELEN'S *palm.*)

O.

(*Her thumb and forefinger extend.*)

L.

(*Same contact repeated.*)

L.

(*She puts* HELEN'S *hand to the doll.*)

Doll.

JAMES. You spell pretty well.

(ANNIE *in one hurried move gets the drawers swiftly back into the suitcase, the lid banged shut, and her head turned, to see* JAMES *leaning in the doorway.*)

Finding out if she's ticklish? She is.

(ANNIE *regards him stonily, but* HELEN *after a scowling moment tugs at her hand again, imperious.* ANNIE *repeats the letters, and* HELEN *interrupts her fingers in the middle, feeling each of them, puzzled.* ANNIE *touches* HELEN'S *hand to the doll, and begins spelling into it again.*)

JAMES. What is it, a game?

ANNIE [*curtly*]. An alphabet.

JAMES. Alphabet?

ANNIE. For the deaf.

(HELEN *now repeats the finger movements in air, exactly, her head cocked to her own hand, and* ANNIE'S *eyes suddenly gleam.*)

Ho. How *bright* she is!

JAMES. You think she knows what she's doing?

(*He takes* HELEN'S *hand, to throw a meaningless gesture into it; she repeats this one too.*)

She imitates everything, she's a monkey.

ANNIE [*very pleased*]. Yes, she's a bright little monkey, all right.

(*She takes the doll from* HELEN, *and reaches for her hand;* HELEN *instantly grabs the doll back.* ANNIE *takes it again, and* HELEN'S *hand next, but* HELEN *is incensed now; when* ANNIE *draws her hand to her face to shake her head no, then tries to spell to her,* HELEN *slaps at* ANNIE'S *face.* ANNIE *grasps* HELEN *by both arms, and swings her into a chair, holding her pinned there, kicking, while glasses, doll, bonnet fly in various directions.* JAMES *laughs.*)

JAMES. She wants her doll back.

ANNIE. When she spells it.

JAMES. Spell, she doesn't know the thing has a name, even.

ANNIE. Of course not, who expects her to, now? All I want is her fingers to learn the letters.

JAMES. Won't mean anything to her.

(ANNIE *gives him a look. She then tries to form* HELEN'S *fingers into the letters, but* HELEN *swings a haymaker instead, which* ANNIE *barely ducks, at once pinning her down again.*)

Doesn't like that alphabet, Miss Sullivan. You invent it yourself?

(HELEN *is now in a rage, fighting tooth and nail to get out of the chair, and* ANNIE *answers while struggling and dodging her kicks.*)

ANNIE. Spanish monks under a—vow of silence. Which I wish *you'd* take!

(*And suddenly releasing* HELEN's *hands, she comes and shuts the door in* JAMES's *face.* HELEN *drops to the floor, groping around for the doll.* ANNIE *looks around desperately, sees her purse on the bed, rummages in it, and comes up with a battered piece of cake wrapped in newspaper; with her foot she moves the doll deftly out of the way of* HELEN's *groping, and going on her knee she lets* HELEN *smell the cake. When* HELEN *grabs for it,* ANNIE *removes the cake and spells quickly into the reaching hand.*)

Cake. From Washington up north, it's the best I can do.

(HELEN's *hand waits, baffled.* ANNIE *repeats it.*)

C, a, k, e. Do what my fingers do, never mind what it means.

(*She touches the cake briefly to* HELEN's *nose, pats her hand, presents her own hand.* HELEN *spells the letters rapidly back.* ANNIE *pats her hand enthusiastically, and gives her the cake;* HELEN *crams it into her mouth with both hands.* ANNIE *watches her, with humor.*)

Get it down fast, maybe I'll steal that back too. Now.

(*She takes the doll, touches it to* HELEN's *nose, and spells again into her hand.*)

D, o, l, l. Think it over.

(HELEN *thinks it over, while* ANNIE *presents her own hand. Then* HELEN *spells three letters.* ANNIE *waits a second, then completes the word for* HELEN *in her palm.*)

L.

(*She hands over the doll, and* HELEN *gets a good grip on its leg.*)

Imitate now, understand later. End of the first les—

(*She never finishes, because* HELEN *swings the doll with a furious energy, it hits* ANNIE *squarely in the face, and she falls back with a cry of pain, her knuckles up to her mouth.* HELEN *waits, tensed for further combat. When* ANNIE *lowers her knuckles she looks at blood on them; she works her lips, gets to her feet, finds the mirror, and bares her teeth at herself. Now she is furious herself.*)

You little wretch, no one's taught you *any* manners? I'll—

(*But rounding from the mirror she sees the door slam,* HELEN *and the doll are on the outside, and* HELEN *is turning the key in the lock.* ANNIE *darts over, to pull the knob; the door is locked fast. She yanks it again.*)

Helen! Helen, let me out of—

(*She bats her brow at the folly of speaking, but* JAMES, *now downstairs, hears her and turns to see* HELEN *with the key and doll groping her way down the steps;* JAMES *takes in the whole situation, makes a move to intercept* HELEN, *but then changes his mind, lets her pass, and amusedly follows her out onto the porch. Upstairs* ANNIE *meanwhile rattles the knob, kneels, peers through the keyhole, gets up. She goes to the window, looks down, frowns.* JAMES *from the yard sings gaily up to her.*)

JAMES.
Buffalo girl, are you coming out tonight,
Coming out tonight,
Coming out—

(*He drifts back into the house.* ANNIE *takes a handkerchief, nurses her mouth, stands in the middle of the room, staring at door and window in turn, and so catches sight of herself in the mirror, her cheek scratched, her hair dishevelled, her handkerchief bloody, her face disgusted with herself. She addresses the mirror, with some irony.*)

ANNIE. Don't worry. They'll find you, you're not lost. Only out of place.

(*But she coughs, spits something into her palm, and stares at it, outraged.*)

And toothless.

(*She winces.*)

Oo! It hurts.

(*She pours some water into the basin, dips the handkerchief, and presses it to her mouth. Standing there, bent over the basin in pain—with the rest of the set dim and unreal, and the lights upon her taking on the subtle color of the past—she hears again, as do we, the faraway voices, and slowly she lifts her head to them; the boy's voice is the same, the others are cracked old crones in a nightmare, and perhaps we see their shadows.*)

BOY'S VOICE. It hurts. Annie, it hurts.

FIRST CRONE'S VOICE.[9] Keep that brat shut up, can't you, girlie, how's a body to get any sleep in this damn ward?

BOY'S VOICE. It hurts. It hurts.

SECOND CRONE'S VOICE. Shut up, you!

BOY'S VOICE. Annie, when are we goin' home? You promised!

ANNIE. Jimmie—

BOY'S VOICE. Forever and ever, you said forever—

(ANNIE *drops the handkerchief, averts to the window, and is arrested there by the next cry.*)

Annie? Annie, you there? Annie! It *hurts!*

THIRD CRONE'S VOICE. Grab him, he's fallin'!

BOY'S VOICE. *Annie!*

DOCTOR'S VOICE [*a pause, slowly*]. Little girl. Little girl, I must tell you your brother will be going on a—

(*But* ANNIE *claps her hands to her ears, to shut this out; there is instant silence.*

As the lights bring the other areas in again, JAMES *goes to the steps to listen for any sound from upstairs.* KELLER *re-entering from left crosses toward the house; he passes* HELEN *en route to her retreat under the pump.* KATE *re-enters the rear door of the family room, with flowers for the table.*)

KATE. Supper is ready, Jimmie, will you call your father?

JAMES. Certainly.

(*But he calls up the stairs, for* ANNIE's *benefit:*)

Father! Supper!

KELLER [*at the door*]. No need to shout, I've been cooling my heels for an hour. Sit down.

JAMES. Certainly.

KELLER. Viney!

(VINEY *backs in with a roast, while they get settled around the table.*)

VINEY. Yes, Cap'n, right here.

KATE. Mildred went directly to sleep, Viney?

VINEY. Oh yes, that babe's a angel.

KATE. And Helen had a good supper?

VINEY [*vaguely*]. I dunno, Miss Kate, somehow she didn't have much of a appetite tonight—

KATE [*a bit guilty*]. Oh. Dear.

KELLER [*hastily*]. Well, now. Couldn't say the same for my part, I'm famished. Katie, your plate.

KATE [*looking*]. But where is Miss Annie?

(*A silence.*)

JAMES [*pleasantly*]. In her room.

KELLER. In her room? Doesn't she know hot food must be eaten hot? Go bring her down at once, Jimmie.

JAMES [*rises*]. Certainly. I'll get a ladder.

KELLER [*stares*]. What?

JAMES. I'll need a ladder. Shouldn't take me long.

KATE [*stares*]. What shouldn't take you—

KELLER. Jimmie, do as I say! Go upstairs at once and tell Miss Sullivan supper is getting cold—

JAMES. She's locked in her room.

KELLER. Locked in her—

KATE. What on earth are you—

JAMES. Helen locked her in and made off with the key.

KATE [*rising*]. And you sit here and say nothing?

JAMES. Well, everyone's been telling me not to say anything.

(*He goes serenely out and across the yard, whistling.* KELLER *thrusting up from his chair makes for the stairs.*)

---

9. **crones,** old women, inmates of the State Infirmary at Tewksbury.

KATE. Viney, look out in back for Helen. See if she has that key.

VINEY. Yes, Miss Kate.

(VINEY *goes out the rear door.*)

KELLER [*calling down*]. She's out by the pump!

(KATE *goes out on the porch after* HELEN, *while* KELLER *knocks on* ANNIE'S *door, then rattles the knob, imperiously.*)

Miss Sullivan! Are you in there!

ANNIE. Oh, I'm in here, all right.

KELLER. Is there no key on your side?

ANNIE [*with some asperity*]. Well, if there was a key in here, I wouldn't be in here. Helen took it, the only thing on my side is me.

KELLER. Miss Sullivan. I—

(*He tries, but cannot hold it back.*)

Not in the house ten minutes, I don't see *how* you managed it!

(*He stomps downstairs again, while* ANNIE *mutters to herself.*)

ANNIE. And even I'm not on my side.

KELLER [*roaring*]. Viney!

VINEY [*reappearing*]. Yes, Cap'n?

KELLER. Put that meat back in the oven!

(VINEY *bears the roast off again, while* KELLER *strides out onto the porch.* KATE *is with* HELEN *at the pump, opening her hands.*)

KATE. She has no key.

KELLER. Nonsense, she must have the key. Have you searched in her pockets?

KATE. Yes. She doesn't have it.

KELLER. Katie, she must have the key.

KATE. Would you prefer to search her yourself, Captain?

KELLER. No, I would not prefer to search her! She almost took my kneecap off this evening, when I tried merely to—

(JAMES *reappears carrying a long ladder, with* PERCY *running after him to be in on things.*)

Take that ladder back!

JAMES. Certainly.

(*He turns around with it.* MARTHA *comes skipping around the upstage corner of the house to be in on things, accompanied by the setter Belle.*)

KATE. She could have hidden the key.

KELLER. Where?

KATE. Anywhere. Under a stone. In the flower beds. In the grass—

KELLER. Well, I can't plow up the entire grounds to find a missing key! Jimmie!

JAMES. Sir?

KELLER. Bring me a ladder!

JAMES. Certainly.

(VINEY *comes around the downstage side of the house to be in on things; she has Mildred over her shoulder, bleating.* KELLER *places the ladder against* ANNIE'S *window and mounts.* ANNIE *meanwhile is running about making herself presentable, washing the blood off her mouth, straightening her clothes, tidying her hair. Another Negro servant enters to gaze in wonder, increasing the gathering ring of spectators.*)

KATE [*sharply*]. What is Mildred doing up?

VINEY. Cap'n woke her, ma'am, all that hollerin'.

KELLER. Miss Sullivan!

(ANNIE *comes to the window, with as much air of gracious normality as she can manage;* KELLER *is at the window.*)

ANNIE [*brightly*]. Yes, Captain Keller?

KELLER. Come out!

ANNIE. I don't see how I can. There isn't room.

KELLER. I intend to carry you. Climb onto my shoulder and hold tight.

ANNIE. Oh, no. It's—very chivalrous of you, but I'd really prefer to—

KELLER. Miss Sullivan, follow instructions! I will not have you also tumbling out of our windows.

(ANNIE *obeys, with some misgivings.*)

I hope this is not a sample of what we may expect from you. In the way of simplifying the work of looking after Helen.

ANNIE. Captain Keller, I'm perfectly able to go down a ladder under my own—

KELLER. I doubt it, Miss Sullivan. Simply hold onto my neck.

(*He begins down with her, while the spectators stand in a wide and somewhat awestricken circle, watching.* KELLER *half-misses a rung, and* ANNIE *grabs at his whiskers.*)

My *neck*, Miss Sullivan!

ANNIE. I'm sorry to inconvenience you this way—

KELLER. No inconvenience, other than having that door taken down and the lock replaced, if we fail to find that key.

ANNIE. Oh, I'll look everywhere for it.

KELLER. Thank you. Do not look in any rooms that can be locked. There.

(*He stands her on the ground.* JAMES *applauds.*)

ANNIE. Thank you very much.

(*She smooths her skirt, looking as composed and ladylike as possible.* KELLER *stares around at the spectators.*)

KELLER. Go, go, back to your work. What are you looking at here? There's nothing here to look at.

(*They break up, move off.*)

Now would it be possible for us to have supper, like other people?

(*He marches into the house.*)

KATE. Viney, serve supper. I'll put Mildred to sleep.

(*They all go in.* JAMES *is the last to leave, murmuring to* ANNIE *with a gesture.*)

JAMES. Might as well leave the l, a, d, d, e, r, hm?

(ANNIE *ignores him, looking at* HELEN; JAMES *goes in too. Imperceptibly the lights commence to narrow down.* ANNIE *and* HELEN *are now alone in the yard,* HELEN *seated at the pump, where she has been oblivious to it all, a battered little savage, playing with the doll*

Annie learns what happened to the lost key in this scene from the film version of The Miracle Worker.

in a picture of innocent contentment. ANNIE *comes near, leans against the house, and taking off her smoked glasses, studies her, not without awe. Presently* HELEN *rises, gropes around to see if anyone is present;* ANNIE *evades her hand, and when* HELEN *is satisfied she is alone, the key suddenly protrudes out of her mouth. She takes it in her fingers, stands thinking, gropes to the pump, lifts a loose board, drops the key into the well, and hugs herself gleefully.* ANNIE *stares. But after a moment she shakes her head to herself, she cannot keep the smile from her lips.*)

ANNIE. You *devil.*

(*Her tone is one of great respect, humor, and acceptance of challenge.*)

You think I'm so easily gotten rid of? You have a thing or two to learn, first. I have nothing else to do.

(*She goes up the steps to the porch, but turns for a final word, almost of warning.*)

And nowhere to go.

(*And presently she moves into the house to the others, as the lights dim down and out, except for the small circle upon* HELEN *solitary at the pump, which ends the act.*)

I

ANNIE ACCEPTS A CHALLENGE

A skillful playwright strives to end each act of a play at a point of such high interest that the audience is eager to find out what happens next. As Act I ends, Annie realizes, with both humor and awe, that in Helen she has a devilish little adversary who feels that she "has won the first round."

Earlier in this first act, Mr. Gibson laid the groundwork for understanding why Helen is the problem she is and how Annie Sullivan had come to her as a teacher. Explain.

1. What frightening discovery did Kate Keller make about the one-and-one-half-year-old Helen in the first scene of the play? How old is Helen when she is next introduced?

2. Why does Captain Keller stubbornly refuse, for a long time, to write to the doctor in Baltimore? How does each member of the household feel about Helen? Through whom are the Kellers put in touch with Anagnos and in turn with Annie Sullivan?

3. What do you learn of Annie Sullivan's background in her conversation with Anagnos? What does she say Perkins Institution has done for her? What is the attitude of Anagnos and the children of Perkins Institution toward Annie? What is the gift the children send to Helen?

4. When do you have the first indication that Annie believes that a child handicapped as Helen should be treated as an ordinary child?

5. Identify the characters who speak the following lines and briefly outline the situation in which the words are spoken:

a. ". . . I'm as shaky inside as a baby's rattle!"

b. "Great improvement. Now we have two of them to look after."

c. "All right, Miss O'Sullivan. Let's begin with doll."

d. "Don't worry. They'll find you, you're not lost. Only out of place. And toothless."

II

IMPLICATIONS

Consider these statements. Determine whether you agree or not.

1. We are most sympathetic or understanding toward those with problems closest to our own.

2. Most people tend to interpret all the events of the world in terms of their own personal experiences.

3. One small grievance can often ruin a lifetime.

III

TECHNIQUES

Characterization

The opening stage directions in Act I tell you only that Kate Keller is a "young gentlewoman with a sweet girlish face," while Captain Keller is "a hearty gentleman in his forties with chin whiskers."

1. Captain Keller's first speech reveals a bluff heartiness which carries with it the impression that he is used to imposing his opinions on others without being sensitive to their feelings. How is this trait of his reflected in other situations throughout Act I?

2. In his dialogue, particularly with Annie, the Captain emerges as an almost comically pompous figure. What ideas does he have about proper behavior for "ladies"? Find lines in which Annie's Irish wit makes him look rather ludicrous. Discuss those lines on page 221 which indicate that sometimes the Captain feels he is not as important as he would like to believe.

3. Although Kate Keller is a "gentlewoman," her gentleness overlays a strength of purpose which is brought out plainly after Helen's tragic illness. In what instances does she demonstrate both strength of character and persistence? While she shows strength of character, she could also be considered "weak." Explain why this is true.

4. Helen is an unrestrained, spoiled, strong-willed child, desperate with the frustration of being unable to communicate. This is evident from that first scene in which she appears. Discuss those incidents in Act I which show that Helen wishes to talk and have eyes that see. Describe her physical appearance. What indicates to Annie that Helen is a "bright" child and has a good mind that needs only to be reached?

5. Find lines from Act I which show that Annie understands her own nature. What does Anagnos say that Annie lacks? What does Annie say about her ability to love other people? Discuss those qualities which equip her best for her struggle with Helen.

6. Why do you think there is no description of Aunt Ev? How would you characterize her?

Significant Details

1. What is the importance of the battered volume which Annie is carrying under her arm when she gets off the train?

2. Locate the line in Act I in which Annie tells Kate that she will try to teach Helen language. Upon whose words is she basing her plan?

3. What does Helen's gesture of touching her cheek mean?

Staging

As the play progressed, it undoubtedly became apparent to the reader why Mr. Gibson specified that the stage should be divided into two areas.

1. What does the area behind the diagonal represent? Describe how this space is divided up. Why is the area in front of the diagonal called "neutral" ground? Discuss the meaning of the author's direction that "locales should be only skeletal suggestions, and the movement from one to another should be accomplishable by little more than lights."

2. Although the stage is kept as uncluttered as possible, certain stage properties are used to indicate where action is taking place. How is the audience made aware that action has shifted (a) to the Perkins Institution in Boston, (b) to the railroad station?

3. What device is used to indicate the passing of five years early in Act I?

4. If *The Miracle Worker* had been planned for conventional scene changing, how many separate scenes would have been necessary for Act I?

TECHNIQUES

The Playwright's Art

CHARACTERIZATION

In a novel, an author has the opportunity to provide detailed descriptions of his characters and their actions. In a drama, the playwright must reveal and develop characters primarily through costuming, action, and dialogue on the stage. Generally, the main characters in a drama will undergo change as a result of the action of the play while the minor characters will not. The minor characters serve to further the action of the play and provide increased possibility for giving the audience more insight into the main characters. Think back over Act I. Discuss how this concept can be illustrated in the character of Aunt Ev.

For Annie Sullivan, things have never been easy. Had she not had a lot of fighting spirit, she very likely would not have survived the horrors of her early childhood and adolescence. Playwright Gibson describes her face as grave and rather obstinate in repose but impudent, combative, and twinkling with life when she is active.

Aunt Ev, Viney, and James all help give insight into the characters of Helen, Kate, and Captain Keller. Discuss the minor characters introduced in Act I who help to establish Annie's character.

SIGNIFICANT DETAILS

Pantomime is one of the oldest forms of drama. For such performances the performers express themselves by mute gestures. The entire personality of Helen must be revealed through statements from other characters about her or their reactions to her, and through her pantomime. Unless one reads the detailed stage directions carefully, much of what is significant in this play would be overlooked.

Why would one have missed a great deal of the dramatic impact at the end of Act I if he had failed to read the stage direction on page 229?

STAGING

The staging of a play must be consistent with mood of the action. The setting not only provides the atmosphere for the play but helps foreshadow the drama that follows the opening scene. Notice the opening scenes of each act of *The Miracle Worker*. Consider how each one is consistent with the act it opens.

Act II

I*t is evening.*

The only room visible in the KELLER *house is* ANNIE's, *where by lamplight* ANNIE *in a shawl is at a desk writing a letter; at her bureau* HELEN *in her customary unkempt state is tucking her doll in the bottom drawer as a cradle, the contents of which she has dumped out, creating as usual a fine disorder.*

ANNIE *mutters each word as she writes her letter, slowly, her eyes close to and almost touching the page, to follow with difficulty her pen-work.*

ANNIE. ". . . and, nobody, here, has, attempted, to, control, her. The, greatest, problem, I, have, is, how, to, disipline, her, without, breaking, her, spirit."

(*Resolute voice*)

"But, I, shall, insist, on, reasonable, obedience, from, the, start—"

(*At which point* HELEN, *groping about on the desk, knocks over the inkwell.* ANNIE *jumps up, rescues her letter, rights the inkwell, grabs a towel to stem the spillage, and then wipes at* HELEN's *hands;* HELEN *as always pulls free, but not until* ANNIE *first gets three letters into her palm.*)

Ink.

(HELEN *is enough interested in and puzzled by this spelling that she proffers her hand again; so* ANNIE *spells and impassively dunks it back into the spillage.*)

Ink. It has a name.

(*She wipes the hand clean, and leads* HELEN *to her bureau, where she looks for something to engage her. She finds a sewing card, with needle and thread, and going to her knees, shows* HELEN's *hand how to connect one row of holes.*)

Down. Under. Up. And be careful of the needle—

(HELEN *gets it, and* ANNIE *rises.*)

Fine. You keep out of the ink and perhaps I can keep out of—the soup.

(*She returns to the desk, tidies it, and resumes writing her letter, bent close to the page.*)

"These, blots, are, her, handiwork. I—"

(*She is interrupted by a gasp:* HELEN *has stuck her finger, and sits sucking at it, darkly. Then with vengeful resolve she seizes her doll, and is about to dash its brains out on the floor when* ANNIE *diving catches it in one hand, which she at once shakes with hopping pain but otherwise ignores patiently.*)

All right, let's try temperance.

(*Taking the doll, she kneels, goes through the motion of knocking its head to the floor, spells into* HELEN's *hand:*)

Bad, girl.

(*She lets* HELEN *feel the grieved expression on her face.* HELEN *imitates it. Next she makes* HELEN *caress the doll and kiss the hurt spot and hold it gently in her arms, then spells into her hand:*)

Good, girl.

(*She lets* HELEN *feel the smile on her face.* HELEN *sits with a scowl, which suddenly clears; she pats the doll, kisses it, wreathes her face in a large artificial smile, and bears the doll to the washstand, where she carefully sits it.* ANNIE *watches, pleased.*)

Very good girl—

(*Whereupon* HELEN *elevates the pitcher and dashes it on the floor instead.* ANNIE *leaps to her feet, and stands inarticulate;* HELEN *calmly gropes back to sit to the sewing card and needle.*)

ANNIE *manages to achieve self-control. She picks up a fragment or two of the pitcher, sees* HELEN *is puzzling over the card, and resolutely kneels to demonstrate it again. She spells into* HELEN's *hand.*

KATE *meanwhile coming around the corner with folded sheets on her arm, halts at the doorway and watches them for a moment in silence; she is moved, but level.*)

KATE [*presently*]. What are you saying to her?

(ANNIE *glancing up is a bit embarrassed, and rises from the spelling, to find her company manners.*)

ANNIE. Oh, I was just making conversation. Saying it was a sewing card.

KATE. But does that—

(*She imitates with her fingers.*)

—mean that to her?

ANNIE. No. No, she won't know what spelling is till she knows what a word is.

KATE. Yet you keep spelling to her. Why?

ANNIE [*cheerily*]. I like to hear myself talk!

KATE. The Captain says it's like spelling to the fence post.

ANNIE [*a pause*]. Does he, now.

KATE. Is it?

ANNIE. No, it's how I watch you talk to Mildred.

KATE. Mildred.

ANNIE. Any baby. Gibberish, grown-up gibberish, baby-talk gibberish, do they understand one word of it to start? Somehow they begin to. If they hear it, I'm letting Helen hear it.

KATE. Other children are not—impaired.

ANNIE. Ho, there's nothing impaired in that head, it works like a mousetrap!

KATE [*smiles*]. But after a child hears how many words, Miss Annie, a million?

ANNIE. I guess no mother's ever minded enough to count.

(*She drops her eyes to spell into* HELEN's *hand, again indicating the card;* HELEN *spells back, and* ANNIE *is amused.*)

KATE [*too quickly*]. What did she spell?

ANNIE. I spelt card. She spelt cake!

(*She takes in* KATE's *quickness, and shakes her head, gently.*)

No, it's only a finger-game to her, Mrs. Keller. What she has to learn first is that things have names.

KATE. And when will she learn?

ANNIE. Maybe after a million and one words.

(*They hold each other's gaze;* KATE *then speaks quietly.*)

KATE. I should like to learn those letters, Miss Annie.

ANNIE [*pleased*]. I'll teach you tomorrow morning. That makes only a half million each!

KATE [*then*]. It's her bedtime.

(ANNIE *reaches for the sewing card,* HELEN *objects,* ANNIE *insists, and* HELEN *gets rid of* ANNIE's *hand by jabbing it with the needle.* ANNIE *gasps, and moves to grip* HELEN's *wrist; but* KATE *intervenes with a proffered sweet, and* HELEN *drops the card, crams the sweet into her mouth, and scrambles up to search her mother's hands for more.* ANNIE *nurses her wound, staring after the sweet.*)

I'm sorry, Miss Annie.

ANNIE [*indignantly*]. Why does she get a reward? For stabbing me?

KATE. Well—

(*Then, tiredly*)

We catch our flies with honey, I'm afraid. We haven't the heart for much else, and so many times she simply cannot be compelled.

ANNIE [*ominous*]. Yes. I'm the same way myself.

KATE *smiles, and leads* HELEN *off around the corner.* ANNIE *alone in her room picks up things and in the act of removing* HELEN's *doll gives way to unmannerly temptation: she throttles it. She drops it on her bed, and stands pondering. Then she turns back, sits decisively, and writes again, as the lights dim on her.*)

(*Grimly*)

"The, more, I, think, the, more, certain, I, am, that, obedience, is, the, gateway, through, which, knowledge, enters, the, mind, of, the, child—"

(*On the word "obedience" a shaft of sunlight hits the water pump outside, while* ANNIE's *voice ends in the dark, followed by a distant cockcrow; daylight comes up over another corner of the sky, with* VINEY's *voice heard at once.*)

VINEY. Breakfast ready!

(VINEY *comes down into the sunlight beam, and pumps a pitcherful of water. While the pitcher is brimming we hear conversation from the dark; the light grows to the family room of the house where all are either entering or already seated at breakfast, with* KELLER *and* JAMES *arguing the war.* HELEN *is wandering around the table to explore the contents of the other plates. When* ANNIE *is in her chair, she watches* HELEN. VINEY *re-enters, sets the pitcher on the table;* KATE *lifts the almost empty biscuit plate with an inquiring look,* VINEY *nods and bears it off back, neither of them interrupting the men.* ANNIE *meanwhile sits with fork quiet, watching* HELEN, *who at her mother's plate pokes her hand among some scrambled eggs.* KATE *catches* ANNIE's *eyes on her, smiles with a wry gesture.* HELEN *moves on to* JAMES's *plate, the male talk continuing,* JAMES *deferential and* KELLER *overriding.*)

JAMES. —no, but shouldn't we give the devil his due, father? The fact is we lost the South two years earlier when he outthought us behind Vicksburg.[10]

KELLER. Outthought is a peculiar word for a butcher.

JAMES. Harness maker, wasn't he?

KELLER. I said butcher, his only virtue as a soldier was numbers and he led them to slaughter with no more regard than for so many sheep.

JAMES. But even if in that sense he was a butcher, the fact is he—

KELLER. And a drunken one, half the war.

JAMES. Agreed, father. If his own people said he was I can't argue he—

KELLER. Well, what is it you find to admire in such a man, Jimmie, the butchery or the drunkenness?

JAMES. Neither, father, only the fact that he beat us.

KELLER. He didn't.

JAMES. Is it your contention we won the war, sir?

KELLER. He didn't beat us at Vicksburg. We lost Vicksburg because Pemberton gave Bragg five thousand of his cavalry and Loring,[11] whom I knew personally for a nincompoop before you were born, marched away from Champion's Hill with enough men to have held them, we lost Vicksburg by stupidity verging on treason.

JAMES. I would have said we lost Vicksburg because Grant was one thing no Yankee general was before him—

KELLER. Drunk? I doubt it.

JAMES. Obstinate.

KELLER. Obstinate. Could any of them compare even in that with old Stonewall? If he'd been there we would still have Vicksburg.

JAMES. Well, the butcher simply wouldn't give up, he tried four ways of getting around Vicksburg and on the fifth try he got around. Anyone else would have pulled north and—

KELLER. He wouldn't have got around if we'd had a Southerner in command, instead of a half-breed Yankee traitor like Pemberton—

(*While this background talk is in progress,* HELEN *is working around the table, ultimately toward* ANNIE's *plate. She messes with her hands in* JAMES's *plate, then in* KELLER's, *both men taking it so for granted they hardly notice. Then* HELEN *comes groping with soiled hands past her own plate, to* ANNIE's; *her hand goes to it, and* ANNIE, *who has been waiting, deliberately lifts and removes her hand.* HELEN *gropes again,* ANNIE *firmly pins her by the wrist, and removes her hand from the table.* HELEN *thrusts her hands again,* ANNIE *catches them, and* HELEN *begins to*

---

10. James is referring to General U. S. Grant, whose Union troops captured Vicksburg on July 4, 1863.
11. **Pemberton, Bragg,** and **Loring,** mentioned by Captain Keller, were Confederate officers.

flail and make noises; the interruption brings KELLER's *gaze upon them.*)

What's the matter there?

KATE. Miss Annie. You see, she's accustomed to helping herself from our plates to anything she—

ANNIE [*evenly*]. Yes, but *I'm* not accustomed to it.

KELLER. No, of course not. Viney!

KATE. Give her something, Jimmie, to quiet her.

JAMES [*blandly*]. But her table manners are the best she has. Well.

(*He pokes across with a chunk of bacon at* HELEN's *hand, which* ANNIE *releases; but* HELEN *knocks the bacon away and stubbornly thrusts at* ANNIE's *plate,* ANNIE *grips her wrists again, the struggle mounts.*)

KELLER. Let her this time, Miss Sullivan, it's the only way we get any adult conversation. If my son's half merits that description.

(*He rises.*)

I'll get you another plate.

ANNIE [*gripping* HELEN]. I have a plate, thank you.

KATE [*calling*]. Viney! I'm afraid what Captain Keller says is only too true, she'll persist in this until she gets her own way.

KELLER [*at the door*]. Viney, bring Miss Sullivan another plate—

ANNIE [*stonily*]. I have a plate, nothing's wrong with the *plate*, I intend to keep it.

(*Silence for a moment, except for* HELEN's *noises as she struggles to get loose; the* KELLERS *are a bit nonplussed, and* ANNIE *is too darkly intent on* HELEN's *manners to have any thoughts now of her own.*)

JAMES. Ha. You see why they took Vicksburg?

KELLER [*uncertainly*]. Miss Sullivan. One plate or another is hardly a matter to struggle with a deprived child about.

ANNIE. Oh, I'd sooner have a more—

(HELEN *begins to kick,* ANNIE *moves her ankles to the opposite side of the chair.*)

—heroic issue myself, I—

KELLER. No, I really must insist you—

(HELEN *bangs her toe on the chair and sinks to the floor, crying with rage and feigned injury;* ANNIE *keeps hold of her wrists, gazing down, while* KATE *rises.*)

Now she's hurt herself.

ANNIE [*grimly*]. No, she hasn't.

KELLER. Will you please let her hands go?

KATE. Miss Annie, you don't know the child well enough yet, she'll keep—

ANNIE. I know an ordinary tantrum well enough, when I see one, and a badly spoiled child—

JAMES. Hear, hear.

KELLER [*very annoyed*]. Miss Sullivan! You would have more understanding of your pupil if you had some pity in you. Now kindly do as I—

ANNIE. Pity?

(*She releases* HELEN *to turn equally annoyed on* KELLER *across the table; instantly* HELEN *scrambles up and dives at* ANNIE's *plate. This time* ANNIE *intercepts her by pouncing on her wrists like a hawk, and her temper boils.*)

For this *tyrant*? The whole house turns on her whims, is there anything she wants she doesn't get? I'll tell you what I pity, that the sun won't rise and set for her all her life, and every day you're telling her it will, what good will your pity do her when you're under the strawberries, Captain Keller?

KELLER [*outraged*]. Kate, for the love of heaven will you—

KATE. Miss Annie, please, I don't think it serves to lose our—

ANNIE. It does you good, that's all. It's less trouble to feel sorry for her than to teach her anything better, isn't it?

KELLER. I fail to see where you have taught her anything yet, Miss Sullivan!

ANNIE. I'll begin this minute, if you'll leave the room, Captain Keller!

KELLER [*astonished*]. Leave the—

ANNIE. Everyone, please.

(*She struggles with* HELEN, *while* KELLER *endeavors to control his voice.*)

*Annie Sullivan struggles with Helen
during the wild breakfast battle
scene from Act II.*

KELLER. Miss Sullivan, you are here only as a
paid teacher. Nothing more, and not to lecture—

ANNIE. I can't *un*teach her six years of pity if
you can't stand up to one tantrum! Old Stonewall, indeed. Mrs. Keller, you promised me
help.

KATE. Indeed I did, we truly want to—

ANNIE. Then leave me alone with her. Now!

KELLER [*in a wrath*]. Katie, will you come outside with me? At once, please.

(*He marches to the front door.* KATE *and*
JAMES *follow him. Simultaneously* ANNIE *releases* HELEN'S *wrists, and the child again
sinks to the floor, kicking and crying her
weird noises;* ANNIE *steps over her to meet*
VINEY *coming in the rear doorway with bis-
cuits and a clean plate, surprised at the general commotion.*)

VINEY. Heaven sakes—

ANNIE. Out, please.

(*She backs* VINEY *out with one hand, closes
the door on her astonished mouth, locks it,
and removes the key.* KELLER *meanwhile
snatches his hat from a rack, and* KATE *fol-*

lows him down the porch steps. JAMES *lingers
in the doorway to address* ANNIE *across the
room with a bow.*)

JAMES. If it takes all summer, general.

(ANNIE *comes over to his door in turn, removing her glasses grimly; as* KELLER *outside
begins speaking,* ANNIE *closes the door on*
JAMES, *locks it, removes the key, and turns
with her back against the door to stare ominously at* HELEN, *kicking on the floor.*

JAMES *takes his hat from the rack, and going
down the porch steps joins* KATE *and* KELLER
talking in the yard, KELLER *in a sputter of
ire.*)

KELLER. This girl, this—cub of a girl—*pre-
sumes!* I tell you, I'm of half a mind to ship
her back to Boston before the week is out.
You can inform her so from me!

KATE [*eyebrows up*]. I, Captain?

KELLER. She's a *hireling!* Now I want it clear,
unless there's an apology and complete
change of manner she goes back on the next
train! Will you make that quite clear?

KATE. Where will you be, Captain, while I am
making it quite—

KELLER. At the office!

(*He begins off left, finds his napkin still in
his irate hand, is uncertain with it, dabs his
lips with dignity, gets rid of it in a toss to*
JAMES, *and marches off.* JAMES *turns to eye*
KATE.)

JAMES. Will you?

(KATE'S *mouth is set, and* JAMES *studies it
lightly.*)

I thought what she said was exceptionally
intelligent. I've been saying it for years.

KATE [*not without scorn*]. To his face?

(*She comes to relieve him of the white napkin, but reverts again with it.*)

Or will you take it, Jimmie? As a flag?

(JAMES *stalks out, much offended, and* KATE
*turning stares across the yard at the house;
the lights narrowing down to the following*

pantomime in the family room leave her motionless in the dark.

ANNIE *meanwhile has begun by slapping both keys down on a shelf out of* HELEN's *reach; she returns to the table, upstage.* HELEN's *kicking has subsided, and when from the floor her hand finds* ANNIE's *chair empty she pauses.* ANNIE *clears the table of* KATE's, JAMES's, *and* KELLER's *plates; she gets back to her own across the table just in time to slide it deftly away from* HELEN's *pouncing hand. She lifts the hand and moves it to* HELEN's *plate, and after an instant's exploration,* HELEN *sits again on the floor and drums her heels.* ANNIE *comes around the table and resumes her chair. When* HELEN *feels her skirt again, she ceases kicking, waits for whatever is to come, renews some kicking, waits again.* ANNIE *retrieving her plate takes up a forkful of food, stops it halfway to her mouth, gazes at it devoid of appetite, and half-lowers it; but after a look at* HELEN *she sighs, dips the forkful toward* HELEN *in a for-your-sake toast, and puts it in her own mouth to chew, not without an effort.*

HELEN *now gets hold of the chair leg, and half-succeeds in pulling the chair out from under her.* ANNIE *bangs it down with her rear, heavily, and sits with all her weight.* HELEN's *next attempt to topple it is unavailing, so her fingers dive in a pinch at* ANNIE's *flank.* ANNIE *in the middle of her mouthful almost loses it with startle, and she slaps down her fork to round on* HELEN. *The child comes up with curiosity to feel what* ANNIE *is doing, so* ANNIE *resumes eating, letting* HELEN's *hand follow the movement of her fork to her mouth; whereupon* HELEN *at once reaches into* ANNIE's *plate.* ANNIE *firmly removes her hand to her own plate.* HELEN *in reply pinches* ANNIE's *thigh, a good mean pinchful that makes* ANNIE *jump.* ANNIE *sets the fork down, and sits with her mouth tight.* HELEN *digs another pinch into her thigh, and this time* ANNIE *slaps her hand smartly away;* HELEN *retaliates with a roundhouse*

fist that catches ANNIE *on the ear, and* ANNIE's *hand leaps at once in a forceful slap across* HELEN's *cheek;* HELEN *is the startled one now.* ANNIE's *hand in compunction falters to her own face, but when* HELEN *hits at her again,* ANNIE *deliberately slaps her again.* HELEN *lifts her fist irresolute for another roundhouse,* ANNIE *lifts her hand resolute for another slap, and they freeze in this posture, while* HELEN *mulls it over. She thinks better of it, drops her fist, and giving* ANNIE *a wide berth, gropes around to her mother's chair, to find it empty; she blunders her way along the table, upstage, and encountering the empty chairs and missing plates, she looks bewildered; she gropes back to her mother's chair, again touches her cheek and indicates the chair, and waits for the world to answer.*

A lull before the continuing storm—Helen and Annie during the breakfast room scene.

ANNIE *now reaches over to spell into her hand, but* HELEN *yanks it away; she gropes to the front door, tries the knob, and finds the door locked, with no key. She gropes to the rear door, and finds it locked, with no key. She commences to bang on it.* ANNIE *rises, crosses, takes her wrists, draws her resisting*

237

back to the table, seats her, and releases her hands upon her plate; as ANNIE herself begins to sit, HELEN writhes out of her chair, runs to the front door, and tugs and kicks at it. ANNIE rises again, crosses, draws her by one wrist back to the table, seats her, and sits; HELEN escapes back to the door, knocking over her mother's chair en route. ANNIE rises again in pursuit, and this time lifts HELEN bodily from behind and bears her kicking to her chair. She deposits her, and once more turns to sit. HELEN scrambles out, but as she passes ANNIE catches her up again from behind and deposits her in the chair; HELEN scrambles out on the other side, for the rear door, but ANNIE at her heels catches her up and deposits her again in the chair. She stands behind it. HELEN scrambles out to her right, and the instant her feet hit the floor ANNIE lifts and deposits her back; she scrambles out to her left, and is at once lifted and deposited back. She tries right again and is deposited back, and tries left again and is deposited back, and now feints ANNIE to the right but is off to her left, and is promptly deposited back. She sits a moment, and then starts straight over the tabletop, dishware notwithstanding; ANNIE hauls her in and deposits her back, with her plate spilling in her lap, and she melts to the floor and crawls under the table, laborious among its legs and chairs; but ANNIE is swift around the table and waiting on the other side when she surfaces, immediately bearing her aloft; HELEN clutches at JAMES's chair for anchorage, but it comes with her, and halfway back she abandons it to the floor. ANNIE deposits her in her chair, and waits, HELEN sits tensed motionless. Then she tentatively puts out her left foot and hand, ANNIE interposes her own hand, and at the contact HELEN jerks hers in. She tries her right foot, ANNIE blocks it with her own, and HELEN jerks hers in. Finally, leaning back, she slumps down in her chair, in a sullen biding.

ANNIE backs off a step, and watches; HELEN

offers no move. ANNIE takes a deep breath. Both of them and the room are in considerable disorder, two chairs down and the table a mess, but ANNIE makes no effort to tidy it; she only sits on her own chair, and lets her energy refill. Then she takes up knife and fork, and resolutely addresses her food. HELEN's hand comes out to explore, and seeing it ANNIE sits without moving; the child's hand goes over her hand and fork, pauses—ANNIE still does not move—and withdraws. Presently it moves for her own plate, slaps about for it, and stops, thwarted. At this, ANNIE again rises, recovers HELEN's plate from the floor and a handful of scattered food from the deranged tablecloth, drops it on the plate, and pushes the plate into contact with HELEN's fist. Neither of them now moves for a pregnant moment—until HELEN suddenly takes a grab of food and wolfs it down. ANNIE permits herself the humor of a minor bow and warming of her hands together; she wanders off a step or two, watching. HELEN cleans up the plate.

After a glower of indecision, she holds the empty plate out for more. ANNIE accepts it, and crossing to the removed plates, spoons food from them onto it; she stands debating the spoon, tapping it a few times on HELEN's plate; and when she returns with the plate she brings the spoon, too. She puts the spoon first into HELEN's hand, then sets the plate down. HELEN discarding the spoon reaches with her hand, and ANNIE stops it by the wrist; she replaces the spoon in it. HELEN impatiently discards it again, and again ANNIE stops her hand, to replace the spoon in it. This time HELEN throws the spoon on the floor. ANNIE after considering it lifts HELEN bodily out of the chair, and in a wrestling match on the floor closes her fingers upon the spoon, and returns her with it to the chair. HELEN again throws the spoon on the floor. ANNIE lifts her out of the chair again; but in the struggle over the spoon HELEN with ANNIE on her back sends her sliding over her head;

HELEN *flees back to her chair and scrambles into it. When* ANNIE *comes after her she clutches it for dear life;* ANNIE *pries one hand loose, then the other, then the first again, then the other again, and then lifts* HELEN *by the waist, chair and all, and shakes the chair loose.* HELEN *wrestles to get free, but* ANNIE *pins her to the floor, closes her fingers upon the spoon, and lifts her kicking under one arm; with her other hand she gets the chair in place again, and plunks* HELEN *back on it. When she releases her hand,* HELEN *throws the spoon at her.*

ANNIE *now removes the plate of food.* HELEN *grabbing finds it missing, and commences to bang with her fists on the table.* ANNIE *collects a fistful of spoons and descends with them and the plate on* HELEN; *she lets her smell the plate, at which* HELEN *ceases banging, and* ANNIE *puts the plate down and a spoon in* HELEN's *hand.* HELEN *throws it on the floor.* ANNIE *puts another spoon in her hand.* HELEN *throws it on the floor.* ANNIE *puts another spoon in her hand.* HELEN *throws it on the floor. When* ANNIE *comes to her last spoon she sits next to* HELEN, *and gripping the spoon in* HELEN's *hand compels her to take food in it up to her mouth.* HELEN *sits with lips shut.* ANNIE *waits a stolid moment, then lowers* HELEN's *hand. She tries again;* HELEN's *lips remain shut.* ANNIE *waits, lowers* HELEN's *hand. She tries again; this time* HELEN *suddenly opens her mouth and accepts the food.* ANNIE *lowers the spoon with a sigh of relief, and* HELEN *spews the mouthful out at her face.* ANNIE *sits a moment with eyes closed, then takes the pitcher and dashes its water into* HELEN's *face, who gasps astonished.* ANNIE *with* HELEN's *hand takes up another spoonful, and shoves it into her open mouth.* HELEN *swallows involuntarily, and while she is catching her breath* ANNIE *forces her palm open, throws four swift letters into it, then another four, and bows toward her with devastating pleasantness.*)

ANNIE. Good girl.

(ANNIE *lifts* HELEN's *hand to feel her face nodding;* HELEN *grabs a fistful of her hair, and yanks. The pain brings* ANNIE *to her knees, and* HELEN *pummels her; they roll under the table, and the lights commence to dim out on them.*

Simultaneously the light at left has been rising, slowly, so slowly that it seems at first we only imagine what is intimated in the yard: a few ghostlike figures, in silence, motionless, waiting. Now the distant belfry chimes commence to toll the hour, also very slowly, almost—it is twelve—interminably; the sense is that of a long time passing. We can identify the figures before the twelfth stroke, all facing the house in a kind of watch: KATE *is standing exactly as before, but now with the baby Mildred sleeping in her arms, and placed here and there, unmoving, are* AUNT EV *in her hat with a hanky to her nose, and the two Negro children,* PERCY *and* MARTHA *with necks outstretched eagerly, and* VINEY *with a knotted kerchief on her head and a feather duster in her hand.*

The chimes cease, and there is silence. For a long moment none of the group moves.

VINEY [*presently*]. What am I gone do, Miss Kate? It's noontime, dinner's comin', I didn't get them breakfast dishes out of there yet.

(KATE *says nothing, stares at the house.* MARTHA *shifts* HELEN's *doll in her clutch, and it plaintively says momma.*)

KATE [*presently*]. You run along, Martha.

(AUNT EV *blows her nose.*)

AUNT EV [*wretchedly*]. I can't wait out here a minute longer, Kate, why, this could go on all afternoon, too.

KATE. I'll tell the Captain you called.

VINEY [*to the children*]. You hear what Miss Kate say? Never you mind what's going on here.

(*Still no one moves.*)

You run along tend your own bizness.

(*Finally* VINEY *turns on the children with the feather duster.*)

Shoo!

(*The two children divide before her. She chases them off.* AUNT EV *comes to* KATE, *on her dignity.*)

AUNT EV. Say what you like, Kate, but that child is a *Keller.*

(*She opens her parasol, preparatory to leaving.*)

I needn't remind you that all the Kellers are cousins to General Robert E. Lee. I don't know *who* that girl is.

(*She waits; but* KATE *staring at the house is without response.*)

The only Sullivan I've heard of—from Boston too, and I'd think twice before locking her up with that kind—is that man John L.[12]

(*And* AUNT EV *departs, with head high. Presently* VINEY *comes to* KATE, *her arms out for the baby.*)

VINEY. You give me her, Miss Kate, I'll sneak her in back, to her crib.

(*But* KATE *is moveless, until* VINEY *starts to take the baby;* KATE *looks down at her before relinquishing her.*)

KATE [*slowly*]. This child never gives me a minute's worry.

VINEY. Oh yes, this one's the angel of the family, no question bout *that.*

(*She begins off rear with the baby, heading around the house; and* KATE *now turns her back on it, her hand to her eyes. At this moment there is the slamming of a door, and when* KATE *wheels* HELEN *is blundering down the porch steps into the light like a ruined bat out of hell.* VINEY *halts, and* KATE *runs in;* HELEN *collides with her mother's knees, and reels off and back to clutch them as her savior.* ANNIE *with smoked glasses in hand stands on the porch, also much undone, looking as though she had indeed just taken Vicksburg.* KATE *taking in* HELEN's *ravaged*

state *becomes steely in her gaze up at* ANNIE.)

KATE. What happened?

(ANNIE *meets* KATE's *gaze, and gives a factual report, too exhausted for anything but a flat voice.*)

ANNIE. She ate from her own plate.

(*She thinks a moment.*)

She ate with a spoon. Herself.

(KATE *frowns, uncertain with thought, and glances down at* HELEN.)

And she folded her napkin.

(KATE's *gaze now wavers, from* HELEN *to* ANNIE, *and back.*)

KATE [*softly*]. Folded—her napkin?

ANNIE. The room's a wreck, but her napkin is folded.

(*She pauses, then:*)

I'll be in my room, Mrs. Keller.

(*She moves to re-enter the house; but she stops at* VINEY's *voice.*)

VINEY [*cheery*]. Don't be long, Miss Annie. Dinner be ready right away!

(VINEY *carries Mildred around the back of the house.* ANNIE *stands unmoving, takes a deep breath, stares over her shoulder at* KATE *and* HELEN, *then inclines her head graciously, and goes with a slight stagger into the house. The lights in her room above steal up in readiness for her.*

KATE *remains alone with* HELEN *in the yard, standing protectively over her, in a kind of wonder.*)

KATE [*slowly*]. Folded her napkin.

(*She contemplates the wild head at her thighs, and moves her fingertips over it, with such a tenderness, and something like a fear*

---

12. **John L. Sullivan** (1858–1918), of Boston, was heavyweight boxing champion from 1882 to 1892.

of its strangeness, that her own eyes close; she whispers, bending to it:)

My Helen—folded her napkin—

(*And still erect, with only her head in surrender,* KATE *for the first time that we see loses her protracted war with grief; but she will not let a sound escape her, only the grimace of tears comes, and sobs that shake her in a grip of silence. But* HELEN *feels them, and her hand comes up in its own wondering, to interrogate her mother's face, until* KATE *buries her lips in the child's palm.*

Upstairs, ANNIE *enters her room, closes the door, and stands back against it; the lights, growing on her with their special color, commence to fade on* KATE *and* HELEN. *Then* ANNIE *goes wearily to her suitcase, and lifts it to take it toward the bed. But it knocks an object to the floor, and she turns back to regard it. A new voice comes in a cultured murmur, hesitant as with the effort of remembering a text:*)

MAN'S VOICE.[13] This—soul—

(ANNIE *puts the suitcase down, and kneels to the object: it is the battered Perkins report, and she stands with it in her hand, letting memory try to speak:*)

This—blind, deaf, mute—woman—

(ANNIE *sits on her bed, opens the book, and finding the passage, brings it up an inch from her eyes to read, her face and lips following the overheard words, the voice quite factual now:*)

Can nothing be done to disinter this human soul? The whole neighborhood would rush to save this woman if she were buried alive by the caving in of a pit, and labor with zeal until she were dug out. Now if there were one who had as much patience as zeal, he might awaken her to a consciousness of her immortal—

(*When the boy's voice comes,* ANNIE *closes her eyes, in pain.*)

BOY'S VOICE. Annie? Annie, you there?

ANNIE. Hush.

BOY'S VOICE. Annie, what's that noise?

(ANNIE *tries not to answer; her own voice is drawn out of her, unwilling.*)

ANNIE. Just a cot, Jimmie.

BOY'S VOICE. Where they pushin' it?

ANNIE. To the deadhouse.

BOY'S VOICE. Annie. Does it hurt, to be dead?

(ANNIE *escapes by opening her eyes, her hand works restlessly over her cheek; she retreats into the book again, but the cracked old crones interrupt, whispering.* ANNIE *slowly lowers the book.*)

FIRST CRONE'S VOICE. There is schools.

SECOND CRONE'S VOICE. There is schools outside—

THIRD CRONE'S VOICE. —schools where they teach blind ones, worse'n you—

FIRST CRONE'S VOICE. To read—

SECOND CRONE'S VOICE. To read and write—

THIRD CRONE'S VOICE. There is schools outside where they—

FIRST CRONE'S VOICE. There is schools—

(*Silence.* ANNIE *sits with her eyes shining, her hand almost in a caress over the book. Then:*)

BOY'S VOICE. You ain't goin' to school, are you, Annie?

ANNIE [*whispering*]. When I grow up.

BOY'S VOICE. You ain't either, Annie. You're goin' to stay here take care of me.

ANNIE. I'm goin' to school when I grow up.

BOY'S VOICE. You said we'll be together, forever and ever and ever—

ANNIE [*fierce*]. I'm goin' to school when I grow up!

DOCTOR'S VOICE [*slowly*]. Little girl. Little girl, I must tell you. Your brother will be going on a journey, soon.

(ANNIE *sits rigid, in silence. Then the boy's voice pierces it, a shriek of terror.*)

---

13. This voice represents that of Dr. Howe reading his report on Laura Bridgman.

BOY'S VOICE. *Annie!*

(*It goes into* ANNIE *like a sword, she doubles onto it; the book falls to the floor. It takes her a racked moment to find herself and what she was engaged in here; when she sees the suitcase she remembers, and lifts it once again toward the bed. But the voices are with her, as she halts with suitcase in hand.*)

FIRST CRONE'S VOICE. Goodbye, Annie.

DOCTOR'S VOICE. Write me when you learn how.

SECOND CRONE'S VOICE. Don't tell anyone you came from here. Don't tell anyone—

THIRD CRONE'S VOICE. Yeah, don't tell anyone you came from—

FIRST CRONE'S VOICE. Yeah, don't tell anyone—

SECOND CRONE'S VOICE. Don't tell any—

(*The echoing voices fade. After a moment* ANNIE *lays the suitcase on the bed; and the last voice comes faintly, from far away.*)

BOY'S VOICE. Annie. It hurts, to be dead. Forever.

(ANNIE *falls to her knees by the bed, stifling her mouth in it. When at last she rolls blindly away from it, her palm comes down on the open report; she opens her eyes, regards it dully, and then, still on her knees, takes in the print.*)

MAN'S VOICE [*factual*]. —might awaken her to a consciousness of her immortal nature. The chance is small indeed; but with a smaller chance they would have dug desperately for her in the pit; and is the life of the soul of less import than that of the body?

(ANNIE *gets to her feet. She drops the book on the bed, and pauses over her suitcase; after a moment she unclasps and opens it. Standing before it, she comes to her decision; she at once turns to the bureau, and taking her things out of its drawers, commences to throw them into the open suitcase.*

In the darkness down left a hand strikes a match, and lights a hanging oil lamp. It is KELLER'S *hand, and his voice accompanies it, very angry; the lights rising here before they*

fade on ANNIE *show* KELLER *and* KATE *inside a suggestion of a garden house, with a bay-window seat towards center and a door at back.*)

KELLER. Katie, I will not *have* it! Now you did not see when that girl after supper tonight went to look for Helen in her room—

KATE. No.

KELLER. The child practically climbed out of her window to escape from her! What kind of teacher *is* she? I thought I had seen her at her worst this morning, shouting at me, but I come home to find the entire house disorganized by her—Helen won't stay one second in the same room, won't come to the table with her, won't let herself be bathed or undressed or put to bed by her, or even by Viney now, and the end result is that *you* have to do more for the child than before we hired this girl's services! From the moment she stepped off the train she's been nothing but a burden, incompetent, impertinent, ineffectual, immodest—

KATE. She folded her napkin, Captain.

KELLER. What?

KATE. Not ineffectual. Helen did fold her napkin.

KELLER. What in heaven's name is so extraordinary about folding a napkin?

KATE [*with some humor*]. Well. It's more than you did, Captain.

KELLER. Katie. I did not bring you all the way out here to the garden house to be frivolous. Now, how does Miss Sullivan propose to teach a deaf-blind pupil who won't let her even touch her?

KATE [*a pause*]. I don't know.

KELLER. The fact is, today she scuttled any chance she ever had of getting along with the child. If you can see any point or purpose to her staying on here longer, it's more than—

KATE. What do you wish me to do?

KELLER. I want you to give her notice.

KATE. I can't.

KELLER. Then if you won't, I must. I simply will not—

(*He is interrupted by a knock at the back door.* KELLER *after a glance at* KATE *moves to open the door;* ANNIE *in her smoked glasses is standing outside.* KELLER *contemplates her, heavily.*)

Miss Sullivan.

ANNIE. Captain Keller.

(*She is nervous, keyed up to seizing the bull by the horns again, and she assumes a cheeriness which is not unshaky.*)

Viney said I'd find you both over here in the garden house. I thought we should—have a talk?

KELLER [*reluctantly*]. Yes, I— Well, come in.

(ANNIE *enters, and is interested in this room; she rounds on her heel, anxiously, studying it.* KELLER *turns the matter over to* KATE, *sotto voce.*)

Katie.

KATE [*turning it back, courteously*]. Captain.

(KELLER *clears his throat, makes ready.*)

KELLER. I, ah—wanted first to make my position clear to Mrs. Keller, in private. I have decided I—am not satisfied—in fact, am deeply dissatisfied—with the manner in which—

ANNIE [*intent*]. Excuse me, is this little house ever in use?

KELLER [*with patience*]. In the hunting season. If you will give me your attention, Miss Sullivan.

(ANNIE *turns her smoked glasses upon him; they hold his unwilling stare.*)

I have tried to make allowances for you because you come from a part of the country where people are—women, I should say—come from who—well, for whom—

(*It begins to elude him.*)

—allowances must—be made. I have decided, nevertheless, to—that is, decided I—

(*Vexedly*)

Miss Sullivan, I find it difficult to talk through those glasses.

ANNIE [*eagerly, removing them*]. Oh, of course.

KELLER [*dourly*]. Why do you wear them, the sun has been down for an hour.

ANNIE [*pleasantly, at the lamp*]. Any kind of light hurts my eyes.

(*A silence;* KELLER *ponders her, heavily.*)

KELLER. Put them on. Miss Sullivan, I have decided to—give you another chance.

ANNIE [*cheerfully*]. To do what?

KELLER. To—remain in our employ.

(ANNIE's *eyes widen.*)

But on two conditions. I am not accustomed to rudeness in servants or women, and that is the first. If you are to stay, there must be a radical change of manner.

ANNIE [*a pause*]. Whose?

KELLER [*exploding*]. Yours, young lady, isn't it obvious? And the second is that you persuade me there's the slightest hope of your teaching a child who flees from you now like the plague, to anyone else she can find in this house.

ANNIE [*a pause*]. There isn't.

(KATE *stops sewing, and fixes her eyes upon* ANNIE.)

KATE. What, Miss Annie?

ANNIE. It's hopeless here. I can't teach a child who runs away.

KELLER [*nonplussed*]. Then—do I understand you—propose—

ANNIE. Well, if we all agree it's hopeless, the next question is what—

KATE. Miss Annie.

(*She is leaning toward* ANNIE, *in deadly earnest; it commands both* ANNIE *and* KELLER.)

I am not agreed. I think perhaps you—underestimate Helen.

ANNIE. I think everybody else here does.

KATE. She did fold her napkin. She learns, she learns, do you know she began talking when she was six months old? She could say "water." Not really—"wahwah." "Wahwah," but she meant water, she knew what it meant, and only six months old, I never saw a child so—bright, or outgoing—

(*Her voice is unsteady, but she gets it level.*)

It's still in her, somewhere, isn't it? You should have seen her before her illness, such a good-tempered child—

ANNIE [*agreeably*]. She's changed.

(*A pause,* KATE *not letting her eyes go; her appeal at last is unconditional, and very quiet.*)

KATE. Miss Annie, put up with it. And with us.

KELLER. Us!

KATE. Please? Like the lost lamb in the parable, I love her all the more.

ANNIE. Mrs. Keller, I don't think Helen's worst handicap is deafness or blindness. I think it's your love. And pity.

KELLER. Now what does that mean?

ANNIE. All of you here are so sorry for her you've kept her—like a pet, why, even a dog you housebreak. No wonder she won't let me come near her. It's useless for me to try to teach her language or anything else here. I might as well—

KATE [*cuts in*]. Miss Annie, before you came we spoke of putting her in an asylum.

(ANNIE *turns back to regard her. A pause.*)

ANNIE. What kind of asylum?

KELLER. For mental defectives.

KATE. I visited there. I can't tell you what I saw, people like—animals, with—*rats*, in the halls, and—

(*She shakes her head on her vision.*)

What else are we to do, if you give up?

ANNIE. Give up?

KATE. You said it was hopeless.

ANNIE. Here. Give up, why, I only today saw what has to be done, to begin!

(*She glances from* KATE *to* KELLER, *who stare, waiting; and she makes it as plain and simple as her nervousness permits.*)

I—want complete charge of her.

KELLER. You already have that. It has resulted in—

ANNIE. No, I mean day and night. She has to be dependent on me.

KATE. For what?

ANNIE. Everything. The food she eats, the clothes she wears, fresh—

(*She is amused at herself, though very serious.*)

—air, yes, the air she breathes, whatever her body needs is a—primer, to teach her out of. It's the only way, the one who lets her have it should be her teacher.

(*She considers them in turn; they digest it,* KELLER *frowning,* KATE *perplexed.*)

Not anyone who *loves* her, you have so many feelings they fall over each other like feet, you won't use your chances and you won't let me.

KATE. But if she runs from you—*to us*—

ANNIE. Yes, that's the point. I'll have to live with her somewhere else.

KELLER. What!

ANNIE. Till she learns to depend on and listen to me.

KATE [*not without alarm*]. For how long?

ANNIE. As long as it takes.

(*A pause. She takes a breath.*)

I packed half my things already.

KELLER. Miss—Sullivan!

(*But when* ANNIE *attends upon him he is speechless, and she is merely earnest.*)

ANNIE. Captain Keller, it meets both your conditions. It's the one way I can get back in touch with Helen, and I don't see how I can be rude to you again if you're not around to interfere with me.

KELLER [*red-faced*]. And what is your intention if I say no? Pack the other half, for home, and abandon your charge to—to—

ANNIE. The asylum?

(*She waits, appraises* KELLER's *glare and* KATE's *uncertainty, and decides to use her weapons.*)

I grew up in such an asylum. The state almshouse.

(KATE's *head comes up on this, and* KELLER

stares hard; ANNIE's *tone is cheerful enough, albeit level as gunfire.*)

Rats—why, my brother Jimmie and I used to play with the rats because we didn't have toys. Maybe you'd like to know what Helen will find there, not on visiting days? One ward was full of the—old women, crippled, blind, most of them dying, but even if what they had was catching there was nowhere else to move them, and that's where they put us. There were younger ones across the hall, . . . mostly with T.B., and epileptic fits, . . . and some insane. Some just had the D.T.'s.[14] . . . The room Jimmie and I played in was the deadhouse, where they kept the bodies till they could dig—

KATE [*closes her eyes*]. Oh, my dear—

ANNIE. —the graves.

(*She is immune to* KATE's *compassion.*)

No, it made me strong. But I don't think you need send Helen there. She's strong enough.

(*She waits again; but when neither offers her a word, she simply concludes.*)

No, I have no conditions, Captain Keller.

KATE [*not looking up*]. Miss Annie.

ANNIE. Yes.

KATE [*a pause*]. Where would you—take Helen?

ANNIE. Ohh—

(*Brightly*)

Italy?

KELLER [*wheeling*]. What?

ANNIE. Can't have everything, how would this garden house do? Furnish it, bring Helen here after a long ride so she won't recognize it, and you can see her every day. If she doesn't know. Well?

KATE [*a sigh of relief*]. Is that all?

ANNIE. That's all.

KATE. Captain.

(KELLER *turns his head; and* KATE's *request is quiet but firm.*)

With your permission?

KELLER [*teeth in cigar*]. Why must she depend on you for the food she eats?

ANNIE [*a pause*]. I want control of it.

KELLER. Why?

ANNIE. It's a way to reach her.

KELLER [*stares*]. You intend to *starve* her into letting you touch her?

ANNIE. She won't starve, she'll learn. All's fair in love and war, Captain Keller, you never cut supplies?

KELLER. This is hardly a war!

ANNIE. Well, it's not love. A siege is a siege.

KELLER [*heavily*]. Miss Sullivan. Do you *like* the child?

ANNIE [*straight in his eyes*]. Do you?

(*A long pause.*)

KATE. You could have a servant here—

ANNIE [*amused*]. I'll have enough work without looking after a servant! But that boy Percy could sleep here, run errands—

KATE [*also amused*]. We can let Percy sleep here, I think, Captain?

ANNIE [*eagerly*]. And some old furniture, all our own—

KATE [*also eager*]. Captain? Do you think that walnut bedstead in the barn would be too—

KELLER. I have not yet consented to Percy! Or to the house, or to the proposal! Or to Miss Sullivan's—staying on when I—

(*But he erupts in an irate surrender.*)

Very well, I consent to everything!

(*He shakes the cigar at* ANNIE.)

For two weeks. I'll give you two weeks in this place, and it will be a miracle if you get the child to tolerate you.

KATE. Two weeks? Miss Annie, can you accomplish anything in two weeks?

KELLER. Anything or not, two weeks, then the child comes back to us. Make up your mind, Miss Sullivan, yes or no?

ANNIE. Two weeks. For only one miracle?

---

14. **D.T.'s**\'dē ▲tēz\ an abbreviation for *delirium tremens*\də ▲lē·rĭ·əm ▲trĕ·mənz\, a violent trembling of the body, often accompanied by visual hallucinations, due to excessive use of alcohol.

(*She nods at him, nervously.*)

I'll get her to tolerate me.

(KELLER *marches out, and slams the door.* KATE *on her feet regards* ANNIE, *who is facing the door.*)

KATE [*then*]. You can't think as little of love as you said.

(ANNIE *glances questioning.*)

Or you wouldn't stay.

ANNIE [*a pause*]. I didn't come here for love. I came for money!

(KATE *shakes her head to this, with a smile; after a moment she extends her open hand.* ANNIE *looks at it, but when she puts hers out it is not to shake hands, it is to set her fist in* KATE's *palm.*)

KATE [*puzzled*]. Hm?

ANNIE. A. It's the first of many. Twenty-six!

(KATE *squeezes her fist, squeezes it hard, and hastens out after* KELLER. ANNIE *stands as the door closes behind her, her manner so apprehensive that finally she slaps her brow, holds it, sighs, and, with her eyes closed, crosses herself for luck.*)

The lights dim into a cool silhouette scene around her, the lamp paling out, and now, in formal entrances, persons appear around ANNIE *with furniture for the room:* PERCY *crosses the stage with a rocking chair and waits;* MARTHA *from another direction bears in a stool,* VINEY *bears in a small table, and the other Negro servant rolls in a bed partway from left; and* ANNIE, *opening her eyes to put her glasses back on, sees them. She turns around in the room once, and goes into action, pointing out locations for each article; the servants place them and leave, and* ANNIE *then darts around, interchanging them. In the midst of this—while* PERCY *and* MARTHA *reappear with a tray of food and a chair, respectively—*JAMES *comes down from the house with* ANNIE's *suitcase, and stands viewing the room and her quizzically;* ANNIE *halts abruptly under his eye, embarrassed, then*

seizes the suitcase from his hand, explaining herself brightly.)

ANNIE. I always wanted to live in a doll's house! (*She sets the suitcase out of the way, and continues;* VINEY *at left appears to position a rod with drapes for a doorway, and the other servant at center pushes in a wheelbarrow loaded with a couple of boxes of* HELEN's *toys and clothes.* ANNIE *helps lift them into the room, and the servant pushes the wheelbarrow off. In none of this is any heed taken of the imaginary walls of the garden house, the furniture is moved in from every side and itself defines the walls.*

ANNIE *now drags the box of toys into center, props up the doll conspicuously on top; with the people melted away, except for* JAMES, *all is again still. The lights turn again without pause, rising warmer.*)

JAMES. You don't let go of things easily, do you? How will you—win her hand now, in this place?

ANNIE [*curtly*]. Do I know? I lost my temper, and here we are!

JAMES [*lightly*]. No touching, no teaching. Of course, you *are bigger*—

ANNIE. I'm not counting on force, I'm counting on her. That little imp is dying to know.

JAMES. Know what?

ANNIE. Anything. Any and every crumb in God's creation. I'll have to use that appetite too.

(*She gives the room a final survey, straightens the bed, arranges the curtains.*)

JAMES [*a pause*]. Maybe she'll teach you.

ANNIE. Of course.

JAMES. That she isn't. That there's such a thing as—dullness of heart. Acceptance. And letting go. Sooner or later we all give up, don't we?

ANNIE. Maybe you all do. It's my idea of the original sin.

JAMES. What is?

ANNIE [*witheringly*]. Giving up.

JAMES [*nettled*]. You won't open her. Why

can't you let her be? Have some—pity on her, for being what she is—

ANNIE. If I'd ever once thought like that, I'd be dead!

JAMES [*pleasantly*]. You will be. Why trouble?

(ANNIE *turns to glare at him; he is mocking.*)

Or will you teach me?

(*And with a bow, he drifts off.*
Now in the distance there comes the clopping of hoofs, drawing near, and nearer, up to the door; and they halt. ANNIE *wheels to face the door. When it opens this time, the* KELLERS—KATE *in travelling bonnet,* KELLER *also hatted—are standing there with* HELEN *between them; she is in a cloak.* KATE *gently cues her into the room.* HELEN *comes in groping, baffled, but interested in the new surroundings;* ANNIE *evades her exploring hand, her gaze not leaving the child.*)

ANNIE. Does she know where she is?

KATE [*shakes her head*]. We rode her out in the country for two hours.

KELLER. For all she knows, she could be in another town—

(HELEN *stumbles over the box on the floor and in it discovers her doll and other battered toys, is pleased, sits to them, then becomes puzzled and suddenly very wary. She scrambles up and back to her mother's thighs, but* ANNIE *steps in, and it is hers that* HELEN *embraces.* HELEN *recoils, gropes, and touches her cheek instantly.*)

KATE. That's her sign for me.

ANNIE. I know.

(HELEN *waits, then recommences her groping, more urgently.* KATE *stands indecisive, and takes an abrupt step toward her, but* ANNIE's *hand is a barrier.*)

In two weeks.

KATE. Miss Annie, I—Please be good to her. These two weeks, try to be very good to her—

ANNIE. I will.

(KATE, *turning then, hurries out. The* KELLERS *cross back of the main house.*

ANNIE *closes the door.* HELEN *starts at the door jar, and rushes it.* ANNIE *holds her off.* HELEN *kicks her, breaks free, and careens around the room like an imprisoned bird, colliding with furniture, groping wildly, repeatedly touching her cheek in a growing panic. When she has covered the room, she commences her weird screaming.* ANNIE *moves to comfort her, but her touch sends* HELEN *into a paroxysm of rage: she tears away, falls over her box of toys, flings its contents in handfuls in* ANNIE's *direction, flings the box too, reels to her feet, rips curtains from the window, bangs and kicks at the door, sweeps objects off the mantelpiece and shelf, a little tornado incarnate, all destruction, until she comes upon her doll and, in the act of hurling it, freezes. Then she clutches it to herself, and in exhaustion sinks sobbing to the floor.* ANNIE *stands contemplating her, in some awe.*)

Two weeks.

(*She shakes her head, not without a touch of disgusted bewilderment.*)

What did I get into now?

(*The lights have been dimming throughout, and the garden house is lit only by moonlight now, with* ANNIE *lost in the patches of dark.*

KATE, *now hatless and coatless, enters the family room by the rear door, carrying a lamp.* KELLER, *also hatless, wanders simultaneously around the back of the main house to where* JAMES *has been waiting, in the rising moonlight, on the porch.*)

KELLER. I can't understand it. I had every intention of dismissing that girl, not setting her up like an empress.

JAMES. Yes, what's her secret, sir?

KELLER. Secret?

JAMES [*pleasantly*]. That enables her to get anything she wants out of you? When I can't.

(JAMES *turns to go into the house, but* KELLER *grasps his wrist, twisting him half to his knees.* KATE *comes from the porch.*)

KELLER [angrily]. She does *not* get anything she—

JAMES [in pain]. Don't—don't—

KATE. Captain.

KELLER. He's afraid.

(*He throws* JAMES *away from him, with contempt.*)

What *does* he want out of me?

JAMES [an outcry]. My God, don't you know?

(*He gazes from* KELLER *to* KATE.)

Everything you forgot, when you forgot my mother.

KELLER. What!

(JAMES *wheels into the house.* KELLER *takes a stride to the porch, to roar after him.*)

One thing that girl's secret is not, she doesn't fire one shot and disappear!

(KATE *stands rigid, and* KELLER *comes back to her.*)

Katie. Don't mind what he—

KATE. Captain, *I* am proud of you.

KELLER. For what?

KATE. For letting this girl have what she needs.

KELLER. Why can't my son be? He can't bear me, you'd think I treat him as hard as this girl does Helen—

(*He breaks off, as it dawns in him.*)

KATE [gently]. Perhaps you do.

KELLER. But he has to learn some respect!

KATE [a pause, wryly]. Do you like the child?

(*She turns again to the porch, but pauses, reluctant.*)

How empty the house is, tonight.

(*After a moment she continues on in.* KELLER *stands moveless, as the moonlight dies on him.*

The distant belfry chimes toll, two o'clock, and with them, a moment later, comes the boy's voice on the wind, in a whisper:)

BOY'S VOICE. Annie. Annie.

(*In her patch of dark* ANNIE, *now in her nightgown, hurls a cup into a corner as though it were her grief, getting rid of its taste through her teeth.*)

ANNIE. No! No pity, I won't have it.

(*She comes to* HELEN, *prone on the floor.*)

On either of us.

(*She goes to her knees, but when she touches* HELEN'S *hand the child starts up awake, recoils, and scrambles away from her under the bed.* ANNIE *stares after her. She strikes her palm on the floor, with passion.*)

I *will* touch you!

(*She gets to her feet, and paces in a kind of anger around the bed, her hand in her hair, and confronting* HELEN *at each turn.*)

How, how? How do I—

(ANNIE *stops. Then she calls out urgently, loudly.*)

Percy! Percy!

(*She moves swiftly to the drapes, at left.*)

Percy, wake up!

(PERCY'S *voice comes in a thick sleepy mumble, unintelligible.*)

Get out of bed and come in here, I need you.

(ANNIE *darts away, finds and strikes a match, and touches it to the hanging lamp; the lights come up dimly in the room, and* PERCY *stands bare to the waist in torn overalls between the drapes, with eyes closed, swaying.* ANNIE *goes to him, pats his cheeks vigorously.*)

PERCY. You awake?

PERCY. No'm.

ANNIE. How would you like to play a nice game?

PERCY. Whah?

ANNIE. With Helen. She's under the bed. Touch her hand.

(*She kneels* PERCY *down at the bed, thrusting his hand under it to contact* HELEN'S; HELEN

248

emits an animal sound and crawls to the opposite side, but commences sniffing. ANNIE *rounds the bed with* PERCY *and thrusts his hand again at* HELEN; *this time* HELEN *clutches it, sniffs in recognition, and comes scrambling out after* PERCY, *to hug him with delight.* PERCY *alarmed struggles, and* HELEN'S *fingers go to his mouth.*)

PERCY. Lemme go. Lemme go—

(HELEN *fingers her own lips, as before, moving them in dumb imitation.*)

She tryin' talk. She gonna hit me—
ANNIE [*grimly*]. She *can* talk. If she only knew, I'll show you how. She makes letters.

(*She opens* PERCY'S *other hand, and spells into it:*)

This one is C. C.

(*She hits his palm with it a couple of times, her eyes upon* HELEN *across him;* HELEN *gropes to feel what* PERCY'S *hand is doing, and when she encounters* ANNIE'S *she falls back from them.*)

She's mad at me now, though, she won't play. But she knows lots of letters. Here's another, A. C, a. C, a.

(*But she is watching* HELEN, *who comes groping, consumed with curiosity;* ANNIE *makes the letters in* PERCY'S *hand, and* HELEN *pokes to question what they are up to. Then* HELEN *snatches* PERCY'S *other hand, and quickly spells four letters into it.* ANNIE *follows them aloud.*)

C, a, k, e! She spells cake, she gets cake.

(*She is swiftly over to the tray of food, to fetch cake and a jug of milk.*)

She doesn't know yet it means this. Isn't it funny she knows how to spell it and doesn't *know* she knows?

(*She breaks the cake in two pieces, and extends one to each;* HELEN *rolls away from her offer.*)

Well, if she won't play it with me, I'll play it with you. Would you like to learn one she doesn't know?

PERCY. No'm.

(*But* ANNIE *seizes his wrist, and spells to him.*)

ANNIE. M, i, l, k. M is this. I, that's an easy one, just the little finger. L is this—

(*And* HELEN *comes back with her hand, to feel the new word.* ANNIE *brushes her away, and continues spelling aloud to* PERCY. HELEN'S *hand comes back again, and tries to get in;* ANNIE *brushes it away again.* HELEN'S *hand insists, and* ANNIE *puts it away rudely.*)

No, why should I talk to you? I'm teaching Percy a new word. L. K is this—

(HELEN *now yanks their hands apart; she butts* PERCY *away, and thrusts her palm out insistently.* ANNIE'S *eyes are bright, with glee.*)

Ho, you're *jealous*, are you!

(HELEN'S *hand waits, intractably waits.*)

All *right*.

(ANNIE *spells into it, milk; and* HELEN *after a moment spells it back to* ANNIE. ANNIE *takes her hand, with her whole face shining. She gives a great sigh.*)

Good! So I'm finally back to where I can touch you, hm? Touch and go! No love lost, but here we go.

(*She puts the jug of milk into* HELEN'S *hand and squeezes* PERCY'S *shoulder.*)

You can go to bed now, you've earned your sleep. Thank you.

(PERCY *stumbling up weaves his way out through the drapes.* HELEN *finishes drinking, and holds the jug out, for* ANNIE; *when* ANNIE *takes it,* HELEN *crawls onto the bed, and makes for sleep.* ANNIE *stands, looks down at her.*)

Now all I have to teach you is—one word. Everything.

(*She sets the jug down. On the floor now* ANNIE *spies the doll, stoops to pick it up, and with it dangling in her hand, turns off the lamp. A shaft of moonlight is left on* HELEN *in the bed, and a second shaft on the rocking chair; and* ANNIE, *after putting off her smoked glasses, sits in the rocker with the doll. She is rather happy, and dangles the doll on her knee, and it makes its momma sound.* ANNIE *whispers to it in mock solicitude.*)

Hush, little baby. Don't—say a word—

(*She lays it against her shoulder, and begins rocking with it, patting its diminutive behind; she talks the lullaby to it, humorously at first.*)

　　Momma's gonna buy you—a mockingbird:
　　If that—mockingbird don't sing—

(*The rhythm of the rocking takes her into the tune, softly, and more tenderly.*)

　　Momma's gonna buy you a diamond ring:
　　If that diamond ring turns to brass—

(*A third shaft of moonlight outside now rises to pick out* JAMES *at the main house, with one foot on the porch step; he turns his body, as if hearing the song.*)

　　Momma's gonna buy you a looking-glass:
　　If that looking-glass gets broke—

(*In the family room a fourth shaft picks out* KELLER, *seated at the table, in thought; and he, too, lifts his head, as if hearing.*)

　　Momma's gonna buy you a billy goat:
　　If that billy goat won't pull—

(*The fifth shaft is upstairs in* ANNIE's *room, and picks out* KATE, *pacing there; and she halts, turning her head, too, as if hearing.*)

　　Momma's gonna buy you a cart and bull:
　　If that cart and bull turns over,
　　Momma's gonna buy you a dog named
　　　　Rover;
　　If that dog named Rover won't bark—

(*With the shafts of moonlight on* HELEN, *and* JAMES, *and* KELLER, *and* KATE, *all moveless, and* ANNIE *rocking the doll, the curtain ends the act.*)

I

A GENERAL DECIDES UPON HER STRATEGY

No one who reads or sees *The Miracle Worker* will soon forget the exhausting breakfast battle which Annie and Helen wage with only two words spoken—those of Annie when she says "Good girl" to Helen. To thank her for the compliment, Helen grabs a fistful of Annie's hair and yanks her to her knees. But in this memorable clash of wills, Annie comes out the victor. Helen *folds* her napkin!

1. Even though Annie has won a battle, she is so weary from it that she starts packing her suitcase to leave the Keller household. Whose voice causes her to stop and reconsider her decision? From what text are the words coming? In her conference with the Kellers, what demand does she make and how is it received? What is the outcome of this interview?

2. Identify the characters who speak the following lines and briefly outline the situation in which the words are spoken:

a. "The, more, I, think, the, more, certain, I, am, that, obedience, is, the, gateway, through, which, knowledge, enters, the, mind, of, the, child—."

b. "Yes, but *I'm* not accustomed to it."

c. "It's the first of many. Twenty-six!"

d. "Maybe you all do. It's my idea of the original sin."

e. "Don't you know? Everything you forgot, when you forgot my mother."

f. "Now all I have to teach you is—one word. Everything."

II

IMPLICATIONS

Do you agree or disagree with the following statements?

1. Intelligence can be recognized by those who understand it even though it is not demonstrated in the usual ways.

2. Pity is a very destructive emotion.

3. There are occasions when it is necessary to be "cruel in order to be kind."

III
TECHNIQUES

Characterization

Annie understood Helen through her own experiences and through her own intelligence, Kate understood Helen with her heart and from watching her closely over the years; why did Captain Keller misinterpret Helen's needs and capabilities so thoroughly?

Significant Details

Since the reader of a play must interpret the lines himself rather than having them interpreted for him by an actor, he must be alert to notice the significance of the punctuation. Why did playwright Gibson place a comma after every word written by Miss Sullivan at the beginning of Act II?

Staging

The ability to visualize the stage and action on it is most essential to get the full dramatic effect of the ending of Act II.

1. Why is lighting of key importance in this closing scene?

2. Briefly discuss the significance of lighting in the staging of the entire play.

Understanding the Play

Just as for a good story, a drama depends on conflict for interest and action. In Act I we have begun to see the tension within the Keller family, and the conflict between Annie and Helen is begun. In Act II this last conflict is acted out wildly but not resolved. Before the breakfast room battle, which other conflicts are carried forward? What are the issues in these minor conflicts?

Act III

T*he stage is totally dark, until we see* ANNIE *and* HELEN *silhouetted on the bed in the garden house.* ANNIE'*s voice is audible, very patient, and worn; it has been saying this for a long time.*

ANNIE. Water, Helen. This is water. W, a, t, e, r. It has a *name.*

(*A silence. Then:*)

Egg, e, g, g. It has a *name*, the name stands for the thing. Oh, it's so simple, simple as birth, to explain.

(*The lights have commenced to rise, not on the garden house but on the homestead. Then:*)

Helen, Helen, the chick *has* to come out of its shell, sometime. You come out, too.

(*In the bedroom upstairs, we see* VINEY *unhurriedly washing the window, dusting, turning the mattress, readying the room for use again; then in the family room a diminished group at one end of the table—*KATE, KELLER, JAMES—*finishing up a quiet breakfast; then outside, down right, the other Negro servant on his knees, assisted by* MARTHA, *working with a trowel around a new trellis and wheelbarrow. The scene is one of everyday calm, and all are oblivious to* ANNIE'*s voice.*)

There's only one way out, for you, and it's language. To learn that your fingers can talk. And say anything, anything you can name. This is mug. Mug, m, u, g. Helen, it has a *name*. It—has—a—*name*—

(KATE *rises from the table.*)

KELLER [*gently*]. You haven't eaten, Katie.

KATE [*smiles, shakes her head*]. I haven't the appetite I'm too—restless, I can't sit to it.

KELLER. You should eat, my dear. It will be a long day, waiting.

JAMES [*lightly*]. But it's been a short two weeks. I never thought life could be so—noiseless, went much too quickly for me.

(KATE *and* KELLER *gaze at him, in silence.* JAMES *becomes uncomfortable.*)

ANNIE. C, a, r, d. Card. C, a—

JAMES. Well, the house has been practically normal, hasn't it?

KELLER [*harshly*]. Jimmie.

JAMES. Is it wrong to enjoy a quiet breakfast, after five years? And you two even seem to enjoy each other—

KELLER. It could be even more noiseless, Jimmie, without your tongue running every minute. Haven't you enough feeling to imagine what Katie has been undergoing, ever since—

(KATE *stops him, with her hand on his arm.*)

KATE. Captain.

(*To* JAMES.)

It's true. The two weeks have been normal, quiet, all you say. But not short. Interminable.

(*She rises, and wanders out; she pauses on the porch steps, gazing toward the garden house.*)

ANNIE [*fading*]. W, a, t, e, r. But it means *this*. W, a, t, e, r. *This*. W, a, t—

JAMES. I only meant that Miss Sullivan is a boon. Of contention, though, it seems.

KELLER [*heavily*]. If and when you're a parent, Jimmie, you will understand what separation means. A mother loses a—protector.

JAMES [*baffled*]. Hm?

KELLER. You'll learn, we don't just keep our children safe. They keep us safe.

(*He rises, with his empty coffee cup and saucer.*)

There are of course all kinds of separation, Katie has lived with one kind for five years. And another is disappointment. In a child.

(*He goes with the cup out the rear door.* JAMES *sits for a long moment of stillness. In the garden house the lights commence to come up;* ANNIE, *haggard at the table, is writing a letter, her face again almost in contact with the stationery;* HELEN, *apart on the stool, and for the first time as clean and neat as a*

button, *is quietly crocheting an endless chain of wool, which snakes all around the room.*)

ANNIE. "I, feel, every, day, more, and, more, in—"

(*She pauses, and turns the pages of a dictionary before her; her finger descends the words to a full stop. She elevates her eyebrows, then copies the word.*)

"—adequate."

(*In the main house* JAMES *pushes up, and goes to the front doorway, after* KATE.)

JAMES. Kate?

(KATE *turns her glance.* JAMES *is rather weary.*)

I'm sorry. Open my mouth, like that fairy tale, frogs jump out.

KATE. No. It has been better. For everyone.

(*She starts away, up center.*)

ANNIE [*writing*]. "If, only, there, were, someone, to, help, me, I, need, a, teacher, as, much, as, Helen—"

JAMES. Kate.

(KATE *halts, waits.*)

What does he want from me?

KATE. That's not the question. Stand up to the world, Jimmie, that comes first.

JAMES [*a pause, wryly*]. But the world is him.

KATE. Yes. And no one can do it for you.

JAMES. Kate.

(*His voice is humble.*)

At least we— Could you—be my friend?

KATE. I am.

(KATE *turns to wander, up back of the garden house.* ANNIE's *murmur comes at once; the lights begin to die on the main house.*)

ANNIE. "—my, mind, is, undisiplined, full, of, skips, and, jumps, and—"

(*She halts, rereads, frowns.*)

Hm.

(ANNIE *puts her nose again in the dictionary, flips back to an earlier page, and fingers down the words;* KATE *presently comes down toward the bay window with a trayful of food.*)

Disinter—disinterested—disjoin—dis—

(*She backtracks, indignant.*)

Disinterested, disjoin— Where's disipline?

(*She goes a page or two back, searching with her finger, muttering.*)

What a dictionary, have to know how to spell it before you can look up how to spell it, disciple, *discipline!* Diskipline.

(*She corrects the word in her letter.*)

Undisciplined.

(*But her eyes are bothering her, she closes them in exhaustion and gently fingers the eyelids.* KATE *watches her through the window.*)

KATE. What are you doing to your eyes?

(ANNIE *glances around; she puts her smoked glasses on, and gets up to come over, assuming a cheerful energy.*)

ANNIE. It's worse on my vanity! I'm learning to spell. It's like a surprise party, the most unexpected characters turn up.

KATE. You're not to overwork your eyes, Miss Annie.

ANNIE. Well.

(*She takes the tray, sets it on her chair, and carries chair and tray to* HELEN.)

Whatever I spell to Helen I'd better spell right.

KATE [*almost wistful*]: How—serene she is.

ANNIE. She learned this stitch yesterday. Now I can't get her to stop!

(*She disentangles one foot from the wool chain, and sets the chair before* HELEN. HELEN *at its contact with her knee feels the plate, promptly sets her crocheting down, and tucks the napkin in at her neck, but* ANNIE *withholds the spoon; when* HELEN *finds it missing, she folds her hands in her lap, and quietly waits.* ANNIE *twinkles at* KATE *with mock devoutness.*)

Such a little lady, she'd sooner starve than eat with her fingers.

(*She gives* HELEN *the spoon, and* HELEN *begins to eat, neatly.*)

KATE. You've taught her so much, these two weeks. I would never have—

ANNIE. Not enough.

(*She is suddenly gloomy, shakes her head.*)

Obedience isn't enough. Well, she learned two nouns this morning, key and water, brings her up to eighteen nouns and three verbs.

KATE [*hesitant*]: But—not—

ANNIE. No. Not that they mean things. It's still a finger-game, no meaning.

(*She turns to* KATE, *abruptly.*)

Mrs. Keller—

(*But she defers it; she comes back, to sit in the bay and lift her hand.*)

Shall we play our finger-game?

KATE: How will she learn it?

ANNIE. It will come.

(*She spells a word;* KATE *does not respond.*)

KATE. How?

ANNIE [*a pause*]. How does a bird learn to fly?

(*She spells again.*)

We're born to use words, like wings, it has to come.

KATE. How?

ANNIE [*another pause, wearily*]. All right. I don't know how.

(*She pushes up her glasses, to rub her eyes.*)

I've done everything I could think of. Whatever she's learned here—keeping herself clean, knitting, stringing beads, meals, setting-up exercises each morning, we climb trees, hunt eggs, yesterday a chick was born in her hands—all of it I spell, everything we do, we never stop spelling. I go to bed with —writer's cramp from talking so much!

KATE. I worry about you, Miss Annie. You must rest.

ANNIE. Now? She spells back in her *sleep,* her

fingers make letters when she doesn't know! In her bones those five fingers know, that hand aches to—speak out, and something in her mind is asleep, how do I—nudge that awake? That's the one question.

KATE. With no answer.

ANNIE. [*long pause*]. Except keep at it. Like this.

(*She again begins spelling—I, need—and* KATE's *brows gather, following the words.*)

KATE. More—time?

(*She glances at* ANNIE, *who looks her in the eyes, silent.*)

Here?

ANNIE. Spell it.

(KATE *spells a word—no—shaking her head;* ANNIE *spells two words—why, not—back, with an impatient question in her eyes; and* KATE *moves her head in pain to answer it.*)

KATE. Because I can't—

ANNIE. Spell it! If she ever learns, you'll have a lot to tell each other, start now.

(KATE *painstakingly spells in air. In the midst of this the rear door opens, and* KELLER *enters with the setter Belle in tow.*)

KELLER. Miss Sullivan? On my way to the office, I brought Helen a playmate—

ANNIE. Outside please, Captain Keller.

KELLER. My dear child, the two weeks are up today, surely you don't object to—

ANNIE [*rising*]. They're not up till six o'clock.

KELLER [*indulgent*]. Oh, now. What difference can a fraction of one day—

ANNIE. An agreement is an agreement. Now you've been very good, I'm sure you can keep it up for a few more hours.

(*She escorts* KELLER *by the arm over the threshold; he obeys, leaving Belle.*)

KELLER. Miss Sullivan, you are a tyrant.

ANNIE. Likewise, I'm sure. You can stand there, and close the door if she comes.

KATE. I don't think you know how eager we are to have her back in our arms—

ANNIE. I do know, it's my main worry.

KELLER. It's like expecting a new child in the house. Well, she *is*, so—composed, so—

(*Gently*)

Attractive. You've done wonders for her, Miss Sullivan.

ANNIE [*not a question*]. Have I.

KELLER. If there's anything you want from us in repayment tell us, it will be a privilege to—

ANNIE. I just told Mrs. Keller. I want more time.

KATE. Miss Annie—

ANNIE. Another week.

(HELEN *lifts her head, and begins to sniff.*)

KELLER. We miss the child. *I* miss her, I'm glad to say, that's a different debt I owe you—

ANNIE. Pay it to Helen. Give *her* another week.

KATE [*gently*]. Doesn't she miss us?

KELLER. Of course she does. What a wrench this unexplainable—exile must be to her, can you say it's not?

ANNIE. No. But I—

(HELEN *is off the stool, to grope about the room; when she encounters Belle, she throws her arms around the dog's neck in delight.*)

KATE. Doesn't she need affection too, Miss Annie?

ANNIE [*wavering*]. She—never shows me she needs it, she won't have any—caressing or—

KATE. But you're not her mother.

KELLER. And what would another week accomplish? We are more than satisfied, you've done more than we ever thought possible, taught her constructive—

ANNIE. I can't promise anything. All I can—

KELLER [*no break*].—things to do, to behave like —even look like—a human child, so manageable, contented, cleaner, more—

ANNIE [*withering*]. Cleaner.

KELLER. Well. We say cleanliness is next to godliness, Miss—

ANNIE. Cleanliness is next to nothing, she has to learn that everything has its name! That words can be her *eyes*, to everything in the world outside her, and inside too, what is she without words? With them she can think, have ideas, be reached, there's not a thought or fact in the world that can't be hers. You publish a newspaper, Captain Keller, do I have to tell you what words are? And she has them already—

KELLER. Miss Sullivan.

ANNIE. —eighteen nouns and three verbs, they're in her fingers now, I need only time to push *one* of them into her mind! One, and everything under the sun will follow. Don't you see what she's learned here is only clearing the way for that? I can't risk her unlearning it, give me more time alone with her, another week to—

KELLER. Look.

(*He points, and* ANNIE *turns.* HELEN *is playing with Belle's claws; she makes letters with her fingers, shows them to Belle, waits with her palm, then manipulates the dog's claws.*)

What is she spelling?

(*A silence.*)

KATE. Water?

(ANNIE *nods.*)

KELLER. Teaching a dog to spell.

(*A pause*)

The dog doesn't know what she means, any more than she knows what you mean, Miss Sullivan. I think you ask too much, of her and yourself. God may not have meant Helen to have the—eyes you speak of.

ANNIE [*toneless*]. I mean her to.

KELLER [*curiously*]. What is it to you?

(ANNIE's *head comes slowly up.*)

You make us see how we indulge her for our sake. Is the opposite true, for you?

ANNIE [*then*]. Half a week?

KELLER. An agreement *is* an agreement.

ANNIE. Mrs. Keller?

KATE [*simply*]. I want her back.

(*A wait;* ANNIE *then lets her hands drop in surrender, and nods.*)

KELLER. I'll send Viney over to help you pack.

ANNIE. Not until six o'clock. I have her till six o'clock.

KELLER [*consenting*]. Six o'clock. Come, Katie.

(KATE *leaving the window joins him around back, while* KELLER *closes the door; they are shut out.*

Only the garden house is daylit now, and the light on it is narrowing down. ANNIE *stands watching* HELEN *work Belle's claws. Then she settles beside them on her knees, and stops* HELEN's *hand.*)

ANNIE [*gently*]. No.

(*She shakes her head, with* HELEN's *hand to her face, then spells.*)

Dog. D, o, g. Dog.

(*She touches* HELEN's *hand to Belle.* HELEN *dutifully pats the dog's head, and resumes spelling to its paw.*)

Not water.

(ANNIE *rolls to her feet, brings a tumbler of water back from the tray, and kneels with it, to seize* HELEN's *hand and spell.*)

Here. Water. *Water.*

(*She thrusts* HELEN's *hand into the tumbler.* HELEN *lifts her hand out dripping, wipes it daintily on Belle's hide, and taking the tumbler from* ANNIE, *endeavors to thrust Belle's paw into it.* ANNIE *sits watching, wearily.*)

I don't know how to tell you. Not a soul in the world knows how to tell you. Helen, Helen.

(*She bends in compassion to touch her lips to* HELEN's *temple, and instantly* HELEN *pauses, her hands off the dog, her head slightly averted. The lights are still narrowing, and Belle slinks off. After a moment* ANNIE *sits back.*)

Yes, what's it to me? They're satisfied. Give them back their child and dog, both housebroken, everyone's satisfied. But me, and you.

(HELEN's *hand comes out into the light, groping.*)

Reach. *Reach!*

(ANNIE *extending her own hand grips*

HELEN's; *the two hands are clasped, tense in the light, the rest of the room changing in shadow.*)

I wanted to teach you—oh, everything the earth is full of, Helen, everything on it that's ours for a wink and it's gone, and what we are on it, the—light we bring to it and leave behind in—words, why, you can see five thousand years back in a light of words, everything we feel, think, know—and share, in words, so not a soul is in darkness, or done with, even in the grave. And I know, I *know*, one word and I can—put the world in your hand—and whatever it is to me, I won't take less! How, how, how do I tell you that *this*—

(*She spells.*)

—means a *word*, and the word means this *thing*, wool?

(*She thrusts the wool at* HELEN's *hand;* HELEN *sits, puzzled.* ANNIE *puts the crocheting aside.*)

Or this—s, t, o, o, l—means this *thing*, stool?

(*She claps* HELEN's *palm to the stool.* HELEN *waits, uncomprehending.* ANNIE *snatches up her napkin, spells:*)

Napkin!

(*She forces it on* HELEN's *hand, waits, discards it, lifts a fold of the child's dress, spells:*)

Dress!

(*She lets it drop, spells:*)

F, a, c, e, face!

(*She draws* HELEN's *hand to her cheek, and pressing it there, staring into the child's responseless eyes, hears the distant belfry begin to toll, slowly: one, two, three, four, five, six.*

On the third stroke the lights stealing in around the garden house show us figures waiting: VINEY, *the other servant,* MARTHA, PERCY *at the drapes, and* JAMES *on the dim porch.* ANNIE *and* HELEN *remain, frozen. The chimes die away. Silently* PERCY *moves the drape-rod back out of sight;* VINEY *steps into the room—not using the door—and unmakes the bed; the other servant brings the wheelbarrow over, leaves it handy, rolls the bed off;* VINEY *puts the bed linens on top of a waiting boxful of* HELEN's *toys, and loads the box on the wheelbarrow;* MARTHA *and* PERCY *take out the chairs, with the trayful, then the table; and* JAMES, *coming down and into the room, lifts* ANNIE's *suitcase from its corner.* VINEY *and the other servant load the remaining odds and ends on the wheelbarrow, and the servant wheels it off.* VINEY *and the children departing leave only* JAMES *in the room with* ANNIE *and* HELEN. JAMES *studies the two of them, without mockery, and then, quietly going to the door and opening it, bears the suitcase out, and housewards. He leaves the door open.*

KATE *steps into the doorway, and stands.* ANNIE *lifting her gaze from* HELEN *sees her; she takes* HELEN's *hand from her cheek, and returns it to the child's own, stroking it there twice, in her mother-sign, before spelling slowly into it:*)

M, o, t, h, e, r. Mother.

(HELEN *with her hand free strokes her cheek, suddenly forlorn.* ANNIE *takes her hand again.*)

M, o, t, h—

(*But* KATE *is trembling with such impatience that her voice breaks from her, harsh.*)

KATE. Let her *come!*

(ANNIE *lifts* HELEN *to her feet, with a turn, and gives her a little push. Now* HELEN *begins groping, sensing something, trembling herself; and* KATE *falling one step in onto her knees clasps her, kissing her.* HELEN *clutches her, tight as she can.* KATE *is inarticulate, choked, repeating* HELEN's *name again and again. She wheels with her in her arms, to stumble away out the doorway;* ANNIE *stands unmoving, while* KATE *in a blind walk carries* HELEN *like a baby behind the main house, out of view.* ANNIE *is now alone on the stage.*

She turns, gazing around at the stripped room, bidding it silently farewell, impassively, like a defeated general on the deserted battlefield. All that remains is a stand with a basin of water; and here ANNIE *takes up an eyecup, bathes each of her eyes, empties the eyecup, drops it in her purse, and tiredly locates her smoked glasses on the floor. The lights alter subtly; in the act of putting on her glasses* ANNIE *hears something that stops her, with head lifted. We hear it too, the voices out of the past, including her own now, in a whisper:*)

BOY'S VOICE. You said we'd be together, forever— You promised, forever and—*Annie!*

ANAGNOS' VOICE. But that battle is dead and done with, why not let it stay buried?

ANNIE'S VOICE [*whispering*]. I think God must owe me a resurrection.

ANAGNOS' VOICE. What?

(*A pause; and* ANNIE *answers it herself, heavily.*)

ANNIE. And I owe God one.

BOY'S VOICE. Forever and ever—

(ANNIE *shakes her head.*)

—forever, and ever, and—

(ANNIE *covers her ears.*)

—forever, and ever, and ever—

(*It pursues* ANNIE; *she flees to snatch up her purse, wheels to the doorway, and* KELLER *is standing in it. The lights have lost their special color.*)

KELLER. Miss—Annie.

(*He has an envelope in his fingers.*)

I've been waiting to give you this.

ANNIE [*after a breath*]. What?

KELLER. Your first month's salary.

(*He puts it in her hand.*)

With many more to come, I trust. It doesn't express what we feel, it doesn't pay our debt. For what you've done.

ANNIE. What have I done?

KELLER. Taken a wild thing, and given us back a child.

ANNIE [*presently*]. I taught her one thing, no. Don't do this, don't do that—

KELLER. It's more than all of us could, in all the years we—

ANNIE. I wanted to teach her what language is. I wanted to teach her yes.

KELLER. You will have time.

ANNIE. I don't know how. I know without it to do nothing but obey is—no gift, obedience without understanding is a—blindness, too. Is that all I've wished on her?

KELLER [*gently*]. No, no—

ANNIE. Maybe. I don't know what else to do. Simply go on, keep doing what I've done, and have—faith that inside she's— That inside it's waiting. Like water, underground. All I can do is keep on.

KELLER. It's enough. For us.

ANNIE. You can help, Captain Keller.

KELLER. How?

ANNIE. Even learning no has been at a cost. Of much trouble and pain. Don't undo it.

KELLER. Why should we wish to—

ANNIE [*abruptly*]. The world isn't an easy place for anyone, I don't want her just to obey but to let her have her way in everything is a lie, to *her*, I can't—

(*Her eyes fill, it takes her by surprise, and she laughs through it.*)

And I don't even love her, she's not my child! Well, You've got to stand between that lie and her.

KELLER. We'll try.

ANNIE. Because *I* will. As long as you let me stay, that's one promise I'll keep.

KELLER. Agreed. We've learned something too, I hope.

(*A pause*)

Won't you come now, to supper?

ANNIE. Yes.

(*She wags the envelope, ruefully.*)

Why doesn't God pay His debts each month?

KELLER. I beg your pardon?

ANNIE. Nothing. I used to wonder how I could—

(*The lights are fading on them, simultaneously rising on the family room of the main house, where* VINEY *is polishing glassware at the table set for dinner.*)

—earn a living.

KELLER. Oh, you do.

ANNIE. I really do. Now the question is, can I survive it!

(KELLER *smiles, offers his arm.*)

KELLER. May I?

(ANNIE *takes it, and the lights lose them as he escorts her out.*

Now in the family room the rear door opens, and HELEN *steps in. She stands a moment, then sniffs in one deep grateful breath, and her hands go out vigorously to familiar things, over the door panels, and to the chairs around the table, and over the silverware on the table, until she meets* VINEY; *she pats her flank approvingly.*)

VINEY. Oh, we glad to have you back, too, prob'ly.

(HELEN *hurries groping to the front door, opens and closes it, removes its key, opens and closes it again to be sure it is unlocked, gropes back to the rear door and repeats the procedure, removing its key and hugging herself gleefully.*

AUNT EV *is next in by the rear door, with a relish tray; she bends to kiss* HELEN'S *cheek.* HELEN *finds* KATE *behind her, and thrusts the keys at her.*)

KATE. What? Oh.

(*To* EV)

Keys.

(*She pockets them, lets* HELEN *feel them.*)

Yes, *I'll* keep the keys. I think we've had enough of locked doors, too.

(JAMES, *having earlier put* ANNIE's *suitcase inside her door upstairs and taken himself*

out of view around the corner, now reappears and comes down the stairs as ANNIE *and* KELLER *mount the porch steps. Following them into the family room, he pats* ANNIE's *hair in passing, rather to her surprise.*)

JAMES. Evening, general.

(*He takes his own chair opposite.*

VINEY *bears the empty water pitcher out to the porch. The remaining suggestion of garden house is gone now, and the water pump is unobstructed;* VINEY *pumps water into the pitcher.*

KATE *surveying the table breaks the silence.*)

KATE. Will you say the grace, Jimmie?

(*They bow their heads, except for* HELEN, *who palms her empty plate and then reaches to be sure her mother is there.* JAMES *considers a moment, glances across at* ANNIE, *lowers his head again, and obliges.*)

JAMES [*lightly*]. And Jacob was left alone, and wrestled with an angel until the breaking of the day; and the hollow of Jacob's thigh was out of joint, as he wrestled with him; and the angel said, Let me go, for the day breaketh. And Jacob said, I will not let thee go, except thou bless me. Amen.[15]

(ANNIE *has lifted her eyes suspiciously at* JAMES, *who winks expressionlessly and inclines his head to* HELEN.)

Oh, you angel.

(*The others lift their faces;* VINEY *returns with the pitcher, setting it down near* KATE, *then goes out the rear door; and* ANNIE *puts a napkin around* HELEN.)

AUNT EV. That's a very strange grace, James.

KELLER. Will you start the muffins, Ev?

JAMES. It's from the Good Book, isn't it?

AUNT EV [*passing a plate*]. Well, of course it is. Didn't you know?

JAMES. Yes. I knew.

KELLER [*serving*]. Ham, Miss Annie?

---

15. James gives a shortened version of the King James translation of Genesis 32:24–26.

258

ANNIE. Please.

AUNT EV. Then why ask?

JAMES. I meant it *is* from the Good Book, and therefore a fitting grace.

AUNT EV. Well. I don't know about *that*.

KATE [*with the pitcher*]. Miss Annie?

ANNIE. Thank you.

AUNT EV. There's an awful *lot* of things in the Good Book that I wouldn't care to hear just before eating.

(*When* ANNIE *reaches for the pitcher,* HELEN *removes her napkin and drops it to the floor.* ANNIE *is filling* HELEN'S *glass when she notices it; she considers* HELEN'S *bland expression a moment, then bends, retrieves it, and tucks it around* HELEN'S *neck again.*)

JAMES. Well, fitting in the sense that Jacob's thigh was out of joint, and so is this piggie's.

AUNT EV. I declare, James—

KATE. Pickles, Aunt Ev?

AUNT EV. Oh, I should say so, you know my opinion of your pickles—

KATE. This is the end of them, I'm afraid. I didn't put up nearly enough last summer, this year I intend to—

(*She interrupts herself, seeing* HELEN *deliberately lift off her napkin and drop it again to the floor. She bends to retrieve it, but* ANNIE *stops her arm.*)

KELLER [*not noticing*]. Reverend looked in at the office today to complain his hens have stopped laying. Poor fellow, he was out of joint, all he could—

(*He stops too, to frown down the table at* KATE, HELEN, *and* ANNIE *in turn, all suspended in midmotion.*)

JAMES [*not noticing*]. I've always suspected those hens.

AUNT EV. Of what?

JAMES. I think they're Papists. Has he tried—

(*He stops, too, following* KELLER'S *eyes.* ANNIE *now stoops to pick the napkin up.*)

AUNT EV. James, now you're pulling my lower extremity, the first thing you know we'll be—

(*She stops, too, hearing herself in the silence.* ANNIE, *with everyone now watching, for the third time put the napkin on* HELEN. HELEN *yanks it off, and throws it down.* ANNIE *rises, lifts* HELEN'S *plate, and bears it away.* HELEN, *feeling it gone, slides down and commences to kick up under the table; the dishes jump.* ANNIE *contemplates this for a moment, then coming back takes* HELEN'S *wrists firmly and swings her off the chair.* HELEN *struggling gets one hand free, and catches at her mother's skirt; when* KATE *takes her by the shoulders,* HELEN *hangs quiet.*)

Helen clinging to her mother to escape Annie's discipline after her return from the garden house.

KATE. Miss Annie.

ANNIE. No.

KATE [*a pause*]. It's a very special day.

ANNIE [*grimly*]. It will be, when I give in to that.

(*She tries to disengage* HELEN'S *hand;* KATE *lays hers on* ANNIE'S.)

KATE. Please. I've hardly had a chance to welcome her home—

ANNIE. Captain Keller.

KELLER [*embarrassed*]. Oh. Katie, we—had a

little talk, Miss Annie feels that if we indulge Helen in these—

AUNT EV. But what's the child done?

ANNIE. She's learned not to throw things on the floor and kick. It took us the best part of two weeks and—

AUNT EV. But only a napkin, it's not as if it were breakable!

ANNIE. And everything she's learned *is?* Mrs. Keller, I don't think we should—play tug-of-war for her, either give her to me or you keep her from kicking.

KATE. What do you wish to do?

ANNIE. Let me take her from the table.

AUNT EV. Oh, let her stay, my goodness, she's only a child, she doesn't have to wear a napkin if she doesn't want to her first evening—

ANNIE [*level*]. And ask outsiders not to interfere.

AUNT EV [*astonished*]. Out—outsi—I'm the child's *aunt!*

KATE [*distressed*]. Will once hurt so much, Miss Annie? I've—made all Helen's favorite foods, tonight.

(*A pause*)

KELLER [*gently*]. It's a homecoming party, Miss Annie.

(ANNIE *after a moment releases* HELEN. *But she cannot accept it, at her own chair she shakes her head and turns back, intent on* KATE.)

ANNIE. She's testing you. You realize?

JAMES [*to* ANNIE]. She's testing you.

KELLER. Jimmie, be quiet.

(JAMES *sits, tense.*)

Now she's home, naturally she—

ANNIE. And she wants to see what will happen. At your hands. I said it was my main worry, is this what you promised me not half an hour ago?

KELLER [*reasonably*]. But she's *not* kicking, now—

ANNIE. And not learning not to. Mrs. Keller, teaching her is bound to be painful, to everyone. I know it hurts to watch, but she'll live

up to just what you demand of her, and no more.

JAMES [*palely*]. She's testing *you.*

KELLER [*testily*]. Jimmie.

JAMES. I have an opinion, I think I should—

KELLER. No one's interested in hearing your opinion.

ANNIE. *I'm* interested, of course she's testing me. Let me keep her to what she's learned and she'll go on learning from me. Take her out of my hands and it all comes apart.

(KATE *closes her eyes, digesting it;* ANNIE *sits again, with a brief comment for her.*)

Be bountiful, it's at her expense.

(*She turns to* JAMES, *flatly.*)

Please pass me more of—her favorite foods.

(*Then* KATE *lifts* HELEN's *hand, and turning her toward* ANNIE, *surrenders her;* HELEN *makes for her own chair.*)

KATE [*low*]. Take her, Miss Annie.

ANNIE [*then*]. Thank you.

(*But the moment* ANNIE *rising reaches for her hand,* HELEN *begins to fight and kick, clutching to the tablecloth, and uttering laments.* ANNIE *again tries to loosen her hand, and* KELLER *rises.*)

KELLER [*tolerant*]. I'm afraid you're the difficulty, Miss Annie. Now I'll keep her to what she's learned, you're quite right there—

(*He takes* HELEN's *hands from* ANNIE, *pats them;* HELEN *quiets down.*)

—but I don't see that we need send her from the table, after all, she's the guest of honor. Bring her plate back.

ANNIE. If she was a seeing child, none of you would tolerate one—

KELLER. Well, she's not, I think some compromise is called for. Bring her plate, please.

(ANNIE's *jaw sets, but she restores the plate, while* KELLER *fastens the napkin around* HELEN's *neck; she permits it.*)

There. It's not unnatural, most of us take some aversion to our teachers, and occasionally another hand can smooth things out.

(*He puts a fork in* HELEN's *hand;* HELEN *takes it. Genially:*)

Now. Shall we start all over?

(*He goes back around the table, and sits.* ANNIE *stands watching.* HELEN *is motionless, thinking things through, until with a wicked glee she deliberately flings the fork on the floor. After another moment she plunges her hand into her food, and crams a fistful into her mouth.*)

JAMES [*wearily*]. I think we've started all over—

(KELLER *shoots a glare at him, as* HELEN *plunges her other hand into* ANNIE's *plate.* ANNIE *at once moves in, to grasp her wrist, and* HELEN *flinging out a hand encounters the pitcher; she swings with it at* ANNIE; ANNIE *falling back blocks it with an elbow, but the water flies over her dress.* ANNIE *gets her breath, then snatches the pitcher away in one hand, hoists* HELEN *up bodily under the other arm, and starts to carry her out, kicking.* KELLER *stands.*)

ANNIE [*savagely polite*]. Don't get up!

KELLER. Where are you going?

ANNIE. Don't smooth anything else out for me, don't interfere in any way! I treat her like a seeing child because I *ask* her to see, I *expect* her to see, don't undo what I do!

KELLER. Where are you taking her?

ANNIE. To make her fill this pitcher again!

(*She thrusts out with* HELEN *under her arm, but* HELEN *escapes up the stairs and* ANNIE *runs after her.* KELLER *stands rigid.* AUNT EV *is astounded.*)

AUNT EV. You let her speak to you like that, Arthur? A creature who *works* for you?

KELLER [*angrily*]. No, I don't.

(*He is starting after* ANNIE *when* JAMES, *on his feet with shaky resolve, interposes his chair between them in* KELLER's *path.*)

JAMES. Let her go.

KELLER. What!

Scene from The Miracle Worker. *Helen being dragged to the well to refill the spilled pitcher.*

JAMES [*a swallow*]. I said—let her go. She's right.

(KELLER *glares at the chair and him.* JAMES *takes a deep breath, then headlong:*)

She's right. Kate's right, I'm right, and you're wrong. If you drive her away from here it will be over my dead—chair, has it never occurred to you that on one occasion you might be consummately wrong?

(KELLER's *stare is unbelieving, even a little fascinated.* KATE *rises in trepidation, to mediate.*)

KATE. Captain.

(KELLER *stops her with his raised hand; his eyes stay on* JAMES's *pale face, for a long hold. When he finally finds his voice, it is gruff.*)

KELLER. Sit down, everyone.

(*He sits.* KATE *sits.* JAMES *holds onto his chair.* KELLER *speaks mildly.*)

Please sit down, Jimmie.

(JAMES *sits, and a moveless silence prevails;* KELLER's *eyes do not leave him.*

ANNIE *has pulled* HELEN *downstairs again by one hand, the pitcher in her other hand, down the porch steps, and across the yard to the pump. She puts* HELEN's *hand on the pump handle, grimly.*)

ANNIE. All right. Pump.

(HELEN *touches her cheek, waits uncertainly.*)

No, she's not here. Pump!

(*She forces* HELEN's *hand to work the handle, then lets go. And* HELEN *obeys. She pumps till the water comes, then* ANNIE *puts the pitcher in her other hand and guides it under the spout, and the water tumbling half into and half around the pitcher douses* HELEN's *hand.* ANNIE *takes over the handle to keep water coming, and does automatically what she has done so many times before, spells into* HELEN's *free palm:*)

Water. W, a, t, e, r. *Water.* It has a—*name*—

(*And now the miracle happens.* HELEN *drops the pitcher on the slab under the spout, it*

Patty Duke as Helen Keller in the dramatic last minutes of The Miracle Worker—*Water!*

shatters. She stands transfixed.* ANNIE *freezes on the pump handle: there is a change in the sundown light, and with it a change in* HELEN's *face, some light coming into it we have never seen there, some struggle in the depths behind it; and her lips tremble, trying to remember something the muscles around them once knew, till at last it finds its way out, painfully, a baby sound buried under the debris of years of dumbness.*)

HELEN. Wah. Wah.

(*And again, with great effort*)

Wah. Wah.

(HELEN *plunges her hand into the dwindling water, spells into her own palm. Then she gropes frantically,* ANNIE *reaches for her hand, and* HELEN *spells into* ANNIE's *hand.*)

ANNIE [*whispering*]. Yes.

(HELEN *spells into it again.*)

Yes!

(HELEN *grabs at the handle, pumps for more water, plunges her hand into its spurt and grabs* ANNIE's *to spell it again.*)

Yes! Oh, my dear—

(*She falls to her knees to clasp* HELEN's *hand, but* HELEN *pulls it free, stands almost bewildered, then drops to the ground, pats it swiftly, holds up her palm, imperious.* ANNIE *spells into it:*)

Ground.

(HELEN *spells it back.*)

Yes!

(HELEN *whirls to the pump, pats it, holds up her palm, and* ANNIE *spells into it.*)

Pump.

(HELEN *spells it back.*)

Yes! Yes!

(*Now* HELEN *is in such an excitement she is possessed, wild, trembling, cannot be still, turns, runs, falls on the porch step, claps it, reaches out her palm, and* ANNIE *is at it instantly to spell:*)

Step.

(HELEN *has no time to spell back now, she whirls groping, to touch anything, encounters the trellis, shakes it, thrusts out her palm, and* ANNIE *while spelling to her cries wildly at the house.*)

Trellis. Mrs. Keller! *Mrs. Keller!*

(*Inside,* KATE *starts to her feet.* HELEN *scrambles back onto the porch, groping, and finds the bell string, tugs it; the bell rings, the distant chimes begin tolling the hour, all the bells in town seem to break into speech while* HELEN *reaches out and* ANNIE *spells feverishly into her hand.* KATE *hurries out, with* KELLER *after her;* AUNT EV *is on her feet, to peer out the window; only* JAMES *remains at the table, and with a napkin wipes his damp brow. From up right and left the servants—*VINEY, *the two Negro children, the other servant—run in, and stand watching from a distance as* HELEN, *ringing the bell, with her other hand encounters her mother's skirt; when she throws a hand out,* ANNIE *spells into it:*)

Mother.

(KELLER *now seizes* HELEN's *hand, she touches him, gestures a hand, and* ANNIE *again spells:*)

Papa— She *knows!*

(KATE *and* KELLER *go to their knees, stammering, clutching* HELEN *to them, and* ANNIE *steps unsteadily back to watch the threesome,* HELEN *spelling wildly into* KATE's *hand, then into* KELLER's, KATE *spelling back into* HELEN's; *they cannot keep their hands off her, and rock her in their clasp.*

Then HELEN *gropes, feels nothing, turns all around, pulls free, and comes with both hands groping, to find* ANNIE. *She encounters* ANNIE's *thighs,* ANNIE *kneels to her,* HELEN's *hand pats* ANNIE's *cheek impatiently, points a finger, and waits; and* ANNIE *spells into it:*)

Teacher.

(HELEN *spells it back, slowly;* ANNIE *nods.*)

Teacher.

(*She holds* HELEN's *hand to her cheek. Presently* HELEN *withdraws it, not jerkily, only with reserve, and retreats a step. She stands thinking it over, then turns again and stumbles back to her parents. They try to embrace her, but she has something else in mind, it is to get the keys, and she hits* KATE's *pocket until* KATE *digs them out for her.*

ANNIE *with her own load of emotion has retreated, her back turned, toward the pump, to sit;* KATE *moves to* HELEN, *touches her hand questioningly, and* HELEN *spells a word to her.* KATE *comprehends it, their first act of verbal communication, and she can hardly utter the word aloud, in wonder, gratitude, and deprivation; it is a moment in which she simultaneously finds and loses a child.*)

KATE. Teacher?

(ANNIE *turns; and* KATE, *facing* HELEN *in her direction by the shoulders, holds her back, holds her back, and then relinquishes her.* HELEN *feels her way across the yard, rather shyly, and when her moving hands touch* ANNIE's *skirt she stops. Then she holds out the keys and places them in* ANNIE's *hand. For a moment neither of them moves. Then* HELEN *slides into* ANNIE's *arms, and lifting away her smoked glasses, kisses her on the cheek.* ANNIE *gathers her in.*

KATE *torn both ways turns from this, gestures the servants off, and makes her way into the house, on* KELLER's *arm. The servants go, in separate directions.*

The lights are half down now, except over the pump. ANNIE *and* HELEN *are here, alone in the yard.* ANNIE *has found* HELEN's *hand, almost without knowing it, and she spells slowly into it, her voice unsteady, whispering:*)

ANNIE. I, love, Helen.

(*She clutches the child to her, tight this time, not spelling, whispering into her hair.*)

Forever, and—

(*She stops. The lights over the pump are taking on the color of the past, and it brings* ANNIE'S *head up, her eyes opening, in fear; and as slowly as though drawn she rises, to listen, with her hands on* HELEN'S *shoulders. She waits, waits, listening with ears and eyes both, slowly here, slowly there: and hears only silence. There are no voices. The color passes on, and when her eyes come back to* HELEN *she can breathe the end of her phrase without fear:*)

—ever.

(*In the family room* KATE *has stood over the table, staring at* HELEN'S *plate, with* KELLER *at her shoulder; now* JAMES *takes a step to move her chair in, and* KATE *sits, with head erect, and* KELLER *inclines his head to* JAMES; *so it is* AUNT EV, *hesitant, and rather humble, who moves to the door.*

Outside HELEN *tugs at* ANNIE'S *hand, and* ANNIE *comes with it.* HELEN *pulls her toward the house; and hand in hand, they cross the yard, and ascend the porch steps, in the rising lights, to where* AUNT EV *is holding the door open for them.*

The curtain ends the play.)

I

EVERYTHING HAS ITS NAME

In finally bringing Helen to understand language, Annie achieves a "miracle" which allows Helen to come to know ". . . everything the earth is full of. . . ." A woman of lesser spirit and determination would have given up long before such dramatic victory, but Annie felt she couldn't settle for less.

1. Act III opens on the final day of the two weeks Annie has had with Helen in the garden house. How have Helen's behavior and appearance changed in the two weeks she has been away from the family?

2. Describe Helen's homecoming meal. Why does Helen act as she does? What had Annie told

Kate earlier in the play that she considered to be Helen's greatest handicap? Why do you think Kate finally decides to let Annie discipline Helen?

3. Identify the characters who speak the following lines and briefly outline the situation in which the words are spoken:

a. "I go to bed with—writer's cramp from talking so much!"

b. "The dog doesn't know what she means, any more than she knows what you mean, Miss Sullivan."

c. ". . . obedience without understanding is a—blindness, too."

d. ". . . she'll live up to just what you demand of her, and no more."

e. "Papa—She *knows!*"

II

IMPLICATIONS

Consider whether you agree or disagree with the following statement.

To devote your life to helping another may be to find it in a very real sense.

III

TECHNIQUES

Characterization

1. How do Kate and James differ as to how long the two weeks has seemed?

2. Described in Act I as "an indolent young man," James seems weak, cynical, and vacillating through much of the play. What in James's situation gives him an excuse to feel abused and left out?

When does James finally stand up to his father and oppose him? How do you think this display of courage might change him and his father's attitude toward him?

3. Throughout the play, Annie hears offstage voices which have a great deal to do with understanding her character and the action in the play. Whose is the boy's voice she hears? Where, in her memories, are the crones' voices coming from? What man's voice is responsible for her decision to keep on trying to help Helen even after the battle in the breakfast room? What is the significance of the fact that she no longer can hear the voices as the play ends?

Significant Details

1. What word is Annie teaching Helen when Act III begins? Why is it necessary that the reader or audience understand that Helen has learned the manual alphabet symbols for this particular word?

2. When Helen returns to the big house, Viney greets her with, "Oh, we glad to have you back too, prob'ly." What does this humorous detail contribute to the tension of the scene?

3. Explain the significance of the business about the keys.

Staging

1. After Captain Keller exits following the opening breakfast scene, James asks Kate to be his friend. Very briefly, she replies, "I am," and leaves. Several different interpretations are possible about her response depending on her gestures and tone of voice. Suggest several of these possibilities and explain how the actress might have conveyed them.

2. In this play, we repeatedly find the Keller family at mealtime. What function does this setting serve for the drama?

IV

WORDS

A. We may be given good clues to the meanings of words when they are contrasted with familiar elements. If we read "his ideas were clear and definite rather than nebulous," we may safely guess that *nebulous* in this sentence may mean *vague, cloudy,* or *ill-formed.* Of course, elements joined by *and* and similar connectives must be compatible with each other, able to fit together without confusion in meaning. If we read "the Asians were dressed in the strange and exotic costumes of their home countries," *exotic* must be at least compatible with *strange* so that there is no contradiction between them. Check over the following for these context clues as you try to guess the meanings of the italicized words:

1. This discussion is at an end! I'll thank you not to *broach* it again.

2. We hear a boy's voice whispering; perhaps we see shadowy *intimations* of these speakers in the background.

3. Keller then *irately* flings his newspaper on the porch floor, stamps into the house past Viney and disappears.

4. KELLER: "I intend to carry you. Climb onto my shoulder and hold tight." ANNIE: "Oh, no. It's —very *chivalrous* of you, but . . ."

5. Is it your *contention* we won the war, sir?

6. Helen is working around the table, *ultimately* toward Annie's plate . . .

7. Annie slaps her hand smartly away; Helen *retaliates* with a roundhouse fist that catches Annie on the ear.

B. *Ab-, ad-, com-,* etc., have been mentioned as situational prefixes. Other similar prefixes include *inter-,* with the general meaning of *among, between; intro-,* or *intra-,* which may mean *inwardly, to the inside, within; ob-,* suggesting *over, against, toward; per-,* often, but not always, meaning *through; pro-,* indicating *forward, forth, favoring; re-,* which is likely to mean *back, away* when it does not mean *again;* and *sub-,* often meaning *under, beneath, down.* Using your dictionary, check the meanings of the prefixes in the following words: *protrude, permission, reproachful, intercept, oblivious, proffer, object* (vb.), *intervene, persist, revert, subside, retaliate, interpose, relinquish, perplex, proposal, opposite?* Write the meaning of the prefix after each word. Underline those that agree with the meanings given above.

C. What are the companion nouns for the following verbs from the first two acts of the play: *divide, designate, emit, approach, restrain, annoy, seize, commence, retrieve, conceal, collide, gratify, maintain, dismay, evade, descend, acquire, manage, remove, perceive?* How many different patterns show up in your list?

D. Notice the pronunciation symbol your dictionary uses to indicate the sound of each italicized vowel: man*a*ge, c*a*ress, mir*a*cle; *e*levate, indulg*e*nt, cr*e*scendo; vis*i*ble, *e*pisodic, vig*i*l; accomm*o*date, pant*o*mime, nincomp*oo*p; s*u*rrender, tantr*u*m, inj*u*ry. In modern dictionaries the sound involved is usually transcribed as ə—called *schwa* or *shwa.* In each of these words where are the main stresses or accents? What conclusions can you draw about the pronunciation of vowels in unstressed syllables and about the spelling of the ə sound?

At the end of *The Miracle Worker*
we see Helen wild with joy and quivering
with the desire to learn, as quickly as possible,
everything about this new world
into which she has been drawn.
This dramatic moment of awakening provided
a natural climax for *The Miracle Worker*.
But a play can only show us Helen Keller
from the *outside*. Now compare an account
of the incident at the pump,
written from the *inside*, by Helen herself.
The following selection from *The Story of My Life*
begins at exactly the moment
when *The Miracle Worker* ended. Miss Keller
goes on to tell of what happened after that—
now that she had this "strange, new sight
that had come to me."

How I Learned
to See

HELEN KELLER

My teacher placed my hand under the
spout. As the cool stream gushed over one hand
she spelled into the other the word *water*, first
slowly, then rapidly. I stood still, my whole
attention fixed upon the motions of her fingers.
Suddenly I felt a misty consciousness as of
something forgotten—a thrill of returning
thought; and somehow the mystery of language
was revealed to me. I knew then that "w-a-t-e-r"
meant the wonderful cool something that was
flowing over my hand. That living word awakened my soul, gave it light, hope, joy, set it
free! There were barriers still, it is true, but
barriers that could in time be swept away.

I left the well-house eager to learn. Everything had a name, and each name gave birth to
a new thought. As we returned to the house
every object which I touched seemed to quiver
with life. That was because I saw everything

with the strange, new sight that had come to
me. On entering the door I remembered the
doll I had broken. I felt my way to the hearth
and picked up the pieces. I tried vainly to put
them together. Then my eyes filled with tears;
for I realized what I had done, and for the first
time I felt repentance and sorrow.

I learned a great many new words that day.
I do not remember what they all were; but I
do know that *mother, father, sister, teacher*
were among them—words that were to make
the world blossom for me, "like Aaron's rod,
with flowers."[1] It would have been difficult to
find a happier child than I was as I lay in my
crib at the close of that eventful day and lived
over the joys it had brought me, and for the
first time longed for a new day to come . . .

I recall many incidents of the summer of
1887 that followed my soul's sudden awakening. I did nothing but explore with my hands
and learn the name of every object that I
touched; and the more I handled things and
learned their names and uses, the more joyous
and confident grew my sense of kinship with
the rest of the world . . .

When the time of daisies and buttercups
came Miss Sullivan took me by the hand across
the fields, where men were preparing the earth
for the seed, to the banks of the Tennessee
River, and there, sitting on the warm grass, I
had my first lessons in the beneficence of nature. I learned how the sun and the rain make
to grow out of the ground every tree that is
pleasant to the sight and good for food, how
birds build their nests and live and thrive from
land to land, how the squirrel, the deer, the lion
and every other creature finds food and shelter.
As my knowledge of things grew I felt more
and more the delight of the world I was in.
Long before I learned to do a sum in arithmetic or describe the shape of the earth, Miss
Sullivan had taught me to find beauty in the
fragrant woods, in every blade of grass, and in
the curves and dimples of my baby sister's

---

1. Aaron's rod or wand blossomed miraculously and
bore almonds in the Biblical story told in Numbers 17:8.

hand. She linked my earliest thoughts with nature, and made me feel that "birds and flowers and I were happy peers."

But about this time I had an experience which taught me that nature is not always kind. One day my teacher and I were returning from a long ramble. The morning had been fine, but it was growing warm and sultry when at last we turned our faces homeward. Two or three times we stopped to rest under a tree by the wayside. Our last halt was under a wild cherry tree a short distance from the house. The shade was grateful, and the tree was so easy to climb that with my teacher's assistance I was able to scramble to a seat in the branches. It was so cool up in the tree that Miss Sullivan proposed that we have our luncheon there. I promised to keep still while she went to the house to fetch it.

Suddenly a change passed over the tree. All the sun's warmth left the air. I knew the sky was black, because all the heat, which meant light to me, had died out of the atmosphere. A strange odor came up from the earth. I knew it, it was the odor that always precedes a thunderstorm, and a nameless fear clutched at my heart. I felt absolutely alone, cut off from my friends and the firm earth. The immense, the unknown, enfolded me. I remained still and expectant; a chilling terror crept over me. I longed for my teacher's return; but above all things I wanted to get down from that tree.

There was a moment of sinister silence, then a multitudinous stirring of the leaves. A shiver ran through the tree, and the wind sent forth a blast that would have knocked me off had I not clung to the branch with might and main. The tree swayed and strained. The small twigs snapped and fell about me in showers. A wild impulse to jump seized me, but terror held me fast. I crouched down in the fork of the tree. The branches lashed about me. I felt the intermittent jarring that came now and then, as if something heavy had fallen and the shock had traveled up till it reached the limb I sat on. It worked my suspense up to the highest point, and just as I was thinking the tree and I should fall together, my teacher seized my hand and

The real Helen Keller at the age of ten talking with her beloved teacher, Annie Sullivan—1890

helped me down. I clung to her, trembling with joy to feel the earth under my feet once more. I had learned a new lesson—that nature "wages open war against her children, and under softest touch hides treacherous claws."

After this experience it was a long time before I climbed another tree. The mere thought filled me with terror . . .

I had now the key to all language, and I was eager to learn to use it. Children who hear acquire language without any particular effort; the words that fall from others' lips they catch on the wing, as it were, delightedly, while the little deaf child must trap them by a slow and often painful process. But whatever the process, the result is wonderful. Gradually from naming an object we advance step by step until we have traversed the vast distance between our first stammered syllable and the sweep of thought in a line of Shakespeare.

At first, when my teacher told me about a new thing I asked very few questions. My ideas were vague, and my vocabulary was inadequate; but as my knowledge of things grew, and I learned more and more words, my field of inquiry broadened, and I would return again and again to the same subject, eager for further information. Sometimes a new word revived an image that some earlier experience had engraved on my brain.

I remember the morning that I first asked the meaning of the word, "love." This was before I knew many words. I had found a few early violets in the garden and brought them to my teacher. Miss Sullivan put her arm gently round me and spelled into my hand, "I love Helen."

"What is love?" I asked.

She drew me closer to her and said, "It is here," pointing to my heart, whose beats I was conscious of for the first time. Her words puzzled me very much because I did not then understand anything unless I touched it.

I smelt the violets in her hand and asked, half in words, half in signs, a question which meant, "Is love the sweetness of flowers?"

"No," said my teacher.

Helen Keller and Annie Sullivan on the lawn of Dr. Alexander Graham Bell's home in Cape Breton, Nova Scotia.

Again I thought. The warm sun was shining on us.

"Is this not love?" I asked, pointing in the direction from which the heat came, "Is this not love?"

It seemed to me that there could be nothing more beautiful than the sun, whose warmth makes all things grow. But Miss Sullivan shook her head, and I was greatly puzzled and disappointed. I thought it strange that my teacher could not show me love.

A day or two afterward I was stringing beads of different sizes in symmetrical groups—two large beads, three small ones, and so on. I had made many mistakes, and Miss Sullivan had pointed them out again and again with gentle patience. Finally I noticed a very obvious error in the sequence and for an instant I concentrated my attention on the lesson and tried to think how I should have arranged the beads. Miss Sullivan touched my forehead and spelled with decided emphasis, "Think."

In a flash I knew that the word was the name of the process that was going on in my head. This was my first conscious perception of an abstract idea.

For a long time I was still—I was not thinking of the beads in my lap, but trying to find a meaning for "love" in the light of this new idea. The sun had been under a cloud all day, and there had been brief showers; but suddenly the sun broke forth in all its southern splendour.

Again I asked my teacher, "Is this not love?"

"Love is something like the clouds that were in the sky before the sun came out," she replied. Then in simpler words than these, which at that time I could not have understood, she explained: "You cannot touch the clouds, you know; but you feel the rain and know how glad the flowers and the thirsty earth are to have it after a hot day. You cannot touch love either; but you feel the sweetness that it pours into everything. Without love you would not be happy or want to play."

The beautiful truth burst upon my mind—I felt that there were invisible lines stretched between my spirit and the spirits of others.

From the beginning of my education Miss Sullivan made it a practice to speak to me as she would speak to any hearing child; the only difference was that she spelled the sentences into my hand instead of speaking them. If I did not know the words and idioms necessary to express my thoughts she supplied them, even suggesting conversation when I was unable to keep up my end of the dialogue.

This process was continued for several years; for the deaf child does not learn in a month, or even in two or three years, the numberless idioms and expressions used in the simplest daily intercourse. The little hearing child learns these from constant repetition and imitation. The conversation he hears in his home stimulates his mind and suggests topics and calls forth the spontaneous expression of his own thoughts. This natural exchange of ideas is denied to the deaf child. My teacher, realizing this, determined to supply the kinds of stimulus I lacked. This she did by repeating to me as far as possible, verbatim, what she heard, and by showing me how I could take part in the conversation. But it was a long time before I ventured to take the initiative, and still longer before I could find something appropriate to say at the right time.

The deaf and the blind find it very difficult to acquire the amenities of conversation. How much more this difficulty must be augmented in the case of those who are both deaf and blind! They cannot distinguish the tone of the voice or, without assistance, go up and down the gamut of tones that give significance to words; nor can they watch the expression of the speaker's face, and a look is often the very soul of what one says . . .

Thus I learned from life itself. At the beginning I was only a little mass of possibilities. It was my teacher who unfolded and developed them. When she came, everything about me breathed of love and joy and was full of meaning. She has never since let pass an opportunity to point out the beauty that is in everything, nor has she ceased trying in thought and action and example to make my life sweet and useful.

Postscript

Destined to become a celebrity before she was ten because of her astounding accomplishments, Helen Keller went on to learn not only to read, to write, to ride a toboggan, to swim, to ride a horse, but also she learned to speak. After only a dozen lessons from a special teacher, she had mastered simple sentences. The one she repeated over and over during the first few days of her triumph was, "I am not dumb now."

So great was her determination to use her voice, rather than the manual alphabet, that she had Miss Sullivan tape her fingers together so that she could not give in to the impulse to use them in communicating. Learning to speak was one of the most difficult of her achievements.

After graduating from college, Miss Keller, accompanied by Anne Sullivan, went on a series of successful lecture tours across the United States. Though her voice and intonation are not like those of a hearing person, she is as easily understood as people who speak with a foreign accent.

For two years she traveled with the Orpheum Circuit (vaudeville) and once played in an early silent Hollywood film entitled *Deliverance*. Her task, as she saw it, was to awaken public interest in helping the handicapped.

She has traveled to many parts of the world at the invitation of various governments and private organizations. Many times she has gone of her own accord to visit hospitals, asylums, and institutions for the physically afflicted, in this country and abroad. Her plea to people everywhere has been for help to liberate, as she was liberated, the blind, the deaf, the mute, from their lonely cells of isolation. One of the founders of the American Foundation of the Blind in 1923, she has helped that organization raise millions of dollars.

How does one act toward a person who is physically handicapped? They wish simply to

*Helen Keller in Africa, 1951, during one
of her journeys for the American Foundation
for the Blind Overseas.*

be treated like other people—without pity. All
of her life, Miss Keller has resented those who
pitied her.

When someone remarked that Helen Keller's
life must be terribly dull with night the same as
day, Mark Twain, a close friend, retorted,
"Blindness is an exciting business, I tell you. If
you don't believe it, get up on some dark night
on the wrong side of your bed when the house
is on fire, and try to find the door!"

Although Anne Sullivan was often in ill
health and underwent several operations trying to save her poor eyesight, Helen's beloved
Teacher was, except for brief periods, always
with her pupil. Even after Miss Sullivan married the literary critic and writer, John Macy,
the Macys at once brought Helen to live with
them.

When Anne Sullivan Macy died in 1936,
Helen Keller felt that part of herself had died,
too. In her diary she wrote, "Always I shall look

about, despite myself, for the sparkle with
which she charmed the dullest person into a
new appreciation of beauty or justice or human
rights."

All of the many honors that have been bestowed upon her, and all of the achievements
she has made, Helen Keller credits to Teacher.
Thus it is appropriate that her latest book is the
one Miss Keller has wanted to write most of her
life—*Teacher: Anne Sullivan Macy.*

In addition to *The Story of My Life, Mid-
stream* and *Helen Keller's Journal* are especially fascinating reading.

I

BREAKING THE BARRIER

One of the interesting things to think about in
"How I Learned to See" is the way Helen Keller
tried to find meanings for words that referred to
things she could not touch or taste or smell. For example, she tells us that at that time "light" to her
meant "heat," like that coming from the sun.

1. Recall her experience in the storm and explain how she knew the sky was *black*.

2. Discuss the way Miss Sullivan explained to Helen what the abstraction "love" meant. Is this different from the way it could be explained to a seeing and hearing child?

II
IMPLICATIONS

Consider and discuss the following statements.

1. "Blindness is an exciting business, I tell you."

2. "Nature 'wages open war against her children.'"

3. To gain something through great personal effort is to appreciate it most fully.

III
TECHNIQUES
Significant Details

Helen Keller had no access to the visible forms of nature and yet she has communicated a spring storm (paragraphs 7 and 8) and her response to it with wonderful clarity. Through the senses of smell and touch she sets a scene filled with atmosphere and emotion. List the details which affected each of these two senses.

IV
WORDS

A. A suffix, as you know, may be added to a word to make it function as a different part of speech. For example, to convert *angel* to an adjective, we add *-ic*, producing *angelic*. And to make *material* into a verb, we add *-ize*, creating *materialize*. In some instances, however, the suffix is not added to the original word; a completely new word, including the necessary suffix, must be used as the new part of speech. Let us look at some examples from "How I Learned To See": *word, house, mother, language,* and *flowers.* Converting these words to new parts of speech, you get the following:

word	verbal	verbalize
language	linguistic	lingual
mother	maternal	matriarchal
house	domestic	domesticate
flower	floral	florid

In each case, the reason that the new word is different from the original word is that the new word comes from Latin and the old word does not. What is the adjectival form that ends in *-al* for each of these words: *mind, mouth, hand, brother, finger, father,* and *foot.* Clue: *death* becomes *mortal.*

B. On the basis of what you have learned about context clues, try to determine the meaning of each *underlined* word in the sentences below:

"...it was the odor that always *precedes* a thunderstorm...."

"I felt the *intermittent* jarring that came now and then...."

"...'nature wages open war against her children, and under softest touch hides *treacherous* claws.'"

"This was my first conscious *perception* of an abstract idea."

C. After "How I Learned To See," there is a postscript in which comments are made about Miss Keller. The prefix *post-* means "after," and *script* means "written." A postscript, therefore, is anything that is written after the main body of material. The meaning "after" can be seen in the words *posterity* and *postgraduate.* When a person leaves something to *posterity*, he is leaving it to those who come after him, that is, future generations. A *postgraduate* is a student who pursues further studies after he has graduated. The very opposite of *post* is the prefix *ante,* "before," as in *anteroom* and *antecedent.* An anteroom is a room that is placed before another room and often serves as an entrance or, sometimes, as a waiting room. In English grammar, an antecedent is the word to which a pronoun refers; it comes before the pronoun. In the sentence "William lost his book," *William* is the antecedent of *his.* Remembering the meanings of the two prefixes *post* and *ante* and using your dictionary, try to answer the following questions:

1. When were *antebellum* homes built?

2. What is a *postmortem* examination?

3. If a person *postdated* a letter, what would he have done?

4. What is the *posterior* side of an insect?

5. What time of the day is referred to by *ante meridiem?*

6. What is an *antechamber?*

271

Dick Gregory

Dick Gregory (1932–   ) was born in St. Louis, Missouri. In high school he was a state track champion, and later he was named Outstanding Athlete at Southern Illinois University. A top-ranked comedian, Gregory has spent much of his adult life working to promote better understanding by all Americans of what it means to be black.

Jack London

Jack London (1876–1916) was born in San Francisco and later moved to Oakland where he spent his high school years in a rough waterfront section. A sailor at eighteen, later a longshoreman, a gold hunter in Alaska, a war correspondent during the Russo-Japanese War, and a world traveler, London used these experiences in writing his short stories and novels. Many of his works reveal his sympathy for the poor and downtrodden. Two of his most widely read novels are *The Call of the Wild* and *The Sea Wolf*.

James Saxon Childers

James Saxon Childers (1899–1965) was born in Birmingham, Alabama. He held degrees from Oberlin College, Oxford University, and Oglethorpe University, and he was a Rhodes Scholar in 1923. He served in both World War I and World War II, and he had been a columnist, feature writer, newspaper editor, college English professor, and lecturer for the U.S. State Department in the Far and Middle East. His last work was *Nation on the Flying Trapeze*.

Jesse Stuart

Jesse Stuart (1907–   ), short story writer, novelist, poet, and teacher, was born in Greenup County, Kentucky, where he now lives. The first of his family to go to high school, he taught in a country school at seventeen and worked his way through Lincoln Memorial University. One of America's most popular writers, Stuart says that he has been writing for as long as he can remember. Many of the stories and poems he wrote in high school and college were later published. His best-known books are *Man with a Bull-Tongue Plow, Taps for Private Tussie, Hie to the Hunters,* and *The Year of My Rebirth,* the last written while he was recovering from a heart attack.

Langston Hughes

Langston Hughes (1902–1967), noted American Negro poet, short story writer, and playwright, was born in Joplin, Missouri, spent his early years in Kansas, went to school in Cleveland, Ohio, and later attended Columbia University and Lincoln University. He traveled extensively, living in Mexico, Paris, and the Far East. He wrote his first short story while in high school and began publishing his poetry shortly after his high school graduation. His first volume of poems, *The Weary Blues,* was published in 1926. Some of his other books are *The Dream Keeper, Shakespeare in Harlem, One-Way Ticket,* and *Montage of a Dream Deferred.* His poems have been translated into many languages and several have been set to music. Often referred to as the "poet laureate of Harlem," Langston Hughes was given several literary awards. His final volume of poems was published after his death.

James A. Emanuel

James A. Emanuel (1921–   ), born and raised in Alliance, Nebraska, attended Howard, Northwestern, and Columbia Universities where he received, respectively, his B.A. (1950), M.A. (1953), and Ph.D. (1962) degrees. He worked on ranches and farms as a teen-ager, and at the age of twenty he became Confidential Secretary to General Benjamin O. Davis, Sr., the Assistant Inspector General of the U.S. Army. He then did wartime duty in the South Pacific with the 93rd Infantry Division. Before accepting a position teaching literature at the City College of the City University of New York in 1957, he taught from 1954–1956 at the YWCA secretarial school in Harlem.

Emanuel's poetry was first published in college periodicals. By 1958 his work began to appear in *Midwest Quarterly, The New York Times, Negro Digest, Freedomways,* and other periodicals. His poetry has been anthologized in several collections and textbooks. A volume of his poetry, *The Treehouse and Other Poems,* was published in 1968.

Carl Wendell Hines, Jr.

Carl Wendell Hines, Jr., (1940–   ), was born in North Carolina. He was graduated from Tennessee Agricultural and Industrial University in 1962. While a student there he formed his own jazz group and wrote poetry. His verses have been hailed as some of the best by contemporary black writers.

Pär Lagerkvist

Pär Lagerkvist (1891–   ), Swedish poet, dramatist, and novelist, is the son of a railway workman. After completing high school he studied for a time at the University of Uppsala. In 1916 publication of a collection of poems entitled *Anguish* won Lagerkvist critical acclaim and marked the beginning of his recognition as a literary figure. Throughout his long literary career he has spoken out against brutality and tried to express modern man's vision of himself and his world. Some of his most important works are his autobiography, *Guest of Reality,* an allegorical novel called *The Dwarf,* and *Barabbas.* In 1940

he was elected to the Swedish Academy, and in 1951 he was awarded the Nobel Prize for Literature.

William Gibson

William Gibson (1914–   ), American poet, short story writer, novelist, and playwright, was born and educated in New York City, which serves as the setting for his first stories. Gibson has also lived in both the Midwest and the Rockies, locales for a number of his poems. His most popular works are *Two for the Seesaw* and *The Miracle Worker.*

Helen Keller

Helen Keller (1880–1968) was born in Tuscumbia, Alabama. After graduation from Radcliffe College in 1904, Miss Keller dedicated her life to working for the blind through lectures, writings, and the Helen Keller Endowment Foundation. Her best-known books are *The Story of My Life,* *Out of the Dark,* and *Teacher.* She was awarded many honorary degrees because of her work in behalf of the handicapped. The Medal of Freedom, the highest honor a President of the United States can bestow on a civilian, was given to her in 1964.

274   THE INNER CIRCLE

THE INNER CIRCLE

in the inner city

in the inner city
or
like we call it
home
we think a lot about uptown
and the silent nights
and the houses straight as
dead men
and the pastel lights
and we hang on to our no place
happy to be alive
and in the inner city
or
like we call it
home

LUCILLE CLIFTON

From *Good Times*, by Lucille Clifton.
Copyright © 1969 by Lucille Clifton.
Reprinted by permission of Random
House, Inc.

*Marisol combines several different media to produce a unique
sculpture that reveals the subtle relationships in this family circle.*

*"The Family" (1962) Marisol
Wood with paint, charcoal, plaster, and other materials, 82⅝ x 65½ x 15½"
Collection, The Museum of Modern Art, New York. Advisory Committee Fund.*

The Father
and His Sons

AESOP FABLE

A father had a family of seven sons who were constantly quarreling among themselves. When he saw that he could not persuade them to change their quarrelsome ways by anything he said, the father determined to give them a practical illustration. For this purpose, he told them one day to bring him a bundle of sticks. When they had done so, he placed the bound bundle into the hands of each son in succession, and ordered him to break it in pieces. Each tried with all his strength, and was not able to do it. He next unbound the bundle, took the sticks separately and, one by one, put them into their hands again; now they broke them easily. Then he addressed them in these words: "My sons, if you are of one mind, and unite to assist each other, you will be as this bundle of sticks, uninjured by all the attempts of your enemies; but if you are divided among yourselves, you will be broken as easily as these separate twigs."

In the sixth century B.C., Aesop told a fable about a father who brought his sons together in order to counsel them against quarreling among themselves. Although this family formed an inner circle of shared lives, the father felt it necessary to give the sons a practical lesson on what happens when family members are not understanding and sympathetic toward one another.

Aesop's fable has survived through the centuries because its theme has always been relevant. Homes and families have been and continue to be torn apart by feelings of rebellion and jealousy, perhaps more at the present time than at any other time in history. And although many people think family patterns may change in the future, it is unlikely that this will happen unless the essential nature of man changes too. There is in each person a need to love and be loved, a need that manifests itself very early in life and continues to be important until death. Therefore, being part of an inner circle is a continuing need of mankind.

Home and family mean different things to different people. Lucille Clifton speaks of her home "in the inner city" as a vital environment where she felt happy to be alive as compared with the houses uptown that seemed to her as "straight as dead men." Similarly, Nikki Giovanni, in "Nikki-Rosa," recalls the happiness of being together with her family. On the other hand, Alfred Higgins in "All the Years of Her Life" and P. S. Wilkinson in "So Much Unfairness of Things" face certain conflicts within their inner circles. A great variety of "inner circle" situations is offered in the selections that follow. From Mrs. Higgins and her son Alfred to Mrs. Whalen and her son Marvin, all are different.

The major selection on this theme is a play that has had an almost unbroken record of performances on the stage for nearly four centuries. What could make this play so deathless? There are many answers to this question, but the most generally accepted one is that the story *Romeo and Juliet* tells never grows old. Here is the kind of once-in-a-lifetime romantic love that, ideally, is the beginning of so many inner circles. Here is a lack of understanding and communication between parents and children, a problem of the past as well as the present. Here is the kind of pressure that prevents people from making decisions that are carefully thought through. Here is a tragedy that might easily have been avoided. And here, also, is a beauty of language combined with dramatic action that holds a fascination for either the reader or the audience.

In the diverse selections in this unit there are many inner circles with the frustrations, pain, laughter, satisfactions, and tragedy that result from the inborn desire people have to form close ties with one another.

Most of us think we understand
the other members of our family group
or our "inner circle." Yet suddenly we may find
ourselves really "seeing" a familiar individual
for the first time.
After you have read the story which follows,
see how well you understand Alfred's mother.

All the Years
of Her Life

MORLEY CALLAGHAN

They were closing the drugstore, and
Alfred Higgins, who had just taken off his white
jacket, was putting on his coat and getting
ready to go home. The little gray-haired man,
Sam Carr, who owned the drugstore, was bending down behind the cash register, and when
Alfred Higgins passed him, he looked up and
said softly, "Just a moment, Alfred. One moment before you go."

The soft, confident, quiet way in which Sam
Carr spoke made Alfred start to button his coat
nervously. He felt sure his face was white. Sam
Carr usually said, "Good night," brusquely,
without looking up. In the six months he had
been working in the drugstore Alfred had never
heard his employer speak softly like that. His
heart began to beat so loud it was hard for him
to get his breath. "What is it, Mr. Carr?" he
asked.

"Maybe you'd be good enough to take a few
things out of your pocket and leave them here
before you go," Sam Carr said.

"What things? What are you talking about?"

"You've got a compact and a lipstick and at

least two tubes of toothpaste in your pockets,
Alfred."

"What do you mean? Do you think I'm
crazy?" Alfred blustered. His face got red and
he knew he looked fierce with indignation. But
Sam Carr, standing by the door with his blue
eyes shining bright behind his glasses and his
lips moving underneath his gray mustache, only
nodded his head a few times, and then Alfred
grew very frightened and he didn't know what
to say. Slowly he raised his hand and dipped it
into his pocket, and with his eyes never meeting
Sam Carr's eyes, he took out a blue compact
and two tubes of toothpaste and lipstick, and he
laid them one by one on the counter.

"Petty thieving, eh, Alfred?" Sam Carr said.
"And maybe you'd be good enough to tell me
how long this has been going on."

"This is the first time I ever took anything."

"So now you think you'll tell me a lie, eh?
What kind of a sap do I look like, huh? I don't
know what goes on in my own store, eh? I tell
you you've been doing this pretty steady," Sam
Carr said as he went over and stood behind the
cash register.

Ever since Alfred had left school he had been
getting into trouble wherever he worked. He
lived at home with his mother and his father,
who was a printer. His two older brothers were
married and his sister had got married last year,
and it would have been all right for his parents
now if Alfred had only been able to keep a job.

While Sam Carr smiled and stroked the side
of his face very delicately with the tips of his
fingers, Alfred began to feel that familiar terror
growing in him that had been in him every time
he had got into such trouble.

"I liked you," Sam Carr was saying. "I liked
you and would have trusted you, and now look
what I got to do." While Alfred watched with
his alert, frightened blue eyes, Sam Carr
drummed with his fingers on the counter. "I
don't like to call a cop in point-blank," he was
saying as he looked very worried. "You're a fool,
and maybe I should call your father and tell
him you're a fool. Maybe I should let them
know I'm going to have you locked up."

"My father's not at home. He's a printer. He works nights," Alfred said.

"Who's at home?"

"My mother, I guess."

"Then we'll see what she says." Sam Carr went to the phone and dialed the number. Alfred was not so much ashamed, but there was that deep fright growing in him, and he blurted out arrogantly, like a strong, full-grown man, "Just a minute. You don't need to draw anybody else in. You don't need to tell her." He wanted to sound like a swaggering, big guy who could look after himself, yet the old, childish hope was in him, the longing that someone at home would come and help him. "Yeah, that's right, he's in trouble," Mr. Carr was saying. "Yeah, your boy works for me. You'd better come down in a hurry." And when he was finished Mr. Carr went over to the door and looked out at the street and watched the people passing in the late summer night. "I'll keep my eye out for a cop," was all he said.

Alfred knew how his mother would come rushing in; she would rush in with her eyes blazing, or maybe she would be crying, and she would push him away when he tried to talk to her, and make him feel her dreadful contempt; yet he longed that she might come before Mr. Carr saw the cop on the beat passing the door.

While they waited—and it seemed a long time—they did not speak, and when at last they heard someone tapping on the closed door, Mr. Carr, turning the latch, said crisply, "Come in, Mrs. Higgins." He looked hard-faced and stern.

Mrs. Higgins must have been going to bed when he telephoned, for her hair was tucked in loosely under her hat, and her hand at her throat held her light coat tight across her chest so her dress would not show. She came in, large and plump, with a little smile on her friendly face. Most of the store lights had been turned out and at first she did not see Alfred, who was standing in the shadow at the end of the counter. Yet as soon as she saw him she did not look as Alfred thought she would look: she smiled, her blue eyes never wavered, and with a calmness and dignity that made them forget that her clothes seemed to have been thrown on her, she put out her hand to Mr. Carr and said politely, "I'm Mrs. Higgins. I'm Alfred's mother."

Mr. Carr was a bit embarrassed by her lack of terror and her simplicity, and he hardly knew what to say to her, so she asked, "Is Alfred in trouble?"

"He is. He's been taking things from the store. I caught him redhanded. Little things like compacts and toothpaste and lipsticks. Stuff he can sell easily," the proprietor said.

As she listened Mrs. Higgins looked at Alfred sometimes and nodded her head sadly, and when Sam Carr had finished she said gravely, "Is it so, Alfred?"

"Yes."

"Why have you been doing it?"

"I been spending money, I guess."

"On what?"

"Going around with the guys, I guess," Alfred said.

Mrs. Higgins put out her hand and touched Sam Carr's arm with an understanding gentleness, and speaking as though afraid of disturbing him, she said, "If you would only listen to me before doing anything." Her simple earnestness made her shy; her humility made her falter and look away, but in a moment she was smiling gravely again, and she said with a kind of patient dignity, "What did you intend to do, Mr. Carr?"

"I was going to get a cop. That's what I ought to do."

"Yes, I suppose so. It's not for me to say, because he's my son. Yet I sometimes think a little good advice is the best thing for a boy when he's at a certain period in his life," she said.

Alfred couldn't understand his mother's quiet composure, for if they had been at home and someone had suggested that he was going to be arrested, he knew she would be in a rage and would cry out against him. Yet now she was standing there with that gentle, pleading smile on her face, saying, "I wonder if you don't think it would be better just to let him come home with me. He looks a big fellow, doesn't he? It takes some of them a long time to get any sense," and they both stared at Alfred, who shifted away with a bit of light shining for a moment on his thin face and the tiny pimples over his cheekbone.

But even while he was turning away uneasily Alfred was realizing that Mr. Carr had become aware that his mother was really a fine woman; he knew that Sam Carr was puzzled by his mother, as if he had expected her to come in and plead with him tearfully, and instead he was being made to feel a bit ashamed by her vast tolerance. While there was only the sound of the mother's soft, assured voice in the store, Mr. Carr began to nod his head encouragingly at her. Without being alarmed, while being just large and still and simple and hopeful, she was becoming dominant there in the dimly lit store. "Of course, I don't want to be harsh," Mr. Carr was saying. "I'll tell you what I'll do. I'll just fire him and let it go at that. How's that?" and he got up and shook hands with Mrs. Higgins, bowing low to her in deep respect.

There was such warmth and gratitude in the way she said, "I'll never forget your kindness," that Mr. Carr began to feel warm and genial himself.

"Sorry we had to meet this way," he said. "But I'm glad I got in touch with you. Just wanted to do the right thing, that's all," he said.

"It's better to meet like this than never, isn't it?" she said. Suddenly they clasped hands as if they liked each other, as if they had known each other a long time. "Good night, sir," she said.

"Good night, Mrs. Higgins. I'm truly sorry," he said.

The mother and son walked along the street together, and the mother was taking a long, firm stride as she looked ahead with her stern face full of worry. Alfred was afraid to speak to her, he was afraid of the silence that was between them, so he only looked ahead too, for the excitement and relief were still pretty strong in him; but in a little while, going along like that in silence made him terribly aware of the strength and the sternness in her; he began to wonder what she was thinking of as she stared

ahead so grimly; she seemed to have forgotten that he walked beside her; so when they were passing under the Sixth Avenue elevated and the rumble of the train seemed to break the silence, he said in his old, blustering way, "Thank God it turned out like that. I certainly won't get in a jam like that again."

"Be quiet. Don't speak to me. You've disgraced me again and again," she said bitterly.

"That's the last time. That's all I'm saying."

"Have the decency to be quiet," she snapped. They kept on their way, looking straight ahead.

When they were at home and his mother took off her coat, Alfred saw that she was really only half-dressed, and she made him feel afraid again when she said, without even looking at him, "You're a bad lot. God forgive you. It's one thing after another and always has been. Why do you stand there stupidly? Go to bed, why don't you?" When he was going, she said, "I'm going to make myself a cup of tea. Mind, now, not a word about tonight to your father."

While Alfred was undressing in his bedroom, he heard his mother moving around the kitchen. She filled the kettle and put it on the stove. She moved a chair. And as he listened there was no shame in him, just wonder and a kind of admiration of her strength and repose. He could still see Sam Carr nodding his head encouragingly to her; he could hear her talking simply and earnestly, and as he sat on his bed he felt a pride in her strength. "She certainly was smooth," he thought. "Gee, I'd like to tell her she sounded swell."

And at last he got up and went along to the kitchen, and when he was at the door he saw his mother pouring herself a cup of tea. He watched and he didn't move. Her face, as she sat there, was a frightened, broken face utterly unlike the face of the woman who had been so assured a little while ago in the drugstore. When she reached out and lifted the kettle to pour hot water in her cup, her hand trembled and the water splashed on the stove. Leaning back in the chair, she sighed and lifted the cup to her lips, and her lips were groping loosely as if they would never reach the cup. She swallowed the hot tea eagerly, and then she straightened up in relief, though her hand holding the cup still trembled. She looked very old.

It seemed to Alfred that this was the way it had been every time he had been in trouble before, that this trembling had really been in her as she hurried out half-dressed to the drugstore. He understood why she had sat alone in the kitchen the night his young sister had kept repeating doggedly that she was getting married. Now he felt all that his mother had been thinking of as they walked along the street together a little while ago. He watched his mother, and he never spoke, but at that moment his youth seemed to be over; he knew all the years of her life by the way her hand trembled as she raised the cup to her lips. It seemed to him that this was the first time he had ever looked upon his mother.

I

A BOY GAINS INSIGHT

Alfred does some growing up as he watches his mother drinking the cup of tea in the kitchen. Suddenly, he sees her not as a pillar of strength and courage, but as an individual beset by uncertainties and feeling old. Do you find it strange that the members of this small inner circle could be so unaware of each other's problems and strengths? Do you suppose this is true of most families? Could it be true of your own family?

1. What is Alfred's first reaction when Mr. Carr accuses him of stealing?

2. How does Mrs. Higgins gain Mr. Carr's sympathy and understanding? Does this seem realistic? What evidence is there that Mrs. Higgins really did not feel the tolerance she pretended?

3. What lines tell the reader that the parents in this household do not work together in helping the children with their problems? Does the reader feel sympathy for Alfred? Why or why not?

II

IMPLICATIONS

Consider and discuss these ideas.

1. Mr. Carr didn't call the boy's father. There was some relationship between the boy's behavior and the father's working hours.

2. Few people ever really understand one another.

III

TECHNIQUES

Characterization

In the short story, the conclusion is of great importance. In the last three paragraphs of this story, the author deepens the characterizations of both Alfred and his mother and determines the reader's feelings toward them.

1. Analyze your feelings toward this mother and son. Do you: (a) pity them, (b) understand them, (c) detest them, (d) condemn them, or (e) admire them?

2. How would the characterizations have been changed if Alfred had seen his mother smiling, seemingly pleased with herself, as she sat alone in the kitchen?

Narrative Viewpoint

If the writer holds himself aloof, probing into the thoughts of his characters and telling his readers how these persons felt and saw, he is said to be writing from an "all-knowing" or "all-seeing" point of view. This is the *narrative viewpoint* from which Morley Callaghan presents the story you have just read, even though he is concerned primarily with revealing how Alfred thinks and feels about things.

You will be reading many short stories in THE INNER CIRCLE. As you read, practice observing the author's skill in creating a single *effect* or impression. To develop a literary appreciation of the short story, you should exercise your ability to pick out the underlying *theme* or idea. Deciding the relative importance of *characterization*, *plot*, or *setting* in the selections should prove challenging. Too, as you become aware of the different *narrative viewpoints* employed in the various stories, you will come to realize why each author found it to his advantage to use one rather than another in a particular situation.

Elements of the Short Story

Effect

The famous French author, Guy de Maupassant (1850–1893), is believed by some literary historians to be the originator of the modern short story. It was he who said that readers are divided into various groups, each saying to the writer:

"Comfort me."	"Make me laugh."
"Amuse me."	"Make me shudder."
"Touch me."	"Make me weep."
"Make me dream."	"Make me think."

Within a limited number of pages, this is really what the short story strives to do—to "comfort," to "amuse," to "touch" the reader in some way, leaving a single overall impression or *effect*.

Edgar Allan Poe, an American author, whose stories and poems you will read later in this book, is given credit for formulating certain principles for writing short stories. In setting forth his method of composing a short story, he said that he always began by considering which *effect* or impression he wished to make upon the reader. Then he used the three ingredients of a story—*action, characters,* and *setting*—to "construct" the desired effect.

The *characters* are the figures who are in the story. The *action* is what they do or what happens to them. The *setting* is the background or surroundings in which the story takes place.

Type of Short Story

Characterization (as for Mrs. Higgins) is of first importance when the writer depends primarily upon the development of a certain character or characters for his effect. The *plot* is most important if the action is tightly organized (see "The Most Dangerous Game"), but the characterization is sketchy. *Setting* is not often the most important element, but it may be very significant when it influences both characters and action.

Theme

When he writes a story, an author usually has a *theme,* or a basic idea which he wishes to set forth. For example, the theme for the short story, "The Most Dangerous Game," in CALL TO ADVENTURE, might be said to be: "A person's judgment of good or evil is influenced by his circumstances." The theme of a story may not be easy for the reader to see and put into words. In deciding upon the theme of a story, it is helpful to use the following formula: "In this story, the author is trying to show that. . . ." When the theme is most significant, the author achieves his effect through setting forth the idea in a memorable way.

Narrative Viewpoint

One problem which always confronts an author is the matter of deciding upon *narrative viewpoint.* The author, of course, is always the one who really tells the story, but he must decide from what viewpoint it would be of advantage to tell it. He must choose whether to tell it in first or third person. If he tells it in first person, the pronoun "I" indicates the narrator. If "I" is understood to be the author himself, he appears to be sharing a true experience.

However, the writer may decide that he wishes to write in third person, thus speaking of the characters as "he" or "she" or using their names. When telling a story in third person, the writer may limit the reader's information to the observations, thoughts, and actions of one character; but he is free to range from one character to another.

Symbolism

Sometimes an author will use a concrete thing to stand for a difficult-to-describe idea that is necessary to his story. This representation of an invisible element by something visible is called symbolism. The symbol is intended to bring a response from the reader with more meaning or overtones than words alone could achieve.

The symbolism may be a very simple illustration of an idea, such as that in the opening fable. You recall that the father used a bundle of sticks as an effective symbol of the unity he wished to teach his sons. Here, the sticks carried the father's meaning much more vividly than all of his lectures.

Although this poem is not very long, it tells you a great deal about what Nikki Giovanni thought was important within the inner circle of her home when she was growing up.

Nikki-Rosa

childhood remembrances are always a drag
if you're Black
you always remember things like living in Woodlawn
with no inside toilet
and if you become famous or something   5
they never talk about how happy you were to have your mother
all to yourself and
how good the water felt when you got your bath from one of those
big tubs that folk in chicago barbecue in
and somehow when you talk about home   10
it never gets across how much you
understood their feelings
as the whole family attended meetings about Hollydale
and even though you remember
your biographers never understand   15
your father's pain as he sells his stock
and another dream goes
and though you're poor it isn't poverty that
concerns you
and though they fought a lot   20
it isn't your father's drinking that makes any difference
but only that everybody is together and you
and your sister have happy birthdays and very good christmasses
and I really hope no white person ever has cause to write about me
because they never understand Black love is Black wealth and they'll 25
probably talk about my hard childhood and never understand that
all the while I was quite happy

NIKKI GIOVANNI

Reprinted by permission of Broadside Press.

NARRATIVE VIEWPOINT

1. Why wouldn't Nikki Giovanni want a white biographer writing about her childhood?

2. What are some of her happy memories?

3. Why did she consider such things as the family's fighting and her father's drinking unimportant?

The Gift of the Magi

O. HENRY

One dollar and eighty-seven cents. That was all. And sixty cents of it was in pennies. Pennies saved one and two at a time by bull-dozing the grocer and the vegetable man and the butcher until one's cheeks burned with the silent imputation of parsimony[1] that such close dealing implied. Three times Della counted it. One dollar and eighty-seven cents. And the next day would be Christmas.

There was clearly nothing to do but flop down on the shabby little couch and howl. So Della did it. Which instigates the moral reflection that life is made up of sobs, sniffles, and smiles, with sniffles predominating.

While the mistress of the home is gradually subsiding from the first stage to the second, take a look at the home. A furnished flat at eight dollars per week. It did not exactly beggar description,[2] but it certainly had that word on the lookout for the mendicancy squad.[3]

In the vestibule below was a letter box into which no letter would go, and an electric button from which no mortal finger could coax a ring. Also appertaining thereunto was a card bearing the name "Mr. James Dillingham Young."

The "Dillingham" had been flung to the breeze during a former period of prosperity when its possessor was being paid thirty dollars per week. Now, when the income was shrunk to twenty dollars, the letters of "Dillingham" looked blurred, as though they were thinking seriously of contracting to a modest and unassuming D. But whenever Mr. James Dillingham Young came home and reached his flat above, he was called "Jim" and greatly hugged by Mrs. James Dillingham Young, already introduced to you as Della. Which is all very good.

Della finished her cry and attended to her cheeks with the powder rag. She stood by the window and looked out dully at a gray cat walking a gray fence in a gray back yard. Tomorrow would be Christmas Day, and she had only $1.87 with which to buy Jim a present. She had been saving every penny she could for months, with this result. Twenty dollars a week doesn't go far. Expenses had been greater than she had calculated. They always are. Only $1.87 to buy a present for Jim. Her Jim. Many a happy hour she had spent planning something nice for him. Something fine and rare and sterling—something just a little bit near to being worthy of the honor of being owned by Jim.

There was a pier glass[4] between the windows of the room. Perhaps you have seen a pier glass in an eight-dollar flat. A very thin and very agile person may, by observing his reflection in a rapid sequence of longitudinal strips, obtain a fairly accurate conception of his looks. Della, being slender, had mastered the art.

Suddenly she whirled from the window and stood before the glass. Her eyes were shining brilliantly, but her face had lost its color

---

1. **imputation of parsimony**\ˈpär·sə ˈmō·nē\ charge of stinginess.
2. **beggar description,** exhaust the powers of description.
3. **mendicancy**\ˈmĕn·dĭ·kən·sē\ **squad,** police unit assigned to arrest those illegally begging. The reference is to the word *beggar.*
4. **pier glass,** tall, narrow mirror.

within twenty seconds. Rapidly she pulled down her hair and let it fall to its full length.

Now, there were two possessions of the James Dillingham Youngs in which they both took a mighty pride. One was Jim's gold watch that had been his father's and his grandfather's. The other was Della's hair. Had the Queen of Sheba lived in the flat across the air shaft, Della would have let her hair hang out the window some day to dry just to depreciate Her Majesty's jewels and gifts. Had King Solomon been the janitor, with all his treasures piled up in the basement, Jim would have pulled out his watch every time he passed, just to see him pluck at his beard from envy.

So now Della's beautiful hair fell about her, rippling and shining like a cascade of brown waters. It reached below her knee and made itself almost a garment for her. And then she did it up again nervously and quickly. Once she faltered for a minute and stood still while a tear or two splashed on the worn red carpet.

On went her old brown jacket; on went her old brown hat. With a whirl of skirts and with the brilliant sparkle still in her eyes she fluttered out the door and down the stairs to the street.

Where she stopped, the sign read, "Mme Sofronie. Hair Goods of All Kinds." One flight up Della ran and collected herself, panting. Madame, large, too white, chilly, hardly looked the "Sofronie."

"Will you buy my hair?" asked Della.

"I buy hair," said Madame. "Take yer hat off and let's have a sight at the looks of it."

Down rippled the brown cascade.

"Twenty dollars," said Madame, lifting the mass with a practiced hand.

"Give it to me quick," said Della.

Oh, and the next two hours tripped by on rosy wings. Forget the hashed metaphor. She was ransacking the stores for Jim's present.

She found it at last. It surely had been made for Jim and no one else. There was no other like it in any of the stores, and she had turned all of them inside out. It was a plati-

num fob chain, simple and chaste in design, properly proclaiming its value by substance alone and not by meretricious[5] ornamentation—as all good things should do. It was even worthy of The Watch. As soon as she saw it, she knew that it must be Jim's. It was like him. Quietness and value—the description applied to both. Twenty-one dollars they took from her for it, and she hurried home with the eighty-seven cents. With that chain on his watch Jim might be properly anxious about the time in any company. Grand as the watch was, he sometimes looked at it on the sly on account of the old leather strap that he used in place of a chain.

When Della reached home her intoxication gave way a little to prudence and reason. She got out her curling irons and lighted the gas and went to work repairing the ravages made by generosity added to love. Which is always a tremendous task, dear friends—a mammoth task.

Within forty minutes her head was covered with tiny, close-lying curls that made her look wonderfully like a truant schoolboy. She looked at her reflection in the mirror long, carefully, and critically.

"If Jim doesn't kill me," she said to herself, "before he takes a second look at me, he'll say I look like a Coney Island chorus girl. But what could I do—oh! what could I do with a dollar and eighty-seven cents?"

At seven o'clock the coffee was made and the frying pan was on the back of the stove, hot and ready to cook the chops.

Jim was never late. Della doubled the fob chain in her hand and sat on the corner of the table near the door that he always entered. Then she heard his step on the stair away down on the first flight, and she turned white for just a moment. She had a habit of saying little silent prayers about the simplest everyday things, and now she whispered, "Please, God, make him think I am still pretty."

---

5. **meretricious**\\'mĕr•ə ▲trĭsh•əs\\ gaudy, cheap looking.

The door opened, and Jim stepped in and closed it. He looked thin and very serious. Poor fellow, he was only twenty-two—and to be burdened with a family! He needed a new overcoat, and he was without gloves.

Jim stopped inside the door, as immovable as a setter at the scent of quail. His eyes were fixed upon Della, and there was an expression in them that she could not read, and it terrified her. It was not anger, nor surprise, nor disapproval, nor horror, nor any of the sentiments that she had been prepared for. He simply stared at her fixedly with that peculiar expression on his face.

Della wriggled off the table and went for him.

"Jim, darling," she cried, "don't look at me that way. I had my hair cut off and sold it because I couldn't have lived through Christmas without giving you a present. It'll grow out again—you won't mind, will you? I just had to do it. My hair grows awfully fast. Say

'Merry Christmas!' Jim, and let's be happy. You don't know what a nice—what a beautiful, nice gift I've got for you."

"You've cut off your hair?" asked Jim, laboriously, as if he had not arrived at that patent fact yet even after the hardest mental labor.

"Cut it off and sold it," said Della. "Don't you like me just as well, anyhow? I'm me without my hair, ain't I?"

Jim looked about the room curiously.

"You say your hair is gone?" he said, with an air almost of idiocy.

"You needn't look for it," said Della. "It's sold, I tell you—sold and gone, too. It's Christmas Eve, boy. Be good to me, for it went for you. Maybe the hairs of my head were numbered," she went on with a sudden serious sweetness, "but nobody could ever count my love for you. Shall I put the chops on, Jim?"

Out of his trance Jim seemed quickly to wake. He enfolded his Della. For ten seconds let us regard with discreet scrutiny some inconsequential object in the other direction. Eight dollars a week or a million a year— what is the difference? A mathematician or a wit would give you the wrong answer. The Magi brought valuable gifts, but that was not among them. This dark assertion will be illuminated later on.

Jim drew a package from his overcoat pocket and threw it upon the table.

"Don't make any mistake, Dell," he said, "about me. I don't think there's anything in the way of a haircut or a shave or a shampoo that could make me like my girl any less. But if you'll unwrap that package, you may see why you had me going a while at first."

White fingers and nimble tore at the string and paper. And then an ecstatic scream of joy; and then, alas! a quick feminine change to hysterical tears and wails, necessitating the immediate employment of all the comforting powers of the lord of the flat.

For there lay The Combs—the set of combs, side and back, that Della had worshiped for long in a Broadway window. Beautiful combs, pure tortoise shell, with jeweled rims—just the shade to wear in the beautiful vanished hair. They were expensive combs, she knew, and her heart had simply craved and yearned over them without the least hope of possession. And now they were hers, but the tresses that should have adorned the coveted adornments were gone.

But she hugged them to her bosom, and at length she was able to look up with dim eyes and a smile and say, "My hair grows so fast, Jim!" And then Della leaped up like a little singed cat and cried, "Oh, oh!"

Jim had not yet seen his beautiful present. She held it out to him eagerly upon her open palm. The dull precious metal seemed to flash with a reflection of her bright and ardent spirit.

"Isn't it a dandy, Jim? I hunted all over town to find it. You'll have to look at the time a hundred times a day now. Give me your watch. I want to see how it looks on it."

Instead of obeying, Jim tumbled down on the couch and put his hands under the back of his head and smiled.

"Dell," said he, "let's put our Christmas presents away and keep 'em a while. They're too nice to use just at present. I sold the watch to get the money to buy your combs. And now suppose you put the chops on."

The Magi, as you know, were wise men— wonderfully wise men—who brought gifts to the Babe in the manger. They invented the art of giving Christmas presents. Being wise, their gifts were no doubt wise ones, possibly bearing the privilege of exchange in case of duplication. And here I have lamely related to you the uneventful chronicle of two foolish children in a flat who most unwisely sacrificed for each other the greatest treasures of their house. But in a last word to the wise of these days let it be said that of all who give gifts these two were the wisest. Of all who give and receive gifts, such as they are wisest. Everywhere they are wisest. They are the Magi.

I

AN EXCHANGE OF LOVE

Paradoxically, anyone willing to sacrifice his greatest treasure to show his love for another person may be unwise, but he is at the same time extremely wise. This would seem to be the theme or central idea of "The Gift of the Magi."

1. Although the theme remains ageless, there are many indications to show that the story took place a number of years ago. Discuss details that date the account.

2. How much money had Della saved? How much does Mme Sofronie pay her for her hair? What does she buy for Jim?

3. How does Jim act when he first sees Della? Why is he so completely at a loss? What does he say when Della shows him the present she bought for him?

4. Discuss how you felt when you learned what Jim has done. Were you disappointed or pleased with the way he acts at the end of the story?

II

IMPLICATIONS

Discuss the following quotations as they relate to the O. Henry story:

1. "It is more blessed to give than to receive" —Acts 20:35.

2. "One must be poor to know the luxury of giving"—George Eliot, *Middlemarch.*

3. "A man there was, though some did count him mad,

The more he cast away the more he had"— John Bunyan, *Pilgrim's Progress.*

III

TECHNIQUES

Effect

"The Gift of the Magi" is so well-known that it is considered a classic. It demonstrates the three general traits of the O. Henry story: its characters are common persons living in a big city; it is sentimental and semirealistic; and it has a surprise ending.

Because he was bound by contract to produce a story a week for the *New York World* and these stories necessarily had to appeal to popular taste, O. Henry's writing was not flawless. Nevertheless, he was a master at producing stories which "touched" the reader so as to leave an overall impression or *effect*. Discuss which of the three traits of O. Henry's writing previously mentioned you think might be most responsible for leaving the reader with a memorable impression or *effect*.

Type of Short Story

The action in most O. Henry stories had to be tightly organized, or contrived, in order to allow for the surprise ending. This meant that *plot* was extremely important. In brief sentences, see if you can outline the plot of "The Gift of the Magi." You may wish to begin with the statement: It is the day before Christmas and Della does not have enough money to buy her husband a worthy Christmas gift.

Narrative Viewpoint

Although O. Henry wrote "The Gift of the Magi" in third person—that is, using "he," "she," or the names of the characters—he did not confine himself simply to the thoughts and actions of the characters themselves. He allowed himself to be present on the scene as an observer who communicated directly with the reader. This was a literary device (known as "Dear Reader") commonly used by writers of a century ago but rarely used now. An example of this device occurs in paragraph two: "Which instigates the moral reflection that life is made up of sobs, sniffles, and smiles, with sniffles predominating."

1. Locate and discuss other passages in which the author makes his presence felt.

2. It is mainly in these passages that the author gives himself free rein in using long, high-sounding words. What do you think was O. Henry's purpose in using such fancy words?

You may have difficulty deciding
who is the "hero"
in this warmly humorous story.
However, you will have no trouble
in seeing that Mr. Whalen's feelings
for his son influence his views
of persons outside his family circle
and his own community—
especially those individuals who come
from a rival basketball town.

The Hero

MARGARET WEYMOUTH
JACKSON

Mr. Whalen came into the kitchen by the back door and closed it softly behind him. He looked anxiously at his wife.

"Is Marv in?" he asked.

"He's resting," she whispered. Mr. Whalen nodded. He tiptoed through the dining room and went into the front hall as quiet as a mouse, and hung his hat and coat away. But he could not resist peeking into the darkened living room. A fire burned on the hearth, and on the couch lay a boy, or young man, who looked, at first glance, as though he were at least seven feet tall. He had a throw pulled up around his neck, and his stocking feet stuck out from the cuffs of his corduroy trousers over the end of the sofa.

"Dad?" a husky young voice said.

"Yes. Did I waken you? I'm sorry."

"I wasn't sleeping. I'm just resting."

Mr. Whalen went over to the couch and looked down at the long figure with deep concern.

"How do you feel?" he asked tenderly.

"Swell, Dad. I feel fine. I feel as though I'm going to be lucky tonight."

"That's fine! That's wonderful!" said his father fervently.

"What time is it, Dad?"

"Quarter to six."

"About time for me to get up and have my supper. Is it ready? I ought to stretch a bit."

"You lie still now, Marv. I'll see about your supper."

Mr. Whalen hurried back into the kitchen.

"He's awake," he informed his wife. "Is his supper ready?"

"In a minute, dear. I'm just making his tea."

Mr. Whalen went back into the living room with his anxious, bustling air.

The young man was up from the couch. He had turned on the light in a table lamp. He was putting on his shoes. He looked very young, not more than sixteen. His hair was thick as taffy and about the same color. He was thin, with a nose a little too big, and with clear blue eyes and a pleasant mouth and chin. He was not especially handsome, except to his father, who thought him the finest-looking boy in the whole wide world. The boy looked up a little shyly and smiled, and somehow his father's opinion was justified.

"I couldn't hit a thing in short practice yesterday," Marvin said. "That means I'll be hot tonight. Red-hot!"

"I hope so. I certainly hope so."

"You're going to the game, aren't you, Dad? You and Mother?"

Wild horses couldn't have kept Mr. Whalen away.

Marvin rose from his chair. He went up and up and up. Six feet four in his stocking feet, a hundred and seventy-six pounds, and sixteen years of age. Marvin flexed his muscles, crouched a little, and made a twisting leap into the air, one arm going up over his head in a swinging circle, his hand brushing the ceiling. He landed lightly as a cat. His father watched him, appearing neither astonished nor amused. There was nothing but the most profound respect and admiration in Mr. Whalen's eyes.

"We've been timing that pivot. Mr. Leach had two guards on me yesterday and they couldn't hold me, but I couldn't hit. Well, Dad, let's eat. I ought to be getting up to the gym."

They went into the kitchen, where the supper was laid on a clean cloth at a small round table. There was steak and potatoes and salad and chocolate cake for his parents, toast and tea and coddled eggs for the boy.

"I don't think you ought to put the cake out where Marv can see it, when he can't have any," fussed Mr. Whalen.

Marvin grinned. "It's okay, Dad. I don't mind. I'll eat some when I get home."

"Did you take your shower? Dry yourself good?"

"Sure, Dad. Of course."

"Was the doctor at school today? This was the day he was to check the team, wasn't it?"

"Yes. He was there. I'm okay. The arch supports Mr. Leach sent for came. You know, my left foot's been getting a little flat. Doc thought I ought to have something while I'm still growing."

"It's a good thing. Have you got them here?"

"Yes. I'll get them."

"No. Just tell me where they are. I'll look at them."

"In my room. In my gym shoes."

Mr. Whalen wasn't eating a bite of supper. It just gave him indigestion to eat on game nights. He got too excited. He couldn't stand it. The boy was eating calmly. He ate four coddled eggs. He ate six pieces of toast. He drank four cups of tea with lemon and sugar. In the boy's room Mr. Whalen checked the things in his bag—the white woolen socks, the clean folded towel, the shoes with their arch supports, and so on. The insets looked all right, his father thought. The fine, heavy satin playing suits would be packed in the box in which they came from the dry cleaner's, to keep them from getting wrinkled before the game.

There, alone in Marvin's room, with Marvin's ties hanging on his dresser, with his windbreaker thrown down in a chair and his high school books on the table, Mr. Whalen felt a little ill. He pressed his hand over his heart. He mustn't show his anxiety, he thought. The boy was calm. He felt lucky. Mustn't break that feeling. Mr. Whalen went back into the kitchen with an air of cheer, a plump, middle-aged man with a retreating hairline and kind, anxious, brown eyes. Mr. Whalen was a few inches shorter than his wife. But he had never regretted marrying a tall woman. Look at his boy!

Marv was looking at the funnies in the evening paper. Mr. Whalen resisted the temptation to look at the kitchen clock. The boy would know when to go. He took the front part of the paper and sat down and tried to put his mind on the news. Mrs. Whalen quietly washed the supper dishes. Marvin finished the funnies in the local paper and handed it to his father. Mr. Whalen took it and read the news that Hilltown High was to play Sunset High, of Stone City, at the local gym that evening. The Stone City team hadn't lost a game. They were grooming for the state championship. Mr. Whalen felt weak. He hoped Marvin hadn't read this. Indignation grew in the father, as he read on down the column, that the odds were against the local team. How dare Mr. Minton print such nonsense for the boys to read —to discourage them? It was outrageous. Mr. Whalen would certainly give the editor a piece of his mind. Perhaps Marvin had read it and believed it! Everything was so important—the psychology wasn't good.

Marvin had finished the funnies in the city paper, and he put it down and rose. He said a little ruefully, "I'm still hungry, but I can't eat more now."

"I'll have something ready for you when you get home," his mother said.

Marvin went into his room and came back in his windbreaker, his hair combed smoothly on his head.

"I'll see you at the gym," he said. "Sit where you always do, will you, Dad?"

"Yes. Yes. We'll be there."

"Okay. I'll be seeing you."

"Don't you want me to take you down in the car?"

"No. Thanks, Dad, but no. It'll do me good to run down there. It won't take me but a minute."

A shrill whistle sounded from the street.

"There's Johnny." Marvin left at once.

Mr. Whalen looked at his watch. "Better hurry, Mother. The first game starts at seven. We won't get our regular seats if we're late."

"I'm not going to the gym at half-past six," said Mrs. Whalen definitely. "We'll be there in time, and no one will take our seats. If you don't calm down, you are going to have a stroke at one of these games."

"I'm perfectly calm," said Mr. Whalen indignantly; "I'm as calm as—as calm as a June day. That's how calm I am. You know I'm not of a nervous temperament. Just because I want to get to the game on time, you say I am excited. You're as up in the air as I am."

"I am not," said Mrs. Whalen. She sat down at the cleared table and looked at the advertisements in the paper. Mr. Whalen looked at his watch again. He fidgeted.

"You can go ahead, if you like," she said. "I'll come alone."

"No, no," he protested, "I'll wait for you. Do you think we had better take the car? I put it up, but I can get it out again."

"We'll walk," she said. "It will do you good—quiet your nerves."

"I'm not nervous," he almost shouted. Then he subsided again, muttered a little, pretended to read the paper, checked his watch against the kitchen clock to see if it had stopped.

"If we're going to walk . . ." he said in a minute.

Mrs. Whalen looked at him with pity. He couldn't help it, she knew. She folded the papers and put them away, took off her white apron, smoothed her hair, and went to get her wraps. Mr. Whalen was at the front door, his overcoat on, his hat in his hand. She deliberately pottered, getting the cat off the piano and putting him out of doors, locking the kitchen door, turning out lights, hunting for her gloves.

Mr. Whalen was almost frantic by the time she joined him on the front porch. They went down the walk together, and when they reached the sidewalk they met neighbors also bound for the gym.

"How's Marv?" asked the man next door. "Is he all right?"

"Marv's fine, just fine. He couldn't be better."

"Boy, oh, boy," said the other enthusiastically, "would I like to see the boys whip Stone City! It would be worth a million dollars—a cool million. Stone City thinks no one can beat them. We'd burn the town down."

"Oh, this game doesn't matter so much," said Mr. Whalen deprecatingly. "The team is working toward the tournaments. Be a shame to show all their stuff tonight."

"Well, we'll see. We'll see."

They went ahead. At the next corner they met other friends.

"How's Marv? How's the big boy?"

"He's fine. He's all right." Mr. Whalen's chest expansion increased. Cars were parked all along the sidewalk before the group of township school buildings—the grade school and the high school, with the fine brick gymnasium between them. The walks were crowded now, for the whole town, except those in wheel chairs or just born, went to the games, and this was an important game with Hilltown's hereditary foe. Mr. Whalen grew very anxious about their seats. If Marvin looked around for them and didn't find them . . . He hurried his wife a little. They went into the outer hall of the gymnasium. The school principal was standing there talking to the coach, Mr. Leach. Mr. Whalen's heart plummeted. Had anything gone wrong? Had something happened to Marvin? He looked at them anxiously, but they spoke in normal tones.

"Good evening, Mrs. Whalen. Good evening, Tom."

Several small boys were running up and down the stairs, and the school principal turned and spoke to them severely. The Whalens had to make room for a young married couple, he carrying a small baby, she holding the hand of a little boy. Then they reached the window where the typing teacher was tearing off ticket stubs. Mr. Whalen paid his half dollar and they went inside the iron bar and up the steps to the gym proper.

The gymnasium wasn't half full. The bleachers which rose on either side of the shining, sacred floor with its cabalistic markings were spotted with people. The Hilltown eighth grade was playing the Sugar Ridge eighth grade. The boys scrambled, fell down, got up, and threw the ball, panted and heaved and struggled on the floor. A basketball flew about. A group of smaller children were seated in a tight knot, and two little girls whose only ambition in life was to become high school cheerleaders led a piercing yell:

> *Hit 'em high,*
> *Hit 'em low;*
> *Come on, eighth grade,*
> *Let's go!*

The voices of the junior high were almost piping. Mr. Whalen remembered how he had suffered when Marvin was in the eighth grade and they had to go to the games at six o'clock to watch him play. The junior-high games were very abbreviated, with six-minute quarters, which was all the state athletic association would let them play. Marvin had been five feet ten at thirteen, but too thin. He had put on a little weight in proportion to his height since then, but his father thought he should be heavier. The present eighth-grade team could not compare with Marvin's, Mr. Whalen decided.

But the boys did try hard. They were winning. The gun sounded, the junior high went to pieces with wild cheering, and the teams trotted off the floor, panting, sweating, happy.

Almost at once another group came on in secondhand white wool tops and the old blue satin trunks from last year. This was the second team. The boys were pretty good. They practiced, throwing the ball from far out, running in under the basket, passing to one another. Mr. and Mrs. Whalen had found their regular seats unoccupied, halfway between the third

and fourth uprights which supported the lofty gymnasium ceiling. Mr. Whalen sat down a little weakly and wiped his forehead. Mrs. Whalen began at once to visit with a friend sitting behind her, but Mr. Whalen could not hear what anyone said.

The Stone City reserves came out on the floor to warm up. They looked like first-string men.

Mr. Leach was talking to the timekeeper. He was a good coach—a mighty good coach. They were lucky to keep him here at Hilltown. The luckiest thing that had ever happened to the town was when Mr. Leach had married a Hilltown girl who didn't want to move away. They'd never have been able to hold him otherwise. It meant so much to the boys to have a decent, kindly man to coach them. Some of the high school coaches felt that their teams had to win, no matter how. It would be very bad to have his boy under such an influence, thought Mr. Whalen, who simply could not bear to see the team defeated, and who was always first to yell "Thief!" and "Robber!"

The officials came out in their green shirts, and Mr. Whalen almost had heart failure. There was that tall, thin man who had fouled Marvin every time he had moved in the tournaments last year. He was always against Hilltown. He had been so unfair that Mr. Leach had complained about him to the state association. The only time Mr. Leach had ever done such a thing. Oh, this was awful. Mr. Whalen twisted his hat in his hands. The other official he had seen often. He was fair—very fair. Sugar Ridge had complained about him for favoring Hilltown, but Mr. Whalen thought him an excellent referee.

The gymnasium was filling fast now. All the high school students—two hundred of them— were packed in the cheering section. The junior high was swallowed up, lost. The cheering section looked as though not one more could get into it, and yet youngsters kept climbing up, squeezing in. The rest of the space was filled with townspeople, from toddlers in snow suits to graybearded dodderers. On the opposite side of the gymnasium, the visiting fans were filling their seats. Big crowd from Stone City. Businessmen and quarrymen and stone carvers and their wives and children. They must feel confident of winning, Mr. Whalen thought. Their cheerleaders were out on the floor. Where were Hilltown's? Ah, there they were—Beth and Mary. Hilltown's cheerleaders were extremely pretty adolescents dressed in blue satin slacks with white satin shirts, the word "Yell" in blue letters over their shoulders—a true gilding of the lily. Mary was Marvin's girl. She was the prettiest girl in town. And she had personality, too, and vigor.

Now the two girls leaped into position, spun their hands, spread out their arms, catapulted their bodies into the air in perfect synchronization, and the breathless cheering section came out in a long roll.

> *Hello, Stone City,*
> *Hello, Stone City,*
> *Hilltown says,*
> *Hello-o-o-o!*

Not to be outdone, the Stone City leaders, in crimson-and-gold uniforms, returned the compliment:

> *Hello, Hilltown . . .*

and the sound came nicely across the big gym. Mr. Whalen got a hard knot in his throat, and the bright lights and colors of the gymnasium swam in a mist. He couldn't help it. They were so young. Their voices were so young!

The whistle blew. The reserves were at it.

Mr. Whalen closed his eyes and sat still. It would be so long; the cheering wouldn't really start, the evening wouldn't begin until the team came out. He remembered when Marvin was born. He had been tall then—twenty-two inches. Mr. Whalen prayed, his lips moving a little, that Marvin wouldn't get hurt tonight. Suppose he had a heart attack and fell dead, like that boy at Capital City years ago. Suppose he got knocked against one of the steel uprights and hurt his head—damaged his brain? Suppose he got his knee injured? Mr. Whalen

opened his eyes. He must not think of those things. He had promised his wife he would not worry so. He felt her hand, light but firm, on his arm.

"Here are the Lanes," she said.

Mr. Whalen spoke to them. Johnny's parents crowded in behind the Whalens. Johnny's father's hand fell on Mr. Whalen's shoulder.

"How's Marv tonight?"

"Fine, fine. How's Johnny?"

"Couldn't be better. I believe the boys are going to take them.

The two fathers looked at each other and away. Mr. Whalen felt a little better.

"How's business?" asked Johnny's father, and they talked about business a moment or two, but they were not interested.

There was a crisis of some kind on the floor. Several players were down in a pile. Someone was hurt. Mr. Whalen bit the edge of his felt hat. The boy was up now. The Stone City coach was out on the floor, but the boy shook his head. He was all right. The game was resumed.

At last it was over. The reserves had won. Mr. Whalen thought that was a bad omen. The eighth grade had won. The reserves had won. No, it was too much. The big team would lose. If the others had lost, he would have considered that a bad omen too. Every omen was bad to Mr. Whalen at this stage. The floor was empty. The high school band played "Indiana," and "Onward, Hilltown," and everyone stood up and sang.

There was a breathless pause, and then a crashing cheer hit the ceiling of the big gym and bounced back. The Team was out. Out there on the floor in their blue satin suits, with jackets over their white tops, warming up, throwing the ball deftly about. What caused the change? Mr. Whalen never knew, but everything was quick now, almost professional in tone and quality. Self-confidence, authority, had come into the gymnasium. Ten or twelve boys out there warming up. But there was really only one boy on the floor for Mr. Whalen, a tall, thin, fair boy with limber legs still faintly brown from summer swimming. Mr. Whalen did not even attempt to tear his eyes from Marvin.

The Stone City team came out. Mr. Whalen looked away from Marvin for a moment to study them. Two or three of them were as tall as Marvin, maybe taller. He felt indignant. They must be seniors, all of them. Or five-year men. He studied the boys. He liked to see if he could pick out the first-string men from the lot. He could almost always do it—not by their skill or their height, but by their faces. That little fellow with the pug nose—he was a first-string man. And the two big ones—the other tall man Mr. Whalen discarded correctly. And the boy with the thick chest. What it was, he wasn't sure—some carelessness, some ease that marked the first-string men. The others were always a little self-conscious, a little too eager.

The referee blew the whistle. The substitutes left the floor, carrying extra jackets. The boy with the pug nose came forward for Stone City. So he was captain? Mr. Whalen felt gratified in his judgment. Marvin came forward for his team. He was captain too. There was a Number 1 in blue on the sleeveless white satin shirt he wore. The referee talked to them. The boys took their positions, the umpire his along the edge of the floor. The cheering section roared:

We may be rough,
We may be tough,
But we're the team
That's got the stuff!
Fight! Fight! Fight!

Mary turned a complete somersault, her lithe young body going over backward, her heels in the air, then hitting the floor to bounce her straight up in a spread eagle. Her pretty mouth was open in a square. The rooting swelled. The substitutes sat down with their coaches. Marvin stood back out of the center ring until the referee, ball in hand, waved him in. The ball went into the air as the whistle blew, and the game was on.

Marvin got the tip-off straight to Johnny. Marv ran down into the corner, where he circled to confuse his guard. Johnny brought the ball down over the line, faked a pass and drew out Marvin's guard, bounced the ball to Perk, who carried it almost to the foul line and passed to Marvin, who threw the ball into the basket. Stone City leaped outside, threw the ball in, a long pass. Perk leaped for it, but missed. The tall Stone City forward dribbled, dodging skillfully. The guards were smothering him, but he pivoted, flung the ball over his head and into the basket. A basket each in the first minute of play!

Mr. Whalen had stopped breathing. He was in a state of suspended animation. The game was very fast—too fast. Stone City scored a second and a third time. Marvin called time out. Someone threw a wet towel from the bench, and it slid along the floor. The boys wiped their faces with it, threw it back. They whispered together. The referee blew the whistle. Yes, they were going to try the new trick play they had been practicing. It worked. Marvin's pivot was wonderful. The score was four to six.

Marvin played with a happy romping abandon. He was skillful, deft, acute. But he was also gay. The youngsters screamed his name. Mr. Whalen saw Mary's rapt, adoring look. Marvin romped down the floor like a young colt.

At the end of the quarter, the score was fourteen to ten in Stone City's favor. At the end of the half, it was still in Stone City's favor, but only fourteen to thirteen. Stone City didn't score in the second quarter.

Mr. Whalen felt a deep disquietude. He had been watching the tall center on the other team, the pivot man. He had thick, black, curly hair and black eyes. Mr. Whalen thought he looked tough. He had fouled Marvin twice in the first half. That is, he had been called for two fouls, but he had fouled him oftener. Mr. Whalen was sure he had tripped Marvin that time Marvin fell on the floor and cracked his elbow. Marvin had jumped up again at once.

The Stone City center was a dirty player and ought to be taken off the floor. The school band was playing, but Mr. Whalen couldn't hear it. He was very upset. If the referees were going to let Stone City foul Hilltown and get away with it . . . He felt hot under the collar. He felt desperate.

"Why don't you go out and smoke?" his wife asked. Mr. Whalen folded his overcoat to mark his place and went out of the gym. He smoked two cigarettes as fast as he could. He would stay out here. The stars were cool and calm above his head. The night air was fresh. He couldn't stand it in the gymnasium. He would wait here until the game was over. If Marvin was hurt, he wouldn't see it. He resolved this firmly. But when the whistle blew and he heard the burst of cheering, he rushed back into the gymnasium like a man going to a fire.

The second half had begun. Again the big center fouled Marvin. Marvin got two free throws and made both good.

Fifteen to fourteen now! The crowd went wild. The game got very fast again. Mr. Whalen watched Marvin and his opponent like a hawk. There! It happened.

Mr. Whalen was on his feet, yelling, "Watch him! Watch him!"

The Stone City center had driven his elbow into Marvin's stomach. Marvin was doubled up. Marvin was down on the floor. A groan went up from the bleachers. Mr. Whalen started out on the floor. Something held him. He looked around blindly. His wife had a firm grip on his coat-tails. She gave him a smart yank and pulled him unexpectedly down on the bench beside her.

"He doesn't want you on the floor," she said fiercely.

Mr. Whalen was very angry, but he controlled himself. He sat still. Marvin was up again. Mary led a cheer for him. Marvin was all right. He got two more free throws. Now Hilltown was three points ahead. Marvin was fouled again, got two more free throws and missed them both. He was hurt! He never missed free throws—well, hardly ever. What

was the matter with the referee? Was he crazy? Was he bribed? Mr. Whalen groaned.

Stone City took time out, and in the last minute of the third quarter they made three quick baskets. It put them ahead again, three points. A foul was called on Marvin—for pushing.

"Why, he never did at all!" yelled Mr. Whalen. "He couldn't stop fast enough—that's not a foul! Just give them the ball, boys! Don't try to touch it!"

"Will you hush?" demanded his wife.

The Stone City forward made one of the two throws allowed. It was the quarter.

The game was tied three times in the last quarter. With five minutes to play, the big center fouled Marvin again. His last personal. He was out of the game. The Hilltown crowd booed him. None so loud as Mr. Whalen, who often talked long and seriously to Marvin about sportsmanship.

Then Marvin got hot. He couldn't miss. Everyone on the team fed him the ball, and he could throw it from anywhere and it went, plop, right into the basket. Marvin pivoted. His height, his spring, carried him away from his guards. Marvin pranced. His long legs carried him where he would. He threw the ball over his head and from impossible angles. Once he was knocked down on the floor, and he threw from there and made the basket. His joy, his perfection, his luck, caused the crowd to burst into continuous wild cheering. Stone City took time out. They ran in substitutes, but they couldn't stop Marvin. Perk would recover the ball; he and Johnny fed it skillfully to Marvin, and Marvin laid it in. The gun went off with Hilltown twelve points ahead.

Mr. Whalen was a wreck. He could hardly stand up. Mrs. Whalen took his arm and half supported him toward the stairs that led down to the school grounds. The Stone City fans were angry. A big, broad-shouldered man with fierce black eyes complained in a loud, quarrelsome voice:

"That skinny kid—that Whalen boy—he fouled my boy! Who cares? But when my boy protects himself, what happens? They put him off the floor. They put my Guido[1] out, so Hill-town wins. I get my hands on that tall monkey and I'll fix him."

"Be careful. That's my son you're talking about." The strength had returned to Mr. Whalen. He was strong as a lion. Mrs. Whalen pulled at his arm, but he jerked away. He turned on the crowded stairs. "Before you do anything to Marvin," he said, his voice loud and high, "you'd better do something to me. Your son fouled repeatedly."

"That's a lie!" yelled the other, and Mr. Whalen hit him. He hit him right in the stomach as hard as he could punch him. Instantly there was a melee. Johnny's father was punching somebody, and for a moment the crowd heaved and milled on the stairs. Someone screamed. Something like a bolt of lightning hit Mr. Whalen in the eye, and he struck back.

Friends were pulling him away. The town marshal shouldered good-naturedly between the combatants. The big man was in the grip of others from Stone City, who dragged him back up the stairs. Mr. Whalen struggled with his captors, fellow townsmen, who sympathized with him but had no intention of letting him fight. Johnny's mother and Marvin's mother hustled their men out into the cold night air.

"Really!" the high school principal was saying anxiously. "Really, we mustn't have any trouble. The boys don't fight. If we could just keep the fathers away from the games! Really, Mrs. Whalen, this won't do."

"I've got a good notion to take a poke at him too," said Mr. Whalen, who was clear above himself.

In the kitchen, Mr. Whalen looked in a small mirror at his reflection. He felt wonderful. He felt marvelous. He was going to have a black eye. He grabbed his wife and kissed her soundly.

"They beat them!" he said. "They beat Stone City!"

"You old fool!" cried Mrs. Whalen. "I declare I'd be ashamed of Marvin if he acted like that. You and Johnny's father—fighting like hoodlums."

"I don't care!" said Mr. Whalen. "I'm glad I hit him. Teach him a lesson. I feel great. I'm hungry. Make some coffee, Mother."

Marvin wouldn't be in for an hour. He would have a date with Mary at the soda parlor, to which the whole high school would repair. They heard the siren blowing, they looked out of the window and saw the reflection of the bonfire on the courthouse lawn. They heard the fire engine. The team was having a ride on the fire engine. Mr. Whalen stood on his front porch and cheered. The town was wild with joy. Not a citizen that wasn't up in the air tonight.

At last Marvin came in. He was cheerful, practical.

"Did you really have a fight, Dad? Someone told me you popped Guido's father. . . . Boy, are you going to have a shiner!" Marvin was greatly amused. He examined his father's eye, recommended an ice pack.

"I want it to get black," said Mr. Whalen stubbornly.

"We sure fixed Guido," said Marvin, and laughed.

"Did you have a fight?" asked his father eagerly.

"Heck, no! I'm going to get him a date with Betty. He noticed her. He's coming up next Sunday. Their team went downtown for sodas because Guido wanted to meet Betty. I wasn't sore at him. I only mean he was easy to handle. I saw right away that I could make him foul me, give me extra shots, get him off the floor. It's very easy to do with a big clumsy guy like that."

Mr. Whalen fingered his swelling eye and watched Marvin eat two hot ham sandwiches and a big slab of chocolate cake and drink a quart of milk. Marvin had already had a soda.

"You must sleep late in the morning," Mr. Whalen said. "Maybe you got too tired tonight. Now, don't eat too much cake."

---

1. **Guido**\ˈgē 'dō\ or \ˈgwē 'dō\.

Mr. Whalen's eye hurt. Mrs. Whalen got him to bed and put a cold compress on it.

"Old ninny," she murmured, and stooped and kissed him. Mr. Whalen sighed. He was exhausted. He was getting too old to play basketball, he thought confusedly.

I

WHO'S THE HERO?

An inner circle of a family can be pulled into a distorted shape by actions from without or emotions within. "All the Years of Her Life" showed an inner circle twisted and pulled by the relationships of those within it. Alfred's father appears to have paid little attention to him; and for lack of guidance, Alfred involved himself in petty thefts that tore his mother's heart apart. But in "The Hero," the situation is a very different one. Mr. Whalen is almost too much involved in his son's life. What effect do you feel this may have on Marv? And what on the relationship between the parents? Mrs. Whalen calls Mr. Whalen an old fool and says she'd be ashamed of Marvin if he had acted as his father did. Do you feel that in spite of this she really understands her husband and is very fond of him?

II

IMPLICATIONS

Consider these statements and discuss the evidence for or against them.

1. There is evidence of real "inner circle" feeling among the members of this family.

2. Marv conceals his tensions and innermost thoughts while his father expresses his.

3. Marv is the "hero" referred to in the title.

4. Mr. Whalen is the "hero" referred to in the title.

5. Mr. Whalen's desire to have his son excel comes from his own self-centeredness.

III

TECHNIQUES

Characterization

Although Mr. Whalen seems like an individual, he is actually more of a *type character*. Think what *type* would mean when it is used to refer to a person. Consider the following characteristics as they apply to Whalen, and then explain what you think a *type character* would be.

1. Physical appearance and disposition

2. Personal habits

3. Attitudes and ideals

4. Status within his family and among his friends

5. Someone like him that you know

Theme

This delightful story leaves us chuckling and yet thoughtful in a way that moves us to say, "You know, there's a lot in this."

1. As to the theme, do you think Margaret Weymouth Jackson was trying to tell you that:

a. Most fathers desire to live through their sons the glories they never achieved themselves?

b. Poor sportsmanship could be eliminated more easily if it were not for the influence of the older generation?

c. There is too much attention centered on sports contests in America?

2. Discuss whether you believe any one of these theme statements would suffice. If not, compose a statement of your own which you feel is more satisfactory.

Narrative Viewpoint

"The Hero" is an example of a story told in third person. Is most of the action viewed through the eyes of:

1. a central character?

2. a minor character?

3. a disinterested spectator?

Effect

This is a story designed to make us laugh, but it also has the effect of making us think and ponder over the relationship between the members of the family and the aspirations of the boy and his father. Study pages 290 and 291. How has the author pointed out that something is reversed in the attitudes of Marvin and his father?

What artist has not tried to capture the bond of unity in a family group or a circle of friends? This gallery emphasizes the great variety of ways in which artists have handled this theme.

LOVERS makes the ultimate statement of this theme. Notice the many ways in which the artist, Charles White, has closed the circle in design as well as content.

LOVERS   *Charles White*

FAMILY GROUP, 1948–49
Henry Moore
Bronze (cast 1950), 59¼ x 46½″
Collection, The Museum of Modern Art,
New York, A. Conger Goodyear Fund

Quite opposite to LOVERS in approach but just as close to the theme of
family unity is Moore's massive sculpture FAMILY GROUP. Contrast the
simplified figures and the overall shape. Notice the way Moore has cut
into his forms. He would remind you that all art is more than its subject:
it is form, space, and a statement about what can be done with the
media, the material with which the artist works.

THE MUSIC LESSON
Thomas Hart Benton

These contrasting pairs offer a fascinating range of differences and similarities. The farmers share a skill in the secure circles of their quiet lives, while the threatened mothers encompass the young in the taut circle of their protecting love. These artists are widely separated in time and culture. Tanner was a black painter of the nineteenth century while Benton painted in our time. Biggers is an American whose harsh realism parallels for his people the intense feelings of Kollwitz, a German woman who knew the horror of World War II.

THE BANJO LESSON
Henry Ossawa Tanner
Huntington Library, Hampton Institute,
Hampton, Virginia

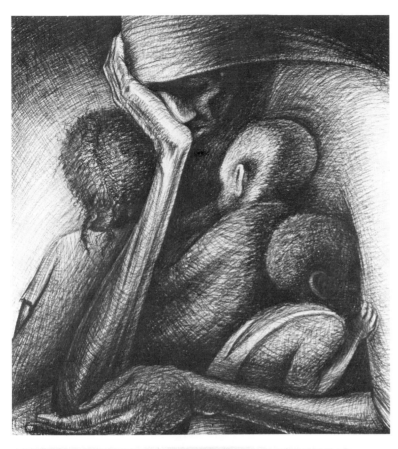

CRADLE
John Biggers
Museum of Fine Arts, Houston

SEEDCORN MUST NOT BE GROUND
Kathe Kollwitz
Courtesy of the Galerie
St. Etienne, New York

MOTHER AND SON
Daniel Garber
Courtesy of the Pennsylvania Academy
of Fine Arts

ROOM IN NEW YORK
Edward Hopper

Look beyond the content of these three paintings to see what each artist has pointed out about light. Each painting has an atmosphere, even a temperature, that a viewer can feel. What things contribute to this quality? Some pictures seem to require that we add our own stories about the circle of the lives glimpsed. MOTHER AND SON and ROOM IN NEW YORK show quiet adult relationships, ones that are perhaps filled with strain and tension. In contrast to these paintings, THE BOATING PARTY shows an entirely different kind of relationship between people. Bright color, strong line, and bold darks stand behind the tender circle of the painting's subject.

THE BOATING PARTY
Mary Cassatt
Chester Dale Collection, National
Gallery of Art, Washington, D.C.

His real name was William Armstrong, which was like "a big tail on a small kite," and he went by the name of Doodle. He was "just about the craziest brother a boy ever had" and one whose courage far outmeasured his size. Only Aunt Nicey, however, realized how special he was from the very beginning.

The Scarlet Ibis

JAMES HURST

It was in the clove of seasons, summer was dead but autumn had not yet been born, that the ibis lit in the bleeding tree. The flower garden was stained with rotting brown magnolia petals and ironweeds grew rank amid the purple phlox. The five o'clocks by the chimney still marked time, but the oriole nest in the elm was untenanted and rocked back and forth like an empty cradle. The last graveyard flowers were blooming, and their smell drifted across the cotton field and through every room of our house, speaking softly the names of our dead.

It's strange that all this is still so clear to me, now that that summer has long since fled and time has had its way. A grindstone stands where the bleeding tree stood, just outside the kitchen door, and now if an oriole sings in the elm, its song seems to die up in the leaves, a silvery dust. The flower garden is prim, the house a gleaming white, and the pale fence across the yard stands straight and spruce. But sometimes (like right now), as I sit in the cool, green-draped parlor, the grindstone begins to turn, and time with all its changes is ground away—and I remember Doodle.

Doodle was just about the craziest brother a boy ever had. Of course, he wasn't a crazy crazy like old Miss Leedie, who was in love with President Wilson[1] and wrote him a letter every day, but was a nice crazy, like someone you meet in your dreams. He was born when I was six and was, from the outset, a disappointment. He seemed all head, with a tiny body which was red and shriveled like an old man's. Everybody thought he was going to die— everybody except Aunt Nicey, who had delivered him. She said he would live because he was born in a caul and cauls were made from Jesus' nightgown. Daddy had Mr. Heath, the carpenter, build a little mahogany coffin for him. But he didn't die, and when he was three months old Mama and Daddy decided they might as well name him. They named him William Armstrong, which was like tying a big tail on a small kite. Such a name sounds good only on a tombstone.

I thought myself pretty smart at many things, like holding my breath, running, jumping, or climbing the vines in Old Woman Swamp, and I wanted more than anything else someone to race to Horsehead Landing, someone to box with, and someone to perch with in the top fork of the great pine behind the barn, where across the fields and swamps you could see the sea. I wanted a brother. But Mama, crying, told me that even if William Armstrong lived, he would never do these things with me. He might not, she sobbed, even be "all there." He might, as long as he lived, lie on the rubber sheet in the center of the bed in the front bedroom where the white marquisette curtains billowed out in the afternoon sea breeze, rustling like palmetto fronds.

It was bad enough having an invalid brother, but having one who possibly was not all there was unbearable, so I began to make plans to kill him by smothering him with a pillow. However, one afternoon as I watched him, my head poked between the iron posts of the foot of the bed, he looked straight at me and grinned. I skipped through the rooms, down the echoing

Reprinted by permission of James Hurst.

---

1. **Woodrow Wilson** (1856–1924), president of the United States from 1913 to 1921.

halls, shouting, "Mama, he smiled. He's all there! He's all there!" and he was.

When he was two, if you laid him on his stomach, he began to try to move himself, straining terribly. The doctor said that with his weak heart this strain would probably kill him, but it didn't. Trembling, he'd push himself up, turning first red, then a soft purple, and finally collapse back onto the bed like an old worn-out doll. I can still see Mama watching him, her hand pressed tight across her mouth, her eyes wide and unblinking. But he learned to crawl (it was his third winter), and we brought him out of the front bedroom, putting him on the rug before the fireplace. For the first time he became one of us.

As long as he lay all the time in bed, we called him William Armstrong, even though it was formal and sounded as if we were referring to one of our ancestors, but with his creeping around on the deerskin rug and beginning to talk, something had to be done about his name. It was I who renamed him. When he crawled, he crawled backwards, as if he were in reverse and couldn't change gears. If you called him, he'd turn around as if he were going in the other direction, then he'd back right up to you to be picked up. Crawling backward made him look like a doodlebug, so I began to call him Doodle, and in time even Mama and Daddy thought it was a better name than William Armstrong. Only Aunt Nicey disagreed. She said caul babies should be treated with special respect since they might turn out to be saints. Renaming my brother was perhaps the kindest thing I ever did for him, because nobody expects much from someone called Doodle.

Although Doodle learned to crawl, he showed no signs of walking, but he wasn't idle. He talked so much that we all quit listening to what he said. It was about this time that Daddy built him a go-cart and I had to pull him around. At first I just paraded him up and down the piazza, but then he started crying to be taken out into the yard and it ended up by my having to lug him wherever I went. If I so much as picked up my cap, he'd start crying to go with me and Mama would call from wherever she was, "Take Doodle with you."

He was a burden in many ways. The doctor had said that he mustn't get too excited, too hot, too cold, or too tired and that he must always be treated gently. A long list of dont's went with him, all of which I ignored once we got out of the house. To discourage his coming with me, I'd run with him across the ends of the cotton rows and careen him around corners on two wheels. Sometimes I accidentally turned him over, but he never told Mama. His skin was very sensitive, and he had to wear a big straw hat whenever he went out. When the going got rough and he had to cling to the sides of the go-cart, the hat slipped all the way down over his ears. He was a sight. Finally, I could see I was licked. Doodle was my brother and he was going to cling to me forever, no matter what I did, so I dragged him across the burning cotton field to share with him the only beauty I knew, Old Woman Swamp. I pulled the go-cart through the saw-tooth fern, down into the green dimness where the palmetto fronds whispered by the stream. I lifted him out and set him down in the soft rubber grass beside a tall pine. His eyes were round with wonder as he gazed about him, and his little hands began to stroke the rubber grass. Then he began to cry.

"For heaven's sake, what's the matter?" I asked, annoyed.

"It's so pretty," he said. "So pretty, pretty, pretty."

After that day Doodle and I often went down into Old Woman Swamp. I would gather wildflowers, wild violets, honeysuckle, yellow jasmine, snakeflowers, and water lilies, and with wire grass we'd weave them into necklaces and crowns. We'd bedeck ourselves with our handiwork and loll about thus beautified, beyond the touch of the everyday world. Then when the slanted rays of the sun burned orange in the tops of the pines, we'd drop our jewels into the stream and watch them float away toward the sea.

There is within me (and with sadness I have watched it in others) a knot of cruelty borne by the stream of love, much as our blood sometimes bears the seed of our destruction, and at times I was mean to Doodle. One day I took him up to the barn loft and showed him his casket, telling him how we all had believed he would die. It was covered with a film of Paris green sprinkled to kill the rats, and screech owls had built a nest inside it.

Doodle studied the mahogany box for a long time, then said, "It's not mine."

"It is," I said. "And before I'll help you down from the loft, you're going to have to touch it."

"I won't touch it," he said sullenly.

"Then I'll leave you here by yourself," I threatened, and made as if I were going down.

Doodle was frightened of being left. "Don't go leave me, Brother," he cried, and he leaned toward the coffin. His hand, trembling, reached out, and when he touched the casket he screamed. A screech owl flapped out of the box into our faces. scaring us and covering us with Paris green. Doodle was paralyzed, so I put him on my shoulder and carried him down the ladder, and even when we were outside in the bright sunshine, he clung to me, crying, "Don't leave me. Don't leave me."

When Doodle was five years old, I was embarrassed at having a brother of that age who couldn't walk, so I set out to teach him. We were down in Old Woman Swamp and it was spring and the sick-sweet smell of bay flowers hung everywhere like a mournful song. "I'm going to teach you to walk, Doodle," I said.

He was sitting comfortably on the soft grass, leaning back against the pine. "Why?" he asked.

I hadn't expected such an answer. "So I won't have to haul you around all the time."

"I can't walk, Brother," he said.

"Who says so?" I demanded.

"Mama, the doctor—everybody."

"Oh, you can walk," I said, and I took him by the arms and stood him up. He collapsed onto the grass like a half-empty flour sack. It was as if he had no bones in his little legs.

"Don't hurt me, Brother," he warned.

"Shut up. I'm not going to hurt you. I'm going to teach you to walk." I heaved him up again, and again he collapsed.

This time he did not lift his face up out of the rubber grass. "I just can't do it. Let's make honeysuckle wreaths."

"Oh yes you can, Doodle," I said. "All you got to do is try. Now come on," and I hauled him up once more.

It seemed so hopeless from the beginning that it's a miracle I didn't give up. But all of us must have something or someone to be proud of, and Doodle had become mine. I did not know then that pride is a wonderful, terrible thing, a seed that bears two vines, life and death. Every day that summer we went to the pine beside the stream of Old Woman Swamp, and I put him on his feet at least a hundred times each afternoon. Occasionally I too became discouraged because it didn't seem as if he was trying, and I would say, "Doodle, don't you *want* to learn to walk?"

He'd nod his head, and I'd say, "Well, if you don't keep trying, you'll never learn." Then I'd paint for him a picture of us as old men, white-haired, him with a long white beard and me still pulling him around in the go-cart. This never failed to make him try again.

Finally one day, after many weeks of practicing, he stood alone for a few seconds. When he fell, I grabbed him in my arms and hugged him, our laughter pealing through the swamp like a ringing bell. Now we knew it could be done. Hope no longer hid in the dark palmetto thicket but perched like a cardinal in the lacy toothbrush tree, brilliantly visible. "Yes, yes," I cried, and he cried it too, and the grass beneath us was soft and the smell of the swamp was sweet.

With success so imminent, we decided not to tell anyone until he could actually walk. Each day, barring rain, we sneaked into Old Woman Swamp, and by cotton-picking time Doodle was ready to show what he could do. He still wasn't able to walk far, but we could wait no longer. Keeping a nice secret is very hard to do, like holding your breath. We chose to reveal all on October eighth, Doodle's sixth birthday, and for weeks ahead we mooned around the house, promising everybody a most spectacular surprise. Aunt Nicey said that, after so much talk, if we produced anything less tremendous than the Resurrection, she was going to be disappointed.

At breakfast on our chosen day, when Mama, Daddy, and Aunt Nicey were in the dining room, I brought Doodle to the door in the go-cart just as usual and had them turn their backs, making them cross their hearts and hope to die if they peeked. I helped Doodle up, and when he was standing alone I let them look. There wasn't a sound as Doodle walked slowly across the room and sat down at his place at the table. Then Mama began to cry and ran over to him, hugging him and kissing him. Daddy hugged him too, so I went to Aunt Nicey, who was thanks praying in the doorway, and began to waltz her around. We danced together quite well until she came down on my big toe with her brogans, hurting me so badly I thought I was crippled for life.

Doodle told them it was I who had taught him to walk, so everyone wanted to hug me, and I began to cry.

"What are you crying for?" asked Daddy, but I couldn't answer. They did not know that I did it for myself; that pride, whose slave I was, spoke to me louder than all their voices, and that Doodle walked only because I was ashamed of having a crippled brother.

Within a few months Doodle had learned to walk well and his go-cart was put up in the barn loft (it's still there) beside his little mahogany coffin. Now, when we roamed off together, resting often, we never turned back until our destination had been reached, and to help pass the time, we took up lying. From the beginning Doodle was a terrible liar and he got me in the habit. Had anyone stopped to listen to us, we would have been sent off to Dix Hill.

My lies were scary, involved, and usually pointless, but Doodle's were twice as crazy. People in his stories all had wings and flew wherever they wanted to go. His favorite lie was about a boy named Peter who had a pet peacock with a ten-foot tail. Peter wore a golden robe that glittered so brightly that when he walked through the sunflowers they turned away from the sun to face him. When Peter was ready to go to sleep, the peacock spread his magnificent tail, enfolding the boy gently like a closing go-to-sleep flower, burying him in the gloriously iridescent, rustling vortex. Yes, I must admit it. Doodle could beat me lying.

Doodle and I spent lots of time thinking about our future. We decided that when we were grown we'd live in Old Woman Swamp and pick dog-tongue for a living. Beside the stream, he planned, we'd build us a house of whispering leaves and the swamp birds would be our chickens. All day long (when we weren't gathering dog-tongue) we'd swing through the cypresses on the rope vines, and if it rained we'd huddle beneath an umbrella tree and play stickfrog. Mama and Daddy could come and live with us if they wanted to. He even came up with the idea that he could marry Mama and I could marry Daddy. Of course, I was old enough to know this wouldn't work out, but the picture he painted was so beautiful and serene that all I could do was whisper Yes, yes.

Once I had succeeded in teaching Doodle to walk, I began to believe in my own infallibility and I prepared a terrific development program for him, unknown to Mama and Daddy, of course. I would teach him to run, to swim, to climb trees, and to fight. He, too, now believed in my infallibility, so we set the deadline for these accomplishments less than a year away, when, it had been decided, Doodle could start to school.

That winter we didn't make much progress, for I was in school and Doodle suffered from one bad cold after another. But when spring came, rich and warm, we raised our sights again. Success lay at the end of summer like a pot of gold,[2] and our campaign got off to a good start. On hot days, Doodle and I went down to Horsehead Landing and I gave him swimming lessons or showed him how to row a boat. Sometimes we descended into the cool greenness of Old Woman Swamp and climbed the rope vines or boxed scientifically beneath the pine where he had learned to walk. Promise hung about us like the leaves, and wherever we looked, ferns unfurled and birds broke into song.

That summer, the summer of 1918, was blighted. In May and June there was no rain and the crops withered, curled up, then died under the thirsty sun. One morning in July a hurricane came out of the east, tipping over the oaks in the yard and splitting the limbs of the elm trees. That afternoon it roared back out of the west, blew the fallen oaks around, snapping their roots and tearing them out of the earth like a hawk at the entrails of a chicken. Cotton bolls were wrenched from the stalks and lay like green walnuts in the valleys between the rows, while the cornfield leaned over uniformly so that the tassels touched the ground. Doodle and I followed Daddy out into the cotton field, where he stood, shoulders sagging, surveying the ruin. When his chin sank down onto his chest, we were frightened, and Doodle slipped his hand into mine. Suddenly Daddy straightened his shoulders, raised a giant knuckly fist, and with a voice that seemed to rumble out of the earth itself began cursing heaven, hell, the weather, and the Republican Party. Doodle and I, prodding each other and giggling, went back to the house, knowing that everything would be all right.

---

2. The author is comparing success at the end of summer to the pot of gold that is said to lie at the end of the rainbow.

And during that summer, strange names were heard through the house: Château Thierry, Amiens, Soissons, and in her blessing at the supper table, Mama once said, "And bless the Pearsons, whose boy Joe was lost at Belleau Wood."[3]

So we came to that clove of seasons. School was only a few weeks away, and Doodle was far behind schedule. He could barely clear the ground when climbing up the rope vines and his swimming was certainly not passable. We decided to double our efforts, to make that last drive and reach our pot of gold. I made him swim until he turned blue and row until he couldn't lift an oar. Wherever we went, I purposely walked fast, and although he kept up, his face turned red and his eyes became glazed. Once, he could go no further, so he collapsed on the ground and began to cry.

"Aw, come on, Doodle," I urged. "You can do it. Do you want to be different from everybody else when you start school?"

"Does it make any difference?"

"It certainly does," I said. "Now, come on," and I helped him up.

As we slipped through dog days, Doodle began to look feverish, and Mama felt his forehead, asking him if he felt ill. At night he didn't sleep well, and sometimes he had nightmares, crying out until I touched him and said, "Wake up, Doodle. Wake up."

It was Saturday noon, just a few days before school was to start. I should have already admitted defeat, but my pride wouldn't let me. The excitement of our program had now been gone for weeks, but still we kept on with a tired doggedness. It was too late to turn back, for we had both wandered too far into a net of expectations and had left no crumbs behind.

Daddy, Mama, Doodle, and I were seated at the dining-room table having lunch. It was a hot day, with all the windows and doors open in case a breeze should come. In the kitchen Aunt Nicey was humming softly. After a long silence, Daddy spoke. "It's so calm, I wouldn't be surprised if we had a storm this afternoon."

"I haven't heard a rain frog," said Mama, who believed in signs, as she served the bread around the table.

"I did," declared Doodle. "Down in the swamp."

"He didn't," I said contrarily.

"You did, eh?" said Daddy, ignoring my denial.

"I certainly did," Doodle reiterated, scowling at me over the top of his iced-tea glass, and we were quiet again.

Suddenly, from out in the yard, came a strange croaking noise. Doodle stopped eating, with a piece of bread poised ready for his mouth, his eyes popped round like two blue buttons. "What's that?" he whispered.

I jumped up, knocking over my chair, and had reached the door when Mama called, "Pick up the chair, sit down again, and say excuse me."

By the time I had done this, Doodle had excused himself and had slipped out into the yard. He was looking up into the bleeding tree. "It's a great big red bird!" he called.

The bird croaked loudly again, and Mama and Daddy came out into the yard. We shaded our eyes with our hands against the hazy glare of the sun and peered up through the still leaves. On the topmost branch a bird the size of a chicken, with scarlet feathers and long legs, was perched precariously. Its wings hung down loosely, and as we watched, a feather dropped away and floated slowly down through the green leaves.

"It's not even frightened of us," Mama said.

"It looks tired," Daddy added. "Or maybe sick."

Doodle's hands were clasped at his throat, and I had never seen him stand still so long. "What is it?" he asked.

Daddy shook his head. "I don't know, maybe it's—"

---

3. **Château Thierry**\shə ▲tō tyĕ 'rē\ **Amiens**\ä·mĭ ▲ĕnz\ **Soissons**\'swä ▲saü\ and **Belleau**\bə ▲lō\ **Wood** were scenes of World War I battles in which U.S. troops took part in 1918.

At that moment the bird began to flutter, but the wings were uncoordinated, and amid much flapping and a spray of flying feathers, it tumbled down, bumping through the limbs of the bleeding tree and landing at our feet with a thud. Its long, graceful neck jerked twice into an S, then straightened out, and the bird was still. A white veil came over the eyes and the long white beak unhinged. Its legs were crossed and its clawlike feet were delicately curved at rest. Even death did not mar its grace, for it lay on the earth like a broken vase of red flowers, and we stood around it, awed by its exotic beauty.

"It's dead," Mama said.

"What is it?" Doodle repeated.

"Go bring me the bird book," said Daddy.

I ran into the house and brought back the bird book. As we watched, Daddy thumbed through its pages. "It's a scarlet ibis," he said, pointing to a picture. "It lives in the tropics—South America to Florida. A storm must have brought it here."

Sadly, we all looked back at the bird. A scarlet ibis! How many miles it had traveled to die like this, in *our* yard, beneath the bleeding tree.

"Let's finish lunch," Mama said, nudging us back toward the dining room.

"I'm not hungry," said Doodle, and he knelt down beside the ibis.

"We've got peach cobbler for dessert," Mama tempted from the doorway.

Doodle remained kneeling. "I'm going to bury him."

"Don't you dare touch him," Mama warned. "There's no telling what disease he might have had."

"All right," said Doodle. "I won't."

Daddy, Mama, and I went back to the dining-room table, but we watched Doodle through the open door. He took out a piece of string from his pocket and, without touching the ibis, looped one end around its neck. Slowly, while singing softly *Shall We Gather at the River,* he carried the bird around to the front yard and dug a hole in the flower garden, next to the petunia bed. Now we were watching him through the front window, but he didn't know it. His awkwardness at digging the hole with a shovel whose handle was twice as long as he was made us laugh, and we covered our mouths with our hands so he wouldn't hear.

When Doodle came into the dining room, he found us seriously eating our cobbler. He was pale and lingered just inside the screen door. "Did you get the scarlet ibis buried?" asked Daddy.

Doodle didn't speak but nodded his head.

"Go wash your hands, and then you can have some peach cobbler," said Mama.

"I'm not hungry," he said.

"Dead birds is bad luck," said Aunt Nicey, poking her head from the kitchen door. "Specially *red* dead birds!"

As soon as I had finished eating, Doodle and I hurried off to Horsehead Landing. Time was short, and Doodle still had a long way to go if he was going to keep up with the other boys when he started school. The sun, gilded with the yellow cast of autumn, still burned fiercely, but the dark green woods through which we passed were shady and cool. When we reached the landing, Doodle said he was too tired to swim, so we got into a skiff and floated down the creek with the tide. Far off in the marsh a rail was scolding, and over on the beach locusts were singing in the myrtle trees. Doodle did not speak and kept his head turned away, letting one hand trail limply in the water.

After we had drifted a long way, I put the oars in place and made Doodle row back against the tide. Black clouds began to gather in the southwest, and he kept watching them, trying to pull the oars a little faster. When we reached Horsehead Landing, lightning was playing across half the sky and thunder roared out, hiding even the sound of the sea. The sun disappeared and darkness descended, almost like night. Flocks of marsh crows flew by, heading inland to their roosting trees, and two egrets, squawking, arose from the oyster-rock shallows and careened away.

Doodle was both tired and frightened, and when he stepped from the skiff he collapsed onto the mud, sending an armada of fiddler crabs rustling off into the marsh grass. I helped him up, and as he wiped the mud off his trousers, he smiled at me ashamedly. He had failed and we both knew it, so we started back home, racing the storm. We never spoke (What are the words that can solder cracked pride?), but I knew he was watching me, watching for a sign of mercy. The lightning was near now, and from fear he walked so close behind me he kept stepping on my heels. The faster I walked, the faster he walked, so I began to run. The rain was coming, roaring through the pines, and then, like a bursting Roman candle, a gum tree ahead of us was shattered by a bolt of lightning. When the deafening peal of thunder had died, and in the moment before the rain arrived, I heard Doodle, who had fallen behind, cry out, "Brother, Brother, don't leave me! Don't leave me!"

The knowledge that Doodle's and my plans had come to naught was bitter, and that streak of cruelty within me awakened. I ran as fast as I could, leaving him far behind with a wall of rain dividing us. The drops stung my face like nettles, and the wind flared the wet glistening leaves of the bordering trees. Soon I could hear his voice no more.

I hadn't run too far before I became tired, and the flood of childish spite evanesced as well. I stopped and waited for Doodle. The sound of rain was everywhere, but the wind had died and it fell straight down in parallel paths like ropes hanging from the sky. As I waited, I peered through the downpour, but no one came. Finally I went back and found him huddled beneath a red nightshade bush beside the road. He was sitting on the ground, his face buried in his arms, which were resting on his drawn-up knees. "Let's go, Doodle," I said.

He didn't answer, so I placed my hand on his forehead and lifted his head. Limply, he fell backwards onto the earth. He had been bleeding from the mouth, and his neck and the front of his shirt were stained a brilliant red.

"Doodle! Doodle!" I cried, shaking him, but there was no answer but the ropy rain. He lay very awkwardly, with his head thrown far back, making his vermillion neck appear unusually long and slim. His little legs, bent sharply at the knees, had never before seemed so fragile, so thin.

I began to weep, and the tear-blurred vision in red before me looked very familiar. "Doodle!" I screamed above the pounding storm and threw my body to the earth above his. For a long long time, it seemed forever, I lay there crying, sheltering my fallen scarlet ibis from the heresy of rain.

I

LITTLE BOY WITH A BIG HEART

Pride has many ways of showing itself. Mr. Whalen had such pride in Marvin that he was willing to punch anyone who dared suggest that Marvin was less than perfect, while Doodle's brother was too proud to accept a handicapped member into his inner circle. Pride drove him to destroy what had become very precious.

Consider and discuss:

1. Why was it such a disappointment to the older boy when the baby was born strange-looking and sickly?

2. What was the first indication that "William Armstrong" had a great deal of courage despite his weak heart? Why was he a burden to his older brother? What was Doodle's reaction when he was first taken to Old Woman Swamp? How did this affect the relationship between the two brothers? Was his older brother unnaturally cruel to Doodle? How did Doodle regard his older brother?

3. Do you feel that this family made a close and pleasant "inner circle"? What is the relationship of the mother and father with the two boys? What place does Aunt Nicey have in the circle?

II

IMPLICATIONS

The following statements are taken directly from the story. Express your ideas concerning their meaning.

1. ". . . pride is a wonderful, terrible thing, a seed that bears two vines, life and death."

2. "There is within me (and with sadness I have watched it in others) a knot of cruelty borne by the stream of love . . ."

III

TECHNIQUES

Theme

Either of the two quotations given in Part II could be considered the theme or basic idea for "The Scarlet Ibis." Select the one you believe to be better and explain why.

Effect

This is a story written with sensitivity and beauty of language. The atmosphere of haunting sadness which unifies the narrative is established in the first paragraph and is felt throughout the story. Amidst this atmosphere, the author makes the relationship between the two brothers seem natural and believable.

In creating his atmosphere, James Hurst uses unusual words and expressions, *imaginative language, symbolism,* and *foreshadowing.*

Consider and discuss:

1. Three unusual words or expressions. Note specifically the identification of the time when the story opens, and the indication of something strange about the baby's birth.

2. Three examples of symbolism, in particular:

a. The many direct and indirect references to a certain color.

b. What the fall season symbolizes.

c. What is symbolic about the coming of the great red bird.

3. Two of the most vivid examples of simile and metaphor.

4. The foreshadowing of the ending.

5. The final effect or impression of this story. In a brief paper, compare its effect with that of "The Hero."

Narrative Viewpoint

From whose viewpoint does the author narrate his story? Discuss the advantage of telling it in first person.

IV

WORDS

A. English is a flexible language, so speakers and writers are often inventive in their use of it. Using hyphens, they sometimes link together two or more words to function as a single word. An example of this linkage can be seen in the sentence "I resent her holier-than-thou attitude." In this sentence, three words serve the purpose of a single-word modifier. And in the preceding sentence, *single-word* functions as one word. Sometimes users of the language connect quite a number of words together: "Ralph had that I-wish-I-knew-what-was-going-on expression on his face." Here eight words are used where one word, *puzzled,* could have been used. Three additional examples of word-combining may be cited from "The Scarlet Ibis": "cotton-picking time," "go-to-sleep flowers," and "tear-blurred vision." When they are used frequently enough, words linked together like those mentioned above become a regular part of our vocabulary and are listed in the dictionary; examples are *round-the-clock* ("continuous"), *back-up* ("substitute"), and *say-so* (informal for "authority"). What is meant by the linked words in each of the following sentences:

1. This team has a *never-say-die* spirit.

2. On every issue he is a *middle-of-the-roader.*

3. He's a great *open-field* football carrier!

B. Some plants and animals are named after people who were in one way or another associated with them. *Magnolia* and *Oriole,* mentioned in "The Scarlet Ibis," are good examples. *Magnolia* owes its name to Pierre Magnol (1638–1715), the French botanist. A magnolia is any of a group of trees and shrubs having showy white, pink, purple, or yellow flowers. The baltimore oriole, an American songbird, was named after Lord Baltimore, the founder of Maryland; his coat of arms was black and orange, the colors of the male oriole. Also based on a person's name is *poinsettia* —from Joel Roberts Poinsett (1799–1851), a U.S. Minister to Mexico. Poinsett developed an interest in this Mexican plant, with its large scarlet bracts surrounding small yellow flowers, and brought it back to his own country. Concentrating just on plants, try to determine the name of the person from which each of the following derives its name: *fuchsia, begonia, camellia, marigold, zinnia, peony, dahlia,* and *narcissus.* (Note that some of these plant names are derived from mythological names.)

At fourteen, P.S. was already six feet tall;
he could conjugate Latin verbs to suit himself,
and he knew all about the Toad Code.
How he could live up
to both his school's Honor Code
and the expectations of his family, however,
were two quite different matters.

So Much Unfairness
of Things

C. D. B. BRYAN

The Virginia Preparatory School lies just off the Shirley Highway between Washington, D.C., and Richmond. It is a small Southern school with dull red brick dormitories and class-room buildings, quiet old school buildings with quiet old Southern names—Page House, Stuart Hall, Randolph Hall, Breckinridge, Pinckney, and Coulter. The high brick wall that surrounds the school is known as the Breastworks, and the shallow pond behind the football field is the Crater. V.P.S. is an old school, with an old school's traditions. A sign commemorates the use of the school by Union troops as a military hospital in 1861, and every October the school celebrates "Liberation Day," in honor of the day in 1866 when the school reopened.

Graduates of the Virginia Preparatory School who have not returned for some years are shocked by the glass-and-steel apartment houses and cinder-block ramblers that have sprung up around the school grounds, but once they have driven along the Breastworks and passed through the ornate wrought-iron East Gate, they see, with satisfaction, that the school

has not changed. Neither have its customs. For example, new boys, or "toads," still must obey the Toad Code. They must be courteous to old boys and faculty. They must know the school song and cheers by the end of the second week. They must know the names of all members of the faculty and the varsity football team. They must hold doors open for old boys and see that old boys are served first in the dining room. And they must "run relay"—meaning that they have to wake up the old boys in the morning when they wish to be awakened and see that they are not disturbed when they wish to sleep.

Philip Sadler Wilkinson was fourteen; he was an old boy. The new boy shook him lightly. "Mr. Wilkinson? Mr. Wilkinson? It's five-thirty, sir. You asked me to wake you up."

Next year the new boy would be permitted to call Philip Sadler Wilkinson "P.S.," like the others. He watched P.S. stretch, turn over, and go back to sleep. "Sir, Hey! Wake up!"

P.S. rolled out of his metal cot, rubbed his eyes, felt around the top of his desk for his glasses, put them on, and looked at the new boy.

"Toad?"

"Yes, sir?"

"What is the date?"

"Thursday, the seventh of June."

"How much longer do we have until the end of the school year?"

"Seven days, twenty-three hours, and"—the new boy looked at his wristwatch—"and thir-teen minutes, sir."

P.S. smiled. "Are you sure?"

"No, sir."

"Ah-hah! Ah-HAH! Toad, assume the posi-tion!"

The new boy locked his knees and bent over and grabbed his ankles.

"What is a 'toad,' toad?" P.S. asked.

"Sir, a toad is a loathsome warty creature who eats insects and worms, sir. A toad is the lowest form of amphibian. A toad is despicable."

"Well, well, now, straighten those knees, toad." P.S. looked at the new boy and saw that his face was turning red with strain. "Toad, are you in pain?"

313

"No, sir," the new boy lied.

"Then you may straighten up."

The new boy massaged his calves. "Honestly, P.S., you're a sadist."

"No, no, wait till next year. You'll be pulling the same thing on some toad yourself. I had it done to me, you had it done to you. And did I detect you calling me by my rightful name?"

The new boy smiled.

"Ah, you toads will never learn. Assume the position."

The new boy started to bend over again.

"Oh, go away," P.S. said. The new boy started out of the door and P.S. called him back. "Hey, toad? You gonna kill the Latin exam?"

"I hope so."

"How do you conjugate the verb 'to spit'?"

"*Exspuo, exspuere, exspui—*"

"Heck, no!" P.S. laughed. It's *spitto, spittere, ach tui, splattus!*"

The new boy groaned and left the room.

P.S. looked at his watch. It was twenty minutes to six. He could hear the new boy waking up the boy in the next room. P.S. picked up his water glass and toothbrush and tiptoed down the corridor. He stopped at Charlie Merritt's room and knocked softly.

"Who is it?"

"It's me, Charlie."

"Oh, hey, P.S. Come on in."

P.S. pushed aside the curtain of the cubicle. Charlie was sitting at his desk studying.

"Morning," P.S. whispered.

"Morning."

"Studying the Latin?"

"Yep."

"You know how to conjugate the verb 'to spit'?"

"Yep," Charlie said. "*Spitto, spittere, ach—*"

"O.K., O.K.!" P.S. laughed. "You gonna kill the exam?"

"I hope so. You think you'll pass it?"

"Doubt it. I haven't passed one yet." P.S. looked over at Charlie's bureau. "Say, Charlie? Can I borrow your toothpaste? I'm out."

"Sure, but roll it from the bottom of the tube, will you?"

P.S. picked up the toothpaste and went down the hall to the bathroom. Mabrey, the head monitor, was shaving. P.S. watched him in the mirror.

"You must have a porcupine for a father," P.S. said. "You've got the heaviest beard in the school."

Mabrey began to shave the length of his neck. "Wilkinson, you're about as funny as a rubber crutch."

"Cut your throat! Cut your throat!" P.S. began to dance around behind Mabrey, sprinkling voodoo potions on the top of the older student's head. "Monkey dust! Monkey dust! Oh, black Pizoola! Great Kubla of the Ancient Curse! Make this bad man cut his throat!"

Mabrey cursed and a small red stain began to seep through the lather on his throat. "P.S., *will you get out of here!*"

P.S. stared, eyes wide open, at the broadening stain.

"Hey! Hey, it worked!"

Mabrey undid the towel from around his waist and snapped P.S.'s skinny behind. P.S. yelped and jumped away. "Hey, Mr. Mabrey, sir? Hey, Mabrey? I'm sorry, I really am. I didn't know it would work."

"What would work?"

"My voodoo curse. I didn't know it would make you cut yourself."

"For Pete's sake, P.S., what're you talking about? I cut a pimple. Will you leave me alone before I throw you out of a closed window?"

P.S. was quiet for a moment. Then he moved over to the washbasin next to Mabrey and looked at himself in the mirror. He ran his fingers through his light-brown hair and pushed his glasses higher on his nose. "Hey, Mabrey? Do you think I'm fresh? I mean, I have great respect for you—you being the head monitor and all. I mean it. Sometimes I worry. I mean, do you think I'm too fresh?"

Mabrey finished rinsing his face. "P.S., kid," he said as he dried himself. "You're all right. You're a nice guy. And I'm willing to bet that if you could only learn to throw a baseball from center field to second base overhand, you might

315

turn out to be a pretty fair little baseball player."

"*Overhand!* Whaddya mean 'overhand'? They call me 'Deadeye Wilkinson.'" P.S. wound up with an imaginary baseball and threw it as hard as he could. Then he pantomimed being the second baseman. He crouched and caught the incoming ball at his knees and thrust his hand down to tag out the runner. "*Safe!*" he shouted. "I mean, out! Out! Out!"

"Too late," Mabrey said, and laughed. "An umpire never changes his decision."

"I meant *out,*" P.S. said.

Mabrey disappeared down the hall.

P.S. brushed his teeth, being careful to squeeze the toothpaste from the bottom of the tube. He looked at himself in the mirror and chanted, "*Fuero, fueris, fuerit, fuerimus, fueritis, fuerint!*" He examined his upper lip and was disappointed. He wished that he didn't have such a young face. He wished he had a heavy beard, like Mabrey. He washed his face, wet his hair down, and walked back into Charlie's room. Charlie was P.S.'s best friend. He was very short. The other boys kidded him about being an engineer for Lionel trains.[1] P.S. was very tall and thin, and he had not yet grown into his height. At fourteen he was already six feet tall, and he had a tendency to stoop to compensate. He and Charlie were known as Mutt and Jeff. When P.S. entered the room, Charlie was curled upon his bed studying his Latin notes. He didn't look up until P.S. dropped the toothpaste tube on his pillow.

"Rolled from the bottom," P.S. said.

"Hey, how do you expect to pass your Latin exam if you don't study? I heard you and Mabrey clowning around in there."

"If I don't study!" P.S. said. "Do you know how long I've studied for this exam? If I flunk it again this year, I get to keep the trophy."

"What trophy?"

"For Pete's sake, I don't know what trophy. But I'll get something for sure. I've spent the last two weeks practically doing nothing but studying Latin. I recopied all my notes. I underlined practically the whole book. And I memorized all the irregular verbs. Come on, come on, ask me anything. If I don't pass it this year, I've had it. Come on, ask me anything."

"O.K., what's the word for 'ridge'?"

"The word for 'ridge'?" P.S. stalled.

"Yep."

P.S. thought for a moment. "Look, I don't know. Make it two for three."

"The word for 'ridge' is '*iugum.*'" Charlie looked at his notes. "O.K., two out of three. What's the word for 'crowd'? And 'troop,' as in 'a troop of cavalry'?"

"The word for 'crowd' is '*turba, turbae.*' . . . What was the other one?"

"'Troop of cavalry.'"

"'Cavalry' is '*equitatus.*' . . . I don't know. What is 'troop'?"

"'Troop' is '*turma.*'" Charlie laughed. "Well, you got one out of three."

"Did I get partial credit for the 'cavalry'?"

"Nope."

"I hope Dr. Fairfax is more lenient than you are."

"He won't be," Charlie said.

"If I flunk the Latin exam again this year . . ."

"How come you flunked it last year?"

"How come anybody flunks an exam? I didn't know the answers. Boy, Charlie, I don't know what I'm going to do with you. If you weren't such a nice guy and lend me your toothpaste and things like that all the time, I'd probably feed you to the—to the what's-their-name fish. Those fish who eat people in South America all the time."[2]

"Well, since you don't know what to do with me, as a start, why don't you let me study?"

"Sure. Sure, O.K. . . . O.K., be a grind. See if I care."

P.S. walked back to his cubicle and pulled his Ullman and Henry "Latin II" from his unpainted bookcase. First he studied the irregular verbs in the back of the book. Then he went over his vocabulary list. He concentrated for as

---

1. **Lionel**\ˈlai·ə·nəl\ trains are a well-known line of toy trains.
2. P.S. is thinking of the **piranha**\pī ˈran·yə\ fish.

316

long as he could; then he leaned out of his window to look at the shadows of the trees directly below, dropped a penny out of the window to see if a squirrel would pick it up, checked his window sill to see if the cookie crumbs he had left for the mockingbird were still there.

He turned back to his Latin book and leafed through the Forestier illustrations of Roman soldiers. He picked up the picture his father had given him last Christmas. Within the frame were four small round photographs of Wilkinsons in uniform. There was his father as an infantry major during the Second World War, his grandfather as a captain in the field artillery during the First World War, his great-great-grandfather as a corporal in a soft gray Confederate uniform and a great-great-great-great something or other in a dark uniform with a lot of bright buttons. P.S. didn't know who the last picture was of. He imagined it to be somebody from the Revolutionary War. P.S. had seen the oil portrait the photograph had been taken from hanging in the hallway of his grandfather's house. P.S. had the long, thin nose of the other Wilkinsons in the pictures, but he still had the round cheeks of youth and the perfect eyebrows. He was the fifteenth of his family to attend the Virginia Preparatory School. Among the buildings at V.P.S. there was a Wilkinson Memorial Library and a Sadler Gymnasium. When P.S. was packing to begin his first year at the school, his father had said, "Son, when your great-grandfather went off to V.P.S., his father gave him a dozen silk handkerchiefs and a pair of warm gloves. When I went off to V.P.S., your grandfather gave me a dozen silk handkerchiefs and a pair of warm gloves. And now here are a dozen silk handkerchiefs and a pair of warm gloves for you."

P.S. looked at the brightly patterned Liberty-silk handkerchiefs and the fuzzy red mittens. No thirteen-year-old ever wore red mittens, except girls, and particularly not fuzzy red mittens. And P.S. knew he would never dare to wear the silk handkerchiefs.

"Well, thank you very much, Dad," he said.

"That's all right, son."

P.S. left the red mittens behind when he went away to V.P.S. He used two of the silk handkerchiefs to cover the top of his bureau and bookcase, gave one other away to a girl, and hid the rest beneath his underwear on the second shelf of his bureau. His father had done very well at the school; he had been a senior monitor, editor-in-chief of the yearbook, and a distance runner in winter and spring track. P.S. hoped he would do as well, but he knew he had disappointed his father so far. When he flunked the Latin examination last year and tried to explain to his father that he just could not do Latin, he could see the disbelief in his father's eyes. "Good Lord, son, you just didn't study. 'Can't do Latin,' what nonsense!" But P.S. knew that studying had nothing to do with it. His father said that no Wilkinson had ever flunked at V.P.S.; P.S. was the first. His father was not the kind to lose his temper. P.S. wished he were. When P.S. had done something wrong, his father would just look at him and smile sadly and shake his head.

The boy had never felt particularly close to his father. He had never been able to talk to or with his father. He had found the best means of getting along with his father was to keep out of his way. He had given up their ever sharing anything. He had no illusions about leading a calendar-picture life with his father—canoeing or hunting together. He could remember trying to get his father to play catch with him and how his father would always say, "Not now, son, not now." But there were certain occasions that his father felt should be shared with P.S. These were the proper father-son occasions that made P.S. feel like some sort of ornament. There would be Father's Day, or the big football game of the season. P.S. would be told to order two tickets, and the afternoon of the game he and his father would watch the first half together. His father remembered all of the cheers and was shocked when P.S. didn't remember some of the words to the school song. At the half, his father would disappear to talk to his friends and P.S. would be left alone to watch the overcoats or umbrellas.

317

After the game P.S. would wander back to the field house, where the alumni tables were set up. He would locate his father and stand next to him until his father introduced him to the persons he was talking to. Then his father would say, "Run along, son. I'll meet you back in your room." So, P.S. would go back to his room and wait for his father to come by. The boy would straighten up the bed, dust the bureau, and sweep the floor. And then after a long wait his father would come in and sit down. "Well, how are you, son?" the conversation would always start. And P.S. would answer, "Fine, thank you, sir." His father would look around the room and remark about its not being large enough to swing a cat in, then there would be two or three anecdotes about the times when he was a boy at V.P.S., and then he would look at his watch and say, "Well, I guess I'd better be pushing off." His father would ask him if there was anything he needed, and P.S. would say that he didn't think there was anything. His father would give him a five-dollar bill and drive away. And P.S., with enormous relief, would go look for Charlie. "Did you and your dad have a good time?" Charlie would ask. "Sure," P.S. would say. And that would end the conversation.

P.S. knew that his father loved him, but he also knew better than to expect any sign of affection. Affection always seemed to embarrass his father. P.S. remembered his first year at school, when his father had first come up to see him. He had been very happy to see his father, and when they were saying goodbye P.S. stepped forward as usual to kiss him and his father drew away. P.S. always made it a point now to shake hands with his father. And at fourteen respect and obedience had taken the place of love.

P.S. picked up his Latin notes and went over the translations he had completed. He wished he knew what questions would be asked. In last year's exam there were questions from all over the book, and it made the exam very difficult to study for, if they were going to do that. He pic-

tured himself handing in the finished examination to Dr. Fairfax and saying, "Sir? Wilkinsons do not flunk. Please grade my exam accordingly."

P.S. looked at his wristwatch. The dining hall would begin serving breakfast in fifteen minutes. He made his bed and put on a clean pair of khakis and a button-down shirt. He slipped into his old white bucks and broke a lace tying them, and pulled out the shorter piece and threaded what was left through the next eyelet up, as the older boys did. He tidied up his room for inspection, picked up his notes, and went back to Charlie's room. Charlie was sweeping the halls and emptying all trash baskets. P.S. entered and sat down on the bed.

"Hey, P.S.! I just made the bed!"

"O.K., O.K., I'll straighten it up when I leave." P.S. ran his fingers across the desk top. "Merritt, two demerits—dust. . . . Hey, you know what, Charlie?"

Charlie dusted the desk and then said, "What?"

"You're such a grump in the morning. I sure'd hate to be married to you."

"Well, I wouldn't worry about that. In the first place, my parents wouldn't approve."

"I'm not so sure that my family would want me to marry a Merritt, either. I think you'd have to take my family name. I mean, you know, you're just not our class."

"P.S., buddy, you're in a class all by yourself." . . .

"Well, you know what I meant."

"I don't know anything at all."

P.S. looked at Charlie for a moment, then he laughed. "I'm not going to take advantage of your last remark. I'm much too good a sport to rake you over the coals when you place your ample foot in your ample mouth."

"*Ample foot!*" Charlie held up his foot. "I've got a very small foot. It's a sign of good breeding."

"Only in horses, Twinkletoes, only in horses."

"Horses, *horses!* What do horses have to do with it?"

"Ask me no questions and I'll tell you no lies."

P.S. leafed through Charlie's notes. "Hey, the exam's at ten-thirty, isn't it?"

"Yep. If you flunk Latin again, will they make you go to summer school?"

"Probably. I really think it's archaic the way they make you pass Latin to get out of this place."

"Boy, I sure hope I pass it," Charlie said.

"You will. You will. You're the brain in the class."

"Come on, let's go to chow."

"That's what I've been waiting for, my good buddy, my good friend, old pal of mine." P.S. jumped off the bed, scooped up his notebook, and started out of the room.

"Hey!" Charlie said. "What about the bed?"

At eight o'clock chapel, P.S. knelt in the pew and prayed: *"Dear God, I pray that I pass my Latin exam this morning. . . . If I can pass this exam, then I'll do anything you want me to do. . . . God, please. If I don't pass this exam, I've really had it. . . .* They must have made these pews for midgets; I never fit in them right. . . . How am I ever going to get out to Colorado this summer unless I pass that exam? . . . *Please God, I don't want a high grade, all I want is to pass . . . and you don't have to help me on the others. . . . I don't want to pass this exam for myself only. I mean, it means a lot to my family. My father will be very disappointed if I flunk the exam. . . .* I wonder if Charlie will be able to go out to Colorado with me. . . . *God bless Mom, God bless Dad, God bless Grandpa Sadler and Grandma Sadler, God bless Grandpa Wilkinson and Granny Wilkinson, God bless all my relatives I haven't mentioned. . . . Amen. And . . . and God? Please, please help me to pass this exam."*

At ten-fifteen, P.S. and Charlie fell in step and walked over to Randolph Hall, where the examination was to be held.

"Well, if we don't know it now, we never will," Charlie said.

"Even if I did know it now, I wouldn't know it tomorrow." P.S. reached into his pants pocket and pulled out his lucky exam tie. It was a stained and unraveled blue knit. As they walked up the path, he was careful to tie the tie backward, the wide end next to his shirt, the seam facing out. Then he checked his watch pocket to see that his lucky silver dollar was there.

"What's the Latin for 'then'?" Charlie asked.

"*'Tum,'*" P.S. answered. "Tums for your *tummy."*

"What's the word for 'thence,' or 'from there'?"

"*'Inde.'*" P.S. began to sing: *Inde* evening *byde* moonlight you could *hearde—*"

"For Pete's sake, P.S.!" Charlie laughed.

"You don't like my singing?"

"Not much."

"You know? I'm thinking of joining the choir and glee club next year. You know why? They've got a couple of dances next fall. One with St. Catharine's and another with St. Tim's. You wanta try out with me?"

"I don't know. I can't sing."

"Who's gonna sing?" P.S. grabbed Charlie's arm and growled, "Baby, I'm no singer, I'm a lover!"

"Lover? Who says you're a lover?"

"Ask me no questions and I'll tell you no lies."

P.S. and Charlie walked up the worn wooden steps of Randolph Hall to the third-floor study hall, where the Latin examination was to be given. They both were in the upper study hall, since they were underclassmen still. P.S.'s desk was in the back corner of the study hall, against the wall. He sat down and brushed the dust off the top of his desk with his palm. Someone had traced a hand into the wood. Others had traced and retraced the hand and deepened the grooves. They had added fingernails and rings. P.S. had added a tattoo. He lifted the desk top and, searching for his pencil sharpener, saw that he had some more Latin translations in his desk. He read them through quickly and decided it was too late to learn anything from them. He pulled out his pencil sharpener and closed his desk. The study hall was filling with boys, who took their places at their desks and called back and forth to each other in their slow

Southern voices. It was a long, thin room with high windows on either side, and the walls were painted a dirty yellow. Between the windows were framed engravings of Roman ruins and Southern generals. The large fluorescent lights above the desks buzzed and blinked into life. A dark, curly-haired boy sat down in the desk next to P.S. and began to empty his pockets of pencils and pens.

"Hey, Jumbo," P.S. said. "You gonna kill the exam?"

"I hope so. If I can get a good grade on it, then I don't have to worry so much about my math exam tomorrow."

"Well, if we don't know it now we never will."

"You're right."

Jumbo had played second-string tackle on the varsity this year. He was expected to be first-string next year, and by his final year, the coaches thought, he might become an All-Virginia High School tackle. Jumbo was a sincere, not very bright student who came from a farm in Virginia and wanted to be a farmer when he finished college. P.S. had sat next to Jumbo all year, but they had never become particularly close friends. Jumbo lived in a different dormitory and had a tendency to stick with the other members of the football team. But P.S. liked him, and Jumbo was really the only member of the football team that he knew at all.

P.S. looked up at the engraving of General Robert E. Lee and his horse, Traveller. He glanced over at Jumbo. Jumbo was cleaning his fingernails with the tip of his automatic pencil.

"Well, good luck," P.S. said.

"Good luck to you."

"I'll need it."

P.S. stood up and looked for Charlie. "Hey! Hey, Charlie?"

Charlie turned around. "Yeah?"

"*Piggo, piggere, squeely, gruntum!*"

"For Pete's sake, P.S.!"

"Hey, P.S.?" someone shouted. "You gonna flunk it again this year?"

"No, no, I don't think so," P.S. answered in mock seriousness. "In point of fact, as the good Dr. Fairfax would say—in point of fact, I might

just come out with the highest grade in class. After all, I'm such a brain."

The noise in the study hall suddenly stopped; Dr. Fairfax had entered. The Latin instructor walked to the back of the study hall, where P.S. was sitting.

"And what was all that about, Wilkinson?"

"Sir, I was telling the others how I'm the brain in your class."

"Indeed?" Dr. Fairfax asked.

"Yes, sir. But I was only kidding."

"Indeed," the Latin instructor said, and the other students laughed.

Dr. Fairfax was a large man with a lean, aesthetic face, which he tried to hide with a military mustache. He had taught at the Virginia Preparatory School since 1919. P.S.'s father had had Dr. Fairfax for a Latin instructor. When P.S. read *Goodbye, Mr. Chips*,[3] he had kept thinking of Dr. Fairfax. The Latin instructor wore the same suit and vest all winter. They were always immaculate. The first day of spring was marked by Dr. Fairfax's appearance in a white linen suit, which he always wore with a small blue bachelor's-button. Before a study hall last spring, someone had placed an alarm clock set to go off during the middle of study hall in one of the tall wastepaper baskets at the rear of the room. The student had then emptied all of the pencil sharpeners and several ink bottles into the basket and covered all this with crumpled-up pad paper. When the alarm clock went off, Dr. Fairfax strode down the aisle and reached into the wastepaper basket for the clock. When he lifted it out, the sleeve of his white linen jacket was covered with ink and pencil shavings. There was a stunned silence in the study hall as Dr. Fairfax looked at his sleeve. And then Dr. Fairfax began to laugh. The old man sat down on one of the desk tops and laughed and laughed, until finally the students had enough nerve to join him. The next day, he appeared in the same linen suit, but it

---

3. **Goodbye, Mr. Chips** is a short novel dealing with an English school instructor; it was written by James Hilton in 1934.

was absolutely clean. Nobody was given demerits or punished in any manner. Dr. Fairfax was P.S.'s favorite instructor. P.S. watched him separate the examination papers and blue books into neat piles at the proctor's desk. Dr. Fairfax looked up at the electric clock over the study-hall door and then at his thin gold pocket watch. He cleared his throat. "Good morning, gentlemen."

"GOOD MORNING, SIR!" the students shouted.

"Gentlemen, there will be no talking during the examination. In the two hours given you, you will have ample time to complete all of the necessary work. When the bell sounds signifying the end of examination, you will cease work immediately. In point of fact, anyone found working after the bell will be looked upon most unfavorably. When you receive your examinations, make certain that the print is legible. Make sure that you place your names on each of your blue books. If you have any difficulty reading the examination, hold your hand above your head and you will be given a fresh copy. The tops of your desks should be cleared of all notes, papers and books. Are there any questions? . . . If not, will Baylor and you, Grandy, and . . . and Merritt . . . will the three of you please pass out the examinations."

P.S. watched Charlie get up and walk over to the desk.

Dr. Fairfax reached into his breast pocket and pulled out a pair of steel-rimmed spectacles. He looked out across the room. "We are nearing the end of the school year," he said. "Examinations always seem to cause students an undue amount of concern. I assure you, I can well remember when I was a student at V.P.S. In point of fact, I was not so very different from some of you—"

The instructor was interrupted by a rasping Bronx cheer. He looked quickly over in the direction of the sound. "Travers, was that you?"

"No, sir."

"Brandon, was that you?"

The student hesitated, then answered, "Yes, sir."

"Brandon, I consider that marked disrespect, and it will cost you ten demerits."

"Aww, sir—"

"Fifteen." Dr. Fairfax cleared his throat again. "Now, if I may continue? . . . Good. There are a few important things to remember when taking an examination. First, do not get upset when you cannot at once answer all of the questions. The examination is designed—"

P.S. stopped listening. Charlie was walking down the aisle toward him.

"Hey, Charlie," he whispered, "give me an easy one."

"There will be no favoritism on my part."

"How does it look?"

"Tough."

"Merritt and Wilkinson?" Dr. Fairfax said. "That last little bit of conversation will cost you each five demerits."

The Latin instructor looked up at the electric clock again. "When you receive your examinations, you may begin. Are there any questions? . . . If not, gentlemen, it might be well for us to remember this ancient Latin proverb: '*Abusus non tollit usum.*'" Dr. Fairfax waited for the laugh. There was none. He cleared his throat again. "Perhaps . . . perhaps we had better ask the class brain what the proverb means. Wilkinson?"

P.S. stood up. "'*Abusus non tollit usum,*' sir?"

"That's right."

"Something like 'Abuse does not tolerate the use,' sir?"

"What does the verb '*tollo, tollere, sustuli, sublatus*' mean?"

"To take away, sir."

"That's right. The proverb, then, is 'Abuse does not take away the use,' or, in the context I was referring to, just because you gentlemen cannot do Latin properly does not mean that it should not be done at all."

"Yes, sir," P.S. said, and he sat down.

Dr. Fairfax unfolded his newspaper, and P.S. began to read the examination. He picked up his pencil and printed in large letters on the cover of his blue book:

PHILIP SADLER WILKINSON
LATIN EXAMINATION
LATIN II—DR. FAIRFAX
VIRGINIA PREPARATORY SCHOOL
7 JUNE 1962—BOOK ONE (1)

Then he put down his pencil, stretched, and began to work.

P.S. read the examination carefully. He saw that he would be able to do very little of it from memory, and felt the first surge of panic moisten his palms. He tried to translate the first Latin-to-English passage. He remembered that it fell on the right-hand side of the page in his Ullman and Henry, opposite the picture of the Roman galley. The picture was a still taken from the silent-movie version of *Ben-Hur*.[4] He recognized some of the verbs, more of the nouns, and finally he began to be able to translate. It was about the Veneti[5] ships, which were more efficient than the Roman galleys because they had prows and flat keels. He translated the entire passage, put down his pencil, and stretched again.

An hour later, P.S. knew he was in trouble. The first translation and the vocabulary section were the only parts of the exam he had been able to do without too much difficulty. He was able to give the rule and examples for the datives of agent and possession. The English-to-Latin sentences were the most difficult. He had been able to do only one of those. For the question "How do you determine the tense of the infinitive in indirect statement?" he wrote, "You can determine the tense by the construction of the sentence and by the word endings," and hoped he might get some credit. The two Latin-to-English passages counted twenty points apiece. If he could only do that second translation, he stood a chance of passing the examination. He recognized the adverb *"inde,"* but he saw that it didn't help him very much. The examination was halfway over. He tried to count how many points he had made so far on the examination. He thought he might have somewhere between fifty and fifty-five. Passing was seventy. If he could just translate that second passage, he would have the points he

needed to pass. Dr. Fairfax never scaled the grades. P.S. had heard that one year the Latin instructor flunked everybody but two.

He glanced over at Jumbo. Then he looked back down at his own examination and swore under his breath. Jumbo looked over at him and smiled. P.S. pantomimed that he could not answer the question, and Jumbo smiled again. P.S. slid his glasses off and rubbed his eyes. He fought down the panic, wiped his hands on his pants legs, and looked at the passage again. He couldn't make any sense out of the blur of the words. He squinted, looked at them, put on his glasses again, and knew that he was in trouble.

He leaned over his desk and closed his eyes. *Dear God, please help me on this examination . . . please, God, please . . . I must pass this examination. . . .* He opened his eyes and looked carefully around to see if anyone had seen him praying. The others were all working hard on the examination. P.S. looked up again at the engraving on the wall above his desk. Beneath the portrait was the caption "Soon after the close of the War Between the States, General Robert E. Lee became the head of a school for young men. General Lee made this statement when he met with his students for the first time: 'We have but one rule in this school, and that is that every student must be a gentleman.' " They left out that other rule, P.S. thought. They left out the one that says you have to have Latin to graduate! Or is that part of being a gentleman, too?

He read the Latin-to-English passage through twice, then he read it through backwards. He knew he had seen the passage before. He even remembered seeing it recently. But where? He knew that the passage dealt with the difficulties the Romans were having in fortifying their positions, but there were so many technical words in it that he could not get more than five of the twenty points from

---

4. **Ben Hur**\bĕn hər\ is a historical novel written by Lew Wallace in 1880 dealing with the times of Christ.
5. **The Veneti**\ᵛvĕ·nə 'tē\ were a people of western France in the first century B.C.

the translation, and he needed at least fifteen to pass. . . . He was going to flunk. *But I can't flunk! I can't flunk!* I've got to pass!

P.S. knew if he flunked he wouldn't be able to face his father. No matter what excuse P.S. gave, his father would not believe he hadn't loafed all term.

He looked at the passage and tried to remember where he had seen it. And then his mouth went dry. He felt the flush burn into the back of his neck and spread to his cheeks. He swallowed hard. *The translation's in my desk! . . . It's in my desk! . . . It's the translation on the top of the stack in my desk . . . in my desk!*

All he would have to do would be to slip the translation out of his desk, copy it, put it away, and he would pass the examination. All of his worries would be over. His father would be happy that he passed the examination. He wouldn't have to go to summer school. He and Charlie could go out to Colorado together to work on that dude ranch. He would be through with Latin forever. The Latin grade would never pull his average down again. Everything would be all right. Everything would be fine. All he would have to do would be to copy that one paragraph. Everyone cheated. Maybe not at V.P.S. But in other schools they bragged about it. . . . Everyone cheated in one way or another. Why should that one passage ruin everything? Who cared what problems the Romans had!

P.S. glanced over at Jumbo. Jumbo was chewing on his pencil eraser as he worked on the examination. Dr. Fairfax was still reading his newspaper. P.S. felt his heart beat faster. It began beating so hard that he was certain Jumbo could hear it. P.S. gently raised his desk top and pretended to feel around for a pencil. He let his blue book slide halfway off his desk so it leaned in his lap. Then he slid the translation under the blue book and slid the blue book and notes back onto his desk. He was certain that everyone had seen him—that everyone knew he was about to cheat. He slowly raised his eyes to look at Dr. Fairfax, who went on

reading. P.S. covered part of the notes with his examination and began to copy the rest into his blue book. He could feel the heat in his cheeks, the dryness in his mouth. *Dear God . . . God, please don't let them catch me! . . . Please!*

He changed the smooth translation into a rough one as he copied, so that it would match his other translation.

From these things the army was taught the nature of the place and how the slope of the hill and the necessity of the time demanded more than one plan and order for the art of war. Different legions, some in one part, others in another, fought the enemy. And the view was obstructed by very thick hedges. Sure support could not be placed, nor could it be seen what work would be necessary in which part, nor could all the commands be administered by one man. Therefore, against so much unfairness of things, various consequences ensued.

He put down his pencil and looked around the study hall. No one was watching. P.S. carefully slid the translation back into his desk. He looked to see if the translation gave him any words that might help him on the rest of the examination. His heart was still beating wildly in his chest, and his hands shook. He licked his lips and concentrated on behaving normally. *It's over. . . . It's over. . . . I've cheated, but it's all over and no one said anything!*

He began to relax.

Fifteen minutes later, Dr. Fairfax stood up at his desk, looked at the electric clock, then down at his pocket watch. He cleared his throat and said, "Stop!"

Several students groaned. The rest gathered up their pencils and pens.

"Make certain you have written out the pledge in full and signed it," Dr. Fairfax said.

P.S. felt the physical pain of fear again. He opened his blue book and wrote, "I pledge on my honor as a gentleman that I have neither given nor received unauthorized assistance on this examination." He hesitated; then he signed his name.

"Place your examination inside your blue book," Dr. Fairfax continued. "Make certain that you put your name on your blue book. . . . Baylor? If you and, uh, Ferguson and Showalter will be good enough to pick up the examinations, the rest of you may go. And, um, gentlemen, your grades will be posted on the front door of my office no sooner than forty-eight hours from now. In point of fact, any attempt to solicit your grade any sooner than that will result in bad temper on my part and greater severity in the marking of papers. Are there any questions? . . . If not, gentlemen, dismissed."

The students stood up and stretched. An immediate, excited hum of voices filled the study hall. P.S. looked down at his exam paper. He slid it into his blue book and left it on his desk.

Charlie was waiting at the door of the study hall. "Well, P.S., how'd the brain do?"

"You know it's bad luck to talk about an exam before the grades are posted."

"I know. I'm just asking how you think you did."

"I don't know," P.S. said.

"Well, well, I mean, do you think you passed?"

"I don't know!"

"Whooey!" Charlie whistled. "And you called *me* a grump!"

They walked down the stairs together. At the bottom, Charlie asked P.S. if he was going to go to lunch.

"No, I don't think so," P.S. said. "I'm not feeling so well. I think I'll lie down for a while. I'll see ya."

"Sure," Charlie said. "See ya."

In his cubicle in Memorial Hall, P.S. took off his lucky exam tie. He put his silver dollar back onto his bookcase. He reached inside the hollow copy of *Gulliver's Travels*[6] for the pack of cigarettes he kept there. Then he walked down the corridor to the bathroom, stepped into one of the stalls and locked the door. He lit the cigarette and leaned his forehead against the cool green marble divider. He was sick with fear and dread. *It's over! It's all over!* he said, trying

to calm himself. He did not like the new knowledge he had of himself. He was a cheater. He rolled his forehead back and forth against the stone, pressing his forehead into it, hurting himself. P.S. had broken the Honor Code of the school, and he was scared.

I shouldn't have cheated! What if someone had seen me! I shouldn't have cheated! Maybe somebody did see me. . . . Maybe Dr. Fairfax will know I cheated when he sees my exam. . . . Maybe somebody will check my desk after the exam and find the copy of the translation. . . . I cheated. I cheated! Stupid fool. . . . What if somebody finds out! . . . Maybe I should turn myself in. . . . I wonder if they'd kick me out if I turned myself in. . . . It would prove that I really am honest, I just made a mistake, that's all. . . . I'll tell them I couldn't help it. . . . Maybe they'll just give me a reprimand.

But P.S. knew that if he turned himself in, they would tell his parents he had cheated, so what good would that do? His father would be just as angry. Even more so, since Wilkinsons don't cheat, either. P.S. knew how ashamed his father would make him feel. His father would have to tell others that P.S. had cheated. It was a part of the Southern tradition. "My son has disgraced me. It is better that you hear it from me than somebody else." His father would do something like that. And having other people know he had cheated would be too much shame to bear. And even if he did turn himself in, the school would make him take another exam. . . . And he'd flunk that one, too. . . . He knew it. . . . *Oh, God, what am I going to do?*

If he didn't turn himself in and no one had seen him, then who would know? He would never cheat again. If he could just get away with it this one time. Then everything would be O.K. Nobody need ever know—except himself. And P.S. knew he would never be able to forget that he had cheated. Maybe if he turned himself in, it would be better in the long run. *What long run? What kind of long run will I have if*

---

6. **Gulliver's** \ˈgə•lə•vərz\ **Travels,** a classic of English literature, written by Jonathan Swift in 1726.

I turn myself in? Everybody in the school will know I cheated, no matter whether I turn myself in or not. . . . They won't remember me for turning myself in. . . . They'll remember that I cheated in the first place. . . .

P.S. wanted to cry, but he couldn't. He dropped the cigarette into the toilet and flushed it down. Then he went over to the sink and rinsed his mouth out. He had some chewing gum in his room; that would cover the smell of his smoking. He looked at himself in the mirror. He couldn't see any change since this morning, and yet he felt so different. He looked at his eyes to see if there were lines under them now. *What shall I do?* he asked his reflection. *What the — shall I do?* He turned on the cold water and rinsed his face. He dried himself on a towel someone had left behind, and walked back down the corridor to his room. He brushed aside the curtain, entered the cubicle, and stopped frozen with fear. Mabrey, the head monitor, was sitting on P.S.'s bed.

"Wilkinson," Mabrey said, "would you mind coming with me? Just outside for a few minutes."

"What about?"

Mabrey got up from the bed. "Come on, P.S."

"What . . . What do you want me for?"

"We want to talk to you."

We! WE! P.S. picked up his jacket and started to put it on.

"You won't need your jacket," Mabrey said, as he walked into the corridor.

"It doesn't matter, I'll wear it anyway."

P.S. followed Mabrey out of the dormitory. *I didn't have a chance to turn myself in,* he thought. *I didn't have a chance to choose. . . .*

"You think you'll make the varsity baseball team next year?" Mabrey asked.

"I don't know," P.S. said. *What is he talking about baseball for?*

The new boy who had wakened P.S. passed them on the walk. He said hello to both Mabrey and P.S. He received no answer and shrugged.

Mabrey and P.S. took the path to the headmaster's office. P.S. could feel the enormous weight of the fear building up inside him again.

Mabrey opened the door for P.S. and ushered him into the headmaster's waiting room. Nelson, a pale, fat-faced senior, was sitting there alone. He was the secretary of the Honor Committee. P.S. had always hated him. The other members of the Honor Committee were Mabrey, the vice-president; Linus Hendricks, the president; Mr. Seaton, the headmaster; and Dr. Fairfax, who served as faculty adviser. Mabrey motioned that P.S. was to sit down in the chair facing the others—the only straight-backed wooden chair in the room. Every now and then, Nelson would look up at P.S. and shake his head. The door to the headmaster's office opened and Mr. Seaton came out, followed by Linus Hendricks, Dr. Fairfax, and— *Gosh, what is Jumbo doing here! Don't tell me he cheated, too! He was sitting right next to me!* Jumbo walked out of the room without looking at P.S.

Linus Hendricks waited for the others to seat themselves, then he sat down himself and faced P.S. "Well, P.S., I imagine you know why you're here."

P.S. looked at Hendricks. Hendricks was the captain of the football team. He and Mabrey were the two most important undergraduates in the school.

"Well, P.S.?" Hendricks repeated.

"Yes, sir," P.S. said.

He could feel them all staring at him. He looked down at his hands folded in his lap. He could see clearly every line in his thumb knuckle. He could see the dirt caught under the corner of his fingernail, and the small blue vein running across the knuckle.

He looked up at Dr. Fairfax. He wanted to tell him not to worry. He wanted to tell him that he was sorry, so very sorry.

The headmaster, Mr. Seaton, was a young man. He had just become the headmaster of V.P.S. this year. He liked the students, and the students liked him. He was prematurely bald, and smiled a lot. He had a very young and pretty wife, and some of the students were in love with her and fought to sit at her table in the dining room. Mr. Seaton liked to play tennis. He would play the students and bet his dessert that he would win. And most of the time he would lose, and the students were enormously pleased to see the headmaster of the school have to get up from the table and pay his bets. Mr. Seaton would walk very quickly across the dining hall, his bald head bent to hide his smile. He would swoop up to a table, drop the dessert—and depart, like a bombing airplane. P.S. could tell that the headmaster was distressed he had cheated.

Linus Hendricks crossed his legs and sank back into the deep leather armchair. Mabrey and Nelson leaned forward as though they were going to charge P.S.

"P.S.," Hendricks said. "You're here this afternoon because the Honor Committee has reason to suspect that you may have cheated on the Latin exam this morning. We must ask you whether or not this is true."

P.S. raised his head and looked at Hendricks. Hendricks was wearing a bright striped tie. P.S. concentrated on the stripes. Thick black, thin white, medium green, thin white, and thick black.

"P.S., did you, or did you not, cheat on the Latin examination?"

P.S. nodded.

"Yes or no, P.S.?" Hendricks asked.

P.S. no longer felt anything. He was numb with misery. "Yes," he said, in a small, tired voice. "Yes, I cheated on the examination. But I was going to turn myself in. I was going to turn myself in, I swear I was."

"If you were going to turn yourself in, why didn't you?" Nelson asked.

"I couldn't . . . I couldn't yet. . . ." P.S. looked at Dr. Fairfax. "I'm sorry, sir. I'm terribly sorry. . . ." P.S. began to cry. "I'm so ashamed. . . . Oh, God. . . ." P.S. tried to stop crying. He couldn't. The tears stung his eyes. One tear slipped into the inside of his glasses and puddled across the bottom of the lens. He reached into his back pocket for a handkerchief, but he had forgotten to bring one. He started to pull out his shirttail, and decided he'd better not. He wiped his face with the side of his hand.

Mr. Seaton walked over to P.S. and gave him his handkerchief. The headmaster rested his hand on P.S.'s shoulder. "Why, P.S.? Why did you cheat?"

P.S. couldn't answer.

"P.S., you were the last boy I expected this of. Why did you feel you had to cheat on this exam?"

"I don't know, sir."

"But P.S., you must have had some reason."

Nelson said, "Answer the headmaster when he's asking you a question, Wilkinson."

P.S. looked up at him with such loathing that Nelson looked away.

Mr. Seaton crouched down next to P.S. "You must have been aware of the penalty for cheating."

P.S. nooded.

"Then why, in heaven's name, did you risk expulsion to pass the examination?"

"Sir—sir, I flunked Latin last year, sir. I knew I'd flunk it this year, too. I—I knew I couldn't pass the Latin exam ever."

"But why did you *cheat?*"

"Because . . . because, sir, I had to pass the exam."

The headmaster ran his hand across his forehead. "P.S., I'm not trying to trick you, I'm only trying to understand why you did this thing. Why did you bring the notes into the exam with you?"

"Sir, Mr. Seaton, I didn't bring the notes in, they were in my desk. If they hadn't been, I wouldn't be here. I didn't want to cheat. I didn't *mean* to cheat. I—it was just the only way I could pass the exam."

Nelson rested his pudgy arms on the sides of his leather armchair and looked at the headmaster and then back to P.S. Then he said, "Wilkinson, you have been in V.P.S. for two years. You must be familiar, I imagine, with the Honor Code. In fact, in your study hall there is a small wooden plaque above the proctor's desk. On it is carved the four points of the Honor Code: 'I will not lie. I will not steal. I will not cheat. I will report anyone I see doing so.' You are familiar with them, aren't you?"

"Of course I'm familiar with them," P.S. said impatiently.

"Why did you think you were so much better than everyone else that you could ignore it?"

"I don't think I'm better than everyone else, Nelson," P.S. said.

"Well, you sure aren't! The others don't cheat." Nelson sat back again, very satisfied with himself.

Dr. Fairfax came from behind the chairs and stood next to P.S. "Unless you hold your tongue, Nelson—unless you hold your tongue, I shall personally escort you out of here."

"But, sir," Nelson whined, "I'm only trying to—"

"SHUT UP!" Dr. Fairfax roared. He returned to the back of the room.

Mr. Seaton spoke again. "P.S., if you had flunked this exam, you would have been able to take another. Perhaps you would have passed the re-examination. Most boys do."

"I wouldn't have, sir," P.S. said. "I just cannot do Latin. You could have given me fifty examinations, sir. And I don't mean any disrespect, but I would have flunked all fifty of them."

Mabrey asked the headmaster if he could speak. Then he turned to P.S. "P.S., we—all of us have been tempted at some time or another to cheat. All of us have either resisted the temptation or, perhaps, we were lucky enough to get away with it. I think that what we want to know is what *made* you cheat. Just having to pass the exam isn't enough. I know you, P.S. I may know you better than anyone in the room, because I've shared the same floor in the dorm with you for this year. And we were on the same floor when you were a toad. You're not the kind who cheats unless he has a damn good—" Mabrey glanced over at the headmaster. "Excuse me, sir. I didn't mean to swear."

The headmaster nodded and indicated that Mabrey was to continue.

"What I mean is this, P.S. I know you don't care how high your grade is, just so long as you keep out of trouble. . . . You're one of the most popular boys in your class. Everybody likes you. Why would you throw all of this over, just to pass a Latin exam?"

"I don't know. I don't know. . . . I had to pass the exam. If I flunked it again, my father would kill me."

"What do you mean he would 'kill' you?" Mr. Seaton asked.

"Oh, nothing, sir. I mean—I don't mean he would hurt me. He would just—Oh, I don't know how to explain it to you. If I flunked the exam again, he'd just make me feel so, I don't know . . . *ashamed* . . . so terrible. I just couldn't take it again."

There was a moment of silence in the room. P.S. began to cry again. He could tell the headmaster still didn't understand why he had cheated. He looked down at his hands again. With his index finger he traced the veins that crossed the back of his hand. He looked over at the wooden arm of his straight-backed chair. He could see the little drops of moisture where his hand had squeezed the arm of the chair. He could make out every grain of wood, every worn spot. He took off his glasses and rubbed his eyes. He tried taking deep breaths, but each time his breath would be choked off.

Hendricks cleared his throat and recrossed his legs. "P.S.," he said, "we have your examination here. You signed your name to the pledge at the end of the exam. You swore on your honor that you had not cheated." Hendricks paused. P.S. knew what he was driving at.

"If I hadn't signed my name to the pledge, you would have known I had cheated right away," P.S. explained. "I didn't want to break my honor again. I was going to turn myself in, honest I was."

"You didn't, though," Nelson said.

"I would have!" P.S. said. But he still wasn't sure whether he would have or not. He knew he never would be certain.

"So, we've got you on lying and cheating," Nelson said. "How do we know you haven't stolen, too?"

Dr. Fairfax grabbed the lapels of Nelson's jacket, pulled him out of the chair, and pushed him out of the room. The old man closed the door and leaned against it. He wiped his brow and said, "Mr. Seaton, sir, I trust you won't find fault with my actions. That young Nelson has a tendency to bother me. In point of fact, he irritates me intensely."

P.S. looked gratefully at Dr. Fairfax. The old man smiled sadly. Mabrey was talking quietly to Hendricks. Mr. Seaton sat down in Nelson's chair and turned to P.S. "I know this is a difficult question. Would you—would you have turned Jumbo in had you seen him cheating?"

P.S. felt the blood drain from his face. *So Jumbo turned me in! . . . Jumbo saw me! . . . Sitting next to me all year! . . . Jumbo turned me in! Why?*

He looked up at the others. They were all waiting for his answer. He had the most curious feeling of aloofness, of coldness. If he said yes, that he would have turned Jumbo in, it would be a lie, and he knew it. If he answered yes, it would please the headmaster, though. Because it would mean that P.S. still had faith in the school system. If he said no, he wouldn't have turned Jumbo in, it would be as good as admitting that he would not obey the fourth part of the Honor Code—"I will report anyone I see doing so." He waited a moment and then answered, "I don't know. I don't know whether I would have turned Jumbo in or not."

"Thank you very much, P.S.," the headmaster said.

P.S. could tell that Mr. Seaton was disappointed in his answer.

"Gentlemen, do you have any further questions you would like to ask Wilkinson?"

"Nothing, sir," Hendricks answered.

The headmaster looked over at Dr. Fairfax, who shook his head. "Well, then, P.S., if you don't mind, we'd like you to sit in my office until we call for you."

P.S. got up and started for the door.

"Have you had any lunch?" Dr. Fairfax asked.

"No, sir. But I'm not very hungry."

"I'll have Mrs. Burdick bring in some milk and cookies."

"Thank you, sir."

The door opened and P.S. stood up as Mr. Seaton walked over to his desk and eased himself into the swivel chair. P.S. had been sitting alone in the headmaster's office for several hours.

"Sit down, please," the headmaster said. He picked up a wooden pencil and began to roll it back and forth between his palms. P.S. could hear the click of the pencil as it rolled across the headmaster's ring. Mr. Seaton laid the pencil aside and rubbed his cheek. His hand moved up the side of his face and began to massage his temples. Then he looked up at P.S. and said, "The Honor Committee has decided that you must leave the school. The penalty for cheating at V.P.S. is immediate expulsion. There cannot be any exceptions."

P.S. took a deep breath and pushed himself back into the soft leather seat. Then he dropped his hands into his lap and slumped. He was beyond crying; there was nothing left to cry about.

"Your father is waiting for you in the other room," Mr. Seaton said. "I've asked him to wait outside for a few minutes, because I want to speak to you alone. I want you to understand why the school had to make the decision to expel you. The school—this school—is only as good as its honor system. And the honor system is only as good as the students who live by it."

P.S. cleared his throat and looked down at his fingernails. He wished the headmaster wouldn't talk about it. He knew why the school had to expel him. It was done. It was over with. What good would it do to talk about it?

"The honor system, since it is based on mutual trust and confidence, no doubt makes it easier for some students to cheat," the headmaster said. "I am not so naïve as to believe that there aren't any boys who cheat here. Unfortunately, our honor system makes it easy for them to do so. These boys have not been caught. Perhaps they will never be caught. But I feel that it was far better for you to have been caught right away, P.S., because you are not a cheater. Notice that I said you *are* not a cheater instead of you *were* not a cheater. . . . Yes, you cheated this one time. I do not need to ask whether you cheated before. I know you haven't. I know also that you will not cheat again. I was frankly stunned when I heard that you had cheated on Dr. Fairfax's examination. You were the last boy I would have expected to cheat. I am still not entirely satisfied by the reasons you gave for cheating. I suppose a person never is. Maybe it is impossible to give reasons for such an act." Mr. Seaton began massaging his temple again. "P.S., the most difficult thing that you must try to understand is that Jumbo did the right thing. Jumbo was correct in turning you in."

P.S. stiffened in the chair. "Yes, sir," he said.

"If no one reported infractions, we would have no Honor Code. The Code would be obeyed only when it was convenient to obey it. It would be given lip service. The whole system would break down. The school would become just another private school, instead of the respected and loved institution it now is. Put yourself in Jumbo's shoes for a moment. You and Jumbo are friends—*believe me,* you are friends. If you had heard what Jumbo said about you in here, and how it hurt him to turn you in, you would know what a good friend Jumbo is. You have been expelled for cheating. You will not be here next fall. But Jumbo will be. Jumbo will stay on at V.P.S., and the other students will know that he was the one who turned you in. When I asked you whether you would have turned Jumbo in, you said that you didn't know. You and I both know from your answer that you wouldn't have turned Jumbo in. Perhaps the schoolboy code is still stronger in you than the Honor Code. Many students feel stronger about the schoolboy code than the Honor Code. No one likes to turn in a friend. A lot of boys who don't know any better, a lot of your friends, will never forgive Jumbo. It will be plenty tough for him. Just as it is tough on anybody who does his duty. I think—I honestly think that Jumbo has done you a favor. I'm not going to suggest that you be grateful to him. Not yet. That would be as ridiculous as

my saying something as trite as 'Someday you will be able to look back on this and laugh.' . . . P.S., you will *never* be able to look back on this and laugh. But you may be able to understand." The headmaster looked at his wristwatch and then said, "I'm going to leave you alone with your father for a few minutes; then I suggest you go back to your room and pack. The other students won't be back in the dormitories yet, so you can be alone." He got up from behind the desk. P.S. rose also. He looked down at the milk and cookies Mrs. Burdick had left him. There was half a glass of milk and three cookies left.

The headmaster looked at P.S. for a moment and then he said, "I'm sorry you have been expelled, P.S. You were a good student here. One of the most popular boys in your class. You will leave behind a great many good friends."

"Thank you, sir," P.S. said.

"I'll see you before you and your father leave."

"Yes, sir."

The headmaster walked into the waiting room. P.S. could hear Dr. Fairfax talking, and then his father. The door closed, and P.S. sat down to wait for his father. He could feel the fear building up inside of him again. He did not know what to say to his father. What could he say? He sipped the last of the milk as the door opened. P.S. put down the glass and stood up.

Stewart Wilkinson closed the door behind him and looked at his son. He wanted to hold the boy and comfort him, but Phil looked so solid, so strong, standing there. Why isn't he crying, he wondered, and then he told himself that he wouldn't have cried, either; that the boy had plenty of time to cry; that he would never cry in front of his father again. He tried to think of something to say. He knew that he often was clumsy in his relations with Phil, and said the wrong thing, and he wondered whether he had been that sensitive at his son's age. He looked down at the plate of cookies and the empty milk glass.

"Where did you get the milk and cookies, son?"

"Mrs. Burdick brought them to me, sir."

He never calls me "Dad" now, Stewart Wilkinson said to himself. Always "sir." . . . My own son calls me "sir." . . .

"Did you thank her?"

"Yes, sir."

Stewart Wilkinson walked over to the couch next to his son and sat down. The boy remained standing.

"Phil, son, sit down, please."

"Yes, sir."

Looking at his son, Stewart Wilkinson could not understand why they had grown apart during the last few years. He had always remained close to his father. Why wasn't it the same between him and the boy who sat so stiff beside him, so still in spite of the horror he must have gone through during the past few hours?

"I'm sorry, sir."

"Yes . . . yes, son, I know you are. . . . I'm terribly sorry myself. Sorry for you. . . . Mr. Seaton told me another boy turned you in, is that right?"

P.S. nodded.

"He also told me that he believes you would have turned yourself in had you been given enough time."

"I don't know whether I would have or not. I never had a chance to find out."

"I think you would have. I think you would have."

He waited for his son to say something; then, realizing there was nothing the boy could say, he spoke again. "I was talking to Dr. Fairfax outside—you knew he was my Latin teacher, too?"

"Yes, sir."

"We always used to be able to tell when the first day of spring came, because Dr. Fairfax put on his white linen suit."

"Yes, sir."

"At any rate, that man thinks very highly of you, Phil. He is very upset that you had to be expelled. I hope you will speak to him before we go. He's a good man to have on your side."

"I want to speak to him."

"Phil . . . Phil . . ." Stewart Wilkinson thought for a minute. He wanted so desperately what he said to be the right thing to say. "Phil, I know that I am partly responsible for what has happened. I must have in some way pressured you into it. I wanted your marks to be high. I wanted you to get the best education that you could. V.P.S. isn't the best school in the country, but it's a very fine one. It's a school that has meant a lot to our family. But that doesn't matter so much. I mean, that part of it is all over with. I'm sorry that you cheated, because I know you're not the cheating kind. I'm also sorry because you are going to have to face the family and get it over with. This is going to be tough. But they'll all understand. I doubt that there is any of us who have never cheated in one way or another. But it will make them very proud of you if you can go see them and look them in the eye."

He picked up one of the cookies and began to bite little pieces out of the edge. Then he shook his head sadly, in the gesture P.S. knew so well. "Ah, son, it's so terrible that you have to learn these lessons when you are young. I know that you don't want me to feel sorry for you, but I can't help it. I'm not angry with you. I'm a little disappointed, perhaps, but I can understand it, I think. I suppose I must appear as an ogre to you at times. But Phil, I—If I'm tough with you, it's just because I'm trying to help you. Maybe I'm too tough." Stewart Wilkinson looked over at his son. He saw that the boy was watching him. He felt a little embarrassed to have revealed so much of himself before his son. But he knew they were alike. He knew that Phil was really his son. They already spoke alike. Already laughed at the same sort of things, appreciated the same things. Their tastes were pretty much the same. He knew that, if anything, he was too much like the boy to be able to help him. And also that the problem was the boy's own, and that he would resent his father's interfering.

"Phil, I'll go speak with Mr. Seaton for a little while, and then I'll come on over and help you pack. If you'd like, I'll pack for you and you can sit in the car."

"No, that's all right, sir, I'll pack. I mean, most of the stuff is packed up already. I'll meet you over there."

Stewart Wilkinson rose with his son. Again he wanted to hold the boy, to show him how much he loved him.

"I'll be through packing in a few minutes. I'll meet you in my room," P.S. said.

"Fine, son."

Together they carried the footlocker down the staircase of Memorial Hall. P.S. stopped at the door, balanced the footlocker with one hand, then pulled the heavy door open. The door swung back before they could get through. Stewart Wilkinson stumbled and P.S. said, "I'm sorry."

They carried the footlocker across the small patch of lawn between the front of Memorial Hall and the main drive and slid the footlocker into the back of the station wagon.

"How much more is there, son?"

"A couple of small boxes, some books, and a couple of pictures."

Stewart Wilkinson pulled a silk handkerchief out of his back pocket and wiped his brow. "You think we can get all of them in one more trip?"

"I think so, sir. At least, we can try."

They turned back toward the dormitory. Stewart Wilkinson rested his hand on his son's shoulder as they walked back across the lawn. "Phil, Mr. Seaton told me that he thinks he might be able to get you into Hotchkiss. How does that sound to you?"

"It's a funny name for a school."

"Hotchkiss, funny? Why?"

"I don't know, it just sounds funny."

"Well, do you think you'd like to go there?"

"Sure. I mean I don't know. I haven't given it much thought."

Stewart Wilkinson laughed. "I guess you haven't."

The boy looked worriedly at his father for a moment. He wondered whether his father was making fun of him. And then he saw the humor in his remark and laughed, too.

They brought the last of the boxes down from the room and slid them into the car and closed the tailgate.

"Did you get a chance to talk to Dr. Fairfax?"

"Yes, sir. He came by the room while I was packing."

"What did he say?"

"I don't know. I mean he was sorry I was going and all that, but he said I'd get along fine anywhere and that it wasn't the end of the world."

"Did he say 'in point of fact'?"

"Yeah." P.S. laughed. "He said, 'Well, boy, you'll do all right. In point of fact, you have nothing to worry about.' I really like old Doc Fairfax."

They went around the side of the car and climbed in.

"Anything you've forgotten? Books out of the library, equipment in the gym? Anybody special you want to see before we go home?"

"No, Dad, thanks, that's all—Hey, wait a minute, could you, Dad?" P.S. got out of the car. "It's Charlie—Charlie Merritt. I'd like to say goodbye to him."

"Sure, son, take your time."

The two boys spoke together for a moment, standing in the road; then they shook hands. Stewart Wilkinson turned off the engine and watched as the boys walked back to the road toward him. As they drew near, he got out of the station wagon.

"Dad, this is Charlie Merritt. . . . Charlie, you remember my father."

"Yes, sir. How are you, sir?"

"Fine, thank you, Charlie."

"Sir, Mr. Wilkinson, I'm sorry about P.S. getting kicked out and all."

Stewart Wilkinson nodded.

"He's just sorry because I won't be around to borrow his toothpaste any more. He likes to lend it to me because I always roll it from the top and lose the cap."

P.S. and Charlie laughed.

"Hey, P.S.?" Charlie said. "Does this mean

you're not going to have to work off the five demerits Doc Fairfax gave us this morning?"

"What did you two get five demerits for?" Stewart Wilkinson asked.

"We were talking about the exam," P.S. said.

Father and son looked at each other, and then P.S. turned away. It was clear that he was thinking about the exam and his cheating again. And then the boy took a deep breath and smiled. "You know? It's funny," he said. "I mean, it seems that exam took place so long ago. . . . Well, Charlie." P.S. stuck out his hand and Charlie took it. "Well, I guess we'd better get going. I'll see you around, O.K.?"

"Sure, P.S.," Charlie said.

The two boys shook hands again solemnly. Then Charlie shook hands with P.S.'s father. P.S. and Stewart Wilkinson got back into the station wagon.

Charlie walked around to P.S.'s window. "Hey, P.S.? Make sure you let me hear from you this summer, O.K.?"

"Sure, Charlie. Take care of yourself."

They drove around the school drive, by the Wilkinson Memorial Library and the Sadler Gymnasium and then they turned down the slight hill toward the Breastworks, and as they passed through the ornate, wrought-iron gate P.S. began to cry.

I

NOT THE KIND WHO CHEATS?

P.S. knew he was disobeying the Honor Code when he reached inside his desk and eased out the translation he needed. Why did he feel he *had* to pass the test? Was Mabrey right when he tried to excuse P.S. by arguing that the boy was not the kind who usually cheated? Is there a "kind" of person who cheats? Consider and discuss:

1. Why was the Honor Code so important to Virginia Preparatory School? Describe some of the traditions and customs there.

2. Why was P.S. well-liked at school? Which of his antics or remarks amused you most? Contrast

the study habits of Charlie and P.S. Do you think that P.S. really couldn't pass a Latin exam or that he merely *thought* he couldn't? Discuss.

3. Jumbo, as the informer, would have a more difficult time at V.P.S. in the period ahead than would P.S., who would be in another school.

4. Describe the relationship between P.S. and his father. How do you think the cheating incident might affect that relationship?

II

IMPLICATIONS

Do you agree or disagree with the following statements?

1. Any person will cheat if the pressure is great enough.

2. It is not honor, but fear of being caught which keeps most people from cheating.

3. You are not a cheater until you are caught.

4. It is good to have students, such as those on the Honor Committee, make judgments of other students.

5. Cheating lowers a person in his own estimation. (A line from the story tells us, on page 324: "He did not like the new knowledge he had of himself. He was a cheater." Is this a common feeling?)

6. The strength of family love and loyalty is not really tested until one member of such an inner circle has done something frowned upon by society.

III

TECHNIQUES

Theme

Set down what you think to be the theme of this selection, beginning with the formula statement, "In this story the author is trying to show us that . . ."

Narrative Viewpoint

No person is identified as the narrator in this story. The author remains out of sight, so to speak, and tells what happens in the third person.

1. Why does making the reader conscious of P.S.'s inner turmoil add to the depth and emotional appeal of this story?

2. What might have happened to the effect of the story if P.S. had told his own story in the first person?

A family circle may be torn
and distorted by outside forces,
but most often the threat comes from within.
Jealousy, lack of affection,
and ridiculous pride are potential dangers.
However, at times an inner circle
must shift and change. How people adjust
to these changes has furnished material
for many stories. Sometimes the adjustment
brings with it maturity. Minta,
in the long-to-be-remembered story
which follows, felt she knew the very morning
in which she "grew up."

From Mother . . . with Love

ZOA SHERBURNE

The day that Minta Hawley grew up was a crisp golden day in early September.

Afterwards she was to remember everything about that day with poignant clarity. She remembered the slapping sound the waves made, the pungent smell of the logs burning, even the gulls that soared and swooped overhead; but most of all she remembered her father's face when he told her.

It began like any other Saturday, with Minta lying in bed an extra hour. Breakfast was always lazy and unhurried on Saturday mornings. The three of them in the breakfast room —Minta's father engrossed in his paper; her mother flying around in a gayly colored housecoat, mixing waffles and frying bacon; Minta setting the table.

They talked, the casual happy talk of people who love each other and don't have to make conversation. About neighborhood doings . . .

Reprinted by permission of Ann Elmo Agency, Inc.

about items in the paper . . . about the clothes Minta would need when she went away to school in a couple of weeks.

It was after the dishes were finished that Minta's father asked her if she would like to go down to the beach for a little while.

"Low tide," he said. "Might get a few clams."

Minta nodded agreement, but her mother made a little face.

"Horrors, clam chowder for another week!"

"Sure you wouldn't like to go, Mary?" Minta's father asked. "The salt air might help your headache."

"No. You two run along. I'll curl up with an apple and a television program." She yawned and stretched, looking almost as young as Minta.

Minta ran upstairs and got into her heavy shoes and jeans. "Shall I call Sally and ask her if she wants to go?" she yelled, leaning far over the bannister.

"Let's just go by ourselves this time," her father answered rather shortly.

He was silent as they drove toward the beach, but it wasn't the companionable silence that Minta had come to expect from him. There was something grim about it.

"He's going to talk to me about school," Minta told herself, "He's going to try to talk me out of it again."

It was funny the way her father had acted when she announced her intention of going to MaryHill this term. It had always been such an accepted thing; her mother had graduated from MaryHill and it followed that Minta should be enrolled there as a matter of course.

Last year was different. With Mother just recovering from that operation it was natural that he should expect Minta to stay home; she had even *wanted* to stay. But now going to MaryHill was something special. She would live in a dormitory and be part of all the campus fun. It wasn't as if MaryHill were clear across the country, either, she'd probably be getting home every month or so . . . and there were the Christmas holidays . . . and then spring vacation.

Minta's chin was lifted in a stubborn line as her father parked the car and went around to get the shovels and pail from the trunk.

It wasn't like him to be so stubborn, usually he was jolly and easygoing and inclined to leave such matters entirely up to Minta's mother.

She followed him down to the beach, her boots squishing in the wet sand. The tide was far out and farther up the beach she could see bent figures busily digging along the water's edge.

A scattered beach fire smoldered near the bank and Minta poked it into place and revived it with splinters of driftwood until she had coaxed back a steady warming blaze. When she sat back on her heels to smile up at her father she felt her throat constrict with a smothering fear. His eyes looked the way they had when . . .

When?

Suddenly she remembered. He was looking at her and trying to smile, just the way he had looked at her the time her appendix burst and they were taking her to the hospital. She could almost hear the wail of the ambulance siren and feel the way he had held her hands tightly, trying to make it easier. His eyes had told her then, as they told her now, that he would a thousand times rather bear the pain than watch her suffer.

It seemed like a long time that she knelt there by the beach fire, afraid to move, childishly willing herself to wake from the nightmarish feeling that gripped her.

He took her hand and pulled her to her feet and they started walking up the beach slowly, not toward the group of people digging clams, but in the other direction, toward the jagged pile of rocks that jutted out into the bay.

She heard a strange voice, her own voice.

"I thought . . . I thought you wanted to talk to me about school, but it isn't that, is it, Father?"

Father.

She never called him Father. It was always "Dad" or "Pops" or, when she was feeling especially gay, "John Henry."

His fingers tightened around hers. "In a way it is . . . about school."

And then, before the feeling of relief could erase the fear he went on. "I went to see Dr. Morton last week, Minta. I've been seeing him pretty regularly these last few months."

She flashed a quick frightened look up at him. "You aren't ill?"

"No." He sighed and it was a heartbreaking sound. "No. It isn't me. It's your mother. That's why I don't want you to go to MaryHill this year."

"But . . . but she's feeling so much better, Dad. Except for these headaches once in a while. She's even taking on a little weight—" She broke off and stopped walking and her hand was steady on his arm. "Tell me," she said quietly.

The look was back in his eyes again but this time Minta scarcely noticed it, she was aware only of his words, the dreadful echoing finality of his words.

Her mother was going to die.

To die.

Her mother.

To die, the doctor said. Three months, perhaps less. . . .

Her mother who was gay and scatterbrained and more fun than anyone else in the world. Her mother who could be counted on to announce in the spring that she was going to do her Christmas shopping early *this* year, and then left everything until the week before Christmas.

No one was worse about forgetting anniversaries and birthdays and things like that; but the easy-to-remember dates, like Valentine's Day and St. Patrick's Day and Halloween were always gala affairs complete with table favors and three-decker cakes.

Minta's mother wore the highest heels and the maddest hats of any mother on the block. She was so pretty. And she always had time for things like listening to new records and helping paste pictures in Minta's scrapbook.

She wasn't ever sick—except for the headaches and the operation last year which she had laughingly dismissed as a rest cure.

"I shouldn't have told you." Her father was speaking in a voice that Minta had never heard from him before. A voice that held loneliness and fear and a sort of angry pain. "I was afraid I couldn't make you understand, why you had to stay home . . . why you'd have to forget about MaryHill for this year." His eyes begged her to forgive him and for some reason she wanted to put her arms around him, as if she were much older and stronger.

"Of course you had to tell me," she said steadily. "Of course I had to know." And then— "Three months, but Dad, that's *Christmas.*"

He took her hand and tucked it under his arm and they started walking again.

It was like walking through a nightmare. The steady squish-squish of the wet sand and the little hollows their feet made filling up almost as soon as they passed.

He talked quietly, explaining, telling her everything the doctor had said, and Minta listened without tears, without comment.

She watched his face as though it were the face of a stranger.

She thought about a thousand unrelated things.

Last winter when he had chased her and her mother around the back yard to wash their faces in the new snow. She could still see the bright red jacket her mother had worn . . . the kerchief that came off in the struggle . . . the way the neighbors had watched from their windows, laughing and shaking their heads.

She remembered all the times they had gone swimming this past summer. Minta and her father loved to swim but her mother had preferred to curl up on a beach blanket and watch them.

"You have the disposition of a Siamese cat," Minta had accused her mother laughingly. "A cushion by the fire in the winter and a cushion in the sun in the summer. . . ."

"And a bowl of cream nearby," her mother had agreed instantly.

She was always good-natured about their teasing.

But in spite of her apparent frailty and her admitted laziness she managed to accomplish an astounding amount of work. Girl Scouts, PTA, Church bazaars, Red Cross. People were always calling her to head a committee or organize a drive. Young people congregated in her home. Not just Minta's gang, but the neighborhood youngsters. She had Easter egg hunts for them; she bought their raffle tickets and bandaged their skinned knees.

It was like coming back from a long journey when her father stopped talking and they turned back toward the car.

"So that's why I can't let you go away, Midge." Her father's voice was very low and he didn't seem to realize that he had called her by the babyish name she had discarded when she started to first grade. "It isn't just your mother I'm thinking about . . . it's me. I need you."

She looked at him quickly and her heart twisted with pity. He did need her. He would need her more than ever.

In the car she sat very close to him.

"We didn't get the clams," she reminded him once, but he only nodded.

Just before they reached home he reached over and took her hand in a tight hurting grip.

"We can't tell her, Minta. The doctor left it up to me and I said not to tell her. We have to let her have this last time . . . this last little time . . . without that hanging over her. We have to go on as if everything were exactly the same."

She nodded to show that she understood. After a moment she spoke past the ache in her throat. "About school. I'll . . . I'll tell her that I decided to wait until next year. Or that I'm afraid I'd be lonesome without the gang. I've been sort of . . . sort of seesawing back and forth, anyway."

It seemed impossible that life could go on exactly as before.

The small private world peopled by the three of them was as snug and warm and happy as though no shadow had touched them.

They watched television and argued good-naturedly about the programs. Minta's friends came and went and there was the usual round of parties and dances and games. Her father continued to bowl two evenings a week and her mother became involved in various pre-holiday pursuits.

"I really must get at my Christmas shopping," she mentioned the day she was wrapping trick-or-treat candy for Halloween.

Minta shook her head and sighed gustily.

Her mother started this "I-must-get-at-my-Christmas-shopping" routine every spring and followed it up until after Thanksgiving but she never actually got around to it until two or three days before Christmas.

It was amazing that Minta could laugh and say, "Oh, *you* . . ." the way she did year after year.

It was a knife turning in her heart when her mother straightened up from the gay cellophane-wrapped candies and brushed a stray wisp of taffy-colored hair back from one flushed cheek.

"Don't laugh," she said, pretending to be stern. "You know you're just exactly like me."

It was a warming thought. She *was* like her mother. Inside, where it really mattered she was like her mother, even though she had her father's dark eyes and straight black hair, even though she had his build and the firm chin of all the Hawleys.

She wanted to put her arm around her mother and hug her, hard. She wanted to say, "I hope I am like you. I want to be."

But instead she got up and stretched and wrinkled her nose.

"Perish forbid," she said, "that I should be such a scatterbrain."

She was rewarded by the flash of a dimple in her mother's cheek.

It seemed to Minta, as week followed week, that the day at the beach had been something out of a nightmare: something that she could push away from her and forget about. Sometimes she looked at her father, laughing, teasing them, or howling about the month-end bills and she thought, "It didn't happen . . . it isn't true."

And then at night she would lie sleepless in her room, the pretty room that had been reconverted from her nursery. She watched the moonlight drift patterns across the yellow bedspread and the breeze billow the curtains that her mother had made by hand, because that was the only way she could be sure of an absolute match.

"Yellow is such a difficult color to match," she had explained around a mouthful of pins.

And in the dark hours of the night Minta had known it wasn't a nightmare. It was true. It was true.

One windy November day she hurried home from school and found her mother in the yard raking leaves. She wore a bright kerchief over her head and she had Minta's old polo coat belted around her. She looked young and gay and carefree and her eyes were shining.

"Hi!" She waved the rake invitingly. "Change your clothes and come help. We'll have a smudge party in the alley."

Minta stopped and leaned on the gate. She saw with a new awareness that there were dark circles under her mother's eyes and that the flags of color in her cheeks were too bright. But she managed a chuckle.

"I wish you could see yourself, Mom. For two cents I'd get my camera and take a picture of you."

She ran into the house and got her camera and they took a whole roll of pictures.

"Good," her mother said complacently. "Now we can show them to your father the next time he accuses me of being a Sally-Sit-by-the-Fire."

They piled the leaves into a huge damp stack, with the help of half a dozen neighborhood children. It wouldn't burn properly but gave out with clouds of thick, black, wonderfully pungent smoke.

Her mother was tired that night. She lay on the davenport and made out her Christmas card list while Minta and her father watched the wrestling matches. It was like a thousand other such evenings but in some unaccountable way it was different.

"Because it's the last time," Minta told herself. "The last time we'll ever rake the leaves and make a bonfire in the alley. The last time I'll snap a picture of her with her arms around the Kelly kids. The last time . . . the last time. . . ."

She got up quickly and went out into the kitchen and made popcorn in the electric popper, bringing a bowl to her mother first, remembering just the way she liked it, salt and not too much butter.

But that night she wakened in the chilly darkness of her room and began to cry, softly, her head buried in the curve of her arm. At first it helped, loosening the tight bands about her heart, washing away the fear and the loneliness, but when she tried to stop she found that she couldn't. Great wracking sobs shook her until she could no longer smother them against her pillow. And then the light was on and her mother was there bending over her, her face concerned, her voice soothing.

"Darling, what is it? Wake up, baby, you're having a bad dream."

"No . . . no, it isn't a dream," Minta choked. "It's true . . . it's true."

The thin hand kept smoothing back her tumbled hair and her mother went on talking in the tone she had always used to comfort a much smaller Minta.

She was aware that her father had come to the doorway. He said nothing, just stood there watching them while Minta's sobs diminished into hiccupy sighs.

Her mother pulled the blanket up over Minta's shoulder and gave her a little spank. "The idea! Gollywogs, at your age," she said reprovingly. "Want me to leave the light on in case your spook comes back?"

Minta shook her head, blinking against the tears that crowded against her eyelids, even managing a wobbly smile.

She never cried again.

Not even when the ambulance came a week later to take her mother to the hospital. Not even when she was standing beside her mother's high white hospital bed, holding her hand tightly, forcing herself to chatter of inconsequential things.

"Be sure that your father takes his vitamin pills, won't you, Minta? He's so careless unless I'm there to keep an eye on him."

"I'll watch him like a beagle," Minta promised lightly. "Now you behave yourself and get out of here in a hurry, you hear?"

Not even at the funeral. . . .

The friends and relatives came and went and it was as if she stood on the sidelines watching the Minta who talked with them and answered their questions. As if her heart were encased in a shell that kept it from breaking.

She went to school and came home afterwards to the empty house. She tried to do the things her mother had done but even with the help of well-meaning friends and neighbors it was hard. She tried not to hate the people who urged her to cry.

"You'll feel better, dear," her Aunt Grace had insisted and then had lifted her handkerchief to her eyes and walked away when Minta had only stared at her with chilling indifference.

She overheard people talking about her mother.

"She never knew, did she?" they asked.

And always Minta's father answered, "No, she never knew. Even at the very last, when she was waiting for the ambulance to come she looked around the bedroom and said, 'I must get these curtains done up before Christmas.' "

Minta knew that her father was worried about her and she was sorry, but it was as if there were a wall between them, a wall that she was too tired to surmount.

One night he came to the door of her room where she was studying.

"I wonder if you'd like to go through those clothes before your Aunt Grace takes them to the church bazaar," he began haltingly. And then when she looked up at him, not understanding, he went on gently, "Your mother's clothes. We thought someone might as well get some good out of them."

She stood up and closed the book and went past him without another word, but she closed the door behind her when she went into her mother's room.

There were some suit boxes by the closet door and Minta vaguely remembered that the women from the bazaar committee had called several times.

Her hands felt slightly unsteady as she pulled open the top dresser drawer and looked down at the stacks of clean handkerchiefs, the stockings in their quilted satin case, the gloves folded into tissue wrappings.

"I can't do it," she told herself, but she got a box and started putting the things into it, trying not to look at them, trying to forget how delighted her mother had been with the pale green slip, trying not to remember.

Once she hesitated and almost lifted a soft wool sweater from the pile that was growing in the suit box. She had borrowed it so often that her mother used to complain that she felt like a criminal every time she borrowed it back again. She didn't mean it though . . . she loved having Minta borrow her things.

Minta put the sweater with the other things and closed the box firmly.

Now, the things in the closet—

Opening the door was almost like feeling her mother in the room beside her. A faint perfume clung to most of her garments. The housecoat . . . the woolly robe . . . the tan polo coat . . . the scarlet jacket . . . her new blue wool with the pegtop skirt.

Minta started folding the things with almost frantic haste, stuffing them into boxes, cramming the lids on and then starting on another box.

At the very back of the closet were the two pieces of matched luggage that had been her mother's last birthday gift from her father. They were heavy when she tried to move them —too heavy.

She brought them out into the room and put them side by side on her mother's bed. Her breath caught in her throat when she opened them.

Dozens and dozens of boxes, all tied with bright red ribbon, the gift tags written out in her mother's careful script. Gayly colored Christmas stickers, sprigs of holly.

To Minta from Mother and Dad . . . to Grace from Mary . . . to John from Mary . . . to the Kelly Gremlins from Aunt Mary . . . to Uncle Art from the Hawley family . . .

"So you knew," Minta whispered the words. "You knew all the time."

She looked down in surprise as a hot tear dropped on her hand and she dashed it away almost impatiently.

She picked up another package and read the tag. To Minta from Mother . . . with love.

Without opening it she knew that it was a picture frame and she remembered the way she had teased her mother to have a good photograph taken.

"The only one I have of you looks like a fugitive from a chain gang," she had pointed out. "I can't very well go away to school next year with *that*."

She put the package back in the suitcase with all the others and carried the cases back into the closet.

Poor Dad, she thought.

"She never knew," she could hear him saying. "Not even at the last."

Minta opened the box beside the bed and took out the sweater and the pale green slip.

"You know perfectly well that you're just exactly like me," she remembered her mother saying.

She brushed the tears away and went down the stairs and out into the cheerless living room.

"I'd like to keep these things, Dad," she said in her most matter-of-fact voice, and she showed him the sweater and slip. "The slip is a little big but I'll grow into it. It . . . it looks like her, I think."

She went around the room, snapping on the lamps, turning on the television that had been silent for so long. She was aware that his eyes followed her, that he could hardly avoid noticing the tear stains on her cheeks.

"I think I'll have an apple," she said. "Want one?"

He nodded. "Sure. Bring me one as long as you're making the trip."

It was natural. It was almost like old times, except that the blue chair by the fireplace was vacant.

She went out into the kitchen hurriedly.

"I'll tell him that I pestered mother to do her shopping early this year," she told herself as she got the apples from the refrigerator. "I'll tell him that it was my idea about the photographs. She wanted him to believe that she didn't know."

The vitamin pills were pushed back on a shelf. She took them out of the refrigerator and put them on the window sill where she would be sure to see them in the morning.

When she came back into the living room she noticed that a light in a Christmas wreath was winking on and off in the Kelly's window across the street.

"I guess we should start thinking about Christmas, Dad." She tossed him an apple as she spoke and he caught it deftly.

She hesitated for just a moment and then walked over and sat down in the blue chair by the fire, as if she belonged there, and looked across at her father, and smiled.

I

THE EMPTY CHAIR

Minta's story seems a complicated one. First, she had to accept the knowledge that her mother was to die; then, learn to live with this aching fear; and in the end, accept the reality of her mother's death. Nevertheless, many "inner circles" are broken apart temporarily or permanently under circumstances as heartbreaking. Why do you suppose that Minta picks the September day as the day she grew up, rather than the one when she found the suitcase of Christmas gifts?

Discuss these in relation to their significance in the story.

1. "They talked, the casual happy talk of people who love each other and don't have to make conversation."

2. "She never cried again. . . . Not even when the ambulance came . . . to take her mother to the hospital. . . . Not even at the funeral."

3. The mother's statement, "You know you're just exactly like me," helped Minta face reality.

II

IMPLICATIONS

Consider and discuss the merits of these statements.

1. The members of this family did the wise thing to pretend to each other that the mother was going to be all right.

2. Actually, whether it is death or some other problem, the best course of action is a frank discussion among those concerned.

III

TECHNIQUES

Effect

Recall the unity of tone or atmosphere in "The Scarlet Ibis." Tone or atmosphere in writing is achieved much as it is in music. The composer combines musical sounds in a particular way and with a particular rhythm to arouse specific feelings in the listener. Similarly, the writer uses descriptive words and phrases to fit a certain pattern and tempo. In this way, he may arouse predetermined feelings such as foreboding and sadness, amusement, or seriousness, or even gaiety.

1. "From Mother . . . with Love" definitely has a unity of tone. What emotional response did you get from reading the story? Do you think your response was the kind the author intended?

2. Has the author created her atmosphere in a cheap and sentimental fashion or did she use restraint? Discuss.

Here is a story concerned with the prejudice
which sometimes holds people apart.
Once in a while, you find a person who believes
in doing something about such prejudice.
Tom and Andy's father was one who had little
patience with it. He knew that his boys would not
grow up until they learned to respect the rights
of others. He could be mighty rough on those
guilty of injustice—even if those persons
were his own sons.

The Strangers
That Came to Town

AMBROSE FLACK

The first of April came dark and stormy, with
silver whips of lightning cracking open the lowering clouds that seemed to skim the treetops.
My brother Tom and I, recovering from chest
colds, tired of reading and listening to the radio, turned to the big living room window of
our house on Syringa Street.

"Here they come, Mother," cried Tom when
a big truck drove up in the teeming rain and
stopped in front of the empty cottage across the
street.

Mother hurried in from the kitchen and we
three looked out. That truck, we knew, contained the Duvitch family and all their earthly
possessions.

Mr. Duvitch and the biggest boy carefully
helped Mrs. Duvitch from the seat and walked
her into the house, supporting her all the way.
Another big boy, carrying a well-bundled baby,
followed. A stream of young Duvitches, accompanied by a big brown houndlike dog, poured
out of the back of the truck and stood in a huddle in the rain.

Reprinted by permission of Ambrose Flack.

The barnyard sounds we heard escaped from
two crates of hens the Duvitches had fetched
along and from a burlap bag in which a small
flock of ducks had been stowed. While the livestock made noises according to its kind, the
Duvitches were quiet—almost solemn. They
showed no elation at finding themselves in a
new neighborhood and a very pretty neighborhood at that.

All afternoon Mother, Tom and myself had
been watching out for them, with rather mixed
emotions. For the Duvitches were immigrants
and the first of their nationality to settle in our
small smug town. Coming to our obscure part
of the state a year before, they had moved into
a rotting old farmhouse two miles north of
town, long abandoned. After the slashing hurricane of mid-March, the moss-rotten dwelling
looked like the house in the fairy tale that remained standing only because it did not know
which way to fall and the Duvitches were
forced to give it up.

"I wonder if Mrs. Duvitch is ill," murmured
Mother, looking through the rain at the dreary
street scene.

"She must be," said Tom. "I wonder if it'll be
all right for Andy and me to help 'em move in
their stuff."

This request, as Mother well knew, was not
inspired by genuine feeling for the Duvitches
but by curiosity and she shook her head. It was
a strict family rule that any illness which kept
us out of school would automatically keep us
indoors.

But the Duvitches got along very well without help from us. As it turned out, they were
old hands at moving. For years before coming
to America they had been on the move, to escape starvation, separation, possible assassina-
tion. Every child capable of two-legged loco-
motion pitched in and helped carry the things
from the truck. In no time at all, it seemed, the
truck was empty and the Duvitches were shut
up tight in their new home.

That was the signal for Mother to step into
the kitchen. She returned swathed in her
hooded raincoat, carrying a basket containing

a vacuum jug of chicken soup, a baked tuna-fish dish, steaming hot; a loaf of fresh bread and a chocolate cake. These she took to the house across the street and gave basket and all to the boy who answered her knock. It wasn't her plan to stop for a visit that day but to wait a week or so and call when the Duvitches were all settled.

The next day when the three of us—Mother, Tom and myself—were having lunch, we heard a faint tap at the back door. I answered it and there stood a pale dark-eyed boy, looking very solemn, holding our basket. It contained the empty vacuum jug, casserole dish and cake plate, all of which shone, and a tiny very shapely potted rose tree, in exquisite pink-tipped bud, the handsomest plant––and the only plant of its kind––ever seen in that neighborhood.

"I send them a few scraps of food," murmured Mother, a few seconds later, deeply touched, "and get this queenly gift!"

That was our last traffic with the Duvitch family for over two years. When Mother stopped to visit them a week after their coming, the little girl who opened the door a few inches said, "Mamma sick; she stay in bed today." Mrs. Duvitch never crossed the street to our house and Mother, a rather formal woman, made no further attempts to see the family. But Father disagreed when she remarked that she thought the Duvitches probably wished to be left alone.

Syringa Street seemed to be a friendly street. It was a crooked maple-shady country lane that wound through the town without losing its charm. The sidewalk here and there was almost lost in weeds and the ditches, in places, were brightened by clumps of orange day lilies. Widely spaced cottages, some of them smothered in vines, only seemed to make the neighborhood more rural. There were brilliant flower gardens, vegetable plots, fruit trees— and a few henhouses. The children, who enjoyed all the benefits of country life while actually living in town, were quite numerous. Behind the façades of the street's dwellings there was probably no more greed, envy, supersti-

tion or intolerance than lurked behind the doors of any average dwelling in any average American town. The cardinal virtues, no doubt, were all represented.[1] Yes, Syringa Street seemed to be a friendly street.

But the Duvitches were marked people. They were the one struggling family in a prosperous community—and poverty, amid prosperity, is often embarrassing and irritating to the prosperous. They were considered unattractive physically. They were so meek! The Duvitches never fought back.

The women started in on Mrs. Duvitch because she "never showed her face." It is true, she was rarely if ever seen in the daytime, emerging from her dwelling only after dark in warm weather, to sit on the veranda, where she found privacy behind the ragged trumpet-creeper. But this gave rise to the rumor that she was the victim of an obscure skin disease and that every morning she shook scales out of the bed sheet. . . .

Mr. Duvitch, too, was classified as an untouchable. His job, a rather malodorous one, was with the local rendering plant as a laborer. It followed that the Syringa Street young, meeting him on the street, sometimes stopped their noses as they passed him by—a form of torment all the more acute when Mr. Duvitch had to share it with the children that happened to be with him.

Black hard luck seemed to be their lot.

A few weeks after they moved to Syringa Street, they suffered a minor tragedy. Mr. Duvitch got sick and lost out on two weeks' pay. It took the family all summer to recover from that blow. Inside of a year and a half, three Duvitch boys had lost, among them, by various mishaps, two fingers, one eye and an ear lobe. They were forever being cut up, bruised, mutilated by things falling, breaking, cracking, and exploding.

A mild case of typhoid, mass cases of whooping cough and measles—all plagued the family

---

1. In theological history the cardinal virtues were prudence, justice, fortitude, and temperance.

within a year of their arrival. Their only bright spot here was Dr. Switzer, one of the town's kindliest souls. He declined to accept fees, but was several times seen leaving the Duvitch cottage, carrying off a handsome house plant and looking very pleased. The Duvitches' dog, Kasimar, acted just like the family to which he belonged—like one of the world's poorest canine relations. He seemed to be afraid of his own shadow and no one had ever heard him bark or growl.

Because they cast their eyes on the sidewalk as one passed them by and spoke only when spoken to, the young Duvitches, like their parents, were considered antisocial. They were regarded as born scavengers too, for they spent hours foraging in the town dump, where they often picked up their footgear, some of their pants and shirts and furnishings for the house as well. They went on country excursions to gather watercress, dandelion greens, mushrooms, and wild berries; and the few apples and tomatoes they occasionally concealed under their blouses didn't make the farmers on whom they poached much poorer. Tom and I raided tomato patches and robbed apple trees just for the fun of it.

That first September four Duvitches—Irving, Benny, Abe, and Esther—registered at the local grammar school. Mrs. Lovejoy, the principal, said they were bright, conscientious, pathetically eager but almost pathologically shy. Before she could put a stop to it, some of their classmates scoffed at the leaf-lard-and-black-bread sandwiches they ate for lunch, huddled in one corner of the recreation room, dressed in their boiled-out ragpickers' clothes. After school they headed straight for home, never lingering on the playground.

Even the tradesmen to whom the Duvitches gave good money were either curt with them or downright rude. Mrs. Frithjof Kinsella, the proprietor of the general store and a big jolly Viking who could be heard two blocks away, extended credit to almost everybody in town and had a way of insulting her customers so heartily that they all loved her for it. The Duvitches,

however, Mrs. Kinsella very carefully *did not insult* (a form of insult in itself) and neither did she extend them credit.

But Mother, remembering the potted rose tree, always had a friendly word and a smile for the young Duvitches when she saw them and she always had a bone for Kasimar when he found courage to venture across the road. Father was the only man on Syringa Street who tipped his hat to sixteen-year-old pock-marked Maria Duvitch, otherwise quite pretty, when he met her coming home from her piece-work job in Miller's Box Factory. It may have been that their European travail made it easy for them to endure such a trifle as humiliation in America.

"I think," said Father one fine Saturday morning in July two years after the Duvitches had come to Syringa Street, "that it would be very pleasant for Andy, Tom, and myself to pitch our tent out at Durston's Pond and spend the night. We could fish and swim. That is," he added, "if Mother can spare us."

"I can spare you very well," Mother said cheerfully.

She had a notion it did menfolk good to get away from their women occasionally and in this instance the sacrifice came easily, because camp life was little to her liking. She packed a hamper of food; Tom and I fetched the tent from the attic and Father looked over his fishing tackle. An hour after lunch we were driving through rolling farm country out to Durston's Pond, four miles north of town.

We often had the serene little lake all to ourselves, but on our arrival that afternoon we found half a dozen male Duvitches in possession. They had been fishing for several hours, casting from the shore, dropping their lines over the wooden bridge that spanned Cat Creek where it flowed into the pond and trolling for bass from a flat-bottomed rowboat.

Tom and I, Philistines like our friends, ignored the Duvitch boys but Father went up to Mr. Duvitch, who was fishing from the shore, and put out his hand.

"Good afternoon, Mr. Duvitch! It's nice to see you and the boys here. What a beautiful day! Are Mrs. Duvitch and the girls all well?"

Mr. Duvitch was a little fellow, a lean starve-
ling of a man with watery blue eyes and a
kicked-about look. Gratitude for being agreeably noticed showed in his mosquito-bitten face
as he took Father's hand, and his tremulous
smile showed broken teeth.

"I know the mosquitoes are biting," Father
went on pleasantly, "but are the fish?"

Proudly, oh, so proudly, Mr. Duvitch exhibited the catch that would probably feed his
family for the better part of a week: a fine mess
of bass, perch, and sunfish all of them alive,
as far as I could see, and swimming around in
the oaken washtub into which they had been
dropped. Father gave Mr. Duvitch hearty congratulations and said we couldn't hope to do as
well but that we'd try.

We three pitched the tent on a little knoll
above the pond, and then Father, with a happy
sigh, lay down on a blanket for a nap in the sun.
Tom and I played a game of chew-the-peg on
the grassy bank above the water and, later on,
made several trips to the tent for the camera,
the field glasses, the sun lotion. On a trip for a
cold drink from the vacuum jug and to fetch
towels and soap, we stopped to look again at
the Duvitches' catch of fish.

Mr. Duvitch and the boys had moved away
and were fishing in a small arm of the pond below us. None of them seemed visible. Tom and
I, our glances meeting over the big cake of
soap in my hand, were similarly and wickedly
inspired—the thing was irresistible. We held a
brief whispering conversation; and then, egged
on by him and quite willing on my own, I
played a shameful trick on the Duvitches, the
memory of which will come back to the end of
my days to plague me. Without considering
further, I dropped the cake of soap into the tub
of fish.

"Let's go," whispered Tom after we had
watched the soap sink to the bottom.

We swam out to the raft, diving and frolicking in the deep water. After a while the Duvitches, calling it a day, assembled at a spot on

the shore below our tent, happy in the knowledge of a good catch to take home.

In a little while Tom and I could hear their
muffled exclamations of disbelief and dismay.
Father woke up and joined our neighbors in a
conclave, looking down at the tub of fish near
his feet. After a few moments he produced the
whistle he carried on all our country excursions
and blew it piercingly three times, the procla-
mation of emergency. This meant that Tom and
I must come at once.

Looking as guilty as we felt, we swam in and
joined the group gathering around the tub. In
the midst of our stricken neighbors stood Father, holding the half-melted cake of soap in
his palm silently but accusingly, for the fish had
perished miserably in the soapy water and were
unfit to eat. Not only had Tom and I snatched
precious food from their mouths but we had
also brazenly advertised the contempt in which
we held them.

Father's eyes were narrow slits of blue fire
in his white face. I had never seen him so angry.
One look at Tom and me told him everything.
Words would have been superfluous and my
brother and I bowed our heads in acknowledge-
ment of our guilt.

"You will begin," Father said in a voice I
didn't recognize, "by saying you're sorry."

Our stunned neighbor wiped his blinking
eyes as he listened to our mumbled words,
which Father made us repeat when they were
inaudible. But there was no hostility, no animosity toward us in the man and it was obvious
also that he considered himself too humble to
receive an apology, finding it, like most of life's
troubles, a mockery to be endured without protest. His sons showed no resentment, either,
only a kind of resignation.

Manny Duvitch, as it turned out, had told
Father he had seen me drop something in the
tub of fish (before he learned that it had been
a cake of soap). Now he looked guiltier than
Tom and I. Because he had been witness and
accuser, it was as if he considered himself to be
the troublemaker, deserving the punishment.

"Do you realize," said Father coldly, looking

from Tom to me, "that in certain primitive communities the sort of stunt you've pulled would be punishable by death?"

Tom and I did not reply.

"Turn over the tub," said Father abruptly, addressing us as if we were strangers.

We turned it over. The gray, soapy water ran away in bubbly rivulets, disappearing in the coarse mat of turf, and the poisoned fish lay exposed on the grass—quiet, strangled, open-mouthed—and somehow looking as if they were mutely protesting their horrid unnatural fate.

"Count the fish," Father ordered us, his voice like steel.

Tom and I got down on our knees.

"How many are there?" demanded Father.

"Sixty-one," I said.

"How many bass?"

"Twelve."

Father handed Mr. Duvitch two dollars, the price of a day's rental of the rowboat. Then, looking both like the avenging angel and executioner, he ordered Tom and me, with our tackle and bait, off the land we had disgraced—into exile, out on Durston's Pond.

"And you are not to come back," he gave out in the same steely tones, "until you've caught sixty-one fish to repay Mr. Duvitch. See to it that among them you bring in at least a dozen bass."

Father stepped up to the tent on the knoll to fetch our shirts and dungarees. These he rolled into a tight ball and shot like a bolt into the rowboat. He then turned his back to us and, thus disowned, Tom and I lost no time in rowing out on the pond. Father's decisions, even with Mother present, were never reversed and swift execution, from which there was no appeal, followed his sentences.

Out in the middle of the big pond we dropped anchor, threaded our steel rods and, baiting our hooks, began to fish. I knew that if it took us all summer to catch them, we dared not set foot ashore without sixty-one fish. Almost at once Tom pulled in a good-sized bass and ten minutes later two yellow perch were added to our string. The crestfallen Duvitches went home.

Father threw himself on the blanket, furiously smoking a cigar. That was about four in the afternoon.

Oh, the mosquitoes! They were bad enough at the time, and while the light held, but after we had been fishing for three hours and had caught eight fish, they swarmed out of the dark Hades of swampland surrounding the pond like Lucifer's angels, in legions.[2]

After an hour of it we wanted to leap overboard. They got into our ears, our noses, our eyes, even into our mouths, and nestling in our hair, they bit through to our scalps. I remembered tales of Indian prisoners in Alaska, stripped by their captors and turned loose on the tundra, where they died of the mosquitoes in two hours. Several times we slipped over the side of the boat, immersing ourselves in the water to escape the blood-thirsty clouds. The night dragged on while the whining swarms grew thicker.

"Andy, what time is it?"

"Ten o'clock, Tom."

"Is that all?" Tom groaned and pulled in another bass and killed six or eight mosquitoes in one slap. Two hours passed and midnight was ghostly on Durston's Pond.

The moon, bright as day, sailed high in the purple sky, dimming the starfire, casting a great white shaft of quivering radiance on the water, but it was all hideous. The big yellow disk sank in a gauzy cloudbank, then disappeared for good and the stars shone out with renewed splendor.

"Andy, what *time* is it?"

"Two o'clock, Tom."

The treetops whispered as if in conspiracy against us. Owls hooted—mockingly we thought—and bats circled over our heads, making us feel thoroughly damned. Our only solace was the campfire Father kept burning near the tent, which flared like a beacon light in the dark. We went on fishing as our tormentors bit

---

2. According to legend the angel **Lucifer**\\ᴧlū·sĭ·fər\\ led many other angels to revolt against the Divinity. They were condemned finally to Hell (or **Hades**\\ᴧhā 'dēz\\).

and sang. Each hour was an eternity of frenzy and I fairly panted for the light of dawn to come, but even now I cannot decide which was worse, that night with the mosquitoes on Durston's Pond or the following day in the blistering heat.

"Andy—"

"It's four o'clock, Tom, and we've got sixteen fish."

Dawn came but even I, a highly impressionable youngster of seventeen, did not enjoy that calm effulgent majesty of daybreak. A long stretch on Durston's Pond, under the July sun, still faced us.

The rising sun was red, casting glimmering circles of rose-colored light on the windless surface of the pond. The mosquitoes thinned, the fish continued to bite. But as we fished the sun mounted steadily and by eleven it had fulfilled its awful prophecy and became a ball of fire in the cloudless skies. Tom and I began to bake in the heat waves that shimmered over the pond and we were steamed in the scalding vapory mist.

"I wish it was night again, Andy," groaned Tom after sweating out two hours of it. "This is worse than the mosquitoes."

"At least we won't get any infections from our bites, Tom," I said feebly. "The sun's cauterizing them."

"We might get sunstrokes, though. We're liable to, without our hats. But I don't care if I do. I'd rather be unconscious."

Tom was only fifteen and I think he hated me that day. I, the older, should have been his protector against participation in crime, not his accomplice. I wanted to row him in, then come back to finish the business alone, but there on the green Edenlike shore stood Father—the archangel bearing the fiery sword, stationed by the Lord at the gates of Paradise to bar the way.[3]

Tom and I weighed our hooks down to the deep cold water. We caught two more bass and half a dozen sunfish.

By one o'clock groups of people gathered on the shore, for word of the drama that was being enacted on Durston's Pond had spread through the town. Some of the visitors praised Father for his stern discipline; others berated him. He went right on reading his magazine and smoking his cigar, as indifferent to their praise as he was to their criticism.

Local fishermen who knew the lake and something about the angling ability of the average youngster made gloomy estimates as to the possible length of our exile on the water. A few had us fishing until the snow flew. They made bets too. Would Tom and I have the guts to stick it out? Most of the bets were against us.

But we sat there in the rowboat, without food, through the hottest day of the summer.

No breeze stirred. No cloud obscured the sun. Even the bird life of the swamp, usually a medley of song, was silent and dead. Tom was drooping visibly in the glare and I tried hard not to look at his scorched face.

Between three and four we dropped lines in a school of yellow perch and pulled up no less than twenty. The bass continued to bite in the deep black holes off the swamp, which bristled with tree trunks. Benumbed, half-blinded, moving like automatons, Tom and I geared ourselves for the home stretch.

When the sun, dropping low, had lost its fury and the hard blue enamel of the sky began to pale, I pulled up the thirteenth bass, which was our sixty-first fish.

Turned lobster-red, fairly devoured, famished and drooping from lack of sleep, we put together our rods and with our remaining strength rowed to where Father was waiting.

He received us coolly, making no comment on our condition. At once he asked to see the fish and we held them up by the strings.

"Count them," he said.

Obviously we would receive permission to

---

3. When Adam and Eve were driven from the Garden of Eden, the Lord stationed an angel with the sword outside the garden to bar their reentry. See Genesis, 3:24.

land only when we had produced the required number, which was the price of our freedom.

"Sixty-one," said Tom.

"Including thirteen bass," I added.

"Very good," said Father in businesslike tones. "We will now restore to Mr. Duvitch his rightful property."

Tom and I took care not to play the part of triumphant heroes, even of redeemed sinners —that would not have suited our parent. Certainly, in appearance, we were more damned than redeemed. But when we tottered out of the rowboat something in me was quietly rejoicing. I guessed that Father was secretly proud of our fortitude and I realized, too, that all through the night he had suffered with us.

We walked through the crowd of visitors on the lake shore, climbed into the car and silently drove to the Duvitch cottage. Mrs. Duvitch and the children were not visible but we found Mr. Duvitch sitting on the porch.

When he saw Tom and me and we silently handed him the strings of fish, he gulped and swallowed hard. For a moment he could not speak. Then, in a voice that was raw with emotion, he protested that he had not wished us to suffer so. Suppose we had fallen overboard in the dark?

"Will you shake hands with the boys?" asked Father.

Instead, Mr. Duvitch broke down. My brother and I did not know where to look and during those moments we suffered more acutely than we had suffered in the clouds of mosquitoes and under the broiling sun. After our neighbor had composed himself, he seized our hands and bowed his head over them. There was something Biblical, like a picture in the Old Testament, in the man's gesture. Anyway, it was my greatest lesson in humility.

When Mother, who had heard about our exile on the pond from a neighbor, saw us she burst into tears. She tried to embrace us but we drew back painfully. While she was rubbing salves and ointments on our seared backs

and necks, somebody knocked at the kitchen door and Father opened it to find Mrs. Duvitch standing there, her face and skin as undefiled as the Virgin's[4]—the first time she had crossed the street to our house.

In her pale swaying hand Mrs. Duvitch held a porcelain teacup, ornamented with pink rosebuds and golden leaves—a relic from the old country and, as it turned out, her most cherished possession.

Her voice, thin and wispy from fright and shock, was difficult to follow. But we gathered that she had brought the teacup over as a peace offering and as a plea for our forgiveness to her family for the living purgatory, no matter whose fault, through which my brother and I had passed. When Mother declined the teacup and assured Mrs. Duvitch that she would not have it otherwise with Tom and me, our neighbor, unable to find her tongue, made a little eloquent sign with her hands that was for thanks and that looked like a silent blessing. She quietly turned and went away; and again I felt that I had witnessed a scene from the Old Testament.

Mother continued her ministrations to Tom and me and put us to bed. Despite our skin, which stuck to sheet and pillowcase, we slept like creatures drugged.

"It is high time," Tom and I heard Father say calmly, sanely, to Mother around noon next day when we woke up, "for this senseless feeling against the Duvitches to stop and I'm willing to do still more to stop it. Tonight we are having supper with them. I've just seen Mr. Duvitch and he remarked that since Andy and Tom caught the fish, he'd feel better if we all shared in them. I suggested a fish-fry picnic supper and with a few hints from me, and some encouragement, he invited us over. It may be an ordeal but we ought to be able to bear it."

We walked across the street at six o'clock, not knowing what to expect. All the Duvitches, dressed in their Sunday best, bright and flushed

---

4. **The Virgin** is the Virgin Mary, the mother of Christ.

and shining as we had never seen them, received us at the door as if we had been royalty. They looked at Tom and me and delicately looked away—I shuddered when I thought of what my brother and I would have had to endure had this been any other family.

Instead of a wretched abode we found a scantily furnished home that shone with cleanliness and smelled of spicy garden pinks. In its almost barren simplicity there was something comely. A few of the stands, chairs and tables had the intimate quality of what is fashioned by the human hand. These, together with odds and ends the family had brought from the old country and others resurrected from the town dump and mended, painted, waxed and polished, made for a kind of native household harmony. The house plants (no window was without several) delighted Mother. Mrs. Duvitch was raising little orange and lemon trees from seed and experimenting with a pineapple plant growing in a butter tub.

At once we were conscious of a remarkable difference in the demeanor of the family. The children, thrilled by their first party, by the family's first recognition in this country, kept showing their pleasure in wide delighted smiles. I couldn't believe they were the same timid downcast youngsters one met on the street and saw in school; they seemed to have been touched by a wand. The Duvitches' home was their castle: sustained and animated by the security of its four walls, shut away from a world of contempt and hostility, they were complete human beings. In their own house their true personalities emerged.

As the host Mr. Duvitch was a man we were seeing for the first time. Overjoyed to have neighbors in his house, he was so full of himself that I was conscious of an invisible stature in him which made him seem quite as tall as Father. He beamed and feasted his eyes on us. Saying very little, he managed to make us feel a great deal and he constantly sought his wife's eyes with glances of delight over the wonder of what was happening.

David, the oldest boy, helped his father serve a bottle of homemade blackberry wine.

We ate fried fish and good food of the American picnic variety at a long plank table set out in the back yard under an apple tree. The young Duvitches passed things politely, never helping themselves first; and their thanks upon receiving a dish were almost ceremonial. They waited patiently for their plates and ate every scrap of food.

Father kept the conversation going. His every word was listened to, every childish eye riveted on him while he spoke.

Tom and I, fascinated by the family's metamorphosis, almost forgot about our blisters and our stings. As Father told stories and jokes, we discovered that the Duvitches had a gift for gaiety, for laughter, all but extinguished but still capable of resurrection. They were merry people who had suffered too much. How strange to see the boys and girls throw back their heads and laugh when Father said something that was funny, but not terribly funny.

After supper we were ushered to the open summer kitchen, the coolest room in the house, for entertainment.

David played folk songs on his accordion. Mr. Duvitch turned out to be an amateur ventriloquist; he made the dog Kasimar talk Polish, the cat Jan talk Russian and a doll named Sophia talk English. Mrs. Duvitch read aloud to us, translating as she went along, a letter her mother had received from the great actress Modjeska, whom her family had known long ago.[5]

I could tell that the Duvitches were a great revelation to Father and that he had enjoyed the evening tremendously.

"To think," he murmured as if talking to himself, while we were crossing the street, "that they should turn out to be gentle people of cultivation and accomplishment. Looked down on and ignored by their inferiors!"

5. **Helena**\ˈhĕ lā·nə\ **Modjeska**\mɔ ᴧjĕs·ka\ (1840–1909) was a world-famous tragic actress.

I like to believe that the oil paintings of George Washington, Abraham Lincoln and Thomas Jefferson, which hung in our living room, helped to establish the Duvitches in our community. Even the fountain tinkling in the lily pool in our garden might have helped. In that town, oil paintings and flowing fountains were the symbols of wealth and aristocracy. Only a few mansions on Sycamore Hill were adorned with such.

Because our home was graced with these symbols, we had always been classified with the town's great, which gave us such prestige in the neighborhood that people often followed our lead. Obviously the Duvitches were important in Father's eyes, shown by the rigorous sentence he had imposed on Tom and me for our misuse of them. Added to that, we had recognized the family by taking a meal with them in their own house. People, often persuaded to accept what we accepted, to believe what we believed, began to think the Duvitches must really count, after all. Most of our neighbors decided that if they were good enough for a highly educated man like Father (the only college graduate on Syringa Street), they were good enough for them. The galvanized community began to look upon things in a different light and it soon became the fashion to give the Duvitches the favorable nod.

Mother invited Mrs. Duvitch to a tea party, where her delicate manners, and the fine needlework which engaged her, won the approval of the local housewives who were present. On hot days our neighbor asked one of her big boys to carry the pineapple plant (which Mother had advertised well), into the back yard; and since botanical rarities were irresistible in that town of gardens, people were soon stopping by the fence for a look at the tropical specimen. After a while Mrs. Duvitch found courage to ask these people into her house and, if Mr. Duvitch was at home, he told the visitors stories about life in the old country. It was then that the neighborhood learned about the family's European past.

The children ceased stopping their noses when Mr. Duvitch passed them by and it wasn't long before the young Duvitches were able to enjoy outside companionship when they found time to play. They blossomed out in school and they were soon shining in school plays and festivals. Even Kasimar began to take on the ways of an American dog, daring to bark and growl on occasion.

Nathan Duvitch, who was seventeen, could throw and hit a baseball as far as anybody his age in town. When I learned this, and let it be known, he was asked to join one of the local ball clubs. David, invited to play his accordion at a country dance, turned out to be a magician with the instrument and ended up being one of the community's most popular players. Mrs. Frithjof Kinsella gave Manny an after-school job in her store and later on told Mother he was worth three boys put together.

The community presently had reason to be grateful for Mrs. Duvitch's presence. It turned out that she had a great gift for nursing, and no fear of death, no fear of disease, contagious or otherwise. In times of severe illness Dr. Switzer often suggested that she be sent for— her own girls could take over at home. There were almost no nurses in town and the nearest hospital was over a hundred miles away. When Mrs. Duvitch quietly slipped into a sickroom, she never failed to bring along a sedative influence, a kind of sanity. After an hour or two of her serene presence, the patient was calmed and comforted and the family reassured.

People began to turn to the Duvitches in all kinds of trouble. A boy who got in a bad scrape, a bitter family quarrel, a baby who had come into the world deformed—the elder Duvitches, with their old-world wisdom and gift for accepting the inevitable, could sit by the hour and argue gently and convincingly against disgrace, false pride, grief, fear.

Most surprising of all, Mr. Duvitch, in one respect, turned out to be characteristically American. One Saturday afternoon when my ball team was playing Nathan's, Father met him in the local ball park.

"Chust like de American boy," Mr. Duvitch exploded when Nathan made a timely hit that drove in two runs. Our neighbor choked with pride and went on: "Nathan's battering averich three hunnert tventy-sevened!"

On a cold snowy afternoon in winter Mr. Duvitch stopped at our house and presented Father (who had enormous hands, much bigger than any of the Duvitches') with a handsome pair of leather mittens, lined with fur, which had a slightly acrid ashy odor.

"No doubt one of the boys resurrected them from a heap of ashes in the dump," remarked Father, drawing on the mittens, which fitted perfectly. "Why should I value them any the less? *Who* would have dreamed that the Duvitches would have so much more to offer us than we have to offer them?"

I
ORDEAL AND UNDERSTANDING

When outsiders such as the Duvitches are not accepted in a community because of social prejudice, in many instances, all it takes to remedy the situation is to have one worthy citizen openly show his respect for them. Being accepted into *one* "inner circle" is like a magic key which opens the door to respect from others.

Consider and discuss:

1. The many ways in which Tom and Andy's father shows that he respects the Duvitches. Why is the fishing incident particularly important?

2. Inside of their own home, the personalities of all the Duvitches seemed to change. Why?

3. How could knowing the Duvitches enrich the "inner circles" of those who accepted them?

II
IMPLICATIONS

Decide whether or not you agree with these statements. Discuss them with relation to the story.

1. If one is to keep his self-respect and be worthy of the respect of others, he must always take responsibility for his own actions.

2. Poverty is embarrassing and irritating to the prosperous.

III
TECHNIQUES
Narrative Viewpoint

This story is told in the first person by Andy, one of the main characters. The use of the first person allows the writer to establish a person-to-person relationship, as though he were sharing an experience with the reader, but it also has some disadvantages. The narrator can't tell you about himself directly, so his actions, thoughts, and words must indicate the kind of person he is. In this short story, when Andy spreads the word that Nathan Duvitch is a good ballplayer, thereby getting him into a local ball club, you know that Andy is not vindictive; he does not hold a grudge.

1. How is it revealed that Andy has genuine concern for his younger brother?

2. What other traits of Andy's character are revealed and how?

SUMMING UP

The Inner Circle

The inner circles in the stories you have just read are of many kinds. In the first circle you saw tense, worried Alfred Higgins, his heartsick, uncertain mother and his unsympathetic, disinterested father. In other circles, real and fictional, you saw such people as the poetess Nikki Giovanni, the slightly foolish Mr. Whalen, and the humble, compassionate Mr. Duvitch. Each person was different, but all were aware of the basic human need for the love and security found most abundantly in a close inner circle of family or friends.

IMPLICATIONS

The following quotations were written over the past twenty-two hundred years. Discuss how each applies to ideas expressed in one or more of the preceding group of selections.

1. "All happy families resemble one another; every unhappy family is unhappy in its own fashion"—Leo Tolstoy, nineteenth century.

2. "Justice is never anything in itself, but, in the dealings of men with one another in any place whatever and at any time, it is a kind of compact not to harm or be harmed"—Epicurus, third century B.C.

3. "If a house be divided against itself, that house cannot stand"—Mark 3:25.

4. "There is nothing more tragic in life than the utter impossibility of changing what you have done"—John Galsworthy, twentieth century.

TECHNIQUES

The fable, ancestor of the short story, is ordinarily quite short and written with the purpose of teaching a useful lesson or moral. Its lesson is summed up in a final statement called a maxim or a proverb. See if you can recall the maxim with which the Aesop fable on the opening page of THE INNER CIRCLE concluded. Check yourself to see how nearly you remembered the exact wording.

Theme and Effect

The modern short story, if it follows the pattern established by such well-known authors as the French writer de Maupassant and the American writer Edgar Allan Poe, has a basic idea or *theme*, and strives for a single *effect*.

1. Discuss in what ways you think a short story presenting a basic idea or theme would differ from a fable.

2. Some of the selections in this section depended heavily upon their appeal to the emotions to achieve the final *effect*. Recall the ways de Maupassant stated (page 282) that the reader wished to be reached. Opposite each category below, list one or more selections from THE INNER CIRCLE which affected you emotionally in that particular way:

a. "Amused me."
b. "Made me weep."
c. "Made me think."

Type of Short Story

In many short stories, *characterization, action, setting,* and *theme* seem to be almost equal in importance. However, in this section, most stories are concerned primarily with *theme* and *characterization*. Select one story and in a brief paper discuss the four elements in it.

Narrative Viewpoint

The point of view from which a story is told is a matter to be considered carefully for both short and long stories. Discuss the possible viewpoints from which an author can narrate a story. What advantages or disadvantages go with each viewpoint?

Symbolism

When an author uses a concrete thing to stand for an idea difficult to describe, he is using symbolism. How did James Hurst use the scarlet ibis as a symbol to convey meaning in his story about the little boy, Doodle?

Romeo and Juliet

Introduction

Perhaps the best-known story in western literature on the theme of tragic young love is *Romeo and Juliet*. When he wrote his drama on this popular theme in 1595, the thirty-one-year-old William Shakespeare could not possibly have known he was creating a masterpiece that would still be appearing on the stage more than three and one-half centuries later. Also, he might have scoffed at the suggestion that his play would have such appeal that it would influence the ideas of millions of young persons about romantic love and inspire the creation of paintings, music, opera, ballet, musicals, and film.

Shakespeare and His Times

No poet and playwright in the history of English literature has a greater reputation than William Shakespeare. That he was an actor undoubtedly helped him to write plays that have real audience appeal.

To fully appreciate a Shakespearean play when reading it, one needs to have some knowledge of what the theater was like in Shakespeare's time. There were none of the elaborate stage sets seen in much present-day theater. For a long time plays had been performed only in inns or taverns. Most of these had an inner courtyard and rooms opening onto balconies overlooking the yard. The performers set up their stage at one end of the yard, and those in the audience who could afford it sat in the balconies, protected from the weather by the balcony roofs. The poorer spectators stood on the ground around the stage. Much of the clowning and buffoonery that was common to stage productions was to keep these "groundlings" from becoming restless.

When theaters began to be built, they generally followed the layout of the inns—roofed rows of seats along all the walls except the one from which the stage extended. The center area was left open to the sky so that action on the stage could be seen plainly. In the beginning there was no artificial lighting, and plays were performed in the afternoon.

The stage was a large platform, at the back of which there were two doors, at the right and the left, with a room or recessed space, sometimes curtained, in between. Action such as that for a street scene or a ball would take place out on the open platform. Action set in a smaller area or room, such as that in Friar Laurence's cell, would take place in the recessed space. Above this space was a raised platform, or balcony, to be remembered as the place where Juliet stood for two of the most famous scenes in the play you are about to read.

The "groundlings," who stood around the stage in the regular theater buildings as they had at the inns or taverns, were the noisy section of the audience. They ate lunch, cracked nuts, threw garbage, and heckled the performers if they didn't like the action on the stage.

Most of the stories dramatized at this time were stories the audience already knew. The audience's familiarity with the story, however, detracted nothing from their enjoyment of, or enthusiasm for, the play.

Another point of interest about the theater of Shakespeare's time is that it used no actresses. The usual theatrical troupe consisted of about fifteen men. With each company of adults there were two or three young boys who played the female roles in the plays while they learned the art of acting. All members of a company had to be versatile performers because among them they had to handle all the different roles that would be required in doing a variety of plays.

The Globe Theater, Bankside, in the days of Shakespeare.

The Playwright's Art

Staging

All of the entrances and exits of the actors in Shakespeare's time had to be made in full view of the audience since there were no outside curtains for the stage. A playwright could not depend on realistic sets or even on very many "props" (stage properties) to create an illusion. Information had to be woven into the actors' lines to help the audience understand the scenes on the stage. A common practice was to use an introductory speech, or prologue, at the beginning of the play and/or at the beginning of separate acts to give the audience a summary of the story or to call attention to the theme. This prologue was usually spoken by a single narrator, or chorus.

As you will note in *Romeo and Juliet*, the chorus enters first to give in the prologue a brief summary of the story. The action begins in Verona, Italy, where two influential families have been feuding for years. From these bitterly feuding households come a boy and a girl who fall in love. Their love is starcrossed, or ill-fated, from the beginning. Only the deaths of the two young people force their parents to realize the folly of their feud.

In the action of the play Shakespeare demonstrates his mastery of the staging techniques necessary to keep the audience's interest. The play moves rapidly. The entire drama spans less than one week in the lives of the characters. In this brief time the two central characters meet, fall in love, and die.

In the two dozen short, action-packed scenes, Shakespeare makes the audience feel the pressure of time and the inevitability of the tragic end.

In addition to fast-paced action to hold his audience, Shakespeare uses contrast—contrast in characters, contrast in mood, contrast in setting. For example, the servants who open the play amuse the audience with their foolish prattle. When Tybalt enters, however, the deadly depth of the hatred between the families is revealed. Shortly after, the entrance of old Capulet in his nightgown, calling for his sword, introduces humor again when Lady Capulet suggests he would do better to call for a crutch.

With the entrance of Prince Escalus, Shakespeare introduces the heavy element of authority. Prince Escalus' decree of death to those who disturb the peace of the streets again creates a feeling of foreboding about what lies ahead. Contrast is offered again in the purity of feeling the young lovers have for each other and the coarse and more matter-of-fact views toward romance offered by Juliet's nurse and Romeo's friend Mercutio.

As you read the play, try to visualize the characters as they would have appeared on Shakespeare's stage and note the fast pace of the action and the way the tragic and comic elements are woven together to keep the drama interesting to the very end.

Language

To playgoers of Shakespeare's time, a successful drama was one that combined variety of action with variety of language. Audiences expected to hear passages of great poetic beauty, dramatic speeches filled with bombast, and coarse, boisterous wordplay. Shakespeare gave them all of these.

Within the play as a whole there are a notable amount of rhyme, many extended conceits (which are farfetched ideas expressed in fanciful language), and a number of musically beautiful passages such as those in the first balcony scene and in the farewell of the lovers at dawn.

Act I, Scene 1 opens with *punning*, a type of wordplay that delighted Shakespeare's audiences. A pun may be defined as a play on words based on the similarity of sound between two words with different meanings. The opening conversation of the play between Sampson and Gregory, the two servants of the Capulet family, is an example of punning. The meanings of many of the expressions are strange to you but would be familiar to people living in Shakespeare's day. The marginal notes will help you quickly understand strange words and expressions.

Characters

ESCALUS (ˇĕs·kə·ləs), *Prince of Verona.*

MONTAGUE (ˇmant·ə·gyū),
CAPULET (ˇkăp·yə·lət), } *heads of two feuding households.*

LADY MONTAGUE,
LADY CAPULET, } *their wives.*

ROMEO, *the son of the Montagues.*

JULIET, *the daughter of the Capulets.*

MERCUTIO ('mər·kyū ˇshē·ō), *kinsman of Prince Escalus and friend of Romeo.*

BENVOLIO (bĕn ˇvō·lē·ō), *nephew of Montague and friend of Romeo.*

TYBALT (ˇtĭ·bəlt), *nephew of Lady Capulet.*

PARIS (ˇpăr·əs), *kinsman of Prince Escalus and suitor of Juliet.*

FRAIR LAURENCE, *Franciscan priest.*

FRIAR JOHN, *messenger of Friar Laurence.*

NURSE, *servant and friend of Juliet.*

SAMPSON,
GREGORY, } *servants of Capulet.*

BALTHASAR, *servant of Romeo.*

ABRAHAM, *servant of Montague.*

PETER, *servant of Juliet's nurse.*

APOTHECARY.

MUSICIANS, MASKERS, WATCHMEN, PAGES, OFFICERS, CITIZENS, *and* ATTENDANTS.

Scene: Verona, Italy; Mantua, Italy.
Time: the fourteenth century.

ROMEO AND JULIET

Prologue

CHORUS. Two households, both alike in dignity,[1]
In fair Verona, where we lay our scene,
From ancient grudge break to new mutiny,[2]
Where civil blood makes civil hands unclean,[3]
From forth the fatal loins of these two foes   5
A pair of star-crossed[4] lovers take their life;
Whose misadventured piteous overthrows
Doth with their death bury their parents' strife.
The fearful passage of their death-marked love,
And the continuance of their parents' rage,   10
Which, but[5] their children's end, naught could remove,
Is now the two hours' traffic of our stage;
The which if you with patient ears attend,
What here shall miss, our toil shall strive to mend.

1. **dignity,** rank.

2. **mutiny,** rioting.

3. **Where . . . unclean,** where citizens' hands are soiled with one another's blood.
4. **star-crossed,** fated for distaster. In Shakespeare's time it was a common belief that the stars controlled people's lives.

5. **but,** with the exception of.

Act I

SCENE 1

A summer morning in a public square in Verona, Italy. SAMPSON *and* GREGORY, *servants of the Capulet family, come into the square, armed with swords and small shields. They carry weapons because in a bloody feud such as that between the Capulets and the Montagues, even the servants must be prepared to fight at any moment.*

SAMPSON. Gregory, on my word, we'll not carry coals.[1]
GREGORY. No, for then we should be colliers.[2]
SAMPSON. I mean, an[3] we be in choler,[4] we'll draw.
GREGORY. Ay, while you live, draw your neck out of collar.[5]   5
SAMPSON. I strike quickly, being moved.
GREGORY. But thou art not quickly moved to strike.
SAMPSON. A dog of the house of Montague moves me.

1. **carry coals,** submit to insults.
2. **colliers** \ˈkŏl·yərs\ coal merchants.
3. **an,** if.
4. **in choler,** angry.
5. **collar,** hangman's noose.

355

GREGORY. To move is to stir; and to be valiant is to stand;
therefore, if thou art moved, thou run'st away.   10

SAMPSON. A dog of that house shall move me to stand.
I will take the wall of⁶ any man of Montague's.   6. take . . . wall of, get the better of.

GREGORY. The quarrel is between our masters and us
their men.

SAMPSON. 'Tis all one. I will show myself a tyrant.   15

GREGORY. (*In warning.*) Draw thy sword! Here comes
two of the house of Montague.

[*Enter* ABRAHAM *and* BALTHASAR, *servants of the
Montagues.*]

SAMPSON. My naked weapon is out; quarrel, I will
back thee.

GREGORY. How? Turn thy back and run?   20

SAMPSON. Fear me not.

GREGORY. No, marry.⁷ I fear thee!   7. marry, by the Virgin Mary, a mild oath.

SAMPSON. Let us take the law of our sides;⁸ let them   8. take . . . sides, keep on the right side of the law.
begin.

GREGORY. I will frown as I pass by, and let them take   25
it as they list.⁹   9. list, please.

SAMPSON. Nay, as they dare. I will bite my thumb¹⁰ at   10. bite my thumb, make an insulting gesture.
them, which is disgrace to them if they bear it.

ABRAHAM. Do you bite your thumb at us, sir?

SAMPSON. I do bite my thumb, sir.   30

ABRAHAM. Do you bite your thumb at us, sir?

SAMPSON. (*Aside to* GREGORY.) Is the law of our side
if I say ay?

GREGORY. (*Aside to* SAMPSON.) No.

SAMPSON. No, sir, I do not bite my thumb at you, sir;   35
but I bite my thumb, sir.

GREGORY. Do you quarrel, sir?

ABRAHAM. Quarrel, sir? No, sir.

SAMPSON. But if you do, sir, I am for you. I serve as
good a man as you.   40

ABRAHAM. No better.

SAMPSON. Well, sir.

[*Enter* BENVOLIO.]

GREGORY. (*Aside to* SAMPSON.) Say "better." Here comes
one of my master's kinsmen.

SAMPSON. Yes, better, sir.   45

ABRAHAM. You lie.

SAMPSON. Draw, if you be men. Gregory, remember
thy swashing¹¹ blow.   11. swashing, smashing.

[*The four servants fight.*]

BENVOLIO. Part, fools! (*Beats down their swords.*)
Put up your swords. You know not what you do.   50

[*Enter* TYBALT.]

TYBALT. (*Contemptuously.*) What, art thou drawn
   among these heartless hinds?[12]
Turn thee Benvolio, look upon thy death.

BENVOLIO. I do but keep the peace. Put up thy sword,
Or manage it to part these men with me.

TYBALT. What, drawn, and talk of peace? I hate the
   word   55
As I hate hell, all Montagues, and thee.
Have at thee, coward! (*They fight.*)

[*Enter an* OFFICER *and three or four* CITIZENS *with
   clubs or partisans.*]

OFFICER. Clubs, bills, and partisans![13] Strike, beat them
   down.

CITIZENS. Down with the Capulets! Down with the
   Montagues!

[*Enter old* CAPULET *in his gown.*[14] LADY CAPULET *is
   trying to hold him back.*]

CAPULET. What noise is this? Give me my long sword,
   ho!   60

LADY CAPULET. A crutch,[15] a crutch! Why call you for a
   sword?

CAPULET. My sword, I say! Old Montague is come
And flourishes his blade in spite[16] of me.

[*Enter old* MONTAGUE *and* LADY MONTAGUE.]

MONTAGUE. Thou villain Capulet!—Hold me not; let
   me go.

LADY MONTAGUE. Thou shalt not stir one foot to seek
   a foe.   65

[*Enter* PRINCE ESCALUS *and his* ATTENDANTS.]

PRINCE. Rebellious subjects, enemies to peace,
Profaners of this neighbor-stainèd steel—
Will they not hear? What, ho! You men, you beasts,
That quench the fire of your pernicious rage
With purple fountains issuing from your veins!   70
On pain of torture, from those bloody hands
Throw your mistempered weapons to the ground
And hear the sentence of your movèd prince.
Three civil brawls, bred of an airy word
By thee, old Capulet, and Montague,   75

12. **heartless hinds,** cowardly servants.

13. **bills . . . partisans,** long-handled weapons tipped with sharp blades.

14. **gown,** a dressing gown.

15. **crutch.** Lady Capulet suggests a crutch is a better weapon for him at his age.

16. **spite,** defiance.

Have thrice disturbed the quiet of our streets
And made Verona's ancient citizens
Cast by their grave beseeming ornaments
To wield old partisans, in hands as old,
Cank'red with peace, to part your cank'red hate.   80
If ever you disturb our streets again,
Your lives shall pay the forfeit of the peace.[17]
For this time all the rest depart away.
You, Capulet, shall go along with me;
And, Montague, come you this afternoon,   85
To know our farther pleasure in this case,
To old Freetown, our common judgment place.
Once more, on pain of death, all men depart.

[*Exeunt*[18] *all but* MONTAGUE, LADY MONTAGUE, *and*
   BENVOLIO.]

17. **forfeit . . . peace,** penalty for creating a disturbance.

18. **Exeunt**\ˈĕk·sē ˈənt\ plural form of *exit.*

MONTAGUE. Who set this ancient quarrel new abroach?[19]
  Speak, nephew, were you by when it began?   90
BENVOLIO. Here were the servants of your adversary
  And yours, close fighting ere I did approach.
  I drew to part them. In the instant came
  The fiery Tybalt, with his sword prepared,
  Which, as he breathed defiance to my ears,   95
  He swung about his head and cut the winds,
  Who, nothing hurt withal,[20] hissed him in scorn.
  While we were interchanging thrusts and blows,
  Came more and more, and fought on part and part,
  Till the Prince came, who parted either part.   100
LADY MONTAGUE. O, where is Romeo? Saw you him
    today?
  Right glad I am he was not at this fray.
BENVOLIO. Madam, an hour before the worshiped sun
  Peered forth the golden window of the east,
  A troubled mind drave me to walk abroad,   105
  Where underneath the grove of sycamore
  That westward rooteth from this city side,
  So early walking did I see your son.
  Towards him I made, but he was ware of me
  And stole into the covert of the wood.   110
  I, measuring his affections[21] by my own,
  That most are busied when they're most alone,
  Pursued my humor[22] not pursuing his,
  And gladly shunned who gladly fled from me.
MONTAGUE. Many a morning hath he there been seen,   115
  With tears augmenting the fresh morning's dew,
  Adding to clouds more clouds with his deep sighs.
  But all so soon as the all-cheering sun
  Should in the farthest east begin to draw
  The shady curtains from Aurora's[23] bed,   120
  Away from light steals home my heavy[24] son
  And private in his chamber pens himself,
  Shuts up his windows, locks fair daylight out,
  And makes himself an artificial night.
  Black and portentous must this humor prove,   125
  Unless good counsel may the cause remove.
BENVOLIO. My noble uncle, do you know the cause?
MONTAGUE. I neither know it nor can learn of him.
BENVOLIO. Have you importuned him by any means?
MONTAGUE. Both by myself and many other friends.   130
  But he, his own affections' counsellor,
  Is to himself—I will not say how true—
  But to himself so secret and so close,[25]
  So far from sounding and discovery,[26]

19. **set ... abroach,** started this old quarrel again.

20. **withal,** with this.

21. **affections,** inclinations.

22. **humor,** mood.

23. **Aurora,** goddess of the dawn.
24. **heavy,** depressed.

25. **close,** not inclined to talk.
26. **sounding and discovery,** responding to efforts to understand his views.

As is the bud bit with an envious worm,   135
Ere he can spread his sweet leaves to the air,
Or dedicate his beauty to the sun.
Could we but learn from whence his sorrows grow,
We would as willingly give cure as know.

[*Enter* ROMEO *lost in thought.*]

BENVOLIO. See where he comes, so please you step aside.   140
I'll know his grievance or be much denied.[27]
MONTAGUE. I would thou wert so happy by thy stay[28]
To hear true shrift.[29] Come madam, let's away.

[*Exeunt* MONTAGUE *and* LADY MONTAGUE.]

BENVOLIO. Good morrow, cousin.
ROMEO.   Is the day so young?
BENVOLIO. But new struck nine.
ROMEO.   Ay me! Sad hours seem
   long.   145
Was that my father that went hence so fast?
BENVOLIO. It was. What sadness lengthens Romeo's
   hours?
ROMEO. Not having that which having makes them
   short.
BENVOLIO. In love?
ROMEO. Out——   150
BENVOLIO. Of love?
ROMEO. Out of her favor where I am in love.
BENVOLIO. Alas that love, so gentle in his view,
   Should be so tyrannous and rough in proof![30]
ROMEO. Alas that love, whose view is muffled still,[31]   155
   Should without eyes see pathways to his will!
   Where shall we dine? O me! What fray was here?
   Yet tell me not, for I have heard it all.
   Here's much to do with hate, but more with love.
   Why then, O brawling love, O loving hate,   160
   O anything, of nothing first create!
   O heavy lightness, serious vanity,
   Misshapen chaos of well-seeming forms,
   Feather of lead, bright smoke, cold fire, sick health,
   Still-waking[32] sleep, that is not what it is!   165
   This love feel I, that feel no love in this.[33]
   Dost thou not laugh?
BENVOLIO.   No, coz,[34] I rather weep.
ROMEO. Good heart, at what?
BENVOLIO.   At thy good heart's
   oppression.
ROMEO. Why, such is love's transgression.

27. **be much denied.** He will find it difficult to refuse me an answer.
28. **happy . . . stay,** fortunate in waiting.
29. **To hear . . . shrift,** as to hear a true confession.

30. **in proof,** in experiencing.
31. **view . . . still,** sight is blindfolded. Cupid was often pictured with a blindfold.

32. **Still-waking,** always wakeful.
33. **that feel . . . this,** that can take no pleasure in this love.
34. **coz\kəz** cousin.

Griefs of mine own lie heavy in my breast,　　　　170
Which thou wilt propagate, to have it pressed
With more of thine; this love that thou hast shown
Doth add more grief to too much of mine own.
Love is a smoke made with the fume of sighs;
Being purged, a fire sparkling in lovers' eyes;　　175
Being vexed, a sea nourished with lover's tears.
What is it else? A madness most discreet,
A choking gall, and a preserving sweet.
Farewell, my coz.
BENVOLIO.　　　　　　Soft![35] I will go along.
And if you leave me so, you do me wrong.　　　180
ROMEO. Tut! I have lost myself; I am not here.
This is not Romeo, he's some other where.
BENVOLIO. Tell me in sadness,[36] who is that you love?
ROMEO. What, shall I groan and tell thee?
BENVOLIO.　　　　　　　　Groan? Why,
　no;
But sadly tell me who.　　　　　　　185
ROMEO. Bid a sick man in sadness make his will!
Ah, word ill urged to one that is so ill!
In sadness, cousin, I do love a woman.
BENVOLIO. I aimed so near when I supposed you loved.
ROMEO. A right good markman. And she's fair I love.　190
BENVOLIO. A right fair mark, fair coz, is soonest hit.
ROMEO. Well in that hit you miss. She'll not be hit
With Cupid's arrow. She hath Dian's wit,[37]
And in strong proof of chastity well armed,
From love's weak childish bow she lives uncharmed.　195
She hath forsworn to love, and in that vow
Do I live dead that live to tell it now.
BENVOLIO. Be ruled by me; forget to think of her.
ROMEO. O, teach me how I should forget to think!
BENVOLIO. By giving liberty unto thine eyes.　　200
Examine other beauties.
ROMEO.　　　　　　'Tis the way
To call hers, exquisite, in question more.
Farewell. Thou canst not teach me to forget.
BENVOLIO. I'll pay that doctrine, or else die in debt.[38]

[*They exit.*]

35. **Soft,** wait a moment.

36. **sadness,** seriousness.

37. **Dian's wit,** wisdom of the goddess Diana.

38. **I'll ... debt.** I'll teach you or die trying.

TYING THE SCENES TOGETHER: SCENE 1

There has been a street brawl. An uneasy peace has been declared. Romeo has made an appearance to moan about an unhappy love affair. From what you have learned thus far about Benvolio, Tybalt, and Romeo, which one would you expect to start the fight again?

A street near the Capulet house. Enter CAPULET, PARIS, *and*
SERVANT.

CAPULET. (*Addressing* PARIS.) But Montague is bound
    as well as I,
  In penalty alike; and 'tis not hard, I think,
  For men so old as we to keep the peace.
PARIS. Of honorable reckoning[1] are you both,
  And pity 'tis you lived at odds so long.   5
  But now, my lord, what say you to my suit?
CAPULET. But saying o'er what I have said before:
  My child is yet a stranger in the world,
  She hath not seen the change of fourteen years;
  Let two more summers wither in their pride   10
  Ere we may think her ripe to be a bride.
  Earth hath swallowed all my hopes but she:
  She is the hopeful lady of my earth.[2]
  But woo her, gentle Paris, get her heart;
  My will to her consent is but a part.[3]   15
  And she agree, within her scope of choice
  Lies my consent and fair according voice.
  This night I told an old accustomed feast,
  Whereto I have invited many a guest,
  Such as I love; and you among the store,   20
  One more, most welcome, makes my number more.
  At my poor house look to behold this night
  Earth-treading stars that make dark heaven light.
  Such comfort as do lusty young men feel
  When well-apparelled April on the heel   25
  Of limping Winter treads, even such delight
  Among fresh female buds shall you this night
  Inherit[4] at my house. Hear all, all see,
  And like her most whose merit most shall be.
  Come, go with me. (*To* SERVANT, *giving him a paper.*)
    Go, sirrah,[5] trudge about   30
  Through fair Verona; find those persons out
  Whose names are written there, and to them say
  My house and welcome on their pleasure stay.

[CAPULET *and* PARIS *exit.*]

SERVANT. Find them out whose names are written here!
  It is written that the shoemaker should meddle with   35
  his yard, and the tailor with his last, the fisher with
  his pencil, and the painter with his nets.[6] But I am
  sent to find those persons whose names are here writ,

---

1. **reckoning,** reputation.

2. **hopeful . . . earth.** She is his only living child.

3. **My will . . . part.** Her consent is more important than my wishes.

4. **Inherit,** enjoy.

5. **sirrah,** a term of familiar address.

6. **It . . . nets.** Confusing tradesmen and their tools was a stock comic routine on the stage at this time.

and can never find what names the writing person
hath here writ. I must to the learned.⁷ In good time!⁸   40

[*Enter* BENVOLIO *and* ROMEO.]

BENVOLIO. Tut man, one fire burns out another's burning;
  One pain is lessened by another's anguish;
  Turn giddy, and be holp by backward turning;
  One desperate grief cures with another's languish.
  Take thou some new infection to thy eye,   45
  And the rank poison of the old will die.
ROMEO. Your plantain leaf⁹ is excellent for that.
BENVOLIO. For what, I pray thee?
ROMEO.   For your broken shin.
BENVOLIO. Why Romeo, art thou mad?
ROMEO. Not mad, but bound more than a madman is;   50
  Shut up in prison, kept without my food,
  Whipped and tormented and—God-den,¹⁰ good fel-
    low.
SERVANT. God gi' god-den. I pray, sir, can you read?
ROMEO. Ay, mine own fortune in my misery.   55
SERVANT. Perhaps you have learned it without book. But,
  I pray, can you read anything you see?
ROMEO. Ay, if I know the letters and the language.
SERVANT. Ye say honestly,¹¹ rest you merry.¹²
ROMEO. Stay fellow; I can read. (*He reads the letter.*)   60
  "Signior Martino and his wife and daughters; County
  Anselme and his beauteous sisters; the lady widow of
  Vitruvio; Signior Placentio and his lovely nieces; Mer-
  cutio and his brother Valentine; mine uncle Capulet,
  his wife and daughters; my fair niece Rosaline;   65
  Livia; Signior Valentio and his cousin Tybalt; Lucio
  and the lively Helena." (*He returns the paper to the*
  SERVANT.)
  A fair assembly. Whither should they come?
SERVANT. Up.
ROMEO. Whither? To supper?   70
SERVANT. To our house.
ROMEO. Whose house?
SERVANT. My master's.
ROMEO. Indeed I should have asked you that before.
SERVANT. Now I'll tell you without asking. My master   75
  is the great rich Capulet, and if you be not of the
  house of Montagues, I pray come and crush a cup¹³
  of wine. Rest you merry. (*He exits.*)
BENVOLIO. At this same ancient¹⁴ feast of Capulet's
  Sups the fair Rosaline whom thou so loves,   80
  With all the admirèd beauties of Verona.

7. **learned,** someone who can read.
8. **In good time.** The servant exclaims at his good fortune that Benvolio and Romeo approach.

9. **plantain leaf,** considered effective in stopping the flow of blood.

10. **God-den,** good evening.

11. **honestly.** He thinks Romeo is joking and starts to leave.
12. **rest you merry,** may you be merry.

13. **crush a cup,** have a drink.

14. **ancient,** traditional.

Go thither, and with unattainted eye,
Compare her face with some that I shall show,
And I will make thee think thy swan a crow.
ROMEO. One fairer than my love? The all-seeing sun   85
Ne'er saw her match since first the world begun.
BENVOLIO. Tut, you saw her fair, none else being by,
Herself poised[15] with herself in either eye.
But in that crystal scales[16] let there be weighed
Your lady's love against some other maid   90
That I will show you shining at this feast,
And she shall scant show well that now shows best.
ROMEO. I'll go along, no such sight to be shown,
But to rejoice in splendor of mine own.[17]

[*Exit* ROMEO *and* BENVOLIO.]

15. **poised,** balanced.
16. **crystal scales,** Romeo's eyes.

17. **splendor . . . own,** my own lady's splendor.

TYING THE SCENES TOGETHER: SCENE 2

Paris has asked Capulet for Juliet's hand. Capulet has sent out invitations for a masked ball. Romeo and Benvolio have learned about this party and plan to attend uninvited. What do you expect will happen at the masked ball?

SCENE 3

A *room in Capulet's house.* LADY CAPULET *and* NURSE *enter.*

LADY CAPULET. Nurse, where's my daughter? Call her
forth to me.
NURSE. I bade her come. What, lamb! What, ladybird!
God forbid, where's this girl? What, Juliet!

[*Enter* JULIET.]

JULIET. How now? Who calls?
NURSE. Your mother.   5
JULIET. Madam, I am here. What is your will?
LADY CAPULET. This is the matter—Nurse, give leave
awhile,
We must talk in secret. Nurse, come back again;
I have remembered me, thou's[1] hear our counsel.
Thou knowest my daughter's of a pretty age.   10
NURSE. Faith, I can tell her age unto an hour.
LADY CAPULET. She's not fourteen.
NURSE. I'll lay fourteen of my teeth, and yet, to my
teen[2] be it spoken, I have but four, she's not four-
teen. How long is it now to Lammastide?[3]   15
LADY CAPULET. A fortnight and odd days.

1. **thou's,** thou shalt.

2. **teen,** sorrow.
3. **Lammastide,** August 1.

NURSE. Even or odd, of all days in the year,
    Come Lammas Eve at night shall she be fourteen.
    Susan and she—God rest all Christian souls—
    Were of an age. Well, Susan is with God,   20
    She was too good for me. But, as I said,
    On Lammas Eve at night shall she be fourteen;
    That shall she, marry, I remember it well.
    'Tis since the earthquake now eleven years;
    And she was weaned—I never shall forget it—   25
    Of all the days of the year, upon that day.
LADY CAPULET. Enough of this. I pray thee hold thy
    peace.
NURSE. Peace, I have done. God mark thee to His grace!
    Thou wast the prettiest babe that e'er I nursed.
    And I might live to see thee married once,   30
    I have my wish.
LADY CAPULET. Marry, that "marry" is the very theme
    I came to talk of. Tell me, daughter Juliet,
    How stands your dispositions to be married?
JULIET. It is an honor that I dream not of.   35
LADY CAPULET. Well, think of marriage now. Younger
    than you,
    Here in Verona, ladies of esteem,
    Are made already mothers. By my count,
    I was your mother much upon these years[4]
    That you are now a maid. Thus then in brief—   40
    The valiant Paris seeks you for his love.
NURSE. A man, young lady! Lady, such a man
    As all the world—why he's a man of wax.[5]
LADY CAPULET. Verona's summer hath not such a flower.
NURSE. Nay he's a flower, in faith a very flower.   45
LADY CAPULET. What say you? Can you love the gentle-
    man?
    This night you shall behold him at our feast.
    Read o'er the volume of young Paris' face,
    And find delight writ there with beauty's pen;
    Examine every married lineament,[6]   50
    And see how one another lends content;[7]
    And what obscured in this fair volume lies
    Find written in the margent of his eyes.
    Speak briefly, can you like of Paris' love?
JULIET. I'll look to like, if looking liking move.[8]   55
    But no more deep will I endart mine eye
    Than your consent gives strength to make it fly.

[*Enter a* SERVANT.]

SERVANT. Madam, the guests are come, supper served

4. **much . . . years,** almost at the same age.

5. **a man of wax,** a man of perfect figure.

6. **married lineament,** harmonious feature.
7. **one . . . content,** all enhance one another.

8. **I'll . . . move.** I agree to look favorably on him, if mere eyesight can produce affection.

up, you called, my young lady asked for, the nurse
cursed in the pantry, and everything in extremity.   60
I must hence to wait. I beseech you follow straight.[9]

LADY CAPULET. We follow thee. (*Exit* SERVANT.) Juliet,
the County stays.[10]

NURSE. Go girl, seek happy days.

[*They exit.*]

TYING THE SCENES TOGETHER: SCENE 3

Juliet and her nurse have made an appearance. Juliet has been
told that Paris seeks her love. The nurse is in favor of such a
match. What is the nurse's character like?

SCENE 4

A street near the Capulet house that same evening. Enter
ROMEO, MERCUTIO, *and* BENVOLIO *along with other*
MASKERS *and* TORCHBEARERS. *Although they have not been
invited, they are on their way to the Capulet masquerade
party, confident that their costumes and masks will keep
them from being recognized.*

ROMEO. What, shall this speech be spoke for our excuse?
Or shall we on without apology?[1]

BENVOLIO. Let them measure us by what they will,
We'll measure[2] them a measure, and be gone.

ROMEO. Give me a torch, I am not for this ambling;[3]   5
Being but heavy, I will bear the light.

MERCUTIO. Nay, gentle Romeo, we must have you dance.

ROMEO. Not I, believe me. You have dancing shoes
With nimble soles; I have a soul of lead
So stakes me to the ground I cannot move.   10

MERCUTIO. You are a lover, borrow Cupid's wings
And soar with them above a common bound.[4]

ROMEO. I am too sore enpierced with his shaft
To soar with his light feathers; and so bound,
I cannot bound a pitch[5] above dull woe.   15
Under love's heavy burden do I sink.

MERCUTIO. And—to sink in it, should you burden love—
Too great oppression for a tender thing.

ROMEO. Is love a tender thing? It is too rough,
Too rude, too boisterous, and it pricks like thorn.   20

MERCUTIO. If love be rough with you, be rough with
love;
Give me a case[6] to put my visage in.

9. **straight,** at once.

10. **the County stays.** Count Paris waits
for you.

1. **without apology,** without the prepared speech with which visiting
maskers usually introduce themselves.
2. **measure,** dance.
3. **ambling,** courtly dancing.

4. **bound,** leap made in some dances.

5. **a pitch,** any height.

6. **case,** mask.

A visor for a visor![7] (*Puts on a mask.*) What care I
What curious eye doth quote[8] deformities?
Here are the beetle brows shall blush for me.   25
BENVOLIO. Come, knock and enter; and no sooner in
    But every man betake him to his legs.
ROMEO. A torch for me! Let wantons light of heart
    Tickle and senseless rushes[9] with their heels;
    For I am proverbed with a grandsire phrase,[10]   30
    I'll be a candle-holder[11] and look on.
MERCUTIO. Come, we burn daylight, ho!
ROMEO. Nay, that's not so.
MERCUTIO.   I mean sir, in delay
    We waste our lights in vain, like lights by day.
ROMEO. We mean well in going to this masque,   35
    But 'tis no wit to go.
MERCUTIO.   Why, may one ask?
ROMEO. I dreamt a dream tonight.
MERCUTIO.   And so did I.
ROMEO. Well, what was yours?
MERCUTIO.   That dreamers often lie.
ROMEO. In bed asleep, while they do dream things true.
MERCUTIO. O, then I see Queen Mab[12] hath been with
    you.   40
    She is the fairies' midwife, and she comes
    In shape no bigger than an agate stone
    On the forefinger of an alderman,
    Drawn with a team of little atomies[13]
    Over men's noses as they lie asleep.   45
    Her wagon spokes made of long spinners'[14] legs,
    The cover, of the wings of grasshoppers;
    Her traces,[15] of the smallest spider web;
    Her collars,[16] of the moonshine's watery beams;
    Her whip, of cricket's bone; the lash, of film;   50
    Her wagoner, a small gray-coated gnat,
    Not half so big as a round little worm,
    Pricked from the lazy finger of a maid.
    Her chariot is an empty hazelnut,
    Made by the joiner squirrel or old grub,[17]   55
    Time out o' mind the fairies' coachmakers.
    And in this state she gallops night by night
    Through lovers' brains, and then they dream of love;
    On courtiers' knees, that dream on curtsies straight;
    O'er lawyers' fingers, who straight dream on fees;   60
    O'er ladies' lips, who straight on kisses dream,
    Which oft the angry Mab with blisters plagues,
    Because their breath with sweetmeats tainted are.

7. **A visor . . . visor,** a mask for an ugly
masklike face.
8. **quote,** take notice of.

9. **senseless rushes,** unfeeling fibers
used as floor coverings.
10. **proverbed . . . phrase,** taught by an
old saying.
11. **candle-holder,** a spectator.

12. **Queen Mab**\măb\ queen of the
fairies.

13. **atomies,** tiny creatures.

14. **spinners',** spiders'.

15. **traces,** harnesses.
16. **collars,** harness collars.

17. **joiner . . . old grub,** both woodwork-
ers and adept at hollowing out nuts.

Sometime she gallops o'er a courtier's nose,
And then dreams he of smelling out a suit;[18]   65
And sometime comes she with a tithe pig's[19] tail
Tickling a parson's nose as 'a lies asleep,
Then he dreams of another benefice.[20]
Sometime she driveth o'er a soldier's neck,
And then dreams he of cutting foreign throats,   70
Of breaches, ambuscadoes,[21] Spanish blades,
Of healths five fathom deep; and then anon
Drums in his ear, at which he starts and wakes;
And being thus frighted, swears a prayer or two,
And sleeps again. This is that very Mab   75
That plats the manes of horses in the night
And bakes the elflocks[22] in foul sluttish hairs,
Which once untangled much misfortune bodes.
This is she—
ROMEO.   Peace, peace, Mercutio, peace!
Thou talk'st of nothing.
MERCUTIO.   True, I talk of dreams;   80
Which are the children of an idle brain,
Begot of nothing but vain fantasy;
Which is as thin of substance as the air,
And more inconstant than the wind, who woos
Even now the frozen bosom of the north   85
And, being angered, puffs away from thence,
Turning his side to the dew-dropping south.
BENVOLIO. This wind you talk of blows us from our-
   selves.
Supper is done, and we shall come too late.
ROMEO. I fear, too early; for my mind misgives   90
Some consequence yet hanging in the stars,
Shall bitterly begin his fearful date
With this night's revels, and expire the term
Of a despisèd life closed in my breast,
By some vile forfeit of untimely death.   95
But he that hath the steerage of my course
Direct my sail. On, lusty gentlemen!
BENVOLIO. Strike, drum.

[*They march about the stage and then exit.*]

TYING THE SCENES TOGETHER: SCENE 4

Romeo, Benvolio, and Mercutio have come masked to the
Capulets' door. Romeo, though, has said that he has misgivings
about crashing this party of their enemies. He feels something
terrible is going to happen. Why do you think Shakespeare has
Romeo say this?

18. **smelling out a suit,** finding someone who will pay for a favor granted.
19. **tithe-pig,** a pig due the parson as
part of a parishioner's contribution.
20. **benefice****bĕn·ə·fəs\\   another assured source of income.

21. **ambuscadoes****ăm·bə 'ska·dəz\\   surprise attacks with swords made of fine
steel from Toledo in Spain.

22. **elflocks,** matted hair.

SCENE 5

The ballroom in Capulet's house where dancing is about to begin. ROMEO, *costumed as a pilgrim returned from the Holy Land, and his friends are among the guests.* CAPU-LET, LADY CAPULET, *and* JULIET *are welcoming the revelers to the dancing.*

CAPULET. Welcome, gentlemen! Ladies that have their toes
Unplagued with corns will walk a bout with you.
Ah ha, my mistresses, which of you all
Will now deny to dance? She that makes dainty,
She I'll swear hath corns. Am I come near ye now?   5
Welcome, gentlemen! I have seen the day
That I have worn a visor¹ and could tell
A whispering tale in a fair lady's ear,
Such as would please. 'Tis gone, 'tis gone, 'tis gone.
You are welcome, gentlemen! Come, musicians, play.   10

1. **visor,** mask.

[MUSICIANS *play and guests dance.*]

A hall, a hall,² give room, and foot it, girls.
(*To* SERVANTS.) More light you knaves, and turn the tables up;³
And quench the fire, the room is grown too hot.
(*To an elderly kinsman.*) Nay sit, nay sit, good cousin Capulet,
For you and I are past our dancing days.   15
How long is't now since last yourself and I
Were in a mask?
SECOND CAPULET.   By'r lady, thirty years.
CAPULET. What man, 'tis not so much, 'tis not so much;
'Tis since the nuptial of Lucentio,
Come Pentecost as quickly as it will,   20
Some five and twenty years, and then we masked.
SECOND CAPULET. 'Tis more, 'tis more, his son is elder sir;
His son is thirty.
CAPULET.   Will you tell me that?
His son was but a ward two years ago.

2. **A hall, a hall,** clear the room for dancing.

3. **turn the tables up.** The tables were flat leaves hinged together and placed on trestles. When they were folded, they took up little space.

[ROMEO, *looking about for* ROSALINE, *sees* JULIET *among the dancers, and he instantly falls in love with her.*]

ROMEO. (*To a* SERVANT.) What lady's that which doth enrich the hand   25
Of yonder knight?

SERVANT. I know not sir.

ROMEO. O, she doth teach the torches to burn bright!
  It seems she hangs upon the cheek of night
  As a rich jewel in an Ethiop's ear;   30
  Beauty too rich for use, for earth too dear.
  So shows a snowy dove trooping with crows,
  As yonder lady o'er her fellows shows.
  The measure done, I'll watch her place of stand,
  And, touching hers, make blessèd my rude hand.   35
  Did my heart love till now? Forswear it sight,
  For I ne'er saw true beauty till this night.

TYBALT. (*Who has overheard* ROMEO.) This by his voice,
    should be a Montague.
  Fetch me my rapier, boy. What, dares the slave
  Come hither covered with an antic face,⁴   40
  To fleer and scorn at our solemnity?⁵
  Now by the stock and honor of my kin,
  To strike him dead I hold it not a sin.

CAPULET. (*Overhearing* TYBALT.) Why, how now, kins-
    man? Wherefore storm you so?

TYBALT. Uncle, this is a Montague, our foe,   45
  A villain that is hither come in spite
  To scorn at our solemnity this night.

CAPULET. Young Romeo is it?

TYBALT.   'Tis he, that villain Romeo.

CAPULET. Content thee, gentle coz, let him alone.
  'A bears him like a portly gentleman,   50
  And, to say truth, Verona brags of him
  To be a virtuous and well-governed youth.
  I would not for the wealth of all this town
  Here in my house do him disparagement.
  Therefore be patient; take no note of him.   55
  It is my will, the which if thou respect,
  Show a fair presence and put off these frowns,
  An ill-beseeming semblance for a feast.

TYBALT. It fits when such a villain is a guest.
  I'll not endure him.

CAPULET.   He shall be endured.   60
  What, goodman boy!⁶ I say he shall. Go to!⁷
  Am I the master here, or you? Go to!
  You'll not endure him, God shall mend my soul!
  You'll make a mutiny among my guests!
  You will set cock-a-hoop.⁸ You'll be the man!   65

TYBALT. Why, uncle, 'tis a shame.

CAPULET.   Go to, go to!
  You are a saucy boy. Is't so, indeed?
  This trick may chance to scathe you. I know what.

4. **antic face,** grotesque mask.

5. **To fleer ... solemnity,** to mock our festivities.

6. **goodman boy,** a scornful term.
7. **Go to!** That's enough!

8. **set cock-a-hoop,** throw off all restraint.

You must contrary me! Marry, 'tis time.

TYBALT. I will withdraw, but this intrusion shall,   70
  Now seeming sweet, convert to bitt'rest gall. (*He
    exits.*)

[*As* TYBALT *exits*, ROMEO *approaches* JULIET *and takes
  her hand. His words are like those of a pilgrim
  who has found the shrine that he is seeking.*]

ROMEO. If I profane with my unworthiest hand
  This holy shrine,[9] the gentle sin is this:
  My lips, two blushing pilgrims, ready stand
  To smooth that rough touch with a tender kiss.   75
JULIET. Good pilgrim, you do wrong your hand too
    much,
  Which mannerly devotion shows in this;
  For saints have hands that pilgrims' hands do touch,
  And palm to palm is holy palmers' kiss.[10]
ROMEO. Have not saints lips, and holy palmers too?   80
JULIET. Ay, pilgrim, lips that they must use in prayer.

9. **shrine**, Juliet's hand.

10. **holy palmers' kiss.** Juliet suggests
that pilgrims usually kiss by touching
palms.

371

ROMEO. O, then, dear saint, let lips do what hands do.
They pray; grant thou, lest faith turn to despair.
JULIET. Saints do not move, though grant for prayers'
sake.[11]
ROMEO. Then move not while my prayer's effect I take. 85
Thus from my lips, by thine, my sin is purged. (*Kisses
her.*)
JULIET. Then have my lips the sin that they have took.
ROMEO. Sin from my lips? O trespass sweetly urged.
Give me my sin again. (*Kisses her.*)
JULIET.   You kiss by th' book.[12]
NURSE. Madam, your mother craves a word with you. 90

[JULIET *goes to her mother.*]

ROMEO. What is her mother?
NURSE.   Marry, bachelor,
Her mother is the lady of the house,
And a good lady, and a wise and virtuous.
I nursed her daughter that you talked withal.
I tell you, he that can lay hold of her   95
Shall have the chinks.[13]
ROMEO.   Is she a Capulet?
O dear account, my life is my foe's debt.[14]
BENVOLIO. Away, be gone; the sport is at the best.
ROMEO. Ay, so I fear, the more is my unrest.
CAPULET. Nay, gentlemen, prepare not to be gone; 100
We have a trifling foolish banquet towards.[15]
Is it e'en so? Why then, I thank you all.
I thank you, honest gentlemen. Good night.
More torches here! Come on then; let's to bed.
Ah, sirrah, by my fay,[16] it waxes late;   105
I'll to my rest.

[*All exit except for* JULIET *and* NURSE.]

JULIET. Come hither, nurse. What is yond gentleman?
NURSE. The son and heir of old Tiberio.
JULIET. What's he that now is going out of door?
NURSE. Marry, that, I think, be young Petruchio.   110
JULIET. What's he that follows here, that would not
dance?
NURSE. I know not.
JULIET. Go ask his name—if he is married,
My grave is like to be my wedding bed.
NURSE. His name is Romeo, and a Montague,   115
The only son of your great enemy.

11. **Saints . . . sake.** Saints do not interfere in human affairs, they only answer prayers.

12. **by th' book,** by formal rules.

13. **chinks,** money.

14. **my life . . . debt.** My life is owed to my foe.

15. **foolish banquet towards,** light refreshments in preparation.

16. **fay,** faith.

JULIET. My only love sprung from my only hate,
Too early seen unknown, and known too late!
Prodigious[17] birth of love it is to me
That I must love a loathèd enemy.   120
NURSE. What's this? What's this?
JULIET.   A rhyme I learnt even
    now
Of one I danced withal. (*A call off-stage: "Juliet."*)
NURSE.   Anon, anon!
Come, let's away; the strangers all are gone.

[JULIET *and* NURSE *leave.*]

17. **Prodigious**\prə ˈdij·əs\ monstrous: promising misfortune.

TYING THE SCENES TOGETHER: SCENE 5

Capulet has made everyone welcome at the party but has had to restrain Tybalt from fighting Romeo. Romeo and Juliet have met briefly and have fallen desperately in love. What do they learn about one another that gives them cause for grief?

I
ENEMIES FALL IN LOVE

1. What penalty does Prince Escalus set for the next Capulet or Montague who breaks the peace?

2. What is Capulet's attitude toward Paris as a future son-in-law?

3. At the masked ball, what is the argument between Tybalt and Capulet?

II
IMPLICATIONS

Discuss the following statements.

1. Young people are in love with the idea of being in love.

2. An inner circle is often held together by dislike or ill-feeling toward another inner circle.

3. People who lack formal education tend to be laughed at or made fun of by those who have education.

III
TECHNIQUES

Staging

1. Why would the "groundlings" be amused in Scene 2 by the speech of the servant told to distribute invitations to the Capulets' ball? What kind of actions would you visualize for him?

2. Why would a masked ball be particularly pleasing to Shakespeare's audiences? How does Benvolio taunt Romeo into going?

Language

Playgoers who went to *Romeo and Juliet* in order to hear wordplay and fanciful language heard much of it in Act I. One of the most famous passages in the play is Mercutio's "Queen Mab" speech in Scene 4. What imaginative pictures does he draw of Queen Mab? Why would Mercutio's description of the fairy queen's activities amuse many in the audience?

Act II

Prologue

CHORUS. Now old desire doth in his deathbed lie,
And young affection gapes to be his heir;
That fair for which love groaned for and would die,
With tender Juliet matched, is now not fair.
Now Romeo is beloved, and loves again,   5
Alike bewitchèd by the charm of looks;
But to his foe supposed he must complain,
And she steal love's sweet bait from fearful hooks.
Being held a foe, he may not have access
To breathe such vows as lovers use to swear;   10
And she as much in love, her means much less
To meet her new belovèd anywhere;
But passion lends them power, time means, to meet,
Temp'ring extremities with extreme sweet.

SCENE 1

*A lane outside the wall of Capulet's orchard, shortly after
the party.* ROMEO *enters alone.*

ROMEO. Can I go forward when my heart is here?
Turn back, dull earth,[1] and find thy center[2] out.

> 1. **earth,** his own body.
> 2. **center,** heart, or, figuratively, Juliet.

[ROMEO *climbs the wall and leaps down into the orchard
as* BENVOLIO *and* MERCUTIO *enter.*]

BENVOLIO. Romeo! My cousin Romeo! Romeo!
MERCUTIO.   He is wise
And, on my life, hath stolen him home to bed.
BENVOLIO. He ran this way and leaped this orchard wall.   5
Call, good Mercutio.
MERCUTIO.   Nay, I'll conjure[3] too.

> 3. **conjure,** call him up by magic.

Romeo! Humors! Madman! Passion! Lover!
Appear thou in the likeness of a sigh,
Speak but one rhyme and I am satisfied;
Cry but "Ay me"; pronounce but "love" and "dove."   10
He heareth not, he stirreth not, he moveth not;
The ape[4] is dead, and I must conjure him.
I conjure thee by Rosaline's bright eyes,

> 4. **ape.** Romeo, hiding, is compared to
> a trained ape that plays dead until his
> master says a special word.

By her high forehead and her scarlet lip,
That in thy likeness thou appear to us.   15

374

BENVOLIO. Come, he hath hid himself among these trees
    To be consorted with[5] the humorous night.
    Blind is his love and best befits the dark.
MERCUTIO. If love be blind, love cannot hit the mark.
    Romeo, good night. I'll to my truckle bed;[6]   20
    This field bed is too cold for me to sleep.
    Come, shall we go?
BENVOLIO.   Go then, for 'tis in vain
    To seek him here that means not to be found.

[BENVOLIO *and* MERCUTIO *exit.*]

5. **be consorted with,** harmonize with or blend into.

6. **truckle bed,** trundle bed.

TYING THE SCENES TOGETHER: SCENE 1

After the party, Romeo has slipped away from his friends and leaped over the wall surrounding Capulet's orchard. Benvolio and Mercutio have tried to find him as they joked about his love affairs. What do you notice about Mercutio's personality that could get him into trouble easily?

SCENE 2

*Inside Capulet's orchard. There is a balcony directly out-
side of Juliet's bedroom.* ROMEO *is standing in the
shadows.*

ROMEO. (*Moving toward the house.*) He jests at scars
    that never felt a wound.

[JULIET *comes out on the balcony. She is unaware of*
    ROMEO *standing below.*]

But soft, what light through yonder window breaks?
It is the East, and Juliet is the sun.
Arise, fair sun, and kill[1] the envious moon,
Who is already sick and pale with grief,   5
That thou her maid[2] art far more fair than she.
Be not her maid, since she is envious.
Her vestal livery[3] is but sick and green,
And none but fools do fear it. Cast it off.
It is my lady. O, it is my love!   10
O, that she knew she were!
She speaks, yet she says nothing. What of that?
Her eye discourses; I will answer it.
I am too bold, 'tis not to me she speaks.
Two of the fairest stars in all the heaven,   15
Having some business, do entreat her eyes

1. **kill,** make disappear.

2. **maid.** Juliet, as an unmarried girl, would be under supervision of Diana, goddess of the moon and patroness of the unmarried.
3. **vestal livery,** virgin dress.

To twinkle in their spheres[4] till they return.
What if her eyes were there, they in her head?
The brightness of her cheek would shame those stars
As daylight doth a lamp; her eyes in heaven 20
Would through the airy region stream so bright
That birds would sing and think it were not night.
See how she leans her cheek upon her hand.
O, that I were a glove upon that hand,
That I might touch that cheek!
JULIET.   Ay me!
ROMEO.   She speaks. 25
O, speak again, bright angel, for thou art
As glorious to this night, being o'er my head,
As is a wingèd messenger of heaven
Unto the white-upturnèd wond'ring eyes
Of mortals that fall back to gaze on him 30
When he bestrides the lazy puffing clouds
And sails upon the bosom of the air.
JULIET. O Romeo, Romeo, wherefore art thou Romeo?
Deny thy father and refuse thy name;
Or, if thou wilt not, be but sworn my love, 35
And I'll no longer be a Capulet.
ROMEO. (*Aside.*) Shall I hear more, or shall I speak at
this?
JULIET. 'Tis but thy name that is my enemy.
Thou art thyself, though not a Montague.
What's Montague? It is nor hand, nor foot, 40
Nor arm, nor face, nor any other part
Belonging to a man. O, be some other name.
What's in a name? That which we call a rose
By any other word would smell as sweet;
So Romeo would, were he not Romeo called, 45
Retain that dear perfection which he owes[5]
Without that title. Romeo, doff thy name,
And for thy name, which is no part of thee,
Take all myself.
ROMEO. (*Speaking loudly enough to be heard by* JULIET.)
I take thee at thy word.
Call me but love, and I'll be new baptized; 50
Henceforth I never will be Romeo.
JULIET. What man art thou, that, thus bescreened in
night,
So stumblest on my counsel?
ROMEO.   By a name
I know not how to tell thee who I am.
My name, dear saint, is hateful to myself 55
Because it is an enemy to thee.

4. **spheres**, the hollow, transparent globes in which, it was believed, the stars and planets were set.

5. **owes**, owns.

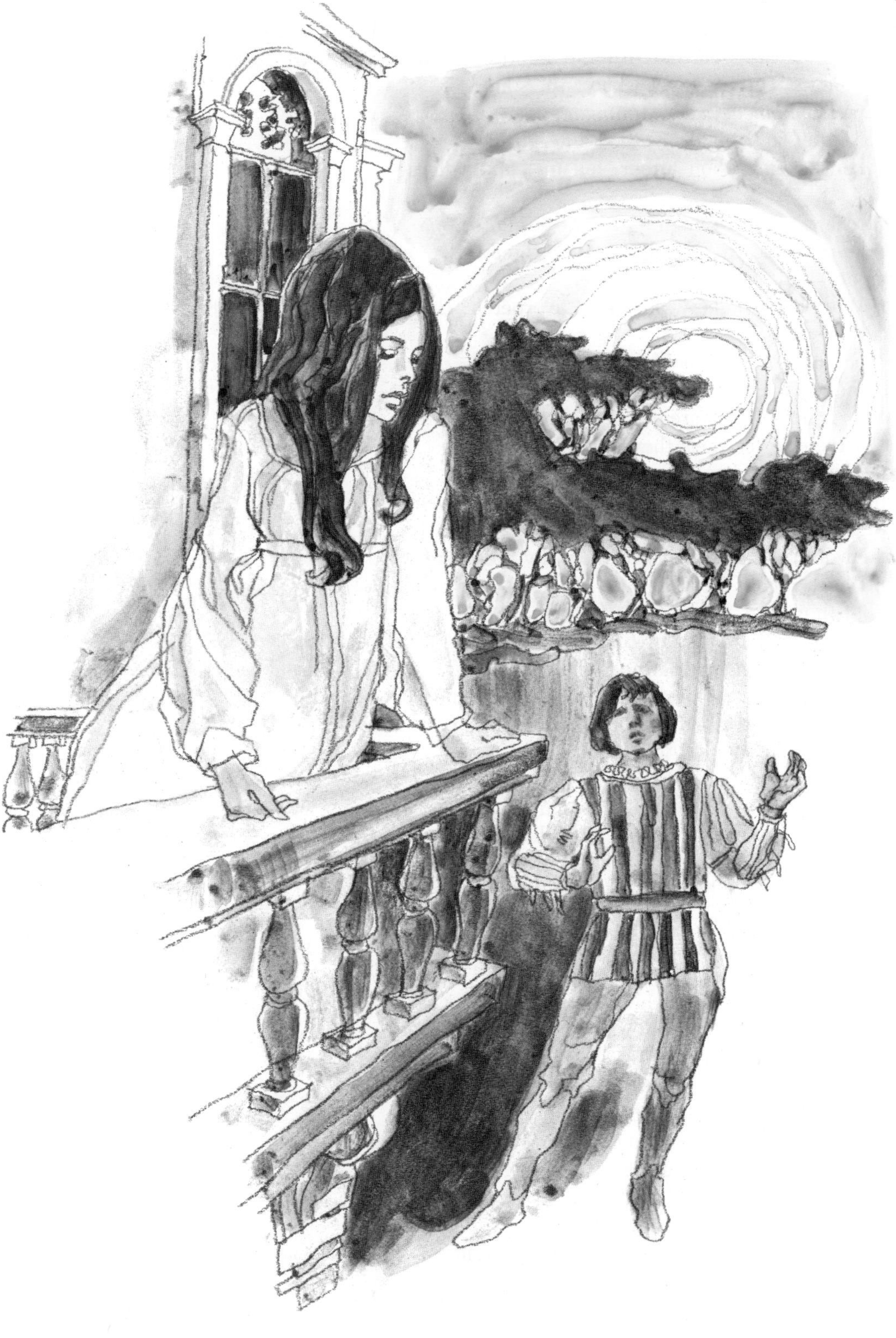

Had I it written, I would tear the word.

JULIET. My ears have yet not drunk a hundred words
    Of thy tongue's uttering, yet I know the sound.
    Art thou not Romeo, and a Montague?   60

ROMEO. Neither, fair maid, if either thee dislike.

JULIET. How camest thou hither, tell me, and where-
    fore?
    The orchard walls are high and hard to climb,
    And the place death, considering who thou art,
    If any of my kinsmen find thee here.   65

ROMEO. With love's light wings did I o'erperch[6] these
    walls;
    For stony limits cannot hold love out,
    And what love can do, that dares love attempt.
    Therefore thy kinsmen are no stop to me.

JULIET. If they do see thee, they will murder thee.   70

ROMEO. Alack, there lies more peril in thine eye
    Than twenty of their swords; look thou but sweet,
    And I am proof[7] against their enmity.

JULIET. I would not for the world they saw thee here.

ROMEO. I have night's cloak to hide me from their eyes;   75
    And but thou love me, let them find me here.
    My life were better ended by their hate
    Than death proroguèd,[8] wanting of thy love.

JULIET. By whose direction found'st thou out this place?

ROMEO. By love, that first did prompt me to inquire.   80
    He lent me counsel, and I lent him eyes.
    I am no pilot; yet, wert thou as far
    As that vast shore washed with the farthest sea,
    I should adventure for such merchandise.

JULIET. Thou knowest the mask of night is on my face,   85
    Else would a maiden blush bepaint my cheek
    For that which thou hast heard me speak tonight.
    Fain would I dwell on form,[9] fain, fain deny
    What I have spoke; but farewell compliment.[10]
    Dost thou love me? I know thou wilt say "Ay,"   90
    And I will take thy word. Yet, if thou swear'st,
    Thou mayst prove false; at lovers' perjuries,
    They say Jove laughs. O gentle Romeo,
    If thou dost love, pronounce it faithfully.
    Or if thou thinkest I am too quickly won,   95
    I'll frown and be perverse and say thee nay,
    So thou wilt woo; but else, not for the world.
    In truth, fair Montague, I am too fond,
    And therefore thou mayst think my havior[11] light.
    But trust me, gentleman, I'll prove more true   100
    Than those that have more cunning to be strange.[12]

6. **o'erperch,** fly over.

7. **proof,** protected.

8. **proroguèd** \p(r)ə ˈrō·gĕd\ postponed.

9. **Fain . . . form.** Happily would I follow the usual rules of courtship.
10. **compliment,** niceties of etiquette.

11. **havior,** behavior.

12. **strange,** shy, reserved.

I should have been more strange, I must confess,
But that thou overheard'st, ere I was ware,
My true love's passion; therefore pardon me,
And not impute this yielding to light love,   105
Which the dark night hath so discoverèd.

ROMEO. Lady, by yonder blessèd moon I vow,
That tips with silver all these fruit tree tops—

JULIET. O, swear not by the moon, th' inconstant moon,
That monthly changes in her circle orb,   110
Lest that thy love prove likewise variable.

ROMEO. What shall I swear by?

JULIET.   Do not swear at all;
Or if thou wilt, swear by thy gracious self,
Which is the god of my idolatry,
And I'll believe thee.

ROMEO.   If my heart's dear love—   115

JULIET. Well, do not swear. Although I joy in thee,
I have no joy of this contract tonight;
It is too rash, too unadvised,[13] too sudden,   13. **unadvised,** heedless.
Too like the lightning, which doth cease to be
Ere one can say "It lightens." Sweet, good night!   120
This bud of love, by summer's ripening breath,
May prove a beauteous flower when next we meet.
Good night, good night! As sweet repose and rest
Come to thy heart as that within my breast.

ROMEO. O, wilt thou leave me so unsatisfied?   125

JULIET. What satisfaction canst thou have tonight?

ROMEO. Th' exchange of thy love's faithful vow for mine.

JULIET. I gave thee mine before thou didst request it.
And yet I would it were to give again.

ROMEO. Wouldst thou withdraw it? For what purpose,
love?   130

JULIET. But to be frank[14] and give it thee again.   14. **frank,** generous.
And yet I wish but for the thing I have.
My bounty is as boundless as the sea,
My love as deep; the more I give to thee,
The more I have, for both are infinite.   135

[NURSE *calls within.*]

I hear some noise within. Dear love, adieu!
Anon, good nurse! Sweet Montague, be true.
Stay but a little, I will come again.

[JULIET *goes into her room.*]

ROMEO. O blessèd, blessèd night! I am afeard,
Being in night, all this is but a dream,   140

Too flattering-sweet to be substantial.

[JULIET *returns to the balcony.*]

JULIET. Three words, dear Romeo, and good night
    indeed.
If that thy bent of love be honorable,
Thy purpose marriage, send me word tomorrow,
By one that I'll procure to come to thee,   145
Where and what time thou wilt perform the rite;
And all my fortunes at thy foot I'll lay
And follow thee my lord throughout the world.
NURSE. (*Within.*) Madam!
JULIET. I come anon.—But if thou meanest not well,   150
I do beseech thee—
NURSE. (*Within.*) Madam!
JULIET.   By and by I come.—
To cease thy strife and leave me to my grief.
Tomorrow will I send.
ROMEO.   So thrive my soul—
JULIET. A thousand times good night! (*She exits.*)   155
ROMEO. A thousand times the worse, to want thy light!
Love goes toward love as schoolboys from their
    books;
But love from love, toward school with heavy looks.

[JULIET *reappears on the balcony.*]

JULIET. Hist! Romeo, hist! O for a falconer's voice
To lure this tassel-gentle[15] back again.   160
Bondage is hoarse and may not speak aloud,[16]
Else would I tear the cave where Echo[17] lies
And make her airy tongue more hoarse than mine
With repetition of my Romeo's name.
Romeo!   165
ROMEO. It is my soul that calls upon my name.
How silver-sweet sound lovers' tongues by night,
Like softest music to attending ears.
JULIET. Romeo!
ROMEO.   My sweet?
JULIET.   At what o'clock tomorrow
Shall I send to thee?
ROMEO.   By the hour of nine.   170
JULIET. I will not fail; 'tis twenty years till then.
I have forgot why I did call thee back.
ROMEO. Let me stand here till thou remember it.
JULIET. I shall forget, to have thee still stand there,
Remembering how I love thy company.   175
ROMEO. And I'll still stay, to have thee still forget,

15. **tassel-gentle,** male falcon.
16. **Bondage ... aloud.** She is held
prisoner by the nearness of her parents
so she must speak softly.
17. **Echo,** in classical mythology, a
mountain nymph who pined away for
love of Narcissus until only her voice
remained.

Forgetting any other home but this.

JULIET. 'Tis almost morning; I would have thee gone,
   And yet no farther than a wanton's[18] bird,
   That lets it hop a little from his hand,   180
   Like a poor prisoner in his twisted gyves,[19]
   And with a silken thread plucks it back again,
   So loving-jealous of his liberty.

ROMEO. I would I were thy bird.

JULIET.   Sweet, so would I;
   Yet I should kill thee with much cherishing.   185
   Good night, good night! Parting is such sweet sorrow
   That I shall say good night till it be morrow.[20] (*Exit.*)

ROMEO. Sleep dwell upon thine eyes, peace in thy
      breast.
   Would I were sleep and peace, so sweet to rest.
   Hence will I to my ghostly[21] father's cell,   190
   His help to crave, and my dear hap[22] to tell. (*Exit.*)

18. **wanton's,** pampered child's.

19. **gyves**\jīvs\ bonds, fetters.

20. **morrow,** morning.

21. **ghostly,** spiritual.
22. **dear hap,** good fortune.

TYING THE SCENES TOGETHER: SCENE 2

Romeo and Juliet have exchanged vows of love. Juliet has
agreed to send a messenger to Romeo the next morning to learn
what plan he has made for their wedding. What character traits
do you see revealed in this scene in both Romeo and Juliet?

SCENE 3

*Early morning in a small room in a Franciscan monastery.
Enter* FRIAR LAURENCE, *carrying a basket of plants and
herbs.*

FRIAR LAURENCE. The gray-eyed morn smiles on the
      frowning night,
   Check'ring the eastern clouds with streaks of light;
   And fleckèd darkness like a drunkard reels
   From forth day's path and Titan's fiery wheels.[1]
   Now, ere the sun advance his burning eye   5
   The day to cheer, and night's dank dew to dry,
   I must up-fill this osier cage[2] of ours
   With baleful weeds and precious-juicèd flowers,
   Many for many virtues excellent,
   None but for some, and yet all different.   10
   O, mickle[3] is the powerful grace that lies
   In plants, herbs, stones, and their true qualities;
   For naught so vile that on the earth doth live,
   But to the earth some special good doth give;
   Nor aught so good but, strained from that fair use,   15
   Revolts from true birth,[4] stumbling on abuse.

1. **Titan's fiery wheels,** the chariot
wheels of the ancient Greek sun god
Titan.

2. **osier**\ˈō·zhər\ **cage,** willow basket.

3. **mickle,** much.

4. **true birth,** its true nature.

Virtue itself turns vice, being misapplied,
And vice sometimes by action dignified.

[ROMEO *enters and stands, unseen, by the door.*]

Within the infant rind of this weak flower
Poison hath residence and medicine power;   20
For this, being smelt, with that part cheers each part;[5]
Being tasted, stays all senses with the heart.[6]
Two such opposèd kings encamp them still
In man as well as herbs—grace[7] and rude will;[8]
And where the worser is predominant,   25
Full soon the canker[9] death eats up that plant.
ROMEO. Good morrow, Father.
FRIAR LAURENCE.   Benedicite![10]
What early tongue so sweet saluteth me?
Young son, it argues a distempered head[11]
So soon to bid good morrow to thy bed.   30
Care keeps his watch in every old man's eye,
And where care lodges, sleep will never lie;
But where unbruisèd youth with unstuffed brain
Doth couch his limbs, there golden sleep doth reign.
Therefore thy earliness doth me assure   35
Thou art up-roused with some distemperature;
Or if not so, then here I hit it right,
Our Romeo hath not been in bed tonight.
ROMEO. That last is true; the sweeter rest was mine.
FRIAR LAURENCE. God pardon sin! Wast thou with
    Rosaline?   40
ROMEO. With Rosaline, my ghostly father? No.
I have forgot that name and that name's woe.
FRIAR LAURENCE. That's my good son; but where hast
    thou been then?
ROMEO. I'll tell thee ere thou ask it me again.
I have been feasting with mine enemy,   45
Where on a sudden one hath wounded me,
That's by me wounded; both our remedies
Within thy help and holy physic[12] lies.
I bear no hatred, blessèd man, for, lo,
My intercession likewise steads my foe.   50
FRIAR LAURENCE. Be plain, good son, and homely in thy
    drift;[13]
Riddling[14] confession finds but riddling shrift.[15]
ROMEO. Then plainly know my heart's dear love is set
On the fair daughter of rich Capulet.
As mine on hers, so hers is set on mine,   55

5. **being smelt . . . each part.** Its odor is a stimulant.
6. **stays . . . heart,** by stopping the heart.
7. **grace,** goodness.
8. **rude will,** lust or evil.

9. **canker,** cankerworm, eater of plants.

10. **Benedicite**\\'ben·ə ˈdĭs·ət·ē\\ God bless you.

11. **distempered head,** troubled mind.

12. **physic,** healing medicine.

13. **homely . . . drift,** simple and direct in your speech.
14. **Riddling,** misleading.
15. **shrift,** forgiveness.

And all combined,[16] save what thou must combine
By holy marriage. When, and where, and how,
We met, we wooed, and made exchange of vow,
I'll tell thee as we pass; but this I pray,
That thou consent to marry us today.   60
FRIAR LAURENCE. Holy Saint Francis, what a change is
    here!
Is Rosaline that thou didst love so dear,
So soon forsaken? Young men's love then lies
Not truly in their hearts, but in their eyes.
Jesu Maria, what a deal of brine   65
Hath washed thy sallow cheeks for Rosaline!
How much salt water thrown away in waste
To season love, that of it doth not taste!
The sun not yet thy sighs from heaven clears,
Thy old groans ring yet in mine ancient ears.   70
Lo, here upon thy cheek the stain doth sit
Of an old tear that is not washed off yet.
If e'er thou wast thyself, and these woes thine,
Thou and these woes were all for Rosaline.
And art thou changed? Pronounce this sentence then: 75
Women may fall when there's no strength in men.
ROMEO. Thou chid'st[17] me oft for loving Rosaline.
FRIAR LAURENCE. For doting, not for loving, pupil mine.
ROMEO. And bad'st me bury love.
FRIAR LAURENCE.   Not in a grave,
To lay one in, another out to have.   80
ROMEO. I pray thee chide me not, her I love now
    Doth grace for grace, and love for love allow.
    The other did not so.
FRIAR LAURENCE.   O she knew well
Thy love did read by rote, that could not spell.
But come, young waverer, come go with me,   85
In one respect I'll thy assistant be;
For this alliance may so happy prove,
To turn your households' rancor to pure love.
ROMEO. O let us hence! I stand on sudden haste.
FRIAR LAURENCE. Wisely and slow, they stumble that
    run fast.   90

[ROMEO *and* FRIAR LAURENCE *exit.*]

16. **all combined.** The arrangement is complete.

17. **chid'st,** scolded.

TYING THE SCENES TOGETHER: SCENE 3

Romeo has talked Friar Laurence into performing the marriage
rites that very day. How does the Friar show himself very human
in his reactions to Romeo's sudden switch in sweethearts?

A street, later in the morning. Enter BENVOLIO *and* MER-
CUTIO.

MERCUTIO. Where the devil should this Romeo be?
  Came he not home tonight?
BENVOLIO. Not to his father's; I spoke with his man.
MERCUTIO. Why that same pale hard-hearted wench,
    that Rosaline,
  Torments him so that he will sure run mad.   5
BENVOLIO. Tybalt, the kinsman to old Capulet,
  Hath sent a letter to his father's house.
MERCUTIO. A challenge,[1] on my life.
BENVOLIO. Romeo will answer it.
MERCUTIO. Any man that can write may answer a letter.   10
BENVOLIO. Nay, he will answer the letter's master, how
  he dares, being dared.
MERCUTIO. Alas, poor Romeo, he is already dead, stab-
  bed with a white wench's black eye, run through
  the ear with a love song, the very pin[2] of his heart   15
  cleft with the blind bow-boy's butt-shaft;[3] and is he
  a man to encounter Tybalt?
BENVOLIO. Why, what is Tybalt?
MERCUTIO. More than Prince of Cats.[4] O, he's the
  courageous captain of compliments.[5] He fights as   20
  you sing, keeps time, distance, and proportion; he
  rests his minim rests,[6] one, two, and the third in
  your bosom! The very butcher of a silk button,[7] a
  duelist, a duelist; a gentleman of the very first house,[8]
  of the first and second cause.[9] Ah, the immortal   25
  passado![10] The punto reverso![11] The hay![12]

[ROMEO *enters in a good mood.*]

BENVOLIO. Here comes Romeo, here comes Romeo!
MERCUTIO. Signior Romeo, bon jour![13] There's a French
  salutation to your French slop.[14] You gave us the
  counterfeit[15] fairly last night.   30
ROMEO. Good morrow to you both. What counterfeit
  did I give you?
MERCUTIO. The slip,[16] sir, the slip; can you not conceive?
ROMEO. Pardon, good Mercutio, my business was great,
  and in such a case as mine a man may strain courtesy.   35
MERCUTIO. That's as much as to say, such a case as
  yours constrains a man to bow in the hams.[17]
ROMEO. Meaning, to curtsy.
MERCUTIO. Thou hast most kindly hit it.

1. **challenge,** that is, challenge to a duel.

2. **pin,** the center of a target.
3. **bow-boy's butt-shaft,** Cupid's blunt arrow. Mercutio suggests that Cupid needed only the least powerful weapon to overwhelm Romeo.
4. **Prince of Cats,** a play on Tybalt's name. In a collection of fables, the name of the Prince of Cats was Tibert or Tibalt.
5. **captain of compliments,** maker of rules of ceremony in dueling.
6. **minim rests,** half rests in music.
7. **butcher . . . button,** one who can select and cut off any button of his adversary's dress.
8. **of . . . house,** of the first rank as a duelist.
9. **of . . . cause,** ready to quarrel over anything or nothing.
10. **passado**\pə ˈsŏd·ō\ a step forward or aside in thrusting.
11. **punto reverso**\ˈpᴜn·tō·rĕ ˈvĕr·sō\ a backward thrust from the left side of the body.
12. **hay,** a home thrust.
13. **Signior . . . bon jour**\sēn ˈyɔr . . . bō(n) ˈzʰᴜr\ Sir Romeo, good-day.
14. **slop,** full trousers, cut French style.
15. **gave . . . counterfeit,** played us a trick.
16. **slip,** escape; counterfeit coin.

17. **hams,** hips.

ROMEO. A most courteous exposition. 40

MERCUTIO. Nay, I am the very pink of courtesy.

ROMEO. Pink for flower.

MERCUTIO. Right.

ROMEO. Why, then is my pump[18] well flowered.

MERCUTIO. Sure wit, follow me this jest now till thou 45
hast worn out thy pump, that, when the single sole
of it is worn, the jest may remain, after the wearing,
solely singular.[19]

ROMEO. O single-soled jest, solely singular for the
singleness![20] 50

MERCUTIO. Come between us, good Benvolio! My wits
faints.

ROMEO. Swits and spurs,[21] swits and spurs, or I'll cry
a match.[22]

MERCUTIO. Why, is not this better now than groaning 55
for love? Now art thou sociable, now art thou Romeo;
now art thou what thou art, by art as well as by
nature.

BENVOLIO. Stop there, stop there!

ROMEO. Here's goodly gear![23] A sail, a sail! 60

[*Enter* NURSE *and* PETER, *her servant.*]

MERCUTIO. Two, two; a shirt and a smock.[24]

NURSE. Peter.

PETER. Anon.

NURSE. My fan, Peter.

MERCUTIO. Good Peter, to hide her face, for her fan's 65
the fairer face.

NURSE. God ye good morrow, gentlemen. Can any of
you tell me where I may find the young Romeo?

ROMEO. I can tell you; but young Romeo will be older
when you have found him than he was when you 70
sought him. I am the youngest of that name, for
fault of a worse.

NURSE. You say well.

MERCUTIO. Yea, is the worst well? Very well took, i' faith,
wisely, wisely. 75

NURSE. If you be he, sir, I desire some confidence with
you.

MERCUTIO. Romeo, will you come to your father's?
We'll to dinner thither.

ROMEO. I will follow you. 80

MERCUTIO. Farewell, ancient lady, farewell. (*Singing.*)
"Lady, lady, lady."

[MERCUTIO *and* BENVOLIO *exit.*]

18. **pump**, shoe; "well flowered" refers to an ornamental flower design punched into the leather.

19. **solely singular,** all alone.

20. **single-soled . . . singleness,** weak joke, outstanding for its feebleness.

21. **Swits and spurs,** switch and spurs; that is, keep your horse running.
22. **cry a match,** claim a victory.

23. **goodly gear,** handsome merchandise (spoken here facetiously).

24. **smock,** lady's blouse.

NURSE. I pray you, sir, what saucy merchant was this that was so full of his ropery?[25]

ROMEO. A gentleman, Nurse, that loves to hear himself talk and will speak more in a minute than he will stand to in a month. 85

NURSE. And 'a speak anything against me, I'll take him down, and 'a were lustier than he is, and twenty such Jacks;[26] and if I cannot, I'll find those that shall. 90 Scurvy knave! I am none of his flirt-gills.[27] (*To* PETER.) And thou must stand by, too, and suffer every knave to use me at his pleasure!

PETER. I saw no man use you at his pleasure. If I had, my weapon should quickly have been out, I warrant 95 you. I dare draw as soon as another man, if I see occasion in a good quarrel, and the law on my side.

NURSE. Now, afore God, I am so vexed that every part about me quivers. Scurvy knave! Pray you, sir, a word; and, as I told you, my young lady bid me 100 inquire you out. What she bid me say, I will keep to myself; but first let me tell ye, if ye should lead her in a fool's paradise,[28] as they say, it were a very gross kind of behavior, as they say; for the gentlewoman is young; and therefore, if you should deal 105 double with her, truly it were an ill thing to be offered to any gentlewoman, and very weak dealing.

ROMEO. Nurse, commend[29] me to thy lady and mistress. I protest[30] unto thee——

NURSE. Good heart, and i' faith I will tell her as much. 110 Lord, lord, she will be a joyful woman.

ROMEO. What wilt thou tell her, Nurse? Thou dost not mark me.

NURSE. I will tell her, sir, that you do protest, which, as I take it, is a gentlemanlike offer. 115

ROMEO. Bid her devise
Some means to come to shrift this afternoon;
And there she shall at Friar Laurence' cell
Be shrived[31] and married. Here is for thy pains.

NURSE. No, truly, sir, not a penny. 120

ROMEO. Go to! I say you shall.

NURSE. This afternoon, sir? Well, she shall be there.

ROMEO. And stay, good Nurse, behind the abbey wall.
Within this hour my man shall be with thee
And bring thee cords made like a tackled stair,[32] 125
Which to the high topgallant[33] of my joy
Must be my convoy in the secret night.
Farewell. Be trusty, and I'll quit thy pains.

25. **ropery,** joking.

26. **Jacks,** rascals.
27. **flirt-gills,** flirtatious women.

28. **lead . . . paradise,** let her think you wish to marry her when you do not.

29. **commend,** recommend.
30. **protest,** vow.

31. **shrived,** cleansed of sin.

32. **tackled stair,** rope ladder.
33. **topgallant,** summit, height.

Farewell. Commend me to thy mistress.

NURSE. Now God in heaven bless thee. Hark you, sir.   130

ROMEO. What say'st thou, my dear Nurse?

NURSE. Is your man secret? Did you ne'er hear say,
Two may keep counsel, putting one away?

ROMEO. Warrant thee my man's as true as steel.

NURSE. Well, sir, my mistress is the sweetest lady. Lord,   135
lord, when 'twas a little prating thing. O, there is a
nobleman in town, one Paris, that would fain lay
knife aboard;³⁴ but she, good soul, had as lief see a
toad, a very toad, as see him. I anger her sometimes,
and tell her that Paris is the properer man, but I'll   140
warrant you, when I say so, she looks as pale as any
clout³⁵ in the versal³⁶ world.

ROMEO. Commend me to thy lady.

NURSE. Ay, a thousand times. (*Exit* ROMEO.) Peter!

PETER. Anon.   145

NURSE. Before, and apace.

[NURSE *and* PETER *exit.*]

34. **fain ... aboard,** gladly seize, in the manner of a pirate, what he desires.

35. **clout,** rag.
36. **versal,** universal.

TYING THE SCENES TOGETHER: SCENE 4

Mercutio and Benvolio have met Romeo in the street that
morning and found that he seems to have recovered his senses.
He no longer moans over Rosaline. Juliet has sent her nurse to
learn the wedding plans from Romeo. How does Mercutio's encounter with the nurse bear out the judgment you have already
made about his character?

SCENE 5

Capulet's orchard. JULIET *enters.*

JULIET. The clock struck nine when I did send the
Nurse;
In half an hour she promised to return.
Perchance she cannot meet him—that's not so.
O, she is lame! Love's heralds should be thoughts,
Which ten times faster glides than the sun's beams,   5
Driving back shadows over louring hills.
Therefore do nimble-pinioned¹ doves draw love,²
And therefore hath the wind-swift Cupid wings.
Now is the sun upon the highmost hill
Of this day's journey, and from nine till twelve   10

1. **nimble-pinioned,** swift-winged.
2. **love,** Venus, the goddess whose chariot was drawn by doves.

Is three long hours, yet she is not come.
Had she affections and warm youthful blood,
She would be as swift in motion as a ball;
My words would bandy³ her to my sweet love,
And his to me.   15
But old folks, many feign⁴ as they were dead,
Unwieldy, slow, heavy, and pale as lead.

[*Enter* NURSE *and* PETER.]

O God, she comes! O honey Nurse, what news?
Hast thou met with him? Send thy man away.
NURSE. Peter, stay at the gate. (PETER *exits.*)   20
JULIET. Now, good sweet Nurse—O Lord, why look'st
    thou sad?
Though news be sad, yet tell them merrily;
If good, thou shamest the music of sweet news
By playing it to me with so sour a face.
NURSE. I am aweary, give me leave⁵ awhile.   25
Fie, how my bones ache! What a jaunce⁶ have I had!
JULIET. I would thou hadst my bones, and I thy news.
Nay, come, I pray thee speak; good, good Nurse,
    speak.
NURSE. Jesu, what haste! Can you not stay awhile?
Do you not see that I am out of breath?   30
JULIET. How art thou out of breath when thou hast
    breath
To say to me that thou art out of breath?
The excuse that thou dost make in this delay
Is longer than the tale thou dost excuse.
Is thy news good or bad? Answer to that.   35
Say either, and I'll stay the circumstance.⁷
Let me be satisfied, is't good or bad?
NURSE. Well, you have made a simple⁸ choice; you know
    not how to choose a man. Romeo? No, not he;
    though his face be better than any man's, yet his   40
    leg excels all men's; and for a hand and a foot, and
    a body, though they be not to be talked on, yet they
    are past compare. He is not the flower of courtesy,
    but I'll warrant him, as gentle as a lamb. Go thy
    ways, wench; serve God. What, have you dined at   45
    home?
JULIET. No, no. But all this did I know before.
What says he of our marriage? What of that?
NURSE. Lord, how my head aches! What a head have I!
It beats as it would fall in twenty pieces.   50
My back a t' other side—ah, my back, my back!

3. **bandy,** speed.

4. **feign\fān** appear.

5. **give me leave,** let me alone.

6. **jaunce,** jolting, rough journey.

7. **stay the circumstance,** wait to hear
the details.

8. **simple,** foolish.

Beshrew[9] your heart for sending me about
To catch my death with jauncing up and down!
JULIET. I' faith, I am sorry that thou art not well.
Sweet, sweet, sweet Nurse, tell me, what says my
love?   55
NURSE. Your love says, like an honest gentleman, and a
courteous, and a kind, and a handsome, and, I war-
rant, a virtuous—— Where is your mother?
JULIET. Where is my mother? Why, she is within.
Where should she be? How oddly thou repliest!   60
"Your love says, like an honest gentleman,
Where is your mother?"
NURSE.   O God's lady dear,
Are you so hot?[10] Marry come up, I trow.[11]
Is this the poultice[12] for my aching bones?
Henceforward do your messages yourself.   65
JULIET. Here's such a coil![13] Come, what says Romeo?
NURSE. Have you got leave to go to shrift today?
JULIET. I have.
NURSE. Then hie you hence to Friar Laurence' cell;
There stays a husband to make you a wife.   70
Now comes the wanton blood up in your cheeks;
They'll be in scarlet straight at any news.
Hie you to church; I must another way,
To fetch a ladder, by the which your love
Must climb a bird's nest soon when it is dark.   75
I am the drudge, and toil in your delight.
Go; I'll to dinner; hie you to the cell.
JULIET. Hie to high fortune! Honest Nurse, farewell.

[*They exit in opposite directions.*]

TYING THE SCENES TOGETHER: SCENE 5

The impatient Juliet has finally managed to get the talkative
nurse to tell her the wedding plans. How does the nurse add
humor to this scene?

SCENE 6

It is afternoon in Friar Laurence's cell. Enter FRIAR
LAURENCE *and* ROMEO.

FRIAR LAURENCE. So smile the heavens upon this holy act
That after hours with sorrow chide us not!
ROMEO. Amen, amen! But come what sorrow can,

9. **Beshrew,** shame upon.

10. **hot,** angry.   11. **trow,** declare.

12. **poultice**\\ˈpōl·təs\\ ointment.

13. **coil,** fuss.

It cannot countervail¹ the exchange of joy
That one short minute gives me in her sight.   5
Do thou but close our hands with holy words,
Then love-devouring death do what he dare;
It is enough I may but call her mine.
FRIAR LAURENCE. These violent delights have violent
    ends
And in their triumph die, like fire and powder,   10
Which, as they kiss, consume. The sweetest honey
Is loathsome in his own deliciousness
And in the taste confounds² the appetite.
Therefore love moderately: long love doth so;
Too swift arrives as tardy as too slow.   15

    [*Enter* JULIET.]

Here comes the lady. O, so light a foot
Will ne'er wear out the everlasting flint.³
A lover may bestride the gossamers⁴
That idles in the wanton summer air,
And yet not fall; so light is vanity.⁵   20
JULIET. Good even to my ghostly confessor.
FRIAR LAURENCE. Romeo shall thank thee, daughter, for
    us both.
JULIET. As much to him, else is his thanks too much.
ROMEO. Ah, Juliet, if the measure of thy joy
    Be heaped like mine, and that thy skill be more   25
    To blazon⁶ it, then sweeten with thy breath
    This neighbor air, and let rich music's tongue
    Unfold the imagined happiness that both
    Receive in either by this dear encounter.
JULIET. Conceit, more rich in matter than in words,   30
    Brags of his substance, not of ornament.⁷
    They are but beggars that can count their worth.
    But my true love is grown to such excess,
    I cannot sum up sum of half my wealth.
FRIAR LAURENCE. Come, come with me, and we will
    make short work;   35
    For, by your leaves, you shall not stay alone
    Till holy Church incorporate two in one.

    [*They exit to perform the simple wedding ceremony.*]

1. **countervail,** outweigh.

2. **confounds,** destroys.

3. **wear . . . flint,** referring to an old proverb: "Small water drops will eventually wear away the stone."
4. **gossamers**\ˈgŏs·ə·mərz\ spider's web.
5. **vanity,** earthly love.

6. **blazon,** describe.

7. **Conceit . . . ornament.** Juliet's love is more important than fancy words.

TYING THE SCENES TOGETHER: SCENE 6
What has just taken place in Friar Laurence's cell?

THE LOVERS MARRY

1. How does Romeo happen to find out that Juliet wishes he had a different name?

2. How does Juliet ask Romeo to prove that he is sincere in his love?

3. Although Friar Laurence is scandalized at the shallowness of Romeo's love for Rosaline, what good does the Friar think might come of Romeo's love for Juliet?

4. By whom does Romeo send word to Juliet?

5. What do you think is the most important single event that occurs in this act?

II

IMPLICATIONS

Identify the following generalizations with the characters who express these beliefs in Act II.

1. A man in love makes a poor fighter.

2. Moderate love is more lasting than love that is sudden and violent.

3. Sincerity of intention and action is more important than fancy language.

III

TECHNIQUES

Staging

1. Why do you think Shakespeare opened Act II with the scene between Benvolio and Mercutio?

2. The balcony scene is one of the most famous in stage history. As you visualize it, what is there about its staging that makes it memorable?

3. In Scene 4, how does Mercutio's presence on the stage add interest when Juliet's nurse comes to see Romeo?

Language

Many of the lines spoken by Romeo and Juliet in the famous balcony scene have been memorized and repeated so often that they are universally recognized whenever they are quoted. What lines did you recognize as you read this scene?

Act III

SCENE 1

The public square. Enter BENVOLIO, MERCUTIO, *and some of their men.*

BENVOLIO. I pray thee, good Mercutio, let's retire.
The day is hot, the Capulets are abroad,
And, if we meet, we shall not 'scape a brawl,
For now, these hot days, is the mad blood stirring.

[*Enter* TYBALT *with other men of the Capulet family.*]

BENVOLIO. By my head, here comes the Capulets.   5
MERCUTIO. By my heel, I care not.
TYBALT. Follow me close, for I will speak to them.
Gentlemen, good den. A word with one of you.
MERCUTIO. And but one word with one of us? Couple
it with something; make it a word and a blow.   10
TYBALT. You shall find me apt enough to that, sir, and
you will give me occasion.
MERCUTIO. Could you not take some occasion without
giving?
TYBALT. Mercutio, thou consortest with Romeo.   15
MERCUTIO. Consort?[1] What, dost thou make us minstrels?
And thou make minstrels of us, look to hear nothing
but discords. Here's my fiddlestick;[2] here's that shall
make you dance. Zounds,[3] consort!
BENVOLIO. We talk here in the public haunt of men.   20
Either withdraw unto some private place,
Or reason coldly of your grievances,
Or else depart. Here all eyes gaze on us.
MERCUTIO. Men's eyes were made to look, and let them
gaze.
I will not budge for no man's pleasure, I.   25

[ROMEO *enters.*]

TYBALT. Well, peace be with you, sir. Here comes my
man.
MERCUTIO. But I'll be hanged, sir, if he wear your
livery.[4]
Marry, go before to field,[5] he'll be your follower!
Your worship in that sense may call him man.
TYBALT. Romeo, the love I bear thee can afford   30
No better term than this—thou art a villain.[6]
ROMEO. Tybalt, the reason that I have to love thee
Doth much excuse the appertaining[7] rage

1. **Consort,** associate with, also term for a musical group.

2. **fiddlestick,** rapier.

3. **Zounds,** by God's wounds.

4. **livery,** servant's uniform.

5. **field,** dueling place.

6. **villain,** one of low birth.

7. **appertaining,** suitable.

To such a greeting—villain am I none.
Therefore farewell. I see thou knowest me not.   35
TYBALT. Boy, this shall not excuse the injuries
  That thou hast done me; therefore turn and draw.
ROMEO. I do protest I never injured thee,
  But love thee better than thou canst devise
  Till thou shalt know the reason of my love.   40
  And so, good Capulet, which name I tender[8]
  As dearly as mine own, be satisfied.
MERCUTIO. O calm, dishonorable, vile submission!
  Alla stoccata[9] carries it away.[10] (*Draws his sword.*)
  Tybalt, you rat catcher,[11] will you walk?   45
TYBALT. What wouldst thou have with me?
MERCUTIO. Good King of Cats, nothing but one of
  your nine lives. That I mean to make bold withal,
  and as you shall use me hereafter, dry-beat[12] the rest
  of the eight. Will you pluck your sword out of his   50
  pilcher[13] by the ears? Make haste, lest mine be about
  your ears ere it be out.

8. **tender,** cherish.

9. **Alla stoccata**\ˈal·la·stɔk ˈka·ta\ at the thrust, a fencing term.
10. **carries it away.** Tybalt's fencing skill has intimidated Romeo.
11. **rat catcher,** a cat.

12. **dry-beat,** bruise.

13. **pilcher,** scabbard.

TYBALT. I am for you. (*Draws his sword.*)
ROMEO. Gentle Mercutio, put thy rapier up.
MERCUTIO. Come, sir, your passado!　　　　　　　　　55

[TYBALT *and* MERCUTIO *fight.*]

ROMEO. Draw, Benvolio, beat down their weapons.
　Gentlemen, for shame! Forbear this outrage!
　Tybalt, Mercutio, the Prince expressly hath
　Forbid this bandying in Verona streets.
　Hold, Tybalt! Good Mercutio!

[ROMEO *tries to separate* MERCUTIO *and* TYBALT *and
　in doing so he blocks* MERCUTIO *from using his
　rapier.* TYBALT *stabs* MERCUTIO *and exits with his
　followers.*]

MERCUTIO.　　　　　　　I am hurt.　　　　60
　A plague a both your houses![14] I am sped.[15]
　Is he gone and hath nothing?
BENVOLIO.　　　　　　What, art thou hurt?
MERCUTIO. Ay, ay, a scratch, a scratch. Marry, 'tis
　enough.
　Where is my page? Go, villain, fetch a surgeon.

[*Exit* PAGE.]

ROMEO. Courage man, the hurt cannot be much.　　65
MERCUTIO. No, 'tis not so deep as a well, nor so wide
　as a church door, but 'tis enough, 'twill serve. Ask
　for me tomorrow, and you shall find me a grave[16]
　man. I am peppered,[17] I warrant, for this world. A
　plague a both your houses! Zounds, a dog, a rat, a　70
　mouse, a cat, to scratch a man to death! A braggart,
　a rogue, a villain, that fights by the book or arithme-
　tic![18] Why the devil came you between us? I was
　hurt under your arm.
ROMEO. I thought all for the best.　　　　　75
MERCUTIO. Help me into some house Benvolio,
　Or I shall faint. A plague a both your houses!
　They have made worms' meat of me. I have it,[19]
　And soundly too. Your houses!

[*Exit* MERCUTIO *supported by* BENVOLIO.]

ROMEO. This gentleman, the Prince's near ally,　　80
　My very friend, hath got this mortal hurt
　In my behalf; my reputation stained
　With Tybalt's slander, Tybalt, that an hour
　Hath been my cousin. O sweet Juliet,
　Thy beauty hath made me effeminate　　　85

14. **houses,** the houses of Capulet and
Montague.
15. **sped,** fatally injured.

16. **grave,** double meaning of "serious"
and "in the grave."
17. **peppered,** finished.

18. **arithmetic,** counting his strokes.

19. **I have it.** I am wounded.

And in my temper softened valor's steel!

[*Enter* BENVOLIO.]

BENVOLIO. O Romeo, Romeo, brave Mercutio is dead!
    That gallant spirit hath aspired[20] the clouds,
    Which too untimely here did scorn the earth.
ROMEO. This day's black fate on moe[21] days doth
    depend;[22]
    This but begins the woe others must end.

[*Enter* TYBALT.]

BENVOLIO. Here comes the furious Tybalt back again.
ROMEO. Alive in triumph, and Mercutio slain?
    Away to heaven respective lenity,[23]
    And fire-eyed fury be my conduct now!
    Now, Tybalt, take the villain back again
    That late thou gavest me, for Mercutio's soul
    Is but a little way above our heads,
    Staying for thine to keep him company.
    Either thou or I, or both, must go with him.
TYBALT. Thou, wretched boy, that didst consort him
    here,
    Shalt with him hence.
ROMEO.   This shall determine that.

[*They fight.* TYBALT *falls.*]

BENVOLIO. Romeo, away, be gone!
    The citizens are up, and Tybalt slain.
    Stand not amazed; the Prince will doom thee death
    If thou art taken. Hence, be gone, away!
ROMEO. O, I am fortune's fool!
BENVOLIO.   Why dost thou stay?

[ROMEO *exits and* CITIZENS *enter.*]

CITIZEN. Which way ran he that killed Mercutio?
    Tybalt, that murderer, which way ran he?
BENVOLIO. There lies that Tybalt.
CITIZEN.   Up, sir, go with me.
    I charge thee in the Prince's name obey.

[*Enter* PRINCE, *old* MONTAGUE, CAPULET, *their wives,
    and all.*]

PRINCE. Where are the vile beginners of this fray?
BENVOLIO. O noble Prince, I can discover[24] all
    The unlucky manage[25] of this fatal brawl.
    There lies the man, slain by young Romeo,
    That slew thy kinsman, brave Mercutio.

90

95

100

105

110

115

20. **aspired,** risen to.

21. **moe,** more.
22. **depend,** cast a frightening shadow.

23. **lenity,** mercy.

24. **discover,** reveal.
25. **manage,** conduct.

LADY CAPULET. Tybalt, my cousin! O my brother's child!
O Prince! O cousin! Husband! O, the blood is spilt
Of my dear kinsman! Prince, as thou art true,
For blood of ours shed blood of Montague.   120
O cousin, cousin!
PRINCE. Benvolio, who began this bloody fray?
BENVOLIO. Tybalt, here slain, whom Romeo's hand did
    slay.
Romeo, that spoke him fair, bid him bethink
How nice the quarrel was, and urged withal   125
Your high displeasure. All this, uttered
With gentle breath, calm look, knees humbly bowed,
Could not take truce with the unruly spleen[26]
Of Tybalt deaf to peace, but that he tilts[27]
With piercing steel at bold Mercutio's breast;   130
Who, all as hot, turns deadly point to point,
And, with a martial scorn, with one hand beats
Cold death aside, and with the other sends
It back to Tybalt, whose dexterity
Retorts it. Romeo he cries aloud,   135
"Hold, friends; friends, part," and swifter than his
    tongue,
His agile arm beats down their fatal points,
And 'twixt them rushes; underneath whose arm
An envious thrust from Tybalt hit the life
Of stout Mercutio, and then Tybalt fled;   140
But by and by comes back to Romeo,
Who had but newly entertained revenge,
And to't they go like lightning; for, ere I
Could draw to part them, was stout Tybalt slain;
And, as he fell, did Romeo turn and fly.   145
This is the truth, or let Benvolio die.
LADY CAPULET. He is a kinsman to the Montague;
Affection makes him false, he speaks not true.
Some twenty of them fought in this black strife,
And all those twenty could but kill one life.   150
I beg for justice, which thou, Prince, must give.
Romeo slew Tybalt, Romeo must not live.
PRINCE. Romeo slew him, he slew Mercutio.
Who now the price of his dear blood doth owe?[28]
MONTAGUE. Not Romeo, Prince; he was Mercutio's
    friend.   155
His fault concludes but what the law should end,
The life of Tybalt.
PRINCE.   And for that offense
Immediately we do exile him hence.
I have an interest in your hate's proceeding,

26. **spleen,** temper.
27. **tilts,** strikes.

28. **Who ... owe?** Who now should give his life?

My blood for your rude brawls doth lie a-bleeding; 160
But I'll amerce[29] you with so strong a fine
That you shall all repent the loss of mine.
I will be deaf to pleading and excuses;
Nor tears nor prayers shall purchase out abuses.[30]
Therefore use none. Let Romeo hence in haste,   165
Else, when he is found, that hour is his last.
Bear hence this body and attend our will.
Mercy but murders, pardoning those that kill.

[They all exit.]

29. **amerce,** punish.

30. **purchase . . . abuses,** buy pardons for crimes.

TYING THE SCENES TOGETHER: SCENE 1

Tybalt has killed Mercutio, and Romeo in revenge has killed Tybalt. The Prince has decreed that Romeo is to be banished rather than put to death. Discuss whether the actions of Mercutio and Tybalt are what you would have expected of them. Which of the two characters do you think is the audience's favorite?

SCENE 2

Capulet's orchard, a short time after the street fight. JULIET *enters.*

JULIET. Gallop apace, you fiery-footed steeds,
Towards Phoebus'[1] lodging; such a wagoner
As Phaëthon[2] would whip you to the west
And bring in cloudy night immediately.
Spread thy close curtain, love-performing night,   5
That runaways' eyes[3] may wink, and Romeo
Leap to these arms untalked of and unseen.
Come night, come Romeo, come thou day in night;
For thou wilt lie upon the wings of night
Whiter than new snow upon a raven's back.   10
Come gentle night, come loving, black-browed night;
Give me my Romeo, and when he shall die,
Take him and cut him out in little stars,
And he will make the face of heaven so fine
That all the world will be in love with night   15
And pay no worship to the garish sun.
O, here comes my nurse,

[NURSE *enters with a rope ladder.*]

And she brings news; and every tongue that speaks
But Romeo's name speaks heavenly eloquence.
Now, Nurse, what news? What hast thou there, the
    cords   20

1. **Phoebus**\\ˈfē·bəs\\ the sun god.
2. **Phaëthon**\\fā·ə 'thŏn\\ son of Phoebus. He was allowed to drive the chariot of the sun for a day. Too weak to control the horses, he nearly destroyed the universe.
3. **runaways' eyes,** eyes of the sun's horses.

That Romeo bid thee fetch?

NURSE.   Ay, ay, the cords.

JULIET. Ay me! What news? Why dost thou wring thy
    hands?

NURSE. Ah, weladay! He's dead, he's dead, he's dead!
    We are undone, lady, we are undone!
    Alack the day! He's gone, he's killed, he's dead!   25

JULIET. Can heaven be so envious?

NURSE.   Romeo can,
    Though heaven cannot. O Romeo, Romeo,
    Who ever would have thought it? Romeo!

JULIET. What devil art thou that dost torment me thus?
    This torture should be roared in dismal hell.   30
    Hath Romeo slain himself? Say thou but "Ay,"
    And that bare vowel "I"[4] shall poison more
    Than the death-darting eye of cockatrice.[5]
    I am not I, if there be such an I,
    Or those eyes' shut[6] that makes thee answer "Ay."   35
    If he be slain, say "Ay"; or if not, "No."
    Brief sounds determine of my weal or woe.

NURSE. I saw the wound, I saw it with mine eyes,
    God save the mark[7]—here on his manly breast.
    A piteous corse,[8] a bloody piteous corse;   40
    Pale, pale as ashes, all bedaubed in blood,
    All in gore-blood. I swounded[9] at the sight.

JULIET. O, break, my heart! Poor bankrupt, break at
    once!
    To prison, eyes; ne'er look on liberty.
    Vile earth, to earth resign; end motion here,   45
    And thou and Romeo press one heavy bier!

NURSE. O Tybalt, Tybalt, the best friend I had!
    O courteous Tybalt; honest gentleman!
    That ever I should live to see thee dead!

JULIET. What storm is this that blows so contrary?   50
    Is Romeo slaughtered, and is Tybalt dead?
    My dearest cousin, and my dearer lord?
    Then, dreadful trumpet, sound the general doom,
    For who is living, if those two are gone?

NURSE. Tybalt is gone, and Romeo banished;   55
    Romeo that killed him, he is banished.

JULIET. O God! Did Romeo's hand shed Tybalt's blood?

NURSE. It did, it did, alas the day, it did!

JULIET. O serpent heart, hid with a flowering face!
    Did ever dragon keep so fair a cave?   60
    Beautiful tyrant, fiend angelical,
    Dove-feathered raven, wolvish-ravening lamb,
    Despisèd substance of divinest show,

4. **I,** used in word play here with "ay"
(yes) or "eye."

5. **cockatrice**\ˈkŏk·ə·trəs\ fabled creature that could kill with a glance of its
eyes.

6. **those eyes' shut,** that is, the nurse's
eyes.

7. **God ... mark.** God have pity on us.

8. **corse,** corpse.

9. **swounded,** swooned.

Just opposite to what thou justly seem'st—
A damned saint, an honorable villain!   65
O nature, what hadst thou to do in hell
When thou didst bower the spirit of a fiend
In mortal paradise of such sweet flesh?
Was ever book containing such vile matter
So fairly bound? O, that deceit should dwell   70
In such a gorgeous palace!
NURSE.   There's no trust,
No faith, no honesty in men; all perjured,
All forsworn,[10] all naught, all dissemblers.
Ah, where's my man? Give me some aqua vitae.[11]
These griefs, these woes, these sorrows make me old.   75
Shame come to Romeo!
JULIET.   Blistered be thy tongue
For such a wish! He was not born to shame.
Upon his brow shame is ashamed to sit;
For 'tis a throne where honor may be crowned
Sole monarch of the universal earth.   80
O, what a beast was I to chide at him!
NURSE. Will you speak well of him that killed your
     cousin?
JULIET. Shall I speak ill of him that is my husband?
Ah, poor my lord, what tongue shall smooth thy
     name
When I, thy three-hours wife, have mangled it?   85
But wherefore, villain, didst thou kill my cousin?
That villain cousin would have killed my husband.
Back, foolish tears, back to your native spring,
Your tributary drops belong to woe,
Which you, mistaking, offer up to joy.   90
My husband lives, that Tybalt would have slain;
And Tybalt's dead, that would have slain my hus-
     band.
All this is comfort, wherefore weep I then?
Some word there was, worser than Tybalt's death,
That murdered me. I would forget it fain;   95
But O, it presses to my memory
Like damnèd guilty deeds to sinners' minds:
"Tybalt is dead, and Romeo—banishèd."
That "banishèd," that one word "banishèd,"
Hath slain ten thousand Tybalts. Tybalt's death   100
Was woe enough, if it had ended there.
Or, if sour woe delights in fellowship,
And needly will be ranked with other griefs,
Why followed not, when she said "Tybalt's dead,"
Thy father, or thy mother, nay, or both,   105

10. **forsworn,** faithless.
11. **aqua vitae**\\'ak•wə ▲vit•ē\\ brandy.

Which modern lamentation might have moved?
But with a rearward following Tybalt's death,
"Romeo is banishèd"—to speak that word
Is father, mother, Tybalt, Romeo, Juliet,
All slain, all dead. "Romeo is banishèd"—   110
There is no end, no limit, measure, bound,
In that word's death; no words can that woe sound.
Where is my father and my mother, Nurse?
NURSE. Weeping and wailing over Tybalt's corse.
Will you go to them? I will bring you thither.   115
JULIET. Wash they his wounds with tears? Mine shall
    be spent,
When theirs are dry, for Romeo's banishment.
Take up those cords. Poor ropes, you are beguiled,
Both you and I, for Romeo is exiled.
NURSE. Hie to your chamber. I'll find Romeo   120
To comfort you. I wot[12] well where he is.   12. **wot,** know.
Hark ye, your Romeo will be here at night.
I'll to him; he is hid at Laurence' cell.
JULIET. O, find him! Give this ring to my true knight
And bid him come to take his last farewell.   125

[JULIET *and* NURSE *exit.*]

TYING THE SCENES TOGETHER: SCENE 2

Juliet, waiting for her husband, has been told by the nurse
that Romeo has killed Tybalt. Her grief for her cousin Tybalt
was less than her joy over the fact that Romeo still lives. The
nurse has promised to find Romeo and bring him secretly to
Juliet before he leaves the city. What is revealed about Juliet's
character in this scene?

SCENE 3

FRIAR LAURENCE *enters his cell.*

FRIAR LAURENCE. Romeo, come forth; come forth, thou
    fearful man.
Affliction is enamored of thy parts,
And thou art wedded to calamity.

[ROMEO *enters.*]

ROMEO. Father, what news? What is the Prince's doom?
What sorrow craves acquaintance at my hand   5
That I yet know not?
FRIAR LAURENCE.   Too familiar
Is my dear son with such sour company.

401

I bring thee tidings of the Prince's doom.

ROMEO. What less than doomsday[1] is the Prince's doom?

FRIAR LAURENCE. A gentler judgment vanished[2] from his
    lips;
  Not body's death, but body's banishment.

ROMEO. Ha, banishment? Be merciful, say "death";
  For exile hath more terror in his look,
  Much more than death. Do not say "banishment."

FRIAR LAURENCE. Hence from Verona art thou banishèd.
  Be patient, for the world is broad and wide.

ROMEO. There is no world without Verona walls,
  But purgatory, torture, hell itself.
  Hence banishèd is banished from the world,
  And world's exile is death. Then "banishèd"
  Is death mistermed. Calling death "banishèd,"
  Thou cut'st my head off with a golden axe,
  And smilest upon the stroke that murders me.

FRIAR LAURENCE. O deadly sin! O rude unthankfulness!
  Thy fault our law calls death, but the kind Prince,
  Taking thy part, hath rushed aside the law,
  And turned that black word "death" to "banishment."
  This is dear mercy, and thou seest it not.

ROMEO. 'Tis torture, and not mercy. Heaven is here,
  Where Juliet lives; and every cat and dog
  And little mouse, every unworthy thing,
  Live here in heaven and may look on her;
  But Romeo may not, he is banishèd.
  And sayest thou yet that exile is not death?
  Hadst thou no poison mixed, no sharp-ground knife,
  No sudden mean of death, though ne'er so mean,
  But "banishèd" to kill me—"banishèd"?
  O Friar, the damnèd use that word in hell;
  Howling attends it! How hast thou the heart,
  Being a divine, a ghostly confessor,
  A sin-absolver, and my friend professed,
  To mangle me with that word "banishèd"?

FRIAR LAURENCE. Thou fond mad man, hear me a little
    speak.

ROMEO. O, thou wilt speak again of banishment.

FRIAR LAURENCE. I'll give thee armor to keep off that
    word;
  Adversity's sweet milk, philosophy,
  To comfort thee, though thou art banishèd.

ROMEO. Yet "banishèd"? Hang up philosophy!
  Unless philosophy can make a Juliet,
  Displant a town, reverse a prince's doom,
  It helps not, it prevails not. Talk no more.

1. doomsday, death.
2. vanished, issued.

10

15

20

25

30

35

40

45

50

FRIAR LAURENCE. O, then I see that madmen have no
    ears.
ROMEO. How should they, when that wise men have
    no eyes?
FRIAR LAURENCE. Let me dispute with thee of thy estate.[3]

3. **estate,** situation.

ROMEO. Thou canst not speak of that thou dost not feel.   55
    Wert thou as young as I, Juliet thy love,
    An hour but married, Tybalt murdered,
    Doting like me, and like me banishèd,
    Then mightst thou speak, then mightst thou tear thy
      hair,
    And fall upon the ground, as I do now,   60
    Taking the measure of an unmade grave.

[NURSE *knocks on the door.*]

FRIAR LAURENCE. Arise, one knocks. Good Romeo, hide
    thyself.
ROMEO. Not I; unless the breath of heart-sick groans
    Mistlike infold me from the search of eyes.

[NURSE *knocks again.*]

FRIAR LAURENCE. Hark, how they knock! Who's there?
    Romeo, arise;   65
    Thou wilt be taken.—Stay awhile!—Stand up;

[*Knocking grows louder.*]

    Run to my study.—By and by!—God's will,
    What simpleness is this.—I come, I come!
    Who knocks so hard? Whence come you? What's
      your will?

[NURSE *enters.*]

NURSE. Let me come in, and you shall know my errand.   70
    I come from Lady Juliet.
FRIAR LAURENCE.   Welcome then.
NURSE. O holy Friar, O, tell me, holy Friar,
    Where is my lady's lord, where's Romeo?
FRIAR LAURENCE. There on the ground, with his own
    tears made drunk.
NURSE. O, he is even in my mistress' case,[4]   75
    Just in her case! O woeful sympathy!
    Piteous predicament! Even so lies she,
    Blubbering and weeping, weeping and blubbering.
    Stand up, stand up; stand, and you be a man.
    For Juliet's sake, for her sake, rise and stand!   80
    Why should you fall into so deep an O?[5]
ROMEO. (*Rises.*) Nurse—

4. **O . . . case.** Romeo is in the same
state as Juliet.

5. **O,** fit of grief.

NURSE. Ah sir, ah sir! Death's the end of all.

ROMEO. Spakest thou of Juliet? How is it with her?
Doth not she think me an old⁶ murderer,   85   6. **old,** calloused.
Now I have stained the childhood of our joy
With blood removed but little from her own?
Where is she? And how doth she! And what says
My concealed lady to our cancelled love?

NURSE. O, she says nothing, sir, but weeps and weeps,   90
And now falls on her bed, and then starts up,
And Tybalt calls, and then on Romeo cries,
And then down falls again.

ROMEO.   As if that name,
Shot from the deadly level⁷ of a gun,   7. **level,** aim.
Did murder her; as that name's cursèd hand   95
Murdered her kinsman. O, tell me, Friar, tell me,
In what vile part of this anatomy
Doth my name lodge? Tell me, that I may sack
The hateful mansion.

[ROMEO *draws his dagger and offers to stab himself.*
    NURSE *snatches it away.*]

FRIAR LAURENCE.   Hold thy desperate hand.
Art thou a man? Thy form cries out thou art;   100
Thy tears are womanish, thy wild acts denote
The unreasonable fury of a beast.
Unseemly woman in a seeming man!
And ill-beseeming beast in seeming both!
Thou hast amazed me. By my holy order,   105
I thought thy disposition better tempered.
Hast thou slain Tybalt? Wilt thou slay thyself,
And slay thy lady that in thy life lives,
By doing damnèd hate upon thyself?
Why railest⁸ thou on thy birth, the heaven, and   8. **railest,** complain.
    earth,   110
Since birth, and heaven, and earth, all three do meet
In thee at once; which thou at once wouldst lose?
What, rouse thee, man! Thy Juliet is alive,
For whose dear sake thou wast but lately dead.
There art thou happy. Tybalt would kill thee,   115
But thou slewest Tybalt; there art thou happy too.
The law, that threatened death, becomes thy friend
And turns it to exile; there art thou happy.
A pack of blessings light upon thy back,
Happiness courts thee in her best array;   120
But like a misbehaved and sullen wench,
Thou pouts up thy fortune and thy love.

Take heed, take heed, for such die miserable.
Go get thee to thy love, as was decreed,
Ascend her chamber, hence and comfort her.   125
But look thou stay not till the watch be set,[9]
For then thou canst not pass to Mantua,
Where thou shalt live till we can find a time
To blaze[10] your marriage, reconcile your friends,[11]
Beg pardon of the Prince, and call thee back   130
With twenty hundred thousand times more joy
Than thou went'st forth in lamentation.
Go before, Nurse. Commend me to thy lady,
And bid her hasten all the house to bed,
Which heavy sorrow makes them apt unto.   135
Romeo is coming.
NURSE. O Lord, I could have stayed here all the night
To hear good counsel. O, what learning is!
My lord, I'll tell my lady you will come.
ROMEO. Do so, and bid my sweet prepare to chide.   140
NURSE. Here, sir, a ring she bid me give you, sir.
Hie you, make haste, for it grows very late.

[NURSE *exits.*]

ROMEO. How well my comfort is revived by this!
FRIAR LAURENCE. Go hence; good night; and here stands
     all your state—
Either be gone before the watch be set,   145
Or by the break of day disguised from hence.
Sojourn in Mantua; I'll find out your man,
And he shall signify from time to time
Every good hap to you that chances here.
Give me thy hand; 'tis late. Farewell; good night.   150
ROMEO. But that a joy past joy calls out on me,
It were a grief so brief to part with thee.
Farewell.

[ROMEO *exits.*]

9. **watch be set,** the night watch takes up its post at the city gates.

10. **blaze,** announce.
11. **friends,** families.

TYING THE SCENES TOGETHER: SCENE 3

Romeo has learned from the Friar that the Prince has ordered banishment rather than death. The Friar has comforted Romeo when he despaired and has suggested he go to Mantua to live until the Prince grants a pardon. The nurse has told Romeo to hurry to comfort Juliet. The Friar has warned him he must leave Verona before daybreak. Does Romeo show himself to be weak or strong in this scene? Is Juliet any stronger emotionally?

Capulet's house, later that night. Enter CAPULET, LADY
CAPULET, *and* PARIS.

CAPULET. Things have fallen out, sir, so unluckily
  That we have had no time to move[1] our daughter.
  Look you, she loved her kinsman Tybalt dearly,
  And so did I. Well, we were born to die.
  'Tis very late; she'll not come down tonight.   5
  I promise you, but for your company,
  I would have been abed an hour ago.
PARIS. These times of woe afford no times to woo.
  Madam, good night. Commend me to your daughter.
LADY CAPULET. I will, and know her mind early tomor-
    row;   10
  Tonight she's mewed up to her heaviness.[2]
CAPULET. Sir Paris, I will make a desperate tender[3]
  Of my child's love. I think she will be ruled
  In all respects by me; nay more, I doubt it not.
  Wife, go you to her ere you go to bed;   15
  Acquaint her here of my son Paris' love
  And bid her, mark you me, on Wednesday next—
  But soft! What day is this?
PARIS.   Monday, my lord.
CAPULET. Monday? Ha, ha! Well, Wednesday is too
    soon.
  A Thursday let it be, a Thursday, tell her,   20
  She shall be married to this noble earl.
  Will you be ready? Do you like this haste?
  We'll keep no great ado—a friend or two;
  For hark you, Tybalt being slain so late,
  It may be thought we held him carelessly,   25
  Being our kinsman, if we revel much.
  Therefore we'll have some half a dozen friends,
  And there an end. But what say you to Thursday?
PARIS. My lord, I would that Thursday were tomorrow.
CAPULET. Well, get you gone. A Thursday be it then.   30
  Go you to Juliet ere you go to bed;
  Prepare her, wife, against this wedding day.
  Farewell, my lord. Light to my chamber, ho!
  Afore me, it is so very late that we
  May call it early by and by. Good night.   35

1. **move,** talk with.

2. **mewed . . . heaviness,** shut up with
her grief.
3. **desperate tender,** rash offer.

TYING THE SCENES TOGETHER: SCENE 4

Capulet decides that Paris and Juliet will marry in three days.
What does this show about him as a father?

SCENE 5

Capulet's orchard. ROMEO *and* JULIET *enter from her room to the balcony.*

JULIET. Wilt thou be gone? It is not yet near day.
　It was the nightingale, and not the lark,[1]
　That pierced the fearful hollow of thine ear;
　Nightly she sings on yond pomegranate tree.
　Believe me, love, it was the nightingale.　　　　　5
ROMEO. It was the lark, the herald of the morn,
　No nightingale. Look, love, what envious streaks
　Do lace the severing clouds in yonder east.
　Night's candles[2] are burnt out, and jocund[3] day
　Stands tiptoe on the misty mountaintops.　　　　10
　I must be gone and live, or stay and die.
JULIET. Yond light is not daylight, I know it, I.
　It is some meteor that the sun exhales,
　To be to thee this night a torchbearer,
　And light thee on thy way to Mantua.　　　　　15
　Therefore stay yet; thou need'st not to be gone.
ROMEO. Let me be ta'en, let me be put to death.
　I am content, so thou wilt have it so.
　I'll say yon gray is not the morning's eye,
　'Tis but the pale reflex of Cynthia's[4] brow;　　20
　Nor that is not the lark whose notes do beat
　The vaulty heaven so high above our heads.
　I have more care to stay than will to go.
　Come, death, and welcome, Juliet wills it so.
　How is't, my soul? Let's talk; it is not day.　　25
JULIET. It is, it is; hie hence, be gone, away!
　It is the lark that sings so out of tune,
　Straining harsh discords and unpleasing sharps.
　Some say the lark makes sweet division;[5]
　This doth not so, for she divideth us.　　　　　30
　Some say the lark and loathèd toad change eyes;[6]
　O, now I would they had changed voices too,
　Since arm from arm that voice doth us affray,[7]
　Hunting thee hence with hunt's-up[8] to the day.
　O, now be gone! More light and light it grows.　35
ROMEO. More light and light, more dark and dark our
　　woes.

[NURSE *enters.*]

NURSE. Madam!
JULIET. Nurse?
NURSE. Your lady mother is coming to your chamber.

1. **nightingale . . . lark.** The nightingale is a night songster, while the lark sings at daybreak.

2. **Night's candles,** the stars.
3. **jocund**\▲jŏk·ənd\ cheery.

4. **Cynthia,** another name for the moon goddess, Diana.

5. **division,** melody.

6. **change eyes,** a folk tale.

7. **affray,** frighten.
8. **hunt's-up,** morning call to awaken hunters.

The day is broke; be wary, look about. (*She exits.*) 40
JULIET. Then, window, let day in, and let life out.
ROMEO. Farewell, farewell! One kiss, and I'll descend.

[*He descends down the ladder.*]

JULIET. Art thou gone so, love, lord, ay husband, friend?
  I must hear from thee every day in the hour,
  For in a minute there are many days. 45
  O, by this count I shall be much in years
  Ere I again behold my Romeo!
ROMEO. Farewell!
  I will omit no opportunity
  That may convey my greetings, love, to thee. 50
JULIET. O, think'st thou we shall ever meet again?
ROMEO. I doubt it not; and all these woes shall serve
  For sweet discourses in our times to come.
JULIET. O God, I have an ill-divining soul![9]
  Methinks I see thee, now thou art so low,[10] 55
  As one dead in the bottom of a tomb.
  Either my eyesight fails, or thou lookest pale.
ROMEO. And trust me, love, in my eye so do you.
  Dry sorrow drinks our blood.[11] Adieu, adieu!

  [ROMEO *exits.*]

JULIET. O fortune, fortune! All men call thee fickle; 60
  If thou art fickle, what dost thou with him
  That is renowned for faith? Be fickle, fortune,
  For then I hope thou wilt not keep him long,
  But send him back.
LADY CAPULET. (*Off-stage.*) Ho, daughter! Are you up? 65
JULIET. Who is't that calls? It is my lady mother.
  Is she not down[12] so late, or up so early?
  What unaccustomed cause procures[13] her hither?

  [LADY CAPULET *enters.*]

LADY CAPULET. Why, how now, Juliet?
JULIET.   Madam, I am not
    well.
LADY CAPULET. Evermore weeping for your cousin's
    death? 70
  What, wilt thou wash him from his grave with tears?
  And if thou couldst, thou couldst not make him live.
  Therefore have done. Some grief shows much of
    love;
  But much of grief shows still some want of wit.
JULIET. Yet let me weep for such a feeling loss. 75

9. **ill-divining soul,** one that foresees evil.
10. **low.** Romeo now stands on the ground.

11. **Dry . . . blood.** Sorrow was believed to dry up the blood.

12. **down,** in bed.
13. **procures,** brings.

408

LADY CAPULET. So shall you feel the loss, but not the
   friend
   Which you weep for.

JULIET.   Feeling so the loss,
   I cannot choose but ever weep the friend.

LADY CAPULET. Well, girl, thou weep'st not so much for
   his death
   As that the villain lives which slaughtered him.   80

JULIET. What villain, madam?

LADY CAPULET.   That same villain Romeo.

JULIET. (*Aside.*) Villain and he be many miles
   asunder.—
   God pardon him; I do with all my heart.
   And yet no man like he doth grieve my heart.

LADY CAPULET. That is because the traitor murderer
   lives.   85

JULIET. Ay, madam, from the reach of these my hands.
   Would none but I might venge my cousin's death!

LADY CAPULET. We will have vengeance for it, fear
   thou not.
   Then weep no more. I'll send to one in Mantua,
   Where that same banished runagate doth live,   90
   Shall give him such an unaccustomed dram,[14]
   That he shall soon keep Tybalt company.
   And then I hope thou wilt be satisfied.

14. **dram**, drink; here, poisoned.

JULIET. Indeed I never shall be satisfied
   With Romeo till I behold him—dead[15]—   95
   Is my poor heart so for a kinsman vexed.
   Madam, if you could find out but a man
   To bear a poison, I would temper it,
   That Romeo should, upon receipt thereof,
   Soon sleep in quiet. O, how my heart abhors   100
   To hear him named, and cannot come to him,
   To wreak the love I bore my cousin
   Upon his body that hath slaughtered him!

15. **dead.** Juliet arranges her words in such a way that Lady Capulet will mistakenly think that Juliet wishes to see Romeo dead.

LADY CAPULET. Find thou the means, and I'll find such
   a man.
   But now I'll tell thee joyful tidings, girl.   105

JULIET. And joy comes well in such a needy time.
   What are they, beseech your ladyship?

LADY CAPULET. Well, well, thou hast a careful father,
   child,
   One who, to put thee from thy heaviness,
   Hath sorted out a sudden day of joy,   110
   That thou expects not nor I looked not for.

JULIET. Madam, in happy time! What day is that?

LADY CAPULET. Marry, my child, early next Thursday morn
  The gallant, young, and noble gentleman,
  The County Paris, at Saint Peter's Church,   115
  Shall happily make thee there a joyful bride.
JULIET. Now by Saint Peter's Church, and Peter too,
  He shall not make me there a joyful bride!
  I wonder at this haste, that I must wed
  Ere he that should be husband comes to woo.   120
  I pray you tell my lord and father, madam,
  I will not marry yet, and when I do, I swear
  It shall be Romeo, whom you know I hate,
  Rather than Paris. These are news indeed!
LADY CAPULET. Here comes your father, tell him so yourself,   125
  And see how he will take it at your hands.

[*Enter* CAPULET *and* NURSE.]

CAPULET. When the sun sets, the earth doth drizzle low;
  But for the sunset of my brother's son
  It rains downright.
  How now? A conduit,[16] girl? What, still in tears?   130   16. **conduit,** fountain.
  Evermore showering? In one little body
  Thou counterfeits a bark, a sea, a wind;
  For still thy eyes, which I may call the sea,
  Do ebb and flow with tears; the bark thy body is,
  Sailing in this salt flood; the winds, thy sighs,   135
  Who, raging with thy tears and they with them,
  Without a sudden calm will overset
  Thy tempest-tossèd body. How now, wife?
  Have you delivered to her our decree?
LADY CAPULET. Ay, sir, but she will none,[17] she gives   17. **will none,** refuses "our decree."
  you thanks.   140
  I would the fool were married to her grave!
CAPULET. Soft! Take me with you, take me with you, wife.
  How will she none? Doth she not give us thanks?
  Is she not proud? Doth she not count her blest,
  Unworthy as she is, that we have wrought   145
  So worthy a gentleman to be her bridegroom?
JULIET. Not proud you have, but thankful that you have.
  Proud can I never be of what I hate,
  But thankful even for hate that is meant love.
CAPULET. How, how, how, how, chop-logic?[18] What is   18. **chop-logic,** quibbling.
  this?   150
  "Proud," and "I thank you," and "I thank you not;"
  And yet "not proud." Mistress minion[19] you,   19. **minion,** spoiled darling.

410

Thank me no thankings, nor proud me no prouds,
But fettle[20] your fine joints 'gainst Thursday next
To go with Paris to Saint Peter's Church,   155
Or I will drag thee on a hurdle[21] thither.
Out, you green-sickness carrion![22] Out, you baggage![23]
You tallow-face![24]

LADY CAPULET. Fie, fie! What, are you mad?

JULIET. Good father, I beseech you on my knees,
Hear me with patience but to speak a word.   160

CAPULET. Hang thee, young baggage! Disobedient
    wretch!
I tell thee what—get thee to church a Thursday
Or never after look me in the face.
Speak not, reply not, do not answer me!
My fingers itch.[25] Wife, we scarce thought us blest   165
That God had lent us but this only child;
But now I see this one is one too much.
And that we have a curse in having her.
Out on her, hilding![26]

NURSE.   God in heaven bless her!

20. **fettle,** prepare.

21. **hurdle,** sled on which criminals were carried to execution.
22. **green-sickness carrion,** pale and sickly creature.
23. **baggage,** worthless woman.
24. **tallow-face,** pale face.

25. **itch,** to strike her.

26. **hilding,** worthless being.

You are to blame, my lord, to rate²⁷ her so.   170   27. **rate,** abuse.

CAPULET. And why, my lady wisdom? Hold your tongue,
 Good prudence. Smatter with your gossips, go!
NURSE. I speak no treason.
CAPULET.   O, God ye god-den.
NURSE. May not one speak?
CAPULET.   Peace, you mumbling fool!
 Utter your gravity o'er a gossip's bowl,   175
 For here we need it not.
LADY CAPULET.   You are too hot.
CAPULET. God's bread!²⁸ It makes me mad.   28. **God's bread,** by the sacrament; a
 Day, night, hour; tide, time; work, play;   mild oath.
 Alone, in company; still my care hath been
 To have her matched; and having now provided   180
 A gentleman of noble parentage,
 Of fair demesnes,²⁹ youthful, and nobly trained,   29. **demesnes**\dĭ·mānz\ demeanor.
 Stuffed, as they say, with honorable parts,
 Proportioned as one's thought would wish a man—
 And then to have a wretched puling³⁰ fool,   185   30. **puling,** whimpering.
 A whining mammet,³¹ in her fortune's tender,³²   31. **mammet,** doll.
 To answer "I'll not wed, I cannot love;   32. **in . . . tender,** in response to her
 I am too young, I pray you pardon me"   good fortune.
 But, and you will not wed, I'll pardon you!
 Graze where you will, you shall not house with me.   190
 Look to't, think on't; I do not use to jest.
 Thursday is near; lay hand on heart, advise.
 An you be mine, I'll give you to my friend;
 An you be not, hang, beg, starve, die in the streets,
 For, by my soul, I'll ne'er acknowledge thee,   195
 Nor what is mine shall never do thee good.
 Trust to't. Bethink you. I'll not be forsworn.

[CAPULET *exits.*]

JULIET. Is there no pity sitting in the clouds,
 That sees into the bottom of my grief?
 O sweet my mother, cast me not away!   200
 Delay this marriage for a month, a week;
 Or if you do not, make the bridal bed
 In that dim monument where Tybalt lies.
LADY CAPULET. Talk not to me, for I'll not speak a
  word.
 Do as thou wilt, for I have done with thee.   205

[*She exits leaving* JULIET *and* NURSE *alone.*]

JULIET. O God! O Nurse, how shall this be prevented?
 My husband is on earth, my faith in heaven;
 How shall that faith return again to earth

Unless that husband send it me from heaven
By leaving earth? Comfort me, counsel me.   210
Alack, alack, that heaven should practice stratagems
Upon so soft a subject as myself!
What say'st thou? Hast thou not a word of joy?
Some comfort, Nurse.
NURSE.   Faith, here it is.
Romeo is banished; and all the world to nothing   215
That he dares ne'er come back to challenge you;
Or if he do, it needs must be by stealth.
Then, since the case so stands as now it doth,
I think it best you married with the County.
O, he's a lovely gentleman!   220
Romeo's a dishclout[33] to him. An eagle, madam,   33. **dishclout,** dishcloth.
Hath not so green, so quick, so fair an eye
As Paris hath. Beshrew[34] my very heart,   34. **Beshrew,** a curse on.
I think you are happy in this second match,
For it excels your first; or if it did not,   225
Your first is dead, or 'twere as good he were
As living here and you no use of him.
JULIET. Speak'st thou from thy heart?
NURSE. And from my soul too; else beshrew them both.
JULIET. Amen!   230
NURSE. What?
JULIET. Well, thou hast comforted me marvelous much.
Go in, and tell my lady I am gone,
Having displeased my father, to Laurence' cell,
To make confession and to be absolved.   235
NURSE. Marry, I will; and this is wisely done. (*Exit.*)
JULIET. Ancient damnation![35] O most wicked fiend!   35. **damnation,** devilish old woman.
Is it more sin to wish me thus forsworn,[36]   36. **forsworn,** guilty of breaking her
Or to dispraise my lord with that same tongue   marriage vow to Romeo.
Which she hath praised him with above compare   240
So many thousand times? Go, counselor!
Thou and my bosom[37] henceforth shall be twain.   37. **bosom,** confidence.
I'll to the Friar to know his remedy.
If all else fail, myself have power to die.

[JULIET *exits.*]

TYING THE SCENES TOGETHER: SCENE 5

Romeo and Juliet have parted at daybreak. Juliet's parents
have told her she is to be married to Paris in three days. If she
does not consent, they will disown her. The nurse has advised
Juliet to go ahead and marry Paris. Juliet has decided to go to
Friar Laurence for help. Do you think Capulet's rage at Juliet's
"ingratitude" is the natural reaction of a father living in his time?

I

ROMEO IS BANISHED

1. Why does Mercutio fight with Tybalt, and how does it happen that Mercutio is killed?

2. What causes the Prince to banish Romeo?

3. What sensible advice does Friar Laurence give when Romeo threatens to kill himself?

4. Before Juliet can recover from the shock of Romeo's banishment, what ultimatum is she given by her father?

5. What advice does the nurse give to Juliet?

6. Why does Juliet go to Friar Laurence as the act ends?

II

IMPLICATIONS

Identify happenings in Scene 1 of Act III that might justify each of the following statements:

1. A great deal of what seems to be bravery is really vanity.

2. The best of intentions often result in tragedy.

3. Some persons are victims of fate and cannot help themselves.

III

TECHNIQUES

Staging

A dramatic bit of "stage business" occurs with the nurse in Act III, just as it does in Act II. In the previous act, the nurse held Juliet in suspense and complained about her aches and pains before finally giving Juliet the information she desired. In Act III, Scene 2, when the nurse comes in bringing the ladder Romeo is to use to get to Juliet's room, how does she throw Juliet into immediate panic?

Act III is long, but Shakespeare displays great skill in sustaining audience interest. One technique he uses is to shift the action around so that all parts and levels of the stage are used. He also opens the act with slashing swordplay that results in the deaths of two important characters and the banishment of the hero. To increase the tension, he introduces the pressure of time. Discuss in which scenes and in what way the pressure of time is revealed to the audience.

Language

Most of the punning found in the play was put in to liven up the speeches and to add comedy. Nevertheless, to persons living in Shakespeare's time, puns were not used solely in humorous situations. This is shown clearly in Scene 2, in the dialogue between Juliet and the nurse when Juliet thinks it is Romeo who is dead. Her agony and fear find expression in a torrent of puns (lines 31–36) based on the like-sounding words "I," and "ay" or "eye." Explain why you think this passage is almost always cut from modern presentations of the play. Would most actresses playing the part of Juliet wish it left in?

414

Act IV

SCENE 1

The cell of Friar Laurence, Tuesday forenoon. Enter FRIAR LAURENCE *with* PARIS.

FRIAR LAURENCE. On Thursday, sir? The time is very
    short.
PARIS. My father Capulet will have it so,
    And I am nothing slow to slack his haste.
FRIAR LAURENCE. You say you do not know the lady's
    mind.
    Uneven is the course; I like it not.   5
PARIS. Immoderately she weeps for Tybalt's death,
    And therefore have I little talked of love;
    For Venus smiles not in a house of tears.
    Now, sir, her father counts it dangerous
    That she do give her sorrow so much sway,   10
    And in his wisdom hastes our marriage
    To stop the inundation of her tears,
    Which, too much minded by herself alone,
    May be put from her by society.
    Now do you know the reason of this haste.   15
FRIAR LAURENCE. (*Aside.*) I would I knew not why it
    should be slowed.
    Look, sir, here comes the lady toward my cell.

[JULIET *enters.*]

PARIS. Happily met, my lady and my wife!
JULIET. That may be, sir, when I may be a wife.
PARIS. That may be, must be, love, on Thursday next.   20
JULIET. What must be shall be.
FRIAR LAURENCE.   That's a certain text.[1]   1. **text,** truth.
PARIS. Come you to make confession to this Father?
JULIET. To answer that, I should confess to you.
PARIS. Do not deny to him that you love me.
JULIET. I will confess to you that I love him.   25
PARIS. So will ye, I am sure, that you love me.
JULIET. If I do so, it will be of more price,[2]   2. **price,** value.
    Being spoke behind your back, than to your face.
PARIS. Poor soul, thy face is much abused with tears.
JULIET. The tears have not got small victory by that,   30
    For it was bad enough before their spite.
PARIS. Thou wrong'st it more than tears with that
    report.
JULIET. That is no slander, sir, which is a truth;

And what I spake, I spake it to my face.

PARIS. Thy face is mine, and thou hast sland'red it.   35

JULIET. It may be so, for it is not mine own.

Are you at leisure, holy Father, now,

Or shall I come to you at evening mass?

FRIAR LAURENCE. My leisure serves me, pensive daughter, now.

My lord, we must entreat the time alone.   40

PARIS. God shield I should disturb devotion!

Juliet, on Thursday early will I rouse ye.

Till then, adieu, and keep this holy kiss.

[PARIS *exits.*]

JULIET. O, shut the door, and when thou hast done so,

Come weep with me, past hope, past care, past help!   45

FRIAR LAURENCE. O Juliet, I already know thy grief;

It strains me past the compass of my wits.[3]

I hear thou must, and nothing may prorogue it,

On Thursday next be married to this County.

JULIET. Tell me not, Friar, that thou hearest of this,   50

Unless thou tell me how I may prevent it.

If in thy wisdom thou canst give no help,

Do thou but call my resolution wise

And with this knife I'll help it presently.[4]

God joined my heart and Romeo's, thou our hands;   55

And ere this hand, by thee to Romeo's sealed,

Shall be the label to another deed,

Or my true heart with treacherous revolt

Turn to another, this shall slay them both.

Therefore, out of thy long-experienced time,   60

Give me some present counsel; or, behold,

'Twixt my extremes and me this bloody knife

Shall play the umpire, arbitrating that

Which the commission of thy years and art

Could to no issue of true honor bring.   65

Be not so long to speak. I long to die

If what thou speak'st speak not of remedy.

FRIAR LAURENCE. Hold, daughter. I do spy a kind of hope,

Which craves as desperate an execution

As that is desperate which we would prevent.   70

If, rather than to marry County Paris,

Thou hast the strength of will to slay thyself,

Then is it likely thou wilt undertake

A thing like death to chide away this shame,

3. **the compass . . . wits,** my wit's end.

4. **presently,** at once.

That cop'st with[5] death himself to scape from it;   75
And, if thou darest, I'll give thee remedy.

JULIET. O, bid me leap, rather than marry Paris,
From off the battlements of any tower,
Or walk in thievish ways, or bid me lurk
Where serpents are; chain me with roaring bears,   80
Or hide me nightly in a charnel house,[6]
O'ercovered quite with dead men's rattling bones,
With reeky[7] shanks and yellow chapless[8] skulls;
Or bid me go into a new-made grave
And hide me with a dead man in his shroud—   85
Things that, to hear them told, have made me
    tremble—
And I will do it without fear or doubt,
To live an unstained wife to my sweet love.

FRIAR LAURENCE. Hold, then. Go home, be merry, give
    consent
To marry Paris. Wednesday is tomorrow.   90
Tomorrow night look that thou lie alone;
Let not thy nurse lie with thee in thy chamber.
Take thou this vial, being then in bed,
And this distilling liquor drink thou off;
When presently through all thy veins shall run   95
A cold and drowsy humor;[9] for no pulse
Shall keep his native progress, but surcease;[10]
No warmth, no breath, shall testify thou livest;
The roses in thy lips and cheeks shall fade
To waned ashes, thy eyes' windows fall   100
Like death when he shuts up the day of life;
Each part, deprived of supple government,[11]
Shall, stiff and stark and cold, appear like death;
And in this borrowed likeness of shrunk death
Thou shalt continue two-and-forty hours,   105
And then awake as from a pleasant sleep.
Now, when the bridegroom in the morning comes
To rouse thee from thy bed, there art thou dead,
Then, as the manner of our country is,
In thy best robes uncovered, on the bier,   110
Thou shalt be borne to that same ancient vault
Where all the kindred of the Capulets lie.
In the meantime, against thou shalt awake,[12]
Shall Romeo by my letters know our drift,[13]
And hither shall he come; and he and I   115
Will watch thy waking, and that very night
Shall Romeo bear thee hence to Mantua.
And this shall free thee from this present shame,

5. **cop'st with,** deals.

6. **charnel house,** vault where the bodies of the dead were placed.

7. **reeky,** reeking. 8. **chapless,** jawless.
8. **chapless,** jawless.

9. **humor,** bodily fluid.
10. **surcease,** cease.

11. **supple government,** ease of movement.

12. **against . . . awake,** in preparation for your waking.
13. **drift,** intention.

   If no inconstant toy[14] nor womanish fear
   Abate thy valor in the acting it.   120

JULIET. Give me, give me! O, tell not me of fear!

FRIAR LAURENCE. Hold! Get you gone, be strong and
    prosperous
   In this resolve. I'll send a friar with speed
   To Mantua, with my letters to thy lord.

JULIET. Love give me strength, and strength shall help
    afford.   125
   Farewell, dear father.

[They exit together.]

14. **toy,** whim.

TYING THE SCENES TOGETHER: SCENE 1

Paris has made arrangements with the Friar to marry him to
Juliet on Thursday. Juliet has come to the Friar for counsel. He
has given her a drug to take the night before the wedding. This
drug will put her into a death-like trance. She is to be placed in
the family burial vault, from which she will be rescued by
Romeo and taken to Mantua. What does Juliet's willingness to
take this powerful drug show about her character?

SCENE 2

A hall in the house of Capulet. Enter CAPULET, LADY CAPU-
LET, NURSE, *and* SERVANTS. CAPULET *hands* SERVANT *a list of
guests to be invited to the wedding.*

CAPULET. So many guests invite as here are writ.

[Exit FIRST SERVANT.*]*

Sirrah, go hire me twenty cunning cooks.

SECOND SERVANT. You shall have none ill, sir; for I'll try
   if they can lick their fingers.

CAPULET. How canst thou try them so?   5

SECOND SERVANT. Marry, sir, 'tis an ill cook that cannot
   lick his own fingers; therefore he that cannot lick
   his fingers goes not with me.

CAPULET. Go, begone.

[Exit SECOND SERVANT.*]*

We shall be much unfurnished for this time.   10
   What, is my daughter gone to Friar Laurence?

NURSE. Ay, forsooth.

CAPULET. Well, he may chance to do some good on her.

[JULIET enters in good spirits.]

NURSE. See where she comes from shrift with merry
    look.

CAPULET. How now, my headstrong? Where have you
    been gadding?   15

JULIET. Where I have learnt me to repent the sin
    Of disobedient opposition
    To you and your behests,[1] and am enjoined   1. **behests,** orders.
    By holy Laurence to fall prostrate here
    And beg your pardon. Pardon, I beseech you!   20
    Henceforward I am ever ruled by you.

CAPULET. Send for the County; go tell him of this.
    I'll have this knot knit up tomorrow morning.

JULIET. I met the youthful lord at Laurence' cell
    And gave him what becomèd[2] love I might,   25   2. **becomèd,** suitable.
    Not stepping o'er the bounds of modesty.

CAPULET. Why, I am glad on't; this is well. Stand up.
    This is as't should be. Let me see the County.
    Ay, marry, go, I say, and fetch him hither.
    Now, afore God, this reverend holy Friar,   30
    All our whole city is much bound to him.

JULIET. Nurse, will you go with me into my closet[3]   3. **closet,** private room.
    To help me sort such needful ornaments
    As you think fit to furnish me tomorrow?

LADY CAPULET. No, not till Thursday. There is time
    enough.   35

CAPULET. Go, Nurse, go with her. We'll to church
    tomorrow.

[JULIET *and* NURSE *exit.*]

LADY CAPULET. We shall be short in our provision;
    'Tis now near night.

CAPULET.   Tush, I will stir about,
    And all things shall be well, I warrant thee, wife.
    Go thou to Juliet, help to deck up her.   40
    I'll not to bed tonight; let me alone.
    I'll play the housewife for this once. What, ho!
    They are all forth. Well, I will walk myself
    To County Paris to prepare up him
    Against tomorrow. My heart is wondrous light,   45
    Since this same wayward girl is so reclaimed.

[CAPULET *and* LADY CAPULET *exit.*]

TYING THE SCENES TOGETHER: SCENE 2

The Capulet household has begun preparations for the wedding. Juliet has pretended a willingness to obey her father's
wishes. In his joy, her father has decided to set the wedding
ahead a day. Why is this decision characteristic of the father?

419

Juliet's room. JULIET *and* NURSE *enter.*

JULIET. Ay, those attires are best; but, gentle Nurse,
  I pray thee leave me to myself tonight,
  For I have need of many orisons[1]
  To move the heavens to smile upon my state,
  Which, well thou knowest, is cross[2] and full of sin.   5

  [*Enter* LADY CAPULET.]

LADY CAPULET. What, are you busy, ho? Need you my
    help?
JULIET. No, madam, we have culled[3] such necessaries
  As are behoveful[4] for our state tomorrow.
  So please you, let me now be left alone,
  And let the nurse this night sit up with you;   10
  For I am sure you have your hands full all
  In this so sudden business.
LADY CAPULET.   Good night.
  Get thee to bed, and rest, for thou hast need.

  [*Exit* LADY CAPULET *and* NURSE.]

JULIET. Farewell! God knows when we shall meet again.
  I have a faint cold fear thrills through my veins   15
  That almost freezes up the heat of life.
  I'll call them back again to comfort me.
  Nurse! What should she do here?
  My dismal scene I needs must act alone.
  Come, vial.   20
  What if this mixture do not work at all?
  Shall I be married then tomorrow morning?
  No, no! This shall forbid it. Lie thou there.

  [*She lays down her dagger.*]

  What if it be a poison which the Friar
  Subtly hath ministered to have me dead,   25
  Lest in this marriage he should be dishonored
  Because he married me before to Romeo?
  I fear it is, and yet methinks it should not,
  For he hath still been tried a holy man.
  How if, when I am laid into the tomb,   30
  I wake before the time that Romeo
  Come to redeem me? There's a fearful point!
  Shall I not then be stifled in the vault,
  To whose foul mouth no healthsome air breathes in,
  And there die strangled ere my Romeo comes?   35

1. **orisons**\ˈȯr•ə•sənz\ prayers.

2. **cross,** irregular.

3. **culled,** chosen.
4. **behoveful,** necessary.

Or, if I live, is it not very like
The horrible conceit[5] of death and night,
Together with the terror of the place—
As in a vault, an ancient receptacle
Where, for this many hundred years the bones   40
Of all my buried ancestors are packed;
Where bloody Tybalt, yet but green in earth,
Lies festering in his shroud; where, as they say,
At some hours in the night spirits resort.
Alack, alack, is it not like that I,   45
So early waking, what with loathsome smells,
And shrieks like mandrakes[6] torn out of the earth,
That living mortals, hearing them, run mad:—
O, if I wake, shall I not be distraught,
Environed with all these hideous fears,   50
And madly play with my forefathers' joints,
And pluck the mangled Tybalt from his shroud,

5. **conceit,** imagination.

6. **mandrake,** plant with a forked root. It resembles a human figure and is believed to shriek when pulled from the ground.

421

And, in this rage, with some great kinsman's bone
As with a club dash out my desperate brains?
O, look! Methinks I see my cousin's ghost   55
Seeking out Romeo, that did spit his body
Upon a rapier's point. Stay, Tybalt, stay!
Romeo, Romeo, Romeo, I drink to thee.

[*She drinks and falls upon her curtained bed.*]

TYING THE SCENES TOGETHER: SCENE 3

Juliet has dismissed her mother and the nurse for the night
and, after thinking of the many things that might go wrong, has
drunk the potion. Why might she have good cause to fear that
the Friar might really have given her a poison?

SCENE 4

*A hall in the house of Capulet on Wednesday morning.
Enter* LADY CAPULET *and* NURSE. *They are busy with
wedding feast preparations.*

LADY CAPULET. Hold, take these keys and fetch more
    spices, Nurse.
NURSE. They call for dates and quinces in the pastry.[1]   1. **pastry,** baking room.

[*Enter* CAPULET.]

CAPULET. Come, stir, stir, stir! The second cock hath
    crowed,
The curfew bell hath rung, 'tis three o'clock.
The County will be here with music straight   5
For so he said he would. (*Music plays.*)
              I hear him near.
Nurse! Wife! What, ho! What, Nurse, I say!
Go waken Juliet; go and trim her up.
I'll go and chat with Paris. Hie, make haste,
Make haste; the bridegroom he is come already;   10
Make haste, I say.

[*They exit.*]

TYING THE SCENES TOGETHER: SCENE 4

All but the very last minute wedding preparations have been
completed in the Capulet household. The nurse has been sent to
help the bride dress. What do you know that the nurse is going
to discover?

SCENE 5

Juliet's room, moments later. NURSE *enters.*

NURSE. Mistress! What, mistress! Juliet! Fast,[1] I warrant
    her. She——
Why, lamb! Why, lady! Fie, you slugabed.
Why, love, I say! Madam! Sweetheart! Why, bride!
I needs must wake her, Madam, madam, madam!

1. **Fast,** fast asleep.

[*She pulls back the curtains around the bed.*]

What, dressed, and in your clothes, and down again?   5
I must needs wake her. Lady! Lady! Lady!
Alas, alas! Help, help! My lady's dead!
O weladay[2] that ever I was born!
Some aqua vitae, ho! My lord! My lady!

2. **O weladay,** alas.

[*Enter* LADY CAPULET.]

LADY CAPULET. What noise is here?
NURSE.   O lamentable day!   10
LADY CAPULET. What is the matter?
NURSE.   Look, look! O heavy
    day!
LADY CAPULET. O me, O me! My child, my only life!
    Revive, look up, or I will die with thee!
    Help, help! Call help.

[*Enter* CAPULET.]

CAPULET. For shame, bring Juliet forth; her lord is
    come.   15
NURSE. She's dead, deceased; she's dead, alack the day!
LADY CAPULET. Alack the day, she's dead, she's dead,
    she's dead!
CAPULET. Ha! Let me see her. Out alas! She's cold,
    Her blood is settled, and her joints are stiff;
    Life and these lips have long been separated.   20
    Death lies on her like an untimely frost
    Upon the sweetest flower of all the field.
NURSE. O lamentable day!
LADY CAPULET.   O woeful time!
CAPULET. Death, that hath ta'en her hence to make me
    wail,
    Ties up my tongue and will not let me speak.   25

[*Enter* FRIAR LAURENCE *and* PARIS.]

FRIAR LAURENCE. Come, is the bride ready to go to
    church?

CAPULET. Ready to go, but never to return.
    Death is my son-in-law, Death is my heir;
    My daughter he hath wedded. I will die
    And leave him all. Life, living,[3] all is Death's.   30
PARIS. Have I thought, love, to see this morning's face,
    And doth it give me such a sight as this?
LADY CAPULET. Accursed, unhappy, wretched, hateful
      day!
    Most miserable hour that e'er time saw
    In lasting labor of his pilgrimage!   35
    But one, poor one, one poor and loving child,
    But one thing to rejoice and solace in,
    And cruel Death hath catched it from my sight.
NURSE. O woe! O woeful, woeful, woeful day!
    Most lamentable day, most woeful day   40
    That ever, ever I did yet behold!
    O day, O day, O day! O hateful day!
    Never was seen so black a day as this.
    O woeful day! O woeful day!
PARIS. Beguiled, divorced, wronged, spited, slain!   45
    Most detestable Death, by thee beguiled,
    By cruel, cruel thee, quite overthrown.
    O love! O life; not life, but love in death!
CAPULET. Despised, distressed, hated, martyred, killed!
    Uncomfortable time, why cam'st thou now   50
    To murder, murder our solemnity?[4]
    O child, O child! My soul, and not my child!
    Dead art thou! Alack, my child is dead,
    And with my child my joys are buried!
FRIAR LAURENCE. Peace, ho, for shame! Confusion's[5] cure
      lives not   55
    In these confusions. Heaven and yourself
    Had part in this fair maid, now heaven hath all,
    And all the better is it for the maid.
    Your part in her you could not keep from death,
    But heaven keeps his part in eternal life.   60
    The most you sought was her promotion,
    For 'twas your heaven she should be advanced;
    And weep ye now, seeing she is advanced
    Above the clouds, as high as heaven itself?
    O, in this love, you love your child so ill   65
    That you run mad, seeing that she is well.
    She's not well married that lives married long,
    But she's best married that dies married young.
    Dry up your tears and stick your rosemary[6]
    On this fair corse, and, as the custom is,   70
    And in her best array bear her to church;

3. living, worldly goods.

4. **To murder . . . solemnity,** to ruin our ceremony.

5. **Confusion's,** disaster's.

6. **rosemary,** a symbol of immortality and enduring love, used at both funerals and weddings.

For though fond nature bids us all lament,
Yet nature's tears are reason's merriment.
CAPULET. All things that we ordained festival
    Turn from their office to black funeral;   75
    Our instruments to melancholy bells,
    Our wedding cheer to a sad burial feast;
    Our solemn hymns to sullen dirges change;
    Our bridal flowers serve for a buried corse;
    And all things change them to the contrary.   80
FRIAR LAURENCE. Sir, go you in; and, madam, go with
    him;
    And go, Sir Paris; everyone prepare
    To follow this fair corse unto her grave.
    The heavens do lower upon you for some ill;
    Move them no more by crossing their high will.   85

[*They exit.*]

TYING THE SCENES TOGETHER: SCENE 5

The nurse has discovered Juliet in her bed. Everyone thinks
she is dead. The Friar urges the family to put aside its grief and
prepare Juliet for burial. The wedding has turned into a funeral.

I
A DESPERATE COURSE IS TAKEN

1. What brings Paris to Friar Laurence's cell?

2. Briefly outline the desperate plan the Friar proposes to Juliet.

3. What change does Capulet make in the wedding plans?

4. What fears beset Juliet before she drinks the potion?

II
IMPLICATIONS

1. One act of deception leads to another.

2. Persons who wish to believe something is true are easily deceived into thinking that it is.

3. Most grief is self-pity.

III
TECHNIQUES

Staging

1. What does the playwright accomplish by having Capulet suddenly decide to set the wedding a day ahead?

2. At the end of Scene 1, the audience is left tense and fearful from the desperate session they have just witnessed in Friar Laurence's cell. Why do you think it was good theater for Shakespeare to open Scene 2 with the gay atmosphere of wedding preparations? What comedy is introduced before Juliet's entrance?

Language

1. The conversation between Paris and Juliet in the Friar's cell is filled with word play and double meanings. The audience finds it particularly interesting because they know what Juliet means when she answers Paris, though he is ignorant of what she is really saying. Re-read this brief conversation (Scene 1, lines 18–43) and discuss.

2. What horrors does Juliet describe that she would endure rather than be married to another man?

Act V

SCENE 1

A street in Mantua on the following day. ROMEO *enters.*

ROMEO. If I may trust the flattering truth of sleep,
My dreams presage[1] some joyful news at hand.
My bosom's lord[2] sits lightly in his throne,
And all this day an unaccustomed spirit
Lifts me above the ground with cheerful thoughts.   5
I dreamt my lady came and found me dead—
Strange dream that gives a dead man leave to
   think—
And breathed such life with kisses in my lips
That I revived and was an emperor.
Ah me, how sweet is love itself possessed,   10
When but love's shadows[3] are so rich in joy.

[*Enter* BALTHASAR.]

News from Verona! How now, Balthasar?
Dost thou not bring me letters from the Friar?
How doth my lady? Is my father well?
How fares my Juliet? That I ask again,   15
For nothing can be ill if she be well.
BALTHASAR. Then she is well, and nothing
   can be ill.
Her body sleeps in Capel's monument,
And her immortal part with angels lives.
I saw her laid low in her kindred's vault,   20
And presently took post[4] to tell it you.
O, pardon me for bringing these ill news,
Since you did leave it for my office, sir.
ROMEO. Is it even so? Then I defy you, stars!
Thou knowest my lodging. Get me ink and paper   25
And hire post horses; I will hence tonight.
BALTHASAR. I do beseech you, sir, have
   patience.
Your looks are pale and wild and do import
Some misadventure.
ROMEO.   Tush, thou art deceived.
Leave me and do the thing I bid thee do.   30
Hast thou no letters to me from the Friar?
BALTHASAR. No, my good lord.
ROMEO.   No matter. Get
   thee gone.
And hire those horses; I'll be with thee straight.

1. **presage,** foretell.
2. **bosom's lord,** heart.

3. **shadows,** dreams.

4. **took post,** rode in haste.

426

[*Exit* BALTHASAR.]

Well, Juliet, I will lie with thee tonight.
Let's see for means. O mischief, thou art swift
To enter in the thoughts of desperate men.   35
I do remember an apothecary—
And hereabouts 'a dwells—which late I noted
In tattered weeds, with overwhelming[5] brows,
Culling of simples;[6] meager were his looks,
Sharp misery had worn him to the bones;   40
And in his needy shop a tortoise hung,
An alligator stuffed, and other skins
Of ill-shaped fishes; and about his shelves
A beggarly account of empty boxes,
Green earthen pots, bladders, and musty seeds,   45
Remnants of packthread,[7] and old cakes of roses,[8]
Were thinly scattered, to make up a show.
Noting this penury,[9] to myself I said,
"An if a man did need a poison now
Whose sale is present death in Mantua,   50
Here lives a caitiff[10] wretch would sell it him."
O, this same thought did but forerun my need,
And this same needy man must sell it me.
As I remember, this should be the house.
Being holiday, the beggar's shop is shut.   55
What, ho, apothecary!

[*Enter* APOTHECARY.]

APOTHECARY.   Who calls so loud?
ROMEO. Come hither, man. I see that thou art poor.
  Hold, there is forty ducats.[11] Let me have
  A dram[12] of poison, such soon-speeding gear[13]
  As will disperse itself through all the veins   60
  That the life-weary taker may fall dead,
  And that the trunk[14] may be discharged of breath
  As violently as hasty powder fired
  Doth hurry from the fatal cannon's womb.[15]
APOTHECARY. Such mortal drugs I have; but Mantua's
    law   65
  Is death to any he that utters[16] them.
ROMEO. Art thou so bare and full of wretchedness
  And fearest to die? Famine is in thy cheeks,
  Need and oppression starveth in thy eyes,
  Contempt and beggary hangs upon thy back.   70
  The world is not thy friend, nor the world's law;
  The world affords no law to make thee rich;
  Then be not poor, but break it and take this.

5. **overwhelming,** overhanging.
6. **simples,** herbs.

7. **packthread,** wrapping string.
8. **cakes of roses,** pressed rose petals used in cosmetics.
9. **penury****pĕn•yə•rē**\\ poverty.

10. **caitiff****kāt•əf**\\ miserable.

11. **ducats****dək•əts**\\ gold coins.
12. **dram,** fluid measure.
13. **gear,** stuff.

14. **trunk,** body.

15. **womb,** barrel.

16. **utters,** distributes.

APOTHECARY. My poverty but not my will consents.

ROMEO. I pay thy poverty and not thy will.   75

APOTHECARY. Put this in any liquid thing you will
  And drink it off, and if you had the strength
  Of twenty men, it would dispatch you straight.

ROMEO. There is thy gold, worse poison to men's souls,
  Doing more murder in this loathsome world,   80
  Than these poor compounds that thou mayst not
    sell.
  I sell thee poison; thou hast sold me none.
  Farewell. Buy food and get thyself in flesh.
  Come, cordial¹⁷ and not poison, go with me
  To Juliet's grave; for there must I use thee.   85

[*He exits.*]

17. **cordial,** reviving liquid.

TYING THE SCENES TOGETHER: SCENE 1

Romeo has learned of Juliet's supposed death and after buying
poison to kill himself, has set out for Verona. How does his conversation with the apothecary show you that Romeo feels there
is a great deal wrong with the social conditions of his time?

SCENE 2

Friar Laurence's cell, that night. FRIAR JOHN *enters.*

FRIAR JOHN. Holy Franciscan Friar, brother, ho!

[*Enter* FRIAR LAURENCE.]

FRIAR LAURENCE. This same should be the voice of Friar
    John.
  Welcome from Mantua. What says Romeo?
  Or, if his mind be writ, give me his letter.

FRIAR JOHN. Going to find a barefoot brother¹ out,   5
  One of our order, to associate² me
  Here in this city visiting the sick,
  And finding him, the searchers³ of the town,
  Suspecting that we both were in a house
  Where the infectious pestilence⁴ did reign,   10
  Sealed up the doors, and would not let us forth,
  So that my speed to Mantua there was stayed.

FRIAR LAURENCE. Who bare my letter, then, to Romeo?

FRIAR JOHN. I could not send it—here it is again—
  Nor get a messenger to bring it thee,   15
  So fearful were they of infection.

FRIAR LAURENCE. Unhappy fortune! By my brotherhood,

1. **barefoot brother,** another friar.
2. **associate,** accompany.

3. **searchers,** health officials.

4. **pestilence,** plague.

428

The letter was not nice,[5] but full of charge,[6]
Of dear import;[7] and the neglecting it
May do much danger. Friar John, go hence,   20
Get me an iron crow[8] and bring it straight
Unto my cell.

FRIAR JOHN. Brother, I'll go and bring it thee. (*Exit.*)

FRIAR LAURENCE. Now must I to the monument[9] alone.
Within this three hours will fair Juliet wake.   25
She will beshrew me much that Romeo
Hath had no notice of these accidents;
But I will write again to Mantua,
And keep her at my cell till Romeo come—
Poor living corse, closed in a dead man's tomb! (*Exit.*)   30

5. **nice,** trifling.
6. **charge,** information.
7. **dear import,** great importance.

8. **crow,** crowbar.

9. **monument,** tomb.

TYING THE SCENES TOGETHER: SCENE 2

Friar Laurence learns that his letter to Romeo has not been
delivered, so he hurries to Juliet's tomb to be there when she
awakens. Is the Friar's reaction to Friar John's news what you
would have expected of him? Explain.

SCENE 3

*A church graveyard where the Capulets' burial vault is
located, late that night. Enter* PARIS *and* PAGE *who is
carrying a torch, flowers, and perfumed water.*

PARIS. Give me thy torch, boy. Hence, and stand aloof.
Yet put it out, for I would not be seen.
Under yond yew trees lay thee all along,
Holding thy ear close to the hollow ground.
So shall no foot upon the churchyard tread—   5
Being loose, unfirm, with digging up of graves—
But thou shalt hear it. Whistle then to me,
As signal that thou hearest something approach.
Give me those flowers. Do as I bid thee, go.

PAGE. (*Aside.*) I am almost afraid to stand alone   10
Here in the churchyard; yet I will adventure.

[*He retires.*]

PARIS. Sweet flower, with flowers thy bridal bed I strew
O woe! Thy canopy is dust and stones
Which with sweet water nightly I will dew;
Or, wanting that, with tears distilled by moans.   15
The obsequies[1] that I for thee will keep
Nightly shall be to strew thy grave and weep.

[PAGE *whistles off-stage.*]

1. **obsequies**\ˈŏb·sə·kwēs\ funeral rites.

429

The boy gives warning something doth approach.
What cursèd foot wanders this way tonight
To cross my obsequies and true love's rite?   20
What, with a torch? Muffle me, night, awhile.

[PARIS *retires as* ROMEO *and* BALTHASAR *enter carrying*
a torch, a mattock, and a crow of iron.]

ROMEO. Give me that mattock² and the wrenching iron.   2. **mattock**, pickaxe.
  Hold, take this letter; early in the morning
  See thou deliver it to my lord and father.
  Give me the light. Upon thy life I charge thee,   25
  Whate'er thou hearest or seest, stand all aloof,
  And do not interrupt me in my course.
  Why I descend into this bed of death
  Is partly to behold my lady's face,
  But chiefly to take thence from her dead finger   30
  A precious ring³—a ring that I must use   3. **precious ring.** A false excuse to keep
  In dear employment. Therefore hence, be gone.   Balthasar from interfering.
  But if thou, jealous,⁴ dost return to pry   4. **jealous**, curious.
  In what I farther shall intend to do,
  By heaven, I will tear thee joint by joint   35
  And strew this hungry churchyard with thy limbs.
  The time and my intents are savage-wild,
  More fierce and more inexorable far,
  Than empty tigers or the roaring sea.
BALTHASAR. I will be gone, sir, and not trouble ye.   40
ROMEO. So shalt thou show me friendship. (*Offering*
    money.) Take thou that.
  Live, and be prosperous, and farewell, good fellow.
BALTHASAR. (*Aside.*) For all this same, I'll hide me
    hereabout.
  His looks I fear, and his intents I doubt. (*He retires.*)
ROMEO. Thou detestable maw,⁵ thou womb of death,   45   5. **maw**, stomach.
  Gorged with the dearest morsel of the earth,
  Thus I enforce thy rotten jaws to open,
  And in despite I'll cram thee with more food.

[ROMEO *opens the tomb.*]

PARIS. This is that banished haughty Montague
  That murdered my love's cousin, with which grief   50
  It is supposed the fair creature died,
  And here is come to do some villainous shame
  To the dead bodies. I will apprehend him.
  Stop thy unhallowèd toil, vile Montague!
  Can vengeance be pursued further than death?   55
  Condemnèd villain, I do apprehend thee.
  Obey, and go with me, for thou must die.

430

ROMEO. I must indeed; and therefore came I hither.
Good gentle youth, tempt not a desperate man;
Fly hence and leave me. Think upon these gone;   60
Let them affright thee. I beseech thee, youth,
Put not another sin upon my head
By urging me to fury. O, be gone!
By heaven, I love thee better than myself,
For I come hither armed against myself.   65
Stay not, be gone. Live, and hereafter say
A madman's mercy bid thee run away.
PARIS. I do defy thy conjurations.[6]
And apprehend thee for a felon[7] here.
ROMEO. Wilt thou provoke me? Then have at thee,
boy!   70
PAGE. O Lord, they fight! I will go call the watch.
(*Exits.*)
PARIS. (*Falls.*) O, I am slain! If thou be merciful,
Open the tomb, lay me with Juliet. (*Dies.*)
ROMEO. In faith, I will. Let me peruse this face.
Mercutio's kinsman, noble County Paris!   75
What said my man when my betossèd soul
Did not attend him as we rode? I think
He told me Paris should have married Juliet.
Said he not so, or did I dream it so?
Or am I mad, hearing him talk of Juliet,   80
To think it was so? O, give me thy hand,
One writ with me in sour misfortune's book!
I'll bury thee in a triumphant grave.
A grave? O, no, a lanthorn,[8] slaughtered youth,
For here lies Juliet, and her beauty makes   85
This vault a feasting presence[9] full of light.
Death, lie thou there, by a dead man interred.

[*He places PARIS in the tomb.*]

How oft when men are at the point of death
Have they been merry! Which their keepers call
A lightning before death. O, how may I   90
Call this a lightning? O my love, my wife!
Death, that hath sucked the honey of thy breath,
Hath had no power yet upon thy beauty.
Thou art not conquered. Beauty's ensign[10] yet
Is crimson in thy lips and in thy cheeks,   95
And death's pale flag is not advancèd there.
Tybalt, liest thou there in thy bloody sheet?
O, what more favor can I do to thee
Than with that hand that cut thy youth in twain
To sunder his that was thine enemy?   100

6. **conjurations,** appeals.

7. **felon,** criminal.

8. **lanthorn,** here, a many windowed tower, as atop a cathedral.

9. **feasting presence,** festive room for royalty.

10. **ensign,** banner.

431

Forgive me, cousin! Ah, dear Juliet,
Why art thou yet so fair? Shall I believe
That unsubstantial Death is amorous,
And that the lean abhorrèd monster keeps
Thee here in dark to be his paramour?[11]   105
For fear of that I still will stay with thee
And never from this pallet of dim night
Depart again. Here, here will I remain
With worms that are thy chambermaids. O, here
Will I set up my everlasting rest   110
And shake the yoke of inauspicious stars[12]
From this world-wearied flesh. Eyes, look your last!
Arms, take your last embrace! And, lips, O you
The doors of breath, seal with a righteous kiss
A dateless bargain to engrossing death!   115
Come, bitter conduct, come, unsavory guide!
Thou desperate pilot, now at once run on
The dashing rocks thy seasick weary bark!
Here's to my love! (*He drinks the poison.*) O true
    apothecary!
Thy drugs are quick. Thus with a kiss I die.   120

[*He kisses* JULIET *and falls. Enter* FRIAR LAURENCE
    with lantern, crowbar, mattock, and spade.]

FRIAR LAURENCE. Saint Francis be my speed! How oft
    tonight
Have my old feet stumbled at graves! Who's there?
BALTHASAR. Here's one, a friend, and one that knows
    you well.
FRIAR LAURENCE. Bliss be upon you! Tell me, good my
    friend,
What torch is yond that vainly lends his light   125
To grubs and eyeless skulls? As I discern,
It burneth in the Capels' monument.
BALTHASAR. It doth so, holy sir; and there's my master,
One that you love.
FRIAR LAURENCE.   Who is it?
BALTHASAR.   Romeo.
FRIAR LAURENCE. How long hath he been there?
BALTHASAR.   Full half
    an hour.   130
FRIAR LAURENCE. Go with me to the vault.
BALTHASAR.   I dare not, sir.
My master knows not but I am gone hence,
And fearfully did menace me with death
If I did stay to look on his intents.

FRIAR LAURENCE. Stay then; I'll go alone. Fear comes
    upon me.   135
   O, much I fear some ill unthrifty[13] thing.   13. **unthrifty,** unlucky.
BALTHASAR. As I did sleep under this yew tree here,
   I dreamt my master and another fought,
   And that my master slew him.
FRIAR LAURENCE.   Romeo!
   Alack, alack, what blood is this which stains   140
   The stony entrance of this sepulcher?
   What mean these masterless and gory swords
   To lie discolored by this place of peace?

[*He enters the tomb.*]

   Romeo! O, pale! Who else? What, Paris too?
   And steeped in blood? Ah, what an unkind hour   145
   Is guilty of this lamentable chance!
   The lady stirs.

[JULIET *slowly rises.*]

JULIET. O comfortable[14] Friar! Where is my lord?   14. **comfortable,** comforting.
   I do remember well where I should be,
   And there I am. Where is my Romeo?   150
FRIAR LAURENCE. I hear some noise. Lady, come from
    that nest
   Of death, contagion, and unnatural sleep.
   A greater power than we can contradict
   Hath thwarted our intents. Come, come away.
   Thy husband in thy bosom there lies dead;   155
   And Paris too. Come, I'll dispose of thee
   Among a sisterhood of holy nuns.
   Stay not to question, for the watch is coming.
   Come, go, good Juliet. I dare no longer stay.

[*He leaves* JULIET *alone.*]

JULIET. Go, get thee hence, for I will not away.   160
   What's here? A cup, closed in my truelove's hand?
   Poison, I see, hath been his timeless[15] end.   15. **timeless,** untimely.
   O churl![16] Drunk all, and left no friendly drop   16. **churl,** miser.
   To help me after? I will kiss thy lips.
   Haply some poison yet doth hang on them   165
   To make me die with a restorative.
   Thy lips are warm!
CHIEF WATCHMAN. (*Off-stage.*) Lead, boy. Which way?
JULIET. Yea, noise? Then I'll be brief. O happy[17] dagger!   17. **happy,** opportune.

[*Snatches Romeo's dagger.*]

This is thy sheath; (*Stabs herself and falls.*) there
   rust, and let me die.   170

[*Enter* WATCH *with the* PAGE *of* PARIS.]

PAGE. This is the place. There, where the torch doth
   burn.
CHIEF WATCHMAN. The ground is bloody. Search about
   the churchyard.
   Go, some of you; whoe'er you find attach.[18]   **18. attach,** arrest.
   Pitiful sight! Here lies the County slain;
   And Juliet bleeding, warm, and newly dead,   175
   Who here hath lain this two days buried.
   Go, tell the Prince; run to the Capulets;
   Raise up the Montagues; some others search.
   We see the ground whereon these woes do lie,
   But the true ground of all these piteous woes   180
   We cannot without circumstance descry.[19]   **19. without ... descry,** without details
                                                      discern.

[*Enter some members of the* WATCH *with* BALTHASAR.]

SECOND WATCHMAN. Here's Romeo's man. We found him
   in the churchyard.
CHIEF WATCHMAN. Hold him in safety till the Prince
   come hither.

[*Enter* FRIAR LAURENCE *with another* WATCHMAN.]

THIRD WATCHMAN. Here is a friar that trembles, sighs,
   and weeps.
   We took this mattock and this spade from him   185
   As he was coming from this churchyard's side.
CHIEF WATCHMAN. A great suspicion! Stay the friar too.

[*Enter* PRINCE ESCALUS *and* ATTENDANTS.]

PRINCE. What misadventure is so early up,
   That calls our person from our morning rest?

[*Enter* CAPULET *and* LADY CAPULET.]

CAPULET. What should it be, that is so shrieked abroad?   190
LADY CAPULET. O, the people in the street cry "Romeo,"
   Some "Juliet," and some "Paris"; and all run
   With open outcry toward our monument.
PRINCE. What fear is this which startles in your ears?
CHIEF WATCHMAN. Sovereign, here lies the County Paris
   slain;   195
   And Romeo dead; and Juliet, dead before,
   Warm and new killed.
PRINCE. Search, seek, and know how this foul murder
   comes.

CHIEF WATCHMAN. Here is a friar, and slaughtered
    Romeo's man.
    With instruments upon them fit to open   200
    These dead men's tombs.
CAPULET. O heavens! O wife, look how our daughter
    bleeds!
    This dagger hath mista'en, for, lo, his house[20]
    Is empty on the back of Montague,
    And it missheathèd in my daughter's bosom!   205
LADY CAPULET. O me, this sight of death is as a bell
    That warns[21] my old age to a sepulcher.

[*Enter* MONTAGUE *and others.*]

PRINCE. Come, Montague; for thou art early up
    To see thy son and heir more early down.
MONTAGUE. Alas, my liege, my wife is dead tonight;   210
    Grief of my son's exile hath stopped her breath.
    What further woe conspires against mine age?
PRINCE. Look, and thou shalt see.
MONTAGUE. O thou untaught! What manners is in this,
    To press before thy father to a grave?   215
PRINCE. Seal up the mouth of outrage[22] for a while,
    Till we can clear these ambiguities[23]
    And know their spring, their head, their true descent;
    And then will I be general of your woes
    And lead you even to death. Meantime forbear,   220
    And let mischance be slave to patience.
    Bring forth the parties of suspicion.
FRIAR LAURENCE. I am the greatest, able to do least,
    Yet most suspected, as the time and place
    Doth make against me, of this direful murder;   225
    And here I stand, both to impeach and purge[24]
    Myself condemned and myself excused.
PRINCE. Then say at once what thou dost know in this.
FRIAR LAURENCE. I will be brief, for my short date of
    breath[25]
    Is not so long as is a tedious tale.   230
    Romeo, there dead, was husband to that Juliet,
    And she, there dead, that's Romeo's faithful wife.
    I married them, and their stol'n marriage day
    Was Tybalt's doomsday, whose untimely death
    Banished the new-made bridegroom from this city, 235
    For whom, and not for Tybalt, Juliet pined.
    You, to remove that siege of grief from her,
    Betrothed and would have married her perforce
    To County Paris. Then comes she to me
    And with wild looks bid me devise some mean   240

20. **his house,** its scabbard.

21. **warns,** summons.

22. **mouth of outrage,** loud outcries.
23. **ambiguities**\'am·bə ᵃgyū·ət·ēz\ mysteries.

24. **impeach and purge,** accuse and clear.

25. **date of breath,** years to live.

To rid her from this second marriage,
Or in my cell there would she kill herself.
Then gave I her, so tutored by my art,
A sleeping potion; which so took effect
As I intended, for it wrought on her   245
The form of death. Meantime I writ to Romeo
That he should hither come as this dire night
To help to take her from her borrowed²⁶ grave,   26. **borrowed,** temporary.
Being the time the potion's force should cease.
But he which bore my letter, Friar John,   250
Was stayed by accident, and yesternight
Returned my letter back. Then all alone
At the prefixèd hour of her waking
Came I to take her from her kindred's vault;
Meaning to keep her closely²⁷ at my cell   255   27. **closely,** secretly.
Till I conveniently could send to Romeo.
But when I came, some minute ere the time
Of her awakening, here untimely lay
The noble Paris and true Romeo dead.
She wakes; and I entreated her come forth   260
And bear this work of heaven with patience;
But then a noise did scare me from the tomb,
And she, too desperate, would not go with me,
But, as it seems, did violence on herself.
All this I know, and to the marriage   265
Her nurse is privy;²⁸ and if aught in this   28. **privy**\ˈprĭv·ē\ in on the secret.
Miscarried by my fault, let my old life
Be sacrificed some hour before his time
Unto the rigor of severest law.
PRINCE. We still have known thee for a holy man.   270
  Where's Romeo's man? What can he say to this?
BALTHASAR. I brought my master news of Juliet's death;
  And then in post²⁹ he came from Mantua   29. **in post,** in haste.
  To this same place, to this same monument.
  This letter he early bid me give his father,   275
  And threatened me with death, going in the vault,
  If I departed not and left him there.
PRINCE. Give me the letter. I will look on it.
  Where is the County's page that raised the watch?
  Sirrah, what made your master in this place?   280
PAGE. He came with flowers to strew his lady's grave;
  And bid me stand aloof, and so I did.
  Anon comes one with light to ope the tomb;
  And by and by my master drew on him;
  And then I ran away to call the watch.   285
PRINCE. This letter doth make good the Friar's words,
  Their course of love, the tidings of her death;

And here he writes that he did buy a poison
Of a poor 'pothecary and therewithal
Came to this vault to die and lie with Juliet.   290
Where be these enemies? Capulet, Montague,
See what a scourge[30] is laid upon your hate,   30. **scourge,** punishment.
That heaven finds means to kill your joys with love.
And I, for winking at your discords too,
Have lost a brace of kinsmen. All are punished.   295

CAPULET. O brother Montague, give me thy hand.
This is my daughter's jointure,[31] for no more   31. **jointure,** dowry.
Can I demand.

MONTAGUE.   But I can give thee more;
For I will raise her staute in pure gold,
That whiles Verona by that name is known,   300
There shall no figure at such rate[32] be set   32. **rate,** value.
As that of true and faithful Juliet.

CAPULET. As rich shall Romeo's by his lady's lie,
Poor sacrifices of our enmity.

PRINCE. A glooming peace this morning with it brings. 305
The sun for sorrow will not show his head.
Go hence, to have more talk of these sad things;
Some shall be pardoned, and some punishèd;
For never was a story of more woe
Than this of Juliet and her Romeo.   310

TYING THE SCENES TOGETHER: SCENE 3

Romeo has killed Paris at the Capulet tomb and has drunk
poison himself before the Friar arrives. Juliet has stabbed herself
upon discovering Romeo dead. The Prince, the Capulets, and
the Montagues have come to the Capulet tomb. Friar Laurence
has explained why Romeo and Juliet are dead, and the families
have agreed to put an end to their senseless feud.

I
A TRAGIC TALE IS ENDED

1. In Scene 1, what desperate course of action does Romeo take after Balthasar brings him the news about Juliet?

2. Why had Friar John been unable to deliver Friar Laurence's letter to Romeo? What does Friar Laurence decide he must do immediately?

3. Explain the presence of Paris at the tomb. What does he think when he sees Romeo come into the burial vault?

4. What dreadful sight meets the eyes of Friar Laurence when he enters the Capulet tomb? Why does he leave the tomb even though Juliet has awakened?

5. Why does Juliet kill herself? Which two people are caught by the watchmen?

6. What causes the Capulets and the Montagues to end their feud? What do the fathers decide to do to commemorate their children's love?

II
IMPLICATIONS

The following list of implications should help you sum up the play as a whole. Many people argue about the central theme, or what Shakespeare was trying to show in *Romeo and Juliet.* Perhaps he had more than one theme. Or he may have had one central theme and a number of less important ones. Discuss the following statements and decide whether you can find support for all of them in the play and which one or ones you would consider important enough to be themes.

1. The road to disaster is paved with good intentions.

2. A person's destiny is determined in the stars or by fate.

3. Grief is a common cause of death.

4. Love triumphs over hate.

5. Youth often must suffer for parents' mistakes.

6. Haste and lack of wise forethought bring about disaster.

7. There is a close connection between the characters of men and the misfortunes they suffer.

8. The force of overwhelming love is bound to result in good.

9. The only way some people learn is through suffering.

10. Most of life's misfortunes are the result of accidental happenings.

III
TECHNIQUES

Staging

Scene 1 of Act V is extremely important in the building of suspense to the final climax and conclusion of the play. Shakespeare first guarantees the attention of the audience through the dramatic contrast of a shift in Romeo's mood. The audience then feels immediate apprehension at Romeo's hasty decision to return to Verona.

1. How do you think you would feel if you were in the audience and heard Romeo say, "No matter," when Balthasar told him he had no letter?

2. Even though the apothecary's shop cannot be shown with a stage set, how does the audience know exactly what the shop and its owner look like?

3. Although the plays were given in daylight, Scenes 2 and 3 both take place at night, as do some scenes in previous acts. What kind of stage props do you think would be used in all these scenes to remind the audience that the action was taking place at night?

Language

1. What main purpose do you think Shakespeare had in mind when he wrote Romeo's last speech? Why would this be an extremely difficult speech for an actor to deliver convincingly?

2. Friar Laurence's final speech is one of the longest speeches in the play. Why do you think it contains no fanciful language or imaginative word play?

439

Morley Callaghan

Morley Callaghan (1903–   ), Canadian novelist and short story writer, was born in Toronto. After graduating from the University of Toronto in 1925, Callaghan became a reporter on the *Toronto Daily Star*. While working on the *Star*, he met Ernest Hemingway, who both encouraged him and introduced him to most of the literary giants and editors of the era. His writing style, which is reminiscent of Hemingway's, is stark and to the point.

Nikki Giovanni

Nikki Giovanni (1943–   ) was born in Knoxville, Tennessee. She attended Fisk University and the University of Pennsylvania and is now teaching literature at Rutgers University. Her prose and poetry have been published in *Negro Digest* (now *Black World*) and other periodicals. A collection of her poetry, *Black Judgment,* was printed in 1968.

O. Henry

O. Henry (1862–1910) is the pen name of William Sydney Porter. Born in Greensboro, North Carolina, he was a school drop-out at fifteen, working first in a drug store, then as a teller in a bank in Austin, Texas. When a shortage was discovered in his accounts at the bank, Porter foolishly fled to Mexico. However, he soon returned, was tried and sentenced to prison. Ironically, it was later determined almost conclusively that he was not an embezzler, but simply the victim of a poor bookkeeping system. It was in prison that he began writing stories and after his release he went to New York City to write for the *New York World*. His stories were very popular and have been widely imitated.

Margaret Weymouth Jackson

Margaret Weymouth Jackson (1895–   ) was born in Eureka, Arkansas. After attending Hillsdale College in Michigan, she married and began her writing career. She has been on the editorial staff of two magazines and has written several widely acclaimed novels—*Elizabeth's Tower, Kindy's Crossing,* and *First Fiddle.*

James Hurst

James Hurst (1922–   ) was born on a North Carolina farm. After studying to be a chemical engineer at North Carolina State College, Hurst turned to the world of opera and began studying voice at New York's Juilliard School of Music and in Rome. When his operatic career failed, he took a job as a bank clerk during the day and became a writer at night. After publishing a number of stories in little-known magazines, he made his first appearance in a national magazine, *The Atlantic,* in 1960 with "The Scarlet Ibis."

C. D. B. Bryan

C. D. B. (Courtland Dixon Barnes) Bryan (1936–   ), stepson of author John O'Hara and son of magazine writer J. Bryan II, is a Yale graduate who now lives in New York City. His first book, *P. S. Wilkinson,* won the $10,000 biennial Harper Prize Novel contest in 1964.

Zoa Morin Sherburne

Zoa Morin Sherburne (1912–   ), American short story writer and novelist, was born in Seattle, Washington and attended Seattle public schools. Chosen woman of the year by Phi Delta Nu, Miss Sherburne has been writing professionally since 1947. *Almost April, The High White Wall,* and *Ballerina on Skates* are her most widely read books.

Ambrose Flack

Ambrose Flack (1902–   ), a native son of Syracuse, New York, has written a number of short stories which have appeared in leading national magazines. He has also written extensively for radio and television.

William Shakespeare

William Shakespeare (1564–1616) was one of the greatest dramatists and poets in Western literature. By the time he wrote *Romeo and Juliet,* it is believed that he had already written more than a half dozen of the thirty-seven plays that were to make him world famous. Very little is actually known about his boyhood, his schooling, or how he happened to become a writer and an actor. One story is that he got started as a dramatist by holding the horses of playgoers outside a theater in London. Eventually an opportunity presented itself, and he was given employment within. But this may be just folklore.

Although many details of his life are obscure, it is known that Shakespeare was born in the town of Stratford-on-Avon, England, in April of 1564, the son of a prosperous shopkeeper and glovemaker. His father held a number of city offices, including those of alderman and mayor. Because of his father's importance in the community, William would have been entitled to go to grammar school free. Many Shakespeare scholars believe that this is what happened. In the grammar school of that time, he would have received all the learning necessary to become a writer. Many cultivated men of Shakespeare's time received all their formal education in grammar school.

The one record of his youth that is undisputed is a marriage license, issued by the Bishop of Worcester in 1582, permitting him to marry Anne Hathaway. He was then eighteen and Anne some seven or eight years older. They had three children, a girl first and twins about two years later.

What Shakespeare first did to make a living is not certain. Some believe he may have been a teacher for a short period in Stratford, but there is no proof that this is true.

It is known that by 1592, he was one of the best-established and most important dramatists in London. As well as being a successful actor and playwright, Shakespeare was a good businessman. Acting troupes were then organized on a business basis and shared the profits they made in producing plays. Shakespeare was a member of a company made up of the greatest actors in England which was known as the King's Men after 1603, when King James I of England became its patron.

The members of the King's Men had their own building, the Globe, one of the handsomest theaters of the time. In the cold English winters, however, its open air center discouraged many people from attending the plays. To overcome this difficulty, Shakespeare's company took over a roomy hall located within the walls of an old monastery building. This hall, protected from the weather, with a stage artificially lighted by candle chandeliers, became a very popular winter playhouse known as the Second Blackfriars Theater.

During his career in London, Shakespeare made enough money to buy a beautiful home for his family in Stratford as well as a good deal of other property. He retired to Stratford about five years before his death to live as a "gentleman," a title which meant he was by that time the possessor of a royal coat of arms.

What is poetry? Who knows?
Not a rose, but the scent of the rose;
Not the sky, but the light in the sky;
Not the fly, but the gleam of the fly;
Not the sea, but the sound of the sea;
Not myself, but what makes me
See, hear, and feel something that prose
Cannot: and what it is, who knows?

ELEANOR FARJEON

442   THE WAYS OF A POET

THE WAYS OF A POET

The pearl is a disease of the oyster,
A poem is a disease of the spirit
Caused by the irritation
Of a granule of Truth
Fallen into that soft gray bivalve
We call the mind.

CHRISTOPHER MORLEY

If I read a book and it makes my whole
    body so cold no fire can warm me,
I know that is poetry.
If I feel physically as if the top of my head
    were taken off,
I know that is poetry.
These are the only ways I know it.
Is there any other way?

EMILY DICKINSON

Letter to Col. T. W. Higginson August, 1870

*Brancusi captures a poetic vision in
sculpture.*

*"Bird in Space" 1925
Constantin Brancusi   Philadelphia
Museum of Art: The Louise and
Walter Arensberg Collection*

When we read a poem, or when we hear one read, we are seeing for a moment through the poet's eyes. It is almost as if he had said to us simply: "Look, I have seen something interesting; I have felt about it in a certain way; I would like to share my experience with you."

If we accept the poet's invitation, if we try to understand his response to life, we may discover new, exciting ways of seeing the world around us. We may increase our understanding of other people and even of ourselves. The poet's purpose is to make his reader see and feel through skillful use of language. The sculptor fashions clay or stone; the painter mixes colors and transfers them to canvas; the poet works with words, arranging and rearranging sounds to convey his meaning.

An effective poem concentrates much thought and feeling into a short space. Consider, for example, the vivid impression the poet Louis MacNeice suggests with the title and first two lines of this poem:

> *Sunday Morning*
> Down the road someone is practicing scales,
> The notes like little fishes vanish with a wink of tails. . . .

Both the title and the lines at once appeal to our senses of time and place, seeing and hearing. We react to the words "Sunday Morning" in terms of our own Sunday mornings, usually a time of quiet. We are reminded of all the times we have heard someone practicing a musical instrument in the distance. We see the black shapes of the notes with their "tails" squirming across a sheet of music. We hear the runs of musical scales as each note dashes through the air of the quiet street like a tiny fish darting in a stream.

MacNeice has made his twenty words count. He calls to mind the reader's own experience in order to create a sharp sense of Sunday morning. The comparison of musical notes to little fishes strikes us with a sense of surprise. Here lies the true test of any poet—*what his poetry does to us.*

Obviously, if a poem is going to have any effect upon us, we must cooperate with the poet. We must allow the poet's words to shape our imaginations. In the poems printed on the next few pages, one poet asks us to see a hungry child staring through a train window; another asks us to see an orange-haired old woman feeding pigeons by the Public Library. We must be willing to see with the poet, feel with him, laugh with him, listen to his stories.

Poetry can be a way of escaping into fantasy and imagination.

"Sunday Morning" from *Collected Poems*, by Louis MacNeice, reprinted by permission of Oxford University Press.

It can be a way of investigating the realities of life. In any case, poetry is not something that is remote from us. It has always been a part of our lives. It is the rollicking jump-rope jingle:

> Needles and pins, needles and pins,
> When a man marries his trouble begins.

It is *Hickory Dickory Dock.* . . . It is the mocking chatter children use to taunt friends:

> Johnny Moses, Johnny Moses.
> Can't get to heaven 'til his big mouth closes!

It is the singing commercial on radio or television. It is the words to a musical comedy song:

> It's only a paper moon
> Hanging over the cardboard sea. . . .

It is the stirring hymn, the solemn anthem:

> Mine eyes have seen the glory of the coming of the Lord;
> He is trampling out the vintage where the grapes of
>   wrath are stored. . . .

It is in a great epic like the *Aeneid:*

> I sing of arms and of the man who. . . .

Poetry is usually printed in a pattern of short, rhythmical lines surrounded by more than the usual amount of white space on the page. Sometimes it is in rhyme, sometimes not. Often it even springs at us from a page of prose, as when, in *The Red Badge of Courage,* Stephen Crane writes: "The red sun was pasted in the sky like a wafer." Poetry, finally, is as much a part of the rhythm of living as is breathing or the beat of the heart.

Although poetry often comes to us through our eyes, it will not give us the greatest pleasure if it does not also strike our ears. In all likelihood, you will read the verses on the following pages silently. However, read some of them *aloud,* not once but two or three times. As you do so, observe carefully the way each poem is punctuated. Failure to do this is like driving through traffic ignoring the traffic signals.

The practice of voicing the rhythm and sound of the lines will help you get more enjoyment from the poems. Studying the poems will also stimulate you to look about you with new eyes and to listen with new ears.

THE POET SEES In this section, "The Poet Sees," each writer has tried to present sharp-edged pictures. The sense of sight—the shapes, the sizes, the colors of things—is dominant in these poems.

But, the poets may appeal to the other senses as well. They call to mind the smell, the taste, the sound, the touch of the world around us.

Mechanical things often seem to have
a life of their own.
This poem lets us see a steam shovel
as a prehistoric beast.

Steam Shovel

The dinosaurs are not all dead.
I saw one raise its iron head
To watch me walking down the road
Beyond our house today.
Its jaws were dripping with a load   5
Of earth and grass that it had cropped.
It must have heard me where I stopped,
Snorted white steam my way,
And stretched its long neck out to see,
And chewed, and grinned quite amiably.   10

CHARLES MALAM

From *Upper Pasture* by Charles Malam. Copyright 1930, ©
1958 by Charles Malam. Reprinted by permission of Holt,
Rinehart and Winston, Inc.

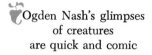 Ogden Nash's glimpses
of creatures
are quick and comic

The Hippopotamus

Behold the hippopotamus!
We laugh at how he looks to us,
And yet in moments dank and grim
I wonder how we look to him.
Peace, peace, thou hippopotamus!
We really look all right to us,
As you no doubt delight the eye
Of other hippopotami.

OGDEN NASH

The Camel

The camel has a single hump;
The dromedary, two;
Or else the other way around.
I'm never sure. Are you?

OGDEN NASH

The Ostrich

The ostrich roams the great Sahara.[1]
Its mouth is wide, its neck is narra.
It has such long and lofty legs,
I'm glad it sits to lay its eggs.

OGDEN NASH

---

1. **The Sahara**\sə ˈhă·rə\ is the great desert of North Africa.

A chance glimpse
of a face you may never see again—why
does it haunt you?

Through a Train Window

Hunger-eyed and sallow-cheeked
The child stared in at me, and
I stared back, full-bellied,
A vintage wine beside my plate.
No despair showed on her face,
None at least that I could see.
Just a trace of disbelief
That I ate there instead of she.

GORDON PARKS

From *Gordon Parks: A Poet and His
Camera* by Gordon Parks. Copyright 1968
in all countries of the International Copyright Union by Gordon Parks. Reprinted by
permission of The Viking Press, Inc.

These verses by Richard Wright follow a pattern
developed by the Japanese centuries ago. Called a
hokku, or haiku, each verse captures a complete
picture or mood in seventeen syllables, with
five syllables in the first line, seven in the second line,
and five in the third.

Hokku Poems

I am nobody
A red sinking autumn sun
Took my name away

In the falling snow
A laughing boy holds out his palms
Until they are white

The crow flew so fast
That he left his lonely caw
Behind in the fields

RICHARD WRIGHT

What did she mean to the pigeons?
What did they mean to her?
Here is a picture more vivid than
most artists could paint with a brush.

Pigeon Woman

Slate, or dirty-marble-colored,
or rusty-iron-colored, the pigeons
on the flagstones in front of the
Public Library make a sharp lake

into which the pigeon woman wades   5
at exactly 1:30. She wears a
plastic pink raincoat with a round
collar (looking like a little

girl, so gay) and flat gym shoes,
her hair square-cut orange.   10
Wide-apart feet carefully enter
the spinning, crooning waves

(as if she'd just learned how
to walk, each step conscious,
an accomplishment) blue knots in the   15
calves of her bare legs (uglied marble),

age in angled cords of jaw
and neck, her pimento-colored hair,
hanging in thin tassels, is gray
around a balding crown.   20

The day-old bread drops down
from her veined hand dipping out
of a paper sack. Choppy, shadowy ripples,
the pigeons strike around her legs.

Sack empty, she squats and seems to rinse   25
her hands in them—the rainy greens and
oily purples of their necks. Almost
they let her wet her thirsty fingertips—

but drain away in an untouchable tide.
A make-believe trade   30
she has come to, in her lostness
or illness or age—to treat the motley

city pigeons at 1:30 every day, in all
weathers. It is for them she colors
her own feathers. Ruddy-footed   35
on the lime-stained paving,

purling to meet her when she comes,
they are a lake of love. Retreating
from her hands as soon as empty,
they are the flints of love.   40

MAY SWENSON

As he describes
a London evening long ago,
the poet creates
a vivid picture.

Prelude

The winter evening settles down
With smell of steaks in passageways.
Six o'clock.
The burnt-out ends of smoky days.
And now a gusty shower wraps   5
The grimy scraps
Of withered leaves about your feet
And newspapers from vacant lots;
The showers beat
On broken blinds and chimney pots,   10
And at the corner of the street
A lonely cab horse steams and stamps.
And then the lighting of the lamps.

T. S. ELIOT

Listen to the sounds that echo in your ears
when you have finished reading the poem below.

The High School Band

On warm days in September the high school band
Is up with the birds and marches along our street,
Boom boom,
To a field where it goes boom boom until eight forty-five
When it marches, as in the old rhyme, back, boom boom,   5
To its study halls, leaving our street
Empty except for the leaves that descend, to no drum,
And lie still.
In September
A great many high school bands beat a great many drums,   10
And the silences after their partings are very deep.

REED WHITTEMORE

Reprinted with permission of The Macmillan Company from *The Self-made Man* by Reed Whittemore. © by Reed Whittemore, 1959.

See the picture
this poet is painting with words.
Is it more than
just a picture?

The Term

A rumpled sheet
of brown paper
about the length

and apparent bulk
of a man was   5
rolling with the

wind slowly over
and over in
the street as

a car drove down   10
upon it and
crushed it to

the ground. Unlike
a man it rose
again rolling   15

with the wind over
and over to be as
it was before.

WILLIAM CARLOS WILLIAMS

The next verses
give us several views of people.
In addition to the quick,
delightful impressions,
what does each poet have to say?

Reflections Dental

How pure, how beautiful, how fine
Do teeth on television shine!
No flutist flutes, no dancer twirls,
But comes equipped with matching pearls.
Gleeful announcers all are born   5
With sets like rows of hybrid corn.
Clowns, critics, clergy, commentators,
Ventriloquists and roller skaters,
M.C.s who beat their palms together,
The girl who diagrams the weather,   10
The crooner crooning for his supper—
All flash white treasures, lower and upper.
With miles of smiles the airwaves teem,
And each an orthodontist's[1] dream.

'Twould please my eye as gold a miser's—   15
One charmer with uncapped incisors.

PHYLLIS MC GINLEY

---

1. **orthodontist**\'ŏr•thə **▲**dŏn•tĭst\ a dentist who special-
izes in straightening teeth.

From *The Love Letters of Phyllis McGinley* by Phyllis Mc-
Ginley. Copyright © 1957 by Phyllis McGinley. Originally
appeared in *The New Yorker*. Reprinted by permission of
The Viking Press, Inc.

Imaginary Portrait

The proofs that photographers send
Are much more revealing than kind.
That's not how I look to myself—
I'm always retouched in my mind.

REBECCA MC CANN

My Pompous Friend

His sense of worth is strong;
   To watch him walk is fun.
He marches forth, a long
   Processional of one.

LAWRENCE EMERSON NELSON

How do *you* visualize spring rain?
How does it sound to *you?* When you have
just the right picture in your mind
and just the right sound in your ears,
read the following poem.

Rain Music

On the dusty earth-drum
   Beats the falling rain;
Now a whispered murmur,
   Now a louder strain.

Slender, silvery drumsticks,   5
   On an ancient drum,
Beat the mellow music
   Bidding life to come.

Chords of earth awakened,
   Notes of greening spring,   10
Rise and fall triumphant
   Over every thing.

Slender, silvery drumsticks
   Beat the long tattoo—
God, the Great Musician,   15
   Calling life anew.

JOSEPH SEAMON COTTER, JR.

No pretense about
this poem, is there? Do you
like it? Why?

Soup

I saw a famous man eating soup.
I say he was lifting a fat broth
Into his mouth with a spoon.
His name was in the newspapers that day
Spelled out in tall black headlines
And thousands of people were talking about him.

   When I saw him,
He sat bending his head over a plate
Putting soup in his mouth with a spoon.

CARL SANDBURG

From *Smoke and Steel* by Carl Sandburg, copyright, 1920, by Harcourt Brace Jovanovich, Inc.; copyright, 1948, by Carl Sandburg. Reprinted by permission of the publishers.

The poet of the following sketch
has given you such exacting facts
to observe that you might not be aware
that he has included
some ideas for you to consider.

The Runaway

Once when the snow of the year was beginning to fall,
We stopped by a mountain pasture to say, "Whose colt?"
A little Morgan[1] had one forefoot on the wall,
The other curled at his breast. He dipped his head
And snorted at us. And then he had to bolt.   5
We heard the miniature thunder where he fled,
And we saw him, or thought we saw him, dim and gray,
Like a shadow against the curtain of falling flakes.
"I think the little fellow's afraid of the snow.
He isn't winter-broken. It isn't play   10
With the little fellow at all. He's running away.
I doubt if even his mother could tell him, 'Sakes,
It's only weather.' He'd think she didn't know!
Where is his mother? He can't be out alone."
And now he comes again with a clatter of stone,   15
And mounts the wall again with whited eyes
And all his tail that isn't hair up straight.
He shudders his coat as if to throw off flies.
"Whoever it is that leaves him out so late,
When other creatures have gone to stall and bin,   20
Ought to be told to come and take him in."

ROBERT FROST

---

1. **Morgan,** one of a famous small, sturdy breed of horses.

Many people have the mistaken idea that poetry
is always about nature, flowers, love, and generally
vague topics. "The Base Stealer," like "Soup,"
shows that a real poet can find something of interest
in the most common event. The subject of this poem
is no farther away than your local ball park.

The Base Stealer

Poised between going on and back, pulled
Both ways taut like a tightrope-walker,
Fingertips pointing the opposites,
Now bouncing tiptoe like a dropped ball
Or a kid skipping rope, come on, come on,   5

Running a scattering of steps sidewise,
How he teeters, skitters, tingles, teases,
Taunts them, hovers like an ecstatic bird,
He's only flirting, crowd him, crowd him,
Delicate, delicate, delicate, delicate—now!   10

ROBERT FRANCIS

TECHNIQUES

Imagery, Rhythm, Poetic Forms

The poet Coleridge declared that poetry is "the best words in their best order." Other people, before and after him, have said so many other things that, finally, it is not easy to say exactly what poetry is. Certainly it isn't just rhyme or meter, because acceptable poetry has been written without one or the other of these. *Blank verse* lacks rhyme and *free verse* lacks a formal beat. However, while no one can say what it is that any one poem must have, there are general characteristics that can be discovered from a study of a large body of poetry. Some of these are:

1. Rich *imagery* resulting from the use of descriptive or *figurative language*. Such imagery serves to bring together the reader's experience and the author's imagination. You are familiar with metaphor and simile from your study of the *Odyssey*.

2. Music and sound pattern coming from the *rhythm* of the words and the choice of rhymes. Most poetry has meter—a beat of accented and unaccented syllables:

Ĭ meant̀/ t̆o dò/ m̆y work̀/ tŏdaỳ./

Longer poems are divided into sections called *stanzas*, which usually have a fixed and repeating pattern. A stanza of two rhyming lines is called a *couplet*.

3. Special ways of using words and rhymes. *Alliteration* is the repetition of beginning sounds: The *tall, tanned Texan*. Another poet's device is *onomatopoeia*, which is the use of words whose sounds suggest their meanings: The *buzz* of a bee.

There are also special kinds of poems such as lyric verse, light and satiric verse, haiku, ballads, and epics.

Lyric verse speaks of the poet's feelings. The name reminds us that such poetry was once sung to the accompaniment of a small, harplike instrument called a lyre.

Ballads, also, were originally for singing. Traditional story poems common during the Middle Ages, many ballads survived by word of mouth for hundreds of years before they were written down. In general, their language is simple, they contain refrains and they celebrate love, bravery, or treachery. *Epics* like the *Odyssey* are longer and more heroic than ballads, but they, too, are narrative, storytelling poetry.

Humorous verse and *light verse* are playful poetry, while *satiric verse* holds its subject up to ridicule.

THE POET SEES

Steam Shovel

The poet observes a common sight—an earth-moving machine in action. His reaction is far from ordinary. What has he done to transform an ordinary subject into a delightful picture?

If you are familiar with the term *metaphor* (review the notes for the *Odyssey*, if necessary), explain how the poet uses this device in "Steam Shovel."

At the time this poem was written, most steam shovels were actually powered by steam. Now, however, they have either gasoline or diesel engines. What mythical monster does the poet suggest when he says the machine "snorted white steam"?

Three Poems by Nash

Ogden Nash was one of America's most popular writers of humorous verse. To make us laugh, he tried to take us by surprise, to catch us off guard. With his unexpected endings and his unusual, even fantastic, rhymes he gives a whimsical view of everyday subjects. Incidentally, how many humps does a dromedary have?

From these verses by Ogden Nash, select an example to show how the poet has stretched the shapes of words to make a rhyme. Discuss how this affects the humor. Consider and discuss this statement: Beauty is in the eye of the beholder.

Through a Train Window

Gordon Parks is a well-known photographer as well as a writer. In his book *A Poet and His Camera*, from which this poem comes, there is a photograph of the little girl he saw through the window. Other people looking out at her might not have seen what Parks saw. They might have been more interested in the way she was dressed or perhaps wondered why she was standing so near the train.

1. What does the fact that he had a "vintage wine" beside his plate indicate about the cost of the meal?

2. What does this poem tell you about the poet?

Hokku Poems

The haiku, with its seventeen syllables, is purposely short enough to be spoken in one breath. It is one tiny scene, one observation, almost like a photograph.

In composing haiku the writer needs to remember that he should remain impersonal—he makes an observation, records an impression through the careful placement of words. Usually each haiku answers three questions: what is the main topic of interest, where it is, and when. Some writers choose to rhyme their first and third lines in order to make each verse seem a complete unit.

Below are two examples of haiku written by ninth-grade students. One has rhyme.

> Through the greening earth
> The purple crocus lifts up
> Arms in sudden birth.

> Across the desert
> Wagons keep moving westward;
> The red man watches.

Discuss the picture or momentary observation you find in each of Richard Wright's poems. Which of the three do you find most vivid? Why?

Pigeon Woman

May Swenson uses imagery combined with colors to paint her picture of the pigeon woman.

1. What detailed metaphor does she use to describe the way the woman approaches and feeds the birds?

2. What colors does she use in making the word picture vivid?

3. What is the woman seeking in her feeding of the birds? Do they give it to her?

Prelude

This quiet poem was written about a time when cab horses were still common. Waiting patiently for their drivers to take someone somewhere, the horses stamped their feet impatiently. Their wet bodies steamed in the cold rain. In the era of cab horses, what kind of lamp is suggested by "And then the lighting of the lamps"?

If you look closely at this poem, you will see that the poet has described five aspects of the winter evening. What are they? Each could be considered as belonging to one of the five senses: sight, hearing, touch, taste, and smell. Assign two or three lines to each sense and defend your choices by pointing out the deciding words and phrases.

The High School Band

On September mornings, when the high school band is practicing, the bursts of sound are broken and irregular. You hear the beat of the drum, the blare of music, silence, and then perhaps a certain section of the band playing alone.

1. Do you recall what *onomatopoeia* is? (See page 459, number 3.) Where can you find an illustration of this poetic device in "The High School Band"?

2. If you have really seen and heard with the poet as you read this poem, you know that the last line is effective. Describe how it leaves you feeling.

The Term

1. Do you think William Carlos Williams intended his poem to amuse you, to make you angry, to make you think?

2. Discuss whether the experience described is one common to many persons.

3. Why did the paper look like a man? How did it show it was different from a man?

4. If it had been a man, what would very likely have happened to the term, or period of life, he had to live?

Imaginary Portrait, My Pompous Friend, Reflections Dental

To help us see more than surface situations in their verses, these poets use a gentle form of *satire*.

1. In a sentence or two, explain what human act or folly each poet has satirized.

2. Choose one verse and discuss what you believe to be the poet's real attitude toward the poem's subject.

3. You might find it fun to try your own hand at humorous verses like these. Look around, think of a funny situation, then write. The following questions may suggest some poetical situations: If you have delivered papers, how is your aim? Do you get confused in making introductions? Who is the most miserly person you know? Why don't parents realize that styles change? What makes people conceited?

Rain Music

Now that you have read the poem "Rain Music," in what ways did Cotter's impressions of spring rain differ from yours? Was the mood of the poem different from yours? Explain.

The poet's purpose was certainly to create a

colorful word picture of sight and sound—the rising symphony of rain. His images, "dusty earth-drum," "slender, silvery drumsticks," "mellow music," "greening spring," appeal to the senses and stir the imagination. But the poet also had something else in mind. What does he suggest about the cycle of life and seasons?

Read the last four lines again. Without this last verse, what idea would have been omitted?

Soup

A famous man looks just like any other man when he's eating a bowl of soup, according to Carl Sandburg.

1. Is the poet's choice of language realistic or imaginative? Why does the title fit the poem so well?

2. Discuss whether you think the reader sees what Sandburg wanted him to see when he has finished reading the poem.

The Runaway

1. Anyone who has observed the ways of colts knows that Robert Frost's description of the little Morgan is true to life. Read the poem again, carefully. Do you think Frost means to suggest a similarity between the behavior of the colt and that of another kind of young animal?

2. Discuss the effects that the poet achieves with the following: *curled at his breast, miniature thunder, winter broken, whited eyes, shudders his coat, stall and bin.*

The Base Stealer

Understanding this poem requires some knowledge of baseball. If you have ever tried to steal a base or have watched someone try it, you know that base stealing is an art. It requires nerve, speed, timing, and the ability to make a split-second decision. It requires, too, the ability to rattle the players on the opposing team so they will be caught off balance when the base stealer finally streaks toward the coveted base.

1. In this lively, one-sentence look at the player's antics, the poet interjects directions and comments to the players. Find these interjections and discuss what effect the poet gains by using them.

2. Look again at the words in the last line. To whom do you think they are spoken? They are spoken in response to what kind of action taking place down on the field?

A SUMMING UP

The Poet Sees

Think back over some of the poems you have read in this section. *Do not turn back to the poems.* Think of each poem in turn. Let the images from each poem come before your eyes like a series of paintings hung in a row. Which images remain sharp in your mind? Which is the most vivid? Here, for your reference, are the titles of some of the poems to consider:

"Through A Train Window"

"Hokku Poems"

"Prelude"

"Soup"

"The Term"

"Pigeon Woman"

"The Base Stealer"

When you have decided which is the most vivid image for you, turn back to the poem in which it occurs. Study the poem and the image. Then write a paragraph of a few sentences explaining why this particular word picture stayed with you.

If possible, exchange papers with others and read them aloud to compare reasons for making choices. It should be interesting, and you will find out that there are many ways of seeing a poem.

THE POET FEELS The first group of poems in THE WAYS OF A POET is titled "The Poet Sees," because the emphasis is upon external things: sights and sounds. In each of the next poems the emphasis comes from the poet's internal world. The central theme is the poet's own feelings. Note, however, that even here poets cannot express their feelings unless they refer to specific things in the world about them. It is not very interesting merely to hear someone say "I am sad" or "I am happy." Good poets express themselves in terms of particular places (as in "Apache Mother"), particular persons (as in "John Doe, Jr."), or particular things. Note the specific objects mentioned in "Days."

Days

Some days my thoughts are just cocoons—all cold, and dull, and blind,
They hang from dripping branches in the gray woods of my mind;
And other days they drift and shine—such free and flying things!
I find the gold dust in my hair, left by their brushing wings.

KARLE WILSON BAKER

"I Meant to Do My Work Today"

I meant to do my work today,
But a brown bird sang in the apple tree,
And a butterfly flitted across the field,
And all the leaves were calling me.

And the wind went sighing over the land,
Tossing the grasses to and fro,
And a rainbow held out its shining hand—
So what could I do but laugh and go?

RICHARD LE GALLIENNE

In the first two stanzas the poet describes
the situation. Not until the third stanza does
he tell you how he feels about it.

Dog, Midwinter

This dog barking at me now—
do I really bother him
or is he acting out
the old faithful watch-dog routine?

Or (and I hope it's this)   5
is he so lonely locked up
in the snow-filled yard that the sight
of another living thing stirs him?

For I can truly say
I'm as lonely now   10
as you, dog, so
speaking for both of us
bark your crazy head off.

RAYMOND SOUSTER

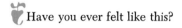Have you ever felt like this?

Empty

No, nothing
passes
through my mind;
it is like a wide sky
empty and white.   5

Yet I am here,
quiet, before you,
and looking at you,
yet I do not see you.

No, nothing   10
passes
through my mind;
it is like a wide sky
empty and white.

MARÍA NÚÑEZ

The speaker in
the next poem
is also looking back
and expressing
a strong feeling
about what happened
to an individual,
but the narrative viewpoint
has shifted.

John Doe, Jr.

Among the Missing . . .
　　　　　　　I think he always was—
Only no one thought to mention it before. . . .

He was the boy who didn't make the team
although, God knows, he tried: his were the fingers,　　5
always too eager, that always fumbled the ball.
He was the fellow
people forgot to invite when they planned a party.
After the party, once in a while, they would say,
"We should have invited John." But that was after;　　10
and most of the time they did not think about it.
John thought about it: thought of the laughter and music.
He was the chap who dreamed that his loneliness
might somehow find in words a redemptive beauty:
the yearning youth who sent his poems and stories,　　15
bundled in hope, to editors—and found them,
paired to rejection slips,[1] in his mail-box, later.
He was the man, defeated by diffidence,
who waited in line—and who did not get the job. . . .

Only war had use for him, and only　　20
long enough to lose him. . . .
　　　　　　　Among the missing. . . .

BONARO W. OVERSTREET

Reprinted from *Hands Laid upon the Wind* by Bonaro W. Overstreet. By permission of W. W. Norton & Co., Inc. Copyright
1955 by W. W. Norton & Co., Inc.

1. A rejection slip is a note from an editor or publisher
to an author rejecting his product.

Place yourself beside
this mother. How would you feel if you were
transplanted to completely new
and strange surroundings?

Apache Mother

Softly round and sensitive,
muted till you learn to trust,
good mother of five, tribe-handsome children,
you are filled with endless fear
in this unfriendly city,   5
distant from the reservation you have known.
You strive to hold your troubled husband,
to keep your home,
to understand the notes
your children bring from school.   10
And all is churned with loneliness.

MARGARET G. HINDES

At times most of us have felt like John Doe, Jr. It has seemed
that no matter what we did we could not succeed. We have been "defeated by diffidence"—
that is, by lack of confidence in ourselves. The author of the next poem expresses
quite a different attitude toward life. W. E. Henley was ill much of his life.
He wrote this famous verse during a twenty-month stay in the hospital
fighting a form of tuberculosis. Henley proclaims that man's spirit
is unconquerable, that his spirit can rise above adversity.

Invictus

Out of the night that covers me,
   Black as the Pit from pole to pole,
I thank whatever gods may be
   For my unconquerable soul.

In the fell[1] clutch of circumstance   5
   I have not winced nor cried aloud.
Under the bludgeonings of chance
   My head is bloody but unbowed.

Beyond this place of wrath and tears
   Looms but the horror of the shade,   10
And yet the menace of the years
   Finds, and shall find me, unafraid.

It matters not how strait[2] the gate,
   How charged with punishments the scroll,
I am the master of my fate;   15
   I am the captain of my soul.

WILLIAM ERNEST HENLEY

---

1. **fell,** cruel, fierce, dreadful.
2. **strait,** narrow.

Here is a song of praise
dating from about the tenth century B.C.

The Twenty-third Psalm

The Lord is my shepherd; I shall not want.
He maketh me to lie down in green pastures;
    he leadeth me beside the still waters.
He restoreth my soul; he leadeth me in the paths
    of righteousness for his name's sake.
Yea, though I walk through the valley of the shadow
    of death, I will fear no evil; for thou art with
    me; thy rod and thy staff,[1] they comfort me.
Thou preparest a table before me in the presence
    of mine enemies; thou anointest my head with
    oil;[2] my cup runneth over.
Surely goodness and mercy shall follow me all the
    days of my life; and I will dwell in the house
    of the Lord for ever.

THE BIBLE

---

1. **the rod and the staff** of a shepherd.
2. **oil,** an ointment used ceremonially by the Hebrews
to dedicate a person or a thing to God.

THE POET FEELS

Two Poems of Changing Mood

1. In "Days" the poet tells us how the world of her thoughts and emotions seems on different days. Le Gallienne tells us how his mood changed on a certain day and why. Make a list of the things Le Gallienne says called him away from his work and explain whether you think his decision was really difficult.

2. Think what cocoons eventually become, then explain why the poet makes a logical development of this metaphor in "Days."

Dog, Midwinter

1. The poet first suggests two reasons why the dog might be barking at him. What are they?

2. How does he reveal in the last stanza that he sympathizes with the dog?

Empty

Do you sometimes find yourself looking at a person, apparently listening to what he is saying, yet not even hearing him? Your mind is empty. Why do you think the first and third stanzas in this poem are the same?

John Doe, Jr.

1. John Doe is an imaginary name used in certain legal procedures and has come to mean generally any fictitious person. Cartoonists refer to the average citizen as John Q. Public, in much the same way. Discuss reasons why the poet chose to use John Doe, Jr., instead of the boy's real name.

2. The first two lines of the poem suggest that the poet has been stirred to remember John. What news has she obviously just heard?

3. Since the poet refers to John's contemporaries as "they," discuss the way she appears to view her own part in the boy's life.

Apache Mother

On the familiar reservation this Apache woman would have felt better able to bring up her family. In the strange, unfriendly city, she feels lonely and lost.

1. From what narrative viewpoint does the poet write? What does she accomplish by this?

2. What are some problems that might trouble the husband?

3. What are some things the notes from school might be about?

An implication to consider:

Most people in a city are lonely.

Invictus

1. "Invictus," which means "unconquered" in Latin, has been popular for well over half a century. It has been a source of inspiration to many people. How did the poet feel about meeting life's troubles? How does this attitude differ from yours?

2. Many of the expressions here are in a style that is seldom used now. Explain what the poet means by the following:

  a. the Pit from pole to pole

  b. the fell clutch of circumstance

  c. this place of wrath and tears

  d. the horror of the shade

An implication to consider and discuss:

A person can never be master of his fate or captain of his soul.

The Twenty-third Psalm

This psalm is one of the best-known poems in all literature. One of the many songs of praise written by the shepherd David, it is found in the Old Testament of the Bible.

1. Explain the metaphor of the shepherd.

2. What images in line 2 give the reader or listener a feeling of comfort and security?

A SUMMING UP

The Poet Feels

1. Review the poems in "The Poet Feels" with an eye to answering this question: Do most of the poets speak of their feelings in general, abstract terms, or do they express emotion through telling of specific objects, places, people, and events? Discuss with examples.

2. Select the poem in this group which seems to you to express the greatest depth of feeling. Explain your choice.

Words

A. In "The Twenty-third Psalm," there are verb endings that are archaic, that is, no longer used in English: *-eth* as in *maketh* and *-est* as in *preparest*. In Old English (449–1100) and in Middle English (1100–1500), *-eth* was used to form the third person singular (he) present tense as in *he leadeth,* and *-est* was used for the second person singular (thou) present tense as in *thou anointest. Thou,* of course, is *you* in modern English. The possessive form of *thou* is *thy,* as in *thy rod.* In contemporary English, *thy* is *your.* Suffixes, then, are not the only archaic forms in the poem. What do *yea, art,* and *mine* mean?

B. A good dictionary not only defines a word but also briefly sketches its derivation, that is, its origin and historical development. If, for example, you looked up the word *victor,* you would find that it means "one who defeats an enemy or opponent"; you would also find that it is derived from the past participle (*victus*) of the Latin word *vincere,* meaning "to conquer." The title of the poem "Invictus" is derived from the same source. Were you to look up the word *invincible,* which means "unconquerable," you would discover that it is also based on this Latin verb. Information about the background of the word *sensitive,* which appears in "Apache Mother," can also be found in the dictionary. *Sensitive* stems from a Latin word meaning "to feel or to perceive by the senses." We generally think of a sensitive person as one who is keenly responsive to the feelings, attitudes, or situations of others. Related to *sensitive* are such words as *sensory, sensation, sensitize,* and *sensible.* For each of the following words from the unit "The Poet Feels," find background information in the dictionary: *diffidence, redemptive, Apache, menace, reservation, scroll, captain,* and *cocoon.*

C. To inform the reader of the status of a word, a good dictionary uses various labels, including *archaic, informal, British, regional,* and *foreign language.* An archaic word is one that once was widely used but now is rarely used. The word *strait,* meaning "narrow," in "Invictus" is archaic. The label *informal* is applied to a word that is appropriate for everyday, ordinary conversations but not suitable for more formal situations. *Chap* in "John Doe, Jr." is an informal word meaning "a man or boy." While in a conversation you might refer to someone as a *chap,* in a serious speech you probably would refer to him as a *person.* If the meaning of a word differs in British English from American English, that word is labeled *chiefly British.* In British English, for example, *tin* means "a container for preserved foodstuff; a can." And a *lift* is an "elevator." A word that is popular in one region of the country but virtually unknown elsewhere is labeled *regional,* and the area where it is common is specified, for example, *Southern U.S., New England,* and *Southwestern U.S.* The word *bayou,* when it means "a marshy, sluggish body of water that is tributary to a river or other body of water," is labeled *Southern U.S.* Foreign words that have not been fully integrated into English—though they may be fairly common—and are regarded by native speakers to be non-English are given the label of the language to which they belong. *Répondez s'il vous plaît,* which is commonly abbreviated R.S.V.P., is used on formal invitations; it means "Please reply." It is labeled *French.* When using your dictionary for the various exercises in this book, be sure to pay attention to the five labels discussed above.

Gallery | THE WAYS OF A POET

POTTERY HORSE
China, T'ang Dynasty

Every good poet,
like every good artist,
lets you see reality through his eyes.
No two will see any object alike,
yet each will offer new insights.
In this gallery, note how each artist
shows you something peculiarly his own
in his view of the form of a horse.

Graceful animals have,
from the beginning of art records,
intrigued the artist and demanded
his response and creativity.
The first works come from antiquity;
the most recent of them is the horse
from what is sometimes called
the Golden Age of China:
T'ang Dynasty, 618–906. This work
has been restored to give you an idea
of how it might have looked when it,
and the art of ceramics, was new.

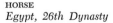

HORSE
Egypt, 26th Dynasty

REARING HORSES
Roman Bronze, First Century A.D.

HORSES AND GROOMS
Japanese screen painting, Ashikaga to Early Momoyama period

HORSES
Study for the Black Countess, Henri Toulouse-Lautrec

These horse pictures point out the changes in style, moving from sixteenth-century Japan through the Expressionist Movement of the early twentieth century. Each of these painters is saying something quite different, though they all start from the same place: the form of the horse.

BLUE HORSES
Franz Marc

THE HORSE, 1928
Alexander Calder
Walnut, 15½ x 34¾" Collection,
The Museum of Modern Art, New York,
Acquired through the Lillie P. Bliss Bequest.

HORSE
Marino Marini

These three horse sculptures
are quite different though contemporary. There is
an element of humor in the wooden piece
by Calder, who is best known for his mobile sculpture.
The startling work of the modern Italian painter
and sculptor, Marino Marini, shows tension.
Obviously, the ceramic WOUNDED HORSE says *pain*.

WOUNDED HORSE
Agenore Fabbri

THE POET TELLS A STORY We have read poems which put an emphasis on external sights and sounds and poems which put an emphasis on emotion and ways of feeling. Now we turn to narrative poems—poems that tell tales. Some of these stories are full of emotion, some have rapid action, some are mysterious, some humorous, and some historical. The emphasis here is on the narration of an event. But note that the elements we have studied already—sharp imagery and emotion—are still present.

This short Greek legend tells one of the best-known stories of the ancient world. According to the myth, King Minos of the island of Crete wished to have a secret labyrinth built. He sent for the master craftsman Daedalus, who brought his son, Icarus, with him. After Daedalus built the maze, the king, fearful that his secret would be revealed, held the father and son prisoners.

The Story of Daedalus and Icarus

Homesick for homeland, Daedalus hated Crete
And his long exile there, but the sea held him.
"Though Minos blocks escape by land or water,"
Daedalus said, "surely the sky is open,
And that's the way we'll go. Minos' dominion   5
Does not include the air." He turned his thinking
Toward unknown arts, changing the laws of nature.
He laid out feathers in order, first the smallest,
A little larger next it, and so continued,
The way that pan-pipes rise in gradual sequence.   10
He fastened them with twine and wax, at middle,
At bottom, so, and bent them, gently curving,
So that they looked like wings of birds, most surely.
And Icarus, his son, stood by and watched him,
Not knowing he was dealing with his downfall,   15
Stood by and watched, and raised his shiny face
To let a feather, light as down, fall on it,
Or stuck his thumb into the yellow wax,
Fooling around, the way a boy will, always,
Whenever a father tries to get some work done.   20

Still, it was done at last, and the father hovered,
Poised, in the moving air, and taught his son:
"I warn you, Icarus, fly a middle course:
Don't go too low, or water will weigh the wings down;
Don't go too high, or the sun's fire will burn them.   25
Keep to the middle way. And one more thing,
No fancy steering by star or constellation,
Follow my lead!" That was the flying lesson,
And now to fit the wings to the boy's shoulders.
Between the work and warning the father found   30
His cheeks were wet with tears, and his hands trembled.
He kissed his son (*Good-bye,* if he had known it),
Rose on his wings, flew on ahead, as fearful
As any bird launching the little nestlings
Out of high nest into thin air. *Keep on,*   35
Keep on, he signals, *follow me!* He guides him
In flight—O fatal art!—and the wings move
And the father looks back to see the son's wings moving.
Far off, far down, some fisherman is watching
As the rod dips and trembles over the water,   40
Some shepherd rests his weight upon his crook,
Some ploughman on the handles of the ploughshare,
And all look up, in absolute amazement,
At those air-borne above. They must be gods!
They were over Samos, Juno's sacred island,   45
Delos and Paros toward the left, Lebinthus
Visible to the right, and another island,
Calymne, rich in honey. And the boy
Thought *This is wonderful!* and left his father,
Soared higher, higher, drawn to the vast heaven,   50
Nearer the sun, and the wax that held the wings
Melted in that fierce heat, and the bare arms
Beat up and down in air, and lacking oarage
Took hold of nothing. *Father!* he cried, and *Father!*
Until the blue sea hushed him, the dark water   55
Men call the Icarian now. And Daedalus,
Father no more, called "Icarus, where are you!
Where are you, Icarus? Tell me where to find you!"
And saw the wings on the waves, and cursed his talents,
Buried the body in a tomb, and the land   60
Was named for Icarus.

OVID

Translated by Rolfe Humphries

There are two swimmers in this poem.
One of them has finished swimming forever.

Swimmers

I took the crazy short-cut to the bay;
Over a fence or two and through a hedge,
Jumping a private road, along the edge
Of backyards full of drying wash it lay.
And now, the last set being played and over,   5
I hurried past the ruddy lakes of clover;
I swung my racket at astonished oaks,
My arm still tingling from aggressive strokes.
Tennis was over for the day—
I took the leaping short-cut to the bay.   10

Then the quick plunge into the cool, green dark,
The windy waters rushing past me, through me;
Filled with a sense of some heroic lark
Existing in a vigor clean and roomy.
Swiftly I rose to meet the cat-like sea   15
That sprang upon me with a hundred claws,
And grappled, pulled me down and played with me.
Then, held suspended in the tightening pause
When one wave grows into a toppling acre,
I dived headlong into the foremost breaker,   20
Pitting against a cold and turbulent strife
The feverish intensity of life.
Out of the foam I lurched and rode the wave,
Swimming, hand over hand, against the wind;
I felt the sea's vain pounding, and I grinned   25
Knowing I was its master, not its slave.
Back on the curving beach I stood again,
Facing the bath-house, when a group of men,
Stumbling beneath some sort of weight, went by.
I could not see the heavy thing they carried;   30
I only heard: "He never gave a cry—"
"Who's going to tell her?" "Yes, and they just married—"
"Such a good swimmer, too . . ." And then they passed,
Leaving the silence throbbing and aghast.

A moment there my frightened heart hung slack,   35
And then the rich, retarded blood came back
Singing a livelier tune; and in my pulse
Beat the great wave that endlessly exults.
Why I was there and whither I must go,
I did not care. Enough for me to know   40
The same persistent struggle and the glowing
Waste of all spendthrift hours, bravely showing
Life, an adventure perilous and gay,
And death, a long and vivid holiday.

LOUIS UNTERMEYER

It was the end of May in 1940. At Dunkirk on the coast of France,
Hitler's Nazi armies, with superior forces and equipment, had trapped
the British Expeditionary Forces and remnants of the French army. The situation appeared
hopeless and tragic until the British government hastily set in motion one of the greatest
rescue operations in history. All branches of the British armed services, assisted by hundreds
of civilian volunteers, manned boats of all types in dashing back and forth
across the English Channel, eventually carrying over 338,000 soldiers away from the beaches
at Dunkirk. Prime Minister Winston Churchill called this feat of World War II
a "miracle of deliverance." How an English boy and his young sister
became part of this "miracle" is a story this poem tells.

Dunkirk

Will came back from school that day,
And he had little to say.
But he stood a long time looking down
To where the gray-green Channel water
Slapped at the foot of the little town,   5
And to where his boat, the *Sarah P,*
Bobbed at the tide on an even keel,
With her one old sail, patched at the leech,[1]
Furled like a slattern[2] down at heel.

---

1. **leech,** the edge of a sail.
2. **slattern,** an untidy, slovenly woman.

He stood for a while above the beach;   10
He saw how the wind and current caught her.
He looked a long time out to sea.
There was steady wind and the sky was pale
And a haze in the east that looked like smoke.

Will went back to the house to dress.   15
He was halfway through when his sister Bess,
Who was near fourteen and younger than he
By just two years, came home from play.
She asked him, "Where are you going, Will?"
He said, "For a good long sail."   20
"Can I come along?"
                         "No, Bess," he spoke.
"I may be gone for a night and a day."
Bess looked at him. She kept very still.
She had heard the news of the Flanders rout,[3]
How the English were trapped above Dunkirk,   25
And the fleet had gone to get them out—
But everyone thought that it wouldn't work.
There was too much fear, there was too much doubt.
She looked at him, and he looked at her.
They were English children, born and bred.   30
He frowned her down, but she wouldn't stir.
She shook her proud young head.
"You'll need a crew," she said.

They raised the sail on the *Sarah P,*
Like a pennoncel[4] on a young knight's lance,   35
And headed the *Sarah* out to sea,
To bring their soldiers home from France.

There was no command, there was no set plan,
But six hundred boats went out with them
On the gray-green waters, sailing fast,   40
River excursion and fisherman,
Tug and schooner and racing M,[5]
And the little boats came following last.

From every harbor and town they went
Who had sailed their craft in the sun and rain,   45

———————
3. **Flanders rout,** the defeat and retreat of the British and French armies
in Flanders.
4. **pennoncel**\ˈpĕ·nən ˈsĕl\ a little flag or pennant.
5. **racing M,** racing boats built to particular specifications.

From the South Downs,[6] from the cliffs of Kent,
From the village street, from the country lane.
There are twenty miles of rolling sea
From coast to coast, by the sea gull's flight,
But the tides were fair and the wind was free,   50
And they raised[7] Dunkirk by the fall of night.

They raised Dunkirk with its harbor torn
By the blasted stern and the sunken prow;
They had raced for fun on an English tide,
They were English children bred and born,   55
And whether they lived or whether they died,
They raced for England now.

Bess was as white as the *Sarah's* sail,
She set her teeth and smiled at Will.
He held his course for the smoky veil   60
Where the harbor narrowed thin and long.
The British ships were firing strong.

He took the *Sarah* into his hands,[8]
He drove her in through fire and death
To the wet men waiting on the sands.   65
He got his load and he got his breath,
And she came about, and the wind fought her.
He shut his eyes and he tried to pray.
He saw his England where she lay.
The wind's green home, the sea's proud daughter,   70
Still in the moonlight, dreaming deep,
The English cliffs and the English loam—
He had fourteen men to get away.
And the moon was clear and the night like day
For planes to see where the white sails creep   75
Over the black water.

He closed his eyes and he prayed for her;
He prayed to the men who had made her great,
Who had built her land of forest and park,
Who had made the seas an English lake;[9]   80
He prayed for a fog to bring the dark;
He prayed to get home for England's sake.
And the fog came down on the rolling sea,

---

6. The **South Downs** are a ridge of hills running down to the coast in southern England; Kent is the southeasternmost of the English shires.
7. **raised Dunkirk,** had Dunkirk in sight over the horizon.
8. He assumed firm and complete control of the vessel.
9. For a long time in their history the English enjoyed such naval supremacy that the ocean could be called "an English lake."

And covered the ships with English mist.
The diving planes were baffled and blind.   85

For Nelson was there in the *Victory*,[10]
With his one good eye, and his sullen twist,
And the guns were out on *The Golden Hind*,[11]
Their shot flashed over the *Sarah P.*
He could hear them cheer as he came about.   90

By burning wharves, by battered slips,[12]
Galleon, frigate, and brigantine,
The old dead captains fought their ships,
And the great dead admirals led the line.
It was England's night, it was England's sea.   95

The fog rolled over the harbor key.[13]
Bess held to the stays and conned[14] him out.
And all through the dark, while the *Sarah's* wake
Hissed behind him, and vanished in foam,
There at his side sat Francis Drake,   100
And held him true and steered him home.

ROBERT NATHAN

---

10. Viscount Horatio **Nelson** (1758–1805) lost his right eye
fighting French forces near Corsica in 1794. His flagship *Victory* led the English fleet in the defeat of the French at Trafalgar, in which battle Nelson was killed.
11. **The Golden Hind** was the ship in which Sir Francis Drake
(1540?–1596) sailed around the world (1577–1580).
12. **slips**, docks.
13. **key**, harbor opening.
14. **conned**, gave directions about the vessel's course.

Born in the woods and cradled on pine, was William Sycamore
a real man or a symbol of all the men who created the Western frontier?

The Ballad of William Sycamore
(1790–1871)

My father, he was a mountaineer,
His fist was a knotty hammer;
He was quick on his feet as a running deer,
And he spoke with a Yankee stammer.

My mother, she was merry and brave,   5
And so she came to her labor,
With a tall green fir for her doctor grave
And a stream for her comforting neighbor.

And some are wrapped in the linen fine,
And some like a godling's scion;[1]   10
But I was cradled on twigs of pine
In the skin of a mountain lion.

And some remember a white, starched lap
And a ewer with silver handles;
But I remember a coonskin cap   15
And the smell of bayberry candles!

The cabin logs, with the bark still rough,
And my mother who laughed at trifles,
And the tall, lank visitors, brown as snuff,
With their long, straight squirrel rifles.   20

I can hear them dance, like a foggy song,
Through the deepest one of my slumbers,
The fiddle squeaking the boots along
And my father calling the numbers.[2]

The quick feet shaking the puncheon floor,   25
And the fiddle squeaking and squealing,
Till the dried herbs rattled above the door
And the dust went up to the ceiling.

There are children lucky from dawn till dusk,
But never a child so lucky!   30
For I cut my teeth on "Money Musk"[3]
In the Bloody Ground of Kentucky![4]

When I grew tall as the Indian corn,
My father had little to lend me,
But he gave me his great, old powder horn   35
And his woodsman's skill to befriend me.

With a leather shirt to cover my back,
And a redskin nose to unravel
Each forest sign,[5] I carried my pack
As far as a scout could travel.   40

Till I lost my boyhood and found my wife,
A girl like a Salem clipper![6]
A woman straight as a hunting knife
With eyes as bright as the Dipper!

We cleared our camp where the buffalo feed,   45
Unheard-of streams were our flagons;
And I sowed my sons like the apple seed
On the trail of the Western wagons.

They were right, tight boys, never sulky or slow,
A fruitful, a goodly muster.   50

The eldest died at the Alamo.[7]
The youngest fell with Custer.[8]

The letter that told it burned my hand.
Yet we smiled and said, "So be it!"
But I could not live when they fenced the land,
For it broke my heart to see it.   55

I saddled a red, unbroken colt
And rode him into the day there;
And he threw me down like a thunderbolt
And rolled on me as I lay there.   60

The hunter's whistle hummed in my ear
As the city men tried to move me,
And I died in my boots like a pioneer
With the whole wide sky above me.

Now I lie in the heart of the fat, black soil,   65
Like the seed of a prairie thistle;
It has washed my bones with honey and oil
And picked them clean as a whistle.

And my youth returns, like the rains of spring,
And my sons, like the wild geese flying;   70
And I lie and hear the meadow lark sing
And have much content in my dying.

Go play with the towns you have built of blocks,
The towns where you would have bound me!
I sleep in my earth like a tired fox,   75
And my buffalo have found me.

STEPHEN VINCENT BENÉT

---

1. **godling's scion**\ˈsī·ən\ descendant of a god.
2. His father called out the numbers that directed various steps in square dances.
3. "**Money Musk**"\məsk\ was a square dance tune.
4. **The Bloody Ground of Kentucky** was so named because of the bitter battles there between Indians and settlers.
5. **redskin nose . . . sign,** the forest knowledge of an Indian.
6. Fast, tall-masted sailing ships from Salem\ˈsā·ləm\, Massachusetts, famous in the mid-nineteenth century.
7. **The Alamo**\ˈă·lə ˈmō\ is a fort at San Antonio, Texas, at which a garrison of 187 Texans was killed by Mexican forces in 1836.
8. **George Custer** (1839–1876) and all his men were killed in a battle with Sioux Indians in Montana in 1876.

481

Naturally a poem can tell a comic story as well as a serious one. The first two poems below are as brief and to the point as a joke or wisecrack. The third poem is a longer, more leisurely "yarn"—such as those told by Mark Twain and other American humorists. No poem could be more typically American than "Casey at the Bat." Celebrating "the great American game," these verses are perhaps the most popular ever written about a sports event.

The Termite

Some primal termite knocked on wood
And tasted it, and found it good,
And that is why your Cousin May
Fell through the parlor floor today.

OGDEN NASH

The Purist

I give you now Professor Twist,
A conscientious scientist.
Trustees exclaimed, "He never bungles!"
And sent him off to distant jungles.
Camped on a tropic riverside,   5
One day he missed his loving bride.
She had, the guide informed him later,
Been eaten by an alligator.
Professor Twist could not but smile.
"You mean," he said, "a crocodile."   10

OGDEN NASH

Casey at the Bat

The outlook wasn't brilliant for the Mudville nine that day;
The score stood four to two, with but one inning more to play;
And so, when Cooney died at first, and Burrows did the same,
A sickly silence fell upon the patrons of the game.

A straggling few got up to go in deep despair. The rest   5
Clung to the hope which springs eternal in the human breast;
They thought, if only Casey could but get a whack at that,
They'd put up even money now, with Casey at the bat.

But Flynn preceded Casey, as did also Jimmy Blake,
And the former was a pudding, and the latter was a fake;   10
So upon that stricken multitude grim melancholy sat,
For there seemed but little chance of Casey's getting to the bat.

But Flynn let drive a single, to the wonderment of all,
And Blake, the much despised, tore the cover off the ball;
And when the dust had lifted, and they saw what had occurred,   15
There was Jimmy safe on second, and Flynn a-hugging third.

Then from the gladdened multitude went up a joyous yell,
It bounded from the mountaintop, and rattled in the dell;
It struck upon the hillside, and recoiled upon the flat;
For Casey, mighty Casey, was advancing to the bat.   20

There was ease in Casey's manner as he stepped into his place,
There was pride in Casey's bearing, and a smile on Casey's face;
And when, responding to the cheers, he lightly doffed his hat,
No stranger in the crowd could doubt 'twas Casey at the bat.

Ten thousand eyes were on him as he rubbed his hands with dirt,   25
Five thousand tongues applauded when he wiped them on his shirt;
Then while the writhing pitcher ground the ball into his hip,
Defiance gleamed in Casey's eye, a sneer curled Casey's lip.

And now the leather-covered sphere came hurtling through the air,
And Casey stood a-watching it in haughty grandeur there;   30
Close by the sturdy batsman the ball unheeded sped.
"That ain't my style," said Casey. "Strike one," the umpire said.

From the benches, black with people, there went up a muffled roar,
Like the beating of the storm-waves on a stern and distant shore;
"Kill him! kill the umpire!" shouted someone on the stand,   35
And it's likely they'd have killed him had not Casey raised his hand.

With a smile of Christian charity great Casey's visage shone;
He stilled the rising tumult; he bade the game go on;
He signaled to the pitcher, and once more the spheroid flew,
But Casey still ignored it, and the umpire said, "Strike two."   40

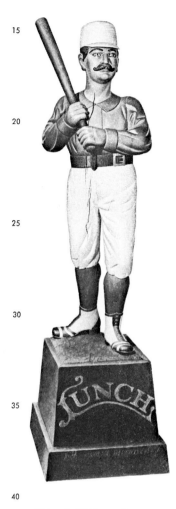

*"Baseball Player,"
early American
cigar store figure.*

"Fraud!" cried the maddened thousands, and the echo answered, "Fraud!"
But a scornful look from Casey, and the audience was awed;
They saw his face grow stern and cold, they saw his muscles strain,
And they knew that Casey wouldn't let that ball go by again.

The sneer is gone from Casey's lips, his teeth are clenched in hate,   45
He pounds with cruel violence his bat upon the plate;
And now the pitcher holds the ball, and now he lets it go,
And now the air is shattered by the force of Casey's blow.

Oh! somewhere in this favored land the sun is shining bright,
The band is playing somewhere, and somewhere hearts are light;   50
And somewhere men are laughing, and somewhere children shout,
But there is no joy in Mudville—mighty Casey has struck out!

ERNEST LAWRENCE THAYER

This is a tale of an evil creature.
Have you ever heard her on a winter's night?

Molly Means

Old Molly Means was a hag and a witch;
Chile of the devil, the dark, and sitch.
Her heavy hair hung thick in ropes
And her blazing eyes was black as pitch.
Imp at three and wench at 'leben   5
She counted her husbands to the number seben.
  O Molly, Molly, Molly Means
  There goes the ghost of Molly Means.

Some say she was born with a veil on her face
So she could look through unnatchal space   10
Through the future and through the past
And charm a body or an evil place
And every man could well despise
The evil look in her coal black eyes.
  Old Molly, Molly, Molly Means   15
  Dark is the ghost of Molly Means.

And when the tale begun to spread
Of evil and of holy dread:
Her black-hand arts and her evil powers
How she cast her spells and called the dead,   20
The younguns was afraid at night
And the farmers feared their crops would blight.
  Old Molly, Molly, Molly Means
  Cold is the ghost of Molly Means.

Then one dark day she put a spell   25
On a young gal-bride just come to dwell
In the lane just down from Molly's shack
And when her husband come riding back
His wife was barking like a dog
And on all fours like a common hog.   30
  O Molly, Molly, Molly Means
  Where is the ghost of Molly Means?

From *For My People* by Margaret Walker, Yale University Press. Copyright © 1942 by Yale University Press.

The neighbors come and they went away
And said she'd die before break of day
But her husband held her in his arms   35
And swore he'd break the wicked charms;
He'd search all up and down the land
And turn the spell on Molly's hand.
   O Molly, Molly, Molly Means
   Sharp is the ghost of Molly Means.   40

So he rode all day and he rode all night
And at the dawn he come in sight
Of a man who said he could move the spell
And cause the awful thing to dwell
On Molly Means, to bark and bleed   45
Till she died at the hands of her evil deed.
   Old Molly, Molly, Molly Means
   This is the ghost of Molly Means.

Sometimes at night through the shadowy trees
She rides along on a winter breeze.   50
You can hear her holler and whine and cry.
Her voice is thin and her moan is high,
And her cackling laugh or her barking cold
Bring terror to the young and old.
   O Molly, Molly, Molly Means   55
   Lean is the ghost of Molly Means.

MARGARET WALKER

Pay particular attention to the punctuation in the next poem. Many of the lines have no end punctuation. Thus, both sound and the sense depend upon alert reading. What actually happens and what does the poet think about this episode at the zoo?

At Woodward's Gardens

A boy, presuming on his intellect,
Once showed two little monkeys in a cage
A burning-glass they could not understand
And never could be made to understand.
Words are no good: to say it was a lens   5
For gathering solar rays would not have helped.
But let him show them how the weapon worked.
He made the sun a pinpoint on the nose
Of first one then the other till it brought
A look of puzzled dimness to their eyes   10
That blinking could not seem to blink away.
They stood arms laced together at the bars,
And exchanged troubled glances over life.
One put a thoughtful hand up to his nose
As if reminded—or as if perhaps   15
Within a million years of an idea.
He got his purple little knuckles stung.
The already known had once more been confirmed
By psychological experiment,
And that were all the finding to announce   20
Had the boy not presumed too close and long.
There was a sudden flash of arm, a snatch,
And the glass was the monkeys', not the boy's.
Precipitately they retired back-cage
And instituted an investigation   25
On their part, though without the needed insight.
They bit the glass and listened for the flavor.
They broke the handle and the binding off it.
Then none the wiser, frankly gave it up,
And having hid it in their bedding straw   30
Against the day of prisoners' ennui,
Came dryly forward to the bars again
To answer for themselves: Who said it mattered
What monkeys did or didn't understand?
They might not understand a burning-glass.   35
They might not understand the sun itself.
It's knowing what to do with things that counts.

ROBERT FROST

The speaker in this free verse story is the cockroach archy, who lives in a newspaper office. Since he has the soul of a poet, each night archy writes on a typewriter by jumping up and down on the keys. But since he isn't big enough to depress the shift key, he uses no capital letters, and he does not bother with punctuation. He makes a lot of sense, though, and what he has to say about warty bliggens really applies to people. Read the poem aloud for the challenge and the meaning.

warty bliggens, the toad

i met a toad
the other day by the name
of warty bliggens
he was sitting under
a toadstool   5
feeling contented
he explained that when the cosmos
was created
that toadstool was especially
planned for his personal   10
shelter from sun and rain
thought out and prepared
for him

do not tell me
said warty bliggens   15
that there is not a purpose
in the universe
the thought is blasphemy

a little more
conversation revealed   20
that warty bliggens
considers himself to be
the center of the said
universe
the earth exists   25
to grow toadstools for him
to sit under
the sun to give him light
by day and the moon

and wheeling constellations   30
to make beautiful
the night for the sake of
warty bliggens

to what act of yours
do you impute   35
this interest on the part
of the creator
of the universe
i asked him
why is it that you   40
are so greatly favored

ask rather
said warty bliggens
what the universe
has done to deserve me   45

if i were a
human being i would
not laugh
too complacently
at poor warty bliggens   50
for similar
absurdities
have only too often
lodged in the crinkles
of the human cerebrum   55
                         archy

DON MARQUIS

The Story of Daedalus and Icarus

In the opening lines of this poem you are given a natural picture of a father and son.

1. What important project is the father working on? What does the boy do while his father works?

2. Discuss the advice the father gives his son before they begin the flight. Although the father scolds, how does he feel about his son?

3. What happens to Icarus? How does this make the father feel?

An implication to consider:

What older people say, young people disregard.

Swimmers

1. This poem expresses vividly the youthful zest for life and the exhilaration of physical exertion. Even the spectacle of a drowning curbs the boy's high spirits only for a moment. Then his "blood came back/ Singing a livelier tune." Why does his gaiety return? Is he merely hardhearted or indifferent to tragedy? How do the last eight lines explain the boy's reaction to the drowning?

2. Explain the image (l. 15) created by the phrase "cat-like sea."

Dunkirk

When Will tries to pray as he and Bess begin their return voyage with their boatload of soldiers, he thinks of his England as home of the wind and proud daughter of the sea. Since his thoughts at this time are filled with emotion, there is a naturalness in his turning to *imagery* to express his love, pride, and longing for his country.

1. How do you know that Will is familiar with the stories of England's great heroes? For what does he pray? How are his prayers answered?

2. Does the poet expect you to believe that Sir Francis Drake actually sat at Will's side and ". . . held him true and steered him home"? Explain how England's "great dead admirals" really figured in the whole rescue operation.

3. The poem has an irregular rhyme scheme which adapts itself well to the pattern of conversation. Discuss whether you find it easy or hard

to read. What one line is repeated in the poem? How does this repetition bear a relation to the theme or basic idea behind the poem?

The Ballad of William Sycamore

1. By placing the dates under the title, the poet suggests that William Sycamore was a real person. However, the details given in the ballad indicate that Will Sycamore is probably a symbol of the American pioneer. Look back through the poem and select lines which support this symbolism.

2. The following are often found in ballads. Find an example in this poem of:

a. a tragic incident

b. an act of physical courage

c. the supernatural

3. One of the earliest forms of literature, the ballad was used to tell a historic or exciting story to music. The poet has written this modern American ballad with a rhythm and a beat like that found in square-dance music. Why is this appropriate? Experiment with reading this poem aloud as you tap your toe to a square-dance rhythm.

Discuss whether or not this ballad would have been more effective had it ended with line 64.

The Termite and The Purist

These are "just for fun" by one of the masters of humorous verse. Try to decide just what it is that makes these two verses funny.

Casey at the Bat

1. Part of the humor of this poem comes from the author's use of unexpected words and expressions. These expressions seem a bit "fancy" or formal for the situation: for example, "gladdened multitude" (l. 17) or "spheroid" (l. 39). Find two more such examples and discuss how they contribute to the humor of the poem.

2. It can be fun to dramatize this poem. The characters are Casey, Blake, Flynn, a catcher, a pitcher, an umpire, and the fans. One of the most expressive readers in the class should narrate the poem, while the cast goes through the action. Any speeches are said by the characters themselves at the appropriate points. Then the narrator picks up the thread of the story.

Molly Means

In this poem the dialect of the storyteller is that

of the people about whom the story is told. This makes the narrative seem as natural as if the poet were speaking directly to the reader.

1. Describe Molly Means. What unnatural powers did she have?

2. What did she do to the "young gal-bride"? What did the husband then do?

3. Do you think the man got his wife back? Explain.

At Woodward's Gardens

1. The poet lets us know how he feels about this incident in the first line of the poem. He says that the boy was "presuming on his intellect." (Look up this meaning of *presume* in the dictionary.) Does this mean that the poet really thought the boy was very bright? What attitude is suggested in line 7 when the poet refers to the lens as a *weapon?*

2. What level of intelligence does the poet assign to the monkeys? What lines show this?

3. There is strong satire in lines 18 and 19. Explain.

4. Explain the last line of the poem. Who really knew "what to do" with the burning-glass? The monkeys or the boy?

5. Discuss the implications of the poet's statement: "It's knowing what to do with things that counts" (l. 37).

warty bliggens, the toad

This is a tale told with a purpose. The punch line, of course, comes in the last stanza.

1. What is warty bliggens' philosophy?

2. Do most people share this philosophy, whether they admit it or not?

3. What *is* the challenge in reading this poem aloud?

4. Why is this poem a good example of personification?

A SUMMING UP
The Poet Tells a Story

The poems in this group do more than tell a story. Each one depends upon the use of imagery and upon the expression of emotions. Explain how this is done in each poem.

Moreover, each story-poem expresses an idea or a theme, as well. Identify the poems which contain any of these main ideas.

1. Overconfidence may bring disaster.

2. Though tragedy strikes some down, the challenge of life for youth remains.

3. People are naturally egotistical.

SUMMING UP
The Ways of a Poet

Poetry, like all forms of art, is a shared experience. Through our involvement with the poet's experience we learn new ways of using our senses.

The ways of the poet are not easy. In order to see truthfully, he must recognize truth and be able to let us see it through his eyes. To do this he must be a most acute observer of life. The poet must incorporate his observations in such vivid imagery that we experience a shock of surprise when we recognize the familiar and the believable in what the poet has written.

Consider and discuss these quotations and statements about poetry.

1. The impact of good poetry does not come from the subject of the poem; it comes from the style and metaphor.

2. Robert Frost said that a poem "begins in delight and ends in wisdom."

3. A poem that expresses strong feeling is quite personal.

4. Simply because a poet writes in the first person, we should not conclude that his poem is autobiographical.

5. An old poem is probably better than a new one.

6. "All slang is metaphor, and all metaphor is poetry"—Chesterton.

7. "All poets are mad"—Burton.

8. "Poetry is certainly something more than good sense, but it must be good sense at all events; just as a palace is more than a house, but it must be a house at least"—Coleridge.

Words

A. In several other sections on words, you learned that there are various processes by which new words are formed. In addition to those you learned about before, there is the combining of words to make self-explaining compounds. *Tight-rope* (in "The Base Stealer"), *headline* (in "Soup"), and *homeland* (in "The Story of Daedalus and Icarus") are good examples of compound words that explain themselves. This kind of compound word must be distinguished from an idiomatic compound, which is not self-explanatory. The words *egghead* and *Molotov cocktail* do not explain themselves, for an egghead has nothing to do with an egg, and a Molotov cocktail is not something to drink. Today, self-explaining compounds make up about 8 per cent of all new word-formations in our language. Some further examples of these compounds are *atomic bomb, appointment book, supermarket, jack-in-the-box, sharpshooter,* and *ingroup.* What compounds can you add to this list?

B. As you may remember, one way of creating new words is by adding suffixes to existing words or roots. Four common verb suffixes are *-en, -ate, -ize,* and *-fy.* Adding these endings to the words *quick, pulse,* and *sense,* all of which appear in "The Swimmers," you get *quicken* and *pulsate* (with the necessary adjustment in spelling). Let's consider some of the meanings for each of the above verb suffixes:

-en   "to cause to be" (*sharpen*); "to cause to have" (*lengthen*); "to come to be" (*steepen*); "to come to have" (*broaden*)

-ate   "act on" (*assassinate*); "cause to become" (*activate*); "furnish with" (*capacitate*)

-ize   "to cause to be" (*regularize*); "to become" (*materialize*); "treat like" (*idolize*)

-fy "to make" (*clarify*); "make similar to" (*citify*)

Suffixes like these are called derivational because they change the part of speech of the word to which they are attached. When they are attached to roots they also determine the part of speech of the new words. Which of the above four verb suffixes may be added to each of these words: *humid, satire, capital, deep, legal, specific, social, liquid, internal,* and *height*? (Note that some spelling adjustment will be necessary in some cases.)

BIOGRAPHICAL NOTES

Charles Malam

Charles Malam (1906–   ) is an American poet whose verses, like "Steam Shovel," often treat everyday objects and happenings with a light, whimsical touch.

Ogden Nash

Ogden Nash (1912–1971), whose hundreds of rib-tickling rhymes have appeared in many magazines and have been collected in several books, was considered the leading American writer of humorous verse. Born in Rye, New York, Nash attended Harvard, then worked in a publishing firm before devoting full time to writing, lecturing, and giving readings.

Gordon Parks

Gordon Parks (1912–   ) was born in Fort Scott, Kansas. Recognized as one of the most creative photographic journalists in the United States, this black writer is a man of many talents. He plays piano well, has composed symphonies that have been performed in the United States and abroad, and has written, produced, and directed motion pictures. Among his books are the novel *The Learning Tree* and an autobiography, *A Choice of Weapons.* His book, *A Poet and His Camera* combines many of Parks's world famous color photographs with his poetry.

Richard Wright

Richard Wright (1908–1960) was born on a farm near Natchez, Mississippi and was taken to Memphis, Tennessee in his early youth. After his father deserted his family, his partially paralyzed mother was forced to put Wright first in an orphanage and later to send him to live with various relatives. At the age of nineteen, in 1927, he went to Chicago where he worked as a street cleaner, dishwasher, post-office clerk, porter, and at other odd jobs. During this period he was writing in fictional form about his childhood in the South and his experiences in Chicago. In 1937, Wright joined the Federal Writer's Project, and his first book of four novellas, *Uncle Tom's Children,* was published in 1938. His novel *Native Son,* published in 1940, was to make him world famous. Wright lived in Paris from 1947 until his death.

May Swenson

May Swenson (1919–   ) was born in Utah and attended Utah State University. After graduation she went to New York to write. Her poetry, which is widely read, has been praised especially for its sharp images, or pictures. In addition to her talent for seeing and recording fresh, stimulating imagery, she has a way of making her verses interesting to the reader. One of her popular collections of poetry is *To Mix With Time.*

T. S. Eliot

T. S. (Thomas Stearns) Eliot (1888–1965) was born in St. Louis, Missouri. Educated at Harvard, the Sorbonne, and Oxford, Eliot settled in England in 1915 and became a British subject. Over the years he won wide acclaim for his poetry, verse plays, and literary criticism. This American-English poet made several visits to the United States to give lectures and to teach in American universities. In 1948 he was awarded the Nobel Prize for Literature.

Reed Whittemore

Reed Whittemore (1919–   ) was born in New Haven, Connecticut. A graduate of Yale University, he has written several books and published widely in magazines. Among his books are *Self-Made Man, Boy from Iowa,* and *From Zero to Absolute.* Much of the subject matter for his poetry is drawn from everyday sights, sounds, and happenings. He is currently a teacher at the University of Maryland.

William Carlos Williams

William Carlos Williams (1883–1963) was born in New Jersey where he grew up and practiced medicine. His poems and stories are popular in the United States and around the English speaking world. For his writings Dr. Williams drew from the everyday, the commonplace. Although at first reading his verses seem to be simple statements, they generally yield a deeper meaning when examined carefully.

Rebecca McCann

Rebecca McCann is an American artist and poet whose short, humorous verses are intended to make people laugh at their own foolish thoughts and actions.

Lawrence Emerson Nelson

Lawrence Emerson Nelson (1893–   ), born in Clinton, Missouri, has written several books of verse and contributed to numerous newspapers and magazines.

Phyllis McGinley

Phyllis McGinley (1905–   ) was born in Ontario, Oregon and grew up in Colorado and Utah. Now a wife and mother living in Larchmont, New York, Mrs. McGinley recalls that she and her brother once attended a rural Colorado school where they were the only pupils. A writer of light verse and stories for children, she writes about day-to-day happenings with such penetrating insight that these events become more than the routine most people think they are. She was awarded the Pulitzer Prize for poetry in 1961.

Joseph Seamon Cotter, Jr.

Joseph Seamon Cotter, Jr. (1895–1919) was born in Louisville, Kentucky. He attended Fisk University but developed tuberculosis in his eighteenth year and was forced to leave school. His poetry, most of which he wrote during the last six years of his illness, is ranked among the best by black poets in the period during World War I.

Carl Sandburg

Carl Sandburg (1878–1967), "poet of the people," was born in Galesburg, Illinois. After "riding the rails" as a hobo and trying his hand at a variety of odd jobs—newspaper reporter, advertising writer, farmhand, and foreign correspondent—Sandburg first tasted fame in 1916 with the publication of *Chicago Poems.* He was known as the "voice of the common man," writing in the vernacular and frequently using both contemporary slang and colloquialisms. Winner of two Pulitzer Prizes, Sandburg is famed for his voluminous and popular biography of Abraham Lincoln.

Robert Frost

Robert Frost (1874–1963) was born in San Francisco. When he was ten years old his father died, and the family moved to Lawrence, Massachusetts, the home of several generations of his family. After attending Dartmouth College for a short time, Frost left to work at a variety of jobs—mill hand, school teacher, and farmer. Following his marriage, he entered Harvard University, but left after two years to become a farmer in New Hampshire. When he failed in this, he took his family to England and devoted three years to writing. His first two books of poetry, *A Boy's Will* and *North of Boston*, were immediately successful; and he returned to the United States.

In New England he continued to write volume after volume of fine poetry, in addition to giving lectures, teaching in various colleges and universities, and farming. Four times Frost was awarded the Pulitzer Prize for poetry and long before his death was regarded as one of the world's foremost modern poets. While most of his verses have a New England setting, Frost was not concerned mainly with this particular section of the country. His basic concern was the drama of people engaged in everyday affairs.

At the ceremony following the inauguration of President John F. Kennedy in January, 1961, Frost became the first poet ever honored on such an occasion by being invited to read one of his poems.

Robert Francis

Robert Francis (1901–   ), poet, lecturer, and teacher, was born in Upland, Pennsylvania. A graduate of Harvard University, he was the Harvard Phi Beta Kappa poet in 1960. His chief interests are writing, reading, music, and gardening.

Karle Wilson Baker

Karle Wilson Baker (1878–   ), poet, short story writer, novelist, and essayist, was born in Little Rock, Arkansas. She attended the University of Chicago. A college professor, Miss Baker was awarded the Southern Prize by the Poetry Society of South Carolina in 1925.

Richard Le Gallienne

Richard Le Gallienne (1866–1947), British poet and essayist, was born in Liverpool, England. He was educated at Liverpool College and then went to work for an accounting firm. In 1891 he became literary critic of the *London Star*. He moved to America in 1898.

Raymond Souster

Raymond Souster (1921–   ) was born in Toronto, Ontario, Canada. He has written several books of poetry and published verse in magazines. One of his latest books is *The Way It Looks From Here*. He has an interest in animals, and one of his hobbies is collecting animal postage stamps.

María Núñez

María Núñez, originally from Almuñécar, Granada, Spain, is now a Canadian citizen and lives in Toronto. Her poetry has been published in magazines in Spain and Argentina. Only recently she began writing poems in English.

Bonaro W. Overstreet

Bonaro W. Overstreet (1902–   ), American poet, teacher, and lecturer, was born in Geyserville, California. Mrs. Overstreet, in addition to her own writing, lecturing, and teaching, has also collaborated with her husband, Harry Allen Overstreet, on many books.

William Ernest Henley

William Ernest Henley (1849–1903), British poet, playwright, and essayist, was born in Gloucester, England. As a youth he contracted tuberculosis, and throughout his lifetime he was plagued by ill health. A friend of Robert Louis Stevenson, he was the supposed model for Long John Silver in Stevenson's *Treasure Island*.

Ovid

Ovid (43 B.C.–A.D. 17), Roman poet, was born in Sulmona, Italy. After training for a legal career, Ovid abandoned law and politics and turned to the literary life. Although a great favorite in Augustan Age society, Ovid was suddenly banished by Augustus to Tomi, a town on the Black Sea. He spent the rest of his life in exile.

Rolfe Humphries

Rolfe Humphries (1894–   ), American educator, translator, and poet, was born in Philadephia.

A graduate of Stanford University, Mr. Humphries has won numerous writing awards, including the Guggenheim creative writing fellowship. His books of verse include *The Wind of Time* and *Out of the Jewel*.

Louis Untermeyer

Louis Untermeyer (1885–   ), American poet, was born in New York. After leaving school at fifteen, he went to work for his father, who was a jewelry manufacturer. In 1923, he left the world of business to become a writer, lecturer, and poet.

Robert Nathan

Robert Nathan (1894–   ) is primarily an American novelist. He was educated in Switzerland and at Phillips Exeter Academy and Harvard. Except for two brief periods when he was a member of a New York advertising firm and in 1924–1925 when he taught at New York University's School of Journalism, he has devoted himself entirely to writing. In 1933 his novel of the depression, *One More Spring*, was nearly a best seller. Nathan's style is highly individual, delicate, and often dealing in fantasy. *Portrait of Jennie*, 1940, is among his best-known novels. "Dunkirk" is an example of his poetry, and his feeling for this medium often comes through in his prose.

Stephen Vincent Benét

Stephen Vincent Benét (1898–1943), poet, short story writer, and playwright, was born in Bethlehem, Pennsylvania. He received both his B.A. and his M.A. from Yale University and did further graduate work at the Sorbonne, where he met his wife, who was a staff member of the *Chicago Tribune*, Paris edition. His epic poem, *John Brown's Body*, was awarded a Pulitzer Prize.

Ernest Lawrence Thayer

Ernest Lawrence Thayer (1863–1940), ballad writer and journalist, was born in Lawrence, Massachusetts. After graduating from Harvard University, where he edited the school paper, he worked for a number of newspapers.

Margaret Walker

Margaret Walker (1915–   ) was born in Birmingham, Alabama. The daughter of a Methodist minister, she was educated in public schools in Alabama, Mississippi, and Louisiana and earned degrees from Northwestern University and Iowa State University. Her first book of poetry, *For My People*, was the result of her winning the Yale University Younger Poets competition. Her long novel of slavery and the Civil War, *Jubilee*, was published in 1966. She is regarded as one of the most talented black American writers.

Don Marquis

Don Marquis (1878–1937) worked at a variety of jobs before he became a successful journalist and humorist. His best-known book is *archie and mehitabel*, a satire on life in the 1920s as seen through the eyes of archie, a cockroach, and mehitabel, an alley cat. This work is still widely read and quoted. In addition to humor, Marquis wrote serious plays, novels, and poetry. He once said that it would be ironic if he should be remembered longest for creating the character of archie, but today his name is most often recalled as the inventor of that philosophical little insect.

IDENTITY

My Beard

IS IT STRANGE IS IT FRIGHTENING TO SEE
DOES IT DERANGE OR BRING CHANGE
TO YOUR RULES OF CONFORMITY?

Why do you frown at my beard—
An item so dear to me?
Does it bring to mind
That I'm trying to find
A thing you may never see—
A thing from the past
To which I hold fast
Known as identity?

JIMMIE SHERMAN

detail from "The Wall of Respect"
Mike Maumey

*Each face depicted in this wall painting
reveals the identity and emotions of
these people.*

I am different. I am also very much like other people. Whether I am young or very old, I still feel the need for a separate identity, to be recognized as an individual or person, a need to let other persons know who I am.

The people in the following pages establish their identities through a variety of means, ranging from wearing a snappy uniform to kicking over a bucket of apricots. As the inner feelings of these individuals are revealed, each of us may understand a little more clearly why he feels hurt if someone he knows passes him in the hall without speaking, or if he is overworked when nominations are being made for student council, or if someone he'd like for a friend snubs him instead of smiling at him.

Our feelings are just as complex as the many parts that go into our physical make-up. One feeling that is always with all of us is that of wanting to be recognized as a person who is in some way different from others.

Are clothes very important to a person? Does it make much difference how he looks? When you find out what a handsome policeman's uniform did for Tango, you may have an answer to the above questions!

Clothes Make the Man

HENRI DUVERNOIS

I don't like it," Tango complained again. "I won't feel right, walking up and down in that."

"Shut up and put it on," Mireault[1] told him, and so, of course, Tango obeyed. Mireault was half the size but he was clever. If they had given Tango a tail, he would have put it between his legs when Mireault spoke.

"Now, see?" Mireault said. "What did I tell you? Looks good, doesn't it? See, you've even got a whistle."

"Not bad," Tango had to admit, surveying himself in the mirror. He pushed out his mighty chest and threw back his broad shoulders. Even the Eel, the quick silent one who was Mireault's working partner and who rarely opened his mouth, was stirred to speech. "Boy, ain't he handsome!" he said.

No doubt about it, Tango made a noble sight. The policeman's uniform might have been cut to his measure by the best tailor in Paris. His little eyes looked brighter beneath the visor of the jaunty cap; they almost looked intelligent.

"Stop gawking at yourself and wipe that dumb grin off your face," Mireault said impatiently, "and listen. This is so simple a half-wit could do it, so maybe if you try hard you can too."

With regret Tango turned away from the mirror. His broad forehead wrinkled in the painful expression that meant he was concentrating.

"All you do is walk up and down the street," Mireault said. "Easy and slow, like a real cop on his beat. Then if anyone hears us working in the house they won't get suspicious, seeing you. Keep walking until we come out, then hang around a few minutes covering us. That's all there is to it. We'll meet back here. Now you understand?"

"Sure," Tango said, his eyes straying to the mirror.

"Then get going!" Mireault snapped.

Tango was a little nervous walking to the street Mireault and the Eel had picked out, but nothing happened. It was a prosperous section, and in the dim glow of the shaded corner light Tango could see what handsome houses they were—sober, solid, well cared for. The house where the job was to be pulled was in the middle of the block, behind a garden wall. Mireault and the Eel had cased it thoroughly; there was a tin-can wall safe upstairs with a very comfortable load inside. Apparently the old-fashioned family didn't believe in banks. Maybe they would, Mireault had said, after tonight.

Tango wondered what it would be like to live in so fine a house, but the effort of imagination was beyond him. He had seldom ever seen a street such as this one. He worked in the shabby quarters of Paris—a little purse-snatching, a little shoplifting; he even panhandled. Yes, he was good at panhandling. Timid businessmen usually came right across when Tango's huge shoulders towered over them; they looked fearfully at the massive hands and dug for whatever change they had.

He sauntered down the pavement, turned at the corner and came back. Halfway, he saw the two shadowy figures slip over the garden wall and disappear. Mireault and the Eel were at work.

Tango fell to thinking of how he had looked

---

1. **Mireault**\mēr ⁺ō\

in the mirror. With the impressive image vivid in his mind, he straightened his shoulders and threw out his chest again. Standing erect, he tried a salute. It felt good. He grinned, oddly pleased, and walked on.

It was while he was turning at the other corner that he saw the police lieutenant.

Such a sight was usually enough to send him traveling as rapidly as his feet would move. He stared in horror. He fancied that the lieutenant, approaching, was gazing at him curiously. Tango's body was rigid; his palms were sweating. With a tremendous effort he restrained the wild impulse to plunge away. He shuddered. Then, stiffly, with the lieutenant no more than a few feet from him, he raised his arm and saluted.

The lieutenant casually acknowledged the salute and passed by.

Tango stood peering after him. After a moment, he felt a peculiar gratification. "Say!" he said to himself. "Say, you see that? I salute,

and he salutes right back. Say, that—that's pretty fine!"

It was extraordinary, the pleasure it gave him. He almost wanted to run up to the lieutenant and salute again. He threw back his shoulders straighter than ever and, erect and proud, walked down the pavement. At the corner he paused and rocked on his heels a moment as all policemen do.

"I guess I looked good to him," he told himself. "I guess he don't see many cops looking so good."

After a few more trips, he found an old lady hesitating on the corner. He saw her make two or three false starts to get across and each time nervously come back.

Tango did not even notice the plump-looking purse in her hand. He poised in front of her, saluted, and offered his arm. She looked at him with a sweet smile. "Oh, thank you, officer!" she said.

There was no traffic visible, but Tango held

up his other arm majestically, as if halting a horde of roaring trucks. With infinite dignity they crossed to the other side. It was a pretty picture indeed.

"Thank you so much, officer!" she said.

"Please madam," Tango said, "don't mention it." He paused. "That's what we're here for, you know," he added. And, gallantly, he saluted again.

He stood proudly watching her retreating figure. Before she had quite disappeared, she glanced back to regard him with another smile. Tango stood so straight the cloth strained across his chest. With a flourish, he saluted once more.

He went down the block, saluting at intervals. An indefinable emotion was stirring in him. In all Paris there could have been no more perfect an example of the calm, strong, resourceful guardian of law and order.

A disheveled figure came weaving toward him out of the shadows. It was a man, waving his arms aggressively, shuffling his feet and muttering savage but unintelligible epithets.[2] His glazed eyes fell upon Tango and he scowled. "Yea!" he cried. "Lousy cop!"

A deep sense of shock ran through Tango. "Here! Here!" he said. "Get along, get along."

"Big cowardly cop!" the drunk yelled. "Big bag of wind in a uniform! Beat up the little fellow and let the big crooks go! Thass all y' good for—beat up the little fellows an'—"

A mingled emotion of outrage and anger grew in Tango. A flush rose to his face.

"I spit on you!" the drunk declared scornfully. "Bah! There!" And he suited the action to the words.

Something popped in Tango's head. His face was purple. He seized the other with one mighty hand, shook him ferociously, and, without any clear idea of what he was going to do with him, dragged him off down the street.

Overawed, shaken out of his wits, the drunk was now passive and silent. But Tango was beside himself, and when, halfway down the block, two figures came skimming over the garden wall and landed on the pavement near him, he was in no mood to stop.

"You fool, what are you doing?" Mireault said in a furious whisper. "You want to ruin the whole job? Let go of him, Blockhead!" And he struck Tango across the cheek.

Indescribable emotions swirled in Tango's head. He remembered the lieutenant answering his salute; he remembered the old lady's look of gratitude and admiration; he remembered the splendid figure of himself in the mirror. And he remembered what the drunk had said.

He arose to the full pitch of a mighty fury. While Mireault and the Eel stared at him in sheer paralyzed horror, he stuffed the shiny whistle in his mouth and blew a salvo[3] of blasts loud and long enough to bring all the police in Paris.

"Crooks, robbers!" he bellowed. "I arrest you! I arrest you in the name of the law!"

I
A MAN TRANSFORMED

Mireault and the Eel give Tango the job of lookout to make sure they are uninterrupted in their burglary attempt.

1. Why doesn't Tango arouse suspicion as he paces back and forth on the street in front of the house?

2. Describe Tango's meeting with the police lieutenant.

3. How does he help the old lady?

4. Why does he become furious with the drunk?

5. How does the story end? What do you suppose happened after this?

II
IMPLICATIONS

1. Fine clothing makes fine persons.

---

2. **epithets**\ˈĕp·ĭ 'thĕts\ uncomplimentary names.
3. **salvo**\ˈsăl·vō\ a series, here, a round of whistle blasts.

2. A weak-minded person is most easily led.

3. All persons wish to feel important.

III

TECHNIQUES

Style

Henri Duvernois' writing style is lively and vivid. His choice of words is especially colorful and expressive. For example, in paragraph four, Tango is described as *"surveying* himself in the mirror." This gives the impression of his turning this way and that to inspect himself in great detail. A less vivid word choice would have been *"looking* at himself in the mirror."

1. In paragraph six, find a similar example of a more expressive word being used in a place where "looking" might have been used.

2. The following lines from the story all exemplify Duvernois' choice of expressive words where commonplace ones would have served. List the word he uses and give the more ordinary synonym for each:

    a. ". . . he saw the two shadowy figures _____ over the garden wall. . . ."

    b. "He _____ down the pavement. . . ."

    c. "He _____ in front of her, saluted. . . ."

    d. "A disheveled figure came _____ toward him. . . ."

    e. ". . . two figures came _____ over the garden wall. . . ."

Giving Insight

Although the story is lightly and humorously told, Tango is actually a pathetic figure, considered almost a half-wit by his accomplices. This is, no doubt, one reason why the reader enjoys the way the story ends. There is the feeling that the crooks, who are simply using poor Tango, have managed to outsmart themselves.

1. Find three statements in the first twelve paragraphs of the story with which the author gives insight concerning Tango's lack of intelligence.

2. How does Tango feel when the lieutenant returns his salute?

3. What feelings swirl through Tango's head after Mireault strikes him? Why is Tango's blowing his whistle consistent with the insight about his character that has been given?

IV

WORDS

Read the following sentences from "Clothes Make the Man," focusing your attention on the *italicized* words:

" 'I don't like it,' Tango *complained*. . . ."

" 'Then get going!' Mireault *snapped*."

" 'Big cowardly cop!' the drunk *yelled*."

The words *complained, snapped,* and *yelled* serve the same purpose as the more general word *said,* but they are more specific and more vivid. They convey the attitude or the tone of the speaker; in other words, they tell in what manner he is speaking. The speaker's state of mind may also be expressed by *said* coupled with a modifier, as in this example:

"Stop gawking at yourself and wipe that dumb grin off your face," Mireault *said impatiently*. . . ."

Yet, a single word like *snapped* is more forceful than *said impatiently;* it is also more economical. In each of the following sentences, *said* is used with an *ly* modifier. In each sentence, substitute a single vivid word for the two *italicized* ones.

1. "Please don't go now," she *said pleadingly*.

2. "I will not compromise!" she *said angrily*.

3. *Bitterly,* he *said,* "And to think that I trusted you."

4. "We must prepare ourselves," he *said urgently*.

5. "Our team has won!" Ralph *said happily*.

TECHNIQUES

Style

One of the most interesting things to look for in a piece of writing is the author's style. Actually most of the elements that have already been discussed in this section are parts of style. The author's word choice—simple and direct or unusual and complicated—his imagery and the things he selects for description, the arrangement of the sentences, and the spirit or outlook of the author himself as it is expressed in his writings all figure in a careful study of a writer's style.

To understand the nature of a writing style it is best to examine the writing of two authors whose styles are in strong contrast to each other. For illustration, read a page of Sir Arthur Conan Doyle's "The Red-Headed League" in CALL TO ADVENTURE where the scholarly, word-loving, observant master sleuth is analyzing a problem for his mystified friend, Dr. Watson. List the unfamiliar words, notice the careful description, sense the haughty attitude of detective Holmes. Now read several of the opening paragraphs of "Thank You M'am" by Langston Hughes in WITH WHAT YOU HAVE. Are there any words that are not familiar? What sort of things are described? What is the attitude of the characters toward each other?

Both of these authors, Doyle and Hughes, have highly individual styles. One is elaborate, the other very simple. Both writing styles are good in that they create a particular effect for the reader. He is conscious of a consistent style without even analyzing it.

The use of words that are exactly right is of great importance in setting forth an idea, arousing emotions, or creating images. Word choice varies according to the effect the writer wants to achieve. Look at the sentence "He hung up his clothes" and substitute a word—apparel, rags, raiment, duds, garments, weeds—for the word clothes. Note how the use of a word that is formal or informal, slangy or humorous can change the effect. Each may be appropriate in a particular situation.

Giving Insight

Insight may be defined as "seeing into inner character or underlying truth." Each of the selections in this anthology was chosen to give the reader insights into life. However, the selections in IDENTITY deal particularly with the inner self, the way a person sees himself, his wish for recognition as an individual. For this reason, in TECHNIQUES, attention will be drawn to the ways the authors give insight into or reveal basic truths about character.

For example, in the story you have just read, Tango was a fellow who had come to accept the idea that he didn't amount to much. The author establishes this very early by his statement, "If they had given Tango a tail, he would have put it between his legs when Mireault spoke." A dog who tucks his tail between his legs is one who is timid, one who is afraid. Through the use of imaginative language, the author very quickly gives an idea of Tango's feelings about himself.

As is true with an author's style, the way an author gives insight is not confined to the use of one specific literary technique. Rather, an author employs many techniques. Observing how the various writers reveal character will serve to re-emphasize many of the literary considerations discussed earlier in the text.

"'They'll never know
you been here,' Alf said."
Why should that have
made such a difference to Jamie?

The Way Up

WILLIAM HOFFMAN

Sitting in the back row of English literature class, Jamie looked through an open window toward a rounded silver water tower which poked up through the woods like a great metal tulip. The tower had recently been painted and appeared immaculate in the spring sunlight. Tubular steel legs were hidden at the bottom by newly greening oaks, sycamores, and poplars that bordered the rear grounds of the suburban Richmond High School.

Jamie had made no brag. He had not even spoken the evening he was at Jawbone's house, loafing in the basement playroom with the others.

"Look at Jamie's," Jawbone said. Jawbone was a dark, wiry boy of eighteen who had a jutting chin. He wanted to go to West Point. He stuck a finger on Jamie's picture in the new yearbook. Under the names of the others were accomplishments—teams, organizations, trophies.

"Not even the Glee Club," Nick said, lying on a sofa, his legs hanging over the arm rest at one end. He was a blond Italian whose father owned a fancy restaurant downtown.

"They'll never know you been here," Alf said. Alf, the top student, was a heavyset, shaggy boy who'd won his letter in baseball.

More sensitive than the rest, he was immediately sorry. He reached across a chair to punch Jamie's arm. Jamie dodged and smiled, though smiling was like cracking rock.

They meant the remarks goodnaturedly. Still, the words made him see what his relationship to them was. He had gone through four years of high school without leaving a mark. He had ridden with them daily, shared their secrets, and eaten in their homes. They considered him a friend. But they expected nothing from him.

At first he was resentful and hurt, as if betrayed. Next he had fantasies of heroic derring-do on the basketball court or baseball diamond —because of his smallness he didn't dream of football glory any longer. After the fantasies, he tried to think of projects. Finally he came up with a plan.

He had spent a lot of time working out details. He was now merely waiting for the right day—or rather night. Recently there had been rain and blustering weather. Even when the sun shone, the wind gusted. This afternoon, however, as he sat in English literature class, Jamie saw that the treetops barely quivered.

His eyes kept returning to the silver water tower. Other students had attempted the climb. A few inventive ones had gone up as far as the catwalk around the fat belly of the tank, where they had painted skulls and crossbones. A sophomore had lost his nerve halfway and got stuck. The Richmond rescue squad had coaxed him down like a kitten from a light pole. The boy had been so ashamed he had tried to join the Army. Nobody had ever made it to the stubby spike on the crown.

Mr. Tharpe, the principal, understood the tower's temptation and had ordered the ladder above the catwalk taken off. He had also directed that the ladder up the leg be cut high above the ground. Lastly, he had made climbing the tower punishable by expulsion.

The toughest problem was getting from the catwalk to the crown. As the tank served only the school, it wasn't large, but without a ladder the rounded sides appeared unscalable.

Jamie concluded that he needed a light hook which could be thrown fifteen to twenty feet.

He found what he wanted in a Richmond boating store—a small, three-pronged, aluminum anchor. Along with the anchor he bought fifty feet of braided nylon line that had a thousand-pound test strength. He also purchased a hacksaw. The clerk packed the things in a strong cardboard box, and as soon as Jamie reached home he hid them in the back of his closet.

He assembled other equipment as well—tennis shoes, a pair of light cotton gloves, a sweat suit which would keep him warm in the night air, yet allow him to move freely, a billed cap, a small flashlight with a holding ring, and a sheath knife to fasten to his leather belt.

Twice he scheduled attempts on the tower. The first night a thunderstorm washed him out. The second, the moon was too bright, increasing the risk that he would be seen.

Delay made him uneasy. He felt that if he didn't go soon, he might lose his nerve. He had been nursing his courage, but it was leaching out in the daily wear of waiting. He had too much opportunity to second-guess himself and find reasons not to carry out his plan.

The bell rang. He went to his locker and then left the building quickly. He wanted to get away without the others seeing him, but Alf called his name. Alf ran down the sidewalk. He adjusted his glasses.

"Want to shoot baskets?" he asked, making an imaginary hook shot. He held up two fingers to indicate a score.

"No, thanks," Jamie answered, moving on.

"You're getting pretty exclusive lately," Alf said.

"I've always been exclusive," Jamie told him, hoping it sounded like a joke.

He spent the afternoon working around the house. He cut the grass and spread some of the lawn fertilizer his father had stored in the garage. When he had a chance, he went up to his room and again checked his equipment.

The check was just nervousness. He knew his equipment was right.

After dinner, as he was sure they would, his parents went next door to play cards. He and his brother David were left in the house. David was a year younger, although already heavier than Jamie. He had been asked to come out for football and liked to flex his muscles before a mirror.

Jamie sat at his desk and pretended to study so he wouldn't be questioned. He listened to sound of the night coming through the open window. There was some wind, but not enough to worry him. The sky was cloudy.

When David went down to the kitchen for a sandwich, Jamie undressed, put on the sweat suit, and pulled pajamas over it. He kept his socks on. He slipped his belt through slots in the leather sheath of the knife and buckled it around his waist. Hearing David approach, Jamie got into bed.

"You sick?" David asked, surprised.

"Just sleepy."

"You look kind of queasy."

"I'm okay."

David watched TV and did his exercises before coming to bed. Jamie listened, as he had for weeks, to the pattern of his brother's breathing. In practice, Jamie had got up several times and moved around the dark room. Once David had waked. Jamie had explained he was after another blanket.

David breathed softly. When he was completely asleep, his mouth opened and he wheezed slightly. Jamie heard the wheezing now. Still he did not move, although he wanted badly to start. He lay on his back, eyes open, waiting for his parents.

They returned at eleven. He heard them in the kitchen. Finally his mother came to his and David's room. Jamie smelled her perfume. She bent over them, lightly adjusting the covers. He kept his eyes shut until she went out.

As soon as she was gone, he swung his legs out of bed. He stood, listening, but David's breathing did not change. Jamie walked to the closet, slipped off his pajamas, and sat on the floor to pull on his tennis shoes. He tied the laces in double knots.

He put on his baseball cap and fastened the large, red bandanna around his neck. The bandanna, too, was part of his plan. He had bought it in a Richmond ten-cent store. For some time he had been carrying it to school and whipping it out to be seen by Jawbone, Nick, and Alf. Though no name was on it, people would identify it as his—the right people, anyway.

Lastly he worked his fingers into the cotton gloves, gathered the hacksaw and aluminum anchor, and tiptoed to the window. It was already half raised. Earlier in the week he'd rubbed soap along the metal tracks to prevent squeaking.

The window slid up noiselessly. He unsnapped the screen and lifted it out. David turned in his bed but did not wake. Jamie climbed onto the window ledge, lowered his equipment to the ground, and stepped down to the grass of the back yard. He stood still and listened. David did not stir. Jamie replaced the screen without hooking it and picked up his equipment.

Crouching, he ran—not fast enough to wear himself out, but with the easy lope of a distance runner. He carried the anchor in his right hand, the saw in his left. The damp grass of neighboring yards brushed his feet softly. He stayed in the shadows.

On reaching the high school, he cut behind the main building and headed toward the athletic field. When he was almost to the other side, a dog snarled close behind him. He was afraid that if he continued running, the dog might jump him. He turned and ducked behind a pile of canvas tackling-dummies.

The dog leaped out of the dark, its hair bristling, its teeth bared. Jamie talked softly, holding his hands at his sides so as not to excite the boxer. The animal circled, sniffed, and growled.

"King!" a voice from the field house called.

It was Carver, the watchman—an erect, dark figure outlined against a door. "Here, boy!"

The dog sprang off toward the field house. Jamie pressed against the ground. Carver leaned over to pat the boxer.

"What's out there?" he asked, turning on his long flashlight. The light brushed across the dummies. Jamie held his breath. Carver talked to the dog. Finally the flashlight went out, and Carver entered the field house. The door slammed.

Jamie pushed up and sprinted. He wanted to be well away in case the boxer was still loose. His arms pumped. By the time he reached the woods, he was winded. There was no use even starting up the tower unless he was fresh. He rested against a tree.

When his breath steadied, he walked on through the woods. He didn't need his flashlight. Clouds had slid away from a sickle moon, which laid a pale sheen on his path. He stopped once to be certain nobody was following.

He walked out of the woods to the tower and under it. Though the tank wasn't large, it was high and seemed to float like a balloon. The silver skin shone eerily. The steel legs were like those of a giant insect poised over him. He touched the steel and kicked a cement footing to rid himself of the sensation. The tank was simply a water tower which could be climbed.

He didn't hurry. Hurrying might tire him. Methodically he unwound the line from the anchor. He looped the saw onto his belt. He adjusted his cap. Standing away from a leg of the tower, he swung the anchor around his head like a lasso and let fly at the ladder.

The hooks missed by inches. The light anchor clanged against tubular steel, which reverberated like a gong. The sound was loud —loud enough, perhaps, to alert the watchman or the family who lived in a board-and-batten house nearby. Quickly Jamie picked up the anchor, swung it, and threw. A prong clattered over a rung.

He had practiced rope climbing. Two or three afternoons a week he had pulled himself to the I-beam at the top of the gym where ropes were attached to swivels. He had learned to go up without using his legs. Basketball players had stood around to watch, impressed that anybody so slight could climb so well.

"You're turning into a regular Atlas," Nick had said.

Jamie had already tied knots every five feet along the nylon line in order to have a better grip on it. He fingered the line and pulled. As he looked up, he felt doubt. The line was thin, the tower great. He jumped before he had time to think further.

Climbing made him feel better. He reached the bottom of the ladder and easily drew himself onto it. He stopped to loosen the anchor. He wrapped the line around the anchor's shank and hooked it over his left shoulder.

He stepped up slowly. He was attempting to pace himself for the distance. He looked neither up nor down. Doing so might cause dizziness. He narrowed his eyes and tried to see no more than his own gloved hands closing over rungs.

After what seemed a long while, he glanced up to get his bearings on the catwalk. He was disappointed at how far it was above him. He estimated that he had come only a quarter of the way. His excitement was giving him a false sense of time.

He kept on. When he again looked up, he had climbed not quite halfway. His breathing was noisy, and he rested. As he clung to the ladder, he thought how easy it would be to go back now. Nobody knew he was here. He could go down and slip into his bed without ever being missed.

He was angry at himself for considering it. His trouble was thinking too much. To block the thoughts, he stepped up, determined to reach the catwalk without stopping again.

He climbed until his arms and legs ached. He sucked at air. He did not raise his eyes lest the distance to the catwalk discourage him. Occasionally a light wind gusted against his face and chest—not hard enough to worry him, but sufficient to slow his step.

His head banged steel. The blow frightened and pained him and he clutched at the ladder. The catwalk door was right over him, its heavy padlock swinging from his having hit it.

He put his right leg through the ladder and hooked the foot over a rung to keep from falling in case he lost his balance. He unbuckled his belt to get the hacksaw. Because of the awkwardness of his position, he had to work slowly. His left hand held the lock, his right the saw.

Cutting was more difficult than he'd anticipated. He had to rest and wipe sweat from his face. When the metal finally snapped, he flung the saw from him. It was a long time hitting the ground.

He threw the padlock down, too, glad he had on gloves in case an investigation checked fingerprints. He raised a hand to the trap door and pushed. The thick iron squeaked but gave only a little. He stepped up another rung in order to hunch his shoulders and the back of his head against it. The door rose, teetered, and fell to the catwalk with a loud clang.

He climbed the rest of the way up the ladder, swung off it to the catwalk, and, holding the railing, closed the trap door. As he straightened to look out over the dark land, he had his first real sense of how high he was. Instinctively, he pressed against the tank. He edged around the catwalk until he faced the school. Lights from houses were faint and twinkling, and he saw the skyline milkiness of Richmond itself.

He grinned, thinking of Alf, Nick, and Jawbone. They wouldn't believe it! They were lying down there, warm in their bunks. He waved a hand over them.

He turned to the tank. He was still a good fifteen feet from the top. As he calculated the distance, a cloud passing over gave him a feeling that the tower was falling. Space shifted under him. He grabbed at the tank.

Leaning against it, he considered tying his bandanna to the railing on the school side. In the morning everybody would see it. Going up this far was certainly a victory, and people would be impressed.

He took off the bandanna and hesitated, fingering it. For tying the bandanna to the railing he might be temporarily honored, but if he was the first to reach the top, he would be remembered for years.

He retied the bandanna around his neck and unwound the nylon line from the anchor. In order to throw to the top of the tank from the proper angle, he had to lean out and flap his arm upward. He forced his thigh hard against the railing. Holding the anchor from him, he threw.

The anchor thumped on top of the rounded tower but slid back when he pulled the line. He jumped to keep from being hit. He stumbled and almost fell. Fear surged in him.

He rested against the tank. When he was calmer, he again threw the anchor. He made half a dozen tries, but each time it came sliding back. He didn't have quite the angle he needed to get the anchor to the crown where the spike was. There was simply no way to do it. He had to tie the bandanna to the railing and climb down.

Another idea nagged him. He shook his head as if he'd been asked. He didn't want to step up onto the railing. He'd be crazy to do it. He could, of course, use part of his line to tie himself. Thus if he slipped, he wouldn't fall far.

He wrapped the nylon line twice around his waist. He knotted the middle section to one of the upright supports of the railing.

Cautiously, like a performer mounting the high wire, he stepped up onto the pipe railing. He rested a hand against the tank so that any fall would be toward the catwalk. His left foot dangled. Though his body wished to bend, he straightened it. He was sweating, and the anchor was wet in his grip. He blinked to clear his eyes, being careful not to turn his head toward where he might look down.

He hefted the anchor, and with a gentle, looping motion arched it over himself. The anchor slid back and struck him in the side of the face. Standing on the railing, he was unable to dodge. His head throbbed and ached. He touched his cheek, and his hand came away bloody.

He pulled the anchor up from the catwalk. This time he didn't throw it directly over him. When he tugged on the line, the anchor came down. He felt weak and sick.

He balanced the anchor, tossed it, and jerked the line. The anchor did not come back. He jumped to the catwalk and pulled. The anchor held.

He couldn't be certain it was caught on the spike. Perhaps a hook tip was in a seam or had snagged a bolt. He hung all his weight on the line, drawing up his feet to do so. Next he untied the line from the railing support. He dried his hands on his sweat suit and wiped his mouth.

With a great effort, he pulled himself up. When he reached the rounded curve of the roof, he worked his hands under the line that his weight stretched tight. Nausea pumped through him as he bruised his knuckles on the steel. Grunting, he made a final thrust of his body and lay flat against the slope.

His heart beat hard. He sweated, yet felt cold in the gusting wind. He raised his head to look at the top of the tower. Two prongs of the anchor had caught the spike.

He crawled up. Because of the slope and his tennis shoes, he could have done it without a line. He lay on his side as he took off the bandanna. He tied the bandanna high on the spike. He tested to make certain the bandanna would not blow loose.

To go down, he merely let his body slide against the steel. He braked himself by gripping the line. His feet jarred against the catwalk. He hated leaving his anchor, but he knew of no way to pull it free. With his knife, he cut the line as high as he could reach. He wound what was left of it around his body and opened the trap door.

As he put a foot on the ladder, a gust of wind caught his cap and blew it off. He snatched for the cap but missed. It fluttered dizzily down and down and down. He couldn't stop looking. The cap seemed to fall forever. He felt the pull of space. He'd tumble the same way if he slipped. He began to shake. He was too weak to climb down that great distance. He backed off.

Fear ballooned in him, and he shook harder. He couldn't stop thinking of the boy who'd gotten stalled halfway up and needed the Richmond rescue squad. The terrible disgrace of it—the sirens, the people gathered around, and the spotlight swinging up. The police would call his parents.

Yet he was unable to force himself to the ladder. The grip was gone from his fingers, and his body was limp. He might climb down a few steps and not be able to hold. He had the sensation of falling, like the cap, of cartwheeling end-over-end to the ground. He lay flat on the catwalk, his face against steel strips. He was shaking so badly that his temple knocked against the metal.

He gave himself up to fear. As if his mouth had a life of its own, yells came out. He couldn't stop the sounds. He shouted for help. He screamed and begged in a rush of terror.

The wind carried his voice away. Even if he was missed at home and searched for, nobody would think of looking on the tower. He'd have to lie on the catwalk all night. He couldn't! With his flashlight he signaled toward the school. There was no response from the watchman. Jamie kept yelling until his voice became faint and hoarse. He wept.

The fright in him was gradually replaced by exhaustion. He lay panting. He felt the heat of shame. He thought of Alf, Nick, and Jawbone seeing him like this. He thought of his parents. Like a person gone blind, he groped for the trap door.

This time he didn't allow himself to look down. Instead he rolled his eyes upward. His fingers measured the position of the hole, and he lowered a trembling foot to a rung. As if decrepit, he shifted his weight onto the ladder.

He went down a step. He was holding the rungs too tightly, and his sweating hands made the steel slippery. He felt the pull of space behind him. His breathing was rapid and shallow. He moved the way a small child would, using the same foot first on each rung.

He closed his eyes. His body functioned with no direction from him. He was a passenger cowering inside.

He rested, hanging his armpits over the ladder and leaning his forehead against the steel. For an instant he was drunkenly comfortable. He wobbled on the ladder, almost letting go. He caught himself and cried out.

Again he started down. In the endlessness of his descent, he didn't believe he would ever get to the bottom. His hands would fail, and he would drop off. He imagined his body curving to the ground.

He stopped on the ladder, not understanding. The fact that his foot swung under him and found no support meant nothing. He believed his tiredness had tricked him. A second time he put out the foot. Like one coming from a cave into sunlight, he opened his eyes and squinted. He saw the dark shapes of trees. He was at the base of the ladder. Lying under the tower was his cap.

Wearily, even calmly now, he untied the line from his waist and knotted it to the bottom rung. He wrapped the line around his wrists. He slid down, but he was too weak to brake himself effectively. The line burned his skin. When he hit the ground, he fell backwards. He lay looking at the silver tower shining above him.

Using one of the tubular steel legs for support, he pulled himself up, staggered, and stooped for his cap. He turned to get his bearings before stumbling into a jogging run. At the trees he wove to a stop and again looked at the tower. He shuddered.

He breathed deeply. Straightening, he entered the dark woods with the step of a man who wouldn't be hurried and walked back toward the house.

I
HE HAD TO LEAVE A MARK

Jamie was determined to do something that would lift him out of obscurity, even if it wouldn't be listed in the school yearbook.

1. What does Jamie plan to do?

2. What measures had the school principal taken to prevent this from happening?

3. What equipment does Jamie assemble?

4. What problem does he have in getting across the athletic field?

5. How had Jamie prepared himself for the rope climbing?

6. What does he have to do to get the anchor to catch in the spike at the top of the tower?

7. When does he lose control of his feelings?

8. How does he feel when he reaches the end of the ladder in his descent?

II
IMPLICATIONS

1. Small size or stature is an excuse for lack of achievement.

2. It is more important to prove to ourselves that we are capable of accomplishing a difficult task than it is to prove it to others.

III
TECHNIQUES

Style

William Hoffman's style throughout "The Way Up" is clear and concise. He makes no attempt at involved imagery and, for the most part, uses words that are common and ordinary. Does he favor simple or more complicated sentence patterns? What do you think this accomplishes, particularly in the very tense moments in the story?

Giving Insight

1. How does the author let the reader know, in paragraph six, that Alf's remark had hit Jamie very hard?

2. What words in the final paragraph of the story lead the reader to believe that Jamie's future may be different because of what he has proved to himself?

In this autobiographical account, Richard Wright said the first test in a new school comes "not in books but in how one's fellows took one. . . ." Would they think you are someone worth knowing?

The Fight

RICHARD WRIGHT

After breakfast, Uncle Clark took me to school, introduced me to the principal. The first half of the school day passed without incident. I sat looking at the strange reading book, following the lessons. The subjects seemed simple, and I felt that I could keep up. My anxiety was still in me; I was wondering how I would get on with the boys. Each new school meant a new area of life to be conquered. Were the boys tough? How hard did they fight? I took it for granted that they fought.

At noon recess I went into the school grounds, and a group of boys sauntered up to me, looked at me from my head to my feet, whispering among themselves. I leaned against a wall, trying to conceal my uneasiness.

"Where you from?" a boy asked abruptly.

"Jackson," I answered.

"How come they make you people so ugly in Jackson?" he demanded.

There was loud laughter.

"You're not any too good-looking yourself," I countered instantly.

"Oh!"

"Aw!"

"You hear what he told 'im?"

"You think you're smart, don't you?" the boy asked, sneering.

"Listen, I ain't picking a fight," I said. "But if you want to fight, I'll fight."

"Hunh, hard guy, ain't you?"

"As hard as you."

"Do you know who you can tell that to?" he asked me.

"And you know who you can tell it back to?" I asked.

"Are you talking about my mama?" he asked, edging forward.

"If you want it that way," I said.

This was my test. If I failed now, I would have failed at school, for the first trial came not in books but in how one's fellows took one, what value they placed upon one's willingness to fight.

"Take back what you said," the boy challenged me.

"Make me," I said.

The crowd howled, sensing a fight. The boy hesitated, weighing his chances of beating me.

"You ain't gonna take what that new boy said, is you?" someone taunted the boy.

The boy came close. I stood my ground. Our faces were four inches apart.

"You think I'm scared of you, don't you?" he asked.

"I told you what I think," I said.

Somebody, eager and afraid that we would not fight, pushed the boy, and he bumped into me. I shoved him away violently.

"Don't push me!" the boy said.

"Then keep off me!" I said.

He was pushed again, and I struck out with my right and caught him in the mouth. The crowd yelled, milled, surging so close that I could barely lift my arm to land a blow. When either of us tried to strike the other, we would be thrown off balance by the screaming boys. Every blow landed elicited shouts of delight. Knowing that if I did not win or make a good showing, I would have to fight a new boy each day, I fought tigerishly, trying to leave a scar, seeking to draw blood as proof that I was not a coward, that I could take care of myself. The bell rang, and the crowd pulled us apart. The fight seemed a draw.

"I ain't through with you!" the boy shouted.

In the classroom the boys asked me questions about myself; I was someone worth knowing. When the bell rang for school to be dismissed, I was set to fight again, but the boy was not in sight.

On my way home I found a cheap ring in the streets, and at once I knew what I was going to do with it. The ring had a red stone held by tiny prongs which I loosened, took the stone out, leaving the sharp tiny prongs jutting up. I slid the ring on to my finger and shadowboxed. Now let a bully come, and I would show him how to fight; I would leave a crimson streak on his face with every blow.

But I never had to use the ring. After I had exhibited my new weapon at school, a description of it spread among the boys. I challenged my enemy to another fight, but he would not respond. Fighting was now not necessary. I had been accepted.

I
HE PASSED THE TEST

1. Why did Richard Wright fight so ferociously when he was challenged by the boy at the new school?

2. How did he know he had "passed the test" when class resumed?

3. What weapon did Wright fashion for himself that he never had to use?

II
IMPLICATIONS

1. Human relations are more important than scholastic achievement.

2. Most people are eager to fight only when they feel they can win.

3. To be someone worth knowing you must be willing to fight to establish a place for yourself.

III
TECHNIQUES

Style

1. Wright's style of writing is straightforward and realistic. What do you think makes the scene on the school grounds at noon recess seem so real and the action move so rapidly?

2. The author indulges in very little imagery. He does say, in describing the fight, that he fought "tigerishly, trying to leave a scar," seeking to draw blood as proof he was not a coward. What image does he give the reader after he finds the ring and takes the stone out?

Giving Insight

The final sentence of the first paragraph gives insight into the way Richard Wright thinks. He has no false notions that what is ahead will be easy. What is this matter-of-fact statement that lets the reader know his attitude?

Man was intended for something more important than the mere gathering of prunes and apricots. Of this Manuel felt sure.

The Confrontation

RAYMOND BARRIO

No matter which way he turned, he was trapped in an endless maze of apricot trees, as though forever, neat rows of them, neatly planted, row after row, just like the blackest bars on a jail. There had to be an end. There had to be. There—trapped. There had to be a way out. Locked. There had to be a respite.[1] Animal. The buckets and the crates kept piling up higher. Brute. He felt alone. Though surrounded by other pickers. Beast. Though he was perspiring heavily, his shirt was powder dry. Savage. The hot dry air. The hot dry air sucking every drop of living moisture from his brute body. Wreck. He stopped and walked to the farthest end of the first row for some water, raised the dented dipper from the brute tank, drank the holy water in great brute gulps so he wouldn't have to savor its tastelessness, letting it spill down his torn shirt to cool his exhausted body, to replenish his brute cells and animal pores and stinking follicles[2] and pig gristle, a truly refined wreck of an animal, pleased to meetcha. Predator.

Lunch.

Almost too exhausted to eat, he munched his cheese with tortillas,[3] smoked on ashes, then lay back on the cool ground for half an hour. That short rest in the hot shade replenished some of his humor and resolve. He felt his spirit swell out again like a thirsty sponge

in water. Then up again. The trees. The branches again. The briary branches. The scratching leaves. The twigs tearing at his shirt sleeves. The ladder. The rough bark. The endlessly unending piling up of bucket upon box upon crate upon stack upon rack upon mound upon mountain. He picked a mountain of cots automatically. An automator. A beast. A ray of enemy sun penetrated the tree that was hiding him and split his forehead open. His mind whirred. He blacked out. Luckily he'd been leaning against a heavy branch. His feet hooked to the ladder's rung. His half-filled bucket slipped from his grasp and fell in slow motion, splattering the fruit he'd so laboriously picked. To the ground. Robert happened by and shook his head. "Whatsamatter, can't you see straight." Manuel was too tired even to curse. He should have had some salt pills.

Midafternoon.

The summer's fierce zenith[4] passed overhead. It passed. Then dropped. It started to light the ocean behind him, back of the hills. Sandy dreams. Cool nights. Cold drinks. Soft guitar music with Lupe sitting beside him. All wafting through his feverish moments. Tiredness drained his spirit of will. Exhaustion drained his mind. His fingers burned. His arms flailed the innocent trees. He was slowing down. He could hardly fill his last bucket. Suddenly the whistle blew. The day's work was at last ended.

Ended!

The contratista[5] Roberto Morales[6] stood there.

His feet straddled. Mexican style. A real robber. A Mexican general. A gentlemanly, friendly, polite, grinning, vicious, thieving brute. The worst kind. To his own people.

---

1. **respite**\ˈrĕs·pət\ an interval of relief or rest.
2. **follicle**\ˈfal·ĭ·kəlz\ small anatomical cavity.
3. **tortillas**\tɔr·tē·(y)as\ flat, unleavened cakes.
4. **zenith,** the point at which a celestial body, in this case the sun, is directly above the observer.
5. **contratista**\kɔn·tra·ˈtēs·ta\ a labor contractor.
6. **Morales**\mɔ·ˈra·lĕs\

From "The Plum Plum Pickers," by Raymond Barrio. © Ventura Press, P. O. Box 2268, Sunnyvale, California 94087.

Despite his being a fellow Mexican, despite his torn, old clothing, everyone knew what kind of clever criminal he was. Despite his crude, ignorant manner, showing that he was one of them, that he'd started with them, that he grew up with them, that he'd suffered all the sordid deprivations with them, he was actually the shrewdest, smartest, richest cannibal in forty counties around. They sure couldn't blame the güeros[7] for this miscarriage.[8] He was a crew chief. How could anyone know what he did to his own people? And what did the güeros care? So the anglo[9] growers and güero executives, smiling in their cool filtered offices, puffing their elegant thin cigars, washed their clean blond bloodless dirtless hands of the whole matter. All they did was hire Roberto Morales. Firm, fair, and square. For an agreed-upon price. Good. How he got his people down to the pickings was no concern of theirs. They were honest, those güeros. They could sleep at night. They fulfilled their end of the bargain, and cheated no one. Their only crime; their only soul crime indeed was that they just didn't care how that migratory scum lived. It was no concern of theirs. Their religion said it was no concern of theirs. Their wives said it was no concern of theirs. Their aldermen[10] said it was no concern of theirs. Their——

Whenever Roberto Morales spoke, Manuel had to force himself not to answer. He had to keep his temper from flaring.

"Now," announced Morales at last, in his friendliest tone. "Now. I must take two cents from every bucket. I am sorry. There was a miscalculation. Everybody understands. Everybody?" He slid his eyes around, smiling, palms up.

The tired, exhausted pickers gasped as one.

Yes. Everyone understood. Freezing in place. After all that hard work.

"Any questions, men?"

Morales grinned, knowing everyone realized that he had the upper hand, that that would mean a loss of two or three dollars out of each picker's pay that day, a huge windfall for Morales.

"You promised to take nothing!" Manuel heard himself saying. Everyone turned in astonishment to stare at Manuel.

"I said two cents, hombre. You got a problem or what?"

"You promised."

The two men, centered in a huge ring of red-ringed eyes, glared at each other. Reaching for each other's jugular. The other exhausted animals studied the tableau through widening eyes. It was so unequal. Morales remained calm, confident, studying Manuel. As though memorizing his features. He had the whole advantage. Then, with his last remaining energy, Manuel lifted his foot and clumsily tipped over his own last bucket of cots. They rolled away in all directions around everyone's feet.

Roberto Morales' eyes blazed. His fists clenched. "You pick them up, Gutierrez."

So. He knew his name. After all. For answer, Manuel kicked over another bucket, and again the fruit rolled away in all directions.

Then an astonishing thing happened.

All the other pickers moved toward their own buckets still standing beside them on the ground awaiting the truck gatherer, and took an ominous position over them, straddling their feet over them. Without looking around, without taking his eyes off Manuel, Roberto Morales said sharply, "All right. All right, men. I shall take nothing this time."

Manuel felt a thrill of power course through his nerves.

He had never won anything before. He would have to pay for this, for his defiance, somehow, again, later. But he had shown de-

---

7. **güeros***gŭe·rōs\\ a Mexican word meaning persons with fair hair.
8. **miscarriage,** a failure in the administration of justice.
9. **anglo,** an English speaking resident of the United States.
10. **aldermen,** members of a governing body.

fiance. He had salvaged his money savagely and he had earned respect from his fellow slaves. The big bosses would never know of this little incident, and would probably be surprised, and perhaps even a little mortified, for a few minutes. But they wouldn't care. It was bread, pan y[11] tortillas out of his children's mouths. But they still wouldn't give a single hoot. Manuel had wrenched Morales' greedy fingers away and removed a fat slug of a purse from his sticky grasp. And in his slow way, in his stupid, accidental, dangerous way, Manuel had made an extravagant discovery, as Don Gaspar had also made two centuries before, in almost exactly the same spot. And that was—that a man counted for something. For men, Manuel dimly suspected, are built for something more important and less trifling than the mere gathering of prunes and apricots, hour upon hour, decade upon decade, insensibly, mechanically, antlike. Men are built to experience a certain sense of honor and pride.

Or else they are dead before they die.

I

A LEADER IS BORN

The contratista, or labor contractor, Morales, was a traitor to his own people, willing to rob them for personal gain.

1. What demand does he make of the fruit pickers after they have finished their day's work?

2. How does Manuel surprise himself?

3. What action does he take in defiance of Morales?

4. How do the other pickers support him?

5. How does Manuel feel about what he has done?

II

IMPLICATIONS

1. Desire for money will corrupt most people.

2. It is more contemptible to rob your own people than to rob others.

3. When man is pushed to his limits, rebellion is instinctive.

4. People become much braver when they have a leader.

III

TECHNIQUES

Style

When an individual is working under nearly intolerable conditions, as for example in extreme heat, and he pushes his body almost past the limit of its endurance, his thoughts become chaotic and disorganized. Raymond Barrio's writing style in "The Confrontation" is choppy and sometimes hard to understand. Why is this style an effective way of revealing Manuel's thoughts?

Giving Insight

1. How are Manuel's feelings about Morales first revealed?

2. How does the reader know that Morales had realized that Manuel was a potential threat to him?

3. Why is Manuel's victory so important to him?

IV

WORDS

It is sometimes possible to tell at a glance that two or more words are related in some way. The words *automatically* and *automaton*, from "The Confrontation," are obviously related; both are derived from the Greek forms *auto*, "self," and *matos*, "willing." Both words, therefore, refer to self-willed or self-controlled action. In the context of the story, automatically means "mechanically," and *automaton* means "machine or robot." Manuel, the writer says, performed his monotonous, back-breaking job mechanically, as if he were a robot, not a human being. Also from the story are two other look-alike words—*cents* and *century*. Both words come from the Latin word *centum*, meaning "hundred." In the United States, a *cent* is one one-hundredth of a dollar, the basic monetary unit. And a *century*, of course, is a hundred years. Keeping in mind what you have just learned and using your dictionary, try to answer the following questions:

1. What is an *autobiography*?

2. Does *automation* increase or decrease jobs in a factory? Explain.

---

11. **pan y** \ˈpan·ē\ bread and.

Even though he failed on the first
big job of his life, Nathan Hale established
his identity and the world remembers who he
was. He did it with a few simple words.

Nathan Hale

NANCY HALE

"The boy was only a couple of years out
of New Haven[1] when he joined up. He'd hardly
got started. He'd been teaching school, you
know, up at East Haddam and then down in
New London, and it looked as if he was shaping up into a fine teacher. He'd made a lot of
friends everywhere he went, and the girls
always liked him. They say he was a good-
looking boy.

"Then the war came. Things had looked
bad to us Americans for a long time, but when
the first gun was fired on that April day[2] it
seemed to light a sudden strong fire in everyone's heart. It seemed to call out—'Americans!'
The boy's brothers, John and Joseph, volunteered first off. It was a patriotic family—the
father'd been a Deputy in the old Connecticut
Assembly. The boy himself had signed up with
the school for a year. He wasn't the kind to let
people down, but he did write and ask to be
released from his contract two weeks early.
He joined up in July, as a Lieutenant in
Webb's Seventh Connecticut.

"Well, you know how things went after
that. The boy was in camp up near Boston all
winter. It wasn't an exciting siege. But there
was a lot to do getting the men to reenlist.
Most of their terms of enlistment ran out in
December. The General was worried about it.

Our boy offered the men in his company his
own pay for a month if they'd stay that much
longer. Anyway the siege was maintained.

"He got a leave in the winter and went
home. Maybe that was when he got engaged.
Alicia Adams. A lovely girl; they would have
made a handsome couple. When Spring came
the enemy evacuated Boston and our army
went down to New York, where real trouble
was threatening. The boy'd been made a captain by that time. He was twenty-one years
old.

"Our Long Island campaign was just this
side of disastrous. Morale was none too good,
afterwards. I don't suppose the General was in
a worse spot in the whole war than he was
for those three weeks right after the Battle of
Long Island. There we lay, facing the enemy
across the East River, and no way of knowing
what they had up their sleeve. Surprise was
what we feared. The answer to that was com-
panies of rangers, to scout around and find out
what was up. Knowlton's Rangers was organized, and our boy switched over to it. He
wanted action, you see.

"But the rangers weren't enough. The General wanted to know two things: when the
enemy was planning to attack, and where. Nobody could tell him. The General let it be
known that he'd welcome volunteers to spy.

"Now, people didn't take kindly to the word
'spy' around these parts. It didn't mean excitement or glamour or any of those things. It
meant something degrading. It was a job they
gave to bums, who didn't care. But the General said he wanted a spy. Well, our boy volunteered. His friends tried to talk him out of it.
They spoke of the indignity; they also told
him he'd make a terrible spy—frank, open boy
like him.

"But his idea was, the job was necessary.
That was the great thing. Its being necessary

From "Nathan Hale" by Nancy Hale from *There Were Giants
in the Land*. Copyright 1942, © 1970 by Holt, Rinehart and
Winston, Inc. Reprinted by permission of Holt, Rinehart and
Winston, Inc.

1. **New Haven**, location of Yale University.
2. **April day**, April 19, 1775, when the American
regular troops fought the British redcoats around
Lexington, Massachusetts.

seemed to him to make it honorable. He was sent through the enemy lines dressed up like a Dutch schoolmaster.

"He didn't make such a bad spy, after all. He got what he went after, and hid the drawings in his shoes. He was on his way back, crossing their lines, when they caught him. They found the information on him. He admitted he was over there to spy. You know what a spy gets. They hanged him in the morning. He wrote some letters to the family at home, but they were destroyed before his eyes, they say. But in his last moment, they let him say what he wanted to. And later one of their officers told one of our officers what he'd said.

"There he was, with the noose around his neck. He hadn't got much done. He'd got caught on the first big job of his life. He wasn't going to marry Alicia Adams, nor to have any children, nor to do any more teaching, nor to finish fighting this war. He stood there in the morning air, and he spoke and said who he was, his commission and all. And then he added, 'I only regret that I have but one life to lose for my country.'"

You could tell the story like that, simply, because it is a simple story, and when you'd finished you'd have told about all there is to tell about Nathan Hale. There isn't even a contemporary picture of him. Most of the friends to whom he wrote didn't keep his letters. He was just a young American who'd gone to war, who'd lived for twenty-one ordinary enough years before—in the day's work —he died for his country.

One of his brothers, Enoch, was my great-great-grandfather.

When I was a child there was a small bronze statue, about four feet high, that stood in the corner of the living room at home. It was just about my height, but it wasn't another child. It was a young man, with his wrists tied behind him and his ankles bound. I passed it several times a day every day of my childhood. Sometimes I used to touch the bronze face. It

was a small-scale replica of the Nathan Hale statue at Yale.

I must have been told his story, because I always knew it. But my father never went on about it, if you know what I mean. There his story was, for what it might mean to you. Some of my other ancestors were the kind of characters that have a whole legend of anecdotes surrounding them, pointed, stirring, or uproarious. But the young man with his hands bound had died at twenty-one, a patriot, as stark and all alone and anecdoteless as young men of twenty-one must be.

Once I was set upon the knees of an old gentleman whose grandmother had been Alicia Adams. She had married and had children, and lived to be eighty-eight, a pretty, sparkling old lady. And when she died she said, "Where is Nathan?" But about the young man himself there were no family reminiscences, no odd little jokes, no tales beyond the short, plain story of his life and death. He had had no time to do anything memorable but die.

Nevertheless. . . . It was my job as a child to fill the kitchen scuttle with coal from the cellar. I was not a brave child, and to me the long corners of the cellar seemed menacing and full of queer, moving shadows—wolves? robbers? I cannot remember when I first started taking the thought of Nathan Hale down cellar with me, for a shield and a buckler.[3] I thought, "If he could be hanged, I can go down cellar." The thing was, he was no impossible hero; he was a member of the family, and he was young too. He was a hero you could take along with you into the cellar of a New England farmhouse. You felt he'd be likely to say, "Aren't any wolves or robbers back there that I can see."

Well, I am grown up now and I know very little more about Nathan Hale than I did then. There are, of course, a mass of details about his short life. A devoted scholar named George Dudley Seymour has spent years in collecting all that can be collected about him. There's a

---

3. **buckler**, a small, round shield.

wartime diary. They know his friends. He played football and checkers at camp. He drank wine at Brown's Tavern and cider at Stone's. But when you add all these little things you only affirm the peculiar simplicity of the story.

Hale is a symbol of all the young American men who fight and who die for us. Partly he is a symbol because he was the first of our heroes in the first of our own wars. He was the first to show the world what Americans are made of. The reason they destroyed his letters home at the time of his death was, they said, so that "the rebels should not know they have a man who can die so firmly." He showed them.

He is no Washington or Jefferson although he ranks with the heroes. Washington was a great general and Jefferson was a genius. All of our nation's heroes are great men who are great by their minds and by their deeds and by their careers. All except Hale. His special gift to his country, and to us who love that country, was the manner of his death.

He is the young American. He is the patron of all the young Americans who have grown up as he did in quiet self-respecting families; who have gone to college and done well, and had fun too; who have started out along their life's careers, well spoken of, promising; and then broken off to join their country's forces in time of war without an instant's hesitation; knowing what must be done and who must do it. He was no different than they. He was an American boy. Everything that can be said of them can be said of him. In the letters of his friends written about him after his death, certain words keep cropping up. They sound oddly familiar. "Promising . . . patriotic . . . generous . . . modest . . . high-spirited . . . devoted . . ." His friends fitted the words to Hale. They fit Americans.

Nothing was more American in Hale than his taking on the duties that led to his death. It was a dirty job, spying. Nobody wanted it. He took it. There's something about that, taking on a dirty job that's got to be done, that rings a bell. It's an American custom of Amer-

ican heroes. He wasn't a remarkably articulate boy. His letters are nothing special. He just jotted things in his diary. But he became the spokesman for young American fighting men who have to die for their country. He chanced to say the thing they think; the thing they mean, when there's not even a split second to think. He stood there at Turtle Bay on Manhattan Island. Don't think he declaimed.[4] He wasn't that kind. He had those few moments, and he was thinking about all the different things that were ending for him. He said and I think it was more like a remark:

"I only regret . . ."

I

A SPOKESMAN FOR YOUNG AMERICANS

1. What was Nathan Hale doing before he joined the Army?

2. Why did he take the job of spying?

3. Describe the scene when he was hanged.

4. In what way did Nathan Hale help Nancy when she was a child?

II

IMPLICATIONS

1. Spying is a dishonorable job.

2. "All of our nation's heroes are great men who are great by their minds and by their deeds and by their careers."

3. Nathan Hale was a typical American boy.

III

TECHNIQUES

Style

1. How do you know where the storyteller breaks off the straight narrative and begins to include personal reminiscences?

2. What words at the beginning of the third paragraph are particularly characteristic of the oral story teller?

---

4. **declaimed,** made a formal speech.

In different ways and at different times we all must answer the question, "Who am I?" In a sense, some painters attempt to do this in self-portraits. This collection includes not only self-portraits but also portraits that artists have made of others that reveal something about who or what these people are.

Everyone is a member of some minority and as such must cope with relating to the world that both affects and conflicts with his life. The young black painter Walker depicts this identity issue in MY THOUGHTS-MY IDEAS.

MY THOUGHTS-MY IDEAS
Larry Walker

SELF PORTRAIT
Max Beckmann
Courtesy of the Art Institute of Chicago

THE ARTIST IN HIS STUDIO
James Whistler
Courtesy of the Art Institute of Chicago

These three very different self-portraits reveal many things about their creators. Pride, even arrogance, is apparent in both the Whistler and the Beckmann, but it is easy for us to see the vast differences in the lives and art forms of these two men. In contrast, the Sheeler says more about the painter's creative identity than about his actual life. The painter shows us himself at work translating a landscape into an industrial design which is typical of much of the work Sheeler is known for.

The formal and traditional portrait of the Hatch Family by Eastman Johnson was painted more than a hundred years ago. For the members of this impressive family there was little question of identity. The family's distinguished position determined for each individual the self-important identity he or she would be expected to assume. In contrast, Soyer attempts more than photographic realism in THE BROWN SWEATER, for he reveals something about the young girl's emerging sense of herself in relation to her family. ANCESTRAL WORSHIP is a very abstract and personal statement of a person's relationship to his heritage.

THE HATCH FAMILY
Eastman Johnson
The Metropolitan Museum of Art,
Gift of Frederic H. Hatch, 1926

THE BROWN SWEATER, 1952
Raphael Soyer
Collection, Whitney Museum of American Art

ANCESTRAL WORSHIP
Theodore Stamos
Pastel, gouache, and ink, Collection,
Whitney Museum of American Art

Identity

A UNIVERSAL DESIRE

What is it that causes a person to want to establish his identity? It would appear that one's nationality or race make little difference. Whether a person is a crook, a school boy, a school teacher, or a fruit picker, he feels the need to establish an identity for himself.

As a person grows up he knows he is changing, that he is not what he was nor yet what he will become. He wants to be himself and to let others know who he is. To do this he often does something out of the ordinary, something that may be spectacularly foolish. For example, Jamie's climb up the tower in "The Way Up" was meaningless to everyone except himself and his small circle of friends. On the other hand Richard Wright's establishment of his identity at school was unquestionably a simple matter of survival. Establishing an identity must be a continuing process. Discuss why this is true.

IMPLICATIONS

1. Who a person "is" depends on the situation.
2. Identity is usually established by accident.
3. There are not as many opportunities for establishing an identity today as there were in frontier times.
4. Establishing an identity is pointless for a person unless it is of benefit to him.
5. Everyone has an identity.

TECHNIQUES

Style

Style includes a writer's choice of words, his sentence structure, his point of view, his use of imagery, and the attitude he adopts toward his subject. Think back over the selections you have read in this unit. Below are given combinations of descriptive terms, each combination applying more directly to the style of one specific selection than to the others. See if you can match the selection with the appropriate set of terms:

1. Choppy, disorganized, obvious sympathy for the main character.
2. Factual, conversational, storytelling manner.
3. Realistic, hard hitting, autobiographical.
4. Light, humorous, tongue-in-cheek attitude.
5. Boyish, suspenseful, straightforward narrative.

Giving Insight

Giving insight is managed by a writer through the use of a variety of techniques. In each of the sentences below there are words that triggered an individual to assert his identity. Without looking back through the unit, see how well you can reconstruct the circumstances in which the following lines were spoken and how they made the character feel.

1. "Now. I must take two cents from every bucket."
2. "They'll never know you been here. . . ."
3. "How come they make you people so ugly in Jackson?"
4. " 'Let go of him, Blockhead!' And he struck Tango across the cheek."

When the Legends Die

Introduction

The last selection on the theme of identity is the short novel *When the Legends Die*. In this absorbing story Tom Black Bull, a Ute Indian, is trapped between two ways of life—the Indian's way and the white man's way—and he searches desperately for answers to the questions of who he is and where he belongs.

On thin strips of land in southwestern Colorado, northwestern New Mexico, and southeastern Utah are clustered Ute and Navaho Indian reservations. On these reservations, which are administered by the Bureau of Indian Affairs of the Department of the Interior, thousands of the original Americans live nearly totally managed lives—the result of the white man's attempt to "civilize" them, to force them to stop being what they were.

As a young man, the author, Hal Borland, knew many Utes and spent considerable time in their homeland. This is an area of rugged mountains and stream-threaded valleys, a place where the highest peaks keep their snow cover even in the heat of summer, where the upland blue-green of aspen, spruce, and pine gradually slope down to the muted green of cedar trees and sage brush, finally leveling out into the red and ochre of sandstone buttes and desert.

It is no secret that the reservation system has been far from successful in achieving assimilation. Turned away by the hostile barriers of bigotry that keep most Indians out of the mainstream of life in the United States, the Indian American clings precariously to the lowest rung of the economic ladder.

Before the white man herded the last Indian Americans onto reservations, the Indians' life style reflected rhythms and rituals that were already ancient at the time of Columbus' discovery of the New World. Never a wanton destroyer of the land and the life upon it, the Indian maintained a balance between himself and his surroundings, a precious balance that has been lost.

This novel is divided into four sections, or chapters, and each chapter can be read much as you would read a short story. However, a novel allows for greater development of character, situations, and theme.

Three Levels of Meaning in a Novel

The reader of a novel must allow the words to create pictures and feelings in his mind; he must let the words create characters so vividly that he actually lives their experience through the words. The duty of the writer, then, is to select words and incidents that will create these pictures, telling just enough, but not too much, to let the reader project himself into the action. As you read *When the Legends Die,* try to share the experience as though you lived it too. Put yourself in the place of Tom Black Bull. Imagine his surroundings. This "substitute experience" is the first level of reading.

However, a well written novel like *When the Legends Die* does more than simply tell a story or take a reader through an experience. The events usually show something worth knowing about human beings and the ways in which they live. This significant comment about people in general is the second level of reading in a novel.

Sometimes in a novel the words are so exactly right that the reader takes pleasure in their remarkable clarity. Sometimes the story itself is arranged so beautifully that the reader can enjoy the sheer skill of the storyteller. Recognizing the beauty of an author's craftsmanship is the third level of reading.

WHEN THE LEGENDS DIE

HAL BORLAND

1   Bessie

He came home in midafternoon, hurrying through the alley. Bessie was sitting on the back step of the unpainted two-room house, peeling willow twigs with her teeth and watching the boy chase butterflies among the tall horseweeds. She looked up and saw her man come toward her. His face was bloody, his shirt torn and bloody down the front. She clapped a hand to her mouth to stifle her cry, and followed him into the house. He whispered, in the Ute[1] tongue, "They will come after me. Bring water to wash. Get the other shirt."

She filled the tin basin and brought it to him. There was a cut over his left eye and a darkening bruise beside his mouth. She got the other shirt while he washed; then she took the pan of red-stained water outside and poured it on the ground among the weeds. It sank into the dry soil and left only a dark, wet spot. When she went inside again he was pulling the clean shirt over his head. He wrapped the torn shirt into a bundle, the bloody places hidden, and said, still in Ute, "I shall go to the stream with black-stem ferns on Horse Moun-

tain. Come to me there." He tucked the bundle under his arm, took his rifle, went to the door and looked, waited. Then he touched her face with his free hand and hurried through the scrub oak toward the river. The magpies screamed for a moment, then were silent.

She searched the floor for spots of blood and dried the basin; then she went to sit on the step again.

The boy, who was five years old and only an inch or so taller than the horseweeds, came and stood at her knee, asking questions with his eyes.

She smiled at him. "Nobody came. Nothing happened. Remember, if they ask." He nodded. She handed him a willow twig. He peeled the bark with his teeth, as she had done, and chewed it, tasting the green bitterness. "Go catch a grasshopper," she said. He went back among the weeds.

She waited half an hour.

Then they came up the street and stood in front of her, the tall sheriff, the short, fat man from the sawmill, and Blue Elk, with his squeaky shoes, black coat and derby hat, his wool-bound braids, his air of importance.

She clapped her hand to her mouth and began to wail. "You bring trouble!" Then, to Blue Elk, in the Ute tongue, "My man is hurt?"

The sheriff said to Blue Elk, "See what she knows."

Blue Elk rubbed his soft hands together. He said in Ute, "Bessie! Stop the wailing. Let the other woman mourn. Your man is not hurt. Where have you hidden him?"

"He is not here. Why do you come here for him?"

"He was here. He came here."

"If you know this, find him." She gestured toward the house.

"What does she say?" the sheriff asked.

"She says he is not here. She says we should look."

The sheriff and the sawmill man went in-

---

1. Ute\yūt\

side. She asked Blue Elk, "Why do you want my man? What happened?"

"He killed a man. He killed Frank No Deer."

"That one." Scorn was in her eyes.

"I know. A thief, a no-good. But George killed him. Where did George go?"

She shrugged.

"Where is the boy?"

She glanced at the weed patch and then waved her hand vaguely. "Boys play, go where they will."

The men came back. "No sign of him."

"They will watch you," Blue Elk said, still in the tongue.

"If they want me, I am here."

The sheriff said, "Tell her we'll find him if we have to run down every little Ute fishing and berry camp in the mountains. He covered his tracks, or she did. But we'll find him."

Blue Elk said to her, "You heard. For the cost of two horses I could settle this."

"I have not the cost of two horses."

"One horse," Blue Elk offered.

She shook her head. "I have not the cost of one goat."

"What does she say?" the sheriff asked.

"She says she has not seen him."

"I think she's lying."

"My people," Blue Elk said in English, "do not lie."

The sheriff grunted. "They just kill each other over a lunch pail. Some day one of them is going to kill you, Blue Elk." He turned to the sawmill man. "Let's go find Frank's squaw. You better tell her you'll pay for the funeral."

"Fifty dollars for a coffin. That's all," the other said.

The woman said scornfully in Ute, "The cost of two ponies!"

"What does she say?" the sheriff asked.

"She says she is glad it was not her man who was killed."

"You know where to find Frank's squaw?"

Blue Elk nodded, and they left.

She sat on the steps another ten minutes. Then she said, "Come now," and there was a movement among the horseweeds. The boy

stood up and came to her and they went indoors. She praised him. She walked about the house, choosing things, not yet taking them from their places. Ammunition. Fishhooks and line. The axe. Knives. Spare moccasins. The boy's coat. Two blankets.

She started a fire in the stove and put meat on to boil. She neatened up the house, to leave it clean, and to occupy the time. It was a company house. For two years, the sawmill had taken money from her man's pay for rent and for the old iron bed, the dresser with the broken leg, the four chairs, the table, the stove. By now, they owned the two blankets, and that was all she was taking. The knives and axe were hers, and she had made the moccasins and the coat. When it was dark, they would pack these things and go. Two summers ago Blue Elk had brought them here from Horse Mountain. Now he was sending them back.

She sat on the step with the boy and thought of that summer of 1910.

They had lived near Arboles on the Southern Ute reservation in southwestern Colorado, and her man had a cornfield. The drought came and the corn burned up. One evening her man said, "We are going fishing. Our friends are going, Charley Huckleberry too, so it is all right." Charley was a member of the council.

The next morning, in six wagons, they went up the Piedra River to the reservation line and camped. All summer they caught and ate fish and packed berries and there were no cornfields to worry about.

It was like the old days. In the evening the men wrestled and ran races and the children threw stones at the magpies and the women sat and talked. It was a happy time.

The day they broke camp someone said they should go into Piedra Town and buy candy for the children. Charley Huckleberry said it was all right to go. So they went to the store and spent all the money they had on the candy.

Then someone said, "Let us go farther up

the river and camp and catch more fish," Charley Huckleberry said he guessed that would be all right, too.

There were plenty of fish and serviceberries were ripe. The women and children picked them, and set up racks and smoked the fish they didn't eat. Then the men killed two fat deer which had come to the river to drink. The venison tasted good after so much fish, and the women told the men to go up on Horse Mountain and get more deer and they would dry it, the old way, for winter.

Nobody remembered how long they were there because it didn't matter. When they had made enough meat, they said, and had smoked fish and dried berries for the winter, they would go back to the reservation.

Then Blue Elk came and told them the police were after them because they had no fishing and hunting permit. Charley said there couldn't be any trouble because he was in charge and he was a member of the council. But Blue Elk said the council had sent him to find them.

Charley said, "Somebody always pays you to come to tell of trouble. The council didn't pay you. Who did?" But everybody knew that Charley was worried.

"I came to warn you," Blue Elk said, "and to tell you that this trouble can be taken care of."

Johnny Sour Water said, "Maybe we should let our women put you on the drying rack, like a fat fish, and smoke you too."

Everybody laughed, because Blue Elk did look like a big, fat fish. But they didn't laugh much. They didn't know how this would come out. Bessie's man, George Black Bull, said, "We dried fish and berries; we made deer meat for the winter. We did not kill sheep or cows. Nobody can make trouble of this." Bessie was proud of him.

But Blue Elk said, "You did it without permits. There will be a fine for that. You are not so foolish as to think you can keep that meat?"

Then he said, "Your cornfields are burned. Your blankets are thin. Your women need new skirts. You already owe money to the trader. But I can get work for you and you will not have to worry about the winter."

"What do the sawmill men in Pagosa pay for you making this talk to us?" Charley Huckleberry asked.

Blue Elk said, "I worry for my people. That is why I tell you now that the sawmill man will give you jobs. He needs more men to work. He will pay two dollars a day, silver."

There was talk at that. Two dollars a day, silver!

Then Charley Huckleberry said Blue Elk was probably right about the fine because they had come too far off the reservation and stayed too long. That was not big trouble, and that was all the trouble there would be, Charley said.

But there still was this matter of two dollars a day, silver. The women said this might be a good thing, and the men said that if all of them went together to Pagosa it would be a happy time, maybe. And they did not have to stay long. In two months, they would have more than a hundred dollars, all silver. . . . So they went back to the reservation, the council took the meat and smoked fish for a fine, and Blue Elk got permits for them to go to work in the sawmill so they would not be hungry that winter.

In Pagosa Blue Elk helped the men to make their sign on the papers that said so much would be kept out of their pay to pay rent and buy furniture. And they could buy what they needed at the company store. The papers said they could not go away while they owed money for these things.

Then, one day, Blue Elk came to the house and told Bessie that she and George must get married.

Bessie said, "George is my man. That is enough. That is married as it always was."

Blue Elk said, "There is the boy. You must be married for the boy, and the preacher must baptize him with holy water and give him a name."

"I wash him with water when he is dirty,"

Bessie said. "I have given him his name. Can the preacher do more than this?"

"It must be done. It will cost five dollars."

"I do not have five dollars," Bessie told him. "They take my man's money and do not pay it to him."

"I will see that he gets five dollars this week," Blue Elk said, and he did. George gave the money to Blue Elk and he took them to the preacher. The preacher said words and wrote on a paper and they were married. Then he asked what they wanted to name the boy. Bessie said, "He is Little Black Bull. He will choose when he needs another name." The preacher said he must have another name now, and that Thomas was a good name. Bessie said it didn't matter because Little Black Bull would pick his own name when the time came. So the preacher sprinkled water on the boy's head and George got no pay at all the next week because of that five dollars.

When the aspens came to leaf the next spring, George told the sawmill man he was going back to the reservation. The man looked in the book and said George owed forty-two dollars at the company store and must work four more weeks. But the next week the man gave George only seven dollars and kept the rest of his wages for rent and furniture. And the next week it was only five because one day the sawmill broke down and didn't run.

In four weeks George had saved only fifteen dollars. He hid the money in his lunch pail, but someone stole his lunch pail. Nobody saw the thief; but Frank No Deer, who was a mixed-blood Apache from the Jicarilla reservation in New Mexico, bought a new hat and boots that cost exactly fifteen dollars. George accused him of stealing his money and Frank laughed and said he had won that money in a dice game. Nobody knew of such a dice game, but George could not prove this thing. So he started again to save his money.

It was August before he had fifteen dollars again. He put it in a bean can and buried it, and when he found someone had dug it up, he told Frank No Deer he had stolen it. Frank only laughed. But he bought a suit of clothes, and the man at the store said it cost exactly fifteen dollars.

They did not go back to the reservation that fall either because now they owed fifty dollars at the store. All that winter George saved money again, this time in paper money which he kept in his pocket. He saved forty dollars, and two days ago he had told Bessie that in two weeks they would go back even if they were hungry next winter. Bessie said that would be a happy time.

Then yesterday, when he had quit work for lunch, someone had taken his lunch pail. He went out to where the other men were eating and Frank No Deer had that lunch pail. George said, "You are a thief. But this time you did not steal my money because it was not in my lunch pail. It is here in my pocket."

Then George tried to take his lunch pail and Frank No Deer tried to take it back and they had a fight. George sat on Frank No Deer and pounded his head on the ground. Then he let him up and Frank No Deer went away and did not come back to work all afternoon. After he had gone, George felt in his pocket. Frank No Deer had stolen his money while they wrestled.

George had told Bessie last night, "Three times Frank No Deer has stolen my money and tomorrow I am going to kill him. . . ."

Bessie remembered all these things. She looked at the boy and thought it would be good to go away from here. The boy should know the old ways.

In her mind was one of the old songs that her mother had sung, a song about the roundness of things, of grass stems and aspens and the sun and the days and the years. Bessie sang it now, softly, and added words of her own about the roundness of a little boy's eyes and arms and legs, and the roundness of a bird's nest and a basket, coiled and complete, a part of the roundness of the whole.

The boy smiled as he heard it.

And then it was sunset, and they ate the meat. She put the boy to bed and he put his head against her and touched her cheek with his hand. Then he went to sleep and she waited for the deep darkness, saying thanks that there would be no moon.

The star that is a hunter with a pack on his back[2] was halfway down the sky in the northwest when she went out on the step and listened. Everything was quiet. She had made no light in the house, so she could see in this darkness. She went down the path to the alley, and nobody was there. She went around the house. Nobody was in the street. Nobody was watching. She knew this.

She wakened the boy, and whispered, "Do not talk. Stay close to me. Hold to my skirt and walk where I walk. We will make a game." They went out and she picked up the pack and the axe.

They went to the alley and turned left, not the way her man had gone, and followed a path to the top of the hill. In the starlight Bessie could see the road that led west toward Piedra Town. If she followed that road seventeen miles she would come to the road to Arboles, and there she would turn north. But half that far would be as far as the boy should walk tonight. In the starlight her eyes also saw an owl, two rabbits, a striped cat from town, a jay sleeping on a branch. She wanted to tell the boy how to see these things in the starlight. But tonight they were not talking.

She felt the boy's tiredness as he walked behind her, and she put down the pack and held him in her arms while they rested. They went on again. The hunter star was down near the horizon, making the big circle the stars made every night. It was good to know the roundness, the completeness, again; not the sharp squareness of houses and streets. They came to a stream and drank and then found a grove of spruces. She pushed the drooping branches aside and went into that green spruce lodge and spread the blankets and they slept.

She wakened soon after sunrise and lay listening. The jays were scolding. A squirrel cried at them and she knew it was only jays and squirrels. She tucked the blankets around the sleeping boy, and took a fishhook and line and a knife and went to a grassy place beside the stream. She caught four grasshoppers, stiff with the night chill, put one on the hook and tossed it into a quiet pool. She caught four fish and went back past the grassy place and thanked the grasshoppers before she cleaned the fish. She gathered wood and built a fire near the stream, so the thin smoke would not be seen in the morning mist from the water, and she put green sticks inside the fish to hold them open and set them beside the fire to cook.

Then she wakened the boy and they ate. They washed themselves in the pool and sat naked on a rock, clean and rested and fed, and watched the sun rise over the mountain. Softly she sang the old song for washing yourself when the sun is rising, and the boy sang a part of it with her. He did not yet know all the words. After that, they put on their clothes and went on again.

That afternoon they came to the place where the two roads met. They sat in the scrub oak on the hillside and watched. Nobody came along either road. Then they went north where there was no road but only the game trails, to the east branch of the Piedra. She found a cave in which to spend the night, and the next afternoon they came to the foot of Horse Mountain.

She turned away from the place where the black-stem ferns grow, and they climbed the mountain till she found a place to watch the valley. They watched until the sun sank. Nobody came.

They stayed there two days, eating berries, building no fire to make smoke or smell; and nobody came. Then they went back down and around the mountain to the place where the black-stem ferns grow. At the spring beyond the ferns, she found his sign, a leafless willow twig that stood in a mossy place. She pulled

---

2. **The star ... back,** actually the constellation of Orion.

it out; it had been peeled at the bottom. She put it back, peeled two more twigs and thrust them into the moss beside it. Then she and the boy climbed to a sheltered place from which she could see the spring.

He came that evening. He stepped out of the deep shadows and took the twigs from the moss, and then he was gone. She said her thanks to the earth and sky and the quarters of the earth, and then she and the boy slept. He knew they had come.

It was not until the second day afterward that he came for them. He held her hand and smiled at the boy. He said, "They have not yet come here." And she knew he had gone back the way she came and made sure nobody had followed her.

That afternoon they went over the shoulder of Horse Mountain. They saw four spruce grouse sitting on a low branch, and while she walked in front of them to keep them watching her he went around behind them and killed two with a stick. When it was dark he built a fire inside an old bear den and she cooked the grouse. They were together. It was a happy time.

The next day they followed the big fork of the Piedra to Bald Mountain. At the far side of the mountain, he built a shelter close beside a spring. It was the first week of August.

They heard a mountain lion's kill-cry in the night and next morning he went up the mountain to look for the deer carcass. He found it in a patch of brush where the lion had dragged it after eating a forequarter. He butchered out the meat and took what was left of the skin and packed them down to the shelter. She built a drying rack, sliced the meat thin to cure; now she had skin to make leather and sinew for sewing. And that night he kept a fire going and sat watching for the lion, which prowled the nearby darkness, growling but fire-wary.

She said that if he would get more deer she could make meat for the winter. He said, "The rifle makes too big a noise. But when I was a boy I killed birds with arrows." And the next day he cut a strip of scrub oak and shaped it and cured it by fire and sun. He made pine shafts and feathered them with grouse feathers and hardened their points in the fire. He hid where the deer came to a pool at dusk to drink and shot all his arrows. But he did not kill one deer.

She said, "We did not sing the song for hunting deer." He said that a rifle was better than a song for killing deer, but he didn't dare use the rifle yet. So she taught him the song for hunting deer, and that night he killed a fat doe. She made meat. She made leather leggings and shirts. It was like the old days.

One morning they saw that Pagosa Peak to the east was white with snow. They moved to the south side of the mountain where the sun would shine when the short days came. He found a place where an old slide had taken down a whole grove of lodgepole pines. He said, "I will make a house of those poles."

She said, "I do not want a house. I want a lodge that is round, like the path of the stars, like good things that have no end." So he cut poles and made a lodge, and piled other poles and brush around it, and when the aspen leaves littered the earth with gold you could not see that lodge. It was a part of the earth itself.

She and the boy gathered wild pea seeds and dug roots of the elk thistle. They gathered acorns and pine nuts. She shaped a grinding stone and ground acorn meal and she wove a willow basket and filled it with water-leached meal.[3] They caught fish and dried them on a rack set over the fire.

The aspen leaves fell and the wind sang a song of wide skies and far mountaintops. The first snow came, fluffy as cotton grass in bloom. He looked about the lodge, stocked with food, snug and safe, and he said, "This is not like having a cornfield on the reservation or the company store at the sawmill." She smiled;

_____
3. **water-leached meal,** acorn meal that has been washed in water.

this was the way it should be. She sang the song of the lodge safe for the winter. The boy sang most of the words with her. He was learning the old ways.

Winter is long in the high country and the white days can bring black hunger. But the Utes have lived many generations, many grandmothers, in that land. They speak its language.

Before ice locked the valleys, Bessie and the boy gathered willow shoots and inner bark and ripe grasses for her winter basketry. She made rawhide, and her man shaped ironwood frames on which she wove snowshoes. He took deer while they still had their fat and taught the boy to set snares for rabbits. Then, when the cold shrank the days, she kept the stewpot full and simmering.

Winter passed, and came again. They lived as their people had always lived. And no one came looking for them.

The third time the aspens turned to gold, he looked at the boy, now almost as tall as his mother. "Soon the boy can go with me and kill deer in the thickets," he said. But that was a winter of much snow. When it was half over, the deer had been driven to lower valleys, and there was little meat in the lodge. One day he said, "I must go and find the deer," and he put on his snowshoes. He said he was going over the ridge into the valley beyond, and he went up the slope to cross the gully, an hour's travel from the lodge. It was a hot-sun morning after a brittle cold night.

He had been gone an hour when she heard the thunder sound, the voice of an avalanche. She went outside and saw a plume of fine snow like a cloud over a big snowslide, and she saw where the slide had come lunging down the mountain. She cried out once in horror, and the boy came and stood beside her, watching, as the snow plume floated away and the thunder echoed into silence down the gully.

She moaned with grief, knowing as clearly as though she had seen it happen. She said to the boy, "We must make mourning. But first we must find him."

They put on snowshoes, and went up the slope, following her man's tracks to the gully. It was swept clean, not one tree left standing. Far down the valley they saw the heap of snow and rocks and broken trees where the slide had piled upon itself. They crossed to the other side of the gully. There were no tracks. He had not crossed the gully.

They went down to the foot of the slide, looking along its jumbled face. Then the boy shouted and pointed to something in the snow. It was the shaft of an arrow. They dug in the snow, and finally they found his body and stood beside it, crying for him; and the boy sang the wailing song for the dead. She had not taught him that; he had it in his heart. Then she got the broken body over her shoulders and, step by heavy step, she carried him home to the lodge. And all that night they made mourning.

The next day she dressed him in new leggings and shirt and wrapped him in blanket and deerskin. She filled baskets with food and looped long thongs to a deerskin, and they hauled him up the mountain to a cave. They set the food beside him, that he might eat on his long journey. Then they sang the death songs for him, with the stars watching them, and they went down the mountain and back to the lodge.

She said to the boy, "Now you are the man."

It was a long winter. Some days the boy's snares had no rabbits and they went hungry. Each day she told him the old tales and sang the old songs, and he watched the way she wove baskets. Each day he strung the bow and drew the bowstring as far as he could. When there were leaves on the aspens again he could draw an arrow almost to the point. Then the deer came back up the valleys and he made his first big meat.

She said, "Soon you will know a name for yourself." He said, "This morning I met a she-bear, a grizzly, and she was not afraid of me. We talked to each other. When I killed the deer I left part of the meat for that she-bear. I shall call myself Bear's Brother."

And that was his name.

Summer passed like a white cloud drifting over the mountain. One day when she was cutting wood the axehead broke. She said to the boy, "We must go to Pagosa for a new axe. They cannot want him now for killing Frank No Deer."

She was not sure this was true, but she knew she had to go. So she took two of her best baskets and they went down to Pagosa, to Jim Thatcher's store. People turned to look, because they wore deerskin clothes. But nobody said, "Where is your man?"

Jim Thatcher had been in that store many years, and his father there before him. He traded salt and sugar and knives and axes and cans of beans for Indian robes and leatherwork and baskets. She set the two baskets on his counter. He looked at them, then at her. "You used to live here, didn't you?" he said.

She made the sign that she did not understand. "How much?" she said, pointing to the baskets.

"Do you want cash or trade?" he asked.

Without answering, she chose an axe and put it on the counter beside the baskets. Then she beckoned to the boy, and together they looked eagerly about the store. The boy stopped at a case of hunting knives. She asked what he would like. He said, in the tongue, "There is nothing." But his eye went back to the knives. Jim Thatcher saw this. He took out a knife and laid it on the counter. "This one?" he asked. The boy closed his eyes. He said again to his mother, "There is nothing."

She turned to Jim and said, "Candy." Jim filled a small bag and set it on the counter. He started to put the knife back in the case, but she made a quick gesture. So Jim Thatcher mentally added up the prices: two dollars for the axe, a dollar and a half for the knife, a nickel for the candy. . . . But the baskets were the best Ute work he had ever seen. He might get three or four dollars apiece for them. He put the knife back on the counter, and she

nodded, satisfied. He asked, "Where is your man?" She looked at him, a flash of fear in her eyes. "I remember you," he said. "Your man is George Black Bull."

She put the things in her pack and started to leave. "No need to run," he said. "That case is all cleared up. Self-defense, they called it. Do you understand?" She stared at him, searching his face. "You understand English. Tell George he can come back. They're not looking for him anymore."

She shook her head, and spoke to the boy in Ute, and they left the store.

Nobody spoke to them. Nobody followed. . . . But it could have been a trick, what Thatcher had said. Maybe they wanted the boy. They left the road and sat hidden in the brush, watching, for an hour. But there was nobody. They went on, following the game trails, walking carefully to leave no track.

One day in the spring when he went to catch fish, he met the she-bear again. He said to her, "I am Bear's Brother and we are friends." She listened as he sang a song of friendship that came to him. Then she went away, but he followed her and saw her uproot an old stump and catch three chipmunks and lick up the swarming ants. He left half the fish he caught for her.

When he told his mother of this, she said, "It is good to have a friend." She told him that the Utes had been friends of everything in the mountains in the old days—bears, deer, mountain lions, jays, ravens. Then she was silent. She could not tell him the things that were in her mind, the things Jim Thatcher had said about her man. She had been so afraid that she hadn't really heard what he said. She wanted to hear these things again. She told the boy she must go on a journey alone. If they took her, she could get away, somehow; but the boy might not know how.

She took two baskets to trade, and Jim liked them, as before. She chose calico for herself in trade and a blue coat with brass buttons for the boy. It was more than he would like to give her for the baskets, but she wanted him to talk. They haggled, taking away, putting back. Finally he said, "Bessie, you didn't tell your man what I said. He hasn't been to town."

"There is this thing about Frank No Deer," she said. Unconsciously, she fell into English.

"I told you that was settled. You didn't believe me? Well, it is. Now where is George?" She made the gesture, "Cut off, finished."

"That's too bad. What happened?"

"The snowslide. Two winters gone."

"I'm sorry, Bessie. And the boy?"

She smiled. Then she held out a hand, high as her head. She put her hand on the blue jacket. "For him," she said. He let her take the calico and jacket, and when she left the store with them she met Blue Elk. He stopped in surprise. "I have waited a long time to see you."

"I am here. You see me." Her voice was cold.

"We must talk," Blue Elk said, and he took her to a vacant lot near the bridge. They sat down and he glanced at her clothes. "You are living in the old way. Where?" She didn't answer.

"Your man can come back," he said. "I settled that thing for the cost of two horses. You owe me the cost of two horses."

"I told you I did not have the cost of one goat."

"I told them he killed Frank No Deer because Frank tried to kill him. That is the way it was settled. Your man owes me for this. Where is your man?" She made the cut-off sign. "Dead?" he asked. She nodded. "And the boy?" She did not answer. "The boy should be in the school at Ignacio."

"No! . . . No!"

He grabbed her pack, pulling it open. The calico and the coat with brass buttons fell out. She caught the coat up and held it away from him. He took the cloth. "You owe me for settling this thing. Give me the coat."

He was on his knees, holding to the pack and her cloth. She turned and ran up the street. She went back to Bald Mountain with no food, no cloth, but with the blue coat with brass buttons. And with the knowledge that it was settled, this thing about Frank No Deer.

The next summer she went alone to Pagosa again. This time she took four baskets and traded them for a red blanket. When she had put it in her pack, Jim said, "Watch out for Blue Elk, Bessie."

"That one!" She said it like a curse.

"He tried to sell your cloth back to me last summer. He made quite a fuss when I wouldn't take it. What happened?"

"He stole that cloth from me. He said I owed him the cost of two horses. For settling that thing about my man."

"Why, the old scoundrel! He wasn't even a witness at the inquest. Well, he's out of town today."

So she went back and gave the blanket to the boy for his bed. He knew that red is the rainbow color for protection.

He had begun to fill out, with the stocky frame of the Utes. He could drive an arrow all the way through a deer and carry its hindquarters on his shoulders. He had braids almost as long as his mother's, and he wore a breechclout[4] and moccasins in the summer, and in the winter, leggings and the winter shirt.

That was a bad winter. Their meat was gone before the days began to lengthen, though Bessie ate little, saving it for the boy. "You must be strong," she said. "When these storms end we must go to the lower valleys for meat."

At last the storms eased and they prepared to get meat. She went with him, though he said she should not, for she remembered what had happened to her man.

She was weak from lack of food and the cold made her cough. When he took a deer, they ate the liver and those parts that make strength. They made packs of the meat and went back to the lodge. It was a long journey

---

4. **breechclout**\ˈbrēch·klaut\ a cloth or animal skin worn to cover the loins.

and when they returned she was so weak she could scarcely stand. He made her lie on her bed and cooked soup for her. She had a pain in her chest.

She said, "Help me to sit up," and he helped her. She tried to work at a basket, but her hands would not do what she told them to do. He sat beside her and made the basket for her. He said, "My hands have watched your hands many times. My hands are your hands now."

The pain became worse. She was so hot she could not have even one robe around her shoulders, then so cold that he put his red banket around her and still she shivered. She said, "I am sick." He said, "I am singing the songs for making you well." She said, "I do not hear these songs." He said, "I am singing them inside." She said, "Sing them outside. I am very sick."

He sang the songs all that night. She said, "I am not going to get over this sickness, my son." He said, "I will not sing the song for going away yet." She said, "No. Not yet."

That afternoon she talked about things he had not known, the sawmill and Blue Elk and Frank No Deer. Then she did not talk. It was night. She said, "Sing the song for going away, my son." She tried to reach up and touch his face, but her arm was too weak. He took her hand and held it to his face. Then she died.

He made mourning all that night, and when it was daylight he put her deerskin dress on her and wrapped her in the red blanket, then in a deerskin robe, so she would be warm on the long journey. He put dried berries and dried meat, the last there was in the lodge, in two baskets. And he took her up the mountains to the cave where they had buried his father. He buried his mother there, and he sang the old songs. Then he went back to the lodge and he was alone.

Spring came again. Strawberries made the grass white with blossom and red anemones were in bloom. The boy caught trout in the pools, and watched for his friend, the bear. Then he saw her one morning in a wild meadow, eating grass and strawberries. She had two cubs with her. He talked to her and she shook her head and growled. A she-bear with cubs is not friendly. Her cubs listened, curious about this boy, but she cuffed them and hurried them away into the brush.

For days he watched them. He found where she went for food, and where she slept. But she was no longer his friend. One day he said to the cubs, "I am Bear's Brother. You are my brother and my sister." But the she-bear growled to him to go away.

So he made friends of the squirrels that lived in a hollow pine tree near the lodge. They sat in his hand and talked to him. Then the chipmunks in the rocks asked to be friends. They came into the lodge and lived with him. A jay said it wanted to be his friend. It rode on his shoulder and pecked at the lobe of his ear. Serviceberries ripened and he dried them. He made meat and smoked it as he had learned from his mother.

Then the man came.

The boy was fishing when his friend the jay called an alarm from a nearby aspen. The boy drew in his line, covered his tracks, and sat in the brush to watch. The jay flew down the valley, screaming, and came back, tree by tree, telling the boy a stranger was coming. Then the man appeared, with his mouse-colored burro. He stopped at pool, picked up a handful of sand and let the water from it trickle between his fingers. He shook his head and threw the sand back. Then he and the burro went on up the creek. The jay sat on the boy's shoulder and was silent.

The boy followed the man all afternoon. He went slowly, scooping a handful of sand from every pool. Toward evening he found some that pleased him. He took a pan from the pack on the burro, put sand and water into it and slowly swished it out again, then rubbed his finger on the bottom of the pan. Then he unpacked the burro and made camp beside the stream.

The boy went back to his lodge. On the way, he met the she-bear and her cubs. He tried to tell her about the stranger, but she told him not to talk to her. He was going out to watch again the next morning when he heard the thunder of a gun. Three times. Then there was silence.

He did not hurry. What happened had happened and could not be changed. But soon he heard the man shouting angrily. Then he saw him at the creek, his left arm red with blood to his fingers. The man washed his arm, but could not stop the blood. And then the boy saw the she-bear, a grizzled brown heap beside the man's fire. The man walked around her, still afraid. He tore his shirt and tied a strip of cloth around his arm and twisted a stick in it, but the blood still ran from his fingers. His talk became fear-talk. He went to get his burro, but it was afraid of the bear and braced its legs, and the man was so weak he almost fell before he got on its back. He shouted and beat the burro with his gun and it went around the bear and down the valley at a trot.

The boy left his watching place. The female cub was dead beside the she-bear; he heard the other cub crying beyond the creek. He found it and talked to it and it went with him to the man's camp. It cried when it nosed at the dead she-bear. He talked to it again, and fed it the man's food. Then he told the cub to come with him to his lodge, and it came.

That is how the boy and the bear cub became brothers and friends. After that the boy was not alone.

Jim Thatcher was checking invoices on a warm July day when he heard the yelps of a dogfight in the street. Then someone shouted, "Get a gun! It's a bear!" Jim ran outside with his .30-30.[5] He couldn't believe his eyes. There was a grizzly cub, hunkered back in the dust, with three dogs yelping and dancing around it. A boy was shouting to the cub in Ute. He was ten or eleven years old, and dressed in the old way, with breechclout, moccasins and braids. The cub started to go to him, only to be attacked by the dogs again. It snarled, and slapped a dog sprawling with a gash along its ribs.

Men were running up from all directions. Someone shouted, "Kill it, Jim, before it kills every dog in town!" The cub licked the boy's hand, then faced the crowd, frightened by the uproar, but ready to fight.

Jim called to the men, "Keep your shirts on. Can't you see it's a pet cub?" He turned to the boy. "Tell your friend to behave himself, son."

The boy looked at him, bewildered. He said something in Ute, caught the bear's scruff in one hand, and picked up his pack. Then he and the cub walked into Jim's store. Jim followed and closed the door behind him. The crowd clustered outside the door.

While the cub stood beside him, the boy set three baskets on the counter. Then he went to a pile of blankets, found a red one and brought it back to the counter.

Jim examined the baskets. They were identical with the last ones Bessie had brought in, though of even better workmanship. He looked at the boy. "Where is your mother?" There was no answer. The boy pushed the baskets toward Jim and drew the blanket toward himself.

Jim shook his head. No use dickering. This boy was a throwback, right out of the old, old days. Jim asked, "Don't you know any English at all?"

The boy's blank look said, truthfully, that he didn't.

Jim went outside and found Blue Elk in the crowd, and Blue Elk came into the store, beaming at being singled out. Jim said, "This is Bessie Black Bull's boy. He doesn't savvy[6] English. Find out where his mother is."

Blue Elk spoke to the boy in the tongue. "We are of the people, we two. I am your friend. The man wants to know where is your mother, where you are living now."

---

5. **.30-30,** a hunting rifle referred to commonly as a "thirty-thirty."

6. **savvy,** a slang term for "understand" or "know"; a corruption of the Spanish word "sabe."

The boy scowled. "My mother—" He made the cut-off sign. "I live in my lodge with my brother."

When Blue Elk said Bessie was dead, Jim exclaimed, "I don't believe it! She made these baskets. When did she die?"

Blue Elk asked the question, but the boy said, "I will not talk of this thing." He made the cut-off sign, sharply.

"Boys do not speak to the old men of their people in this way!" Blue Elk said impatiently.

But the boy folded the blanket into his pack, put his hand on the cub's scruff and went out through the crowd, the cub beside him. Nobody tried to stop them as they went back to the hills.

As Blue Elk went off, puzzling over this matter, the preacher caught up with him. "Who was that boy, Blue Elk?"

Blue Elk glanced at him. "Thomas Black Bull."

"Thomas Black Bull? Then that's the boy I baptized. Why is he running around in a clout like a savage? Where are his parents?"

"His parents are dead. He lives with his brother."

"I didn't know he had a brother. Does he mean an uncle?"

Blue Elk looked at him shrewdly. "I could find out."

"I wish you would. I baptized him. I feel responsible."

"I worry for my people," Blue Elk said. "But it is a hard trip, and I am old. I have no money for this trip."

The preacher felt in his pocket, and Blue Elk heard the clink of silver dollars. The preacher offered him one, but Blue Elk shook his head. "This will be a very hard trip. Ten dollars."

"All I have is the mission money, but I might make it five. And if you bring the boy in to the reservation school, the Indian agent might give you five more dollars of government money."

"I do this for my people." Blue Elk held out his hand.

Blue Elk tracked the boy and the bear into the mountains, and on the third day he rode into the hollow below the lodge. A jay screamed at him; a squirrel chattered. He waited, letting the jay and the squirrel say he was there, and soon the boy appeared. He said, "I did not ask you to come here."

"I have come to help you. I am tired and hungry."

The boy looked at him, the jay on his shoulder. Then he said, "You may rest and eat. Then you must go." He led the way to the lodge.

Inside, in the coolness and dimness, Blue Elk remembered his grandmother's lodge. The boy set dried meat in front of him, and it had the taste of meat he had eaten in his boyhood. He saw the bows and arrows, the venison on the drying rack, the tanned robes on the walls, the sewing basket with its coil of dry sinew and its bone awls.[7] He saw the willow twigs and ferns for baskets. There was a coil of strips in a bowl of water, pliant for weaving, and a partly finished basket. It was a lodge such as only the old people remembered.

He said, "When I was young I knew a lodge such as this. When the short white days came we were hungry."

"That is the way it is."

"That is the way it was. The old days are gone." The boy did not answer. "Your father was my friend," Blue Elk said. "Now your father is gone, I am a grandfather to you. I must tell you what to do."

The boy looked at Blue Elk and sang the beginning of the mourning song. He stopped. "If you are a grandfather," he said, "you will sing the mourning song." But Blue Elk was silent. The boy said, "How can you tell me what to do when you do not know the songs?"

"I sing the song inside."

"My mother and father will not know if you sing the song inside." He sang again, and Blue Elk closed his eyes and sang with him. His

---

7. **bone awls,** pointed tools of bone used for making holes in leather.

memory did not know the words, but his tongue remembered, and tears came to his eyes. It was a song for Blue Elk's own mother. Then Blue Elk opened his eyes, and forgot the old people. He said, "When did your mother go away?"

"In the winter before the winter that is past."

Blue Elk stared at him. "You have been alone too many days." The boy made no answer. "My ears are listening," Blue Elk said. "It is good to talk of what happened."

The boy looked into the ashes. It was a long time since he had talked to anyone except the bear cub, the jay and the squirrels. He was a boy, with things to tell, not a man who can contain all the things that happen. At last he said, "I will tell of these things." But there was a whine at the doorway. He said, "Come in, Brother. We have one of the grandfathers with us."

The bear cub came in, sniffing warily. Blue Elk sat quietly and let it know his smell. It bristled and turned to the boy. The boy said, "Come, I shall tell this grandfather about you." The cub went to him and lay down, and the boy told Blue Elk about the bear and about his father and mother. When he had done, Blue Elk said, "The old days are gone, ended."

"How can there be an end?" the boy asked. "There is the roundness." He made the gesture for the circle, the no-end.

"There is the roundness. But our people have forgotten it." He studied the boy's face. "Do you know the song for remembering?" The boy sang it. When he was through, Blue Elk said, "You will sing that song to our people who have forgotten, in Ignacio."[8]

The boy sat silent for a long time. Then he said, "You will go and tell them of the songs. I will stay here."

"They should hear these songs," Blue Elk said. "It is good for a people to change but it is not good for them to forget."

He believed this as he said it. Then he remembered the Indian agent, who might give him five more dollars, and the preacher who felt responsible for this boy. He told himself he must do this thing. He said, "Tomorrow we will go to Ignacio."

The boy said, "Tomorrow I will talk of this."

The next morning they went down to the pool and bathed. Blue Elk gasped in the icy coldness, but he was warm inside as he had not been since he was a boy. When they had bathed, they sat on a rock that faced the rising sun. The boy sang the song to the sun, and Blue Elk's tongue remembered. He said again, "Our people should hear these songs."

The boy thought. He asked, "How long is it to Ignacio?" and Blue Elk said, "Less than three days' journey."

After breakfast, still considering, the boy called the jay and the squirrels. When the jay sat on his shoulder and one of the squirrels in his hand, he whispered a question and they seemed to answer.

Blue Elk was looking around the lodge at all the things worth silver dollars. He could return. Even if the agent did not pay him five dollars, he could be well paid for the journey. Then he told himself: I came for the boy's good. This boy should not be here alone in the winter.

The boy turned from the doorway. "I will come. The jay and the squirrels will watch till I return." He turned to the bear cub. "But you will go with me, Brother."

That is how it happened.

DISCUSSION FOR UNDERSTANDING

1. Why do George Black Bull, Bessie, and the boy go back to living in the old ways?

2. Why does Bessie want a lodge that is round?

3. Describe the circumstances under which the boy is given a name by the white man. What name does he later choose for himself and why?

4. Why does Blue Elk follow the boy back to his lodge? How does he persuade the boy to go with him to Ignacio?

---

8. **Ignacio**\ĭg ▲na·syō\

2 The School

When they came in sight of the agency Blue Elk wished he had left the bear on the mountain. The Utes respected bears, but the agency people did not understand these things.

There were many buildings at the agency: the headquarters and the school, the dormitory and the barns and stables. There was a flagpole, with a red, white, and blue flag at the top. The boy wondered what it meant. There were Indians hurrying from one building to another, but the men and boys had short hair, which was a strange thing to see. Blue Elk said, "We will talk to the head man. He will hear what you have to say, but first you must do as he says."

The boy understood Blue Elk's words, but he did not know what Blue Elk meant by those words. He said to the bear, "We will talk to the head man in this big lodge."

Inside the headquarters Blue Elk led the way to a white man at a desk. The man looked up. "Hello, Blue Elk," he said. Then he saw the boy and the bear. "What's that bear doing here?" he demanded sharply.

"The bear belongs to the boy," Blue Elk said uneasily. "The boy wouldn't come without him. He should be put in a strong pen." Then he added, "The boy does not understand your talk. He speaks only Ute. The preacher said he should be in school."

The man hurried out. He came back with a strong collar and a chain, and handed them to Blue Elk. The bear was wrinkling its nose as though it did not like the man's smell. But it stood quietly, the boy's hand on its neck.

Blue Elk turned to the boy. "The man wants you to put this collar on the bear. It is so he will not be hurt. These people are afraid of bears."

Reluctantly, the boy fastened the collar on the bear cub, and the man led them to a pen for breaking wild horses. The man fastened the chain to a post in the middle of the pen.

"My brother will not like this thing," the boy said.

"The head man cannot hear what you have to say if he is afraid of the bear. Come." The boy spoke into the bear's ear before he went with Blue Elk and the man to the agent's office.

The government agent was a fat, red-faced man with freckles, sandy hair, and eyes so light blue they looked milky. He said, "Well, Blue Elk, what have you got up your sleeve this time? I understand you brought a bear cub with you." He looked at the boy. "And why is this boy running around in a clout? Who is he?"

"The preacher christened him Thomas Black Bull. He has been living alone, in the old way. He has no English, and his father and mother are dead."

The agent frowned. "Go get Benny Grayback. You wait outside, Blue Elk. I want to talk to this boy alone."

Benny Grayback was a stocky Ute, perhaps thirty years old. He wore a white shirt and a blue necktie, like the agent. He was in charge of the carpentry shop.

The agent said, "Benny, I want to talk to this boy. Blue Elk says he speaks no English. Is that true?"

Benny asked the question. "It is true," he said, and then he questioned the boy in Ute.

"He says his name is Bear's Brother and he lives with his brother," Benny said finally. "His friends, a jay and the squirrels and chipmunks, also live with him." Benny smiled. "He has lived this way since his mother died, the winter before last. I think he must be wrong, but that is what he says."

"Tell him he will live here now, with other boys and girls. He will go to school and learn the things he should know."

"He says he did not come here to live, he came to tell us of the old ways." Benny smiled again. "Blue Elk told him we would want to know these things."

"Sounds like Blue Elk. Tell him we will hear about the old ways at a proper time. First he must learn the new ways."

"He says he will go back to his own lodge until you want to listen to him."

"No. He *must* stay here for a while."

Benny said this. The boy did not answer.

The agent sighed. "Go get him some clothes, Benny. And look after him a few days, get him started. He looks like a bright boy. And Benny, don't let him turn that bear cub loose. I'll hold you responsible. Now send Blue Elk in again."

Benny left with the boy and Blue Elk came in, all smiles and expectancy. "This Thomas Black Bull," the agent said, "is he George Black Bull's son? The one who hid back in the hills?"

"That is right."

"Who told you to bring him in?"

"The preacher in Pagosa. He said he should be in school. He said you would pay me for the trip. It was a hard trip and I am an old man."

"I haven't any funds for that kind of thing. If you had come and told me, I would have sent my own men after him. You would sell your own grandmother, wouldn't you, Blue Elk?"

"My grandmother," Blue Elk said, "is dead."

He waited, but the agent dismissed him, and Blue Elk went out, hurt and angry. Well, if the agent would not pay him, there were other ways. As he rode past the horse-breaking pen, he thought it was good that the bear was here, not loose on Bald Mountain guarding the lodge.

They put Thomas Black Bull in a room with Luther Spotted Dog, who was fourteen and had been at the school several years. Luther helped Thomas put on the stiff new agency pants and shirt. Thomas tried one shoe, threw it aside, and kept his moccasins. When Luther showed him how soft the cot was, Thomas tore the bed apart and arranged the blankets on the floor. When Luther began to praise the school and the teachers, Thomas looked out the window and ignored him.

The supper bell rang, and they went down to the dining room. Thomas made a face at the cooking smells and when he tasted the meat he spat it out.

"It stinks," he said to Luther, and got up and went out.

Benny Grayback had been watching. He followed Thomas to the horse-breaking pen. "Where are you going?"

Thomas didn't answer. He opened the gate and the bear cub ran toward him. It was snubbed by the chain and jerked from its feet. Benny caught the boy by the shoulder.

"I am going back to my lodge!" the boy shouted.

"No," Benny said, holding his arms. "You are staying here."

"I shall take my brother and go!" The boy bit Benny's hand. Benny slapped him, closed the gate and hauled him away. "You are an evil person!" the boy cried, trying to wrench free. "I hate you! My brother hates you!"

But Benny twisted his arms behind him and forced him back to his dormitory room. There Benny made him sit down and told him he must learn to live the new way. The boy sat in defiant silence, and when Luther Spotted Dog came from supper Benny said, "Thomas is to stay here until breakfast time. I will hold you responsible."

Luther looked at Thomas dubiously, but he nodded.

Then Benny told Neil Swanson, the man in charge of livestock, to secure the bear. Neil lassoed the bear cub, choked it into submission, and padlocked the chain around its neck and to the snubbing post. Benny pocketed the keys.

The next morning Luther's face was scratched and his right eye almost closed. Thomas limped and his wrists were raw. After breakfast, which Thomas pushed away, Benny said to Luther, "You had a hard time last night."

"He would have killed me. I had to tie him up."

"Bring him to my class," Benny ordered.

When Benny introduced Thomas to the fifteen boys in the carpentry class, he stared at them coldly, then went to a window and stood with his back to the room. Two boys whispered, in Ute, about his braids. One of them took two long shavings and hung them behind his ears. All the boys laughed except Luther Spotted Dog. Benny told them to be quiet. Then a boy near Thomas whined like a bear and said in falsetto, "My name is Bear Meat." Without a word Thomas picked up a wooden mallet from the nearest bench and flung it at him. The boy dodged and the mallet clattered the length of the room.

"Stop it!" Benny ordered. "All of you! Get back to work." He took Thomas by the arm, led him to his desk. "Why did you do that?" he demanded in Ute. "These boys want to be your friends."

"I have no friends here," Thomas said.

So Benny took Thomas to Miss Rowena Ellis, who taught English. A plump woman who spoke several Indian tongues, she was unofficial mother to every homesick child in the school. To Thomas she said, in Ute, "We should know each other. This place is full of strangeness. I will tell you about it."

"I came here," he said, "to tell them of the old ways."

"I want to hear," she said, "but first I will tell you of the new ways." She started to tell him about the school.

He cut her off. "I do not need these things."

She was a patient woman. She smiled, and as her class filed into the room, she said: "We have a new boy, Thomas Black Bull. He will tell us about his interesting life, but first we must teach him some English. We will start today with oral review." The boys groaned, but she kept them at vocabulary drill while Thomas stood by the window. When it was over, Miss Ellis went to him. "You see, it is

not so hard to learn new things. You learned something today. I know this."

"I do not need these things," Thomas said. "You do not understand."

He left the room and ran outside to the breaking pen. The bear whined, and he tore angrily at the padlocks with his fingers. At last he gave up and stood silent while the bear licked his hands. Then he saw Benny Grayback waiting at the gate. "I will do these things you tell me to do if you will let my brother live with me."

Benny said, "Luther Spotted Dog would not be happy with a bear living in his room."

"Luther Spotted Dog can live in another place."

Benny said, "I am busy; but if you will go to your room after lunch, we will talk later."

Luther did not return to the room until after his last class. He opened the door and saw all his belongings piled in one corner. Thomas said, "Take your things and go." He threw Luther's things into the hall and closed the door. Luther ran for Benny Grayback, and together they forced the door. "What does this mean?" Benny demanded.

"Now there is room here for my brother," Thomas said.

Benny took Thomas by the arm. "Come with me. There is another room where you are going to live."

"First we will talk."

"We will go to this other room. Then we will talk."

He took Thomas downstairs to a room so small there was space for only a cot and a washstand. It had one small window, with bars on the outside, and it had a heavy door with a lock. Thomas said, "My brother will not like this place."

"We will not talk about the bear today," Benny said. He went out, and locked the door. The boy beat on the door with his fists, and then began to chant. It was a sorrow song, a song that Benny had never heard because it was the boy's own song. Benny did not want to listen but he heard, and although he wanted to go away he stayed there. He began to say the words softly, and to sway with the rhythm. It was a song from far back, not only in the boy but in Benny's own people. Its rhythm was his own heartbeat.

Then he heard his own voice, and forced himself to stop. This was nonsense. The old ways were gone. He hurried away and went to see the agent.

The agent was annoyed and said, "It is all because of that bear cub. We'll have to shoot it."

Benny Grayback gasped. "No!" he exclaimed. "You cannot kill the bear!" Then he clapped his hand over his mouth.

The agent frowned. He had tried to understand these people for twenty-five years, but there still were things that he could not fathom, emotions and superstitions that he couldn't reach, even in someone like Benny Grayback, who was civilized and educated.

"I know the feeling about bears," he said, carefully. "But when one is a troublemaker you kill it, don't you?" Benny nodded. "And this one is making trouble, isn't it?"

Benny hesitated. "There is trouble, yes."

"Because of the bear."

"I do not know this," Benny said, falling into the old speech pattern even though he spoke English. He paused. "If you kill the bear," he said, "then you will kill the boy."

"What makes you think that, Benny?"

"My grandmother—" Benny broke off. The boy's sorrow chant had beaten at him again. He shrugged away his grandmother and the old ways. "I know it," he said. "That is all."

The agent sighed. "Very well, Benny. Do the best you can for a day or two. And find Blue Elk; I think he can help us."

"Where have you been?" the agent asked when Blue Elk at last arrived. "I sent for you three days ago."

Blue Elk looked smug. "I have been busy," he said.

"I want you to take that bear back to the mountains."

Blue Elk shook his head. "I cannot do this. It is not my bear. It does not know me."

The agent smiled grimly. "The boy will take the bear. You will go along and bring the boy back without the bear."

Blue Elk seemed to be worrying something in his mind. "I cannot take the bear back to Bald Mountain," he said.

"The other side of Horse Mountain will be far enough."

Blue Elk seemed to relax somewhat. "That is a long journey."

"I will pay you ten dollars, silver."

Blue Elk sighed. "I do not like this job, but I need this money."

After supper he went to see the boy. "I have come to take you back to the mountains," he said. "Your brother will go with us."

"I do not need you to take us back. I can find the way."

"The agent says I go with you because I brought you here."

"Your mouth," the boy said bitterly, "is like Benny Grayback's. It is full of lies." And he began to chant his sorrow song.

"Be quiet," Blue Elk ordered. But the boy went on chanting, and before long Blue Elk was swaying to the rhythms and saying words that he remembered. Then darkness came, and the boy's hoarse voice died away, and Blue Elk fell asleep on the cot.

They started at dawn the next day, the bear dragging the chain still locked around its neck. They traveled two days, and each night Blue Elk padlocked the bear to a tree. The third morning they came to the foot of Horse Mountain. Again Blue Elk chained the bear to a tree. Then he said, "We will leave the bear here."

"My brother wants to go with me to my lodge."

"The bear can go," Blue Elk said. "But you must come back to the school with me."

Then the boy knew what they had done to him. Without a word, he came at Blue Elk, kicking, clawing, trying to take the keys from him. But Blue Elk was too strong for him. He took a rope and tied the boy's arms and ankles. "Let us have no more trouble," he said, when he had caught his breath. "The bear must go away. You must go back with me."

"No."

Blue Elk shrugged. "If you do not tell the bear to go, we will leave him chained to that tree. If that is the way you want it to be—" He waited, but the boy did not answer. Finally Blue Elk untied the boy's ankles. "We will go back now," he said. He took the end of the rope that bound the boy's arms, tied it to his pony's saddle horn and got into the saddle.

The boy looked at the bear, and he looked at Blue Elk. He said, "I will tell my brother to go home."

Blue Elk freed the boy's hands and gave him the keys, but he held on to the end of the rope. The boy said to the bear, "They have made me do this, Brother." He took off the chain, hugged the cub's head to him and buried his face in its neck. Then he stepped back. "Go home," he ordered. "Go!" And he turned away.

The bear stood for a moment, then took a step toward him. The boy cried, "Go—before they put the chain on you again!" And the bear turned, uncertain, and walked away from him. The boy said to Blue Elk, "I wish you were dead for this thing you have done."

Back at school, Thomas seemed finally to accept the routine. He ate the food and went back to a regular room in the dormitory. Rowena Ellis thought he had learned more than he let on in everything; but he was useless in the stables, and the slowest in the class in carpentry. He did better in the cobbler's shop, where the teacher noticed his unusual skill with his fingers and suggested that he might be a basketmaker. So Thomas was sent to the basketry class of Dolly Beaverfoot, a Paiute[1] from Utah.

Dolly gave Thomas the conventional basket materials, but he pushed the coarse reeds aside and said, "These are no good." He went outside and came back with an armful of willow stems. Dolly smiled with pleasure as he began stripping the bark from them with his teeth, in the old way. When he had the material to suit him he wove a basket that not even Dolly could match.

The girls in the basketry class—Thomas was the only boy—had whispered that he was handsome; and the boys, of course, heard about this. They began talking about "the new girl" and saying, "She makes better baskets than the teacher," and "Her name is really Bear's Sister."

Thomas ignored these things until one afternoon when he and Luther and two other boys were cleaning the horse barn. One of the boys said to Luther, "Was Bear's Sister nice to you, Luther, when she lived in your room?"

Luther grinned broadly. "No. She was a very poor squaw." He pretended to trip on his pitchfork and threw a forkful of dirty straw at Thomas.

Thomas said, "Don't do that again."

Luther laughed. "Bear's Sister is getting mad."

Thomas knocked Luther down, but another boy leaped on his back. He caught that boy by the hair and threw him to the floor. The fourth boy ran to find Neil Swanson, but when Neil got there Thomas had backed both his tormentors into a corner and was pounding their faces in turn.

Neil dragged him off, and ordered the other boys to their rooms. Then he asked, "Why did you start this fight?"

Thomas was silent.

"All right," Neil said, "I'll have to teach you a lesson." He got a harness strap and flogged him, and Thomas took it tight-lipped, without a sound. Neil said, "Now go to your room."

Thomas went to the basketry room instead and tore his baskets to shreds. Then he went to his room and locked the door. Neither Benny nor Rowena could make him unlock it.

---

1. **Paiute**\ˈpai·yūt\ an Indian tribe.

The agent said, "Leave him alone. He'll starve out in a day or two."

He didn't starve out. The second night he put on his breechclout, took a blanket and climbed out the window. He slid down a drain spout to the ground, forced his way into the kitchen and took a knife, a ball of strong cord and a two-pound remnant of pot roast. Then he started north, eating the meat as he traveled.

He went first to Horse Mountain. There he looked for bear sign and sang the bear song, but there was no sign and no answer, so he went on to their lodge on Bald Mountain.

He drank at his stream, and washed in his pool, and started up the path his moccasins had helped to make. Bushes already were overgrowing it. He called to the jay, but it screamed and flew off. The chipmunks ran and hid among the rocks. The squirrels scurried up the pines, scolding at his intrusion.

He came to the last turn in the path, and he put a hand to his mouth to stop the cry of pain. There was no lodge. Where it had been was a charred place, a circle of ashes.

He poked among the ashes. Nothing, not even a knife blade.

And then he knew. It was no accident. Someone had come and taken everything, even the battered cooking pot, and burned the lodge. He stood among the ashes and whispered his sorrow chant, not even saying it aloud. For small griefs you shout, but the big griefs must be borne alone, inside.

When he had finished he looked up the mountainside for a long time, thinking of his father and his mother. Then he sang his bear song as loud as he could sing. There was no answer. At dusk he sang it again. There was no answer.

It was as though he had never been here.

He lay in his blanket and slept, and the next morning clouds hung low over the mountain and the valley was filled with mist as cold as sleet. He bathed at the pool, but he sang no song for a new day. He did not even whisper the sorrow song. There was no song in him. Only a numbness, a nothing. . . .

The next day, he met them at the foot of

545

Horse Mountain. There were only two of them, Benny Grayback and an old tracker called Fish. Benny said, "We came to take you back to the reservation."

"I will go back," Thomas said, in English.

The day after he returned to school, Thomas had his braids cut off. The next morning he put on shoes. And after his return, he spoke only in English. He worked in the cobbler's shop, designing and plaiting quirts[2] and bridles. He was as skillful at this as he had been at basketry. He still made no friends, though several girls would have liked to be his friends. The boys who had taunted him left him alone, for he often carried one of the quirts he made.

Winter passed, and late March came. There were catkins[3] on the willows and tassels on the aspens. Thomas knew the bears would soon be leaving their winter dens to claim their old ranges.

A moonlit night came and he sat in his room and knew what was going to happen. He hoped it would happen, and he wished it would not. He waited, and the cattle bawled in their pens. The horses snorted and raced about their corrals. He opened his window, and in the moonlight he saw the bear beside the horse-breaking pen. It stood there nosing the air, then shuffled its feet like a great shaggy dog. It whined softly.

Other windows opened. Someone shouted an alarm.

Thomas picked up a quirt and ran through the moonlight to the corral, singing the bear song. The bear came to meet him. He stopped singing and shouted warning words, then angry words. The bear stopped and growled, then came on, whining again. He went up to it, swished the quirt in its face and screamed in Ute, "Go away! Go home to the mountains!"

The bear rose on its hind legs and spread its forepaws as though to tear him to pieces. Its teeth were white in the moonlight. It was a two-year-old now and stood taller than the boy. The boy lashed it across the face with

the quirt, again and again, screaming, "Go! Go! Go!" The bear dropped to all fours, whimpering. It nosed the boy's hands, and it cried like a child. And the boy put an arm around its neck, buried his face in its fur and wept. He wept until the bear drew away and licked his face and whimpered again.

The boy backed away. "You are no longer my brother," he cried. "When I went to find my brother and sang my song he would not listen. Now there is nobody."

He stood silent in the moonlight, his head bowed, and the bear swayed from side to side, from foot to foot, moaning.

"Go, or they will kill you," the boy said. "They do not need guns to kill. They kill without guns." He put a hand on the bear's neck and he said, "Come. I will go a little way with you." And they walked slowly across the grounds in the moonlight, toward the aspens with catkins like chipmunk tails. They walked among the trees and into the shadows, and after a little while there was the sound of a song so desolate that the coyotes answered it from the gullies beyond.

After another little while the boy came back out of the shadows of the trees, walking alone. Men and boys were standing beside the doorway. They stepped aside, making way for him, and later they said it was like seeing a remote and terrible man, not a boy.

The next day he went to his classes as though nothing had happened, but in his eyes people saw something that made them afraid. Nobody spoke of what had happened in the moonlight.

That spring Neil Swanson tried to make a farmer out of him. He learned, readily enough, to hitch a team to a plow, but plowing seemed senseless to him. Why should anyone rip up grass and make the earth grow something else? If left to itself, the earth would grow grass

---

2. **quirts,** riding whips with short handles and lashes of braided leather.
3. **catkins,** dense, drooping clusters of small, scale-like flowers.

and many other things. When you plowed up the grass you were making the earth into something it did not want to be.

After two weeks of crooked furrows, Swanson said, "Since you won't learn to plow, you'll have to learn to milk."

The smell of warm milk made him feel sick, but he learned to milk a cow. And that summer Neil sent him out with the horse herd each day. He learned to ride the old herd horse, and the long hours in the open were a relief. There was sunshine, sky, distance and a degree of freedom.

Soon Thomas began to wonder what it would be like to ride an unbroken horse. One day he roped a two-year-old colt and got on its back. He was thrown after the first two jumps. He caught the colt and tried again. That time he landed in a bed of cactus and spent the rest of the afternoon pulling out thorns. But the next day he rode another colt for several minutes before it bucked him off. He soon learned that each horse has its own rhythm—not only in its gaits,[4] but in the way it bucks and pitches. If he rode the horse with its own rhythm, gripped with his knees and thighs and kept his balance, he could ride every horse in the herd. He began to feel a sense of mastery, something he had not felt since the day he stood in front of his burned lodge and knew that everything that had ever mattered to him was gone.

Toward the end of August he was riding a particularly mean two-year-old pinto when Benny Grayback rode out to the grazing ground. He was so intent on the pinto that he rode it to a standstill before he knew that Benny was there.

Benny glared at him. "How long have you been riding the colts? They are supposed to graze. Neil says they are all too thin, and I came to find out why."

"The grass is poor," Thomas said.

"You give them no time to eat it. It is not for you to tame them. When they are needed, they will be tamed by those who know how to break horses." Which was true. Each spring

the horses were driven into the breaking pen, beaten, choked and water-starved until there was no fight in them. In the old days the Utes had respected their horses and tamed them. Now they broke the horses, broke their spirit.

Thomas gathered the herd, and he and Benny took them back to the agency. And that was the end of his horse-herding.

Classes started and Thomas went back to leatherwork and the hated cow barn. When the winter began to thin away, Benny said, "Albert Left Hand needs a helper for the lambing season, and Thomas Black Bull isn't good for anything else; he might make a sheep-herder."

The agent said, "It's worth a try."

So they took him to Albert Left Hand out at the edge of the reservation. Albert was a short, fat man who smelled of rancid mutton tallow. When he was not napping or sitting in silence beside his tent, he spent his time hunting prairie dogs, and he seemed to eat nothing but prairie dog stew. He was a surly old man of few words, and those usually were abusive.

Despite this, Thomas found a degree of peace and contentment with Albert Left Hand. It was spring and the arid sage flats came to life in purple ground plum, starry cactus, white lilies and larkspur, the gold of pucker-petaled sundrops and the fragrant moonglow of primroses. Meadowlarks greeted the sunrise and cheered the evening. Horned larks spilled song all day in their spiraling flight. In the prairie dog towns, burrowing owls tilted on their long, slim legs and hissed and screeched.

When the ewes[5] began to drop their lambs, Albert Left Hand showed Thomas how to help a ewe in the birth struggle, how to get a lamb on its feet and sucking. When a lamb or ewe failed to survive, Albert skinned it. "Pelt's worth a quarter," he said. Then, when all the

---

4. **gaits,** a series of foot movements such as walk, trot, pace, or canter by which a horse moves forward.
5. **ewes\yūz** female sheep.

lambs were born, Albert went back to hunting prairie dogs.

But Thomas was busier than ever, for the lambs had even less sense than their foolish mothers. They strayed, they fell into canyons, they thrust stupid noses at buzzing rattlesnakes. And at dusk, the coyotes got one now and then.

July came and they had saved forty-five out of sixty lambs. The ewes had put on fat and were showing prime fleeces when Thomas helped Albert herd them to the shearing pens near the agency. After they were penned, Albert said, "Now we will go to Bayfield. I will sell the skins. I will buy you a bottle of pop."

Drowsy Bayfield had its Saturday afternoon crowd. A dozen horses were hitched at the long rack in front of the general store; the two saloons spilled loud talk and laughter onto the board sidewalk. When they had unloaded the stinking pelts Albert gave Thomas a nickel, but Thomas didn't know where to get pop. Looking, he came to the saddlery shop. In the window was the most beautiful saddle he had ever seen, polished and ornately tooled. He stared at it, admiring with all his heart.

Then he saw the black-and-white bridle hanging from the saddle horn. It was one he had made, with a pattern he had thought up. He read the price tag and gasped. Five dollars! He hadn't got anything for it because the money went to pay for his keep. If he could sell bridles for five dollars, then some day he could buy that saddle.

He was still staring at it when two cowhands came out of the nearest saloon. The tall, slim one jabbed a thumb into Thomas's ribs and said, "You know how to ride a horse—all Indian kids do. Look, you go get my horse and ride it back here and I'll give you this quarter."

Tom looked at the man wide-eyed. A quarter just to ride a horse! "Get the black gelding down there in the cottonwoods," the cowhand said. "And *ride* him. He don't lead very well." His companion laughed.

Thomas found the horse, hitched by a neck rope. It was so skittish he had to drive it around the tree until the rope was wound tight. Then he snubbed the reins to the saddle horn, so it couldn't get its head down, untied the rope, got his foot in the stirrup and swung into the saddle as the horse began buckjumping. When he had its rhythm and his own balance, he gave it a little slack in the reins and it bucked viciously a time or two before he got it headed up the street. Holding its head high with the snubbed reins, he rode it to the waiting cowhand, got off and handed the reins to its owner.

The cowhand growled, "You snubbed the reins."

"He brought the horse, didn't he?" his companion said. "Pay up, Slim. And let's see *you* ride him. Unless you're afraid."

"I can ride anything with hair and four legs," Slim said, giving Tom the quarter. He swung into the saddle, but before he hit the seat the horse had ducked its head and begun to buck. Three jumps and Slim was loose. The fourth jump sent him sprawling. He got to his feet, cursing, and someone in the crowd that had gathered caught the horse and brought it back.

The other cowhand turned to Thomas. "I'll give you a dollar if you ride that horse again—without snubbing the reins."

Thomas hesitated. But a dollar, a whole dollar!

He took the reins, gave them one turn around his left hand, and swung up. He held the horse's head up for one jump while he settled himself, then tightened his knees, let the reins go slack and rode with the buck. The horse came down stiff-legged, went into a series of twisting bucks, and side-lunged halfway up the block. Tom kept his seat and put it to a stiff-legged trot. It tossed its head and wanted to run, but he held it in to the end of the block, then came back in a series of short, jolting jumps.

A moment later, proud and embarrassed, he was squirming away through the crowd with his silver dollar when an unshaven redhaired man in levis and worn, fancy-stitched boots stopped him.

"You're quite a rider, son," he began. Then, edging down the street with Thomas, he asked many questions, and Thomas told him his name and why he was herding sheep.

The man grinned. "A boy like you herding sheep! You just throw in with Red Dillon and we'll *both* go places. How'd you like to be a real bronc twister? I got a place down in New Mexico, the other side of the reservation, with a whole string of bad horses you can ride."

Thomas hesitated. "I haven't got a permit."

"I'll tend to that. The agency's right on our way."

They found Albert Left Hand in the café and Red told him he was taking Thomas home with him. Albert Left Hand didn't even look up. He took a bite of raisin pie, chewed for a moment, then growled, "Boys come, boys go. That one's no good."

Red grinned as they turned away. "We ought to eat before we go," he said to Thomas. "Me giving you a job, you ought to treat. Money's no good in your pocket."

So they found stools at the other end of the counter, and Red ordered chili and coffee for both of them, until they had an even dollar's worth. Then Thomas gave Red his dollar and Red paid.

Red's horses, a black and a sorrel,[6] were waiting. Both were saddled, but the saddle on the black had no horn. Red saw Thomas puzzling. "This here's a bronc saddle, for rodeo-ing," he said. "If a bronc comes over backwards onto you, there's no horn to punch a hole in your guts. If you get throwed frontwards by a mean bucker there's no horn to hang you up by your chap strings. You're going to see a lot of this saddle, Tom." He swung onto the sorrel and Tom mounted the black, and they headed for the agency.

DISCUSSION FOR UNDERSTANDING

1. What makes Blue Elk decide to return to the lodge on Bald Mountain?

2. How do the agent and Blue Elk trick Tom into parting with the bear?

3. How does Tom change when he returns to school after running away to Bald Mountain? How is he different after his second parting with the bear?

3   The Arena

Red got the permit without any trouble. For the agent, it solved the whole problem of Thomas Black Bull.

Tom and Red Dillon rode south to New Mexico. The second day they rode across rolling flats, mirages shimmering and vanishing ahead of them, and Red made a sweeping gestures. "Now we're on my range. Grass enough here for a thousand head of horses. But help eats up all the profits, so I keep my layout small. Me and old Meo handle it. You'll like Meo. Used to be quite a rider himself, till a bronc fell on him eight, ten years ago. Broke something in his back. Ever seen a rodeo, Tom?"

"No."

"Things go right, we'll go to the show in Aztec next month. And we'll get paid for it, Tom. We'll *make* them pay." He laughed. "I've got a feeling my luck's turned."

In the midafternoon they came to the sharp-walled canyon of the San Juan,[1] which swept in a great arc down through a corner of New Mexico before it swung north again into Utah and the incredible canyons of the Colorado.[2] They rode down a trail where the river twisted like a silver snake in its canyon, and came to a weathered cabin, a log barn and some corrals among huge old cottonwoods. A man was hoeing a patch of beans and pepper plants beyond the cabin, and when they had taken care of

---

6. **sorrel,** a horse with a reddish-brown colored coat.

---

1. **San Juan,** a river.
2. **Colorado,** a river.

their horses he came to meet them. He was a gnomish,[3] leather-faced old Mexican with a hump on his shoulders.

"This is Tom, Meo," Red said. "We're going to teach him to be a bronc twister."

Meo looked at Tom. Then he asked Red, "You win at Mancos?"

Red shook his head. "Cleaned out. But my luck's changed. Me and Tom are going to Aztec and take their shirts."

"Maybe," Meo said, and he went back to the garden.

The cabin was one long room with bunks against one wall, and assorted riding gear on pegs on the other. A string of red chilies hung from a beam, and on the ashes in the fireplace stood a coffeepot and a simmering iron kettle. Red filled two bowls with beans and chili from the kettle.

"Well, Tom," he said, "the agent asked would I see to it that you had a home and learned a trade. I don't know what he'd say about this place, but you won't starve. As for a trade, well, I never been in the poorhouse, and I don't plan to be. You stick with me and we'll both make out. Now eat up. Put some gristle in your gut. You'll need it, because you're going to start learning that trade tomorrow."

The next morning Tom got his first lesson as a bronc rider. Red had nine horses out on the range, all buckers and outlaws.[4] "You learn to ride my string of outlaws, you can ride any horse you'll draw in the kind of shows we'll work," Red said.

He told Tom to put on a pair of chaps[5] he had soaked in the horse trough to make them cling, and then they roped a horse, cinched[6] on a bronc saddle and Tom mounted. He rode only four jumps before he was thrown.

"Too much rein," Red said. "Try again." Tom rode a few jumps longer that time. "Not enough rein," Red announced. "Now do it right."

Tom got into the saddle again, bruised and angry. He was loosened in the saddle twice, but the wet chaps clung and he rode the horse to a standstill. "That's better," Red said grudgingly, and Meo brought a fresh horse.

Tom was thrown five times the first day, but he began to learn how to fall as well as how to ride. The second day he found his timing, began to gauge a horse's pattern in its first few jumps. At the end of the week he rode two horses in succession to a standstill.

Then they built a rodeo chute in the corral; a plank pen with walls just wide enough to take a horse, gates at each end that crowded a horse so it could neither lunge nor buck, and a narrow runway on each side from which to saddle the horse and mount. The first horse Tom rode out of the chute was a big roan[7] as mean as a tomcat with its tail on fire. When Meo opened the gate, it lunged out, fighting like a fiend. The rein slipped in Tom's sweaty hands; he lost a stirrup and went head over heels onto the hard-packed corral. Red caught the roan and shouted, "Come back in and ride him right this time!"

Tom dried his hands on his shirt, straddled the chute and lowered himself into the saddle again. The roan went out just as viciously as before, rearing and coming down with jolts that made Tom's teeth hurt. But Tom rode him, for ages it seemed, though once he had to grab the saddle with his free right hand. When the horse, gasping, slowed to a crow-hop, he eased out of the saddle, his legs quivering, his belly drum-tight. "You pulled leather," Red accused. "You didn't ride him clean."

"I rode him." Tom started for the corral fence but couldn't make it before he threw up.

---

3. **gnomish,** dwarf-like, shriveled.
4. **outlaws,** horses that are vicious.
5. **chaps,** heavy leather trousers without a seat that are worn over ordinary trousers to protect the legs from brush and cacti.
6. **cinched,** secured the saddle to the horse. Cinches are the straps on a saddle that are secured around the belly of a horse.
7. **roan,** a horse with a reddish-brown or brown coat thickly sprinkled with white or gray.

Red said, "You've done your puking. Now you ride like I tell you to." He had a fresh horse in the chute.

Two more weeks and Tom had ridden every horse in Red's string to a standstill. "We're almost ready for Aztec," Red said. "But there's still a thing or two you've got to learn."

The next morning they put a gray mare in the chute. She was a ducker and a dodger but Tom knew her tricks. He was buckling on his chaps when Red asked unexpectedly, "How does the saddle suit you? Cinches tight enough?"

Tom shook the saddle. It seemed right—front cinch tight, back cinch just snug. "It'll do," he said. He mounted and set his spurs at the base of the horse's neck, and Meo swung the gate open. The gray lunged out. She bucked twice and the saddle began to turn. Tom kicked free of the stirrups just in time to be thrown clear as the saddle fell.

He landed hard, and as he got up he saw Red laughing. Tom looked at the saddle and saw that both straps that held the cinches were broken. They had been cut halfway through with a knife. He looked at Red. "You did that!" he said.

"Sure I did," Red said, still laughing.

Tom was thirty pounds lighter than Red Dillon, but he lunged at him with both fists. Red dodged, hit him one quick blow, knocked him down and held him down by the shoulders. "Cool off," he said. "I told you yesterday you still had to learn a thing or two. First one is, don't trust anybody when it comes to your saddle and your gear. Not even me. Check everything."

He let go, and Tom got to his feet, still glowering.

"Second thing you just learned," Red said, "is not to jump somebody bigger than you. When you get mad like that, take it out on a horse, where you've got a chance to win." He turned and walked away.

Tom caught the gray mare, tied a rope around her for a surcingle,[8] mounted her and rode her to a standstill. When she finally came to a stop, snorting bloody foam, he got off and went to the house.

Red was at the table, drinking coffee. "Get it out of your system?" he asked.

"I rode her," Tom said.

"Sure. I knew you could." Red stirred his coffee and watched him for a moment. "You can ride the horses they'll have at Aztec, too. But you're going to lose, just the same."

"No, I'm not."

"I say you are. They'll figure you're just another Indian kid who thinks he can ride; and that's what I'll tell them you are. So you enter the saddle bronc riding, and you score high in the first two go-rounds. But you lose the final. Understand?"

"No."

"You better understand, because that's what you're going to do. You lose the final go-round. After that you ride again. Never mind how come. You ride again, and you ride that horse right into the ground."

"But—"

"Don't but me! You didn't think I just wanted to make a hero out of you, did you? Not with that Aztec bunch just aching to bet. *Now* do you understand?" Tom hesitated, and Red rubbed his knuckles. "You got one beauty of a shiner. No need getting another one like it. Now, you're going to do what I say, aren't you?"

Tom nodded. "Yes," he said.

Aztec was just a wide place in the road, but its rodeo drew ranch folk from the whole area. The contestants were mostly ranch hands; purses were small, but betting free-handed. It was a two-day show with the preliminary rounds the first afternoon, the semifinals and finals the next day. The main event was the bronc riding, man against horse, the historic reason for rodeo itself.

Red had ridden there the year before, but

---

8. **surcingle,** cinch.

he told people he'd just come this time to see the show. "And to see if the boy, here, can ride. He thinks he can, and I guess this is a good time to find out."

His listeners looked at Tom, just another Indian boy in faded levis, with hair that looked as though it had been cut with dull sheep shears. Several men grinned and asked Red if he'd like to lay a few bets on the kid.

Red laughed. "I said he *thinks* he can ride. Let's wait for the first go-round."

According to rodeo rules, Tom would have to ride holding the rein in one hand, not touching saddle or horse with the other. He must rake with his spurs, keep his feet moving, and ride ten full seconds. Then the horn would blow, a mounted pickup man would come alongside, take his rein and let him pivot out of the saddle to the ground.

The ride was scored on points based on skill in the saddle and the difficulty of the horse. If a rider was thrown or committed a foul he lost the go-round. At Aztec, as in most small rodeos, each go-round was an elimination contest, leaving only the five top riders for the finals. "So start right out riding rough and tough," Red told Tom.

The first day Tom drew a snaky, wide-winding black that bucked in a tight circle. He had no special trouble and was surprised to realize that the crowd was applauding him. He placed second.

That evening there was a good deal of talk about this Indian kid who didn't look more than twelve or thirteen but rode like a man. Red made a few small bets for the second go-round in the morning, but refused to bet on the finals. "Tom's luck may run out," he said.

Next morning Tom drew a big roan that went out of the chute in a series of spectacular lunges that brought an instant roar from the crowd. After two jumps Tom knew he could ride him, so he raked and gouged with his spurs, the roan bellowed and fought, and Tom punished him every legal way he knew. When the horn blew, the crowd was in an uproar. Tom won the round.

At lunchtime Red had several drinks and began to brag as though he'd had one too many. The betting crowd winked at each other. A few of them placed bets with him on the finals, but again Red kept the bets low. The minute he and Tom started back to the rodeo grounds Red sobered up. "Well, Tom," he said, "you've been a hero. Like it?"

"Yes," Tom said.

"I thought so. Well, you're going to be a bum in the finals. I've got the deadfall all set up. You're going to give your horse slack in the rein after the first few jumps and look for a soft place to land."

"No I'm not. I can—"

"You do like I say, or I'll break your neck! But then you're going to ride again. A special event. And then you'd *better* be a hero or start running. Now do you understand?"

"I guess so," Tom said reluctantly.

Back in the arena Red played the drunken braggart again, but as Tom mounted the big black he had drawn, there was threat in Red's eyes. Then the announcer bellowed, "Coming out of Chute Number Three, on Tar Baby, Tom Black Bull!" and the crowd began to roar. The black lunged out bucking. It side-jumped and Tom raked with his spurs. He knew he could ride this horse, but after a few bucks he let the rein slip as the black ducked its head. It got six inches of slack, came up in another buck, and Tom kicked his feet free and went sprawling hard.

The crowd groaned. Tom lay for a moment, gasping, aching with pain, and hurting inside because he could have ridden that horse to a standstill. He hunched to his knees till the pain eased and then got slowly to his feet. He limped back to the chutes, head bowed.

Red came to meet him. He put an arm around Tom's shoulders and said loudly, "Tough luck, kid! What happened?"

Tom looked at him, hating him, and didn't answer. They went back to the chutes. Tom sat down in the shade, head in his hands, and heard the chute open and the last rider's horse go out squealing. A few minutes later the announcer was bellowing the final results. Tom Black Bull, because of his spectacular rides in the first two go-rounds, placed fourth.

The men who had bets with Red came to collect, and he paid them off. "You took me," he said. "But I still say the boy is the best rider here. He just had bad luck with that big black." When the others laughed, he added, "I say Tom can ride any horse here—*any* of them."

"That's big talk, Dillon," a stocky black-haired ranchman said. "Maybe we could set up a special event for him. What odds would you give?"

"Odds?" Red laughed derisively. "The boy just got thrown and you want me to give odds!"

The announcer had come over to see what was happening. Now he bellowed to the crowd, "Don't hurry off, folks! We may have a special event in the making. Stick around!"

Red turned to Tom. "Want to make another ride, Tom?"

Tom knew the answer he had to make. Anyway, he wanted to ride again, to prove himself. "Yes," he said.

Red turned to the men around him. "You heard him. Give me two-to-one odds and the boy'll ride any horse you pick, not just to the ten-second horn, but all the way. Now what do you say?"

"That," the black-haired man said, "I want to see."

Red covered the bets, using his saddle and two horses as collateral, and the bettors went to the corral and picked out a big bay horse which had thrown its first rider in six seconds.

The announcer bellowed to the crowd, "Well, folks, we've got us a special event. Tom Black Bull is going to ride that big bay they're bringing to the chutes right now. And listen to this, folks! Tom is going to try to ride this horse to a standstill!" There was a roar of approval from the crowd.

Red and Tom checked everything from stirrups to reins. Then the bay was put in the chute and saddled. Tom dried his hands,

jammed his hat tight and mounted, and the gate swung open.

The bay took two steps and went into the air; it zigzagged, bucked, reared and spun. Tom felt as though his head were being driven down between his shoulders; his left arm seemed about to be torn from its socket. But he rode, and he rode clean.

The ten-second horn blew. The crowd was in an uproar, but Tom heard nothing. He was riding for himself now. The blood drummed in his ears, his teeth ached with the pounding. He gouged the horse with his spurs, shifted his weight, brought it down with every jump, punishing the horse; he snapped the rein as though trying to break the horse's neck. The bay was grunting with every leap. Finally it bellowed and came up in a pawing, dancing leap of fury, and then it came down with a jolt that jarred the earth and began to buck in a tight circle. But the bellows became gasps of pain. It bucked again, came down spraddle-legged, staggered, began to cough, took a few steps and stood trembling. It tried to buck once more and failed.

The crowd was yelling, and a pickup man was alongside, shouting to Tom. "Get clear! He's going down!" Tom felt the horse sagging; he grabbed the pickup man's shoulder and kicked free just as the bay fell from under him. His feet struck the ground and his knees buckled. He went down, and looked around to see the fallen horse jerking convulsively. There was a gush of blood from its mouth, and its head fell down. Tom heard the crowd gasp. He got to his feet and walked to the chute, clung to the planks and began to retch.

"Give him air!" Red ordered. "All right?" he asked Tom. Tom nodded, clinging to the chute, and Red went to collect his winnings. A man brought Tom's saddle over, staring at Tom in awe. "Bay's dead," he said. "Ruptured its lungs."

Red came back stuffing money into his pockets. "Come on, Tom," he said. "Let's get out of here." They started toward the corrals and their own saddle horses, but the black-haired ranchman followed them. "Just a minute, Dillon," he said. "That was a setup!" He was flushed with anger.

"You picked the horse, and the boy rode him, didn't he?"

"He did. But he could have ridden the black in the final go-round, too. Only he had orders not to. Didn't you, son?"

"Leave him alone!" Red snapped. "He made his ride!"

The man turned to Tom. "You had your orders, didn't you?"

Red cocked his fist. "I said leave him alone!"

The man stepped back. "All right, Dillon. You took us. But don't you ever show up at an Aztec rodeo again!"

"Aztec!" Red laughed derisively. "Why, you two-bit tinhorn! We're going where there's *real* money! . . . Come on, Tom."

They rode at a lope the first five miles and Red kept watching the road behind them. Then, since nobody was following them, they slowed to a trot and Red began gloating. Tom heard his braggart voice, his jeering laugh, and remembered the way he had ridden the bay to death, punishing not the horse but something that Red Dillon represented. He had killed the horse, but Red's grating laughter was still right here beside him. He felt queasy again, got off his horse, and began to retch.

Red grinned. "You're kind of shook-up, I guess."

Just at dark they rode up to a trading post and Red went in. He came back with three bottles, stowed two of them in his bedroll, opened the third and took a long drink. After that he drank as he rode, talking and laughing to himself. Tom would fall asleep in the saddle, then wake up feeling the queasiness again, as Red's voice rasped at his ears.

It was almost midnight when they reached home. Red bellowed for Meo, and when the old man appeared, lantern in hand, he said, "Meo, you old chili-eater, I took 'em!" His words were slurred. Meo steadied him as he dismounted, and he wove his way to the cabin.

Then Tom himself almost fell as he pulled his saddle off.

"I'll finish," Meo said. "Go get food and coffee."

Red was sprawled in his bunk, already asleep, and Tom was sitting at the table, staring at his beans and coffee, when Meo came in. "You won?" Meo said.

Tom shook his head. "I lost."

"And then you rode again?"

"Yes." Tom wondered how he knew. "I killed a horse."

"Ah-h-h." Meo nodded. He glanced toward Red, snoring in his bunk, and pointed with his chin. "*He* won." Tom nodded, and Meo went over to Red. He took the money from his pockets, counted it, then put back a few bills. He thrust the rest into his own pocket. Then he sat down opposite Tom with a cup of coffee. "Tell me about it," he said.

Tom told him, and at last Meo said, "Some day they will kill that one. Or he will kill himself." He sipped his coffee. "Why did you come here, Tom?" he asked.

"One must live somewhere. I lived in the mountains in the old way. They took me away."

"The mountains are still there," Meo said after a time.

"The old way is finished." Unconsciously Tom made the cut-off sign. "I have no one. So I came to be a rider."

Meo grunted. "Why?" he asked again.

Tom wondered how to tell him what he had felt when he was riding the big bay at Aztec, but it was deeper than words. At last he said, knowing it was not the whole truth, but still a part of it, "To be the boss. I am the boss, on the horse."

"Sometimes. When *he* tells you to be." Meo finished his coffee.

"Tomorrow," he said, "we will harvest the frijoles,[9] you and I. Go to bed now."

They harvested the beans in the old way,

---

9. **frijoles**\frē ˄hkɔ·lĕs\ beans.

piling the vines on a tarp, flailing them with a stick. Then they picked the chilies. On the fourth afternoon Red came out of the cabin, pale, weak-kneed, but sober. The next morning he told Meo to bring the horses in.

"Week after next we're going to hit the road," he said to Tom. "But before we go you're going to learn how to lose a go-around without getting thrown. Let a horse throw you, you may break an arm or something. Then we're out of business for a month." Tom was staring at him, his mouth set angrily. "You got ideas?" Red flared. "If you have, get rid of them. Heroes are a dime a dozen, little two-bit heroes everywhere you go. And they all wind up broke, especially Indians and Mexes. Meo was a hero once." He laughed. "Now take a look at him. Just an other broken down old chili-eater."

Tom made no comment.

Red said, "There's a dozen ways to lose a go-round. You're going to learn them all. And you're going to learn how to look like you're doing your best *not* to lose." He saw the look in Tom's eyes, and added, "And if you try double-crossing me, I'll break your neck."

So Tom entered the world of small-time rodeo, a world of hot, dusty little cow-country towns, vicious, unpredictable horses, ambitious country riders and jealous third-rate professionals, and, with Red Dillon, a world of noisy saloons, smoky pool halls, ratty hotels and flyspecked chili parlors.

The night before a rodeo opened Red would give Tom his orders. Then, with variations, it would be the same story as that first time at Aztec. And when Red had collected his winnings, they would get out of town before the bettors knew what hit them.

The system wasn't foolproof. Red got jumped occasionally by irate bettors, and once they were chased out of town by a posse. Now and then a horse outguessed Tom and he was thrown when Red had ordered him to win, and twice he was so badly hurt that they had

to call it quits until Meo could nurse him back to health at home. But, as Red said, things averaged out pretty well.

For two years they worked the rodeos in eastern New Mexico and the Oklahoma Panhandle and northern Texas, and then Red bought a pickup truck with a two-horse trailer so they could cover more ground. Wherever they went, Tom drifted through the routine and didn't even think; what he really lived for were the winning top-form rides that Red eventually ordered. The other riders paid him little attention. In fact, time after time, some gay-shirted, arrogant rider mistook him for a stableboy and ordered him out of the arena. Tom had grown a couple of inches, put on twenty pounds of muscle and sinew, and was almost as big as Red, but he still played the part of a backcountry Indian kid with ragged hair and shabby work clothes.

In the fall season of their third year, Red struck north into Colorado and Wyoming. But now bettors were suspicious. Red wouldn't admit it, but Tom had outgrown his role. On foot, he might look like a novice, but once in the saddle, his skill and experience couldn't be hidden. The next spring Red headed for southern Arizona where he said there was more sucker money. But except for one good cleanup, he couldn't raise a bet, and even Tom's luck seemed to be running out. He couldn't seem to win even when Red ordered him to. Sometimes he knew he was going to lose as soon as he got in the saddle.

"I'm getting tired," he said. "My timing's off. Let's go home, Red."

"We're not going home broke! You can still ride when you want to. There's a show in Uvalde County next week. If we win, we go home. But if you lose—" Red rubbed his fist and laughed, a short, ugly laugh.

So they drove north, to Uvalde County. They took a room at the hotel and Red went out to set things up. It was after midnight when he came back, stumbling drunk. He was still sleeping the next morning when Tom got up and went out to the arena to look at the horses and listen to the old, familiar talk about horses and women. Finally he climbed into the empty stands and sat in the sun. And the questions came: Who am I? Where do I belong?

As in a dream, he saw a boy he once knew who lived in the old way, a boy called Bear's Brother. Then there was another boy, Thomas Black Bull, who lived on the reservation, herded sheep and braided hair ropes and bridles. He remembered those boys. But he wasn't Bear's Brother and he wasn't Thomas Black Bull. Then he saw another boy, at Red Dillon's place, learning how to ride clean or dirty, how to do what he was told. That boy was partly himself but still a stranger. That was the boy who had told old Meo he rode so he could be the boss.

He sat there, remembering, and he saw a little whirlwind pick up a puff of dust down in the arena and swirl it past the loafers beside the empty chutes. The dust hid them for a moment and in their place he saw a crowd of riders, shouting, swearing at the horses, laughing. He heard the horses grunting, squealing, heard the crowd cheering. He felt the tightness in his belly as he sat in the saddle, braced, just before the gate opened, the quiver in his legs. The feel of the horse you got through the rein; the feel of his ribs beneath your calves. The feel of the stirrups, the rake of the spurs, the rhythm. The exhilaration, the sense of mastery. The contest won, not over the other riders but over the horse, the violence, the elemental force. The sense of triumph.

He left the stands and went back to the hotel.

Red was up and dressed, bleary-eyed with a hangover. "Where have you been?" he demanded truculently.[10] Tom didn't answer. "Get over being tired? You'd better. I'm setting up the deadfall,[11] so start figuring how to lose the first go-round and make it look good."

Tom shook his head. "No, Red. Bet it straight."

Red gasped. "Don't you say no to me!"

"I'm going to ride this one clean and for keeps, Red."

"Why, you dirty, double-crossing, lousy little Indian!" Red made a lunge at him. Tom sidestepped and knocked Red down. He scrambled to his feet, and Tom knocked him down again, then quickly left the room. He went out onto the street and walked for half an hour, letting his anger cool.

Red wasn't there when he went back. He waited ten minutes, then went out to the rodeo grounds, got his gear, checked his saddle and took it out to the chutes. There was still no sign of Red when the announcer bellowed, "Coming out of Chute Number Three, on Black Star—Tom Black!"

The bronc lunged out, and for the first few jumps Tom didn't know whether he could make it or not. Then something happened inside. He was riding a hurt, a hate. He had walked away from Red this morning because, though he hated him, he didn't want to kill him. Now he wanted to hurt and maim. His timing came back, all his skill. He gouged and fought, and the horse fought back. The stands roared, but Tom didn't hear them. He didn't hear the ten-second horn. The pickup man yelled, "Time! Time, you fool!" He grabbed the rein, and Tom automatically pivoted to the ground. He left the arena, not waiting for the score. He had made his ride. The score didn't matter.

Red was back at the hotel, deep in drunken sleep. Tom went through his pockets, and found more than seven hundred dollars. He took all but ten, then went out again. He walked along the street until he came to a clothing store and caught sight of himself in a mirror in the window. He stared, unbelieving. With his beat-up old hat, his long, ragged hair, his faded work shirt and worn levis, he looked like an overgrown reservation kid.

He went inside and bought a whole new

---

10. **truculently**\ˈtrək·yə·lənt·lē\ in a threatening manner.
11. **deadfall**, a trap, in this instance for unwary bettors.

outfit: cream-colored hat, pink-striped silk shirt, purple neckerchief, copper-riveted levis, fancy-stitched boots. He put everything on, and left his old clothes in the fitting room, except for his boots. They are the one thing a bronc rider never throws away, for he feels the horse, senses every move it makes, through his feet in the stirrups, through his old, soft, worn boots.

Then Tom sat in a barber chair for the first time in his life, and when the barber had finished he stared at himself in the mirror. He was no longer a boy. He looked like a ranch hand fresh in town, with two months' wages on his back. He looked to be eighteen or nineteen years old.

Still marveling, he went to a restaurant for supper. The waitress smiled at him, though waitresses usually gave him one look and turned away, sniffing. As he walked back in the dusk to the hotel he saw two girls watching him. One of them came up to him, smiling. "Don't I know you? Isn't your name—" She paused, her eyes inviting. "What *is* your name?" she asked.

He wanted to run, and yet he wanted to stay. "Tom," he said. "Tom Black."

She put a hand on his arm. "My," she said softly, "you are sure good-looking. I'll bet you're here with the rodeo." He nodded. "I just love rodeo men!" She smiled. "And I'm not busy tonight." She pressed against him, and his sensitive nose caught a musky smell. His pulse throbbed in his temples. Then he saw the crow's-feet, the blotches beneath her makeup and the hard look in her eyes. And he knew what she was. He pushed her away and hurried on, hoping Red would still be there. But the room was empty.

He stood at the window a long time, letting his pulse ebb. He was sure now that there was only one thing that mattered to him—the arena, the battle with the broncs. Today it had been a good ride. Tomorrow his draw was a leggy bay called Sleepwalker. A big horse, mean as they come. Which suited him right down to the ground. "The devil with them!"

he said aloud. "Red, and the women and . . . all of them!"

Red had not reappeared by morning, and he was not at the arena. An old man helped Tom saddle Sleepwalker, and he went out of the chute to make one of the best, most brutal rides of his life—vicious, hard, superbly skillful. When the day's totals were announced, Tom Black was top man again. He was packing his gear when the head judge, a gaunt old-timer with a white mustache, came over. He said, "You must have a crawful of cockleburs, son. What are you trying to do? Kill yourself, or kill every horse you straddle?"

"I rode clean, didn't I?" Tom demanded.

The judge sucked his teeth a moment. "Look, son, forget it, whatever it is. Yes, you rode clean. You could be a champion. But if you keep on this way you won't live to see the day."

"Does it matter?" Tom asked.

The judge saw the look in his eyes and walked away.

Late that night there was a banging at the door. It was the old man who had helped Tom saddle up. "Your redheaded partner," he said, "is in the hoosegow. Dead drunk."

"Thanks."

"You going to leave him there?"

"Yes," Tom said.

The next morning Tom drove the truck to a garage and traded it in on a secondhand Buick convertible, paying the difference with some of Red's money. He drove the Buick to the livery stable and had the horse trailer hitched to it. Then he went to the arena.

He won the finals with another horse-killing ride and gave the old man who had helped him twenty-five dollars from his purse money. Then he went to the livery stable for the Buick-trailer outfit, drove it to the jail, paid Red's fine and loaded him, still in a stupor, into the back seat and headed for home. It was the second day before Red came to. He licked his dry lips, and asked, eyes shut, "Where are we?"

"On the way home."

Red opened his eyes and looked at Tom. His mouth fell open; then he grinned, a silly grin. "A haircut. A pink shirt. You stinking dude!" Tom drove in silence, and Red looked around, felt the Buick upholstery. "Where did you get this? Did you sell the horses and the trailer?"

"No, they're hitched on. I didn't even sell your saddle."

"Good." Then Red felt in his pockets. "Somebody rolled me."

"I did."

Red was silent a long time. At last he said, "Meo used to roll me." He covered his eyes with his hands. "I never could save a dime. Somebody always took it off of me. Now it's you." He wasn't complaining. He was stating sad, unemotional fact.

They were beyond Pecos when Red spoke again. "We'd have made a fortune, back there in Uvalde County, if you hadn't got so stiff-necked, Tom. We could still clean up, out in California."

"No, Red. I'm through with that. I'm riding for keeps now."

"What you got in mind, Tom? The big time?"

"Yes."

Red sighed. "Always wanted to see that Odessa show." He reached for the big names. "And Calgary, Denver, Albuquerque . . . I'm glad you didn't sell my saddle, Tom. Fellow sells his saddle, he's just about at the end of his rope."

In October Tom brought the horses into the corral and began working with them alone. Red had become mean as a rabid coyote, wanting excitement, riding away and returning with a hangover. Meo said he was *malo*, meaning either sick or mean, or both.

Then one day Red rode off and didn't come back. A week later a Mexican rode down to the cabin. Red, he said, was sick, very sick, in the hotel in Aztec.

The road was only a trail, but Tom made the thirty miles in less than an hour. He found Red lying gaunt and listless in a chipped iron bed.

Red caught a shallow breath at sight of him. "I'm sick, Tom. Doc Wilson—" He gasped. "Take me home. Don't let me die in this rathole."

Tom took one of Red's hands. The hot fingers gripped his. "Take me home," Red said again.

"Pretty soon," Tom said. "After I see the doctor."

Tom found Doc Wilson's house and went in the door marked OFFICE without knocking. He said, "I'm Tom Black. I want to know how sick Red Dillon is."

The doctor's voice was a tired growl. "Dillon," he said, "has a bad heart, his kidneys are riddled, and his liver is shot. I saw him three hours ago and figured he'd be dead by dark. He's still alive, I take it."

"Yes. I'm going to take him home."

"Don't son. He'll be dead before you get there."

Only Red's eyes moved when Tom came back into his room. He watched Tom a moment, his expression vague, then he rasped, "Tell Meo to make a fresh pot of coffee. Got an awful hangover." Then his eyes seemed to clear. "Take me home, Tom."

He tried to sit up, and Tom put an arm around him. Red stared at him and whispered, "Better luck next time." His lips moved and Tom leaned close. "Game's over," Red gasped. Then the breath seemed to ease out of him, and Tom let him back gently onto the pillow.

Two days later he and Meo buried Red in a dusty little graveyard in Aztec, and Meo paid all the expenses with money that was really Red's. When they got home, Meo said, "Now it is my place."

"Yes," Tom said. "It's your place now, Meo."

Meo seemed surprised at having no argument about it. "When my times comes," he said, "then it is your place."

"Don't worry about that, Meo. I won't be here long. I'm riding at Odessa in a few weeks.

Do you want to come along?"

Meo shook his head. "I rode my horses. I am an old man."

It didn't matter to Tom whether Meo went along or not. You have to ride your own furies.

"You come, you go, just like him," Meo said.

Odessa was just a small southwest Texas town, but its show opened the season for the big rodeos. Veteran riders went there to test their reflexes, newcomers to see if youth and hunger for glory could outweigh experience in the arena. Many newcomers were weeded out at Odessa; a fortunate few rode to glory. Tom's hands were sweating as he sat in his saddle awaiting the signal for his first ride, and he made a mediocre showing. He did better in the second go-round, but he was still too tense, and he knew it.

Then in the finals he drew a horse so mean and full of fight that he had no time to think of anything, and for the first time he rode the way he knew he could ride. He placed second in the final round, won enough place money to pay his hotel bill. The money mattered little. He had begun to find himself. That *did* matter.

From Odessa he went on to the next show, and the next. The newcomers began to drop out, but at the end of the season Tom was named the best first-year man on the circuit, and the next season, after some time home with Meo, he took up where he had left off.

For three months he was in the money in every show; the crowd began to know him by name, and rodeo people said Tom Black was on his way to the championship, something practically unheard of for a second-year man.

It was hot, sweaty June when a horse went crazy under him, lunged back into an empty chute, and impaled itself, screaming, on a splintered gate. Tom was thrown heavily against the chute, his left shoulder crushed. The doctor said it would be two months before he could ride again.

Four days later, driving with one arm, he headed west, for home, for Meo. But when he got to the cabin he had the uneasy feeling that something was wrong. He pushed open the door; no one was there. The barn was empty, too, and Meo's saddle missing.

At Doc Wilson's house in Aztec, he banged on the office door and walked in. "Where's Meo?" he asked.

The doctor said, "Meo is dead."

"When?" Tom asked. "What happened?"

"About a month ago. He rode into see me one afternoon and said, 'I am going to die.' He didn't look sick to me, and his pulse and blood pressure were normal. I told him he'd live another twenty years. But he just said, 'No. Tonight,' as if he knew all about it. And he gave me a roll of bills and said I should see that he was buried right, with a coffin and a priest." The doctor paused. "He died that night, in his sleep." He looked at Tom, frowning. "I've known some of these people to *wish* themselves to death, but that was when they were dying anyway. I swear there wasn't anything wrong with Meo."

"He just knew," Tom said.

"What do you mean, he knew?"

Tom shrugged and made no comment.

Dr. Wilson shifted uneasily in his chair. . . . "Now, let's have a look at that shoulder of yours."

He examined it gently. "Young bones knit fast. What are you going to do now?"

"Go out to the place till this is all right. Then rodeo."

The doctor looked at him, speculating. "I'd think you'd want to settle down. Put a little herd of sheep out there, or a few cattle—" Tom was shaking his head. "Look, I know you're a reservation boy, but you're smart; you could make something of yourself. Dillon was a tin-horn gambler and Meo illiterate, but you've got a chance, if you'll take it."

He stopped. Time after time he had seen an Indian just draw the curtains and retreat into a kind of pride that was all mixed up with hurt and resentment. Tom Black was doing it now. The doctor shrugged again. "Well," he said, "I suppose . . ." He got to his feet, and Tom thanked him and left. The doctor had reminded him of the Indian agent. He didn't want to think about those things.

He went back to the cabin and tried to settle in, but for all its familiar corners, it was a strange place, alien. He thought: I do not belong here.

He walked on the flats to keep his legs strong. He saw falcons and a few jackrabbits, and once he saw four of Red's broncs, wild as deer. Cobwebbed memories of Albert Left Hand, of Benny Grayback and Blue Elk drifted through his mind, like shadows, leaving a dull ache.

He was a stranger on Red's land. All he had here was a hatful of memories. Scars of old hurts.

He looked at the empty corral. He saw himself there, learning to fight a bronc, learning to punish. The moon rose and the corral became a breaking pen with a bear cub chained to a snubbing post. And the barn became a barn where a tormented boy was flogged for turning on his tormentors.

He got to his feet, and went into the cabin for an axe and matches. He cut the rails of the corral and piled them against the barn. Then he set fires in the litter of old hay inside it. Within minutes, flames leaped through the roof; it fell in with a roar and a great billowing of embers. Tom loaded his car. Then he split kindling and lit it on the cabin floor. He sat in his car almost an hour, watching the flames consume the cabin, seeing Meo's garden turn into a patch of charred ground. When the fire had subsided into smoldering ashes, Tom looked at the circuit schedule. The next show was at Wolf Point, on the Missouri River, up in Montana. He had four days to get there.

Before Tom's ride in the first go-round at Wolf Point, the announcer said, "The next man out is just back in business. A bronc put him in the hospital, and could be he's out for revenge! Here he comes, out of Chute Number Two, on High Tension—the old devil-killer himself, Tom Black!"

The crowd roared as he came out. Three jumps and he was dizzy with pain from his arm. Every jolt drove the pain deeper, but he fought it down with raking spurs. His shoulder was healed but so stiff that he couldn't trust the rein in his left hand; from now on he would be an unorthodox right-handed rider. At Wolf Point this put him off balance at first. But in anger and pain, he rode each go-round like a fiend, and he kept the crowd in turmoil.

He rode every remaining show on the circuit. The pain eased, and as he got used to riding right-handed, his balance and timing came back.

But his whole riding style had changed. He was still a slick, skillful rider who could pile up points when he wanted to, but now he wasn't riding for points. He was riding for the ride, for the punishment he could give a horse, and he was riding that way consistently. He still won enough purse money to pay his expenses but he would not make a clean, high-scoring ride if he could choose a rule-defying one that brought out the worst in a horse. And he knew a dozen ways to drive a bronc into a frenzy.

He didn't even come close to the championship that year. But he left no doubt that he rode for revenge, though nobody was quite sure why. He was the devil-killer, and no one seemed to wonder who the real devil was whom he was trying to kill. The crowds went wild when Killer Tom Black was announced, and when he rode, the silence was so tense, so profound, that some even said they could hear Devil Tom cursing his horse. That wasn't true. Tom rode tight-lipped, even more quietly venomous in the saddle than he was on foot. And he was known as a hostile, silent man who had no friends.

As the seasons went by, Tom Black became a living legend. Whenever rodeo folk gathered to swap stories they would talk of the great broncs—Steamboat, Midnight, War Paint, Iron

Mountain, Tipperary. Then they would mention the great riders. And almost at once someone would say, "Well, for my money, Tom Black . . ." And there would be a pause. The name was always spoken with respect that verged on awe.

A first-year man, brash in his ignorance, might ask, "What year did Black win the championship?" And one of the veterans would say with rebuke in his voice. "Tom never won the championship. He never went after it." And if the first-year man persisted, "Why not, if he's so good?" the answer would be: "Old Man Satan never had to win a title to prove how good *he* was."

"How long has Tom Black been up?"

"I couldn't say. He was here when I came up, six years ago."

"Why, I saw him ride at Odessa eight years ago!"

If anyone had asked Tom Black himself, he would have had to stop and figure to know how long he had been riding on the big circuit. Time no longer mattered to him. Between shows he merely went through the motions of living. Nothing but the rodeo mattered because there *was* nothing else. Ride three times, pack, go. . . . Ride three times, pack, go. . . . It was a rhythm, almost like the rhythm of a bronc. He was stomped by horses; he was thrown. He was stuck together with tape and catgut. But still he rode.

Time had no meaning.

That's the way the years passed.

It was almost noon when he wakened, and for a few minutes he didn't know where he was. All cities sounded pretty much alike. Then he remembered: this was New York. He stared at the ceiling. It was sky-blue. Blue, the female color. He was surprised to be thinking in the old way. Blue for the south, the gentle, the female. Black for the north, the harsh, the male.

He put the thought away. Blue was blue. He yawned and stretched, and felt the deep, old aches. His right knee throbbed, the knee that was smashed in Denver. There was a dull ache in his left shoulder, the stiff one. The aches you live with. He dressed, went downstairs and bought a paper. He found the feature story on an inside page. The photograph of a scowling face with a slit mouth, crooked nose, wide cheekbones, the scar across the chin. And the headline read: THE KILLER RIDES AGAIN.

The first few lines, written by the show publicity man, were so familiar he could have read them with his eyes shut:

> Tom Black is back in the Garden[12] with the rodeo, and the crowds are waiting for him to kill another horse. Black, a full-blooded Indian, is known to rodeo buffs as Killer Tom, Devil Tom, and an assortment of other grim nicknames. He has earned them all. A veteran bronc rider, Tom Black has ridden nine horses to death in the rodeo arena. . . .

The story was full of vivid detail, only half true. Actually, he had been involved in the death of only six broncs, including that first one at Aztec. But he had to admit, to himself at least, that several others had been retired, wind or spirit broken, after he rode them.

The bull riding was going on when he got to the Garden. After that came the girls, who might just as well have been Broadway show girls except that they had learned to ride a horse and do stunts on a special saddle. The bronc riding was next.

Tom had drawn tonight's number-three ride. He went over to the chute as the number-one rider was announced. A helper was there, holding a big roan's head. Tom stepped up onto the chute runway, saddle in hand, and let it down easily, cinches dangling. The roan flinched, but didn't even hunch its back. Some

---

12. **Garden**, Madison Square Garden, a huge enclosed arena in New York City for sporting events and other large gatherings.

broncs tried to fight the saddle. Others saved their fight for the rider.

The crowd was roaring. Number one, a newcomer who had made a spectacular ride last night, was doing all right for himself again. Tom didn't look up from snugging the cinches, but he could hear the stomp of hoofs, the grunting wheezes. Then the horn blew and the crowd cheered and whistled. Tom glanced up and saw the rider grin at the crowd and wave his hat. He was good, and he knew it, a boy on his way up.

Tom let himself down into the saddle, sensed the taut muscles of the bronc beneath his calves. The crowd groaned as the number-two rider was thrown. A moment later, the announcer was bellowing, "And now, ladies and gentlemen, here comes a rider you all know. Some call him Devil Tom, some call him Black Death—he has a whole string of names like that." The crowd had begun to cheer. The announcer waited for the cheers to ease off. "I don't have to tell you any more about him, I see. Anyway, here he is, coming out of Chute Number Three—I give you Tom Black, on Sky Rocket!"

The crowd roared again, then tensed into silence.

Sky Rocket went out with a bellow. Rein taut, spurs raking, Tom Black began his ride. He had made that ride a thousand times. Sky Rocket was a pattern bucker: three lunges, a side jump, a half spin, then three lunges again.

Tom rode with the rhythm, punishing with spurs, brutal with rein. Three times the roan followed the pattern: lunge, lunge, lunge, side jump, spin. Then, frantic, it tried to duck left. Tom shifted his weight for leverage, and a stab of pain shot through his right knee and streaked to his ankle. To keep from losing the stirrup he jabbed his spur deeper. The roan squealed and bunched, neck bowed for another lunge. Tom powered its head around as it left the ground. Off-balance, it seemed to tangle its feet in the air, and Tom felt it begin to fall. He tried to thrust himself clear, but his numb right foot didn't respond. He was still in

the saddle as the roan came down with a crash on its right side. . .

Tom felt one crushing blow across his hips before his head struck the arena. Then the whole world seemed to explode in a burst of light and pain. Then darkness, nothing. . . .

In the hospital, most of the first week Tom existed in the half-world of the critically hurt where there is neither night nor day, but only overlapping periods of confused consciousness and dreams, and always for Tom, the chilling nightmare of falling, trapped in the saddle on a bronc that was forever falling but never landing. His body fought its battles quite apart from his mind, with the help of transfusions, injections, surgery.

Then slowly his vitality reasserted itself. The first morning of his second week, he wakened at dawn and saw the flame of sunrise in his window. The memory of another dawn came to him, the dawn when he and his mother, fleeing from Pagosa, bathed in an icy brook, then sat naked on the rocks and sang the chant to a new day. The rhythm of that chant throbbed in his memory. He tried to move, but pain stabbed at his chest and hips, and bitterness rose in him at his helplessness.

He was still rankling when a nurse came in. She had coppery hair and blue eyes, and when she said, "Good morning! How are we today?" he immediately resented her ready smile and bubbly air. She set down a tray, lowered the window shade and started to put a thermometer into this mouth. "Put up that shade," he ordered.

"But the sun is right in your eyes."

"I like the sun. Put it up!"

She laughed at him, raised the shade, then took his pulse and temperature. She put the breakfast tray on the bed table, saw that he took two capsules—"Happy pills, to sweeten your disposition"—and went away. The coffee tasted the way burning hay smelled, and he remembered the strong, bitter coffee Meo used to make; but he ate hungrily.

"What's your name?" he asked the nurse next morning.

"Mary Redmond." She moved to lower the window shade.

"Leave that shade alone! Where are you from?"

"Massachusetts." She came back to his bedside.

"That's New England." It was an accusation. "I used to have a mealymouthed schoolteacher who talked like you. She was from New England."

She laughed. "You're talkative this morning. You must be feeling better." She took his temperature and then asked, "Where did you know this charming teacher from New England?"

"In Colorado, on the reservation."

"Oh?" She poured him fresh water.

He repeated sharply, "On the reservation."

"I heard you the first time. Look, Chief, put away your tomahawk and take the feathers out of your hair. You're just another man to me. . . . Anything else I can do for you?"

"No. Leave me alone."

That afternoon Dr. Ferguson, the surgeon, came in to see him. "How many ribs?" Tom asked as Ferguson checked him.

"Several—plus a lung puncture, a deep concussion, a broken femur and a broken pelvis."

"How long will I be laid up?"

"We've pinned your femur—that's the big bone in your thigh. You can walk as soon as your pelvis knits. I'd say six weeks."

"How soon can I ride again?"

"Never, if you take my advice."

"I didn't ask for advice. And I'll ride again."

"It's up to you." Dr. Ferguson shrugged and left.

He watched Mary Redmond every morning with rising resentment. Her gentle efficiency emphasized his helplessness, his need for care.

"I hear it's beautiful out in Colorado," she said one day.

"You wouldn't like it. It's all mountains and trees."

"I like mountains and trees." Most men, she was thinking, were grumpy when they were sick. Then they began to get well and appreciated what you did for them. She filled his water glass and made his bed, humming softly. "Now, what more can I do for you?"

"Get me a glass of fresh water."

"I just filled your glass. See?"

He drank the water and held out the glass. "I said fresh water." His voice was testy. "Don't you know who I am?"

She filled the glass. "Of course I do. You're the man who rode ten horses to death. Aren't you proud of that?"

"So they say it's ten, now?"

"Yes, ten, counting the one that put you in here."

"So that one's dead too? I didn't know."

"Well, now you know." She said it sharply. He didn't seem to be sorry at all, and suddenly she was angry at him.

He wasn't listening. He was thinking about the big roan, though he didn't want to think about it—or the others.

That night he had the nightmare again, of being trapped in the saddle and the big roan falling, falling, never coming down. He wakened and, lying in the darkness, he was able, for the first time, to remember the ride from the moment the chute gate opened right through to the end. He remembered his anger; then his fear, the fear that made him so desperate that he jerked the roan off balance.

And now he knew why he hadn't been able to remember anything but that sensation of falling. He had refused to face the fact that fear had caused the fall. *Fear.* According to the code of the arena, a bronc rider isn't afraid of man, beast, or devil. You don't admit fear, even to yourself. Instead, you get up off the ground and back in the saddle, and you ride the bronc to a standstill, and the fear with it. Tom had known he had to ride again, but he hadn't known why. Now he did, and he slept, free of the nightmare at last.

Mary Redmond did not appear the next day, or the next. He wondered why, but it wasn't important. He had plans to make. He would get out of here, go somewhere for a while, get back in shape, then catch up with the circuit by the end of the summer.

Mary was back the third morning; she had simply taken her regular two days off. "Where have you been?" he demanded.

"Why, Chief!" she exclaimed. "Don't tell me you missed me. The last time I saw you, you hated everybody in sight."

"I still do."

"Some folks," she said as she began to make the bed, "are just too mean to die. You'll live a long, long time." He's mad at life, she was thinking, not at me.

That afternoon Dr. Ferguson took the stitches out of his thigh, and a morning came when Mary triumphantly brought a wheelchair. He managed it so well that a few days later she said, "Doctor may let you try the walker in a week."

When she had left him in the sun porch, Tom wheeled himself to a window frame and pulled himself onto his feet. He took a few tentative steps, almost fell, and sweated with the effort. But the next morning he managed a dozen steps, balancing carefully on his weak legs. He could walk again.

He was halfway down the room when Mary came in.

"What are you doing!" she exclaimed, running toward him. "Suppose you had fallen!" He let her help him back to the chair, and she ran for Dr. Ferguson.

"So," said the surgeon, "you pulled a Lazarus."[13] He smiled. "All right, let's see you do it again. If you've damaged those bones, a few more steps won't matter."

Carefully, Tom crossed to the window, turned, and came back. His forehead was beaded but there was triumph in his eyes. "How soon can I get out of here?" he demanded.

"That depends. You're walking on sheer will power now." Dr. Ferguson considered. "I want some X rays and I want to run a few tests. Meanwhile you get those muscles toughened up. Maybe next Tuesday or Wednesday. But you'll need a few weeks in some place where you can be taken care of. I'll send you a list of convalescent homes." He held out his hand. "Stout fellow."

Next morning, Tom was looking at the list when Mary came in. He didn't like the sound of any of them. "Well, stout fellow!" she said. "I thought you'd be up and have your bed made."

"Where is White Plains?" he asked.

"Out in Westchester. Why?" She looked over his shoulder and saw the list. "Oh, those homes —most of them are pretty terrible. What you need is just a quiet place and somebody to see that you get good meals and plenty of rest." He was silent and Mary went on. "I wish you had a place like my apartment! It's just two blocks from the Drive. You could walk along the river." Her hands seemed even more deft and gentle than usual as she gave him an alcohol rub.

The next day she said triumphantly, "I've found just the place for you. It's near Nyack, just up the Hudson. You'll love it. I called the woman who runs it last night and she'll save a room for you. Isn't that wonderful?"

"I'll have to think about it." Something in this situation added up wrong. Tom tried to puzzle it out, forgot to concentrate on his walking, and almost fell. Mary ran to take his arm. He snapped, "Leave me alone." He was angry at himself, not at her; but when she said, "You'd better rest," he flared again. "Leave me alone!"

That afternoon she came into his room before she went off duty. "I have to call my friend in Nyack," she said. "Shall I tell her to hold that room?" When he didn't answer, she said, "I'm not trying to talk you into anything." She hesitated, then hurried on. "When I mentioned my apartment yesterday I didn't mean a thing. I was just thinking you would have a nice place to walk. So don't get any wrong ideas. If you go to Nyack I may go up there on a day off to see that you are doing all right. But beyond that—"

---

13. **Lazarus**\ˈlaz•(ə)•rəs\ a biblical character.

Then the whole pattern fell into place. Blue Elk, Benny, Red, Rowena Ellis—they had trapped him, every one of them. And now Mary Redmond. "Tell your friend," he said, "I've made other plans."

"Oh . . . Well, I hope the place is what you need."

When she had gone, he got a pencil and set down figures and added them up. He had never saved his money; he had lived it up, and, in the past few years, spent a lot on hospitals. There wasn't much left but he figured that after he had sold his car, settled with the surgeon and the hospital, paid train fare and bus fare, he would have maybe two hundred dollars. Enough for a while. "Heroes die broke," he could hear Red say. Well, he wasn't dead, and he wasn't broke. Not quite.

Mary was almost as gay as ever the next morning. She chattered and hummed to herself as she made his bed. She seemed as impersonal as though he were someone who had just walked in off the street. She made him feel like an absolute stranger.

When she left, he was tempted to tell her that he would go to the place in Nyack, that he wanted to be taken care of, comforted. Then he said to himself angrily, You big fool! You've been taken care of for almost six weeks.

That afternoon, just before going off duty, she came to his room again. "I just stopped in to say good-by. I do with all my patients before they go."

"I'm not leaving till tomorrow."

"I'm off duty then. Well—" She hesitated. "Well, good-by. And good luck."

He was still listening to her footsteps down the hall when Dr. Ferguson came in to say that the X rays and tests were all right. "Where did you decide to go, by the way?" he asked.

"I'm going back home," Tom said.

"Good!" said the doctor.

After he left, Tom went out into the corridor and walked toward the sun porch, without the wheelchair and with no one at his elbow. He almost wished someone would try to stop him. But nobody did.

DISCUSSION FOR UNDERSTANDING

1. In addition to fine points of bronc riding, what two lessons does Dillon teach Tom?

2. What reasons does Tom give Meo for having come to Red Dillon's place? Why?

3. How does Tom change significantly while he and Red are at the Uvalde County Rodeo? What happens to Red shortly after they return home?

4. Why does Tom burn Meo's cabin? How does he acquire fame as Killer Tom Black?

5. Why is he hospitalized in New York City? Why does he reject Mary Redmond's offer of friendship?

4   The Mountains

He was the only passenger to get off at Pagosa. As the bus roared on toward Bayfield, he looked up and down the street. It had stores on only one side, above a slope and the tumbling mountain stream of the upper San Juan River. He wondered why he had come. It was only vaguely familiar, like a place in a long-forgotten dream. It wasn't home. But he had to come somewhere.

The few passersby, men in work clothes, stared at him, and he was conscious of his tan sport jacket, striped shirt, fancy-stitched boots. For years he had been stared at, but that was a part of being what he was. Now he felt self-conscious.

Two Indians were sitting on the curb in front of the hardware store. They, too, stared at him; and he had walked on past before he thought that he knew one of them. He reached back, found a name. Luther . . . Luther Spotted Dog. The boy he had thrown out of the room. Luther Spotted Dog, looking like a skid-row character!

He came to a market, Thatcher's Market, the sign said. He stared through the new, big window. The place was changed, but he was tempted to go in, to see if Jim Thatcher was still there. But even if he were, he probably wouldn't remember Bessie and little Tom.

Tom crossed the street, went down the slope to the San Juan and sat down. A startled magpie flew squawking from a nearby aspen. He watched the stream glinting in the sun.

He had wondered all the way from Denver to Wolf Creek Pass what it would be like. Then, as the road wound steeply down from the pass through the pines and aspens, the smells began to touch the quick of his being, the resinous pine smell, the damp woods smell, the clean smell of fast water. It was almost painful, the way it cut down through the layers of the years. He had finally had to close his eyes and make himself aware of the bus smells to ease it.

After half an hour he climbed back up the slope. He must find a cheap room somewhere. But first he had to get some other clothes. In these he looked like a millionaire dude.

In the clothing store, a clerk showed him a pair of tight-cut, fancy-stitched denim pants. "No. Work clothes," Tom said. He glanced down at himself and smiled. "I've got the dude kind."

Another man came in, a man in dusty levis and a sweat-stained black hat. He waited while the clerk showed Tom some levis cut for ease not style. Tom nodded. "And a couple of shirts, work boots and a brush jacket."

While he was trying on the boots, the clerk asked, "You staying around here?" It was only a conversational question.

"I used to live around here." Then, with a smile, "I used to herd sheep, over near Bayfield."

The clerk chuckled, knowing it was a joke. He knew the dress boots Tom had just taken off cost eighty-five dollars a pair.

When Tom paid his bill and turned to leave, the man in the dusty levis stopped him. "Did I hear you say you used to herd sheep? You wouldn't know where I could find a good herder?"

Tom shook his head. Then, trying to make

contact with someone, something, here, he asked, "Why do you need a herder this time of year? Your flocks must be out on grass."

"They are. Up on summer range. But I lost one of my herders, name of Manuel, last week —fool shot himself in the foot. His flock's on the Piedra, up Horse Mountain. Know that country?"

"I've been there."

"Your face looks familiar," the man said. "Do I know you? My name's Jim Woodward."

"I'm Tom Black Bull." He said the name without thinking.

Woodward shook his head. "No, I guess not."

Tom started out of the store. Then, on impulse, he turned back. "I'll take that flock for you," he said.

Woodward stared at him, unbelieving. "You mean that?"

"Yes."

"Well, I'll be doggoned!" Woodward laughed. "I was thinking you were probably an actor from that movie crowd at Durango. If you don't mind my asking, what do you want to herd sheep for?"

"I broke a leg; doctor says it's all right to walk on, but I want something that's not too hard work for a while now."

"Well, come on! I've got a man from the home ranch up there holding the flock, but I need him in the hayfield. Throw your things in the jeep over there. I'll be right with you."

They headed west on the highway, and Woodward answered Tom's questions. He said the home ranch was in the San Luis Valley, over near Antonito. He ran twelve to fifteen thousand head of sheep, parceled out in flocks of two thousand head, and sent them out into the high country for summer range. He sold the lambs, after they were fattened, in the fall, wintered the ewes at the home ranch. "My supply man makes the rounds once a week," Woodward said. "If you know that Horse Mountain country, you'll make out."

At Piedra Town the jeep turned north into the hills on a track that couldn't even be called a wagon trail. Before Tom could believe it, remembering his trips on foot, they were making their way around Horse Mountain. They found the flock grazing at the far end of a big natural meadow edged by aspens and scattered pines.

Woodward drove past a tent beside a small creek, and across the meadow toward the sheep. A tall, sinewy youngster got to his feet and waved. Two dogs barked, and a saddle horse lifted its head.

"Dave," Woodward shouted, "this is Tom. He's going to take the flock. Come on in to camp and show him where things are."

Dave kept a neat camp. The Dutch oven beside the cooking fireplace was clean, the coffeepot airing, the skillet scoured. Dave showed Tom the tin-covered grub box, the cooler in the creek with meat and butter, the kerosene can for the lantern. He flipped open the tent flaps, pointed to the blankets neatly drawn up on the canvas cot. . . . "No bugs. Anything I hate is a lousy bed." He turned to the dogs. "Shep and Spot know the hand signals. And old Mac"—nodding toward the bay gelding—"is a lazy old plug, but he doesn't wander. You don't have 'to hobble him."

Woodward was getting restless. He handed Tom his clothes bag from the jeep, then picked up two boxes of .30-30 shells. "Almost forgot these. You may need them."

Dave nodded. "Manuel said there's a bear or two around. The rifle's in the saddle boot. She's sighted in at a hundred yards and shoots good and flat."

Dave and Woodward got into the jeep. "Anything comes up, ask Charley, the supply man. He'll be around Thursday," Woodward said. "Or is it Wednesday up here?"

"Thursday," Dave said.

Woodward was gunning the motor. Dave shouted, "Good luck!" as the jeep swung toward the valley.

Tom watched them out of sight, heard the motor a few minutes longer. Then he just stood and listened to the silence. It was un-believable. He had forgotten. He heard the burbling of the creek, the whispering of the aspens, but those sounds were like a part of the silence, the peace.

One of the dogs nosed his hand. He rubbed its ear, then looked at the flock, beginning to scatter into the edge of the timber. He ordered the dogs to go pull the flock together, but they were baffled by his words. Without thinking, he made the hand signals Albert Left Hand had used so long ago, and the dogs raced across the meadow.

He walked after them, leading the horse, and the grass underfoot felt strangely soft. It had been a long time since he walked on grass. His legs were stiff, but he walked all the way to the flock; then he let the horse graze.

He sat down, savoring the thin, pine-scented air, resting his eyes on the nearby green, the distant blue. He heard lambs bleating, ewes blatting their answers, and he smiled. He had come to rest, to work his way back to the arena. But he hadn't expected to go all the way back to his beginnings. He was a sheepherder again, right back where he started.

The sun slipped down beyond the peaks to the west; he watered the sheep, then unsaddled the horse and hung the saddle from a rope over a low branch of a pine to keep it out of reach of porcupines.[1] When he had eaten a can of beans and fed the dogs, he walked around the flock. The stars glinted, the aspens whispered to the night. The sheep were quiet. He went back to the tent and was asleep in five minutes.

It was dawn when he wakened. The dogs, curled up beside the fireplace, stretched and whined a greeting. He went to the creek, washed in the icy water and noticed the dew dripping from the bushes. He had forgotten how wet everything was in a mountain dawn, and how chilly. He built a fire, cooked bacon and pancakes. Jays screamed and one came

---

1. **to keep . . . porcupines,** attracted by the salt from the horse's sweat in the leather, the porcupines would chew on the saddle.

close, expecting a handout. He tossed it a piece of pancake. Then he fried the last of the batter and flipped it out for the birds and chipmunks.

He got the stew meat from the cooler and set it to cook with onions and potatoes in the Dutch oven. Then, with old Mac and the dogs, he gathered the scattered sheep. Afterward he circled the meadow, orienting himself.

He couldn't remember this particular meadow, but he was sure he had been in the valley just below. He would recognize many places once he let the layers of time slip off. Time, he thought, was like the onions he had just peeled. Layer on layer, and to get down to the heart of things, you let the layers peel off, one by one.

He came to a place where the timbered slope fell away steeply and a wide vista opened to the northwest. The mountains in the distance seemed to stand in ranks, but two peaks loomed above the others. He smiled, knowing them: Granite Peak and Bald Mountain. He felt another layer of time peeling off.

The gossipy, friendly supply man, Charley, came and went. Tom put the fresh meat and butter in the cooler, stowed the groceries, and was glad to be alone. But that night he dreamed about Blue Elk. In the dream Tom was no longer a boy. He was a man, come back after the long years, but Blue Elk, wearing his derby and squeaky shoes, talked as though Tom were still a boy. "The old ways are gone," Blue Elk said. "You must learn the white man's reading and writing. You must learn to plow and plant." And Tom asked, "Did you learn to plow and plant, Blue Elk? Did you learn to read and write?"

"I am old," Blue Elk said. "I speak for your own good."

Tom said to him, "I learned. Don't you know who I am? I am Devil Tom, the Killer. I killed you, Blue Elk, and I would have killed Red Dillon, but he killed himself. Do you know that, Blue Elk?"

And the man in his dream wasn't Blue Elk at all. It was Red Dillon, laughing at him. "When you feel that way," Red said, "take it out on the horses."

"I took it out on the horses!" Tom cried.

Then there was Blue Elk again, and Tom was a boy chanting a song long forgotten of the rhythm of the earth and the days and the seasons. He chanted and Blue Elk began to sway and chant, humming the words he couldn't remember. His voice rose to a mournful howl that swelled and then faded. And Tom wakened to hear one of the dogs howling outside the tent.

At dawn next morning, Tom bathed in the icy creek, wondering why he did not wait, as usual, until the air was warm. But as he rubbed warmth into his body, he felt a glow that made him glad he had done it.

Riding out to the flock, he thought out why he had had that dream. The supply man reminded him of Red, and Red reminded him of Blue Elk. Nothing mysterious about that. This was just another day, he told himself sensibly, another day of getting ready to go back to the arena. Suddenly he smelled the arena, heard the sounds. He remembered the jolt of a bronc, sensed the pattern: lunge, lunge, lunge, half spin, side jump, lunge, lunge, lunge.

And caught himself. No need to go over that ride in the Garden again. He got to his feet, walked along the edge of the flock. He laughed to himself. Killer Tom herding sheep!

Weeks passed, marked only by Charley's visits. Jays came to share Tom's breakfast each morning, and chipmunks sat on his knee and ate crumbs from his hand. He plucked grass stems and wove a basket half the size of his fist, his fingers remembering a forgotten skill. Then he knew it was childish. But he hung it on a bush where a field mouse looking for a winter haven might find it.

One day he realized that the fawns he saw at the creek were losing their spots; the season was passing. A few mornings later he saw a white cap of snow on Pagosa Peak, far off to the northeast.

Then Woodward arrived again, alone in his jeep. After he had had a look at the sheep, he said, "Found some rodeo pictures the other day in an old magazine." Tom said nothing. "One bronc rider," Woodward said, "was a dead ringer for you. His name was Tom Black. Ever know him?"

"Yes."

"Quite a rider, I judge." Woodward smiled. "What ever happened to him?"

"He's still around."

Woodward seemed pleased with his discovery and didn't press Tom further. "We'll move the sheep down in a couple of weeks," he said. "I keep good herders on for the winter. Want to stay?"

"I've got other plans."

"So you think you're ready to ride again. Well, you've done a good job here. See you in a couple of weeks."

Now that he had committed himself, Tom studied the rodeo schedule. He decided Albuquerque was the place to start. He'd always had good luck there, and it was close by.

Two more weeks. He wished he had a string of horses to tune up with. But he hadn't, so he would have to start cold. You don't forget, though. It would all come back, just as soon as he straddled a bronc.

The final week he took the flock to a small north meadow from which he could see Granite Peak and Bald Mountain. Another month and they would be beautiful, with aspen gold and scrub-oak red. Then the leaves would fall and you would see forty miles on those perfect days when you felt that the whole world was yours, and you had been here forever. Mountains did that to you, these mountains. Then winter would come, snow and silence, and the deep, deep green of pine and spruce. He'd like to know winter here again. But he'd be in California then, getting ready to open the circuit in January.

He was looking at the sheep, not really seeing them, when old Mac snorted, and began to dance sideways, watching a tongue of brush that spilled out into the meadow from the uphill side. The dogs leaped up, bristling and growling.

Tom started to get to his feet, but he was still on his knees when the bear lunged out of the brush, moving with deceptive speed, into a little band of sheep. It slapped with one big paw. The herd blatted and ran in every direction, but a lamb lay there quivering, its neck broken.

Tom was on his feet now, shouting. The bear lifted its head, heaved itself up onto its hind legs for a better look, then dropped to all four again and nosed the lamb. Tom ran toward it, the dogs just ahead of him. The bear hesitated, then picked up the lamb in its jaws, and turned back into the brush.

Tom shouted to the dogs, "Gather them! Bring them in!" They hesitated and he gave the hand signals, and the dogs raced to try to pull the panicky flock together.

Tom hurried on after the bear, now crashing through the underbrush. The trail up the slope was easy to follow. In a hundred yards he came to a little opening in the timber, and there, not fifty yards away, he saw the bear. It stopped, the lamb in its jaw, and faced him across the clearing.

He stepped into the open and paused. The bear dropped the lamb, rumbled a deep growl, and took a few steps toward him. He shouted, "Stop that! Get out of here!" The bear stopped and seemed to bunch its muscles for a rush. It swung its head from side to side, backed away a few steps. Then it picked up the lamb, turned and went on up the mountain.

Tom watched it go, then wiped his face. He felt sweat flowing down his neck. His actions had been incredible. Following a bear that had just made a kill, into brush, without even a belt knife! Then walking out into the open with the bear not fifty yards away and hollering at it! What a fool he had been.

When he went back down the slope, the blatting sheep were still charging about, running from their own shadows, and the dogs were trying desperately to bunch them, almost as frantic as the sheep themselves. It was an hour before he had the flock back on the home meadow.

That evening, as he drank his coffee, the meadow shimmered peacefully in the moonlight with rolling puffs of mist, white as smoke, in the hollows, and the quivering aspen leaves reflecting the moonlight like spangles. But something nagged at Tom. It had been a big bear, high in the shoulders. Its head was broad and he was sure its face was dished. It had a grizzled look, almost frosty. Then he thought maybe it was the light that made it look grizzled. And he thought: You're telling yourself crazy stories. Forget it.

He rolled up in a blanket beside the fire, rifle at hand, and he told himself that if the bear came back he would shoot it.

Next morning, watching the sheep, he realized that he had been putting off something he had to do, something he had to know before he left here. And finally he rode old Mac to the little meadow of the afternoon before.

He went on foot into the brush, taking the rifle this time, and searched for tracks. In the little clearing he found it, the mark of a bear's hind paw. There was the long triangular sole print, the mark of five toes, but only four claw marks. The print was six inches across and at least ten inches long. He looked at it a long time. Then he rode back to the flock.

That evening, sitting beside the fire, he wished he hadn't found the track. Things kept coming back, and he knew why he hadn't gone into Thatcher's Market. Why rake up the old memories?

Sure, he was an Indian, a Ute. But he wasn't a clout Indian or a reservation Indian. He'd made something of himself, forced them to accept him. They would remember Killer Tom Black a long time.

Well, he had found the bear track, and he had gone over the memories, and that was that. He put the whole thing out of his head, and went to bed. And dreamed about his mother, and chanted the death chant and waked himself up. He went outside and looked at the peaceful night till the chill got to him.

Woodward arrived in the jeep with two men. The men would herd the flock on foot to the valley. There the jeep would meet them with the horse trailer and mounts for the herders. They'd camp that night and Woodward would drive Tom to Pagosa in the morning.

So Tom took one last look at Granite Peak and Bald Mountain and helped the others herd the flock down the valley, keeping the drags moving while the others, on the flanks of the flock, kept strays out of the deep timber. That night Woodward brought his plate and sat beside Tom at supper. "Meant to ask, did you have any bear trouble up there?"

"No trouble. I only saw one bear. It got a lamb—I didn't even get a shot—but it never came back."

"Probably the one Manuel saw. A big old cinnamon?"

"It could have been, maybe."

"It *had* to be," Woodward said. "There aren't any grizzlies left. Jim Boone shot the last one years ago over near Granite Peak."

"A big devil," Charley, the supply man, said. "Old as the hills. Scared the daylights out of me, just looking at the hide."

"Every now and then," Woodward said, "somebody still reports a grizzly. Always turns out to be a big cinnamon. See one in the right light, though, he can fool you. You ever see a grizzly?"

"Years ago."

"Dish-faced, high in the shoulder. Leaves tracks that long." He held his hands a foot apart.

Then the talk turned to wild game in general, but Tom was almost unaware of it. Everything had changed. He didn't know why. All he knew was that he had no choice. It was clear what he had to do now to end that last, nagging hurt.

The next morning he told Woodward he would go only as far as Piedra Town. Woodward paid him off there and said, "Well, good luck. I'll plan on watching you ride in Denver."

Woodward headed east toward Antonita, and Tom looked around for the grocery and the hardware store. Half an hour later, shoul-

dering a pack, he picked up his rifle, and took the trail back to Horse Mountain.

He tried the old campsite but had to move to the little meadow because, even with the sheep gone, their smell persisted. He had been so used to it all summer that he hadn't noticed, but now it seemed to taint the air. He thought wryly that a good many things were like the sheep. You thought you got free of them, but the smell kept coming back. Well, that's why he was here. He had to get rid of the last memory smell before he went back to the arena. He was going to run that bear down, and if it was a grizzly, he was going to kill it.

The next morning he climbed the old trail. Half a mile beyond the clearing where he'd seen the bear, he found the remains of the lamb; two hoofs, a scattering of bones. He went on and in early afternoon found a big pine with claw marks as high on the trunk as he could reach. But the bear had rolled a rock away to get at ants and grubs; it could have stood on that rock first to make its claw marks. Tom circled the mountain without finding another sign.

He tried to figure it. A big cinnamon would have left more signs, for a cinnamon is just a black bear in a cinnamon color phase. All bears are wanderers, but blacks and cinnamons keep to a smaller range than grizzlies. If this had been a cinnamon, it would have come back for another lamb, or at least stayed around for a few days, hopeful. But an old grizzly will travel until it makes a big kill, like a deer. Then it eats, hides its kill, sleeps, and gorges again before moving on. It didn't add up either way.

In spite of Woodward, there might still be a wise old grizzly around that had outwitted the hunters; but the chance that it was the cub Tom had known was less than one in a hundred. A grizzly cub doesn't reach full growth till it is six or seven years old, and there would be special hazards for a cub that had been a pet. Some grizzlies live to be thirty, or more, but the chances of survival this long were slim, between hunters and bear-hating ranchmen.

All the odds said that the bear Tom saw was a big cinnamon. But he was going to run it down anyway.

Late the next day Tom found a place where a bear had rolled two rotting logs aside looking for beetles, then had dug out a den of marmots or chipmunks. It must have been a big bear to have moved those big logs. But it had been there several days before and its tracks were smudged.

Up West Fork a little way, he found a rotten stump that had been ripped apart, more of the bear's work. But again, no recognizable tracks. By all the signs, the bear was going northwest, away from Horse Mountain. Tom was already two hours from his camp, and as he worked his way wearily back there, he thought that if he were doing this the old way he would forget about camp, take his rifle and knife and stay with the trail till he caught up with the bear. And, he thought, sing the bear chant! But that's why he had come back—to be free at last of such things.

He took his gear down to West Fork, but during the next two or three days all he found was a place where the bear had dug camas roots. Then a chill wind blew up and a cold rain began. He rigged his small tarp under a clump of spruces and sat there miserably, before a smoky, wet-wood fire, trying to make sense of what he was doing. He had hunted for a week and was no closer to the bear than when he started. Why, if it was a cinnamon, didn't it stay in one place? And why, if it was a grizzly, didn't it either move out or make a big kill? There were deer tracks around.

Thinking of deer, he was suddenly hungry for venison. He was sick of soggy pancakes, bacon and trout. He would take a deer tomorrow. Butcher out a loin; one loin, that's all he needed. . . .

Then something deep inside said that it wasn't right to waste meat. "Waste meat, and what you take to use will soon begin to stink," said the grandmothers. He shook his head angrily. Superstition! What was he anyway? A clout Indian?

He felt the damp under him and moved to a drier place. He put more wet wood on the smoldering fire. No, he decided wryly, he wasn't a clout Indian or he would have picked a better campsite and watched the weather signs. All right, so he had made a mistake. Another mistake. His first mistake was in coming back here.

Why had he come back, anyway? Because he saw a bear that might be a grizzly and he had to kill it. Why? Because he was Killer Tom Black and wanted to forget that he was an Indian, that's why!

He laughed at that, in derision. Devil-Killer Tom was just newspaper stuff. All right, so he had a grudge and took it out on the broncs. He lived up to his reputation, gave the crowds what they wanted. But he had got that out of his system now. He was going back to ride for points, for money. He would wind up his career with a record they would be shooting at for a long time to come.

The more he thought about what he was doing here in the woods, the more he felt like a fool. He had lived with everything that bear represented for a long time. He could go on living with it. As soon as this rain stopped he would pack up and get out.

Next day the sky cleared, and as Tom started out he saw a doe and two fawns come out of the brush to the stream. He raised his rifle, fired, and killed the doe with one clean shot while the fawns whirled back into the brush.

He butchered out a loin and took it back to his camp, exulting. He cooked a slice of venison. The first few mouthfuls tasted wonderful. Then the taste began to change, he didn't know why. Something was bothering him, and he was angry at himself for being bothered. He exclaimed aloud, "I didn't sing the deer chant, either!" Then he was silent, abashed.[2]

He cooked enough slices to last him on the

_____

2. **abashed,** uneasy.

trip back to Pagosa, stowed them in his pack, and left the rest of the loin on the ground, where the carrion eaters would soon dispose of it. Then he started down the trail beside the creek through crisp, almost frosty air.

He came to a place where the creek made a small mud flat, and his eyes caught something: bear tracks, big ones, full of water. They must have been made during the rain yesterday. One track was clean and plain; it was identical with the print he had seen on Horse Mountain.

He climbed the mountainside, away from the creek, finding signs here and there. A quarter of a mile up the slope he found a stump that had been ripped apart. Beside it was the mark of a forepaw, the rough half-moon of the palm, the round heel print, the round toe and claw prints. There was no doubt now. No cinnamon ever had such paws, such claws.

The trail wasn't more than thirty-six hours old. He forgot time until it was midafternoon and he was hungry and the pack straps were cutting into his shoulders. He went to a nearby rise and took his bearings.

To the southeast he saw Horse Mountain; to the northeast, Bald Mountain. He must be on the first bench of Granite Peak. He worked his way along the bench till he came to a place where a small creek bubbled across an opening with a thicket of lodgepole pines at the back, the kind of campsite he should have chosen in the first place. He cut poles and slung his tarp, made a fireplace, built a fire and warmed some venison. It didn't taste fresh, but it was food. That night he slept soundly, dog-tired.

The sun wakened him the next morning. After breakfast, he stowed everything except his knife and rifle and a small pack of venison under the tarp, and went back to where he had left the trail yesterday.

It was a cold trail now, but his eyes were sharpening and he saw little signs he had missed the day before: a broken bush here, a scuffed patch of gravel there. By afternoon he

was able to lay out a line to follow; the bear had stopped wandering and was going somewhere. He forced himself to stop thinking like a man and began to think the way a bear would. It hadn't made a big kill since he had been on the trail, and it was getting hungry for something more than grubs and camas[3] roots and chipmunks. It would go down into the valley where the deer were. He laid out a line and followed it, and knew he was right, for down the slope he came to a pine tree where the bear had stopped to scratch its back. A few white-tipped hairs were still caught in the bark of a low branch. He would have missed that sign yesterday.

Then it was dusk, and he made a cold camp and ate some of the venison, though he didn't like the smell of it. Next morning he ate more of it before he went on. Then, following the bear's trail up Los Pinos Creek, he began to have cramps. He vomited, and felt better, but before he went on he opened the packet of meat. It had begun to stink. He threw the meat away, found a serviceberry bush and chewed a few twigs. The taste cleaned out his mouth and cleared his nose so that he could go on, following the bear tracks to the lower reaches of Bald Mountain.

The next morning he found where the bear had slept, beside a deer run, and that afternoon he found the place where the bear had made a kill. It had hidden in the brush until four deer came along—two does and two fawns. The bear had struck down a doe. The whole story was written unmistakably in frantic hoofprints, drying blood, broken brush, and in blood and deer hair on the brush through which the bear had dragged its kill up the mountainside.

He followed the trail, wary now, every sense alert. It was only a few hours old. Less than a hundred yards up the mountainside he found a cache. The bear had eaten its fill, then hid-

---

3. **camas**\ˈkam·əs\ a plant of the lily family that has edible roots.

den the rest of the carcass under a heap of scratched-up dirt and leaves.

Cautiously he made his way around the edge of the clearing. The bear, gorged, would be sleeping nearby, but later it would return and eat again. Halfway around the clearing he found a tumbled heap of boulders. Moving like a shadow, he searched among them to make sure the bear wasn't there, then settled down, hidden in the rocks, to wait. The cache was in clear sight, not thirty yards away. His rifle would be deadly at that range.

At first the sun felt comfortably warm, but as the rocks caught and reflected the heat his head ached and his mouth was parched with thirst. He was hungry, too, but he could fast; thirst was the torture. He sucked a few pebbles, but that was little help.

His muscles were cramped from lying in one position, and he tried to stretch his legs; but that made a noise among the dry twigs lodged in the rocks, so he lay still again, enduring the aches. Nothing came to the cache but a squawking magpie. Then the sun slid down behind the shoulder of the mountain and he felt the quick chill of early autumn evening.

As the first stars appeared, a cold breeze flowed down the mountainside. He edged closer to the rocks to share the warmth they still held.

Night came. He tried to remember where the moon stood in its cycle, and knew that he hadn't really seen the moon in a long time. And knew that was wrong, since a man should have a friendship with the moon, the sun, the earth. He looked up and saw familiar stars. At least he hadn't forgotten the stars he once knew.

He waited, staring at the dark mound of the cache. Nothing moved, and his eyes wearied, lost their focus. He was tired. He dozed, jerked himself awake, then drifted into sleep.

He didn't know how long he slept, but when he wakened, a starved half-moon was in the sky and he could see the cache clearly through the moon shadows. It was undisturbed. He waited, but nothing came, and he drifted into weary half-sleep again.

Then something was there, just beyond him in the moonlight. He tensed, gripped his rifle —and knew it was not the bear. It was a woman.

He couldn't see her features, but something deep inside him knew who she was. She was the mother; not his own mother but the All-Mother, the mothers and grandmothers all the way back to beginning. She was chanting in a sad and pleading voice, and before he knew it, he was chanting with her. But time after time he forgot the words before he came to the meaningful parts. He was singing softly, as she sang, and at last he knew he was singing the bear chant. He closed his eyes and chanted, his voice remembering now, and when he had finished he opened his eyes and she was gone.

Only the moon was there, directly overhead. And his voice went on singing as though apart from him.

Then he saw the bear.

It came out of the shadows and crossed the opening, pausing to look and listen and nose the air. It was frosty in the moonlight, and its face was dished, not long and straight like a cinnamon bear's. It came slowly toward the cache, then stopped and stared at the rocks where he was hidden. It lifted its massive head and uttered a throaty growl and shifted its forefeet, lifting one, then the other.

He paused in his humming song and the bear's ears stiffened, alert. It rumbled the deep growl again, took two steps toward the rocks. He sang the low, humming song again, came to the meaningful part, sang it. The bear stopped, waited.

Still humming the bear chant, he carefully raised the rifle, resting it on the rocks. His eyes tried to sight it, but the light was dim. Wait, he told himself. Wait for more light.

And, the beat of the chant in his pulse, he waited, and the bear turned away and went to the cache. It tossed leaves and dirt aside with sweeps of its powerful paws and, dragging the carcass into the open, it began to eat.

He watched, and his humming slowly died away, but the beat was still in him. The bear paused in its eating from time to time and looked at the rocks, now accepting his silence as a part of the night. His pulse drummed the beat of the chant and time passed. At last, first light of dawn dimmed the stars overhead, and the moon began to fade. He could see the rifle's sights clearly. It was time to kill.

He pressed his cheek to the rifle's stock, aimed low in the shoulder where the heart lay. He tried to squeeze the trigger, but his finger refused.

He closed his eyes, fighting with himself. "I came to kill the bear!" His throbbing pulse asked, "Why?" He answered, "I must!" And again his pulse beat, "Why?" He answered, "To be myself!" And the pulse asked, "Who—are—you?" He had no answer. Angrily he said, "This bear has made trouble!" The question beat back, "To—whom?" And his own bitter answer, "To me!" Then the question, as before, "Who—are—you?" And he, having no answer he could face, said, whispering the words aloud, "This bear did not make trouble. The trouble is in me." And he lowered the rifle.

It was almost sunrise. The bear nosed the carcass, looked at the rocks, lifted its lip and sniffed the air. Then it turned and crossed the clearing to the trees whence it had come in the moonlight.

He watched it go, and when it was gone he asked himself if he had seen a bear at all. He looked at the rocks and trees and sky and he felt a stranger here. He waited, expecting the feeling to pass, but when he touched the rocks with his hand they were cold and unfriendly. When he moved his cramped legs the dry twigs made a harsh, rasping sound. When he got to his feet a jay screamed at him, saying he did not belong here.

He rubbed life into his numb legs and went down the slope. The bushes resented him and the rocks bruised his knees as he knelt at the creek to drink. The water made him feel sick.

I am weak from hunger, he told himself.

He watched beside the deer run for a time but nothing came, so he stumbled noisily, like a drunken man, across the valley. He found nothing to eat, not even dried berries, and the twigs he chewed were bitter in his mouth.

Darkness came, and the stars appeared. He tried to find one to guide him to his camp, but they wavered in the sky. As he waited for them to settle into place again, he heard the All-Mother singing the star chant, the chant to the night. He began to sing with her and after a little while the stars were steady again. He chose one to guide by, and at last he was going up the long slope of Granite Peak, climbing through aspens and pines which still said silently that he was a stranger there.

But he hoarsely whispered the star chant, and the stars stayed in their places.

It was almost morning when he came to his camp. He drank from the creek, lay down, wrapped his blanket around him and dozed. Then, when dawn lightened the sky he sat up, knowing what he must do. He stripped himself naked and went to a rocky pool in the creek.

The cold, black water drove fiery needles into his legs. He splashed it on his belly and chest as he sat in the knee-deep pool. The cold was like knives; pain sliced at his very vitals. Then it eased, and he scrubbed himself with handfuls of sand. As the sun was about to rise he got out and rubbed life back into his legs. Then he sat on a rock facing the east. He chanted the song to a new day, to the sun and the earth and everything between. Then, naked and unarmed, he started up the mountain.

All morning he made his way through brush and timber, over rocks and gravelly slopes. Noon came and he stopped to rest, and he looked up at the sun and thought how round it is and how round is the path it follows. He looked at the blue roundness of the sky and the roundness of the aspen trunks. He closed his eyes and sang a silent chant to the great roundness of life. When he had finished he lay close to the earth and let the sun beat on his back. He lay there a long time, the earth and the sun holding him between them. Then he went on.

The last part was a difficult climb. It was already deep dusk in the valleys when he reached the top. He stood there and watched the sun sink behind a cloud on the horizon and send flaming colors racing across the sky, gold, then pink, then purple. But he sang no song. He had come to listen, not to talk.

When the first stars appeared he went down the mountainside till he came to a clump of junipers with a mat of prickly needles beneath them. He crawled in and lay down, weak with fasting and fatigue. His muscles ached, and chill bit at his flesh. The prickles in his bed bit into his skin. But he slept.

Dreams came—first, unwanted ones. He was in the corral at the agency, riding a huge, frosty bear, and he lashed it with a rawhide quirt. It lunged three times and side-jumped, and now it was a big roan bronc. It fell and he was trapped; but he crawled free, and there was Red Dillon, saying, "You do like I say, or I'll break your neck!" He struck Red with his fist, and Red was not there. A bronc was struggling on the ground; it sighed and was dead.

He wakened, so tense his muscles screamed with pain. Then he felt the cold and the fiery bite of the needles and he drew his knees up to his chest to feel his own warmth and slept again, and dreamed.

And now he was alone, walking over the earth in the night. He came to a mountain and he said, "I have forgotten who I am." There was no answer. He said, "I was the boy who did what Blue Elk said I must do." Again there was no answer. "I went with Red Dillon and did what he said I must do." Still there was no answer.

"I killed as they taught me to kill!" he cried.

And at last the mountain's voice asked, "Why?"

He was silent a long time. Then he said, "I had to kill the past. I had to be myself. And now there is nothing left to kill except myself, for I did not kill the bear."

And the mountain asked, "Who are you?"

He could not answer, but a voice answered for him. "He is my son." It was the voice of the All-Mother.

Then he wakened and the white light of truth and understanding was all around him. And he saw frost on all the juniper branches, shining in the light of dawn.

He lay there, at first not knowing where he was, then remembering. He crept out from the junipers, too stiff with cold to stand until he had rubbed his legs with handfuls of frosty needles. He washed himself with the needles, and when the sun rose he stared at it till his eyes were blinded, and then sang the chant to the new day. Then he went back down the mountain, so weak from fasting that he had to stop often and rest.

At his camp he opened his pack of supplies, but he did not eat. He took a handful of flour and went down the creek to a place where deer might come to drink. He smoothed a patch of sand with his palm, then took a stick and drew a picture of a deer. He spoke to the picture, calling it by name, and said he needed its help. He said he had killed its sister and wasted her parts because he had forgotten who he was. He said that a man's memory is a faltering thing, but that he had purified himself and now he remembered. He scattered the flour over the picture, his offering to it, and he sang the deer chant.

He said, "I will be quick and merciful, Brother Deer, and I will use your parts as I should."

He slept till late afternoon, still fasting. Then he put on a breechclout, took the rifle and the knife and returned to the place where he had drawn the picture in the sand. He sat down in the brush and made himself a part of the earth and the evening.

Just before the light was too dim to see the rifle's sights they came to drink, two does and a buck. His hands were quivering, but he forced himself to steadiness, and the shot shook the earth. The does were gone in one quick rush, but the buck went to its knees and fell with a long sigh of expended breath. Then there was silence.

He crossed the stream and slit the buck's throat, and he whispered, "Earth, drink this blood that now belongs to you." He butchered the buck the old way and carried every part back to his camp. Then he broke his fast. He cooked and ate, and he slept.

He built his lodge on Granite Peak, but first he set up a drying rack, sliced the venison into thin strips and hung it to cure in the smoke of a smudged fire. He fleshed the hide and started the tanning with a mixture of liver and brains. He put aside sinews for sewing, saved antlers and bones from which to make awls, scrapers and other tools, boiled out and saved marrow fat.

Then he cut lodgepoles in the pine thicket, leaving no obvious gaps. He built the lodge and banked it with brush and earth and leaves to make it winter-warm and to mask it on the mountainside. Then he took another deer, cured more meat for the winter; and he made rawhide for moccasin soles and snowshoe webbing, leather for winter moccasins and leggings. He caught trout and smoked them. He gathered sweet acorns and piñon nuts[4] and wild white pea seeds and elk-thistle roots. He cut and trimmed ironwood for snowshoe frames. He stowed firewood in the lodge.

Aspen leaves fell and the dark flame of the scrub oaks faded to the brown of their bitter little acorns. The season turned to that pause when the mountains rest between summer and winter and a man knows, if there is any understanding in him, the truth of his own being.

And one afternoon, sitting in the sun, sewing the sole on a moccasin, he thought again of the bear. He began examining why he was driven to the hunt in the first place, why he had acted as he did.

Searching for the whys, he reached back to beginnings. To the cub, to Blue Elk, to the school, to the quirting and the denial in the moonlight.[5] That was where the hunt began. That was when he began hunting down all the painful things of the past, to kill them.

And one by one, over the years, he did kill them. All except the bear. All except his childhood, his own heritage. Blue Elk, Benny Grayback, Neil Swanson, Red Dillon, Meo—he paused, considering Meo; then nodded, knowing he killed Meo too when he burned his garden patch.

No, he didn't shoot or knife any of them to death. There are other ways to kill. He killed them, the memory of them, in the arena, when he became Killer Tom Black.

And then he had come back to the mountains, come back to heal his body so he could go on trying to kill the one thing left—the bear, his own boyhood. And he met the bear, and tried to go away again thinking he could forget the bear; and had to come back knowing he couldn't forget.

He had thought he could make an end to his childhood with a bullet, only to find, when the moment came, that he had done his killing. He had killed so many memories that there was nothing left to kill except himself. And not knowing who he was, forgetting even his own identity, he didn't kill the bear. He went in search of himself.

He sewed to the end of the sinew and took another strand, remembering the penance trip up the mountain. He had been so weak from fasting that he had done what he had to do by instinct, knowing that this was the answer, the ultimate hunt. And he had accomplished on that trip what he had set out to accomplish, unknowing, on the bear hunt. He had killed the self he had been for so long. He had killed Tom Black.

And now he remembered a chipmunk he had had as a small boy. He had asked his mother the meaning of the stripes on the chip-

---

4. **piñon**\ˆpĭn·yŏn\ **nuts,** refers to the edible seeds of various low-growing nut pines.
5. **denial . . . moonlight,** refers to the time when Tom had used the quirt and chased away the bear when it came back to him at the school in Ignacio.

577

munk's back. Those stripes, she said, were the paths from its eyes, with which it sees now and tomorrow, to its tail, which is always behind it and a part of yesterday.

He had laughed at that and said he wished he, too, had a tail. His mother had said, "When you are a man you will have a tail, though you will never see it. You will always have something behind you."

Now he understood. Time lays scars on a man like the chipmunk's stripes, paths that lead from where he is now back to where he came from, from the eyes of his knowing to the tail of his remembering.

He had had a long journey; the long and lonely journey a man must make when he denies his own past, refuses to face his own identity. There was no question now who he was. The All-Mother's words, in his vision, stated it beyond denial: "He is my son." He was a Ute, an Indian, and nothing would ever change that. Blue Elk's way and Red Dillon's way could not erase the simple truth of the chipmunk's stripes, the ties that bind a man to his own small part of the enduring roundness.

He finished the moccasin and examined it, satisfied because his hands remembered and his mind had begun to accept. The moccasin was a part of the acceptance. He could never again be a clout Indian, but for a time he had to go back to the old ways, to make his peace with himself. He had begun to feel that peace, at last. In time, he would go down to Pagosa, talk with Jim Thatcher, if he was still alive, learn what happened to Blue Elk, and try to understand why he sold his own people as he did. He would go to the school eventually, and see what was happening there now, try to understand that, too.

But never again would he go back to the arena. He was no longer Tom Black. He was Tom Black Bull, a man who knew and was proud of his own inheritance, who had come to the end of his long hunt.

He went into the lodge, put the moccasin carefully with its mate. Then he went out into the evening and up the slope a little way to a big rock where he could see Horse Mountain and Bald Mountain and the whole tumbled range. He sat there and watched the shadows darken in the valleys; when the sun had set he whispered the chant to the evening. It was an old chant, a very old one, and he sang it not to the evening but to himself, to be sure he would never again forget.

DISCUSSION FOR UNDERSTANDING

1. Why does Tom return to Pagosa? What work does he find there? Describe his feelings and dreams at the sheep camp.

2. Why doesn't he leave the area after he turns down Woodward's job offer?

3. Why can't Tom bring himself to shoot the bear? What admission does he make to himself at this time?

4. Who or what finally answers Tom's question as to his identity?

5. What did Tom decide was his reason for becoming a horse-killer? What did the bear symbolize? What did the penance trip up the mountain accomplish?

6. What do you suppose are Tom's plans for the future?

I

BACK TO HIS BEGINNINGS

It was from his mother, Bessie, that Tom Black Bull learned the old ways of his people. She gave him his birthright by teaching him the songs and rituals that were in the tradition of the Ute. Tricked by Blue Elk, a member of his own tribe, into leaving his home, Tom loses his sense of identity. After years of being spiritually lost, he regains his identity in a dream, when the All-Mother claims him by saying, "He is my son."

When The Legends Die is a story filled with symbolic meaning. It is an odyssey in that Tom

Black Bull travels far from the land of his beginnings and then returns. In his early years, those who influence him most are his mother and father. Later on, Blue Elk and Red Dillon both play major roles in shaping his attitudes. In addition to these two people, Tom Black Bull encounters a number of others who contribute to the shaping of his life. Identify the following characters and discuss their significance in Tom Black Bull's life.

1. Charley Huckleberry
2. Jim Thatcher
3. Benny Grayback
4. Luther Spotted Dog
5. Miss Rowena Ellis
6. Albert Left Hand
7. Doc Wilson
8. Meo
9. Dr. Ferguson
10. Jim Woodward

II
IMPLICATIONS

Discuss the following as they relate to the novel.

1. The white man is by nature more deceitful than the Indian.

2. Indian Americans should be encouraged to live in the "old ways" on reservations.

3. The surest way for anyone from a minority group to achieve success in the white man's world is in professional sports or entertainment.

4. Man becomes lost when he rejects the spiritual side of his nature.

5. A period of questioning and unrest is necessary to confirm any individual's belief in his own identity.

III
TECHNIQUES

Style

A number of qualities are obvious in Hal Borland's writing. He has a deep knowledge of the people and the country he writes about. The vivid imagery he uses particularly demonstrates his familiarity with the locale. He knows the terrain, the plant life, and the seasonal changes. His attitude toward his subject matter is almost immediately obvious, too. He presents his story from the point of view of the Indian American, and does so with compassion.

1. In writing from the Indian point of view, Hal Borland adopts a style that the reader accepts as being Indian-like. Quickly skim the opening scene with George and Bessie. How does the dialogue strike you as being typically Indian?

2. Look at the last line of part 1 (p. 539). How does this support the conclusions you reached in your answer to Question 1?

3. From what source are almost all of Hal Borland's images drawn? Discuss one example that you find particularly vivid.

4. Explain how the author's attitude is revealed in the following passages:

a. "For two years, the sawmill had taken money from her man's pay for rent and for the old iron bed, the dresser with the broken leg, the four chairs, the table, the stove. By now, they owned the two blankets, and that was all she was taking." (p. 528)

b. "George gave the money to Blue Elk and he took them to the preacher. The preacher said words and wrote on a paper and they were married. Then he asked what they wanted to name the boy. Bessie said, 'He is Little Black Bull. He will choose when he needs another name.' The preacher said he must have another name now, and that Thomas was a good name. Bessie said it didn't matter because Little Black Bull would pick his own name when the time came. So the preacher sprinkled water on the boy's head and George got no pay all the next week because of that five dollars." (p. 530)

c. "'I came here,' he said, 'to tell them of the old ways.'

'I want to hear,' she said, 'but first I will tell you of the new ways.' She started to tell him about the school.

He cut her off. 'I do not need these things.'

She was a patient woman. She smiled, and as her class filed into the room, she said: 'We have a new boy, Thomas Black Bull. He will tell us about his interesting life, but first we must teach him some English. We will start today with oral review.' The boys groaned, but she kept them at vocabulary drill while Thomas stood by the window. When it was over, Miss Ellis went to him. 'You see, it is not so hard to learn new things. You learned something today. I know this.'" (p. 542)

Giving Insight

To review, insight is defined as "seeing into inner character or underlying truth." Discuss what the following excerpts tell you about Indian character and beliefs:

1. "It was good to know the roundness, the completeness, again; not the sharp squareness of houses and streets." (p. 531)

2. "She caught four fish and went back past the grassy place and thanked the grasshoppers before she cleaned thes fish." (p. 531)

3. "He said, 'This morning I met a she-bear, a grizzly. . . . We talked to each other. When I killed the deer I left part of the meat for that she-bear. I shall call myself Bear's Brother.'" (p. 533)

4. "For small griefs you shout, but the big griefs must be borne alone, inside." (p. 545)

5. "Why should anyone rip up grass and make the earth grow something else? . . . When you plowed up the grass, you were making the earth into something it did not want to be." (p. 546)

6. "He lay there for a long time, the earth and the sun holding him between them." (p. 576)

7. "He came to a mountain and he said, 'I have forgotten who I am.'" (p. 576)

IV
WORDS

A. In the following sentences, the italicized words are said to be to slang:

"'Why, you dirty, doublecrossing, *lousy* little Indian!'"

"'Your redheaded partner,' he said, 'is in the *hoosegow*.' . . ."

"Dillon was a *tinhorn* gambler. . . ."

The above sentences, as you probably realize, are from *When the Legends Die*. Slang refers to a nonstandard vocabulary consisting largely of coined words, arbitrarily changed words, and extravagant, forced, or humorous figures of speech.

Generally speaking, slang develops from the attempt to find fresh, catchy, vigorous, vivid, or funny expressions. Frequently, a slang expression has only temporary circulation, possibly because of overuse. But sometimes it gains formal status and enters into the standard vocabulary. However, some slang words retain their nonstandard position even though they are frequently used. Language scholars generally agree that slang has a rightful place in English. They point out that whether or not slang is appropriate depends on several factors, including the following:

a. the occasion,

b. the person who is spoken to,

c. the person who is speaking,

d. the circumstances under which one is speaking,

As a general rule, slang is used in casual, everyday situations rather than in more formal ones. Keeping the above information in mind, see whether you can answer these questions: What popular slang words do you currently use? What other examples of slang can you find in *When the Legends Die*? How are argot, cant, shoptalk, and jargon related to slang?

B. As you may have learned from previously reading in this book, Spanish has contributed to the word stockpile of English. The Spanish word may be integrated into English in its original form or it may be changed somewhat to make it more English-sounding. In *When the Legends Die*, there are several words of Spanish origin, for example, *canyon, cinch, rodeo, corral,* and *bronc[o]*. Most of these words, as you can see, are related to ranch life. Some other Spanish loanwords in this category are *buckaroo, lariat, lasso, wrangler, ranch, stampede,* and *quirt* ("riding whip"). Try to determine the meaning of the italicized Spanish loanword in each of the following sentences:

1. In the old West, *vigilantes* often did more harm then good.

2. The posse tracked down the *desperado*.

3. Held *incommunicado*, the suspect refused to talk to the authorities.

4. For breaking the law, he was detained in the *calaboose*.

5. He had just been released from the *hoosegow* in another town.

C. Like other ethnic groups—for example, the Spanish, as you saw earlier—American Indians have enriched American English through numerous words. These words, many of which have been changed from their original form, come from a variety of Indian languages. Some examples may be cited from *When the Legends Die: moccasin, tomahawk, Ute, chipmunk,* and *squaw.* Some other Indian words are *papoose, persimmon, moose, raccoon, pone, hickory,* and *wigwam.* Using your dictionary, try to answer the following questions which involve Indian words:

1. In what state(s) would you be most likely to find a *sequoia*?

2. What is a *mackinaw* used for?

3. What kind of activity goes on in a *caucus*?

BIOGRAPHICAL NOTES

Henri Duvernois

Henri Duvernois (1875–1937), a Frenchman, wrote under the pen name of Henri Simon Schwabacher. His novels, stories, and plays have been translated into several languages. His writings in translation were popular in American magazines in the first quarter of this century.

William Hoffman

William Hoffman (1925–   ) was born in Charleston, West Virginia. Educated at Hampden-Sydney College, Washington and Lee University, and the University of Iowa, he has been a college teacher, soldier, and horse breeder. *The Dark Mountains* (1966) is one of his best known novels. His stories have appeared in *Cosmopolitan, McCall's,* and *Scholastic Magazine.*

Richard Wright

For a biography of Richard Wright, see p. 490.

Raymond Barrio

Raymond Barrio (1921–   ) was born in New Jersey but has lived in California most of his life. A combat veteran of World War II, he attended various colleges in New York, Connecticut, and California. He now teaches at West Valley Junior College in California. His works include numerous articles in art and travel magazines and short fiction in literary periodicals. He has written several novels and is looked upon by some critics as one of the leading Mexican American writers.

Nancy Hale

Nancy Hale (1908–   ) was born in Boston. Her stories and novels have been published widely both here and abroad. She is from a New England family famous in American life and letters. In addition to Nathan Hale, her relatives include Edward Everett Hale, who wrote *The Man Without a Country,* Harriet Beecher Stowe, author of *Uncle Tom's Cabin,* and Lucretia Hale, author of *The Peterkin Papers.*

Hal Borland

Hal Borland (1900–   ) was born in Sterling, Nebraska and moved with his family when he was nine years old to a homestead farm on the prairie of eastern Colorado. As a result of his life in this environment he became interested in wildlife, conservation, and the history of the West. A regular contributor to magazines and newspapers, he has written many books, several in collaboration with his wife, Barbara Dodge Borland. Among the books they have written together are *The Dog Who Came to Stay, The Seventh Winter,* and *The Amulet.* He has recounted his own early days in *High, Wide, and Lonesome.* One of his most recent volumes is a book of essays, *Homelands: A Report from the Country.* For the past several years the Borlands have lived on a farm in northwestern Connecticut.

THE STRANGE AND EERIE

In this etching Goya depicts the nightmarish visions of the unconscious mind.

"The Dream of Reason Produces Monsters"
Francisco Goya
National Gallery of Art, Washington, D.C.
Rosenwald Collection

The Coming of the Plague

September was when it began.
Locusts dying in the fields; our dogs
Silent, moving like shadows on a wall;
And strange worms crawling; flies of a kind
We had never seen before; huge vineyard
    moths;
Badgers and snakes, abandoning
Their holes in the field; the fruit gone rotten;
Queer fungi sprouting; the woods
Covered with spiderwebs; black vapors
Rising from the earth—all these,
And more, began that fall. Ravens flew
    round
The hospital in pairs. Where there was water,
We could hear the sound of beating clothes
All through the night. We could not count
All the miscarriages, the quarrels, the jeal-
    ousies.
And one day in a field I saw
A swarm of frogs, swollen and hideous.
Hundreds upon hundreds, sitting on each
    other,
Huddled together, silent, ominous,
And heard the sound of rushing wind.

WELDON KEES

"The Coming of the Plague" by Weldon Kees from *The Collected Poems of Weldon Kees*, by permission of The University of Nebraska Press.

The eyes grow wide! Breathing almost stops! But the eyes continue to move across that first page and to the next. This is a picture of self-torture, a torture enjoyed by all who like to read stories of the unknown, the mystifying, the terrifying, the strange and eerie.

Weldon Kees tells of unusual things happening in "The Coming of the Plague"—dying locusts, black vapors rising from the earth, a swarm of hideous, bloated frogs, everywhere omens of horror to come. Beginning with this poem, the selections in THE STRANGE AND EERIE have been chosen deliberately for the effect they will have upon the reader. For this reason, the unit concludes with a group of selections by Edgar Allan Poe, an author who believed the most important consideration when writing a story or poem was the effect it would have upon the reader. And the effect he was a master at achieving was that of horror.

But lest the reader be too horrified—before he reaches the Poe section, *Once Upon A Midnight*—he will find a number of selections that will leave him wondering: Could this be? Will this ever happen? What lies in the unknown?

When you begin reading,
be sure to notice the name of the
man who says he is writing this account.
Could it have been only coincidence
that took him where another man
was making gravestones?

August Heat

W. F. HARVEY

PHENISTONE ROAD, CLAPHAM, *August 20th, 190–*. I have had what I believe to be the most remarkable day in my life, and while the events are still fresh in my mind, I wish to put them down on paper as clearly as possible.

Let me say at the outset that my name is James Clarence Withencroft.

I am forty years old, in perfect health, never having known a day's illness.

By profession I am an artist, not a very successful one, but I earn enough money by my black-and-white work to satisfy my necessary wants.

My only near relative, a sister, died five years ago, so that I am independent.

I breakfasted this morning at nine, and after glancing through the morning paper I lighted my pipe and proceeded to let my mind wander in the hope that I might chance upon some subject for my pencil.

The room, though door and windows were open, was oppressively hot, and I had just made up my mind that the coolest and most comfortable place in the neighborhood would be the deep end of the public swimming bath, when the idea came.

I began to draw. So intent was I on my work that I left my lunch untouched, only stopping work when the clock of St. Jude's struck four.

The final result, for a hurried sketch, was, I felt sure, the best thing I had done.

It showed a criminal in the dock immediately after the judge had pronounced sentence. The man was fat—enormously fat. The flesh hung in rolls about his chin; it creased his huge, stumpy neck. He was clean shaven (perhaps I should say a few days before he must have been clean shaven) and almost bald. He stood in the dock, his short, clumsy fingers clasping the rail, looking straight in front of him. The feeling that his expression conveyed was not so much one of horror as of utter, absolute collapse.

There seemed nothing in the man strong enough to sustain that mountain of flesh.

I rolled up the sketch, and without quite knowing why, placed it in my pocket. Then with the rare sense of happiness which the knowledge of a good thing well done gives, I left the house.

I believe that I set out with the idea of calling upon Trenton, for I remember walking along Lytton Street and turning to the right along Gilchrist Road.

From there onward I have only the vaguest recollections of where I went. The one thing of which I was fully conscious was the awful heat, that came up from the dusty asphalt pavement as an almost palpable wave. I longed for the thunder promised by the great banks of clouds that hung low over the western sky.

I must have walked five or six miles, when a small boy roused me from my reverie by asking the time.

It was twenty minutes to seven.

When he left me I began to take stock of my bearings. I found myself standing before a gate that led into a yard bordered by a strip of thirsty earth, where there were flowers, purple stock and scarlet geranium. Above the

From the book *The Beast With Five Fingers* by William Fryer Harvey. Copyright 1947 by E. P. Dutton & Co., Inc., publishers, and reprinted with their permission.

entrance was a board with the inscription—

CHAS. ATKINSON
MONUMENTAL MASON
WORKER IN ENGLISH AND ITALIAN MARBLES

From the yard itself came a cheery whistle, the noise of hammer blows, and the cold sound of steel meeting stone.

A sudden impulse made me enter.

A man was sitting with his back toward me, busy at work on a slab of curiously veined marble. He turned round as he heard my steps and stopped short.

It was the man I had been drawing, whose portrait lay in my pocket.

He sat there, huge and elephantine, the sweat pouring from his scalp, which he wiped with a red silk handkerchief. But though the face was the same, the expression was absolutely different.

He greeted me smiling, as if we were old friends, and shook my hand.

I apologized for my intrusion.

"Everything is hot and glary outside," I said. "This seems an oasis in the wilderness."

"I don't know about the oasis," he replied, "but it certainly is hot. Take a seat, sir!"

He pointed to the end of the gravestone on which he was at work, and I sat down.

"That's a beautiful piece of stone you've got hold of," I said.

He shook his head. "In a way it is," he answered; "the surface here is as fine as anything you could wish, but there's a big flaw at the back, though I don't expect you'd ever notice it. I could never make really a good job of a bit of marble like that. It would be all right in the summer like this; it wouldn't mind the blasted heat. But wait till the winter comes. There's nothing quite like frost to find out the weak points in stone."

"Then what's it for?" I asked.

The man burst out laughing.

"You'd hardly believe me if I was to tell you it's for an exhibition, but it's the truth. Artists have exhibitions, so do grocers and butchers; we have them too. All the latest little things in headstones, you know."

He went on to talk of marbles, which sort best withstood wind and rain, and which were easiest to work; then of his garden and a new sort of carnation he had bought. At the end of every other minute he would drop his tools, wipe his shining head, and curse the heat.

I said little, for I felt uneasy. There was something unnatural, uncanny, in meeting this man.

I tried at first to persuade myself that I had seen him before, that his face, unknown to me, had found a place in some out-of-the-way corner of my memory, but I knew that I was practicing little more than a plausible piece of self-deception.

Mr. Atkinson finished his work, spat on the ground, and got up with a sigh of relief.

"There! what do you think of that?" he said, with an air of evident pride.

The inscription which I read for the first time was this—

SACRED TO THE MEMORY
OF
JAMES CLARENCE WITHENCROFT.
BORN JAN. 18TH, 1860.
HE PASSED AWAY VERY SUDDENLY
ON AUGUST 20TH, 190–
"In the midst of life we are in death."

For some time I sat in silence. Then a cold shudder ran down my spine. I asked him where he had seen the name.

"Oh, I didn't see it anywhere," replied Mr. Atkinson. "I wanted some name, and I put down the first that came into my head. Why do you want to know?"

"It's a strange coincidence, but it happens to be mine."

He gave a long, low whistle.

"And the dates?"

"I can only answer for one of them, and that's correct."

"It's a rum go!" he said.

But he knew less than I did. I told him of

my morning's work. I took the sketch from my pocket and showed it to him. As he looked, the expression of his face altered until it became more and more like that of the man I had drawn.

"And it was only the day before yesterday," he said, "that I told Maria there were no such things as ghosts!"

Neither of us had seen a ghost, but I knew what he meant.

"You probably heard my name," I said.

"And you must have seen me somewhere and have forgotten it! Were you at Clacton-on-Sea last July?"

I had never been to Clacton in my life. We were silent for some time. We were both looking at the same thing, the two dates on the gravestone, and one was right.

"Come inside and have some supper," said Mr. Atkinson.

His wife is a cheerful little woman, with the flaky red cheeks of the country-bred. Her husband introduced me as a friend of his who was an artist. The result was unfortunate, for after the sardines and watercress had been removed, she brought me out a Doré Bible,[1] and I had to sit and express my admiration for nearly half an hour.

I went outside, and found Atkinson sitting on the gravestone smoking.

We resumed the conversation at the point we had left off.

"You must excuse my asking," I said, "but do you know of anything you've done for which you could be put on trial?"

He shook his head.

"I'm not a bankrupt, the business is prosperous enough. Three years ago I gave turkeys to some of the guardians at Christmas, but that's all I can think of. And they were small ones, too," he added as an afterthought.

He got up, fetched a can from the porch, and began to water the flowers. "Twice a day regular in the hot weather," he said, "and then the heat sometimes gets the better of the delicate ones. And ferns, they could never stand it. Where do you live?"

I told him my address. It would take an hour's quick walk to get back home.

"It's like this," he said. "We'll look at the matter straight. If you go back home tonight, you take your chance of accidents. A cart may run over you, and there's always banana skins and orange peel, to say nothing of fallen ladders."

He spoke of the improbable with an intense seriousness that would have been laughable six hours before. But I did not laugh.

"The best thing we can do," he continued, "is for you to stay here till twelve o'clock. We'll go upstairs and smoke; it may be cooler inside."

To my surprise I agreed.

We are sitting in a long, low room beneath the eaves. Atkinson has sent his wife to bed. He himself is busy sharpening some tools at a little oilstone, smoking one of my cigars the while.

The air seems charged with thunder. I am writing this at a shaky table before the open window. The leg is cracked, and Atkinson, who seems a handy man with his tools, is going to mend it as soon as he has finished putting an edge on his chisel.

It is after eleven now. I shall be gone in less than an hour.

But the heat is stifling.

It is enough to send a man mad.

I

YOU WRITE THE ENDING

When this story opens, James Clarence Withencroft is writing down what has happened during what he calls the most remarkable day of his life.

1. Where is he when he is writing this account?

2. Describe the picture he had drawn that morning.

---

1. **Doré Bible,** a Bible illustrated by Paul Gustave Doré (1833–1883), the French artist.

3. How does he discover the identity of the man he had drawn?

4. What is inscribed on the gravestone that Atkinson was finishing?

5. What ending would you provide for this story?

II
IMPLICATIONS

Discuss the following statements.

1. It is useless to struggle against fate.

2. The human mind is capable of sending and receiving mental images without conscious effort.

III
TECHNIQUES

Foreshadowing

1. Beginning with the title and continuing throughout this account, the reader is constantly reminded of the thing that is to bring about tragedy at the story's end. With what two lines does the author foreshadow what must have happened in the short time before Withencroft was to have left to return home?

2. When did you first feel certain that there was something uncanny or unnatural about the way things were happening in this story?

TECHNIQUES

Suspense, Foreshadowing, Imaginative Language

The techniques emphasized in this first section of THE STRANGE AND EERIE are ones with which you are already familiar. They are introduced and explained near the beginning of the text (pp. 17–18) with the selections in CALL TO ADVENTURE.

Exploring the strange and eerie is a form of adventure. In writing stories on this theme, authors must build *suspense,* "a state of excited uncertainty." Although in "August Heat" the main character states his purpose to be a straightforward accounting of events as they had taken place on a certain day, the opening line deliberately sets a trap to catch the reader's interest by describing that day as having been "the most remarkable" in his life. Because the reader feels this statement promises that something truly unusual is to be told, he in interested in learning more about the character who is telling the story.

In maintaining suspense as the story progresses, the author makes use of the technique of *foreshadowing,* "planting hints of dangers and perils that lie ahead." Even before Withencroft begins to describe the man he has drawn, for example, he classifies the man as a criminal. The mere use of the word "criminal" deepens interest, even though this is too early for the reader to under-

stand the significance the term will later have.

"August Heat" demonstrates the use of foreshadowing to an extraordinary extent. Even the explanation the mason gives as to the effect weather has upon flawed marble foreshadows the effect weather may have upon a person less than perfect "beneath the surface" with regard to emotional stability. Discuss those things about the gravestone and its inscription that make it an excellent example of foreshadowing.

In most stories that have appeal because they are about things which are haunting, fearsome, or unexplainable, there is *imaginative language,* "words used so that they arouse the reader's feelings." This is exemplified when the author describes the awful heat that came up from the dusty asphalt pavement as "an almost palpable wave." Many persons have experienced the sensation of being drowned in waves of heat. For this reason, the author's comparison helps the reader *feel* what the character feels.

In the same paragraph that the author describes the heat as rising from the pavement as an almost palpable wave, he also uses imaginative language to help his reader *see* the clouds. Do you recall how he described them? Discuss.

Something *is* if you think
it is, or something *isn't* if
you think it isn't. This was Bishop
Berkeley's theory of acosmism. Whose theory
it was didn't make a particle of
difference to little Nancy.
She believed in it.

The Little Terror

WILL F. JENKINS

There was no crashing roll of thunder when the principles of psychological acosmistic idealism[1] became practicalities in the world inhabited by Nancy. Her mother had no twinge of uneasiness, and her father was reading his newspaper. There was no breathless hush over the earth at the bloodcurdling instant, though possibly Bishop Berkeley[2] (1685–1753), up in heaven, was pleasantly interested. Joe Holt, who was a practicing psychiatrist and might be presumed to have a feeling for such things, hadn't the trace of an intuition of it. The skies did not darken suddenly, nor were there deep rumblings underground. There was not even an unnatural gray twilight in which birds chirped faintly and cattle affrightedly rolled their eyes. There was no sign whatever that the most alarming moment in history was at hand. But still . . .

Nancy went to the gate with her grandfather. She was six and he was sixty, and they were very congenial. Nancy skipped, because she never walked when she could skip or, preferably, run. It was nearing dusk, but there was still a ruddy sunshine in the air, yet the sky was perceptibly darkening.

At the gate Nancy permitted her grandfather to kiss her good-bye, in the benign, smug condescension of little girls who know they are irresistible.

Then she said, "Make a penny go away, Granddaddy."

Her grandfather obediently took a copper penny from his pocket. He put it between his thumb and middle finger and offered it gravely for Nancy's inspection. She held her breath. Her grandfather snapped his fingers. The penny vanished.

Nancy beamed. "Do it again, Granddaddy!"

Her grandfather prepared to repeat. Nancy put her eyes within inches of the coin. She watched with rapt fascination.

The penny vanished a second time.

"It's real magic?" asked Nancy hopefully. She was beginning to discover that one could not count on fairy godmothers—not confidently, at any rate—in moments of despair. But still she hoped.

"It's real magic," agreed her grandfather.

"Show me how!" begged Nancy. "Please!"

Her grandfather whispered confidentially in her ear, "I say 'Oogledeboo' and it vanishes. Can you say that?"

Nancy whispered, "Oogledeboo."

"Splendid!" said her grandfather. He straightened up. "Now you say 'Oogledeboo' at this penny, and see what happens!" He held the penny as before, between thumb and middle finger.

Nancy giggled at it. She said, "Oogledeboo!"

Her grandfather's fingers snapped. The penny vanished.

Nancy beamed. "Again, Granddaddy?"

"Once more," conceded her grandfather. He proffered the penny. It was the same one, but Nancy did not reflect upon that. He took it in his fingers. Her eyes sparkled. She said, "Oogledeboo!"

1. **acosmistic idealism,** the theory that reality exists only in the mind.
2. **Bishop Berkeley,** philosopher and Anglican bishop who was active in the United States from 1728–1731.

The penny vanished. Her grandfather looked slightly surprised. But it was natural. He had never heard of Bishop Berkeley's dictum that *esse* is *percipi*,[3] nor drawn inferences from the statement. However, he beamed at Nancy.

"Now I have to go, Nancy. Good night."

Nancy waved cheerfully as he walked down the street. When he was out of sight, she skipped back to where she had been playing. She did not notice that her grandfather was shaking his coat sleeve absently, as if to make something come out of it—something that did not come.

Nancy settled down placidly to play alone. There was a caterpillar on the doll she had neglected for her grandfather. Nancy regarded it with disfavor. She said sternly, "Oogledeboo!"

The caterpillar vanished. Nancy played with her doll. The sunset proceeded. Twilight fell. Nancy's mother called her, and she went in cheerfully, dragging the doll by one arm. She ate her supper with excellent appetite and beamed at her father and mother. There was only one alarming incident, and it happened to pass unnoticed. Nancy did not want to finish her milk. Her mother said firmly that she must. Then the telephone rang, and her mother got up to answer it.

Nancy looked confidently at the milk in her glass and said, "Oogledeboo."

The milk vanished.

Nancy went happily to bed later, after kissing her father and mother with extravagant affection. She went dreamlessly and placidly to sleep. She slept blissfully all night long.

All was serene through all the cosmos.[4] There was no hint of the appalling thing that had happened. Nobody cringed in nameless horror. Nobody trembled in justified apprehension. Nobody, it appears, happened to be thinking of the Right Reverend George Berkeley, of the Anglican Church, who wrote books of philosophy and died in 1753.

Nancy woke next morning in her customary ebullient mood. She sang lustily as she was dressed, and there was no hint of disturbance until breakfast was served. Then there was a slight collision of wills over Nancy's reluctance to eat her cereal. But just then the milkman came to collect, and her mother went to pay him. When her mother came back, the cereal bowl was quite empty. Nancy's mother praised her warmly. Nancy giggled.

It was a charming morning. Nancy, scrubbed to radiance and wearing a playsuit of healthful brevity, went out to play in her sandbox behind the house. She sang as she played. She was a delightfully happy child. Presently Charles, the little boy next door, came over to play with her. She greeted him with that cordial suspicion with which little girls regard little boys. He stepped on a sand house she had decorated with small stray sticks and cherished bottle caps. She scolded.

"Huh!" said Charles scornfully. "That's no fun! Let's play going to the moon. Let's fight the cat men. Rnnnnnnnh! Bang-bang!"

Nancy demurred.

"Let's play spaceship," insisted Charles. He began to hop excitedly. He shouted, "Whooooooooom! Three gravs! Four! Turn on the stern rockets! Whoooooooooooom! There come the space pirates! Warm up the disintegrators! Shoot the space warp! Bang! Bang! Rnnnnnnnnnnnh! Bang!"

He rushed about madly, fighting a spendid space battle with space pirates from the rings of Saturn, while Nancy placidly practiced interior decorating in her sandpile. She set a wilted buttercup on a dab of sand which to her represented a sideboard—undoubtedly Sheraton.[5] She reflectively arranged another dab of sand into a luxurious sofa. She began to smooth out wall-to-wall carpeting, with the

---

3. esse\ˈĕs•ə\ is percipi\pər ˈkĭ•pē\ to be is to be perceived, that is, things exist only as perceptions in the mind.

4. **cosmos,** an orderly, harmonious, systematic universe.

5. **Sheraton,** a style of English furniture originated by Thomas Sheraton (1751–1806), marked by straight lines and graceful proportions.

intent to add a grandfather's clock next to her sandpile scheme for gracious living.

Charles got into difficulties. A fleet of black spaceships from Sirius[6] winked into existence from the fourth dimension over by the back-porch steps. They sped toward him, disintegrator rays flaming. He flashed into faster-than-light attack, throwing out atomic bombs and with tractor and pressor beams busy. Then came a despairing call from an Earth passenger spaceliner under attack by pirates near the hydrangea bush.

"Whooooooooom!" shouted Charles ferociously. "Coming, Earthship, with all jets firing! Rnnnnnnnnh! Take that! And that! Bang! Bang! Here's an H-bomb for you! Boom!"

Disaster struck. Charles, rushing to the defense of the helpless passenger craft, cut across the sandpile. One sandaled foot landed in the kitchen of Nancy's ranch-type sand-house. Kitchen sink, dishwaster, and breakfast nook—they were marked by rather wobbly lines of pebbles—were obliterated as if by collision with a giant meteor in space. Sand sprayed on Nancy.

"Bang, bang!" roared Charles in his high treble. "Rnnnnnnnh! Take that, you old pirates! Calling Earth! Space patrol ship reporting pirates wiped out! I'm taking off for Pluto!"

Nancy trembled with indignation. She said sternly, "You go home!"

"Huh?" said Charles. He stopped short. "I'm Captain Space! I've got to fight space pirates and things, haven't I?"

"You go home!" said Nancy sternly. "You stepped on my house! You go home or I'll say something at you!"

If she had threatened to tell her mother on him, it might have been effective. But this threat had no meaning to Charles. He shouted. "Whoooooooom! Taking off for Pluto! Invaders from space! Coming, Earth garrison! Hold on, I'm coming with all jets firing! Whooooom!"

He started for Pluto. Unfortunately it appeared that Pluto lay somewhere in the general direction of a yellow tea-rose bush at the edge of the lawn. Charles's orbit would coincide with the sandpile again.

Nancy said vengefully, "Oogledeboo!"

Charles vanished.

Silence fell, and Nancy returned to the building of a sandpile ranchhouse. Presently she sang happily as she worked. Presently, again, she went into the house and asked for cookies. Having skipped her breakfast cereal, she was hungry.

Her mother said, "Where's Charles? Didn't I hear him playing with you?"

Nancy bit into a cooky and said placidly, "I said 'Oogledeboo' at him and he went away."

Nancy's mother smiled absently and went about what she thought were more important affairs. Which was a mistake. There were no more important affairs. According to the principles laid down by Bishop Berkeley between 1685 and 1753, things exist because a mind thinks of them as existing. Nancy had acquired the ability to think confidently of things as ceasing to exist—a gift no adult can acquire. So—by a natural extrapolation of Bishop Berkeley's principle—when she thought of something as ceasing to exist, it did. All of us have wished for such a talent at some time or another, but Nancy had it.

When she was at lunch, the voice of Charles's mother could be heard, calling him. He did not answer, and presently she was at the door. Nancy had arrived at the custard-with-strawberry-jam stage of her lunch then, and she worked zestfully with a spoon. Her mother went to confer with Charles's mother about his whereabouts.

"Why, no," Nancy heard her say. "He was playing with Nancy, but he left." She called, "Nancy! Do you know where Charles went?"

"No, Mother-r!" Nancy sang out happily. She worked further on the custard. She was absorbed.

There was talk at the door. Nancy got some

---

6. **Sirius**\ˈsĭr·ē·əs\ a star in the constellation **Canis major.**

strawberry jam on the large napkin her mother spread over her at mealtime. She was enjoyably licking it off when her mother returned.

"Charles's mother is worried," said Nancy's mother. She frowned a little. "He doesn't usually wander away. You're sure you didn't notice which way he went?" Nancy shook her head. "He didn't go with anybody?" her mother asked uneasily.

Nancy got a big spoonful of custard. "No," she said placidly. "I said 'Oogledeboo' at him and he went away."

Her mother did not inquire further. But she looked unhappy. A parent of a small child always shares the anguish of another parent when a small child can't be found. But it didn't occur to Nancy's mother that she might have heard a complete and accurate description of Charles's disappearance.

Immediately after lunch Nancy's mother dressed her up to go downtown. There was to be a parade, and Nancy's mother was making the sacrifice of an afternoon to Nancy's pleasure. Of course Nancy loathed being dragged through stores, but since her mother was devoting an entire afternoon to her, it was only reasonable that they should start early, to do some shopping, and do more shopping later. This is what is called thinking only of one's children.

Nancy had no forebodings. She adored being dressed up, and wriggled with pleasure as her mother attired her in a very frilly dress, a very frilly hat, a smart little coat, and tiny white gloves which to Nancy were the ultimate of bliss. She sang and paraded before a mirror as her mother prepared for the outing.

She sang, also, as her mother drove downtown. When the traffic grew thick and they stopped at traffic lights, Nancy continued to sing lustily and without self-consciousness. People looked at her and smiled, thinking of innocent and happy childhood.

There were mobs in every store. Other self-sacrificing mothers were out to show their children the parade. They constituted an outrageous crush by a ladies' purse counter. A fat woman jammed Nancy against a counter. She was enraged. Somebody protested, and the fat woman turned indignantly, and in pivoting, that protruding part of her body which was at the height of Nancy's six-year-old head sent Nancy reeling.

Nancy said wrathfully, "Oogledeboo!"

There was no fat woman.

Somebody screamed in a stifled fashion. But nobody believed it. There was a surging of bodies to fill the space where a fat woman had been, and Nancy was banged again and wailed, and grabbed her mother hysterically by the legs.

Her mother completed the purchase of a handbag and harassedly got Nancy out of the crowd. Nancy's frilly hat was dangling and she was very unhappy.

"There, darling!" said her mother penitently. "I shouldn't have brought you into such a crowded place! We'll go upstairs where there won't be so many people."

They got into an elevator. Then a mob charged it. A horde of women resolutely thrust and pushed and shoved, while small children howled. Women are less than ladylike when there are no men around. The elevator operator tried to stem the flood, to no avail.

Nancy was crushed ruthlessly. She became terrified. She gasped, "Oogledeboo!"

There were only five people in the elevator. There was not even a crowd trying to push in.

Nancy's mother trembled for a considerable time after that. Of course it could not possibly be true. Even the elevator operator merely stammered unintelligibly when a floorwalker questioned him. There was nothing to tell. The elevator had been crowded, and suddenly it wasn't. There had been no outcry. The crowd hadn't even visibly faded. It just was— and then it wasn't. So the elevator operator, completely overwrought, was relieved of duty and the floorwalker apologized to the few passengers remaining. They were all remarkably pale, and they all went quickly out of the

store. But of course they didn't believe it either. Not even Nancy's mother.

But Nancy felt much better. More confident. Now, she knew placidly, she could always get room around her if people pushed. Her mother drank a cup of tea in the nearest tea room, and tried tremblingly to remember the psychiatric meaning of the delusion that people vanished before one's eyes. But while her mother trembled, Nancy ate a small plate of vanilla ice cream, with relish.

Nancy's mother really wanted to go straight home then. Already she had made up her mind to ask Joe Holt about the experience. He was the only psychiatrist she knew personally, but he and his wife were fairly close friends. She could mention it in an offhand manner, perhaps. But Nancy had been promised the parade. So they saw it.

It began appropriately with motorcycle policemen, at whom Nancy waved enthusiastically. Her mother had been able to get a place at the very curb, so nothing would interfere with Nancy's view. There came a high school band, with drum majorettes strutting in costumes which would have caused their great-grandmothers to die of heart failure. There came a cadet corps. And then the floats.

Nancy was thrilled by a float in the shape of a swan, decorated by young girls in tinsel dresses and fixed smiles. There was a float showing embarrassed Boy Scouts about a campfire. A float resembling a battleship. A Girl Scout float.

There came a traveling squealing down the street. Children's shrill voices shrieked and shouted. Nancy squirmed to look. Her mother held her tightly. But Nancy's mother was thinking desperately that she'd never expected to call on Joe Holt professionally, but after all, he was a psychiatrist and he played golf with—

Nancy squealed in pure excitement. Her mother looked numbly at the float which caused all the high-pitched tumult. It represented a dragon. It was a very ambitious job.

The body of the beast completely hid the truck on which it was built, and a long and ungainly hooped-canvas tail trailed three car-lengths behind. But it was what went on before that caused the excitement.

The dragon had a twenty-foot movable neck of hooped canvas painted red, with a five-foot head at the end of it. The head had short, blunt horns. It had eyes the size of saucers, and an expression of imbecilic amiability,[7] and smoke came lavishly out of its nostrils. And its head moved from side to side on the movable neck, and it turned coquettishly and seemed to gaze at the spectators wherever it turned with an admirable look of benign imbecility.

Children squealed and shrieked and cheered as the dragon proceeded down the main street. Those at whom it seemed to look shrank back in delighted terror. Those from whom it looked away yelled in sheer excitement.

Nancy trembled in delicious thrill. She jumped up and down. She squealed.

Opposite her, the long, articulated neck swung in her direction. The dragon's head turned toward her. It seemed to look directly at her, in a sort of wall-eyed cordiality. Smoke welled from its nostrils. It swung still closer, as if to take an even closer and even more admiring look.

Nancy said zestfully, "Oogledeboo!"

A smoke pot fell to the pavement and smashed. It scattered strangling, smoldering stuff over five yards of asphalt. A man fell with a clank, landing astride the hood of a battered motor truck which had been hidden by the dragon's body. His expression was that of stunned bewilderment, and he stared at his hands. They had held ropes by which he moved the dragon's neck and head. Now they were empty. There were four men in their undershirts, riding in the truck, and they re-

---

7. **imbecilic**\\'ĭm·bə ˄sĭl·ĭk\\ amiability, empty minded friendliness.

garded their public incredulously, because there was no longer a dragon to hide them.

There was, though, an impressive smoldering conflagration on the street. It called for fire engines. They came.

Nancy's mother was in a chaotic state of mind when she managed to fight her way, with Nancy, to where her car was parked. Her expression tended to be on the wild-eyed side, but she got Nancy into the car and herself behind the wheel. Then she doubted frenziedly whether she was in a fit state to drive. She started off, finally, on the dubious premise that somebody who is really crazy never suspects it.

They were late getting home, and Nancy's father was beginning to be worried. He'd been informed of the disappearance of Charles, next door, and of the feverish hunt for him by police and all the neighbors.

He was relieved when Nancy and her mother turned up, but Nancy's mother got out of the car and said tautly, "Get Joe Holt to come here at once." Nancy's mother spoke in the level, tense tone of one who is likely to scream in another split second. "He's a psychiatrist. I have to see a psychiatrist. Everything's happened today! Charles disappeared. An elevatorful of people vanished before my eyes, and a dragon faded to nothingness while I was looking at it. Things like that don't happen! I'm going crazy, but maybe Joe Holt can do something! Get him, quick!"

Then she collapsed, blubbering. She was thinking of Nancy. Already she envisioned a broken home, herself a madwoman and divorced, Nancy's father remarried to someone who would be cruel to Nancy, and Nancy haunted by the specter of madness looming ever before her. Nancy's mother did not worry about her husband. Perhaps that was significant.

But Nancy's father knew when not to try to be reasonable. Also, he was frightened. He grabbed the telephone and spoke with such desperate urgency that in five minutes Joe Holt, that rising young psychiatrist, had got into his car, raced the necessary five blocks, and was looking anxiously at Nancy's mother, in his houseslippers and without a necktie.

"What the devil?" asked Joe Holt unprofessionally.

Nobody noticed Nancy. Her mother began to tell her wholly incredible story. Her tone was pure desperation. She suddenly remembered the fat woman. She told about it, shrilly.

Nancy said reassuringly, "But that was all right, Mother-r! I said 'Oogledeboo' at her!"

Her mother paid no heed. Nancy's father moved to take her out of the room. She clung convulsively to her mother, and her mother to her. Nancy's father was in an unenviable spot for a moment, there.

"Don't take her away!" panted her mother despairingly. "Not yet! Wait! . . . And five minutes later an elevatorful of people vanished before my eyes!"

She sobbed suddenly. Nancy's father ran his hands through his hair.

Nancy's voice said consolingly, "But Mother-r, they were crowding us! That's why I said 'Oogledeboo' at them. Like Charles was bothering me and I said 'Oogledeboo' at him and made him go away."

Her mother's whole body jerked. She stared at Nancy. And then her anguished face smoothed out suddenly. She said in a quiet and interested tone, "Did you, darling?" But she turned tragic eyes upon Joe Holt. "You see, Joe? Listen to her! The things that've happened have turned her little brain too! Don't bother about me, Joe! Do something for Nancy!"

Joe breathed a small sigh of professional relief. All this business was completely bewildering, but he did know that sometimes a woman will do anything for her child—even stay sane, if necessary.

So he said cheerfully to Nancy, "So you made things go away? That's interesting, Nancy. Tell us about it."

Nancy beamed at him. She liked people. They found her irresistible. So she told how her granddaddy had told her how to do magic. One said "Oogledeboo" at things and they went away.

"I said it to the penny," she finished happily, "and to a caterpillar on my doll, and my milk last night, and my cereal this morning, and Charles, and a fat woman, and the people in the elevator, and the dragon. It's easy," she finished generously. "Want me to show you?"

Her mother gasped. But Joe Holt noticed that she wasn't thinking of herself any longer but of Nancy. And as a practical matter, nobody is neurotic who sincerely cares about anybody else. Joe didn't understand anything, but he began to have hope.

"Why, yes, Nancy!" he said blithely. "Make this—h'm—this vase of flowers go away, will you?"

Nancy's mother said involuntarily, "That's my best vase." But then she said calmly, "Yes, darling, make that go away."

So Nancy, blithe and beaming and six years old, looked at her mother's most-prized almost-Ming vase and said happily, "Oogledeboo."

And of course the vase went away.

It was two o'clock in the morning and raining heavily when they got Nancy's grandfather out of bed to answer the bell. Then Nancy's father and Joe Holt crowded inside the door to talk desperately to him with rain-wet, disheveled faces. He stared.

"You've got to come to the house, sir!" said Nancy's father feverishly. "Nancy's got a psychological acosmistic idea from you, and it's got to be cured!"

Joe Holt said reprovingly, if harassedly, "Not idea. Ability. It's a psychokinetic[8] ability."

Nancy's grandfather said in a rising tone, "Nancy's sick? Sick? And you talk? Come on!"

He grabbed an overcoat and flung out of the house, pulling the coat on over his pajamas. Rain poured down. Lightning glinted on it as it fell. They piled into Joe's convertible and he started it off at frantic speed.

Nancy's grandfather snapped, "How's she sick? When did it start?"

"She says 'Oogledeboo' at things!" panted Nancy's father. "And they vanish! We've got her to bed now, but she's got to be cured! Think what she may do next! She says 'Oogledeboo'!"

Nancy's grandfather barked, "Oogledeboo? What's the matter with saying 'Oogledeboo'? I say 'Oogledeboo' if I feel like it! I taught her to say it!"

"That's just it," said Joe Holt, swallowing. He turned to gesticulate. "You showed her that a penny vanished when she said it. She believed it! It's—idealistic immaterialism![9] . . . Oops!"

He yanked at the wheel and pulled the car out of skid as it headed for a telephone pole aglitter with wetness.

"It was Bishop Berkeley," panted Nancy's father. "Joe just showed me! In a book! Bishop Berkeley said that matter cannot exist without mind. A mind has to perceive something in order for it to exist. It's been a big argument for years. Locke, Hume, Kant, Hegel and all the rest."

The car plunged through a black puddle on the pavement, pockmarked with falling rain under an arc light. Sheets of water, like shining wings, rose on either side of the car.

"*Esse,*" said Joe Holt, gulping, "is *percipi*. If a thing isn't perceived by some mind somewhere, it isn't. But when we know something is, we have to let it go at that. Nancy doesn't. You fixed it so she doesn't. When she says 'Oogledeboo' at something, she's able to think of it as ceasing to exist. So it does cease to exist. Nobody else in the world except God can do that! But Nancy can!"

In the racing, leaking car, Nancy's grandfather stared suspiciously at the water-soaked and nerve-racked individuals beside him. His pajama collar rose out of his overcoat. His white hair bristled.

---

8. **psychokinetic**\'sī·kō·kə ᴧnet·ĭk\ the movement of physical objects by the exercise of mental power.
9. **idealistic immaterialism,** the theory that objects have no reality except as they exist as ideas in the mind.

"And you're telling me Nancy's sick!" he roared. "You two lunatics!"

They babbled further details. Preposterous details. They explained what he had to do. Then suddenly Joe Holt swung into the driveway of the house Nancy lived in. As if on signal, the rain stopped. The two younger men piled out of the car and raced into the house. Nancy's grandfather plodded after them. He entered to hear the chattered query, "She's—still asleep?"

"Yes, the darling!" said Nancy's mother in a warm, throaty voice. She hugged Nancy's grandfather. "Daddy! I'm so glad—"

The living room looked like a shambles. The piano was gone. The almost-Ming vase—of course. The picture over the mantel. Two chairs. A scatter rug.

"We experimented!" babbled Joe Holt desperately. "She made the vase vanish. We couldn't believe it. So she said 'Oogledeboo' at the piano. It wasn't there. The picture over the fireplace! It got to be a happy game! She stood there beaming and saying 'Oogledeboo.' She looked at me once—" He shuddered violently.

Nancy's grandfather could not believe. Naturally! But Nancy's mother pleaded with him. The three of them—Nancy's parents and the psychiatrist—argued hysterically. Their voices rose.

Then there was a delighted giggle from the doorway. Nancy stood there, smiling brightly at her grandfather. She wore her very favorite blue pajamas with Mickey Mouse figures printed on them.

She was sleepy-eyed, but very glad to see her grandfather.

"Hello, Granddaddy!" she said happily. "You waked me up. I can do magic like you told me. Want to see?"

Her grandfather gulped suddenly. He had a moment of dreadful doubt. His daughter had turned wholly pale. Nancy's father was speechless. Joe Holt wrung his hands.

"Wait, now," said Nancy's grandfather shakily. "Just try it on a little thing, Nancy. Just a little thing."

With the sure instinct of a grandfather, he remembered that his overcoat was wet. He put it down on a remaining chair before he took Nancy in his arms. Stout elderly man and beaming six-year-old, they made a pleasant picture in their pajamas.

"There, there," said Nancy's grandfather fondly.

"Su-su-suppose," said Joe Holt, "you make your granddaddy's overcoat go away, Nancy?"

Nancy giggled. Her soft, happy voice pronounced the fateful syllables. Her grandfather's overcoat abruptly was not. Her grandfather sat down suddenly. Nancy slipped from his arms to his knee.

She said benignly, "Are you cold, Granddaddy? You're shivering!"

Nancy's grandfather swallowed loudly. Then he said with infinite care, "Why, yes, Nancy. I am cold. I shouldn't have taken off my overcoat. I need it back. Will you get it back for me, Nancy?"

Nancy said fondly, "But I don't know how, Granddaddy!"

"Why—er—you say 'Oogledeboo' backwards, Nancy. But you have to say it. You made my overcoat go away, so you have to make it come back. 'Oogledeboo' backwards is—ah—is—"

" 'Oobedelgoo,' " said Nancy's father hoarsely. " 'Oogledeboo' spelled backwards is 'Oobedelgoo.' Oobedelgoo!"

Nancy considered, and snuggled against her grandfather. "You say it, Granddaddy!"

"It's no good when I say it," said her grandfather, with false heartiness. "See? Oobedelgoo! But it will work for you! And now— Wait a moment, Nancy! When you say it, don't say it at just my overcoat. You say it at all the things you said 'Oogledeboo' at, all at the same time, and they'll all come back at once. Won't that be nice?"

"No," said Nancy. "Charles bothers me."

Joe Holt moaned.

Nancy's mother said softly, "But he won't any more, darling! Just say 'Oobe—Oobedelgoo' nicely, darling, for mother, at all the things you said the other word to!"

Nancy considered again. Her mother stroked her hand. And presently Nancy said, without enthusiasm, without verve, but with a sort of resigned acquiescence, "Oobedelgoo."

The almost-Ming vase came back, and her grandfather's overcoat, and the piano, and the picture over the mantelpiece and a scatter rug, and two chairs. Out on the lawn there was suddenly the howling wail of a scared small boy, "Wa-a-a-ah!" That was Charles, who found himself suddenly in the dark on a rain-wet lawn. He howled. Those in Nancy's house heard doors open next door and shrieks of joy. Nancy's mother closed her eyes and imagined other screams: a fat woman suddenly finding herself alone in the ladies' purse department of a closed-up department store, an elevatorful of people finding themselves parked in the cellar of the same store, to wait for morning. The nightwatchman of that store would have a busy half hour.

The policeman who suddenly found a dragon in the middle of the street would be upset too, as would the hard-working detectives now busily hunting for a small boy who would insist frantically that he hadn't been anywhere. And he hadn't. He'd been nowhere.

Even a caterpillar, which had been crawling on Nancy's doll until she said "Oogledeboo" at it, would have a difficult time finding a proper place to hide from the rain. It happened to be a diurnal[10] caterpillar, not used to being out at night.

Then Nancy's grandfather spoke with very great care and painstaking charm.

"I forgot to tell you, Nancy," he said with seeming ruefulness, "that now you've said 'Oobedelgoo,' saying 'Oogledeboo' won't work for you any longer. That's why I can't work that magic anymore myself. But you won't mind things not going away when you say 'Oogledeboo,' will you?"

"Won't they?" asked Nancy disappointedly. She said loudly, "Oogledeboo!"

Her father and mother and Joe Holt jumped a foot.

But nothing happened. The four grownups sat still, weak with relief. Nancy cuddled against her grandfather. She sighed. Presently her eyelids drooped sleepily.

There had been no rolling of thunder or flashing of lightning, or earthquakes when the most bloodcurdling instant in history began. But, now that everything was all over, there was a blinding flash of lightning and a reverberating roar of thunder, and the rain began to pour down again.

I
A SMALL BUT MIGHTY MAGICIAN

1. What word does Nancy say when she wishes something to disappear?

2. Why does Nancy dispose of Charles?

3. What finally occurs downtown that causes Nancy's mother to believe that she needs the immediate attention of Joe Holt, the psychiatrist?

II
IMPLICATIONS

1. The theory of acosmism or idealistic immaterialism is ridiculous.

2. Grownups do not really listen to their children.

III
TECHNIQUES

Foreshadowing

Great supernatural events are usually marked, according to legend, by such signs as a breathless hush over the earth, darkening skies, unnatural twilight, strangely chirping birds, and frightened cattle. You are told in the first paragraph of "The Little Terror" that none of these things happened. What concluding words in the first paragraph arouse foreboding?

---

10. **diurnal**\dī ˈərn·(ə)l\ active during the day.

Gallery | THE STRANGE AND EERIE

For centuries painters and draftsmen have been exploring the nightmarish visions of their imaginations. This gallery will introduce you to a few works of art that parallel the effect of the stories in this unit.

THE NIGHTMARE
Henry Füssli

THE PRISONS
Giovanni Piranesi
Achenbach Foundation for Graphic Arts

The darker side of the imagination is very important in the works of the three artists represented here. NIGHTMARE is an eighteenth-century painting that is so grotesque as to be almost comic. In his etching, Piranesi imaginatively evokes the horror of prison. And in the detail from a panel painting by Bosch, a fifteenth-century Flemish painter, the notions of demons and mischief are at once sinister and humorous, ancient and modern.

TEMPTATION OF
ST. ANTHONY,
C. 1500: THE BLACK MASS
Hieronymous Bosch

NIGHT AND CLOUDS
Albert Pinkham Ryder
The St. Louis Art Museum

Because his eyes had been damaged during his youth, Ryder took long walks in the moonlight. It is obvious from his painting NIGHT AND CLOUDS that Ryder was fascinated by the mysterious effects of night light. Berman achieves a similar mood of ominous gloom and bleakness in PROSERPINA. Condemned to live half her life in the underworld, Proserpina broods in spiritual darkness.

PROSERPINA
Eugene Berman
The St. Louis Art Museum

FIVE DRAGONS
Ch'en Jung
Chinese handscroll

From thirteenth century China comes the smoky dragon scroll by a famous painter of dragons. It reminds us of the many weird monsters that exist in Oriental and Western mythology. Many artists have been fascinated by the monstrous and chilling images of age-old fears. In FEAR by Tanguy what seems at first to be an ordinary landscape on closer inspection is a depiction of age-old fears of another kind. It contains symbols suggesting fearful things—the strange empty spaces, the forms like dried bones, the element of pain and danger in the flaming red shape.

FEAR
Yves Tanguy
oil on canvas, Collection,
Whitney Museum of Art

605

Leo Rosten was only nine or ten when he first heard this story. In following years he told it to many people, hoping to find someone who would recognize it and remember the original author's name. He was disappointed in this hope, but here is the story as he remembers it. Like him, you will probably never forget its subtle horror.

Cemetery Path

LEO ROSTEN

Ivan was a timid little man—so timid that the villagers called him "Pigeon" or mocked him with the title, "Ivan the Terrible." Every night Ivan stopped in at the saloon which was on the edge of the village cemetery. Ivan never crossed the cemetery to get to his lonely shack on the other side. The path through the cemetery would save him many minutes, but he had never taken it—not even in the full light of noon.

Late one winter's night, when bitter wind and snow beat against the saloon, the customers took up the familiar mockery. "Ivan's mother was scared by a canary when she carried him in her womb." "Ivan the Terrible— Ivan the Terribly Timid One."

Ivan's sickly protest only fed their taunts, and they jeered cruelly when the young Cossack lieutenant flung his horrid challenge at their quarry.

"You are a pigeon, Ivan. You'll walk all around the cemetery in this fiendish cold—but you dare not cross the cemetery."

Ivan murmured, "The cemetery is nothing

to cross, Lieutenant. It is nothing but earth, like all the other earth."

The lieutenant cried, "A challenge, then! Cross the cemetery tonight, Ivan, and I'll give you five rubles—five gold rubles!"

Perhaps it was the vodka. Perhaps it was the temptation of the five gold rubles. No one ever knew why Ivan, moistening his lips, said suddenly: "Yes, Lieutenant, I'll cross the cemetery!"

The saloon echoed with their disbelief. The lieutenant winked to the men and unbuckled his saber. "Here Ivan. When you get to the center of the cemetery, in front of the biggest tomb, stick the saber into the ground. In the morning we shall go there. And if the saber is in the ground—five gold rubles to you!"

Ivan took the saber. The men drank a toast: "To Ivan the Terrible!" They roared with laughter.

The wind howled around Ivan as he closed the door of the saloon behind him. The cold was knife-sharp. He buttoned his long coat and crossed the dirt road. He could hear the lieutenant's voice, louder than the rest, yelling after him, "Five rubles, pigeon! *If you live!*"

Ivan pushed the cemetery gate open. He walked fast. "Earth, just earth . . . like any other earth." But the darkness was a massive dread. "Five gold rubles . . ." The wind was cruel and the saber was like ice in his hands. Ivan shivered under the long, thick coat and broke into a limping run.

He recognized the large tomb. He must have sobbed—that was the sound that was drowned in the wind. And he kneeled, cold and terrified, and drove the saber into the hard ground. With his fist, he beat it down to the hilt. It was done. The cemetery . . . the challenge . . . five gold rubles.

Ivan started to rise from his knees. But he could not move. Something held him. Something gripped him in an unyielding and implacable hold. Ivan tugged and lurched and pulled—gasping in his panic, shaken by a monstrous fear. But something held Ivan. He cried out in terror, then made senseless gurgling noises.

They found Ivan, next morning, on the ground in front of the tomb that was in the center of the cemetery. His face was not that of a frozen man's, but of a man killed by some nameless horror. And the lieutenant's saber was in the ground where Ivan had pounded it—through the dragging folds of his long coat.

I
A SENSELESS CHALLENGE

1. What caused Ivan to cross the cemetery?
2. What killed Ivan?

II
IMPLICATIONS

1. Fear or panic is stronger than reason.
2. Some persons are doomed by their own natures or dispositions.

III
TECHNIQUES

Foreshadowing

Brief as this account is, with what italicized words does the author foreshadow the ending?

Suspense

Suspense builds from the moment Ivan accepts the young lieutenant's dare, but it is felt even more strongly after he pushes open the gate to the cemetery. Where do you think the suspense ends? Why?

Here is one of the famous "secret tales" of the Arctic trails, calculated to "make your blood turn cold."

The Cremation of Sam McGee

There are strange things done in the midnight sun
By the men who moil[1] for gold;
The Arctic trails have their secret tales
That would make your blood run cold;
The Northern Lights have seen queer sights,   5
But the queerest they ever did see
Was that night on the marge[2] of Lake Lebarge
I cremated Sam McGee.

Now Sam McGee was from Tennessee, where the cotton blooms and blows.
Why he left his home in the South to roam 'round the Pole, God only knows.   10
He was always cold, but the land of gold seemed to hold him like a spell;
Though he'd often say in his homely way that "he'd sooner live in hell."

Reprinted from *Collected Poems of Robert Service* by Robert W. Service by permission of The Ryerson Psess.

1. **moil**\mɔil\ work hard in the dirt.
2. **marge**\marj\ shore.

On a Christmas Day we were mushing our way over the Dawson trail.
Talk of your cold! through the parka's fold it stabbed like a driven nail.
If our eyes we'd close, then the lashes froze till sometimes we couldn't see;   15
It wasn't much fun, but the only one to whimper was Sam McGee.

And that very night, as we lay packed tight in our robes beneath the snow,
And the dogs were fed, and the stars o'erhead were dancing heel and toe,
He turned to me, and "Cap," says he, "I'll cash in this trip, I guess;
And if I do, I'm asking that you won't refuse my last request."   20

Well, he seemed so low that I couldn't say no; then he says with a sort of moan:
"It's the cursed cold, and it's got right hold till I'm chilled clean through to the bone.
Yet 'taint being dead—it's my awful dread of the icy grave that pains;
So I want you to swear that, foul or fair, you'll cremate my last remains."

A pal's last need is a thing to heed, so I swore I would not fail;   25
And we started on at the streak of dawn; but God! he looked ghastly pale.
He crouched on the sleigh, and he raved all day of his home in Tennessee;
And before nightfall a corpse was all that was left of Sam McGee.

There wasn't a breath in that land of death, and I hurried, horror-driven,
With a corpse half-hid that I couldn't get rid, because of a promise given;   30
It was lashed to the sleigh, and it seemed to say: "You may tax your brawn and brains.
But you promised true, and it's up to you to cremate these last remains."

Now a promise made is a debt unpaid, and the trail has its own stern code.
In the days to come, though my lips were dumb, in my heart how I cursed that load.
In the long, long night, by the lone firelight, while the Huskies, round in a ring,   35
Howled out their woes to the homeless snows—O God! how I loathed the thing.

And every day that quiet clay³ seemed to heavy and heavier grow;
And on I went, though the dogs were spent and the grub was getting low;
The trail was bad, and I felt half mad, but I swore I would not give in;
And I'd often sing to the hateful thing, and it harkened with a grin.   40

Till I came to the marge of Lake Lebarge, and a derelict there lay;
It was jammed in the ice, but I saw in a trice it was called the *Alice May.*
And I looked at it, and I thought a bit, and I looked at my frozen chum;
Then "Here," said I, with a sudden cry, "is my cre-ma-to-re-um."⁴

Some planks I tore from the cabin floor, and I lit the boiler fire;   45
Some coal I found that was lying around, and I heaped the fuel higher;
The flames just soared, and the furnace roared—such a blaze you seldom see;
And I burrowed a hole in the glowing coal, and I stuffed in Sam McGee.

Then I made a hike, for I didn't like to hear him sizzle so;
And the heavens scowled, and the Huskies howled, and the wind began to blow. 50

---

3. **quiet clay,** Sam's body.
4. **crematorium**\'krē·mə ▲tō·rē·əm\ a building or other place in which bodies are cremated.

It was icy cold, but the hot sweat rolled down my cheeks, and I don't know why;
And the greasy smoke in an inky cloak went streaking down the sky.

I do not know how long in the snow I wrestled with grisly fear;
But the stars came out and they danced about ere again I ventured near;
I was sick with dread, but I bravely said: "I'll just take a peep inside.   55
I guess he's cooked, and it's time I looked"; . . . then the door I opened wide.

And there sat Sam, looking cool and calm, in the heart of the furnace roar;
And he wore a smile you could see a mile, and he said: "Please close that door.
It's fine in here, but I greatly fear you'll let in the cold and storm—
Since I left Plumtree down in Tennessee, it's the first time I've been warm."   60

There are strange things done in the midnight sun
By the men who moil for gold;
The Arctic trails have their secret tales
That would make your blood run cold;
The Northern Lights have seen queer sights,   65
But the queerest they ever did see
Was that night on the marge of Lake Lebarge
I cremated Sam McGee.

ROBERT W. SERVICE

FORESHADOWING AND SUSPENSE

While working in a bank in the Yukon during the gold rush at the end of the last century, Robert W. Service began turning out rhymes in a half-jesting manner about the life of the sour-doughs (gold miners). These poems struck "pay dirt" immediately and he became famous. This poem was a great favorite with the men and women who went to Alaska to "moil for gold."

1. The poem builds awesome suspense. In the first forty lines, we have visions of the storyteller going stark, raving mad. However, from line forty-one on, the poet lets us know that events will take a grimly humorous turn. He does this by such words and phrases as "frozen chum" and "stuffed in Sam McGee." Find two other such cues. Explain how these are used to change the tone of the poem from one of horror to one of gruesome comedy.

2. Give your feelings about this poem. Explain why it does or does not have an appeal for you. Remember that such an explanation is more interesting if you refer to specific words and phrases.

Are we doomed because
we are human beings?

The Large Ant

HOWARD FAST

There have been all kinds of notions and guesses as to how it would end. One held that sooner or later there would be too many people; another that we would do each other in, and the atom bomb made that a very good likelihood. All sorts of notions, except the simple fact that we were what we were. We could find a way to feed any number of people and perhaps even a way to avoid wiping each other out with the bomb; those things we are very good at, but we have never been any good at changing ourselves or the way we behave.

I know. I am not a bad man or a cruel man; quite to the contrary, I am an ordinary, humane person, and I love my wife and my children and I get along with my neighbors. I am like a great many other men, and do the things they would do and just as thoughtlessly. There it is in a nutshell.

I am also a writer, and I told Lieberman, the curator, and Fitzgerald, the government man, that I would like to write down the story. They shrugged their shoulders. "Go ahead," they said, "because it won't make one bit of difference."

"You don't think it would alarm people?"

"How can it alarm anyone when nobody will believe it?"

"If I could have a photograph or two."

"Oh, no," they said then. "No photographs."

"What kind of sense does that make?" I asked them. "You are willing to let me write the story—why not the photographs so that people could believe me?"

"They still won't believe you. They will just say you faked the photographs, but no one will believe you. It will make for more confusion, and if we have a chance of getting out of this, confusion won't help."

"What will help?"

They weren't ready to say that, because they didn't know. So here is what happened to me, in a very straightforward and ordinary manner.

Every summer, some time in August, four good friends of mine and I go for a week's fishing on the St. Regis chain of lakes in the Adirondacks. We rent the same shack each summer; we drift around in canoes and sometimes we catch a few bass. The fishing isn't very good, but we play cards well together, and we cook out and generally relax. This summer past, I had some things to do that couldn't be put off. I arrived three days late, and the weather was so warm and even and beguiling that I decided to stay on by myself for a day or two after the others left. There was a small flat lawn in front of the shack, and I made up my mind to spend at least three or four hours at short putts. That was how I happened to have the putting iron next to my bed.

The first day I was alone, I opened a can of beans and a can of beer for my supper. Then I lay down in my bed with *Life on the Mississippi*, a pack of cigarettes and an eight-ounce chocolate bar. There was nothing I had to do, no telephone, no demands and no newspapers. At that moment, I was about as contented as any man can be in these nervous times.

It was still light outside, and enough light came in through the window above my head for me to read by. I was just reaching for a fresh cigarette, when I looked up and saw it on the foot of my bed. The edge of my hand was touching the golf club, and with a single motion I swept the club over and down, struck it a savage and accurate blow and killed it. That was what I referred to before. Whatever kind of a man I am, I react as a man does. I think that any man, black, white or yellow, in China, Africa or Russia, would have done the same thing.

First I found that I was sweating all over, and then I knew I was going to be sick. I went outside to vomit, recalling that this hadn't happened to me since 1943, on my way to Europe on a tub of a Liberty ship.[1] Then I felt better and was able to go back into the shack and look at it. It was quite dead, but I had already made up my mind that I was not going to sleep alone in this shack.

I couldn't bear to touch it with my bare hands. With a piece of brown paper, I picked it up and dropped it into my fishing creel. That, I put into the trunk of my car, along with what luggage I carried. Then I closed the door of the shack, got into my car and drove back to New York. I stopped once along the road, just before I reached the Thruway, to nap in the car for a little over an hour. It was almost dawn when I reached the city, and I had shaved, had a hot bath and changed my clothes before my wife awoke.

During breakfast, I explained that I was never much of a hand at the solitary business, and since she knew that, and since driving alone all night was by no means an extraordinary procedure for me, she didn't press me with any questions. I had two eggs, coffee and a cigarette. Then I went into my study, lit another cigarette, and contemplated my fishing creel, which sat upon my desk.

My wife looked in, saw the creel, remarked that it had too ripe a smell, and asked me to remove it to the basement.

"I'm going to dress," she said. The kids were still at camp. "I have a date with Ann for lunch—I had no idea you were coming back. Shall I break it?"

"No, please don't. I can find things to do that have to be done."

Then I sat and smoked some more, and finally I called the Museum, and asked who the curator of insects was. They told me his name was Bertram Lieberman, and I asked to talk to him. He had a pleasant voice. I told him that my name was Morgan, and that I was a writer, and he politely indicated that he had seen my name and read something that I had written. That is formal procedure when a writer introduces himself to a thoughtful person.

I asked Lieberman if I could see him, and he said that he had a busy morning ahead of him. Could it be tomorrow?

"I am afraid it has to be now," I said firmly.

"Oh? Some information you require."

"No. I have a specimen for you."

"Oh?" The "oh" was a cultivated, neutral interval. It asked and answered and said nothing. You have to teach at least five semesters at a college to develop that particular "oh."

"Yes. I think you will be interested."

"An insect?" he asked mildly.

"I think so."

"Oh? Large?"

"Quite large," I told him.

"Eleven o'clock? Can you be here then? On the main floor, to the right, as you enter."

"I'll be there," I said.

"One thing—dead?"

"Yes, it's dead."

"Oh?" again. "I'll be happy to see you at eleven o'clock, Mr. Morgan."

My wife was dressed now. She opened the door to my study and said firmly. "Do get rid of that fishing creel. It smells."

"Yes, darling. I'll get rid of it."

"I should think you'd want to take a nap after driving all night."

"Funny, but I'm not sleepy," I said. "I think I'll drop around to the Museum."

My wife said that was what she liked about me, that I never tired of places like museums, police courts and third-rate night clubs.

Anyway, aside from a racetrack, a museum is the most interesting and unexpected place

---

1. **Liberty ship,** a large American cargo ship built in large numbers during World War II.

in the world. It was unexpected to have two other men waiting for me, along with Mr. Lieberman, in his office. Lieberman was a skinny, sharp-faced man of about sixty. The government man, Fitzgerald, was small, dark-eyed and wore gold-rimmed glasses. He was very alert, but he never told me what part of the government he represented. He just said "we," and it meant the government. Hopper, the third man, was comfortable-looking, pudgy, and genial. He was a United States senator with an interest in entomology,[2] although before this morning I would have taken better than even money that such a thing not only wasn't, but could not be.

The room was large and square and plainly furnished, with shelves and cupboards on all walls.

We shook hands, and then Lieberman asked me, nodding at the creel, "Is that it?"

"That's it."

"May I?"

"Go ahead," I told him. "It's nothing that I want to stuff for the parlor. I'm making you a gift of it."

"Thank you, Mr. Morgan," he said, and then he opened the creel and looked inside. Then he straightened up, and the two other men looked at him inquiringly.

He nodded. "Yes."

The senator closed his eyes for a long moment. Fitzgerald took off his glasses and wiped them industriously. Lieberman spread a piece of plastic on his desk, and then lifted the thing out of my creel and laid it on the plastic. The two men didn't move. They just sat where they were and looked at it.

"What do you think it is, Mr. Morgan?" Lieberman asked me.

"I thought that was your department."

"Yes, of course. I only wanted your impression."

"An ant. That's my impression. It's the first time I saw an ant fourteen, fifteen inches long. I hope it's the last."

"An understandable wish," Lieberman nodded.

Fitzgerald said to me, "May I ask how you killed it, Mr. Morgan?"

"With an iron. A golf club, I mean. I was doing a little fishing with some friends up at St. Regis in the Adirondacks, and I brought the iron for my short shots. They're the worst part of my game, and when my friends left, I intended to stay on at our shack and do four or five hours of short putts. You see—"

"There's no need to explain," Hopper smiled, a trace of sadness on his face. "Some of our very best golfers have the same trouble."

"I was lying in bed, reading, and I saw it at the foot of my bed. I had the club—"

"I understand," Fitzgerald nodded.

"You avoid looking at it," Hopper said.

"It turns my stomach."

"Yes—yes, I suppose so."

Lieberman said, "Would you mind telling us why you killed it, Mr. Morgan."

"Why?"

"Yes—why?"

"I don't understand you," I said. "I don't know what you're driving at."

"Sit down, please, Mr. Morgan," Hopper nodded. "Try to relax. I'm sure this has been very trying."

"I still haven't slept. I want a chance to dream before I say how trying."

"We are not trying to upset you, Mr. Morgan," Lieberman said. "We do feel, however, that certain aspects of this are very important. That is why I am asking you why you killed it. You must have had a reason. Did it seem about to attack you?"

"No."

"Or make any sudden motion toward you?"

"No. It was just there."

"Then why?"

"This is to no purpose," Fitzgerald put in. "We know why he killed it."

"Do you?" I nodded. "You're clearer on the subject than I am."

---

2. **entomology**\ent·ə ▲mŏl·ə·jē\ the scientific study of insects.

"The answer is very simple, Mr. Morgan. You killed it because you are a human being."

"Oh?" I borrowed that from Lieberman.

"Yes. Do you understand?"

"No, I don't."

"Then why did you kill it?" Hopper put in.

"I saw it," I answered slowly, "and somehow I knew that I must kill it. I didn't think or decide. I just grabbed the iron and hit it."

"Precisely," Fitzgerald said.

"You were afraid?" Hopper asked.

"I was scared to death. I still am, to tell the truth."

Lieberman said, "You are an intelligent man, Mr. Morgan. Let me show you something." He then opened the doors of one of the wall cupboards, and there stood eight jars of formaldehyde and in each jar a specimen like mine—and in each case mutilated by the violence of its death. I said nothing. I just stared.

Lieberman closed the cupboard doors. "All in five days," he shrugged.

"A new race of ants," I whispered stupidly.

"No. They're not ants. Come here!" He motioned me to the desk and the other two joined me. Lieberman took a set of dissecting instruments out of his drawer, used one to turn the thing over, and then pointed to the underpart of what would be the thorax in an insect.

"That looks like part of him, doesn't it, Mr. Morgan?"

"Yes, it does."

Using two of the tools, he found a fissure and pried the bottom apart. It came open like the belly of a bomber; it was a pocket, a pouch, a receptacle that the thing wore, and in it were four beautiful little tools or instruments or weapons, each about an inch and a half long. They were beautiful the way any object of functional purpose and loving creation is beautiful—the way the creature itself would have been beautiful, had it not been an insect and myself a man. Using tweezers, Lieberman took each instrument out of the brackets that held it, offering each to me. And

I took each one, felt it, examined it, and then put it down.

I had to look at the ant now, and I realized that I had not truly looked at it before. We don't look carefully at a thing that is horrible or repugnant to us. You can't look at anything through a screen of hatred. But now the hatred and the fear were diluted, and as I looked, I realized it was not an ant although like an ant. It was nothing that I had ever seen or dreamed of.

All three men were watching me, and suddenly I was on the defensive. "I didn't know! What do you expect when you see an insect that size?"

Lieberman nodded.

"What is it?"

From his desk, Lieberman produced a bottle and four small glasses. He poured it and we drank it neat. I would not have expected him to keep good Scotch in his desk.

"We don't know," Hopper said. "We don't know what it is."

Lieberman pointed to the broken skull, from which a white substance oozed. "Brain material—a great deal of it."

"It could be a very intelligent creature," Hopper nodded.

Lieberman said, "It is an insect in developmental structure. We know very little about intelligence in our insects. It's not the same as what we call intelligence. It's a collective phenomenon—as if you were to think of the component parts of our bodies. Each part is alive, but the intelligence is a result of the whole. If that same pattern were to extend to creatures like this one—"

I broke the silence. They were content to stand there and stare at it.

"Suppose it were?"

"What?"

"The kind of collective intelligence you were talking about."

"Oh? Well, I couldn't say. It would be something beyond our wildest dreams. To us —well, what we are to an ordinary ant."

"I don't believe that," I said shortly, and

Fitzgerald, the government man, told me quietly:

"Neither do we. We guess. We comfort ourselves, too."

"If it's that intelligent, why didn't it use one of those weapons on me?"

"Would that be a mark of intelligence?" Hopper asked mildly.

"Perhaps none of these is a weapon," Lieberman said.

"Don't you know? Didn't the others carry instruments?"

"They did," Fitzgerald said shortly.

"Why? What were they?"

"We don't know," Lieberman said.

"But you can find out. We have scientists, engineers—good heavens, this is an age of fantastic instruments. Have them taken apart!"

"We have."

"Then what have you found out?"

"Nothing."

"Do you mean to tell me," I said, "that you can find out nothing about these instruments—what they are, how they work, what their purpose is?"

"Exactly," Hopper nodded. "Nothing, Mr. Morgan. They are meaningless to the finest engineers and technicians in the United States. You know the old story—suppose you gave a radio to Aristotle? What would he do with it? Where would he find power? And what would he receive with no one to send? It is not that these instruments are complex. They are actually very simple. We simply have no idea of what they can or should do."

"But there must be a weapon of some kind."

"Why?" Lieberman demanded. "Look at yourself, Mr. Morgan—a cultured and intelligent man, yet you cannot conceive of a mentality that does not include weapons as a prime necessity. Yet a weapon is an unusual thing, Mr. Morgan. An instrument of murder. We don't think that way, because the weapon has become the symbol of the world we inhabit. Is that civilized, Mr. Morgan? Or are the weapon and civilization in the ultimate sense incompatible? Can you imagine a mentality to which the concept of murder is impossible—or let me say absent. We see everything through our own subjectivity. Why shouldn't some other—this creature, for example—see the process of mentation out of his subjectivity. So he approaches a creature of our world—and he is slain. Why? What explanation? Tell me, Mr. Morgan, what conceivable explanation could we offer a wholly rational creature for this," pointing to the thing on his desk. "I am asking you the question most seriously. What explanation?"

"An accident?" I muttered.

"And the eight jars in my cupboard? Eight accidents?"

"I think, Dr. Lieberman," Fitzgerald said, that you can go a little too far in that direction."

"Yes, you would think so. It's a part of your own background. Mine is as a scientist. As a scientist, I try to be rational when I can. The creation of a structure of good and evil, or what we call morality and ethics, is a function of intelligence—and unquestionably the ultimate evil may be the destruction of conscious intelligence. That is why, so long ago, we at least recognized the injunction, 'Thou shalt not kill!' even if we never gave more than lip service to it. But to a collective intelligence, such as that of which this might be a part, the concept of murder would be monstrous beyond the power of thought."

I sat down and lit a cigarette. My hands were trembling. Hopper apologized. "We have been rather rough with you, Mr. Morgan. But over the past days, eight other people have done just what you did. We are caught in the trap of being what we are."

"But tell me—where do these things come from?"

"It almost doesn't matter where they come from," Hopper said hopelessly. "Perhaps from another planet—perhaps from inside this one—or the moon or Mars. That doesn't matter. Fitzgerald thinks they come from a smaller planet, because their movements are apparently slow on earth. But Dr. Lieberman thinks that they move slowly because they have not discovered the need to move quickly. Meanwhile, they have the problem of murder and what to do with it. Heaven knows how many of them have died in other places—Africa, Asia, Europe."

"Then why don't you publicize this? Put a stop to it before it's too late!"

"We've thought of that," Fitzgerald nodded. "What then—panic, hysteria, charges that this is the result of the atom bomb? We can't change. We are what we are."

"They may go away," I said.

"Yes, they may," Lieberman nodded. "But if they are without the curse of murder, they may also be without the curse of fear. They may be social in the highest sense. What does society do with a murderer?"

"There are societies that put him to death—and there are other societies that recognize his sickness and lock him away, where he can kill no more," Hopper said. "Of course, when a whole world is on trial, that's another matter. We have atom bombs now and other things, and we are reaching out to the stars—"

"I'm inclined to think that they'll run," Fitzgerald put in. "They may just have that curse of fear, Doctor."

"They may," Lieberman admitted. "I hope so."

But the more I think so, the more it seems to me that fear and hatred are the two sides of the same coin. I keep trying to think back, to recreate the moment when I saw it standing at the foot of my bed in the fishing shack. I keep trying to drag out of my memory a clear picture of what it looked like, whether behind that chitinous[3] face and the two gently waving antennae there was any evidence of fear and anger. But the clearer the memory becomes, the more I seem to recall a certain wonderful dignity and repose. Not fear and not anger.

And more and more, as I go about my work, I get the feeling of what Hopper called "a world on trial." I have no sense of anger my-self. Like a criminal who can no longer live with himself, I am content to be judged.

I

A CREATURE OF MYSTERY

This is a strange story—one that leaves the reader wondering greatly about some of the beliefs and standards of conduct that man has accepted for so long without question.

1. How did Morgan happen to be at the cabin in the Adirondacks by himself?

2. How many specimens identical to Morgan's had already been turned in to the museum?

3. What was unusual about the underpart of the thorax of the insect-like creature Morgan killed?

4. Why is the possibility that the theory of collective intelligence might apply to the "large ant" alarming?

5. Why might this place the whole world on trial?

6. What impression does Morgan retain after he searches his memory as to the attitude of his mysterious visitor?

II

IMPLICATIONS

Find evidence in "The Large Ant" to support the following statements.

1. Ordinary man is not so much deliberately cruel as thoughtless.

2. Man's instinctive fear causes him to kill many small and quite harmless creatures.

3. Hatred or repugnance keeps us from seeing many things as they really are.

4. Weapons are a prime necessity to civilization.

5. The greatest evil is the destruction of conscious intelligence.

---

3. **chitinous**\\ˈkīt·(ə)n·əs\\ hard, shell-like.

III
TECHNIQUES

Foreshadowing

What will eventually happen to the human race? Will we destroy ourselves or be destroyed by others? Such disturbing questions, asked indirectly in the beginning paragraphs, warn the reader that the story to follow will undoubtedly be frightening. In the paragraph in which Morgan is refused permission to use pictures on the excuse that doing this would cause more confusion, what clause, beginning with the word "if," arouses particular apprehension in the reader?

Suspense

Suspense is aroused and maintained at a sharp pitch by the author's not revealing what he had struck with his golf club.

1. Describe his reaction after he had killed "it." Why does he use a piece of brown paper to get it into his fishing creel?

2. Who else is waiting with Lieberman at the museum? Why does this make the reader apprehensive?

SUMMING UP

The Strange and Eerie

Two subjects that fascinate people and arouse terror in them at the same time are death and the unfamiliar. These topics are both repugnant and enthralling. For this reason, reading strange and eerie stories involves a victory of mind over emotions. Most people go ahead and read what they know was expressly written to frighten them.

It is true that not everyone is afraid of the unfamiliar or of death under ordinary circumstances. Scientists constantly seek answers to the unknown or unfamiliar, and many people accept the fact of death with courage and composure. But in stories written expressly to thrill and chill the reader, the unfamiliar is introduced or the threat of death appears when the reader is totally unprepared to cope with either. Thus he becomes involved in an enjoyable form of self-torture as he shares the fears and apprehensions of the characters in such stories.

Think back over the selections "August Heat," "The Little Terror," "Cemetery Path," "The Cremation of Sam McGee," and "The Large Ant." Which one dealt with the unfamiliar or supernatural in a lighthearted manner? Which treated death in a humorous way? Which aroused fear about the future of mankind? Which was the only selection that did not actually involve the unfamiliar, or supernatural? Which story depended most heavily upon a principle sometimes referred as to ESP or extrasensory perception?

IMPLICATIONS

Consider and discuss the following statements.

1. It's fun to be scared.

2. We tend to value strange experiences as worthy of being told again and again.

3. Telling a mysterious experience is satisfying to the ego of the storyteller.

4. There are more things to be frightened of within man's makeup than in his environment.

TECHNIQUES

Authors who specialize in writing about the strange and eerie are masters at creating *suspense*, using *imaginative language*, and *foreshadowing* events to come. You awaken at midnight to see a horrible creature from the unknown creeping toward your bed. See if within the space of a single paragraph you can describe the situation, using all three of the literary techniques of *suspense, foreshadowing,* and *imaginative language*.

ONCE UPON A MIDNIGHT

FIVE SELECTIONS BY EDGAR ALLAN POE

Over a hundred years ago a strange, darkly handsome, tormented man wrote a body of stories and poems that have haunted people ever since. This man, Edgar Allan Poe (1809–1849), never seemed able to find success or happiness. He was two years old when his actor parents died. A wealthy tobacco exporter of Richmond, Virginia, took him into his home, although he never really adopted the boy.

Poe was sent to the University of Virginia where, symbolically enough, his room assignment was number 13. Because of gambling debts, however, he was forced to leave before the year was over. He published a small volume of verse in 1827, tried the Army for a few years, and then was admitted to West Point. After a few months there, he was discharged for neglect of duty and disobedience. He worked tirelessly at his writing, but he lost a series of jobs on magazines because of his compulsive drinking.

His cousin, fourteen-year-old Virginia Clemm, a pale-skinned, dark-haired, fragile beauty, became his bride, but she eventually died from tuberculosis. During her life Poe did his most inspired writing and was probably as happy as he ever was. Virginia's death plus financial problems bit by bit wore at his mind until he went through periods of mental imbalance. He died at a comparatively young age, ending a life of anguished suffering.

The writing Edgar Allan Poe left behind has made him one of the best-known American authors outside the United States. He is read and admired throughout the world for the weird and terrifying visions that he managed to trap in words.

A mind like Poe's, brilliant and sensitive though distorted by drinking, failure, and despair, was fascinated by the devious and dark elements in man's nature. Such facets of life attracted him as a moth is attracted by light or a mouse by the cobra's eye. Poe was a master at finding the combination of words and events to send shudders up the spine of the reader. Most of us enjoy toying with possibilities of things just beyond the edge of reality. We like to imagine monsters that are distortions of human beings or to horrify ourselves with frightening, terrifying events. Poe does these things for us with an artistry and skill that can be found in few other writers.

Join with him as a madman creeps down a dark passageway, mysterious subterranean catacombs open up in flickering lights, or a strange bird croaks mournfully, once upon a midnight.

Warning!
Do not read this story
when you are alone in a shadowy room
with the wind howling outside.
Never read it at night!

The Tell-Tale Heart

True!—nervous—very, very dreadfully nervous I had been and am! but why *will* you say that I am mad? The disease had sharpened my senses—not destroyed—not dulled them. Above all was the sense of hearing acute. I heard all things in the heaven and in the earth. I heard many things in hell. How, then, am I mad? Hearken! and observe how healthily— how calmly I can tell you the whole story.

It is impossible to say how first the idea entered my brain; but once conceived, it haunted me day and night. Object there was none. Passion there was none. I loved the old man. He had never wronged me. He had never given me insult. For his gold I had no desire. I think it was his eye! yes, it was this! One of his eyes resembled that of a vulture—a pale blue eye, with a film over it. Whenever it fell upon me, my blood ran cold; and so by degrees—very gradually—I made up my mind to take the life of the old man, and thus rid myself of the eye for ever.

Now this is the point. You fancy me mad. Madmen know nothing. But you should have seen *me*. You should have seen how wisely I proceeded—with what caution—with what foresight—with what dissimulation I went to work!

I was never kinder to the old man than during the whole week before I killed him. And every night, about midnight, I turned the latch of his door and opened it—oh, so gently! And then, when I had made an opening sufficient for my head, I put in a dark lantern, all closed, closed, so that no light shone out, and then I thrust in my head. Oh, you would have laughed to see how cunningly I thrust it in! I moved it slowly— very, very slowly, so that I might not disturb the old man's sleep. It took me an hour to place my whole head within the opening so far that I could see him as he lay upon his bed. Ha!—would a madman have been so wise as this? And then, when my head was well in the room, I undid the lantern cautiously—oh, so cautiously—cautiously (for the hinges creaked) —I undid it just so much that a single thin ray fell upon the vulture eye. And this I did for seven long nights—every night just at midnight—but I found the eye always closed; and so it was impossible to do the work; for it was not the old man who vexed me, but his Evil Eye. And every morning, when the day broke, I went boldly into the chamber, and spoke courageously to him, calling him by name in a hearty tone, and inquiring how he had passed the night. So you see he would have been a very profound old man, indeed, to suspect that every night, just at twelve, I looked in upon him while he slept.

Upon the eighth night I was more than usually cautious in opening the door. A watch's minute hand moves more quickly than did mine. Never before that night had I *felt* the extent of my own powers—of my sagacity. I could scarcely contain my feelings of triumph. To think that there I was, opening the door, little by little, and he not even to dream of my secret deeds or thoughts. I fairly chuckled at the idea; and perhaps he heard me; for he moved on the bed suddenly, as if startled. Now you may think that I drew back—but no. His room was as black as pitch with the thick darkness, (for the shutters were close fastened, through fear of robbers,) and so I knew that he could not see the opening of the door, and I kept pushing it on steadily, steadily.

I had my head in, and was about to open the lantern, when my thumb slipped upon the tin fastening, and the old man sprang up in the bed, crying out—"Who's there?"

I kept quite still and said nothing. For a whole hour I did not move a muscle, and in the meantime I did not hear him lie down. He was still sitting up in the bed listening—just as I have done, night after night, hearkening to the death watches in the wall.

Presently I heard a slight groan, and I knew it was the groan of mortal terror. It was not a groan of pain or of grief—oh, no!—it was the low stifled sound that arises from the bottom of the soul when overcharged with awe. I knew the sound well. Many a night, just at midnight, when all the world slept, it has welled up from my own bosom, deepening, with its dreadful echo, the terrors that distracted me. I say I knew it well. I knew what the old man felt, and pitied him, although I chuckled at heart. I knew that he had been lying awake ever since the first slight noise, when he had turned in the bed. His fears had been ever since growing upon him. He had been trying to fancy them causeless, but could not. He had been saying to himself—"It is nothing but the wind in the chimney—it is only a mouse crossing the floor," or "It is merely a cricket which has made a single chirp." Yes, he had been trying to comfort himself with these suppositions; but he had found all in vain. *All in vain;* because Death, in approaching him, had stalked with his black shadow before him, and enveloped the victim. And it was the mournful influence of the unperceived shadow that caused him to feel—although he neither saw nor heard—to *feel* the presence of my head within the room.

When I had waited a long time, very patiently, without hearing him lie down, I resolved to open a little—a very, very little crevice in the lantern. So I opened it—you cannot imagine how stealthily, stealthily—until, at length, a single dim ray, like the thread of the spider, shot from out the crevice and fell upon the vulture eye.

It was open—wide, wide open—and I grew furious as I gazed upon it. I saw it with perfect distinctness—all a dull blue, with a hideous veil over it that chilled the very marrow in my bones; but I could see nothing else of the old man's face or person: for I had directed the ray, as if by instinct, precisely upon the damned spot.

And now have I not told you that what you mistake for madness is but over-acuteness of the senses?—now, I say, there came to my ears a low, dull, quick sound, such as a watch makes when enveloped in cotton. I knew *that* sound well, too. It was the beating of the old man's heart. It increased my fury, as the beating of a drum stimulates the soldier into courage.

But even yet I refrained and kept still. I scarcely breathed. I held the lantern motionless. I tried how steadily I could maintain the ray upon the eye. Meantime the hellish tattoo of the heart increased. It grew quicker and quicker, and louder and louder every instant. The old man's terror *must* have been extreme! It grew louder, I say, louder every moment!—do you mark me well? I have told you that I am nervous: so I am. And now at the dead hour of the night, amid the dreadful silence of that old house, so strange a noise as this excited me to uncontrollable terror. Yet, for some minutes longer I refrained and stood still. But the beating grew louder, louder! I thought the heart must burst. And now a new anxiety seized me —the sound would be heard by a neighbor! The old man's hour had come! With a loud yell, I threw open the lantern and leaped into the room. He shrieked once—once only. In an instant I dragged him to the floor, and pulled the heavy bed over him. I then smiled gaily, to find the deed so far done. But, for many minutes, the heart beat on with a muffled sound. This, however, did not vex me; it would not be heard through the wall. At length it ceased. The old man was dead. I removed the bed and examined the corpse. Yes, he was stone, stone dead. I placed my hand upon the heart and held it there many minutes. There was no pulsation. He was stone dead. His eye would trouble me no more.

If still you think me mad, you will think so no longer when I describe the wise precautions

I took for the concealment of the body. The night waned, and I worked hastily, but in silence. First of all I dismembered the corpse. I cut off the head and the arms and the legs.

I then took up three planks from the flooring of the chamber, and deposited all between the scantlings. I then replaced the boards so cleverly, so cunningly, that no human eye—not even *his*—could have detected anything wrong. There was nothing to wash out—no stain of any kind—no blood-spot whatever. I had been too wary for that. A tub had caught all—ha! ha!

When I had made an end of these labors, it was four o'clock—still dark as midnight. As the bell sounded the hour, there came a knocking at the street door. I went down to open it with a light heart—for what had I *now* to fear? There entered three men, who introduced themselves, with perfect suavity, as officers of the police. A shriek had been heard by a neighbor during the night; suspicion of foul play had been aroused; information had been lodged at the police office, and they (the officers) had been deputed to search the premises.

I smiled—for *what* had I to fear? I bade the gentlemen welcome. The shriek, I said, was my own in a dream. The old man, I mentioned, was absent in the country. I took my visitors all over the house. I bade them search—search *well*. I led them, at length, to *his* chamber. I showed them his treasures, secure, undisturbed. In the enthusiasm of my confidence, I brought chairs into the room, and desired them *here* to rest from their fatigues, while I myself, in the wild audacity of my perfect triumph, placed my own seat upon the very spot beneath which reposed the corpse of the victim.

The officers were satisfied. My *manner* had convinced them. I was singularly at ease. They sat, and while I answered cheerily, they chatted familiar things. But, ere long, I felt myself getting pale and wished them gone. My head ached, and I fancied a ringing in my ears: but still they sat and still they chatted. The ringing became more distinct: it continued and became more distinct: I talked more freely to get rid of the feeling: but it continued and gained defini-

tiveness—until, at length, I found that the noise was *not* within my ears.

No doubt I now grew *very* pale; but I talked more fluently, and with a heightened voice. Yet the sound increased—and what could I do? It was *a low, dull, quick sound—much such a sound as a watch makes when enveloped in cotton.* I gasped for breath—and yet the officers heard it not. I talked more quickly—more vehemently; but the noise steadily increased. I arose and argued about trifles, in a high key and with violent gesticulations, but the noise steadily increased. Why *would* they not be gone? I paced the floor to and fro with heavy strides, as if excited to fury by the observation of the men—but the noise steadily increased. O God! what *could* I do? I foamed—I raved— I swore! I swung the chair upon which I had been sitting, and grated it upon the boards, but the noise arose over all and continually increased. It grew louder—louder—*louder!* And still the men chatted pleasantly, and smiled. Was it possible they heard not? Almighty God! —no, no! They heard!—they suspected! they *knew!*—they were making a *mockery* of my horror!—this I thought, and this I think. But anything was better than this agony! Anything was more tolerable than this derision! I could bear those hypocritical smiles no longer! I felt that I must scream or die!—and now—again— hark! louder! louder! louder! *louder!*—"Villains!" I shrieked, "dissemble no more! I admit the deed!—tear up the planks!—here, here!— it is the beating of his hideous heart!"

I

MURDER AT MIDNIGHT

Although this account is actually of a brutal, premeditated murder, the madman telling the story seems concerned mainly with convincing his listeners of his sanity.

Discuss the "reasons" the murderer gives for the following:

1. His heightened sense of hearing
2. His decision to kill the old man

3. His manner toward the old man each morning

4. His understanding of the old man's terror

5. His invitation to the police officers to sit and visit with him

6. His belief that the police knew of his crime before he confessed

II

IMPLICATIONS

Consider and discuss these statements:

1. Insane people think that they are sane.

2. The senses of an insane person are more acute than are those of a normal person.

III

TECHNIQUES

Atmosphere

In an essay entitled "Tale-Writing," published in 1847, Poe discussed how the "skilful artist" should go about inventing incidents and establishing mood to produce a single effect. He stated: "If his [the short-story writer's] very first sentence tends not to the outbringing of this effect, then in his very first step has he committed a blunder."

With this in mind, reread the opening lines of "The Tell-Tale Heart," and consider the details which have an effect of creating atmosphere and inspiring terror.

1. Who appears to be telling the story? What is the advantage to using first person as the narrative viewpoint?

2. What is there about the way the words are put together which makes the reader feel that this is truly the raving of a madman? What is the reaction of most persons toward anyone who seems dangerously insane?

As the story unfolds, Poe uses imaginative language to deepen the atmosphere of terror. Discuss:

a. Poe's personification of death;

b. the figure of speech used to describe the sound of the old man's heart.

3. After the lengthy, detailed description of the care and cunning with which the old man's room was entered and the endless minutes while the old man strained to hear any sound, the reader's feeling of horror is deepened by the very brevity and lack of detail surrounding the actual murder and the disposal of the body.

Why do you think Poe chose to give so few details on these matters?

TECHNIQUES

The Art of Edgar Allan Poe

Edgar Allan Poe believed that in writing a short story an author should decide upon the emotional *effect* that he wished to produce in his reader (THE INNER CIRCLE, page 282) and then deliberately set out to put together a tale that would produce that effect. Thus if he wished his effect to be that of terror, as is true with "The Tell-Tale Heart," he took care to choose every detail of setting, characterization, and action so that it blended to give a feeling of terror. Such a general feeling or mood which pervades a story from beginning to end is called *atmosphere*.

We might think of the atmosphere in a literary selection as being much like the atmosphere in a restaurant in which the proprietor has installed fortune tellers, serenading musicians, special lighting, and costumed waiters. Each touch has been deliberately chosen to create certain attitudes and expectations in the patrons. Similarly, the writer builds atmosphere to achieve a particular emotional response from his readers.

Poe knew that people are fascinated by the horrible, the terrible, and the fantastic. Because he wished his stories to have popular appeal, he skillfully developed an atmosphere of terror or horror in many of them.

To create his popular stories, Poe took deliberate advantage of *narrative viewpoint, significant detail, imaginative language, diction* (word choice), and *irony*. These terms, already familiar to you, will be reemphasized in the discussions for this section. In the study notes following the poetry selections, *alliteration, onomatopoeia, rhyme scheme,* and *rhythm* will be discussed again.

In the days when all kings and courts
had their "fools" to amuse them,
Hop-Frog was a triplicate treasure.
In him, all in one person,
his master had a jester to laugh *with*
and a cripple and dwarf to laugh *at.*
When you read this story,
you may be reminded of the often quoted words,
"He who laughs last, laughs best."

Hop-Frog

I never knew any one so keenly alive to a joke as the king was. He seemed to live only for joking. To tell a good story of the joke kind and to tell it well, was the surest road to his favor. Thus it happened that his seven ministers were all noted for their accomplishments as jokers. They all took after the king, too, in being large, corpulent, oily men, as well as inimitable jokers. Whether people grow fat by joking, or whether there is something in fat itself which predisposes to a joke, I have never been quite able to determine; but certain it is that a lean joker is a *rara avis in terris.*[1]

About the refinement, or, as he called them, the "ghosts" of wit, the king troubled himself very little. He had an especial admiration for *breadth* in a jest, and would often put up with *length,* for the sake of it. Overniceties wearied him. He would have preferred Rabelais' "*Gargantua,*" to the "*Zadig*" of Voltaire:[2] and, upon the whole, practical jokes suited his taste far better than verbal ones.

At the date of my narrative, professing jesters had not altogether gone out of fashion at court. Several of the great continental "powers" still retained their "fools," who wore motley, with caps and bells,[3] and who were expected to be always ready with sharp witticisms, at a moment's notice, in consideration of the crumbs that fell from the royal table.

Our king, as a matter of course, retained his "fool." The fact is, he *required* something in the way of folly—if only to counterbalance the heavy wisdom of the seven wise men who were his ministers—not to mention himself.

His fool, or professional jester, was not *only* a fool, however. His value was trebled in the eyes of the king, by the fact of his being also a dwarf and a cripple. Dwarfs were as common at court, in those days, as fools; and many monarchs would have found it difficult to get through their days (days are rather longer at court than elsewhere) without both a jester to laugh *with,* and a dwarf to laugh *at.* But, as I have already observed, your jesters, in ninety-nine cases out of a hundred, are fat, round, and unwieldy—so that it was no small source of self-gratulation with our king that, in Hop-Frog (this was the fool's name), he possessed a triplicate treasure in one person.

I believe the name "Hop-Frog" was *not* that given to the dwarf by his sponsors at baptism, but it was conferred upon him, by general consent of the seven ministers, on account of his inability to walk as other men do. In fact, Hop-Frog could only get along by a sort of interjectional gait—something between a leap and a wriggle,—a movement that afforded illimitable amusement, and of consolation, to the king, for (notwithstanding the protuberance of his stomach and a constitutional swelling of the head) the king, by his whole court, was accounted a capital figure.

But although Hop-Frog, through the distortion of his legs, could move only with great pain and difficulty along a road or floor, the prodigious muscular power which nature seemed to have bestowed upon his arms, by way of compensation for deficiency in the

---

1. **rara avis in terris**\ˈrä·rä ä·wĭs in ˈtĕ·rĭs\ "a rare bird in the land."
2. **Rabelais**\ˈra·bə ˈlā\ (d. 1553) French satirist who wrote a coarse and extreme book in which the giant king **Gargantua**\'gar ˈgăn·chu·a\ figured. The character **Zadig**\ˈza·dĭg\ in the work of **Voltaire**\ˈvōl·târ\ (1694–1778) is very polished.
3. **motley with cap and bells,** the traditional costume of the jester.

lower limbs, enabled him to perform many feats of wonderful dexterity, where trees or ropes were in question, or anything else to climb. At such exercises he certainly much more resembled a squirrel, or a small monkey, than a frog.

I am not able to say, with precision, from what country Hop-Frog originally came. It was from some barbarous region, however, that no person ever heard of—a vast distance from the court of our king. Hop-Frog, and a young girl very little less dwarfish than himself (although of exquisite proportions, and a marvelous dancer), had been forcibly carried off from their respective homes in adjoining provinces, and sent as presents to the king, by one of his ever-victorious generals.

Under these circumstances, it is not to be wondered at that a close intimacy arose between the two little captives. Indeed, they soon became sworn friends. Hop-Frog, who, although he made a great deal of sport, was by no means popular, had it not in his power to render Trippetta many services; but *she*, on account of her grace and exquisite beauty (although a dwarf), was universally admired and petted; so she possessed much influence; and never failed to use it, whenever she could, for the benefit of Hop-Frog.

On some grand state occasion—I forget what —the king determined to have a masquerade; and whenever a masquerade, or anything of that kind, occurred at our court, then the talents both of Hop-Frog and Trippetta were sure to be called in play. Hop-Frog, in especial, was so inventive in the way of getting up pageants, suggesting novel characters and arranging costume, for masked balls, that nothing could be done, it seems, without his assistance.

The night appointed for the *fête* had arrived. A gorgeous hall had been fitted up, under Trippetta's eye, with every kind of device which could possibly give *éclat*[4] to a masquerade. The whole court was in a fever of expectation. As for costumes and characters, it might well be supposed that everybody had come to a decision on such points. Many had made up their minds (as to what *rôles* they should assume) a week, or even a month, in advance; and, in fact, there was not a particle of indecision anywhere—except in the case of the king and his seven ministers. Why *they* hesitated I never could tell, unless they did it by way of a joke. More probably, they found it difficult, on account of being so fat, to make up their minds. At all events, time flew; and, as a last resource, they sent for Trippetta and Hop-Frog.

When the two little friends obeyed the summons of the king, they found him sitting at his wine with the seven members of his cabinet council; but the monarch appeared to be in very ill humor. He knew that Hop-Frog was not fond of wine; for it excited the poor cripple almost to madness; and madness is no comfortable feeling. But the king loved his practical jokes, and took pleasure in forcing Hop-Frog to drink and (as the king called it) "to be merry."

"Come here, Hop-Frog," said he, as the jester and his friend entered the room; "swallow this bumper to the health of your absent friends [here Hop-Frog sighed] and then let us have the benefit of your invention. We want characters—*characters*, man—something novel—out of the way. We are wearied with this everlasting sameness. Come, drink! the wine will brighten your wits."

Hop-Frog endeavored, as usual, to get up a jest in reply to these advances from the king; but the effort was too much. It happened to be the poor dwarf's birthday, and the command to drink to his "absent friends" forced the tears to his eyes. Many large, bitter drops fell into the goblet as he took it, humbly, from the hand of the tyrant.

"Ah! ha! ha! ha!" roared the latter, as the dwarf reluctantly drained the beaker. "See what a glass of good wine can do! Why, your eyes are shining already!"

Poor fellow! his large eyes *gleamed*, rather than shone; for the effect of wine on his excitable brain was not more powerful than instan-

---

4. éclat\'ā ▴kla\ renown, splendor.

taneous. He placed the goblet nervously on the table, and looked round upon the company with a half-insane stare. They all seemed highly amused at the success of the king's "*joke.*"

"And now to business," said the prime minister, a *very* fat man.

"Yes," said the king. "Come, Hop-Frog, lend us your assistance. Characters, my fine fellow; we stand in need of characters—all of us—ha! ha! ha!" and as this was seriously meant for a joke, his laugh was chorused by the seven.

Hop-Frog also laughed, although feebly and somewhat vacantly.

"Come, come," said the king, impatiently, "have you nothing to suggest?"

"I am endeavoring to think of something *novel,*" replied the dwarf, abstractedly, for he was quite bewildered by the wine.

"Endeavoring!" cried the tyrant, fiercely; "what do you mean by *that?* Ah, I perceive. You are sulky, and want more wine. Here, drink this!" and he poured out another goblet full and offered it to the cripple, who merely gazed at it, gasping for breath.

"Drink, I say!" shouted the monster, "or by the fiends——"

The dwarf hesitated. The king grew purple with rage. The courtiers smirked. Trippetta, pale as a corpse, advanced to the monarch's seat, and, falling on her knees before him, implored him to spare her friend.

The tyrant regarded her, for some moments, in evident wonder at her audacity. He seemed quite at a loss what to do or say—how most becomingly to express his indignation. At last, without uttering a syllable, he pushed her violently from him, and threw the contents of the brimming goblet in her face.

The poor girl got up as best she could, and, not daring even to sigh, resumed her position at the foot of the table.

There was a dead silence for about half a minute, during which the falling of a leaf, or of a feather, might have been heard. It was interrupted by a low, but harsh and protracted *grating* sound which seemed to come at once from every corner of the room.

"What—what—*what* are you making that noise for?" demanded the king, turning furiously to the dwarf.

The latter seemed to have recovered, in great measure, from his intoxication, and looking fixedly but quietly into the tyrant's face, merely ejaculated:

"I—I? How could it have been me?"

"The sound appeared to come from without," observed one of the courtiers. "I fancy it was the parrot at the window, whetting his bill upon his cage-wires."

"True," replied the monarch, as if much relieved by the suggestion; "but, on the honor of a knight, I could have sworn that it was the gritting of this vagabond's teeth."

Hereupon the dwarf laughed (the king was too confirmed a joker to object to any one's laughing), and displayed a set of large, powerful, and very repulsive teeth. Moreover, he avowed his perfect willingness to swallow as much wine as desired. The monarch was pacified; and having drained another bumper with no very perceptible ill effect, Hop-Frog entered at once, and with spirit, into the plans for the masquerade.

"I cannot tell what was the association of idea," observed he, very tranquilly, and as if he had never tasted wine in his life, "but *just after* your majesty had struck the girl and thrown the wine in her face—*just after* your majesty had done this, and while the parrot was making that odd noise outside the window, there came into my mind a capital diversion—one of my own country frolics—often enacted among us, at our masquerades: but here it will be new altogether. Unfortunately, however, it requires a company of eight persons, and——"

"Here we *are!*" cried the king, laughing at his acute discovery of the coincidence; "eight to a fraction—I and my seven ministers. Come! what is the diversion?"

"We call it," replied the cripple, "the Eight Chained Ourang-Outangs, and it really is excellent sport if well enacted."

"*We* will enact it," remarked the king,

drawing himself up, and lowering his eyelids.

"The beauty of the game," continued Hop-Frog, "lies in the fright it occasions among the women."

"Capital!" roared in chorus the monarch and his ministry.

"I will equip you as ourang-outangs," proceeded the dwarf; "leave all that to me. The resemblance shall be so striking, that the company of masqueraders will take you for real beasts—and of course, they will be as much terrified as astonished."

"Oh, this is exquisite!" exclaimed the king. "Hop-Frog! I will make a man of you."

"The chains are for the purpose of increasing the confusion by their jangling. You are supposed to have escaped, *en masse*, from your keepers. Your majesty cannot conceive the *effect* produced, at a masquerade, by eight chained ourang-outangs, imagined to be real ones by most of the company; and rushing in with savage cries, among the crowd of delicately and gorgeously habited men and women. The *contrast* is inimitable."

"It *must* be," said the king: and the council arose hurriedly (as it was growing late), to put in execution the scheme of Hop-Frog.

His mode of equipping the party as ourang-outangs was very simple, but effective enough for his purposes. The animals in question had, at the epoch of my story, very rarely been seen in any part of the civilized world; and as the imitations made by the dwarf were sufficiently beast-like and more than sufficiently hideous, their truthfulness to nature was thus thought to be secured.

The king and his ministers were first encased in tight-fitting stockinet shirts and drawers. They were then saturated with tar. At this stage of the process, some one of the party suggested feathers; but the suggestion was at once overruled by the dwarf, who soon convinced the eight, by ocular demonstration, that the hair of such a brute as the ourang-outang was much more efficiently represented by *flax*. A thick coating of the latter was accordingly plastered upon the coating of tar. A long chain

was now procured. First, it was passed about the waist of the king, *and tied;* then about another of the party, and also tied; then about all successively, in the same manner. When this chaining arrangement was complete, and the party stood as far apart from each other as possible, they formed a circle; and to make all things appear natural, Hop-Frog passed the residue of the chain, in two diameters, at right angles, across the circle, after the fashion adopted, at the present day, by those who capture chimpanzees, or other large apes, in Borneo.[5]

The grand saloon in which the masquerade was to take place, was a circular room, very lofty, and receiving the light of the sun only through a single window at top. At night (the season for which the apartment was especially designed) it was illuminated principally by a large chandelier, depending by a chain from the centre of the sky-light, and lowered, or elevated, by means of a counterbalance as usual; but (in order not to look unsightly) this latter passed outside the cupola and over the roof.

The arrangements of the room had been left to Trippetta's superintendence; but, in some particulars, it seems, she had been guided by the calmer judgment of her friend the dwarf. At his suggestion it was that, on this occasion, the chandelier was removed. Its waxen drippings (which, in weather so warm, it was quite impossible to prevent) would have been seriously detrimental to the rich dresses of the guests, who, on account of the crowded state of the saloon, could not *all* be expected to keep from out its centre—that is to say, from under the chandelier. Additional sconces were set in various parts of the hall, out of the way; and a flambeau, emitting sweet odor, was placed in the right hand of each of the Caryatides[6] that stood against the wall—some fifty or sixty all together.

5. **Borneo**\ˈbȯr·nē·ō\ is a large tropical island in the East Indies.
6. **flambeau, emitting . . . Caryatides**\ˈflăm·bō\ a torch; \ˈkă·rĭ̄ə ˈtĭdz\ a pillar designed in the form of a draped female figure.

The eight ourang-outangs, taking Hop-Frog's advice, waited patiently until midnight (when the room was thoroughly filled with masqueraders) before making their appearance. No sooner had the clock ceased striking, however, than they rushed, or rather rolled in, all together—for the impediments of their chains caused most of the party to fall, and all to stumble as they entered.

The excitement among the masqueraders was prodigious, and filled the heart of the king with glee. As had been anticipated, there were not a few of the guests who supposed the ferocious-looking creatures to be beasts of *some* kind in reality, if not precisely ourang-outangs. Many of the women swooned with affright; and had not the king taken the precaution to exclude all weapons from the saloon, his party might soon have expiated their frolic in their blood. As it was, a general rush was made for the doors; but the king had ordered them to be locked immediately upon his entrance; and, at the dwarf's suggestion, the keys had been deposited with *him*.

While the tumult was at its height, and each masquerader attentive only to his own safety (for, in fact, there was much *real* danger from the pressure of the excited crowd), the chain by which the chandelier ordinarily hung, and which had been drawn up on its removal, might have been seen very gradually to descend, until its hooked extremity came within three feet of the floor.

Soon after this, the king and his seven friends having reeled about the hall in all directions, found themselves, at length, in its centre, and, of course, in immediate contact with the chain. While they were thus situated, the dwarf, who had followed noiselessly at their heels, inciting them to keep up the commotion, took hold of their own chain at the intersection of the two portions which crossed the circle diametrically and at right angles. Here, with the rapidity of thought, he inserted the hook from which the chandelier had been wont to depend; and, in an instant, by some unseen agency, the chandelier-chain was drawn so far upward as to take the hook out of reach, and, as an inevitable consequence, to drag the ourang-outangs together in close connection, and face to face.

The masqueraders, by this time, had recovered, in some measure, from their alarm; and, beginning to regard the whole matter as a well-contrived pleasantry, set up a loud shout of laughter at the predicament of the apes.

"Leave them to *me!*" now screamed Hop-Frog, his shrill voice making itself easily heard through all the din. "Leave them to *me*. I fancy *I* know them. If I can only get a good look at them, *I* can soon tell who they are."

Here, scrambling over the heads of the crowd, he managed to get to the wall; when, seizing a flambeau from one of the Caryatides, he returned, as he went, to the centre of the room—leaped, with the agility of a monkey, upon the king's head—and thence clambered a few feet up the chain—holding down the torch to examine the group of ourang-outangs, and still screaming, "*I* shall soon find out who they are!"

And now, while the whole assembly (the apes included) were convulsed with laughter, the jester suddenly uttered a shrill whistle; when the chain flew violently up for about thirty feet—dragging with it the dismayed and struggling ourang-outangs, and leaving them suspended in mid-air between the sky-light and the floor. Hop-Frog, clinging to the chain as it rose, still maintained his relative position in respect to the eight maskers, and still (as if nothing were the matter) continued to thrust his torch down toward them, as though endeavoring to discover who they were.

So thoroughly astonished were the whole company at this ascent, that a dead silence, of about a minute's duration, ensued. It was broken by just such a low, harsh, *grating* sound, as had before attracted the attention of the king and his councillors when the former threw the wine in the face of Trippetta. But, on the present occasion, there could be no question as to *whence* the sound issued. It came from the fang-like teeth of the dwarf, who ground

"The Vengence of Hop-Frog," by James Ensor, collection, The Museum of Modern Art, New York. Gift of Victor S. Riesenfeld.

them and gnashed them as he foamed at the mouth, and glared, with an expression of maniacal rage, into the upturned countenances of the king and his seven companions.

"Ah, ha!" said at length the infuriated jester. "Ah, ha! I begin to see who these people *are*, now!" Here, pretending to scrutinize the king more closely, he held the flambeau to the flaxen coat which enveloped him, and which instantly burst into a sheet of vivid flame. In less than half a minute the whole eight ourang-outangs were blazing fiercely, amid the shrieks of the multitude who gazed at them from below, horror-stricken, and without the power to render them the slightest assistance.

At length the flames, suddenly increasing in virulence, forced the jester to climb higher up the chain, to be out of their reach; and, as he made this movement, the crowd again sank, for a brief instant, into silence. The dwarf seized his opportunity, and once more spoke:

"I now see *distinctly*," he said, "what manner of people these maskers are. They are a great king and his seven privy-councillors,—a king who does not scruple to strike a defenseless girl, and his seven councillors who abet him in the outrage. As for myself, I am simply Hop-Frog, the jester—and *this is my last jest*."

Owing to the high combustibility of both the flax and the tar to which it adhered, the dwarf had scarcely made an end of his brief speech before the work of vengeance was complete. The eight corpses swung in their chains, a fetid, blackened, hideous, and indistinguishable mass. The cripple hurled his torch at them, clambered leisurely to the ceiling, and disappeared through the sky-light.

It is supposed that Trippetta, stationed on the roof of the saloon, had been the accomplice of her friend in his fiery revenge, and that, together, they effected their escape to their own country: for neither was seen again.

I

A FIERY REVENGE

As a poor unfortunate creature whose duty it was to amuse the court, Hop-Frog was denied the right to express the feelings and emotions of a man. He could stand the abuse heaped upon himself, but when the king mistreated Trippetta, the cunning mind of the "fool" conceived a daring scheme of revenge. Actually, of course, the slave was much more intelligent than the master.

1. How does the reader come to realize that the king is really a very stupid person? For what qualities had the king chosen his ministers?

2. How and why had the lighting been changed in the great room where the masquerade was held?

3. Although Hop-Frog was unable to walk as most men do, he had great strength in his arms and shoulders. Why does Poe mention this detail early in the story?

4. When does it become evident that the "low, harsh, *grating* sound" is made by the dwarf?

II

IMPLICATIONS

Consider and discuss these statements:

1. A loud laugh usually covers a vacant mind.

2. Revenge may be sweet, but each time a person gains revenge he loses some part of his own humanity.

3. Revenge is never justified.

III

TECHNIQUES

Foreshadowing Atmosphere

This story of Poe's is based upon the theme of revenge. In creating an atmosphere which carries the reader along to a final reaction of horror, Poe's first sentence is significant. He opens his story with the statement: "I never knew anyone so keenly alive to a joke as the king was."

What word here foreshadows the fact that all is no longer well with the king—that something has happened either to him or to his sense of humor?

Irony

Review the study notes for Part Four of the *Odyssey*. Ironic statements which reverse the known facts or pretend to ignorance have many variations.

1. A crude or biting kind of irony is called sarcasm. Poe carefully employs both irony and sarcasm to make the king seem contemptible.

Discuss the irony and sarcasm in the quotations below:

a. *Our* king . . . *required* something in the way of folly—if only to counterbalance the heavy wisdom of the seven wise men who were his ministers—not to mention himself.

b. "Oh, this is exquisite!" exclaimed the king. "Hop-Frog! I will make a man of you!"

c. "I now see *distinctly*," he said, "what manner of people these maskers are. They are a great king and his seven privy-councillors. . . ."

2. With the corpses of the king and his ministers hanging ". . . a fetid, blackened, hideous, and indistinguishable mass," Poe leaves the reader with a last horrible image in mind. However, it is grimly satisfying. Discuss why this should be so.

The dark mysteries of death intrigued Poe in his poetry as well as in his stories.
In an article for *Graham's Magazine*, April, 1846, he wrote, "The death, then, of a beautiful woman
is, unquestionably, the most poetical topic in the world—and equally is it beyond doubt
that the lips best suited for such a topic are those of a bereaved lover."
Two of Poe's most famous poems, "The Raven" and "Annabel Lee,"
are based upon this theme. "The Raven" was written about two years before his young wife's death,
during the time when she was so frail and sickly that Poe, who loved her very much,
probably suffered her death in his imagination many times.
A playing back and forth of sounds in the poem creates the atmosphere,
a feeling of dark shadows moving in from the corners. Poe felt that poetry was not only
truth or emotions, but also music. "The Raven" is a poem to be accompanied
by the even, pounding rhythm of a bass drum and the wailing notes of a bassoon.
At midnight, we look into the study of a man whose sweetheart has died.

◇ *The Raven*

Once upon a midnight dreary, while I pondered, weak and weary,
Over many a quaint and curious volume of forgotten lore—
While I nodded, nearly napping, suddenly there came a tapping,
As of someone gently rapping, rapping at my chamber door.
" 'Tis some visitor," I muttered, "tapping at my chamber door—   5
Only this and nothing more."

Ah, distinctly I remember it was in the bleak December;
And each separate dying ember wrought its ghost upon the floor.
Eagerly I wished the morrow;—vainly I had sought to borrow
From my books surcease of sorrow—sorrow for the lost Lenore—   10
For the rare and radiant maiden whom the angels name Lenore—
Nameless here for evermore.

And the silken, sad, uncertain rustling of each purple curtain
Thrilled me—filled me with fantastic terrors never felt before;
So that now, to still the beating of my heart, I stood repeating   15
" 'Tis some visitor entreating entrance at my chamber door,
Some late visitor entreating entrance at my chamber door:
This it is and nothing more."

Presently my soul grew stronger; hesitating then no longer,
"Sir," said I, "or Madam, truly your forgiveness I implore: 20
But the fact is I was napping, and so gently you came rapping,
And so faintly you came tapping, tapping at my chamber door,
That I scarce was sure I heard you"—here I opened wide the door;—
Darkness there and nothing more.

Deep into that darkness peering, long I stood there wondering, fearing,   25
Doubting, dreaming dreams no mortals ever dared to dream before:
But the silence was unbroken, and the stillness gave no token,
And the only word there spoken was the whispered word, "Lenore?"
This I whispered, and an echo murmured back the word, "Lenore!"
    Merely this and nothing more.   30

Back into the chamber turning, all my soul within me burning,
Soon again I heard a tapping somewhat louder than before.
"Surely," said I, "surely that is something at my window lattice;
Let me see, then, what thereat is, and this mystery explore;
Let my heart be still a moment and this mystery explore: 35
    'Tis the wind and nothing more!"

Open here I flung the shutter, when, with many a flirt and flutter,
In there stepped a stately Raven of the saintly days of yore;
Not the least obeisance made he; not a minute stopped or stayed he;
But with mien of lord or lady, perched above my chamber door,   40
Perched upon a bust of Pallas[1] just above my chamber door:
    Perched, and sat, and nothing more.

Then this ebon bird beguiling my sad fancy into smiling
By the grave and stern decorum of the countenance it wore,
"Though thy crest be shorn and shaven, thou," I said, "art sure no craven,   45
Ghastly grim and ancient Raven wandering from the Nightly shore—
Tell me what thy lordly name is on the Night's Plutonian[2] shore!"
    Quoth the Raven, "Nevermore."

Much I marveled this ungainly fowl to hear discourse so plainly,
Though its answer little meaning—little relevancy bore;   50
For we cannot help agreeing that no living human being
Ever yet was blessed with seeing bird above his chamber door,
Bird or beast upon the sculptured bust above his chamber door,
    With such name as "Nevermore."

But the Raven, sitting lonely on the placid bust, spoke only   55
That one word, as if his soul in that one word he did outpour.
Nothing further then he uttered, not a feather then he fluttered,
Till I scarcely more than muttered,—"Other friends have flown before;
On the morrow *he* will leave me, as my Hopes have flown before."
    Then the bird said, "Nevermore."   60

---

1. **Pallas**\ˈpă·ləs\ or Pallas Athene was goddess of the arts and industry in classical Greek mythology.
2. **Plutonian**\ˈplü ˈtō·nē·ən\ pertaining to the realm of Pluto, or Hades, the god of the underworld, the gloomy abode of the ghosts of the dead.

Startled at the stillness broken by reply so aptly spoken,
"Doubtless," said I, "what it utters is its only stock and store,
Caught from some unhappy master whom unmerciful Disaster
Followed fast and followed faster till his songs one burden bore—
Till the dirges of his Hope that melancholy burden bore
    Of 'Never—nevermore.' "

                                                  65

But the Raven still beguiling all my fancy into smiling,
Straight I wheeled a cushioned seat in front of bird and bust and door;
Then, upon the velvet sinking, I betook myself to linking
Fancy unto fancy, thinking what this ominous bird of yore,
What this grim, ungainly, ghastly, gaunt, and ominous bird of yore
    Meant in croaking, "Nevermore."

                                                  70

This I sat engaged in guessing, but no syllable expressing
To the fowl whose fiery eyes now burned into my bosom's core;
This and more I sat divining, with my head at ease reclining
On the cushion's velvet lining that the lamplight gloated o'er,
But whose velvet violet lining with the lamplight gloating o'er
    She shall press, ah, nevermore!

                                                  75

Then, methought, the air grew denser, perfumed from an unseen censer
Swung by Seraphim[3] whose footfalls tinkled on the tufted floor.
"Wretch," I cried, "thy God hath lent thee—by these angels he hath sent thee
Respite—respite and nepenthe from thy memories of Lenore,
Quaff, oh, quaff this kind nepenthe, and forget this lost Lenore!"
    Quoth the Raven, "Nevermore."

                                                  80

"Prophet!" said I, "thing of evil! prophet still, if bird or devil!
Whether Tempter sent, or whether tempest tossed thee here ashore,
Desolate yet all undaunted, on this desert land enchanted—
On this home by Horror haunted—tell me truly, I implore:
Is there—*is* there balm in Gilead?[4]—tell me—tell me, I implore!"
    Quoth the Raven, "Nevermore."

                                                  85

"Prophet!" said I, "thing of evil—prophet still, if bird or devil!
By that Heaven that bends above us, by that God we both adore,
Tell this soul with sorrow laden if, within the distant Aidenn,[5]
It shall clasp a sainted maiden whom the angels name Lenore—
Clasp a rare and radiant maiden whom the angels name Lenore!"
    Quoth the Raven, "Nevermore."

                                                  90

                                                  95

---

3. **Seraphim**\\ˆsĕ•rə ˈfĭm\\ plural of seraph, the highest ranking angels.
4. **"Is there balm in Gilead?"**—is there cure or healing? Balm is a soothing oil, an ancient product of the Biblical land Gilead. Jeremiah 8:22, in the Old Testament.
5. **Aidenn**\\ˆā•dĭn\\ paradise; a variant spelling of the Arabic word for Eden.

"Be that word our sign of parting, bird or fiend!" I shrieked, upstarting:
"Get thee back into the tempest and the Night's Plutonian shore!
Leave no black plume as a token of that lie thy soul hath spoken!
Leave my loneliness unbroken!—quit the bust above my door!   100
Take thy beak from out my heart, and take thy form from off my door!"
    Quoth the Raven, "Nevermore."

And the Raven, never flitting, still is sitting *still* is sitting
On the pallid bust of Pallas just above my chamber door;
And his eyes have all the seeming of a demon's that is dreaming,   105
And the lamplight o'er him streaming throws his shadow on the floor;
And my soul from out that shadow that lies floating on the floor
    Shall be lifted—nevermore!

I

A MIDNIGHT VISITOR

It is a dark and gloomy midnight. A man who has lost his beloved Lenore is trying to forget her by burying himself in his books. Suddenly he hears a mysterious tapping at the door. Did you follow the story from there? What happens:

1. When he opens the door?
2. When he returns to his books?
3. When he opens the window and the lattice?
4. When the Raven comes in?
5. When he asks the Raven its name?
6. When he asks the Raven to leave?

II

IMPLICATIONS

Consider these statements. Explain why you agree or disagree.

1. The man discovers that the bird has been trained to say one word. So when he asks questions, he really knows what the answer will be. Thus he is asking things that really increase his unhappiness.

2. The compulsive desire to suffer is a common one, and many people find pleasure in thus punishing themselves.

3. Grief is an emotion that never lessens.

III

TECHNIQUES

Imaginative Language

Poe apparently felt that the word *nevermore* had as melancholy a sound as any in the English language. Thus, he uses the word as the sound of gloom and despair. What other words in the poem seem to have been chosen to give a quality of gloom?

1. This poem is rich in the use of *alliteration*, a term you have used before. Find examples of alliteration and explain what effect they have in the poem.

2. This poem is one the reader remembers, because of the sound of words in it, and because of its original rhyme scheme. Within its intricate and varied pattern the poet uses both parallelism and refrain to produce memorable effects.

a. When two or more poetic lines or portions of lines near one another have a similar structure and express a similar meaning, they are considered *parallel*. Find examples of such parallelism in "The Raven."

b. What words repeated in the refrain are often quoted because once a person has read them he finds them hard to forget?

3. Read through the poem again, noting the imagery chosen for light, color, and texture. List the descriptive words for each group in separate columns. Discuss what each group contributes to the atmosphere of the poem.

Like the singing of violins
in a minor key, the rhythms of "Annabel Lee" pulse
through the reader's heart. Though the poem
may have been inspired by the death
of his wife, Poe did not give it the dark,
somber quality of "The Raven."
But, like "The Raven," this poem is built
on Poe's contention
that the most suitable subject for poetry
is the grief of a man
over the death of a beautiful woman.

Annabel Lee

It was many and many a year ago,
  In a kingdom by the sea,
That a maiden there lived whom you may know
  By the name of Annabel Lee;
And this maiden she lived with no other thought   5
  Than to love and be loved by me.

I was a child and *She* was a child,
  In the kingdom by the sea,
But we loved with a love that was more than love,
  I and my Annabel Lee;   10
With a love that the wingéd seraphs of heaven
  Coveted her and me.

And this was the reason that, long ago,
  In this kingdom by the sea,
A wind blew out of a cloud, chilling   15
  My beautiful Annabel Lee;
So that her highborn kinsmen came
  And bore her away from me,
To shut her up in a sepulcher
  In this kingdom by the sea.   20

The angels, not half so happy in heaven,
  Went envying her and me;
Yes! That was the reason (as all men know,
  In this kingdom by the sea)
That the wind came out of the cloud by night,   25
  Chilling and killing my Annabel Lee.

But our love was stronger by far than the love
    Of those who were older than we,
    Of many far wiser than we;
And neither the angels in heaven above,   30
    Nor the demons down under the sea,
Can ever dissever my soul from the soul
    Of the beautiful Annabel Lee:

For the moon never beams without bringing me dreams
    Of the beautiful Annabel Lee;   35
And the stars never rise, but I feel the bright eyes
    Of the beautiful Annabel Lee;
And so, all the night-tide, I lie down by the side
Of my darling—my darling—my life and my bride,
    In the sepulcher there by the sea,   40
    In her tomb by the sounding sea.

THEME AND TECHNIQUES

Mood and Pattern

"Annabel Lee" is one of the favorite poems of the English language. Its lines are so melodic that people have memorized them almost without trying. The shadowy outline of a story teases the imagination of the reader, urging him to try filling in the details. But the poem is interesting mainly because words are used to create a mood almost the way sound is used in music. The rhythm imitates the melancholy sound of quiet breakers rolling gently upon the seashore, an effect achieved by the pattern of repetition and variation.

What do you discover about the following:

1. The number of lines in the stanzas?

2. The regularity of the rhyme scheme?

3. The repetition of rhyming words from one stanza to the next?

4. The variation in the length of lines?

5. The repetition of the rhythm of lines?

A town is enveloped
in the madness that is carnival.
Raucous laughter, flickering light of torches,
gayly costumed and masked figures
are contrasted with the bitter hate
and horrible thoughts in the mind of one man.
Slowly, slowly, the plot unravels.
Prepare for a chill as penetrating
as that of the cold, dank earth
in the catacombs.

The Cask of Amontillado

The thousand injuries of Fortunato I had borne as best I could, but when he ventured upon insult, I vowed revenge. You, who so well know the nature of my soul, will not suppose, however, that I gave utterance to a threat. *At length* I would be avenged; this was a point definitely settled—but the very definiteness with which it was resolved precluded the idea of risk. I must not only punish, but punish with impunity. A wrong is unredressed when retribution overtakes its redresser. It is equally unredressed when the avenger fails to make himself felt as such to him who has done the wrong.

It must be understood that neither by word nor deed had I given Fortunato cause to doubt my good will. I continued, as was my wont, to smile in his face, and he did not perceive that my smile *now* was at the thought of his immolation.

He had a weak point—this Fortunato—although in other regards he was a man to be respected and even feared. He prided himself on his connoisseurship in wine. Few Italians have the true virtuoso spirit. For the most part their enthusiasm is adopted to suit the time and opportunity, to practice imposture upon the British and Austrian millionaires. In painting and gemmary, Fortunato, like his countrymen, was a quack, but in the matter of old wines he was sincere. In this respect I did not differ from him materially. I was skillful in the Italian vintages myself and bought largely whenever I could.

It was about dusk, one evening during the supreme madness of the carnival season, that I encountered my friend. He accosted me with excessive warmth, for he had been drinking much. The man wore motley. He had on a tight-fitting parti-striped dress, and his head was surmounted by the conical cap and bells. I was so pleased to see him that I thought I should never have done wringing his hand.

I said to him, "My dear Fortunato, you are luckily met. How remarkably well you are looking today! But I have received a pipe [large barrel] of what passes for Amontillado,[1] and I have my doubts."

"How?" said he. "Amontillado? A pipe? Impossible! And in the middle of the carnival!"

"I have my doubts," I replied; "and I was silly enough to pay the full Amontillado price without consulting you in the matter. You were not to be found, and I was fearful of losing a bargain."

"Amontillado!"

"I have my doubts."

"Amontillado!"

"And I must satisfy them."

"Amontillado!"

"As you are engaged, I am on my way to Luchesi. If anyone has a critical turn,[2] it is he. He will tell me—"

"Luchesi cannot tell Amontillado from Sherry."

"And yet some fools will have it that his taste is a match for your own."

"Come, let us go."

"Whither?"

---

1. **Amontillado**\ə ˈmŏn·tĭ ˈla·dō\ a fine Spanish sherry wine.
2. **"If anyone has a critical turn"**—if anyone is able to criticize.

"To your vaults."

"My friend, no; I will not impose upon your good nature. I perceive you have an engagement. Luchesi—"

"I have no engagement—come."

"My friend, no. It is not the engagement, but the severe cold with which I perceive you are afflicted. The vaults are insufferably damp. They are incrusted with niter."

"Let us go nevertheless. The cold is merely nothing. Amontillado! You have been imposed upon. And as for Luchesi, he cannot distinguish Sherry from Amontillado."

Thus speaking, Fortunato possessed himself of my arm. Puting on a mask of black silk, and drawing a *roquelaure*[3] closely about my person, I suffered him to hurry me to my palazzo.[4]

There were no attendants at home; they had absconded to make merry in honor of the time. I had told them that I should not return until the morning, and had given them explicit orders not to stir from the house. These orders were sufficient, I well knew, to insure their immediate disappearance, one and all, as soon as my back was turned.

I took from their sconces [holders] two flambeaux, and giving one to Fortunato, bowed him through several suites of rooms to the archway that led into the vaults. I passed down a long and winding staircase, requesting him to be cautious as he followed. We came at length to the foot of the descent and stood together on the damp ground of the catacombs of the Montresors.

The gait of my friend was unsteady, and the bells upon his cap jingled as he strode.

"The pipe," said he.

"It is farther on," said I; "but observe the white webwork which gleams from these cavern walls."

He turned toward me, and looked into my eyes with two filmy orbs that distilled the rheum[5] of intoxication.

"Niter?"[6] he asked at length.

"Niter," I replied. "How long have you had that cough?"

"Ugh! ugh! uhg!—ugh! ugh! ugh!—ugh! ugh! ugh!—ugh! ugh! ugh!—ugh! ugh! ugh!"

My poor friend found it impossible to reply for many minutes.

"It is nothing," he said at last.

"Come," I said, with decision, "we will go back; your health is precious. You are rich, respected, admired, beloved; you are happy, as once I was. You are a man to be missed. For me it is no matter. We will go back; you will be ill, and I cannot be responsible. Besides, there is Luchesi—"

"Enough," he said; "the cough is a mere nothing; it will not kill me. I shall not die of a cough."

"True—true," I replied; "and, indeed, I had no intention of alarming you unnecessarily—but you should use all proper caution. A draught of this Médoc[7] will defend us from the damps."

Here I knocked off the neck of a bottle which I drew from a long row of its fellows that lay upon the mold.

"Drink," I said, presenting him the wine.

He raised it to his lips with a leer. He paused and nodded to me familiarly, while his bells jingled.

"I drink," he said, "to the buried that repose around us."

"And I to your long life."

He again took my arm, and we proceeded.

"These vaults," he said, "are extensive."

"The Montresors," I replied, "were a great and numerous family."

"I forget your arms."

"A huge human foot *d'or*,[8] in a field azure; the foot crushes a serpent rampant whose fangs are embedded in the heel."

"And the motto?"

---

3. **roquelaure**\'rō·kə ▴lar\ cloak.
4. **palazzo**\pə ▴la·zō\ a palace.
5. **rheum**\rūm\ tears.
6. **niter**\▴nai·tər\ the white webbing was a potassium or sodium salt—saltpeter—commonly collected on the walls of wet, dark places.
7. **Médoc**\mā·dŏk\ a French wine.
8. **d'or**\dōr\ golden, of gold. This describes the coat of arms of Montresor's family.

"Nemo me impune lacessit."[9]

"Good!" he said.

The wine sparkled in his eyes and the bells jingled. My own fancy grew warm with the Médoc. We had passed through walls of piled bones, with casks and puncheons intermingling, into the inmost recesses of the catacombs. I paused again, and this time I made bold to seize Fortunato by an arm above the elbow.

"The niter!" I said. "See, it increases. It hangs like moss upon the vaults. We are below the river's bed. The drops of moisture trickle among the bones. Come, we will go back ere it is too late. Your cough—"

"It is nothing," he said; "let us go on. But first, another draft of the Médoc."

I broke and reached him a flagon of De Grâve.[10] He emptied it at a breath. His eyes flashed with a fierce light. He laughed, and threw the bottle upward with a gesticulation I did not understand.

I looked at him in surprise. He repeated the movement—a grotesque one.

"You do not comprehend?" he said.

"Not I," I replied.

"Then you are not of the brotherhood."

"How?"

"You are not of the masons."

"Yes, yes," I said. "Yes, yes."

"You? Impossible! A mason?"

"A mason," I replied.

"A sign," he said.

"It is this," I answered, producing a trowel from beneath the folds of my *roquelaure.*

"You jest," he exclaimed, recoiling a few paces. "But let us proceed to the Amontillado."

"Be it so," I said, replacing the tool beneath the cloak and again offering him my arm. He leaned upon it heavily. We continued our route in search of the Amontillado. We passed through a range of low arches, descended, passed on, and, descending again, arrived at a deep crypt, in which the foulness of the air caused our flambeaux rather to glow than flame.

At the most remote end of the crypt there appeared another, less spacious. Its walls had been lined with human remains, piled to the vault overhead, in the fashion of the great catacombs of Paris. Three sides of this interior crypt were still ornamented in this manner. From the fourth the bones had been thrown down, and lay promiscuously upon the earth, forming at one point a mound of some size. Within the wall thus exposed by the displacing of the bones we perceived a still interior crypt or recess, in depth about four feet, in width three, in height six or seven. It seemed to have been constructed for no especial use within itself, but formed merely the interval between two of the colossal supports of the roof of the catacombs, and was backed by one of their circumscribing walls of solid granite.

It was in vain that Fortunato, uplifting his dull torch, endeavored to pry into the depth of the recess. Its termination the feeble light did not enable us to see.

"Proceed," I said; "herein is the Amontillado. As for Luchesi—"

"He is an ignoramus," interrupted my friend, as he stepped unsteadily forward, while I followed immediately at his heels. In an instant he had reached the extremity of the niche, and finding his progress arrested by the rock, stood stupidly bewildered. A moment more, and I had fettered him to the granite. In its surface were two iron staples, distant from each other about two feet, horizontally. From one of these depended a short chain, from the other a padlock. Throwing the links about his waist, it was but the work of a few seconds to secure it. He was too much astounded to resist. Withdrawing the key, I stepped back from the recess.

"Pass your hand," I said, "over the wall; you cannot help feeling the niter. Indeed it is *very* damp. Once more let me *implore* you to return. No? Then I must positively leave you. But I must first render you all the little attentions in my power."

---

9. **Nemo me impune lacessit**\\'nĕ·mō mā ĭm ▲pū·nĕ la·kĕ·sĕt\\ "No one attacks me without being punished for it."

10. **De Grâve**\\də grav\\wine.

"The Amontillado!" ejaculated my friend, not yet recovered from his astonishment.

"True," I replied. "The Amontillado."

As I said these words I busied myself among the pile of bones of which I have before spoken. Throwing them aside, I soon uncovered a quantity of building stone and mortar. With these materials and with the aid of my trowel, I began vigorously to wall up the entrance of the niche.

I had scarcely laid the first tier of the masonry when I discovered that the intoxication of Fortunato had in a great measure worn off. The earliest indication I had of this was a low moaning cry from the depth of the recess. It was *not* the cry of a drunken man. There was then a long and obstinate silence. I laid the second tier, and the third, and the fourth; and then I heard the furious vibrations of the chain. The noise lasted for several minutes, during which, that I might hearken to it with the more satisfaction, I ceased my labors and sat down upon the bones. When at last the clanking subsided, I resumed the trowel, and finished without interruption the fifth, the sixth, and the seventh tier. The wall was now nearly upon a level with my breast. I again paused, and holding the flambeaux over the masonwork, threw a few feeble rays upon the figure within.

A succession of loud and shrill screams, bursting suddenly from the throat of the chained form, seemed to thrust me violently back. For a brief moment I hesitated, I trembled. Unsheathing my rapier, I began to grope with it about the recess; but the thought of an instant reassured me. I placed my hand upon the solid fabric of the catacombs, and felt satisfied. I re-approached the wall; I replied to the yells of him who clamored. I re-echoed—I aided—I surpassed them in volume and in strength. I did this, and the clamorer grew still.

It was now midnight, and my task was drawing to a close. I had completed the eighth, the ninth, and the tenth tier. I had finished a portion of the last and the eleventh; there remained but a single stone to be fitted and plastered in.

I struggled with its weight; I placed it partially in its destined position. But now there came from out the niche a low laugh that erected the hairs upon my head. It was succeeded by a sad voice, which I had difficulty in recognizing as that of the noble Fortunato. The voice said:

"Ha! ha! ha!—he! he! he!—a very good joke indeed—an excellent jest. We will have many a rich laugh about it at the palazzo—he! he! he!—over our wine—he! he! he!"

"The Amontillado!" I said.

"He! he! he!—he! he! he!—yes, the Amontillado. But is it not getting late? Will not they be awaiting us at the palazzo—the Lady Fortunato and the rest? Let us be gone."

"Yes," I said, "let us be gone."

"For the love of God, Montresor!"

"Yes," I said, "for the love of God!"

But to these words I hearkened in vain for a reply. I grew impatient. I called aloud,—

"Fortunato!"

No answer. I called again,—

"Fortunato!"

No answer still. I thrust a torch through the remaining aperture and let it fall within. There came forth in return only the jingling of the bells. My heart grew sick—on account of the dampness of the catacombs. I hastened to make an end of my labor. I forced the last stone into its position; I plastered it up. Against the new masonry I re-erected the old rampart of bones. For the half of a century no mortal has disturbed them. *In pace requiescat.*[11]

I

AN UNSUSPECTING VICTIM

The story leads the reader along just as Fortunato is led along. Neither the reader nor Fortunato is aware of the horrible plan being unwound. The final horror is so shocking that the reader's mind rejects the truth just as Fortunato tries to believe it is all a joke.

---

11. **In pace requiescat**\ĭn 'pa·kə 'rē·kwē·ᵃĕs·kat\ "May he rest in peace."

Consider the following:

1. Why is carnival season a good time for Montresor to carry out his diabolical plot?

2. How does Montresor work on Fortunato's vanity to lure him into the trap?

3. What details are given of the catacombs which make them seem particularly depressing?

4. How does Montresor keep Fortunato from any suspicion of his intention?

II

IMPLICATIONS

The two statements below are quotations from the story. Discuss the meaning in each.

1. "A wrong is unredressed when retribution overtakes its redresser."

2. "It is equally unredressed when the avenger fails to make himself felt as such to him who has done the wrong."

III

TECHNIQUES

Atmosphere

Poe manages a fiendish irony throughout the story making it grimly humorous in places and adding to the final impact of horror. Discuss why each of the following is ironic:

a. The victim's name, Fortunato

b. Montresor's apparent concern for Fortunato's health

c. Montresor's toast to Fortunato's long life

d. Fortunato's wearing a cap with bells that tinkle as he walks

e. Montresor's urging the chained Fortunato to return to the street with him

f. Montresor's saying in the final paragraph: "My heart grew sick—on account of the dampness of the catacombs"

g. *In pace requiescat*

IV

WORDS

Edgar Allan Poe was a nineteenth-century literary figure, and, naturally, he wrote in the literary language of his time. His choice of words may seem bookish and rather formal to you, especially when compared to other selections in this book. Find a number of illustrations to back up your own ideas on this subject.

A. Poe selections offer a happy hunting ground for context clue situations. Notice near the beginning of "The Tell-Tale Heart," this sentence: "It is impossible to say how first the idea entered my brain; but once conceived, it haunted me day and night." We get a fairly good notion of the meaning of *conceive* as it is used here. Context clues also give us reasonable meanings for the following: *dissimulation, profound, sagacity, supposition, crevice, stimulate, tattoo, pulsation, dismember, scantlings, wary, suavity, premises, vehemently, dissemble.* Check these words yourself. Verify your guesses by using your dictionary. When we read (in "The Raven,") "vainly I had sought to borrow/ From my books surcease of sorrow . . ." we may guess that surcease means something like "cessation, stopping." Notice how the poem tells you the meanings of *entreating, mien, decorum, ominous, censer, nepenthe.* The wording of "Annabel Lee" is very informative in regard to *seraph, sepulcher,* and *dissever.* Context clues in "The Cask of Amontillado" lead you to good guesses *ghouls* should be clear enough to you after you read "The Bells." Notice how context clues in "The Cask of Amontillado" lead you to good guesses about the meanings of *preclude, retribution, impunity, virtuoso, imposture, vintage, motley, abscond, explicit, catacombs, crypt, ejaculate, rapier, aperture.* Make up your own list of words in "Hop-Frog" in which context clues are most informative.

B. Analyze the following for prefixes and suffixes, indicating what light is cast by your analysis on spelling or meaning: *healthily, foresight, courageously, unperceived, definitiveness, obeisance, clamorous, redresser, immolation, connoisseurship, imposture, insufferably, intermingling, circumscribing, inimitable, illimitable, dexterity, perceptible, maniacal.* What does the *sur-* prefix mean in *surcease?* Notice that in "The Raven" one finds the form *seraphim,* but in "Annabel Lee" the form *seraphs.* The *-im* of *seraphim* is an old plural form coming from the Hebrew language. What is peculiar about the effect of the prefix *dis-* in *dissever?*

English has relatively few verb suffixes. The limited list includes *-en,* as in *darken,* from Old English, and *-ate,* as in *separate, -fy,* as in *glorify,* and *-ize,* as in *sterilize,* from foreign languages. What words do you find in the Poe selections that illustrate use of these suffixes? To what words or word parts can you add these suffixes naturally in English?

Once Upon a Midnight

For more than a century, Poe has been one of the most popular American writers. His stories and poems appeal directly to the reader's emotions and imagination. He has seldom been equaled in his sense of the horrible, the haunting, and the mysterious.

What are the two major topics or subjects with which authors who write of the strange and eerie seem preoccupied? Which of these two do you think held the greater fascination for Poe? (Limit your discussion to Poe's stories and poems that appear in this text.)

IMPLICATIONS

Consider and discuss the following statements.

1. A creative writer usually has an uhappy, searching nature.

2. Man is a fearful, superstitious creature.

3. One reason man is so fascinated by the strange, the eerie, and the unreal is that deep down he believes such things could happen.

TECHNIQUES

It was through his control of *atmosphere* that Poe himself usually made the strong single effect in his stories.

Consider the atmospheres of the three Poe stories in ONCE UPON A MIDNIGHT. What do they have in common? In which way is the atmosphere of each story distinct from that of the other stories?

BIOGRAPHICAL NOTES

W. F. Harvey

William Fryer Harvey (1885–1937) was a British physician whose hobby was writing horror stories. He also wrote essays on the Quakers. During World War I he served in the British Navy and was decorated for bravery when he risked his life to save a fellow seaman trapped in the flooded engine room of a destroyer. Twenty of his best tales have been collected in the book, *The Beast With Five Fingers.*

Will F. Jenkins

Will F. Jenkins (1896–   ) was born in Norfolk, Virginia. One of the most widely published writers of science fiction, mystery, and adventure stories, he published his first work while he was still in high school. Science fiction buffs know his work as it appears under his pen name, Murray Leinster. Many national magazines have presented his stories, and several movies and television dramas have been made from his writings. Among his later novels are *Operation Terror, The Time Tunnel,* and *The Other Side of Nowhere.*

Leo Rosten

Leo Rosten (1908–   ) was born in Poland and brought to the United States when he was two years old. Growing up in a poor neighborhood in Chicago, he worked at odd jobs to help defray school expenses, and earned his Ph.D. from the University of Chicago in 1937. His series of humorous stories about Hyman Kaplan, a student in a night school for adults, was published in book form in 1937 with the title *The Education of Hyman Kaplan,* under the pseudonym Leonard Q. Ross. Many of his suspense stories have been made into movies, and his books and magazine articles are widely read.

Robert W. Service

Robert W. Service (1876–1958), Canadian poet and novelist, was born in Preston, England. After attending Glasgow University and training for a career in banking, Service emigrated to Canada in 1897. His travels for the Canadian Bank of Commerce to the Yukon and Vancouver served as background for many of his verses.

Howard Fast

Howard Fast (1914–   ) was born in New York City. A writer and artist, he published his first novel at seventeen. Best known for his stories, novels, and plays that vividly recreate America's past and deal with problems of human freedom, Mr. Fast is recognized as one of the ablest interpreters of the American way of life. He was given the Screen Writer's Annual Award in 1960 and the annual book award of the Secondary Education Board in 1962. His book *April Morning* is an exciting story of the American Revolution.

*In Roualt's depiction of these two judges he leaves the viewer
wondering what kind of decisions these men might make.*

*"The Judges" from the collection
of the Portland Art Museum,
Portland, Oregon.*

MOMENTS OF DECISION

The Road Not Taken

Two roads diverged in a yellow wood,
And sorry I could not travel both
And be one traveler, long I stood
And looked down one as far as I could
To where it bent in the undergrowth;

Then took the other, as just as fair,
And having perhaps the better claim,
Because it was grassy and wanted wear;
Though as for that the passing there
Had worn them really about the same,

And both that morning equally lay
In leaves no step had trodden black.
Oh, I kept the first for another day!
Yet knowing how way leads on to way,
I doubted if I should ever come back.

I shall be telling this with a sigh
Somewhere ages and ages hence:
Two roads diverged in a wood, and I—
I took the one less traveled by,
And that has made all the difference.

ROBERT FROST

From *The Poetry of Robert Frost* edited by Edward
Connery Lathem. Copyright 1916, 1923, © 1969 by
Holt, Rinehart and Winston, Inc. Copyright 1936,
1944, 1951 by Robert Frost. Copyright © 1964 by
Lesley Frost Ballantine. Reprinted by permission of
Holt, Rinehart and Winston, Inc.

There are many decisions people feel ambivalent about—
everyday choices such as: Should I have my hair cut or let it
grow? Should I order a hamburger or some pizza? Should I
watch television or get my homework done? But sometimes people are ambivalent when they have important decisions to make,
and they have very little to guide them. This is the kind of decision Robert Frost was thinking about when he wrote that sometimes it may be "the road not taken" that makes an important
difference in the way a person's life turns out.

How are decisions made? Is there any sort of magic formula
or pattern that could help a person who is trying to make a difficult choice?

In the selections that follow, you will meet a great variety of
people faced with difficult decisions. John Bagley in the short
story, "The Decision," believes that a scientific appraisal of a situation is necessary before a decision can be made. In the play
The Devil and Daniel Webster, Jabez Stone feels driven to make
a choice that he knows will bring him to disaster. And in the
short novel, *Winter Thunder,* a young teacher, Lecia Terry, is
forced to make a series of desperate decisions, any and all of
which could mean the difference between life and death for her
students and herself.

As a reflection of life, literature naturally contains much that
shows people wavering between courses of action, feeling the
anguish of being unable to decide. In sharing their moments of
decision, we may discover some of the general patterns of
decision-making.

First the hypothesis,
then examination of the facts.
That was the way John Bagley had been trained
to come to a decision. Then, suddenly,
he was faced with a decision that meant
"plunging ahead in darkness."

The Decision

TOM BURNAM

That looks like a nice spot," said Myra Bagley hopefully. She was tired, and the boy Kit was irritable; the day's ride had been long and dusty.

"Well, I don't know," said her husband, slowing the car as they studied the grassy meadow ahead. "Maybe we're not supposed to camp there."

"For Heaven's sake, we're in *Montana*," said Myra. "They told us we could camp anywhere that wasn't posted. You know that." She had not meant to sound quite so sharp.

"We'll flip a nickel," said John Bagley, but then Kit wailed, "Oh, Dad, make up your mind."

John set his lips and stepped on the gas; and though it was too late now, Myra wanted to say, "Kit, *keep quiet!*"

Then a miracle happened. A mile farther, beyond a curve, was a Forest Service marker, "Camp Ground Ahead," and then a triangular sign with an arrow pointing down a narrow winding road which led from the highway to the bank of the stream below.

John slowed the car.

"Will this do?" he asked. Myra bit her lip and didn't answer. The trouble with being married to a scientist, she had long ago decided, was

that everything had to be so scientific. First the Hypothesis: This camp ground will serve us well. Then the Examination of the Facts: Is there water? Do poisonous snakes abound? Are there adequate toilet facilities? Will the slope provide surface drainage in case of rain?

Sometimes she protested while they were trying to buy a new car (this one has a good transmission, he would say, but that one has better brakes) or new furniture (will foam rubber stand up?)—or even a new can-opener for the kitchen (the consumer people say it drops metal shavings into the soup). Then John would withdraw in offended silence after pointing out that he had been *trained* to think on all sides of a question before making a decision.

But for once she had no cause for alarm. "We'll camp here," John said, and both Myra and Kit sighed in relief.

Somewhat downstream from the Bagley's camp ground, though on the other side of the large creek, a huge rock had for uncounted years squatted on the brow of the narrow defile at the bottom of the canyon where now the railroad ran. The train crews sometimes used it as a kind of informal check-point: "There's the rock. Two minutes behind today."

Near the point where the rock hung over the tracks was a small fault.[1] Over the years, this fault had resulted in a slight slippage and settling, so that the rock began to tip just a trifle more toward the tracks some sixty feet below. None of the train crews noticed the almost imperceptible increase in the angle of the rock's inclination; and certainly none of them knew that the rock was now very precariously balanced, so that the slightest further movement in the fault—indeed, perhaps just the right vibration set up by a passing truck on the highway or a locomotive on the tracks—might send it hurtling down.

At such locations as this small canyon where the rock was, the railroad maintained protec-

---

First published in *Harper's Magazine*. Copyright, 1957, by Tom Burnam. Reprinted by permission of Brandt & Brandt.

---

1. **a fault,** a deep crack in the earth's crust.

tive fences; any slides or falling chunks would break one or more of the electric wires, setting into operation certain warning devices. An hour or two before the Bagleys found their camp ground, a boy who lived on a nearby backwoods ranch had aimed his new .22 rifle at an insulator atop the electric fence. The bullet shattered the insulator but did not sever the wire, which merely hung an inch or two lower, the electric circuit remaining unbroken.

"Let's not try to push on too fast tomorrow," Myra said after they had pitched the umbrella tent and Kit had set up his own pup tent close by. "I'm tired."

"But—" John started to say. Then he grinned. "Suits me," he said. "I'm tired too. And maybe tomorrow Kit and I can get in a little fishing. This *is* a nice spot."

The camp ground—they were a little surprised to have it all to themselves—was secluded from the highway. Close by tumbled the large creek which rushed through the canyon; on the opposite side were the railroad tracks, and the rock above them.

"Come on, son," said John the next morning. "Let's cross the bridge and see if we can stir up a trout or two."

The bridge was of heavy but ancient timbers; once used by logging trucks, it was now placarded "Unsafe for Vehicles."

"Be careful," said Myra Bagley. "Don't get run over by a train."

"Oh, Mom," said Kit, but he saw that she was joking, or at least mostly joking.

The man and his son picked up their fishing rods and set off.

"Did you hear that old train go past last night, Dad?" said Kit. "*I* thought it was going right through my pup tent."

John Bagley grimaced. "I think it did go through our tent," he said. "It woke your mother up in fine fashion, I can tell you."

"I bet it did," said Kit, and they grinned together, sharing companionably their masculine delight at the way the noise of the train had alarmed Mother.

"I'll bet that's why we had the camp ground to ourselves," said Kit. "Probably all the natives around here know about the trains."

"Probably," agreed his father.

They had reached the other side. The old truck crossing was barricaded now, though a footpath remained, and a sign said "NOTICE. Property of Montana & Pacific Railway. Permission to Cross Revocable at Any Time."

"What's that mean?" said Kit.

"It means the railroad doesn't want to lose its legal title to the right-of-way," said John.

"Oh," said Kit, who was willing to accept his father's explanation even though he did not wholly understand it. "Can we walk up the tracks?"

"I guess the railroad won't care," said his father, laughing. "It's certainly easier than scrambling along the bank."

"Let's go toward that big rock," said Kit. "See? The one above the tracks, there. I'll bet there's some good fishing right about there."

"Why?" said his father.

"Well," said Kit, "well, that rock makes a shadow on the water, and the trouts like to stay there."

"Trout," said his father. "It's the same, singular or plural."

"O.K.," said Kit, who secretly could not see that it mattered much.

Together father and son walked up the track. It was straight only for a short distance; at either end of the straight stretch the tracks curved away, following the S sweep of the stream and the canyon.

"Better keep our eyes open," said Kit, proud of remembering caution like an adult. "If a train came roaring along, we wouldn't see it."

John looked ahead and behind. For only a quarter-mile or so, until the tracks curved around rock cliffs at either end, did one have a clear view. He smiled at his son. "We'd hear it in plenty of time," he said. The thought of the shattering, surrounding roar the train had made last night caused him only half-consciously to prick up his ears a little. Evidently the trains came through here fast, faster than one would think for mountain country. On a sudden impulse he stopped, went down on one knee, and placed his ear on one of the rails.

"What are you doing?" asked Kit, astonished.

"An old trick I learned when I was about your age," his father said. "Didn't you ever try it?" Then he realized that of course Kit, raised in the city, had never learned how to listen for the trains. Kit at once laid his own ear to a rail. "I don't hear nothing."

"Good heavens," said his father. "*Anything.*"

"Anything," said Kit. "What are you supposed to listen for?"

"It's a kind of humming," his father said. "I didn't hear anything either, as a matter of fact. But if a train were coming, maybe even five miles or so away, you'd hear it."

"Gee," said Kit. "Five miles?"

"Maybe even more," said his father.

"Here's that old rock," said Kit, pointing up. It did indeed cast a shadow on the stream; John noted that there was a small indentation in the bank, and the water looked quite deep. There just might be trout, at that.

"Hey, Dad," said Kit. "What's that fence for?"

John looked where Kit was pointing. "Why, I don't know," he said. "It must be electric, from the look of those insulators. Maybe to keep animals off the track."

"Like bears?" said Kit.

"More likely cows," said his father. "Montana's an open-range state. Though I don't know what a cow would be doing on this side of the creek, or what good a fence would do there, between the canyon wall and the track. Anyway, don't touch it."

"O.K., Dad," said Kit. "Let's put some bait on." He pulled out of his pocket the tin of worms he had dug from the bank of the stream before they started. They were standing in the middle of the track directly beneath the rock, Kit intent on impaling a wriggling worm on his hook, his father tying on a Black Gnat.[2]

At that moment a huge truck with M.A.D. on its side, for "Montana and Dakota"—the "mad trucks" were a regional joke—hit a sizable chuck hole in the road across the stream out of sight behind the tall thick pines on the opposite bank. The driver swore and slammed into a lower gear.

John Bagley felt, or thought he felt, the slightest tremor in the cross-tie under his feet. And something, in a brief split second, struck him as odd about the shadow in which they stood. It was—it was moving, and Kit's scream and John Bagley's instinctive leap as he tried to grab Kit but instead, because his foot hit a small pebble, he got only empty air, were all a part of a kaleidoscopic nightmare of confusion, alarm, and incoherent noise as the great boulder above crashed mightily down, splitting in two with a great cracking sound as it did so, one large chunk stopping inches short of the electric fence in such position that the other and larger piece falling immediately behind struck it, hurtled into the air, and cleared the fence by the merest fraction of an inch.

Had the bottom chunk not stopped where it did, had the other half not happened to strike it exactly as it did, or had the shattered insulator not permitted just enough slack in the electric wire to enable the rock to leap it without touching it, the electric fence would have flashed its warning.

For a confused moment John Bagley stared wildly around. Rock dust hung in the air and he had fallen as he slipped on the pebble and *where was* Kit?

"Dad! Dad!" he heard, and he whirled around. Kit was half-lying on the track. The great split-off chunk of rock, resting partly on one rail, was across his leg.

John Bagley moved swiftly to his son. With horror in his eyes, he knelt down and took Kit's hand.

"I can't move, Dad!" cried Kit. "I can't move."

John looked at the boulder. Maybe, maybe it had not crushed or broken his son's leg; it appeared to be resting on the rail and a cross-tie.

---

2. **a Black Gnat,** a fishing lure made from feathers and colored silk, and meant to resemble an insect.

"Does it hurt much?" he asked softly, but Kit was weeping hysterically and could not answer.

"Kit!" He was ashamed of speaking so sharply, but it did what he hoped: Kit stopped crying.

"It doesn't hurt," Kit said. "Not much, anyway. But I can't pull loose. Move the rock, Dad. Please move it!"

John Bagley looked at the rock. "Move it, Dad," Kit whimpered. John put his shoulder to the rock, knowing the futility of it, knowing that no one man could budge it, but knowing too that for his son he had to try. He pushed until his heart pounded and his eyes misted. The rock did not budge, and John hated it for its stolid resistance to his human muscles.

He realized that he must not succumb to hysteria. What he could see of Kit's leg showed no obvious deformation, and thank God there was no blood. He would need to proceed calmly, efficiently, exploring every possibility. Don't lose your head, he said to himself, don't, don't.

Again he knelt beside his son. Apparently the boulder was resting on a rail and the firm ballast beneath the ties, or on a tie itself. The lower part of Kit's leg disappeared beneath the boulder in the small space between the bottom of the boulder, the rail, and the ground.

"I think it's my foot, Dad," whispered Kit. "My leg's all right, but I can't move my foot, I can't pull it out."

Then the horror struck his father, and his face turned white as he thought, Oh, God, let me keep Kit from thinking of it.

"Dad!" cried Kit. "Oh, Dad, what if—what if—"

It was too late. Kit had thought of it too.

"Come on, son," said John. "Let's pull you loose." He seized Kit by the shoulders.

"You're hurting me," said Kit, sobbing again.

It was no use. Only if help could be found, enough help to take the weight of the rock off the rail and open up what (thank the good Lord for this, at least) must be the small pocket in which Kit's foot was caught, would Kit be free.

"Dad," Kit said, "what are you going to do?" He had stopped crying, but he was shaking, shaking all over, violently.

At that moment they both heard, from some indeterminate distance and direction, the faint hoarse blat of a diesel locomotive's air-horn.

"It's a train," whispered Kit, his eyes wide with terror. "Oh, Daddy, it's a train." He had not called his father "Daddy" for a long time.

Get control of yourself, thought John Bagley. Don't throw yourself at the rock, don't try to move it, you can't move it. You can't pull him loose, you've tried to the limit of your strength, and more. You haven't even got a knife, or a hatchet. . . . But he could not pursue this thought further.

"Kit," said John, "I'm going to have to leave you here and run up the track and stop the train." He spoke as rapidly as he could, knowing at the same time that he must not communicate the full extent of his fear to the boy. "Then we'll get help from the trainmen and push the rock off."

The hoarse blat of the horn came again. It seemed noticeably closer.

"Dad!" cried Kit. "Where's it coming from? What if you run the wrong way?" He twisted and wriggled as he spoke, pushing and crying as he tried to free himself. "*Where's it coming from?*" Faintly, in the distance, they could hear now a dull rumbling clattering roar, echoing and re-echoing through the canyon.

"It's from that way," said John, and he started swiftly to run toward the direction from which the sound seemed to come when his son's cry stopped him.

"No, Dad, no! From there, from there!" Kit pointed in the opposite direction. If only they could see! If only the tracks did not curve out of sight in either direction! If only every rock and tree did not twist and distort and bounce the sound, now seeming much louder, of the train approaching fast and invisible, approaching—but from where? If only diesels made smoke. . . . Now he could not tell at all where the sound originated, and he was afraid his son knew he could not tell, and no matter what happened this, at least, his son must not know.

Sweating, John Bagley put his ear to the rail, and fought down his fear as the loud humming sounded so close by his head.

"You can tell that way, Daddy, can't you?" said Kit. "You can tell where it's coming from?"

John straightened and looked at his son. All his life he had dreaded some such moment as this. He knew—had always known—how to make decisions in the laboratory. Always there was something to go on, a collection of data to assess, or a logical corollary to what had gone before, or a table of figures which, even though capable of misinterpretation, was nevertheless *there*. But always he had feared that the time might come when the data or the corollary or the figures simply did not exist, and yet a step had to be taken even though taking it meant plunging ahead in darkness.

"You *can* tell, Daddy?" Kit was nearly hysterical again. John Bagley had tried never to lie, to himself or others.

"Yes, Kit," said John. "Now I know. Don't worry." Then he was running desperately up the track, as fast as he could in the direction from which he and Kit had come, and he prayed incoherently as he ran.

Another bleat of the horn. Was it louder? Less loud? And the rising-fading-rising rumble . . . it seemed farther away. John Bagley almost stopped, but it was too late now, too late: his course was set, the step in the dark had been taken, and for the first time in his life he knew fully what it was to be committed irrevocably to action without evidence, without the slightest shred of proof that the decision was correct. Yet he knew he must go on. There flashed into his mind a crazy picture of himself running frantically first one way, then the other, betrayed by the mountain echoes, like a foolish base-runner trapped between second and third.

His feet pounded on the cinders between the ties, which he cursed for being so spaced that now and then he stumbled. Once he fell, tearing the knees out of his trousers, then scrambling to his feet, pounding on. Again the horn, and

his heart almost stopped, for it seemed much less loud. But he forced himself on. The decision had been made. Right or wrong, it had been made.

He reached the curve somewhere beyond which—if he was right—would be the train. Would have to be the train. Over his shoulder he caught a last quick look at Kit, pinned by the rock, seeming much too close behind (surely he had covered more ground than that!) and he ran faster, blood-pounding, heart-pounding, sweat-streaming faster. He had hoped that once into the curve he would be able to see (and be seen) a long distance. But the curve was sharp enough, or the walls of the cut through which it ran were close enough to the tracks, so that still he could see nothing.

He stopped, sobbing with exhaustion. He could run no farther. Here he must stand if he was to have even enough strength to wave his arms. But there was no train at which to wave. The train tracks, shining in the sun, curved mockingly away until they disappeared behind the canyon wall, and they were empty. He strained with terrible intensity to hear something, to hear anything, but only the pounding rush of exhaustion filled his ears. He felt himself waver at the edge of consciousness; and for the first time, trying to fight it off but losing ground, he knew that futility and despair were beginning at last utterly to overwhelm him.

Then suddenly above the roaring in his ears sounded a tremendous alien noise, the rasping blast of an air-horn, very close, and three hundred yards away, its great steel snout roaring into view, he saw the train bearing down, and standing squarely in the middle of the track he mustered his final reserves to wave and, foolishly, yell, and he stayed where he was as he heard the increasing roar of the horn, jumping aside so late that for a fright-filled moment he was afraid he himself would be the one to be ground beneath the wheels.

Thank God, now, that it *was* a diesel, for that meant a clear view ahead for both engineer and fireman: they *must* have seen him. Then he heard the grinding squeal of brakes, and he saw the sparks fly as wheel after wheel locked and slid on the rails, and before he fainted he thought dimly: I got through to them, they're going to flatten every wheel. Thank God they saw me, they saw me, and they're stopping.

He returned to consciousness as the last of the cars ground to a shuddering halt and a trainman, leaping down, ran to him.

"My son," he gasped, pointing. "My son . . . down there."

Later, after the train crew had pried the rock up enough so that Kit could be pulled free, and the brakeman had put a small splint on Kit's ankle, though it seemed only to be bruised, and they were all back at the camp ground together (the burly brakeman had insisted on carrying Kit all the way), Myra Bagley looked at her husband and whispered, "Oh, John, how could you tell which direction the train was coming from? How could you tell, in mountains like these where everything echoes so?"

"Myra," John started to say, "I—"

Then he stopped. How could he tell her? The imponderable brooding fact of chance, of Fate, the dark reminder that beyond the shining realm of the controlled experiment, the offer of proof, the calculated risk, lay something incalculable—it was too much now for her. Later, maybe, later. Let Myra (and Kit) think now that he *had* known.

"I used an old Boy Scout trick," he said, smiling a little, feeling his strength return. "I put my ear to the rail."

"And you could tell the *direction?*" Myra asked.

"Sure," he lied. "Sure, if you know how."

"I'm so relieved," Myra said. "Oh, John, if you'd had to *guess. . . .*"

He knew then that he could never tell her.

I
A BLIND CHOICE

No matter what processes a person normally goes through before making a decision, there are times when he seems to have nothing to indicate which direction to take. John Bagley found himself deserted by all the formulas that he had grown accustomed to using, yet his decision *had* to be the right one.

Consider and discuss the significance of the following details:

1. The location of the rock

2. The locomotive's being a diesel

3. The railroad track's winding through a narrow canyon

4. The father's placing his ear to the rails

5. The untruth John Bagley tells his wife

II
IMPLICATIONS

A. Consider and discuss:

1. Thoughtlessness brings as much damage to society as deliberate, malicious action.

2. The best decisions are those made in emergency situations.

3. The greatest mistake is being afraid to make a mistake.

B. Certain often repeated maxims or proverbs seem directly contradictory. Discuss which of this pair contains the best advice:

1. Never change horses in the middle of the stream.

2. A wise man changes his mind, but a fool never does.

III
TECHNIQUES

Suspense

From the point in the story where the thought enters the minds of the father and son that a train *might* come before they can move the huge rock from the boy's leg, the author carefully includes details to increase the anxiety of the reader. Discuss three of these details.

Ending

When the train grinds to a halt in the exciting climax to an agony of suspense, the reader feels intense relief. "Now," he thinks, "they'll rescue Kit and everything will be all right."

Why do you think the author goes beyond this point in drawing the story to its conclusion? Think back to the title of the story when you answer.

Beginnings and Endings

Attention is centered in this group of selections upon *beginnings* and *endings*. Unless a story begins in a fashion which catches our interest, we often do not bother to continue; and unless it ends in a satisfying, dramatic, or interesting way, it leaves us with a disappointed feeling. In some respects, reading a story is like becoming acquainted with a person. First impressions and last ones are of great importance.

Beginnings

There are two common methods for beginning a story. One interest-catching way is to start with some of the characters engaged in a conversation. If the author begins in this fashion, he must be careful to see that he furnishes the reader with background information for understanding *who* is talking and *why* without being obvious or awkward.

In the story you have just read, for example, author Tom Burnam catches the reader's attention by beginning with conversation. In the first few paragraphs, he skillfully lets you know that the characters are a woman named Myra; her husband, whose name is not given until later; and their son, Kit. They are traveling through Montana in a car, tired and looking for a place to camp. *What* they say and *how* they say it tells you much about their personalities.

A second method commonly used is for the writer to begin by simply telling the reader what is happening. He introduces the characters and the background information without conversation. This type of opening may discourage the reader if it is dull or uninteresting, but it need not be that.

Edgar Allan Poe made little use of conversation, but by presenting many of his straight narrative accounts as personal experiences, he made them interest-catching from the beginning.

Endings

There are two common methods for ending stories also. One closes the story at the highest point of emotional interest. The *conflict* is settled and *suspense* ended at the same time that the story concludes (pp. 650–651). The way "The Most Dangerous Game" (p. 16) ends exemplifies this very well. Here the last line is: "He had never slept in a better bed, Rainsford decided." These few words tell you the outcome of the life-and-death struggle between General Zaroff and Rainsford, release you from the strain of sustained suspense, and, at the same time, end the story.

The second type of ending occurs when the author continues his narrative past the high point and "rounds it off." He tells you what happened after the climax had passed and the suspense lessened. If, for example, Richard Connell had gone on to tell how Rainsford managed to leave the island and get home, he would have given his story this kind of conclusion. The "rounded-off," rather than abrupt, ending may be very brief or may take as much as a third of the story.

To give the reader a satisfied feeling when he finishes a story, its ending must be as carefully planned as its beginning.

Since this section includes short stories, an essay, a one-act play, and a short novel, many literary terms discussed earlier are considered again as a review.

The Parsley Garden

WILLIAM SAROYAN

One day in August Al Condraj was wandering through Woolworth's without a penny to spend when he saw a small hammer that was not a toy but a real hammer and he was possessed with a longing to have it. He believed it was just what he needed by which to break the monotony and with which to make something. He had gathered some first-class nails from Foley's Packing House where the box-makers worked and where they had carelessly dropped at least fifteen cents' worth. He had gladly gone to the trouble of gathering them together because it had seemed to him that a nail, as such, was not something to be wasted. He had the nails, perhaps a half pound of them, at least two hundred of them, in a paper bag in the apple box in which he kept his junk at home.

Now, with the ten-cent hammer he believed he could make something out of box wood and the nails, although he had no idea what. Some sort of a table perhaps, or a small bench.

At any rate he took the hammer and slipped it into the pocket of his overalls, but just as he did so a man took him firmly by the arm without a word and pushed him to the back of the store into a small office. Another man, an older

From *The Assyrian and Other Stories,* copyright, 1949, 1950, by William Saroyan. Reprinted by permission of William Saroyan.

one, was seated behind a desk in the office, working with papers. The younger man, the one who had captured him, was excited and his forehead was covered with sweat.

"Well," he said, "here's one more of them."

The man behind the desk got to his feet and looked Al Condraj up and down.

"What's *he* swiped?"

"A hammer." The young man looked at Al with hatred. "Hand it over," he said.

The boy brought the hammer out of his pocket and handed it to the young man, who said, "I ought to hit you over the head with it, that's what I ought to do."

He turned to the older man, the boss, the manager of the store, and he said, "What do you want me to do with him?"

"Leave him with me," the older man said.

The younger man stepped out of the office, and the older man sat down and went back to work. Al Condraj stood in the office fifteen minutes before the older man looked at him again.

"Well," he said.

Al didn't know what to say. The man wasn't looking at him, he was looking at the door.

Finally Al said, "I didn't mean to steal it. I just need it and I haven't got any money."

"Just because you haven't got any money doesn't mean you've got a right to steal things," the man said. "Now, does it?"

"No, sir."

"Well, what am I going to do with you? Turn you over to the police?"

Al didn't say anything, but he certainly didn't want to be turned over to the police. He hated the man, but at the same time he realized somebody else could be a lot tougher than he was being.

"If I let you go, will you promise never to steal from this store again?"

"Yes, sir."

"All right," the man said. "Go out this way and don't come back to this store until you've got some money to spend."

He opened a door to the hall that led to the alley, and Al Condraj hurried down the hall and out into the alley.

The first thing he did when he was free was laugh, but he knew he had been humiliated and he was deeply ashamed. It was not in his nature to take things that did not belong to him. He hated the young man who had caught him and he hated the manager of the store who had made him stand in silence in the office so long. He hadn't liked it at all when the young man had said he ought to hit him over the head with the hammer.

He should have had the courage to look him straight in the eye and say, "You and who else?"

Of course he *had* stolen the hammer and he had been caught, but it seemed to him he oughtn't to have been so humiliated.

After he had walked three blocks he decided he didn't want to go home just yet, so he turned around and started walking back to town. He almost believed he meant to go back and say something to the young man who had caught him. And then he wasn't sure he didn't mean to go back and steal the hammer again, and this time *not* get caught. As long as he had been made to feel like a thief anyway, the least he ought to get out of it was the hammer.

Outside the store he lost his nerve, though. He stood in the street, looking in, for at least ten minutes.

Then, crushed and confused and now bitterly ashamed of himself, first for having stolen something, then for having been caught, then for having been humiliated, then for not having guts enough to go back and do the job right, he began walking home again, his mind so troubled that he didn't greet his pal Pete Waw-chek when they came face to face outside Graf's Hardware.

When he got home he was too ashamed to go inside and examine his junk, so he had a long drink of water from the faucet in the back yard. The faucet was used by his mother to water the stuff she planted every year: okra, bell peppers, tomatoes, cucumbers, onions, garlic, mint, eggplants and parsley.

His mother called the whole business the parsley garden, and every night in the summer she would bring chairs out of the house and put them around the table she had had Ondro, the neighborhood handyman, make for her for fifteen cents, and she would sit at the table and enjoy the cool of the garden and the smell of the things she had planted and tended.

Sometimes she would even make a salad and moisten the flat old-country bread and slice some white cheese, and she and he would have supper in the parsley garden. After supper she would attach the water hose to the faucet and water her plants and the place would be cooler than ever and it would smell real good, real fresh and cool and green, all the different growing things making a green-garden smell out of themselves and the air and the water.

After the long drink of water he sat down where the parsley itself was growing and he pulled a handful of it out and slowly ate it. Then he went inside and told his mother what had happened. He even told her what he had *thought* of doing after he had been turned loose: to go back and steal the hammer again.

"I don't want you to steal," his mother said in broken English. "Here is ten cents. You go back to that man and you give him this money and you bring it home, that hammer."

"No," Al Condraj said. "I won't take your money for something I don't really need. I just thought I ought to have a hammer, so I could make something if I felt like it. I've got a lot of nails and some box wood, but I haven't got a hammer."

"Go buy it, that hammer," his mother said.

"No," Al said.

"All right," his mother said. "Shut up."

That's what she always said when she didn't know what else to say.

Al went out and sat on the steps. His humiliation was beginning to really hurt now. He decided to wander off along the railroad tracks to Foley's because he needed to think about it some more. At Foley's he watched Johnny Gale nailing boxes for ten minutes, but Johnny was too busy to notice him or talk to him, although one day at Sunday school, two or three years ago, Johnny had greeted him and said, "How's the boy?" Johnny worked with a boxmaker's hatchet and everybody in Fresno said he was the fastest boxmaker in town. He was the closest thing to a machine any packing house ever saw. Foley himself was proud of Johnny Gale.

Al Condraj finally set out for home because he didn't want to get in the way. He didn't want somebody working hard to notice that he was being watched and maybe say to him, "Go on, beat it." He didn't want Johnny Gale to do something like that. He didn't want to invite another humiliation.

On the way home he looked for money but all he found was the usual pieces of broken glass and rusty nails, the things that were always cutting his bare feet every summer.

When he got home his mother had made a salad and set the table, so he sat down to eat, but when he put the food in his mouth he just didn't care for it. He got up and went into the three-room house and got his apple box out of the corner of his room and went through his junk. It was all there, the same as yesterday.

He wandered off back to town and stood in front of the closed store, hating the young man who had caught him, and then he went along to the Hippodrome and looked at the display photographs from the two movies that were being shown that day.

Then he went along to the public library to have a look at all the books again, but he didn't like any of them, so he wandered around town some more, and then around half-past eight he went home and went to bed.

His mother had already gone to bed because she had to be up at five to go to work at Inderrieden's, packing figs. Some days there would be work all day, some days there would be only half a day of it, but whatever his mother earned during the summer had to keep them the whole year.

He didn't sleep much that night because he couldn't get over what had happened, and he went over six or seven ways by which to adjust the matter. He went so far as to believe it would be necessary to kill the young man who had caught him. He also believed it would be necessary for him to steal systematically and successfully the rest of his life. It was a hot night and he couldn't sleep.

Finally, his mother got up and walked barefooted to the kitchen for a drink of water and on the way back she said to him softly, "Shut up."

When she got up at five in the morning he was out of the house, but that had happened many times before. He was a restless boy, and he kept moving all the time every summer. He was making mistakes and paying for them, and he had just tried stealing and had been caught at it and he was troubled. She fixed her breakfast, packed her lunch and hurried off to work, hoping it would be a full day.

It was a full day, and then there was overtime, and although she had no more lunch she decided to work on for the extra money, anyway. Almost all the other packers were staying on, too, and her neighbor across the alley, Leeza Ahboot, who worked beside her, said, "Let us work until the work stops, then we'll go home and fix a supper between us and eat it in your parsley garden where it's so cool. It's a hot day and there's no sense not making an extra fifty or sixty cents."

When the two women reached the garden it was almost nine o'clock, but still daylight, and she saw her son nailing pieces of box wood together, making something with a hammer. It looked like a bench. He had already watered the garden and tidied up the rest of the yard, and the place seemed very nice, and her son seemed very serious and busy. She and Leeza went straight to work for their supper, picking bell peppers and tomatoes and cucumbers and a great deal of parsley for the salad.

Then Leeza went to her house for some bread which she had baked the night before, and some white cheese, and in a few minutes they were having supper together and talking pleasantly about the successful day they had had. After supper, they made Turkish coffee over an open fire in the yard. They drank the coffee and smoked a cigarette apiece, and told one another stories about their experiences in the old country and here in Fresno, and then they looked into their cups at the grounds to see if any good fortune was indicated, and there was: health and work and supper out of doors in the summer and enough money for the rest of the year.

Al Condraj worked and overheard some of the things they said, and then Leeza went home to go to bed, and his mother said, "Where you get it, that hammer, Al?"

"I got it at the store."

"How you get it? You steal it?"

Al Condraj finished the bench and sat on it. "No," he said. "I didn't steal it."

"How you get it?"

"I worked at the store for it," Al said.

"The store where you steal it yesterday?"

"Yes."

"Who give you job?"

"The boss."

"What you do?"

"I carried different stuff to the different counters."

"Well, that's good," the woman said. "How long you work for that little hammer?"

"I worked all day," Al said. "Mr. Clemmer gave me the hammer after I'd worked one hour, but I went right on working. The fellow who caught me yesterday showed me what to do, and we worked together. We didn't talk, but at the end of the day he took me to Mr. Clemmer's office and he told Mr. Clemmer that I'd worked hard all day and ought to be paid at least a dollar."

"That's good," the woman said.

"So Mr. Clemmer put a silver dollar on his desk for me, and then the fellow who caught me yesterday told him the store needed a boy like me every day, for a dollar a day, and Mr. Clemmer said I could have the job."

"That's good," the woman said. "You can make it a little money for yourself."

"I left the dollar on Mr. Clemmer's desk," Al Condraj said, "and I told them both I didn't want the job."

"Why you say that?" the woman said. "Dollar a day for eleven-year-old boy good money. Why you not take job?"

"Because I hate the both of them," the boy said. "I would never work for people like that. I just looked at them and picked up my hammer and walked out. I came home and I made this bench."

"All right," his mother said. "Shut up."

His mother went inside and went to bed, but Al Condraj sat on the bench he had made and smelled the parsley garden and didn't feel humiliated any more.

But nothing could stop him from hating the two men, even though he knew they hadn't done anything they shouldn't have done.

I

A GESTURE OF INDEPENDENCE

Al Condraj's decision to leave the silver dollar on Mr. Clemmer's desk and refuse the job which, in those depression years, paid good money, illustrates his almost fantastic spirit of independence. Just by looking at the two men and refusing to take what they had agreed was owed him for his labor, he felt that he had evened the score and left them feeling uncomfortable. Many people will go to great lengths to bolster their damaged pride. Al was one of these.

II

IMPLICATIONS

React to the following statements either affirmatively or negatively. Give reasons for your answer.

1. Al's mother was indifferent to what Al thought or did.

2. Both Mr. Clemmer and the young man who worked for him were very unfair to Al.

3. Al should have been grateful rather than resentful about his treatment.

4. Al wanted and needed the companionship of a father or someone who would take the place of a father.

5. The title doesn't fit this story well at all.

III

TECHNIQUES

Style and Characterization

Lauded by admirers and critics as the first writer in many years to write in a form truly his own, William Saroyan comes from Armenian parentage and *knows* the people he writes about. His short stories and sketches are impressionistic. They reflect strongly his own ideas of personal freedom and independence even amid poverty. The forthright way he reveals the thoughts and reactions of his characters gives the reader a picture of what they are like. Although they may be different in their ways of thinking, they are all vivid and alive. They are not at all artificial.

1. Consider and discuss passages in the story which build up an understanding of Al's character. Summarize in a brief paragraph what he is like.

2. Saroyan's language is as plain and undecorated as his characters. Locate and discuss two passages from the story in which the word choice is particularly realistic.

3. Note the repeated use of the word *hate* or *hatred*. One definition of hate is "to regard with a strong or passionate dislike." Why does the frequent use of this term help explain Al's view of himself?

4. Al Condraj's mother is depicted in the descriptions of the things she likes. Reread the descriptions on page 654 and give an explanation of the character that emerges. When the mother says "Shut up," she is expressing feelings she cannot put into words. What do you suppose she means each time she says "Shut up" in the story?

Beginning

William Saroyan makes his opening sentence count. In it he introduces the central character, tells where he is, and what he is doing. The actual story is set moving at once because the reader can sense that Al may be tempted to take the hammer.

What information does the author supply in the rest of this first paragraph and in the second one to explain why Al is particularly interested in the hammer?

Ending

The author tells us in the next to last paragraph that Al was sitting on the bench he had made, smelling the good smells of the parsley garden, and he "didn't feel humiliated any more."

These words would seem to conclude the story. Why then do you think that William Saroyan added his last paragraph? Is the feeling it expresses in keeping with the author's characterization of Al? Explain.

Gallery | MOMENTS OF DECISION

Since it depends so much on events that went before, the Moment of Decision
is not an easy thing to picture. Yet the drama of this moment has intrigued painters
as well as writers. Often the artist has had to select the decisive moment
from some well-known story of a famous decision from which to create his picture. Occasionally,
as in the picture FRIENDS OR ENEMIES? and in the steamboat watercolor SNAGS, the artist
pictures a situation that must bring about a Moment of Decision.

THE JUDGEMENT OF SOLOMON
Nicolas Poussin

SAMSON
Roger Vieillard

The Hebrew king Solomon was called upon to
decide the fate of a baby. In this famous
Biblical story a baby had died and two women
claimed the living child. Solomon concluded that
the mother of the live baby would not permit it
to be hurt. Therefore he said: "Divide the child
in half and give each woman her share." He awarded
the baby to her who protested. Above, the
judgment has been given; you can judge who is
the real mother.

Also from the Old Testament comes the story
for this modern print. Mighty Samson, separated
from his source of strength by the treachery of
Delilah, blinded and chained to public pillars,
finds new strength. Pulling down the pillars, he
destroys himself and his tormentors.

In the delicate provincial painting of
fifteenth-century Siena, Italy, St. Anthony
acts on his decision to share his wealth.

SAINT ANTHONY DISTRIBUTING HIS WEALTH TO THE POOR
Sasetta and Assistant
Samuel H. Cress Collection, National Gallery of Art, Washington, D.C.

DECLARATION OF INDEPENDENCE
John Trumbull
Courtesy Yale University Art Gallery

John Trumbull painted
the momentous historical decision
of the American people while the original
signers were still alive. Their heads
are portraits from life. The painter had been
on General Washington's staff at the beginning
of the Revolutionary War.

Bingham was the painter of many moments
of decision on the American frontier.
Campaigning in an election, of course,
is designed to bring about decision-making.

CANVASSING FOR A VOTE
George Caleb Bingham

Eakins was a realistic painter
with a scholarly interest in anatomy.
He had attended just such
demonstration surgery as he depicts
in his picture. In the nineteenth
century, when the picture
was painted, surgery was not
the skillful practice it is today,
but then, as now, every moment
must be one of decision.

In À VINGT ANS
("At Twenty Years"),
the young lady is being asked
for a momentous decision.

The Senate etching
from the last century
tells of the steady stream of decision-making
that goes into creating
the nation's laws.
In HUNG JURY,
the lithographer has caught
the frustration of indecision.
The moment of decision
must come soon.

THE CHESS GAME
Lucas Von Leyden

The poor lady
is receiving a good deal
of help in her
decision-making
for the game of chess.
Notice the many
dramatic details
in this rich
sixteenth-century
Dutch painting.

HUNG JURY
William Sharp

SNAGS
*early American aquatint
from a Carl Bodmer painting*

The steamboat pilot has danger ahead.
His job required of him a constant series
of decisions on which his life
and that of his passengers depended.

661

Mike Flannery, the Westcote
express agent, was a man of iron will. But
even a strong man can only stand so much,
or perhaps it would be better to say,
so many.

Pigs Is Pigs

ELLIS PARKER BUTLER

Mike Flannery, the Westcote agent of
the Interurban Express Company, leaned over
the counter of the express office and shook his
fist. Mr. Morehouse, angry and red, stood on
the other side of the counter, trembling with
rage. The argument had been long and
heated, and at last Mr. Morehouse had talked
himself speechless. The cause of the trouble
stood on the counter between the two men. It
was a soap box across the top of which were
nailed a number of strips, forming a rough
but serviceable cage. In it two spotted guinea
pigs were greedily eating lettuce leaves.

"Do as you like, then!" shouted Flannery,
"pay for them and take them, or don't pay for
them and leave them be. Rules is rules, Mister
Morehouse, and Mike Flannery's not going to
be called down for breaking them."

"But, you everlastingly stupid idiot!"
shouted Mr. Morehouse, madly shaking a
flimsy printed book beneath the agent's nose,
"can't you read it here—in your own plain
printed rates? 'Pets, domestic, Franklin to
Westcote, if properly boxed, twenty-five cents
each.'" He threw the book on the counter in
disgust. "What more do you want? Aren't they
pets? Aren't they domestic? Aren't they properly boxed? What?"

He turned and walked back and forth
rapidly, frowning ferociously.

Suddenly he turned to Flannery and, forcing his voice to an artificial calmness, spoke
slowly but with intense sarcasm.

"Pets," he said. "P-e-t-s! Twenty-five cents
each. There are two of them. One! Two! Two
times twenty-five are fifty! Can you understand that? I offer you fifty cents."

Flannery reached for the book. He ran his
hand through the pages and stopped at page
sixty-four.

"And I don't take fifty cents," he whispered
in mockery. "Here's the rule for it. 'When the
agent be in any doubt regarding which of two
rates applies to a shipment, he shall charge
the larger. The consignee may file a claim for
the overcharge.' In this case, Mister Morehouse, I be in doubt. Pets them animals may
be, and domestic they are, but pigs I'm blame
sure they are, and my rules say plain as the
nose on your face, 'Pigs, Franklin to Westcote,
thirty cents each.' And, Mr. Morehouse, by my
arithmetical knowledge two times thirty
comes to sixty cents."

Mr. Morehouse shook his head savagely.
"Nonsense!" he shouted, "confounded nonsense, I tell you! Why, you poor ignorant foreigner, that rule means common pigs, domestic pigs, not guinea pigs!"

Flannery was stubborn.

"Pigs is pigs," he declared firmly, "Guinea
pigs or Irish pigs is all the same to the Interurban Express Company and to Mike Flannery. The nationality of the pig creates no
differential in the rate, Mister Morehouse! It
would be the same if they were Dutch pigs or
Russian pigs. Mike Flannery," he added, "is
here to tend to the express business and not to
hold conversation with pigs in seventeen languages for to discover if they're Chinese or
Tipperary[1] by birth and nativity."

Mr. Morehouse hesitated and then flung out
his arms wildly.

"Very well!" he shouted, "you shall hear of

---

1. **Tipperary,** a county in south central Ireland.

this! Your president shall hear of this! It is an outrage! I have offered you fifty cents. You refuse it! Keep the pigs until you are ready to take the fifty cents, but, by George, sir, if one hair of those pigs' heads is harmed, I will have the law on you!"

He turned and stalked out, slamming the door. Flannery carefully lifted the soap box from the counter and placed it in a corner. He was not worried. He felt the peace that comes to a faithful servant who has done his duty and done it well.

Mr. Morehouse went home raging. His boy, who had been awaiting the guinea pigs, knew better than to ask him for them. He was a normal boy and therefore always had a guilty conscience when his father was angry. So the boy slipped quietly around the house. There is nothing so soothing to a guilty conscience as to be out of the path of the avenger.

Mr. Morehouse stormed into the house. "Where's the ink?" he shouted at his wife as soon as his foot was across the doorsill.

Mrs. Morehouse jumped, guiltily. She never used ink. She had not seen the ink, nor moved the ink, nor thought of the ink, but her husband's tone convicted her of the guilt of having borne and reared a boy, and she knew that whenever her husband wanted anything in a loud voice, the boy had been at it.

"I'll find Sammy," she said meekly.

When the ink was found, Mr. Morehouse wrote rapidly, and he read the completed letter and smiled a triumphant smile.

"That will settle that crazy Irishman!" he exclaimed. "When they get that letter, he will hunt another job, all right!"

A week later Mr. Morehouse received a long official envelope with the card of the Interurban Express Company in the upper left corner. He tore it open eagerly and drew out a sheet of paper. At the top it bore the number A6754. The letter was short. "Subject— Rate on guinea pigs," it said, "Dr. Sir—We are in receipt of your letter regarding rate on guinea pigs between Franklin and Westcote, addressed to the president of this company.

All claims for overcharge should be addressed to the Claims Department."

Mr. Morehouse wrote the Claims Department. He wrote six pages of choice sarcasm, vituperation, and argument, and sent them to Claims.

A few weeks later he received a reply from the Claims Department. Attached to it was his last letter.

"Dr. Sir," said the reply. "Your letter of the 16th inst., addressed to this Department, subject rate on guinea pigs from Franklin to Westcote, rec'd. We have taken up the matter with our agent at Westcote, and his reply is attached herewith. He informs us that you refused to receive the consignment or to pay the charges. You have therefore no claim against this company, and your letter regarding the proper rate on the consignment should be addressed to our Tariff Department."

Mr. Morehouse wrote to the Tariff Department. He stated his case clearly and gave his arguments in full, quoting a page or two from the encyclopedia to prove that guinea pigs were not common pigs.

With the care that characterizes corporations when they are systematically conducted, Mr. Morehouse's letter was numbered, O.K.'d, and started through the regular channels. Duplicate copies of the bill of lading, manifest, Flannery's receipt for the package, and several other pertinent papers were pinned to the letter, and they were passed to the head of the Tariff Department.

The head of the Tariff Department put his feet on his desk and yawned. He looked through the papers carelessly.

"Miss Kane," he said to his stenographer, "take.this letter. 'Agent, Westcote, N.J. Please advise why consignment referred to in attached papers was refused domestic pet rates.'"

Miss Kane made a series of curves and angles on her notebook and waited with pencil poised. The department head looked at the papers again.

"Huh! guinea pigs!" he said. "Probably

starved to death by this time! Add this to that letter: 'Give condition of consignment at present.'"

He tossed the papers on the stenographer's desk, took his feet from his own desk, and went out to lunch.

When Mike Flannery received the letter he scratched his head.

"Give present condition," he repeated thoughtfully. "Now what do them clerks be wanting to know, I wonder! 'Present condition,' is it? Them pigs, praise St. Patrick, are in good health, so far as I know, but I never was no veterinary surgeon to pigs. Maybe them clerks want me to call in the pig doctor and have their pulses taken. One thing I do know, however, which is they've glorious appetites for pigs their size. Eats? They'd eat the brass padlocks off of a barn door! If the paddy pig, by the same token, ate as hearty as these pigs do, there'd be a famine in Ireland."

To assure himself that his report would be up to date, Flannery went to the rear of the office and looked into the cage. The pigs had been transferred to a larger box—a dry goods box.

"One, —two, —three, —four, —five, —six, —seven, —eight!" he counted. "Seven spotted and one all black. All well and hearty and all eating like raging hippopotamuses." He went back to his desk and wrote.

"Mr. Morgan, Head of Tariff Department," he wrote. "Why do I say guinea pigs is pigs because they is pigs and will be 'til you say they ain't which is what the rule book says stop your jollying me you know it as well as I do. As to health they are all well and hoping you are the same. P.S. There are eight now the family increased all good eaters. P.S. I paid out so far two dollars for cabbage which they like shall I put in bill for same what?"

Morgan, head of the Tariff Department, when he received this letter, laughed. He read it again and became serious. He looked up and thought it over.

"By George!" he said, "Flannery is right, 'pigs is pigs.' I'll have to get authority on this thing. Meanwhile, Miss Kane, take this letter: Agent, Westcote, N.J. Regarding shipment guinea pigs, File No. A6754. Rule 83, General Instructions to Agents, clearly states that agents shall collect from consignee all costs of provender, etc., etc., required for live stock while in transit or storage. You will proceed to collect same from consignee."

Flannery received this letter next morning, and when he read it he grinned.

"Proceed to collect," he said softly. "How them clerks do like to be talking! *Me* proceed to collect two dollars and twenty-five cents off Mister Morehouse! I wonder do them clerks *know* Mister Morehouse? I'll get it! Oh, yes! 'Mister Morehouse, two and a quarter, please.' 'Certainly, my dear friend Flannery. Delighted!' *Not!*"

Flannery drove the express wagon to Mr. Morehouse's door. Mr. Morehouse answered the bell.

"Ah, ha!" he cried as he saw it was Flannery. "So you've come to your senses at last, have you? I thought you would! Bring the box in."

"I have no box," said Flannery coldly. "I have a bill against Mister John C. Morehouse for two dollars and twenty-five cents for cabbages eaten by his pigs. Would you wish to pay it?"

"Pay—Cabbages—!" gasped Mr. Morehouse. "Do you mean to say that two little guinea pigs—"

"Eight!" said Flannery. "Papa and mamma and the six children. Eight!"

For answer Mr. Morehouse slammed the door in Flannery's face. Flannery looked at the door reproachfully.

"I take it the consignee don't want to pay for them cabbages," he said. "If I know signs of refusal, the consignee refuses to pay for one dang cabbage leaf and be hanged to me!"

Mr. Morgan, head of the Tariff Department, consulted the president of the Interurban Express Company regarding guinea pigs, as to whether they were pigs or not pigs. The president was inclined to treat the matter lightly.

"What is the rate on pigs and on pets?" he asked.

"Pigs thirty cents, pets twenty-five, said Morgan.

"Then of course guinea pigs are pigs," said the president.

"Yes," agreed Morgan, "I look at it that way, too. A thing that can come under two rates is naturally to be classed as the higher. But the guinea pigs, pigs? Aren't they rabbits?"

"Come to think of it," said the president, "I believe they are more like rabbits. Sort of halfway station between pig and rabbit. I think the question is this—are guinea pigs of the domestic pig family? I'll ask Professor Gordon. He is an authority on such things. Leave the papers with me."

The president put the papers on his desk and wrote a letter to Professor Gordon. Unfortunately the Professor was in South America collecting zoological specimens, and the letter was forwarded to him by his wife. As the Professor was in the highest Andes, where no white man had ever penetrated, the letter was many months in reaching him. The president forgot the guinea pigs, Morgan forgot them, Mr. Morehouse forgot them, but Flannery did not. One half of his time he gave to the duties of his agency; the other half was devoted to the guinea pigs. Long before Professor Gordon received the president's letter, Morgan received one from Flannery.

"About them guinea pigs," it said, "what shall I do they are great in family life, no race suicide for them, there are thirty-two now shall I sell them do you take this express office for a menagerie, answer quick."

Morgan reached for a telegraph blank and wrote:

"Agent, Westcote. Don't sell pigs."

He then wrote Flannery a letter calling his attention to the fact that the pigs were not the property of the company but were merely being held during a settlement of a dispute regarding rates. He advised Flannery to take the best possible care of them.

Flannery, letter in hand, looked at the pigs and sighed. The dry goods box cage had become too small. He boarded up twenty feet of the rear of the express office to make a large and airy home for them, and went about his business. He worked with feverish intensity when out on his rounds, for the pigs required attention and took most of his time. Some months later, in desperation, he seized a sheet of paper and wrote "160" across it and mailed it to Morgan. Morgan returned it asking for explanation. Flannery replied:

"There are now one hundred sixty of them pigs, for heavens sake let me sell off some, do you want me to go crazy, what."

"Sell no pigs," Morgan wired.

Not long after this the president of the express company received a letter from Professor Gordon. It was a long and scholarly letter, but the point was that the guinea pig was the *Cavia aparoea*[2] while the common pig was the genus *Sus* of the family *Suidae*. He remarked that they were prolific and multiplied rapidly.

"They are not pigs," said the president, decidedly, to Morgan. "The twenty-five cent rate applies."

Morgan made the proper notation on the papers that had accumulated in File A6754 and turned them over to the Audit Department. The Audit Department took some time to look the matter up and, after the usual delay, wrote Flannery that as he had on hand one hundred and sixty guinea pigs, the property of consignee, he should deliver them and collect charges at the rate of twenty-five cents each.

Flannery spent a day herding his charges through a narrow opening in their cage so that he might count them.

---

2. **Cavia aparoea**\ˈka·vē·ə·a·pə ˈrē·ə\ the genus and species to which the guinea pig belongs.

"Audit Dept." He wrote, when he had finished the count, "you are way off there may be was one hundred and sixty guinea pigs once, but wake up don't be a back number. I've got even eight hundred, now shall I collect for eight hundred or what, how about sixty-four dollars I paid out for cabbages."

It required a great many letters back and forth before the Audit Department was able to understand why the error had been made of billing one hundred and sixty instead of eight hundred, and still more time for it to get the meaning of the "cabbages."

Flannery was crowded into a few feet at the extreme front of the office. The pigs had all the rest of the room and two boys were employed constantly attending to them. The day after Flannery had counted the guinea pigs there were eight more added to his drove, and by the time the Audit Department gave him authority to collect for eight hundred Flannery had given up all attempts to attend to the receipts of the delivery of goods. He was hastily building galleries around the express office, tier above tier. He had four thousand and sixty-four guinea pigs to care for. More were arriving daily.

Immediately following its authorization the Audit Department sent another letter, but Flannery was too busy to open it. They wrote another and then they telegraphed:

"Error in guinea pig bill. Collect for two guinea pigs, fifty cents. Deliver all to consignee."

Flannery read the telegram and cheered up. He wrote out a bill as rapidly as his pencil could travel over the paper and ran all the way to the Morehouse home. At the gate he stopped suddenly. The house stared at him with vacant eyes. The windows were bare of curtains, and he could see into the empty rooms. A sign on the porch said, "To Let." Mr. Morehouse had moved. Flannery ran all the way back to the express office. Sixty-nine guinea pigs had been born during his absence. He ran out again and made feverish inquiries in the village. Mr. Morehouse had not only

moved, but he had left Westcote. Flannery returned to the express office and found that two hundred and six guinea pigs had entered the world since he left. He wrote a telegram to the Audit Department.

"Can't collect fifty cents for two guinea pigs consignee has left town address unknown what shall I do? Flannery."

The telegram was handed to one of the clerks in the Audit Department, and as he read it he laughed.

"Flannery must be crazy. He ought to know that the thing to do is to return the consignment here," said the clerk. He telegraphed Flannery to send the pigs to the main office of the company at Franklin.

When Flannery received the telegram, he set to work. The six boys he had engaged to help him also set to work. They worked with the haste of desperate men, making cages out of soap boxes, cracker boxes, and all kinds of boxes, and as fast as the cages were completed, they filled them with guinea pigs and expressed them to Franklin. Day after day the cages of guinea pigs flowed in a steady stream from Westcote to Franklin, and still Flannery and his six helpers ripped and nailed and packed—relentlessly and feverishly. At the end of the week they had shipped two hundred and eighty cases of guinea pigs, and there were in the express office seven hundred and four more pigs than when they began packing them.

"Stop sending pigs. Warehouse full," came a telegram to Flannery. He stopped packing only long enough to wire back, "Can't stop," and kept on sending them. On the next train up from Franklin came one of the company's inspectors. He had instructions to stop the stream of guinea pigs at all hazards. As his train drew up at Westcote station, he saw a cattle car standing on the express company's siding. When he reached the express office he saw the express wagon backed up to the door. Six boys were carrying bushel baskets full of guinea pigs from the office and dumping them into the wagon. Inside the room Flannery, with his coat and vest off, was shoveling guinea pigs into bushel baskets with a coal scoop. He was winding up the guinea pig episode for once and for all.

He looked up at the inspector with a snort of anger.

"One wagonload more and I'll be quit of them, and never will you catch Flannery with no more foreign pigs on his hands. No, sir! They near was the death of me. Next time I'll know that pigs of whatever nationality is domestic pets—and go at the lowest rate."

He began shoveling again rapidly, speaking quickly between breaths.

"Rules may be rules, but you can't fool Mike Flannery twice with the same trick—when it comes to live stock, dang the rules. So long as Flannery runs this express office—pigs is pets —and cows is pets—and horses is pets—and lions and tigers and Rocky Mountain goats is pets—and the rate on them is twenty-five cents."

He paused long enough to let one of the boys put an empty basket in the place of the one he had just filled. There were only a few guinea pigs left. As he noted their limited number, his natural habit of looking on the bright side returned.

"Well, anyhow," he said cheerfully, "it's not so bad as it might be. What if them guinea pigs had been elephants!"

I

A BATTLE OF WILLS

Anyone who has raised guinea pigs will understand Mike Flannery's problem very well. He could have saved himself bushels of trouble by being a little less stubborn.

1. Why does Mr. Morehouse refuse to take home the two guinea pigs he had ordered for his boy?

2. What does Mr. Morehouse do as soon as he reaches home? What result does his action have?

3. Why does the Claims Department refer him to the Tariff Department?

4. Why does Flannery try to collect $2.25 from Morehouse?

5. How does it happen that it is months before any decision is reached about the guinea pigs?

6. What happens to Flannery and the guinea pigs during this delay?

7. What does Flannery finally do with the guinea pigs?

II

IMPLICATIONS

Discuss how this story indirectly endorses all of the following timeworn sayings or adages.

1. Mighty oaks from little acorns grow.

2. Experience is a hard teacher.

3. Every cloud has a silver lining.

III

TECHNIQUES

This highly humorous story is a gentle satire that spoofs or pokes fun at the red tape of big business. It shows how a ridiculously simple decision concerning the express rate for two guinea pigs can become very complicated when processed through bureaucratic channels.

Beginnings

In this classically humorous story, Ellis Parker Butler sets the stage for developing the plot very quickly and skillfully.

1. How do the first two sentences immediately catch the reader's interest?

2. What have you learned by the end of the first paragraph?

3. What device does Butler begin using in the second paragraph to sustain interest?

Endings

Even while the reader realizes that what the author has done is to create an exaggerated, highly improbable situation, the action is built so logically on accepted business routines that it makes the ending even funnier.

1. Where do you think the high point of interest occurs?

2. From which point on would you say the author is simply concerned with rounding off his story to leave the reader with a satisfied feeling?

It was just
a "lousy snapper." Did it
have a right to live?

The Turtle

GEORGE VUKELICH

They were driving up to fish the White Creek for German Browns[1] and the false dawn was purpling the Wisconsin countryside when they spotted the huge hump-backed object in the middle of the sandroad and Jimmy coasted the station wagon to a stop.

"Pa," he said. "Turtle. Lousy snapper."

Old Tony sat up.

"Is he dead?"

"Not yet," Jimmy said. "Not yet he isn't." He shifted into neutral and pulled the handbrake. The snapper lay large and darkgreen in the headlight beams, and they got out and went around to look at it closely. The turtle moved a little and left razorlike clawmarks in the wet sand, and it waited.

"Probably heading for the creek," Jimmy said. "They kill trout like crazy."

They stood staring down.

"I'd run the wagon over him," Jimmy said. "Only he's too big."

He looked around and walked to the ditchway, and came back with a long finger-thick pine branch. He jabbed it into the turtle's face and the snakehead lashed out and struck like springsteel and the branch snapped like a stick of macaroni, and it all happened fast as a matchflare.

"Looka that!" Tony whistled.

"You bet, Pa. I bet he goes sixty pounds. Seventy maybe."

The turtle was darting its head around now in long stretching movements.

"I think he got some branch stuck in his craw," Jimmy said. He got out a cigaret and lighted it, and flipped the match at the rock-green shell.

"I wish now I'd brought the twenty-two," he said. "The pistol."

"You going to kill him?"

"Why not?" Jimmy asked. "They kill trout, don't they?"

They stood there smoking and not talking, and looking down at the unmoving shell.

"I could use the lug wrench on him," Jimmy said. "Only I don't think it's long enough. I don't want my hands near him."

Tony didn't say anything.

"You watch him," Jimmy said. "I'll go find something in the wagon."

Slowly Tony squatted down onto his haunches and smoked and stared at the turtle. Poor Old One, he thought. You had the misfortune to be caught in the middle of a sandroad, and you are very vulnerable on the sandroads, and now you are going to get the holy life beaten out of you.

The turtle stopped its stretching movements and was still. Tony looked at the full webbed feet and the nail claws and he knew the truth.

"It would be different in the water, turtle," he said. "In the water you could cut down anybody."

He thought about this snapper in the water and how it would move like a torpedo and bring down trout, and nobody would monkey with it in the water—and here it was in the middle of a sandroad, vulnerable as a baby and waiting to get its brains beaten out.

He finished his cigaret and field-stripped[2] it, and got to his feet and walked to the wagon and reached into the glove compartment for

---

1. **German Browns,** trout having yellow-brown sides with reddish spots.
2. **field-stripped,** peeled off the remaining cigaret paper and scattered the tobacco.

the thermos of coffee. What was he getting all worked up about a turtle for? He was an old man and he was acting like a kid, and they were going up to the White for German Browns, and he was getting worked up about a turtle in the middle of a sandroad. He walked back to the turtle and hunched down and sipped at the strong black coffee and watched the old snapper watching him.

Jimmy came up to him holding the bumper jack.

"I want to play it safe," he said. "I don't think the lug wrench is long enough." He squatted beside Tony. "What do you think?"

"He waits," Tony said. "What difference what I think?"

Jimmy squinted at him.

"I can tell something's eating you. What are you thinking, Pa?"

"I am thinking this is not a brave thing."

"What?"

"This turtle—he does not have a chance."

Jimmy lit a cigaret and hefted the bumper jack. The turtle moved ever so slightly.

"You talk like an old woman. An old tired woman."

"I can understand this turtle's position."

"He doesn't have a chance?"

"That's right."

"And that bothers you?"

Tony looked into Jimmy's face.

"That is right," he said. "That bothers me."

"Well of all the dumb stupid things," Jimmy said. "What do you want me to do? Get down on all fours and fight with him?"

"No," Tony said. "Not on all fours. Not on all fours." He looked at Jimmy. "In the water. Fight this turtle in the water. That would be a brave thing, my son."

Jimmy put down the bumper jack and reached for the thermos jug and didn't say anything. He drank his coffee and smoked his cigaret, and he stared at the turtle and didn't say anything.

"You're crazy," he said finally.

"It is a thought, my son. A thought. This helpless plodding old one like a little baby in this sandroad, eh? But in the water, his home . . ." Tony snapped his fingers with the suddenness of a switch blade. "In the water he could cut down anyone, anything . . . any man. Fight him in the water, Jimmy. Use your bumper jack in the water . . ."

"I think you're nuts," Jimmy said. "I think you're honest to goodness nuts."

Tony shrugged. "This does not seem fair for you, eh? To be in the water with this one." He motioned at the turtle. "This seems nuts to you. Crazy to you. Because in the water he could cripple you. Drown you. Because in the water you are not a match."

"What are you trying to prove, Pa?"

"Jimmy. This turtle is putting up his life. In the road here you are putting up nothing. You have nothing to lose at all. Not a finger or a hand or your life. Nothing. You smash him with a long steel bumper jack and he cannot get to you. He has as much chance as a ripe watermelon."

"So?"

"So I want you to put up something also. You should have something to lose or it is no match."

Jimmy looked at the old man and then at the turtle.

"Any fool can smash a watermelon," Tony said. "It does not take a brave man."

"Pa. It's only a turtle. You're making a federal case."

Old Tony looked at his son. "All right," he said. "Finish your coffee now and do what you are going to do. I say nothing more. Only for the next five minutes put yourself into this turtle's place. Put yourself into his shell and watch through his eyes. And try to think what he is thinking when he sees a coward coming to kill him with a long steel bumper jack."

Jimmy got to his feet and ground out his cigaret.

"All right, Pa," he said. "All right. You win."

Tony rose slowly from his crouch.

"No," he said. "Not me. You. You win."

"But Pa, they do kill trout."

"So," Tony said. "They kill trout. Nature put

them here, and they kill trout. To survive. The trout are not extinct, eh? We kill trout also, we men. To survive? No, for sport. This old one, he takes what he needs. I do not kill him for being in nature's plan. I do not play God."

Jimmy walked to the rear of the wagon then and flung down the bumper jack and closed up the door and came back.

"Pa," he said. "Honest to goodness you got the nuttiest ideas I ever heard."

Old Tony walked around behind the snapper and gently prodded it with his boot toe, and the turtle went waddling forward across the road and toppled over the sand shoulder and disappeared in the brushy growth of the creek bank. Tony and his son climbed into the wagon and sat looking at each other. The sun was coming up strong now and the sky was cracking open like a shell and spilling reds and golds and blues, and Jimmy started the engine.

Tony put the thermos away and got out his cigarets and stuck one in his son's mouth.

"So?" he said.

They sat smoking for a full minute watching each other, and then Jimmy released the emergency and they rolled slowly along the drying sandroad and down past the huge cleansing dawn coming, and the pine forests growing tall in the rising mists, and the quickly quiet waters of the eternal creek.

II

IMPLICATIONS

Discuss the following statements.

1. The old feel sympathy for the old; the young feel impatience.

2. Man has no right to play God.

3. Wisdom comes with age.

III

TECHNIQUES

Beginnings

Although "The Turtle" is short, it tells a story clearly and forcefully. The author uses only one long sentence to let the reader know what the situation is before he introduces conversation. Careful consideration of this beginning conversation shows that it served a definite purpose.

1. What does the reader learn from Jimmy's first speech?

2. Describe the incident near the beginning of the story that shows that the turtle could be a dangerous fighter.

Endings

"The Turtle" is an excellent illustration of the second type of ending described in Techniques, page 652.

1. Where does the climax occur and the suspense lessen?

2. What does the reader learn about Tony and the relationship between him and his son in the last paragraphs of the story after the climax has occurred?

I

A DEBATED DECISION

Tony felt compassion for the old turtle. He thought his son should fight him fairly.

1. Why does Jimmy feel that he should kill the turtle?

2. What ways to kill the old snapper does Jimmy consider?

3. How does the father suggest that his son should fight the turtle? Why?

> The boy found himself in blackness
> that could "terrify a flame"
> and "drench a mind with madness."
> Yet once he had made the decision,
> there was no turning back.

An Underground Episode

EDMUND WARE

Three figures leaned against the slanting rain—Alamo Laska, Nick Christopher, and the boy who had run away from home. They rested on their long-handled shovels, and, as they gazed into the crater which by their brawn they had hollowed in the earth, the blue clay oozed back again, slowly devouring the fruits of their toil.

Laska, the nomad, thought of the wild geese winging southward to warm bayous. Nick's heart, under the bone and muscle of his great chest, swelled with sweet thoughts of his wife and child who lived in a foreign city across an ocean. The boy felt the sting of rain against his cheeks and dreamed of his mother, who seemed lovely and far away.

It was Sunday. The regular deep-trench gang lounged in their warm boardinghouse, while out on the job the three men toiled alone. They breathed heavily, and the gray steam crawled upon their backs, for it was cold.

"Look at 'er filling in," growled Laska, "faster than a man could dig."

"Mud's get inna pipe," said Nick. "The inspector make us tear him out if she fill any more."

Backed close to the edge of the crater stood a giant trench-digging machine. In the dusk it appeared as a crouched and shadowy animal—silent, gloomy, capable. But a broken piston had crippled its engines and they were swathed in tarpaulin.

A long gray mound stretched away from the crater opposite the machine. Buried thirty feet below the mound was the new-laid sewer pipe. From the bottom of the pit at the machine, the pipe ran a hundred yards horizontally under the surface, opening in a manhole. This hundred yards of new-laid pipe was the reason for the three men digging in the rain. They had dug eleven hours trying to uncover the open end of the pipe in order to seal it against the mud. But rain and ooze and storm had bested them. The bank had caved, and the mud had crawled into the mouth of the pipe, obstructing it.

"It's getting dark fast," said Laska, "an' we're licked."

"We can't do nothing more," said the boy.

Nick Christopher scraped the mud from his shovel. He looked up into the whirlpools of the sky. "In a year I go old country. I see my wife. I see my kid."

"Nick," said Laska, "go over to the shanty and get a couple of lanterns and telephone Stender. Tell him if he don't want the inspector on our tail to get out here quick with a gang."

Nick stuck his shovel in the mud and moved away across the plain toward the shanty.

The cold had crept into the boy. It frightened him, and in the darkness his eyes sought Laska's face. "How could we clean out the pipe, even when the gang got down to it?"

"Maybe we could flush her out with a fire hose," said Laska.

"There's no water plug within a mile."

Laska said nothing. The boy waited for him to reply, but he didn't. Picking up his damp shirt, the boy pulled it on over his head. He did not tuck in the tails, and they flapped in the wind, slapping against him. He looked like a gaunt, serious bird, striving to leave the ground. He was bare-headed, and his yellow hair was matted and stringy with dampness. His face was thin, a little sunken, and fine drops of moisture clung to the fuzz on his cheeks. His lips were blue with cold. He was seventeen.

Laska stared into the pit. It was too dark to see bottom, but something in the black hole fascinated him. "If we could get a rope through the pipe, we could drag sandbags through into the manhole. That would clean her out in good shape."

"How could we get a rope through?"

"I dunno. Stender'll know." Laska walked over to the digging machine and leaned against its towering side. The rain had turned to sleet. "It's cold," he said.

The boy followed Laska and went close to him for warmth and friendship. "How could we get a rope through?"

Laska's shoulders lifted slowly. "You'll see. You'll see when Stender gets here. Say, it's freezing."

After a long time of waiting, a yellow light flamed into being in the shanty, and they heard the muffled scraping of boots on the board floor. The shanty door opened. A rectangle of light stood out sharply.

Swart figures crossed and recrossed the lighted area, pouring out into the storm.

"Ho!" called Laska.

"Ho!" came the answer, galloping to them in the wind.

They heard the rasping of caked mud on dungarees, the clank of shovels, the voice of Stender, the foreman. Lanterns swung like yellow pendulums. Long-legged shadows reached and receded.

The diggers gathered about the rim of the pit, staring. Stender's face showed in the lantern light. His lips were wrinkled, as if constantly prepared for blasphemy. He was a tall, cursing conqueror. Orders shot from his throat, and noisily the men descended into the pit and began to dig. They drew huge, gasping breaths like mired beasts fighting for life.

The boy watched, his eyes bulging in the dark. Hitherto he had thought very briefly of sewers, regarding them as unlovely things. But Laska and Nick and Stender gave them splendor and importance. The deep-trench men were admirable monsters. They knew the clay, the feel and pattern of it, for it had long been heavy in their minds and muscles. They were big in three dimensions, and their eyes were black and barbarous. When they ate, it was with rough-and-tumble relish, and as their bellies fattened, they spoke tolerantly of enemies. They played hard and they worked hard. They were diggers in clay, transformed by lantern light into a race of giants.

Through the rain came Stender, his black slicker crackling. "They're down," he said. "Angelo just struck the pipe."

Laska grunted.

Stender blew his nose with his fingers, walked away, and climbed down into the hole. They lost sight of him as he dropped over the rim. The sound of digging had ceased, and two or three men on the surface rested on their shovels, the light from below gleaming in their flat faces. Laska and the boy knew that Stender was examining the pipe. They heard him swearing at what he had found.

After a moment he clambered up over the rim and held up a lantern. His cuddy, gripped firmly between his teeth, was upside down to keep out the wet.

"Someone's got to go through the pipe," he said, raising his voice. "There's fifty bucks for the man that'll go through the pipe into the manhole with a line tied to his foot. Fifty bucks!"

There was a moment of quiet. The men thought of the fifty dollars and furtively measured themselves against the deed at hand. It seemed to the boy that he was the only one who feared the task. He did not think of the fifty dollars, but thought only of the fear. Three hundred feet through a rathole, eighteen inches in diameter. Three hundred feet of muck, of wet black dark, and no turning back. But, if he did not volunteer, they would know that he was afraid. The boy stepped from behind Laska and said uncertainly: "I'll go, Stender," and he wished he might snatch back the words; for, looking about him, he saw that not a man among those present could have wedged his shoulders into the mouth of an eighteen-inch pipe. He was the only volunteer. They had known he would be the only one.

Stender came striding over holding the lantern above his head. He peered into the boy's face. "Take off your clothes," he said.

"Take off my clothes?"

"That's what I said."

"You might get a buckle caught in a joint," said Laska. "See?"

The boy saw only that he had been trapped very cunningly. At home he could have been openly fearful, for at home everything about him was known. There, quite simply, he could have said: "I won't do it. I'm frightened. I'll be killed." But here the diggers in clay were lancing him with looks. And Laska was bringing a ball of line, one end of which would be fastened to his ankle.

"Just go in a sweater," said Laska. "A sweater an' boots over your woolens. We'll be waiting for you at the manhole."

He wanted so desperately to dive off into the night that he felt his legs bracing for a spring, and a tight feeling in his throat. Then, mechanically, he began to take off his clothes. Nick had gone clumping off to the shanty and shortly returned with a pair of hip boots. "Here, kid. I get 'em warm for you inna shanty."

He thrust his feet into the boots, and Laska knelt and tied the heavy line to his ankle. "Too tight?"

"No. It's all right, I guess."

"Well—come on."

They walked past Stender, who was pacing up and down among the men. They slid down into the crater, deepened now by the diggers. They stood by the partly covered mouth of the pipe. They were thirty feet below the surface of the ground.

Laska reached down and tugged at the knot he had tied in the line, then he peered into the mouth of the tube. He peered cautiously, as if he thought it might be inhabited. The boy's glance wandered up the wet sides of the pit.

Over the rim a circle of bland yellow faces peered at him. Sleet tinkled against lanterns, spattered down and stung his flesh.

"Go ahead in," said Laska.

The boy blanched.

"Just keep thinking of the manhole, where you'll come out," said Laska.

The boy's throat constricted. He seemed to be bursting with a pressure from inside. He got down on his belly in the slush-ice and mud. It penetrated slowly to his skin and spread over him. He put his head inside the mouth of the pipe, drew back in horror. Some gibbering words flew from his lips. His voice sounded preposterously loud. Laska's voice was already shopworn with distance. "You can make it! Go ahead."

He lay on his left side and, reaching out with his left arm, caught a joint and drew himself in. The mud oozed up around him, finding its way upon him, welling up against the left side of his face. He pressed his right cheek against the ceiling of the pipe to keep the muck from covering his mouth and nose. Laska's voice was far and muffled. Laska was in another world—a sane world of night, of storm, and the mellow glow of lanterns.

"Are you makin' it all right, kid?"

The boy cried out, his ears ringing with his cry. It re-echoed from the sides of the pipe. The sides hemmed him, pinned him, closed him in on every side with their paralyzing circumference.

There is no darkness like the darkness underground that miners know. It borrows something from night, from tombs, from places used by bats. Such fluid black can terrify a flame, and suffocate, and drench a mind with madness. There is a fierce desire to struggle, to beat one's hands against the prison. The boy longed to lift his pitiful human strength against the walls. He longed to claw at his eyes in the mad certainty that more than darkness curtained them.

He had moved but a few feet on his journey when panic swept him. Ahead of him the mud had built into a solid wave. Putting forth his left hand, he felt a scant two inches between the wave's crest and the ceiling of the pipe. There was nothing to do but go back. If he moved ahead, it meant death by suffocation. He tried to back away, but caught his toe in a joint of the pipe. He was entombed! In an hour he would be a body. The cold and dampness would kill him before they could dig down to him. Nick and Laska would pull him from the muck, and Laska would say: "Huh, his clock's stopped."

He thrashed with delirious strength against his prison. He felt the skin tearing away from the backs of his hands as he flailed the rough walls. And some gods must have snickered, for above the walls of the pipe were thirty feet of unyielding clay, eight thousand miles of earth below. A strength, a weight, a night, each a thousand times his most revolting dream, leaned upon the boy, depressing, crushing, stamping him out. The ground gave no cry of battle. It did no bleeding, suffered no pain, uttered no groans. It flattened him silently. It swallowed him in its foul tyranny. It dropped its merciless weight upon his mind. It was so inhuman, so horribly incognizant[1] of the God men swore had made it.

In the midst of his frenzy, when he had beaten his face against the walls until it bled, he heard a ringing voice he knew was real, springing from human sympathy. It was Laska, calling: "Are you all right, kid?"

In that instant the boy loved Laska as he loved his life. Laska's voice sheered the weight from him, scattered the darkness, brought him new balance and a hope to live.

"Fine!" he answered in a crackling yell. He yelled again, loving the sound of his voice, and thinking how foolish yelling was in such a place.

With his left hand he groped ahead and found that the wave of mud had settled, leveled off by its own weight. He drew his body together, pressing it against the pipe. He straightened, moved ahead six inches. His fingers found a loop of oakum[2] dangling from a joint, and he pulled himself on, his left arm forward,

his right arm behind over his hip, like a swimmer's.

He had vanquished panic, and he looked ahead to victory. Each joint brought him twenty inches nearer his goal. Each twenty inches was a plateau which enabled him to vision a new plateau—the next joint. The joints were like small deceitful rests upon a march.

He had been more than an hour on the way. He did not know how far he had gone, a third, perhaps even a half of the distance. He forgot the present, forgot fear, wet cold, blackness; he lost himself in dreaming of the world of men outside the prison. It was as if he were a small superb island in hell.

He did not know how long he had been counting the joints, but he found himself whispering good numbers: "Fifty-one, fifty-two, fifty-three . . ." Each joint, when he thought of it, appeared to take up a vast time of squirming in the muck, and the line dragged heavily behind his foot.

Suddenly, staring into the darkness so that it seemed to bring a pain to his eyes, he saw a pallid ray. He closed his eyes, opened them, and looked again. The ray was real, and he uttered a whimper of relief. He knew that the ray must come from Stender's lantern. He pictured Stender and a group of the diggers huddled in the manhole, waiting for him. The men and the manhole grew magnificent in his mind, and he thought of them worshipfully.

"Seventy-six, seventy-seven, seventy-eight—"

The ray grew slowly, like a worthwhile thing. It took an oval shape, and the oval grew fat, like an egg, then round. It was a straight line to the manhole, and the mud had thinned.

Through the pipe, into the boy's ears, a voice rumbled like half-hearted thunder. It was Stender's voice: "How you makin' it?"

"Oh, just fine!" His cry came pricking back into his ears like a shower of needles.

---

1. **incognizant**\ĭn ᴀkŏg·nĭ·zənt\ not knowing or recognizing.
2. **oakum**\ᴀō·kəm\ untwisted rope fibers used for packing and caulking.

There followed a long span of numbness. The cold and wet had dulled his senses, so that whenever the rough ceiling of the pipe ripped his face, he did not feel it; so that struggling in the muck became an almost pleasant and normal thing, since all elements of fear and pain and imagination had been removed. Warmth and dryness became alien to him. He was a creature native to darkness, foreign to light.

The round yellow disk before him gave him his only sense of living. It was a sunlit landfall, luring him on. He would close his eyes and count five joints, then open them quickly, cheering himself at the perceptible stages of progress.

Then, abruptly, it seemed, he was close to the manhole. He could hear men moving. He could see the outline of Stender's head as Stender peered into the mouth of the pipe. Men kneeled, pushing each other's heads to one side, in order to watch him squirm toward them. They began to talk excitedly. He could hear them breathing, see details—and Stender and Laska reached in. They got their hands upon him. They hauled him to them, as if he were something they wanted to inspect scientifically. He felt as if they thought he was a rarity, a thing of great oddness. The light dazzled him. It began to move around and around and to dissolve into many lights, some of which danced locally on a bottle. He heard Stender's voice: "Well, he made it all right. What do you know?"

"Here, kid," said Laska, holding the bottle to his mouth. "Drink all of this that you can hold."

He could not stand up. He believed calmly that his flesh and bones were constructed of putty. He could hear no vestige of the song of victory he had dreamed of hearing. He looked stupidly at his hands, which bled painlessly. He could not feel his arms and legs at all. He was a vast sensation of lantern light and the steam of human beings breathing in a damp place.

Faces peered at him. The faces were curious and surprised. He felt a clouded, uncomprehending resentment against them. Stender held him up on one side, Laska on the other. They looked at each other across him. Suddenly Laska stooped and gathered him effortlessly into his arms.

"You'll get covered with mud," mumbled the boy.

"Darned if he didn't make it all right," said Stender. "Save us tearing out the pipe."

"Heck with the pipe," said Laska.

The boy's wet head fell against Laska's chest. He felt the rise and fall of Laska's muscles and knew that Laska was climbing with him up the iron steps inside the manhole. Night wind smote him. He buried his head deeper against Laska. Laska's body became a mountain of warmth. He felt a heavy sighing peace, like a soldier who has been comfortably wounded and knows that war for him is over.

I

NO OTHER WAY

As soon as he had uttered the words, "I'll go, Stender," the boy wished he might snatch them back. He had felt compelled to volunteer so that he wouldn't be thought a coward. His was a choice made because he felt it was the only thing he could do.

The author, Edmund Ware, himself, was this boy who made the terrifying choice. Pulling, pushing, and squirming, he fought his way through the mud-filled sewer pipe on Thanksgiving Day, 1921.

Because we usually write best about what we know best, the author was able to describe this underground episode with such clarity that the reader seems to be going into the pipe with him. One almost *feels* the trapped boy's terror as he presses his cheek against the ceiling of the pipe to keep the muck from covering his mouth and nose.

Consider and discuss the following details:

1. The situation which led to the foreman's call for a man to crawl through the pipe

2. The boy's attitude toward sewers

3. The way the boy is dressed for his ordeal

4. The danger involved in going through the pipe

5. The psychological effect on the boy of Laska's voice as he shouted, "Are you all right, kid?"

6. The boy's feelings when he first sees the ray of light from the lantern and again when he reaches the manhole and safety

II
IMPLICATIONS

Consider these statements.

1. The type of man found directing most heavy construction jobs is not as concerned with the value of human life as with saving time and work in fulfilling a contract.

2. The difference between success and failure is made up of a word of encouragement.

III
TECHNIQUES

Beginning

What information does the author give you in his first two sentences? Who is named first among the characters? Can you think of a reason why Edmund Ware listed him first? Why do you suppose he identified the boy as having run away from home? How does he get the story moving within the first paragraph?

Atmosphere

This story has its special impact or effect because the author has successfully saturated it in an atmosphere of cheerless gloom. You are continually conscious of the slimy mud, the dreary rain, and the damp chill.

The paragraphs which describe the boy's entry into and passage through the pipe effectively deepen the oppressive atmosphere. Discuss two descriptive passages from this section of the story which are particularly expressive.

IV
WORDS

A. Use context clues to try to determine the meanings of the underlined words in the following sentences:

1. "His lips were wrinkled as if constantly prepared for blasphemy."

2. "The boy saw only that he had been trapped very cunningly."

3. "Some gibbering words flew from his lips."

4. "He thrashed with delirious strength against his prison."

5. "He could hear no vestige of the song of victory he had dreamed of hearing."

6. "He would close his eyes and count five joints, then open them quickly, cheering himself at the perceptible stages of progress."

7. "He felt a clouded, uncomprehending resentment against them."

B. Read the following sentence from "An Underground Episode," paying special attention to the word *incognizant:* "It was so inhuman, so horribly incognizant of the God men swore had made it." *Incognizant* is a good example of how a prefix, a base form, and a suffix come together to form a word. The prefix *in-* means "not." It becomes *il-* before *l* (*illegal*), *im-* before *p, m,* and *b* (*impossible, immobile,* and *imbalance*), and *ir-* before *r* (*irregular*). This prefix, which has a negative meaning, must be distinguished from the prefix *in-* that means "in" or "into" (*input*). The base form of *incognizant* comes from the Latin word *cognoscere,* meaning "to know." Derived from the same source is the familiar word *recognize,* which means, of course, "to know someone on sight." *Ant-* is an adjective suffix having the general sense of doing or being something, as in *relevant, pleasant,* and *ascendant.* A noun suffix with the identical spelling is *ant-,* as in *servant, tenant,* and *contestant.* With all three parts together, *incognizant* means "not being aware of or knowing something." See whether you can figure out the meaning of each of the following words: *insurmountable, cognition, irresponsible, incognito savant, registrant,* and *irreverent.*

A Fantasy

This one-act play, "The Devil and Daniel Webster," is called a *fantasy* because it does not try to stay within the limits of reality. A fantasy may draw from the world of make-believe for characters, setting, or plot; but usually there is enough reality mixed with the unreal to make it interesting.

While "The Devil and Daniel Webster" is printed here in one-act play form, Stephen Vincent Benét first wrote it as a short story, published in the *Saturday Evening Post*. It was so enthusiastically received that Benét soon followed the story with movie and radio versions, and this one-act stage play. More recently it has been made into a television drama, all of which shows that this tale has found a permanent place in American folk legends.

The play opens with the wedding celebration of Mary and Jabez Stone and centers attention on the steadfast love they have for one another, but it is quite evident that the strongest character in the play is Daniel Webster. A skilled statesman and outstanding orator who lived from 1782 to 1852, Webster could be called an American folk hero. A staunch believer in the ideals of freedom and democracy, he was a passionate defender of the Union. Whenever needed, he stood ready to come to the aid of a neighbor, and was a man who would fight for what he thought was right.

Because Webster was so admired, many tales of his powers and exploits came to be told. There were people who believed that he was downright superhuman. Benét's short-story version, patterned after the traditional folk tale, begins with a lengthy recitation of Webster's legendary powers and exploits. Webster was a man "with a mouth like a mastiff, a brow like a mountain, and eyes like burning anthracite." Thousands trusted Webster " . . . right next to

The Devil and Daniel Webster.

God Almighty . . . and when he stood up to speak, stars and stripes came right out of the sky. . . ." He once spoke against a river and made it disappear; he could make trout jump right out of the water into his pockets because they knew there was no use in putting up a fight against him; and the chickens he raised on his big farm called Marshfield were all white meat. These are only a few of the marvelous things told about Webster in the story.

In the play, long, descriptive passages are not practicable, and conveying Webster's awesome reputation presents more of a problem. While reading, be alert to see how Benét manages to give you some concept of Webster's stature as an American.

◆ When Jabez Stone said out loud
　　　that he'd sell his soul,
　　Mr. Scratch didn't waste much time
in coming 'round to make a deal. Perhaps Jabez
　　might have changed his mind, but a New
　　Hampshire man never goes back on his word.
　　　Is Stephen Vincent Benét's purpose
　　　in this play simply to entertain,
　　or does he wish to present serious ideas
　　in a dramatic and arresting way?
See what conclusion you have drawn about this
　　by the time you've finished reading
about Dan'l Webster's memorable contest
with the devil over the soul of Jabez Stone.
This was a tussle which ended in a decision.

The Devil
and Daniel Webster

STEPHEN VINCENT BENÉT

Characters

JABEZ STONE

MARY STONE

DANIEL WEBSTER

MR. SCRATCH

THE FIDDLER

JUSTICE HATHORNE

JUSTICE HATHORNE'S CLERK

KING PHILIP

TEACH

WALTER BUTLER

SIMON GIRTY

DALE

Men and Women of Cross Corners,
　　New Hampshire

Scene: JABEZ STONE's *farmhouse*
Time: 1841

The setting is the main room of a New Hampshire farmhouse in 1841, a big comfortable room that hasn't yet developed the stuffiness of a front parlor. A door, right, leads to the kitchen—a door, left, to the outside. There is a fireplace, right. Windows, in center, show a glimpse of summer landscape. Most of the furniture has been cleared away for the dance which follows the wedding of JABEZ[1] *and* MARY STONE, *but there is a settle or bench by the fireplace, a table, left, with some wedding presents upon it, at least three chairs by the table, and a cider barrel on which the* FIDDLER *sits, in front of the table. Near the table, against the side wall, there is a cupboard where there are glasses and a jug. There is a clock. (See Note A for production hints.) A country wedding has been in progress—the wedding of* JABEZ *and* MARY STONE. *He is a husky young farmer, around twenty-eight or thirty. The bride is in her early twenties. He is dressed in stiff store clothes, but not ridiculously—they are of good quality and he looks important. The bride is in a simple white or cream wedding dress and may carry a small, stiff bouquet of country flowers.*

Now the wedding is over and the guests are dancing. The FIDDLER *is perched on the cider barrel. He plays and calls square-dance figures. The guests include the recognizable types of a small New England town: doctor, lawyer, storekeeper, old maid, schoolteacher, farmer, etc. There is an air of prosperity and hearty country mirth about the whole affair.*

At rise, JABEZ *and* MARY *are up left center, receiving the congratulations of a few last guests, who talk to them and pass on to the dance. The others are dancing. There is a buzz of conversation that follows the tune of the dance music.*

---

1. **Jabez** \ˈjā·bĕz\.

FIRST WOMAN. Right nice wedding.

FIRST MAN. Handsome couple.

SECOND WOMAN. [*Passing through crowd with dish of oyster stew.*] Oysters for supper!

SECOND MAN. [*Passing cake.*] And layer cake— layer cake—

AN OLD MAN. [*Hobbling toward cider barrel.*] Makes me feel young again! Oh, by jingo!

AN OLD WOMAN. [*Pursuing him.*] Henry, Henry, you've been drinking cider!

FIDDLER. Set to your partners! Dosy-do!²

WOMEN. Mary and Jabez.

MEN. Jabez and Mary.

A WOMAN. Where's the State Senator?

A MAN. Where's the lucky bride?

[*With cries of "Mary—Jabez—strike it up, fiddler—make room for the bride and groom," the crowd drags* MARY *and* JABEZ, *pleased but embarrassed, into the center of the room and* MARY *and* JABEZ *do a little solo dance, while the crowd claps, applauds and makes various remarks.*]

A MAN. Handsome steppers!

A WOMAN. She's pretty as a picture.

A SECOND MAN. Cut your pigeon-wing, Jabez!

THE OLD MAN. Young again, young again, that's the way I feel! [*He tries to cut a pigeon-wing himself.*]

THE OLD WOMAN. Henry, Henry, careful of your rheumatiz!

A THIRD WOMAN. Makes me feel all teary—seeing them so happy.

[*The solo dance ends, the music stops for a moment.*]

THE OLD MAN. [*Gossiping to a neighbor.*] Wonder where he got it all—Stones was always poor.

HIS NEIGHBOR. Ain't poor now—makes you wonder just a mite.

A THIRD MAN. Don't begrudge it to him—but I wonder where he got it.

THE OLD MAN. [*Starting to whisper.*] Let me tell you something—

THE OLD WOMAN. [*Quickly.*] Henry, Henry, don't you start to gossip. [*She drags him away.*]

FIDDLER. [*Cutting in.*] Set to your partners! Scratch for corn!

[*The dance resumes, but as it does so, the crowd chants back and forth.*]

WOMEN. Gossip's got a sharp tooth.

MEN. Gossip's got a mean tooth.

WOMEN. She's a lucky woman. They're a lucky pair.

MEN. That's true as gospel. But I wonder where he got it.

WOMEN. Money, land and riches.

MEN. Just came out of nowhere.

WOMEN AND MEN. [*Together.*] Wonder where he got it all.—But that's his business.

FIDDLER. Left and right—grand chain!

[*The dance rises to a pitch of ecstasy with the final figure—the fiddle squeaks and stops. The dancers mop their brows.*]

FIRST MAN. Whew! Ain't danced like that since I was knee-high to a grasshopper!

SECOND MAN. Play us "The Portland Fancy," fiddler!

THIRD MAN. No, wait a minute, neighbor. Let's hear from the happy pair! Hey, Jabez!

FOURTH MAN. Let's hear from the State Senator!

[*They crowd around* JABEZ *and push him up on the settle.*]

OLD MAN. Might as well. It's the last time he'll have the last word!

OLD WOMAN. Now, Henry Banks, you ought to be ashamed of yourself!

OLD MAN. Told you so, Jabez!

THE CROWD. Speech!

JABEZ. [*Embarrassed.*] Neighbors—friends— I'm not much of a speaker—spite of your 'lecting me to State Senate—

THE CROWD. That's the ticket, Jabez. Smart man, Jabez. I voted for ye. Go ahead, Senator, you're doing fine.

JABEZ. But we're certainly glad to have you here—me and Mary. And we want to thank you for coming and—

---

2. **dosy-do**\ˈdō·sē ˈdō\ back to back. This and "cut your pigeon-wing" are directions for square-dance steps.

A VOICE. Vote the Whig ticket!³

ANOTHER VOICE. Hooray for Daniel Webster!

JABEZ. And I'm glad Hi Foster said that, for those are my sentiments, too. Mr. Webster has promised to honor us with his presence here tonight.

THE CROWD. Hurray for Dan'l! Hurray for the greatest man in the U.S.!

JABEZ. And when he comes, I know we'll give him a real New Hampshire welcome.

THE CROWD. Sure we will—Webster forever—and down with Henry Clay!⁴

JABEZ. And meanwhile—well, there's Mary and me [*Takes her hand.*]—and, if you folks don't have a good time, well, we won't feel right about getting married at all. Because I know I've been lucky—and I hope she feels that way, too. And, well, we're going to be happy or bust a trace!⁵ [*He wipes his brow to terrific applause. He and* MARY *look at each other.*]

A WOMAN. [*In kitchen doorway.*] Come and get the cider, folks!

[*The crowd begins to drift away—a few to the kitchen—a few toward the door that leads to the outside. They furnish a shifting background to the next little scene, where* MARY *and* JABEZ *are left alone by the fireplace.*]

JABEZ. Mary.

MARY. Mr. Stone.

JABEZ. Mary.

MARY. My husband.

JABEZ. That's a big word, husband.

MARY. It's a good word.

JABEZ. Are you happy, Mary?

MARY. Yes. So happy, I'm afraid.

JABEZ. Afraid?

MARY. I suppose it happens to every girl—just for a minute. It's like spring turning into summer. You want it to be summer. But the spring was sweet. [*Dismissing the mood.*] I'm sorry. Forgive me. It just came and went, like something cold. As if we'd been too lucky.

JABEZ. We can't be too lucky, Mary. Not you and me.

MARY. [*Rather mischievously.*] If you say so, Mr. Stone. But you don't even know what sort of housekeeper I am. And Aunt Hepsy says—

JABEZ. Bother your Aunt Hepsy! There's just you and me and that's all that matters in the world.

MARY. And you don't know something else—

JABEZ. What's that?

MARY. How proud I am of you. Ever since I was a little girl. Ever since you carried my books. Oh, I'm sorry for women who can't be proud of their men. It must be a lonely feeling.

JABEZ. [*Uncomfortably.*] A man can't always be proud of everything, Mary. There's some things a man does, or might do—when he has to make his way.

MARY. [*Laughing.*] I know—terrible things—like being the best farmer in the county and the best State Senator—

JABEZ. [*Quietly.*] And a few things, besides. But you remember one thing, Mary, whatever happens. It was all for you. And nothing's going to happen. Because he hasn't come yet—and he would have come if it was wrong.

MARY. But it's wonderful to have Mr. Webster come to us.

JABEZ. I wasn't thinking about Mr. Webster. [*He takes both her hands.*] Mary, I've got something to tell you. I should have told you before, but I couldn't seem to bear it. Only, now that it's all right, I can. Ten years ago—

A VOICE. [*From off stage.*] Dan'l! Dan'l Webster!

[JABEZ *drops* MARY's *hands and looks around. The crowd begins to mill and gather toward the door. Others rush in from the kitchen.*]

---

3. **The Whig party** was the American political party opposing the Democrats about 1834. It was the one to which Webster belonged.
4. **Senator Henry Clay** (1777–1852) was a frequent opponent of Daniel Webster in the United States Senate.
5. **bust a trace,** break a piece of harness.

Daniel Webster arrives. Scene from a production at Old Sturbridge Village.

ANOTHER VOICE. Black Dan'l! He's come!

ANOTHER VOICE. Three cheers for the greatest man in the U.S.!

ANOTHER VOICE. Three cheers for Daniel Webster!

[*And, to the cheering and applause of the crowd,* DANIEL WEBSTER *enters and stands for a moment upstage, in the familiar pose, his head thrown back, his attitude leonine. He stops the cheering of the crowd with a gesture.*]

WEBSTER. Neighbors—old friends—it does me good to hear you. But don't cheer me—I'm not running for President this summer. [*A laugh from the crowd.*] I'm here on a better errand—to pay my humble respects to a most charming lady and her very fortunate spouse.

[*There is the twang of a fiddle-string breaking.*]

FIDDLER. 'Tarnation! Busted a string!

A VOICE. He's always bustin' strings.

[WEBSTER *blinks at the interruption but goes on.*]

WEBSTER. We're proud of State Senator Stone in these parts—we know what he's done. Ten years ago he started out with a patch of land that was mostly rocks and mortgages and now—well, you've only to look around you. I don't know that I've ever seen a likelier farm, not even at Marshfield—and I hope, before I die, I'll have the privilege of shaking his hand as Governor of this State. I don't know how he's done it—I couldn't have done it myself. But I know this—Jabez Stone wears no man's collar.[6] [*At this statement there is a discordant squeak from the fiddle and* JABEZ *looks embarrassed.* WEBSTER *knits his brows.*] And what's more, if I know Jabez, he never will. But I didn't come here to talk politics—I came to kiss the bride. [*He does so amid great applause. He shakes hands with* JABEZ.] Congratulations, Stone—you're a lucky man. And now, if our friend in the corner will give us a tune on his fiddle—

[*The crowd presses forward to meet the great man. He shakes hands with several.*]

A MAN. Remember me, Mr. Webster? Saw ye up at the State House at Concord.

ANOTHER MAN. Glad to see ye, Mr. Webster. I voted for ye ten times.

[WEBSTER *receives their homage politely, but his mind is still on music.*]

WEBSTER. [*A trifle irritated.*] I said, if our friend in the corner would give us a tune on his fiddle—

FIDDLER. [*Passionately, flinging the fiddle down.*] Excuse me, Mr. Webster. But the very devil's got into that fiddle of mine. She was doing all right up to just a minute ago. But now I've tuned her and tuned her and she won't play a note I want.

[*And, at this point,* MR. SCRATCH *makes his appearance. He has entered, unobserved, and mixed with the crowd while all eyes were upon* DANIEL WEBSTER. *He is, of course, the devil—a New England devil, dressed like a rather shabby attorney but with something just a little wrong in clothes and appearance. For one thing, he wears black gloves on his hands. He carries a large black tin box, like a botanist's collecting-box, under one arm. Now he slips through the crowd and taps the fiddler on the shoulder.*]

SCRATCH. [*Insinuatingly.*] Maybe you need some rosin[7] on your bow, fiddler?

FIDDLER. Maybe I do and maybe I don't. [*Turns*

and confronts the stranger.] But who are you? I don't remember seeing you before.

SCRATCH. Oh, I'm just a friend—a humble friend of the bridegroom's. [*He walks toward* JABEZ. *Apologetically.*] I'm afraid I came in the wrong way, Mr. Stone. You've improved the place so much since I last saw it that I hardly knew the front door. But, I assure you, I came as fast as I could.

JABEZ. [*Obviously shocked.*] It—it doesn't matter. [*With a great effort.*] Mary—Mr. Webster—this is a—a friend of mine from Boston—a legal friend. I didn't expect him today but—

SCRATCH. Oh, my dear Mr. Stone—an occasion like this—I wouldn't miss it for the world. [*He bows.*] Charmed, Mrs. Stone. Delighted, Mr. Webster. But—don't let me break up the merriment of the meeting. [*He turns back toward the table and the* FIDDLER.]

FIDDLER. [*With a grudge, to* SCRATCH.] Boston lawyer, eh?

SCRATCH. You might call me that.

FIDDLER. [*Tapping the tin box with his bow.*] And what have you got in that big tin box of yours? Law-papers?

SCRATCH. Oh—curiosities for the most part. I'm a collector, too.

FIDDLER. Don't hold much with Boston curiosities, myself. And you know about fiddling too, do you? Know all about it?

SCRATCH. Oh— [*A deprecatory shrug.*]

FIDDLER. Don't shrug your shoulders at me—I ain't no Frenchman. Telling me I needed more rosin!

MARY. [*Trying to stop the quarrel.*] Isaac—please—

FIDDLER. Sorry, Mary—Mrs. Stone. But I been playing the fiddle at Cross Corners weddings for twenty-five years. And now here comes a stranger from Boston and tells me I need more rosin!

---

6. **wears no man's collar,** is independent, takes orders from no one.

7. **rosin**\rŏz·ĭn\ hard resin, an amber-colored vegetable substance used to wax violin bows.

SCRATCH. But, my good friend—

FIDDLER. Rosin indeed! Here—play it yourself then and see what you can make of it! [*He thrusts the fiddle at* SCRATCH. *The latter stiffens, slowly lays his black collecting-box on the table, and takes the fiddle.*]

SCRATCH. [*With feigned embarrassment.*] But really, I— [*He bows toward* JABEZ.] Shall I —Mr. Senator?

[JABEZ *makes a helpless gesture of assent.*]

MARY. [*To* JABEZ.] Mr. Stone—Mr. Stone—are you ill?

JABEZ. No—no—but I feel—it's hot—

WEBSTER. [*Chuckling.*] Don't you fret, Mrs. Stone. I've got the right medicine for him. [*He pulls a flask from his pocket.*] Ten-year-old Medford, Stone—I buy it by the keg down at Marshfield. Here— [*He tries to give some of the rum to* JABEZ.]

JABEZ. No—[*He turns.*]—Mary—Mr. Webster —[*But he cannot explain. With a burst.*] Oh, let him play—let him play! Don't you see he's bound to? Don't you see there's nothing we can do?

[*A rustle of discomfort among the guests.* SCRATCH *draws the bow across the fiddle in a horrible discord.*]

FIDDLER. [*Triumphantly.*] I told you so, stranger. The devil's in that fiddle!

SCRATCH. I'm afraid it needs special tuning. [*Draws the bow in a second discord.*] There —that's better. [*Grinning.*] And now for this happy—this very happy occasion—in tribute to the bride and groom—I'll play something appropriate—a song of young love—

MARY. Oh, Jabez—Mr. Webster—stop him! Do you see his hands? He's playing with gloves on his hands.

[WEBSTER *starts forward, but, even as he does so,* SCRATCH *begins to play and all freeze as* SCRATCH *goes on with the extremely inappropriate song that follows. At first his manner is oily and mocking—it is not till he reaches the line "The devil took the words away" that*

he really becomes terrifying and the crowd starts to be afraid.]

SCRATCH. [*Accompanying himself fantastically.*]

Young William was a thriving boy.
(Listen to my doleful tale.)
Young Mary Clark was all his joy.
(Listen to my doleful tale.)

He swore he'd love her all his life.
She swore she'd be his loving wife.

But William found a gambler's den
And drank with livery-stable men.

He played the cards, he played the dice.
He would not listen to advice,

And when in church he tried to pray,
The devil took the words away.

[SCRATCH, *still playing, starts to march across the stage.*]

The devil got him by the toe,
And so, alas, he had to go.

"Young Mary Clark, young Mary Clark,
I now must go into the dark."

[*These last two verses have been directed at* JABEZ. SCRATCH *continues, now turning on* MARY.]

Young Mary lay upon her bed.
"Alas my Will-i-am is dead."

He came to her a bleeding ghost—

[*He rushes at* MARY, *but* WEBSTER *stands between them.*]

WEBSTER. Stop! Stop! You miserable wretch— can't you see that you're frightening Mrs. Stone? [*He wrenches the fiddle out of* SCRATCH's *hands and tosses it aside.*] And now, sir—out of this house!

SCRATCH. [*Facing him.*] You're a bold man, Mr. Webster. Too bold for your own good, perhaps. And anyhow, it wasn't my fiddle. It belonged to— [*He wheels and sees the* FIDDLER *tampering with the collecting-box that has been left on the table.*] Idiot! What are you doing with my collecting-box? [*He*

683

rushes for the FIDDLER *and chases him round the table, but the* FIDDLER *is just one jump ahead.*]

FIDDLER. Boston lawyer, eh? Well, I don't think so. I think you've got something in that box of yours you're afraid to show. And, by jingo — [*He throws open the lid of the box. The lights wink and there is a clap of thunder. All eyes stare upward. Something has flown out of the box. But what? (See Note B for production hints.)* FIDDLER, *with relief.*] Why, 'tain't nothing but a moth.

MARY. A white moth—a flying thing.

WEBSTER. A common moth—*telea polyphemus—*[8]

THE CROWD. A moth—just a moth—a moth—

FIDDLER. [*Terrified.*] But it ain't. It ain't no common moth! I seen it! And it's got a death's-head on it! [*He strikes at the invisible object with his bow to drive it away.*]

VOICE OF THE MOTH. Help me, neighbors! Help me! *(See Note C for production hints.)*

WEBSTER. What's that? It wails like a lost soul.

MARY. A lost soul.

THE CROWD. A lost soul—lost—in darkness—in the darkness.

VOICE OF THE MOTH. Help me, neighbors!

FIDDLER. It sounds like Miser Stevens.

JABEZ. Miser Stevens!

THE CROWD. The Miser—Miser Stevens—a lost soul—lost.

FIDDLER. [*Frantically.*] It sounds like Miser Stevens—and you had him in your box. But it can't be. He ain't dead.

JABEZ. He ain't dead—I tell you he ain't dead! He was just as spry and mean as a woodchuck, Tuesday.

THE CROWD. Miser Stevens—soul of Miser Stevens—but he ain't dead.

SCRATCH. [*Dominating them.*] Listen!

[*A bell off stage begins to toll a knell, slowly, solemnly.*]

MARY. The bell—the church bell—the bell that rang at my wedding.

WEBSTER. The church bell—the passing bell.

JABEZ. The funeral bell.

THE CROWD. The bell—the passing bell—Miser Stevens—dead.

VOICE OF THE MOTH. Help me, neighbors, help me! I sold my soul to the devil. I'm not the first or the last. Help me. Help Jabez Stone!

SCRATCH. Ah, would you! [*He catches the moth in his red bandanna, stuffs it back into his collecting-box, and shuts the lid with a snap.*]

VOICE OF THE MOTH. [*Fading.*] Lost—lost forever, forever. Lost, like Jabez Stone.

[*The crowd turns on* JABEZ. *They read his secret in his face.*]

THE CROWD. Jabez Stone—Jabez Stone—answer us—answer us.

MARY. Tell them, dear—answer them—you are good—you are brave—you are innocent.

[*But the crowd is all pointing hands and horrified eyes.*]

THE CROWD. Jabez Stone—Jabez Stone. Who's your friend in black, Jabez Stone? [*They point to* SCRATCH.]

WEBSTER. Answer them, Mr. State Senator.

THE CROWD. Jabez Stone—Jabez Stone. Where did you get your money, Jabez Stone?

[SCRATCH *grins and taps his collecting-box.* JABEZ *cannot speak.*]

JABEZ. I—I— [*He stops.*]

THE CROWD. Jabez Stone—Jabez Stone. What was the price you paid for it, Jabez Stone?

JABEZ. [*Looking around wildly.*] Help me, neighbors! Help me!

[*This cracks the built-up tension and sends the crowd over the edge into fanaticism.*]

A WOMAN'S VOICE. [*High and hysterical.*] He's sold his soul to the devil! [*She points to* JABEZ.]

OTHER VOICES. To the devil!

THE CROWD. He's sold his soul to the devil! The devil himself! The devil's playing the fiddle! The devil's come for his own!

JABEZ. [*Appealing.*] But, neighbors—I didn't know—I didn't mean—oh, help me!

---

8. **telea polyphemus**\tĕ ▲lā·ə ′pa·lē ▲fē·məs\ Webster is supplying the scientific name for the moth.

THE CROWD. [*Inexorably.*] He's sold his soul to the devil!

SCRATCH. [*Grinning.*] To the devil!

THE CROWD. He's sold his soul to the devil! There's no help left for him, neighbors! Run, hide, hurry, before we're caught! He's a lost soul—Jabez Stone—he's the devil's own! Run, hide, hasten! [*They stream across the stage like a flurry of bats, the cannier picking up the wedding-presents they have given to take along with them.*]

[MR. SCRATCH *drives them out into the night, fiddle in hand, and follows them.* JABEZ *and* MARY *are left with* WEBSTER. JABEZ *has sunk into a chair, beaten, with his head in his hands.* MARY *is trying to comfort him.* WEBSTER *looks at them for a moment and shakes his head, sadly. As he crosses to exit to the porch, his hand drops for a moment on* JABEZ's *shoulder, but* JABEZ *makes no sign.* WEBSTER *exits.* JABEZ *lifts his head.*]

MARY. [*Comforting him.*] My dear—my dear—

JABEZ. I—it's all true, Mary. All true. You must hurry.

MARY. Hurry?

JABEZ. Hurry after them—back to the village—back to your folks. Mr. Webster will take you—you'll be safe with Mr. Webster. You see, it's all true and he'll be back in a minute. [*With a shudder.*] The other one. [*He groans.*] I've got until twelve o'clock. That's the contract. But there isn't much time.

MARY. Are you telling me to run away from you, Mr. Stone?

JABEZ. You don't understand, Mary. It's true.

MARY. We made some promises to each other. Maybe you've forgotten them. But I haven't. I said, it's for better or worse. It's for better or worse. I said, in sickness or in health. Well, that covers the ground, Mr. Stone.

JABEZ. But, Mary, you must—I command you.

MARY. "For thy people shall be my people and thy God my God." [*Quietly.*] That was Ruth, in the Book.[9] I always liked the name of Ruth—always liked the thought of her. I always thought—I'll call a child Ruth, some

time. I guess that was just a girl's notion. [*She breaks.*] But, oh, Jabez—why?

JABEZ. It started years ago, Mary. I guess I was a youngster then—guess I must have been. A youngster with a lot of ambitions and no way in the world to get there. I wanted city clothes and a big white house—I wanted to be State Senator and have people look up to me. But all I got on the farm was a crop of stones. You could work all day and all night but that was all you got.

MARY. [*Softly.*] It was pretty—that hill-farm, Jabez. You could look all the way across the valley.

JABEZ. Pretty? It was fever and ague—it was stones and blight. If I had a horse, he got colic—if I planted garden truck, the woodchucks ate it. I'd lie awake nights and try to figure out a way to get somewhere—but there wasn't any way. And all the time you were growing up, in the town. I couldn't ask you to marry me and take you to a place like that.

MARY. Do you think it's the place makes the difference to a woman? I'd—I'd have kept your house. I'd have stroked the cat and fed the chickens and seen you wiped your shoes on the mat. I wouldn't have asked for more. Oh, Jabez—why didn't you tell me?

JABEZ. It happened before I could. Just an average day—you know—just an average day. But there was a mean east wind and a mean small rain. Well, I was plowing, and the share broke clean off on a rock where there hadn't been any rock the day before. I didn't have money for a new one—I didn't have money to get it mended. So I said it and I said loud, "I'll sell my soul for about two cents," I said. [*He stops.* MARY *stares at him.*] Well, that's all there is to it, I guess. He came along that afternoon—that fellow from Boston—and the dog looked at him and ran away. Well, I had to make it more than two cents, but he was agreeable to that. So I

---

9. Mary quotes from the Book of Ruth, 1:16, in the Old Testament; **the Book,** the Bible.

pricked my thumb with a pin and signed the paper. It felt hot when you touched it, that paper. I keep remembering that. [*He pauses.*] And it's all come true and he's kept his part of the bargain. I got the riches and I've married you. And, oh, God Almighty, what shall I do?

MARY. Let us run away! Let us creep and hide!

JABEZ. You can't run away from the devil—I've seen his horses. Miser Stevens tried to run away.

MARY. Let us pray—let us pray to the God of Mercy that He redeem us.

JABEZ. I can't pray, Mary. The words just burn in my heart.

MARY. I won't let you go! I won't! There must be someone who could help us. I'll get the judge and the squire—

JABEZ. Who'll take a case against old Scratch? Who'll face the devil himself and do him brown? There isn't a lawyer in the world who'd dare do that.

[WEBSTER *appears in the doorway.*]

WEBSTER. Good evening, neighbors. Did you say something about lawyers—

MARY. Mr. Webster!

JABEZ. Dan'l Webster! But I thought—

WEBSTER. You'll excuse me for leaving you for a moment. I was just taking a stroll on the porch, in the cool of the evening. Fine summer evening, too.

JABEZ. Well, it might be, I guess, but that kind of depends on the circumstances.

WEBSTER. H'm. Yes. I happened to overhear a little of your conversation. I gather you're in trouble, Neighbor Stone.

JABEZ. Sore trouble.

WEBSTER. [*Delicately.*] Sort of law case, I understand.

JABEZ. You might call it that, Mr. Webster. Kind of a mortgage case, in a way.

MARY. Oh, Jabez!

WEBSTER. Mortgage case. Well, I don't generally plead now, except before the Supreme Court, but this case of yours presents some very unusual features and I never deserted a neighbor in trouble yet. So, if I can be of any assistance—

MARY. Oh, Mr. Webster, will you help him?

JABEZ. It's a terrible lot to ask you. But—well, you see, there's Mary. And, if you could see your way to it—

WEBSTER. I will.

MARY. [*Weeping with relief.*] Oh, Mr. Webster!

WEBSTER. There, there, Mrs. Stone. After all, if two New Hampshire men aren't a match for the devil, we might as well give the country back to the Indians. When is he coming, Jabez?

JABEZ. Twelve o'clock. The time's getting late.

WEBSTER. Then I'd better refresh my memory. The—er—mortgage was for a definite term of years?

JABEZ. Ten years.

WEBSTER. And it falls due—?

JABEZ. Tonight. Oh, I can't see how I came to be such a fool!

WEBSTER. No use crying over spilt milk, Stone. We've got to get you out of it, now. But tell me one thing. Did you sign this precious document of your own free will?

JABEZ. Yes, it was my own free will. I can't deny that.

WEBSTER. H'm, that's a trifle unfortunate. But we'll see.

MARY. Oh, Mr. Webster, can you save him? Can you?

WEBSTER. I shall do my best, madam. That's all you can ever say till you see what the jury looks like.

MARY. But even you, Mr. Webster—oh, I know you're Secretary of State—I know you're a great man—I know you've done wonderful things. But it's different—fighting the devil!

WEBSTER. [*Towering.*] I've fought John C. Calhoun,[10] madam. And I've fought Henry Clay. And, by the great shade of Andrew Jackson,

---

10. **John C. Calhoun**\ˈkăl ˈhūn\ (1782–1850) was another frequent opponent of Daniel Webster in the United States Senate.

I'd fight ten thousand devils to save a New Hampshire man!

JABEZ. You hear, Mary?

MARY. Yes. And I trust Mr. Webster. But—oh, there must be some way that I can help!

WEBSTER. There is one, madam, and a hard one. As Mr. Stone's counsel, I must formally request your withdrawal.

MARY. No.

WEBSTER. Madam, think for a moment. You cannot help Mr. Stone—since you are his wife, your testimony would be prejudiced. And frankly, madam, in a very few moments this is going to be no place for a lady.

MARY. But I can't—I can't leave him—I can't bear it!

JABEZ. You must go, Mary. You must.

WEBSTER. Pray, madam—you can help us with your prayers. Are the prayers of the innocent unavailing?

MARY. Oh, I'll pray—I'll pray. But a woman's more than a praying machine, whatever men think. And how do I know?

WEBSTER. Trust me, Mrs. Stone.

[MARY *turns to go, and, with one hand on* JABEZ's *shoulder, as she moves to the door, says the following prayer.*]

MARY.

Now may there be a blessing and a light betwixt thee and me, forever.

For, as Ruth unto Naomi, so do I cleave unto thee.

Set me as a seal upon thy heart, as a seal upon thine arm, for love is strong as death.

Many waters cannot quench love, neither can the floods drown it.

As Ruth unto Naomi, so do I cleave unto thee.

The Lord watch between thee and me when we are absent, one from the other.

Amen. Amen.

[*She goes out.*]

WEBSTER. Amen.

JABEZ. Thank you, Mr. Webster. She ought to go. But I couldn't have made her do it.

WEBSTER. Well, Stone—I know ladies—and I wouldn't be surprised if she's still got her ear

to the keyhole. But she's best out of this night's business. How long have we got to wait?

JABEZ. [*Beginning to be terrified again.*] Not long—not long.

WEBSTER. Then I'll just get out the jug, with your permission, Stone. Somehow or other, waiting's wonderfully shorter with a jug. [*He crosses to the cupboard, gets out jug and glasses, pours himself a drink.*] Ten-year-old Medford. There's nothing like it. I saw an inch-worm take a drop of it once and he stood right up on his hind legs and bit a bee. Come —try a nip.

JABEZ. There's no joy in it for me.

WEBSTER. Oh, come, man, come! Just because you've sold your soul to the devil, that needn't make you a teetotaller. [*He laughs and passes the jug to* JABEZ, *who tries to pour from it. But at that moment the clock whirs and begins to strike the three-quarters, and* JABEZ *spills the liquor.*]

JABEZ. Oh, God!

WEBSTER. Never mind—it's a nervous feeling, waiting for a trial to begin. I remember my first case—

JABEZ. 'Tain't that. [*He turns to* WEBSTER.] Mr. Webster—Mr. Webster—for God's sake harness your horses and get away from this place as fast as you can!

WEBSTER. [*Placidly.*] You've brought me a long way, neighbor, to tell me you don't like my company.

JABEZ. I've brought you the devil's own way. I can see it all, now. He's after both of us— him and his collecting-box! Well, he can have me, if he likes—I don't say I relish it but I made the bargain. But you're the whole United States! He can't get you, Mr. Webster—he mustn't get you!

WEBSTER. I'm obliged to you, Neighbor Stone. It's kindly thought of. But there's a jug on the table and a case in hand. And I never left a jug or a case half-finished in my life. [*There is a knock at the door.* JABEZ *gives a cry.*] Ah, I thought your clock was a trifle slow, Neighbor Stone. Come in!

[SCRATCH *enters from the night.*]

SCRATCH. Mr. Webster! This is a pleasure!

WEBSTER. Attorney of record for Jabez Stone. Might I ask your name?

SCRATCH. I've gone by a good many. Perhaps Scratch will do for the evening. I'm often called that in these regions. May I? [*He sits at the table and pours a drink from the jug. (See Note D for production hints.) The liquor steams as it pours into the glass while* JABEZ *watches, terrified.* SCRATCH *grins, toasting* WEBSTER *and* JABEZ *silently in the liquor. Then he becomes businesslike. To* WEBSTER.] And now I call upon you, as a law-abiding citizen, to assist me in taking possession of my property.

WEBSTER. Not so fast, Mr. Scratch. Produce your evidence, if you have it.

[SCRATCH *takes out a black pocketbook and examines papers.*]

SCRATCH. Slattery—Stanley—Stone. [*Takes out a deed.*] There, Mr. Webster. All open and aboveboard and in due and legal form. Our firm has its reputation to consider—we deal only in the one way.

WEBSTER. [*Taking deed and looking it over.*] H'm. This appears—I say, it appears—to be properly drawn. But, of course, we contest the signature. [*Tosses it back, contemptuously.*]

SCRATCH. [*Suddenly turning on* JABEZ *and shooting a finger at him.*] Is that your signature?

JABEZ. [*Wearily.*] You know very well it is.

WEBSTER. [*Angrily.*] Keep quiet, Stone. [*To* SCRATCH.] But that is a minor matter. This precious document isn't worth the paper it's written on. The law permits no traffic in human flesh.

SCRATCH. Oh, my dear Mr. Webster! Courts in every state in the Union have held that human flesh is property and recoverable. Read your Fugitive Slave Act. Or, shall I cite Brander versus McRae?

WEBSTER. But, in the case of the State of Maryland versus Four Barrels of Bourbon—

SCRATCH. That was overruled, as you know, sir. North Carolina versus Jenkins and Co.

WEBSTER. [*Unwillingly.*] You seem to have an excellent acquaintance with the law, sir.

SCRATCH. Sir, that is no fault of mine. Where I come from, we have always gotten the pick of the Bar.[11]

WEBSTER. [*Changing his note, heartily.*] Well, come now, sir. There's no need to make hay and oats of a trifling matter when we're both sensible men. Surely we can settle this little difficulty out of court. My client is quite prepared to offer a compromise. [SCRATCH *smiles.*] A very substantial compromise. [SCRATCH *smiles more broadly, slowly shaking his head.*] Hang it, man, we offer ten thousand dollars! [SCRATCH *signs "No."*] Twenty thousand—thirty—name your figure! I'll raise it if I have to mortgage Marshfield![12]

SCRATCH. Quite useless, Mr. Webster. There is only one thing I want from you—the execution of my contract.

WEBSTER. But this is absurd. Mr. Stone is now a State Senator. The property has greatly increased in value!

SCRATCH. The principle of *caveat emptor*[13] still holds, Mr. Webster. [*He yawns and looks at the clock.*] And now, if you have no further arguments to adduce—I'm rather pressed for time—[*He rises briskly as if to take* JABEZ *into custody.*]

WEBSTER. [*Thundering.*] Pressed or not, you shall not have this man. Mr. Stone is an American citizen and no American citizen may be forced into the service of a foreign prince. We fought England for that, in '12, and we'll fight for it again!

SCRATCH. Foreign? And who calls me a foreigner?

WEBSTER. Well, I never yet heard of the dev—of your claiming American citizenship.

SCRATCH. And who with better right? When the

---

11. **the Bar,** the legal profession.
12. **Marshfield,** Webster's own farm.
13. **caveat emptor**\\ˈka·vē·at ˈĕmp·tər\\ legal term meaning "let the buyer beware."

first wrong was done to the first Indian, I was there. When the first slaver put out for the Congo, I stood on her deck. Am I not in your books and stories and beliefs, from the first settlements on? Am I not spoken of, still, in every church in New England? 'Tis true, the North claims me for a Southerner and the South for a Northerner, but I am neither. I am merely an honest American like yourself—and of the best descent—for, to tell the truth, Mr. Webster, though I don't like to boast of it, my name is older in the country than yours.

WEBSTER. Aha! Then I stand on the Constitution! I demand a trial for my client!

SCRATCH. The case is hardly one for an ordinary jury—and indeed, the lateness of the hour—

WEBSTER. Let it be any court you choose, so it is an American judge and an American jury. Let it be the quick or the dead, I'll abide the issue.

SCRATCH. The quick or the dead! You have said it! [*He points his finger at the place where the jury is to appear. There is a clap of thunder and a flash of light. The stage blacks out completely. All that can be seen is the face of* SCRATCH, *lit with a ghastly green light as he recites the invocation that summons the jury. As, one by one, the important jurymen are mentioned, they appear. (See Note E for production hints.)*]

I summon the jury Mr. Webster demands.
From churchyard mould and gallows grave,
Brimstone pit and burning gulf,
I summon them!
Dastard, liar, scoundrel, knave,
I summon them! Appear!
There's Simon Girty,[14] the renegade,
The haunter of the forest glade
Who joined with Indian and wolf
To hunt the pioneer.
The stains upon his hunting-shirt
Are not the blood of the deer.
There's Walter Butler,[15] the loyalist,
Who carried a firebrand in his fist
Of massacre and shame.
King Philip's[16] eye is wild and bright.
They slew him in the great Swamp Fight,
But still, with terror and affright,

The land recalls his name.
Blackbeard Teach, the pirate fell,
Smeet the strangler, hot from hell,
Dale, who broke men on the wheel,
Morton, of the tarnished steel,
I summon them, I summon them
From their tormented flame!
Quick or dead, quick or dead,
Broken heart and bitter head,
True Americans, each one,
Traitor and disloyal son,
Cankered earth and twisted tree,
Outcasts of eternity,
Twelve great sinners, tried and true,
For the work they are to do!
I summon them, I summon them!
Appear, appear, appear!

[*The jury has now taken its place in the box —*WALTER BUTLER *in the place of foreman. They are eerily lit and so made up as to suggest the unearthly. They sit stiffly in their box. At first, when one moves, all move, in stylized gestures. It is not till the end of* WEBSTER'S *speech that they begin to show any trace of humanity. They speak rhythmically, and, at first, in low, eerie voices.*]

JABEZ. [*Seeing them, horrified.*] A jury of the dead!

JURY. Of the dead!

JABEZ. A jury of the damned!

JURY. Of the damned!

SCRATCH. Are you content with the jury, Mr. Webster?

WEBSTER. Quite content. Though I miss General Arnold[17] from the company.

SCRATCH. Benedict Arnold is engaged upon other business. Ah, you asked for a justice, I believe. [*He points his finger and* JUSTICE HATHORNE, *a tall, lean, terrifying Puritan, appears, followed by his* CLERK.] Justice Ha-

---

14. **Simon ˈGirty**\ˈgər·tē\ deserted the Americans to serve the Indians and British in 1778.
15. **Walter Butler** led Indians and British in attacks on American settlements in northern New York.
16. **King Philip** (d. 1676) was an Indian chief who fought against English settlers in eastern New England.
17. **General Arnold**, Benedict Arnold, general during the American Revolution who betrayed his country by spying for the British.

thorne is a jurist of experience. He presided at the Salem witch trials.[18] There were others who repented of the business later. But not he, not he!

HATHORNE. Repent of such notable wonders and undertakings? Nay, hang them, hang them all! [*He takes his place on the bench.*]

[*The* CLERK, *an ominous little man with claw-like hands, takes his place. The room has now been transformed into a courtroom.*]

CLERK. [*In a gabble of ritual.*] Oyes, oyes, oyes.[19] All ye who have business with this honorable court of special session this night, step forward!

HATHORNE [*With gavel.*] Call the first case.

CLERK. The World, the Flesh, and the Devil versus Jabez Stone.

HATHORNE. Who appears for the plaintiff?

SCRATCH. I, Your Honor.

HATHORNE. And for the defendant?

WEBSTER. I.

JURY. The case—the case—he'll have little luck with this case.

HATHORNE. The case will proceed.

WEBSTER. Your Honor, I move to dismiss this case on the grounds of improper jurisdiction.

HATHORNE. Motion denied.

WEBSTER. On the grounds of insufficient evidence.

HATHORNE. Motion denied.

JURY. Motion denied—denied. Motion denied.

WEBSTER. I will take an exception.

HATHORNE. There are no exceptions in this court.

JURY. No exceptions—no exceptions in this court. It's a bad case, Daniel Webster—a losing case.

WEBSTER. Your Honor—

HATHORNE. The prosecution will proceed—

SCRATCH. Your Honor—gentlemen of the jury. This is a plain, straightforward case. It need not detain us long.

JURY. Detain us long—it will not detain us long.

SCRATCH. It concerns one thing alone—the transference, barter and sale of a certain piece of property, to wit, his soul, by Jabez Stone, farmer, of Cross Corners, New Hampshire. That transference, barter, or sale is attested by a deed. I offer that deed in evidence and mark it Exhibit A.

WEBSTER. I object.

HATHORNE. Objection denied. Mark it Exhibit A.

[SCRATCH *hands the deed—an ominous and impressive document—to the* CLERK, *who hands it to* HATHORNE. HATHORNE *hands it back to the* CLERK, *who stamps it. All very fast and with mechanical gestures.*]

JURY. Exhibit A—mark it Exhibit A. [SCRATCH *takes the deed from the* CLERK *and offers it to the* JURY, *who pass it rapidly among them, hardly looking at it, and hand it back to* SCRATCH.] We know the deed—the deed—it burns in our fingers—we do not have to see the deed. It's a losing case.

SCRATCH. It offers incontestable evidence of the truth of the prosecution's claim. I shall now call Jabez Stone to the witness-stand.

JURY. [*Hungrily.*] Jabez Stone to the witness-stand, Jabez Stone. He's a fine, fat fellow, Jabez Stone. He'll fry like a battercake, once we get him where we want him.

WEBSTER. Your Honor, I move that this jury be discharged for flagrant and open bias!

HATHORNE. Motion denied.

WEBSTER. Exception.

HATHORNE. Exception denied.

JURY. His motion's always denied. He thinks himself smart and clever—lawyer Webster. But his motion's always denied.

WEBSTER. Your Honor! [*He chokes with anger.*]

CLERK. [*Advancing.*] Jabez Stone to the witness-stand!

JURY. Jabez Stone—Jabez Stone.

---

18. About twenty persons were executed as witches during a hysterical period in 1692 in Salem, Massachusetts.

19. In the early Middle Ages the French language was used in English law courts. **Oyes** or **oyez**\ˈō•yĕz\ is the French for "listen." This is a standard formula for calling a court room to order at the beginning of its proceedings.

[WEBSTER *gives* JABEZ *an encouraging pat on the back, and* JABEZ *takes his place in the witness-stand, very scared.*]

CLERK. [*Offering a black book.*] Do you solemnly swear—testify—so help you—and it's no good, for we don't care what you testify?

JABEZ. I do.

SCRATCH. What's your name?

JABEZ. Jabez Stone.

SCRATCH. Occupation?

JABEZ. Farmer.

SCRATCH. Residence?

JABEZ. Cross Corners, New Hampshire.

[*These three questions are very fast and mechanical on the part of* SCRATCH. *He is absolutely sure of victory and just going through a form.*]

JURY. A farmer—he'll farm in hell—we'll see that he farms in hell.

SCRATCH. Now, Jabez Stone, answer me. You'd better, you know. You haven't got a chance and there'll be a cooler place by the fire for you.

WEBSTER. I protest! This is intimidation! This mocks all justice!

HATHORNE. The protest is irrelevant, incompetent, and immaterial. We have our own justice. The protest is denied.

JURY. Irrelevant, incompetent, and immaterial—we have our own justice—oh, ho, Daniel Webster! [*The* JURY'S *eyes fix upon* WEBSTER *for an instant, hungrily.*]

SCRATCH. Did you or did you not sign this document?

JABEZ. Oh, I signed it! You know I signed it. And, if I have to go to hell for it, I'll go!

[*A sigh sweeps over the* JURY.]

JURY. One of us—one of us now—we'll save a place by the fire for you, Jabez Stone.

SCRATCH. The prosecution rests.

HATHORNE. Remove the prisoner.

WEBSTER. But I wish to cross-examine—I wish to prove—

HATHORNE. There will be no cross-examination. We have our own justice. You may speak, if you like. But be brief.

JURY. Brief—be very brief—we're weary of earth—incompetent, irrelevant, and immaterial—they say he's a smart man, Webster, but he's lost his case tonight—be very brief—we have our own justice here.

[WEBSTER *stares around him like a baited bull. Can't find words.*]

MARY'S VOICE. [*From off stage.*] Set me as a seal upon thy heart, as a seal upon thine arm, for love is strong as death—

JURY. [*Loudly.*] A seal!—ha, ha—a burning seal!

MARY'S VOICE. Love is strong—

JURY. [*Drowning her out.*] Death is stronger than love. Set the seal upon Daniel Webster—the burning seal of the lost. Make him one of us—one of the damned—one with Jabez Stone!

[*The* JURY'S *eyes all fix upon* WEBSTER. *The* CLERK *advances as if to take him into custody. But* WEBSTER *silences them all with a great gesture.*]

WEBSTER.

Be still!

I was going to thunder and roar. I shall not do that.

I was doing to denounce and defy. I shall not do that.

You have judged this man already with your abominable justice. See that you defend it. For I shall not speak of this man.

You are demons now, but once you were men. I shall speak to every one of you.

Of common things I speak, of small things and common.

The freshness of morning to the young, the taste of food to the hungry, the day's toil, the rest by the fire, the quiet sleep.

These are good things.

But without freedom they sicken, without freedom they are nothing.

Freedom is the bread and the morning and the risen sun.

It was for freedom we came in the boats and the ships. It was for freedom we came.

It has been a long journey, a hard one, a bitter one.

But, out of the wrong and the right, the sufferings and the starvation, there is a new thing, a free thing.

The traitors in their treachery, the wise in their wisdom, the valiant in their courage—all, all have played a part.

It may not be denied in hell nor shall hell prevail against it.

Have you forgotten this? [*He turns to the* JURY.] Have you forgotten the forest?

GIRTY. [*As in a dream.*] The forest, the rustle of the forest, the free forest.

WEBSTER. [*To* KING PHILIP.] Have you forgotten your lost nation?

KING PHILIP. My lost nation—my fires in the wood—my warriors.

WEBSTER. [*To* TEACH.] Have you forgotten the sea and the way of ships?

TEACH. The sea—and the swift ships sailing—the blue sea.

JURY. Forgotten—remembered—forgotten yet remembered.

WEBSTER. You were men once. Have you forgotten?

JURY. We were men once. We have not thought of it nor remembered. But we were men.

WEBSTER.

Now here is this man with good and evil in his heart.

Do you know him? He is your brother. Will you take the law of the oppressor and bind him down?

It is not for him that I speak. It is for all of you.

There is sadness in being a man, but it is a proud thing, too.

There is failure and despair on the journey—the endless journey of mankind.

We are tricked and trapped—we stumble into the pit—but, out of the pit, we rise again.

No demon that was ever foaled can know the inwardness of that—only men—bewildered men.

They have broken freedom with their hands and cast her out from the nations—yet shall she live while man lives.

She shall live in the blood and the heart—she shall live in the earth of this country—she shall not be broken.

When the whips of the oppressors are broken and their names forgotten and destroyed,

I see you, mighty, shining, liberty, liberty! I see free men walking and talking under a free star.

God save the United States and the men who have made her free.

The defense rests.

JURY. [*Exultantly.*] We were men—we were free—we were men—we have not forgotten —our children—our children shall follow and be free.

HATHORNE. [*Rapping with gavel.*] The jury will retire to consider its verdict.

BUTLER. [*Rising.*] There is no need. The jury has heard Mr. Webster. We find for the defendant, Jabez Stone!

JURY. Not guilty!

SCRATCH. [*In a screech, rushing forward.*] But, Your Honor—[*But, even as he does so, there is a flash and a thunderclap, the stage blacks out again, and when the lights come on,* JUDGE *and* JURY *are gone. The yellow light of dawn lights the windows.*]

JABEZ. They're gone and it's morning—Mary, Mary!

MARY. [*In doorway.*] My love—my dear. [*She rushes to him.*]

[*Meanwhile* SCRATCH *has been collecting his papers and trying to sneak out. But* WEBSTER *catches him.*]

WEBSTER. Just a minute, Mr. Scratch. I'll have that paper first, if you please. [*He takes the deed and tears it.*] And, now, sir, I'll have you!

SCRATCH. Come, come, Mr. Webster. This sort of thing is ridic—ouch—is ridiculous. If you're worried about the costs of the case, naturally, I'd be glad to pay.

WEBSTER. And so you shall. First of all, you'll

Daniel Webster, daguerreotype.

promise and covenant never to bother Jabez Stone or any other New Hampshire man from now till doomsday. For any hell we want to raise in this State, we can raise ourselves, without any help from you.

SCRATCH. Ouch! Well, they never did run very big to the barrel but—ouch—I agree!

WEBSTER. See you keep to the bargain! And then—well, I've got a ram named Goliath. He can butt through an iron door. I'd like to turn you loose in his field and see what he could do to you. [SCRATCH *trembles.*] But that would be hard on the ram. So we'll just call in the neighbors and give you a shivaree.[20]

SCRATCH. Mr. Webster—please—oh—

WEBSTER. Neighbors! Neighbors! Come in and see what a long-barrelled, slab-sided, lantern-jawed, fortune-telling note-shaver I've got by the scruff of the neck! Bring on your kettles and your pans! [*A noise and murmur outside.*] Bring on your muskets and your flails!

JABEZ. We'll drive him out of New Hampshire!

MARY. We'll drive old Scratch away!

[*The crowd rushes in, with muskets, flails, brooms, etc. They pursue* SCRATCH *around the stage, chanting.*]

THE CROWD.

We'll drive him out of New Hampshire!
We'll drive old Scratch away!
Forever and a day, boys;
Forever and a day!

[*They finally catch* SCRATCH *between two of them and fling him out of the door, bodily.*]

A MAN. Three cheers for Dan'l Webster!

ANOTHER MAN. Three cheers for Daniel Webster! He's licked the devil!

WEBSTER [*Moving to center stage, and joining* JABEZ's *hands and* MARY's.] And whom God hath joined let no man put asunder. [*He kisses* MARY *and turns, dusting his hands.*] Well, that job's done. I hope there's pie for breakfast, neighbor Stone.

[*Some of the women, dancing, bring in pies from the kitchen.*]

Staging such a play as this,
with its elements of fantasy,
would present many problems, particularly
to the amateur director. Here are the author's
production suggestions, which should prove
interesting and enlightening
to the general reader as well as to those
actually concerned with putting on the play.

Note A

The set must be arranged so that it can be transformed, in short notice, from the living room of a farmhouse into a courtroom. In an elaborate production, the back-wall of the set, between the two windows, can be flown during the first black-out and a practical jury box, with the jurors concealed within it, can be rolled on. The fireplace can also revolve and turn into the judge's stand. In a simpler production, a pair of long benches, one higher than the other, at the back of the set, can be used as a jury box and the jurors steal on during the black-out, to be gradually lit at the end of Scratch's invocation, while the Judge enters and takes his seat on the high settle by the fireplace, his Clerk sitting on a stool below him. The table, left, becomes the lawyer's table,

---

20. **shivaree**\\'shĭ·və ▲rē\\ a mock serenade, with banging pots and pans; frontier horseplay customary at weddings.

where Scratch and Webster sit. There is no need of an actual dock or witness box—Jabez, during his interrogation, merely stands to the right of the jury, lit by a spot.

Note B

As a practical moth-effect would be difficult, the whole business of the moth can be suggested by the Crowd turning, staring and pointing, first up, then right, then left, following the flight of an imaginary moth. The stage begins to darken at the first letting of the moth out of the box, and the following scene is played in dim light.

Scratch can recite his song instead of singing it, though music for this song, if desired, can be obtained by special arrangement with Brandt and Brandt, 101 Park Avenue, New York City. The fiddle accompaniment can be faked, off stage, if necessary. All it needs is to be eerie and discordant.

Note C

The speeches of the Moth should come in a high, shrill voice from somebody concealed among the Crowd where he will not be seen by the audience. If desired, the speeches can be spoken from off stage. But the words are important and must be heard. During this scene, the Crowd speaks in a definite, beating rhythm.

Note D

Alka-Seltzer or dry ice—or a combination of both, will make the devil's glass steam. But, if dry ice is used, Mr. Scratch must be careful not to try to drink from the glass.

Note E

The moment the stage blacks out, Mr. Scratch removes a flashlight with a green bulb from the inside pocket of his voluminous coat and, holding it carefully in his black-gloved hands, lets the green light play on his face during the invocation. On the last line, he switches off the flashlight and sticks it back in his pocket. This can be done so the audience does not see it.

List of Properties

Glasses
Jug
Clock
Violin and bow
Bouquet of flowers
Dish (for oyster stew)
Dish (with cake)
Black tin box
Flask
Gavel
Black book
Pies

A few wedding presents of various kinds
Black pocketbook with a few documents and other papers, including a large and impressive deed

---

I
A FAIR PRICE?

1. Fantasies are usually written for one of two reasons—either to take the reader into a make-believe world where he can escape from reality, or to point up basic ideas. What do you believe is the purpose of this fantasy? Before answering, think about the two questions below.

a. What does the play say about the importance of freedom and democracy?

b. What are you told about the struggle between good and evil in man? (The expression that someone has "sold his soul to the devil" is based upon an old superstition. What does the saying mean when it is used to describe what someone has done?)

2. Some knowledge of American history is helpful in understanding the full significance of certain lines in the play. Consider and discuss the following topics briefly. Relate each to action in the drama.

a. The political views of John C. Calhoun and Henry Clay as contrasted to those of Webster

b. Slave laws around the time 1841

c. The Salem Witch Trials

d. The meaning of Webster's words on page 689: "Then I stand on the Constitution! I demand a trial for my client!"

e. The background of the jury members

3. To fully appreciate the course of action in the play, the reader must be aware of certain specific details. Consider and discuss the following questions:

a. What is the reaction of Jabez when Mary says she feels sorry for women who can't be proud of their men?

b. How does Mr. Scratch first make his presence felt? What is strange about his attire? What is the meaning of the song he sings and of his use of the violin?

c. What reasons does Webster give for deciding to take the case of Jabez Stone? What does he say later about a law case or a jug?

d. What are the four legal ways Webster tries to save Jabez Stone before he finally demands a trial by jury? How does Scratch thwart him in each of the four attempts?

e. Where is poetic form used in the play? Why is it particularly effective?

f. Why does Webster accept the jury Scratch produces? About which other famous traitor did Webster inquire? Who presided at the trial as judge?

g. What indications are there that the devil and his jury wanted the soul of Webster as well as that of Stone? How does Webster manage to win freedom for Jabez Stone? Describe his final appeal to the jury in detail.

h. What are the characteristics of New Hampshire men as revealed during the course of the play?

i. How is fantasy used in the play as a whole? Which fantastic happening would be particularly hard to stage?

4. There are many MOMENTS OF DECISION in this play other than the controversial one which occurred when Jabez aligned himself with the devil. Point out two particularly important ones.

II
IMPLICATIONS

Here are some statements made by famous men over the years, beginning with the Roman historian Tacitus. Which of these ideas do you believe apply to the play? Consider and discuss the relationships.

1. Liberties and masters are not easily combined.—Tacitus

2. Man is born free and everywhere he is in irons.—Rousseau

3. In giving freedom to the slave, we assure freedom to the free—honorable alike in what we give and what we preserve.—Abraham Lincoln

4. Democracy . . . is a condition where people believe that other people are as good as they are. —Stuart Chase

5. The love of money is the root of all evil. —New Testament

6. The web of our life is of a mingled yarn, good and ill together.—Shakespeare

III
TECHNIQUES

Beginning

A one-act play might be thought of as having a similar relationship to a three-act play as a short story has to a novel. The one-act play must get under way immediately without lengthy introduction of the characters and their backgrounds. Its production must be compressed within a short space of time, just as a short story is limited in the number of pages it may cover.

The opening lines must not only set the story in motion toward its climax, they must also capture the interest of the audience.

1. Why do you think Benét used the characters of the old man and the old woman in the opening wedding scene? How do you know that Jabez is an important fellow in his part of the state? Do these opening lines give any indication of something questionable about Jabez' success? How?

2. What does this opening scene tell you about Daniel Webster? What does it tell about the way Jabez and Mary feel about each other?

Plot

In the opening scene, the author sets up a rather idealistic picture of the successful young man marrying the beautiful girl—but the suspicions of the audience are aroused that things are not as blissful as they appear.

1. What is the first clue as the wedding celebration progresses that all is not going to run smoothly?

2. Which of the following happenings that occur after the wedding scene could be called the high point or climax in the action of the plot? Explain your choice.
    a. Jabez is found not guilty.
    b. Scratch is thrown out.
    c. The lovers are reunited.

Ending

How do Webster's closing lines fit the characterization he has been given throughout the play? Discuss.

When the leadsman on a river
steamer sang out "M-A-R-K T-W-A-I-N,"
it meant that the river depth was two fathoms
(two times six feet). Samuel Langhorne
Clemens, as a boy growing up in the
village of Hannibal, Missouri, on the west
bank of the Mississippi River, loved
the river and liked to hear this call, which
meant that the water there was deep enough
to be safe for any river boat.
He longed to follow the river,
and after working briefly in his brother's
printshop, he ran away to serve an
apprenticeship as a cub pilot. For four years
thereafter he piloted steamers.
After he had been writing for some
time, he took the haunting call of the leadsman
for his pen name. As Mark Twain, Clemens
became recognized as one of the world's
great writers.
In the following selection from the
book *Life on the Mississippi,* Mark Twain tells
us that even more than a good memory
a river pilot must have "good and quick judgment
and decision, and a cool, calm courage
that no peril can shake."

A Pilot's
Needs

MARK TWAIN

There is one faculty which a pilot must in-
cessantly cultivate until he has brought it to
absolute perfection. Nothing short of perfection will do. That faculty is memory. He cannot stop with merely thinking a thing is so and

From *Life on the Mississippi* by Mark Twain. Reprinted by permission of Harper & Row, Publishers.

so; he must *know* it; for this is eminently one
of the "exact" sciences. With what scorn a pilot
was looked upon, in the old times, if he ever
ventured to deal in that feeble phrase "I think,"
instead of the vigorous one "I know!" One cannot easily realize what a tremendous thing it is
to know every trivial detail of twelve hundred
miles of river and know it with absolute exactness. If you will take the longest street in New
York, and travel up and down it, conning its
features patiently until you know every house
and window and door and lamppost and big
and little sign by heart, and know them so accurately that you can instantly name the one
you are abreast of when you are set down at
random in that street in the middle of an inky
black night, you will then have a tolerable notion of the amount and the exactness of a pilot's
knowledge who carries the Mississippi River
in his head. And then if you will go on until
you know every street crossing, the character,
size, and position of the crossing stones, and the
varying depth of mud in each of those numberless places, you will have some idea of what the
pilot must know in order to keep a Mississippi
steamer out of trouble. Next, if you will take
half of the signs in that long street, and *change
their places* once a month, and still manage to
know their new positions accurately on dark
nights, and keep up with these repeated
changes without making any mistakes, you will
understand what is required of a pilot's peer-
less memory by the fickle Mississippi.

I think a pilot's memory is about the most
wonderful thing in the world. To know the Old
and New Testaments by heart, and be able to
recite them glibly, forward or backward, or
begin at random anywhere in the book and
recite both ways and never trip or make a mistake, is no extravagant mass of knowledge, and
no marvelous facility, compared to a pilot's
massed knowledge of the Mississippi and his
marvelous facility in the handling of it. I make
this comparison deliberately, and believe I
am not expanding the truth when I do it. Many
will think my figure too strong, but pilots will
not.

Currier and Ives Lithograph, "Through the Bayou by Torchlight"

And how easily and comfortably the pilot's memory does its work; how placidly effortless is its way; how *unconsciously* it lays up its vast stores, hour by hour, day by day, and never loses or mislays a single valuable package of them all! Take an instance. Let a leadsman cry, "Half twain![1] Half twain! Half twain! Half twain! Half twain!" until it becomes as monotonous as the ticking of a clock; let conversation be going on all the time, and the pilot be doing his share of the talking, and no longer consciously listening to the leadsman; and in the midst of this endless string of half twains let a single "quarter twain!" be interjected, without emphasis, and then the half twain cry go on again, just as before: two or three weeks later that pilot can describe with precision the boat's position in the river when that quarter twain was uttered, and give you such a lot of head-marks, stern-marks, and side-marks to guide you, that you ought to be able to take the boat there and put her in that same spot again yourself! The cry of "quarter twain" did not really take his mind from his talk, but his trained faculties instantly photographed the bearings, noted the change of depth, and laid up the important details for future reference without requiring any assistance from *him* in the matter. If you were walking and talking with a friend, and another friend at your side kept up a monotonous repetition of the vowel sound A, for a couple of blocks, and then in the midst interjected an R, thus, A, A, A, A, A, R, A, A, A, etc., and gave the R no emphasis, you would not be able to state, two or three weeks afterward, that the R had been put in, nor be able to tell what objects you were passing at the moment it was done. But you could if your memory had been patiently and laboriously trained to do that sort of thing mechanically.

Give a man a tolerably fair memory to start with, and piloting will develop into a very co-

---

1. **leadsman . . . twain,** the leadsman of a riverboat took soundings of the water depth by a lead-weighted rope (plummet); **twain\twān** means two fathoms—twelve feet; the sounding line was marked in fathom lengths.

lossus of capability. But *only in the matters it is daily drilled in.* A time would come when the man's faculties could not help noticing landmarks and soundings, and his memory could not help holding on to them with the grip of a vise; but if you asked that same man at noon what he had had for breakfast, it would be ten chances to one that he could not tell you. Astonishing things can be done with the human memory if you will devote it faithfully to one particular line of business.

Samuel Clemens as a pilot, approximately 1859.

At the time that wages soared so high on the Missouri River, my chief, Mr. Bixby, went up there and learned more than a thousand miles of that stream with an ease and rapidity that were astonishing. When he had seen each division *once* in the daytime and *once* at night, his education was so nearly complete that he took out a "daylight" license; a few trips later he took out a full license, and went to piloting day and night,—and he ranked A-1, too.

Mr. Bixby placed me as steersman for a while under a pilot whose feats of memory were a constant marvel to me. However, his memory was born in him, I think, not built. For instance, somebody would mention a name. Instantly Mr. Brown would break in:

"Oh, I knew *him.* Sallow-faced, red-headed fellow, with a little scar on the side of his throat, like a splinter under the flesh. He was only in the Southern trade six months. That was thirteen years ago. I made a trip with him. There was five feet in the upper river then; the *Henry Blake* grounded at the foot of Tower Island drawing four and a half; the *George Elliott* unshipped her rudder on the wreck of the *Sunflower—*"

"Why, the *Sunflower* didn't sink until—"

"*I* know when she sunk; it was three years before that, on the 2nd of December; Asa Hardy was captain of her, and his brother John was first clerk; and it was his first trip in her, too; Tom Jones told me these things a week afterward in New Orleans; he was first mate of the *Sunflower.* . . ."

And so on, by the hour, the man's tongue would go. He could *not* forget anything. It was simply impossible. The most trivial details remained as distinct and luminous in his head, after they had lain there for years, as the most memorable events. His was not simply a pilot's memory; its grasp was universal. If he were talking about a trifling letter he had received seven years before, he was pretty sure to deliver you the entire screed from memory. And then without observing that he was departing from the true line of his talk, he was more than likely to hurl in a long-drawn parenthetical biography of the writer of that letter; and you were lucky indeed if he did not take up that writer's relatives, one by one, and give you their biographies, too.

Such a memory as that is a great misfortune. To it, all occurrences are of the same size. Its possessor cannot distinguish an interesting circumstance from an uninteresting one. As a talker, he is bound to clog his narrative with tiresome details and make himself an insufferable bore. . . .

A pilot must have a memory; but there are two higher qualities which he must also have. He must have good and quick judgment and decision, and a cool, calm courage that no peril can shake. Give a man the merest trifle of pluck to start with, and by the time he has become a pilot he cannot be unmanned by any danger a steamboat can get into; but one cannot quite say the same for judgment. Judgment is a matter of brains, and a man must *start* with a good stock of that article or he will never succeed as a pilot.

The growth of courage in the pilothouse is steady all the time, but it does not reach a high and satisfactory condition until some time after the young pilot has been "standing his own watch," alone and under the staggering weight of all the responsibilities connected with the position. When an apprentice has become pretty thoroughly acquainted with the river, he goes clattering along so fearlessly with his steamboat, night or day, that he presently begins to imagine that it is *his* courage that animates him; but the first time the pilot steps out and leaves him to his own devices he finds out it was the other man's. He discovers that the article has been left out of his own cargo altogether. The whole river is bristling with exigencies in a moment; he is not prepared for them; he does not know how to meet them; all his knowledge forsakes him; and within fifteen minutes he is as white as a sheet and scared almost to death. Therefore pilots wisely train these cubs by various strategic tricks to look danger in the face a little more calmly. A favorite way of theirs is to play a friendly swindle upon the candidate.

Mr. Bixby served me in this fashion once, and for years afterward I used to blush even in my sleep when I thought of it. I had become a good steersman; so good, indeed, that I had all the work to do on our watch, night and day; Mr. Bixby seldom made a suggestion to me; all he ever did was to take the wheel on particularly bad nights or in particularly bad crossings, land the boat when she needed to be landed, play gentleman of leisure nine-tenths of the watch, and collect the wages. The lower river was about bank full, and if anybody had questioned my ability to run any crossing between Cairo[2] and New Orleans without help or instruction, I should have felt irreparably hurt.

The Pilot House. Illustration from early edition of Life on the Mississippi.

The idea of being afraid of any crossing in the lot, in the *daytime,* was a thing too preposterous for contemplation. Well, one matchless summer's day I was bowling down the bend above island 66, brimful of self-conceit and carrying my nose as high as a giraffe's, when Mr. Bixby said—

"I am going below a while. I suppose you know the next crossing?"

This was almost an affront. It was about the plainest and simplest crossing in the whole river. One couldn't come to any harm, whether he ran it right or not; and as for depth, there never had been any bottom there. I knew all this, perfectly well.

"Know how to *run* it? Why, I can run it with my eyes shut."

"How much water is there in it?"

2. **Cairo**\\ᴬkā•rō\\ a river town at the southern tip of Illinois.

The captain of a steamboat.

"Well, that is an odd question. I couldn't get bottom there with a church steeple."

"You think so, do you?"

The very tone of the question shook my confidence. That was what Mr. Bixby was expecting. He left, without saying anything more. I began to imagine all sorts of things. Mr. Bixby, unknown to me, of course, sent somebody down to the forecastle with some mysterious instruction to the leadsmen, another messenger was sent to whisper among the officers, and then Mr. Bixby went into hiding behind a smoke stack where he could observe results. Presently the captain stepped out on the hurricane deck; next the chief mate appeared; then a clerk. Every moment or two a straggler was added to my audience; and before I got to the head of the island I had fifteen or twenty people assembled down there under my nose. I began to wonder what the trouble was. As I started

across, the captain glanced aloft at me and said with a sham uneasiness in his voice—

"Where is Mr. Bixby?"

"Gone below, sir."

But that did the business for me. My imagination began to construct dangers out of nothing, and they multiplied faster than I could keep the run of them. All at once I imagined I saw shoal water ahead! The wave of coward agony that surged through me then came near dislocating every joint in me. All my confidence in that crossing vanished. I seized the bell rope; dropped it, ashamed; seized it again; dropped it once more; clutched it tremblingly once again, and pulled it so feebly that I could hardly hear the stroke myself. Captain and mate sang out instantly, and both together—

"Starboard lead there! And quick about it!"

This was another shock. I began to climb the wheel like a squirrel; but I would hardly get the boat started to port before I would see new dangers on that side, and away I would spin to the other; only to find perils accumulating to starboard, and be crazy to get to port again. Then came the leadsman's sepulchral cry:

"D-e-e-p four!"

Deep four in a bottomless crossing! The terror of it took my breath away.

"M-a-r-k three! . . . M-a-r-k three[3] . . . Quarter less three! . . . Half twain!"

This was frightful! I seized the bell ropes and stopped the engines.

"Quarter twain! Quarter twain! *Mark* twain!"

I was helpless. I did not know what in the world to do. I was quaking from head to foot, and I could have hung my hat on my eyes, they stuck out so far.

"Quarter *less* twain! Nine and a *half!*"

We were drawing nine![4] My hands were in a nerveless flutter. I could not ring a bell intelligibly with them. I flew to the speaking tube and shouted to the engineer—

---

3. **The water mark is at three fathoms.** The following quarters are points between three and two (mark twain).

4. **drawing nine,** the boat sat nine feet into the water.

"Oh, Ben, if you love me, *back* her! Quick, Ben! Oh, back the immortal *soul* out of her!"

I heard the door close gently. I looked around, and there stood Mr. Bixby, smiling a bland, sweet smile. Then the audience on the hurricane deck sent up a thundergust of humiliating laughter. I saw it all, now, and I felt meaner than the meanest man in human history. I laid in the lead, set the boat in her marks, came ahead on the engines, and said:

"It was a fine trick to play on an orphan, *wasn't* it? I suppose I'll never hear the last of how I was ass enough to heave the lead[5] at the head of 66."

"Well, no, you won't, maybe. In fact I hope you won't; for I want you to learn something by that experience. Didn't you *know* there was no bottom in that crossing?"

"Yes, sir, I did."

"Very well, then. You shouldn't have allowed me or anybody else to shake your confidence in that knowledge. Try to remember that. And another thing: when you get into a dangerous place, don't turn coward. That isn't going to help matters any."

It was a good enough lesson, but pretty hardly learned. Yet about the hardest part of it was that for months I so often had to hear a phrase which I had conceived a particular distaste for. It was, "Oh, Ben, if you love me, back her!"

I

NO PLACE FOR INDECISION

That there was no place for indecision during the working day of a river pilot was brought home so forcibly to this "orphan" that he was not likely to forget the lesson very soon. As Mr. Bixby told him, when you *know* something, you should not allow anything or anyone to shake your confidence in that knowledge.

---

5. **heave the lead,** even taking measures at this well-known, deep channel was unheard of.

1. Through comparisons, Mark Twain impresses upon the reader's mind the magnitude of what is required of a pilot's memory if he is to keep a steamer out of trouble on the Mississippi. Discuss two of these comparisons.

2. Describe the peculiarities of the way a pilot's mind worked. In what respect was Mr. Brown's phenomenal memory a misfortune?

3. What are the two qualities Twain sets down as even more necessary to a good pilot than memory?

4. What was the reason for the "friendly swindle" played upon the young cub pilot by Captain Bixby and the crew?

5. How did Clemens react in the "emergency"? What was the phrase which he heard repeated so often after the incident that he came to dislike it heartily?

II

IMPLICATIONS

Do you agree or disagree with the following statement?

A test such as this, in which the instructor deliberately attempts to upset the learner, is not good. Such experiences would weaken rather than strengthen one's ability to make decisions.

III

TECHNIQUES

Style

Mark Twain wrote with unusual clarity and simplicity. Many persons believe that his influence on later American writers was greater than that of any other American author.

While he might appear to be a careless writer who simply "wrote as he talked," actually, Twain was a very painstaking workman who spent hours scribbling and revising.

1. Although a number of Twain's sentences are lengthy, they are so well organized and so simply worded that the reader has no difficulty getting the meaning. Look back over paragraph one for examples of this and discuss them.

2. Mark Twain's writing was of such variety that it is hard to classify, but most of it is sprinkled with his humor. Select one situation or statement from the account you have just read and tell what makes it funny.

Here are two stories
to be read one immediately following the other.
Each concerns a beautiful princess
faced with a momentous decision.
After you have read the first selection,
long considered a classic,
you will understand why it became the subject
for so much conjecture and controversy.
With James Thurber as the author
of the second story, of course
you can expect anything, so don't be surprised.
Remember, however, that Thurber used humor
as a way of saying something serious.

The Lady
or the Tiger?

FRANK R. STOCKTON

In the very olden times, there lived a semi-barbaric king, whose ideas, though somewhat polished and sharpened by the progressiveness of distant Latin neighbors, were still large, florid, and untrammeled, as became the half of him which was barbaric. He was a man of exuberant fancy, and, withal, of an authority so irresistible that, at his will, he turned his fancies into facts. He was greatly given to self-communing; and, when he and himself agreed upon anything, the thing was done. When every member of his domestic and political systems moved smoothly in its appointed course, his nature was bland and genial; but whenever there was a little hitch, and some of his orbs got out of their orbits, he was blander and more genial still, for nothing pleased him so much as to make the crooked straight, and crush down uneven places.

Among the borrowed notions by which his barbarism had become semified[1] was that of the public arena, in which, by exhibitions of manly and beastly valor, the minds of his subjects were refined and cultured.

But even here the exuberant and barbaric fancy asserted itself. The arena of the king was built, not to give the people an opportunity of hearing the rhapsodies of dying gladiators, nor to enable them to view the inevitable conclusion of a conflict between religious opinions and hungry jaws, but for purposes far better adapted to widen and develop the mental energies of the people. This vast amphitheater, with its encircling galleries, its mysterious vaults, and its unseen passages, was an agent of poetic justice, in which crime was punished, or virtue rewarded, by the decrees of an impartial and incorruptible chance.

When a subject was accused of a crime of sufficient importance to interest the king, public notice was given that on an appointed day the fate of the accused person would be decided in the king's arena—a structure which well deserved its name; for, although its form and plan were borrowed from afar, its purpose emanated solely from the brain of this man, who, every barleycorn[2] a king, knew no tradition to which he owed more allegiance than pleased his fancy, and who ingrafted on every adopted form of human thought and action the rich growth of his barbaric idealism.

When all the people had assembled in the galleries, and the king, surrounded by his court, sat high up on his throne of royal state on one side of the arena, he gave a signal, a door beneath him opened, and the accused subject stepped out into the amphitheater. Directly opposite him, on the other side of the enclosed space, were two doors, exactly alike and side by side. It was the duty and the privilege of the person on trial to walk directly to these doors and open one of them. He could open either door he pleased; he was subject to

---

1. **semified,** cut in half. The reference is to "semi-barbaric" in the opening sentence.
2. **barleycorn,** an ancient measure equal to one third of an inch. The phrase is a mockery of "every inch a king," and means that this particular king was very small-minded.

no guidance or influence but that of the aforementioned impartial and incorruptible chance. If he opened the one, there came out of it a hungry tiger, the fiercest and most cruel that could be found, which immediately sprang upon him and tore him to pieces as a punishment for his guilt. The moment that the case of the criminal was thus decided, doleful iron bells were clanged, great wails went up from the hired mourners posted on the outer rim of the arena, and the vast audience, with bowed heads and downcast hearts, wended slowly their homeward way, mourning greatly that one so young and fair, or so old and respected, should have merited so dire a fate.

But, if the accused person opened the other door, there came forth from it a lady, the most suitable to his years and station that His Majesty could select among his fair subjects; and to this lady he was immediately married, as a reward of his innocence. It mattered not that he might already possess a wife and family, or that his affections might be engaged upon an object of his own selection; the king allowed no such subordinate arrangements to interfere with his great scheme of retribution and reward. The exercise, as in the other instance, took place immediately and in the arena. Another door opened beneath the king, and a priest, followed by a band of choristers, and dancing maidens blowing joyous airs on golden horns and treading an epithalamic measure[3] advanced to where the pair stood, side by side; and the wedding was promptly and cheerily solemnized. Then the gay brass bells rang forth their merry peals, the people shouted glad hurrahs, and the innocent man, preceded by children strewing flowers on his path, led his bride to his home.

This was the king's semi-barbaric method of administering justice. Its perfect fairness is obvious. The criminal could not know out of which door would come the lady; he opened either he pleased, without having the slightest idea whether, in the next instant, he was to be devoured or married. On some occasions the tiger came out one door; and on some, out of the other. The decisions of this tribunal were not only fair, they were positively determinate; the accused person was instantly punished if he found himself guilty; and, if innocent, he was rewarded on the spot, whether he liked it or not. There was no escape from the judgments of the king's arena.

The institution was a very popular one. When the people gathered together on one of the great trial days, they never knew whether they were to witness a bloody slaughter or a hilarious wedding. This element of uncertainty lent an interest to the occasion which it could not otherwise have attained. Thus, the masses were entertained and pleased; and the thinking part of the community could bring no charge of unfairness against this plan, for did not the accused person have the whole matter in his own hands?

This semi-barbaric king had a daughter as blooming as his most florid fancies and with a soul as fervent and impervious as his own. As is usual in such cases, she was the apple of his eye and was loved by him above all humanity. Among his courtiers was a young man of that firmness of blood and lowness of station common to the conventional heroes of romance who love royal maidens. This royal maiden was well satisfied with her lover, for he was handsome and brave to a degree unsurpassed in all this kingdom; and she loved him with an ardor that had enough of barbarism in it to make it exceedingly warm and strong. This love affair moved on happily for many months, until one day the king happened to discover its existence. He did not hesitate nor waver in regard to his duty in the premises. The youth was immediately cast into prison, and a day was appointed for his trial in the king's arena. This, of course, was an especially important occasion; and His Majesty, as well as all the people, was greatly interested in the workings and development of this trial. Never before had such a case occurred; never before had a subject dared to love the daughter of a king.

---

3. **epithalamic measure**\ĕ·pĭ·thal ▴a·mĭc\ a wedding song.

In after years such things became commonplace enough; but then they were, in no slight degree, novel and startling.

The tiger cages of the kingdom were searched for the most savage and relentless beasts, from which the fiercest monster might be selected for the arena; and the ranks of maiden youth and beauty throughout the land were carefully surveyed by competent judges in order that the young man might have a fitting bride in case fate did not determine for him a different destiny. Of course, everybody knew that the deed with which the accused was charged had been done. He had loved the princess, and neither he, she, nor anyone else thought of denying the fact; but the king would not think of allowing any fact of this kind to interfere with the working of the tribunal, in which he took such great delight and satisfaction. No matter how the affair turned out, the youth would be disposed of; and the king would take an aesthetic pleasure in watching the course of events, which would determine whether or not the young man had done wrong in allowing himself to love the princess.

The appointed day arrived. From far and near the people gathered and thronged the great galleries of the arena; and crowds, unable to gain admittance, massed themselves against its outside walls. The king and his court were in their places, opposite the twin doors—those fateful portals, so terrible in their similarity.

All was ready. The signal was given. A door beneath the royal party opened, and the lover of the princess walked into the arena. Tall, beautiful, fair, his appearance was greeted with a low hum of admiration and anxiety. Half the audience had not known so grand a youth had lived among them. No wonder the princess loved him! What a terrible thing for him to be there!

As the youth advanced into the arena, he turned, as the custom was, to bow to the king; but he did not think at all of that royal personage; his eyes were fixed upon the princess who sat to the right of her father. Had it not been for the moiety[4] of barbarism in her nature, it is probable that lady would not have been there; but her intense and fervid soul would not allow her to be absent on an occasion in which she was so terribly interested. From the moment that the decree had gone forth, that her lover should decide his fate in the king's arena, she had thought of nothing, night or day, but this great event and the various subjects connected with it. Possessed of more power, influence, and force of character than anyone who had ever before been interested in such a case, she had done what no other person had done—she had possessed herself of the secret of the doors. She knew in which of the two rooms that lay behind those doors stood the cage of the tiger, with its open front, and in which waited the lady. Through these thick doors, heavily curtained with skins on the inside, it was impossible that any noise or suggestion should come from within to the person who should approach to raise the latch of one of them; but gold, and the power of a woman's will, had brought the secret to the princess.

And not only did she know in which room stood the lady ready to emerge, all blushing and radiant, should her door be opened, but she knew who the lady was. It was one of the fairest and loveliest of the damsels of the court who had been selected as the reward of the accused youth, should he be proved innocent of the crime of aspiring to one so far above him; and the princess hated her. Often had she seen, or imagined that she had seen, this fair creature throwing glances of admiration upon the person of her lover; and sometimes she thought these glances were perceived and even returned. Now and then she had seen them talking together; it was but for a moment or two, but much can be said in a brief space; it may have been on most unimportant topics, but how could she know that? The girl was lovely, but she had dared to raise her eyes to the loved one of the princess; and, with all the intensity of the savage blood transmitted to

---

4. **moiety**\ˈmɔi·ə·tē\ half portion.

her through long lines of wholly barbaric ancestors, she hated the woman who blushed and trembled behind the silent door.

When her lover turned and looked at her, and his eyes met hers as she sat there paler and whiter than anyone in the vast ocean of anxious faces about her, he saw, by that power of quick perception which is given to those whose souls are one, that she knew behind which door crouched the tiger and behind which stood the lady. He had expected her to know it. He understood her nature; and his soul was assured that she would never rest until she had made plain to herself this thing, hidden to all other lookers-on, even to the king. The only hope for the youth in which there was any element of certainty was based upon the success of the princess in discovering this mystery; and the moment he looked upon her, he saw she had succeeded, as in his soul he knew she would succeed.

Then it was his quick and anxious glance asked the question: "Which?" It was as plain to her as if he shouted it from where he stood. There was not an instant to be lost. The question was asked in a flash; it must be answered in another.

Her right arm lay on the cushioned parapet before her. She raised her hand, and made a slight, quick movement toward the right. No one but her lover saw her. Every eye but his was fixed on the man in the arena.

He turned, and with a firm and rapid step he walked across the empty space. Every heart stopped beating, every breath was held, every eye was fixed immovable upon that man. Without the slightest hesitation, he went to the door on the right and opened it.

Now, the point of the story is this: Did the tiger come out of that door, or did the lady?

The more we reflect upon this question the harder it is to answer. It involves a study of the human heart which leads us through devious mazes of passion, out of which it is difficult to find our way. Think of it, fair reader, not as if the decision of the question depended upon yourself, but upon that hot-blooded, semi-barbaric princess, her soul at a white heat beneath the combined fires of despair and jealousy. She had lost him, but who should have him?

How often, in her waking hours and in her dreams, had she started in wild horror and covered her face with her hands as she thought of her lover opening the door on the other side of which waited the cruel fangs of the tiger!

But how much oftener had she seen him at the other door! How in her grievous reveries had she gnashed her teeth and torn her hair when she saw his start of rapturous delight as he opened the door of the lady! How her soul had burned in agony when she had seen him rush to meet that woman, with her flushing cheek and sparkling eye of triumph; when she had seen him lead her forth, his whole frame kindled with the joy of recovered life; when she had heard the loud shouts from the multitude and the wild ringing of the happy bells; when she had seen the priest with his joyous followers advance to the couple and make them man and wife before her very eyes; and when she had seen them walk away together upon their path of flowers, followed by the tremendous shouts of the hilarious multitude, in which her one despairing shriek was lost and drowned!

Would it not be better for him to die at once and go to wait for her in the blessed regions of semi-barbaric futurity?

And yet, that awful tiger, those shrieks, that blood!

Her decision had been indicated in an instant, but it had been made after days and nights of anguished deliberation. She had known she would be asked; she had decided what she would answer; and without the slightest hesitation, she had moved her hand to the right.

The question of her decision is not one to be lightly considered, and it is not for me to presume to set myself up as the one person able to answer it. And so I leave it all with you: Which came out of the opened door—the lady, or the tiger?

". . . it is the most valuable of all the gifts. . . ."

The Princess
and the
Tin Box

JAMES THURBER

Once upon a time, in a far country, there lived a king whose daughter was the prettiest princess in the world. Her eyes were like the cornflower, her hair was sweeter than the hyacinth, and her throat made the swan look dusty.

From the time she was a year old, the princess had been showered with presents. Her nursery looked like Cartier's window.[1] Her toys were all made of gold or platinum or diamonds or emeralds. She was not permitted to have wooden blocks or china dolls or rubber dogs or linen books, because such materials were considered cheap for the daughter of a king.

When she was seven, she was allowed to attend the wedding of her brother and throw real pearls at the bride instead of rice. Only the nightingale, with his lyre of gold, was permitted to sing for the princess. The common blackbird, with his boxwood flute, was kept out of the palace grounds. She walked in silver-and-samite slippers to a sapphire-and-topaz bathroom and slept in an ivory bed inlaid with rubies.

On the day the princess was eighteen, the king sent a royal ambassador to the courts of five neighboring kingdoms to announce that he would give his daughter's hand in marriage to the prince who brought her the gift she liked the most.

The first prince to arrive at the palace rode a swift white stallion and laid at the feet of the princess an enormous apple made of solid gold which he had taken from a dragon who had guarded it for a thousand years. It was placed on a long ebony table set up to hold the gifts of the princess's suitors. The second prince, who came on a gray charger, brought her a nightingale made of a thousand diamonds, and it was placed beside the golden apple. The third prince, riding on a black horse, carried a great jewel box made of platinum and sapphires, and it was placed next to the diamond nightingale. The fourth prince, astride a fiery yellow horse, gave the princess a gigantic heart made of rubies and pierced by an emerald arrow. It was placed next to the platinum-and-sapphire jewel box.

Now the fifth prince was the strongest and handsomest of all the five suitors, but he was the son of a poor king whose realm had been overrun by mice and locusts and wizards and mining engineers so that there was nothing much of value left in it. He came plodding up to the palace of the princess on a plow horse, and he brought her a small tin box filled with mica and feldspar and hornblende which he had picked up on the way.

The other princes roared with disdainful laughter when they saw the tawdry gift the fifth prince had brought to the princess. But she examined it with great interest and squealed with delight, for all her life she had been glutted with precious stones and priceless metals, but she had never seen tin before or mica or feldspar or hornblend. The tin box was placed next to the ruby heart pierced with an emerald arrow.

"Now," the king said to his daughter, "you must select the gift you like best and marry the prince that brought it."

The princess smiled and walked up to the table and picked up the present she liked most. It was the platinum-and-sapphire jewel box, the gift of the third prince.

"The way I figure it," she said, "is this. It is

1. **Cartier's**\\ˈkär·tē·āz\ a famous jeweler in New York.

a very large and expensive box, and when I am married, I will meet many admirers who will give me precious gems with which to fill it to the top. Therefore, it is the most valuable of all the gifts my suitors have brought me and I like it the best."

The princess married the third prince that very day in the midst of great merriment and high revelry. More than a hundred thousand pearls were thrown at her and she loved it.

Moral: All those who thought the princess was going to select the tin box filled with worthless stones instead of one of the other gifts will kindly stay after class and write one hundred times on the blackboard "I would rather have a hunk of aluminum silicate than a diamond necklace."

I
TWO GIRLS MAKE UP THEIR MINDS

By far the most popular thing Frank Stockton ever wrote was the short story first titled "In the King's Arena." Originally, it was intended to be read as part of an evening's entertainment at a party for friends. However, the party turned out to be one of gay confusion, and Stockton decided not to read his story. Later, he reworked it a bit and sent it to *Century Magazine*, which bought it for $50.

Eventually his story was published under the title, "The Lady, or the Tiger?" Almost immediately it became a literary sensation, with the solution to the problem it presented being discussed all over the country.

Robert Browning, famous British writer, after being asked to read the story and give his opinion, decided without hesitation that the princess directed her lover to the tiger's door.

1. There are many who believe that Stockton himself suggested the decision the princess made. In debating whether or not you believe this to be true, consider and discuss:

a. Stockton's repeated reference to the girl as hot-blooded and semi-barbaric;

b. Lines which indicate that the princess was uncertain that her love was fully returned;

c. The feeling the princess had for the damsel who was behind the closed door;

d. The fact that Stockton was regarded as a realist who used his fairy tales to put across truths which he felt he could not do otherwise.

2. Find any passages that seem to support the opposite theory—that the princess would choose to let her lover live, even though she lost him. Discuss.

3. Discuss the ways in which Stockton's description of the king and his methods of dispensing justice are slyly humorous or satirical.

4. What was the decision which Thurber's princess had to make? How did she explain her choice? With what moral did Thurber conclude his fable? What does he suggest is all-important to most people at the present time?

II
IMPLICATIONS

Consider and discuss.

The tremendous popularity of "The Lady, or the Tiger?" stemmed almost entirely from the unanswered, perhaps unanswerable, human problems which Stockton set forth. He was deluged with so many thousands of letters begging a solution that he finally answered with a puzzling statement which brought satisfaction to very few: "If you decide which it was—the lady, or the tiger—you find out what kind of a person you are yourself."

1. Consider Stockton's statement carefully and discuss whether you agree that when you decide whether jealousy or love was the stronger influence on the princess, you reveal your own character.

2. The young man knew from the princess's nod which door he was opening.

III
TECHNIQUES
Beginnings and Endings

Thurber's aim in "The Princess and the Tin Box" is to make the reader *think* at the same time that he is being entertained. How does the author accomplish his purpose?

In the first place, Thurber knew quite a little bit about the ways people think and act. He knew that human beings are most comfortable doing things that fall into certain familiar patterns.

1. Explain why the four familiar words at the very beginning of Thurber's story lead the reader to assume that the tale will end with four other equally well-known words.

2. Much of Thurber's humor depends on using some expression, comparison, or idea that seems out of place or not in harmony with what has gone before. For example, in the second sentence, why does the comparison ". . . and her throat made the swan look dusty" seem to be not quite what one might expect in such a story? Find one other example and discuss why it, too, seems out of place.

3. Thurber describes how the princess had been reared in great and exaggerated luxury, yet the reader is not prepared to accept the rather logical decision the princess finally makes. Why?

4. Stockton's story has been said to have no ending. Discuss. Which of the two stories do you believe you will remember longer? Why?

SUMMING UP

Moments of Decision

THEME

The decisions read about in MOMENTS OF DECISION are as varied as the personalities of the individuals who made them. Yet in looking back over the selections, one can discover some of the general patterns into which decisions fall.

By far the greatest number of decisions are *routine* and are made without much thought; many are *planned* and take a great deal of thought; some are *emergency* decisions and arise from the need for immediate action with no time for the lengthy consideration of various possibilities. Choices made under any of these conditions, of course, might be thought of as either morally good or morally bad, and might win approval or disapproval.

Whether, like Robert Frost, a person must decide which road to take, or whether, like John Bagley, he is suddenly thrust into a position where he must make many critical decisions quickly, his background of experience will determine to a large extent the kinds of choices he will make and the ease with which he will make them.

IMPLICATIONS

Summary Statements

One of the following should be selected as a topic for a paper of some length. In enlarging upon the subject chosen, you will probably want to use ideas gained from the unit selections, the study materials, outside research, and personal experience.

About People

1. "There is no more miserable human being than one in whom nothing is habitual but indecision."—William James (American psychologist and philosopher)

2. Excessive ambition brings moral decay.

3. Most people would make a better decision if they were given a second chance.

4. Since what is to be, will be, any decision an individual makes is of little consequence.

5. The decisions an individual makes are influenced by reading literary selections which deal with making decisions.

6. Any person in an official capacity should be held personally responsible for any decisions he makes.

7. Most individuals have a set of values established early in life which determine the kinds of decisions they make.

TECHNIQUES

1. Compare Aesop's fable, of father and sons, THE INNER CIRCLE, page 276, with Thurber's fable in this section, "The Princess and the Tin Box." In what ways do they differ with respect to: (a) purpose, (b) language, (c) ending?

2. Decide which character from the preceding group of selections is most memorable for you. Discuss why this is true, keeping in mind the author's skill and your own background of experience.

3. The use of deliberate exaggeration is one of the most frequently used ways of achieving humor. However, using exaggeration well is a most difficult feat. So many times when one tries it the result is not humorous, but ludicrous. Note the ways the authors James Thurber and Ellis Parker Butler employ this technique, then try your hand at writing a paper in which you use exaggeration to add humor. These papers should prove interesting to read aloud in class.

Was the strength and wisdom
of her twenty-three years enough to help her
make the desperate decisions demanded
of her? Lecia Terry, a young schoolteacher,
found herself beset by fears.
Based on the true experience
of the author's niece during the terrible
blizzard of 1949, this short novel presents a
realistic picture of what might have
happened to any group of boys and girls
going to a country school located in an isolated
section of the Nebraska plains during
this time.
Winter Thunder begins quietly.
Read carefully so that you will not fail to
feel the atmosphere of loneliness,
isolation, and impending disaster that
Mari Sandoz builds from the start.

WINTER THUNDER

MARI SANDOZ

The snow began quietly this time, like an afterthought to the gray Sunday night. The moon almost broke through once, but toward daylight a little wind came up and started white curls, thin and lonesome, running over the old drifts left from the New Year storm. Gradually the snow thickened, until around eight-thirty the two ruts of the winding trails were covered and undisturbed except down in the Lone Tree district, where an old yellow bus crawled heavily along, feeling out the ruts between the choppy sand hills.

As the wind rose the snow whipped against the posts of a ranch fence across the trail, and

caked against the bus windows, shutting in the young faces pressed to the glass. The storm increased until all the air was a powdery white and every hill, every trace of road, was obliterated. The bus wavered and swayed in its direction, the tracks filling in close upon the wheels as they sought out the trail lost somewhere far back, and then finally grasped at any footing, until it looked like some great snowy, bewildered bug seen momentarily through the shifting wind. But it kept moving, hesitating here, stalling there in the deepening drifts, bucking heavily into them, drawing back to try once more while the chains spun out white fans that were lost in the driving snow which seemed almost as thick, as dense. Once the bus had to back down from a steep little patch that might have led into a storm-lost valley with a ranch house and warmth and shelter. It started doggedly around, slower now, but decisive, feeling cautiously for traction on the drifted hillside. Then the wheels began to slip, catch, and then slip again, the bus tipping precariously in the push of the wind, a cry inside lost under the rising noise of the storm.

For a long time it seemed that the creeping bus could not be stopped. Even when all discernible direction or purpose was finally gone, it still moved, backing, starting again, this way and that, plowing the deepened slope, swaying, leaning until it seemed momentarily very tall and held from toppling only by the thickness of the flying snow. Once more a wheel caught and held under the thunder of the red-hot smoking exhaust. It slipped, and held again, but now the force of the wind was too great. For a moment the tilting bus seemed to lift. Then it pivoted into a slow skid and turned half around, broadside. Slowly it went over, almost as though without weight at all, settling lightly against a drift, to become a part of it at that thickening place where the white storm turned to snowbanks, lost except that there were frightening cries from inside, and a hiss of steam and smoke from the hot engine against the snow.

In a moment the door was forced outward,

the wind catching a puff of smoke as dark, muffled heads pushed up and were white in an instant. They were children, mostly in snow-suits and in sheepskin coats, thrust down over the bus side, coughing and gasping as the force of the blizzard struck them, the older ones hunching their shoulders to shield themselves and some of the rest.

Once more the engine roared out and the upper back wheel spun on its side, free and foolish in its awkward caking of snow. Then the young woman who had handed the children down followed them, her sheepskin collar up about her head, her arms full of blankets and lunch boxes.

"You'll have to give it up, Chuck," she called back into the smoking interior. "Quick! Bring the rest of the lunches—"

With Chuck, sixteen and almost as tall as a man, beside her, Lecia Terry pushed the frightened huddle of children together and hurried them away downwind into the wall of storm. Once she tried to look back through the smother of snow, wishing that they might have taken the rope and shovel from the toolbox. But there was no time to dig for them on the under side now.

Back at the bus thick smoke was sliding out the door into the snow that swept along the side. Flames began to lick up under the leaning windows, the caking of ice suddenly running from them. The glass held one moment and burst, and the flames whipped out, torn away by the storm as the whole bus was suddenly a wet, shining yellow that blistered and browned with the heat. Then there was a dull explosion above the roar of the wind, and down the slope the fleeing little group heard it and thought they saw a dark fragment fly past overhead.

"Well, I guess that was the gas tank going," Chuck shouted as he tried to peer back under his shielding cap. But there was only the blizzard closed in around them, and the instinctive fear that these swift storms brought to all living creatures, particularly the young.

There was sobbing among the children now, a small one crying out, "Teacher! Teacher!"

inside the thick scarf about her face, clutching for Lecia in her sudden panic.

"Sh-h, Joanie. I'm right here," the young woman soothed, drawing the six-year-old to her, looking around for the others, already so white that she could scarcely see them in the powdery storm.

"Bill, will you help Chuck pack all the lunches in two, three boxes, tight, so nothing gets lost? Maggie's big sirup bucket'll hold a lot. Throw all the empties away. We'll have to travel light—" she said, trying to make it sound a little like an old joke.

"My father will be coming for me soon—" the eight-year-old Olive said primly. "So you need not touch my lunch."

"Nobody can find us here," Chuck said shortly, and the girl did not reply, too polite to argue. But now one of the small boys began to cry. "I want my own lunch box too, Teacher," he protested, breathless from the wind. "I—I want to go home!"

His older brother slapped him across the ear muffs with a mittened hand. "Shut up, Fritz," he commanded. "You can't go home. The bus is—" Then he stopped, looked toward the teacher, almost lost only an arm's length away, and the full realization of their plight struck him. "We can't go home," he said, so quietly that he could scarcely be heard in the wind. "The bus is burned and Chuck and Miss Lecia don't know where we are—"

"Sure we know!" Chuck shouted against him without looking up from the lunch packing, his long back stooped protectively over his task. "Don't we know, Lecia? Anyway, it won't last. Radio this morning said just light snow flurries, or Dad wouldn't have let me take the bus out 'stead of him, even sick as he was." The tall boy straightened up, the lunch boxes strung to the belt of his sheepskin to bang together in the wind until they were snow-crusted. "Baldy Stever'll be out with his plane looking for his girl friend soon's it clears a little, won't he, Lecia?" he said. "Like he came New Year's, with skis on it."

But the bold talk did not quiet the sobbing,

and the teacher's nod was lost in the storm as she tied scarves and mufflers across the faces of the younger children, leaving only little slits for the eyes, with the brows and lashes already furred with snow. Then she lined up the seven, mixing the ages from six-year-old Joanie to twelve-year-old Bill, who limped heavily as he moved in the deepening snow. One of the blankets she pinned around the thinly dressed Maggie, who had only a short outgrown coat, cotton stockings, and torn overshoes against the January storm. The other blanket she tied around herself, ready to carry Joanie on her back, Indian fashion, when the short little legs were worn out.[1]

Awkwardly, one after another, Lecia pulled the left arm of each pupil from the sleeve, buttoned it inside the coat and then tied the empty sleeve to the right arm of the one ahead. She took the lead, with little Joanie tied to her belt, where she could be helped. Chuck was at the tail end of the clumsy little queue, just behind Bill with the steel-braced ankle.

"Never risk getting separated," Lecia remembered hearing her pioneer grandfather say when he told of burying the dead from the January blizzard of 1888 here, the one still called the school children's storm. "Never get separated and never stop moving until you find shelter—"

The teacher squinted back along the line, moving like some long snowy winter-logged animal, the segmented back bowed before the sharpening blizzard wind. Just the momentary turn into the storm took her breath and frightened her for these children hunched into themselves, half of them crying softly, hopelessly, as though already lost. They must hurry. With not a rock anywhere and not a tree within miles to show the directions, they had to seek out the landmark of the ranch country—the wire fence. So the girl started downwind again, breaking the new drifts as she searched for valley ground where fences were most likely, barbed-wire fences that might lead to a ranch, or nowhere except around some hay meadow. But it was their only chance the girl from the sand hills

knew. Stumbling, floundering through the snow, she kept the awkward string moving, the eyes of the older ones straining through frozen lashes for even the top of one fence post, those of the small ones turned in upon their fear as the snow caked on the mufflers over their faces and they stumbled blindly to the pull from ahead.

Once there was a bolt of lightning, milky white in the blizzard, and a shaking of thunder, ominous winter thunder that stopped the moving feet. Almost at once the wind grew sharper, penetrating even Chuck's heavy sheepskin coat, numbing the ears and feet as panting, sobbing, the children plowed on again, the new drifts soon far above Lecia's boots, and no visibility, no way to avoid them.

With their hands so awkwardly useless, someone stumbled every few steps, but the first to fall was the crippled Bill, the others, the crying ones too, standing silent in the storm, not even able to slap one frozen hand against another while the boy was helped up. After that others went down, and soon it was all that the teacher and the boy Chuck could do to keep the children moving as they pushed through the chop hills and found themselves going up what seemed a long wind-swept, wind-frozen slope, Lecia carrying Joanie on her back most of the time now. But they kept moving somehow, barely noticing even the jack rabbit that burst out among their feet and was gone into the storm. Otherwise there was nothing.

After a long, long time they reached what seemed a high ridge of hills standing across the full blast of the north wind that bent them low and blinded. Suddenly Chuck's feet slid off sideways into a hole, a deep-cupped blowout hidden by the storm. Before he could stop, he had drawn the rest tumbling in after him, with an avalanche of snow. Crying, frightened, the smaller ones were set to their feet and brushed off a little. Then they all crouched together under the bank to catch their breath out of the

---

1. She was ready to carry Joanie on her back as an Indian squaw carried a baby.

wind, shivering, wet from the snow that had fallen inside their clothes, which were already freezing hard as board.

"With the blowouts always from the northwest to the southeast," Chuck shouted into the teacher's covered ear, "the wind's plainly from the north, so we're being pushed about due south. That direction there can't be a house for five, six miles, even if we could find it—unless we got clear out of our home country—"

The girl shivered, empty with fear. "—So that's why we haven't found a fence," she said slowly. "We're probably in the old Bar M summer range, miles and miles across. But we can't go any other direction—"

"I could alone; I could make it out alone!" Chuck shouted suddenly, angrily.

For a moment the teacher was silent, waiting, but when he added nothing more, she said: "You can't leave these little ones now, Chuck. Even if you were sure you could find a ranch—"

There was no reply, except that the crippled boy began to cry, a reddening from his ankle coming up through the snow that was packed into his overshoes around the brace. Others were sobbing too, and shaking with cold, but the younger ones were very quiet now, already drowsing, and so the young teacher had to get to her feet and help lift the children out of the blowout. Slapping the muffler-covered cheeks, shaking the smaller ones so hard that the caked snow fell from them, she got the line moving again, but very slowly. She was worn out too, from the path-breaking and with Joanie in her arms to warm the child, keep her from the sleep of freezing that came upon her on Lecia's back, with only the thin blanket against the ice of the wind.

They seemed to be going down now, through a long deep-drifted slope, plowing into buried yucca clumps, the sharp spears penetrating the snowsuits, even the boot tops. Here a few head of cattle passed them, less than three feet away and barely to be seen. They were running, snow-caked, blinded, bawling, and Lecia squinted anxiously back into the storm for others, for a herd that might be upon them, trample them as surely as stampeding buffaloes. But there were no more now, and she could see that Chuck was shouting, "Little chance of its clearing up soon, with that snow thunder and those cattle already drifting so fast—all the way from the winter range!"

Yes, drifting fast with the force and terror of the storm, even hardy, thick-haired range cattle running!

Then suddenly one of the younger boys cried out something. "Teacher!" he repeated, "I saw a post!"

But it must have been a trick of the wind, for there was only the driving snow, except that the sharp-eyed Maggie saw one too, ahead and to the right—a snowy post with only the upper foot or so out of the drifts, holding up a strand of gray wire taut and humming in the cold.

For a moment Lecia could not see through the blurring of her eyes. At least this was something to follow, but which way? To her signal Chuck lifted his arm and dropped it. He didn't recognize the fence either, and so the teacher took the easier direction, leftward, only sideface to the wind, although it might lead to the hills, to some final drift as the fleeing cattle would end.

Moving slowly along the fence, Lecia knew that it could not be much farther anyway. Her arms were wooden with cold and the weight of the child, her legs so weary in the deepening drifts that with each step it seemed that she could never lift a snow-caked boot again.

Then suddenly Chuck was doubling up the line. "I think I know where we are! That old split post just back there's where we made a take-down running coyotes with Dad's hounds this fall. If I'm right, this is Miller's north meadow, and there's a strip of willows down ahead there, off to the right—"

For a moment the girl set Joanie into the deep snow, panting, and even when she caught her breath, she was afraid to speak.

"How far to a house?" she finally asked, her lips frozen.

"There's no house along this fence if it's the

Miller," Chuck had to admit. "It just goes around the meadow, three, four miles long."

"You're sure—" the teacher asked slowly, "—sure there's no cross fence to the ranch? You might get through, find help in time—"

The boy could only shake his snowy head and then, thinking that the storm hid this, he shouted the words on the wind. No, no cross fence, and the ranch was five miles south. Not even a haystack left in the valley here. Miller had had his hay balers in this fall, hauled it all out for his fancy Angus herd.

Then they must take a chance on the willows, with Bill hardly able to limp along, Joanie too heavy to carry, and several others worn out. So they wallowed through the drifted fence and tried to keep parallel to its direction, but far enough in the meadow to see any willows. There must be willows now.

Suddenly Lecia went down in what must have been a deep gully, the ground gone, the girl sinking into soft powdery snow to her shoulder. Panting, choking, she managed to get Joanie and the rest back out and the frightened ones quieted a little. Then she swung off right along the barer edge of the gully, seeking a place to cross. The wind was blowing in powerful gusts now, so that she could scarcely stand up. Bent low she dragged at the line behind her, most of the children crawling in the trench she plowed for them. There was no crying now—only the slow, slow moving. Perhaps they should dig into the snow here below the gully bank. Indians and trappers had done that and survived. But they had thick-furred buffalo robes to shut out the cold and snow, and they were grown men, tough, strong—not helpless, worn-out children, their frozen feet heavy as stone, with only an overgrown boy and a twenty-three-year-old girl to lead them, keep them alive.

More and more often Lecia had to stop, her head down, her arms dropping the weight of the little girl. But there seemed to be a shallowing in the gully now, and so it was time she tried to break a path through it and turned back toward the fence if they were not to wander

lost as so many did that other time, long ago, when a teacher and her nine pupils were lost, finally falling to die on the prairie. They must cling to the fence here, if it went no farther than around the meadow. At least it was proof that something existed on the earth except the thick, stinging blizzard, with a white, freezing, plodding little queue caught in the heart of it, surrounded.

Once when the girl looked up from the running snow it seemed there was something darkish off to the right, little farther than arm's reach away. She saw it again, something rounded, perhaps a willow clump, low, snow filled, and possibly with more near by. Signaling to Chuck, Lecia turned down to it—a willow covered as in sleep, but with at least two more bushes just beyond, larger, darker, and standing closer together, their longer upper arms snow-weighted, entwined over the drifts. There, between the clumps, out of the worst of the storm, she left the children squatted close, the blankets held over them. With the belts of her coat and Chuck's, they tied the longer brushy tops of the two clumps together as solidly as they could. Then, fighting the grasping wind, they managed to fasten the blankets across the gap between the willows, to hold awhile. Behind this protection Lecia dug through the snow to the frozen ground while Chuck gathered dead wood. Inside a close little kneeling circle of children they built a fire pile with some dry inner bark and a piece of sandwich paper for the lighting. Awkwardly, with freezing hands the teacher and Chuck hurried, neither daring to think about matches, dry ones, in any pocket after this stumbling and falling through the snow.

The two smaller children were dropping into the heavy sleep of exhaustion and cold and had to be held in their places by the older ones while Chuck dug swiftly through his pockets, deeper, more awkwardly, then frantically, the circle of peering eyes like those of fearful young animals, cornered, winter-trapped.

Down to his shirt, Chuck found some in his pocket, six in a holder made of two rifle cartridges slipped together. Hurrying clumsily he struck one of the matches. It sputtered and went out, the flames sucked away. They had to try again, making a closer circle, with the coat-tails of the children thrown up over their heads to shut out the storm. This time the match caught on the waxed paper and the diamond willow began to snap and sizzle in the snow, throwing a dancing light up to the circle of crouching children.

But it seemed even colder now that they had stopped walking and Lecia thought of the night ahead, with the temperature surely down to twenty-five or thirty below zero. Beyond that she would not look now; but to get through this night they must have a great pile of wood, and they must have shelter even to hold the fire.

"We can't both go out at one time," the teacher told Chuck in their planning, somehow making it seem as for a long, long time. "It's too risky for the children. We might not get back."

The boy looked around from the fire he was nursing, and upward, but there was still no thinning of the storm, the area of snowy visibility almost as small as the confines of their new meat-freeze room[2] at the ranch. Even so he gave the girl no sign of agreement.

Lecia set willow poles into the snowbanks as she went to look for wood, none farther apart than the outstretched reach of her arms. She found more willows, each clump sitting alone in the isolation of the driving storm, so cold now that the green wood snapped off like glass. Each time it was only by the row of sticks in the drifts that she managed to stagger her blinded and panting way back against the wind with her load of wood.

The brushier portions she piled behind the blankets of the shelter to catch the snow and shut out the wind. Some, long as fish poles, she pushed through the willow clumps and across the opening between, in a sort of lattice inside the bellying blankets that Eddie and Calla tried to hold in place. They were the first of the children to separate themselves from the snowy

composite, the enforced co-ordinate that had been the queue driven by the storm, the circle that shielded the sprouting fire. Now they were once more individuals who could move alone, hold the blankets from blowing inward, pile the dry powdery snow from the ground against and between the sticks, trying to work it like plaster, building a wall between the clumps of willows. Even Bill helped a little, as far as he could reach without moving the bad ankle. They worked slowly, clumsily, pounding their freezing hands at the fire, but returning.

By one o'clock the north wind was cut off so that the fire fattened and burned higher, soften-ing the ice caked to the clothing until it could be knocked off, and softening the face of the drift reached by the wind-blown heat. The children packed this against the north wall too, and into the willow clumps both ways, draw-ing the rounded wall inward toward the top along the bend of the willows, making what looked like half of an Indian snow shelter, or the wickiup Calla had seen at the county fair, just high enough at the center for a seven-year-old to stand up, the snow walls glistening rosy in the firelight as the wind was shut off.

"That's a good job!" Chuck shouted over the roar of the storm as he tried to rub circulation into Joanie's waxen feet. The small girl was be-ginning to cry out of her sleep with the first pain; others began too, their ears and hands swollen and purpling, their toes painful as their boots thawed. But it seemed that the feet of nine-year-old Maggie must be lost, the ragged old overshoes and cotton stockings so frozen that she had to cut them away with Eddie's knife. Under them her feet were like stone, dead white stone, although the girl was work-ing hard to rub life into them. She worked silently and alone, as had become natural long ago, her thin face pinched and anxious with the pain and the alarm.

Of them all only Olive seemed untouched. She was dry in her heavy waterproofed snow-

---

2. **The meat-freeze room** was the compartment in which meat was frozen for keeping.

suit with attached rubber feet inside the snow
boots. And she was still certain that her father
would soon come for her.

"He would not care to leave me in such an
unpleasant place—"

When they had the semicircular wall of the
shelter drawn in as far as the snow would hold,
Lecia decided to pull the blankets away from
the outside and use one over the top, with the
belt-tied willows sticking through a smoke hole
cut in the center. But as the blankets came
down, part of the loose snow wall was blown
in by the force of the blizzard, the huddle of
children suddenly white again, the fire almost
smothered. So the wall had to be rebuilt in discouragement, but with care, using more brush
and sticks, more fire-softened snow to freeze
in place as soon as it was struck by the storm.
Lecia had to stop several times for her hands
too, pounding them hard, holding them over
the fire, the diamond sparkling. She tried to
turn the ring off before the swelling became
too great and then gave it up. The wall must
be finished, and when it was solid, Calla came
to whisper under the roar of the wind. "Bill's
been eating the lunch," she said.

"Oh, Bill! That's not fair to the others, to
your own little sister Joanie!" Lecia cried. Suddenly not the good teacher, she grabbed up the
containers and hung them on high branches
out in plain sight for watching, for reminders
and derision from the other children. "Why, it
may be days before we are found!" she scolded,
in her exasperation saying what should have
been kept hidden in silence.

Before the boy could defend himself with a
plea of hunger or his usual complaint about
the crippled foot, some realization of their
plight had struck the others. Even little Fritz,
with the security of an older sister and brother
like Calla and Eddie along, began to sob. Only
the round-cheeked Olive was calm, the others
angered to see it, wanting to shout against her
outsider's assurance, to tell her she was too
stupid and green to know that her father could
not come for her in such a blizzard, that he
would never find her if he could get through.

But they were silent under the teacher's admonitory eye. And, as in the schoolhouse and
on the playground, Bill had withdrawn, except
that now it could not be more than a foot or
two.

As the frozen earth between the willow
humps became soggy, Calla and Eddie helped
move the others around so that there was room
to draw the fire first one way and then another,
to dry and warm the ground. Lecia watched to
see that they set no one afire and then bowed
her head out into the storm again. Chuck was
dragging in willows for the night. They drove
sticks into the hardening drifts around the front
of the shelter and piled brush against them to
catch the snow. It filled in as fast as they
worked until there was no more than a little
crawling hole left. Then Chuck laid a mat of

715

brushy sticks on the ground and packed soft snow into them to freeze, making a handled slab big enough to close the low doorway. Now, so long as the blanket with the smoke hole stayed tied over the top they could be as warm as they wished in the little shelter that was scarcely longer than a tall man—a close cramping for the teacher, Chuck, and the seven pupils, but easily warmed with a few fingers of wood, an Indian fire.[3] Safe and warm so long as the shelter stood against the rising ferocity of the blizzard, and the willows lasted.

By now the cold stung the nose and burned the lungs, the snow turned to sharp crystals that drew blood from the bare skin. It drove the teacher and Chuck in to the fire, shaking, unable, it seemed, ever to be warmed through again. Lecia opened her sheepskin coat, hung up her frozen scarf and cap and shook out her thick brown hair that gleamed in the firelight. Even with her tawny skin red and swollen, her gold-flecked hazel eyes bloodshot, she was still a pretty girl, and the diamond on her hand flashed as she hunted for her stick of white salve to pass around for the raw, bleeding lips. It was all she could do.

Now they tried to plan for what was to come, but here they were as blind as in the flight through the storm. There would be sickness, with the noses already running, Joanie coughing deep from her chest, and, worst of all, Maggie's feet that seemed to be dying. Besides, the fire must be kept going and the food spread over three, perhaps four, days.

Here Bill raised his complaining voice. "You ain't our boss outside of school! We'll do what we want to. There ain't enough to eat for everybody."

"You mean *isn't*, not *ain't*," the teacher corrected firmly. "And talking like that—when you've barely missed one lunch time!"

"You ain't never my boss," Chuck said casually, "—only about the kids while in the bus, like you do with my dad when he's driving. I sure can do what I want to here, and I'll do it."

Slowly the girl looked around the ring of drowsy, firelit eyes upon her, some uneasy at this bold talk to their teacher, but some smaller ones aping the defiance of the big boys. Chuck, who sat almost a head taller than Lecia, grinned down at the pretty young teacher but with an arrogance that was intended to remind her he saw nothing here as his responsibility, nothing this side of the bus except saving himself.

Unable to reply in words that would not frighten the children more, the teacher looked past the fire into the boy's broad, defiant face, into his unblinking, storm-red eyes, the look commanding at first, then changing to something else in spite of herself, into a sort of public test, until it seemed she dared not turn her gaze away or at that instant the sixteen-year-old boy must assert his victory by plunging out into the storm and perhaps destroy himself, perhaps bring death to all of them.

Before this silent, incomprehensible struggle the children were uneasy and afraid, even the coughing stilled, so that the storm seemed very loud outside the smoke hole. But little Fritz was too young to be held so for long. "I'm hungry!" he shouted against the restraining hand of his sister. "I want my lunch!"

As though freed, released, Chuck sat back and grinned a little at the small boy. Matter of factly the teacher washed her raw hands with snow and held them over the fire. Then she spread her napkin on her lap and set out all there was in the eight lunches now: fourteen sandwiches, most of them large, six pieces of Sunday cake, a handful of cookies, a few pieces of candy, and six apples and two oranges, frozen hard. There were two thermos bottles of milk, and these Lecia pushed away into the snow wall.

"If somebody gets sick and can't eat solid food," she said to the owners, their eyes following her hands in consternation. Even with the best management, there would be no food of any kind in a few days, but this the small owners could not yet understand.

---

3. **An Indian fire** is a small fire near which one can crouch or huddle for warmth.

The frozen fruit she handed to Chuck and, without meeting the girl's eyes, he set it around the coals for toasting, to be eaten now because it would not keep well, and might sicken leaner stomachs. In the meantime Lecia set one lunch box filled with snow near the fire and packed away all except four of the big sandwiches into the others, the eyes of the children following her hands here too, even as she hung the containers back above her head. Then she divided the four sandwiches into halves and passed them around.

"Eat very slowly," she cautioned. "Blizzards usually last three days, so we must make what we have here last too, probably clear to Thursday, or longer."

But Bill seemed not to be listening. "Chuck's eating!" he suddenly protested. "He ain't, *isn't*, in on the lunches."

For a moment the teacher looked sternly at the boy. "After Chuck carried them all from the bus, helped you through the bad places, and helped to make the shelter and the fire!" the girl said in astonishment. "Now we'll have no more of this bickering and complaint. Here we are equal partners, and not one of us will get out of this alive unless we keep working together. Even your comic books should have taught you that much! And don't think this is play. You remember what the storm of 1888 was called in your history book—because so many school children died in it. That storm was short, not over two days most places, nothing for length like the one we had holiday time this year, and no telling about this one. Most of the children in 1888 died because somebody got panicky, didn't think, or they didn't stick together—"

There was silence all around the fire now, the storm seeming to rise, the children edging closer to each other, glancing fearfully over their shoulders as though toward night windows with terrible things stalking outside.

"Oh, we're O.K.," Chuck said optimistically. "We can last three days easy here—" the rebellion gone from him, or hidden for the moment.

Thinking of a five-day storm, the teacher looked around the frightened, sooty faces, the children coughing and sniffling, their pocket tissue gone, the few handkerchiefs hung to dry and wondered if any, even the man-tall Chuck, would be here by then.

But Olive, the newcomer, was unconcerned. "I should like another sandwich, Miss Terry. From my own lunch, please," she said, with the formality of an old-fashioned boarding school for eight-year-olds. "I won't need the remainder. My father will come for me when it is time."

"He won't find you—" Maggie said as she rubbed at her feet, color seeping into them now, an angry gray-splotched purple, with pain that twisted the thin face.

"My father will come," Olive repeated, plainly meaning that he was not like the fathers of the others here, particularly Maggie's, who had done nothing since the war except make a little South Pacific bug juice,[4] as he called it, for himself from chokecherries, wild grapes, or raisins in the way they did in the war. He had only a little piece of copper tubing, and so he couldn't make more than enough for himself, yet he got into jail just the same, for crashing his old truck through the window of the county assistance office.[5] But things had not been good before that. Often this fall Maggie was at school when the bus arrived, not waiting at the stop near their crumbling old sod shack but walking the three miles. Sometimes her face was bruised, but she was silent to any questioning. If Maggie lost her feet now, it was because she had no warm snowsuit and high boots like the others, only the short old coat above her skinny knees, the broken overshoes with the soles flopping.

But there was still a cheerful face at the fire. Although little Fritz's cheeks seemed swollen to bursting and his frosted ears stood away

---

4. **South Pacific bug juice** is a designation for a homemade brandy of high alcoholic content.
5. **The county assistance office** is the relief office caring for the needy or the unemployed.

under the flaps of his cap, he could still show his gap-toothed grin in mischief.

"If we don't get home till Thursday, Teacher, Baldy'll be awful mad at you when he comes flying out Wednesday—"

The rest laughed a little, drowsily. "Maybe Baldy won't be flying around that soon," Eddie said, and was corrected by Calla's sisterly concern. "Don't say Baldy. Say Mr. Stever."

But the teacher busied herself hanging up everything loose. Then with Chuck's knife she slit the remaining blanket down the middle and fastened half around each side against the snow wall, like a tipi lining. By the time the white blizzard darkness came, the smaller children had all been taken outside for the last time and lay in fretful, uneasy sleep. Olive had been the last, waiting stubbornly for her father until she toppled forward. Calla caught her and made room for the girl still murmuring, "Papa—"

Finally the last sob for parent and home was stilled, even Joanie asleep, her feverish head in the teacher's lap, her throat raw and swelling, with nothing except hot snow water to ease the hollow cough. There were half a dozen lozenges in Lecia's pocket but these must be saved for the worse time that would surely come.

The children were packed around the fire like little pigs or puppies on a very cold night. Chuck was at the opposite side from Lecia, the boys on his side, the girls on hers, with Calla and her brothers around the back. The older ones lay nearer the wall, their arms over the younger to hold their restlessness from the fire.

But Bill was still up, drawn back under the willows, his head pulled into his sheepskin collar, his ankle bent to him. He watched the teacher doze in fatigue, met her guilty waking gaze sullenly. But finally he reached down into his pocket and drew out something in waxed paper.

"I didn't eat the piece you gave me—" he said, holding out his half of the sandwich.

"Bill! That was fine of you," the girl said, too worn out for more as she reached up to put it away.

"No—no, you eat it. I guess you didn't take any."

A moment Lecia looked at the boy, but he avoided her as he edged himself around Chuck closer to the fire, turning his chilled back to the coals, and so she ate the buttered bread with the thick slice of strengthening cold beef, while more snow was driven in through the smoke hole and settled in sparkling dust toward the little fire. There were white flashes too, and the far rumble of winter thunder.

"Is—is there lots of willows left?" the crippled boy asked.

The teacher knew what he meant—how many clumps, and if so far out that someone might get lost.

"I think there are quite a few," she replied, needing to reassure the boy, but unable to make it a flat lie.

A long time he sat silent. Finally he pulled his cap off and shook the long yellowish hair back from his petulant face. "I wonder what Mother's doing—" he said slowly, looking away, his hand seeking out the tortured ankle. Lecia motioned him to hold it over to her and so she did not need to reply, to ask what all the mothers of these children must be doing, with the telephone lines still down from the other storm and surely nobody foolish enough to try bucking this one, unless it might be Olive's father, the new Eastern owner of the little Box Y ranch.

With snow water heated in the lunch tin, Lecia washed the poor stick that was the boy's ankle, gently sponging the bone laid almost bare where the frozen snow and the iron brace wore through the scarred and unhealthy skin.

"It looks pretty bad, Bill, but you probably won't have to put the brace back on for days—" Lecia started to comfort, but it was too late, and she had to see fear and anger and self-pity darken the face in the firelight. Because nothing could be unsaid, the girl silently bandaged the ankle with half of the boy's handkerchief. "Now get a little sleep if you can," she said gently.

The boy crawled in next to Eddie as though

718

Ed were the older, and for a long time the teacher felt the dark eyes staring at her out of the shadowy coat collar as though she had deliberately maneuvered this plunge into the blizzard.

Several times before midnight the girl started to doze but jerked herself awake at the frozen creak of the willow shelter, to push the out-tossed arms back and replenish the fire.

Eddie's cough began to boom deep as from a barrel. He turned and moaned, digging at his chest, Calla helpless beside him, her sleep-weighted eyes anxious on the teacher. Maggie too was finally crying now. Her feet had puffed up and purpled dark as jelly bags, with the graying spots that would surely break and slough off, perhaps spread in gangrene. Yet all Lecia could do was turn the girl's feet from the fire and push them behind the blanket against the snow to relieve the pain and itching a little. Perhaps only freeze them more. Lecia touched the girl's forehead to calm her but felt her stiffen and start to pull away from this unaccustomed kindly touch. Then Maggie relaxed a little and as the teacher stroked the hot temples, she wondered how many days it might be before help could get through. Suddenly their plight here seemed so hopeless, the strength and wisdom of her twenty-three years so weak and futile, that she had to slip out into the storm for calm. And finally Maggie slept, worn out, but still tearing at her feet.

To the weary girl watching, half asleep, at the fire, the roar of the storm rose and fell like the panting of a great live thing, sometimes a little like many great planes warming up together. If only she had married Dale Stever New Year's, they would be in the Caribbean now, these children all safe at home, with probably no other teacher available so soon. Once Lecia turned her swollen hand to the fire, watching the ring catch and break the light into life, and tried to recall the fine plans Dale had made for them. He wasn't a rancher's son like those who usually took her to parties and dances—like Joe, or Wilmo, or even Ben, of the local bank. Dale had come from outside last summer and bought up the sale pavilion in town. Since then he flew all around the surrounding ranch country in a plane the color of a wild canary rising from a plum thicket, gathering stock for the sales. Fairtime he took Lecia and her friend Sallie down to the state fair, and several times on long trips since, to Omaha to the ballet and to Denver. At first it seemed he was all jolly big-talk, with windy stories of his stock in an oil company down in Dallas and in a Chicago commission house. He had a touch of gray at his temples that he thought made him look distinguished when he had his hat on, and to their fathers he called himself the Dutch uncle of the two girls. But gradually he concentrated on Lecia, and at Christmas there was the big diamond and the plane ready to fly south. He even took her to the school board to ask for a release from her contract.

"No," the old school director told the girl. "Bill Terry was a friend of mine, brought me into the country. I can't help his granddaughter marry no man in a rush hurry."

Dale laughed confidently and put his arm about the girl's shoulder as they left, but somehow Lecia couldn't break her contract. They must wait until school was out. Dale had been angry. "This is no life for a girl as pretty as you," he said. Truly he was right. Today it was no life for any girl.

Soon after midnight Lecia was startled out of a doze by the sound of cattle bawling somewhere in the roar of the storm, like the herds that passed her home in the night of the May blizzard three years ago, when so many died in the drifts and lakes that the whole region was a stench far into the summer. Then suddenly the girl realized where she was, and hurried bareheaded out into the storm. The bawling was very close; any moment hundreds of storm-blinded cattle might be running over the little willows, over their own two clumps.

Lecia dragged burning sticks from the fire, but in an instant the storm had sucked their flame away. So, with her arms up to shield her eyes from the snow that was sharp as steel

easily it could overcome the little circle of children here if it were not for the handful of fire, for the walls of the storm's own snow.

Toward morning the weary girl knew that she could not keep awake. She had stirred Chuck to sit up a while, but he was unable to shake off the weight of sleep so heavy on an overgrown boy. Trying to remember how the Indians carried their fire—something about moss and damp, rotted wood—Lecia pulled old dead roots from the willow butts and laid them into the coals with the ends sticking far out. Even with waxed paper handy it would be a desperate chance. Willows burned fast as kindlings and there were only five matches, including the one from Eddie's pocket, and no telling how many spoiled by dampness.

Even so it was sweet to let herself sink into darkness, but it seemed that she awoke at once, stiff and cold from the nightmare that reached into the waking black, even the ashes of the fire spot cold. With the waxed paper held ready, the girl blew on the ends of the unburnt roots her hands found, carefully, breathless in her fear. At last a red spark glowed deep in one, and when the fire was going again, she slipped outside for calm in the cold that was like thin, sharp glass in the nose.

There was still no earth and no sky, only the white storm of late dawn blowing hard. But the wood had lasted and now Lecia put on a few extra sticks and heated water to wash the goose mush from the inflamed eyes of the children. She started a rousing song: "Get up! Get up, you sleepyhead!" but even before it was done, Joanie began to whimper, "I'm hungry—"

So the teacher laid out four sandwiches on sticks over the coals and then added another half for herself when she saw Bill watching. "There won't be anything more today except a pinch of cake unless the sun breaks through."

"If it does, we can stomp out a message on the snow," Calla said cheerfully.

dust, she stood behind the shelter shouting the "Hi-ah! Hi-ah!" she had learned when she helped the cowboys push cattle[6] to market. It was a futile, lost little sound against cattle compelled to run by an instinct that could not be denied, compelled to flee for survival before the descent of the arctic storm, never stopping until trapped in some drift, or boldly overtaken in some open fence corner to freeze on their feet, as Lecia had seen them stand.

Realizing her danger as a warmth crept over her, the girl stumbled back into the shelter and crouched at the fire. She barely noticed the sting of returning blood in her ears and face while she listened until the drifting herd was surely past, made more afraid by the knowledge of this thing that drove cattle galloping through the night, the power of it, and how

---

6. **To push cattle** is to drive or herd cattle.

"Yes, even if people can't travel for a whole week, Baldy'll come flying over to see about his girl friend," Bill said, boldly.

The younger boys laughed a little, but Chuck was more serious. "If the sky lightens at all and there's no blowing, I'll do the stomping before I leave."

"You'd run away now?" the teacher asked softly as she combed at Joanie's fine brown hair.

"Somebody's got to get help," he defended in loud words.

The children around the fire were suddenly quiet, turning their eyes to follow the tall boy as he pulled up his sheepskin collar and crawled out into the storm. And silent a long time afterward—all except Joanie, who sobbed softly, without understanding. Even Olive looked up once, but Maggie grated her feet hard along the snow wall and tore at their congestion as though she heard nothing.

Then suddenly there was stomping outside and Chuck came back in, snowy, thick frost all over his collar and cap, his brows and lashes in ice, the children pushing over toward him, as to one gone, lost. He brought more wood, and the teacher seemed to have forgotten that he had said anything about leaving. But the children watched him now, even when they pretended they didn't, and watched Lecia too, for suspicion had come in.

The teacher started as for a school day, except that the arithmetic was rote learning of addition and multiplication tables and a quick run through some trick problems: "If I had a fox, a goose, and some corn to get across a river in a boat—" and then, "If I had a dollar to buy a hundred eggs—no, I should take something that won't make us hungry."

"Like a hundred pencils?"

"Well, yes, let's take pencils. I want to buy a hundred for a dollar. Some are five cents each, poor ones two and a half cents, and broken ones half a cent. How many of each kind must I buy?"

In history and nature study they talked about the Indians that still roamed the sand hills when Lecia's grandfather came into the country. They lived the winter long in skin tipis something like the shelter here, and almost as crowded, but with piles of thick-furred buffalo robes for the ground and the beds. The girls sat on one side, the boys on the other.

"Like we are here—" Fritz said, his eyes shining in the discovery. "We're Indians. Whoo-oo-oo!" he cried, slapping his mouth with his palm.

They talked about the food too, the piles of dried and pounded meat, the winter hunts, how the village and lodges were governed, and what the children did, their winter games, one almost like "button, button." The boys learned from the men—such things as arrow-making, and later bullet-making, hunting, fighting; and particularly the virtues of resourcefulness, courage, fortitude, and responsibility for all the people. A girl learned from the women—beading, tanning hides, and all the other things needed to live well with modesty, steadfastness, and generosity, and with courage and fortitude and responsibility too, for it was thought that the future of the people lay in the palms of the women, to be cherished or thrown away.

"What does that mean, Teacher?" Fritz asked, hitting out in mischief at his brother Eddie, despite Calla and the teacher both watching, then shouting he was hungry again.

The rest tried to laugh a little as Calla whispered to her small brother, trying to make herself heard against the storm, while Lecia taught them a poem about Indians. Even Joanie repeated a few lines for her, although the child leaned weak and feverish against Calla while Bill comforted his bound ankle and Maggie tried hard to pull herself out of the curious drowsiness that had the teacher frightened.

After a while the children played "button, button," and tried to tell each other poems. When Eddie got stuck on "Snowbound,"[7] Bill

---

7. "**Snowbound**" was a poem written in 1866 by John Greenleaf Whittier (1807–1892).

nudged Fritz and they laughed as easily at his discomfiture as at school, perhaps because Chuck was back and this was the second day of the storm, with tomorrow the third. Then it would clear up and somebody with a scoop shovel would get his horse along the barer ridges to a telephone.

"Maybe somebody'll just come running over the hills to find us," Eddie teased, looking at Olive, turning his face from the teacher.

"Well, even if nobody came and Baldy couldn't find a place to land with skis on his plane, he would have sacks of food and blankets and stuff dropped like in the movies and the newspapers."

"I saw it in a movie once, I did," Joanie cried.

So they talked, pretending no one was looking up at the hanging lunch buckets, or sick and afraid. But Lecia did not hear them.

"Oh-oo, Teacher's sleeping like one of those old Indian women up to Gordon, just sitting there!" Eddie exclaimed.

"Sh-h," Calla said, in her way. "Let her stretch out here," and with a polite smile Olive moved aside.

That night Joanie was delirious, and once Maggie slipped past the teacher out into the storm to relieve the fire of her feet. By midnight she couldn't stand on them, and the grayish spots were yellow under the thick skin of a barefoot summer, the swelling creeping above the girl's thin ankles, with red streaks reaching almost to the knees. Her eyes glistened, her cheeks were burning, and she talked of wild and dreadful things.

Lecia tried to remember all that she had read of frost-bite, all that her grandfather had told, but she knew that the inflammation spreading past the frozen area was like the cold overtaking the fleeing cattle, and she had to make a desperate decision. She dug two holes deep into the snow wall and laid Maggie with her feet in them almost to her knees, wishing they had something waterproof for covering. The cold would probably freeze the girl more, but it would numb the nerves and

perhaps slow the congestion and tissue starvation. Later, when the girl was restless again and crying, Lecia found the yellow spots spreading, painful and hard as boils. She burned the end of a safety pin and while Maggie's frightened eyes became caverns in her thin face, Lecia opened one of the spots. Bloody pus burst down over her hand. Holding the foot aside she wiped it away on the snow, from her ring too, and then slipped it from her shrunken finger and hung it on a twig overhead, where it swayed a little, like a morning dewdrop while she opened the rest of the festering.

When the girl's feet were bathed and bound in the sleeves torn from Lecia's white shirt blouse, she thrust them back into the snow. Then she gave Maggie half a cup of the milk, very quietly, hoping none would awaken to see, although none needed it more. Almost at once the girl was asleep, to rest until the pus gathered again. But the first time Lecia returned with firewood she saw the thermos bottle half out. She jerked it from the hole. The milk was all gone, and across the little fire Olive stared at her teacher.

"It was mine," the girl said flatly.

So the time had come when the little food left must be hidden. Now, with all but Olive sleeping, was the time. When Lecia came back in, the girl held out something—the ring that had been left hanging on the twig and forgotten.

The next day and the next were the same, only colder, the drifts deeper and harder along the willows, the wind so sharp with snow that it froze the eyeballs. Lecia and Chuck covered their faces as they fought their way back against it, the wood dragging from their shoulders, tied by a strap of cloth cut off around the bottom of Lecia's coat. One at a time they went out and came back, a hand stretched ahead feeling for the next guide pole in the snow before the other let go of the last, the covered face turned from the storm to save the breath from being torn away by the wind.

All the third day there was watching out of the smoke hole for the sky that never appeared. When night finally came without star or stillness, even Lecia, who had tried to prepare herself for this eventuality, felt that she could not face another day of blizzard. Maggie no longer sat up now and both Joanie and Eddie were so sick—their fever high, their chests filling—that the teacher had to try something. She seemed to remember that the early settlers used willow bark to break a fever, so she steeped a handful in Maggie's tin cup until the liquid was strong and dark. She made the two children drink it, first experimentally, then more, and after a while they began to sweat. When they awoke they were wet, their hair clinging to their vulnerable young foreheads, but they seemed better all the next day, except weak. Then at night it was the same with Joanie.

The fourth day was like the rest, colder, with the same white storm outside, the children hunching silent upon themselves inside. Sometimes a small one sobbed a little in sickness and hunger, but it was no more than a soft moaning now, even when Lecia divided most of the little food that was left. The children, even Chuck, took it like animals, and then sat silent again, the deep-socketed eyes watching, some slyly gnawing at willow sticks and roots hidden in the palm.

Everybody around the fire was coughing and fevered now, it seemed to Lecia, the bickering going beyond childish things to quarrels about real or fancied animosities between their families. Once even Calla spoke angrily to Bill, defending her brothers.

"At least they aren't mama babies like you!"

"Mama babies! I wouldn't talk if everybody knew that my family got a start in cattle by stealing calves—"

"You can't say such things!" Calla cried, up and reaching for Bill, caught without his brace and unable to flee into the storm, Joanie crying: "Don't! Don't hit my brother!"

When Lecia returned, Chuck was holding the two apart, shaking them both. The teacher spoke in anger and impatience too now, and Bill's face flushed with embarrassment and shame, the sudden red like fever in his hunger-grayed cheeks.

Only Maggie with her poor feet was quiet, and Olive, sitting as though stunned or somewhere far away. The teacher knew that she should do something for this girl, only eight yet apparently so self-contained. Olive never spoke of her father now, as none of the boys teased Lecia about Baldy any more. Olive was as remote about him as everything else since the night she drank the milk, and found the ring on a twig.

Too weary to think about it, and knowing she must keep awake in the night, Lecia stretched out for a nap. When she awoke Olive was sitting exactly the same, but the places of Chuck and Eddie were empty—Eddie out in the blizzard after his night of sweating. Then the boys returned with wood, weak, dragging, almost frozen, and with something that Lecia had to be told outside. There seemed only one willow clump left.

One clump? Then they must start digging at the frozen butts, or even pull down their shelter to keep the fire alive, for now the boys too were believing that the storm would blow forever. Yet toward evening there was a thinning above the smoke hole, the sun suddenly there like a thin disk of milky ice from the bottom of a cup. It was almost a promise, even though the storm swept the sun away in a few minutes and the wind shifted around to the south, whipping in past the block the boys had in the hole of the shelter. The children shivered, restless. Once Eddie rose from his sleep and fought to get out, go home. When he finally awakened, he lay down in a chill, very close to the fire, and would not move until a stench of burning cloth helped rouse him. Then he drank the bitter willow bark tea too and finally he slept.

Friday morning the sun came out again toward ten o'clock, the same cold, pale disk, with the snow still running along the earth, running higher than the shelter or Chuck, shutting out everything except the veiled sun. The boy came in, looked around the starved, listless circle at the fire, at the teacher too, with her face that had been so pretty Monday morning gaunt and sooty now.

He laid two red-tipped matches, half of all he had, in the girl's lap. "I'm getting out," he said, and without a protest from anyone crawled through the hole and was gone.

The children were almost past noticing his desertion now, barely replying when spoken to. If the colds got worse or pneumonia struck, it would be over in a few hours. Maggie hadn't sat up since yesterday, lying flat, staring at the white storm blowing thin above the smoke hole. If any of them wondered how Lecia could keep the fire going alone, with nothing much except the willow butts left, none spoke of it. The teacher sat with her arms hanging between her knees, hopeless.

She finally stirred and put the matches away in waxed paper in her shirt pocket where her ring lay, buttoning the flap down carefully now. Joanie started to cough again, choking, turned red and then very white under the grime and grayness of her face, lying very still. Now Bill made the first gesture toward his small sister.

"Come here, Doll," he said gently, drawing her awkwardly from Lecia's lap, the child lifting her head slowly, holding herself away, looking up at him as a baby might at a stranger, to be weighed and considered. Then she snuggled against him and in a moment she was asleep.

After a long time there seemed a dull sound outside, and then Chuck was suddenly back, crawling in almost as though he had not left, panting in his weakness from the fight against the wind that had turned north again, and colder.

"Scared an eagle off a drift out there," he finally managed to say. "And there's a critter stuck in the snow—beyond the far willows. Small spring calf. Froze hard, but its meat—"

Then the realization that Chuck was back struck the teacher. She was not alone with the children, and he too was safe for now. But there was something more. The boy who had resented them and his involvement in their plight—he had escaped and come back.

"Oh, Chuck!" the girl exclaimed. Then what he said reached her mind. "A calf? Maybe we could build a fire there so we can cut some off, if we can't get it all out." She reached for her boots. "But we'll have to go work at it one at a time—" looking around the firelit faces that were turned toward her as before, but the eyes alert, watching as though a morsel might be dropped, even thrown.

"I'll go with Chuck, Miss Lecia," Bill said softly. "He can show me and I'll show you. Save time hunting—"

The teacher looked at the crippled boy, already setting Joanie gently aside and reaching for his brace. She felt pride in him, and unfortunate doubt.

"He can probably make it," Chuck said, a little condescending. "It's not over an eighth of a mile, and I found more willows farther along the way, the drifts mostly frozen hard too. I blazed the willows beyond our poles—"

"You'll be careful—mark everything," the girl pleaded.

"We've got to. It's snowing again, and the sun's gone."

It seemed hours since the boys went out and finally the teacher had to go after them, appalled that the younger ones had to be left alone, yet it must be done. She moved very carefully, feeling her way in the new storm, going sideways to it, from pole to pole. Then she came to a place where the markers were gone, probably blown down and buried by the turning wind. The boys were out there, lost, in at least fifteen, perhaps twenty, below zero. Without sticks to guide her way back, the girl dared go no farther but she crouched there, bowed before the wind, cupping her mouth with her mittens, shouting her hopeless: "Boys! Chuck! O-hoo!" the wind snatching it away.

She kept calling until she was shaking and frozen and then to a frightening warmth.

But now she had to keep on, for it seemed that she heard something, a vague, smothered sound, and yet a little like a reply. Tears freezing on her face she called again and again until suddenly the boys were at her feet, there before she could see them, so much like the snow, like white dragging animals, one bowed, half carrying the other. For a few minutes they crouched together in desperate relief, the snow running over them as something immovable, like an old willow butt. Then, together, they pulled themselves up and started back. When they finally reached the shelter, out of breath and frozen, they said nothing of what had happened, nor spoke at all for a while. Yet all, even little Joanie, seemed to sense that the boys had almost been lost.

As soon as the teacher was warmed a little, she started out alone, not certain that she could make it against the storm, but knowing that she must try to get meat. She took Chuck's knife, some dry bark, waxed paper, the two matches in her shirt pocket, and a bundle of poles pulled from their shelter. Moving very carefully beyond the gap in the willow markers, she set new sticks deep, and tipped carefully with the new storm. She found the farther willow clumps with Chuck's blazing, and the brush pile the boys had made, and beside it the ice-covered head of the calf still reaching out of the snow. The hole they had dug around the red hindquarters was drifted in loosely, but easily dug out. Lecia set a fire pile there and felt for a match with her numb fingers, fishing in the depths of her pocket, something round in the way, her ring. But she got the match and lighted the fire under her shielding sheepskin coat. For a long time she crouched protectively over the flame, the wind carrying away the stench of burning calf hair. As the skin thawed, she hacked at it the way Indians must have done here a thousand years ago, their stone knives sharper and more expertly handled.

At a sound she looked over her shoulder and saw a coyote not three feet away, gaunt-bellied too, and apparently no more afraid than a hungry dog. But suddenly he caught the human smell, even against the wind, and was gone. He would have made a soft rug at the fire, Lecia thought, and wondered if he might not return to watch just beyond the wall of storm. But she was too busy to look. As the heat penetrated the meat, she cut off one slice after another until she had a little smoky pile, not much for nine people who had lived five days on one lunch apiece, but enough to bring tears that were not all from the storm. In this meat, perhaps three pounds, might lie the life of her pupils.

Lecia scattered the fresh ashes over the calf to keep the coyotes away and piled brush into the fire hole. Then she headed sideways into the storm, so violent that it was a good thing she had the strength of a little cautious meat inside her, for it seemed no one could face the wounding snow. Numb and frightened, she managed to hold herself, not get hurried, panicked, never move until the next broken willow, the next marker was located. So she got back, to find Chuck out near the shelter digging wood from the old clumps, watching, uneasy.

It was hard for the children to wait while the thinner slices of meat roasted around the sticks. When the smell filled the little shelter, Lecia passed out toasted bits to be chewed very slowly and well. It tasted fine and none asked for bread or salt—not even Olive, still silent and alone. She accepted the meat, but returned only distant gravity for the teacher's smile.

By now the white blizzard darkness was coming back, but before they slept there was a little piece of boiled veal for each and a little hot broth. It was a more cheerful sleeping time, even a confident one, although in the night they were struck by the diarrhea that Lecia had expected. But that was from the fresh meat and should not last.

By now Lecia could build a coal bed with rotten wood and ashes to hold a fire a long time, even with diamond willows, and so she dressed Maggie's feet, the girl light as a sack of bird bones, and prepared the night fire. For a while Chuck and Eddie kept each other awake with stories of coyote hunts and with plans for another morning of storm, the sixth. The two boys met the day with so much confidence that Lecia had to let them go out into the storm. Eddie, only ten, suddenly became a little old man in his seriousness as he explained their plans carefully. They would make a big brush pile so that they could settle out of the wind and work the fire until they got a whole hindquarter of the calf hacked off. So the teacher watched them go out very full of hope, the hope of meat, one of the half blankets along to drag their prize in over the snow, like great hunters returning.

Bill had looked sadly after the disappearing boot soles, but without complaint. He helped Lecia with the smaller children, washing at the grime of their faces that would never yield except to soap, and took them out into the storm and back while the teacher soaked Maggie's great swollen feet and tried to keep the girl from knowing that the bone ends of her toes could be seen in the suppurating pits of dying flesh. There were holes on the tops of the toes too, along the edges of her feet, and up the heels as high as the ankle. But above there the swelling seemed looser, the red streaks perhaps no farther up the bony legs. Once Bill looked over the teacher's shoulder and then anxiously into her face. Others had chilblains —his own feet were swollen from yesterday— but not like this.

"Will she lose—" he started to whisper, but he could not put the rest into words, not with a crippled foot himself.

The air was thick and white with new snow whipped by a northwest wind when Lecia went out for a little wood and to watch for the boys. But they were once more within touching distance before she could see them—very cold and backing awkwardly into the storm through the soft, new drifts, but dragging a whole hindquarter of the calf. It was a lot of

meat, and surely the wind must finally blow itself out, the clouds be drained.

By the time Eddie and Chuck were warm they knew they had eaten too much roasted veal while they worked. Next Olive became sick, and Fritz, their deprived stomachs refusing the sudden meat, accepting only the broth. During the night the nausea struck Lecia too, and left her so weak that she could scarcely lift her head all the next day. That night Chuck lost his voice for a while, and Joanie was worse again, her mind full of terrors, the cough so deep, so exhausting that Bill made a little tent over her face with the skirt of his coat to carry steam from a bucket of boiling snow water to her face. Then sometime toward morning the wind turned and cut into the southeast corner of the shelter, crumbling the whole side inward.

The boys crawled out to patch it with brush and snow softened at the fire, Lecia helping dry off the children, as much as she could. Then when they were done and she laid her swimming head down, she heard a coyote's thin, high howl and realized that the wind was dying. Through the smoke hole she saw the running snow like pale windrows of cloud against the sky, and between them stars shining, far pale stars. As one or another awoke, she directed sleepy eyes to look up. Awed, Joanie looked a second time. "You mean they're really stars—?"

"Yes, and maybe there will be sunshine in the morning."

Dawn came early that eighth day, but it seemed that nothing could be left alive in the cold whiteness of the earth that was only frozen scarves of snow flung deep and layered over themselves. The trailing drifts stretched down from the high ridge of hills in the north, so deep that they made a long, sliding slope of it far over the meadow and up the wind-whipped hills beyond, with not a dark spot anywhere to the horizon—not a yucca or fence post or willow above the snow. In the first touch of the sun the frozen snow sparkled in the deep silence following a long, long storm.

Then out of the hills a lone grouse came cackling over the empty meadow, gleaming silver underneath as she flew, her voice carrying loud in the cold stillness.

But the meadow was not completely empty, for out of a little white mound of drifted willows a curl of smoke rose and spread thin and blue along the hill. There was another sound too, farther, steadier than the cackle of the grouse, a sound seeming to come from all around and even under the feet.

"A plane!" Chuck shouted hoarsely, bursting out into the blinding sunlight.

Several other dark figures crept out behind him into the frosty air, their breath a cloud about them as they stood looking northward. A big plane broke from the horizon over the hills, seeming high up, and then another, flying lower. Foolishly Chuck and Eddie started to shout. "Help! Hello! Help!" they cried, waving their arms as they ran toward the planes, as though to hasten their sight, their coming.

But almost at once the sky was empty, the planes circling and gone. For a long time the boys stared into the broad, cold sky, pale, with nothing in it except wind streaks that were stirring along the ground too, setting feather curls of snow to running.

"Quick! Let's make a big smudge!" Lecia called out, her voice loud in the unaccustomed quiet, and fearful. She threw water on the fire inside, driving smoke out of the hole while the boys set the snowy woodpile to burning.

Before the smoke could climb far, there were planes up over the north hills again, coming fast. Now even Fritz got out into the stinging cold—everybody except Joanie, held back by Lecia, and Olive, who did not move from her place. Maggie was lifted up by the teacher to watch through the smoke hole as something tumbled from the higher plane, came falling down. Then it opened out like the waxy white bloom of the yucca, and settled toward the snow, with several other smaller chutes, bright as poppies, opening behind.

There was shouting and talk outside the shelter and while Lecia was hurrying to get the children into their caps and boots, a man came crawling into the shelter with a bag—a doctor. In the light of the fire and a flashlight he looked swiftly at Joanie and then at Olive, considered her unchanging face, lifted the lids of her eyes, smiled, and got no response. Then he examined the poor feet of Maggie, the girl like a skin-bound skeleton in this first sharp light, her eyes dark and fearful on the man's face.

The doctor nodded reassuringly to Lecia, and smiled down at Maggie.

"You're a tough little girl!" he said. "Tough as the barbed wire you have out in this country. But you're lucky somebody thought to try snow against the gangrene—" He filled a little syringe and fingered cotton as he looked around to divert the child.

"All nine of you alive, the boys say. Amazing! Somebody got word to a telephone during the night, but we had no hope for any of you. Small children lost eight days without food, with fifty inches of snow at thirty-eight below zero. Probably a hundred people dead through the country. The radio in the plane picked up a report that six were found frozen in a car stalled on the highway—not over five miles from town. I don't see how you managed here."

The doctor rubbed the punctured place in the child's arm a little, covered it, smiling into her fearful eyes, as men with a stretcher broke into the front of the shelter.

When they got outside, the air was loud with engine roar, several planes flying around overhead, two with skis already up toward the shelter and a helicopter, hovering like a brownish dragonfly, settling. Men in uniform were running toward the children, motioning where they should be brought.

They came along the snow trail broken by the stretcher men, but walking through it as through the storm. Lecia, suddenly trembling, shaking, her feet unsteady on the frozen snow, was still in the lead, the others behind her, and Chuck once more at the end. Bill, limping awkwardly, carried little Joanie, who clung very close to her brother. They were followed by

Calla and Eddie, with Fritz between them, and then the stretcher with Maggie. Only Olive of all the children walked alone, just ahead of Chuck, and brushing aside all help.

There were men running toward the bedraggled, sooty little string now, men with cameras and others, among them some who cried, joyous as children, and who must be noticed, must be acknowledged soon—Olive's father and Dale Stever of the yellow plane—

But for now, for this little journey back from the smoke-holed shelter of snow, the awkward queue stayed together.

I

AN INDOMITABLE COMMANDER

Lecia Terry was a person capable of making decisions. Even though she sometimes felt fearful, she was careful not to let this show. Had she been subject to hopeless indecision, it would have meant disaster for her little group.

1. List at least three quiet decisions Lecia Terry makes between the time the bus overturns and she and the children reach the willows.

2. What advice from her pioneer grandfather helps her make decisions?

3. How does Chuck happen to be driving the bus?

4. Describe the willow shelter they fashion.

5. What decision does Lecia make about the food they have?

6. How does the story get its name?

7. About whom do the children tease Lecia?

8. Why do Maggie's feet freeze?

9. What source of food does Chuck discover that keeps them from starving?

10. How long is it before the storm abates and they are rescued?

11. Why is the doctor so amazed that they are all still alive?

II

IMPLICATIONS

Consider and discuss these statements.

1. In many groups, there are loners like Olive.

In the story her development is logical and yet terrifying.

2. Of all the children in the makeshift shelter, Olive was the most in need of help.

3. Bill had the crippled personality that often develops when a person is physically imperfect. He felt sorry for himself and wanted sympathy. Obviously he could never change.

4. The author shows Chuck as most sixteen-year-old boys really are—rebellious and self-centered.

5. Odd bits of information, such as the things Lecia's grandfather had taught her about storms, often are remembered by people in times of emergency.

6. People such as Maggie who are used to hardship have a better chance of survival than those who are used to good care.

7. Nothing destroys morale in a group so quickly as the realization that there is disagreement among the leaders. The struggle between Chuck and Lecia for authority is a case in point.

8. An experience such as that described in *Winter Thunder* would leave more damaging effects than good ones.

9. In *Winter Thunder*, Lecia is brave because she has to be; the children depend upon her. Most brave actions are a result of necessity.

10. When a person becomes part of an interdependent group, he surrenders part of his own liberty.

11. We should rely more often upon simple, homemade medicines.

III

TECHNIQUES

Although this story is based on the experience of Mari Sandoz's niece, Mari Sandoz herself knew the country, its storms, and its people from her own years of teaching in the rural schools of Nebraska. This is an important factor in her ability to make the story so real.

Miss Sandoz stated that in writing *Winter Thunder* she had a larger purpose than simply to show nine people battered, numbed, and pounded by a terrible storm. She wanted to make it a thrilling and moving study of the will to survive and of "the dignity of courage."

Beginnings

Particularly in the opening paragraphs of this story, the language stirs the reader's imagination by bringing vivid pictures into focus. There is something ominous about the snow, which she says began quietly that Monday morning "like an afterthought to the gray Sunday night." Even the name of the school district, Lone Tree, adds to the impression of isolation.

1. What is the only thing moving in the thickening snow? How does the author describe its movements in paragraph one? With what simile does she sharpen the focus of this picture in paragraph two?

2. The storm is more than just the setting for this story. The storm actually is the adversary or enemy in the plot. All the action grows out of this conflict between man and nature. How soon does the reader realize that the teacher and children are in a desperate situation?

Endings

From the time the planes return, the reader knows the valiant little group is to be rescued. They have survived! But there is still interest and curiosity as to who the rescuers are, what news they will have, and how Lecia, Chuck, and the children will react after their ordeal. What is significant about the way the children go to meet the plane? Did you feel satisfied with the ending?

phoneme-grapheme correspondence may be demonstrated by the *ch* sound and its graphic symbols: *ch* (*chief*), *c* (*cello*), *t* (*culture*), *tch* (*patch*), and *ti* (*question*). Note that the letters *ch* represent the *k* sound in *character* and the *sh* sound in *machine*. With the help of your dictionary, see whether you can determine which letters symbolize the *s* sound in the following words: *cent, psalm, muscle, schism, moss, glisten, sword, waltz,* and *site*.

B. Read the following sentences from *Winter Thunder*, paying special attention to the italicized verbs:

". . . the snow *whipped* against the posts. . . ."
"Once more the engine *roared* out. . . ."
"The teacher *squinted* back along the line. . . ."

Verbs like *whipped, roared,* and *squinted* specify the action (that is, they tell in what manner the action takes place), economize on words, and invigorate the writer's prose. To gauge the effectiveness of these verbs, one may substitute other words and then compare the new words with the original ones:

. . . the snow *blew hard* against the posts. . . .
Once more the engine *sped up loudly*. . . .
The teacher *looked with difficulty* back along the line. . . .

What other verbs in *Winter Thunder* can you find that are specific, vivid, and economical to the same degree that *whipped, roared,* and *squinted* are?

IV

WORDS

A. From a previous lesson, you may remember that a grapheme is a letter or combination of letters that represents an individual sound in the language, or phoneme. A phoneme may be symbolized, you may also recall, by a number of different graphemes. A good example of the phoneme-grapheme relationship can be illustrated by the *f* sound in *enough, defiant,* and *often,* all of which appear in *Winter Thunder*. This sound may be represented by *f* (*father*), *ff* (*offer*), *ft* (*soften*), *gh* (*enough*), *lf* (*half*), and *ph* (*sphere*). Sometimes one grapheme symbolizes two different phonemes; for example, *gh* at times represents the *f* sound and at other times the *g* sound, as in *ghost*. Another example of the

BIOGRAPHICAL NOTES

Tom Burnam

Tom Burnam (1913–   ), short story writer and English professor, was born in Montana. After doing undergraduate work at the University of Idaho, he received his Ph.D. from the University of Washington. Burnam, who was a Visiting Professor of American Literature at the University of Helsinki in Finland in 1961, has taught literature and writing at Colorado State College.

William Saroyan

William Saroyan (1908–   ), American short story writer and playwright, was born in Fresno,

California. After quitting school in his second year of junior high, Saroyan worked as a telegraph messenger, office worker, farm laborer, and newspaper man. When *Story Magazine* accepted his "Daring Young Man on the Flying Trapeze," in 1934, Saroyan's literary career was well on its way. A true individualist in every sense of the word, Saroyan refused the Pulitzer Prize for drama for *The Time of Your Life*. His most widely read work is *The Human Comedy*.

Ellis Parker Butler

Ellis Parker Butler (1869–1937) grew up on an Iowa farm. Influenced by Mark Twain, who lived for a time in Butler's home town, the Iowa humorist was a popular writer for over forty years, turning out great numbers of essays, sketches, and stories. His story, "Pigs Is Pigs," was an immediate success when it was published in 1905 and is now considered a classic of American humor.

Edmund Ware

Edmund Ware (1900–   ), whose real name is Edmund Ware Smith, was born in Connecticut. When he was sixteen, Ware ran away from home and tried his hand as cook, guide, packer, cowpuncher, and sandhog. These experiences serve as background material for several of his books. Ware's books, *One-Eyed Poacher, The Maine Woods,* and *For Maine Only,* hold great appeal for all lovers of nature.

Stephen Vincent Benét

For a biography of Stephen Vincent Benét, see page 493.

Mark Twain

Mark Twain (Samuel L. Clemens, 1835–1910), short story writer, humorist, and novelist, was born in the Mississippi River town of Hannibal, Missouri. After trying his hand at being a printer, river pilot, prospector, and reporter, Twain's education for his writing career was completed. His stories and books, based upon his own experiences both in Hannibal and in the West, quickly put him at the top of American writers. *Huckleberry Finn, Tom Sawyer,* and *Life on the Mississippi* are some of his better-known works.

Frank R. Stockton

Frank R. Stockton (1834–1902), short story writer, was born in Philadelphia, Pennsylvania. After graduating from high school, he learned the trade of woodcarving, a skill he later utilized when he used his own engravings as illustrations for some of his writings. After turning to writing as a full-time career, he worked for his brother's newspaper and for several magazines, eventually rising to the position of assistant editor of *St. Nicholas* magazine.

Mari Sandoz

Mari Sandoz (1901–1966), American novelist and biographer, was born in Sheridan County, Nebraska. Her first stories were published in the junior page of the *Omaha Daily News*. While attending the University of Nebraska, she wrote numerous short stories, winning honorable mention in a *Harper's* contest in 1926. She was associate editor of *Schools Executive Magazine* for several years and taught school in Nebraska. Among fiction and nonfiction that she has written are *The Horsecatcher, The Buffalo Hunters, Crazy Horse,* and *Old Jules,* the story of her father which won the *Atlantic* nonfiction prize in 1935.

James Thurber

James Thurber, American novelist and illustrator, was born in Columbus, Ohio, in 1894. Educated at Ohio State University, Thurber worked on both the *Columbus Dispatch* and the Paris edition of the *Chicago Tribune*. He also served as managing editor and staff writer for *The New Yorker*. One of the great American humorists, Thurber is best known for his classic short story, *The Secret Life of Walter Mitty*. In 1960, Thurber acted in a dramatic revue (*The Thurber Carnival*) of several of his essays and short stories. He died in 1961.

Glossary

This glossary contains difficult words which are not in the vocabularies of average ninth-grade students. The definitions apply to the uses of the words in this text. For more complete study of the range of meanings for these words, the student must consult his dictionary. Many other specific and uncommon terms have been footnoted with the selections.

Pronunciation Guide

A key to the pronunciation symbols is given at the bottom of every other page. By consulting the most recent dictionaries, the student may notice that the symbols here represent a series of compromises between current scholarly interpretations of sounds and less precise symbols which continue to have wide acceptance. A few minutes' study of the pronunciation key before using this glossary will make it possible for the student to use the pronunciation transcriptions with the greatest ease and efficiency.

The same key is used for pronunciations given here and in the footnotes. Foreign terms and names are transcribed so as to be acceptable in standard American speech rather than precise in terms of their original languages.

Accent marks precede the stressed syllables. The mark ᴧ indicates the heaviest stress and the mark ' indicates an intermediate stress.

Abbreviations indicate parts of speech and special spellings. The following are used:

n.	noun
v.	verb
adj.	adjective
adv.	adverb
pl.	plural

abash\ə ᴧbăsh\ v. To shame, make timid or shy. (n. -ment)

ab·er·ra·tion\'ă·bə ᴧrā·shən\ n. A mental turn or lapse from normal, a mental deviation. (adj. -al)

ab·hor·rence\əb ᴧhōr·əns\ n. Loathing, detestation, strong dislike. (adj. abhorrent, v. abhor)

ab·ject\ᴧăb 'jĕkt\ adj. Hopeless, downcast, utterly dispirited. (n. -ness, adv. -ly)

abom·i·na·ble\ə ᴧbŏ·mĭ·nĭ·bəl\ adj. Hateful, detestable. (v. abominate, n. abomination)

abor·tive\ə ᴧbŏr·tĭv\ adj. Without effective result, ending in nothing. (adv. -ly)

abridge·ment\ə ᴧbrĭj·mənt\ n. A reduced or condensed version. (v. abridge)

ab·scond\əb ᴧskŏnd\ v. To leave or run away secretly or stealthily. (n. -er)

ab·sorp·tion\əb ᴧsŏrp·shən\ n. A state of intense interest in and concern about one particular thing. (v. absorb, adj. absorbing)

ab·stain\əb ᴧstān\ v. To withhold oneself from, refrain. (n. -er, abstention; adj. abstentive)

ab·sti·nent\ᴧăb·stĭ·nənt\ adj. Abstaining (voluntarily or not) from food or drink. (n. abstinence, adv. -ly)

ab·stract\əb ᴧstrăkt\ adj. 1. Not material and concrete. 2. Not narrow and specific. (also n., and v., n. -ion, adv. -ly)

ab·stract·ed\əb ᴧstrăk·təd\ adj. Withdrawn from attention to the immediate situation, preoccupied with something else. (v. abstract, n. abstraction, and adv. -ly)

ab·struse\əb ᴧstrūs\ adj. Hard to understand, marked by mysterious learning or lore. (n. -ness, adv. -ly)

abut\ə ᴧbət\ v. -ted, -ting. To touch, be situated next to. (n. -ment)

abyss\ə ᴧbĭs\ n., pl. -es. A bottomless or very deep and sheer gulf, chasm, or pit.

ac·cel·er·a·tion\ək 'sĕ·lə ᴧrā·shən\ n. Increase in rate of speed. (v. accelerate)

ac·cen·tu·a·tion\ăk 'sĕn·chu ᴧā·shən\ n. Utterance, pronunciation. (v. accentuate. To emphasize.)

ac·claim\ə ᴧklām\ v. To praise and applaud highly and widely. (also n.)

ac·com·plice\ə ᴧkəm·plĭs\ n. One who aids another in something criminal, illegal, or wrong.

ac·cost\ə ᴧkŏst\ v. To greet and speak to (sometimes for some evil purpose).

ac·cred·it\ə ᴧkrē·dĭt\ v. To think of as having, assign to, credit with, consider as having. (n. -ation)

ac·qui·esce\ă·kwē ᴧĕs\ v. To agree, consent. (n. -nce, adj. -nt)

ac·rid\ᴧăk·rəd\ adj. Sharp and irritating. (n. -ness, adv. -ly)

ac·ti·vate\ᴧăk·tə 'vāt\ v. To cause to be in active operation. (n. activation)

ad·age\ᴧă·dĭj\ n. A proverb, common saying.

ad·duce\ə ᴧdūs\ v. To show or bring forth (especially as evidence or proof).

adept\ə ᴧdĕpt\ adj. Particularly skilled or capable. (also n. -ness, adv. -ly)

ă bad, ā bake, a father, ĕ sell, ē equal, aɪ mile, ĭ sit, ŏ cot, ō note, ɔ law, ū boom, ʊ wood, yū you, yʊ fury, aʊ cow, ɔɪ boy. The schwa is used for both stressed and unstressed sounds: ə mud, word, even; ch chase, itch; sh shell, wish; th path, thin; th the, either; ŋ wing; w wet, wheat; zh pleasure.

ad·mo·ni·tion\\'ăd·mə ‸nĭ·shən\ n. Warning, advice by way of caution. (v. admonish, adj. admonitory)

ad·ren·al·in\əd ‸rĕ·nə 'lĭn\ n. A glandular hormone likely to flow at times of fear and danger.

ad·ver·sary\\'ăd·vər 'sä·rē\ n., pl. -ies. One with whom one is fighting or competing.

ad·ver·si·ty\əd ‸vər·sǐ·tē) n. Misfortune, difficulty, trouble. (adj. adverse)

aero·nau·tics\\'ă·rə ‸no·tĭks\ n. The study or science of navigation through the air. (adj. aeronautical)

aes·thet·ic\əs ‸thĕ·tĭk\ adj. Marked by sensitivity, taste, and judgment. (adv. -ally)

af·fa·ble\\'ă·fə·bəl\ adj. Pleasant, congenial, easy-going, and considerate. (n. affability, adv. affably)

af·fec·ta·tion\\'ă·fĕk ‸tā·shən\ n. Unnatural or artificial behavior, with pretense or show in order to impress. (adj. affected)

af·fix\ə ‸fĭks\ v. To attach, fasten. (n. -ation)

af·flic·tion\ə ‸flĭk·shən\ n. Suffering, pain, distress. (v. afflict)

aghast\ə ‸găst\ adj. Feeling dismay or terror.

agil·i·ty\ə ‸jĭ·lǐ·tē\ n. Quick, light, dexterous nimbleness. (adj. agile)

alien\\'ā·lē·ən\ adj. Foreign, strange, unknown. (also n.)

al·lay\ə 'lā\ v. To calm, soothe.

al·lege\ə ‸lĕj\ v. To say or state (often without proof or certainty). (n. allegation)

al·lude\ə ‸lūd\ v. To refer to, mention (especially in passing) without being detailed or explicit.

al·lu·sion\ə ‸lū·zhən\ n. A suggestion, reference (often made indirectly or in passing).

am·big·u·ous\\'ăm ‸bĭ·gyū·əs\ adj. Unclear in expression, capable of expressing different meanings. (n. ambiguity, adv. -ly)

am·bro·sia\\'ăm ‸brō·zhēa\ n. The wonderful and delicious food of the Greek and Roman gods. (adj. ambrosial)

amend\ə ‸mĕnd\ v. To correct, add corrections. (n. -ment)

ame·ni·ty\ə ‸mĕ·nǐ·tē or ə ‸mē·nǐ·tē\ n. Manner or behavior leading to a smooth and pleasant social relationship.

anach·ro·nism\ə ‸năk·rə·nĭzm\ n. Something mentioned or implied as existing at the wrong time (as a television set in ancient Rome). (adj. anachronistic)

an·a·lyt·i·cal\\'ă·nə ‸lĭ·tǐ·kəl\ adj. Given to or marked by thoughtful analysis. (n. analysis, adv. -ly)

an·ec·dote\‸ă·nək 'dōt\ n. A short humorous story about a person. (adj. anecdotal)

an·es·the·sia\\'ă·nəs ‸thē·zhēa\ n. A numbing, daze, unconsciousness in which no pain is felt.

an·i·mate\‸ă·nǐ· 'māt\ v. 1. To make brisk or active. 2. To give life purpose to. (n. animation, adj. animated)

an·i·mos·i·ty\\'ă·nǐ ‸mŏ·sǐ·tē\ n. Blended resentment, hatred, and dislike.

an·ni·hi·late\ə ‸nai·hǐ 'lāt\ v. To bring to nothingness, destroy, end utterly. (n. annihilation)

an·nu·ity\ə ‸nū·ǐ·tē\ n. A financial arrangement guaranteeing a certain yearly income.

anoint\ə ‸noint\ v. To smear with oil or an oily substance, rub with oil by way of soothing, pour oil on or rub ointment on as a ritual.

anom·a·lous\ə ‸nŏ·mə·ləs\ adj. Not typical; unusual, unexpected, and contrary to the usual type or pattern. (n. anomaly)

anon·y·mous\ə ‸nŏ·nǐ·məs\ adj. Nameless, having no significance attached to the name. (n. anonymity)

an·te·ri·or\\'ăn ‸tē·rē·ər\ adj. Front, toward the front. (adv. -ly)

an·tic·i·pa·tion\ăn 'tǐ·sǐ ‸pā·shən\ n. Expectation or imaginative foresight of the future. (v. anticipate, adj. anticipatory)

an·tith·e·sis\\'ăn ‸tǐ·thə·sǐs\ n., pl. antitheses. A contrast, a contrasting or contradicting statement. (adj. antithetical)

ap·er·ture\\'ă·pər·chər\ n. An opening or hole permitting passage or sight.

apex\\'ā 'pĕks\ n. Tip, topmost point.

apoth·e·cary\ə ‸pŏ·thə 'kă·rē\ n., pl. -ies. A druggist, pharmacist.

ap·pal or **ap·pall**\ə ‸pol\ v. To cause shock, dismay, or fear.

ap·pend\ə ‸pĕnd\ v. To attach so as to hang. (n. -age. An arm, a leg.)

ap·per·tain\\'ă·pər ‸tān\ v. To relate, have some connection.

ap·po·site\\'ă·pə·sǐt\ adj. Appropriate, fit, suitable. (n. -ness, adv. -ly)

ap·pre·cia·ble\ə ‸prē·shə·bəl\ adj. Noticeable, perceptible. (v. appreciate)

ap·pre·hend\\'ă·prē ‸hĕnd\ v. 1. To perceive and comprehend. 2. To anticipate with dread. (n. apprehension, adj. apprehensive)

apt\ăpt\ adj. Appropriate, suitable. (n. -ness, adv. -ly)

ap·ti·tude\‸ăp·tǐ 'tūd\ n. A disposition or ability.

ar·bo·re·al\\'ar ‸bŏ·rē·əl\ adj. Living in trees, suited to life in trees.

ar·chae·ol·o·gist\\'ar·kē ‸ŏ·lə·jǐst\ n. A student or expert at human life in ages long past. (n. archaeology, adj. archaeological)

ar·cha·ic\\'ar ‸kā·ǐk\ adj. Out of date, showing old-fashioned procedures or values. (adv. -ally)

ar·dor\\'ar·dər\ n. Warm and enthusiastic feeling, passion.

ar·ray\ə ‸rā\ n. An impressive regular arrangement or display. (also v.)

ar·ro·gance\\'ă·rə·gəns\ n. Haughty pride and unpleasant scorn for others. (adj. arrogant)

ar·te·ry\\'ar·tə·rē\ n., pl. -ies. A main thoroughfare for traffic.

ar·tic·u·late\\'ar ‸tǐk·yə·lət\ adj. Said so as to be clearly understood. (also v., n. articulation)

ar·ti·fice\\'ar·tǐ·fǐs\ n. A tricky device or measure.

as·cer·tain\\'ă·sər ‸tān\ v. To find out, learn certainly, learn and make sure. (n. -ment)

as·i·nin·i·ty\\'ă·sǐ ‸nǐ·nǐ·tē\ n. Stupidity and foolishness. (adj. asinine)

as·pect\‸ăs·pĕkt\ n. A phase, appearance.

as·per·i·ty\əs ‸pā·rǐ·tē\ n. Sharpness or bitterness of temper.

as·sail\ə ⁴sāl\ v. To attack fiercely (either physically or verbally). (n. -ant)

as·sem·blage\ə ⁴sĕm·blĭj\ n. A set, group, or collection brought together. (v. assemble)

athe·is·tic\'ā·thē ⁴ĭs·tĭk\ adj. Showing disbelief in the existence of a god. (n. atheist, atheism; adv. -ally)

atroc·i·ty\ə ⁴trŏ·sĭ·tē\ n. A very evil, cruel, or shocking action. (adj. atrocious)

at·tri·bute\⁴ă·trĭ'byūt\ n. A distinguishing trait or characteristic. (v. \ə ⁴trĭ·byūt\ To assign, consider as resulting from; n. attribution.)

au·dac·i·ty\'ɔ ⁴dă·sĭ·tē\ n. Reckless or insolent daring that tempts fate. (adj. audacious)

aug·ment\'ɔg ⁴mĕnt\ v. To add to. (n. -ation)

au·tom·a·ton\ɔ ⁴tŏ·mə 'tŏn\ n., pl. -s or automata. A mechanical man or robot, one acting in a purely mechanical way.

aux·il·ia·ry\ɔg ⁴zĭ·lə·rē\ adj. Supplementary but aiding when necessary. (also n.)

avail\ə ⁴vāl\ n. Success, successful accomplishment. (also v.)

avert\ə ⁴vərt\ v. To turn aside.

av·id\⁴ă·vĭd\ adj. Marked by eager enthusiastic interest. (n. -ity, adv. -ly)

azure\⁴ă·zhər\ adj. Sky blue. (also n.)

bal·last\⁴bă·ləst\ v. To supply with weights in order to stabilize. (also n.)

ban·dy\⁴băn·dē\ v. To pass or throw back and forth.

ban·ter\⁴băn·tər\ v. To tease, joke with, jest at good-humoredly. (also n.)

be·deck\bē ⁴dĕk\ v. To adorn, decorate (especially in a loud or showy way).

be·fall\bē ⁴fal\ v. irreg., befell, befallen. To happen to.

be·guile\bē ⁴gail\ v. 1. To coax or charm with coy or comic conduct. 2. To pass pleasantly. (n. -ment)

bel·lig·er·ent\bə ⁴lĭ·jə·rənt\ adj. Quarrelsome or warlike, inclined to fight or argue. (also n., n. belligerence, and adv. -ly)

be·mused\bē ⁴myūzd\ adj. Stunned or absorbed to the point of losing normal perception and reaction.

bene·fac·tor\⁴bĕ·nə 'făk·tər\ n. One who aids another (especially with money, grants, or influence). (n. benefaction)

be·nef·i·cence\bə ⁴nĕ·fĭ·səns\ n. Kindly generosity. (adj. beneficent)

be·nev·o·lent\bə ⁴nĕ·və·lĭnt\ adj. Kindly, well-intentioned, well-wishing. (n. benevolence)

be·nign\bə ⁴nain\ adj. Marked by good-natured friendliness. (n. -ity, adv. -ly)

be·queath\bē ⁴kwēth\ v. To give by will as an inheritance.

be·rate\bē ⁴rāt\ v. To scold, rebuke.

be·reave\bə ⁴rēv\ v. To deprive of by death. (n. -ment)

be·seech\bē ⁴sēch\ v. irreg., besought. To implore, beg.

be·stow\bē ⁴stō\ v. To give, endow. (n. -al)

bi·as\⁴bai·əs\ n., pl. -es. 1. Mental attitude, inclination, preference. 2. Prejudice, lack of fairness. (also v., adj. -ed)

bi·zarre\bĭ ⁴zar\ adj. Striking, unusual, outlandish; quaint, grotesque, and demanding attention. (adv. -ly)

blanch\blănch\ v. To become pale.

blas·phe·my\⁴blăs·fə·mē\ n. Profanity, mockery of things sacred. (v. blaspheme, adj. blasphemous)

blaze\blāz\ v. To mark (as a trail) by cutting notches or gashes in trees.

blight\blait\ v. To cause lack of growth, withering, or death of plants. (also n.)

blithe\blaith\ adj. Glad, happy, carefree.

blow·out\⁴blō 'aut\ n. A rut or gulch eroded by the wind.

bode\bōd\ v. To show as an indication of a future development.

bo·tan·i·cal\bə ⁴tă·nĭ·kəl\ adj. Of or pertaining to plants, flowers, or botany. (n. botany, adv. -ly)

boun·te·ous\⁴baun·tē·əs\ adj. Showing generous abundance. (n. bounty, adv. -ly)

bout\baut\ n. A period of activity like a round in boxing.

brawn\brɔn\ n. Strength, muscular development. (adj. brawny)

bra·zen\⁴brā·zən\ adj. 1. Made of brass. 2. Marked by insolence or contempt openly expressed. (adv. -ly)

broach\brōch\ v. To bring up in conversation.

brusque\brəsk\ adj. Showing marked shortness of manner verging on rudeness. (n. -ness, adv. -ly)

bur·den\⁴bər·dən\ n. Chorus, summarizing refrain.

cache\kăsh\ v. To conceal, hide away for future use. (also n.)

ca·dence\⁴kā·dəns\ n. 1. A sequence of musical notes (often showing a falling or concluding effect). 2. A measured series of tones in speech.

ca·lam·i·ty\kə ⁴lă·mĭ·tē\ n., pl. -ies. A great misfortune or tragedy. (adj. calamitous)

cal·ci·fy\⁴kăl·sĭ 'fai\ v. To make or become hard or brittle through deposits of calcium. (n. calcification)

cal·i·bra·tion\'kă·lĭ ⁴brā·shən\ n. Exact checking of the accuracy of any scale, gage, or instrument. (v. calibrate)

cam·phor\⁴kăm·fər\ n. A crystalline compound with a strong smell used in medicine and in preserving textiles.

can·dor\⁴kăn·dər\ n. Frankness, truthfulness. (adj. candid)

can·kered\⁴kaŋ·kərd\ adj. Blighted, eaten at, con-

ă b*a*d, ā b*a*ke, a f*a*ther, ĕ s*e*ll, ē *e*qual, ai m*i*le, ĭ s*i*t, ŏ c*o*t, ō n*o*te, ɔ l*a*w, ū b*oo*m, ʊ w*oo*d, yū *you*, yʊ f*u*ry, aʊ c*ow*, ɔi b*oy*. The schwa is used for both stressed and unstressed sounds: ə m*u*d, w*o*rd, *e*ven; ᴄh *ch*ase, i*tch*; sh *sh*ell, wi*sh*; th p*a*th, *thin*; t̪h *the*, ei*ther*; ŋ wi*ng*; w *w*et, *wh*eat; zh plea*s*ure.

sumed as by a cancer. (v. and n. canker, adj. cankerous)

can·tle\kăn·təl\ n. The ascending part at the back of a saddle.

ca·price\kə ˄prēs\ n. An unpredictable notion or turn of thoughts, whim. (adj. capricious)

ca·reen\kə ˄rēn\ v. To go or run in a wild lurching course.

car·i·ca·ture\˄kă·rĭ·kə 'ehur\ n. A likeness or imitation showing grotesque exaggerations. (also v.)

car·niv·o·rous\'kar ˄nĭ·və·rəs\ adj. Eating and subsisting on flesh rather than on grains and vegetables. (n. carnivore)

caul\kɔl\ n. A membrane sometimes enclosing the head of a child at birth.

cau·ter·ize\˄kɔ·tə 'raiz\ v. To clean or sterilize by (or as if by) burning. (n. cauterization, cautery)

cav·al·cade\˄kă·vəl 'kād\ n. 1. A parade of horsemen. 2. Any dramatic procession.

ce·ler·i·ty\sə ˄lă·rĭ·tē\ n. Rapidity, speed.

cen·ser\˄sĕn·sər\ n. A decorated or elaborate incense burner.

cen·trif·u·gal\sen ˄trĭ·fyə·gəl\ adj. Acting by a movement away from the center.

ces·sa·tion\sĕ ˄sā·shən\ n. Ceasing, stopping.

chafe\ehāf\ v. To become impatient, to fret, worry.

cha·grin\shə ˄grĭn\ n. A feeling of irritated embarrassment and disappointment. (v. chagrined or chagrinned, chagrining or chagrinning. To feel chagrin.)

champ\ehămp\ v. To chew with noisy vigor as a horse does on grass.

charg·er\˄ehar·jər\ n. A large and heavy warhorse.

char·nel\˄ehar·nəl\ adj. Pertaining to death, corpses, and tombs.

chase\ehās\ v. To engrave, emboss.

chasm\kăzm\ n. A deep gorge or gorgelike opening in the earth, a large long pit.

chas·tise\˄ehăs 'taiz\ v. To whip, punish. (n. -ment)

chat·tels\˄ehă·təlz\ n. plural. Possessions.

chem·ur·gist\kĕ ˄mər·jĭst\ n. A chemist who seeks to find new uses for farm materials and products. (n. chemurgy, adj. chemurgic)

chide\ehaid\ v. To scold, rebuke.

chil·blains\˄ehĭl 'blānz\ n. plural. Painful swelling caused by exposure to extreme cold.

chiv·al·ry\˄shĭ·vəl·rē\ n., pl. -ies. 1. The medieval knightly code of courtliness, gentlemanliness, and fairness. 2. Blended courtesy and protectiveness toward one weaker (especially a girl or woman). (adj. chivalric, chivalrous)

chlo·ro·form\˄klō·rə 'fôrm\ n. A colorless and quickly evaporating liquid used as an anesthetic. (also v.)

chol·era\˄kŏ·lə·rə\ n. Any of several infectious intestinal diseases common in Asia. (adj. -ic)

cho·ris·ter\˄kō·rĭs·tər\ n. A member of a chorus.

chor·tle\˄ehôr·təl\ v. To chuckle loudly.

chuck·hole\˄ehək 'hōl\ n. A hole in the surface of a road.

ci·pher\˄sai·fər\ n. Secret writing, cryptogram. (v. To do arithmetic problems.)

cir·cum·scribe\˄sər·kəm 'skraib\ v. To encircle, surround, encompass. (n. circumscription)

cir·cum·spect\˄sər·kəm 'spĕkt\ adj. Alert, wary, vigilant. (adv. -ly)

ci·vil·i·ty\sĭ ˄vĭ·lĭ·tē\ n., pl. -ies. 1. A comment or gesture suggesting courtesy. 2. Courtesy and affability. (adj. civil)

clam·ber\˄klăm·bər\ v. To climb awkwardly, scramble.

clam·or\˄klă·mər\ v. To make a noisy sustained outcry. (also n., adj. -ous)

clan·gor\˄klăŋ·ər\ n. A loud clanging sound (as of bells). (also v., adj. -ous)

cler·i·cal\˄klĕ·rĭ·kəl\ adj. Pertaining to the church or the clergy. (also n.)

clin·i·cal\˄klĭ·nĭ·kəl\ adj. Involving direct observation of the patient. (n. clinic, adv. -ly)

clove\klōv\ n. Division, dividing time or point.

co·ad·ju·tor\'kō·ə ˄jū·tər\ n. A helper, assistant. (also adj.)

cod·dle\˄kŏ·dəl\ v. To cook gently at a temperature below boiling.

cog·ni·zant\˄kŏg·nĭ·zənt\ adj. Aware, having perception and knowledge. (n. cognizance)

co·lic\˄kŏ·lĭk\ n. Extreme stomach pain.

col·la·tion\kə ˄lā·shən\ n. A listing together systematically and carefully. (v. collate)

col·lo·ca·tion\'kŏ·lə ˄kā·shən\ n. A complete arrangement in careful order. (v. collocate)

col·lo·quy\˄kŏ·lə·kwē\ n., pl. -ies. Conversation or dialogue. (adj. colloquial)

co·los·sus\kə ˄lŏ·səs\ n., pl. -es or colossi. A giant, gigantic figure or statue. (adj. colossal)

com·bat·ive\kəm ˄bă·tĭv\ adj. Given to fighting or opposing and arguing. (n. and v. combat, adv. -ly)

com·bus·ti·bil·i·ty\kəm 'bəs·tĭ ˄bĭ·lĭ·tē\ n. Power or capacity to burn. (n. combustion, adj. combustible)

com·mem·or·ate\kə ˄mĕ·mə 'rāt\ v. To preserve the memory of, remind of, insure remembrance of. (n. commemoration, adj. commemorative)

com·mend·able\kə ˄mĕn·də·bəl\ adj. Worthy of being praised. (adv. commendably)

com·mis·er·ate\kə ˄mĭ·zə 'rāt\ v. To sympathize; show pity, kindliness, and understanding. (n. commiseration)

com·mu·nion\kə ˄myūn·yən\ n. A close and intimate sharing by conversation about inner thoughts and moods. (v. commune)

com·pas·sion\kəm ˄pă·shən\ n. Sympathetic pity or sorrow. (adj. -ate)

com·pen·sate\˄kŏm·pən 'sāt\ v. To repay, substitute. (n. compensation, adj. compensatory)

com·pe·tence\˄kŏm·pə·təns\ n. Knowledge and judgment. (adj. competent.)

com·pla·cent\kəm ˄plā·sənt\ adj. Self-satisfied and self-assured. (n. complacence, adv. -ly)

com·ple·ment\˄kŏm·plə·mənt\ n. A full quota or crew of men.

com·pli·ance\kəm ˄plai·əns\ n. Submission and obedience. (adj. compliant, v. comply)

com·plic·i·ty\kəm ˄plĭ·sĭ·tē\ n. Participation in something wrong.

com·ply\kəm ˄plai\ v. To act in conformity or accord with another's wishes. (n. compliance)

com·po·nent\kəm ⁺pō·nənt\ n. An essential part.

com·pos·ite\kəm ⁺pŏ·zĭt\ n. A unit or group composed of several things. (also adj., v. compose)

com·po·sure\kəm ⁺pō·zhər\ n. Calm and unruffled self-possession. (v. compose)

com·pre·hend\'kŏm·prē ⁺hĕnd\ v. To understand. (n. comprehension)

com·press\⁺kŏm·prĕs\ n., pl. -es. A pad over a wound or inflammation.

com·pro·mise\⁺kŏm·prə 'maiz\ v. To endanger by laying open to suspicion, doubt, or bad reputation.

com·punc·tion\kəm ⁺pəŋ·shən\ n. A feeling of pity, regret, or remorse in connection with a hostile act.

com·pu·ta·tion\'kŏm·pyə ⁺tā·shən\ n. 1. The act of reckoning or calculating. 2. The calculation. (v. compute, n. computer)

con·cave\kən ⁺kāv\ adj. Hollow, shaped with a curve inward. (n. concavity)

con·cede\kən ⁺sēd\ v. To grant, acknowledge, admit, as in a claim or argument. (adj. concessive)

con·cen·tra·tion\'kŏn·sĭn ⁺trā·shən\ n. Intense attention. (v. concentrate)

con·ces·sion\kən ⁺sĕ·shən\ n. 1. The right to make sales or offer services at a center of recreation. 2. An act of conceding or granting, what is conceded or granted.

con·clave\⁺kŏn 'klāv\ n. A meeting; especially, an important private meeting of leaders.

con·coc·tion\kən ⁺kŏk·shən\ n. Something made by cooking together or otherwise mixing various ingredients. (v. concoct)

con·de·scend\'kŏn·də ⁺sĕnd\ v. 1. To descend voluntarily to a less dignified position, stoop. 2. To seem to defer to another but at the same time acting in a haughty or superior way. (n. condescension)

con·done\kən ⁺dōn\ v., To forgive, sanction, view lightly and tolerantly.

con·fec·tion\kən fĕk·shən\ n. A fancy dish; especially, a sweet.

con·fir·ma·tion\'kŏn·fər ⁺mā·shən\ n. Demonstration, proof, verification. (v. confirm)

con·flu·ence\⁺kŏn·flū·əns\ n. A place where two streams flow together. (adj. confluent)

con·ge·nial\kən ⁺jēn·yəl\ adj. Pleasing, pleasant, sociable. (n. -ity)

con·gest\kən ⁺jĕst\ v. To crowd thickly so as to check free motion or activity.

con·ges·tion\kən ⁺jĕst·chən\ n. An unwholesome accumulation; especially, a bodily condition marked by much swelling.

con·i·cal\⁺kŏ·nĭ·kəl\ adj. In the shape of a cone.

con·jec·ture\kən ⁺jĕk·chər\ n. Guessing, surmising, speculating. (also v., adj. conjectural)

con·ju·gate\⁺kŏn·jə 'gāt\ v. To arrange the parts or forms of in order (as to conjugate a verb). (n. conjugation)

con·jure\⁺kŏn·jər\ v. To call or summon into being or appearance (often by or as if by magic).

con·ju·ror\⁺kŏn·jə·rər\ n. A magician or performer of magic by charms and spells.

con·nois·seur\'kŏ·nə ⁺sər\ n. One with detailed knowledge, easy familiarity, and keen critical perception. (n. -ship)

con·sci·en·tious\kŏn 'shē ⁺ĕn·shəs\ adj. Carefully guided by conscience, in strict accordance with conscience. (adv. -ly)

con·se·quen·tial\'kŏn·sə ⁺kwĕn·shəl\ adj. 1. Important, significant. 2. With much show of importance or self-importance. (adv. -ly)

con·sole\⁺kŏn 'sōl\ n. A frame or cabinet equipped with dials, gauges, and buttons. (v. \kən ⁺sōl\ To cheer or comfort after a disappointment or loss, n. consolation.)

con·sort\kən ⁺sōrt\ v. To agree, fit.

con·spic·u·ous\kən ⁺spĭk·yū·əs\ adj. Attracting much attention, striking and impossible to overlook. (adv. -ly)

con·ster·na·tion\'kŏn·stər ⁺nā·shən\ n. Blended fright, dismay, amazement, and inability to think (v. consternate)

con·strict\kən ⁺strĭkt\ v. To contract, narrow. (n. -ion)

con·sum·mate\⁺kŏn·sə·mət\ adj. Complete, entire, utter. (also v., n. consummation, and adv. -ly)

con·ten·tion\kən ⁺tĕn·shən\ n. An argument maintained or advanced; an argument, dispute, conflict. (v. contend, adj. contentious)

con·text\⁺kŏn 'tĕkst\ n. Surrounding materials, either circumstances or accompanying writing. (adj. -ual)

con·tin·gen·cy\kən ⁺tĭn·jən·sē\ n., pl. -ies. Chance, chance development, any possible accidental development. (adj. contingent)

co·nun·drum\kə ⁺nən·drəm\ n. A puzzling problem like a riddle.

con·verge\kən ⁺vərj\ v. To run together, meet and join. (n. -nce, adj. -nt)

con·vex\kən ⁺vĕks\ adj. Shaped with a curve outward. n. -ity)

con·viv·i·al\kən ⁺vĭ·vē·əl\ adj. Sociable and jovial (especially during eating and drinking). (n. -ity, adv. -ly)

con·vo·lu·tion\'kŏn·və ⁺lū·shən\ n. A fold, twist. (adj. convoluted)

con·vul·sive\kən ⁺vəl·sĭv\ adj. Marked by sudden abnormally strong activity, or violent muscular spasms, (v. convulse, n. convulsion, and adv. -ly)

co·ping\⁺kō·pĭŋ\ n. A protecting and draining top layer on a masonry wall.

co·pi·ous\⁺kō·pē·əs\ adj. Plentiful, abundant. (adv. -ly)

cor·al\⁺kŏ·rəl\ n. A hard substance formed of skeletons of tiny marine animals and used in jewelry.

cor·dial\⁺kŏr·jəl\ adj. Hearty, warm, and sincere. (n. -ity, adv. -ly)

ă bad, ā bake, a father, ĕ sell, ē equal, ai mile, ĭ sit, ŏ cot, ō note, ɔ law, ū boom, ʊ wood, yū you, yʊ fury, aʊ cow, ɔi boy. The schwa is used for both stressed and unstressed sounds: ə mud, word, even; ch chase, itch; sh shell, wish; th path, thin; th the, either; ŋ wing; w wet, wheat; zh pleasure.

cor·ol·lary\ˆkȯ·rə ˈlä·rē\ n., pl. -ies. An idea that logically follows and holds good when another idea has been proved. (also adj.)

cor·pu·lent\kȯr·pyə·lənt\ adj. Portly and stout. (n. corpulence)

cor·ro·sion\kə ˆrō·shən\ n. Wearing away or being destroyed as by rust. (v. corrode)

cor·ru·gate\ˆkȯ·rə ˈgāt\ v. To shape with ridges or grooves. (n. corrugation).

cos·mop·o·lite\kȯz ˆmȯ·pə ˈlait\ n. A well-traveled, smooth, and urbane person. (adj. and n. cosmopolitan)

cote\kōt\ n. A shelter for birds.

coun·te·nance\ˆkaʊn·tə·nəns\ n. Face, facial expression. (also v.)

coun·ter·point\ˆkaʊn·tər ˈpȯint\ n. Balancing of opposites, contrast.

cou·ri·er\ˆku·rē·ər\ n. Special messenger.

cov·e·nant\ˆkə·və·nənt\ v. To pledge or agree to by solemn compact. (n. -er)

co·vert\ˆkə·vərt\ adj. Secret, secretive, concealed. (also n.)

cov·et\ˆkə·vət\ v. To feel strong envious want or craving for something of another's. (adj. -ous)

cow·er\ˆkaʊ·ər\ v. To shrink back in complete fear.

crave\krāv\ v. To wish for very strongly (sometimes compulsively).

crease\krēs\ v. To wound slightly or to stun by grazing with a bullet.

cre·scen·do\krē ˆshěn·dō\ n. A steady rise in loudness or tone. (also adj.)

crimp\krǐmp\ To snarl together.

crook\kruk\ n. A sheperd's staff with a curved top or handle.

cru·ci·ble\ˆkrü·sǐ·bəl\ n. A laboratory utensil capable of withstanding great heat.

crys·tal·line\ˆkrǐs·tə·lǐn\ adj. Suggesting the light glittering quality of crystal. (n. crystal)

crys·tal·lize\ˆkrǐs·tə ˈlaiz\ v. To become definite and clear. (n. crystallization)

cul·mi·nate\ˆkəl·mǐ ˈnāt\ v. To reach a climax or highest point. (n. culmination)

cul·prit\ˆkəl·prǐt\ n. One who is suspected, accused, or found guilty of an offense or crime.

cum·ber\ˆkəm·bər\ v. To inconvenience.

cur·ric·u·lum\kə ˆrǐ·kyu·ləm\ n., pl. -s or curricula. An organized program of courses of study. (adj. curricular)

curt\kərt\ adj. Discourteously or abruptly brief. (n. -ness, adv. -ly)

cut·back\ˆkət ˈbăk\ n. A portion of a path or trail marked by a sharp reversal of direction.

cyn·i·cal\ˆsǐ·nǐ·kəl\ adj. Inclined to disbelief as to another's honesty, good faith, or goodness; strongly inclined to doubt or to pessimism. (n. cynic, cynicism; adv. -ly)

dal·ly\ˆdă·lē\ v. To play, trifle, dawdle. (n. dalliance)

dank\dăŋk\ adj. Damp, chilly, and unpleasant. (n. -ness)

dap·per\ˆdă·pər\ adj. Brisk and stylishly dressed.

dap·pled\ˆdă·pəld\ adj. Spotted or streaked with different colors or shades. (v. dapple)

dearth\dərth\ n. Scarcity, lack. (adj. dear)

de·ba·cle\də ˆba·kəl\ n. A complete ruinous downfall, utter defeat.

de·bris\də ˆbrē\ n. Ruined fragments, rubble, rubbish.

de·cep·tive\də ˆsěp·tǐv\ adj. Tending to deceive, trick, or mislead. (n., v. deceive, and adv. -ly)

de·ci·pher\də ˆsai·fər\ v. To make out the meaning of, read and interpret.

de·cliv·i·ty\də ˆclǐ·vǐ·tē\ n., pl. -ies. A downward slope, low place.

dec·o·rous\ˆdě·kə·rəs\ adj. Proper, well-behaved, quiet. (adv. -ly)

de·co·rum\də ˆkō·rəm\ n. Stiff propriety and soberness.

de·duce\də ˆdūs\ v. To judge and conclude from known principles, determine or conclude after thought and consideration. (n. deduction)

deem\dēm\ v. To judge, think.

de·fer\də ˆfər\ v. To put off, postpone. (n. -ment)

def·er·ence\ˆdě·fə·rəns\ n. Courteous respect for merit or position. (v. defer, adj. deferential)

de·file\ˈdē ˆfail\ n. A narrow valley, gorge. (v. \ˈdē ˆfail\ To march or ride in a line; especially, in single file.)

de·flated\də ˆflā·təd\ adj. Suffering from loss of confidence, poise, or self-possession. (v. deflate, n. deflation)

de·for·ma·tion\ˈdē·fər ˆma·shən\ n. State of being deformed, contortion. (v. deform, n. deformity)

deft\děft\ adj. Showing neat quick performance. (n. -ness, adv. -ly)

deg·ra·da·tion\ˈdě·grə ˆdā·shən\ n. The state or process of being lowered in position, status, capacity, or possessions. (v. degrade)

de·lec·ta·ble\də ˆlěk·tə·bəl\ adj. Delicious, extremely pleasing or satisfying, most enjoyable. (adv. delectably)

de·lin·e·ate\də ˆlǐ·nē ˈāt\ v. To outline, sketch, draw. (n. delineation)

de·lin·quent\də ˆlǐŋ·kwənt\ n. One who is tardy or remiss about some task or duty. (also adj., n. delinquency)

de·lir·i·ous\də ˆlē·rē·əs\ adj. 1. Showing delirium, disoriented and wandering mentally. 2. Marked by or as if by wild irrational excitement connected with delirium. (n. delirium, adv. -ly)

de·lude\də ˆlūd\ v. To mislead, deceive. (n. delusion, adj. delusive)

del·uge\ˆděl ˈyūj\ n. Flood.

de·mean·or\də ˆmē·nər\ n. Behavior, conduct. (v. demean)

de·ment\dē ˆměnt\ v. To drive crazy or insane. (adj. -ed)

de·mo·ni·ac\dē ˆmō·nē·ăk\ adj. Hellish, fiendish. adj. -al, adv. -ally)

de·mur\də ˆmər\ n. Hesitancy, drawing back, unwillingness to go ahead. (also v.)

de·nom·i·na·tion·al\də ˈnȯ·mǐ ˆnā·shə·nəl\ adj. Pertaining or belonging to a religious sect or denomination. (n. denomination)

de·pict\dē ▴pĭkt\ v. To show by drawing, painting, or describing; picture. (n. -ion)

de·plor·a·ble\də ▴plō·rə·bəl\ adj. To be deplored, regrettable, bad. (v. deplore, adv. deplorably)

de·ploy\dē ▴plɔi\ v. To spread out or extend unduly. (n. -ment)

dep·re·cate\▴dĕ·prə 'kāt\ v. To find fault with and argue against, disapprove and find lacking in value. (n. deprecation)

dep·re·ca·to·ry\▴dĕ·prə·kə 'tō·rē\ adj. Tending to deprecate, hold as of little value. (v. deprecate, adv. deprecatorily)

dep·ri·va·tion\'dĕ·prĭ ▴vā·shən\ n. State of being deprived, dispossessed, hindered from having. (v. deprive)

der·e·lict\▴dĕ·rə 'lĭkt\ n. An abandoned ship. (also adj.)

de·ride\dē ▴raid\ v. To mock, ridicule, jeer at. (adj. derisory, derisive)

des·o·la·tion\'dĕ·sə ▴lā·shən\ n. Disheartening loneliness along with abandonment as useless or waste. (adj. and v. desolate)

des·pi·ca·ble\dĕs ▴pĭ·kə 'bəl\ adj. Worthy of scorn and contempt. (adv. despicably)

de·spond·en·cy\də ▴spŏn·dən·sē\ n. Dejection, hopeless sorrow. (n. despond, adj. despondent)

des·ti·tute\dĕs·tĭ 'tūt\ adj. Marked by lack or want, lacking in necessities of life. (n. destitution)

de·tract\dē ▴trăkt\ v. To take away merit or value. (n. -ion)

de·vas·tat·ing\▴dĕ·vəs 'tā·tĭŋ\ adj. Overwhelming and subduing. (n. devastation, v. devastate)

de·vi·a·tion\'dĕ·vē ▴ā·shən\ n. Departure from a straight course.

de·vise\də ▴vaiz\ v. To think out, plan, evolve. (n. device)

de·void\də ▴vɔid\ adj. Showing complete lack or absence, empty, lacking.

de·vout\də ▴vaut\ adj. Showing deep devotion. (n. -ness, adv. -ly)

dex·ter·i·ty\'dĕks ▴tā·rĭ·tē\ n. Blended skill, grace, neatness, and effectiveness in action or accomplishment. (adj. dexterous)

di·a·bol·i·cal\'dai·ə ▴bŏ·lĭ·kəl\ adj. Devilishly cruel and evil. (adv. -ly)

di·a·logue\▴dai·ə 'lŏg\ n. A conversation between two persons.

dif·fi·dence\▴dĭ·fĭ·dəns\ n. Lack of confidence in oneself, shy timidity. (adj. diffident)

dif·fuse\dĭ ▴fyūz\ v. To spread out widely and thinly. (n. diffusion)

dil·i·gent\▴dĭ·lĭ·jənt\ adj. Carefully and conscientiously industrious. (n. diligence, adv. -ly)

di·min·u·tive\dĭ ▴min·yu·tĭv\ adj. Very small or tiny. (adv. -ly)

dint\dĭnt\ n. Forceful means of effect.

dire\dair\ adj. Fearful, terrible.

dirge\dərj\ n. A funeral hymn (or similar mournful poem).

dis·arm·ing\dis ▴ar·mĭŋ\ adj. Intended or tending to allay suspicion, hostility, or attack. (v. disarm, adv. -ly)

dis·cern·i·ble\dĭ ▴sər·nĭ·bəl\ adj. Capable of being discerned, of being perceived or recognized. (v. discern, adv. discernibly)

dis·com·fi·ture\dis ▴kəm·fĭ·chur\ n. Frustrated embarrassment. (v. discomfit)

dis·con·cert\'dĭs·kən ▴sərt\ v. To upset, embarrass, baffle.

dis·con·so·late\'dĭs ▴kŏn·sə·lət\ adj. Sad and dejected and hard to comfort or console. (adv. -ly)

dis·course\'dĭs ▴kōrs\ v. To talk, converse. (also n.)

dis·creet\dĭs ▴krēt\ adj. Close-mouthed, prudent, cautious about saying the wrong thing or saying too much. (n. discretion, adv. -ly)

dis·dain\dĭs ▴dān\ v. To refuse or abstain from through pride or scorn. (also n., adj. -ful)

dis·em·bow·el\'dĭs·əm ▴bau·əl\ v. To cut or tear out the entrails of.

dis·en·gage\'dĭs·ən ▴gāj\ v. To free, unloosen. (n. -ment)

dis·grun·tled\'dĭs ▴grən·təld\ adj. Disappointed, vexed, and irritated.

di·shev·eled\dĭ ▴shĕ·vəld\ adj. Loosened and falling about in disorder.

dis·in·te·grate\'dĭs ▴ĭn·tə 'grāt\ v. To break or fall into separate fragments. (n. disintegration)

dis·mem·ber\dĭs ▴mĕm·bər\ v. To cut off or tear out the limbs, divide into parts. (n. -ment)

dis·perse\dĭs ▴pərs\ v. To scatter and drive away. (n. dispersal)

dis·po·si·tion\'dĭs·pə ▴zĭ·shən\ n. Location, placement. (v. dispose)

dis·qui·et\dĭs ▴kwai·ət\ n. Worry, anxiety, concern. (also v.)

dis·sem·ble\dĭ ▴sĕm·bəl\ v. To mask one's own true thoughts or feelings.

dis·sev·er\dĭ ▴sĕ·vər\ v. To separate, divide. (n. -ance)

dis·sim·u·la·tion\dĭ 'sĭ·mə ▴lā·shən\ n. Crafty deception and pretending, concealment of true motives and intentions. (v. dissimulate)

dis·si·pate\▴dĭ·sĭ 'pāt\ v. To thin out and evaporate, thin and spread away. (n. dissipation)

dis·so·lu·tion\'dĭs·sə ▴lū·shən\ n. A dire and final ending (as by death or decay).

dis·suade\'dĭ ▴swād\ v. To persuade or coax to a different decision. (n. dissuasion)

dis·tinct\dĭ ▴stĭŋkt\ adj. Clear and definite. (n. -ness, adv. -ly)

dis·tor·tion\dĭs ▴tōr·shən\ n. A grotesque, abnormal, or perverted representation; a twisted deviation from normal. (v. distort)

dis·tract\dĭs ▴trăkt\ v. To confuse, frighten and disarrange one's thoughts. (n. -ion)

ă b*a*d, ā b*a*ke, a f*a*ther, ĕ s*e*ll, ē *e*qual, ai m*i*le, ĭ s*i*t, ŏ c*o*t, ō n*o*te, ɔ l*a*w, ū b*oo*m, ʊ w*oo*d, yū y*ou*, yʊ f*u*ry, aʊ c*ow*, ɔi b*oy*. The schwa is used for both stressed and unstressed sounds: ə m*u*d, w*o*rd, *e*ven; ch *ch*ase, it*ch*; sh *sh*ell, wi*sh*; th pa*th*, *th*in; th *th*e, ei*th*er; ŋ wi*ng*; w *w*et, *wh*eat; zh plea*s*ure.

di·verge\dĭ ▲vərj\ v. To split and go on in different directions. (n. -nce, adj. -nt)

di·ver·sion\dĭ ▲vĕr·zhən\ n. Anything intended to divert or take away from serious purposive activity, a recreation or pastime. (v. divert)

di·vine\dĭ ▲vain\ v. To guess, come to know intuitively or without thoughtful reasoning. (n. diviner)

doc·ile\dŏ·sĭl\ adj. Readily obedient and easy to teach, lead, or guide. (n. docility, adv. -ly)

dole·ful\dōl·fəl\ adj. Sad, sorrowful. (adv. -ly)

dom·i·nant\dŏ·mĭ·nənt\ adj. Controlling, showing force or effectiveness leading to governing or controlling. (n. dominance, v. dominate, and adv. -ly)

do·min·ion\də ▲mĭn·yən\ n. The area under a ruler's control.

doo·dle·bug\dū·dəl 'bəg\ n. The young of the ant lion, a digging insect.

du·al\dū·əl\ adj. Having two natures or two counterparts. (n. -ity)

du·bi·ous\dū·bē·əs\ adj. Doubtful, without full belief or confidence. (adv. -ly)

du·pli·cate\dū·plĭ 'kāt\ v. To copy exactly. (also v. and adj., n. duplication)

du·ra·tion\dʊ ▲rā·shən\ n. The length of time that something lasts or endures.

dy·nam·ic\'dai ▲nă·mĭk\ adj. Showing great energy, force, activity, or drive. (adv. -ally)

eb·o·ny\ĕ·bə·nē\ adj. Deep black. (also n.)

ec·cen·tric\ĕk ▲sĕn·trĭk\ adj. Marked by odd, strange, individual traits and inclinations. (n. -ity, adv. -ally)

ec·sta·sy\ĕk·stə·sē\ n., pl. -ies. Most extreme joy or pleasure. (adj. ecstatic)

ee·rie\ē 'rē\ adj. eerier, eeriest. Weird, uncanny, and fearful. (adv. eerily)

ef·face\ə ▲fās\ v. To withdraw from notice, to make quite inconspicuous. (n. -ment)

ef·fec·tu·al\ə ▲fĕk·chəl\ adj. Having a definite and positive effect. (adv. -ly)

ef·ful·gent\ə ▲fəl·jənt\ adj. Marked by a colorful gleaming brightness. (n. effulgence, adv. -ly)

ef·fu·sion\ə ▲fyū·zhən\ n. An escaping of fluids from natural vessels in body tissues. (v. effuse, adj. effusive)

egret\ē 'grēt\ n. A heron with long white plumes.

elapse\ə ▲lăps\ v. To pass, occur.

ela·tion\ē ▲lā·shən\ n. Extreme joy or happiness (as at a victory or success). (v. elate)

ele·gi·ac\'ĕ·lə ▲jai·ək\ adj. Dignified, contemplative, and fit for an elegy (a poem praising the dead). (n. elegy)

elim·i·nate\ə ▲lĭ·mĭ 'nāt\ v. 1. To insure absence, nonexistence, or nonappearance. 2. To rule out, exclude, prevent. 3. To drop out in defeat. (n. elimination)

el·o·quent\ĕ·lə·kwənt\ adj. Extremely expressive in communication. (n. eloquence, adv. -ly)

elude\ē ▲lūd\ v. To escape or get away from. (adj. elusive)

em·a·nate\ĕ·mə 'nāt\ v. To issue forth from a source. (n. emanation)

emerge\ə ▲mərj\ v. To come out into view. (n. -nce)

em·i·nence\ĕ·mĭ·nəns\ n. Height, elevation.

em·i·nent\ĕ·mĭ·nənt\ adj. Outstanding, surpassing.

em·is·sary\ĕ·mĭ 'sā·rē\ n., pl. -ies. Messenger.

emit\ē ▲mĭt\ v. To give out, send out, utter. (n. emission)

em·phat·ic\əm ▲fă·tĭk\ adj. Showing force, stress, and certainty. (adv. -ally)

en·com·pass\ĕn ▲kəm·pəs\ v. To surround, encircle.

en·deav·or\ən ▲dĕ·vər\ n. A sustained strong attempt or effort. (also v.)

en·gen·der\ĕn ▲gĕn·dər\ v. To cause to exist.

en·gross\ĕn ▲grōs\ v. To interest completely, absorb.

enig·ma\ə ▲nĭg·mə\ n. A mystery or puzzle, a situation very hard to understand or explain. (adj. -tic)

en·join\ən ▲jɔin\ v. To prohibit strictly and authoritatively.

en·mi·ty\ĕn·mĭ·tē\ n., pl. -ies. Dislike, hatred, state of being enemies.

en·sue\ĕn ▲sū\ v. To happen, occur (usually as a result or consequence).

en·to·mo·log·i·cal\'ĕn·tə·mə ▲lŏ·jĭ·kəl\ adj. Of or pertaining to insect life. (n. entomology)

en·treat\ən ▲trēt\ v. To ask, beg. (n. entreaty)

en·try\ĕn·trē\ n., pl. -ies. One entered in a contest or competition. (v. enter)

en·vi·ron\ən ▲vai·rən\ v. To surround and encompass and also to condition as one's neighborhood or circumstances do. (n. -ment)

en·vi·sion\ən ▲vĭ·zhən\ v. To imagine the sight of.

ep·i·sode\ĕ·pĭ·sōd\ n. A single incident in a longer narrative.

ep·i·thet\ĕ·pĭ 'thĕt\ n. A descriptive word or phrase attached to a person's name; a distinctive nickname, alternate name, or descriptive phrase.

epit·o·mize\ə ▲pĭ·tə 'maiz\ v. To serve as characteristic or typical as of a complex whole. (n. epitome)

ep·och\ĕ·pək\ n. A period of time marked by certain particular developments.

equa·nim·i·ty\'ē·kwə ▲nĭ·mĭ·tē\ n., pl. -ies. Even and calm mental composure.

er·rat·ic\ə ▲ră·tĭk\ adj. Irregular, inconsistent, and unpredictable. (adv. -ally)

etch\ĕch\ v. To engrave or design by or as if by letting acids eat away marked lines or areas. (n. -ing)

eter·ni·ty\ē ▲tər·nĭ·tē\ n., pl. -ies. An endless period of time. (adj. eternal)

eu·pho·ny\yū·fə·nē\ n., pl. -ies. The quality of pleasing, attractive, or melodic sound effect. (adj. euphonious)

ev·a·nesce\ĕ·və ▲nĕs\ v. To fade away and vanish (n. -nce)

eva·sion\ə ▲vā·zhən\ n. A trick or device to escape having to answer a question or face a situation. (v. evade, adj. evasive)

evolve\ē ▲vŏlv\ v. To produce or develop gradually. (n. evolution)

ew·er\yūr\ n. A large wide-mouthed pitcher.

ex·ac·er·bate\ĕks ▲ă·sər 'bāt\ v. To intensify, aggravate. (n. exacerbation)

ex·cru·ci·at·ing\ĕks ▲krū·shē 'ā·tĭŋ\ adj. Marked by unbearable pain or intense agony.

ex·empt\ək ⁴zĕmpt\ adj. Freed, loosed, spared from. (also v., n. -ion)

ex·hil·a·rate\ĕks ⁴hĭ·lə 'rāt\ v. To bring excited lively pleasure or joy to. (n. exhilaration)

ex·i·gen·cy\⁴ĕk·sĭ·jən·sē\ n., pl. -ies. A pressing situation calling for action or decision. (adj. exigent)

ex·on·er·ate\əg ⁴zŏ·nə 'rāt\ v. To free completely from blame or guilt. (n. exoneration)

ex·ot·ic\ĕk ⁴sŏ·tĭk\ adj. Very new or strange.

ex·pe·di·en·cy\ək ⁴spē·dē·ən·sē\ n., pl. -ies. Suitable and practical wisdom. (adj. expedient)

ex·pe·dite\⁴ĕks·pə 'dait\ v. To hasten, speed up by eliminating delays.

ex·pi·ate\⁴ĕks·pē·āt\ v. To atone for, pay for. (n. expiation)

ex·plic·it\əks ⁴plĭ·sĭt\ adj. Expressed very clearly and definitely. (adv. -ly)

ex·ploit\⁴ĕks·ploit\ n. A noteworthy or meritorious deed or adventure.

ex·pos·tu·la·tion\əks 'pŏs·tyu ⁴lā·shən\ n. An effort to reason earnestly and explain objections. (v. expostulate)

ex·qui·site\⁴ĕks·kwĭ·zĭt\ adj. Beautiful, lovely, as if the product of very delicate skill. (adv. -ly)

ex·ter·mi·nate\ĕks ⁴tər·mĭ 'nāt\ v. To wipe out or destroy totally. (n. extermination, exterminator)

ex·tinct\ĕks ⁴tĭŋkt\ adj. No longer existent, having ended or died out. (n. -ion)

ex·tort\əks ⁴tōrt\ v. To force out, wring or draw out by force or threat. (n. -ion)

ex·tract\ĕks ⁴trăkt\ v. To draw, press, heat, or distill out. (n. -ion)

ex·trav·a·gant\ĕks ⁴tră·və·gənt\ adj. Excessive, most unusual in passing ordinary bounds or limits. (n. extravagance, adv. -ly)

ex·tri·cate\⁴ĕks·trĭ 'kāt\ v. To set free, disentangle. (n. extrication)

ex·u·ber·ant\ĕk ⁴sū·bə·rənt\ adj. Wildly joyful. (n. exuberance)

ex·ult\əg ⁴zəlt\ v. To show great joy at some victory or accomplishment (n. -ation, adj. -tant)

fa·çade\fə ⁴sad\ n. The part of a building seen from the front.

fac·et\⁴fă·sət\ n. Side or surface viewed, aspect.

fa·ce·tious\fə ⁴sē·shəs\ adj. Showing joking lightness and lack of serious concern. (n. -ness, adv. -ly)

fa·cial\⁴fā·shəl\ adj. Of or pertaining to the face.

fa·cil·i·ty\fə ⁴sĭ·lĭ·tē\ n., pl. -ies. 1. Available equipment or other resources, available means. 2. Assured ease in knowing and using.

fac·ul·ty\⁴fă·kəl·tē\ n., pl. -ies. Ability to see, feel, and use other senses and to interpret their messages.

fal·la·cy\⁴fă·lə·sē\ n., pl. -ies. Falsehood, error, lack of truth. (adj. fallacious)

fal·ter\⁴fal·tər\ v. To move uncertainly, stop in hesitation or fear.

fam·ished\⁴fă·mĭsht\ adj. Very hungry, as though half starved. (v. famish)

fa·nat·i·cism\fə ⁴nă·tĭ·sĭzm\ n. Show of intense feeling, wild action, and lack of reason. (n. and adj. fanatic, adj. fanatical)

fan·tas·tic\făn ⁴tăs·tĭk\ adj. Utterly unreal, imaginary, or weird; not realistic or factual; so surprising as to seem unreal. (n. fantasy, adv. -ally)

farce\fars\ n. A ridiculous or nonsensical sequence of actions. (adj. farcical)

fas·tid·i·ous\fas ⁴tĭ·dē·əs\ adj. Carefully dainty and particular. (n. -ness, adv. -ly)

fa·tal·ism\⁴fā·tə·lĭzm\ n. A feeling of powerlessness before fate and an inclination to accept it without struggle. (adj. fatalistic)

fawn·ing\⁴fɔ·nĭŋ\ adj. Overmodest, too submissive and attentive. (v. fawn)

fea·si·bil·i·ty\'fē·zə ⁴bĭ·lət·ē\ n. The quality of being possible.

feign\fān\ v. To pretend, fake.

feint\fānt\ v. To pretend, mislead by a pretended motion. (also n.)

fer·ret\⁴fĕ·rət\ v. To search out, find, detect.

fer·vent\⁴fər·vənt\ adj. Showing warm expression and intensity, enthusiasm, or conviction. (n. fervency, adv. -ly)

fer·vor\⁴fər·vər\ n. Intensity, enthusiasm, and conviction.

fet·id\⁴fĕ·tĭd\ adj. Ill-smelling, stinking. (n. -ness, adv. -ly)

fet·lock\⁴fĕt 'lŏk\ n. The point of horse's leg just above the hoof.

fet·ter\⁴fĕ·tər\ v. To bind with a chain. (also n.)

feu·dal\⁴fyū·dəl\ adj. Of or pertaining to the social and legal system of the Middle Ages. (n. -ism)

fic·ti·tious\fĭk ⁴tĭ·shəs\ adj. From or in fiction, imaginary, made up. (adv. -ly)

fi·let mi·gnon\'fĭ ⁴lā mēn ⁴yŏn\ n. Fine broiled steak.

fi·nal·i·ty\fai ⁴nă·lĭ·tē\ n., pl. -ies. Final last decision or choice (adj. final)

fire·lock\⁴fīr 'lŏk\ n. An early musket fired by flintlock sparks.

fis·sure\⁴fĭ·shər\ n. A crack, crevice.

fla·grant\⁴flā·grənt\ adj. Very conspicuous, impossible not to notice. (n. flagrancy, adv. -ly)

flail\flāl\ n. A threshing tool composed of a free-swinging stick mounted on a handle. (v. To make wild forceful waving or striking motions.)

flank\flăŋk\ v. To be stationed at the side of. (also n.)

fledg·ling\⁴flĕj·lĭŋ\ adj. Having just acquired the capacity for flight (as a young bird).

flor·id\⁴flŏ·rĭd\ adj. 1. Red, rosy, flushed. 2. Extreme, romantic, and showy. (n. -ness, adv. -ly)

floun·der\⁴flaun·dər\ v. To struggle, slip, stumble awkwardly and heavily.

ă b*a*d, ā b*a*ke, a f*a*ther, ĕ s*e*ll, ē *e*qual, ai m*i*le, ĭ s*i*t, ŏ c*o*t, ō n*o*te, ɔ l*a*w, ū b*oo*m, ʊ w*oo*d, yū *you*, yʊ f*u*ry, aʊ c*ow*, ɔi b*oy*. The schwa is used for both stressed and unstressed sounds: ə m*u*d, w*o*rd, *e*ven; ch *ch*ase, i*tch*; sh *sh*ell, wi*sh*; th p*a*th, *th*in; th *the*, ei*th*er; ŋ wi*ng*; w *w*et, *wh*eat; zh plea*s*ure.

fluc·tu·ate\\⁴flək·chu 'āt\ v. To vary back and forth or up and down. (n. fluctuation)

flu·ent\\⁴flū·ənt\ adj. Marked by easy, rapid, smooth speech. (n. fluency, adv. -ly)

flu·id·i·ty\flū ⁴ĭ·dĭ·tē\ n., pl. -ies. The characteristic of expressing or suggesting flowing motion. (n. and adj. fluid)

flush\fləsh\ v. To discover and drive from a hiding place.

foal\fōl\ v. To give birth to (as a mare does a colt).

for·bear\fŏr ⁴bār\ v. irreg., forbore, forborn. To refrain, hold off. (n. -ance)

fore·bod·ing\fər ⁴bō·dĭŋ\ n. Worried concern and expectation of tragic or unfortunate events.

fore·know\fŏr ⁴nō\ v. irreg., foreknew, foreknown. To know in advance. (n. foreknowledge)

fore·sight\fŏr 'sait\ n. Prudent and careful consideration of the future. (adj. -ed)

for·mi·da·ble\⁴fŏr·mĭ·də·bəl\ adj. Large, powerful, and dangerous to attack or oppose; inducing awe, fear, or hesitation in an opponent. (adv. formidably)

for·ti·tude\⁴fŏr·tĭ·tūd\ n. Bravery and determination to endure.

fran·chise\⁴frăn·chaiz\ n. An especial right or privilege given by a governmental agency to engage in a certain stated activity. (also v.)

fri·vol·i·ty\frĭ ⁴vŏ·lĭ·tē\ n., pl. -ies. Lack of intent or earnest seriousness. (adj. frivolous)

frond\frŏnd\ n. A leaf, leaflike shoot.

fur·tive\⁴fər·tĭv\ adj. With sly and quiet stealth, like a thief. (adv. -ly)

fu·tile\⁴fyū·tĭl\ adj. Useless, without any good result or noticeable effect, vain and sure to fail. (n. futility, adv. -ly)

gad·fly\⁴găd 'flai\ n., pl. -ies. A stinging irritating fly (especially one that bites cattle and horses).

gal·axy\⁴gă·lək·sē\ n., pl. -ies. A mass of stars. (adj. galactic)

gal·ley\⁴gă·lē\ n. 1. A low ship driven by oars (or oars and sails) used in early times. 2. A ship's kitchen.

gal·li·vant\⁴gă·lĭ 'vănt\ v. To go around seeking pleasure and wasting time.

gal·van·ic\găl ⁴vă·nĭk\ adj. Produced by, producing, or pertaining to electricity (especially from batteries).

gal·va·nize\⁴găl·və 'naiz\ v. To electrify into recognition or activity.

gam·bol\⁴găm·bəl\ n. Playful leaping or frolicking about. (also n.)

gam·ut\⁴gă·mət\ n. A complete range or series.

gan·grene\⁴găŋ 'grēn\ n. Decay of bodily tissue occurring when flow of blood is checked. (adj. gangrenous)

gaunt\gŏnt\ adj. 1. Grimly unattractive, angular, and unadorned. 2. Thin and bony. 3. Thin and worn from lack of food.

ge·nial\jē·nē·əl\ adj. Marked by cheerful, companionable good humor. (n. -ity, adv. -ly)

ge·nius\⁴jē·nē·əs\ n., pl. -es. Particular character or identifying essence.

gen·teel\'jĕn ⁴tēl\ adj. Marked by avoidance of anything rude, vulgar, or crude; respectable, polite, upper-class.

ge·nus\⁴jē·nəs\ n., pl. -es or genera. A class or type scientifically determined.

ges·tic·u·la·tion\'jĕs 'tĭk·yu ⁴lā·shən\ n. A demonstrative or impassioned gesture, usually one accompanying speech. (v. gesticulate)

ghoul\gūl\ n. An evil spirit that robs graves and does other horrible things. (adj. -ish)

gib·ber·ish\⁴jĭ·bə·rĭsh\ n. Foolish meaningless talk.

glaze\glāz\ v. To cover with (or as with) glass.

glib\glĭb\ adj. Fluent and easy. (n. -ness, adv. -ly)

glow·er\⁴glau·ər\ n. An angry expression, scowl, frown. (also v.)

gnarled\narld\ adj. Knotted or knobby and twisted and rough.

gra·di·ent\⁴grā·dē·ənt\ n. Grade, inclination.

gran·dil·o·quent\'grăn ⁴dĭ·lə·kwənt\ adj. Lofty, grand, and highflown in utterance. (n. grandiloquence, adv. -ly)

gran·u·lar\⁴grăn·yə·lər\ adj. Having the shape or form of a grain, marked by grains.

graph·ic\⁴gră·fĭk\ adj. 1. Vivid and lifelike in calling up a clearly defined picture. 2. Of or pertaining to drawing or sketching. (adv. -ally)

grav·i·ty\⁴gră·vĭ·tē\ n. 1. The force drawing objects to the earth. 2. Extreme seriousness. (adj. grave)

gro·tes·que·rie\grō ⁴tĕs·kə·rē\ n. A grotesque circumstance or occurrence.

gul·ly\⁴gə·lē\ n., pl. -ies. A large ditch or little ravine formed by flowing water.

gy·ro·scope\⁴jai·rə 'skōp\ n. A device consisting of a spinning wheel mounted in a ring used to insure stability of ships and airplanes. (adj. gyroscopic)

hab·it·ed\⁴hă·bĭ·təd\ adj. Dressed, costumed. (n. and v. habit)

hag·gard\⁴hă·gərd\ adj. Looking worn or wasted as by struggle, suffering, or want. (adv. -ly)

hap·haz·ard\'hăp ⁴hă·zərd\ adj. Marked by lack of system, consistency, or steadiness; random, hit-or-miss. (adv. -ly)

hap·less\⁴hăp·ləs\ adj. Miserably unfortunate, tragically luckless. (n. -ness, adv. -ly)

ha·rangue\hə ⁴răŋ\ v. To speak in a sustained noisy way in order to persuade. (also n.)

ha·rass\hə ⁴răs\ v. To trouble or torment by repeated onset. (n. -ment)

har·py\⁴har·pē\ n., pl. -ies. A greedy, grasping person (especially when an old woman).

haunch\hŏnch\ n., pl. -es. Hip or buttock.

ha·ven\⁴hā·vən\ n. A harbor or place of refuge.

hawk·er\⁴hɔ·kər\ n. Seller, vendor. (v. hawk)

hay·mak·er n. A wild swing or blow with full motion of the whole arm.

haz·ard\⁴hă·zərd\ n. Risk, danger, peril, a dangerous chance. (also v., adj. -ous)

ha·zel\⁴hā·zəl\ adj. Yellowish, grayish brown.

her·ald\⁴hĕ·rəld\ n. An official messenger; especially, one sent peaceably to enemies or strangers.

herb·age\\ˈhər·bĭj\ n. Vegetation (especially grass).

he·red·i·tary\hə·ˈrĕ·dĭ·tā·rē\ adj. As described or indicated because of the effect of long tradition.

hes·i·tan·cy\ˈhĕ·zĭ·tən·sē\ n., pl. -ies. Inclination to hesitate, uncertainty and indecision preventing going ahead. (adj. hesitant, v. hesitate)

hi·a·tus\ˈhai·ˈā·təs\ n., pl. -es or hiatus. Gap, omission.

hol·o·caust\ˈhŏ·lə·ˈkɔst\ n. 1. A very large and destructive fire taking many lives and causing much damage. 2. A scene of death and destruction.

hom·age\ˈhŏ·mĭj\ n. Show of honor and respect.

hor·ti·cul·tur·ist\ˈhŏr·tĭ·ˈkəl·ehə·rĭst\ n. Gardener, one expert at growing plants. (n. horticulture, adj. horticultural)

hos·tel\ˈhŏs·təl\ n. An inn, a lodging or shelter for the night.

hov·er\ˈhə·vər\ v. To stay more or less in the same position while in the air.

hu·mil·i·ty\hyū·ˈmĭ·lĭ·tē\ n., pl. -ies. Humble meekness and submissiveness.

Hus·ky\ˈhəs·kē\ n., pl. -ies. A strong Eskimo dog.

hy·brid\ˈhai·brĭd\ adj. Crossbred, bred or produced from different strains. (also n.)

hyp·o·crit·i·cal\ˈhĭ·pə·ˈkrĭ·tĭ·kəl\ adj. Marked by a pretense at being other than one is, masking one's true thoughts. (n. hypocrite, hypocrisy; adv. -ly)

hy·poth·e·sis\ˈhai·ˈpŏ·thə·sĭs\ n., pl. hypotheses. An idea or group of ideas advanced tentatively for later acceptance or rejection. (adj. hypothetical)

hys·te·ria\hĭs·ˈtĕ·rē·ə\ n. Blended extreme emotion and lack of calm rationality. (n. hysterics, adj. hysterical)

ibis\ˈai·bĭs\ n., pl. -es. A colorful long-legged wading bird related to the heron.

ide·al·ism\ˈai·ˈdē·ə·lĭzm\ n. Belief in or adherence to ideals. (n. idealist, adj. idealistic)

id·i·om\ˈi·dĭ·əm\ n. 1. A set arrangement or sequence of words sanctioned in a language. (adj. -atic) 2. Language or dialect.

ig·no·min·i·ous\ˈĭg·nə·ˈmĭ·nē·əs\ adj. Utterly shameful or contemptible. (n. ignominy)

il·leg·i·ble\ĭ·ˈlĕ·jĭ·bəl\ adj. Practically impossible to read because of indistinct writing or printing. (n. illegibility, adv. illegibly)

il·lim·it·able\ĭ·ˈli·mĭ·tə·bəl\ adj. 1. Endless, measureless. (adv. illimitably)

il·lu·sion\ĭ·ˈlū·zhən\ n. An ill-based or unreal notion or belief.

im·mac·u·late\ĭ·ˈmăk·yu·lət\ adj. Quite clean and fresh and utterly spotless. (adv. -ly)

im·merse\ĭ·ˈmərs\ v. To dip or plunge below a surface. (n. immersion)

im·mi·nent\ˈi·mĭ·nənt\ adj. Evidently about to happen in the near future. (n. imminence, adj. -ly)

im·mo·la·tion\ˈi·mə·ˈlā·shən\ n. Sacrifice, sacrificial death of a victim. (v. immolate)

im·mune\ĭ·ˈmyūn\ adj. 1. Protected, safe, not susceptible. 2. Not touched or influenced, exempt. (n. immunity)

im·pact\ˈĭm·ˈpăkt\ n. A striking, hitting, or colliding forcefully.

im·pair\ĭm·ˈpār\ v. To damage, mar, make imperfect. (n. -ment)

im·par·tial\ĭm·ˈpar·shəl\ adj. Without partiality, advance favor, or bias. (n. -ity, adv. -ly)

im·pass·ive\ĭm·ˈpă·sĭv\ adj. With no show of emotion or feeling. (adv. -ly)

im·pede\ĭm·ˈpēd\ v. To hinder. (n. impedance)

im·pel\ĭm·ˈpĕl\ v. To drive forward.

im·pend\ĭm·ˈpĕnd\ v. To threaten in the near future, hang over one.

im·pen·e·tra·ble\ĭm·ˈpĕ·nə·trə·bəl\ adj. Impossible to penetrate or find a way through. (adv. impenetrably)

im·per·a·tive\ĭm·ˈpĕ·rə·tĭv\ adj. 1. Demanding as with authority, showing strong command. 2. Completely necessary or urgent. (adv. -ly)

im·per·cep·ti·ble\ĭm·pər·ˈsĕp·tĭ·bəl\ adj. Impossible or very hard to sense or perceive. (adv. imperceptibly)

im·pe·ri·ous\ĭm·ˈpĕ·rē·əs\ adj. Demanding (often in an overbearing way). (adv. -ly)

im·per·ish·able\ĭm·ˈpĕ·rĭ·shə·bəl\ adj. Enduring, not wearing away or fading to nothing. (adv. imperishably)

im·per·ti·nent\ĭm·ˈpər·tĭ·nənt\ adj. Saucy, impudent, without due respect for authority. (n. impertinence, adv. -ly)

im·per·turb·able\ĭm·pər·ˈtər·bə·bəl\ adj. Calm and impassive despite anything disturbing or alarming. (adv. imperturbably)

im·per·vi·ous\ĭm·ˈpər·vē·əs\ adj. Not open to influence or suggestion from others. (adv. -ly)

im·pi·ous\ˈĭm·pē·əs\ adj. Irreverent, unreligious, blasphemous. (n. impiety, adv. -ly)

im·plic·it\ĭm·ˈplĭ·sĭt\ adj. Without question or doubt. (adv. -ly)

im·ply\ĭm·ˈplai\ v. To hint or suggest without making a direct comment, tell or show without saying openly or clearly. (n. implication)

im·pon·der·a·ble\ĭm·ˈpŏn·dər·ə·bəl\ adj. Impossible to consider, evaluate, or analyze.

im·port\ˈĭm·ˈpōrt\ n. 1. Importance. 2. Significance, meaning.

im·pru·dent\ĭm·ˈprū·dənt\ adj. Unwise, rash, foolish. (n. imprudence, adv. -ly)

im·pu·ni·ty\ĭm·ˈpyū·nĭ·tē\ n. Gloating freedom from detection, punishment, or harm.

in·a·ni·tion\ĭ·ˈnă·ˈnĭsh·ən\ n. Near starvation.

in·ar·tic·u·late\ĭn·ar·ˈtĭk·yu·lət\ adj. 1. Marked by lack of clear distinctness in speech. 2. Unable to speak, as because of great anger. (adv. -ly)

in·au·di·ble\ĭn·ˈɔ·dĭ·bəl\ adj. Not loud or clear enough to be heard. (adv. inaudibly)

ă bad, ā bake, a father, ĕ sell, ē equal, ai mile, ĭ sit, ŏ cot, ō note, ɔ law, ū boom, ʊ wood, yū you, yʊ fury, aʊ cow, ɔi boy. The schwa is used for both stressed and unstressed sounds: ə mud, word, even; ch chase, itch; sh shell, wish; th path, thin; th the, either; ŋ wing; w wet, wheat; zh pleasure.

in·cal·cu·la·ble\ĭn ᐧkăl·kyu·lə·bəl\ adj. Impossible or difficult to calculate or estimate. (adv. incalculably)

in·car·nate\ĭn ᐧkar·nət\ adj. Bodily, in the flesh.

in·ces·sant\ĭn ᐧsĕ·sənt\ adj. Continuing ceaselessly, going on without break or rest. (adv. -ly)

in·ci·den·tal\ĭn·sĭ ᐧdĕn·təl\ adj. In an accidental, minor, or unimportant way. (adv. -ly)

in·ci·sor\ĭn ᐧsai·zər\ n. A sharp front tooth, a tooth with a sharp cutting edge.

in·cite\ĭn ᐧsait\ v. To persuade and encourage (often to a bad action). (n. -ment)

in·cog·ni·zant\ĭn ᐧkŏg·nĭ·zənt\ adj. Without thought, knowledge, or recognition.

in·com·pre·hen·si·ble\ĭn 'kŏm·prē ᐧhĕn·sĭ·bəl\ adj. Impossible to comprehend or understand. (n. incomprehensibility, adv. incomprehensibly)

in·con·se·quen·tial\ĭn 'kŏn·sə ᐧkwĕn·shəl\ adj. Unimportant, trivial. (n. -ity, adv. -ly)

in·con·spic·u·ous\ĭn·kən ᐧspĭk·yu·əs\ adj. Not conspicuous, not commanding special attention. (adv. -ly)

in·cred·i·ble\ĭn ᐧkrĕ·dĭ·bəl\ adj. Unbelievable, too extreme to be believed. (adv. incredibly)

in·cred·u·lous\ĭn ᐧkrĕd·yu·ləs\ adj. Withholding belief, unwilling or unable to believe. (n. incredulity, adv. -ly)

in·di·go\ĭn·dĭ 'gō\ adj. Deep (or violet) blue. (also n.)

in·di·vis·i·ble\ 'ĭn·də ᐧvĭs·ə·bəl\ adj. Not possible to divide.

in·do·lent\ 'ĭn·də·lənt\ adj. Showing carefree laziness and idleness. (n. indolence, adv. -ly)

in·dom·i·ta·ble\ĭn ᐧdŏ·mĭ·tə·bəl\ adj. Incapable of being defeated or daunted. (adv. indomitably)

in·du·bi·ta·ble\ĭn ᐧdū·bĭ·tə·bəl\ adj. Certain, impossible to question or doubt. (adv. indubitably)

in·duce\ĭn ᐧdūs\ v. To persuade or influence to some course or decision. (n. -ment)

in·ef·fec·tu·al\ĭn·ə ᐧfĕk·chəl\ adj. Not effectual, unsuccessful in efforts or duties. (adv. -ly)

in·ept\ĭn ᐧĕpt\ adj. Unfit and hence poor and unsuccessful. (n. -itude, adv. -ly)

in·ev·i·table\ĭn ᐧĕ·vĭ·tə·bəl\ adj. Necessarily bound to happen. (n. inevitability, adv. inevitably)

in·ex·o·ra·ble\ĭn ᐧĕk·sə·rə·bəl\ adj. Sternly bound to go on or to happen in spite of any appeal. (n. inexorability, adv. inexorably)

in·fal·li·bil·i·ty\ĭn 'fă·lĭ ᐧbĭ·lĭ·tē\ n. The characteristic of never being wrong or making a mistake. (adj. infallible)

in·fer·nal\ĭn ᐧfər·nəl\ adj. Hellish, hateful. (adv. -ly)

in·frac·tion\ĭn ᐧfrăk·shən\ n. A breaking or violation (as of a rule or order).

in·fu·sion\ĭn ᐧfyū·zhən\ n. A curative liquor with various ingredients. (v. infuse)

in·ge·nious\ĭn ᐧjē·nē·əs\ adj. Showing keen and resourceful inventiveness or cleverness. (adv. -ly)

in·ge·nu·ity\ĭn·jə ᐧnū·ĭ·tē\ n., pl. -ies. The characteristic of being ingenious, cleverness at inventing or discovering.

in·gen·u·ous\ĭn ᐧjĕn·yu·əs\ adj. With simple frankness and honesty. (n. -ness, adv. -ly)

in·im·i·ta·ble\ĭn ᐧĭ·mĭ·tə·bəl\ adj. So superior as to defy being imitated. (adv. inimitably)

in·i·tia·tive\ĭ ᐧnĭ·shə·tĭv\ n. Confidence and energy in starting a process or procedure. (v. initiate)

in·junc·tion\ĭn ᐧjəŋ·shən\ n. A court order prohibiting a certain action or procedure, an official or professional warning. (v. enjoin)

in·oc·u·late\ĭn ᐧŏk·yu 'lāt\ v. To introduce into the body by medical injection. (n. inoculation)

in·quis·i·to·ri·al\ĭn 'kwĭ·zĭ ᐧtō·rē·əl\ adj. Of or pertaining to an inquisitor or stern persistent questioner. (n. inquisitor)

in·sen·si·bil·i·ty\ĭn 'sĕn·sĭ ᐧbĭ·lĭ·tē\ n., pl. -ies. Unconsciousness; absence of perception, feeling, or thought. (adj. insensible)

in·sid·i·ous\ĭn ᐧsĭ·dē·əs\ adj. Operating in an unseen way hard to detect. (adv. -ly)

in·sin·u·ate\ĭn ᐧsĭn·yu 'āt\ v. To hint or suggest slyly. (adv. insinuatingly)

in·so·lence\ 'ĭn·sə·ləns\ n. Insulting or contemptuous disrespect. (adj. insolent)

in·sol·u·ble\ĭn ᐧsŏl·yu·bəl\ adj. Impossible or extremely difficult to solve. (adv. insolubly)

in·su·late\ 'ĭn·sə 'lāt\ v. To set apart, separate from others. (n. insulation)

in·su·per·a·ble\ĭn ᐧsū·pə·rə·bəl\ adj. Impossible to overcome, impossible or difficult to pass or climb over. (adv. insuperably)

in·sur·mount·able\ 'ĭn·sər ᐧmaunt·ə·bəl\ adj. Insuperable.

in·ter·mi·na·ble\ 'ĭn ᐧter·mĭ·nə·bəl\ adj. Endless, going on forever. (adv. interminably)

in·ter·mit·tent\ 'ĭn·tər ᐧmĭ·tənt\ adj. Recurring, happening at intervals. (adv. -ly)

in·ter·pose\ 'ĭn·tər ᐧpoz\ v. To thrust between so as to interrupt, to put forward in order to interfere. (n. interposition)

in·ter·ro·gate\ 'ĭn ᐧtĕ·rə 'gāt\ v. To ask, query, seek for an answer. (n. interrogation)

in·ter·sperse\ 'ĭn·tər ᐧspərs\ v. To place here and there among other things.

in·ter·vene\ 'ĭn·tər ᐧvēn\ v. To go in or among, often by way of hindrance or interference. (n. intervention)

in·ti·mate\ 'ĭn·tĭ·mət\ adj. Marked by very close connection, with deep personal knowledge and familiarity. (n. intimacy, adv. -ly; v. \ 'ĭn·tĭ 'māt\ To hint or imply, to express indirectly, n. intimation.)

in·tol·er·a·ble\ĭn ᐧtŏ·lə·rə·bəl\ adj. Not to be borne or endured. (adv. intolerably)

in·trac·ta·ble\ĭn ᐧtrăk·tə·bəl\ adj. Not yielding readily to guidance, teaching, or suggestion. (adv. intractably)

in·tre·pid·i·ty\ 'ĭn·trə ᐧpĭ·dĭ·tē\ n. Dauntless bravery. (adj. intrepid)

in·tro·spec·tive\ 'ĭn·trə ᐧspĕk·tĭv\ adj. Marked by or leading to analysis of one's own mind or feelings. (n. introspection)

in·vin·ci·ble\ĭn ᐧvĭn·sĭ·bəl\ adj. Unconquerable, sure to be victorious over any opposition. (n. invincibility, adv. invincibly)

in·vo·ca·tion\ 'ĭn·və ᐧkā·shən\ n. A recitation used in conjuring. (v. invoke)

in·vo·lute\\ˆĭn·və 'lūt\ adj. In a spiral close around an axis.

io·ta\ai ˆō·tə\ n. A very small quantity, a bit.

irate\ai ˆrāt\ adj. Showing anger, vexation, or rage. (adv. -ly)

ir·i·des·cent\'ĭ·rĭ ˆdĕ·sənt\ adj. Having a sheen of many changing colors. (n. iridescence, adv. -ly)

ir·rep·a·ra·ble\ĭ ˆrĕ·pə·rə·bəl\ adj. Beyond repair, mending, or bettering. (adv. irreparably)

ir·res·o·lute\ĭ ˆrĕ·zə 'lūt\ adj. Not resolute or determined, hesitating. (adv. -ly)

ir·re·vo·ca·ble\ĭ ˆrĕ·və·kə·bəl\ adj. Without possibility of revoking or changing. (adv. irrevocably)

itin·er·ary\ĭ ˆtĭ·nə 'rā·rē\ n., pl. -ies. Travel route, list of places passed through.

jad·ed\ˆjā·dəd\ adj. Tired and worn out.

jamb\jăm\ n. The casing or post alongside a door.

jar·gon\ˆjar·gən\ n. Nonsensical, unintelligible, or incoherent nonsense.

jaunt\jɔnt\ n. A carefree pleasure trip, a casual short excursion.

jaun·ty\ˆjɔn·tē\ adj. Showing gayety, assurance, and carelessness. (adv. jauntily)

jet·ti·son\ˆjĕ·tĭ·sən\ v. To throw overboard or drop off in order to lighten. (n. The act or fact of dropping overboard or hurling off.)

jo·vial\ˆjō·vē·əl\ adj. Marked by hearty jollity and good will. (n. -ity, adv. -ly)

jowl\jaul\ n. Jaw.

ju·bi·lant\ˆjū·bĭ·lənt\ adj. Showing triumphant joy. (n. jubilation, adv. -ly)

junc·tion\ˆjən·shən\ n. A place or point at which things cross or intersect.

ju·ris·dic·tion\'ju·rĭs ˆdĭk·shən\ n. Established legal authority over an area.

jux·ta·po·si·tion\'jəks·tə·pə ˆzĭ·shən\ n. Placement side by side. (v. juxtapose)

kins·man\ˆkĭnz·mən\ n., pl. kinsmen. Relative.

knave\nāv\ n. A dishonest or tricky person.

la·bo·ri·ous\lə ˆbō·rē·əs\ adj. Showing or causing much labor or exertion. (n. and v. labor, adv. -ly)

lac·er·ate\ˆlă·sə 'rāt\ v. To tear or rip deeply or badly. (n. laceration)

lam·en·ta·tion\'lă·mən ˆtā·shən\ n. Outcry, wailing, or other noisy sign of grief. (n. and v. lament)

lan·guid\ˆlăŋ·gwĭd\ adj. Marked by tired, indifferent, or listless inactivity. (n. languor, adv. -ly)

lank\lăŋk\ adj. Lean, spare.

lapse\lăps\ n. A falling away through error or omission. (v. To fall or sink.)

la·tent\ˆlā·tənt\ adj. Hidden or undisclosed, often as not yet developed. (n. latency)

lat·er·al\ˆlă·tə·rəl\ adj. At, from, of, or along the side; in a sideways direction or course; projecting to the side. (adv. -ly)

lat·i·tude\ˆlă·tĭ·tūd\ n. A section or area considered according to its north-south location. (adj. latitudinal)

lat·tice\ˆlă·tĭs\ n. A construction of wood or metal horizontal strips fitting over a window, a form of shutter or venetian blind.

lead·er\ˆlē·dər\ n. A short piece of catgut or other line connecting hook and fishing line.

leer\lēr\ n. A contorted look or grimace often showing some unpleasant characteristic. (also v.)

le·gion\ˆlē·jən\ n. A great number, a multitude (as of soldiers).

le·nient\ˆlē·nē·ənt\ adj. Mild, gentle, and permissive; not stern and demanding. (n. lenience, adv. -ly)

leth·ar·gy\ˆlĕ·thər·jē\ n., pl. -ies. Indifferent, listless, continued drowsiness. (adj. lethargic)

lieu\lū\ n. Stead, place.

lilt\lĭlt\ v. To rise and fall in a pleasing musical way. (also n.)

lin·eage\ˆlĭ·nē·əj\ n. Family line, line of descent. (adj. lineal)

liq·ui·da·tion\lĭ·kwĭ ˆdā·shən\ n. The process of settling, closing, or ending financial holdings or transactions. (v. liquidate)

list·less\ˆlĭst·ləs\ adj. Indifferent and languid through weariness or illness. (adv. -ly)

lithe\laith\ adj. Active, supple, graceful, and athletically proportioned. (n. -ness)

lo·co·mo·tion\'lō·kə ˆmō·shən\ n. Natural movement forward (as on legs or wheels).

lo·cu·tion\lō ˆkyū·shən\ n. A particular way of speaking.

lon·gi·tu·di·nal\'lɔŋ·jĭ ˆtū·dĭ·nəl\ adj. Lengthwise, considered as running along the length. (n. longitude, adv. -ly)

lope\lōp\ n. Step, stride. (also v.)

lore\lōr\ n. Knowledge; especially, old, bookish, or folk knowledge.

loz·enge\ˆlŏ·zĕnj\ n. A figure with four equal sides making two obtuse and two acute angles, a candy or cough drop made in this form.

lu·cid\ˆlū·sĭd\ adj. Clear, sound, and rational. (n. -ity, adv. -ly)

lu·di·crous\ˆlū·dĭ·krəs\ adj. Ridiculous, absurdly laughable. (adv. -ly)

lu·mi·nous\ˆlū·mĭ·nəs\ adj. 1. Emitting soft, clear, steady, reflected light. 2. Bright, clear. (n. luminosity, adv. -ly)

lure\lūr\ n. Whatever strongly appeals, attracts or arouses strong desire. (also v.)

lu·rid\ˆlū·rĭd\ adj. Hazily or murkily colorful or vivid, showing a vivid but dark smoky glow. (n. -ness, adv. -ly)

lyr·i·cal\ˆlĭ·rĭ·kəl\ adj. Marked by unrestrained expression of such emotions as pleasure and enthusiasm. (adv. -ly)

ă bad, ā bake, a father, ĕ sell, ē equal, ai mile, ĭ sit, ŏ cot, ō note, ɔ law, ū boom, ʊ wood, yū you, yʊ fury, aʊ cow, ɔi boy. The schwa is used for both stressed and unstressed sounds: ə mud, word, even; ch chase, itch; sh shell, wish; th path, thin; th the, either; ŋ wing; w wet, wheat; zh pleasure.

mag·ni·tude\\ˈmăg·nĭ 'tūd\ n. Noticeably great size.

mal·a·dy\\ˈmă·lə·dē\ n., pl. -ies. Ailment, disease.

ma·lig·nant\mə 'lĭg·nənt\ adj. Hateful, ill-wishing. (n. malignance, adv. -ly)

mal·odor·ous\\ˈmăl ˈō·də·rəs\ adj. Ill-smelling. (adv. -ly)

ma·neu·ver\mə ˈnū·vər\ v. To move or conduct skillfully, despite obstructions and difficulties; to plan and execute in a careful step-by-step way.

man·i·fest\\ˈmă·nĭ 'fĕst\ adj. Evident, apparent, clear. (n. -ation, adv. -ly, and v. To show clearly.)

ma·nip·u·late\mə ˈnĭ·pyə 'lāt\ v. To treat, guide, or operate with various motions of the hands. (n. manipulation)

man·u·mit\\ˈmăn·yu ˈmĭt\ v. To free from slavery by voluntary proper legal action. (n. manumission)

ma·raud\mə ˈrɔd\ v. To roam about and loot, steal, or destroy. (n. -er)

mar·row\\ˈmă·rō\ n. The soft whitish pulpy tissue inside bones.

mas·sive\\ˈmă·sĭv\ adj. Composed of a large mass; big, solid, and bulky. (adv. -ly)

mat·tock\\ˈmă·tək\ n. A heavy tool for digging and cutting roots.

me·di·ate\\ˈmē·dē·āt\ v. To come between opposing parties to try to adjust differences. (n. mediation, mediator)

med·ley\\ˈmĕd·lē\ n. A mixed combination.

me·lee\\ˈmā 'lā or 'mā ˈlā\ n. A brisk confused general fight or skirmish.

me·nag·er·ie\mĕ ˈnă·jə·rē\ n. A considerable collection of different animals (at least some of them undomesticated).

mesh\mĕsh\ n., pl. -es. A network capable of ensnaring. (also v.)

meta·mor·pho·sis\\ˈmĕ·tə ˈmŏr·fə·sĭs\ n., pl. metamorphoses. Complete change.

me·thod·i·cal\mĕ ˈthŏ·dĭ·kəl\ adj. Systematic, in accordance with orderly methods. (n. method, adv. -ly)

me·tic·u·lous\mə ˈtĭk·yu·ləs\ adj. Marked by painstaking care about details. (adv. -ly)

mien\mēn\ n. Bearing, manner, composure.

mil·li·me·ter\\ˈmĭ·lĭ 'mē·tər\ n. A thousandth part of a meter, a little less than four one-hundredths of an inch.

min·ion\\ˈmĭn·yən\ n. A servant or follower.

min·is·tra·tion\\ˈmĭ·nĭ ˈstrā·shən\ n. An act of care or attention. (v. ministrate)

min·strel\\ˈmĭn·strəl\ n. A traveling poet or singer in old times. (n. -sy)

mi·nute\mai ˈnyūt or mĭ ˈnyūt\ adj. 1. Very small, tiny. 2. Marked by concern about tiny details. (adv. -ly)

mis·an·thro·py\mĭ ˈsăn·thrə·pē\ n., pl. -ies. Dislike and distrust of one's fellow men. (n. misanthrope, adj. misanthropic)

mis·car·riage\mĭs ˈkă·rĭj\ n. Mischance, misfortune, accident. (v. miscarry)

mis·giv·ing\mĭs ˈgĭ·vĭŋ\ n. Doubt.

mod·u·late\\ˈmŏ·ju 'lāt\ v. To vary the tone or pitch of, avoiding unpleasant extremes. (n. modulation)

mo·men·tous\mō ˈmĕn·təs\ adj. Extremely significant, of major importance. (n. moment, adv. -ly)

mo·men·tum\mō ˈmĕn·təm\ n., pl. -s or momenta. The impetus or force that keeps and object moving.

mono·tone\\ˈmŏ·nə 'tōn\ n. A single dull unvaried tone. (adj. monotonous)

mo·rale\mə ˈrăl\ n. Resolution to go on in some undertaking or struggle.

mor·al·ize\\ˈmō·rə 'laiz\ v. To consider and draw morals and conclusions. (n. moralization)

mo·rose\mə ˈrōs\ adj. Marked by ill-tempered gloom. (adv. -ly)

mor·ti·fi·ca·tion\\ˈmŏr·tĭ·fĭ ˈkā·shən\ n. Deep embarrassment. (v. mortify)

mo·sa·ic\mō ˈzā·ĭk\ n. A floor, walk, or other flat area decorated by setting various colored stones in mortar. (also adj.)

mot·ley\\ˈmŏt·lē\ n. A cloth of many different colors. (also adj.)

mull\məl\ v. To consider, ponder.

murky\\ˈmər·kē\ adj. Dark, gloomy, and indistinct (often because of fog or smoke). (n. murk, murkiness)

muse\myūz\ n. 1. A goddess or spirit directing some phase of literature or the arts. 2. A period of deep thought. (adv. musingly, v. To meditate or think deeply about in a preoccupied way.)

mu·ti·late\\ˈmyū·tĭ 'lāt\ v. To injure so as to cause loss of a limb or member or to wound similarly. (n. mutilation)

mys·tic\\ˈmĭs·tĭk\ n. One who experiences or professes intuitive knowledge of great truths. (also adj., adj. -al)

mys·ti·fi·ca·tion\\ˈmĭs·tĭ·fĭ ˈkā·shən\ n. Baffling, puzzling, bewildering. (v. mystify)

na·ïve\\ˈna·ēv\ adj. Simple, inexperienced, unsophisticated. (n. -te, adv. -ly)

nar·ra·tive\\ˈnă·rə·tĭv\ n. A story, account. (also adj., v. narrate)

nat·u·ral·ize\\ˈnă·chə·rə· 'laiz\ v. To give citizenship to. (n. naturalization)

niche\nĭch\ n. A recess or indenture in a wall (as for a statue).

noc·tur·nal\nŏk ˈtər·nəl\ adj. Taking place, operating, or performed at night. (adv. -ly)

no·mad\\ˈnō·măd\ n. A wanderer, drifter. (adj. -ic)

nom·i·nal\\ˈnŏ·mĭ·nəl\ adj. Named or designated but yet not actually as named, in name only rather than in fact. (adv. -ly)

non·cha·lant\\ˈnŏn·chə ˈlŏnt\ adj. Marked by lack of concern, care, or emotion; with cool or confident unconcern. (n. nonchalance, adv. -ly)

non·plussed\\ˈnŏn ˈpləst\ adj. Baffled and made uncertain how to act. (v. nonplus)

non·sen·si·cal\nŏn ˈsĕn·sĭ·kəl\ adj. Foolish, lacking sense, marked by nonsense. (n. nonsense, adv. -ly)

nos·tal·gic\nə ˈstăl·jĭk\ adj. Marked by longing and love for home or by yearning for the past. (adv. -ally)

no·ta·tion\\ˈnō ˈtā·shən\ n. An act of noting or writing (especially by means of strange symbols).

nov·el\\ˆnŏ·vəl\ adj. New, unusual, and interesting. (n. -ty)

obei·sance\ō ˆbā·səns\ n. A bow or other indication of respect. (adj. obeisant)

obese\ō ˆbēs\ adj. Unwholesomely stout, having unattractive excessive flesh. (n. obesity)

oblique\ō ˆblēk\ adj. Slanted, inclined, between level and vertical. (n. obliquity)

oblit·er·ate\ŏb ˆlĭ·tə 'rāt\ v. To erase, blot, wear, wash out. (n. obliteration)

obliv·i·ous\əb ˆlĭ·vē·əs\ adj. Not mindful or conscious, completely unaware. (adv. -ly)

ob·scure\əb ˆskyūr\ adj. Minor and very little known. (n. obscurity, adv. -ly, and v. To make dark and indistinct.)

ob·so·lete\'ŏb·sə ˆlēt\ adj. Out of date and no longer of use or value, no longer in use. (n. -ness)

ob·sti·nate\ˆŏb·stĭ·nət\ adj. Stubborn and determined not to yield to others, hard to pass through. (n. obstinacy, adv. -ly)

ob·strep·er·ous\əb ˆstrĕ·pə·rəs\ adj. Noisy and disobedient or unruly. (adv. -ly)

ob·struc·tion\əb ˆstrək·shən\ n. Anything that hinders or blocks the way. (v. obstruct.)

ob·tuse\əb ˆtūs\ adj. Not pointed, blunter and approaching straightness more than a right angle.

oc·u·lar\ˆŏ·kyu·lər\ adj. By or pertaining to the eyes or eyesight. (adv. -ly)

ol·fac·to·ry\ɔl ˆfăk·tə·rē\ adj. Of or pertaining to the sense of smell.

omen\ˆō·mĕn\ n. A sign of something to come.

om·i·nous\ˆŏ·mĭ·nəs\ adj. Showing characteristics foretelling or suggesting evil or unhappy developments, threatening and fearful. (adv. -ly)

opaque·ness\ō ˆpāk·nəs\ n. Not transparent, too solid to see through. (adj. opaque)

opi·ate\ˆō·pē·ət\ n. An opium drug, anything that tends to produce a drugged reaction.

op·ti·mis·tic\'ŏp·tĭ ˆmĭs·tĭk\ adj. Showing a happy or bright attitude whereby one expects a favorable outcome. (n. optimist, optimism; adv. -ally)

or·deal\ōr ˆdēl\ n. A series of painful or difficult experiences, a severe series of tests.

or·nate\ōr ˆnāt\ adj. Highly or elaborately ornamented, marked by extravagant flowery effects. (n. -ness, adv. -ly)

os·ten·ta·tion\'ŏs·tən ˆtā·shən\ n. Showy self-display. (adj. ostentatious)

out·go·ing\'aut 'gō·ĭŋ\ adj. Genuinely or seemingly interested in matters outside one's self.

over·tone n. Suggestion, implication.

over·wrought\'ō·vər ˆrɔt\ adj. Fatigued with nervous strain, overtired and worried.

pac·i·fy\ˆpă·sĭ 'faı\ v. To make calm and peaceful. (n. pacification)

pag·eant\ˆpă·jənt\ n. A colorful procession featuring costume and display. (n. -ry)

pains·tak·ing\ˆpānz 'tā·kĭŋ\ adj. Taking great care, showing conscientious attention. (adv. -ly)

pa·la·tial\pə ˆlā·shəl\ adj. Like a palace; grand, spacious, and imposing.

pal·lid\ˆpă·lĭd\ adj. 1. Pale and wan, looking exhausted or faint. 2. Pale and just visible. (adv. -ly)

pal·lor\ˆpă·lər\ n. Paleness, lack of color.

pal·pa·ble\ˆpăl·pə·bəl\ adj. Readily clear and easily perceived by the senses. (n. palpability, adv. palpably)

pal·pi·tate\ˆpăl·pĭ 'tāt\ v. To tremble, throb, flutter, pulsate. (n. palpitation)

pal·sey or **pal·sy**\ˆpɔl·zē\ n. Paralysis or other crippling sickness.

pan·pipe n. A primitive musical instrument of different length reeds bound side by side.

par·a·ble\ˆpă·rə·bəl\ n. A short narrative from which one may learn some lesson.

par·a·pet\ˆpă·rə 'pĕt\ n. A wall or bulwark to keep people from falling, a railing.

par·en·thet·i·cal\'pă·rən ˆthĕ·tĭ·kəl\ adj. Fit for placing within parentheses, an explanation not grammatically important to the basic sentence. (n. parenthesis, pl. -ses)

Par·is green n. A poisonous bright-green powder used as an insecticide or as a coloring pigment.

par·o·dy\ˆpă·rə·dē\ v. To make a humorous imitation of in order to mock or ridicule. (also n.)

par·ox·ysm\ˆpăr·ək·sĭzm\ n. A wild convulsive fit or seizure.

patho·log·i·cal\'pă·thə ˆlŏ·jĭ·kəl\ adj. Caused by sickness, as though caused by or related to sickness. (n. pathology, adv. -ly)

peer\pēr\ n. An equal in rank, condition, or quality.

peer·less\ˆpēr·ləs\ adj. Unequaled, unrivaled.

pee·vish\ˆpē·vĭsh\ adj. Fretfully cross, impatiently ill-humored. (adv. -ly)

pend·ant\ˆpĕn·dənt\ adj. Hanging suspended.

per·cep·ti·ble\pər ˆsĕp·tĭ·bəl\ adj. Capable of being perceived, of being seen or otherwise sensed. (adv. perceptibly)

per·cep·tion\pər ˆsĕp·shən\ n. Capacity to perceive; action of perceiving, understanding, or realizing. (v. perceive, adj. perceptive)

pe·ri·od·ic\'pē·rē ˆŏ·dĭk\ adj. Given frequently from time to time, happening from time to time. (adv. -ally)

per·se·vere\'pər·sə ˆvēr\ v. To continue steadfastly in some effort or enterprise. (n. perseverance)

per·sis·tence\pər ˆsĭs·təns\ n. Determined steady continuing, especially against difficulty or discouragement. (adj. persistent)

per·son·age\ˆpər·sə·nəj\ n. A person; especially, a person of importance.

per·spec·tive\pər ˆspĕk·tĭv\ n. Proportion or scope

ă bad, ā bake, a father, ĕ sell, ē equal, aı mile, ĭ sit, ŏ cot, ō note, ɔ law, ū boom, ʊ wood, yū you, yʊ fury, aʊ cow, ɔı boy. The schwa is used for both stressed and unstressed sounds: ə mud, word, even; ȼh chase, itch; sh shell, wish; th path, thin; t̲h̲ the, either; ŋ wing; w wet, wheat; zh pleasure.

permitting correct evaluation.

pert\pərt\ adj. Looking saucy, bold, or smart. (adv. -ly)

per·ti·nac·i·ty\'pər·tĭ ˄nă·sĭ·tē\ n. Firm or stubborn persistence. (adj. pertinacious)

per·turb\pər ˄tərb\ v. To worry, agitate. (n. -ation)

per·vade\pər ˄vād\ v. To spread or seep all through. (n. pervasion, adj. pervasive)

per·verse\'pər ˄vərs\ adj. Stubbornly unreasonable and hard to explain. (n. perversity, adv. -ly)

pe·ti·tion·er\pə ˄tĭ·shə·nər\ n. One offering a petition; one seeking some grant or right. (n. and v. petition)

pet·u·lance\˄pĕ·chə·ləns\ n. Fretful impatient complaining. (adj. petulant)

pho·bia\˄fō·bē·ə\ n. A strong and everpresent irrational fear.

pi·az·za\pē ˄a·zə\ n. 1. An open public square. 2. A large open porch or verandah.

pic·tur·esque\'pĭk·tyu ˄rĕsk\ adj. Unusual, colorful, or striking and commanding interest. (adv. -ly)

pig·ment\˄pĭg·mənt\ n. A coloring material; especially, a paste or powder to be mixed with oil in making paint.

pine\pain\ v. 1. To pass time in regret, sorrow, grief, or pain. 2. To long for, yearn.

pin·na·cle\˄pĭ·nə·kəl\ n. 1. Top, topmost point. 2. A small spire or turret.

pir·ou·ette\'pĭr·ə ˄wĕt\ n. A whirling step made on the toes in dancing. (also v.)

piv·ot\˄pĭ·vət\ n. A basketball maneuver involving turning without dribbling the ball. (v. To turn on one foot or on one wheel.)

plac·ard\˄plă·kərd\ n. A printed notice on a large cardboard or similar sheet. (v. To announce by placards.)

pla·cate\˄plā 'kāt\ v. To appease, soothe the anger or irritation of.

plac·id\˄plă·sĭd\ adj. Marked by complete unconcerned calm and peace. (n. -ity, adv. -ly)

plain·tive\˄plān·tĭv\ adj. Marked by mournful complaint. (adv. -ly)

plaque\plăk\ n. A thin plate inscribed with a message and designed for mounting.

pli·ant\˄plai·ənt\ adj. Bending easily and smoothly, supple and athletic. (adv. -ly)

plum·met\˄plə·mət\ v. To fall or sink straight down rapidly.

ply\plai\ v. To work at, execute.

poach\pōch\ x. To hunt or pick without permission on private land. (n. -er)

pock·marked adj. Showing on one's face the scars of a pox (as smallpox or chicken pox).

poi·gnant\˄pɔin·yənt\ adj. Deeply painful, marked by sad deep emotion. (n. poignancy, adv. -ly)

pon·der·ous\˄pŏn·də·rəs\ adj. Heavy and massive.

por·ten·tous\pŏr ˄tĕn·təs\ adj. Foreshadowing or foretelling evil or misfortune to come. (v. portend, n. portent, and adv. -ly)

port·ly\˄pōrt·lē\ adj. Showing stoutness but also dignity, presence, or command. (n. portliness)

pos·tern\˄pŏs·tərn\ adj. Located at the back or rear of a building. (also n.)

pot·ter\˄pŏ·tər\ v. To perform aimless, trivial, and time-consuming small actions.

pre·car·i·ous\prē ˄kă·rē·əs\ adj. Risky, dangerous; especially, likely to fall. (adv. -ly)

prec·e·dent\˄prĕ·sə·dənt\ n. A procedure or event serving as a pattern or example for similar items following. (v. precede)

pre·cip·i·tate\prē ˄sĭ·pĭ 'tāt\ v. To cause to fall or drop, hurl or dash down. (n. precipitation)

pre·ci·sion\prē ˄sĭ·zhən\ n. The quality of being very precise, minutely accurate, or exactly true.

pre·clude\prē ˄klūd\ v. To shut out, prevent, prohibit.

pre·co·cious\prē ˄kō·shəs\ adj. Showing very early or premature development. (n. precocity, adv. -ly)

pre·con·ceived\'prē·kən ˄sēvd\ adj. Formed or thought out in advance, before consideration of the evidence. (n. preconception)

pre·dic·a·ment\prē ˄dĭ·kə·mənt\ n. Dangerous or difficult situation, plight.

pred·i·cate\˄prĕ·dĭ 'kāt\ v. To imply or include as a necessary condition. (n. predication)

pre·dom·i·nate\prē ˄dŏ·mĭ 'nāt\ v. To be dominant over others, be superior to or more important than others. (n. predominance, adj. predominant)

pre·lim·i·nary\prē ˄lĭ·mĭ 'nā·rē\ adj. Done or happening as a necessary preparation or as a necessary first step.

pre·lude\˄prĕl·yūd or ˄prā·lūd\ n. A preliminary section, opening musical movement.

pre·ma·ture\prē·mə ˄chūr\ adj. In advance of the expected or usual time. (adv. -ly)

prem·is·es\˄prĕ·mĭ·səs\ n. *plural.* 1. The details of a situation requiring a decision. 2. A building or part of a building. 3. Areas adjacent to a building. 4. Rooms, quarters, accommodations.

pre·mo·ni·tion\'prē·mə ˄nĭ·shən\ n. Forewarning, advance knowledge of evil, sense of impending trouble.

pre·oc·cu·pa·tion\prē 'ŏk·yu ˄pā·shən\ n. Absorption with one thing resulting in inattention to others. (v. preoccupy)

pre·pos·ter·ous\prē ˄pŏs·tə·rəs\ adj. Ridiculous, absurd. (adv. -ly)

pre·sen·ti·ment\prē ˄zĕn·tə·mĭnt\ n. A notion or hunch about approaching fate or fortune.

pre·sump·tion\prē ˄zəm·shən\ n. An assuming of greater privilege, status, or importance than one really has. (v. presume, adj. presumptuous)

pre·tense\˄prē 'tĕns\ n. Reason, cause, excuse. (v. pretend)

pre·var·i·ca·tion\prə 'vă·rĭ ˄kā·shən\ n. Evasion of the truth, falsehood, lie. (v. prevaricate)

pri·mal\˄prai·məl\ adj. Primeval, very early. (adv. -ly)

pri·me·val\prai ˄mē·vəl\ adj. Of, from, or suggesting a very ancient period. (adv. -ly)

probe\prōb\ v. To test or investigate deeply and thoroughly. (also n.)

proc·tor\˄prŏk·tər\ n. A school aide or instructor who maintains discipline or supervises tests. (also v.)

pro·cure\prō ˄kyūr\ v. To get, obtain. (n. procurer, -ment)

prod·i·gal\˄prŏ·dĭ·gəl\ adj. Not economical or saving,

given to spending generously or wastefully. (n. -ity, adv. -ly)

pro·di·gious\prə ˈdĭ·jəs\ adj. Huge, massive. (adv. -ly)

prof·fer\ˈprŏ·fər\ v. To offer, extend for acceptance.

pro·found\prō ˈfaʊnd\ adj. Deeply wise, deep and intense. (n. profundity, adv. -ly)

pro·fuse\prə ˈfyūs\ adj. Copious, abundant, excessive, poured out without restraint. (n. profusion, adv. -ly)

pro·mis·cu·ous\prə ˈmĭs·kyu·əs\ adj. Showing a variety mixed together without sorting or order. (n. promiscuity, adv. -ly)

prom·on·to·ry\ˈprŏ·mən 'tō·rē\ n., pl. -ies. A high body of land jutting out into water, a headland.

prone\prōn\ adj. Lying flat, with face and stomach pressed against floor or ground.

prop·a·ga·tion\'prŏ·pə ˈgā·shən\ n. Increase, growth, or extension (especially by births). (v. propagate)

pro·pen·si·ty\prō ˈpĕn·sĭ·tē\ n., pl. -ies. Temperamental inclination or tendency.

proph·e·sy\ˈprŏ·fə 'sai\ v. To make a prophecy. (n. prophecy)

pro·pi·tious\prō ˈpĭ·shəs\ adj. Promising success, giving favorable indications. (adv. -ly)

pro·pul·sion\prə ˈpəl·shən\ adj. The propelling, the kind of forward drive or push.

pro·scribe\prō ˈskraib\ v. To write down as outlawed or condemned. (n. proscription)

pros·pect\ˈprŏs 'pĕkt\ n. An anticipation or anticipatory viewpoint. (adj. -ive)

pros·trate\ˈprŏs 'trāt\ adj. Flat, prone. (also v.)

pro·tract\prō ˈtrăkt\ v. To prolong, draw out. (n. -ion)

pro·tu·ber·ance\prō ˈtū·bə·rəns\ n. A part that bulges, sticks out, or projects; the fact of sticking out. (adj. protuberant)

prov·i·dence\ˈprŏ·vĭ·dəns\ n. A kindly protective force or agency, (cap.) the Divinity.

prov·i·dent\ˈprŏ·vĭ·dənt\ adj. Careful, prudent, foresighted.

prox·im·i·ty\prŏk ˈsĭ·mĭ·tē\ n., pl. -ies. Nearness.

pul·sa·tion\pəl ˈsā·shən\ n. Beating or throbbing, pulse. (v. pulsate, n. pulse)

pum·ice\ˈpə·mĭs\ n. Light volcanic rock or powder.

pum·mel\ˈpə·məl\ v. To beat, strike repeatedly with the fists.

pun·gent\ˈpən·jənt\ adj. Sharp, peppery, spicy. (n. pungency, adv. -ly)

pur·ga·to·ry\ˈpər·gə 'tō·rē\ n., pl. -ies. A part of the afterworld in which sins are purged; hence, a place or period of punishment.

pur·ist\pyū·rĭst\ n. A person who is artificially fussy about the correctness of his speech.

purse\pərs\ v. To press together closely.

quack\kwăk\ n. A fraud or impostor, an ignorant person who pretends to knowledge and skill. (n. -ery)

quad·ran·gle\ˈkwad 'răŋ·gəl\ n. An open space enclosed by buildings on all four sides.

quench\kwĕnch\ v. To extinguish, put out.

queue\kyū\ n. A line of people or vehicles. (also v.)

quill\kwĭl\ n. A feather, a pen made by cutting a feather.

quiz·zi·cal\ˈkwĭ·zĭ·kəl\ adj. Marked by teasing and bantering or amused, searching, speculative questioning. (adv. -ly)

rack\răk\ n. A torture device on which the limbs of a prostrate victim were stretched. (also v.)

rad·i·cal\ˈră·dĭ·kəl\ adj. Extreme or complete. (adv. -ly)

rail\rāl\ v. 1. To scold or reproach violently or bitterly. 2. To mock, jest.

rail·lery\ˈrā·lə·rē\ n., pl. -ies. Sarcastic jesting.

rai·ment\ˈrā·mĭnt\ n. Dress, clothing.

raise\rāz\ v. To come in sight of and sail toward.

ran·cid\ˈrăn·sĭd\ adj. Strong, stale, and unpleasant. (adv. -ly)

rank\răŋk\ adj. 1. Strong, unwholesome, and unpleasant. 2. Complete, utter. (adv. -ly)

rap·ture\ˈrăp·chər\ n. A state of greatest joy, most intense happiness. (adj. rapturous)

rar·i·ty\ˈră·rĭ·tē\ n., pl. -ies. Something quite rare or uncommon. (adj. rare)

rate\rāt\ v. To scold, rebuke, upbraid.

ra·ti·o·ci·na·tion\'ră·shē 'ŏ·sĭ 'nā·shən\ n. The process of reasoning in logical ways. (v. ratiocinate)

ra·tion·al\ˈră·shə·nəl\ adj. Sensible, reasonable. (n. -ity, adv. -ly)

ra·tion·ale\'ră·shə ˈnăl\ n. Reasonable or logical basis for development or procedure.

rau·cous\ˈrɔ·kəs\ adj. Harsh, rough, and coarse. (adv. -ly)

rav·age\ˈră·vəj\ v. To lay waste to, harm, destroy as though by a hostile army. (also n.)

rav·en·ous\ˈră·və·nəs\ adj. Showing famished hunger or greed. (adv. -ly)

rav·ish·ing\ˈră·vĭ·shĭŋ\ adj. Very beautiful. (adv. -ly)

realm\rĕlm\ n. A region or area (especially one ruled by a king).

re·buke\rē ˈbyūk\ n. An act or speech indicating strong disapproval. (also v.)

re·cep·ta·cle\rē ˈsĕp·tə·kəl\ n. A container, whatever is used to hold or contain something.

re·cluse\rē ˈklūs\ n. One living by himself and having and seeking little company.

re·coil\rē ˈkɔil\ v. To draw back, retreat, often in fright, confusion, or defeat. (n. Tendency to spring back.)

rec·on·cile\ˈrĕ·kən 'sail\ v. To make content with, dispel doubt. (n. reconciliation)

re·con·vert\'rē·kən ˈvərt\ v. To change back. (n. reconversion)

re·cur·rence\rē ˈkə·rəns\ n. A repetition, a repeated

ă bad, ā bake, a father, ĕ sell, ē equal, ai mile, ĭ sit, ŏ cot, ō note, ɔ law, ū boom, ʊ wood, yū you, yʊ fury, aʊ cow, ɔi boy. The schwa is used for both stressed and unstressed sounds: ə mud, word, even; ch chase, itch; sh shell, wish; th path, thin; th the, either; ŋ wing; w wet, wheat; zh pleasure.

occurrence or incidence. (v. recur, adj. recurrent)

re·cu·sant\\'rĕk·kyə·zənt\ *or* rĭ ▲kyūz·ənt\ n. One withholding allegiance or conformity to an established church or institution. (n. recusancy)

re·demp·tive\rə ▲dĕmp·tĭv\ adj. Serving to redeem, compensate, or repay. (n. redemption, v. redeem)

re·doubt\rē ▲daut\ n. A temporary advance fortification.

re·dress\rē ▲drĕs\ v. To requite, repay.

reek\rēk\ v. To smell very strongly.

re·fec·to·ry\rē ▲fĕk·tə·rē\ n., pl. -ies. A monastery dining hall or a long narrow rectangular table fit for use in it.

ref·or·ma·tion\\'rĕf·fər 'mā·shən\ n. An action of reforming for the better, the results of such an action. (v. reform)

reg·i·men·ta·tion\\'rĕ·jĭ·mĕn ▲tā·shən\ n. Subjection to discipline and control destroying individuality. (v. regiment)

re·in·sti·tute\\'rē ▲ĭn·stĭ 'tūt\ v. To start up again.

re·it·er·ate\\'rē ▲ĭ·tə 'rāt\ v. To repeat (especially with certainty or emphasis). (n. reiteration)

rel·e·van·cy\\'rĕ·lə·vən·sē\ n., pl. -ies. Connection or relationship to the situation. (adj. relevant)

re·lin·quish\rē ▲lĭŋ·kwĭsh\ v. To yield, deliver, give up or over. (n. -ment)

re·luc·tant\rē ▲lək·tənt\ adj. Marked by unwilling hesitancy. (n. reluctance, adv. -ly)

re·mand\rē ▲mănd\ v. To order back (as to a place of confinement).

re·mon·strance\rē ▲mŏn·strəns\ n. Protest, objection, complaint. (v. remonstrate)

re·morse\rē ▲mōrs\ n. Deep regret and sorrow for one's actions. (adj. -ful)

rend\rĕnd\ v. To split, tear, or rip forcefully.

ren·der\\'rĕn·dər\ v. To melt down fast from animal tissue.

re·nounce\rē ▲nauns\ v. To change away from, give up finally. (n. renunciation)

re·past\rē ▲păst\ n. An ample meal.

re·pen·tance\rē ▲pĕn·təns\ n. Sorrow felt for previous misdeeds. (v. repent, adj. repentant)

rep·e·ti·tious\\'rĕ·pə ▲tĭ·shəs\ adj. Strongly marked by repetition, repeating a good deal. (n. repetition, adv. -ly)

re·plen·ish\rē ▲plĕ·nĭsh\ v. To resupply, bring up to a full or adequate quantity.

re·pug·nance\rē ▲pəg·nəns\ n. Dislike, objection. (adj. repugnant)

re·qui·em\\'rĕ·kwē·əm\ n. A dirge, hymn for the dead.

res·i·due\\'rĕ·zĭ 'dū\ n. Remainder, part left over.

re·source·ful\rē ▲zōrs·fəl\ adj. Able to find ways to cope with whatever may arise. (n. resource, adv. -ly)

re·spite\\'rĕs·pət\ n. An interval period free from work, exertion, trouble, or pain; cessation from trouble and pain.

re·splen·dent\rē ▲splĕn·dənt\ adj. Colorful, shining, dazzling, splendid. (n. resplendence)

re·straint\rē ▲strănt\ n. Check or control over display of emotion or desire, control over action or speed. (v. restrain)

re·tal·i·ate\rē ▲tă·lē 'āt\ v. To return or requite (as in getting even). (n. retaliation)

re·tort\rē ▲tōrt\ v. To reply with sharpness, challenge, or defiance. (also n.)

ret·ri·bu·tion\\'rĕ·trĭ ▲byū·shən\ n. Merited punishment or evil in return for a wrong one has done.

re·trieve\rē ▲trēv\ v. To recover, obtain again. (n. retriever)

rev·el·ry\\'rĕ·vəl 'rē\ n. Gaiety and merriment.

re·ver·ber·a·tion\rē 'vər·bə ▲rā·shən\ n. Continued echoing or resounding. (v. reverberate)

rev·er·ie\\'rĕ·və 'rē\ n. Dreamy musing, daydreaming, fanciful contemplation.

re·vo·ca·ble\\'rĕ·və·kə·bəl\ adj. Subject to being revoked or annulled. (v. revoke, n. revocation)

rhap·so·dy\\'răp·sə 'dē\ n., pl. -ies. An utterance marked by lofty and extreme feeling. (adj. rhapsodic)

rid·i·cule\\'rĭ·dĭ 'kyūl\ n. Mocking or joking scorn. (also v., adj. ridiculous)

rife\raif\ adj. Common.

rift\rĭft\ n. An opening, break.

rig·or·ous\\'rĭ·gə·rəs\ adj. Marked by much severity and sternness, hard and oppresive. (n. rigor, adv. -ly)

rit·u·al\\'rĭch·wəl\ n. An established form for procedure in church or court. (also adj., n. -ism)

riv·u·let\\'rĭv·yu·lət\ n. A small stream.

ro·bust\\'rō ▲bəst\ adj. Strong, muscular, and sturdy. (adv. -ly)

rote\rōt\ adj. Accomplished by repeating and memorizing rather than thinking and analyzing. (also n.)

rud·dy\rə·dē\ adj. -ier, -iest. Dark red. (n. ruddiness)

ru·di·ment\\'rū·dĭ·mĭnt\ n. An undeveloped beginning. (adj. rudimentary)

rue·ful\\'rū·fəl\ adj. Marked by mournful sorrow or dejection. (n. rue, adv. -ly)

rup·ture\\'rəp·chər\ v. To break. (also n.)

sa·ble\\'sā·bəl\ adj. Black, dark.

sack\săk\ v. To loot, harry, destroy.

sa·gac·i·ty\sə ▲gă·sĭ·tē\ n., pl. -ies. Deep or cunning wisdom. (adj. sagacious)

sal·low\\'să·lō\ adj. Showing an unwholesome, pale, or yellowish color.

sal·ly\\'să·lē\ n., pl. -ies. A witty or provocative bit of conversation designed to call forth a response.

sa·loon\sə ▲lūn\ n. A large and spacious hall.

sal·u·ta·tion\\'săl·yu ▲tā·shən\ n. A courteous or formal greeting. (v. salute)

sanc·ti·ty\\'săŋ·tĭ·tē\ n., pl. -ies. Holiness, sacredness.

san·guine\\'săŋ·gwĭn\ adj. Optimistic, hopeful, confident. (adv. -ly)

sap·phire\\'să 'fair\ n. A clear deep-blue precious stone.

sar·don·ic\sar ▲dŏ·nĭk\ adj. With sarcastic or lofty disdain. (adv. -ally)

sat·u·rate\\'să·chə 'rāt\ v. To soak very thoroughly. (n. saturation)

sa·vor\\'să·vər\ v. To perceive and enjoy with relish and appreciation, enjoy and fully appreciate. (also n.)

scathe\skāth\ v. Injury, damage, hurt.

scav·en·ger\'skă·vən·jər\ n. 1. An animal that feeds on and hence disposes of dead bodies. 2. One who examines and collects junk and rubbish as of possible use. (v. scavenge)

scru·ple\'skrū·pəl\ v. To hesitate or refrain from because of conscience. (n. A compelling conscientious feeling for rightness or morality.)

scru·pu·lous\'skrū·pyə·ləs\ adj. Having many scruples; extremely honest, just, and upright. (adv. -ly)

scru·ti·nize\'skrū·tǐ 'naiz\ v. To examine or inspect very closely.

scru·ti·ny\'skrū·tǐ·nē\ n., pl. -ies. Close and thorough examination and inspection.

sear\sēr\ v. To burn or scorch with an intense heat.

sed·a·tive\'sě·də·tǐv\ adj. Tending to calm and soothe. (n. sedation)

seer\sēr\ n. One who foretells the future.

seg·ment\'sěg·mǐnt\ n. A well-marked division or section, as of the human body. (adj. -ed)

self-con·ceit\sělf·kən 'sēt\ n. Pride, vanity.

sem·blance\'sěm·bləns\ n. Surface appearance, likeness, similarity.

se·nile\'sē·nīl\ adj. Of unsound judgment because of the effects of old age. (n. senility, adv.-ly)

sen·su·ous\'sěnshu·əs\ adj. Appealing strongly to the senses. (adv. -ly)

sen·tient\'sěn·shənt\ adj. Having feeling and perception. (n. sentience, adv. -ly)

se·pul·chral\sě 'pəl·krəl\ adj. Befitting a grave, as from a tomb. (n. sepulcher, adv. -ly)

se·quel\'sē·kwəl\ n. A continuation, a narrative giving developments that followed.

se·quence\'sē·kwěns\ n. A continuing order with one item following another. (adj. sequent, sequential)

se·ques·ter\sě 'kwěs·tər\ v. To seclude, station away or apart. (n. sequestration)

se·rene\sə 'rēn\ adj. Marked by complete calm, peace and lack of trouble. (n. serenity, adv. -ly)

sev·er\'sě·vər\ v. To cut, cut off, separate. (n. -ance)

sheer\shēr\ adj. Very steep.

shut·tle\'shə·təl\ n. A means of transportation employing short runs back and forth between two points. (also v.)

si·mul·ta·neous\'sai·məl 'tā·nē·əs\ adj. Existing, performed, or occurring at exactly the same time. (adv. -ly)

sin·ew\'sĭn·yū\ n. A tendon. (adj. sinewy)

sin·gu·lar·i·ty\'sĭŋ·gyu 'lă·rǐ·tē\ n., pl. -ies. Strangeness, unusual quality. (adj. singular)

sin·is·ter\'sǐ·nǐs·tər\ adj. Suggesting or indicating harm or evil in some dread or mysterious way. (adv. -ly)

skep·tic\'skěp·tǐk\ n. One given to doubt and disbelief, one suspending judgment and withholding belief. (also adj., n. -ism, and adj. -al)

skulk\skəlk\ v. To show a sullen, fearful, stealthy manner in moving about.

slath·er·ing\'slă·thə·rǐŋ\ n. Slobbering, slavering.

slat·tern\'slă·tərn\ n. An unkempt, dirty, or slovenly woman. (adj. -ly)

sleuth\slūth\ n. A detective.

slith·er\'slǐ·thər\ v. To go with a sliding or gliding motion.

slov·en·ly\'slǒ·vən·lē\ adj. Marked by careless disorder, sloppiness, and dirt. (n. slovenliness)

soar\sōr\ v. To fly or sail high aloft.

so·lace\'sŏ·ləs\ n. Comfort; something that eases, comforts, soothes, or cheers. (v. To comfort, ease, cheer.)

sole\sōl\ adj. Single, only. (adv. -ly)

so·lem·ni·ty\sə 'lěm·nǐ·tē\ n., pl. -ies. Solemnness; sober, grave, or dignified feeling or appearance. (adj. solemn)

so·lic·it\sə 'lǐ·sǐt\ v. To seek to obtain, usually by appeal or entreaty. (n. -ation)

so·lic·i·tor\sə 'lǐ·sǐ·tər\ n. An English lawyer who pleads in the lower courts.

so·lic·i·tous\sə 'lǐ·sǐ·təs\ adj. Showing earnest care and attentive or anxious concern. (n. solicitude, adv. -ly)

so·lil·o·quy\sə 'lǐ·lə·kwē\ n., pl. -ies. A speech delivered as though only to oneself.

sol·u·ble\'sŏl·yu·bəl\ adj. Capable of being solved. (n. solubility)

som·ber\'sŏm·bər\ adj. Dark, gloomy, and depressing. (adv. -ly)

sound\saund\ v. To search into, examine, seek to determine.

spas·mod·ic\'spăz 'mŏ·dĭk\ adj. Of, like, or marked by a spasm; a sudden, violent, abnormal motion. (n. spasm, adv. -ally)

spa·tial\'spā·shəl\ adj. Pertaining to or showing space.

spat·u·la\'spă·chə·lə\ n. A broad-bladed instrument like a knife (used for spreading).

spe·cies\'spē 'sēz\ n., pl. species. Kind or class (especially in a scientific classification).

spec·i·fy\'spě·sǐ 'fai\ v. To state definitely, mention specifically, itemize. (n. specification)

spec·tral\'spěk·trəl\ adj. Like, suggestive of, or appropriate to a specter or ghost. (also adj.)

spec·u·late\'spěk·yu 'lāt\ v. To reflect on and seek to guess about. (n. speculation)

spew\spyū\ v. To vomit.

spin·ster\'spĭn·stər\ n. An older unmarried woman.

sta·bi·li·za·tion\'stā·bə·lə 'zā·shən\ n. The process or state of being steady or resistant to waving.

stac·ca·to\stə 'ka·tō\ adj. Sharp, abrupt, and distinct in sound.

stam·i·na\'stă·mǐ·nə\ n. Strength and endurance.

starve·ling\'starv·lĭŋ\ n. A person or animal chronically ill-fed and showing effects of insufficient diet.

stat·ic\'stă·tǐk\ adj. Marked by stationary electrical charges.

sta·tus\'stă·təs\ n., pl. -es. Position, rating, rank.

stat·ute\'stăt·yūt\ n. Law. (adj. statutory)

ă bad, ā bake, a father, ě sell, ē equal, ai mile, ǐ sit, ŏ cot, ō note, ɔ law, ū boom, ʊ wood, yū you, yʊ fury, au cow, ɔi boy. The schwa is used for both stressed and unstressed sounds: ə mud, word, even; ch chase, itch; sh shell, wish; th path, thin; th the, either; ŋ wing; w wet, wheat; zh pleasure.

staunch\stɔnch\ adj. Marked by firm resolution.

sti·fle\ˆstai·fəl\ v. To stop from breathing, smother.

stim·u·late\ˆstĭm·yə 'lāt\ v. To inspire, motivate, incite to some action or reaction. (adj. and n. stimulant, stimulation)

stim·u·lus\ˆstĭm·yə·ləs\ n., pl. stimuli. A force or agency that excites an action or response.

stint\stĭnt\ v. 1. To serve, issue, or use in a grudging or miserly way. 2. To deprive oneself.

stol·id\ˆstŏ·lĭd\ adj. Without emotion, reaction, or marked activity. (n. -ity, adv. -ly)

stoop\stūp\ n. A small front porch or platform.

strat·a·gem\ˆstră·tə·jəm\ n. A scheme or maneuver to mislead or conceal.

stra·te·gic\strə ˆtē·jĭk\ adj. Beneficial through clever planning or maneuvering. (n. strategy)

stren·u·ous\ˆstrĕn·yu·əs\ adj. Marked by taxing activity and sustained vigorous effort. (adv. -ly)

stu·pen·dous\stu ˆpĕn·dəs\ adj. Astonishing in size, scope, or force; striking in immensity. (adv. -ly)

stu·por\ˆstū·pər\ n. Mental insensibility or extreme dullness and lack of perception.

styl·ize\ˆstai 'laiz\ v. To make conform to a stiff formal style.

sua·vi·ty\ˆswa·vĭ·tē\ n., pl. -ies. Smooth, calm, well-mannered composure. (adj. suave)

sub·lime\sə ˆblaim\ adj. Calling forth deep reverent admiration or awed wonder. (n. sublimity, adv. -ly)

sub·se·quent\ˆsəb·sə·kwənt\ adj. Following, succeeding. (adv. -ly)

sub·side\səb ˆsaid\ v. To recede or abate (as into comparative inactivity).

sub·stan·tial\səb ˆstăn·chəl\ adj. Showing a degree of mass, solidity, and capacity to endure. (n. substance, -ity; adv. -ly)

sub·ter·fuge\ˆsəb·tər·fūj\ n. A plan, scheme, or device to evade or escape.

sub·ter·ra·nean\'səb·tə ˆrā·nē·ən\ adj. Underground, under the earth.

sub·tle\ˆsə·təl\ adj. Hard to understand or perceive, mysterious. (n. -ty, adv. subtly)

suc·cor\sə·kər\ n. Help, aid. (also v.)

suc·cu·lent\ˆsək·yu·lənt\ adj. Juicy and fresh. (n. succulence, adv. -ly)

suc·cumb\sə ˆkəm\ v. To give way to, yield.

suf·fer·ance\ˆsə·fə·rəns\ n. Tolerance, permission to exist. (v. suffer)

suf·fice\sə ˆfais\ v. To be adequate, sufficient. (adj. sufficient, n. sufficiency)

suf·fuse\sə ˆfyūz\ v. To show an additional tinge or quality spreading through. (n. suffusion)

su·per·flu·ous\sū ˆpər·flū·əs\ adj. Unnecessary, capable of being omitted as unnecessary. (n. superfluity, adv. -ly)

sup·ple\ˆsə·pəl\ adj. Showing easy, smooth, more-or-less graceful action; not clumsy or muscle-bound. (n. -ness, adv. -ly)

sup·pli·ant\ˆsə·plē·ənt\ n. One who begs or entreats for help or mercy. (also adj.)

sup·pli·ca·tion\'sə·plĭ ˆkā·shən\ n. Humble and earnest entreaty, request, or prayer.

sup·po·si·tion\'sə·pə ˆzĭ·shən\ n. Something supposed, whether true or not; a notion or guess. (v. suppose)

sup·press\sə ˆprĕs\ v. To put down, check, keep back. (n. -ion)

sup·pu·rate\ˆsə·pə 'rāt\ v. To form pus because of infection. (n. suppuration)

sur·cease\'sər ˆsēs\ n. End, ceasing. (also v.)

sur·cin·gle\ˆsər·sĭŋ·gəl\ n. A girdle, belt.

sure·ty\ˆshū·rə·tē\ n., pl. -ies. Certainty. (adj. sure)

sur·ly\ˆsər·lē\ adj. Marked by or as though by rude and curt bad humor. (n. surliness)

sur·mount\sər ˆmaunt\ v. To overcome, climb, rise, mount over or above.

sur·name\ˆsər 'nām\ n. A last or family name (in contrast to a first or given name).

sur·pass\sər ˆpăs\ v. To exceed, go beyond.

sur·pass·ing\sər ˆpă·sĭŋ\ adj. Exceeding. (adv. -ly)

sus·tain\sə ˆstān\ v. To continue, go on for a notable time.

swathe\swath\ v. To wrap (as with a bandage, blanket, or coat).

swine·herd\swīn 'hərd\ n. One who tends swine or pigs.

swiv·el\ˆswĭ·vəl\ n. A device permitting something (as the seat of a chair) to turn readily. (also v.)

sym·bol·ic\sĭm ˆbŏ·lĭk\ adj. Serving as a sign, token, or symbol. (n. symbol, adv. -ally)

sym·met·ri·cal\sə ˆmĕ·trĭ·kəl\ adj. Showing evenness or equality in paired or contrasting parts, showing balanced exact correspondences. (n. symmetry, adv. -ly)

syn·chro·ni·za·tion\'sĭn·krə·nĭ ˆzā·shən\ n. An arrangement involving perfectly equal or simultaneous timing. (v. synchronize)

tab·u·lar\ˆtă·byu·lər\ adj. Arranged in a table or a convenient orderly listing. (v. tabulate)

taint\tānt\ v. To affect with evil, infect, deprave. (also n.)

tan·gi·ble\ˆtăn·jĭ·bəl\ adj. Readily perceived or understood, quite clear to such a sense as that of touch. (n. tangibility, adv. tangibly)

taunt\tɔnt\ n. A mocking scornful comment or gesture (v. To mock scornfully with sarcastic reproach, mock at, gloat at).

taut\tɔt\ adj. Tight; stretched or pulled tight so that there is no slack; not loose, slack, or lax. (adv. -ly)

taw·dry\ˆtɔ·drē\ adj. Cheap and gaudy. (n. tawdriness)

taw·ny\ˆtɔ·nē\ adj. Tannish brown.

te·dious\ˆtē·dē·əs\ adj. Boresome, monotonous, uninteresting. (n. tedium, adv. -ly)

tem·per·a·men·tal\'tĕm·pə·rə ˆmĕn·təl\ adj. Given to unpredictable moods and capricious choices, likely to be moody or irritable if crossed or opposed. (n. temperament, adv. -ly)

tem·per·ance\ˆtĕm·pə·rəns\ n. Restrained moderation. (adj. temperate)

te·na·cious\tə ˆna·shəs\ adj. Resolute, determined, going on against difficulty or opposition. (n. tenacity, adv. -ly)

tense\tĕns\ v. To become tense, nervous, fearful. (also adj., n. tension)

ten·ta·cle\\ˆtĕn·tə·kəl\ n. A long flexible armlike or hairlike growth.

ten·ta·tive\\ˆtĕn·tə·tĭv\ adj. Performed or made experimentally as a try or test. (adv. -ly)

ter·mi·nol·o·gy\\'tər·mĭ ˆnŏ·lə·jē\ n., pl. -ies. Words used in a particular activity or study. (adj. terminological)

teth·er\\ˆtĕ·t͟hər\ n. A chain or rope to restrict an animal to a certain area. (also v.)

the·o·ret·i·cal\\'t͟hē·ə ˆrĕ·tĭ·kəl\ adj. Showing concern with or dependence on theory or supposition instead of facts and realities. (adv. -ly)

the·sis\\ˆt͟hē·sĭs\ n., pl. theses. A main proposition or idea in an argument.

throw\t͟hrō\ n. A scarf, covering worn around the neck.

thwart\t͟hwɔrt\ v. To check, defeat and baffle.

thwart\t͟hwɔrt\ n. A seat or bench for a rower.

tier\tēr\ n. Layer, row.

til·ler\\ˆtĭ·lər\ n. A lever on a boat or ship to control the rudder.

tim·o·rous\\ˆtĭ·mə·rəs\ adj. Timid, readily inclined to fear. (adv. -ly)

tol·er·a·ble\\ˆtŏ·lə·rə·bəl\ adj. Fair, adequate. (adv. tolerably)

tol·er·ance\\ˆtŏ·lə·rəns\ n. An attitude of ready acceptance of and forgiveness for others. (v. tolerate, adj. tolerant)

to·paz\\ˆtō 'păz\ n., pl. -es. A yellow gem.

tor·tu·ous\\ˆtōr·chu·əs\ adj. Crooked, twisted, hard to cope with. (adv. -ly)

tote\tōt\ v. To carry.

tran·quil\\ˆtrăn·kwĭl\ adj. Peaceful, calm, and unconcerned. (n. -lity, adv. -ly)

tran·scribe\trăns ˆkraib\ v. To write down, copy, recopy. (n. transcription)

trans·fix\trăns ˆfĭks\ v. To pierce through and render motionless.

tran·si·tion\trăn ˆzĭ·z͟hən\ n. Change, passing from one condition to another. (adj. -al)

tran·son·ic\trăn ˆsŏ·nĭk\ adj. Of or pertaining to crossing the sound barrier in flying.

trans·verse\trăns ˆvərs\ adj. Diagonal, crossing from side to side.

tra·vail\\ˆtrə 'văl\ n. Combined very hard work and discouraging difficulty. (also v.)

tra·verse\trə ˆvərs\ v. To go, move, travel over. (n. traversal)

tre·ble\\ˆtrĕ·bəl\ v. To multiply by three. (also adj. and n.)

trek\trĕk\ n. A long, sustained, often slow journey; especially one on foot or by horse and wagon. (also v.)

trem·or\\ˆtrĕ·mər\ n. A vibrating quivering or trembling.

trem·u·lous\\ˆtrĕm·yu·ləs\ adj. Tending to tremble or to waver apologetically. (adv. -ly)

trep·i·da·tion\\'trĕ·pĭ ˆdā·shən\ n. Fearful alarm.

trib·u·la·tion\\'trĭ·byu ˆlā·shən\ n. Oppressive trial, distress, suffering.

tri·bu·nal\trai ˆbyū·nəl\ or trĭ ˆbyū·nəl\ n. A court of justice.

trib·ute\\ˆtrĭ·byūt\ n. A show of respect, admiration, or gratitude.

trite\trait\ adj. Completely stale, totally lacking in freshness or novelty. (n. -ness, adv. -ly)

triv·i·al\\ˆtrĭ·vē·əl\ adj. Entirely minor and unimportant. (n. -ity, adv. -ly)

tro·phy\\ˆtrŏ·fē\ n., pl. -ies. An object serving to commemorate and celebrate some victory or achievement.

tryst\trĭst\ n. A meeting or appointment to meet (especially secretly or romantically). (also v.)

tu·mult\\ˆtū·məlt\ n. Wild, unruly, very noisy activity. (adj. -uous)

tu·nic\\ˆtū·nĭk\ n. A loose-fitting gownlike or blouselike garment worn in Greek and Roman times.

tur·bu·lence\\ˆtər·byu·ləns\ n. Agitated disturbance, with swirling activity. (adj. turbulent)

tur·moil\\ˆtər 'mɔil\ n. Noisy and confused commotion.

twain\twān\ n. Two.

typ·i·fy\\ˆtĭ·pĭ 'fai\ v. To present as a type, symbolize. (n. typification)

ul·ti·mate\\ˆəl·tĭ·mət\ adj. Final, after all other considerations and developments. (adv. -ly)

ul·ti·ma·tum\\'əl·tĭ ˆmā·təm\ n., pl. -s or ultimata. Final warning.

un·as·sum·ing\\'ən·ə ˆsū·mĭŋ\ adj. Modest, not proudly or vainly forward or demanding.

un·can·ny\ən ˆkă·nē\ adj. Seeming supernatural or superhuman for skill, knowledge, or intuition. (adv. uncannily)

un·capped\ən ˆkăpt\ adj. Without the artificial cap prepared by a dentist to cover a jagged tooth.

un·co·or·di·nat·ed\\'ən·kō ˆōr·dĭ 'nā·təd\ adj. Without smooth coordination and harmony.

un·daunt·ed\ən ˆdɔn·təd\ adj. Not checked, discouraged, or made fearful or hesitant. (adv. -ly)

un·der·stud·y\\ˆən·dər 'stə·dē\ n. One who substitutes when a main actor or actress is unable to appear. (also v.)

un·du·la·tion\\'ən·də ˆlā·shən\ n. Irregular wavy motion. (v. undulate)

un·du·ly\ən ˆdū·lē\ adv. Excessively, immoderately. (adj. undue)

un·en·cum·bered\\'ən·ən ˆkəm·bərd\ adj. Not impeded by hindrances.

un·glazed\ən ˆglāzd\ adj. Not equipped with glass panes.

un·in·tel·li·gi·ble\\'ən·ĭn ˆtĕ·lĭ·jĭ·bəl\ adj. Not intelligible, impossible to understand or interpret. (adv. unintelligibly)

ă bad, ā bake, a father, ĕ sell, ē equal, ai mile, ĭ sit, ŏ cot, ō note, ɔ law, ū boom, ʊ wood, yū you, yʊ fury, aʊ cow, ɔi boy. The schwa is used for both stressed and unstressed sounds: ə mud, word, even; ch chase, itch; sh shell, wish; th path, thin; t͟h the, either; ŋ wing; w wet, wheat; zh pleasure.

unique\yu ˄nēk\ adj. Very uncommon or unusual, unmatched or unparalleled, rare. (adv. -ly)

uni·son\˄yū·nĭ·sən\ n. Acting in harmony, with full participation and without discord.

un·kempt\ən ˄kĕmpt\ adj. Showing complete lack of care about clothes and appearance, not carefully combed and otherwise made neat and presentable.

un·per·turbed\'ən·pər ˄tərbd\ adj. Not perturbed, concerned, or agitated.

un·rav·el\ən ˄ră·vəl\ v. To untangle, unfold, simplify.

un·sa·vory\ən ˄sā·və·rē\ adj. Unpleasant, suspicious, repelling.

un·scru·pu·lous\ən ˄skrū·pyu·ləs\ adj. Dishonest, unethical, without moral principles.

un·tram·meled\ən ˄tră·məld\ adj. Not restrained or limited.

un·tres·passed\ən ˄trĕs·pəst\ adj. Not visited or traversed without consent or permission.

ur·gent\˄ər·jənt\ adj. Pressing, needing immediate action or attention. (n. urgency, adv. -ly)

usurp·er\yu ˄sər·pər\ n. One who seizes a kingship or other high rank wrongfully. (v. usurp)

va·ga·ry\˄vā·gə·rē or və ˄gă·rē\ n., pl. -ies. A strange, freakish, or whimsical idea or notion.

va·grant\˄vā·grənt\ adj. Wandering freely in a random and uncontrolled way. (also n., n. vagrancy)

vale·dic·to·ri·an\'vă·lə 'dĭk ˄tō·rē·ən\ n. A top-ranking student who gives a commencement speech. (adj. valedictory)

val·et\˄vă·lət\ n. A man's personal servant.

val·iant\˄văl·yənt\ adj. Courageous, marked by bravery. (adv. -ly)

val·or\˄vă·lər\ n. Bravery in combat. (adj. -ous)

van·tage\˄văn·təj\ n. Advantageous or favorable position.

ve·he·ment\˄vē·ə·mənt\ adj. Showing fervent intense utterance. (n. vehemence, adv. -ly)

ven·er·a·ble\˄vĕ·nə·rə·bəl\ adj. Quite old and worthy of respect. (adv. venerably)

ven·geance\˄vĕn·jəns\ n. Revenge.

venge·ful\˄vĕnj·fəl\ adj. Wanting revenge, vindictive. (adv. -ly)

ver·bal\˄vər·bəl\ adj. Of or by means of words. (adv. -ly)

ver·ba·tim\vər ˄bā·tĭm\ adv. With exactly the same words, word-for-word.

ver·dict\˄vər 'dĭkt\ n. A decision or judgment (especially at the end of a legal case).

verge\vərj\ n. Edge, border, boundary. (v. To approach, come near to).

ver·i·fy\˄vā·rĭ 'fai\ v. To substantiate as true, demonstrate to be true. (n. verification)

veri·si·mil·i·tude\'vĕ·rĭ 'sĭ ˄mĭ·lĭ·tūd\ n. Appearance of truth and reality given to a story.

ver·mil·ion\vər ˄mĭl·yən\ adj. Bright red tinged with yellow. (also n.)

ver·min\˄vər·mĭn\ n. A dirty, destructive, or troublesome insect, worm, or small animal. (adj. -ous)

ver·sa·tile\˄vər·sə·tĭl\ adj. Showing a wide range of abilities or knowledge. (n. versatility, adv. -ly)

ves·tige\˄vĕs·tĭj\ n. Trace, mark, remnant, especially one from which inferences could be made about the past. (adj. vestigial)

vex·a·tious\vĕk ˄sā·shəs\ adj. Troublesome and annoying. (v. vex, n. vexation, and adv. -ly)

vi·car·i·ous\vai ˄kă·rē·əs\ adj. Experienced or done by another but felt or interpreted as though experienced oneself. (adv. -ly)

vi·cin·i·ty\vĭ ˄sĭ·nĭ·tē\ n., pl. -ies. Neighborhood, nearby area.

vi·cis·si·tude\vĭ ˄sĭ·sĭ 'tūd\ n. Change, variation.

vic·tim·ize\˄vĭk·tĭ 'maiz\ v. To cause to be a victim. (n. victimization)

vig·il\˄vĭ·jĭl\ n. A period of careful wakeful watching. (adj. vigilant, n. vigilance)

vil·la\˄vĭ·lə\ n. A large country dwelling with its accompanying buildings (usually belonging to an important or noble figure).

vin·dic·tive\vĭn ˄dĭk·tĭv\ adj. Vengeful and vicious, eager to repay injury. (adv. -ly)

vin·tage\˄vĭn·təj\ n. A particular wine crop; especially, a reference to wine quality and age.

vir·tu·al\˄vər·ehəl\ adj. Being as stated for all practical purposes, but not in strict fact. (adv. -ly)

vir·tue\˄vər·ehū\ n. A specific good character trait, a merit, a good or valuable feature. (adj. virtuous)

vir·tu·o·so\'vər·ehu ˄ō·sō\ n. A person familiar with finer things, a person with sensitive talent for appreciating and criticizing finer things.

vir·u·lence\˄vĕr·yu·ləns\ n. Dangerous or threatening force or intensity. (adj. virulent)

vi·sa\˄vē·sə\ n. A statement of official approval stamped on a passport in a foreign country.

vis·age\˄vĭ·zəj\ n. Face, countenance.

vi·su·al·ize\˄vĭ·zhə 'laiz\ v. To envision, picture mentally. (n., visualization).

vi·tals\˄vai·təlz\ n. plural. Vital organs (as heart, lungs, stomach). (adj. vital)

vi·va·cious\vĭ ˄vā·shəs\ adj. Marked by unusual liveliness and activity. (n. vivacity)

vo·cif·er·ate\vō ˄sĭ·fə 'rāt\ v. To utter or speak loudly or forcefully, shout, cry out. (adj. vociferous, n. vociferation)

vol·a·tile\˄vŏ·lə·tĭl\ adj. Evaporating quickly, changing quickly from liquid to vapor. (n. A vapor, gas.)

vo·li·tion\vō ˄li·shən\ n. Free use of one's own will in choosing or determining. (adj. -al)

vo·lu·mi·nous\və ˄lu·mə·nəs\ adj. 1. Marked by much material (often in many folds). 2. Having copious volume (as of sound). (n. volume)

vo·rac·i·ty\vō ˄ră·sĭ·tē\ n., pl. -ies. Intense wolfish hunger. (adj. voracious)

vouch\vaueh\ v. To affirm or maintain (especially with evidence of authority).

vouch·safe\'vaueh ˄sāf\ v. 1. To deign to utter. 2. To grant, consent.

vul·ner·a·ble\˄vəl·nə·rə·bəl\ adj. Open to attack, injury, or damage; without good protection or defense. (n. vulnerability, adv. vulnerably)

wan\wan\ adj. Pale, faint, and unwholesome in color. (adv. -ly)

wane\wān\ v. To diminish, decline in power. (also n.)

wary\⁴wă·rē\ adj. Very cautious and careful about possible dangers. (adv. warily)

whee·dle\⁴wē·dəl\ v. To coax, cajole, entreat.

wince\wĭns\ v. To start back (as with pain, alarm, or fear).

wist·ful\⁴wĭst·fəl\ adj. Marked by futile yearning or regret. (adv. -ly)

wit·ti·cism\⁴wĭ·tĭ·sĭzm\ n. A clever, witty, or humorous comment.

wont\wɔnt\ n. Custom, habit. (adj. -ed)

wrench\rĕnch\ n., pl. -es. A violent twist or tug away from a usual or accustomed situation. (also v.)

wry\rai\ adj. Marked by ironic gesture or intonation. (adv. wrily)

year·ling\⁴yēr·lĭŋ *or* ⁴yər·ləŋ\ n. An animal about a year old.

yuc·ca\⁴yə·kə\ n. A southwestern plant of the lily family with stiff leaves and white flowers.

zeal\zēl\ n. Ardent, enthusiastic interest and devotion. (adj. -ous)

Literary Terms Index

Literary Types Index

Autobiography and Biography

Drama

Fable

Nonfiction

Novel

Poetry

Short Story

Fine Art Index

Illustration Sources

Acknowledgment is gratefully made to the following museums, galleries, collectors, libraries, photo collections, etc., for their gracious and generous assistance, making possible the reproduction of the art and documentary material for this text.

Key for positions: T (top), L (left), C (center), R (right), B (bottom), and any combination of these, such TRC (top right center).

Achenbach Foundation for Graphic Arts

American Foundation for the Blind: 267, 268, 270

American Museum of Natural History, Courtesy of The: 34

Art Institute of Chicago: 41T; 472C; 520L; 520R; 521, Gift of the Society for Contemporary Art

Art Reference Bureau: 116, 130, 162, 661T

Bayeaux Library, Bayeaux Caltreda, France: 41B

Bettmann Archive Inc., The: 353

Black Star: 494

British Museum, Trustees of the: 118

Brown Brothers: 86, 698

Mac Conner: 13, 22, 69, 192, 197, 202, 205

Gerry Contreras: 64, 498, 505, 516

Constance Lebrun Crown: 162

Fogg Art Museum, Courtesy of, Harvard University: 140, Bequest of David M. Robinson

Freies Deutsches Hochstift, Frankfurter Goethesmuseum: 600L

Hal Frenck: 88, 95, 166, 286, 305, 314, 345, 358, 371, 377, 388, 394, 411, 421, 434, 512, 526, 545, 568

Galerie St. Etienne, Courtesy of, New York: 301B

George Eastman House: 42T

Graphic Presentation Services, Inc.: 61

Grunwald Graphic Arts Foundation, University of California, Los Angeles: 40B; 658TR

Dick Hanley Photography: 677, 681

Heritage Gallery, Los Angeles: 163; 298, and Mr. Charles White

Huntington Library, Hampton Institute, Hampton, Virginia: 300B

Jefferson Medical College, Courtesy of, Thomas Jefferson University: 660TL

Joslyn Art Museum, Omaha, Nebraska: 661CR

Mrs. Fred Chase Koch: 300T

Kröller-Müller Stichting, Otterlo, Holland: 164

The Louvre: 658TL

Metropolitan Museum of Art: 117, Gift of Amelia E. White, 1941; 125, Fletcher Fund, 1930; 160, Bequest of Mrs. H. O. Havemeyer, 1929, The H. O. Havemeyer Collection; 471, Museum Excavations, 1922-23, Rogers Fund, 1923; 522, Gift of Frederic H. Hatch, 1926; 600R, Rogers Fund, 1920; 693, Gift of I. N. Phelps Stokes, Edward S. Hawes, Alice Mary Hawes, Marion Augusta Hawes, 1937

Museum of Fine Arts, Houston: 301T

Museum of Modern Art: 43, Gift of Mrs. Simon Guggenheim; 274, Advisory Committee Fund; 299, A. Conger Goodyear Fund; 473T, Acquired Through the Lillie P. Bliss Bequest; 628, Gift of Victor S. Riesenfeld

Museum of the City of New York: 48; 697, The Harry T. Peters Collection

National Gallery, London: 40T

National Gallery of Art, Washington, D.C.: 39T, Andrew Mellon Collection; 42B, Gift of W. L. and May T. Mellon Foundation; 303, Chester Dale Collection; 582, Rosenwald Collection; 658B, Samuel H. Kress Collection

National Museum of Art, Lisbon, Portugal: 601

Nelson Gallery-Atkins Museum, Kansas City, Missouri: 471TL; 472T, 604, 659B, Nelson Fund

Oestreicher's Prints, Inc.: 661BL

Pennsylvania Academy of Fine Arts: 302T

Philadelphia Museum of Art: 442, The Louise and Walter Arensberg Collection

Portland Art Museum: 641

Royal Ontario Museum, Toronto, Canada: 115

St. Louis Art Museum: 38, 132, Gift of J. Lionberger Davis; 106, 143, 473BR, 602, 603

St. Marylebone Borough Council: 53, Reconstructed by Michael Wright

Santa Barbara Museum of Art: 39B

SAS Scandinavian Airlines: 3

Sheldon Memorial Art Gallery, The University of Nebraska: 302B

Smithsonian Institution, National Air and Space Museum: 436

Collection, James Thrall Soby: 161

Staatliche Museum, Berlin: 110

Edward Steichen: 33

Tuskegee Institute: 187

United Artists Corporation: 229, 236, 237, 259, 261, 262

Wadsworth Atheneum, Hartford: 471BR; 473CL

Larry Walker: 519

Walker Art Center, Minneapolis: 472B

Whitney Museum of American Art, New York: 165, 523T, 523B, 605

Witchita Art Museum: 151

World: 82

Yale University Art Gallery, Courtesy of: 659T

1 2 3 4 5 6 7 8 9 10 KPKP 82 81 80 79 78 77 76 75 74 73